UNIVERSITY CASEBOOK SERIES®

THE LAW OF SUCCESSION: WILLS, TRUSTS, AND ESTATES

by

DANAYA C. WRIGHT
Clarence J. TeSelle Professor of Law
University of Florida
Levin College of Law

Contributing Authors

LEE-FORD TRITT
Professor of Law
Director, Center for Estate Planning
University of Florida
Levin College of Law

PATRICIA STALLWOOD-KENDALL
Indiana Bar

FOUNDATION PRESS

University Casebook Series is a trademark registered in the U.S. Patent and Trademark Office.

© 2013 by LEG, Inc. d/b/a West Academic Publishing
    610 Opperman Drive
    St. Paul, MN 55123
    1–800–313–9378

Printed in the United States of America

ISBN: 978–1–60930–234–4

Mat #41349538

© SHOE–NEW BUSINESS 2010 MACNELLY
DISTRIBUTED BY KING FEATURES SYNDICATE

ACKNOWLEDGMENTS

This has been a massive project taking more than four years to complete. In that time I have accrued debts to countless people. My contributing authors, Lee-ford Tritt and Patty Stallwood-Kendall have been amazingly patient with me, explaining the nuances of tax and trusts law, as well as the interesting details of practice. I have had a wonderful army of research assistants, from Beth DeBarba whose knowledge of Elizabethan English law and history is unmatched in enthusiasm, to LaKesha Thomas and Justin Callaham whose tax skills hopefully kept me from saying something too terribly incorrect. The Georgetown Law Center supported me during my visiting year there, including providing invaluable research and library assistance. And I owe a huge debt to the deans of the University of Florida, Levin College of Law who gave me an extra sabbatical to complete the book. My colleagues George Dawson, Dennis Calfee, Berta Hernandez, Mark Fenster, Lee-ford Tritt, Michael Wolf, Grayson McCouch, and Christine Klein patiently assisted in various ways. And the librarians at the University of Florida found all sorts of interesting sources. I am also indebted to the many people who teach and practice in this area, who have encouraged this project, and whose work I have relied on heavily. I know that I am standing on the shoulders of many experts in the field and I humbly acknowledge my debt to them. I am thankful to the editorial board at Foundation Press who took a chance on this new kind of case book, and to John Bloomquist and Tessa Boury who have been diligent, attentive, and fun editors. And finally, I can never thank my family enough, my parents for all the quirky things they taught me, my in-laws for thinking I walk on water, and Kendal, Teya, and Jeremy, for whom I do everything, and because of whom all I do is enriched. Despite everyone's efforts to keep me straight, all errors are mine.

INTRODUCTION

This is a book about the law of succession—i.e. what happens to a person's property when she dies. For many centuries, and in many countries even today, the property owner has very little control over what happens to her possessions upon her death. They either pass directly to specified family members or the possessions are so few that they are simply divided up among the survivors with little reference to the formal legal rules on inheritance. Despite the great wealth in this country, most people die with a relatively small estate. We tend to use up much of our wealth, even if we had it, just surviving during our lives, raising our children to adulthood, and paying medical bills for end-of-life care.

For those lucky enough to have surplus wealth at their death, the law provides for a bewildering array of options. Most of the laws in the United States involving the estates of decedents (a decedent is the person who dies owning property that must be transferred to some living owners) evolved from England, where there were strict laws of primogeniture (the eldest son inherited to the exclusion of other children) and where, until 1540, land legally could not be devised by will. Ecclesiastical courts had jurisdiction over the transmission of personal property while the common law courts had jurisdiction over real property, leading to numerous conflicts of law and procedural difficulties. Complex estate planning for the wealthy was done by the lawyers who devised ingenious future interests, uses, settlements, and jointures to help ease the inter-generational transfer of property and essentially create wills where none were legally allowed.

Most of these devices, however, were aimed primarily at avoiding certain fees that would accrue upon the inheritance of property, fees payable to the crown. Those fees operated much like estate taxes today. Every time land descended to the next generation, the crown got its percentage, at least for the relatively large estates. Most of English feudal land law was written by the wealthy to protect the landed estates of an aristocratic society, and the non-propertied population was ignored. As our society has become more complex, and legal rules governing all sorts of otherwise private relations have become ubiquitous, the law of the wealthy has been applied downward onto the middle and working classes whose interests at death may be quite different from the interests of the wealthy.

With the vast changes in wealth of the twentieth century, a profound revolution in the laws of succession has occurred, usually with an eye toward providing default rules for the average person of modest means. But nearly every legal rule began rooted in wealth preservation and tax avoidance for the wealthy, and even the most egalitarian changes today carry within them the seeds of their original aristocratic origins. It is the responsibility of the estate planning lawyer, therefore, to determine the best mechanisms for an effective wealth transfer at death and to be sensitive to how the default rules may contradict a client's true intentions.

In the past, very few estates were sizeable enough to warrant what we would call "estate planning." Perhaps 1% or 2% of the population had sufficient wealth to need a complex trust or to require planning to minimize estate tax liabilities. With the rise of the middle class in the mid-twentieth century that changed. As more decedents left moderate estates that required sometimes complex administration at death, we also began seeing a dramatic increase in retirement and pension funds, life insurance, living trusts and spendthrift trusts to protect against creditors. Charitable giving exploded as charitable gifts were given exemptions from estate taxes. Why give your money to the government when you can give it to the charity of your choice?, reasoned many.

The feminist revolution of the 1960s also dramatically altered the law of succession as wives began moving into the work force, began acquiring their own wealth, and second and third marriages became more common. The feudal protection for the widow, a dower interest in the real estate owned by the husband, was replaced with numerous more complicated but egalitarian family protections through elective shares, homestead, family allowances, and other statutory protections from disinheritance. As families became more complex, wealth grew, and estate planning descended among the middle and working classes, numerous devices arose to give decedents better control after their deaths to provide for their loved ones.

Some devices, like the power of appointment and the trust, have been around for centuries, but had not been utilized by the average person for estate planning purposes until the mid- to late-twentieth century. Similarly, life insurance was a luxury for the wealthy. And very few people beyond wealthy industrialists had significant wealth in stock and bond portfolios until the late twentieth century. But today a sizable proportion of the population has at least some stock holdings that may require administration or probate at death.

We can identify two periods of profound change in the needs of decedents, and laws responding to those needs. The first occurred in the late 1960s and 1970s as the probate revolution expanded and the living trust became a staple in average estate plans. People hoping to avoid court-supervised administration of their estates used simple trusts to bypass courts and give themselves more power to control the descent and management of their property. The second change is still occurring with the re-emergence of the perpetual private trust through the abolition of the Rule Against Perpetuities. A larger percentage of the population, beyond the super-rich, are likely to be beneficiaries of dynasty trusts by the end of the twenty-first century. In addition, the rise in complex asset protection and Medicare trusts to deal with the escalating health care costs of end-of-life care, and the predominance of private retirement plans, IRAs, and stock brokerage accounts to supplement social security as the safety net for seniors has led to an explosion in creative mechanisms for estate planning. Changes in savings practices, the prevalence of home ownership among a wider sector of society, the increased burden of consumer debt, and non-traditional family patterns have all brought about a true revolution in this area of law.

Most casebooks center on the default rules of intestate succession and the sometimes quite arcane rules involving will execution and interpretation. While these are important rules to understand, most estate planning today uses a very simple will with a pour-over into a trust.

I hereby bequeath all property I own at death to the trustee of my living trust, to be disposed of according to the terms of the trust.

Trusts, life insurance, retirement accounts, joint bank accounts, and a variety of other forms of investment comprise the average estate of today. Consequently, with the decline of the importance of wills, and the rise in other legal mechanisms for transferring wealth at death, this book focuses primarily on the tools of sound estate planning. Each mechanism (wills, trusts, powers, PODs, TODs, joint tenancies, insurance, and the like) has certain advantages and disadvantages. A sound estate plan recognizes that no two people are alike—that each person has different ambitions, responsibilities, and desires with regard to where her property goes upon her death. Lawyers who rely only on formbook wills and trusts are probably committing malpractice if they do not understand their clients' personal and family needs. Streamlining estate administration at death and avoiding probate litigation is the first sign of a successful estate plan.

At the same time, even the most careful estate plan can go awry if beneficiaries predecease the testator and gifts lapse, if beneficiaries disclaim certain interests, if tax laws change to make certain trusts less favorable, if people marry, divorce, or have children. There is no end of uncertainties, and so most people wish to build some flexibility into their estate plans. People with children and grandchildren may wish to benefit successive generations; others may be more interested in providing for their own comfortable retirement and end of life care for themselves and their spouses. Effectuating the intent of the donor has risen in importance as we have removed many of the mandatory inheritance rules of the past.

The wealthy may wish to minimize tax consequences at all costs; others may wish to disinherit close family members in favor of friends, partners, or charities. All of these are valid desires and the client-oriented lawyer must understand the variety of tools available to allow her to protect her client's interests while conforming to important public policies promoting family stability and individual autonomy.

In a rapidly changing world, it is hard to imagine life 50 years from now, much less 350 years from now, when the forms of wealth and the needs of individuals may be as different from today as ours are from those of Henry VIII's England. What you learn today may change significantly before you even pass the bar and are drafting your first will. It truly is not the same world of our parents or grandparents, and our children's estate planning needs will be different from our own. But what is unlikely to change anytime soon is the assumption that our ownership of property during our life confers on us at least some rights to control the disposition of that property at our death. The powers and limitations associated with that right are the subject of this book.

Philosophy of the Book

Most trusts and estates casebooks were written when the vast library of cases and rules on wills dominated estate planning. Thus, they spent as much as 75% of the book on will doctrines, on everything from mental capacity to will execution problems to disclaimer and lapse of bequests. But that is not the world in which we are currently living. Today, as mentioned above, most wills are very simple—they pour all of a decedent's remaining assets into a revocable trust that becomes irrevocable upon the decedent's death and the trust controls present and future disposition of the estate's property through mechanisms outside of court-supervised administration. Avoiding probate is one of the primary goals most clients seek in planning their estate.

Other clients of great wealth, over $5.25 million for 2013, may have estate tax minimization goals, but the number of clients in that category are fewer than 1% of the U. S. population.[1] Nevertheless, many clients may

---

[1] My colleague Grayson McCouch has done some rough calculations based on estate tax returns filed, number of estates with estate tax liabilities, compared to the yearly death rate

visit a lawyer convinced that they need the newest tax preferred plan. Many other clients are uncomfortable talking with their children or spouses about how they want their property to pass, and will often end up dropping a bombshell on their bereaved family when, after grandpa's funeral, the family discovered that he left everything to his gay lover of 40 years. Everyone has a secret, and everyone has a skeleton in his closet; the estate lawyer's job is to find out the secrets and skeletons so some can be given a proper burial and others dealt with to protect the client and the family.

Lawyers come at the subject of wills, trusts, and estates from a variety of different vantage points. Some organize the material in terms of understanding the different devices for transferring wealth. Thus, they might think of wills, trusts, powers of appointment, or joint bank accounts as discrete subjects, each with its own set of common law and statutory rules. You need to know them all, but you don't need to learn them in a particular order. Others might think of the subject from a planning perspective; i.e. figuring out a client's needs and drafting a plan to satisfy those needs. Others might come at the subject from the perspective of administration, after the decedent's death, when the estate must be administered and the first thing to do is pay the funeral expenses and last minute medical bills, then hit homestead and family allowance provisions, and then move to court-supervised probate, and finally to litigation if there is a glitch in the estate plan.

Most trusts and estates casebooks adopt the first approach. This book adopts a blend of the second and third approaches. We discuss some issues, like homestead and family allowance, that apply to all estates, then talk about the default rules of intestacy, then we move into the basic devices and mechanisms of estate planning (the toolbox), and then we turn toward planning for different types of situations. In the planning section we consider different family needs and examine which mechanisms or devices will best achieve our client's goals. Then we turn to ways in which estate plans can be changed, and then what happens when everything turns sour and litigation ensues. Entering almost any legal field is like learning to swim. You can learn the breathing, the kick, and the arm strokes, but until you just jump into the pool and try to put it all together you feel like you are barely treading water. The order in which you cover the subjects should not matter so long as you take the plunge and get wet.

We three authors also have put our own imprints on this book. I (Danaya Wright) am a property law professor and legal historian who first started teaching estates and trusts as a service. It needed to be taught and it was at least somewhat tangential to my other research and teaching interests to make it a plausible addition. Over time, however, I grew to love the subject but was dissatisfied with the other case books in the field. The decision to write my own book was not taken lightly, and it has been quite an exercise in trying to find the right balance of theory and practice. To that end, I brought on board Patricia Stallwood-Kendall, a small firm and sole practitioner who has practiced trusts and estates for ten years. She has dealt with everything from clients who are being abused by their spouses to non-traditional family planning to the client who wanted to leave her skull to her lifetime partner. She has added countless practice tips and real-life problems while being responsible for keeping the book focused on the eve-

---

and come up with the staggering statistic of .2% of estates are likely to face estate tax liabilities under the current $5.25 million credit.

ryday issues of people's important secrets and family dynamics. Lee-ford Tritt worked in a large New York law firm drafting wills and trusts for the rich and the super-rich. He is a tax expert who has drafted countless complex wills and trusts and has never met a tax minimization trust he didn't like. Lee-ford teaches advanced estate planning and transfer tax courses. He has brought to the book his wealth of knowledge and experience in estate planning and administration. All of us, however, are excited about the new direction this book has taken and how it looks toward the future, not the past. It is traditional and revolutionary at the same time.

Because we focus primarily on good estate planning, there are fewer cases than traditional casebooks. We spend a lot of time analyzing a variety of statutes and how they have modified the traditional common-law rules. We offer cases primarily to understand the origins of important common-law rules and to illustrate what not to do. Every probate litigation is an estate planner's failure. And although one cannot always convince one's clients to follow one's advice, and estates may suffer as a result, there is no excuse for many of the common mistakes lawyers make in drafting wills and trusts, recommending certain will substitutes over others, or injecting ambiguities where none existed in the testator's mind.

Besides the revolution in the use of will substitutes and the changing demographics of work and family, technology has profoundly changed the way people think about their property. Unless you are over 50 years old, you probably don't purchase music on a cd anymore. You probably download it from iTunes or have your entire music library stored in the cloud. But what happens when you die? Can you bequeath your cloud files to someone else? What if some of the music on your computer's hard drive was pirated? Does your executor have a duty to figure out what was pirated before passing it to your beneficiaries? And no one has photo albums anymore. We all have our pictures on our computers, where they can be easily uploaded to friends or to social networking sites. Are those photos property? No longer do you have to divide up the old, yellowing photo albums; an executor could simply copy all of grandma's photos onto a thumb drive for everyone.

Facebook now offers a new service: it will send a message to all your Facebook friends if you die suddenly. You simply assign a good friend the right to authorize the notice and then, if you perish climbing Mt. Everest, your agent will post your private message to everyone you have friended on Facebook. Should that message have any kind of testamentary power? Is the next generation of testators going to write and execute their wills on their smart phones? These questions make the old ones, like how should the law deal with computer signatures or video-taped execution ceremonies, sound simple. As we declutter our lives and go green, how will our executors even know what our property is if it is all password protected or encrypted? Do lawyers have a duty to protect a client's passwords, or are they property passing to the executor?

These are the issues of the next generation of wills and trust lawyers. We have often asked questions in the following chapters to which there simply are no answers because the questions have not been asked before. Even if a testator left all of her encrypted music in a trust for her children and grandchildren, will they even be able to access it 10, 50 or 100 years from now? How do you dispose of property that is constantly changing shape? Fifty years from now we may not have marriage the way we know it, and parenthood may be a very different process. Children might have eight parents, from biological to surrogate to adoptive to step-parents. The brave new world is before you. But to know where we are going, you must know from whence we have come. It is a fascinating journey and we only hope you get the breathing, the kicking, and the arm strokes together to reach the other end. Then, Olympic gold is just over the horizon, after you master the American transfer tax system.

The Sources of Succession Law

Before moving into the body of the material, there are two prefatory matters we need to address—the sources and the terminology of estates and trusts law. The sources alone can be quite complex. A wide variety of common-law rules evolved over the centuries as England, and its colony the United States, moved from their feudal forms to modern industrial societies. Many of the English rules were adopted in this country at the founding, and are still in effect today. Others have been repudiated as not befitting an egalitarian, hard-working society like ours.

Even where the rules have been modified to respond to new times, they form the initial starting point in any analysis of estates and trusts law. Many of these judge-made rules remain valid today and always serve as the default position when there are gaps in statutory provisions. Every state, however, has legislated its own probate code for defining the default rules of estate distribution and they can be remarkably diverse. In addition, each state has laws to ensure that certain popular mechanisms, like unfunded stand-by trusts, are valid where they had been invalid under the English and early American common law. Probate codes can differ widely, making it impossible to give a thorough grounding in the state laws of all 50 states. Eight states are community property states, whose legal origins rest in the civil law rules of Spain and France, rather than the common law rules of England. Two other states, Wisconsin and Alaska, have recently amended their marital property rules to more closely resemble the community property regimes of the Western states. The 40 common law states and the three territories follow English law but with significant amendments.

In 1969, the National Conference of Commissioners on Uniform State Laws (ULC) promulgated the Uniform Probate Code (UPC), a compilation of rules that the Commissioners felt best served the needs of our modern, complex society. The 1969 UPC was adopted in full in 18 states, and in part by many of the other common law states in the 1970s and 1980s. A major revision of the UPC was enacted in 1991, keeping many of the probate procedure provisions of the 1969 UPC, but modernizing the substantive rules to keep up with changes in wealth accumulation practices, tax laws, non-traditional and two-income families, and egalitarian and family protectionist reform policies.

Amendments to the 1991 UPC were made in 1997, 1998, 2002, 2003, and 2008 to deal with particular issues the Commissioners thought needed attention. Since 1991, a majority of states have adopted the UPC in whole or in large part, making individual revisions to suit state needs. Many more states have adopted large parts of the UPC, and others have adopted certain provisions and rejected others. But states do not have automatic update mechanisms, so when the UPC changes, few states change their probate codes in a timely manner. Many "UPC States" are out of touch with many of the post-1991 revisions.

The UPC provides the general starting point for our discussion of state probate laws, even though it has been adopted in only 19 states. We then offer examples in each section of the book of illustrative state laws as points of comparison. Where one state stands out as being unusual, we might examine that state's laws and discuss the motives and policies underlying the differences. We make no effort to give a 53-state analysis of the probate codes (including the District of Columbia, Puerto Rico, and the Virgin Islands); rather, we use individual state statutes to illustrate different ways of approaching similar legal problems.

In 2000, the Uniform Law Commission promulgated the Uniform Trust Code (UTC) to deal with a wide variety of emerging trust issues and to promote uniformity among states since wills and trusts are ambulatory. Like the UPC, the UTC has aspirational elements. Because trust law is primarily judge made, adoption of the UTC is seen by many as an important aspect of law reform in those states otherwise governed primarily by case law, often still referring to eighteenth and nineteenth century English precedents. As trusts have become ubiquitous estate planning devices, differences between the laws of trusts and the laws of wills have posed serious conundrums for courts seeking to further the intentions of testators. The UTC has been adopted in 25 states and territories (not necessarily the same states that have adopted the UPC). As we do with the UPC, we will also provide state examples to highlight UTC provisions of interest.

Other uniform laws figure at times in the book. The Uniform Transfers to Minors Act; the Uniform Testamentary Addition to Trusts Act; the Uniform Statutory Rule Against Perpetuities; the Uniform Simultaneous Death Act; the Uniform Real Property Transfer on Death Act; the Uniform Parentage Act; the Uniform Multiple-Person Accounts Act; Nonprobate Transfers on Death Act; the Uniform Health Care Decisions Act; the Uniform Guardianship and Protective Proceedings Act; the Uniform Durable Power of Attorney Act; the Uniform Disclaimer of Property Interests Act; the Uniform Determination of Death Act; the Uniform Custodial Trust Act; the Uniform Anatomical Gift Act; and other uniform acts make brief or substantial appearances.

A second source is particularly important in this area of law: *The Restatement of the Law (Third) of Property: (Wills and Other Donative Transfers)* (referred to herein as the *Restatement 3d of Property*) is a four-volume set (the 4th still in draft) which purports to restate the majority and preferred common-law rules that have evolved over time in all fifty states. The *Restatement* is an amalgam of judge-made rules that often provides model rules and reasoning when courts are faced with new issues or are asked to change the law in their state and there is no direct legislation on point. Volume 1 covers intestacy, execution and revocation of wills, and post-execution events affecting wills. Volume 2 covers gifts, will substitutes, and a variety of doctrines designed to deal with construction and modification of donative documents. Volume 3 covers future interests and powers.

There is also the *Restatement of the Law (Third) of Trusts (*referred to herein as the *Restatement 3d of Trusts)*, which is a 2 volume set. Volume 1 covers the nature, characteristics and types of trusts, and the creation of trusts. Volume 2 covers elements of trusts, beneficiaries' rights, and modification and termination of trusts. Additional volumes of the *Restatement 3d of Trusts* are underway.

Because this area of law is heavily rule-based and heavily statutory, we have deemphasized cases in this book. That is not to say, however, that the kinds of public policy issues that often drive judicial decisions are not relevant. Quite the contrary. To the greatest extent possible, we raise those policy issues in our discussion of the rules and push the reader to think about the purposes behind relatively generous wealth transmission rules or limitations on those rules.

We also need to explain our approach to the cases. In most casebooks, there are primary cases, reproduced in full or short note cases to elaborate on recent developments or unusual factual situations. The point of the cases is to learn how to read a case, differentiate dicta from holdings, extrapolate the appropriate rules, and work through the legal analysis. By the time you are in this class, however, we assume you know how to read cases carefully. Therefore, we use numerous cases to illustrate a particular legal point, often where there are deviations in applicable rules, or when the facts really drive the decisions. Many of these cases are only one or two paragraphs long and consist of summaries that we have drafted. Because we have distilled the cases to such an extent, it would be distracting to the reader if we included all of the brackets, ellipses, and quotation marks that are necessary to properly attribute authorship. Thus, we have adopted a style where any language pulled directly from the court's opinion is presented in italics, and any language that we have drafted, either as a summary or explanation, is in standard print. We have omitted citations from the cases except where the court quotes directly from another source. And we have elided sentences and paragraphs from the court's opinion to minimize the distractions of sentence and paragraph breaks. We apologize to any judge out there who feels we have misrepresented or mistakenly stated the court's opinion. We hope that the educational value of the text compensates for its lack of strict editorial citations.

We have also chosen to minimize the references to law review articles and other cases that would normally appear in a treatise or scholarly article. We have done this, in part, because the focus of the book is educational, and it is not designed to provide the kind of authoritative sourcing we expect from a treatise. We have also done this to minimize the distractions for students who, in our experience, do not generally find those elaborate notes helpful. Perhaps, after they have graduated law school and are in practice, they might look back to a casebook for references for further study, but there are far better sources than casebooks, and the benefit does not seem worth the cost of cluttering the text with citations and references that will be ignored. This is not to say that those kinds of sources are not tremendously valuable and we encourage students to reach out to other sources if they have questions or want additional information about a subject. We have chosen not to include them because, at 1000 pages the book is already too long, and we hope that the focus on the multitude of short case summaries and statutes, along with lengthy authorial descriptions, will provide the right balance for students at this level.

The book is also replete with discussions of the historical origins of many important succession law doctrines. Again, the complex scholarly literature on the legal history of inheritance is beyond the scope of this book, and we have omitted many of the nuances and citations that make this subject so interesting. Some professors may find this material helpful, and others will find it excessive. We believe that it is easier to understand where the law is going by understanding from whence it has come. But if the historical material is distracting, it can be easily omitted from class reading assignments.

As always, however, we encourage comments from students and teachers using this book and we look forward to making the book even more user-friendly in the next edition.

The Terminology of Succession Law

Also, we must begin our study of the law of decedents' estate with an understanding of the basic vocabulary. Here are a few terms that we will use right from the beginning. More technical terms will be introduced as they arise. One of the most important terms, however, is *donative freedom*, the right of a donor of property to make a gift, either before death or after death, to a recipient. Most books use the term *testamentary freedom* to refer to this power, but in light of the near-universal shift away from wills and toward will substitutes as mechanisms for making most substantial gifts, we use the more generic term *donative freedom* instead.

Administration—the process of identifying and collecting a decedent's property and dispersing it to the appropriate successors. This may be done with or without a court's supervision.

Beneficiary—a person who is the recipient of a gift, either *inter vivos* or testamentary, either by intestacy or under the provisions of a will, trust, or other will substitute. We use the term beneficiary throughout this book to refer to any person who benefits from a gift, regardless of whether it is real or personal property or arises via a will or intestacy.

Bequeath (Bequest)—originally referred to the act of giving personal property via a will and had the same legal meaning as the term legacy.

Codicil—a validly executed testamentary document used to modify a will.

Collateral Relatives—persons related to the decedent through an ancestor such as a parent or grandparent and includes siblings, nieces and nephews, aunts and uncles, cousins, parents, grandparents and the like.

Community Property—a system of property ownership in which property acquired during a marriage is generally held in undivided half interests by each spouse and each share can be entirely managed and individually disposed of at death.

Conservator—a person appointed by a court to manage the estate of someone who is legally unable to manage her estate herself. A conservator can be appointed for a minor child or for an incapacitated adult, and usually deals only with that person's property. In some states a conservator is appointed to manage the person as well (but the term is usually reserved for managing adults only). Most states use the term guardian to refer to someone who is appointed to make decisions for the care of a person. Both guardians and conservators are fiduciaries.

Decedent—the person whose property is being administered after his or her death.

Deed—a written document used to convey property during life (*inter vivos*), usually real property.

Descendant—synonymous with the terms *issue* or *lineal descendant*. Descendants are children, grand-children, great-grandchildren, and so on, but does not include collateral relatives like siblings, nieces and nephews, cousins, and the like.

Descend—the process whereby property passes to legal heirs under the laws of intestate succession. Property that passes by a will or other will substitute does not descend (it is devised) and property that descends can pass to collateral relatives (not limited to descendants).

Devise (Devisee)—the process whereby property passes to successors by virtue of a will or other will substitute. Originally a devise was for real property only, and a bequest was for personal property.

Disclaimer—a refusal to accept a gift, usually required to occur within a relatively short time of the making of the gift.

Distribute—the process whereby the administrator or personal representative of an estate conveys a decedent's property to successors (devisees, legatees, heirs, kin).

Domicile—the state or territory in which a person has primary residence, which is important for administration purposes as the law of the domicile usually governs the distribution of an estate, regardless of the location of the property, except real property will be governed by the law of the situs.

Escheat—process whereby property passes to the state in the absence of legal heirs to take by intestacy and in the absence of a valid will devising the property to others.

Estate—the property of a decedent owned by her at her death, and sometimes including property over which she has a life estate, a power of appointment, or held in trust depending on the origin of the property and her level of dominion and control. The Internal Revenue Code distinguishes between the *gross estate*, which consists of all property over which the decedent exercised sufficient control, and the *net* or *taxable estate*, which consists of all property that passes minus the applicable credits, deductions, and exclusions from taxation.

Executor—person or persons designated in a will to administer a decedent's estate. Also sometimes referred to as a personal representative. Executors have no power to act until appointed by a court.

Fiduciary—a person entrusted with the property of another who has a duty of care in the management and control of that property. Trustees, executors, personal representatives, guardians, and conservators are all fiduciaries.

Gift Cause Mortis—a conditional transfer of property that occurs during life but is made in anticipation of death and is revocable if the donor survives.

Guardian—a person with the duty of care and management of the person of another, usually a minor.

Heir—person(s) who qualify under a state's laws of intestate succession to take the property of a decedent. Heirs are identifiable only at the death of the decedent; prior to death they are *heirs apparent*. An heir must survive the death of the decedent to qualify as an heir. Although persons who succeed to property under a will are called devisees or legatees, a testator may bequeath property in her will to her *heirs*, whose identity will be determined by reference to the laws of intestacy. Historically heirs were those designed to take real property and kin or kindred were those designated to take personal property (a spouse could be kin but not an heir for instance), but that distinction has generally disappeared.

Inter Vivos Gift—a transfer of ownership in property that occurs during the transferor's life. *Inter vivos* means, literally, *between the living.*

Intestate—to die without having made a will or other testamentary disposition, so that one's property passes according to the default rules of intestate succession. In certain circumstances, will provisions that lapse or fail may also pass by the default rules of intestate succession.

Issue—see descendant.

Joint Tenancy—a manner of holding property by more than one person in undivided shares, with a right of survivorship by which the shares of joint tenants automatically pass to surviving tenants. The term is sometimes used to refer to any form of co-ownership, like a tenancy in common or tenancy by the entirety, but is usually used in the context of succession law as a form of co-ownership with a right of survivorship.

Kin or Kindred—originally used to distinguish those who took personal property under the default rules of intestate succession from an heir who took real property. The term is rarely used today except as a synonym for the term heir (which has a strict legal meaning) or the term relation or relative (which has a very broad, inexact meaning).

Legacy (Legatee)—originally used to denote a gift of personal property made in a will, distinguishable from a devise which was a gift of real property. Today devise is the more accepted term to refer to both, but many lawyers still use the term legacy in addition to devise just to cover all their bases.

Notary Public—a person authorized by law to administer oaths and authenticate signatures and documents.

Personal Property—usually distinguished from real property, personal property corresponds somewhat closely to the concept of moveable (as opposed to immoveable) property. The distinction is important in a number of situations, including the separate writing doctrine and choice of law rules in the context of administration of an estate. It includes money, tangible and intangible personal property, securities, and other moveable property. Intangible personal property consists of securities, legal rights and claims, debts, notes, copyrights, patents, and other non-physical legal rights.

Personal Representative—a somewhat universal term covering executors, administrators, and other fiduciaries appointed to administer an estate.

POD—meaning *payable on death*, this is a way to hold certain intangible property such that ownership will pass to a designated beneficiary pursuant to contract provisions in place between the owner and the party who has possession and control over the property (e.g. a bank, a brokerage company, a business).

Power of Appointment—authority given to a person (called a donee) to make decisions about where a decedent's property shall go, usually at a point in time later than the death of the decedent.

Probate—from the Latin *probare*, means to prove or validate a will and thereby allow it to have legal effect. The term is also used to describe a set of courts, probate courts, that supervise the administration of decedents' estates. And the term also modifies the term estate, as in probate estate, to refer to the estate of a decedent that requires administration, but is distinguishable from property a decedent owned that passes outside the probate process through a trust, a joint tenancy, or other will substitute.

Representation—the term used to describe the substitution of more remote relatives to take the property of a parent or other ancestor who predeceased the decedent but who would have been an heir or devisee had that person survived.

Testament (Testamentary, Testator)—means a person's written will and a testator is one who executes a will. The adjective *testamentary* can also refer to devices like a trust that are created through a will or a gift that takes effect at the death of the testator even if they are not made through a written will (see *testamentary gift*).

Testamentary Gift—a transfer of ownership in property to take place only upon the death of the current owner.

Testate—to die with a will or other testamentary instrument and is distinguished from dying without a will, which is to die intestate.

Trust—a method of holding property whereby title is split such that legal title is held by one person (the trustee) for the benefit of another (the beneficiary) who holds the equitable title. The trust derived from the medieval use whereby land would be owned by one person for the *use* of another (called the *cestui que use* or *cestui que trust*). The trustee has a fiduciary responsibility toward the beneficiary(ies) and the property of the trust and must manage the property for the benefit of the beneficiaries.

TOD—meaning *transfer on death*, this is a way of holding property such that ownership transfers on the death of the current owner to a named beneficiary pursuant to a contract (see POD). TOD accounts usually consist of stocks, bonds, and other securities, the transfer on death of which is governed by statute.

Ward—a person for whom a guardian or conservator has been appointed.

Will—a document, properly executed according the statutory requirements, that disposes of a person's property at her death.

Will Substitute—a generic term referring to a variety of instruments other than a will, such as a trust, a TOD, a POD, a joint tenancy, or a power of appointment, according to which property of a decedent will pass at her death. Will substitutes generally do not need to be executed according to the statutory requirements for a will and allow the property to transfer without the need for court supervision (i.e. outside of probate).

———————

With these basic terms in mind, we can now embark on our study of decedent's estates. But we must keep in mind the overarching public policy behind any system of private property, which is that property ultimately must serve the needs of the living. There are many good reasons for allowing people to control their property after their death, but there are also limitations that must come into play to allow property to serve human ends and to adjust for the needs of today and tomorrow, not the dreams of yesterday.

SUMMARY OF CONTENTS

SECTION 4. CHANGING THE PLAN, LITIGATING THE PLAN, AND ATTORNEY DUTIES

TABLE OF CONTENTS

SECTION 4. CHANGING THE PLAN, LITIGATING THE PLAN,
     AND ATTORNEY DUTIES

Chapter 10. Revocation, Modification, and Termination of Testamentary Documents

TABLE OF CASES

The principal cases are in bold type.

TABLE OF STATUTES

THE LAW OF SUCCESSION: WILLS, TRUSTS, AND ESTATES

DECEDENTS' ESTATES, DONATIVE FREEDOM, AND THE DEFAULT RULES

CHAPTER 1

DONATIVE FREEDOM AND GIFTS

A. DONATIVE FREEDOM

The study of trusts and estates usually begins with the concept of testamentary freedom or, as we call it here, *donative freedom.*[1]

But what is donative freedom exactly? Except for King Tut, who literally could entomb himself with all his wives, slaves, gold, and other possessions (except his land), the rest of us ordinary people cannot really take it with us when we pass into the netherworld. We can't even make a good bargain and sell our stuff[2] before we go because our currency isn't of much use in the hereafter. And of course, even King Tut ultimately did not get to keep his stuff—it's all now *owned* by the British Museum *in trust* for the people of the world. But that sure doesn't mean that I get to take any of it home with me, even if I am a beneficiary of that trust.

My father used to say that he wanted to spend his last dollar (that was back before inflation) on the margarita that would drop him into the grave. In other words, he wanted to spend everything he owned before he died. But I would ask him, "what if the last margarita didn't drop you into the grave, instead it just sealed your liver sclerosis and you could have 20 more years if you had the money for a liver transplant?" His answer was usually that we should let him just wander off, like an elephant, when he thought his time was near, to die somewhere without the care or intervention of modern medicine. My answer to that was usually "thanks dad, I really want to spend the rest of my life feeling guilty for letting you be neglected and die in some cave or ancient elephant burial ground."

Unlike my father, most people are risk averse, and would rather know that they will have enough wealth to provide for themselves up to their last day of life, even if that means sacrificing during life to save, and having some left over to give what isn't spent to others. Another way to deal with death is to give all one's stuff away during life, with promises from the recipients that they will use the wealth we give them to provide for us in our old age. But we all know how well that worked for King Lear, whose ungrateful daughters could not be bothered caring for dear old dad once they had his money and his regal responsibilities. Like Blanche DuBois, we have generally learned not to rely on the kindness of strangers,[3] or relatives, unless we have no other choice.

---

[1] We use the term donative freedom to encompass not just gifts that pass by will (testament), but gifts that pass by joint tenancies, trusts, powers, and other will substitutes, either during life or at death.

[2] I use the term *stuff* rather than *property* because, as we all know, *property* is really an adjective describing a set of legal rights that we have in our things, and not the objects themselves. *Stuff* is a good generic term for all of the objects and clutter that we accumulate during our lives.

[3] Tennessee Williams, *A Streetcar Named Desire (Dec. 3, 1947) (Broadway play)*.

So if you have to give your stuff away at death, for death does make us all profoundly generous in that regard, it is probably better that we have laws providing for the smooth intergenerational transfer of wealth that will avoid costly litigation, heavy lawyer fees, or painful emotional scars on our surviving family rather than leave the matter up to death-bed proclamations and promises when fears of eternal damnation might make us less than rational in our generosity. At the same time, even if Grandpa was perfectly rational when he conditioned the succession of his estate on his beneficiaries never marrying anyone by the name of Murphy, there is a point at which the dead are long gone and following their whims, while meaningful for survivors, eventually shackles the living. That is the subject before us: analyzing the laws and procedures of Succession Law to determine if it strikes the right balance between donative freedom (known colloquially as *dead hand control*) and the rights and needs of the living.

Before 1540, an English landowner could not devise his land by will. He could give it away during life, in which case he suffered the King Lear problem, or he could keep control over it until his death when the law mandated that it would pass to his eldest son through primogeniture.[4] But if he had more than one child, or his eldest son was a spendthrift or intemperate scoundrel, he could not devise his land to his other children.[5] He could make a will regarding personal property that would be administered in the ecclesiastical courts, but those courts had no enforcement power if one child took possession of the stuff and refused to give it up to the one to whom it was devised. We could say that there was little *testamentary* freedom in those days.

In 1540, however, King Henry VIII, who was not particularly concerned with the testamentary interests of his subjects, except insofar as they frustrated his collection of feudal revenues, signed into law the Statute of Wills[6] that allowed for the testamentary transfer (by will) of up to two-thirds of a subject's land held in military tenure and all of the land held in socage tenure,[7] while the remaining one-third had to continue to pass by the statutory laws of descent to the legal heir. Why did he do this?

---

[4] There were a few exceptions, like gavelkind, which treated the youngest son as the heir, or equitable partition, which treated all sons equally. But most of England used primogeniture. See JOHN BAKER, AN INTRODUCTION TO ENGLISH LEGAL HISTORY 266–268 (London: Butterworths, 4th ed. 2002).

[5] Of course, this isn't entirely true as he could transfer the land during life to an entity that would not die, like the Church or a group of joint tenants, and impose a use on the transfer, thus requiring the legal title holders hold the property for the use of a set of beneficiaries and then transfer title to whoever the donor designated. This somewhat convoluted imposition of a contractual obligation on the title holder was the precursor to the modern trust and was unrecognized in the common law courts but could be enforced in the Chancery. More of this will follow in Chapter 4.

[6] 32 Hen. 8, c. 1 (1540).

[7] Land held in Military Tenure required the tenant to provide knights for his lord's service, or guards for border patrol or garrison duty. Military Tenure also carried with it the possibility that if the land descended to the tenant's underage heir, the lord could reclaim possession of the land (primer seisin) until the heir came of age and could pay one or two years' income to reclaim it (relief), and until the heir came of age the lord could take custody of the child heir and sell his or her marriage rights to the highest bidder. Land held in Socage Tenure carried with it fixed agricultural duties, like providing a certain amount of grain or livestock. Over time, the Socage fees were heavily regulated and disappeared as inflation made them virtually worthless while the services of relief, primer seisin, and marriage for lands held in Military Tenure were quite valuable up until the Civil War. The Statute of Wills of 1540 allowed for transfer of two-thirds of land held in military tenure and all of the land held in socage tenure. See Baker, Introduction to English Legal History, supra n. 4 at 226–227, 255–257.

He had learned that those cunning common lawyers had devised numerous complex strategies for their clients to avoid the statutory descent of land. This was because when land passed to the legal heir it was subject to a wide variety of government fees (call them estate taxes if you will). Most of those pesky future interests that you learned about in Property are the direct result of the pre-1540 common law prohibition on making a will for land and the requirement of primogeniture, which was not abolished in England until 1925.[8] This lack of testamentary freedom forced people who wanted their land to pass differently from the statutory formula to devise some of the most complex legal machinations that still plague lawyers and law students today.

So what common law subjects got in 1540, and what was later extended to cover all land in 1660, which was when military tenures were abolished,[9] was what we would call *testamentary freedom*.[10] That is, they received the power to dictate, through some form of document or other mechanism, where their stuff would go upon their death, while retaining full ownership and control up to the last moment of life, and their stated wishes would be enforced by courts of law when interlopers tried to take possession upon their death. Everyone pretty much agrees that we all have testamentary freedom, the power to make a will with regard to all of our property and, upon failure to make a will, to know that our property will descend by the default rules of statutory descent and that, subject to some important limitations, courts will enforce those wishes.

Since 1540, when English landowners received the right to make a will, they have been busy devising numerous legal mechanisms to avoid the workings of primogeniture, the default rules of intestate succession, and transfer taxes—those inconveniences that were not abolished with the Statute of Wills. Giving property away during life, creating future interests, using joint tenancies with rights of survivorship, establishing trusts or powers, or buying life insurance were all mechanisms eventually devised to avoid many of the undesirable effects of traditional succession law and the public probate of wills. Because the law has become far more accepting of these different ways of setting up one's property to pass at death or during life, we use the term *donative* freedom here, because testamentary freedom refers only to the right to make a will. Today's property owners have the right to make virtually unlimited donative choices in how they will give away their property and plan for their death. But all of those choices involve one or another limitation or consequence that some property owners may wish to avoid.

Even today, however, the limitations and consequences of the multitude of estate succession mechanisms should make us ponder whether we have donative freedom, or whether we should have it. If our estate is over the threshold for the federal estate tax exemption,[11] up to one half of the

---

[8]   See The Administration of Estates Act 1925, 15 & 16 Geo. 5, c. 23. A decedent could avoid primogeniture, however, by writing a will.

[9]   The Abolition of Military Tenures Act, 12 Car. 2, c. 24 § 8 (1660).

[10]   Although in 1660 the common lawyers would have called it testamentary freedom, because the statute gave the full rights to devise land by will, the freedom to gift land by *inter vivos* transfer, trust, or will, was quite important, and led to a much more vibrant land economy than existed on the continent at the time.

[11]   The estate tax exemption was $1,000,000 in 2003, it slowly increased to $3,500,000 by 2009, then was unlimited in 2010, then set to $5,000,000 in 2011, went up to $5,120,000 in 2012, and $5.25 million in 2013 with yearly adjustments for inflation. Maximum tax rates

surplus could be taken by the federal government in estate taxes. This confiscation of wealth by the government is far greater and more intrusive than anything devised by the Tudors. The government in the fifteenth and early sixteenth centuries usually only took two year's worth of the income on some (not even all) real property and nothing on personal property. So while we think of ourselves as having donative freedom, the modern scheme of estate taxation is far more destructive of wealth accumulation and dead hand control than the inability to make a will for the late Medieval landed elite who could have hired a conveyancer to work around the laws with a *use*.[12]

Similarly, in all but one state, a person cannot disinherit a spouse.[13] Of course, there are numerous ways to try to limit the spouse's entitlement, but the law has taken pretty serious steps to avoid the intentional and unintentional disinheritance of a lawful surviving spouse. Is that consistent with donative freedom? In Louisiana one cannot disinherit one's dependent children.[14] Is that consistent with donative freedom? I may have the freedom to make a will, but if I have to excuse myself to take a phone call during the execution process, or one witness signs my will in the dining room and another in the drawing room, my will can be invalidated and all my testamentary plans set to naught. Is that donative freedom?

Among estates and trusts scholars there is also great debate about just how much donative freedom should be permitted. Some argue that any limits on a donor's freedom, like taxes and the elective share, are impermissible takings of private property. Others argue quite strenuously that property must serve the needs of the living and that the communitarian values of civilized society demand that non-owners have equitable claims to certain property. Spouses and children, in particular, are favored in the law. Even though scholars often assert that donative freedom is necessary to inspire industry and investment by donors, they often disagree about the merits of inheriting property for promoting industry and progress in beneficiaries.

The leading case usually cited for the proposition that the right to determine how your property will pass is a constitutionally protected property right is *Hodel v. Irving*, decided in 1987 by the U.S. Supreme Court. Usually the federal courts don't get involved in estates cases because the law of property, and its posthumous transmission, is the subject of state law. But in the following case, Justice O'Connor treated the right of a decedent to control the descent and devise of land using language that has been cited in countless trusts and estates contexts as supporting the idea that donative freedom is a *property* right that is protected by the Fifth Amendment of the Constitution. Think about who has the rights, how they can be exercised, and the implications of this case for ordinary Americans.

---

during that same period were as high as 50% in 2003, dropped to 35% in 2011 and 2012, and increased to 40% in 2013.

[12] A use was a device whereby property would be held by one person for the use or benefit of another. It is the predecessor to the modern-day trust. More on the history of the use is provided in Chapter 4B.

[13] As you will learn in Chapter 7, spouses in all common law states are entitled to a forced share of a decedent spouse's estate, except in the State of Georgia, that has not chosen to tie up a portion of a decedent's estate. In the ten community property states the spouse already owns half of all marital property, despite who earns it and how it is titled.

[14] LA. CIV. CODE ANN. art. 1493 (1996).

Hodel v. Irving

481 U.S. 704 (1987)

■ JUSTICE O'CONNOR delivered the opinion of the Court.

The question presented is whether the original version of the "escheat" provision of the Indian Land Consolidation Act of 1983, Pub.L. 97–459, Tit. II, 96 Stat. 2519, effected a "taking" of appellees' decedents' property without just compensation.

Towards the end of the 19th century, Congress enacted a series of land Acts which divided the communal reservations of Indian tribes into individual allotments for Indians and unallotted lands for non-Indian settlement. . . . In order to protect the allottees from the improvident disposition of their lands to white settlers, the Sioux allotment statute provided that the allotted lands were to be held in trust by the United States. Id., at 891. Until 1910, the lands of deceased allottees passed to their heirs "according to the laws of the State or Territory" where the land was located, ibid., and after 1910, allottees were permitted to dispose of their interests by will in accordance with regulations promulgated by the Secretary of the Interior. 36 Stat. 856, 25 U.S.C. § 373. Those regulations generally served to protect Indian ownership of the allotted lands.

The policy of allotment of Indian lands quickly proved disastrous for the Indians. Cash generated by land sales to whites was quickly dissipated, and the Indians, rather than farming the land themselves, evolved into petty landlords, leasing their allotted lands to white ranchers and farmers and living off the meager rentals. . . . The failure of the allotment program became even clearer as successive generations came to hold the allotted lands. Thus 40-, 80-, and 160-acre parcels became splintered into multiple undivided interests in land, with some parcels having hundreds, and many parcels having dozens, of owners. Because the land was held in trust and often could not be alienated or partitioned, the fractionation problem grew and grew over time.

A 1928 report commissioned by the Congress found the situation administratively unworkable and economically wasteful. . . . In discussing the Indian Reorganization Act of 1934, Representative Howard said:

> "It is in the case of the inherited allotments, however, that the administrative costs become incredible. . . . On allotted reservations, numerous cases exist where the shares of each individual heir from lease money may be 1 cent a month. Or one heir may own minute fractional shares in 30 or 40 different allotments. The cost of leasing, bookkeeping, and distributing the proceeds in many cases far exceeds the total income. The Indians and the Indian Service personnel are thus trapped in a meaningless system of minute partition in which all thought of the possible use of land to satisfy human needs is lost in a mathematical haze of bookkeeping." 78 Cong.Rec. 11728 (1934).

In 1934, in response to arguments such as these, the Congress acknowledged the failure of its policy and ended further allotment of Indian lands.

But the end of future allotment by itself could not prevent the further compounding of the existing problem caused by the passage of time. Ownership continued to fragment as succeeding generations came to hold the property, since, in the order of things, each property owner was apt to have more than one heir. . . . [In] 1983 . . . Congress [took] action to ameliorate the problem of fractionated ownership of Indian lands.

Section 207 of the Indian Land Consolidation Act—the escheat provision at issue in this case—provided:

"No undivided fractional interest in any tract of trust or restricted land within a tribe's reservation or otherwise subjected to a tribe's jurisdiction shall descendent [sic] by intestacy or devise but shall escheat to that tribe if such interest represents 2 per centum or less of the total acreage in such tract and has earned to its owner less than $100 in the preceding year before it is due to escheat." 96 Stat. 2519.

Congress made no provision for the payment of compensation to the owners of the interests covered by § 207. The statute was signed into law on January 12, 1983, and became effective immediately.

The three appellees—Mary Irving, Patrick Pumpkin Seed, and Eileen Bissonette—are enrolled members of the Oglala Sioux Tribe. They are, or represent, heirs or devisees of members of the Tribe who died in March, April, and June 1983. Eileen Bissonette's decedent, Mary Poor Bear–Little Hoop Cross, purported to will all her property, including property subject to § 207, to her five minor children in whose name Bissonette claims the property. Chester Irving, Charles Leroy Pumpkin Seed, and Edgar Pumpkin Seed all died intestate. At the time of their deaths, the four decedents owned 41 fractional interests subject to the provisions of § 207. App. 20, 22–28, 32–33, 37–39. The Irving estate lost two interests whose value together was approximately $100; the Bureau of Indian Affairs placed total values of approximately $2,700 on the 26 escheatable interests in the Cross estate and $1,816 on the 13 escheatable interests in the Pumpkin Seed estates. But for § 207, this property would have passed, in the ordinary course, to appellees or those they represent.

Appellees filed suit in the United States District Court for the District of South Dakota, claiming that § 207 resulted in a taking of property without just compensation in violation of the Fifth Amendment. The District Court concluded that the statute was constitutional. It held that appellees had no vested interest in the property of the decedents prior to their deaths and that Congress had plenary authority to abolish the power of testamentary disposition of Indian property and to alter the rules of intestate succession.

The Court of Appeals for the Eighth Circuit reversed. Although it agreed that appellees had no vested rights in the decedents' property, it concluded that their decedents had a right, derived from the original Sioux allotment statute, to control disposition of their property at death. The Court of Appeals held that appellees had standing to invoke that right and that the taking of that right without compensation to decedents' estates violated the Fifth Amendment. The Congress, acting pursuant to its broad authority to regulate the descent and devise of Indian trust lands, enacted § 207 as a means of ameliorating, over time, the problem of extreme fractionation of certain Indian lands. By forbidding the passing on at death of small, undivided interests in Indian lands, Congress hoped that future generations of Indians would be able to make more productive use of the Indians' ancestral lands. We agree with the Government that encouraging the consolidation of Indian lands is a public purpose of high order. The fractionation problem on Indian reservations is extraordinary and may call for dramatic action to encourage consolidation. . . .

This Court has held that the Government has considerable latitude in regulating property rights in ways that may adversely affect the owners.

[The Court then explained that the economic impact was fairly minor, and the interference with investment backed expectations was negligible—two of the three prongs of the Penn Central balancing test for determining whether a governmental action works a taking of property without just compensation.]

If we were to stop our analysis at this point, we might well find § 207 constitutional. But the character of the Government regulation here is extraordinary. [T]he regulation here amounts to virtually the abrogation of the right to pass on a certain type of property—the small undivided interest—to one's heirs. In one form or another, the right to pass on property—to one's family in particular—has been part of the Anglo-American legal system since feudal times. The fact that it may be possible for the owners of these interests to effectively control disposition upon death through complex inter vivos transactions such as revocable trusts is simply not an adequate substitute for the rights taken, given the nature of the property. Even the United States concedes that total abrogation of the right to pass property is unprecedented and likely unconstitutional. Moreover, this statute effectively abolishes both descent and devise of these property interests even when the passing of the property to the heir might result in consolidation of property—as for instance when the heir already owns another undivided interest in the property.[15] Since the escheatable interests are not, as the United States argues, necessarily de minimis, nor, as it also argues, does the availability of inter vivos transfer obviate the need for descent and devise, a total abrogation of these rights cannot be upheld.

In holding that complete abolition of both the descent and devise of a particular class of property may be a taking, we reaffirm the continuing vitality of the long line of cases recognizing the States', and where appropriate, the United States', broad authority to adjust the rules governing the descent and devise of property without implicating the guarantees of the Just Compensation Clause. See, e.g., Irving Trust Co. v. Day, 314 U.S. 556, 562, 62 S.Ct. 398, 401, 86 L.Ed. 452 (1942); Jefferson v. Fink, 247 U.S., at 294, 38 S.Ct., at 518. The difference in this case is the fact that both descent and devise are completely abolished; indeed they are abolished even in circumstances when the governmental purpose sought to be advanced, consolidation of ownership of Indian lands, does not conflict with the further descent of the property.

■ JUSTICE STEVENS, with whom JUSTICE WHITE joins, concurring in the judgment.

The Government has a legitimate interest in eliminating Indians' fractional holdings of real property. Legislating in pursuit of this interest, the Government might constitutionally have consolidated the fractional land interests affected by § 207 of the Indian Land Consolidation Act of 1983 in three ways: It might have purchased them; it might have condemned them

---

[15] Justice STEVENS argues that weighing in the balance the fact that § 207 takes the right to pass property even when descent or devise results in consolidation of Indian lands amounts to an unprecedented importation of overbreadth analysis into our Fifth Amendment jurisprudence. Post, at 2085. The basis for this argument is his assertion that none of appellees' decedents actually attempted to pass the property in a way that might have resulted in consolidation. But the fact of the matter remains that before § 207 was enacted appellees' decedents had the power to pass on their property at death to those who already owned an interest in the subject property. This right too was abrogated by § 207; each of the appellees' decedents lost this stick in their bundles of property rights upon the enactment of § 207. It is entirely proper to note the extent of the rights taken from appellees' decedents in assessing whether the statute passes constitutional muster under the Penn Central balancing test.

for a public purpose and paid just compensation to their owners; or it might have left them untouched while conditioning their descent by intestacy or devise upon their consolidation by voluntary conveyances within a reasonable period of time.

Since Congress plainly did not authorize either purchase or condemnation and the payment of just compensation, the statute is valid only if Congress, in § 207, authorized the third alternative. In my opinion, therefore, the principal question in this case is whether § 207 represents a lawful exercise of the sovereign's prerogative to condition the retention of fee simple or other ownership interests upon the performance of a modest statutory duty within a reasonable period of time. . . .

Section 207 differs from more conventional escheats in another important way. It contains no provisions assuring that the property owner was given a fair opportunity to make suitable arrangements to avoid the operation of the statute. Legislation authorizing the escheat of unclaimed property, such as real estate, bank accounts, and other earmarked funds, typically provides as a condition precedent to the escheat an appropriate lapse of time and the provision of adequate notice to make sure that the property may fairly be treated as abandoned. Similarly, interpleader proceedings in District Court provide procedural safeguards, including an opportunity to appear, for those whose rights will be affected by the judgment. The statute before us, in contrast, contained no such mechanism, apparently relying on the possibility that appellees' decedents would simply learn about the statute's consequences one way or another. . . .

It follows, I believe, that § 207 deprived decedents of due process of law by failing to provide an adequate "grace period" in which they could arrange for the consolidation of fractional interests in order to avoid abandonment. Because the statutory presumption of abandonment is invalid under the precise facts of this case, I do not reach the ground relied upon by the Court of Appeals—that the resulting escheat of abandoned property would effect a taking of private property for public use without just compensation.[16]

The conclusion that Congress has failed to provide appellees' decedents with a reasonable opportunity for compliance implies no rejection of Congress' plenary authority over the affairs and the property of Indians. The Constitution vests Congress with plenary power "to deal with the special problems of Indians."

In *Hodel,* Justice O'Connor opined that the right to descent and devise was a *fundamental stick* in the bundle of property rights protected by the Fifth Amendment's just compensation provision. On the other hand, Justice

---

[16] I am unable to join the Court's largely inapposite Fifth Amendment takings analysis. As I have demonstrated, the statute, analogous to those authorizing the escheat of abandoned property, is rooted in the sovereign's authority to oversee and supervise the transfer of property ownership. Instead of analyzing § 207 in relation to our precedents recognizing and limiting the exercise of such authority, however, the Court ignores this line of cases, implicitly questions their validity, and appears to invite widespread challenges under the Fifth Amendment Takings Clause to a variety of statutes of the kind that we upheld in *Texaco v. Short.* Critical to our decision in *Texaco* was the fact that an owner could readily avoid the risk of abandonment in a variety of ways, and the further fact that the statute afforded the affected property owners a reasonable opportunity to familiarize themselves with its terms and to comply with its provisions. . . .

Stevens countered that property rights can be regularly adjusted and even terminated if the property owner is given adequate notice and a mechanism for protecting those rights. All manner of escheat provisions are perfectly constitutional, after all, if property owners can avoid them through deliberate actions. In fact, if a decedent has no legal heirs and makes no will, his property may escheat to the state.[17] That is a universal rule and certainly not one with Constitutional implications.

Nonetheless, *Hodel*, and its companion, *Babbit v. Youpee*, 519 U.S. 234 (1997), have been cited often for the proposition that donative freedom, defined as the right of a decedent to determine the descent and devise of her property, is a constitutionally-protected property right. As you read through the material in the rest of this book, keep in mind the nature of this right that underlies the law of succession.

Most casebooks begin with a discussion of testamentary freedom in order to get students to think about how the laws should balance the rights of a property owner to designate how his stuff will pass after his death (i.e., dead hand control) with the rights of children, spouses, other relatives, and society (i.e., the living) who become the new owners of the stuff and may have different needs or priorities. Only since *Hodel*, in 1987, has it been suggested that there might be a Constitutional right to dead hand control. But this case is somewhat unique even in the takings context, involving Indian trust land, quite extraordinary federal legislation, and was decided in a year the Court was looking to expand property protections through the Just Compensation Clause, a position from which it has arguably retreated in recent years.

Consider the following cases and the courts' determination as to the extent, or lack, of donative freedom allowed the decedents. After *Hodel*, do you think the cases should be decided differently? If not, is *Hodel* of much use?

In re Succession of Collett

11 So.3d 724, 2009–70 (La.App. 3 Cir. 6/3/09)

In this case George Collett died testate on August 14, 2007 leaving his widow and three adult children surviving. At the time he executed his will in 1988 Louisiana law required that all children receive a mandatory share of a parent's estate (forced heirship). The law was changed between the time of execution of his will and his death.[18] Collett's will bequeathed to Marjorie Collett "the disposable portion of all of the property" of which he died possessed, "of any kind, whether movable or immovable, wherever located." Collett also bequeathed to his three children "the forced portion of the property" of which he died possessed, "of whatever nature, and wherever the same is located, share and share alike, subject to the lifetime usufruct in favor of Marjorie L. Collett." In the probate proceedings, two of Collett's children claimed entitlement to the forced portion as the will directed.

---

[17] See Chapter 3.

[18] At the time of execution the law provided that all children, adult or underage, were entitled to a share of a parent's estate. That law was changed in 1997 after the Louisiana Constitution was amended to abolish forced heirship except for descendants of the first degree under age 23, or any such descendants who are incapacitated. See LA. CONST. art. 12 § 5; LA. REV. STAT. § 9:2501 (2001). The 1997 transition rule was then amended in 2001. LA. CIV. CODE ANN. art. § 870 (1981), § 1493 (1996).

The court disagreed, however, and held that because at the time of George Collett's death forced heirship was abolished, the disposable portion bequeathed to Marjorie Collett was one hundred percent of George's estate. The court stated that: *We also find without merit the contention that George Collett manifested a specific desire to leave a portion of his estate to his children by stating that he wished to leave the forced portion to them. George Collett's testament employed terminology that has legal meaning. Thus, instead of using a numerical value, such as one-half or some other fraction or portion of the estate, which would indeed signify a desire to leave something to the children, the testament used legal terms, i.e., "forced portion" and "disposable portion." What is "forced portion" and what is "disposable portion" is to be decided according to the law in effect on the date of the testator's death. At the time of George Collett's death, his estate had no forced portion. Indeed, George Collett's use of this legal phraseology manifests his desire to leave his children only that which the law required him to leave, whatever the law may be at the time of his death. Had George Collett, in fact, wanted to leave his children some portion of his estate and not simply that which the law required him to leave, he would have used terminology that does not vary with the fluctuations in the law. Moreover, the absence of something other than these legal terms demonstrates George Collett's desire to leave his wife the maximum portion of his estate the law allows.*

Query: If the law in Louisiana at the time George Collett executed his will had not provided for a forced share for children, do you think George would have made a separate provision for them? Do you think he would have preferred to have them entirely disinherited because the law changed between the execution of the will and his death? In contrast, would he have preferred that the court read his will literally to give them the portion that would have been their forced share? Would your opinion of the case change if you knew that Marjorie Collett was George's second wife, and that his children were by his first wife? What if Marjorie Collett was George's only wife and she was the mother of the children who brought suit?[19]

Practice Point: The Importance of Your Words

The court in *Collett* reasoned that if George had wanted to provide for his children under his will, he would have used "terminology that does not vary with the fluctuations in the law." Yikes! Are you reading this as a law student, or as a potential estate planning attorney? Because once you begin thinking of this case (and all of the following cases, for that matter) from a *planning* perspective, the effect can be somewhat staggering. For example, it is true that George Collett *could* have drafted his own will in 1988. But isn't it likely that an attorney drafted it for him? And if so, what happened? Why didn't the will have a provision clarifying what George's intentions were? And, if the law changed, did George's attorney try (or was the attorney able or required to try under the Rules of Professional Responsibility) to encourage him to amend his will?

As you read the countless mishaps relating to wills, trusts, and estates that are included in this casebook, begin thinking about what could have been done in the planning phase to avoid the litigation in the first place. Because from an estate

---

[19] In fact, Marjorie was the mother of the children who brought suit. Can you think why they would sue their own mother?

planning attorney's perspective, the very best estate plans are, after all, the ones you never hear about in law school.

In re Hutchin's Estate

147 Misc. 462; 263 N.Y.S. 896 (N.Y. Sur. 1933)

In a proceeding to construe the last will and testament of Jennie M. Hutchins the court invalidated a condition in the residuary clause. Hutchins' will stated: *Third. All of the rest, residue and remainder of my property of every name and nature I hereby give, devise and bequeath . . . in trust, [to] use the interest and income therefrom . . . , for the support and maintenance of my daughter, Ethel Hutcheon (but only if she be separate and apart from her husband, John Hutcheon) and for the support and maintenance of my grand-daughter Marguerite Fredericka Van Guildar Hutcheon.* Ethel Hutcheon, was happily married to John Hutcheon several years prior to the execution of the will and continued happily united in the city of New York. The court stated: *There is no doubt in my mind but that the design of the testatrix was that her daughter, Ethel Hutcheon, should inherit the estate only in the event that she be separate and apart from her husband, John Hutcheon. No other conclusion can be drawn from the language of the will.*

However, the court refused to give effect to the condition, stating: *While the testatrix had the right to give her property to whomsoever she chose, she could not do that which has a tendency to be injurious to the public good. A contract which binds one of the parties to do that which is contrary to the policy of the law is void, no matter how solemnly it may have been made. So a testamentary disposition designed to carry into effect some purpose which the law regards as immoral, illegal or indiscreet, will be held void. Our modern society is built about the home. Its perpetuation is essential to the welfare of the community. The law looks with disfavor upon any contract by which a husband and wife agree to separate and live apart from each other in the future, because such an agreement breaks up the home, and tends to dissolve or alter the marriage relation. The testatrix by her will did not restrain the continuation of the marriage relation between her daughter, Ethel Hutcheon, and her husband in so many words, but if the condition in her will were carried out the result would be the same. The condition attempted to be imposed by the testatrix had no other object than to effectuate a design to separate her daughter from her husband. Therefore, the necessary conclusion is that the condition was wholly void and the daughter, Ethel Hutcheon, takes under the will the same as if the condition had not been sought to be made in the will.*

Query: What would the testator have likely done had she known that the court would not enforce the provision in her will that gave trust benefits to her daughter only on the condition she was separated from her husband? Would she prefer the daughter take the entire trust outright without limitation, or would she prefer to provide for a granddaughter who did not have a husband to support her? Would it matter if the daughter had discussed her marital difficulties with her mother, or if the daughter and her husband had just returned from a cruise where they had reaffirmed their vows just a week before the will was executed? How could the attorney have drafted this clause differently to ensure it would be effective? Is there a way?

Munroe v. Basinger

58 Ga. 118; 1877 WL 2940 (1877)

Mrs. Densler died in 1857, leaving a last will and testament by which she bequeathed to Basinger a certain sum of money for the use of Selina Munroe during her life, then to the use of Selina's children. Selina and her children were slaves at the date of the will. Basinger paid the interest to her regularly until 1861; then going into the war, he turned over the fund to another, who took it with the trust. Selina Munroe brought suit for the interest due, in the city court of Savannah. The court held that the bequest was void when made, under the act of 1818, and that even though the plaintiff was now free, the pre-war law voiding the bequest would continue to operate. Selina and her children received nothing and Mrs. Densler's intestate heirs took all of this money instead.

Cochreham v. Kirkpatrick

48 Tenn. 327, 1870 WL 2662 (Tenn.), 1 Heisk. 327 (1870)

In this case William Smith, by will, gave a part of his land to his daughter and the remainder to his son, the latter with the condition that his widow be allowed to remain on the son's land and he stated as follows: *"It is also my will and desire that my black girl, Eliza be free at my death, and that she is not to be subject to be sold by any of my heirs, and that none of my children nor wife is to have any claim on her as being a slave; and she is to have the privilege of living on the land that I have given to my son, Sevier, or living with any of the connection, as the case may be."* In a subsequent codicil, Smith changed his mind somewhat about Eliza and provided: *"It is also my will that my black girl, Eliza, be not free until the death of my wife."* At the time of suit, Smith's wife was still alive. When a successor purchased the land the son had inherited upon the son's death, Smith's wife and Eliza sued to be allowed to remain on the land.

The court held, however, that: *Under the provisions of the Code, sections 2692 to 2710, the assent of the State to the emancipation of slaves could 'be given only on condition of immediate removal from the State,' and provisions were made for their transportation to the Western coast of Africa. None were allowed to remain, 'unless, from age or disease, they were unable to go.' It does not appear that the complainant, Eliza, ever obtained, or attempted to obtain, the assent of the State to her emancipation. It was manifestly the intention of the testator that she should remain in the State, and that the bequest of freedom, on this condition, was unlawful and void, not only under the Code, but under previous laws of a similar character. And if any doubt can exist as to the true construction of the original will, there can be no doubt that, under the codicil, the right of complainant, Eliza, to emancipation, was only to take effect upon the death of the testator's wife, and as it appears from the bill that she is still living, this would be only an inchoate and imperfect right, that could not be enforced until after the demise of Mrs. Smith. The privilege of living upon the land was void, as being contrary to the policy of the State at the date of the will, and the time of the death of the testator, and could not have been enforced if Mrs. Smith had died before the late civil war. The rights of the complainant, Eliza, so far as the questions raised in the bill are involved, depend upon the will and codicil, and not upon her subsequent freedom, under Article 13 of the Constitution of the United States, and later provisions in the Constitution of Tennessee, neither of which could so operate as to vest an interest in the land, or its use and enjoyment, contrary to the will of the testator, and the laws and policy of the State, existing at the time when it took effect.*

Query: If legal property rights could not be bequeathed to slaves prior to emancipation, and those will provisions that attempted to give them rights were deemed invalid, should those rights have revived upon repeal of the laws that denied the slaves themselves to be property? What would these testators have likely wanted? It seems that when we compare *Collett* with *Munroe* and *Cochreham* that the *law taketh* and the *law taketh*. Can you offer a rational reason for its apparent one-sidedness when it comes to changes in the law?

In re Succession of Glynn

167 So.2d 533 (La. App. 4th Cir. 1964)

Louis Glynn, Sr., died in New Orleans, his domicile, on June 28, 1961 leaving a will that left everything to Ellen Morgan, his caretaker. Children of the decedent's predeceased sister filed an opposition to the probate of the will on the grounds that Morgan lived in open concubinage with decedent and was therefore prohibited from being his legatee by LSA–C.C. art. 1481. Morgan *freely admitted having lived in open concubinage with testator for six or seven years prior to 1941 . . . as husband and wife, without being married, and without any effort to conceal the true nature of their relationship and this fact was generally known. The cause of the termination of the concubinage in 1941 was decedent's decision to marry a third party. Morgan at that time moved to California . . . and married another third party. Decedent's spouse thereafter died* and in 1958 he asked Morgan to return to New Orleans to care for him after he had a stroke, which she agreed to do (apparently she and her spouse had terminated their relationship by that time). There was no evidence that the parties resumed their relationship of concubinage.

Article 1481 of the LSA–Civil Code reads: "Those who have lived together in open concubinage are respectively incapable of making to each other, whether Inter vivos or mortis causa, any donation of immovables; and if they make a donation of movables, it can not exceed one-tenth part of the whole value of their estate." The law excepts those who are later married. In interpreting the statute, the court explained that: *"The first paragraph of the article limits the capacity of persons who 'have lived together', and not merely those who 'live together', or 'are living together' at the death of the testator, to make donations to each other. We deem it immaterial, under the language of the Code, that the concubinage may have ceased even several years prior to the attempted donation; once persons 'have lived together' in open concubinage, they will forever 'have lived together' in open concubinage."* The court further held that the marriage exception only applied to persons who marry each other. Therefore, because Morgan and the decedent had lived in concubinage at one time, the decedent was legally incapable of making any gift to her except of movables to the extent of 1/10 part of the whole value of his estate.

Query: Should wills and trusts laws attempt to promote particular family structures and relations by prohibiting certain devises? Although states have now abolished many such meddlesome laws, non-traditional decedents, especially gay and lesbian testators, have found courts willing to invalidate their wills on the grounds of insane delusion or undue influence when they disinherit blood relatives in favor of intimate partners. See In re: Kaufmann's Will, 247 N.Y.S.2d 664 (App. Div. 1964), aff'd 205 N.E.2d 864 (N.Y. 1965); E. Gary Spitko, *Gone but Not Conforming: Protecting the Abhorrent Testator from Majoritarian Cultural Norms through Minority Culture Arbitration*, 49 CASE W. RES. L. REV. 275 (1999). Is there any way Louis Glynn could have gotten around the law and given his estate to Ellen Morgan despite the prior concubinage?

Kennewick Public Hospital Dist. v. Hawe

151 Wash.App. 660, 214 P.3d 163 (2009)

Albert M. Luth devised all of his real property in Benton County, Washington, to the Kennewick Public Hospital District (Hospital) in perpetuity so long as the property was not "transferred, incumbered [sic] or otherwise alienated from the purposes herein expressed and intended." The property was to go to Benton County (County) or the State of Washington (State) if this direction was violated. That provision violates the rule against perpetuities and is therefore void. The question before us is whether the interest that remains is fee simple absolute (as the Hospital maintains) or whether, instead, it is fee simple determinable (in which case the Diocese of Olympia, Inc. (Diocese) would have an interest under the will of one of Mr. Luth's beneficiaries). We conclude that the resulting interest is fee simple absolute in the Hospital, and we affirm the summary judgment in favor of the Hospital.

Query: Certainly testators should not be able to draft will provisions that violate clear rules like the Rule Against Perpetuities. However, if a will provision does violate the RAP and is voided, should the result be a reversion in the testator's estate or a simple removal of the offending condition? The answer profoundly affects the future disposition of the property.

————————

These examples should give you some insight regarding the complexity of the legal questions raised in the context of decedents' estates. Should the law be a tool to enforce particular moral or public policy agendas by preventing decedents from devising property freely? When the law changes, should rights be revived? Just the simple question of ascertaining the intent of a testator who makes a will under a particular legal regime and then, when the laws change, does not amend the will can be quite difficult. Does this mean the testator wanted the *new law* to apply, *preferred the old law* but didn't have time to make a new will, or was *unaware* the law had changed? The standard rubric is that judges attempt to ascertain the intent of testators to the best of their ability, but sometimes testamentary intent is a concept judges feel uncomfortable respecting, like freeing slaves or giving all to a gay lover or one's favorite televangelist or concubine. Moreover, when courts invalidate provisions of wills, they are faced with deciding how to distribute the property that no longer passes according to the testator's written instructions.

Knowing the parameters of the law and how a testator's intent can be accomplished through the various wills and will substitutes we study here, is only half of the duty of the skillful estate planner. The other half is to thoroughly ascertain a client's wishes and draft them through the estate plan as clearly and cleanly as possible. Litigation is an estate planner's failure, and one of the most important takeaways is that it is always easier to redraft documents or clarify ambiguous terms, even to the extent of annoying redundancy, than to litigate a testator's intent after she has died.

Donative freedom has its limits, however. Courts will not enforce donative freedom if doing so violates a clear legal rule, like the Rule Against Perpetuities or the Rule Against Unreasonable Restraints on Alienation.[20] They also will not follow the testator's intent if that intent is against public policy (I leave my child my entire estate if he murders my ex-husband, or if he promises to burn the house down, or only if he divorces his no-good wife). There are even some non-legal reasons why we might not want to follow a testator's instructions blindly. Think of the numbers of authors and composers who have left their estates to loved ones with the instructions to burn all their unfinished manuscripts,[21] or testators who have requested that their estates be used for frivolous or discriminatory purposes.[22] The world has certainly benefitted by administrators who did not follow their testators' intentions.[23] Sometimes courts are hesitant to enforce socially unpleasant provisions if there is another socially acceptable interpretation that can be successfully applied. An important question facing courts and lawmakers, and consequently you as planners and lawyers, is when should donative freedom end and social engineering begin? Your own personal aversion to a testator's plan to leave her estate to a particular religious or political group is no reason to talk your client out of her plan. But if you think the devise is likely to raise questions about her mental state, or you think a will contest suit is likely to arise by disgruntled children, your duty is to talk candidly with your client about the risks of making what are called "unnatural" dispositions.

One important element of succession law is to prevent fraud and undue influence, especially if we can protect against the unscrupulous caretakers or gold-digging second spouses who befriend grandma or grandpa in their declining years. Should we let them keep the money they inherit from elderly testators? If there are no friends or family paying attention to grandma or grandpa as they get older, is it right to void their wills in favor of distant heirs just because the will beneficiaries are motivated by greed? I often think that if someone is willing to put up with me when I get eccentric and crabby, then they deserve the money, and I sure don't want some neglectful children or grandchildren contesting my will when they haven't bothered to visit me in the nursing home for the past five years. Besides,

---

[20] We discuss these rules further in Chapter 10.

[21] The Roman Poet Virgil and English Poet Philip Larkin, and novelists Thomas Hardy and Franz Kafka all left such instructions. Some were dutifully followed and others not. Nikolai Gogol and Elizabeth Inchbald, however, were more successful, the latter insisting that her memoirs be destroyed in front of her as she lay on her deathbed, too weak to do it herself.

[22] Consider the wills of Harry Houdini who asked that a séance be performed every year on the anniversary of his death; Gene Roddenberry who asked that his ashes be scattered in outer space; Mark Gruenwald who asked that his ashes be mixed with ink and be used to print comic books; or Ernest Digweed who left £26,000 to Jesus on condition that he proves his identity to the British Government.

[23] George Bernard Shaw left a portion of his estate to fund the creation of a phonemic alphabet for the English language, that would rationalize the spelling of English words, but the project failed. He complained that you could spell fish, "ghoti" ("gh" is pronounced like it is in "enough," "o" like it is pronounced in "women," and "ti" as it is pronounced in "ration.") On the other side of this divide was Mark Twain who claimed that anyone who could only think of one way to spell a word was indeed poor in imagination.

it's my money. On the other hand, there are plenty of unscrupulous people willing to take advantage of a person's loneliness, physical incapacity, or failing memories. Laws should protect those who are weakened by age and infirmity, even if they won't protect people from their own stubbornness or stupidity. Your job is to discover and fulfill your client's wishes, even if they are eccentric, while protecting her from her own frailties and the greed of others.

These are by no means easy tasks, and probate courts must struggle to balance the needs and wishes of testators with those of potential beneficiaries.

Further Thinking

What would you do if you were the judge in the following cases, and can you come up with a principled justification for allowing donative freedom in some of these cases and not in others?

- Luis Carlos de Noronha Cabral da Camara, a Portuguese aristocrat, chose 70 people at random from the Lisbon phone directory to inherit his estate, 13 years before he died. He made the choices in front of two witnesses at the registry office because he had no close relatives who were entitled to inherit.[24] (Court affirmed the bequest.)

- Beverly Hills socialite Sandra West, 37, left most of her $3 million fortune to her brother-in-law on condition that she be buried reclining in her baby-blue Ferrari and dressed in her favorite lace nightgown. Her wish was granted after her death in 1977, and after a will challenge by her brother-in-law who hoped to inherit without having to lose the Ferrari.[25] (Court affirmed the bequest.)

- Leona Helmsley left $12 million in trust to her dog, *Trouble*. After the New York court reduced the amount of the trust, it was held to be valid, even though Trouble then required a security detail because she had been receiving death threats by people upset that so much money was being spent on a dog when people were starving.[26] (Court affirmed the bequest.)

- Senator A.O. Bacon, of Georgia, left land in trust to the City of Macon to be developed and used as "a park and pleasure ground" for white people only, the Senator stating in the will that, while he had only the kindest feeling for the Negroes, he was of the opinion that, "in their social relations, the two races (white and negro) should be forever separate."[27] (Court affirmed the will provision, but eventually caused the park to be forfeited when the condition became illegal as a result of a U.S. Supreme Court decision that desegregation was required under the 14th Amendment.)

- Louisa Strittmater wrote on books and pictures around her house that "My father was a corrupt, vicious, and unintelligent savage, a typical specimen of the majority of his sex. Blast his wormstinking carcass and his whole damn breed." And she inscribed on a portrait

---

[24] Patrick Jackson, *Where There's a Will, There's a Whim*, BBC NEWS (Jan. 17, 2007), http://news.bbc.co.uk/2/hi/europe/6268015.stm.

[25] See http://en.wikipedia.org/wiki/Sandra_West.

[26] Sewell Chan, *Leona Helmsley's Unusual Last Will*, THE NEW YORK TIMES (Aug. 29, 2007), http://cityroom.blogs.nytimes.com/2007/08/29/leona–helmsleys–unusual–last–will/.

[27] Evans v. Abney, 396 U.S. 435 (1970).

of her mother "That Moronic she-devil that was my mother." She also smashed a clock and killed a pet kitten. When she left everything to the National Women's Party, distant heirs challenged her will claiming she suffered from insane delusion.[28] (Court struck down her will.)

- Charles Vance Millar, a Canadian lawyer, left the residue of his estate to whatever Canadian woman gave birth to the most number of children in ten years, and to be split in case there was a tie. After years of litigation, the will bequest was upheld and the $750,000 estate was split 4 ways between women who each gave birth to nine children during the ten years. It was known as the *Great Stork Derby* and a TV movie of that name was later made about the race to have as many children as possible.[29] Do you think the women should have been excluded if they got pregnant solely in order to inherit?

- R.A. Drake married twice, the first producing 8 children and the second producing 2 children. His second marriage, made in 1935, was unhappy and resulted in divorce 4 years later. Drake's will, written during this second marriage in 1938, provided: "All of my property real personal or mixed I will devise and bequeath unto my children in equal shares, . . . If any of my children should be awarded to my present wife, or raised by her after 1 year of age, I will such child the sum of One Dollar." Drake died 30 years later in 1967, after divorcing his second wife in 1939, and knowing that his two children by her remained in her custody after the age of 1 year.[30] (Court affirmed the will's disinheritance of Drake's two children by his second wife.)

Take any one of these scenarios and suppose that you are the lawyer for the testator. What would you ask your client about his or her motives? What advice would you give to help your client avoid a will contest suit? What if you were the lawyer for the opponents of the will. What advice would you give them? How would you decide these cases if you were the judge concerned with creating precedents that would discourage socially undesirable behavior?

B. GIFTS

One of the most important characteristics of the law involving estates and trusts is that it is based on the law of gifts, also called *donative transfers*. One might think gifts would be quite simple: a birthday or graduation present, or something larger such as a car, land, or an interest in a business. What the recipient likes about gifts is that they are *free* and *irrevocable*, or at least they cannot be revoked without some exceptional circumstance. And for many donors, gifts are ways to show they care about someone and they are happy making irrevocable transfers of real or personal property.

The law of gifts is characterized primarily by the fact that an item of property is transferred from one person to another *without consideration*. Precisely because it isn't a contract, in which goods of value are exchanged

---

[28] *In re* Strittmater, 53 A.2d 205 (1947).

[29] See http://en.wikipedia.org/wiki/Charles_Vance_Millar.

[30] Brown v. Drake, 275 S.C. 299 (1980).

for money or services, a gift does not involve an exchange. It is an act of true generosity.

Once made, gifts cannot be revoked except under limited circumstances. The *property sticks* are deemed to have transferred from the donor (giver) to the donee (recipient) once the three elements of a gift have been met:

1. *delivery* (or *constructive delivery*),
2. *acceptance* by the donee, and
3. *intent* on the part of the donor to make an irrevocable transfer of the property rights in the object.

Considering the elements, gifts seem relatively straightforward, but you have learned by now that few things are simple in law. One can make a gift conditioned on a future event in which the donor would want the gift back if the event does not take place. Consider the engagement ring if the engagement is broken off.[31] Similarly, people give away possessions in anticipation of possible death, and want those possessions returned should they survive. Someone facing risky surgery or enlisting in the military may be generous in the light of immediate danger, but regret his haste once the danger is past. Gifts in anticipation of death are called gifts *causa mortis*, and they can be revoked by the giver if the anticipated death does not occur. Failure to revoke within a reasonable time after the gift is delivered, however, may estop the donor from revoking a gift *causa mortis*. Furthermore, all sorts of legal problems can arise if the giver, thinking she is not going to survive delicate brain surgery, does indeed survive the procedure but is killed in an automobile accident returning from the hospital. What happens when persons die but not from the anticipated cause have been the subject of a handful of lawsuits.[32] Gifts *causa mortis* should never result from a lawyer's advice, but lawyers may be called in to resolve disputes once they are made.

Gifting can get more complicated, too, when future interests are the subject of the gift. Consider the father who wants to give his son a valuable painting as a graduation present, but does not want to give up possession until his own death.[33] Owners who give away a *remainder interest* but keep *a life estate* in an item of property do not make actual delivery. It is often difficult to discern the giver's intent without the clear evidence of delivery. Is the donor's intent to give away an irrevocable remainder interest, or is his intent simply a promise to make a gift sometime in the future? Because the law focuses on the *timing* of the transfer of the property sticks, which is the event that makes the gift irrevocable, complex gift tax issues can arise.

Regarding the future interest in the painting; imagine it was valued at $5,000.00 at the time the future interest vested in the son. Capital gains taxes on the painting would be payable by the son when he sells it, for the increase in value from when he acquired the future interest to when he sold it. However, the son did not acquire possession of the painting until his father's death some forty years later. At that time the painting was worth much more, perhaps $500,000. If he received ownership of the painting only

---

[31] Albinger v. Harris, 310 Mont. 27, 48 P.3d 711 (Mont. 2002); Fanning v. Iversen, 535 N.W.2d 770 (S.D. 1995); Brown v. Thomas, 127 Wis.2d 318, 379 N.W.2d 868 (Wis. Ct. App. 1985); Lyle v. Durham, 473 N.E.2d 1216 (Ohio Ct. App. 1985).

[32] Antos v. Bocek, 452 P.2d 533 (Az. App. 1969); In re Presender's Est., 285 A.D. 109, 135 N.Y.S.2d 418 (N.Y.A.D. 1954); Ridden v. Thrall, 125 N.Y. 572, 26 N.E. 627 (N.Y. 1891).

[33] Gruen v. Gruen, 496 N.E.2d 869 (N.Y. 1986).

upon his father's death, he would only have to pay capital gains taxes on the increase in value between the time his father died and the time he sold it. In Chapter 9 we discuss in more detail the taxation of donative transfers. For our purposes now, however, it is enough to recognize that the time value of money means that it matters, both economically when the gift occurs, and legally for purposes of dominion and control.

Additional complex questions can arise regarding gifts of future interests, like how would the insurance proceeds be split if the painting was destroyed and it was still hanging on dad's wall? Could King Lear have avoided his fate had he given his daughters a future interest rather than a present estate in his kingdom? Could he even do that with a kingdom? What about gifts of ongoing or intangible property like a business, a race horse, or next season's crops? Gifts of future interests are irrevocable once made, and the person who retains the life estate may be subject to claims of waste if she harms the remainderman's interest in the property. People who give away remainders to avoid probate or taxes often have a hard time letting go of full dominion and exclusive control, but without relinquishing some important property sticks, no gift will be deemed complete.

Other problems that arise in the context of gifts, besides future interests and valuation, involve fraud, undue influence, or misrepresentation. Elderly persons often are presumed to have a weaker state of mind, and thus be more susceptible to overreaching by schemers. The gold-digging second or third spouse, the abusive nurse or caretaker, the remote heir who appears and convinces her frail relative to disinherit his own children, the overreaching televangelist threatening eternal damnation if a check isn't in the mail by sundown, the scam artist, the lottery salesman, and the computer hacker all pose threats to the property of those with, or even without, a weakened sense of self-preservation.

Because of the unique nature of gifts, and because death ultimately makes every one of us generous givers, the law allows people to make written dispositions of their property while they are still of sound and commanding mind for gifts to take place in the future. That is the beauty of the will; it allows one to designate who will take one's property at one's death without requiring that the testator give up any dominion and control over the property during life. These gifts will be enforced unless the donor changes her mind and revokes her will, and she can rest assured that the gifts will be effective even if she later becomes incapacitated and susceptible to the machinations of fortune hunters. Gifts that take place at death are called *testamentary gifts* whether they are made in a will, other document, or pass by intestacy.

For hundreds of years, the will served as the principal instrument to preserve one's true gifting intentions against a world of schemers. As such, an almost mystical ritual has arisen around the will and the making of wills that perpetuate a rather mythic dichotomy between true intentions and false intentions. But what distinguishes the testator's true or false intentions? One merely need consider the case of the late Anna Nicole Smith, the model and *Playboy* centerfold who, at age 26, married 89 year old oil tycoon J. Howard Marshall II. When her octogenarian husband died thirteen months later, Anna Nicole found herself locked in a lengthy court battle over her deceased husband's $1.6 billion estate, against her stepson, E. Pierce Marshall, nearly 30 years her senior.

Although Anna Nicole was not mentioned in her husband's will, he allegedly promised her half of his estate if she would marry him. Assuming that he did intend for her to take half of his estate upon his death, was J. Howard Marshall a victim of Anna Nicole's greed? Was he a strong-willed, independent businessman who wanted to go out of this world with a *Playboy* centerfold at his side? Was he angry with his own children, one of whom he intentionally disinherited, because Mr. Marshall believed they were privileged snobs who assumed a right to inherit wealth that they had no role in creating?

Was Mr. Marshall deluded, eccentric, calculating and intentional, or reckless as a man would be facing a hereafter where material wealth is unimportant? Or was he simply unconcerned about what happened to his wealth once he no longer needed it? We will never know. But the decade-long court battle and the public opinion polls reveal more about the psychology of the living than the character of the dead. Speculation has been rampant that Anna Nicole was a gold-digger who flaunted the ideals of true love, and Smith's name will always be associated with the worst form of marrying for lucre. Yet how many people in the history of time have, by choice or circumstance or even force, placed economic motives higher than true love? We even refer to marriage in economic terms, as a *partnership* and expect each spouse to *endow* the other with his or her worldly goods. What were J. Howard's intentions and were they *unduly* influenced by Anna Nicole?

As you no doubt realize from watching a single season of network television, countless family situations, emotions, and events can affect donative intentions. Second and third marriages often create terrible rifts between children of a prior spouse and the surviving widow (it is usually the widow who survives, though not always). When mom or dad remarries and bestows gifts on a second spouse, many children feel slighted. Is it because they feel the second spouse is imposing on the loneliness and kindness of mom or dad, or because they feel secretly guilty that they care more about their inheritance than their parent's happiness?

The good estate lawyer needs to ferret out the underlying emotions and potential family rifts before an estate plan can be successful. And be conscious that furthering your client's intentions means being able to distinguish true from false intentions. If a client walks in and suddenly seeks to change a long-standing estate plan, what should you do to protect your client's right to change her mind and her right not to be subjected to duress or undue influence? Distinguishing between true and false intentions can only happen if you have a thorough knowledge of your client and take the time to build a relationship of trust.

1. GIFTS TESTAMENTARY AND GIFTS *INTER VIVOS*

There are a number of important issues to consider when distinguishing *testamentary* gifts (those that are made at the giver's death) from *inter vivos* gifts (those made during the giver's life). In this course we generally focus on three characteristics of gifts, remembering that gifts underlie basically everything we do in this area of succession law.

1. Were the elements of a valid gift met—i.e. did the giver form the intent to make a gift to the recipient and did the giver actually do so through delivery and acceptance?
2. Was the giver's intent to make an immediate *inter vivos* gift, a postponed testamentary gift, or perhaps a conditional gift *causa mortis*?

   3.   Was the giver subject to any fraud, undue influence, or did she simply change her mind regarding that gift?

Let's think first about the elements. Usually, the *inter vivos* gift requires all three elements be met at the time the gift is made. Thus, the birthday present wrapped and delivered to the birthday boy is a valid gift upon acceptance by the recipient. Possession of the item was transferred, the item was accepted, and the giver had the intent to make an irrevocable gift. The fact that the recipient may not have wanted socks or underwear does not change the nature of the gift. If the recipient does not like the gift, he may pass it along to someone else, or return it to the giver if the giver agrees to retake possession. *Inter vivos* gifts of presently possessory property interests, therefore, fit the typical requirements of a gift. But note that if the recipient doesn't like the socks and gives them back, there are two transfers of the property. And since each transfer of property can give rise to tax liabilities, you need to start thinking now about whether a completed gift has been made and whether you can achieve the same goals with fewer transfers.

Tax Tip: Three-Card Monte[34]

The current tax laws in the U.S. resemble the game of 3 Card Monte, only arguably without the con men. Once you understand the basic categories and parameters, you can begin to shuffle your client's property to minimize tax liabilities. First, taxes generally accrue upon the transfer of property from one person or entity to another. Transfers can be either gratuitous (i.e. gifts), non-gratuitous (i.e. transfers for value, like sales or contracts for services), or a hybrid (e.g. a sale for less than the full market value, which is part non-gratuitous and part gift). In this class we are focusing on the gratuitous transfer and its tax implications. Taxes on non-gratuitous transfers are things like income taxes, sales taxes, capital gains taxes, and others.

Taxes that accrue on the gratuitous transfer of property are called, quite cleverly, *transfer taxes*. But only some gratuitous transfers are taxable while others are not. Gifts to a spouse and to qualified charities are not taxed (this is accomplished through either a deduction, an exemption, or a credit—which differences we discuss more fully in Chapter 9). In addition, money spent on someone's college tuition or medical expenses are non-taxable gratuitous transfers. And small gifts, like a pair of socks or a remote-controlled car, that are too small to be worth the administrative costs of keeping track of them, are exempted through an annual exclusion amount in the neighborhood of $14,000 per year.

The tax rate on gratuitous transfers is generally the same regardless of whether the gift is made during life or at death, although the transfer taxes may be called different things, like *gift taxes*, *estate taxes*, or *generation skipping transfer taxes,* and complex rules buried in the multiple volumes of the Internal Revenue Code and its Regulations will govern the details of the taxation of the transfer. As a general rule, however, the federal government only taxes the transferor (the person

---

[34] These tax tips will occur throughout the book and are meant to reflect general principles and issues, and are not meant to replace a comprehensive course in the taxation of gratuitous transfers, income tax, or any of the many other important tax classes that you might want to take. The Internal Revenue Code is long and complex, and its Regulations are even longer. Moreover, with the fluctuations in tax laws of recent years, it's difficult to speak with any certainty about many aspects of the tax regime in the U.S. But the basic categories and principles, that are grossly oversimplified here, should be kept in the back of your mind as you work through the material in this course.

gifting the property) and not the transferee (the person receiving the gift). States may also tax the transferee through inheritance taxes, or the transferor through state estate taxes, but state tax laws are too diverse to focus on here.

So three points should be jumping out at you. The first is that if there is the possibility of a tax liability accruing as a result of a gratuitous transfer of property, you will want to minimize the number of transfers necessary to get the property from the owner to the final recipient. If grandma has a set of priceless Chinese Ming vases and she wants them to go to her favorite granddaughter at her death, it would be silly for grandma to give them to her son and then ask him to give them to his daughter. Or, if grandma wills the vases to her son, but her daughter really wants them, we don't generally want the property to pass from grandma to the son, and then from the son to the daughter. So reducing the number of transfers can be very important.

That leads to the second point, which has to do with valuation. Transfer taxes are based on the value of the property being transferred at the time of transfer. Thus, you will need to begin to think about how fluctuations in the value of property might affect whether a client should make a gift during life, or wait until death. Because taxes may be due on the increased value of certain property (like capital gains taxes), you have to pay attention to the tax consequences of many gratuitous transfers.

That leads to the third point, which is how you shuffle the gift pack. If for valuation reasons a donor wants to give away valuable property during life, but she still wants to have the benefit of the use of the property for the rest of her life, she needs to figure out a way to make a gift that looks like a transfer but may not require giving up possession. Or she may want to give it away now but actually have it look like title to the property didn't pass until her death, or some later point. The IRS is logically going to be skeptical of so-called gifts that don't really look like gifts. So understanding what actions are required to make a completed gift, putting that together with an understanding of how the value of the property may motivate the timing of the gift, and understanding the tax liabilities of the type of gift is necessary for advising clients about the different options they have when they are thinking of transferring property gratuitously to another.

We discuss taxes in greater detail in Chapter 9. For now, realize that the timing and number of gifts is as important as the value of the the items being given.

Complications arise when the item is too big to fit in a gift-box, is intangible, is illegal, or is not yet in existence. How does one give away land, or a car still owned by the bank, ownership interest in a business, or future royalties on one's book? Typically, the law allows for *constructive delivery* (such as the deed to the land or the keys to the car). Further, the law permits one to make an authentic statement of intention to *presently* give the legal rights to *future* property so long as the property is in existence or there are legally recognizable rights to the property. For example, I can make an *inter vivos* gift of future mortgage payments or rights in a cooperative apartment before the coop board approves the transfer. I can also make an *inter vivos* gift of the future royalties on my production, if any, of a Broadway show that isn't yet written.[35] But I cannot generally make a gift

---

[35] Jennings v. Cutler, 672 A.2d 1215 (App.Div. 1996) (a mortgage can be the subject of a gift even though the payments will occur in the future); Chiaro v. Chiaro, 213 A.D.2d 369 (2d Dept. 1995) (as can a cooperative apartment that isn't yet in existence); Will of Katz, 142 Misc.2d 1073. (N.Y.Surr.Ct.1989) (the cooperative apartment's board hasn't yet voted to ap-

of property that is not in existence, like the next masterpiece I might paint or the vast wealth I am hoping to earn next year speculating in the stock market. And I may not be able to make a gift of certain property if it is against public policy, like a gift of genetic material for assisted reproduction, an AK–47, or a case of vodka to my 16-year-old nephew.[36]

There is generally no reason not to recognize the gift of future property if we can be adequately convinced that the giver had the intention of making a gift at the *present time* of property *to be acquired in the future.* For instance, I might want to sign away a big inheritance I am likely to receive from an elderly relative before I get divorced and have to produce evidence of all my assets to the court to determine how much alimony I am going to owe my soon-to-be ex-spouse. Gifting future property can have all sorts of tax and creditor implications.

Affixing the recipient's name on the legal documents identifying ownership of property is a typical indication of intent to make a gift, especially when those documents are recorded or handed to the recipient. But signing a deed transferring the farm to one's daughter is *not* a valid transfer if the deed is retained by the donor and placed in his safe deposit box to be recorded only after his death. The daughter is in an especially precarious position if dad does not transfer possession of the farm to her before he dies by making delivery of the deed or possession of the land itself.

Testamentary gifts are gifts that become effective upon death. There are several reasons why people would rather not make *inter vivos* gifts when they can make testamentary gifts, not the least being the ability to change their mind. A *will* is a *testamentary* document expressing the writer's intent to devise gifts of her property to certain beneficiaries, but she retains control and ownership of that property until her death. A great advantage in making a will is that it can be changed at any time before death if the testator alters her intent about who should benefit from her property.

Because the testamentary gift is not valid until the donor's death, beneficiaries under a will have no legally-enforceable property rights to the items listed in the will (remember *Hodel v. Irving*?). At most, the beneficiary has an unvested, inchoate, interest in the property covered by the will, subject to the will's not being revoked. It is an *expectancy.* A testator has no duty to the beneficiaries of a will. She may change her mind, waste the property, or give it to another recipient. J. Howard Marshall had no legal obligation to leave any property to his son, despite that son's devotion to his father's interests.

Also, delivery and acceptance are not usually made prior to death and thus are not necessary elements of a valid testamentary gift. Instead, the donor must form an intent to make a valid testamentary gift, comply with the requisite will formalities manifesting that intent, and not subsequently revoke that intent. The will formalities require that *the will must be in writing, signed, witnessed, and the testator must be of sound mind and appropriate age* to be effective precisely because delivery and acceptance are not present to signify the Testator's intent—see Chapter 4A. Testamentary intent, therefore, is the most important issue to be decided in most will

---

prove the transfer it is still complete); Speelman v. Pascal, 10 N.Y.2d 303 (1961) (regarding the future royalties on My Fair Lady).

[36] *In re* Est. of Kievernagel, 166 Cal.App.4th 1024 (Cal. App. 3 Dist. 2008).

challenges. The testator must have formed the intent to make the particular testamentary disposition reflected in her will, be free from the undue influence or fraudulent pressure of others, she must have the mental capacity to form the intent to make a gift, and she must comprehend that she is making a gift (an uncompensated transfer of property) that will become effective upon her death. Finally, she must not revoke her will or otherwise dispose of the property prior to her death.

If the will is deemed valid, the executor or personal representative of the decedent's estate is responsible for making delivery of the property (actual delivery or executing the necessary documents to transfer title) but, as with *inter vivos* gifts, the recipient is not required to accept the gift. Whether the gift is an ugly painting, great-grandma's salt and pepper shaker collection, the inoperable model-A Ford, ownership in an unprofitable business, or stock in companies that have deplorable environmental records, a recipient can always refuse a gift. No reason is required to refuse *any* gift.

Most donees simply dispose of the worthless 8-track tape collections, or donate grandpa's 1950s bowling shirts to the consignment shop if they don't want to keep the stuff left to them in a will. Such actions are of little consequence for property that has fairly low value. But property that is very valuable can have tax consequences if the recipient accepts the items only to pass them on to others. Hence, many people might opt to *disclaim* the property rather than accept it, causing the property to pass to successor beneficiaries or back to the donor's estate, usually people the recipient would have given the property to anyway. We discuss disclaimers more extensively in Chapter 5.

Distinguishing between testamentary and *inter vivos* gifts is very important. If a donor intends to make an *inter vivos* gift but fails to make delivery properly, the gift fails and the property remains in the ownership of the donor. It then likely will pass to devisees under the donor's will where it will be included in the probate of the donor's estate. Similarly, if a donor intends to make certain testamentary gifts and the will fails for one reason or another, the gifts fail and the property passes by the default rules of intestate succession to the donor's legal heirs. Getting the gift wrong can have significant consequences, certainly to the donee who doesn't receive the hoped-for gift, but also for the donor whose estate may face higher taxes or probate costs associated with the failed gift. At the same time, if a gift fails, someone else, not the intended beneficiary, will get it and that person will likely be willing to exploit every legal argument to make sure the intended gift isn't effective.

2. GIFTS *CAUSA MORTIS*

Gifts *causa mortis*, as above mentioned, are *inter vivos* gifts made in anticipation of death. They do not require the will formalities of a testamentary gift because they entail immediate transfers of possession. However, they are made on the legally-implied condition that the giver must die in the near future from whatever peril motivated the gift. Gifts *causa mortis* are therefore revocable if the giver survives the delicate brain surgery, returns from hiking Mt. Everest, or survives the suicide mission assigned by his commanding officer. Gifts *causa mortis* often are made on the spur of the moment by those facing imminent death, and can be made by handing over one's wedding ring, car keys or safe deposit box key, or by writing a letter or making an oral declaration. Gifts *causa mortis*, however, require the donor give up possession in a manner appropriate to the property.

Gifts *causa mortis* can be particularly problematic, however, when the dying person is not able to hand over possession of the actual items. Usually there are few witnesses to the decedent's instructions, and people very near death may not be lucid enough to clearly think about final dispositions of property. While such sad cases typically are limited to property physically on the decedent's person, there may be instances where a dying patient might instruct her doctors and nurses that she is giving all her worldly possessions to the patient in the bed next to her or the hospital chaplain who just visited. Because gifts made in the last few moments of life closely resemble testamentary gifts, judges are reluctant to validate last minute gestures of generosity.[37] This is particularly true if the dying patient has left a valid will which contradicts the death-bed disposition of that patient's personal property.

Gifts causa mortis are often challenged in three circumstances: 1) when the gift is so close to death as to essentially constitute a testamentary gift that would be invalid for lacking the will formalities, 2) when the giver recovers and wishes to revoke the gift, and 3) when the giver dies shortly after making the gift, but not by the feared cause. Usually, in the case of a typical *inter vivos* gift, the donor parts with possession at a time and in a manner that makes it clear that the gift was intended to be permanent. Gifts *causa mortis*, however, are often made in circumstances where one could reasonably argue the donor was not lucid or did not relinquish full possession and, if the gift fails, then intestate takers or will devisees will get the property instead. With the donor deceased, such disputes often turn into he-said, she-said conflicts that can have quite substantial financial implications for the winners and losers.

Consider the following cases and whether you believe the court was correct in its determination of the type of gift that was intended.

Convy v. Loftin

970 So.2d 104, 2007–668 (La.App. 3 Cir. 2007)

In anticipation of their son's wedding, James and Beth Convy gave the couple $20,000 for a down payment and furnishings for a house. Seven weeks after their elaborate wedding, the son moved out and left the state while their daughter-in-law continued to reside in the home. They eventually divorced, never having resumed cohabitation. The Convys sued to revoke the $20,000 gift. The trial court did not find grounds for revocation. Citing Louisiana Civil Code Article 1559 that an *inter vivos* donation may only be revoked due to ingratitude of the donee, the non-fulfillment of a suspensive condition, the non-performance of a potestative condition, or the legal or conventional return, the court of appeals affirmed. The court stated: *In order to revoke a donation for ingratitude, the donor must show that the donee attempted to take the donor's life, has refused the donor food when he was in distress, or the donee has been guilty of cruel treatment, crimes, or*

---

[37] Mortmain statutes were passed in the eighteenth century to prevent overreaching by charitable and religious organizations preying on the weak and dying. These have been abolished, but the law against overreaching remains. See discussion of Mortmain Statutes in Chapter 10B. Noncharitable organizations or private individuals who prey on dying donors may find their gifts voided for a variety of reasons, from lack of donative intent to fraud and duress to undue influence. For more on these doctrines, see Chapter 11.

grievous injuries toward the donor. La.Civ.Code Art. 1560. After reviewing the record, we find no error in the trial court's conclusion that there is no basis for revocation based on ingratitude. In response to the argument that the gift should be subject to the condition that the parties would remain married, the court stated: *Clearly, the donation was not subject to a suspensive condition of a long marriage, because the donation was made prior to the actual marriage and, thus, could not be the basis for revocation. See La.Civ.Code art. 1565.*

Query: Should there be a presumption that wedding gifts are revocable if the marriage dissolves within the first year? If engagement rings can be revoked, why not wedding gifts?

Samuel v. Northern Trust Co.

34 Ill.App.3d 500, 340 N.E.2d 162 (Ill. App. Ct. 1st Dist. 1975)

Suffering from cirrhosis of the liver, *the decedent, Alfred C. Knudson, told the plaintiff,* Bernyce Samuel, *that he had set aside money for her in his safe deposit box.* Shortly after his death, *an envelope marked 'Property of Bee (the plaintiff's nickname) Samuel', containing $10,000 in cash was found in the decedent's safe deposit box. The words 'Property of' were form-printed and were followed by the hand-printed name 'Bee Samuel'. The name, 'Alfred C. Knudson' was written on the envelope. The decedent's will did not mention the plaintiff; and the executor included the money in the envelope as part of the assets of the estate.* Samuel sued the executor claiming the money was a gift *causa mortis.* The court held that to be a gift *causa mortis,* the following conditions must be met: *The donor must be stricken with some disorder which makes death imminent; death of the donor must ensue as a result of the disorder existing at the time the gift was made without any intervening perfect recovery; the gift must have been made to take effect only in the event of the donor's death by his existing disorder; and there must have been an actual delivery of the subject of the donation to the donee.* The court found that no effective gift was made because neither actual nor constructive delivery had occurred. *The thing must be delivered to the donee or a third person for the donee's benefit in such a way that the donor parts with all control over it. The only act of delivery that can be inferred from the allegations is the placing of the money in a safe deposit box in an envelope with the plaintiff's name on it. The decedent did not give the key to the safe deposit box to the plaintiff nor to any third party in her behalf; nor did the decedent give any written authority to the plaintiff or anyone else to exercise control over the box. At any time the decedent could have gone into the box and disposed of the money in any way he saw fit. Thus, he did not part with all control over the money and thus did not make a delivery. While it appears that the decedent intended that the plaintiff receive this property, intent alone is not sufficient proof of a gift Causa mortis.* Gift denied.

Query: How should the decedent have indicated his intent that the plaintiff would receive this money? Could the money be an intended testamentary gift that would therefore not require delivery? If not, why?

Hatcher v. Buford

27 L.R.A. 507, 60 Ark. 169, 29 S.W. 641 (Ark. 1895)

T. A. Hatcher, a prosperous merchant of Forrest City, Ark., died December 10, 1891. He left a widow, M. E. Hatcher, who seeks to have her dower interest include a share of property he purportedly gifted prior to his death. *About one month before his death, Hatcher directed his agent to buy $4,000 of bank stock, and, about 10 days before, $1,000 more. This stock was issued in the name of his sister Mrs. Buford, and was delivered by Hatcher's agent to her son Walter. Hatcher made a will, in which, among other bequests, was a provision for his wife, and Mrs. Buford was declared residuary legatee and devisee.* The law on dower stated that: *A widow shall be entitled, as a part of her dower, absolutely and in her own right to one-third part of the personal estate, including cash on hand, bonds, bills, notes, book accounts and evidences of debt whereof the husband died seised or possessed.* The question for the court was whether the donor was seised or possessed of the bank stock at the time of his death or had he given up possession to his sister?

The court explained: *The terms 'seised' or 'possessed,' as thus used with reference to personalty, mean simply ownership, which carries with it the actual possession, or a right to the immediate possession. The real inquiry, then, is as to when the title or property in the subject-matter of a* donatio causa mortis *passes. We are aware that there is conflict and confusion in the authorities upon this point, doubtless growing out of the modes of* donatio causa mortis *recognized originally by the Roman jurisprudence, whence the doctrine is derived. Under one of these, the subject-matter of the gift became at once the property of the donee, but on condition that he should return it to the donor in the event of his recovery. Under another, the gift was made upon condition that the thing given should become the property of the donee only in the event of the donor's death. Under the former, delivery was essential; under the latter, it was not.* Following Justinian, the court believed the latter definition was the proper one. *We think the better doctrine upon the transfer of the title to gifts* causa mortis *is that which accords with Justinian's definition, and recognizes the subject-matter of the gift as becoming the property of the donee in the event of the donor's death; i. e. the donor's death is a condition precedent to the vesting of the title to the thing given in the donee. This seems to be the rule adopted by the English courts of chancery, and is supported also by eminent American courts and text writers.*

Because gifts *causa mortis* consequently look an awful lot like testamentary gifts, the court further explained: *Many authorities do speak of the* donatio causa mortis *as but another form of testamentary disposition, and liken it unto the testamentary disposition, for the reason that it is revocable during the donor's life, is subject to his debts if there be a deficiency of assets, and does not become an absolute gift until the donor's death. But while, in these particulars, it resembles a testamentary disposition, it differs from it, in that the subject-matter of the gift is delivered to the donee during the life of the donor, and at his death does not pass into the hands of the executor or administrator, but remains with the donee. This is not because the property or title has passed to the donee during the life of the donor, or that the donor is not actually seised in law at the time of his death, but because it is one of the peculiar characteristics of this species of gift that, at the donor's death, the donee takes, instead of the heir, according to the intention of the donor, as manifested during his life by delivery to the donee.* The court then held that the decedent could not use a gift *causa mortis* to defeat the widow's dower.

Query: If the gift *causa mortis* is interpreted to convey the property rights at the time of delivery, then it is essentially an irrevocable *inter vivos gift*. In contrast, if the gift *causa mortis* is interpreted to convey the property rights only at death, despite a transfer of actual possession, then it resembles a testamentary gift. Is there a valid reason for allowing gifts *causa mortis* if the court interprets them to be subject to the decedent's debts and spousal forced shares just like testamentary gifts?

Huskins v. Huskins

134 N.C. App. 101, 517 S.E.2d 146 (N.C. App. 1999)

In September 1996, David H. Huskins mailed an envelope to his son Scott containing a check payable to his wife, Elizabeth V. Huskins, in the amount of $220,000.00. *The envelope also contained a handwritten note which gave the combination to a safe in their apartment with the statement, "the contents belong to your mother" underneath the combination. In addition, a separate entry on the note stated "cash the check before my will is probated."* Later that day Huskins committed suicide. Four days after his death, Huskins' wife and children opened the safe, with the combination provided by the housekeeper, and found approximately $220,000.00 in cash. The next day, Scott returned to his home in Georgia and received the envelope mailed by his father containing the check payable to his mother and the combination to the safe. Huskins' will gave all his household furnishings to his wife, then established two trusts for the benefit of his wife and children with the residue. Elizabeth Huskins claims that the amount of the check should not be placed in the trust pursuant to the will (and subject only to her life estate) but is hers outright as an *inter vivos* gift. The court found that the evidence was ambiguous, that *there was some evidence of donative intent from the written notation that 'the contents belong to your mother.'. . . There is, however, a serious question about whether mailing the combinations and the note to Scott was a constructive delivery of the contents of the safe to Mrs. Huskins. Had the combinations of the safe and the accompanying note been mailed to Mrs. Huskins, or left for her in the apartment which she shared with decedent, her argument would be far stronger.* The court concluded that *there was no valid delivery of the contents of the safe. While we agree with Mrs. Huskins that one cannot easily deliver a safe, that same consideration does not apply to the delivery of the contents of the safe, especially when the parties in this case resided together in the apartment in which the safe was located. Considering the large amount of money found in the safe, decedent could have also delivered the combinations directly to Mrs. Huskins with an express statement of his intent that she have the contents.*

Query: Would a decedent do better to make *inter vivos gifts* directly to the recipient, rather than dictate his intent through a third party who can attest to the decedent's donative intent?

Matter of Wilson

26 Misc. 2d 839, 206 N.Y.S.2d 323 (N.Y. Sur. Ct. 1960)

In this case, the decedent, who was seriously ill and about to undergo surgery, telephoned the wife of a family friend who was a dealer in jewelry and who was in possession of two valuable pieces of the decedent's jewelry. The decedent told the jeweler's wife to give the jewelry to her sister. When the dealer telephoned the sister the next day to tell her about the jewels, the sister asked the dealer to retain the jewelry until she could fetch them. The decedent died a few days later, before the sister could pick up the jewelry. The question was raised whether delivery and acceptance had occurred. The decedent's will bequeathed all of her property in trust with the income thereof payable to the decedent's sister during her lifetime. Upon the death of the sister the trust remainder would be distributable to six charitable organizations. If the jewelry was deemed a valid *inter vivos* gift, it would not be subject to the trust but would pass to the sister directly. The court held that the gift was a valid *inter vivos* gift to the sister despite the sister pleading that the gift was *causa mortis*. It also held that, because the dealer retained the jewelry upon the instructions of the sister, he acted as an agent for the property owner.

Query: Why was delivery in this case sufficient and not in *Huskins*? Note that in neither case did the decedent speak directly to the recipient of the gift.

Massey v. Hrostek

186 Vt. 211, 980 A.2d 768, 2009 VT 70 (2009)

In November 1996, Daniel Massey and Lucille Hrostek took title in fee simple absolute to their vacation house by warranty deed as joint tenants with rights of survivorship. *Massey, however, paid the entire $270,000 purchase price for the property.* In addition, Massey *paid every expense associated with the property, including all taxes, insurance, utilities, and necessary maintenance costs.* In 2003 the parties' relationship soured and they broke up, at which time Massey changed the locks and alarm codes on the house and denied Hrostek access to the home. In 2004, Massey filed an action to partition the property, and denied that he had given Hrostek any interest in the home. The trial court found that *"[a]lthough [Massey] was the purchaser, he included [Hrostek] as an owner as a sentimental gesture," and that Massey "did not intend this as an outright gift", but only intended that Hrostek would be provided some measure of security if Massey should die while they were still romantically involved. Massey, the court found, "just assumed that" if the parties broke up, Hrostek "would simply sign over the house to him because he had paid for everything." In seeming contrast, however, the court also found that Massey, because of an earlier contentious divorce, "was extremely conservative with putting names on property" and for this reason never had his primary home in Connecticut titled in Hrostek's name.*

The court of appeals reversed, finding that an *inter vivos* gift had been made because *our law establishes a rebuttable presumption 'that the act of titling property in another's name establishes intent to convey a present interest in the property.'* Because the evidence about Massey's intent was ambiguous (he kept Hrostek's name off the primary residence but not the vacation home), the evidence was not enough to rebut the presumption.

Because Massey could have drafted the deed to give them unequal shares, the court attributed half the value of the house to Hrostek, and then offset the maintenance and improvement costs Massey paid against Hrostek's share. Further, Massey was held to have ousted Hrostek when he changed the locks, and therefore Massey's share of the partition proceeds were set off by the rental value of the ousted cotenant's interest for the period of the ouster and he did not receive credit for the expenses incurred during the ouster.

Query: How should the law treat the inclusion of someone's name on a deed as a co-tenant when the prospective co-tenant has not contributed to the purchase price of the property? With a *joint tenancy with right to survivorship*, should the gift be deemed to have occurred at the time the co-tenant's name is added or at the death of the other co-tenant when the right to survivorship results in the survivor taking the entire property? As you will see later, the answer is "it depends." It depends on the intent of the donor and the relationship of the parties.

Worrell v. Lathan

324 S.C. 368, 478 S.E.2d 287 (S.C. Ct. App. 1996)

Barbara Worrell enjoyed a long-term friendship with the decedent, Elizabeth Brisendine. Brisendine often spent time at the beach with Worrell's family. The two ladies saw each other at social events and occasionally travelled together. During Brisendine's terminal illness, Worrell drove Brisendine to and from the hospital and doctors' appointments. On previous occasions, Brisendine had attempted to give Worrell money, but Worrell never accepted it. Worrell visited Brisendine at her home in early September, 1993, during Brisendine's terminal illness. Brisendine wrote a check, made an entry in her checkbook, and attempted to present the check to Worrell. Worrell refused the check, telling Brisendine she looked after her out of friendship and did not desire payment for helping a friend. Brisendine returned the check and checkbook to her pocketbook. Worrell did not see the actual check and she did not know the amount for which it was written. She was later told the check would "be in the mail to [her]."

Brisendine died a few days later, and Worrell thought nothing more about the check until she learned from Brisendine's personal representative that someone had tried to cash a $10,000 check made out to Worrell. Deciding to lay claim to the check, Worrell filed a claim against the estate for $10,000, but it was refused by the personal representative. The trial court denied her claim and the court of appeals affirmed, stating: *Acceptance by the donee of a gift* inter vivos *or causa mortis is generally held to be an essential element of a gift. Acceptance is sufficient if the gift is accepted before revocation by the donor, or before revocation by the death of the donor. In this case, the unexplained circumstances surrounding Worrell's not receiving the check could indicate Brisendine either revoked or intended to revoke the gift before her death. In any event, Brisendine's death effectively revoked the gift.* Citing precedent, the court explained that *[An* inter vivos *gift] operates, if at all, in the donor's lifetime."*

Query: Although courts generally presume acceptance on the part of a donee for property of any sizable value, why didn't the court do so here? Do you think

Brisendine changed her mind or revoked the gift when Worrell declined to take the check? If not, do you think the court reached the right result? Would your opinion change if you learned that the person who tried to cash the check was Brisendine's housekeeper? What if the person was Worrell's mail delivery carrier? What if Brisendine's daughter was her principle heir and beneficiary?

Gartin v. Taylor

577 N.W.2d 410 (Iowa, 1998)

In 1989, John and Ora Gartin loaned their daughter, Carol Taylor, $16,000. There was no promissory note or other writing witnessing the terms of the debt, but Carol made three monthly payments in May, June, and July, 1989, on the loan. After that, no further payments were made. Four years later, in 1993, both John and Ora were placed under conservatorship, and in April, 1994, the conservator commenced an action against Carol for repayment of the debt. Carol claims the loan was forgiven in July, 1989 and her husband testified that he received assurances from Carol's parents in August, 1989 that the loan had been forgiven. Carol also presented a diary entry of her mom's stating "Dad doesn't want her sending checks to repay us." She claims a valid *inter vivos* gift was made of the remainder of the loan. In 1993, however, John Gartin made a will that recognized Carol's obligation under the loan and imposed a timeline subject to a penalty of being disinherited. A later will by John did disinherit Carol.

The trial court held that no effective gift had been made; the court of appeals reversed, and the Iowa Supreme Court reversed again, holding that no effective gift was made. It cited the trial court which had written that: *The court is sympathetic to Carol's position, based on clear evidence of donative intent by her parents. If a valid gift of forgiveness of the loan could be established, it would be irrevocable. The fact that Carol and her parents later developed a strained relationship could not divest Carol of the gift of the loan balance. The gift would be a defense in these proceedings. However, the clear weight of legal authority requires either an instrument in writing to effectuate donative intent when the underlying obligation is oral, or evidence of acts or conduct which operated to place the debt beyond the control of the donors. Here, no such evidence has been presented.* The court further explained: *The court of appeals concluded that the delivery requirement for a completed gift was satisfied by the written notation in Ora's diary. We are persuaded that this is not the case. The diary entry is only that which it purports to be, i.e., an acknowledgment that John Gartin and perhaps Ora Gartin intended to forgive appellant's indebtedness at the time the diary entry was made. As such, it only shows the intention of the obligees, which, standing alone, is insufficient to establish an irrevocable discharge of the obligation.* The problem was lack of delivery. As the court explained: *We are not persuaded that the requirement of delivery should be eliminated with respect to establishing the discharge of duties not based on a legal consideration. To do so would substantially abrogate traditional contract principles.*

Query: Delivery requires both the relinquishment of control by the donor and acceptance of control by the donee. In the case of an oral contract, something beyond intention to forgive the loan was required. What would that have likely been? How many times have you "borrowed" money from your parents with the promise to repay it, only to forget, or have your parent forgive the debt? Did you put any of it in writing? How do you show proof of delivery of an intangible asset? How could you prove intent to forgive the debt?

––––––––––

Courts grapple with identifying what evidence of intent is necessary in order to show whether a gift is *inter vivos, causa mortis,* or testamentary. And since most litigation in this area occurs after the death of the giver, it is particularly difficult to discern with certainty the giver's intent with regard to the gift. In many instances, the most equitable solution for courts is to infer intent from certain *objective* actions and the use of certain legal terms. In other instances, courts rely on presumptions that favor one type of gift or another, even if the presumption results in a ruling that those closest to the decedent believe was not the decedent's true intent.

Courts are especially concerned with fraud, undue influence, insane delusion, incapacity, and misrepresentation when it comes to gifts of all sorts. Consequently, in the case of testamentary gifts, when the decedent cannot correct errors, courts are particularly vigilant about trying to determine whether a will or other testamentary document accurately reflects the testator's true intentions. While delivery and acceptance are critical for *inter vivos* gifts, *all* gifts require *donative intent.*

Considering the cases above, what evidence of intent do you think was most reliable? In which cases would you be most suspicious of the evidence of the testator's intent?

PROBLEMS

1.1. Grandma Cleda mails a surprise present to her niece, Sasha, whom she lost contact with 15 years ago. Sasha signs for the package but later, when she notices the return address, she marks "return to sender" and promptly drops the unopened package off at the shipper. A few days later, Sasha receives a call from her cousin who says, "I can't believe you sent back Grandma Cleda's necklace! She is heartbroken. And, there was one on Antiques Roadshow just like it that appraised for over One Hundred and Fifty Thousand Dollars!" Horrified, Sasha suddenly feels remorseful and calls Grandma Cleda but no one answers the phone. She leaves a message on voicemail stating that she very much wants the necklace—and, that, of course, she loves her Grandma. The following day, Grandma Cleda dies. Her will leaves her entire estate to her friend Marcus. Who gets the necklace?

1.2. Bill shows his three adult children his will, so that they can see that he is leaving his house and bank accounts to them in equal shares. After the meeting, the three children agree that since they own the home now, the best thing for their dad would be to sell it and move him into a studio apartment. Dad catches wind of this and says he has no intention of moving. Can the children force him out?

1.3. Keri and Tom race motorcycles as amateurs. Five minutes before their race, Keri gathers a group of fellow racers together and says, arm around Tom's shoulder, "You know if I die out there today, I want this man to get all the bikes I own." Among the by-standers, Steve says to Kevin, "Same to you, buddy," much to the delight of the crowd. During the race, Keri and Steve are involved in an accident which Keri does not survive. Steve miraculously walks away unscathed, but while driving his truck home from the track, however, he has a heart attack and dies. Who receives their bikes?

1.4. Clarence drafted a will in 2009 which left his entire estate to his temple. Shortly thereafter, he became ill and was tended to with constant attention and care by a nurse named Pat. In hospice, hours before his death, he gave the doctor a check made out to Pat in the amount of $100,000.00. The memo line stated "for all you have done for me." He instructed the doctor to "give this check to Pat," who was out running an errand. Clarence died. An hour later, Pat arrived and was handed the check by the doctor. Is she entitled to the money?

1.5. Minka owns a coffee shop. She sends the following group message to three college buddies who are her Friends on Facebook: "Just saw a commercial trying to sell a will for $59.95. I need to do that. You guys know that if something happens to me, that I want you to have the shop, right?" A week later, Minka is killed in an automobile accident. She dies without a will. Do the friends get the coffee shop?

1.6. Ted tells his friend Garrett over the phone that he is giving Garrett his grill. Garrett replies, "Perfect! Thanks, man. I will pick it up this weekend." On Thursday, Ted dies unexpectedly. His will directs that "any grill and patio furniture in my possession at the time of my death shall go to my daughter Kylie." Who gets the grill?

1.7. Marta is in critical care. Her son brings in a document and 2 witnesses, asking Marta to sign. She does. Then, Marta asks, "What was that?" Her son replies, "Mom, this just makes sure everything goes smoothly in case you don't make it." Marta looks relieved, but one of the more observant witnesses asks her, "Marta, are you sure this is what you want?" Marta says yes and drifts off to sleep. She passes away later that day. The document, entitled "Last Will and Testament," specifically disinherits Marta's three daughters and leaves the entire estate to her only son. What do you think the result would be?

1.8. Apply the reasoning in *Samuel vs. Northern Trust Co.* to the following scenario: Aunt Alex tells her niece she wants her to have all the money in her savings account as a graduation gift since her niece just finished college. She gives her niece her debit card but neglects to give her the PIN. Aunt Alex dies that night. Aunt Alex's will divides everything between her three children, but the savings account is the only asset of significant value. Is her niece entitled to the money in the account?

C. LIMITATIONS ON DONATIVE FREEDOM

Despite grand judicial statements about the importance of donative freedom, every state has legislated numerous restraints on the dead hand, i.e., on a decedent's ability to fully control testamentary, and sometimes even *inter vivos*, gifts. The most obvious are the default rules of intestate succession. A decedent who dies without making any testamentary gifts (through a will, trust, joint tenancy, or other will substitute) will find her estate passes according to strict mathematical percentages to spouses and/or relatives by blood or adoption (usually children and parents before siblings or other collateral relatives.) Although we don't consider the rules of intestate succession to be limitations *per se* on donative freedom, they will govern regardless of testamentary intent if the donor fails to make a will or it fails to meet the strict requirements for validity.

There are numerous other restrictions on donative freedom, even for testators who execute valid wills. The most common restriction on the testator is the *elective share* (the modern version of dower), the right of a spouse to take a statutorily-set percentage of a decedent's estate, often as much as one-half, even if the decedent expressly wanted to leave her spouse less than that amount. Depending on the state, the spouse may be entitled to one-half of a decedent's probate estate, the property owned by the decedent at death, even if the decedent provided ample life insurance, joint tenancy property, or made lifetime gifts to her spouse that exceeded her entire probate estate. In Chapter 7 we discuss elective shares in more detail; just be aware now that spouses have very extensive rights in a decedent's estate in large part because lawmakers assume a spouse contributed significantly to the accumulation of marital wealth.[38]

Nine states are community property states (Arizona, California, Idaho, Louisiana, Nevada, New Mexico, Texas, Washington and Wisconsin.) And Alaska, Puerto Rico, and some Indian nations allow people to opt into a community property regime. In community property states, most property acquired during the marriage is owned jointly by the spouses, with each owning an undivided one-half interest that is freely alienable during life and devisable at death. Thus, one-half of each spouse's income during the marriage is owned by the other during life, and thus can be devised by that spouse at death. If a wife has a 50% ownership interest in all of her husband's property acquired during the marriage, the husband will be free to devise his remaining 50% (plus 50% of the property his wife acquired in which he has an interest) upon his death to anyone, free of claims by the wife. To some extent, this is an overgeneralization; no two community property states have exactly the same rules. Some states presume that income from property owned prior to marriage, and held separately during the marriage, is also separate property. Others states presume that same income is community property.[39] Some states permit the first spouse to die to freely devise his or her share of the community property. Still other states permit the parties to designate the community property as having a right of survivorship in the surviving spouse. This right of survivorship negates the ability of the decedent spouse to devise the property away from the surviving spouse. But community property laws, like the elective share, significantly restrict the donative freedom of married persons.

One state, Louisiana, provides for mandatory inheritances for both children and spouses. In Louisiana, 25% (if there is one qualified child) or 50% (if there is more than one qualified child) of a decedent's estate must pass to qualified children—children under 24, disabled children of any age, and certain grandchildren. Decedents are legally incapable of devising this

---

[38] There are two theories generally cited for why a surviving spouse should be entitled to a share of a deceased spouse's estate. The first is the partnership theory that protects a surviving spouse's interest is the deceased spouse's estate because both spouses worked in tandem to create the wealth. The second is the support theory, which simply provides a surviving spouse with sufficient wealth to support the survivor until her own death. The latter arises from the common law doctrine that husbands were legally bound to support their wives, even after their own death.

[39] Gifts, inheritances, and property owned separately before marriage may be held separately even after marriage. However, complications arise when separate property, such as a business, increases in value during the marriage due to the efforts of both spouses, or if there is an addition of community assets to the separate property. The basic community property regime is a form of protection for spouses and operates as a significant barrier to donative freedom. In Chapter 2 we discuss community property on a more detailed basis.

portion of their estate, called the *legitime*.[40] There are also strict rules allowing certain lifetime gifts to be voided because the gifts reduced the le-legitime.

In Florida, decedents with minor children are entirely unable to devise their homestead. Homestead is defined by the Florida Constitution as the family home or 160 acres of rural land with a farmhouse. Instead, the homestead must descend to the descendants jointly, reserving a life estate to a surviving spouse.[41] Homestead protections are prevalent in most states, though Florida provides one of the most generous. But even in the majority of states, homestead protections mean that a testator is excluded from devising either the real property or cash that is set aside by homestead laws to permit the family to remain in the family home. In Chapter 2 we explore homestead more fully. But recognize that homestead acts as another limitation on donative freedom in many instances.

In addition to the homestead, most states have adopted rules allowing close family members, usually spouses and/or children, the right to take a sum of money from the decedent's estate for support during the administration of the decedent's estate. There also are rules that exempt certain property from testation—cars, tools of a trade, or certain other personal property usually limited to a certain cash value. Family allowances and exempt property are first subtracted from a decedent's estate before even payment of the personal representative or the lawyer. The effect of such protections is to disable decedents from devising this property away from the family.

A person who divorces his spouse, but dies before changing a will that leaves property to the spouse, will not see his estate pass as he directed, because the divorced spouse will be excluded from taking under the will by operation of law. Children born after a will is made are typically given a statutory share of a parent's estate, even if the will purports to leave the property to others. In Chapter 7 we discuss pretermitted spouses and children. A pretermitted child or spouse is one who is not mentioned in a will because the will was written before the marriage or birth of the child. But the law mandates that the spouse or children receive a forced share despite the absence of such a provision in the will. These events can profoundly change a testamentary plan and may often go against a decedent's donative intent.

There are other limitations on donative freedom that are not related to family protections, but rather reflect the likely intentions of most testators. Thus, even if a decedent devises all of his estate to his son, the son will not be entitled to take *any* property if he kills his father in order to speed up his inheritance. And even such arcane rules as the Rule Against Perpetuities frustrates donative freedom when testators wish to establish future interests that might take too long to vest in a beneficiary.

It is not an exaggeration to say that many testators want complete, unbridled freedom to devise their estates to whomever they choose, regardless of marital or affinal relationships. Testators generally feel they are quite capable of providing for the people for whom they have affection, and believe they should be able to dictate where *their* property will go upon

---

[40] LA. CIV. CODE ANN. art. 1493 (1996).

[41] FLA. CONST. art. X, § 4(c); FLA. STAT. Ann. § 732.401 (West 1974). The Florida homestead law was revised in 2010 to give a surviving spouse a right to elect a half share of the homestead, rather than a life estate in the whole, even if there are minor children.

their death. Most testators also choose to leave the lion's share of their estates to their spouses and/or children, and when they deviate from that norm, they usually have fairly good reasons for doing so. They might be in a short second or third marriage and may wish to leave most of their property to their children and not to their spouse, or *vice versa*. Some testators feel that they don't need to provide for their spouses because the latter have sufficient wealth of their own; others would rather provide for spouses because their children are all capable adults who don't need handouts. However, the laws of all states limit the ability of testators to freely devise their property, completely without regard for family relationships and family needs.[42] It seems that most lawmakers, despite desiring unbridled donative freedom themselves, believe others are not trustworthy enough to provide adequately for those who are legally dependent on them.

All states also limit devises that are against public policy, are punitive, or are illegal ("I give $50,000 to whoever kills my ex-spouse"). Donative freedom is a myth even when it comes to opting out of the default rules of intestate succession if the opt-out method fails. And when we consider estate taxes, or limitations on certain kinds of trusts or other testamentary mechanisms, the myth of donative freedom is truly shattered. And yet we still believe it is best to allow testators at least a portion of their estates to devise as they choose.

This limited donative freedom is particularly important for non-traditional or blended families, gay and lesbian families, and for people who elect to donate their wealth to support unpopular political or public causes. Such a testator may find his estate challenged and his mental capacity questioned when he disinherits his children to leave everything to his mistress, or to an unpopular coalition or association. But the freedom to leave one's wealth to one's gay partner, rather than one's disapproving parents, is a critical value which underlies donative freedom. Thus, in evaluating the rules of estate administration and distribution, we must balance the various mechanisms available to testators to structure their giving as they choose, against certain rules that tip the balance in favor of family protections. These rules can have devastating intended or unintended effects on close family members. These rules also can frustrate the non-traditional testator, who wishes full donative freedom to devise her property as she wishes. It is the job of the estate lawyer to maximize testamentary flexibility with the appropriate family protections and minimize the risk of estate litigation.

PROBLEMS

How might donative freedom be affected in the following situations?

1.9. Chen's 2006 will leaves his entire estate to his wife. In 2009, they divorced but he neglected to change his will prior to his death in 2011.

1.10. Drake's 2006 will leaves his entire estate to his wife. In 2011, he files for divorce and executes a new will leaving his entire estate to his sister. He dies before the divorce is final.

1.11. Tera drafts a will at a time when she is single with no children which leaves her entire estate to charity. She later adopts twins but dies before execution of a new will.

---

[42] See Chapter 7 on the Elective Share.

1.12. Ashley has terminal lung cancer and is in extensive pain. Her will leaves all her property to her husband, Brad. One night, when the pain is particularly bad, Ashley convinces Brad to put cyanide in her morphine drip so she can end her life on her terms. He does so.

1.13. Ted Kaczynski, the Unabomber, leaves all the royalties from his Manifesto, worth about $2 million, to anyone who will:

    a.   assassinate the President,

    b.   assassinate the Director of the FBI,

    c.   assassinate the judge who sentenced him to prison,

    d.   assassinate the warden of the prison in which he resides,

    e.   write a book advocating the violent overthrow of the government.

————————

We will discuss all of these limitations on donative freedom in much greater detail as we progress through our study of the law of succession. For now, keep your eyes open for arguments that limit donative freedom either to benefit the living, or to promote public policy. In particular, ask yourself whether they are justified and, perhaps more importantly, whether they mask unacceptable stereotypes or disadvantage disfavored groups. One of the most staggering statistics is that as many as 70% of today's children are being raised in non-traditional families.[43] To the extent our succession laws remain mired in 1950s attitudes protecting traditional family relationships, they will disadvantage millions of innocent people. As we think about donative freedom and limitations on donative freedom in the name of family protections, we must cast a critical glance at whose interests are being promoted and whose interests are being limited.

D. CHANGING DEFINITIONS OF FAMILY

We tend to think we know what is meant by "family." They are those with whom you spend Thanksgiving. If you don't do so, they are the people who can make you feel guilty for years. But legal definitions of family greatly differ, depending on the purpose for which the definition is required. Probate purposes differ from family-law purposes, and may differ from criminal law purposes.

Family relationships are usually centered on the marital unit of wife and husband. But same-sex marriages can throw a wrench into that definition, even though states that have recognized the validity of same-sex marriage simply treat the couple like all other married persons. They are spouses and have the same legal rights to elective shares, intestate portions, homestead and family allowances, exempt property, and other protections provided by state law.

However, because same sex-marriage is not recognized under federal law, same-sex couples don't receive the federal tax benefits of marriage.[44]

————————

[43] Rainbows, http://rainbows.org/statistics.html.

[44] See U.S. v. Windsor, a case before the U.S. Supreme Court on the constitutionality of §3 of the Defense of Marriage Act, which denies a same sex spouse the unlimited marital deduction for estate tax purposes. The case is on appeal from a decision striking the federal law that holds that marriage is only between and a man and a woman. See Windsor v. U.S., 699 F.3d 169 (2d Cir, 2012).

In many situations, this isn't a huge problem because state law mandates many of the most important non-economic rights, like preferential treatment as a personal representative of an estate, the power to designate organ donations, hospital visitation, the elective share, and the homestead protections. But state law marital deduction trusts, designed to take advantage of certain federal tax provisions, don't function in the same way for same-sex spouses as they would for heterosexual spouses.

We also tend to think we know the definition of children. Certainly, biological children who live with their biological parents are children. However, step-children, adopted children, and foster children receive different levels of protection under different state laws. And it can get worse. Legal and scientific advancements have muddied the definition of a child. Thus, children in the process of adoption and children born from artificial reproductive techniques using sperm donors, egg donors, or surrogate mothers may be difficult to classify. Should the law treat them as children of their biological parents until adoption has been completed, or should they be treated as children of their adoptive or intended parents before the legal paperwork as been completed? The 2008 amendments to the Uniform Probate Code dramatically complicated the parent–child rules of the *UPC*. In Chapter Two, we fully analyze the *UPC* as it relates to parents and children, but you need to be sensitive to the fact that many people have parent/child relations with others who the law would not consider children, and others have no relation with people the law considers their children.

One solution to the former situation are rules recognizing virtual adoptions, or adoption by estoppel, in situations where the adopted child was led to believe an adoption took place, that child has performed as a child, and relied on the claims of adults that he/she is legally adopted. However, the child that was produced from both a donated egg and sperm, and implanted into a different woman's womb is, in a very real sense, the child of no parent. Marriage no longer is an impediment to the status of parent, and biological parents will be charged with child support even if the parents are unmarried, and one or both parents spend no time rearing the children. However, an adult can be deemed not a parent of his biological children for probate purposes if he has never recognized the child as his own.

The late Michael Jackson's children likely were never adopted, and were created through artificial means using donor eggs and sperm. Yet Michael reared them from their birth. Should they be removed from his family after his death, or should the intended parental relationship be recognized? Legal presumptions, such as the presumption that a child born to a married couple is the offspring of that couple, may be unnecessary with DNA testing, calling into question cases like *Michael H. v. Gerald D.*[45] in which the Supreme Court affirmed the mother's husband's rights to custody of a child against the biological father.

Even the non-traditional families like the Brady Bunch are easy in the face of the tremendously complicated non-traditional families that are being established today. Gay men using surrogates to create biological children, people with children from multiple partners, grandparents or aunts and uncles raising children, lesbians seeking to adopt the biological children of their partners, older and even post menopausal women using artificial technologies to give birth to children from adopted embryos are all

---

[45] Michael H. v. Gerald D., 491 U.S. 110 (1989).

part of our complex modern world. Think about the children of the anonymous sperm donor who, as half-siblings, get together for annual reunions and keep up with each other on Facebook. And all pose challenges in administrating decedents' estates from the simple default rules of intestate succession to homestead, family allowance, and exempt property protections to complex trusts and class gifts. Should Grandma's trust provision to "my lineal descendants" include grandchildren born from adopted embryos by a granddaughter's lesbian partner?

The complications that have entered the arena of parent/child relationships are further compounded as those generations age, and we must make complex calculations to determine aunts, uncles, cousins, grandparents, and other collateral relatives. Adding to this complexity is the abolition in some states of the Rule Against Perpetuities, which allow for perpetual trusts. Imagine determining legal heirs six or seven generations in the future for making trust distributions. The fertile octogenarian is no longer a humorous anomaly of sixteenth-century legal minds. She, along with children born twenty years after the biological parent has died, will be present in your brave new world. And we cannot even begin to imagine what technology will allow people to do 200 or 300 years from now when some of the dynasty trusts being created today are still in effect. How the skillful estate planner provides appropriately for these non-traditional situations is going to become more and more important to those lawyers seeking to build a practice in this area in the twenty-first century.

It's not just the random love-child here and there who seeks a share of a family trust that we need to accommodate. The ubiquity of blended, same-sex, and other non-traditional families demands laws that respond to and respect the needs of all. In the end, my mother was probably right and her dietary advice can be extended to the law of succession. "Eat in moderation, exercise daily, vary your routine, take the stairs, and eat your spinach." As individuals we should be able to craft our own estate plans, and as members of society we should promote the greater good, even if we don't want to pay taxes or provide for our spouses. Balancing dead hand control with the interests of the living may seem like we are trying to defy the laws of physics and levitate ourselves above our human foibles. The tragedy of modern life may just be the tremendous disconnect between the numbers of planned and privileged children that the wealthy can sculpt in their own images; contrasted with the unplanned, unwanted, and redundant children that fill our foster homes and homeless shelters because they have no family that cares. Should the law of succession tip the balance toward children who have needs or toward the power of testators to use their property to influence a future that they do not inhabit? Keep this question in mind as you progress through this course. In many ways, it is the $500,000 question.

Practice Point: The Importance of Planning for the Non-Traditional Family

If we once thought that intestacy laws could save the integrity of the family unit if a parent neglected to put together an estate plan, we might now argue that in many non-traditional family situations intestacy laws could actually work to erode it. Take, for example, the traditional nuclear family: if mom and dad have mingled all of their assets together during life as Joint Tenants with Rights of Survivorship, or as Tenants by the Entirety (discussed further in later chapters), and die without a plan, intestacy laws would kick in at the second death to help pass along property to their children (and possibly grandchildren), under the assumption that just because mom and dad died without wills didn't mean that they didn't want to provide for their children. It might not be exactly what they wanted, but, hopefully it would be close.

Contrast this outcome to that of the modern family, where it is now likely that mom or dad (or both) has had a prior marriage or two. If each spouse has grown children of their own as well as some minor children, and then they give birth to a child together, what happens to their property at death if *they* have owned everything together as Joint Tenants with Rights of Survivorship or Tenants by the Entirety? We will get to the specifics of this question in later chapters, but let's just say for now that if mom and dad die at separate times without a will in this scenario, intestacy laws would likely NOT protect the children of the first spouse if the step-parent inherits the parent's property and then dies later. In order to get a share of the estate, those children would probably have to submit a claim and fight it out in court—or, depending on the state and the circumstances, they just might be out of luck altogether.

From a planning perspective, sharing this information with clients usually encourages them to go ahead and get their plan drafted—and quickly! But, those are the ones who are already contemplating putting together a plan anyway. That's why they are in your office. Those who don't know and haven't given it any thought are often the ones at greatest risk for a potential disaster at death. And, unfortunately, their estate administrations often demonstrate how the intestacy structure can fail the surviving children of the modern family. So, how can you as an attorney effectively reach the client who is in desperate need of an estate plan but who just doesn't realize it?

If you have flipped through the local newspaper, you have undoubtedly seen announcements for "Wills Seminars" or "Basic Estate Planning Workshops" hosted by law firms that are open to the public. The specifics on advertising as it relates to the estate planning attorney vary from state to state, but typically the goal of the session is to provide education to the public (NOT to give legal advice) about how estate plans work. The result is that some of those in attendance who really need a plan might be startled into awareness, and therefore into action.

But potential clients are sometimes tipped off by other professionals that they need to seek legal counsel. Examples of those professionals include life insurance agents, stock brokers, accountants and financial planners who can identify the potential problem and steer the clients in the attorney's direction.

But, for varying reasons, including lack of money, many nontraditional family members will neglect to put together any kind of a plan. Because our intestacy structure was designed to work with a very traditional notion of the family, the results can run quite contrary to what the decedent would have wanted at all. Can you think of other ways to reach these people?

E. CONCLUSION

This chapter has introduced you to the underlying tensions between donative freedom and family protections that permeate the law of succession. Non-traditional families and non-traditional decedents require flexibility in the laws of estate planning to allow them to provide for the people closest to them. Simultaneously, dependent spouses and children can suffer greatly from the improvidence or ignorance of testators who believe their dependants don't need special consideration in their wills. Legislation that aims to correct social problems is often both underprotective and overprotective at the same time. Decedents who rely on the default rules will generally be satisfied if they want their spouses and biological children to inherit their estates. But decedents who want to deviate from the default rules, for both socially prudent and socially unattractive reasons, have numerous mechanisms for constructing their own estate plans. The lawyer who doesn't have a good understanding of the limits and the totality of powers available for estate planning will do a disservice to her clients. The focus of the remainder of the book, therefore, is on the tools of estate planning and avoiding the pitfalls of inflexible rules where possible.

But as you progress through the material, ask yourself whether the laws we are stydying appropriately balance donative freedom and the dead hand with family protections or the needs of the living. Or do you think changes in the laws are moving in the right direction? Are they too slow to change, or too quick to change? If you cannot satisfy all the people all of the time, who should the law try to benefit?

CHAPTER 2

ADMINISTRATION, PROBATE, AND FAMILY PROTECTIONS

When a person dies, the last thing the surviving family members want to be concerned about are mortgage payments, paying utility bills, selling the house, making insurance payments, notifying Social Security of the decedent's passing, or reviewing any documents in the safe deposit box. This is particularly difficult if the decedent was the principal income-earner or was the person who handled most of the family's financial matters. Because late fees can be assessed if bills are not paid when due, and surviving family members may be legally unable to access bank accounts to pay the bills, it is important that someone assume responsibility for the family's financial matters. That person should locate the decedent's will, if there is one, alert any credit card companies to cancel cards, and notify creditors of the decedent's death. If the estate contains real property, or if there is a will, the estate will probably need to be *probated,* though the estate will certainly require some kind of administration. Administration of an estate does not necessarily require the assistance of a lawyer, but retaining one is wise if the estate is at all complex, or the surviving family members are rather inexperienced in dealing with legal and financial issues.

Every estate must be *administered.* That means that all property owned by the decedent has to be distributed to someone else. Where the only property the decedent owned consisted of a few items of personal property, some clothes, a television, a few books, mementos, and a Social Security check, administration of the estate is rather simple. Family members distribute the items of personal property, and a death certificate is sent to the Social Security office notifying it to stop payments. However, many people have more assets when they die, sometimes a significant estate that must be administered. For many family members, a death means going through attics or basements full of boxes of old documents, wedding clothes, the family china, toys, cutlery, cookware, and trying to find someone to take that out-of-tune piano. But even where the decedent may have owned securities, perhaps had life insurance, and was still able to drive her own car, the estate may be administered out of court.

In contrast, family members of a decedent who owned real property, who wrote a will, who had substantial creditors, whose wealth consisted of ownership interests in a business, or who had other complex financial affairs will most certainly need the assistance of a probate lawyer and a court to assist with the administration of the estate. And if the surviving family members cannot agree on how to dispose of the decedent's possessions, court-supervised administration is critical.

It is quite common, however, not to have a court involved in the administration of a deceased person's estate when all assets are owned jointly with the surviving spouse. The surviving spouse simply retains all the assets and slowly goes about taking the decedent spouse's name off the joint accounts and jointly-held property. In fact, fewer than a third of estates are administered through the probate courts.[1]

But once funeral arrangements are made and the bills start coming in, it's a good idea to begin administration as soon as possible.

This Chapter introduces you to a variety of things you need to know before we get into the details of estate planning and the technical rules of wills, trusts, and other testamentary documents. It introduces you to the administration process, differences between common-law and community property states, and the protections of homestead, family allowance, and exempt property that apply to all estates, regardless of size or manner of administration, whether the decedent had a will or a trust, and whether the property is simple or complex. It then explores the extensive changes to the UPC around the issues of family creation and the parent/child relationship, especially adoption, artificial reproductive techniques, and same-sex marriage because many of the legal rights we discuss throughout this course turn on definitions of family.

A. ADMINISTRATION

When a court is involved in administering an estate, the procedure is usually called *probate*, and most states have special probate courts that handle all aspects of estate administration (also called surrogates courts, orphans courts, or chancery courts in some states). The term *probate* is especially confusing, however, as it has a number of different meanings. It means, first, *the process for proving the validity of a will*—i.e. the judicial process whereby a probate court affirms that a particular will is valid and enforceable. "We need to probate this will," or "the will was probated," or "the 1994 will was probated and not the 1990 will." In this sense of the term, *probate* refers to a very specific process of determining that a will is valid and then distributing the decedent's property accordingly.

Second, the term *probate* is used often to describe *the entire administration process* when supervised by a court, that can be misperceived by many to be costly and time-consuming. In this sense, we often speak of "avoiding the probate process," which generally means avoiding the courts altogether. Because court proceedings are public, and lawyers and personal representatives are entitled to fees out of an estate, many people try to avoid the court-supervised administration process by using a variety of different instruments to allow property to pass to others automatically upon death. Trusts and joint tenancies are the most common mechanisms, but many others exist as well.

Third, we use the term *probate* to distinguish between property titled in the decedent's name that needs to be administered after death, and property that passes to a joint owner or beneficiary without any legal process. Hence, the law distinguishes between the *probate estate* and the *non-probate estate* of a decedent to classify different forms of property. It is mis-

---

[1] Although compiling statistics of this sort is difficult and has not been done systematically, one can correlate the number of deaths in a given year against probate filings. For example, in the State of Florida there were 49,332 probate filings in FY 2010–2011 (see Florida Office of the State Courts Administrator, *FY 2010–11 Statistical Reference Guide*, 6.2, http://www.flcourts.org/gen_public/stats/ReferenceGuide10–11/Ch6.pdf) and 172,509 deaths in calendar year 2010 (see http://www.flpublichealth.com/VSBOOK/VSBOOK.aspx referencing Florida Vital Statistics Annual Report (2010), 73, http://www.flpublichealth.com/VSBOOK/pdf/2010/Deaths.pdf) for a rough probate rate of 28.5%. The probate filings exclude guardianships, custodianships, challenges to trusts, or other civil probate-related actions.

leading to believe that non-probate property does not have to be adminis-tered; though it is true that non-probate property passes by virtue of an instrument that is not a will, and probate property passes according to a will or the default rules of intestacy. An important part of any trusts and estates practice involves distinguishing between *probate* and *non-probate* property.

Most states have a variety of options available for administering es-tates. For estates that are relatively small, usually below a certain dollar value and containing no real property, there is a *summary administration* process that is relatively quick and inexpensive. In Alabama the estate can't be over $3,000 to qualify for summary administration[2]; in Arizona it cannot exceed the costs of funeral expenses and homestead and family al-lowance[3]; and in Arkansas it cannot exceed $100,000.[4] In addition, there is a mechanism for the process of administration *by affidavit* for even smaller estates.[5] States also distinguish between formal and informal procedures,[6] or probating in *solemn form* and *common form*. *Solemn form* requires notice to all interested parties and entails litigation, while *common form* is an *ex parte* proceeding that moves along primarily through affidavits of the exec-utor/personal representative. A final judgment of a solemn form procedure cannot be reopened once the appeals period has passed, while common form procedures may be reopened by an interested party even after distribution of the decedent's property for a period of years. If reopened, the case must then follow the solemn form procedure. Estates that are likely to be con-tested should follow the formal, solemn form procedure to ensure adequate closure and finality.

Probate, or court supervised administration, performs three important functions:

1. It protects decedents who want their wishes followed in the distri-bution of their property. Of course, one might not want great-aunt Edna's tea-cozy collection, but Aunt Edna can feel comfort knowing that a court will enforce her wishes as to who is to receive her prop-erty upon her death.

2. It gives recipients of property evidence of clear title to manage their new property as new owners. Failure to transfer title to the living can cause overwhelming barriers to successor owners. Indeed, clouded title is a persistent problem in minority and working-class communities that often do not utilize the probate process.[7]

3. It offers a method to settle the rights and claims of creditors to pro-vide closure for the living. This includes taxes. The last issue a survivor wishes is to have a creditor appear years after the dece-dent has died, claiming that Uncle Fred's IOU was never paid.

---

[2] ALA.CODE § 43–2–692 (1975).

[3] ARIZ. REV. STAT. ANN. § 14–3973 (1974).

[4] ARK. CODE ANN. § 28–41–101(a)(3) (West 2011).

[5] UPC § 3–1201.

[6] UPC §§ 3–301 and 3–401.

[7] One of the most difficult and time-consuming aspects of post-Katrina relief in the low-er 9th ward was the fact that many of the homeowners whose homes were destroyed had inherited their homes over the years, all completely paid off and in fee simple absolute, but had never changed the title documents upon the deaths of the prior owners. Thus, when it was time to apply for relief funds to rebuild they could not prove their title and were not eligible for replacement funds.

But probate is essentially a process for the living. Probate is self-policing in the sense that survivors are not required to follow a decedent's will if they can agree to distribute the property differently among themselves.[8] The law assumes that anyone who feels cheated by an informal distribution can always bring a probate action to challenge the way a decedent's property was distributed.

If Grandpa decides to disinherit one of his children, and his will expresses that intention, his children can simply decide among themselves to distribute the property equally and disregard Grandpa's dying wishes. If the children are pleased with an equal distribution, the effect is the same as if the will was followed and the children subsequently decided to give part of their inheritance to their disinherited sibling. With regard to the property rights, there is no difference, though there may be tax implications of distributing the property unequally and the children subsequently redistributing it to suit their own sensibilities. A good estate plan, therefore, should not put beneficiaries in the position of having to consider tax or other legal implications if they choose to distribute the property differently than what was in the language of the decedent's will.

This raises the question of *standing*. Only interested parties may open a probate proceeding or intervene in one. Interested parties are creditors or possible beneficiaries that have a stake in the administration of a decedent's estate. Just because Uncle Fred is angry at the way his nephews ignored his brother's will and decided to give all the property to one child, doesn't entitle Uncle Fred to intervene or to file a probate action to force his nephews to follow his brother's stated wishes. Unless he is a creditor or possible beneficiary, either under the will or under the default intestacy statutes, or unless he is a guardian or trustee for a possible beneficiary, Uncle Fred has no standing and cannot contest the disposition of assets.

In most instances, plain old human greed on the part of the beneficiary who would lose property if the decedent's will is not adhered to is enough to ensure that most estates are administered along the decedent's intentions. But regardless how determined a decedent is to disinherit one of her children, the surviving children are able to put aside that wish in order to treat each other equitably and maintain their own relationship among the living if they so choose.

No judge, attorney general, or representative of the state has a stake in demanding that a decedent's wishes are followed, and therefore the probate process is remarkably free of state oversight except in the role of the probate judge who settles disputes between beneficiaries. The UPC even provides that a representative is not entitled to offer a will for probate if all the devisees disagree.[9] Thus, if the beneficiaries don't like a particular distribution, they can actually agree among themselves, prior to distribution, that Grandpa's estate will be distributed differently, and only the beneficiaries and creditors have standing to complain.

---

[8] The District of Columbia code, ironically, provides a fine of $500 to survivors who withhold a will knowingly, and possible imprisonment for destroying a will. See D.C. Code §§ 18–111, 18–112 (1965).

[9] UPC § 3–720.

Tax Tip: Family Settlements, Testator Intent, and the Taxman

Although we have not discussed tax issues in any great detail yet, you already know that gratuitous transfers of valuable property can have tax implications. Gift tax returns may need to be filed and transfer taxes may be due on lifetime or testamentary gratuitous transfers of property. So you want to be thinking about minimizing property transfers whenever tax liabilities call for it. What if Dad has three children: Alice, Bob, and Carol. Because Alice married well and doesn't need any money, dad decides to split his entire estate into only two shares, one for Bob and one for Carol, leaving Alice nothing. After dad's death, Bob and Carol learn of dad's plan and feel terrible (and perhaps Alice just got divorced and had to give up her timeshare in Des Moines). To keep harmony in the family, they could simply each give one-third of their inheritances to Alice, but now we've got two transfers happening to raise potential tax liabilities: the first from dad to Bob and Carol, and the second from Bob and Carol to Alice.

Now many estate planners consulting with dad would probably explain to him that his distribution scheme may cause hard feelings and his children may want to rearrange things, but that doing so might have tax implications he should consider. He might say, "oh, in that case let's give one-third to Alice," or he might say "that's their problem—this is how I want to do it." If he says it is their problem, however, they might go to court for a family settlement rather than simply rearranging the property distribution to suit them and face the extra transfer taxes. Many states allow the heirs and distributees of an estate to enter into an agreement to distribute the property differently than the decedent specified. This court-supervised, legally binding agreement among the relevant competent parties can completely change dad's testamentary disposition, thus avoiding the potential of additional transfer tax liabilities by reducing the number of transfers to one.

But what does the IRS think about family settlements? Despite the supervision and signature of a state probate judge on the settlement agreement, the IRS may not accept the new distribution scheme, especially if the settlement was designed solely to avoid transfer tax liabilities. The IRS will accept the settlement only if it resolves a legitimate *case or controversy* that threatens the estate with litigation. Thus, if Alice was going to challenge dad's will on the grounds of undue influence or lack of mental capacity, and the settlement eliminated the will challenge, the IRS will accept the new distribution pattern without imposing additional tax liabilities. But if the kids entered into the settlement just because they felt sorry that Alice got divorced and disinherited the same week, the IRS probably won't allow the settlement to reduce the tax liabilities.

But what about dad? What about donative freedom and testamentary intent? Should we care more about promoting testamentary intent or reducing costs for the living recipients of testamentary gifts? It's the age-old problem of dead hand control. One solution, however, would be for dad (and his estate planner) to foresee the possibility of a family settlement and structure the instruments so that a careful use of a disclaimer could result in the distribution pattern that the heirs and devisees would likely want. This means that if Bob and Carol don't want to give anything to Alice they don't have to but, if they do, they could each disclaim one-third of their inheritances and it would pass to Alice pursuant to dad's will if he provided that upon disclaimer the property would pass in a manner more likely to appeal to the needs (and tax avoidance preferences) of his devisees.

Typically, the person designated in a will, or the next of kin, will be appointed by the court to be the administrator of the estate (usually called an *executor* if the decedent died testate and a *personal representative* if the decedent died intestate). We will use the term *personal representative* or *representative* throughout the remainder of this book to include executors, administrators, and personal representatives unless the distinctions matter in a particular context. Some states have abolished the different terminology and use a single term to refer to the administrators of all estates, regardless of type.[10]

Upon appointment of a personal representative, *letters of administration*, or *letters testamentary* will be issued by the court and the representative may commence the tedious process of collecting and doing inventory of the decedent's property (called *marshalling the assets*), notifying creditors, paying the bills, and distributing the assets through transfer of title to the heir or beneficiary. If the decedent's preferred representative is not appointed, the court will appoint someone else, usually someone with personal knowledge of the decedent's property, someone agreed to by a majority of the beneficiaries, but even a stranger if necessary. All states have statutes identifying a preferred order for appointing personal administrators, beginning with spouses, then adult children, then parents, siblings, or other heirs.[11] The representative is a *fiduciary* and has obligations to the property of the decedent and the beneficiaries. Further, the representative must make proper accountings to the court as required. The representative is entitled to a commission for her services which are segregated out of the estate, and she must also pay the attorney, court fees, and sometimes other guardian or appraiser's fees. Where the representative's fees are set by state statute, it is usually an amount based on the size of the probate estate, and in most states the commission must be reasonable.

Although court supervised administration may seem expensive and wearisome, it is vital for complex estates. And even though an estate planner realizes an estate will be probated, she should still make sensible use of probate-avoidance mechanisms where they are appropriate. The trusts and estates lawyer should understand where and when a client can reasonably avoid probate and when the client should not. There are advantages to probate, not the least of which is the permanent settling of the estate and the barring of creditors' claims. But much litigation can be avoided through a judicious use of probate and non-probate instruments for managing property. Real property that is not held jointly or in trust will almost always require court-supervised administration in order to completely transfer the title documents, and real property held in other states than the state of domicile will require *ancillary administration*.[12] Bank accounts that are not held jointly or with payable on death (*POD*) designations will also require letters of administration to manage and distribute. Banks are particularly

---

[10] FLA. STAT. § 731.201(28) (2012) and N.J. STAT. ANN. § 3B:1–2 (West 2005).

[11] At least since the 1971 decision in *Reed v. Reed*, 404 U.S. 71, states have been unable to use gender preferences in choosing between persons to be appointed administrators of an estate.

[12] Ancillary administration is a process for dealing with a decedent who owned real property or personal property in a non-domiciliary state. Ancillary administration usually is fairly expeditious, but it usually requires evidence that a will was probated, or letters testamentary issued, in the decedent's domiciliary state. Tangible personal property located in another state may often be collected by the administrator and distributed along with the rest of a decedent's estate. But intangible personal property like bank accounts or trusts will require ancillary administration, as may motor vehicles or other tangible personal property that requires the transfer of title documents.

careful about restricting access to the decedent's bank accounts or safe deposit boxes unless the person claiming entry has the appropriate judge-signed documents.

To facilitate administration of simple estates, many states have adopted statutes allowing for the relatively easy transfer of title for motor vehicles to the next of kin without the necessity of court-supervised probate.[13] And personal property can be easily distributed among survivors without difficulty so long as the survivors agree on the distribution.

The important thing to remember, however, is that one always can avoid probate by giving away all of one's property before death, but that leaves one, like King Lear, vulnerable to the generosity of family and friends. Holding onto every penny may make the decedent feel more independent and secure, but doing so is likely to require more complex admin-administration at death. Most decedents would do well with an estate plan that includes a judicious blend of *inter vivos* and testamentary gifts, reducing the size and complexity of the probate estate without sacrificing the security and the independence of property ownership. For the basic Trusts and Estates course, just knowing that probate is not the endless litigation of *Jarndyce and Jarndyce*,[14] and that we don't need to be afraid of it, is important. The average estate can be closed within a year or two if the personal representative acts diligently. Many estates linger, however, because relatives or family friends, with their own busy lives, decide they can save money by doing all the legwork themselves to administer an estate and forego those expensive probate lawyers.

PROBLEM

2.1. Carla drafts a will one month before she dies. It leaves her entire estate, equally, in separate testamentary trust shares, for the benefit of her brother Michael and her best friend Vita during their lifetimes, with the remainder of each trust share to be distributed to their children at the death of Michael and Vita. Carla names her father, Austin, as Trustee of both trust shares.

When Carla dies, she has a spouse, Noel, whom she was in the process of divorcing. She owes $15,000.00 in credit card debt to American Express, and $5,000 evidenced by a Promissory Note to her mother, Sharron. Michael has one adult child, Thomas, and Vita has no children. Clara's sister insists that Clara really intended to leave her estate to her. To further complicate matters, Springdale Elementary school, which owns land adjacent to Carla's home, claims that Carla promised the principal on a number of occasions that she would leave her real estate to the school at her death so that they could expand their campus.

Who would have standing to contest this probate proceeding?

---

[13]   See, e.g. CAL. Vehicle Code § 5910 (West 1985); FLA. STAT. § 320.0609(7) (2011).

[14]   Jarndyce v. Jarndyce was the mythical endless probate suit in Charles Dickens' novel, *Bleak House.*

**Technology Trend: The Techno-Illiterate Client or
"What's That Ringing Coming from My Handbag?"**

With the increase in online banking, e-filing of tax returns, and electronic discovery in litigation, many law firms and courts are moving toward paperless practices and procedures. But if your clients are like my parents, they never turn their cell phones on except to make a call and leave a message, and then they turn them off before you can call them back. Everything they do is on a piece of paper and their will notes are probably on the back of a grocery list. They may have kept every will they have ever executed, even after it has been revoked by a new one, and it may take you months just to go through their files. Do you send them home with a paper will, or do you try to get it executed on their smart phones and upload it to the cloud so it isn't lost? As courts move toward e-filing, you will likely find yourself caught somewhere between the 19th and the 21st centuries as your clients cling to paper and your office and the court demands everything electronically. You may be required to have the most recent electronic equipment just to manage the electronic data you need.

Just as paper wills, letters, memoranda, and receipts can get lost or destroyed, electronic wills can be accidentally deleted or lost when your hard-drive crashes. Think for a few minutes how you as a lawyer will handle the file-keeping you need for your practice, how you will instruct your client when she goes home with her neat will stapled into the will cover, and how you will advise the personal administrator who is trying to marshal all of a decedent's assets about where to look.

Managing paper by finding it, filing it, and distributing the property accordingly is becoming easier and harder as technologies change. Automatic recurring payments of bills can help alleviate the need for a power of attorney if the client becomes incapacitated. But the personal representative needs to stay on top of those electronic bank statements and credit card bills in order to cancel many services once the client has died. And if we follow the advice of our Information Technology experts, we should have unusual passwords and never leave them lying about, making management of those accounts very difficult by a personal representative.

In the U.K., the courts offer a probate document repository where documents can be placed for safe keeping. In the U.S. there is no federal or state sponsored will repository, although there is a private company, the National Will Depository, with locations in Washington, DC; Missoula, MT; and Eureka, CA. The NWD offers safe-keeping guarantees for 100 years for individuals who may be worried their wills and other probate documents may be swept away in the latest superstorm, or lawyers whose clients have been out of touch for decades but who left their wills with them for safekeeping. However, as simple as it might seem to just send those files to Eureka for hard copy storage and easy identification on the internet, it may in fact be a breach of an attorney's duty of confidentiality to register a will with a depository. See discussion of will depositories in Chapter 12.

B. HOMESTEAD

Often the most important asset of a decedent, and the item of property that needs most to be managed well, is the family home. Most states have provisions protecting the homestead from creditors during life,[15] and many limit the transferability of the homestead at death, or provide surviving spouses and children a right to continue to reside in the home. Florida, Texas, and Kansas have some of the most generous homestead protections in the country—exempting the family home from creditors regardless of the value of the home, while some states completely bar the devising of the homestead if the decedent has a spouse or minor children.

Homestead protections benefit debtors in bankruptcy and are often criticized as ways to defraud legitimate creditors. When O.J. Simpson left California and moved to Florida, purchasing a very expensive home in Miami, he likely understood that the home would be protected from potential tort creditors, besides gaining property tax advantages.[16] And many survivors want the creditor protections to extend to the home as it passes from the decedent to the survivors.

While the generous nature of the Florida and Texas homestead laws have attracted a tremendous amount of criticism for providing shelters for wealthy tax-evaders to keep their ill-gotten gains, the homestead laws also provide a very important function for the average American: protecting the family home, domicile, place of residence, or family farm from creditors who could force a sale and leave a family homeless.[17] Most establish a dollar value that is protected from creditors, or protect the physical home itself. Although all state homestead laws allow the mortgage company to foreclose on the home, or the local government to force a sale for non-payment of property taxes related to the property, a decedent's business creditors, or credit card companies may not attach homestead property and evict the debtor or his family if the homeowner went on a shopping spree in Paris.

But homestead would not be an effective protection if the death of the primary property holder, particularly in common law states,[18] resulted in the rest of the family being evicted by creditors. Concern over evicting widows and minor children prompted states to pass homestead legislation throughout the nineteenth century, and the laws permit the creditor protections to transfer with the property if the homestead passes to a spouse and/or children, particularly minor children. As you will see later in this chapter, in community property states this is less of a concern because the family home is likely to be owned in part by the surviving spouse.

Homestead is particularly important in states that have generous creditor protections, because they shelter enough value to protect the home

---

[15] Forty six states protect some amount of value, or the entire residence, through creditor protections. Delaware, New Jersey, Pennsylvania, and Rhode Island are the states that do not provide any protections against forced sale of the family home by creditors unrelated to the purchase or maintenance of the home itself.

[16] *O.J. Simpson in Jail, But Still Gets Tax Break*, Miami Herald, Sunday, December 12, 2010. For those of you who don't recall the case, O.J. Simpson was found liable under wrongful death tort statutes but his house could not be attached because it was protected under Florida's generous homestead laws.

[17] A quick search of the web will bring up dozens of websites with information on the homestead protections available in each state for bankruptcy proceedings.

[18] This is less a concern in community property states where all marital property is deemed to be owned jointly by both spouses. Even the community property states, however, also provide homestead protections.

from forced sale.[19] Kansas, Florida and Texas shelter the family home of any value, while Minnesota shelters a residential home up to $300,000 in value and agricultural land up to $750,000 in value,[20] and Massachusetts shelters homestead property up to $500,000 in value.[21] Thus, the multi-million dollar mansion in Palm Beach is protected from creditors, just like the $10,000 shack. Indeed, some states have updated their homestead laws to add mobile homes or manufactured homes for living situations that previously had no protection.[22]

Many states affix the protections to particular pieces of real property, like 40 acres (Iowa, Michigan, Wisconsin); 80 acres (Arkansas); 160 acres (Kansas, Florida, Minnesota, Mississippi, Nebraska, Oklahoma, South Dakota); or 200 acres (Texas) of rural land, or ¼ acre (Arkansas); ½ acre (Florida, Iowa, Minnesota); 1 acre (Kansas, Oklahoma, South Dakota, Texas); one city lot (Michigan), or two city lots (Nebraska) of urban land. Some states provide greater homestead protections for married couples than for single persons (California, Illinois, Oregon, Tennessee, Utah). Other states define homestead protections by age (California, Hawaii, Maine, Massachusetts). Still others give preferences if there are minor children living in the home (Maine, Massachusetts).

Most states limit the value that can be sheltered in each of these categories, and some are quite insubstantial. For instance, North Carolina protects only the first $1,000 of an urban residence[23] and Michigan protects only up to $3,500 of the value of a city lot or 40 acres of rural land[24] which isn't going to do a lot these days. Four states have no homestead protections at all (Delaware, New Jersey, Pennsylvania, Rhode Island).

Most states, but not all, require the designation of the particular property as homestead (e.g. Alaska and Kentucky do not require a designation of homestead), and designation may serve multiple functions, such as giving the owner a property tax benefit, as well as protections from creditors who cannot seize the homestead. Arkansas, Florida, Louisiana, Kansas, Michigan, Minnesota and North Carolina's homestead laws are founded in their constitutions,[25] but only those of Florida and Kansas are written with no reference to value limitations on the homestead protections offered. Because there is no dollar value limitation, a homeowner can shelter an unlimited amount of money in the homestead against non-homestead creditors.

Mortgages on the homestead, liens for improvements to the homestead, property taxes, and other debts associated with the purchase and

---

[19] FLA. CONST. art. 10, § 4A; Tex. Interests in Land Exempt from Seizure CODE, ANN. § 41.001 (West 2001).

[20] See MINN. STAT. ANN. § 510.02 (West 1969).

[21] MASS. GEN. LAWS ANN. ch. 188, § 1 (West 2011).

[22] FLA. CONST. art. 10 § 4, cl 47; FLA. STAT. ANN. § 222.05 (West 1869) (amended 1977); ALA. CODE § 6–10–2 (1975) (amended 1980).

[23] N.C. CONST. art. X, § 2.

[24] MICH. CONST. art. X, § 3.

[25] *See, e.g.*, ARK. CONST. art. 9, §§ 4–6 (providing homestead protections for 1 acre of urban or 60 acres of rural land); LA. CONST. art. 12, § 9 (requiring the legislature provide for homestead protections up to a minimum of $15,000); KAN. CONST. art. 15, § 9 (providing for homestead protections for 1 urban or 160 rural acres with no value limitation); FLA. CONST. art. 10, § 4(a) (providing homestead protection for .5 urban acres or 160 rural acres including improvements); MINN. CONST. art. I, § 12 (protecting a "reasonable amount of property" from forced seizure); N.C. CONST. art. X, § 2 (providing an exemption from forced sale for every homestead up to a value no less than $1,000).

maintenance of the homestead cannot be avoided, but unsecured creditors may not force the sale of a homestead. See *Havoco of America, Ltd. v. Hill*, 790 So.2d 1018 (Fla. 2001), and *Palm Beach Savings & Loan Ass'n v. Fishbein*, 609 So.2d 267 (Fla. 1993) (allowing an equitable lien against the homestead where fraudulently obtained funds were used to pay off mortgages on the homestead).

Despite the stories of failed Wall Street executives like Stephen Fuld, financial investors like Bernie Madoff, and tortfeasors like O.J. Simpson being able to shelter vast sums of wealth in their homestead, there are countless numbers of ordinary people whose family home is their principal asset, and who rely on that homestead for providing for their dependants after their death because the family home is protected against unsecured creditors.

Homestead property is also usually exempt property in bankruptcy proceedings, allowing people to keep their homes even when their credit cards or unexpected tort claims threaten their hard-earned assets. An interesting legal question arises as to whether state statutes limiting home-homestead protections where illegally obtained funds are used to purchase the homestead can prevail over the constitutional protections of homestead.[26]

However, for purposes of estate planning, we focus less on the creditor protections, though they are quite important in the estate administration process, and more on the limitations, if any, on the descent and devise of homestead, and the rights of surviving spouses and children to acquire the home or continue to reside there. For purposes of what is called *probate homestead*, there are three basic types of homestead laws.

1. HOMESTEAD PROTECTION TIED TO PARTICULAR REAL ESTATE WITH LIMITATIONS ON DESCENT AND DEVISE

Several states provide a surviving spouse or surviving children with some type of real property right in a particular piece of real estate. This interest may be a life estate, a remainder, a homestead right, a term of years, or even some estate not traditionally recognized by the common law. For instance, Florida, gives a surviving spouse a life estate in the family home, with a forced remainder in the descendants if there are minor children at the time of the home owner's death.[27] Most importantly, the property may not be devised at all if there are minor children; it must pass through intestate succession as a life estate followed by a remainder, although if there is a surviving spouse the spouse may elect a one-half share in the homestead in lieu of a life estate. Regardless of whether the spouse elects, however, problems can arise if some of the decedent's children are minors. Whether there is a spouse or not, the property must pass directly to the minor children, thus necessitating a trust or guardianship.[28]

---

[26] *See Havoco of America, Ltd. v. Hill,* 26 Fla. L. Weekly S416 (Fla. June 21, 2001); *Havoco of America, Ltd. v. Hill,* 790 So. 2d 1018 (Fla. 2001) (providing that the homestead exemption protects a homestead acquired by a debtor using nonexempt assets with the intent to hinder, delay, or defraud creditors; such actions do not qualify for any of the three exceptions to the homestead exemption).

[27] FLA. STAT. ANN. § 732.4015 (West 2010). The statute also permits the spouse to elect a one-half interest in the homestead property in lieu of the life estate, with the other half passing to the descendants.

[28] *See* Unif. Transfers to Minors Act §§ 3, 9(5) (1983).

Other states, however, grant an interest in the family home to the surviving spouse or children that resembles an estate for years, but it is often limited to the time it takes the youngest child to reach age eighteen. For instance, Massachusetts provides that the spouse receives a homestead interest in the property until any minor children have reached age 18, or the spouse dies or remarries, at which time the homestead lien is removed and the property can pass according to the decedent's wishes.[29] In Massachusetts, the homestead right is the right to "use, occupy, and enjoy" the property, and it operates as a kind of lien against the owner's title to prevent the sale of the land until the minor children come of age or move out of the home.[30] The surviving spouse is also entitled to live in the decedent's home rent-free for six months, whether homestead or not.[31]

In Minnesota, descent is limited as well. The Minnesota Homestead Statute provides as follows:

MINN. STAT. 524.2–402

(a) If there is a surviving spouse, the homestead, including a manufactured home which is the family residence, descends free from any testamentary or other disposition of it to which the spouse has not consented in writing or as provided by law, as follows:

(1) if there is no surviving descendant of decedent, to the spouse; or

(2) if there are surviving descendants of decedent, then to the spouse for the term of the spouse's natural life and the remainder in equal shares to the decedent's descendants by representation.

(b) If there is no surviving spouse and the homestead has not been disposed of by will it descends as other real estate.

(c) If the homestead passes by descent or will to the spouse or decedent's descendants or to a trustee of a trust of which the spouse or the decedent's descendants are the sole current beneficiaries, it is exempt from all debts which were not valid charges on it at the time of decedent's death except that the homestead is subject to a claim filed. . . for medical assistance benefits. If the homestead passes to a person other than a spouse or decedent's descendants or to a trustee of a trust of which the spouse or the decedent's descendants are the sole current beneficiaries, it is subject to the payment of expenses of administration, funeral expenses, expenses of last illness, taxes, and debts. . . .

For those of you who remember the lesson from your property class, that life estates in real property are generally a bad idea, there can be problems with homestead protections if they are not managed well. For instance, Florida will allow a testator to place the life interest in the homestead in trust, but not the remainder interests in the children.[32] Thus, where husband and wife die simultaneously, leaving minor dependent children, those children must acquire free and clear fee simple title to the

---

[29] MASS. GEN. LAWS ANN. ch. 188, § 4 (West 2011).

[30] *Id.* at § 3.

[31] MASS. GEN. LAWS ANN. ch. 190B, § 2–403(b) (2012).

[32] *See* Est. of Donovan, 550 So. 2d 37 (Fla. 2d DCA 1989).

homestead, thus necessitating a guardianship for the property.[33] Minnesota will allow either interest to be placed in a trust.[34]

2. LIMITED VALUE HOMESTEAD PROTECTIONS TIED TO PARTICULAR REAL ESTATE

Most states provide a dollar value exemption for homestead, and may tie this value to the particular real estate that was the family home. This means that creditors may be able to force a sale of the property but only if the property is valued above the value of the statutory limitation and if the homeowner has equity in the house up to that value. These values sometimes vary dramatically. For instance, Maine protects homestead up to $10,000 (18–A M.R.S.A. § 2–401), Wyoming up to $30,000 (Wy. St. §§ 2–7–504 & 2–7–508), and New Hampshire up to $100,000 in value (N.H. § 480:1). Minnesota has a recently updated valuation of $300,000 for residences or $750,000 if the property is used for agricultural purposes and the value must update periodically in conformance with state statutes.[35]

In many of these states, the surviving spouse and/or minor children are entitled to continue to live in the homestead, and the value of the homestead is protected from the decedent spouse's creditors up to the value indicated in the statutes. These states generally do not limit the ability of testators to devise the homestead away from surviving family members (though some states do so, like Minnesota and Florida); but if the testator does devise the homestead to protected family members, the home will not be available for execution up to the protected value for paying the estate's debts. But if the home is devised to *another party*, the home then becomes available for attachment to pay the testator's or the donee's debts.

Homestead rights that give the survivors either a life estate in the real property declared as homestead, or some rights to remain in the home, closely resemble *Dower* and *Curtesy* rights (discussed below in Chapter 7) that were widely abolished in the early 20th century and replaced with an elective share. California gives the surviving spouse and children the right, **if the court orders it**, to remain in the homestead during administration, and until the children reach majority, though without any specific real property interest.[36] Where homestead rights do not constitute freehold interests in land, courts often view creditors or devisees of the home as remaindermen.[37]

Differences among the states also exist in determining when a creditor can force a sale of homestead, i.e. whether the surviving spouse is entitled to the protected homestead value (such as $300,000) or the value of a life estate in property worth $300,000. See, e.g. *Stolldorf v. Stolldorf*, 384 P.2d 969 (Wyo. 1963) which held that where a surviving widow was entitled to homestead protections of $4,000, she could receive $4,000 from the proceeds of the sale of the house if it sold for greater than that amount, or the full free and clear ownership of the property if the house would not sell for the full $4,000.

---

[33] FLA. STAT. ANN. § 732.401 (West 2012).

[34] MINN. STAT. ANN. § 524.2–402(c) (West 1994).

[35] MINN. STAT. ANN. § 510.02 (West 1969).

[36] CAL. PROB. CODE. ANN. §§ 6500, 6520–6527 (West 1990).

[37] See 6 A.L.R.2d 515.

Consider the West Virginia Code in this regard:

W.Va. § 38–9–1

Any husband, wife, parent or other head of a household residing in this State, or the infant children of deceased or insane parents, owning a homestead shall by operation of law have a homestead exemption therein to the value of five thousand dollars, subject to the provisions of section forty-eight, article six of the Constitution of this State.

W.Va. § 38–9–4

Any creditor of the person owning such homestead may assert a claim in a civil action, alleging that the value of the homestead is of greater value than five thousand dollars, and if the court shall be satisfied, from the proofs in the cause, that the allegations are true, it shall make such order or decree as may be necessary to subject such excess of value, above the sum of five thousand dollars, to the payment of the debt, or demand of such creditor. If more than one creditor shall join in such judicial proceeding, and their debts or claims be of equal priority, such excess shall be paid pro rata upon the debt or claim of each.

W.Va. § 38–9–5

In case of the death of a husband, wife or parent owning such homestead, the benefit thereof shall descend to his or her minor children, and shall be held and enjoyed by them as such homestead, until all of such infants attain the age of twenty-one years unless they sooner die.

A surviving spouse or child entitled to homestead protections in West Virginia is only protected against creditors up to the value of $5,000 and only until the children reach age 21. Such protection provides very little help toward keeping surviving family members in a family home, and the 2008 housing crisis, increase in the number of bankruptcies, and homelessness show the need for states to revisit their homestead protections.

In Iowa, any homeowner may declare a homestead, and his surviving spouse and/or minor children will be entitled to remain in the home until it is otherwise disposed of by law, but the surviving spouse may choose to take a life estate in the homestead in lieu of any dower interest in the decedent's other real estate.[38] This power to take a life estate in the homestead can dramatically defeat a decedent's estate plan and must be contemplated in advance if the decedent chooses to leave her surviving spouse anything less than the homestead itself.

Preparing estate plans in any state protecting the homestead property itself, or giving a surviving spouse or minor children the right to occupy and possess the family home, can be a trap for the unwary estate lawyer. Whether the surviving spouse is entitled to a particular value or actual possession of the property, and whether the homestead right is in addition to other spousal rights, or in lieu of them, are all issues with which a skilled estate lawyer must become familiar. These states with blended

---

[38] IOWA CODE ANN. §§ 561.11, .12 (West 2012).

homestead laws, especially if the value is reasonably high, can provide important spousal and family protections, but only if they are understood and managed well.

3. A CASH AMOUNT OR HOMESTEAD ALLOWANCE

The third kind of homestead protection consists of a cash allowance from the estate to be applied toward housing or other expenses that is free of claims of creditors. However, this amount only can be allocated to the surviving family members to cover lease payments or other necessary housing expenses. The Uniform Law Commissioners recognized the diversity of state homestead restrictions and benefits and sought to provide a uniform benefit for all surviving spouses and minor children through a simple cash allowance that was not tied to home ownership (thus benefitting families who rent or live in co-ops or mobile homes[39]).

The UPC currently provides that up to $22,500 is to be immediately available to the surviving spouse or children and is payable after the expenses of administration but before creditors or specific bequests. This cash allowance may be good for a year or more of rent to allow the survivors to settle the estate and pay debts. Depending on the circumstances, it may allow the survivors to remain in the family home long enough to resolve whatever financial affairs the decedent left for the survivors to settle. Under the UPC, the cash allowance is in addition to whatever other benefits the surviving spouse receives through an elective share or under a will. A number of states have adopted the UPC allowance approach (Arizona, Alaska, Hawaii, Michigan, Montana, Missouri, and Nebraska).[40] And some have adopted blended approaches that give both the allowance and some additional rights to particular homestead property (Alabama and Wyoming).[41]

The UPC is wonderful in its simplicity, and in recognizing that some allowance should be made for survivors of decedents who did not own their own homes. However, compared to some of the more generous protections noted above, the UPC is rather parsimonious in the allowance it provides. Yet, considering how many people's homes are under water, where they owe more on the mortgage than the home is worth, the UPC's allowance not only provides much needed cash, but is protected from all creditor claims.

---

[39] Because rights in leaseholds and co-ops are generally considered personal property, and not real property, residents in these types of properties often do not receive homestead protections. See Savage v. Pierson, 123 Nev. 86, 157 P.3d 697 (2007); Blankenau v. Landess, 261 Neb. 906 (2001). Florida, however, recognizes 99-year leases and co-op interests for homestead protections. See Higgs v. Warrick, 994 So. 2d 992 (Fla. 3rd DCA 2008); Southern Walls, Inc. v. Stillwell Corp., 810 So. 2d 566 (Fla. 5th DCA 2002).

[40] Examples of states having homestead allowances and their respective amounts include the following: $27,000—ALASKA STAT. ANN. § 13.12.402 (West 2012); $20,000—MONT. CODE ANN. § 72–2–412 (2001); $18,000—ARIZ. REV. STAT. ANN. § 14–2402A (West 2001); $15,000—HAW. REV. STAT. § 560:2–402 (West 2001); MICH. COMP. LAWS § 700.2402 (West 2002); MO. REV. STAT. § 474.290 (2001); $10,000—ME. REV. STAT. tit. 18–A, § 2–401 (2001); $7,500—NEB. REV. STAT. § 30–2322 (2001).

[41] See WYO. STAT. ANN. §§ 2–5–103 and 2–7–501 to 2–7–509 (2002) ($30,000); ALA. CODE § 43–8–110 (2002) ($6,000). For more information on Probate Homestead, see Gregory Duncan, Home Sweet Home? Litigation Aspects to Minnesota's descent of Homestead, 29 WM. MITCHELL L. REV. 185, 194–197 (2002).

UPC § 2–402. Homestead Allowance.

A decedent's surviving spouse is entitled to a homestead allowance of [$22,500]. If there is no surviving spouse, each minor child and each dependent child of the decedent is entitled to a homestead allowance amounting to [$22,500] divided by the number of minor and dependent children of the decedent. The homestead allowance is exempt from and has priority over all claims against the estate. Homestead allowance is in addition to any share passing to the surviving spouse or minor or dependent child by the will of the decedent, unless otherwise provided, by intestate succession, or by way of elective share.

Alt. § 2–402A. Constitutional Homestead.

The value of any constitutional right of homestead in the family home received by a surviving spouse or child must be charged against the spouse or child's homestead allowance to the extent the family home is part of the decedent's estate or would have been but for the homestead provision of the constitution.

Homestead allowances are helpful for the majority of people who do not own their homes and need an allowance for rent and utilities or to pay the mortgage if they do own it. Others may live in a home owned by another or by a trust, and still be able to claim homestead, even though they are not the fee owners of the property.[42] In most states, if the decedent did not own the homestead, the surviving family members are vulnerable to being evicted from their home. One important exception is rent-controlled apartments which usually may not be turned over by landlords when the primary tenant dies.[43]

In general, homestead is provided in addition to any bequests for the surviving spouse or children and is in addition to intestate or testate shares, the elective share, and other exempt property and family allowances.[44] Where probate courts are allowed to set aside real property as a homestead, the physical premises are protected for the surviving family. This is true even if the dollar amounts are not as high as the value of the homestead property itself. The key is in the ability of courts to guarantee that surviving family members are entitled to remain living in the family home, at the very least through the administration process, and preferably longer. But not all states treat the homestead property as additional to elective share or other bequests to family members. Thus, some states will deduct the value of homestead from elective share or testamentary bequests. Consider the Iowa statutes on this subject:

---

[42] Cargill v. Hedge, 358 N.W.2d 490 (Minn. Ct. App. 1984); Southern Walls, Inc. v. Stillwell Corp., 810 So. 2d 566 (Fla. 5th DCA 2002); Grimes v. McCrary, 211 S.W.2d 1005 (Tex. Civ. App. 1948). See Redmond v. Kester, 284 Kan. 209, 159 P.3d 1004 (2007) for homestead protections remaining on residential property placed into self-settled trusts.

[43] *In re* Davidson, 903 N.Y.S.2d 685 (Sup. Ct. 2010); Pick v. Cohen, 83 Cal. App. 4th Supp. 6, 100 Cal. Rptr. 2d 839 (Cal. App. Dep't Super. Ct. 2000).

[44] See 22 A.L.R. 437 (1923); Jeffrey A. Schoenblum, Multistate and Multinational Estate Planning, Table 6.01.

Iowa Code 561.11 OCCUPANCY BY SURVIVING SPOUSE.

Upon the death of either spouse, the survivor may continue to possess and occupy the whole homestead until it is otherwise disposed of according to law, but the setting off of the distributive share of the survivor in the real estate of the deceased shall be such a disposal of the homestead as is herein contemplated.

Iowa Code 561.12 LIFE POSSESSION IN LIEU OF DOWER.

The survivor may elect to retain the homestead for life in lieu of such share in the real estate of the deceased.

Iowa Code 561.14 DEVISE.

Subject to the rights of the surviving spouse, the homestead may be devised like other real estate of the testator.

The Homestead doctrine is not a simple one to absorb, particularly because the deviations among the states are so great. And of course, differences among the protected classes add to the complexity. In most states, the creditor protections are the subject of most litigation, and probate attorneys have to work hard to determine exactly how the homestead protections work to benefit surviving heirs. In this day of high tort judgments, homestead can make a relatively simple lawsuit quite complex. Consider the following case:

Middleton v. Lockhart

344 Ark. 572, 43 S.W.3d 113, (Ark. 2001)

On February 22, 1991, Kenneth G. Middleton was convicted of the first-degree murder of his wife, Katherine, and sentenced to life without parole for the murder plus 200 years for armed criminal action. A week later he entered into a contract to convey a tract of land known as the Middleton homeplace to his brother, which he deeded a week after that. Eight months earlier Katherine's family had filed a wrongful death suit against Kenneth, which went to trial after his criminal conviction and after the homeplace was deeded to his brother. He failed to defend the action and a judgment was entered against him for $1,350,000. In a suit by Katherine's family to set aside the transfer of the homestead, the trial court held that Kenneth had abandoned any homestead right when he murdered his wife. The Arkansas Supreme Court affirmed, explaining:

It is well established that as to a homestead there are no creditors. . . . The object of homestead laws is the protection of the family from dependence and want. It is intended to preserve the family home. Further, the law is to be liberally construed in the interest of the family home. [O]nce acquired, a homestead right is not terminated by death of a spouse or departure of children by reaching the age of majority. Additionally, divorce will not terminate the homestead right in the head of household who continues to occupy the homestead. . . . The question of what, if any, effect the murder of one spouse by the other in the context of a homestead right arising from marriage has on a homestead has not been considered by this court. . . .   The protection of a homestead exemption that Kenneth now seeks to assert came to him only as a consequence of his marriage to Katherine. The existence of a family is necessary to the acquisition of a homestead. Additionally, apart from his family, a debtor seeking a homestead exemption is entitled to no special consideration. Further, a spouse will retain his or her homestead by marriage even if through no fault of his or her own he or she is deserted, or his or her children leave. When Kenneth murdered his wife, he was the sole reason the marriage giving rise to his homestead right was terminated. Upon his wife's murder, all public policy reasons to uphold a homestead right evaporated.

We hold that where a person murders his or her spouse, any homestead rights that person enjoys personally by reason of the marriage to the murdered spouse are extinguished by the murder. The murder would not, however, affect any homestead rights arising from the murderer's status as head of household where such rights are necessary to provide the homestead protections to children or other dependents of the murderer.

Query: Do you think the court would have ruled the same way had Kenneth and Katherine had children who were still minors at the time of the suit? Why do you think that might matter? Furthermore, what if Kenneth and Katherine were not married, but were same-sex partners living with Katherine's biological child and the homestead was in Kenneth's name? Would he even be entitled to the *family* protections of homestead?

Chang v. Lederman

172 Cal. App. 4th 67, 90 Cal. Rptr. 3d 758, (Cal. App. 2d Dist. 2009)

Raphael Schumert, a physician, and Chang, a registered nurse, met in 1994. They lived together for several years before marrying on August 27, 2004. Approximately six months before his marriage to Chang, but while living with her, Schumert, who had been diagnosed with terminal cancer, retained Lederman, a probate attorney and estate planner, to prepare a revocable trust. The trust provided for two specific distributions upon Schumert's death: $30,000 plus some furniture to Chang and $10,000 to a friend. The residue of the trust estate was left to Schumert's only child, Roy Schumert, in trust. The trust also provided that, following Schumert's death, the Sherman Oaks residence was to be sold by his successor trustee or leased to a third party for a fair market rent. The trust specified: "Chang must vacate [the Sherman Oaks residence] within thirty (30) days of my death." Schumert died after amending the trust to reduce the sum for Chang from $30,000 to $15,000 and after executing a new will that did not provide in any way for Chang. After Schumert's death, Lederman wrote Chang requesting she vacate the Sherman Oaks residence, as provided in the trust.

Chang first sought to have the trust revoked and she be awarded a ½ interest in Schumert's entire estate under the omitted spouse doctrine. The trial court rejected her action and further held that her intervention violated the no-contest provision in the trust, which revoked the $15,000 bequest to Chang. Chang then filed a lawsuit against Lederman asserting breach of fiduciary duty, breach of ethical duties of attorney, professional negligence and intentional infliction of emotional distress, claiming that Lederman's demand that Chang move out of the Sherman Oaks residence shortly after the death of her husband "was extreme, outrageous and humiliating." The trial court again ruled against Chang, so she filed an amended complaint asserting, in pertinent part, that Lederman knew the probate homestead provision would protect her from having to move from the Sherman Oaks residence shortly after her husband's death,[45] but nonetheless failed to advise her of that provision and insisted she leave the residence. The trial court again found no duty by Lederman to Chang since Chang was not Lederman's client.

The court of appeals affirmed, explaining: *Chang had never been Lederman's client, and Lederman had no duty to provide legal advice to her simply because she was Schumert's widow. In light of these facts, none of the conduct alleged in the second amended complaint can reasonably be regarded as extreme or outrageous. The letter Lederman sent directing Chang to move from the Sherman Oaks residence, in his capacity as counsel for Hadar, the successor trustee, in connection with the administration of the Raphael Schumert 2004 Revocable Trust, was faithful to the express terms of the trust. Although Chang may have had some right to continued possession of the residence as Schumert's surviving spouse under the homestead provisions of the Probate Code, Lederman had no duty to advise her of those rights.*

Query: Though the court did not consider Attorney Lederman's actions malpractice or intentional infliction of emotional distress, do you believe it was unethical for him not to inform Chang of her right to homestead, not to account for it in the trust, or not to inform his client that upon his remarriage his new spouse would be entitled to homestead? Do you think Lederman was hoping Chang would not assert her homestead rights, or do you think he just didn't know about them?

Practice Point: Identifying Your Client—When the Simple Things Are Not So Simple

In *Chang*, the court highlights the fact that Lederman was not Chang's attorney, and therefore owed her no duty to provide legal advice. And that statement seems clear enough, doesn't it? After all, if attorneys were obligated to give legal advice to non-clients, wouldn't that make them, well, *clients*?

But, like most topics in this casebook, even simple matters like identifying your client can quickly become muddled when we throw in real life scenarios. Take for example, the fairly typical case of mom and dad who arrive at their planning meeting with you along with their two adult children. The parents share with you that they would like to draft will-based plans that would leave everything to these children, equally. We will delve into the ins-and-outs of Professional Responsibility later in the book, but for now, it's easy enough to see whom you would identify in your Engagement Letter as your clients, right? Clearly mom and dad.

---

[45]   CAL. PROB. CODE § 6500 provides, until the inventory is filed in a pending probate proceeding and for a period of 60 days thereafter, the decedent's surviving spouse and minor children are entitled to remain in possession of the family dwelling. CAL. PROB. § 6520 provides, during the administration of a probate estate, the court may set apart one probate homestead for the use of the surviving spouse and the minor children of the decedent. We need not decide the extent to which these provisions protect a widow in Chang's position, that is, in a situation in which there apparently is no community property or quasi-community property, the decedent and the surviving widow did not own property in common, and the widow is the express beneficiary of a gift of cash and personal property in an *inter vivos* trust and is otherwise excluded from any participation in the decedent's estate.

But, this might not be as easy as it seems. What if the children start asking technical questions about how the plan works? What if the oldest child shares with you that she is in the midst of a messy divorce and about to declare bankruptcy and wants to make sure that her inheritance won't be seized by creditors? As an attorney, you can never be too clear about articulating who is your client and to whom you are giving legal advice (after all, what would happen if that child's spouse happened to ask you to take over representation in that messy divorce?). At this point, you would also most likely be making a mental note to proactively explain to future clients that the planning meeting should just be between themselves and you to avoid this situation all together.

Sometimes identification of the client is clear, but balancing your duties between the clients when their circumstances change can also be a tricky maneuver. Imagine drafting wills for a long-time couple who is not married. After a discussion with you, they both insist that they would like their planning and execution meetings to be together. As it turns out, they each direct that their plan leave the other a substantial portion of their estate. And you are very careful about clarifying your role in your Engagement Letter. Assume that the execution goes smoothly and everyone is very happy. Now, fast forward to the following year, when you get a call from one of them who wants to amend his plan by removing the other partner altogether as a beneficiary. Are you in a conflict situation? Can you draft the changes? Do you have an obligation to tell the other partner, or, in contrast are you absolutely prohibited from telling the other partner?

Your exact duties in potential conflict situations will vary from state to state, but in all jurisdictions, you will have to consider these scenarios quite carefully in order to ensure that you are properly maintaining an ethical practice. Because estate planners enjoy the unusual situation of drafting client plans that may not come into play until many years later, your practice will necessarily involve a repeated exercise over time in looking at the same families and re-evaluating who your clients are in every new life situation.

Being careful and knowledgeable means hopefully you won't be sued by your client's survivors, as Attorney Lederman was, or have your case become an example of what not to do in future Trusts and Estates casebooks. Can you think of ways Lederman could have avoided the lawsuit Chang filed?

King v. Ellison

648 So. 2d 666, 19 Fla. L. Weekly S 557 (Fla. 1994)

Florence and Hubert Calhoun, a married couple, purchased property in Indian River County. The couple's respective wills, executed in 1973, bequeathed their entire estates to each other. Hubert's will also provided that if he outlived Florence, his property would pass to his children and stepchildren, share and share alike. Florence's will contained a like provision. The petitioners are the adult lineal descendants of Florence and the stepchildren of Hubert; the respondents are the adult lineal descendants of Hubert and the stepchildren of Florence.

In 1975 Florence died. Hubert married Rosemarie, established homestead in the Indian River property, and within two years of the remarriage passed away. Hubert's will, unchanged from 1973, left his property to his children and stepchildren, share and share alike. However, since the Indian River property was his homestead, its descent was governed by section 732.401(1), Florida Statutes (1991), notwithstanding any provision in his will to the contrary. Pursuant to section 732.401(1), Rosemarie, as surviving spouse, received a life estate in the homestead and Hubert's lineal descendants received a vested remainder. Florence's children (petitioners) brought suit, alleging that section 732.401(1) is unconstitutional because it conflicts with article X, section 4(c) of the Florida Constitution,[46] improperly vests a remainder interest in Hubert's adult lineal descendants, and imposes an improper restraint on the alienation of property. The trial court dismissed the complaint with prejudice.

The Florida Supreme Court found no conflict, explaining: Unlike prior precedent, *the challenged statute is not meant to be a restraint on the right to devise homestead property. The statute prescribes how property shall descend when not devised as permitted under Florida law or the constitution.*

Since Hubert died leaving a surviving spouse, his attempt to devise his homestead fails; therefore the homestead descends pursuant to section 732.401(1), i.e., the spouse takes a life estate and the lineal descendants take a vested remainder.

Query: Prior precedent had held that a complete prohibition on the right to devise homestead was unconstitutional. Consequently, Florida modified its statute to permit the homestead to be devised to the owner's spouse, as per the Constitution. But a testator may not devise the homestead to anyone but the owner's spouse. Although technically in accord with the Florida constitution, does the statute still seem an excessive restraint on the right to devise property? Work out who the petitioners and respondents are and which outcome benefits each party.

If you haven't already figured it out, homestead can be a very powerful mechanism for protecting family interests from creditors, including the decedent's creditors, and it can prove a wily trap for the unwary or unskilled estate planner. In *King v. Ellison*, the entire testamentary plan was set aside because of the failure of the decedent to consider how his second marriage, and his new spouse's homestead rights, would alter his original testamentary intentions. In a state with strict limitations on the ability to devise homestead property, estate lawyers, as well as bankruptcy lawyers, must be informed about and must inform their clients of the advantages and disadvantages of homestead. Because Hubert remarried, Florence's children received nothing, contrary to Hubert and Florence's wills. The home simply could not be devised by will. Do Florence's children have any remedy?

---

[46] FLA. STAT. § 732.401(1) (1991), reads:

(1) If not devised as permitted by law and the Florida Constitution, the homestead shall descend in the same manner as other intestate property; but if the decedent is survived by a spouse and lineal descendants, the surviving spouse shall take a life estate in the homestead, with a vested remainder to the lineal descendants in being at the time of the decedent's death.

Article X, section 4(c) of the Florida Constitution provides:

(c) The homestead shall not be subject to devise if the owner is survived by spouse or minor child, except the homestead may be devised to the owner's spouse if there be no minor child.

PROBLEMS

Identify the type of Homestead described in the following examples:

2.2. Tyra's husband Leo dies in an automobile accident while driving drunk. The other driver received significant injuries and sues Leo's estate to recover damages. Tyra's attorney tells her that the creditors may be able to force the sale of her home if it appraises above $300,000 because the state provides a $300,000 statutory homestead limitation but if the home appraises below that amount, a forced sale cannot occur.

2.3. When planning for her estate, Doris expresses her intent to leave her home to her sister when she dies because it was their parents' home. Doris was married with 3 minor children, but explained she was providing for those family members with ample life insurance policies instead. Her attorney explains that under state law, the home must pass to her spouse during his lifetime and then to her children, regardless of Doris' wishes to the contrary.

2.4. Gordon and Melissa were killed simultaneously in an accident. They had been married for 4 years and had 3 minor children at the time of their death. Fearful that the children would be evicted from their apartment, the appointed guardian was relieved to learn that each child could receive $7,500 which could be used to cover lease payments and necessary living expenses.

Can you think of any ways to better effectuate the clients' wishes in these scenarios and either avoid or utilize the state's homestead limitations?

C. FAMILY ALLOWANCE AND EXEMPT PROPERTY

Every state allows the probate courts to award an allowance, up to a maximum amount, for the maintenance of the surviving spouse and, usually, dependent children during the period of estate administration. The UPC does not mandate a dollar value on the amount of family allowance. Rather, the UPC allows "a reasonable allowance" out of the estate up to a maximum of $27,000. Other states also allow an amount up to a maximum value or a period of support: Fla. Stat. § 732.403 ($18,000); New Mexico § 45–2–402 ($30,000); Ga. § 53–3–1 (a year's support).

The UPC provision on family allowance provides:

UPC § 2–404. Family Allowance.

(a) In addition to the right to homestead allowance and exempt property, the decedent's surviving spouse and minor children whom the decedent was obligated to support and children who were in fact being supported by the decedent are entitled to a reasonable allowance in money out of the estate for their maintenance during the period of administration, which allowance may not continue for longer than one year if the estate is inadequate to discharge allowed claims. The allowance may be paid as a lump sum or in periodic installments. It is payable to the surviving spouse, if living, for the use of the surviving spouse and minor and dependent children; otherwise to the children, or persons having their care and custody. If a minor child or dependent child is not living with the surviving spouse, the allowance may be made partially to the child or his [or her] guardian or other person having the child's care and custody, and partially to the spouse, as their needs may appear. The family allowance is exempt from and has priority over all claims except the homestead allowance.

> (b) The family allowance is not chargeable against any benefit or share passing to the surviving spouse or children by the will of the decedent, unless otherwise provided, by intestate succession or by way of elective share. The death of any person entitled to family allowance terminates the right to allowances not yet paid.

Oregon gives the court very wide discretion in awarding a family allowance for support. The amount is not limited to any maximum amount and may include the transfer of real or personal property, including the entirety of the decedent's estate. If the court deems it appropriate, it may allow the spouse and dependent children to continue to occupy the principal place of abode for up to a year or award support for a period not to exceed two years.[47]

> **Ore. Rev. Stat. § 114.085. Setting apart whole estate for support; termination of administration.**
>
> If it appears, after the expiration of four months after the date of the first publication of notice to interested persons, that reasonable provision for support of the spouse and dependent children of the decedent, or any of them, warrants that the whole of the estate, after payment of claims, taxes and expenses of administration, be set apart for such support, the court may so order. There shall be no further proceeding in the administration of the estate, and the estate shall summarily be closed.

Most states also allow the surviving spouse and dependent children to receive certain personal property, or personal property up to a particular value, from the estate before administration. These exempt property set asides are usually limited to a particular value ($15,000 under the UPC § 2–403) but may include particular items of personal property such as the family automobiles, tools of a trade, household furniture, family mementos, appliances, and personal clothing and effects without reference to value. Ohio allows for the surviving spouse to take one watercraft and one outboard motor;[48] Florida allows the family to retain two automobiles which do not have a gross vehicle weight in excess of 15,000 lbs.;[49] and New Jersey allows the surviving spouse to take the decedent's and the survivor's wearing apparel.[50]

Where the statutes allow for certain specific property to pass to the surviving spouse as exempt property, like automobiles or watercraft, a testator is usually precluded from devising that property to someone else in her will. But when the testator devises the exempt property to the surviving spouse, it may pass by virtue of the exempt property statute and not the will, and thus might not be counted in valuing the estate for elective share or intestacy purposes, though it will be considered the decedent's property at death for estate tax purposes.

---

[47] See Oregon Revised Statutes, §§114–005 to 114–085.

[48] OHIO REV. CODE ANN. § 2106.18–19 (West 1990).

[49] FLA. STAT. ANN. § 732–402 (West). The gross vehicle weight limitation prevents people using large recreational vehicles or valuable motor homes as set asides under the exempt property provisions.

[50] N.J. STAT. ANN. § 3B:16–5 (West 1982). Under the doctrine of coverture, which prevailed in all of the common law states throughout the nineteenth century, all of a wife's personal property became the property of her husband upon the marriage. Thus, many states still allow the surviving wife to regain title to her clothing, jewelry, or other paraphernalia upon the death of her husband.

The UPC provision on Exempt Property states:

UPC § 2–403. Exempt Property.

In addition to the homestead allowance, the decedent's surviving spouse is entitled from the estate to a value, not exceeding $15,000 in excess of any security interests therein, in household furniture, automobiles, furnishings, appliances, and personal effects. If there is no surviving spouse, the decedent's children are entitled jointly to the same value. If encumbered chattels are selected and the value in excess of security interests, plus that of other exempt property, is less than $15,000, or if there is not $15,000 worth of exempt property in the estate, the spouse or children are entitled to other assets of the estate, if any, to the extent necessary to make up the $15,000 value. Rights to exempt property and assets needed to make up a deficiency of exempt property have priority over all claims against the estate, but the right to any assets to make up a deficiency of exempt property abates as necessary to permit earlier payment of homestead allowance and family allowance. These rights are in addition to any benefit or share passing to the surviving spouse or children by the decedent's will, unless otherwise provided, by intestate succession, or by way of elective share.

It is also important to determine the source of homestead, exempt property, and family allowances, for conflicts can arise if the decedent gave his watercraft to his grandson, but his surviving spouse or child wants the boat as exempt property. The UPC sets out the rules for determining what property is available and the priorities of claims.

UPC § 2–405. Source, Determination, and Documentation.

(a) If the estate is otherwise sufficient, property specifically devised may not be use to satisfy rights to homestead allowance or exempt property. Subject to this restriction, the surviving spouse, guardians of minor children, or children who are adults may select property of the estate as homestead allowance and exempt property. The personal representative may make those selections if the surviving spouse, the children, or the guardians of the minor children are unable or fail to do so within a reasonable time or there is no guardian of a minor child. The personal representative may execute an instrument or deed of distribution to establish the ownership of property taken as homestead allowance or exempt property. The personal representative may determine the family allowance in a lump sum not exceeding $27,000 or periodic installments not exceeding $2,250 per month for one year, and may disburse funds of the estate in payment of the family allowance and any part of the homestead allowance payable in cash. The personal representative or an interested person aggrieved by any selection, determination, payment, proposed payment, or failure to act under this section may petition the court for appropriate relief, which may include a family allowance other than that which the personal representative determined or could have determined.

(b) If the right to an elective share is exercised on behalf of a surviving spouse who is an incapacitated person, the personal representative may add any unexpended portions payable under the homestead allowance, exempt property, and family allowance to the trust established under Section 2–212(b).

Homestead, family allowance, and exempt property usually pass to the beneficiaries, *in addition to* other statutory entitlements, like the elective share or *legitime*. Thus, in most states, a surviving spouse may be entitled to the homestead, family allowance, and exempt property and still take an elective share, an intestate share, or a devised share, from the remaining property. For modest estates, these statutory set-asides can comprise a significant portion of the estate, and they come off the top, before any other devises can be satisfied. A surviving spouse who is then entitled to an elective share of one-third of the remainder of the probate estate or half of an intestate estate can upset an estate plan, like we saw in *King v. Ellison*. Ignoring the effect of these set asides can wreak havoc on most modest estate plans. At the same time, homestead can be a very important part of an estate plan in a jurisdiction that protects such property from the decedent's creditors, even if the donative freedom of the testator is drastically limited. Any estate planner who ignores homestead does so at her peril, for no attorney wants to be in Attorney Lederman's shoes, even if he was eventually vindicated.

PROBLEMS

Consider the following estate plan:

2.5. Testator died possessed of the following property:

Family Home	$100,000
Cash in Bank Accounts	$ 20,000
Personal Property	$ 50,000
Automobile	$ 10,000
Stocks and Bonds Portfolio	$120,000
Total Estate at Death	$300,000

Assuming the testator is survived by a spouse who is entitled to $100,000 homestead, $18,000 family allowance, and $15,000 in exempt property, the net probate estate would consist of $167,000 ($300,000 minus $100,000HS, $18,000FA, & $15,000EP). Take out debts and costs of administration and it is likely that less than half of this estate will be freely devisable by the testator.

Now recalculate the net probate estate by deducting the homestead, family allowance, and exempt property set-asides under the UPC, and for the statutes in your own state.

2.6. Using the same estate and homestead, family allowance, and exempt property set-asides as you used in Problem 2.5, calculate the surviving spouse's *total* share if debts and costs of administration are $30,000 and if:

a. the decedent died with a will that devised to the surviving spouse one-half of the net probate estate,

b. the decedent died with a will that left nothing to the spouse, and the state's elective share statute entitles the surviving spouse to a minimum of one-third of the net probate estate.

Now figure out how much is left to pass to children or other devisees that the testator may have wanted to benefit.

As you can see from this simple example, if the homestead allowance is fairly large, the surviving spouse will be entitled to the lion's share of a modest estate. Although most testators realize they must give their surviving spouse one-third to one-half of their estates, once we factor in the set-asides, the testator might be surprised to discover that his surviving spouse could take as much as 80–90% of his estate. While most testators choose to give their surviving spouse the majority of their estates, there are others who, for a variety of reasons, may want to limit the spouse's share. We will learn more about ways to do that when we discuss the elective share and ways to plan for the living in Chapter 7. Here, however, think about ways to limit, or minimize, the set-asides. One should also note that pre- or post-nuptial agreements may be used to allow spouses to waive or disclaim various statutory rights, including these statutory set-asides. We discuss the use of such contracts in Chapter 7 as well. Be aware, however, that some states are more lenient in allowing spouses to waive these rights, while others interpret ambiguities or omissions strictly against waiver or disclaimer.

When Bernie Madoff was originally charged with running a Ponzi scheme, and Richard Fuld was under investigation for the Lehman Brothers collapse, their wives were applying for homestead protections for their Florida vacation homes.[51] The image of wealthy capitalists shielding their ill-gotten gains through the use of Florida's generous homestead law generated a lot of public criticism. But besides modest tweaking to the bankruptcy code after OJ Simpson shielded his assets from the wrongful death suit filed by his ex-wife's family, no legal changes have been made to limit the creditor protections of the homestead laws in Florida, or elsewhere. In fact, where reforms have occurred, they have been to increase the value of homestead protections or make them applicable to more than fee ownership interests in real property. These creditor protections also pass to the donee after the death of the owner if the property is given to a family member. Thus, the Madoff and Fuld children and grandchildren can retain the family mansions without fear that creditors of Bernie's or Dickie's estates will be able to attach the property. Do you think homestead protections and limitations still make sense today, or are they even more necessary in light of the economic downturn and the mortgage crisis? How would you balance the rights of creditors with the needs of families in today's world? How would you balance the protections of family members in particular status relationships (spouse, child) with the lack of protections for those in functional, but not legally-recognized relationships (domestic partner, foster child)? If there is going to be a line, where would you draw it?

---

[51] See Catey Hill, *Ruth Madoff Files Homestead Exemption in Palm Beach on same day Authorities Announce Investigation*, New York Daily News (March 17, 2009), http://articles.ny dailynews.com/2009–03–17/news/17917349_1_ruth–madoff–homestead–exemption–ponzi;
Megan Mcardle, How OJ Simpson may help Dick Fuld from stiffing his Shareholders, The Atlantic (Jan 27, 2009), http://www.theatlantic.com/business/archive/2009/01/how–oj–simpson–may–help–keep–dick–fuld–from–stiffing–his–shareholders/4625/#disqus_thread.

D. Community Property

Currently ten states, containing roughly 25% of the country's population, allocate property rights under the community property rules developed in France and Spain, and not the common law regime of England. Eight of those states (Arizona, California, Idaho, Louisiana, Nevada, New Mexico, Texas, and Washington) were community property states from their inception. Wisconsin and Alaska have recently put into place statutes treating marital property at divorce and death as though it were community property. Alaska allows married couples to choose whether to hold their property separately or as community property.[52] Wisconsin treats marital property as co-owned regardless of how it is titled as between spouses,[53] but not as between one spouse and a third party.[54]

Community property is a relatively straightforward concept. Property owned separately by the spouses before marriage remains separate property unless intentionally commingled, but all property earned during the marriage, and even most income on separate property earned during the marriage, is owned jointly in undivided one-half shares. Thus, at death or dissolution, each spouse is entitled to devise or control his or her one-half of the community property. There is less need for elective shares or other spousal protections because, in community property states, each spouse is entitled to one-half of the marital estate. It is a more streamlined method to settle an estate. The UPC's new elective share provisions (2008 amendments) purport to replicate this outcome through a rather convoluted calculation that is anything but straightforward and simple, as you will see in Chapter 7.

Community property regimes reflect what, in trusts and estates scholarship, is referred to as the *partnership theory of marriage*. Because spouses work together to create and amass wealth, regardless of who is the principal wage-earner, community property regimes treat both spouses as joint owners of all marital property.[55] Because the presumption is in favor of community property, income from separate property will often be treated as community property, if earned during the marriage, unless it is kept distinct and separate from the commingled marital property.

Common law regimes, by contrast, focus primarily on the title-holder. Thus, income earned by one spouse is considered that spouse's sole and separate property to be disposed of however he or she thinks appropriate. To compensate for inequalities in wage earning and to recognize the non-economic contributions of non-wage-earning spouses, common law states put in place relatively generous provisions for distribution of assets upon dissolution and death. The equitable distribution rights (upon dissolution) and elective share rights (upon death) may purport to redistribute marital wealth in an equitable way, but they do not give the non-title holding spouse any control over the property during the marriage, and often cannot prevent the propertied spouse from disposing of all of the property prior to

---

[52] Alaska Stat. Ann. § 34.77.030(a) (West 1998).

[53] Wis. Stat. Ann. § 766.31(1), (2) (West 2012).

[54] *Id.* at 766.70(3)(e), (8).

[55] See Peter Harrington, Untying the Knot: Extending Intestacy Benefits to non-Traditional Families by Severing the Link to Marriage, 25 J. Civ. Rts. & Econ. Dev. 323 (2011); J. Thomas Oldham, You Can't Take it with you, and Maybe you Can't Even Give it Away: The Case of Elizabeth Baldwin Rice, 41 U. Mem L. Rev. 95 (2010). See also Shari Motro, Labor, Luck and Love: Reconsidering the Sanctity of Separate Property, 102 NW. U. L. Rev. 1623 (2008).

dissolution or death.[56] In certain states, a husband who wants to prevent his wife from taking any property at his death may, with some skillful planning, decrease his probate estate so dramatically as to essentially disinherit his wife. In other states, the surviving spouse will take a significant portion of the decedent's estate regardless of *inter vivos* gifts, life insurance, or other provisions made outside of the probate estate for the spouse. Understanding all of the spousal rights recognized in your state is critical for an effective estates and trusts practice.

Classification of property as *community* or *separate* can be difficult. If one spouse owned land prior to marriage, the states are split on whether income from that land during the marriage (say rent or income from timber or minerals) is community or separate.[57] But the appreciation in value of the land would be treated as separate in all community property states, unless community assets were invested in the land to improve its value. But upon divorce such appreciation may be treated as community property.[58] If a spouse's separate property is subject to a mortgage that is paid using community funds, some states simply credit the value of the mortgage payments back to the community, while others treat a portion of the property as community property.[59]

Some of the most complicated problems arise, however, when married couples move from a common-law to a community property state, or vice versa. Fourteen common law states have adopted the *Uniform Disposition of Community Property at Death Act,* which allows each spouse to dispose of half of the property that was acquired as community property. Essentially, the statute allows the property to retain its community character in the form of a *joint tenancy* or *tenancy in common.* In some states, the surviving spouse may be able to take a share of property as community property, and also take an elective share, essentially double-dipping.

On the other hand, community property states generally do not have adequate safeguards to protect the less wealthy partner if the couple moves from a common law to a community property state. Because the latter states do not have elective share or equitable distribution provisions, the surviving spouse who was not the principal title-holder of the marital property will not be entitled to much if the title-holding spouse disinherits her in his will. In this situation, the surviving spouse is entitled to no assets from the estate and has very little community property of her own because they have only recently moved to a community property state.

California, for one, has tried to solve at least some of these disparities. First, the California Probate Code defines community property as all property (real property within the state and personal property wherever situated) acquired during the marriage by a California domiciliary. The definition excludes property acquired by gift or inheritance, but includes all

---

[56] Of course, disinherited spouses can challenge *inter vivos* transactions that they believe defraud them of their marital property rights.

[57] Several states, including Idaho and Texas, would treat the income as community property. E.g., IDAHO CODE ANN. § 32–906(1) (West 1980), § 32–712(10) (West 1875); 3 TEX. FAM. L. SERV. § 24:6 (West 2007) citing TEX. CONST. art. 16 § 15. New Mexico and Washington would not. E.g., N.M. Stat. Ann. § 40–3–12 (West 1973); WASH. REV. CODE ANN. § 26.16.020 (West 2008).

[58] In re Balanson, 25 P.3d 28 (Colo. 2001).

[59] Cf. Pringle v Pringle, 712 P.2d 727 (Idaho App. 1985) (community property investments credited back to the community) with Lindemann v. Lindemann, 960 P.2d 966 (Wash. App. 1998) (increase in value attributable to labor during marriage divided among spouses at dissolution).

property acquired in exchange for community property.[60] The California Family Code, however, includes as community property for purposes of dissolution or legal separation any property held in joint tenancy,[61] *but the probate code does not.* Thus, where a spouse owns real property in joint tenancy with someone not her spouse, and the property transfers to the other joint tenant upon death, the surviving spouse has no interest, though the survivor would have an interest if the parties were divorcing.

Finally, California, like some community property states, does protect the surviving spouse of a couple that moved from a common law state to California by designating certain property as *quasi-community property.* Quasi-community property is all personal property (in California or outside) and real property located within California that was acquired by a decedent who was domiciled out of California, that would have been community property of both spouses if the decedent had been domiciled in California at the time of its acquisition.[62] At death, therefore, one half of the community property and one-half of the quasi-community property may be disposed of by the decedent, and the other half remains the property of the surviving spouse.[63]

Even with such detailed provisions, complications can occur. Consider a couple that moves from Indiana to California in which the husband had acquired the lion's share of the property and had recently married his third wife, who had very little property of her own. Shortly after the move, the wife dies, devising her half of the quasi-community property to her children by a prior marriage. Although her share of the quasi-community property may not be that large, if the marriage had not been long, her ability to devise half of all property acquired during their short marriage could have dramatic effects if the surviving husband's property was in the form of a business, or the property had recently undergone a dramatic increase in value.

On the other hand, what if the husband in this example predeceased his new wife, but shortly before his death had transferred out of his ownership significant pieces of property with the intent of preventing his wife from claiming her quasi-community share? California may allow the spouse to reclaim some of the transferred property from the transferee in certain circumstances, but provisions in the statute can be evaded with proper planning.[64]

Whatever logic exists in these code provisions for treating community property in the average couple, all bets are off when parties have separated, are living apart, or are in the process of divorce, but the legal dissolution is not yet final.

Despite the complexities (and deceptive simplicity) of community property regimes, the Uniform Probate Code has attempted to endorse more forcefully the partnership theory of marriage in its 2008 amendments to the elective share by treating a portion of the decedent's property as "marital property" and then allowing the surviving spouse a 50% share. The idea behind the UPC is that a certain amount of income accruing to a married couple should be considered the product of their joint effort and should be

---

[60] CAL. PROB. CODE § 28 (West 1990).

[61] CAL. FAM. CODE § 2581 (West 1993).

[62] CAL. PROB. CODE § 66 (West 1990).

[63] CAL. PROB. CODE §§ 100, 101 (West 1990).

[64] CAL. PROB. CODE § 102 (West 1990).

owned equally by both. The UPC has a complex calculation in which the "marital property" portion of a decedent's estate increases with length of marriage, so that a decedent married 15 years would have her entire estate considered marital property under the UPC.

One important aspect of community property laws that has yet to be addressed in most states is whether same-sex domestic partners will be entitled to hold property as community property. California provides that registered domestic partners may hold their property in the community, but Washington does not allow domestic partners the full equivalent of marital property rights by denying community property status for marital income. With the haphazard rules on same-sex marriage, domestic partnerships, and civil unions pasted onto the complexities of differences in common law and community property regimes, non-traditional couples need sound estate planning when they change domiciles.

Finally, Wisconsin, which was a former common law state, thoroughly revised its probate code to effectuate community property rights by adopting the Model Marital Property Act in 1997 (eff. 1998). The Act treats certain property acquired during the marriage as jointly owned property. Because the adoption was relatively recent, however, there are complex calculations that must be made regarding property acquired by married couples before the Act and after the Act for determining shares of surviving spouses.

Community property rules will make more sense when contrasted to the outmoded rules on dower and curtesy and the newer doctrines of the elective share, and we explore these differences more fully in the chapter on Planning for Current Generations (see Chapter 7 *infra*.) For now, the important point to remember is that once a person marries, most states will give the non-earning spouse some rights to the earnings and income of the other, even to the point of deeming half the property to belong to the non-earning spouse. And in common law states, although the non-earning spouse has little control over the property during the marriage, he or she has significant rights at death or dissolution.

Common law states that do not give the non-earning spouse half of the property when it is earned, instead allow the wage-earner spouse to control and manage that wealth, but give the non-earning spouse an equitable claim at dissolution or death, up to one-half or even more of the property acquired during the marriage. For purposes of homestead, exempt property, and family allowance, it's irrelevant whether the decedent died intestate or testate. These statutory rights attach to all estates regardless of size or manner of succession. Other rights, like the elective share, however, are relevant only in the testacy context, while some are unique to the intestacy context, and so we postpone discussion of other statutory rights until later.

PROBLEM

2.7. Arti and Raj married young, when they owned next to nothing. They had no children over the course of their marriage, but were very socially and financially involved in the lives of both of their parents, whom they supported happily. Over time, Raj purchased several commercial buildings in the name of his single member LLC, and began receiving considerable rental income. Arti found success as a writer of mystery novels. One of these made the New York Times Bestseller List and yielded over $1M in royalties to Arti, which she put in a separate savings account in her name. All other assets they owned as Tenants by the Entirety. She and Raj discussed their finances and were both comfortable knowing that the other would provide for his/her parents in the event of an untimely death. Unfortunately, Arti died from complications arising from surgery at the age of 35.

How would Raj's rights likely be affected during life and at Arti's death in a community property state? How would this likely differ in a common law state?

E. CHANGING DEFINITIONS OF FAMILY

1. SPOUSES AND QUASI-SPOUSES

As you can already see from what should be the relatively straightforward issues of Homestead, Exempt Property, Family Allowance, and Community Property, the laws in all 50 states privilege spouses and children or lineal descendants (children, grandchildren, great-grandchildren, etc.) for purposes of wealth transmission at death. But in our brave new world of sperm and egg donors, artificial reproductive techniques, same-sex domestic partnership and civil unions, and even the seemingly old-fashioned adoption, who gets counted as a spouse or child for these benefits may not be so straightforward.

When child-actor Gary Coleman died in 2010, the only outstanding will he had was one that gave everything to his wife, Shannon Price, who he had met in early 2007 and married a few months later. They divorced in August, 2008 and he died in May, 2010, from complications from a fall down the stairs of his home, having made no later will or other provision for his estate. In the probate court, Shannon Price petitioned to be named executor of his estate and to have his pre-divorce will probated because, according to her, she was his common-law wife under the laws of Utah, one of the few states that still recognizes common-law marriages. The Utah statute allows persons who were not married by state license to be deemed spouses if they resided together and had the "uniform and general reputation as being husband and wife."[65] Were they, like Elizabeth Taylor and Richard Burton, over being mad at each other and planning on remarrying? Was Shannon simply living there because they still had commingled lives, or was the divorce permanent? Should it matter to the court? Are states that have laws like Utah's recognizing common law marriages simply asking for litigation, are they purposefully providing ways around the bright-line rules of civil marriage for some public policy reason, or are they trying to provide equitable options because they realize that marriage is not a one-size-fits-all arrangement for many people?

We might think that being married is a lot like being pregnant, either you are or you aren't, but the unbelievable diversity of laws on same-sex partnerships, marriage, and civil unions belies this otherwise straightforward status question. Same-sex couples who marry in a state that recognizes same-sex marriage will face great uncertainty if they move to a state that doesn't recognize their status at all, or a state that grants them certain benefits through analogy to civil unions, but not other benefits. They might be spouses for inheritance purposes but not for community property purposes, or *vice versa*. Probably not since the mid-nineteenth

---

[65] See UTAH CODE ANN. § 30–1–4.5 (West 1987).

century have the laws on marriage in this country been so diverse and so hotly contested.

Although finding the loopholes in the arcane rules of marriage used to be the stuff of law school exams and lawyerly cocktail parties, they are now quite common and problematic. Begin first with the legally married couple who had a service, signed their marriage license, and filed it with their local state officer. Although their marriage may seem clear, it will be deemed void *ab initio* if one of the spouses was previously married and had not obtained a legal divorce. Bigamy remains a crime in most states and renders all future marriages void. And there are people like Norman Lewiston, a respected lung transplant specialist and Stanford medical professor, who had three wives unbeknownst to each other. Not until his death in 1991 did they discover the existence of the others.[66] Though he had defrauded the second and third wives by showing them phony divorce papers, is there a good reason to deny these women some, if not all, of the benefits of marriage? Or are we opening Pandora's box if all three wives are allowed pension benefits, some share of his inheritance, and the preference for being appointed personal administrator of his estate?

No longer can couples jump backwards over a broom stick to undo their marriages; they must get a divorce, sign a division of property agreement, and settle on custody of minor children. This is a far more complicated process than the one that got them hitched and, for somewhat obvious reasons, many people do not get an official divorce, leaving them and their intimate associates and family in a bind if they move on to other relationships.

There are also *putative* spouses, that is, people who think they are married but because of some defect in the process are not legally married. For most purposes, putative spouses are treated as legal spouses because the parties assumed they were married, acted accordingly, and there is no good public policy reason to upset a legal arrangement that they believed existed. In fact, if they knew their marriage was defective, they would probably have fixed it.[67] The *Uniform Marriage and Divorce Act*, § 209, gives a court authority to award some of the decedent's estate to his or her putative spouse. But in most instances, courts must use equitable remedies to grant rights to putative spouses.

There are also *voidable* marriages, marriages that were illegal when entered into, like marriages between underage persons or persons who are already married, but which are treated as valid if, upon reaching full age, or when the prior spouse dies, they continued to live as husband and wife and did not renounce their marriages. These persons would be treated as putative spouses even though the disability may have continued throughout the marriage, such as being unable to consummate the marriage.

Same-sex marriages are particularly complicated for estate planners today, as it seems that every few weeks a state legislature either prohibits same-sex marriage or approves it, and it's hard to predict what the law will

---

[66] Richard C. Paddock, *Doctor Led Three Lives with Three Wives*, L.A. TIMES, (Oct. 14, 1991), http://articles.latimes.com/1991–10–14/news/mn–436_1_stanford–professor.

[67] Marriage within the prohibited degrees of relationship, as between cousins, or aunt and nephew, cannot be fixed and yet courts will use their equitable powers to protect the surviving partner at death, especially if the parties were unaware of the defect. If that's the case, why not just let them get married? See Bedard v. Corliss, 82 Mass.App.Ct. 360, 973 N.E.2d 691 (Mass.App.Ct., 2012); Choa Yang Xiong v. Su Xionq, 800 N.W.2d 187, (Minn.App., 2011).

be next week, much less next year. At the time of writing this book, there are nine states and the District of Columbia that permit gay marriage.[68] Rhode Island recognizes same-sex marriages performed in other states but don't allow them within their state. Colorado, Delaware, Hawaii, Illinois, and New Jersey allow civil unions. California, Oregon, Nevada, and Rhode Island grant nearly all the rights of marriage to domestic partners. Hawaii and Wisconsin provide some of the rights of marriage to domestic partners.

Thirty-seven states, however, prohibit by either statute or constitution same-sex marriage, though some of those have recognized civil unions or domestic partnerships. And of course, the 1996 Defense of Marriage Act is under legal challenge in numerous federal cases across the country, as well as being deemed unconstitutional by the Obama administration's Justice Department. On July 1, 2011, the Justice Department filed a brief, in Karen Golinski's federal challenge to the denial of her California wife's rights to health benefits, stating that the suit should not be dismissed because the Defense of Marriage Act is unconstitutional. This unprecedented move will only spark more surprising developments in the battle for same sex marriage in this country. When Ted Olsen and David Boies, the lawyers on opposite sides in Bush v. Gore, joined forces to challenge California's Proposition 8, banning same-sex marriage, you knew the stakes were escalating. After a victory in the Ninth Circuit, in *Perry v. Brown*,[69] the Supreme Court has accepted cert and it is anyone's guess how they will rule on the federal constitutional question of prohibitions on same-sex marriage. By the time you read this, that answer may be settled. Or, as we suspect, there will continue to be many lingering questions even after the Court has spoken on California's law.

The patchwork of laws is particularly complicated for couples that move. Though they might be married in one state, a move to another state that doesn't recognize their marriage means they won't have the same state-law rights that they had before. And even if they move to a state that grants many of the rights of marriage to persons in civil unions or domestic partnerships, many state statutes use the term *spouse* to identify status for certain benefits that would not be available to couples in civil unions or domestic partnerships. For instance, the UPC cuts off the inheritance rights of children by and through their natural parents upon adoption, except when the child is adopted by the *spouse* of the natural parent (i.e. a step-parent).[70] A person might be the spouse of her lesbian partner in Massachusetts, but not in Nebraska, and if she chooses to adopt her partner's biological children, she may end up disinheriting them from their biological mother and her family because she is not recognized as a step-parent for inheritance purposes. *See* Nancy Polikoff, *A Mother Should Not Have to Adopt Her Own Child: Parentage Laws for Children of Lesbian Couples in the Twenty-First Century*, 5 Stan. J. C.R. & C.L. 201, 211–12 (2009).

A model statute has been proposed by Professor Thomas Gallanis that would grant full inheritance rights to domestic partners. See T.P. Gallanis, *Inheritance Rights for Domestic Partners*, 79 TUL. L. REV. 55 (2004). But even if same-sex marriage is available, until it becomes universally recog-

---

[68] Connecticut, Iowa, Maine, Maryland, Massachusetts, New Hampshire, New York, Vermont, Washington and the District allow same sex marriage. California allowed it for a period, and those marriages entered into during a period in 2008 are considered valid. But as of this writing, Californians today have only domestic partnerships available to them.

[69] 671 F.3d 1052 (9th Cir. 2012).

[70] UPC § 2–119.

nized across the 50 states and by the federal government, estate planning for LGBT couples must be done very carefully. As the Wall Street Journal explains:

> *Same-sex couples can get married in five states and the District of Columbia—and in New York starting July 25 [2011]. But the happily-ever-after part doesn't necessarily extend to their personal finances. Such couples still can't file a joint federal tax return, share retirement benefits, shield each other's assets from estate taxes or benefit from many other tax breaks provided through federal law. As a result, same-sex couples who marry have to stay on guard, doing even more financial and legal planning, in some cases, than those who don't choose to tie the knot.[71]*

Despite being granted inheritance rights under state law, same-sex couples lose out on over 1000 federal benefits, including valuable estate and gift tax deductions and pension and social security rights. This means that if Sally pays for more than $14,000 annually in support of her wife, Jane, she might have to file a gift tax return and pay gift taxes. Spouses don't have to keep track of property transfers between spouses because they are exempt from transfer taxes, but not so with domestic partners, unmarried heterosexual couples, or same-sex spouses. Same-sex couples, however, can take advantage of certain other tax benefits. They can set up a Grantor Retained Income Trust or seek the federal adoption credit for adopting their partner's children, both of which are denied to married couples.[72]

One could take an entire course devoted just to the estate planning issues for same-sex couples. And because of the steep learning curve and constantly changing rules, lawyers specializing in LGBTQ estates are appearing in most states. If you are not up to date on these legal issues, you would do your clients a disservice if you simply assumed that all state and federal rights of spouses are, or will be made, available to same-sex couples. Sadly, the UPC punted on the issue when it came to the inheritance penalty for second parent adoptions, simply reiterating the bright-line rule of the past—that spouses get privileged treatment not available for others in similarly-committed relationships.

2. CHILDREN AND QUASI-CHILDREN

Just when you think you've got spouses figured out, the next problem to face is identifying the children. For thousands of years, the only real issue for inheritance law purposes was the difference between marital and non-marital children. Illegitimate children were not entitled to inherit from their parents under the common law, and were considered *fillius nullius* (the son of nobody) in the laws of most of the United States in the early Republic. Although mothers of illegitimate children had exclusive custodial rights, they too could not pass property on to those same children under the laws of some states. See Paula Monopoli, *Non-Marital Children and Post-Death Parentage: A Different Path for Inheritance Law?* 48 SANTA CLARA L. REV. 857 (2008).

---

[71] Kelly Greene, *Marriage Brings Headaches for Same Sex Couples*, WALL STREET JOURNAL (July 9, 2011), http://online.wsj.com/article/SB10001424052702303982504576428341158786506.html.

[72] Raymond Prather, *Advising Same-sex Couples*, 28 No. 2 GPSolo 14, March, 2011, http://www.americanbar.org/publications/gp_solo/2011/march/advising_same_sex_couples0.html. See 46 U.S.C. § 23 (1983), detailing the adoption credit.

Although every state today has given the illegitimate child full legal status as a result of equal protection cases establishing that laws disadvantaging illegitimate children are subject to heightened scrutiny, the preferential treatment of marriage and social barriers against illegitimacy still result in significant differential treatment for marital and non-marital children.[73] See Solangel Moldonado, *Illegitimate Harm: Law, Stigma, and Discrimination against Non-Marital Children*, 632 FLA. L. REV. 345 (2011).

One difference that remains is the continued adherence to the legal fiction that a man is presumed to be the father of all children born to his wife. In 1784 Sir William Murray took this presumption to its extreme end. In 1782 Murray, who had been away for over two years, divorced his wife by private act of Parliament on the proof that she had borne a child while he was overseas. This result was deemed clear evidence of adultery and the House of Lords? gladly released Sir William from the conjugal tie that threatened to impose spurious offspring into his noble lineage. But not satisfied with divorcing his errant wife and leaving her destitute (while keeping all property she brought to the marriage under the laws of coverture), he then filed suit for exclusive custody of the child she had borne, and it was granted to him on the legal fiction that the husband of the mother is deemed, at law, to be the father of all children born to her during the marriage.[74]

The fiction of paternity has not gone the way of many onerous gender-based disabilities, but persists today, with the blessing of the Supreme Court. Consider the following case from Constitutional Law.

Michael H. v. Gerald D.

491 U.S. 110 (1989)

■ JUSTICE SCALIA gave the judgment of the Court and an opinion:

The facts of this case are, we must hope, extraordinary. On May 9, 1976, in Las Vegas, Nevada, Carole D., an international model, and Gerald D., a top executive in a French oil company, were married. The couple established a home in Playa del Rey, California, in which they resided as husband and wife when one or the other was not out of the country on business. In the summer of 1978, Carole became involved in an adulterous affair with a neighbor, Michael H. In September 1980, she conceived a child, Victoria D., who was born on May 11, 1981. Gerald was listed as father on the birth certificate and has always held Victoria out to the world as his daughter. Soon after delivery of the child, however, Carole informed Michael that she believed he might be the father [and she and Gerald split].

In the first three years of her life, Victoria remained always with Carole, but found herself within a variety of quasi-family units. [Sometimes they lived with Gerald, sometimes with Michael, and sometimes with another man, Scott K. When they lived with Michael, he held Victoria out as his child.] . . . In June 1984, Carole reconciled with Gerald and joined him

---

[73] Levy v. Louisiana, 391 U.S. 68, 70 (1968). See also Trimble v. Gordon, 430 U.S. 762 (1977) (prohibiting differential treatment in intestacy for marital and non-marital children).

[74] Consider the following discussions of the marital presumption: Rebecca Moulton, *Note, Who's Your Daddy?: The Inherent Unfairness of the Marital Presumption for Children of Unmarried Parents*, 47 FAM. CT. REV. 698 (2009) and Jana Singer, *Marriage, Biology and Paternity, The Case for Revitalizing the Marital Presumption*, 65 MD. L. REV. 246 (2006).

in New York, where they now live with Victoria and two other children since born into the marriage. [In Michael's 1984 suit for visitation rights, the court-appointed psychologist recommended that Victoria have continued contact with Michael and the trial court ordered limited visitation privileges *pendent lite*. Gerald intervened and moved for summary judgment on the ground that, under CAL. EVID. CODE § 621 "the issue of a wife cohabiting with her husband, who is not impotent or sterile, is conclusively presumed to be a child of the marriage." The Superior Court granted Gerald's motions and denied Michael's motions for continued visitation. The court found] that allowing such visitation would "violat[e] the intention of the Legislature by impugning the integrity of the family unit."

On appeal, Michael asserted, inter alia, that the Superior Court's application of § 621 had violated his procedural and substantive due process rights . . . the California Court of Appeal affirmed the judgment of the Superior Court and upheld the constitutionality of the statute [and] the California Supreme Court denied discretionary review. . . .

Michael raises two related challenges to the constitutionality of § 621. First, he asserts that requirements of procedural due process prevent the State from terminating his liberty interest in his relationship with his child without affording him an opportunity to demonstrate his paternity in an evidentiary hearing. We believe this claim derives from a fundamental misconception of the nature of the California statute. While § 621 is phrased in terms of a presumption, that rule of evidence is the implementation of a substantive rule of law. California declares it to be, except in limited circumstances, irrelevant for paternity purposes whether a child conceived during, and born into, an existing marriage was begotten by someone other than the husband and had a prior relationship with him. As the Court of Appeal phrased it:

> 'The conclusive presumption is actually a substantive rule of law based upon a determination by the Legislature as a matter of overriding social policy, that given a certain relationship between the husband and wife, the husband is to be held responsible for the child, and that the integrity of the family unit should not be impugned.'

Of course the conclusive presumption not only expresses the State's substantive policy but also furthers it, excluding inquiries into the child's paternity that would be destructive of family integrity and privacy.

This Court has struck down as illegitimate certain "irrebuttable presumptions." Those holdings did not, however, rest upon procedural due process. A conclusive presumption does, of course, foreclose the person against whom it is invoked from demonstrating, in a particularized proceeding, that applying the presumption to him will in fact not further the lawful governmental policy the presumption is designed to effectuate. But the same can be said of any legal rule that establishes general classifications, whether framed in terms of a presumption or not. In this respect there is no difference between a rule which says that the marital husband shall be irrebuttably presumed to be the father, and a rule which says that the adulterous natural father shall not be recognized as the legal father. Both rules deny someone in Michael's situation a hearing on whether, in the particular circumstances of his case, California's policies would best be served by giving him parental rights. We therefore reject Michael's procedural due process challenge and proceed to his substantive claim.

Michael contends as a matter of substantive due process that, because he has established a parental relationship with Victoria, protection of Gerald's and Carole's marital union is an insufficient state interest to support termination of that relationship. This argument is, of course, predicated on the assertion that Michael has a constitutionally protected liberty interest in his relationship with Victoria.

It is an established part of our constitutional jurisprudence that the term "liberty" in the Due Process Clause extends beyond freedom from physical restraint. Without that core textual meaning as a limitation, defining the scope of the Due Process Clause "has at times been a treacherous field for this Court," giving "reason for concern lest the only limits to . . . judicial intervention become the predilections of those who happen at the time to be Members of this Court." . . .

In an attempt to limit and guide interpretation of the Clause, we have insisted not merely that the interest denominated as a "liberty" be "fundamental" (a concept that, in isolation, is hard to objectify), but also that it be an interest traditionally protected by our society. As we have put it, the Due Process Clause affords only those protections "so rooted in the traditions and conscience of our people as to be ranked as fundamental." Our cases reflect "continual insistence upon respect for the teachings of history [and] solid recognition of the basic values that underlie our society. . . ."

This insistence that the asserted liberty interest be rooted in history and tradition is evident, as elsewhere, in our cases according constitutional protection to certain parental rights. Michael reads the landmark case of Stanley v. Illinois, 405 U.S. 645, 92 S.Ct. 1208, 31 L.Ed.2d 551 (1972), and subsequent cases as establishing that a liberty interest is created by biological fatherhood plus an established parental relationship-factors that exist in the present case as well. We think that distorts the rationale of those cases. As we view them, they rest not upon such isolated factors but upon the historic respect—indeed, sanctity would not be too strong a term—traditionally accorded to the relationships that develop within the unitary family. As Justice Powell stated for the plurality in Moore v. East Cleveland, supra, 431 U.S., at 503, 97 S.Ct., at 1938: "Our decisions establish that the Constitution protects the sanctity of the family precisely because the institution of the family is deeply rooted in this Nation's history and tradition."

Thus, the legal issue in the present case reduces to whether the relationship between persons in the situation of Michael and Victoria has been treated as a protected family unit under the historic practices of our society, or whether on any other basis it has been accorded special protection. We think it impossible to find that it has. In fact, quite to the contrary, our traditions have protected the marital family (Gerald, Carole, and the child they acknowledge to be theirs) against the sort of claim Michael asserts.[4]

---

[4]   Justice BRENNAN insists that in determining whether a liberty interest exists we must look at Michael's relationship with Victoria in isolation, without reference to the circumstance that Victoria's mother was married to someone else when the child was conceived, and that that woman and her husband wish to raise the child as their own. See *post,* at 2353. We cannot imagine what compels this strange procedure of looking at the act which is assuredly the subject of a liberty interest in isolation from its effect upon other people—rather like inquiring whether there is a liberty interest in firing a gun where the case at hand happens to involve its discharge into another person's body. The logic of Justice BRENNAN's position leads to the conclusion that if Michael had begotten Victoria by rape, that fact would in no way affect his possession of a liberty interest in his relationship with her.

The presumption of legitimacy was a fundamental principle of the common law. . . . We have found nothing in the older sources, nor in the older cases, addressing specifically the power of the natural father to assert parental rights over a child born into a woman's existing marriage with another man. Since it is Michael's burden to establish that such a power (at least where the natural father has established a relationship with the child) is so deeply embedded within our traditions as to be a fundamental right, the lack of evidence alone might defeat his case. But the evidence shows that even in modern times—when, as we have noted, the rigid protection of the marital family has in other respects been relaxed—the ability of a person in Michael's position to claim paternity has not been generally acknowledged.

Moreover, even if it were clear that one in Michael's position generally possesses, and has generally always possessed, standing to challenge the marital child's legitimacy, that would still not establish Michael's case. As noted earlier, what is at issue here is not entitlement to a state pronouncement that Victoria was begotten by Michael. It is no conceivable denial of constitutional right for a State to decline to declare facts unless some legal consequence hinges upon the requested declaration. What Michael asserts here is a right to have himself declared the natural father and thereby to obtain parental prerogatives. What he must establish, therefore, is not that our society has traditionally allowed a natural father in his circumstances to establish paternity, but that it has traditionally accorded such a father parental rights, or at least has not traditionally denied them. Even if the law in all States had always been that the entire world could challenge the marital presumption and obtain a declaration as to who was the natural father, that would not advance Michael's claim. Thus, it is ultimately irrelevant, even for purposes of determining current social attitudes towards the alleged substantive right Michael asserts, that the present law in a number of States appears to allow the natural father—including the natural father who has not established a relationship with the child—the theoretical power to rebut the marital presumption. What counts is whether the States in fact award substantive parental rights to the natural father of a child conceived within, and born into, an extant marital union that wishes to embrace the child. We are not aware of a single case, old or new, that has done so. This is not the stuff of which fundamental rights qualifying as liberty interests are made.

We do not understand why, having rejected our focus upon the societal tradition regarding the natural father's rights vis-à-vis a child whose mother is married to another man, Justice BRENNAN would choose to focus instead upon "parenthood." Why should the relevant category not be even more general—perhaps "family relationships"; or "personal relationships"; or even "emotional attachments in general"? Though the dissent has no basis for the level of generality it would select, we do: We refer to the most specific level at which a relevant tradition protecting, or denying protection to, the asserted right can be identified. If, for example, there were no societal tradition, either way, regarding the rights of the natural father of a child adulterously conceived, we would have to consult, and (if possible) reason from, the traditions regarding natural fathers in general. But there is such a more specific tradition, and it unqualifiedly denies protection to such a parent.

In accord with our traditions, a limit is also imposed by the circumstance that the mother is, at the time of the child's conception and birth, married to, and cohabitating with, another man, both of whom wish to raise the child as the offspring of their union. It is a question of legislative policy and not constitutional law whether California will allow the presumed parenthood of a couple desiring to retain a child conceived within and born into their marriage to be rebutted.

We do not accept Justice BRENNAN's criticism that this result "squashes" the liberty that consists of "the freedom not to conform." It seems to us that reflects the erroneous view that there is only one side to this controversy—that one disposition can expand a "liberty" of sorts without contracting an equivalent "liberty" on the other side. Such a happy choice is rarely available. Here, to provide protection to an adulterous natural father is to deny protection to a marital father, and vice versa. If Michael has a "freedom not to conform" (whatever that means), Gerald must equivalently have a "freedom to conform." One of them will pay a price for asserting that "freedom"—Michael by being unable to act as father of the child he has adulterously begotten, or Gerald by being unable to preserve the integrity of the traditional family unit he and Victoria have established. Our disposition does not choose between these two "freedoms," but leaves that to the people of California. Justice BRENNAN's approach chooses one of them as the constitutional imperative, on no apparent basis except that the unconventional is to be preferred.

The judgment of the California Court of Appeal is Affirmed.

Lengthy dissents by Justices Brennan and White criticized the plurality opinion's reliance on a narrow view of parenthood and tradition.

This decision was handed down in 1989, two years after the Court held that the right to descent and devise was a constitutionally protected property right in *Hodel v. Irving*. The California law treating Victoria as the child of her mother's husband, Gerald, instead of her biological father, Michael, is part of the Family Law Code, which sets out all the laws on marriage, divorce, child custody, child support, adoption, property division at divorce, and, the issue here, the procedures for determining paternity. In most cases, the reasons for bringing a paternity suit are to either obtain child support for a non-marital child, or to allow the child to partake in the biological parent's estate at death. Most states tie their family codes to their probate codes, thus relying on the family code to define who is a child and who is a parent for all purposes, including for inheritance and probate purposes.

But in many ways the family codes and the probate codes have very different policy goals and many judges and lawmakers are not willing to be as expansive and liberal in the probate arena as in the family law arena. Too many innocent children would be negatively affected if the family law codes did not recognize and protect functional parenthood or expansively interpret domestic relations laws that were written a hundred years ago and relied on bright-line status relationships like marriage or biological parentage. In family law, we have moved away from the old common law rules of *fillius nullius* that served only to punish children without deterring adulterous intercourse among adults. With the sexual revolution and the advent of no-fault divorce, family code definitions of parent and child had to move into the twentieth century and recognize that penalizing non-marital children violated their constitutional rights and imposed a moral strait-jacket on parents that they seemed incapable of or unwilling to abide.

Probate codes, on the other hand, are more mired in nineteenth century social values, protecting biological inheritance rights from spurious offspring or, as you will see shortly, the claims of functional children, like foster children. *Hodel v. Irving* reaffirmed the importance of the right to devise one's property, or to have it pass to one's children. But most lawmakers and judges have resisted the tendency of the family codes to expansively interpret parent/child relationships for probate and inheritance purposes. Can you see why that might be? Can you also make an argument for why it should not be, why probate codes should protect functional children as well as biological children? And you should be thinking already about the contradictions raised by this case. If Michael H is denied parental rights under the family law code, will Victoria be able to inherit from or through him on his death, or upon the death of his parents? Do you think Gerald D's family, his biological children or grandchildren, or his siblings, will allow Victoria to inherit from and through Gerald without challenging her rights? To the extent the probate and family law codes are aligned, there are likely to be more opportunities for children to inherit from and through adults who are not their biological parents (as in the foster children situation) and from and through biological parents who are not involved in their care and upbringing. Do you think that is a move in the right direction? Or do you think the Court's finding of no constitutional right to a parent/child relationship, because states have traditionally made laws that favor traditional marriage, bodes ill or well for inheritance rights or testamentary freedom?

As you can see from *Michael H. v. Gerald D.*, the non-traditional family creates a number of difficult problems for dealing with the inheritance rights of children and lineal descendants. Should Victoria be able to inherit from both Michael and Gerald, just one or the other, or neither? Prior to 2008, the UPC defined the parent/child relationship for purposes of intestate succession solely in terms of biological and/or adoptive status, and both were seen as bright-line determinations. If the adoption wasn't final, there wasn't a parent/child relationship and the adopted child was out of luck if his soon-to-be adoptive parent died before the paperwork was final. Consider Victoria's inheritance rights if the pre-2008 UPC is in effect. Consider what her rights might have been under the parent/child provision of your state.

UPC § 2–114. Parent and Child Relationship [2006].

(a) Except as provided in subsections (b) and (c), for purposes of intestate succession by, through, or from a person, an individual is the child of his [or her] natural parents, regardless of their marital status. The parent and child relationship may be established under [the Uniform Parentage Act] [applicable state law] [insert appropriate statutory reference].

(b) An adopted individual is the child of his [or her] adopting parent or parents and not of his [or her] natural parents, but adoption of a child by the spouse of either natural parent has no effect on (i) the relationship between the child and that natural parent or (ii) the right of the child or a descendant of the child to inherit from or through the other natural parent.

> (c) Inheritance from or through a child by either natural parent or his [or her] kindred is precluded unless that natural parent has openly treated the child as his [or hers], and has not refused to support the child.

This provision was adopted in many states and continues in operation, despite recent changes to the UPC and the tremendous technological changes that have occurred since it was originally promulgated in 1969. In 2008, however, the Uniform Law Commission amended the parent/child provisions of the UPC to delete § 2–114 and replace it with the following eight provisions. At this time, Colorado, New Mexico, North Dakota, Utah, and the Virgin Islands have adopted these amendments, and other states are poised to follow. These provisions are aimed at modernizing the probate code definitions of parent and child for those states that have rigid definitions in their probate codes. But some scholars have criticized the amendments for further unlinking the probate code definitions from the family codes.[75]

> **UPC § 2–114. Parent Barred from Inheriting in Certain Circumstances.**
>
> (a) A parent is barred from inheriting from or through a child of the parent if:
>
> (1) the parent's parental rights were terminated and the parent–child relationship was not judicially reestablished; or
>
> (2) the child died before reaching [18] years of age and there is clear and convincing evidence that immediately before the child's death the parental rights of the parent could have been terminated under law of this state other than this [code] on the basis of nonsupport, abandonment, abuse, neglect, or other actions or inactions of the parent toward the child.
>
> (b) For the purpose of intestate succession from or through the deceased child, a parent who is barred from inheriting under this section is treated as if the parent predeceased the child.

This provision bars a parent from inheriting from his or her child if the parent abandoned the child or had parental rights terminated. Would Michael H. not be entitled to inherit from Victoria under this provision if Michael is not paying child support?

> **UPC § 2–115. Definitions. In this [subpart]:**
>
> (1) "Adoptee" means an individual who is adopted.
>
> (2) "Assisted reproduction" means a method of causing pregnancy other than sexual intercourse.
>
> (3) "Divorce" includes an annulment, dissolution, and declaration of invalidity of a marriage.
>
> (4) "Functioned as a parent of the child" means behaving toward a child in a manner consistent with being the child's parent and performing functions that are customarily performed by a parent, including fulfilling parental responsibilities toward the child, recognizing or holding out the child as the individual's child, ma-

---

[75] See Lee-ford Tritt, *Sperms and Estates: An Unadulterated Functionally Based Approach to Parent–Child Property Succession*, 62 SMU L. REV. 367 (2009).

terially participating in the child's upbringing, and residing with the child in the same household as a regular member of that household.

(5) "Genetic father" means the man whose sperm fertilized the egg of a child's genetic mother. If the father–child relationship is established under the presumption of paternity under [insert applicable state law], the term means only the man for whom that relationship is established.

(6) "Genetic mother" means the woman whose egg was fertilized by the sperm of a child's genetic father.

(7) "Genetic parent" means a child's genetic father or genetic mother.

(8) "Incapacity" means the inability of an individual to function as a parent of a child because of the individual's physical or mental condition.

(9) "Relative" means a grandparent or a descendant of a grandparent.

Note how the definitions now focus on *genetic* relationship rather than *natural* relationship, the latter is a term that has less scientific meaning but is used throughout most state's inheritance and probate laws. Adopting the more accurate term genetic relationship may call into question rules like the putative father presumption. Gerald D. might qualify as a natural parent under most state laws, but he would not qualify as a genetic parent.

UPC § 2–116. Effect of Parent–Child Relationship.

Except as otherwise provided in Section 2–119(b) through (e), if a parent–child relationship exists or is established under this [subpart], the parent is a parent of the child and the child is a child of the parent for the purpose of intestate succession.

UPC § 2–117. No Distinction Based on Marital Status.

Except as otherwise provided in Sections 2–114, 2–119, 2–120, or 2–121, a parent–child relationship exists between a child and the child's genetic parents, regardless of the parents' marital status.

So would Victoria be able to inherit from Michael H. even though he is prohibited by law from having a parental relationship with his daughter? Should she be able to?

UPC § 2–120. Child Conceived by Assisted Reproduction Other Than Child Born to Gestational Carrier.

(a) [Definitions.] In this section:

(1) "Birth mother" means a woman, other than a gestational carrier under Section 2–121, who gives birth to a child of assisted reproduction. The term is not limited to a woman who is the child's genetic mother.

(2) "Child of assisted reproduction" means a child conceived by means of assisted reproduction by a woman other than a gestational carrier under Section 2–121.

(3) "Third-party donor" means an individual who produces eggs or sperm used for assisted reproduction, whether or not for consideration. The term does not include:

(A) a husband who provides sperm, or a wife who provides eggs, that are used for assisted reproduction by the wife;

(B) the birth mother of a child of assisted reproduction; or

(C) an individual who has been determined under subsection (e) or (f) to have a parent–child relationship with a child of assisted reproduction.

(b) [Third-Party Donor.] A parent–child relationship does not exist between a child of assisted reproduction and a third-party donor.

(c) [Parent–Child Relationship with Birth Mother.] A parent–child relationship exists between a child of assisted reproduction and the child's birth mother.

(d) [Parent–Child Relationship with Husband Whose Sperm Were Used During His Lifetime by His Wife for Assisted Reproduction.] Except as otherwise provided in subsections (i) and (j), a parent–child relationship exists between a child of assisted reproduction and the husband of the child's birth mother if the husband provided the sperm that the birth mother used during his lifetime for assisted reproduction.

(e) [Birth Certificate: Presumptive Effect.] A birth certificate identifying an individual other than the birth mother as the other parent of a child of assisted reproduction presumptively establishes a parent–child relationship between the child and that individual.

(f) [Parent–Child Relationship with Another.] Except as otherwise provided in subsections (g), (i), and (j), and unless a parent–child relationship is established under subsection (d) or (e), a parent–child relationship exists between a child of assisted reproduction and an individual other than the birth mother who consented to assisted reproduction by the birth mother with intent to be treated as the other parent of the child. Consent to assisted reproduction by the birth mother with intent to be treated as the other parent of the child is established if the individual:

(1) before or after the child's birth, signed a record that, considering all the facts and circumstances, evidences the individual's consent; or

(2) in the absence of a signed record under paragraph (1):

(A) functioned as a parent of the child no later than two years after the child's birth;

(B) intended to function as a parent of the child no later than two years after the child's birth but was prevented from carrying out that intent by death, incapacity, or other circumstances; or

(C) intended to be treated as a parent of a posthumously conceived child, if that intent is established by clear and convincing evidence.

(g) [Record Signed More than Two Years after the Birth of the Child: Effect.] For the purpose of subsection (f)(1), neither an individual who signed a record more than two years after the birth of the child, nor a relative of that individual who is not also a relative of the birth mother, inherits from or through the child unless the individual functioned as a parent of the child before the child reached [18] years of age.

(h) [Presumption: Birth Mother Is Married or Surviving Spouse.] For the purpose of subsection (f)(2), the following rules apply:

(1) If the birth mother is married and no divorce proceeding is pending, in the absence of clear and convincing evidence to the contrary, her spouse satisfies subsection (f)(2)(A) or (B).

(2) If the birth mother is a surviving spouse and at her deceased spouse's death no divorce proceeding was pending, in the absence of clear and convincing evidence to the contrary, her deceased spouse satisfies subsection (f)(2)(B) or (C).

(i) [Divorce Before Placement of Eggs, Sperm, or Embryos.] If a married couple is divorced before placement of eggs, sperm, or embryos, a child resulting from the assisted reproduction is not a child of the birth mother's former spouse, unless the former spouse consented in a record that if assisted reproduction were to occur after divorce, the child would be treated as the former spouse's child.

(j) [Withdrawal of Consent Before Placement of Eggs, Sperm, or Embryos.] If, in a record, an individual withdraws consent to assisted reproduction before placement of eggs, sperm, or embryos, a child resulting from the assisted reproduction is not a child of that individual, unless the individual subsequently satisfies subsection (f).

(k) [When Posthumously Conceived Child Treated as in Gestation.] If, under this section, an individual is a parent of a child of assisted reproduction who is conceived after the individual's death, the child is treated as in gestation at the individual's death for purposes of Section 2–104(a)(2) if the child is:

(1) in utero not later than 36 months after the individual's death; or

(2) born not later than 45 months after the individual's death.

UPC § 2–121. Child Born to Gestational Carrier.

(a) [Definitions.] In this section:

(1) "Gestational agreement" means an enforceable or unenforceable agreement for assisted reproduction in which a woman agrees to carry a child to birth for an intended parent, intended parents, or an individual described in subsection (e).

(2) "Gestational carrier" means a woman who is not an intended parent who gives birth to a child under a gestational agreement. The term is not limited to a woman who is the child's genetic mother.

(3) "Gestational child" means a child born to a gestational carrier under a gestational agreement.

(4) "Intended parent" means an individual who entered into a gestational agreement providing that the individual will be the parent of a child born to a gestational carrier by means of assisted reproduction. The term is not limited to an individual who has a genetic relationship with the child.

(b) [Court Order Adjudicating Parentage: Effect.] A parent–child relationship is conclusively established by a court order designating the parent or parents of a gestational child.

(c) [Gestational Carrier.] A parent–child relationship between a gestational child and the child's gestational carrier does not exist unless the gestational carrier is:

(1) designated as a parent of the child in a court order described in subsection (b); or

(2) the child's genetic mother and a parent–child relationship does not exist under this section with an individual other than the gestational carrier.

(d) [Parent–Child Relationship with Intended Parent or Parents.] In the absence of a court order under subsection (b), a parent–child relationship exists between a gestational child and an intended parent who:

(1) functioned as a parent of the child no later than two years after the child's birth; or

(2) died while the gestational carrier was pregnant if:

(A) there were two intended parents and the other intended parent functioned as a parent of the child no later than two years after the child's birth;

(B) there were two intended parents, the other intended parent also died while the gestational carrier was pregnant, and a relative of either deceased intended parent or the spouse or surviving spouse of a relative of either deceased intended parent functioned as a parent of the child no later than two years after the child's birth; or

(C) there was no other intended parent and a relative of or the spouse or surviving spouse of a relative of the deceased intended parent functioned as a parent of the child no later than two years after the child's birth.

(e) [Gestational Agreement after Death or Incapacity.] In the absence of a court order under subsection (b), a parent–child relationship exists between a gestational child and an individual whose sperm or eggs were used after the individual's death or incapacity to conceive a child under a gestational agreement entered into after the individual's death or incapacity if the individual intended to be treated as the parent of the child. The individual's intent may be shown by:

(1) a record signed by the individual which considering all the facts and circumstances evidences the individual's intent; or

(2) other facts and circumstances establishing the individual's intent by clear and convincing evidence.

(f) [Presumption: Gestational Agreement after Spouse's Death or Incapacity.] Except as otherwise provided in subsection (g), and unless there is clear and convincing evidence of a contrary intent, an individual is deemed to have intended to be treated as the parent of a gestational child for purposes of subsection (e)(2) if:

(1) the individual, before death or incapacity, deposited the sperm or eggs that were used to conceive the child;

(2) when the individual deposited the sperm or eggs, the individual was married and no divorce proceeding was pending; and

(3) the individual's spouse or surviving spouse functioned as a parent of the child no later than two years after the child's birth.

 (g) [Subsection (f) Presumption Inapplicable.] The presumption under subsection (f) does not apply if there is:

(1) a court order under subsection (b); or

(2) a signed record that satisfies subsection (e)(1).

(h) [When Posthumously Conceived Gestational Child Treated as in Gestation.] If, under this section, an individual is a parent of a gestational child who is conceived after the individual's death, the child is treated as in gestation at the individual's death for purposes of Section 2–104(a)(2) if the child is:

(1) in utero not later than 36 months after the individual's death; or

> (2) born not later than 45 months after the individual's death.
>
> **(i) [No Effect on Other Law.]** This section does not affect law of this state other than this [code] regarding the enforceability or validity of a gestational agreement.

As is immediately apparent, these 2008 amendments are quite complex. They deal with the real-life events that happen in people's lives, like artificial reproductive technologies, the adoption that isn't completed when the adoptive parent dies, posthumously conceived children, non-marital children, and parents who do not acknowledge their genetic offspring. They do not, however, treat the problems facing the growing number of children of same-sex couples except to the extent they fit within the surrogacy or adoption situations described here. They continue to rely on traditional status relations of *spouses* at a time when the marriage laws in this country are very unstable and without recognizing that one's relation to one's children is not necessarily tied to one's relation to one's spouse or the genetic parent of one's child. With more and more individuals demanding legal recognition of and protection for non-traditional relationships, we will see the inheritance laws and public policies of the diverse states coming under increased pressure to either expand the protections to more people or limit them for all, as we have seen with the same-sex marriage debate.

Same sex couples, and gay individuals generally, face a number of obstacles in all aspects of reproduction and family-creation. On the one extreme are states that prohibited adoption entirely by homosexual persons (Florida's gay adoption ban, the last in the country, was struck down in September, 2010)[76] or have reinstituted virtual bans by providing for marriage preferences.[77] On the other hand, there are states like California, Connecticut, Massachusetts and the District of Columbia that allow second parent adoptions by the non-biological parent in a same-sex relationship. These statutes may work for lesbian parents, where one is the biological parent but may be unable to marry her partner and therefore allow the partner to qualify as a step-parent. But in those states without a specific statute allowing second parent adoptions, the biological parent runs the risk of having all of her legal relationships to her children severed when her partner adopts her children. And in many states, the legality of second parent adoptions is unclear.[78]

Gay men have even more difficulty legalizing their parent/child relations if they do not have children through "natural means." A number of states outlaw surrogacy contracts altogether, thus prohibiting gay men from contracting with a surrogate to provide both an egg and the gestational services.[79] Instead, these men often find themselves faced with hundreds of thousands of dollars in expenses to arrange for a separate egg donor and

---

[76] Fla. Dep't of Children & Families v. X.X.G., 45 So.3d 79 (Fla. 3d DCA 2010).

[77] Mississippi prohibits adoption by couples of the same gender (MISS. CODE ANN. § 93–17–3(2) (West 1955)); Utah prohibits adoptions by any person "in a relation that is not a legally valid and binding marriage under the laws of the state" (UTAH CODE ANN. § 78B–6–117(3)(b) (West 2008)); Arkansas prohibited any person from adopting if cohabiting with an unmarried partner. In April 2011, the Arkansas Supreme Court struck down the Arkansas statute as unconstitutionally burdening the rights of prospective foster and adoptive parents. Ark. Dept. of Human Servs. v. Cole, 2011 Ark. 145 (2011).

[78] See National Center for Lesbian Rights, *Adoption by Lesbian, Gay, and Bisexual Parents: An Overview of Current Law*, available at: http://www.nclrights.org/site/DocServer/adptn0204.pdf?docID=1221.

[79] See Carla Spivak, *The Law of Surrogate Motherhood in the U.S.*, 58 AM. J. COMP. LAW 97 (2010).

gestational surrogate in order to get around the default rule that the biological mother (who provides both genetic material and gestation) will be deemed the legal mother.[80] And if they use the sperm from one partner, the other partner will need to complete a second parent adoption if he is not a genetic parent. And the second parent adoption risks terminating the child's inheritance rights from his genetic father.

Also, many states use different standards to determine who is a child for purposes of family law and succession law, leading to the problem of children being unable to inherit from a functional parent who has all the legal rights of parent. Who qualifies as a relative for purposes of succession to a rent-controlled apartment may be different from who qualifies as a relative for intestate succession purposes. And with the tremendous numbers of children in the foster care system, living with relatives, living in non-traditional blended families, or simply abandoned, children and parents in many instances without the resources to undertake formal adoption procedures, the UPC provides very little help. By continuing to rely on the formal status-based measurements of marriage and legal adoption, the 2008 UPC amendments provide virtually no remedy. Parents and children are left relying on expensive litigation to try to protect their inheritance rights.

Consider the following cases and whether or not the 2008 UPC parent-child amendments would have provided for a different outcome.

Bean v. Ford

32 Cal. 4th 160, 8 Cal. Rptr. 3d 541, 82 P.3d 747, 2004 Cal. Daily Op. Service 363, 2004 D.A.R. 461 (2004)

Terrold Bean was in the foster care system when he was placed with Kathleen and Arthur Ford at the age of 2. Bean lived with the Fords for 20 years, until he married and left home. He still maintained his relationship with Arthur Ford and their natural daughter, Mary Catherine Ford, and served as the administrator of Mary Catherine's estate after her death in 1999. Upon the death of Arthur Ford, a nephew and a niece, who had not seen Ford in over 15 years, and had not attended his funeral, petitioned the court to be determined his heirs and entitled to his entire estate. Bean also filed a statement of interest to be determined Ford's heir. The court ruled that Bean was not entitled to Ford's estate because he had not been formally adopted and the court refused to extend the doctrine of equitable adoption to this case stating: *Although the evidence showed the Fords and Bean enjoyed a close and enduring familial relationship, evidence was totally lacking that the Fords ever made an attempt to adopt Bean or promised or stated their intent to do so; they neither held Bean out to the world as their natural or adopted child . . . nor represented to Bean that he was their child.*

Query: Is there anything Terrold Bean could have done to ensure his right to inherit? At what point should equity intervene when the child has performed all the duties of a child? Is that what inheritances are for?

---

[80] See Lee-ford Tritt, *Sperms and Estates: An Unadulterated Functionally Based Approach to Parent–Child Property Succession*, 62 SMU L. REV. 367 (2009).

In re Martin B.

17 Misc. 3d 198, 841 N.Y.S.2d 207, 2007 NY Slip Op 27306, 238 N.Y.L.J. 25 (2007)

Two grandchildren born from cryopreserved semen of the [trust] set-tlor's son claimed a right to inherit as the "issue" of their grandfather from a trust he established, even though they were born 5 years after the death of their father and their grandfather, but before the death of the interven-ing life tenant. In deciding whether posthumously-born children should count as the grandfather's "issue," the court explained the problem and its solution as follows: *Compounding the problem, . . . decisions and enact-ments from earlier times—when human reproduction was in all cases a natural and uniform process—do not fit the needs of this more complex era. . . . In this case legislative action has not kept pace with the progress of science. In the absence of binding authority, courts must turn to less im-mediate sources for a reflection of the public's evolving attitude toward assisted reproduction—including statutes in other jurisdictions, model codes, scholarly discussions and Restatements of the law. . . . As can clear-ly be seen from all the above, the legislatures and the courts have tried to balance competing interests. On the one hand, certainty and finality are critical to the public interests in the orderly administration of estates. On the other hand, the human desire to have children, albeit by biotechnology, deserves respect, as do the rights of the children born as a result of such scientific advances. To achieve such balance, the statutes, for example, re-quire written consent to the use of genetic material after death and establish a cut-off date by which the child must be conceived. . . . Indeed, it is noted that the Restatement of Property suggests that "[u]nless the language or circumstances indicate that the transferor had a different intention, a child of assisted reproduction [be] treated for class-gift purposes as a child of a person who consented to function as a parent to the child and who func-tioned in that capacity or was prevented from doing so by an event such as death or incapacity" (Restatement [Third] of Property [Wills and Other Donative Transfers] 14.8 [Tentative Draft No. 4 204]). . . . The rationale of the Restatement. . . should be applied here, namely, if an individual consid-ers a child to be his or her own, society through its laws should do so as well. . . . Accordingly, in the instant case, these post-conceived infants should be treated as part of their father's family for all purposes. Simply put, where a governing instrument is silent, children born of this new bio-technology with the consent of their parent are entitled to the same rights 'for all purposes as those of a natural child.'*

Query: Do you think the court would have ruled that children adopted by the father after the death of the grandfather could inherit from the latter? What if the children were adults when they were adopted? Is the court more willing to allow these children to inherit because they were genetically true grandchil-dren?

Astrue v. Capato

566 U.S. __, 132 S.Ct. 2021 (2012)

Eighteen months after her husband, Robert Capato, died of cancer, Karen Capato gave birth to twins conceived through *in vitro* fertilization using her deceased husband's frozen sperm. Karen applied for social secu-rity survivor's benefits on behalf of the twins, but it was denied by the

Social Security Administration. The District Court affirmed, holding that because the twins could not inherit under the Florida intestacy law of the father's domicile, they were not children for purposes of Social Secuirty. The Third Circuit reversed, holding that 42 U.S.C. § 416(h)(2)(A) defines child to mean the biological or adopted child of an insured individual, and does not refer to state law definitions of child. The Supreme Court reversed again, holding that despite the definition of a child as including the uncontested biological twins here, other provisions of the Social Security Act limited benefits to those persons qualified to inherit under the state intestacy laws of the insured's domicile. And because Florida law would not allow these children to inherit from their biological father, they were denied federal Social Security benefits as well. Justice Ginsberg explained the relationship between state law definitions of parent/child and husband/wife and federal law.

Reference to state law to determine an applicant's status as a "child" is anything but anomalous. Quite the opposite. The Act commonly refers to state law on matters of family status. For example, the Act initially defines "wife" as "the wife of an [insured] individual," if certain conditions are satisfied. § 416(b). Like § 416(e), § 416(b) is, at least in part, tautological (" 'wife' means the [insured's] wife"). One must read on, although there is no express cross-reference, to § 416(h) (rules on "[d]etermination of family status") to complete the definition. Section 416(h)(1)(A) directs that, " for purposes of this subchapter," the law of the insured's domicile determines whether "[the] applicant and [the] insured individual were validly married," and if they were not, whether the applicant would nevertheless have "the same status" as a wife under the State's intestacy law. (Emphasis added.) The Act similarly defines the terms "widow," "husband," and "widower." See § 416(c), (f), (g), (h)(1)(A).

Indeed, as originally enacted, a single provision mandated the use of state intestacy law for "determining whether an applicant is the wife, widow, child, or parent of [an] insured individual." 42 U.S.C. § 409(m) (1940 ed.). All wife, widow, child, and parent applicants thus had to satisfy the same criterion. To be sure, children born during their parents' marriage would have readily qualified under the 1939 formulation because of their eligibility to inherit under state law. But requiring all "child" applicants to qualify under state intestacy law installed a simple test, one that ensured benefits for persons plainly within the legislators' contemplation, while avoiding congressional entanglement in the traditional state-law realm of family relations.

Query: Does it seem fair to allow differences among state probate laws to result in differential treatment of similarly situated beneficiaries of federal entitlements? It's not that Robert Capato paid less in social security taxes because he was a domiciliary of Florida than domiciliaries of states that would allow these children to inherit. The Court relied in part on the stated policy of the SSA that benefits are provided to those dependents who the insured was supporting. Assuming Robert Capato left his entire estate to his wife, in trust, for the benefit of any posthumously-conceived children, should the definition and the policy be better nuanced?

Matter of Brewington's Estate

173 Mont. 458, 568 P.2d 133, (Mont. 1977)

Raymond Brewington died intestate in the 1950's. His wife, Helen Harmon Brewington, survived him. Raymond had several brothers and sisters, but under the laws of intestate succession Helen inherited the entire estate. Helen did not remarry and died intestate September 12, 1975. Several cousins survived her. During the probate of Helen's estate, her cousins were listed as heirs in a petition for adjudication of intestacy. At the time of Helen's death several brothers and sisters of her deceased husband Raymond were still living. One of them, Lawrence Brewington, filed a petition in Helen's estate proceedings asking the district court to amend the determination of heirs, claiming he was one of her next of kin under Montana's laws of succession. . . .   Lawrence does not contend he is entitled to inherit all of Helen's estate, to the exclusion of her cousins. Rather, he contends under the common law doctrine of "ancestral succession", he is entitled to inherit that portion of her estate which came to her when her husband Raymond died. He contends he should be allowed to trace this property. . . .   Under the common law doctrine of ancestral succession, property reverted to the line of family from which property was descended or devised. Because "next of kin" is not defined in the Montana version of the Uniform Probate Code, and the doctrine of ancestral succession has not expressly been abrogated by statute or overruled by court decision, Lawrence argues that collateral relatives of a predeceased spouse should be included among next of kin as to property which descended from that spouse . . . .

The court denied Lawrence's claim on the ground that the Montana Probate Code did not define the term "kindred," but that earlier versions and case law defined it narrowly to include only relatives by consanguinity, and not by affinity. It explained its conclusion as follows: *Lawrence correctly states the 'law favors one's own blood relatives as the natural object of one's bounty'. He does not allege, however, that he was entitled to priority over his brother's wife on the death of his brother 20 years ago, and by statute, Raymond's "bounty" passed in full to Helen at that time. Raymond's estate should not be open to new claims 20 years later. Lawrence also argues that in equity less distant relatives through marriage should receive the benefit of an estate over more distant cousins by blood. In this connection, this Court recognizes the general comments of the Uniform Probate Code, 8 U.L.A. Probate Intestate Succession, pp. 322, 323: 'While the prescribed patterns may strike some as rules of law which may in some cases defeat intent of a decedent, this is true of every statute of this type. In assessing the changes it must therefore be borne in mind that the decedent may always choose a different rule by executing a will.'*

Query: If Raymond and Helen had died simultaneously, her property would have passed directly to her blood relatives and Raymond's would have passed to his blood relatives. Should there be a presumption that when a husband and wife die intestate, especially in states where the surviving spouse takes 100% of the first spouse's estate, a portion of the second spouse's estate should pass back to the first spouse's family upon her death? Laws tracing ancestral property and returning it to the family of origin go back for centuries in many European countries and were slowly changed in the 18th and 19th centuries as a result of increasing mobility of the population, a growing land and securities market, and beliefs that the conjugal tie is more important than ancestral ties.

In re Est. of Bennett

255 Mich. App. 545, 662 N.W.2d 772, (2003)

In this case the decedent left a will, leaving his entire estate to his wife if she survived him, and if she did not, then his entire estate in equal shares to his four natural children and four step-children (natural children of his predeceased wife). His wife, however, did not survive him, but he remarried after the death of his first wife, without changing his will. At his death, therefore, his second wife was entitled to an intestate share as a pretermitted spouse. The Michigan pretermitted spouse statute, M.C.L. § 700.2301, provided that:

> *(1) Except as provided in subsection (2), if a testator's surviving spouse marries the testator after the testator executes his or her will, the surviving spouse is entitled to receive, as an intestate share, not less than the value of the share of the estate the surviving spouse would have received if the testator died intestate as to that portion of the testator's estate, if any, that is not any of the following; . . . (a) Property devised to a child of the testator who was born before the testator married the surviving spouse and who is not the surviving spouse's child.*

In the context of the facts of the case, the surviving spouse's share was taken only from the step-children's portion of the bequeathed estate, and not the natural children's portion, because the latter was protected under the statute. As a result, all of the step-children's portions abated in order to pay the surviving spouse's share, and none of the natural children's portions were reduced. Thus, the surviving second spouse received 50% of the estate, the four natural children split the remaining 50%, and the step-children received nothing.

Query: How should the law treat dispositions under a will made before a person marries? Would your answer change if the marriage was a first marriage for both parties and it lasted 50 years, or if it was a third marriage and lasted for only two years? Here the decedent chose to treat his natural children and his step-children the same, but he was prevented from doing so because the law treated the step-children as strangers, thus protecting the devise to the natural children and causing the devise to the step-children to fail. We will see many other examples in which the legal distinctions between children and non-children or spouses and non-spouses will cause some or all of a testator's estate plan to fail. If this decedent had known that his new wife would be entitled to a share of his estate, do you think he realized it would all come at the expense of his step-children and not be abated ratably across all of his testamentary devises?

For most people, the complexities of the new UPC parent/child provisions may look more like the stuff of law school exams than issues to be faced in a routine estates and trusts practice. As technology changes, however, and states begin to adopt these new provisions, the practicing bar should provide guidance to legislatures and clients about inheritance issues for the non-traditional family. If 70% of children today are being raised in non-traditional families, should courts leave it to legislatures to fix things, or fill the breach using their equity powers?

PROBLEMS

2.8. Luke has three children over the course of his 15 year marriage to Lena (Lucy, Lacey, and Lewis). He calls you to tell you that he just revoked his will (which left everything to Lena at his death and if Lena predeceases him, then everything passes equally to his three children) because a friend told him that intestacy would be much easier for the family after death. He goes on to share the following with you, "By the way, in case you get wind of it, you should know: My friend Gina is claiming that I am her son's real father. I don't know if she's right or not, but he does look an awful lot like me. She is getting a DNA test done. Can you imagine? What a mess. The only other children I thought I might have would be the ones that might come about through Lena's *in vitro* procedures. Can you believe it? Oh, and Lena was pregnant with our first child, Lucy, before we married and I'm beginning to think Lucy might not be genetically mine, though I love her as much as the others."

If Luke happened to die just after his call with you (and before he could execute the new will that you are already drafting for him and before Gina could complete the DNA test), who would be his likely heirs under the UPC and under the parent/child statute of your state? Assume that 45 days after Luke's death, Lena finds out that she is three weeks pregnant. (By the way, if this seems like a crazy scenario, remember that in estate planning, truth is actually often stranger than fiction).

2.9. Switch the facts and assume that Lena had revoked her will and dies intestate, leaving fertilized embryos that Luke has placed into a gestational surrogate 8 months after her death. Twins are born nine months later! Who are the potential legal heirs?

Practice Point: The Doctrine of the Fertile Octogenarian

Despite the fact that every client is unique and truly has her own story to tell in the estate planning meeting (and by now, you should be picking up on the fact that sometimes the stories can be quite interesting), I always relied on one particular moment when I could deliver a line that would make my older female client's smile.

Here's how it would generally play out: in discussing how she wanted her property to pass at death, I would say, "Okay, so we want everything to pass to (heirs names) and if they predecease you, then their shares should pass to (heirs' names). But we have to address another important possibility: under the theory of the Fertile Octogenarian, we should assume that you might still have children well into your eighties and beyond!" At which point, she would usually smile and say something along the lines of, "only if miracles truly exist," or "over my dead body," depending on her level of terror at that particular moment.

This legal fiction of the Fertile Octogenarian has actually been the subject of more than a little derision over the years, with some scholars believing its origins (possibly the Biblical story of Sarah giving birth at age 90), serve to render it absurd or even "antediluvian" in present times.[81] And, even ten years ago, it seemed like good old common sense to *know* that a woman conceiving a child in her eighties and beyond was just the stuff of fiction (and The Rule Against Perpetuities, incidentally).

---

[81] Nancy Knauer, *Legal Fictions and Juristic Truth*, 23 ST. THOMAS L. REV. 1, 2 (2010).

Ah, but times do change, and quickly. In 2008, for example, a 72 year old Indian woman and her 75 year old husband reportedly gave birth to twins.[82] The same year, Rajo Devi, a 70 year old Indian woman gave birth to a daughter.[83] Both families conceived through in vitro fertilization. Similarly, in 2010, the CBS documentary "World's Oldest Moms" examined the lives of four women who used technology to have children well into their post-menopause years.

Of course this has dramatic implications in the area of estate planning, more details of which will be discussed in later chapters. But for now, suffice to say that estate planners everywhere are genuinely thankful that this silly little legal fiction of the Fertile Octogenarian has been a necessary part of solid plans, even in the days when it was, actually, impossible.

F. ADOPTION, ADULT ADOPTION, EQUITABLE ADOPTION, AND FOSTERING

The UPC treats adopted children as genetic children for all inheritance purposes from, through, and by the adopted parents. Thus, an adopted child will be able to inherit from his adoptive parents, grandparents, and collateral relatives, and the latter will be able to inherit from and through the adopted child. And in many adoptions, the natural or genetic parents relinquish their parental rights in order to allow the adoption to take place. One of those parental rights is the right to inherit from the child and for the child to inherit from and through the genetic parent. UPC § 2–119 provides that all inheritance rights cease between an adopted child and her genetic parents unless the child is adopted by a *spouse* of a genetic parent (a step-parent), a relative of a genetic parent, or the child is adopted after the death of both genetic parents. And, UPC § 2–118 provides that a parent–child relationship exists between an adoptive child and the adoptive parents for purposes of inheritance and succession.

Reading these two provisions carefully, can you think of instances of non-traditional family relations that would result in unintended disinheritance or unintended inheritance under the new UPC provisions.

UPC § 2–118. Adoptee and Adoptee's Adoptive Parent or Parents.

(a) [Parent–Child Relationship Between Adoptee and Adoptive Parent or Parents.] A parent–child relationship exists between an adoptee and the adoptee's adoptive parent or parents.

(b) [Individual in Process of Being Adopted by Married Couple; Stepchild in Process of Being Adopted by Stepparent.] For purposes of subsection (a):

(1) an individual who is in the process of being adopted by a married couple when one of the spouses dies is treated as adopted by the deceased spouse if the adoption is subsequently granted to the decedent's surviving spouse; and

(2) a child of a genetic parent who is in the process of being adopted by a genetic parent's spouse when the spouse dies is treated as adopted by the deceased spouse if the genetic parent survives the deceased spouse by 120 hours.

---

[82] Karen Russo, *World's Oldest Mom*, ABC NEWS (July 4, 2008), http://abcnews.go.com/Health/ActiveAging/story?id=5309018 & page=1#.UFaFMmdDD3E.

[83] *Another 70-year-old in India has IVF Baby*, Msnbc (Dec. 8, 2008),, http://www.msnbc.msn.com/id/28112285/ns/health–pregnancy/t/another—year–old–india–has–ivf–baby/.

(c) [Child of Assisted Reproduction or Gestational Child in Process of Being Adopted.] If, after a parent–child relationship is established between a child of assisted reproduction and a parent under Section 2–120 or between a gestational child and a parent under Section 2–121, the child is in the process of being adopted by the parent's spouse when that spouse dies, the child is treated as adopted by the deceased spouse for the purpose of subsection (b)(2).

UPC § 2–119. Adoptee and Adoptee's Genetic Parents.

(a) [Parent–Child Relationship Between Adoptee and Genetic Parents.] Except as otherwise provided in subsections (b) through (e), a parent–child relationship does not exist between an adoptee and the adoptee's genetic parents.

(b) [Stepchild Adopted by Stepparent.] A parent–child relationship exists between an individual who is adopted by the spouse of either genetic parent and:

(1) the genetic parent whose spouse adopted the individual; and

(2) the other genetic parent, but only for the purpose of the right of the adoptee or a descendant of the adoptee to inherit from or through the other genetic parent.

(c) [Individual Adopted by Relative of Genetic Parent.] A parent–child relationship exists between both genetic parents and an individual who is adopted by a relative of a genetic parent, or by the spouse or surviving spouse of a relative of a genetic parent, but only for the purpose of the right of the adoptee or a descendant of the adoptee to inherit from or through either genetic parent.

(d) [Individual Adopted after Death of Both Genetic Parents.] A parent–child relationship exists between both genetic parents and an individual who is adopted after the death of both genetic parents, but only for the purpose of the right of the adoptee or a descendant of the adoptee to inherit through either genetic parent.

(e) [Child of Assisted Reproduction or Gestational Child Who Is Subsequently Adopted.] If, after a parent–child relationship is established between a child of assisted reproduction and a parent or parents under Section 2–120 or between a gestational child and a parent or parents under Section 2–121, the child is adopted by another or others, the child's parent or parents under Section 2–120 or 2–121 are treated as the child's genetic parent or parents for the purpose of this section.

Section 2–122. Equitable Adoption. This [subpart] does not affect the dotrine of equitable adoption.

Notably, the 2008 UPC amendments continue to rely on traditional marriage status for the step-parent adoption exception, thus potentially precluding the child from inheriting from her genetic parent if she is adopted by the same-sex, or unmarried heterosexual partner of that genetic parent. And although some states allow foster children to inherit from foster parents, the UPC made no provision whatsoever for foster children or other functional children in the 2008 amendments. California law, for example, allows a foster child to inherit if the parent–child relationship began during the child's minority and continued throughout the joint lifetime of the parent and child, and it is established by clear and convincing evidence that the foster parent would have adopted the foster child but for a legal barrier.[84]

Children who have been legally adopted, except perhaps those adopted by their genetic parent's same-sex partner, should have a relatively easy time convincing a court that they should inherit from their adoptive parents. And the new UPC provisions provide that a child in the process of adoption also can inherit from the parent who was trying to adopt her if the parent dies before the process is complete. But the UPC makes no provision for foster children, even those who become permanent family members and for whom a meaningful parent/child relationship exists. Terrold Bean would have been out of luck under the UPC, just as he was under the California law, even though California had a provision allowing foster children to inherit in narrow circumstances. Because there had been no *legal* impediment to Bean's adoption, the foster child provision did not apply and the state had no other provision to give functional children inheritance rights. There is no provision for foster children under the UPC.

The most common way to get around the strict rules of legal adoption is the doctrine of *equitable adoption*. Equitable adoption doctrine permits a person to inherit from another who either had contracted to adopt the child and never followed through, or who should be deemed an adoptive parent for intestacy purposes because the child performed her duties as a child and relied on the adult's representations that he would adopt the child. But despite being an equitable remedy to allow a person to inherit where the equities would demand it, courts have been very hesitant to apply the doctrine, especially in the context of step-parents. How would you advise a parent or child after reading the following cases?

Est. of Chambers

175 Cal. App. 4th 891, 96 Cal. Rptr. 3d 651, (Cal. App. 2d Dist. 2009)

Earnest Chambers, Jr. (Chambers), died intestate on January 2007 at the age of 83. Darren Wayne Chambers (Ernest's nephew) filed a petition alleging that he was the adopted son of Chambers' deceased brother, entitling him to a determination that he was Chambers' sole heir by intestate succession. Dorvail Money (son) challenged that petition and asked that he be determined as the sole heir because he was Chambers' natural son. Money, who was born in 1978, claimed he was the product of Chambers' extramarital affair with his mother, Diana Williams. Chambers divorced his first wife and married Williams in 1982 (4 years after Money was born) but they divorced in 1984. Nephew challenged the son's claim, arguing that the latter was a mere step-son and can only prevail if he proves equitable adoption. The son claimed that he was the natural son and merely had to prove paternity under Texas law. The evidentiary standard for proving equitable adoption is clear and convincing, and the evidentiary standard for proving paternity under the Family Law Code is a preponderance of the evidence. The probate court agreed with the son, and ruled that he had met the paternity requirement by a preponderance of the evidence, and that the nephew had failed to rebut that evidence by showing clear and convincing evidence to the contrary. On appeal, the court reversed and remanded, explaining that the probate court erroneously relied on the wrong provisions of the family code and probate code.

---

[84] CAL. PROB. CODE § 6454 (West 2009).

The probate court's reliance on Family Code section 7611(d) by way of Probate Code section 6453, subdivision (a) was misplaced. Instead, the issue was governed by subdivision (b) of Probate Code section 6453, which calls for proof by clear and convincing evidence in cases falling under Family Code section 7630, subdivision (c) (section 7630(c)). Section 7630(c) describes who has standing to bring actions to determine the existence of a father and child relationship "with respect to a child who has no presumed father under Section 7611 or whose presumed father is deceased. . . . " In other words, when a child born out of wedlock wants to show he is the natural child of a man who died without leaving a will, if the child relies on proof that the alleged father openly held him out as his own child, he must do so by clear and convincing evidence. (Prob. Code, § 6453, subd. (b)(2) . . . . The legislative history, as discussed at length by other appellate courts, shows the Legislature had good reason to impose this higher burden of proof: to discourage dubious paternity claims made after a man's death for the sole purpose of inheritance.

Respondent is trying to establish paternity after Chambers's death based on a claim that Chambers openly held respondent out as his son while Chambers was alive. That is precisely the scenario encompassed by Probate Code section 6453, subdivision (b)(2) that calls for proof by clear and convincing evidence. Because the probate court acted under the wrong statutory provisions and applied the incorrect (and lesser) standard of proof, we reverse and remand for a new hearing where the proper standard of proof is applied.

Query: This case shows one unintended consequence when different standards for paternity are required under the probate code and the family code. Because the probate court applied the family code standard of preponderance of the evidence, and not the probate code's clear and convincing standard, the issue was remanded for a new hearing. Does it make sense to you that a child claiming paternity should have a higher bar to pass if seeking an inheritance rather than child support? Note too how the Texas probate code uses a different standard to prove paternity if the putative father is dead and a lesser standard if the father is alive. Does this distinction make sense?

Est. of Thompson

760 N.W.2d 208, 2008 WL 4877762 (Iowa Ct. App. 2008)

When Pamela Jones was four years old, her father married Christine Thompson and, subsequently, Christine and Pamela shared a close and loving mother–daughter relationship. The district court found that Christine *treated Pamela as she would have treated her own child and that Pamela treated [Christine] as if she were [her] own mother. Christine Thompson died intestate and with no surviving issue; consequently, her estate passes to her relatives in Germany who had little contact with her, including property Christine received from Pamela's father's estate, unless Pamela can show that she was equitably adopted by Christine.* The court explained that a *person claiming to inherit under the theory of adoption by estoppel or equitable adoption has the burden to prove (1) an unexecuted agreement or contract to adopt entered into by the decedent, and (2) performance by the adopted child.* The court of appeals agreed with the district court that Pamela did not establish an equitable adoption as she failed to prove that Christine entered into an agreement or contract to adopt Pamela. The court then cited cases discussing that it is against public interest to apply the doctrine of equitable adoption to stepparents. It continued: *While this seems unfair, considering the decades-long, close relationship Christine and Pamela enjoyed, we cannot fix this problem as there is no Iowa case law or statutory authority to do so. Any changes to our law must be done by the legislature. The district court set forth a very thorough recitation of the appropriate facts and applied the appropriate law; thus, we affirm.*

Query: Should courts be more reluctant to apply equitable adoption to stepchildren than to children who were strangers to their adoptive parents? If so, why? Should there be a policy allowing functional children to inherit if the closest other legal heirs are non-citizens or particularly remote?

Est. of Lucas

Not Reported in A.2d, 2005 WL 674682 (D.C.Super. 2005)

Marilyn Lucas petitioned to be appointed personal representative of the estate of Hattie Dean Lucas, as her adopted daughter. The petition was opposed by Donald Thompson-Thornton who claimed to be Hattie's nephew and entitled to take if Marilyn could not. After determining that the parties had standing, the court turned to the primary issue—whether Marilyn was Hattie's daughter. The court recited the facts as follows:

Marilyn was born on February 12, 1954, to Joyce Theresa Fletcher, who was 31, lived on Mt. Vernon Place, N.W., and already had two living children. Marilyn's birth certificate, filed March 3, 1954, did not identify the father and did not name the baby. On August 14, 1958, a "Supplemental Report of Birth" was filed over the signature of Joyce Fletcher. In that document, Joyce Fletcher certified that the child born to her on February 12, 1954 "has been named Marilyn Renee Lucas." The copy of the birth certificate issued to Marilyn on April 12, 2004 states in pertinent part: "Name of child should read Marilyn Renee Lucas. Info, taken from Supp. Dated August 14, 1958." In her 1958 certification, Joyce Fletcher listed her address as 1105 Clifton Street, N.W. The court then recited evidence given by numerous relatives that Marilyn was considered Hattie's baby and that Marilyn called Hattie "mother." *Marilyn grew up in the family home at 1105 Clifton Street, N.W., where, according to her, she lived from birth until she left home after graduating from high school. A District of Columbia Public School records search indicates that Marilyn was enrolled in kindergarten at the Mott Elementary School on September 9, 1959 under the name Marilyn Renee Lucas. The record shows the name of her father as Aaron, the name of her mother as Joyce, and the name of her guardian as "Hattie Lucas Miller". Marilyn was baptized at aged 11 under the name Marilyn Lucas, "daughter of Mr. and Mrs. Avery Lucas." Elementary school report cards from the years 1960, 1961, 1964 and 1965 were signed, under the heading "Parent", sometimes by Hattie, sometimes by her husband, and sometimes by Maude J. Miller. Hattie and Avery called Marilyn their daughter when they claimed her as an exemption on several of their tax returns. Marilyn believed Hattie and her husband were her parents. In Marilyn's presence, they always referred to her as their daughter and later to Marilyn's son as their grandson. They supported her financially and otherwise until she was an adult. She left home after high school. In 2003, Marilyn petitioned to be appointed as guardian for Hattie, alleging that*

Hattie was her mother. She was at Hattie's bedside for two weeks before her death.

Marilyn avers:

My mother and father never discussed with me the facts and circumstances surrounding my birth, nor did they ever discuss with me how they gained custody of me from birth. To be sure, my mother and father never discussed the particulars of the adoption process, and whether or not they ever legally and/or statutorily adopted me.

The court then discussed the issue of equitable adoption. *The issue presented in this case has not been decided by appellate courts in the District of Columbia. . . .   In the present case, Marilyn does not ask the court to "effect an adoption" in the sense of declaring that she is Hattie's adopted daughter. She asks that, solely for the purpose of determining heirship, the Court rule that she has presented sufficient evidence to warrant the Court's deeming her an heir on the theory that Hattie contracted with her mother to adopt her.*

After discussing the statutory and common law schemes in DC and in Maryland regarding intestate succession, parenthood, and adoption, and the preponderance of the doctrine of equity in the intestacy context in most other states, the court rejected Marilyn's claim, stating: *This Court is of the opinion that it should not use its equity power to disturb the District's statutory scheme. "[I]t is well established that courts of equity can no more disregard statutory and constitutional provisions than can courts of law." Whether to permit inheritance by one who is neither the natural nor the adopted child of an intestate is a policy issue for the legislative branch.*

The court concluded: *Even assuming, however, that the Court should apply the doctrine of equitable adoption in this case, the Court concludes that Marilyn has not presented sufficient evidence to warrant a reasonable fact finder in inferring an implied contract to adopt.*

Under the Maryland law on which Marilyn relies, she must prove that Joyce Fletcher and Hattie Lucas entered into a contract whereby Hattie would adopt Marilyn. While the agreement need not have been written, and could be proved by the statements and conduct of the parties, "the proof must be clear, cogent and convincing, so as to leave no reasonable doubt in the mind of the chancellor." While the court is doubtful that Maryland would apply the reasonable doubt standard to this type of case, it would be consistent with . . . the law of many other jurisdictions to insist on proof by clear and convincing evidence. In re Estate of Ford, supra, 82 P.3d at 754 ("Most courts that have considered the question require at least clear and convincing evidence to prove an equitable adoption.") Reciting additional facts, the court explained:

The undisputed evidence is that Joyce Fletcher did not name Marilyn at birth. At some point when Marilyn was an infant, Hattie assumed care for her. Sometime between 1954 and 1958, Joyce Fletcher moved to the address at which Hattie resided. In 1958, Joyce Fletcher signed a supplemental birth certificate stating that the baby born to her in 1954 was named Marilyn Renee Lucas. Marilyn always referred to Hattie as her mother, and thought that Hattie was her mother. Hattie raised Marilyn as her daughter and published to the world—at her baptism, in her school, and in her tax returns—that Marilyn was her daughter. She was not consistent, however, in her representations. When Marilyn was sent to kindergarten in 1959, one year after her name was placed on her birth certificate, Hattie, using the name Hattie Lucas Miller, called herself Marilyn's guardian, and named Joyce as Marilyn's mother and Aaron as her father. Some of Marilyn's report cards were signed by Maude J. Miller as "parent".

The issue is whether a reasonable fact finder could conclude that Hattie and Joyce Fletcher agreed that Hattie would adopt Marilyn. The issue is not whether a fact finder could reasonably infer an agreement that Hattie would raise Marilyn as her daughter and treat her as if she were Hattie's natural or adopted daughter. There must be an agreement to adopt. The best evidence for Marilyn is Joyce Fletcher's naming her Marilyn Renee Lucas on the supplemental birth certificate. Marilyn argues rhetorically: "What other reason would a biological mother give her child the surname of a third person except for the express purpose of putting her child up for adoption?" The Court disagrees with the implied argument that a reasonable fact finder could infer from this evidence that Joyce Fletcher was "put[ting] her child up for adoption," if by "adoption" Marilyn means a formal adoption. A reasonable fact finder could infer from this evidence that Joyce assumed that Marilyn would be raised as Hattie's daughter, and perhaps intended that result. But to go further and infer, by clear and convincing evidence, a meeting of the minds that Hattie would go through the prescribed procedures for adoption would be speculation. The evidence is equally consistent with no agreement,[7] or an agreement to raise and treat Marilyn as a daughter, without formally adopting her.

Query: The court here rejected the claim for equitable adoption because the D.C. Probate Code provided for intestate heirship only by natural and/or adopted children. Because the Code did not recognize equitable adoption, the court would not create that choice. Is that how equitable adoption works? Further, the court stated that even if it recognized equitable adoption, Marilyn had not shown sufficient proof to meet the clear and convincing standard. Do you agree? What proof would she have needed to show?

Est. of Seader

2003 WY 119, 76 P.3d 1236, (Wyo. 2003)

Julie L. Schroeder (Julie) was born on August 13, 1943 to Mary Allen Cirksana (Mary) and Louis Sylvester Burke. When Julie was two years old, Mary married Neil Adam Seader (Neil). At the time of the marriage, Neil agreed to adopt Julie. Over the years, Neil voiced his intention to adopt Julie, and he treated her as if she were his natural daughter. At one time, Mary and Neil discussed adoption with an attorney, but decided not to follow through because of the expense. Neil never did adopt Julie. Nevertheless, she used the surname "Seader" as a youth. Neil and Mary had two sons, Neil J. Seader (Neil J.) and Charles Lee Seader (Charles). Mary died in 1966, leaving her entire estate to Neil. Julie had two children, Kim Sanderson (Kim) and Kirk Olive (Kirk). In his Last Will and Testament, dated August 30, 1996, after a few specific bequests, Neil left the residue of his estate to Neil J., Charles, and Julie. Julie died on May 7, 2000. Neil died on July 10, 2000. The district court refused to apply the

---

[7] Weighing against a conclusion that there was a contract to adopt is Hattie's use of the name "Hattie Lucas Miller" where, as Marilyn's guardian, she enrolled Marilyn in kindergarten as "Marilyn Renee Lucas". "Miller" is the last name of the person who sometimes signed Marilyn's report card as her "parent."

doctrines of equitable adoption, adoption by estoppel, and virtual adoption to avoid the operation of the anti-lapse statute. The district court also concluded that the testator's will did not evidence an intention that the share of a predeceased devisee pass to that devisee's children. The devisee's children appealed. We affirm. . . .

The Adoption Issues

Julie died two months before Neil died. Had she survived him, she would have taken one-third of his residuary estate under his will. Had she been his biological daughter or his legally adopted daughter, her share of his estate would have gone to Kim and Kirk pursuant to [Wyoming's anti-lapse statute]. Likewise, had she been his biological daughter or his legally adopted daughter, and had he died intestate, her share of his estate would have gone to Kim and Kirk. She was not, however, legally adopted. As a result, in an effort to take in her stead under Neil's will, Kim and Kirk now seek equitable recognition of adoptive status for their mother.[6]

Equitable adoption has been described as follows:

> While a child to be adopted pursuant to an agreement between his natural parent and the adoptive parent cannot specifically enforce its adoption by the deceased adoptive parent, nevertheless, because of the agreement, he can obtain specific enforcement of the benefits that would accrue from such adoption—this remedy is sometimes referred to as an equitable adoption.

The terms "equitable adoption," "virtual adoption," and "adoption by estoppel," have been used interchangeably by the courts. Generally speaking, the theory of recovery in an equitable adoption case is founded upon either equitable principles or upon the theory of estoppel. In the former it is a judicial remedy for an unperformed contract of legal adoption or, in the alternative, the ordering of specific performance of an implied contract to adopt. The estoppel theory operates to preclude a party from asserting the invalidity of a status of an "adopted" child for inheritance purposes. It has been said that a so-called "equitable adoption" is no more than a legal fiction permitting specific performance of a contract to adopt. Furthermore, the descriptive phrase "adoption by estoppel" has been described as a shorthand method of saying that because of the promises, acts and conduct of an intestate deceased, those claiming under and through him are estopped to assert that a child was not legally adopted or did not occupy the status of an adopted child. . . .

Equitable adoption must be distinguished from adoption by contract, deed, or notarial act, a process recognized by statute in some jurisdictions. Where such methods of adoption are legislatively sanctioned, they result in a legal adoption status that is no different from the status that arises from a decree of adoption in a judicial proceeding. Equitable adoption, on the other hand, "is never viewed as the equivalent of a formal adoption, in terms of establishing a parent–child relationship, and is merely a status invented by courts of equity as a means of allowing a child in an appropriate case to enjoy part of the advantage of adoptive status."

The elements of equitable adoption are (1) an implied or express agreement to adopt the child; (2) reliance on that agreement; (3) perfor-

---

[6] Equitable adoption does not create an adoption; rather, it merely recognizes its existence for limited purposes. Holt v. Burlington Northern R. Co., 685 S.W.2d 851, 858 (Mo. Ct. App. 1984).

mance by the natural parents in giving up custody; (4) performance by the child in living in the home of, and in acting as the child of, the adoptive parents; (5) partial performance by the foster parents in taking the child into their home and treating the child as their child; and (6) the intestacy of the foster parents.

The majority of states recognize equitable adoption in one form or another, although the doctrine has been explicitly rejected in others. Almost exclusively, the application of the doctrine has been limited to intestate estates. It generally has not been applied to testate estates.[10] In addition, the doctrine is generally limited to the equitably adopted person's attempt to inherit from an intestate adoptive parent, and is not used to enforce the right of the adoptee to inherit from collateral kindred nor to enforce the right of collateral kindred to inherit from the adoptee.

Wyoming has not incontrovertibly recognized equitable adoption, even in intestate estates. . . .   A court of equity has no more right than has a court of law to act on its own notion of what is right in a particular case; it must be guided by the established rules and precedents. Where rights are defined and established by existing legal principles, they may not be changed or unsettled in equity. A court of equity is thus bound by any explicit statute or directly applicable rule of law, regardless of its views of the equities.

Kim and Kirk oversimplify the task presented to this Court. They argue, correctly, that the question is whether their mother should be considered Neil's adopted daughter for purposes of the anti-lapse statute. But they incorrectly characterize that statute as allowing the "children" of a predeceased "family member" to take the share of an estate that was bequeathed to the deceased family member under a will, but denying such treatment to "non-family members." If that were the question, we would only have to determine whether Julie was a "family member." But the statutory construct is much more complex than that.

Neil left the residuary portion of his estate to Julie, Neil J., and Charles. Julie died before Neil did. As applied to the facts of this case, Wyo. Stat. Ann. § 2–6–107(b) provides that, if Julie's residuary devise lapsed, then the entire residue is to be divided equally between Neil J. and Charles. Whether or not the devise to Julie lapsed depends on Wyo. Stat. Ann. § 2–6–106, which provides, in effect, that if Julie is a lineal descendent of Neil's grandparent, the residuary devise to her did not lapse, and her share will go to Kim and Kirk. The question is whether the legislature intended that result. . . .

The primary function of equitable adoption is to enforce a child's right to inherit from someone who promised, but failed, to adopt that child, and then died intestate. Because the putative adoptive parent died without a will, there was neither a testamentary inheritance nor a testamentary disinheritance, either of which was an available option for the decedent (unless there was also a specific promise to make a will or leave an inheritance). Equitable adoption is used to fill that intent "gap" by allowing the child to inherit as if she had been adopted. Where a will has been made, however, there is no gap to be filled. We know the decedent's intent from

---

[10] *But see* Thomas v. Malone, 142 Mo.App. 193, 126 S.W. 522, 523–24 (1910), where an equitably adopted child was allowed to pursue a claim against a will as a pretermitted heir. Further, some courts have begun to apply the doctrine to other claims, such as life insurance benefits, inheritance tax considerations, wrongful death actions, worker's compensation benefits, child support, and will contests. George A. Locke, supra, 97 A.L.R.3d at 353.

the terms of the will. In the instant case, we do not need equitable adoption to enforce Neil's intent to leave a portion of his estate to Julie—Neil did that himself in his will.[15]

This case serves as a good example of why the doctrine of equitable adoption should not be applied to testate estates—the result may negate both legislative and testamentary intent. The specific facts of this case also raise another consideration: when the child seeking recognition of adoptive status is a step-child brought into the home by the marriage of her mother to the putative adoptive father, the inference does not necessarily follow that there was a promise to adopt. A court may infer such a promise in cases where biological parents relinquish their child to others. The same inference may not be appropriate, however, when a mother brings her child into the home of her new husband. In that situation, there may be an equal inference that the father–child or stepfather–stepchild relationship merely arose out of the domestic status of the parties.

As for the stepparent–stepchild relationship in this case, that relationship calls for particular circumspection before recognizing an equitable adoption. Courts have seldom applied the doctrine of equitable adoption or its equivalents to treat a stepparent as an adoptive parent. . . . One reason is the appreciation that it is in the public interest for stepparents to be generous and loving with their stepchildren. Such conduct could be discouraged if a consequence of such kindness toward a stepchild would be the imposition on the stepparent of the legal incidents of parenthood, such as a duty to provide child support after divorce or a reallocation of the stepparent's estate after death.

Finally, although it is part of the probate code chapter dealing with intestate succession, Wyo. Stat. Ann. § 2–4–104 should also be considered when determining the intent of the legislature as to the inheritance rights of children who have not been legally adopted: "Persons of the half-blood inherit the same share they would inherit if they were of the whole blood, but stepchildren and foster children and their descendents do not inherit."

[The court then denied Kim and Kirk's argument that Neil's will evidenced an intent to treat Julie like a child, which would suggest that he would have wanted his step-grandchildren to take their mother's share if she predeceased him. As explanation, the court said:] The will does not even refer to Julie as "my child" or to Julie, Neil J., and Charles as "my children." There is nothing within the language of the will from which we can infer that Julie was intended to be considered a "lineal descendent." It must be remembered that we cannot create an ambiguity within the will by application of the knowledge that Neil did not adopt Julie or by the assertions of others that he had allegedly previously intended to adopt her.

Even if we were to accept the contention that, at the time of his marriage to Julie's mother, Neil agreed to adopt Julie, that adds nothing to our assessment of Neil's testamentary intent. An adopted child, like a natural child, could have been left out of the will altogether. We would have to speculate to conclude that, because Neil included Julie in his will, he meant for the gifts to her to pass to her children if she predeceased him. Such

---

[15] Alternatively, what Kim and Kirk are asking this Court to do is to presume that Neil made his will in ignorance of the adoption statute and in ignorance of the anti-lapse statute, and that he actually intended a result opposite from the statutory results. There is no evidence to support that theory.

speculation is simply not justified; the terms of the will and the statutory provisions are equally unambiguous.

CONCLUSION

We decline to apply the doctrine of equitable adoption to affect the distribution of a testate estate. Equity should not be available to countermand clear legislative mandates. Adoption and probate are both statutory procedures, with formalities designed to ensure certainty. Where neither the applicable statutes nor the last will and testament are ambiguous, neither legislative intent nor testamentary intent depend upon resort to equity. Furthermore, there is no language within the unambiguous Last Will and Testament of Neil Adam Seader from which we can discern an intent that the provisions of Wyo. Stat. Ann. §§ 2–6–106 and 2–6–107 not apply to the testamentary gift to Julie L. Schroeder.

■ GOLDEN, J., dissenting, with whom HILL, C.J., joins.

Because I believe there is room for equity under the unique facts of this case, I dissent. With regards to the first issue, the application of the principles of equity to these facts, I disagree with the reasoning of the majority opinion. The Wyoming Probate Code specifically provides that principles of equity should be applied to supplement Code provisions to the extent the equitable principles do not directly contradict express probate provisions. Wyo. Stat. Ann. § 2–1–102(b). The majority opinion finds such an express contradiction where I believe none exists. . . . A reading of the Wyoming Probate Code as a whole reveals that the legislature intends and expects Wyoming courts to apply equity when necessary to "discover and make effective the intent of a decedent in distribution of his property." § 2–1–102(a)(ii).

Thus, equity may be applied when necessary unless prohibited by an express probate provision. The majority opinion finds such an express prohibition in the anti-lapse statute. To save a bequest from lapsing, the anti-lapse statute requires the deceased devisee be a lineal descendant. The majority opinion claims that the term "lineal descendant" is unambiguous and this Court cannot apply equity to "broaden the class of persons identified by the statute." "Lineal descendant" means no more, or less, than in a direct line, e.g. a child or grandchild. The definition of "child" remains to be supplied. In In re Cadwell's Estate, this Court quoted with approval a definition of "lineal descendant" that included "an adopted child." "Child" is defined by Wyo. Stat. Ann. § 2–1–301(v) as including "an adopted child." No definition expressly states, or even implies, that the definition of "adopted child" is limited to a legally adopted child, to the exclusion of an equitably adopted child. As such, I see no direct conflict in reading "equitably adopted child" into the definition of lineal descendant.

Which brings me back to the initial enquiry—should equity be applied to these facts? I would approach the question in a slightly different manner. Certainly this case does not present the standard set of facts for the application of equitable adoption. Because Neil died testate, equitable adoption in the traditional sense does not apply. The Wyoming Probate Code clearly directs that "[t]he intention of a testator as expressed in his will controls the legal effect of his dispositions." Wyo. Stat. Ann. § 2–6–105. Thus, the critical inquiry is Neil's intentions as expressed in his will.

In determining the intent of a testator, it is important to note that the Wyoming Probate Code is set up as an "opt out" code. In other words, the provisions of the probate code apply unless the testator evinces a contrary intention in the will. Thus, the anti-lapse statute automatically applies unless the testator indicates otherwise in his will. In this case, Neil's will provides no indication that he did not want the anti-lapse statute to apply. Thus, Neil's intent is for the anti-lapse statute to apply. There is no question that if one or both of the biological sons had predeceased their father, their heirs would have taken "in place" of the deceased devisee.

It is critical to note that the anti-lapse statute is not a statute of devise, but rather only limits the conditions upon which an inheritance will lapse. The inheritance does not lapse if it is made to a lineal descendent. If made to a lineal descendant, the "issue of the deceased devisee take in place of the deceased devisee." Wyo. Stat. Ann. § 2–6–106. Thus, Kim and Kirk are not attempting to inherit in their own name or in their own right; they will only take in the place of Julie. It is still Julie's inheritance that is at stake.

Neil's will clearly indicated that he did want Julie to receive an inheritance from him. The question is: did he want her to receive the inheritance as his daughter or as a non-relative? The majority opinion decides the issue against Julie based upon the lack of any express language in the will referring to Julie as his daughter. I believe this oversimplifies the process. Neil never clarified anyone's status in his will. I believe this lack of clarification renders the terms of the will ambiguous.

"[T]he construction of the will is to be resolved by determining the intent of deceased as such appears from a full and complete consideration of the entire will when read in the light of the surrounding circumstances." The circumstances in this case indicate that Neil consistently treated and referred to Julie as his daughter. Julie was his wife's daughter. When Julie's mother died, she left her entire estate to Neil, leaving nothing to Julie. Then Neil executed his will, treating all three children equally in at least two provisions of the will, including the residuary clause. I believe the family context creates a strong implication that Neil considered Julie his daughter, thus creating an ambiguity in his will requiring extrinsic evidence to resolve his true intent.

The complication in this case is that, even if Neil intended Julie to take as his daughter, Julie was never legally adopted by Neil. Julie is legally not a lineal descendant of Neil. I do not believe, however, that the inquiry is automatically at an end with the determination of Julie's legal status. This case is presented to this Court as a plea to recognize Julie as adopted in equity. If Julie is recognized as adopted in equity, for purposes of inheritance only, Julie would be a lineal descendant, her share would not lapse, and her children would take her share as her representatives. This, I believe, is where there is room for the application of equity to affect Neil's testamentary intent.

Query: Should equitable adoption simply not apply when the complex laws of wills are applicable? Is there a valid reason not to treat Julie as an adopted child for purposes of the anti-lapse statute? (We discuss anti-lapse more fully in Chapter 5.) What do you think Neil would have wanted had he known Julie would predecease him? Should Neil's lawyer have discussed that possibility with him?

Ironically, the courts have generally been more receptive to adult adoptions, the adoption of one adult by another, than equitable adoptions, despite provisions like UPC § 2–122 reaffirming by statute the common law doctrine of equitable adoption. But adult adoptions have posed difficulties for many courts as well. Some permit the adoption so long as the adult adoptee consents. But others view an adult adoption when the parties are not in a parent/child relationship to be against public policy. Consider the following cases:

In re P.B. for Adoption of L.C.

392 N.J. Super. 190, 920 A.2d 155, (Ch.Div. 2006)

A married couple, P.B. and S.B., ages fifty and fifty-three, respectively, seek to adopt an unmarried fifty-two-year-old female, L.C. L.C. has resided with the couple for over ten years and wishes to formalize her familial relationship with P.B. and S.B. through adoption and changing her last name to theirs. At the adoption hearing on July 14, 2006, the parties testified as to how they operate as a "team" and desire the adoption in order to make their relationship permanent. L.C. testified that she had been married twice previously, had a troubled relationship with her birth parents and siblings, is currently disabled, and has no valuable personal property. P.B. and S.B. currently rent a two-bedroom mobile home, and testified that they are childless, do not seek to adopt L.C. for inheritance, tax, or other such purposes, but instead seek to make their "family unit" official in the eyes of the law. The parties are assumed to have a platonic relationship, although it should be noted that there was testimony indicating S.B. and L.C. share a bedroom. P.B., S.B., and L.C. presented themselves as a team of three equals.

The court denied the adoption on the grounds that the N.J. statute requiring an age difference of at least 10 years would be waived only where there was adequate evidence that a parent/child relationship existed. The court explained: *This court believes that the age difference requirement was intended by the New Jersey Legislature as a method of ensuring that at least a semblance of a parent–child relationship existed between the adult parties. In fact, this court cannot conceive of any other reason why the Legislature would mandate such a requirement but to ensure such a parent–child relationship. Indeed, it is widely accepted that adult adoption law in most states derives from the ancient Roman principle of adoptio naturam imitatur, i.e., adoption imitates nature. This principle has formed the basis of legislative safeguards such as the age difference requirement which disallow adoptions between those persons not old enough to be the adoptee's natural parent. It seems reasonable to surmise then that the New Jersey Legislature enacted this requirement to safeguard against illogical adult adoptions, where there is no semblance of a parent–child relationship.* In denying the adoption, the court explained: *The court understands that this adoption factored as an important emotional milestone in the parties' relationship, and that the parties appear to want nothing more than to have their relationship made "official" in the eyes of the law. This court's denial of the adoption does not lessen the significance of the parties' relationship. Indeed, "[t]he law does not require or prohibit love or kindness. It deals only with legal rights and duties." P.B. and S.B. have the right to treat L.C. as a family member of equal standing without adopting her. They may also provide her with love and affection or provide for her in their wills. If L.C. wants to change her last name to theirs, she may do so without an adoption decree.*

Query: Does New Jersey have a valid state interest in prohibiting the adult adoption in this case? Does it need one?

One of the primary reasons for requirements like the age differential, or the parent/child relationship of the New Jersey Statute, is to disallow adoption by persons in intimate relationships. Numerous gay and lesbian couples turned to adoption to give each other certain legal rights in the absence of the right to marry. And some states were fine with that. Delaware allows adult adoptions of one lover by another, gay or straight, even if done for purely economic reasons. *In re the Adoption of James A. Swanson, an adult,* 623 A.2d 1095, (Del. 1993). New York, on the other hand, requires a parent/child relationship and will reject an adoption if the parties are in a sexual relationship, even if the age differential is met. *In the Matter of the Adoption of Robert Paul P.,* 63 *N.Y.*2d 233, 481 *N.Y.S.*2d 652, 471 *N.E.*2d 424 (1984). Because adoptions generally cannot be undone, unlike marriage, there are significant policy issues with creating a legal regime in which a homosexual couple feels compelled to resort to adoption in order to obtain legal rights that are otherwise denied them. Assuming the mechanism is not ideal, is the solution to impose a parent/child restriction on adoptions, like New Jersey does, or to not intervene in the private decisions of residents, like Delaware? Same-sex marriage may resolve many of these issues, but it won't resolve the situation for heterosexual couples who prefer adoption to marriage, nor will it undo the thousands of adult adoptions that have already been done for homosexual couples who couldn't wait for marriage.

Often, adult adoptions are done to allow persons to inherit from a relative, when that person would not ordinarily qualify. In 1959 Alfred Minary adopted his wife of 25 years, Myra Minary, in the hopes of allowing her to qualify for benefits from Alfred's mother's trust. Amelia Minary had died in 1932 leaving her estate in trust to pay the income to her husband for his life, then to her three sons for their lives, and upon the death of the last son, to pay the remainder of the trust corpus to Amelia's "surviving heirs, according to the laws of descent and distribution then in force in Kentucky." Two of Amelia's sons had no children, James and Alfred, and Alfred sought to have his wife Myra take a share as his lineal descendant by adopting her. The court rejected the adoption, stating: "Adoption of an adult for the purpose of bringing that person under the provisions of a pre-existing testamentary instrument when he clearly was not intended to be so covered should not be permitted and we do not view this as doing any great violence to the intent and purpose of our adoption laws." *Minary v. Citizens Fidelity Bank & Trust, Co.,* 419 S.W.2d 340 (Ky.App. 1967).

Doris Duke, at age 75, adopted a young woman of 35, Chandi Heffner, she had met at a dance class. Doris was the life beneficiary to trusts established by her father, making her one of the richest women in the world. When Duke died without descendants in 1993 at age 80, she was a billionaire. Having regretted the adoption of Chandi, she executed a document renouncing the adoption, stating that she regretted it, that she believed Chandi's primary motive for the adoption was financial gain, and that she didn't believe her father would have wanted Chandi to benefit from his trusts set up for Doris and her descendants. Consequently, she left most of her fortune to a charitable foundation, but Chandi filed suit to be recognized as a beneficiary of Duke's father's trusts. The New Jersey Superior Court ruled against Chandi, *In re Trust of Duke*, 702 A.2d 1008 (N.J. Super, 1995), but she received a reported $60 million in a settlement of her suit against the trusts.[85]

In many states, an adoption purely for financial reasons may be upheld, especially if, by adopting a person, other potential heirs lose their standing to object because they have been displaced by the adoptee.[86] But some testators and trust settlors may take steps to avoid an adopted beneficiary being able to take in the place of, or in addition to, blood relations. In the Matter of The TRUST UNDER AGREEMENT OF VANDER POEL, 396 N.J.Super. 218, 933 A.2d 628 (N. J. Super, 2007) the court did not allow the adopted child of a trust beneficiary to benefit from a trust established by his mother, even though the trust beneficiary had raised the child since she was 4, had married her mother, and had sought numerous times to adopt her during her minority. She was eventually adopted after she reached adulthood and the adoption was perfectly valid for her to inherit from her adoptive father. The court rejected her right to inherit under her adoptive grandmother's trusts, however, because the trust language restricted its applicability to genetic children with the following restriction:

> The words "descendant" or "issue" as used in this Agreement shall not include any adopted child or children or issue of any adopted child or children, and the words "child" or "children" as used in this Agreement shall not include an adopted child or children.

Do you think such a provision is wise; should it be boilerplate in most trusts, or excluded in most trusts?

Courts use the doctrine of *stranger to the adoption* to prevent both adopted children and adopted adults from taking under the testamentary instruments of relatives of the adopted parent. Thus, if Doris Duke wanted to adopt Chandi Heffner so she could qualify as a child for purposes of taking under Doris' own estate, that would be fine. But if she adopted Chandi so she could inherit property under Doris' father's estate, courts would often not permit the financial incentives of adoption to be used to benefit from those who were strangers to the adoption.

Besides financial motives, however, there are numerous other motives for adult adoptions. In *Hays v. Hays*, 946 So.2d 867 (Ala. Civ. App. 2006), the court rejected an adoption petition by a step-mother to adopt her adult step-daughter after the death of her husband, the daughter's father, even with the step-daughter's consent, in part because the biological mother objected to the adoption. But the court explained that "Alabama law permits adult adoptions [only] when an adult 'consents in writing to be adopted and is related in any degree of kinship, as defined by the intestacy laws of Alabama, or *is a stepchild by marriage.*'" Because the daughter's father had recently died, the step-child relationship ceased to exist, and an adult adoption could not be performed without it.

---

[85] *See* N.Y. Times, May 16, 1996, at B8; *In re* Duke, 663 N.E.2d 202 (N.Y. 1996).

[86] *See, e.g., In re* Estate of Tafel, 449 Pa. 442, 296 A.2d 797 (Pa. 1972); *In re* Estate of Coe, 42 N.J. 485, 201 A.2d 571 (N.J. 1964), *But see, e.g., In re* Estate of Ketcham, 343 Pa. Super. 534, 495 A.2d 594 (1985) (stating adoptee not entitled to inherit under trust where sole purpose of adoption was to secure inheritance); Estate of Coe, 201 A.2d 571 at 575–76 (Appellees' brief summarizing that "equitable principles" should be employed to deal with the "fraud" that would occur if someone were adopted "solely to enable him to take under the will of another").

All sorts of reasons may exist for an adult adoption. For instance, an adult brother sought to adopt his adult sister, who was living in Germany, because she wanted to change her name to the original family name and was not allowed to do so under German law. The adoption was allowed in *In re P.A.L.* 5 P.3d 390 (Colo. App. 2000). And a grandfather sought to adopt his adult grandson in order to confer upon him entitlement to educational financial aid available to the children, but not grandchildren, of disabled veterans. The adoption was allowed in *In re Adoption of Holland*, 965 So.2d 1213 (Fla. 5th DCA 2007).

Adult adoptions are particularly thorny, as courts may disallow adoptions where a parent/child relationship actually existed, as in *Hays* and *Vander Poel*, and permit them where purely financial motives or subterfuge were the sole motives. Adopting one's intimate partner in order to cut off the claims of parents, siblings, or collateral relatives to one's estate, or adopting a grandchild so he can receive educational benefits may seem crass exploitation of the legal promise of adoption. This may seem especially so when a state will not allow second-parent adoptions by the same-sex partner of a natural parent, even though the partner helped plan for the couple's children and has cared for them since birth. See *In re: Adoption of Luke*, 263 Neb. 365 (Neb. 2002). You will learn a lot more about adoption in Family Law. But to the extent adoption affects, or is motivated by, inheritance, the adoption laws of many states appear to be rather arbitrary.

Practice Point: The Importance of Asking "Now, Why Do You Want to Do That?"

Adoption and marriage seem like common-enough events in an estate planning practice. Upon a client's announced intention to do either, we might certainly be safe in saying "Congratulations!" But before jumping in to help with the adult adoption proceeding or the prenuptial agreement, it is really important to often ask another question (which in past years might not have seemed as important)—"Why are you doing this?" That is, sometimes the best thing that we can do for our clients is to help them weigh the legal consequences of their actions to see how their ultimate goals can be met.

Of course, I am not advocating that we should insult our clients' good wishes and feelings of affection for another person when they are sitting before you, gushing with love. The need for further clarification often manifests in situations that just seem, well, strange to you as a planner.

For example, you have a lesbian client who suddenly announces her intention to marry the man who has lived next door to her (and her partner) for the last 20 years. This is the sort of scenario that might make us scratch our heads and say, "Okay, let's talk about this a little bit."

Upon further questioning, we might very well discover that the client just realized that if her very large pension is not given to a spouse or child at her death, then it can pass to no one. She would marry her partner, she says, but it is illegal in your state and she has no children. She also comments that the man next door has always been nice to them. So, her thinking is, why not marry him and have an informal agreement that he will share the proceeds with her partner at death?

Wow! Do you think that this client needs some legal advice regarding how this decision might affect her own partner at death (think: spousal and elective share)? And what about the idea of marriage fraud, or other possible will contests?

Understanding the family dynamic is just as much a part of the estate planner's job as understanding the estate's property and tax implications. If you are a people-person, then this aspect of planning will probably feel like second nature to you. If you are more of a "numbers" person, then you might have to learn a few tricks in order to delve more deeply than face-value and taxes when dealing with your clients. But either way, with the constantly evolving notion of "family," we can help our clients make sure that their goals are met, even if the law hasn't caught up yet to protect them on its own.

G. CONCLUSION

Since the colonial period, and dating back to the English common law, certain status relations have received considerable preferential treatment in the inheritance context. Spouses and legitimate children have been the subject of preferential laws for centuries, besides having caused many heads to roll as Henry VIII struggled to sire a dynasty that would satisfy the strict rules of primogeniture and legitimacy. The troubles Henry faced with infertility, adultery, or legitimacy would be dealt with today through reproductive science and contract law, with a pre-nup or two thrown in for good measure. But the claim that people have complete donative freedom is as much a fiction as the claim that Henry VIII was free to marry and divorce his wives all he wanted because he was king. Social and legal constraints have governed family and succession law for centuries, at a tremendous cost to the lower classes, blended families, and those who do not conform to the traditional family ideal.

As we embark onto our detailed study of inheritance law, keep in mind the long-standing privileging of certain status relations, the purposes behind set-asides like homestead and family allowances, and the clash of those laws with the new world of high-tech family formation. Should we permit greater donative freedom in order to allow non-traditional families to structure their relations and property rights as they see fit? Should we impose certain default assumptions about the wishes of deceased property holders who failed to make their wishes known? Should we protect the O.J. Simpsons of the world who use legal mechanisms designed to protect vulnerable family members to shelter wealth from deserving creditors? Should we penalize the non-traditional LGBTQ families by denying them the kinds of privileged status we recognize for traditional legal marriage? Does the constitutional requirement of equal treatment before the law require doing away with status protections or enlarging them to cover additional persons and relations? We all have different answers to these questions, but we hope you will keep these policy matters in mind as we progress through the rest of the book.

CHAPTER 3

INTESTACY

The law of intestate succession is the default plan for the distribution of a decedent's property upon his death if he fails to make a will. Intestacy also applies if a decedent makes a will but the will is ineffective to pass all or a part of the decedent's estate. Between 50% and 80% of Americans will die without making a will, and their estates will pass according to the default rules of intestate succession in their state of domicile or distributed among family relations according to their own preferences.[1]

The intestate schemes in most states reflect the presumed intent of most decedents, that the surviving spouse should take a significant portion (if not all) of the estate, followed by shares for children or other lineal descendants. Most commonly, only if there is no spouse and no lineal descendants do parents, siblings, or other collateral relatives take any portion of an intestate estate. There are exceptions, of course, where parents might share with a surviving spouse if there are no lineal descendants, but the general plan is relatively consistent across the country: spouses first, children second, parents and siblings third, other collateral relatives last. And if there are no remote heirs, the property escheats to the state.

Interestingly, spouses were not always the principal heir; in fact, for centuries a spouse was not recognized as a legal heir at all, a situation that is still reflected in many wills statutes.[2] Before 1540 in England, however, land had to pass by intestacy to the eldest son (or jointly to all daughters if there was no son), under the law of primogeniture. The inheritance was subject only to a *dower* estate in the widow, which consisted of a life estate in up to one-third of the real property owned by the husband at his death which was to support her until her death. But dower gave her no ownership interests in the couple's land.[3] Even after the 1540 Statute of Wills, by which a landowner could devise up to two-thirds of his real property by will, the remaining one-third had to pass by intestacy[4] to the children or collateral relatives and the widow was entitled only to her dower estate. A widow was also entitled only to a life estate in one-third of the personal property of her husband if there were surviving issue and one-half if there were none.[5]

---

[1] Jeffrey Schoenblum, *Will Contests—An Empirical Study*, 22 Real Prop. Prob. & Tr. J. 607 (1987), and a 2007 survey found that over half of adult Americans do not have a will. See *Majority of American Adults Remain Without Wills*, N.Y. PRESS (Apr. 3, 2007), http://press-room.lawyers.com/Majority-of-American-Adults-Remain-Without-Wills.html.

[2] For instance, most state anti-lapse statutes will save a testamentary devise to a descendant or collateral relative, but not to a spouse if the devisee predeceases the testator. For a further discussion of anti-lapse see Chapter 5.

[3] Dower also attached to land the husband sold or conveyed during life unless the wife had released her dower interest. Dower was viewed by many real property lawyers to be a hindrance to free alienation of land and was abolished by statute in 1833 in England, although the use and later the trust had been used to avoid dower. See EILEEN SPRING, LAW, LAND AND FAMILY: ARISTOCRATIC INHERITANCE IN ENGLAND, 1300–1800 (1997).

[4] A landowner could devise only 2/3rds of his real estate held in military tenure (100% of land held in socage tenure) until 1660 when military tenures were abolished and he could devise all of it. The Tenures Abolition Act 1660, 12 Car. II, c. 24.

[5] Statute of Distributions 1670, 22 & 23 Car. II., Ch. 10.

The English common law was certainly not egalitarian, however, until the twentieth century, for a widower was entitled to a life estate in *all* of the real property his wife brought to the marriage (called *curtesy*) if a child had been born to the union, and there was no provision for personal property because the husband owned all of the wife's personal property upon marriage under the doctrine of coverture.[6] Notably, widows and widowers were not the legal *heirs* of their deceased spouses; they were only entitled to the use of marital property until they too passed away. Husbands could make wills but wives could not until 1882 in England, and during the late nineteenth century in most of the United States.[7] Because the spouse was not considered an heir, statutory and contractual provisions for surviving spouses generally gave the surviving spouse a mere life estate to provide for his or her support until death.

With the demise of dower and curtesy in most states, which was aimed at improving alienability of land,[8] and the advent of married women's property rights by which married women could hold their own real and personal property, intestate succession laws in most states were amended throughout the twentieth century to provide that the surviving spouse would take an outright fee interest in one-third to one-half of the decedent spouse's estate. Only North Carolina retains a distinction between real and personal property, giving the surviving spouse only as much as half the real property while potentially all of the personal property.[9] Today, however, the vast majority of common law states give the surviving spouse an outright share of the decedent spouse's property, though most retain the one-third or one-half share that originated in the early common law. The spouse is now deemed the principal heir in the common law states, an heir who cannot be disinherited even by making a will.

Originally, the community property states did not give the surviving spouse any portion of a decedent spouse's intestate estate because the surviving spouse already controlled half of the community property held by the couple. But recent changes in many of those states now give surviving spouses a portion or even all of the community property owned by a decedent spouse at death.[10] In community property states a decedent spouse can make a will leaving all of her share of the community property to oth-

---

[6] Coverture gave all of a woman's personal property to her husband upon marriage in exchange for a legally-enforceable right to be supported by him. It also gave him legally-enforceable rights to her body, the right to determine her domicile, the right to have her physically restrained or committed to an institution of any kind, and the right to custody of all children she bore to him. She could not enter into a contract with her husband, either before or after marriage, and she could not be convicted of most crimes because it was assumed that all her actions were done at the behest of her husband. See William Blackstone, Commentaries on the Laws of England, Bk 1, ch. 15 (1765) (available at http://www.lonang.com/exlibris/blackstone/bla–115.htm).

[7] The right to make a will was allowed to married women under many Married Women's Property Acts, which gave married women a right to dispose of their own separate property. Of course, these Acts did not allow them to dispose of marital property, which continued to be owned by their husbands. And not all Married Women's Property Acts gave full rights of testation to married women.

[8] Dower and Curtesy continue to exist in Arkansas, (see ARK. CODE ANN. § 28–11–101 (West 2005)), Kentucky (KY. REV. STAT. ANN. § 392.020 (West 1956)), New Jersey (N.J. STAT. ANN. § 3B:28–1 (West 1981)) and Ohio providing for dower only (see OHIO REV. CODE ANN. § 2103.02 (West 2012)). Virginia recently abolished dower for estates created after 1991 (VA. CODE ANN. § 64.1–19.2 (West 2012)) and Massuchesetts repealed dower and curtesy laws in 2008 (MASS. GEN. LAWS ANN. Ch. 191 § 17 (West 2012)).

[9] N.C. GEN. STAT. ANN. § 29–14 (West 1959).

[10] CAL. PROB. CODE § 6401 (West 1990) (amended 2002).

ers, but if she does not make a will, the property will generally pass to the surviving spouse.

Thus, common law states have moved toward giving the surviving spouse at least an out-right one-half share of a decedent spouse's property, and sometimes all of it, while community property states have moved toward giving the surviving spouse all of the community property if a decedent spouse does not make a will.

The priorities between descendants and collateral relatives are remarkably similar between common law and community property states as well. Children take priority over collateral relatives, and then property escheats to the state if there are no legal heirs. Nonetheless, despite the apparent similarity of intestate schemes, the devil is in the details.

There are a number of relatively minor considerations that can make the calculations of intestate shares quite complicated. In this chapter, we begin with the spouse's share, then discuss the shares of descendants, and then parents, siblings or other collateral heirs. The calculations can be quite complex when we consider the three different intestate schemes that have been adopted (*per stirpes*, *per capita*, and hybrid *per stirpes*) and the set asides and priority shares taken out for the surviving spouse that we covered in Chapter 2. But it is not just a matter of remembering the fractions you learned about in 7th grade. Intestacy only gets more complex in our modern society when we consider the place of ex-spouses, step-children, adopted children, foster children, non-biological children of gay parents, children in the process of being adopted, step-siblings and other quasi-relatives who could legitimately claim that an intestate decedent would have wanted to provide for them just as much as or more than traditional blood relatives. We then talk about what happens when certain heirs receive very large lifetime gifts that siblings or other relatives believe should be considered *advancements* against their inheritances. Even after death, the *mom loved you more* phenomenon can complicate an otherwise straightforward calculation of an estate's distribution.

A.   IDENTIFYING THE NET PROBATE ESTATE

Before we move to the intestate share itself, we must begin by determining the property that comprises the intestate estate. Not all of a decedent's estate will be available for final distribution under intestacy (or according to a will for that matter). Most decedents will die holding a variety of different property interests in a variety of different types of forms. Some of that property will pass according to what are called will substitutes, documents and conveyances by which property will shift to a different owner as a result of the death of the decedent. Thus, money held in a joint bank account with a right of survivorship will pass outside probate to the surviving joint tenant and will not be included in the probate estate. Similarly, real property held in joint tenancy with right of survivorship or in tenancy by the entirety will pass outside probate. Retirement accounts or stock brokerage accounts that have designated beneficiaries will pass directly to those beneficiaries outside of probate. Property held in a revocable living trust will most likely pass outside probate. The intestate estate (usually called the **probate estate**), consists only of property owned by the decedent at his death and excludes all property that passes to successors by the various non-probate mechanisms that are available. And the **net probate estate** is the sum of that property after family set-asides (homestead, exempt property, and family allowance), debts, and administration costs are deducted.

We discuss how these other forms of property pass in Chapter 4, below, so at this point, we will consider only a very simple estate. Calculate the **probate estate** and the **net probate estate** for Herman Smith if he owned the following property, subject to the following debts, at his death:

Family house titled in his own name and valued at	$300,000
Personal property valued at	$150,000
Two cars whose combined value is	$ 30,000
Cash in a bank account in his own name	$ 50,000
Cash in a bank account held in joint tenancy with right of survivorship with his wife Wila	$ 50,000
Stock Brokerage account naming their 2 children, Seth and Doris, as beneficiaries	$100,000
Life Insurance naming his wife Wila as beneficiary	$500,000
Total Assets	**$1,180,000**

Herman also has the following debts:

Personal loan from his brother	$100,000
Credit card balances	$ 10,000
Balance on car loan for one of his cars	$ 5,500
Total Debts	**$115,500**

The first thing we need to do is identify the property in Herman's estate that will pass outside of probate and is not to be included in his **probate estate**. This includes the $50,000 in the joint account with his wife Wila that passes directly to her, the $500,000 in life insurance that also passes directly to Wila, and the $100,000 in the stock account that will pass directly to Seth and Doris. The property that remains owned by Herman at his death, and which will comprise his **probate estate**, is the house, personal property, cars, and cash in his bank account—a total of $530,000.

Family house titled in his own name and valued at	$300,000
Personal property valued at	$150,000
Two cars whose combined value is	$ 30,000
Cash in a bank account in his own name	$ 50,000
Probate Estate	**$530,000**

Next we need to subtract the value of Wila's homestead, exempt property, and family allowance from Herman's **probate estate**. Under the UPC, the following family set-asides would be subtracted (assuming the maximum allowable):

Homestead	$22,500
Exempt Property	$15,000
Family Allowance	<u>$27,000</u>
Total set asides	**$64,500**

Subtracting the homestead, exempt property, and family allowance from the **probate estate** results in:

$530,000

<u>−$64,500</u>

$465,500

From that amount we then subtract Herman's debts to determine his **Net Probate Estate** (assume that Seth is a probate lawyer and will administer Herman's estate for free[11]):

$465,500

<u>−$115,500</u>

$350,000 = **Net Probate Estate**

Note that less than 30% of Herman's estate will be subject to probate and distribution under the default intestacy rules. And under modern intestacy rules, Wila will receive a significant portion, if not all, of Herman's net probate estate as his principal heir. Assuming that Seth and Doris are adult children,[12] Wila will be receiving the lion's share of Herman's estate before we even calculate her intestate share. Wila will receive:

Joint Bank Account (outside probate)	$ 50,000
Life Insurance (outside probate)	$500,000
Homestead	$ 22,500
Exempt Property	$ 15,000
Family Allowance	<u>$ 27,000</u>
Wila's Share before probate	**$614,500**

If you are worried you might be missing some property, then check your calculations by adding up the categories of property to get back to the original amount.

---

[11] Both the fees of the lawyer to probate the estate and the court costs would come off at this time. But many states set a relatively modest fee for administration costs based on the size of the estate. *See e.g.*, FLA. STAT. ANN. § 733.6171 (West 1993), MINN. STAT. ANN. § 525.515 (West 1971).

[12] If the children are adults then Wila is likely to receive the total amount of the set-asides. If some of the children are minors and living with a parent who is not the surviving spouse, they may be entitled to some portion of the set-asides. It depends on the law of your state.

Set-asides (Homestead, Family Allowance, and Exempt Property)	$ 64,500
Debts	$115,500
Net Probate Estate	$350,000
Non-Probate Transfers to Surviving Spouse	$550,000
Non-Probate Transfers to Others (Children)	$100,000
Herman's Total Estate at Death	**$1,180,000**

PROBLEMS

3.1. Calculate Herman's net probate estate under the Homestead, Exempt Property, and Family Allowance laws of your state.

3.2. As we progress through our study of the different intestacy schemes, go back and calculate how much Wila, Seth, and Doris will be entitled to of Herman's $350,000 **net probate estate** under the UPC rules discussed below and the rules of your state. What if Seth and Doris are Herman's children, but not Wila's? What if they are Wila's children and not Herman's?

Practice Point: Is Intestacy a Good Estate Plan?

It is very rare that an estate lawyer will tell a client that intestacy should be the basis of the client's estate plan, and yet there is no reason to have a will if the decedent wishes all of her property to pass to her spouse and/or children, in accord with the default rules. The more important issue, usually, is to ensure that the estate passes smoothly, without hiccups or unexpected snags. Thus, intestacy might be part of the plan. But even simple estates often can benefit from a simple will because wills do other things besides simply dispose of property. They usually appoint the personal administrator, identify preferred guardians for minor children, may give funeral instructions,[13] and rank gift preferences in case unexpected debts threaten to eat up a chunk of the estate.

For many people, the fact that a beneficiary may be a minor is cause enough to proceed with drafting a will, which can both prevent unnecessary guardianship issues and provide for distribution of funds over time (which is the way that many clients wish to provide for their children). The default rules of intestacy are back-ups, not usually the main plan, especially when you begin to consider all the other documents that go along with estate planning, like providing a solid Power of Attorney and assorted health care documents. Accordingly, many attorneys are able to create simple "bundles" of those ancillary documents to accompany a simple will plan that will help to achieve the client's goals in ways that might fail if intestacy is the only "plan."

---

[13] As you will see in Chapter 6, these are not necessarily binding, and are often better located not in the will, but in a document that need not wait until probate before it becomes effective.

B. SPOUSAL SHARES

Ironically, in an era in which divorce was rare and marriage was a life-time bond, the tradition of intestacy laws was to give the surviving spouse only between one-third and one-half of the decedent spouse's net probate estate, and some states only gave a life estate to support the surviving spouse until her death. Today, many states have reformed their intestacy laws to give the surviving spouse a minimum of half, often more, and very often all of the intestate estate in recognition of the partnership theory of marriage. The partnership theory of marriage views marital wealth as the joint assets of both parties, even if they are titled in one spouse's name. This recognizes the contributions of stay-at-home spouses who devote their peak earning years to raising children or maintaining a home, rather than earning money or improving property. The shift also recognizes that most decedents of long marriages want their surviving spouse to take all or most of the net probate estate because the spouse helped earn it and may need it for his or her end of life care.[14]

These legal reforms, expanding the surviving spouse's estate from a life estate to outright ownership, make sense if the marriage was of long duration and the children are the offspring of both spouses; i.e. a tradition-al marriage. The shift makes less sense, however, in the case of the second or third marriage, the blended family where each spouse has children from previous relationships, or the relatively short marriage, especially if the surviving spouse has more wealth of her own than the decedent spouse.

Nevertheless, many states have followed the UPC in giving the surviv-ing spouse 100% of a decedent spouse's net probate estate if there is no surviving parent or children, or if all of the children are also the offspring of the surviving spouse. The trend has been to slowly increase the spousal share in the past thirty years, from one-third, to half, to all of the estate, and it is the rare state, like Florida, that has actually reduced the spousal share.[15] Where Florida used to give the first $60,000 plus half, it now gives just half. One can only speculate at the reasons, as state legislative history is difficult to acquire. But in a state that has a rather high population of second and third marriages, it may reflect growing concerns that a late-in-life remarriage should not result in a decedent's children being essentially disinherited. However, the shift certainly fails to recognize the needs of relatively poor couples where that first $60,00 or $100,000 plus half of the net probate estate may mean the difference between losing a house and being evicted or remaining in the family home that the couple worked to acquire.

The expectations of decedents have also changed over the years. Alt-hough many couples may have viewed providing an inheritance for their children to be one of their prime concerns, the trend today is to invest in children early, during college years, and spend the remainder of their hard-earned savings on a comfortable retirement for themselves. For most people of modest estates in their first marriage, their spouse is the beneficiary they care most about. As people acquire more wealth, however, they tend to look around for additional recipients of their bounty. They logically want to provide for their surviving spouse until his or her death, but then also pro-

---

[14] UPC § 2–102, *see e.g.,* ALASKA STAT. ANN. § 13.12.102 (West 1996), COLO. REV. STAT. ANN. § 15–11–102 (West 1994), HAW. REV. STAT. § 560:2–102 (West 1996) for states enacting similar provisions.

[15] FLA. STAT. ANN. § 732.102 (West 1974) (amended 2011).

vide for their children and grandchildren, and if there are assets remaining, perhaps make a charitable gift or provide for friends or other relatives.

But life in the twenty-first century simply isn't the same as it was three decades ago, much less a century ago. Two important changes of the past thirty years have profoundly redirected the expectations of decedents and the factors that affect their judgment about who should take their property. The first is the growing number of second, third, or fourth marriages which may raise the possibility that the surviving spouse contributed very little to the decedent spouse's wealth and may have significant wealth of his own and not need the support of a sizable inheritance. And if the surviving spouse is a second or third spouse, the decedent is likely to have children by a prior relationship that the decedent might prefer to take more of the property. In conjunction with changing marriage patterns are changes in laws to reflect the equal protection mandate that succession laws treat husbands and wives equally, thus abolishing differential treatment of widows and widowers despite the fact that their economic situations usually are not equal.

The second is the tremendous increase in wealth held in other forms, like trusts, life insurance, PODs and TODs, and joint tenancies, that are not included in the probate estate and therefore are not subject to the intestate rules of succession. Even the decedent who owns a modest estate is likely to hold property in ways that would not be subject to intestate succession rules, and so a spousal share could in fact be quite inadequate to provide for the survivor's living expenses if all the non-probate property is directed elsewhere. Similarly, if most of the non-probate property is directed to the surviving spouse, then a relatively small intestate inheritance would be sufficient. These two factors have led to statutory modifications that can be quite technical and confusing. As you will see, the default rule might fit certain individuals well, and others quite poorly, so be aware of how your state's intestacy rules fit in the general pattern of state rules.

We will use the UPC intestacy provisions which have been substantially adopted in many states as our benchmark, and then discuss a variety of other kinds of rules.

UPC § 2–101. Intestate Estate

(a) Any part of a decedent's estate not effectively disposed of by will passes by intestate succession to the decedent's heirs as prescribed in this Code, except as modified by the decedent's will.

(b) A decedent by will may expressly exclude or limit the right of an individual or class to succeed to property of the decedent passing by intestate succession. If that individual or a member of that class survives the decedent, the share of the decedent's intestate estate to which that individual or class would have succeeded passes as if that individual or each member of that class had disclaimed his [or her] intestate share.

UPC § 2–102. Share of Spouse

The intestate share of a decedent's surviving spouse is:

(1) the entire intestate estate if:

(i) no descendant or parent of the decedent survives the decedent; or

(ii) all of the decedent's surviving descendants are also descendants of the surviving spouse and there is no other descendant of the surviving spouse who survives the decedent;

(2) the first [$300,000], plus three-fourths of any balance of the intestate estate, if no descendant of the decedent survives the decedent, but a parent of the decedent survives the decedent;

(3) the first [$225,000], plus one-half of any balance of the intestate estate, if all of the decedent's surviving descendants are also descendants of the surviving spouse and the surviving spouse has one or more surviving descendants who are not descendants of the decedent;

(4) the first [$150,000], plus one-half of any balance of the intestate estate, if one or more of the decedent's surviving descendants are not descendants of the surviving spouse.

Although you might think intestate provisions for a surviving spouse would be quite simple—like "the surviving spouse gets one-half of the net probate estate"—the modern trend is to adjust the spouseal share based on the presence of children and the relative size of the estate. Therefore, the UPC provides for the modest estate by giving the surviving spouse the entire estate if it is a) below the dollar value indicated in the statute, b) if there are no lineal descendants or parents of the decedent, or c) all the decedent's lineal descendants are descendants of the surviving spouse and the surviving spouse has no other lineal descendants (i.e. traditional nuclear family with no step-children).

The UPC then provides that a parent will share with the surviving spouse if the decedent leaves no descendants. Imagine a probate estate worth $800,000 where the surviving spouse takes the homestead and family allowance and exempt property, which is valued at, let's say, $200,000, leaving $600,000 to pass by intestacy.[16] The surviving spouse takes the next $300,000 plus ¾ of the remainder, which is $525,000, leaving $75,000 to pass to the parents. In total, the surviving spouse will take $725,000 (or 90.5%) of the estate and the parents $75,000.

Things get even more complicated when there are step-children. Where the decedent spouse has children that are unrelated to the surviving spouse, the spouse takes the first $150,000 plus half the remainder of the estate. Where the surviving spouse has children that are unrelated to the decedent spouse, the surviving spouse takes the first $225,000 plus half the remainder of the estate. Why the difference? Comments to the UPC explain that the difference is based on the likelihood that the decedent's descendants are unlikely to be the exclusive beneficiaries of the surviving spouse's estate if the surviving spouse has other descendants (so the surviving spouse gets more so as to distribute more to both sets of descendants). And if the decedent spouse has other descendants besides those with the surviv-

---

[16]   Assume no debts or administration costs just to make the math simple.

ing spouse, then the surviving spouse takes less, leaving more to the descendants not related to the surviving spouse, who are not natural objects of the bounty of the surviving spouse.[17]

The following table makes these distinctions easier to follow. Notice there are overlapping categories in the statute.

	Surviving Spouse's Share	UPC Provision
Decedent and spouse have **no** children and decedent has **no** parents	100%	§ 2–102(1)(A)
Decedent and spouse have **no** children and decedent has at least **one** parent[18]	First $300,000 + ¾	§ 2–102(2)
Decedent and spouse have **no** children together but **decedent** has children by a different partner	First $150,000 + ½	§ 2–102(4)
Decedent and spouse have **no** children together but **spouse** has children by a different partner	100%	§ 2–102(1)(A)
Decedent and spouse have **no** children together but **both** have children by a different partner	First $150,000 + ½	§ 2–102(4)
Decedent and spouse have children together and **neither** has children by a different partner	100%	§ 2–102(1)(B)
Decedent and spouse have children together and **decedent** has children by a different partner	First $150,000 + ½	§ 2–102(4)
Decedent and spouse have children together and **spouse** has children by a different partner	First $225,000 + ½	§ 2–102(3)
Decedent and spouse have children together and **both** have children by a different partner	First $150,000 + ½	§ 2–102(4)

Many other states, following the lead of the UPC, instituted a complex formula like this for dealing with blended families, but one must be very careful reading through the statute as the overlapping categories may be different. Notice that the last, the third from the last, and the fifth from the last categories in the table above result in the same spousal share (first $150,000 plus ½) yet the factual categories are quite distinct. Thus, one must be very attentive to the language of the surviving spouse's share un-

---

[17] You are probably wondering why the presence or absence of step-children would affect the spousal share under intestacy, especially where step-children don't share in an estate. That is a very good question. See the comments to UPC § 2–102 for some clarification.

[18] Note that a parent only takes a share if there are no children.

der the intestacy statute to determine which provision applies. Reproduce this table using your own state's intestacy statute (it will come in very useful when you are studying for the bar!).

PROBLEMS

3.3. Continuing from the facts of Problems 3.1 and 3.2, what share of Herman's $350,000 Net Probate Estate will *Wila* be entitled to take under the UPC if Seth and Doris:

  a.   are the children of both?

  b.   are the children of Herman but not Wila?

  c.   are the children of Wila but not Herman?

3.4. Do the same calculations for Wila's share of Herman's estate under the intestacy laws of your state, and remember to deduct homestead, family allowance, and exempt property.

Although most intestacy statutes have relatively similar provisions for the surviving spouse, Mississippi will put your statutory construction skills to the test:

Miss. Code § 91–1–7. Descent of property as between husband and wife.

If a husband die intestate and do not leave children or descendants of children, his widow shall be entitled to his entire estate, real and personal, in fee simple, after payment of his debts; but where the deceased husband shall leave a child or children by that or a former marriage, or descendants of such child or children, his widow shall have a child's part of his estate, in either case in fee simple. If a married woman die owning any real or personal estate not disposed of, it shall descend to her husband and her children or their descendants if she have any surviving her, either by a former husband or by the surviving husband, in equal parts, according to the rules of descent. If she have children and there also be descendants of other children who have died before the mother, the descendants shall inherit the share to which the parent would have been entitled if living, as coheirs with the surviving children. If she have no children or descendants of them, then the husband shall inherit all of her property.

Query: Can you figure out if the Mississippi intestacy statute treats husbands and wives equally?

Most community property states originally provided that each spouse's share of the community property would pass to other relatives, either descendants, parents, or collateral relatives, regardless of the existence of a spouse. In other words, there was no automatic right of survivorship for spouses who died intestate to simply pass the decedent spouse's half share of the community property to the surviving spouse. Most states now, however, provide that the surviving spouse's intestate share is the decedent spouse's entire share of the community property and the quasi-community property, regardless of the presence of children, and a portion of the separate property along similar lines as the UPC.[19]

Cal. Prob. Code § 6401. Surviving Spouse or Domestic Partner Intestate Share of Decedent's Estate

(a) As to community property, the intestate share of the surviving spouse is the one-half of the community property that belongs to the decedent under Section 100.

(b) As to quasi-community property, the intestate share of the surviving spouse is the one-half of the quasi-community property that belongs to the decedent under Section 101.

(c) As to separate property, the intestate share of the surviving spouse or surviving domestic partner, as defined in subdivision (b) of Section 37, is as follows:

(1) The entire intestate estate if the decedent did not leave any surviving issue, parent, brother, sister, or issue of a deceased brother or sister.

(2) One-half of the intestate estate in the following cases:

(A) Where the decedent leaves only one child or the issue of one deceased child.

(B) Where the decedent leaves no issue but leaves a parent or parents or their issue or the issue of either of them.

(3) One-third of the intestate estate in the following cases:

(A) Where the decedent leaves more than one child.

(B) Where the decedent leaves one child and the issue of one or more deceased children.

(C) Where the decedent leaves issue of two or more deceased children.

California and Arizona recently adopted provisions allowing spouses to state that they want their share of the community property to pass to the surviving spouse by right of survivorship rather than to pass by intestacy, thus avoiding probate, but the parties must declare this intention by taking title to property as "community property with rights of survivorship." Survivorship is not the default.[20] Although we will get to the benefits of joint tenancies in the next chapter, can you see why the right to survivorship is preferable to intestacy? When might it not be?

The UPC also gives a provision for surviving spouse's rights in community property. UPC Alt. § 2–102A.

---

[19] *See e.g.,* CAL. PROB. CODE § 6–401(a) & (b) (West 1990) (amended 2002), TEX. PROB. CODE ANN. § 45 (West 1955) (amended 1991), WASH. REV. Code ANN. § 11.02.070 (West 2008) giving half of the decedent's community property to the surviving spouse.

[20] CAL. CIV. CODE § 682.1 (West 2000), ARIZ. REV. STAT. ANN. § 33–431 (1995) (West). If you do not remember how joint tenancies with rights of survivorship work, we discuss them in more detail in Chapter 4.

UPC § 2–102A. Share of Spouse.

(a) The intestate share of a decedent's surviving spouse in separate property is:

(1) the entire intestate estate if:

(A) no descendant or parent of the decedent survives the decedent; or

(B) all of the decedent's surviving descendants are also descendants of the surviving spouse and there is no other descendant of the surviving spouse who survives the decedent;

(2) the first [$300,000], plus three-fourths of any balance of the intestate estate, if no descendant of the decedent survives the decedent, but a parent of the decedent survives the decedent;

(3) the first [$225,000], plus one-half of any balance of the intestate estate, if all of the decedent's surviving descendants are also descendants of the surviving spouse and the surviving spouse has one or more surviving descendants who are not descendants of the decedent;

(4) the first [$150,000], plus one-half of any balance of the intestate estate, if one or more of the decedent's surviving descendants are not descendants of the surviving spouse.

(b) The one-half of community property belonging to the decedent passes to the [surviving spouse] as the intestate share.]

As you can see, the UPC provision recommends that community property pass to the surviving spouse as a default, unless the decedent spouse makes a will. The UPC has the same provision for children in a community property state as in a common law state. Thus, whatever community property does not pass to the spouse would pass to children or lineal descendants first, then to collateral relatives if there are no descendants.

PROBLEMS

Calculate the spousal share in the following scenarios under the UPC intestate provisions.

3.5. Henry and Janice marry in 2006. They have no children together but Henry's only child, Sherard, lived with them off and on during his college years until graduation in 2010. Henry dies intestate in 2011 with a probate estate worth $500,000. Of that, assume that homestead, family allowance, and exempt property are valued at $100,000 and Henry died with $50,000 in debts.

3.6. Tamika and Tom are married, raising five children together. Tamika also has one adult child from a prior marriage. When Tom dies intestate, his probate estate has a value of $600,000. Assume that homestead, family allowance and exempt property are valued at $200,000 and his debts are $100,000.

Problems with the Spousal Share

Although we might think we know who is a surviving spouse, courts still have to grapple with quite a few unexpected difficulties simply to determine who is entitled to a spousal intestate share. The following are some of the difficulties:

1. What happens when spouses die simultaneously? In *Janus v. Tarasewicz* (482 N.E.2d 418 (Ill.App.Ct. 1985)) Stanley and Teresa Janus had recently returned from their honeymoon when they gathered with family members to mourn the death of Stanley's brother, Adam Janus, who had died from ingesting cyanide-laced Tylenol capsules. Feeling out of sorts, they both unknowingly took some of the contaminated Tylenol from Adam's medicine cabinet and shortly thereafter collapsed with seizures. Paramedics were called to the scene and both were taken to the hospital. Stanley was declared dead almost two hours after arriving at the hospital, never having developed blood pressure or a pulse since arriving. Hospital personnel, however, were able to get Teresa's heart beating on its own after arrival and she was put on a mechanical respirator. Teresa remained hooked up to life support for two days until it was terminated. Both died intestate, and in a suit involving the question of whether the two died simultaneously (and therefore should be treated as each having predeceased the other for purposes of administering each estate) or whether Teresa survived Stanley and was therefore entitled to an intestate share of his estate, the court held that Teresa survived Stanley.

This case is troubling for multiple reasons. One reason is that the couple had been married only a few weeks, and yet Teresa's estate took Stanley's entire net probate estate. This meant that since neither had children nor a spouse, all of Stanley's **and** all of Teresa's estate passed to Teresa's parents, and none to Stanley's parents. Had the parties been married longer, the outcome might have seemed less inequitable. Also, had Teresa's medical expenses been significantly greater, so that the addition to her estate of Stanley's property would have helped pay her bills, the outcome would have made sense. The problem with simultaneous death of spouses, especially when they die within a relatively short period of each other, is that the important support aspect behind intestacy laws becomes irrelevant. And in a short marriage it is unlikely that either spouse contributed much to the other spouse's wealth. Had Illinois adopted the Uniform Simultaneous Death Act, then Teresa would have been required to survive Stanley by at least 120 hours before she could inherit from him. The USDA helps to reconcile problems that can arise by virtue of greater and greater medical intervention.[21] What happens when one spouse is kept alive on life support to allow family members time to come pay their last respects while the other is terminated more quickly? Should the "survivor" inherit all from the other and then pass that property to the survivor's relatives to the exclusion of the relatives of the first spouse to die?

2. What about the separated spouses who never completed or never even filed for a dissolution of their marriage, yet have lived estranged for many years? For instance, in *Est. of Goick*, 275 Mont. 13, 909 P.2d 1165 (Mt. 1996), Barbara and Michael Goick, who had married in 1981, began dissolution proceedings in December, 1990 when Michael filed for divorce. In April, 1991 a hearing was held on the dissolution and the parties agreed to all issues except the division of household goods, which the parties were to settle within two weeks. Unable to agree on the division of property eight months later, Barbara filed a motion to divide the property in December, 1991. In January, 1992 Michael's attorney withdrew and no further action was taken on the divorce. Michael died intestate on November 30, 1992. The Montana Supreme Court held that Barbara was a surviving spouse for intestate succession purposes because no final divorce decree had been is-

---

[21] We discuss simultaneous death in Chapter 5.

sued nor had a final settlement been reached as to the marital property rights. The court was influenced by the fact that had the dissolution been completed, Barbara would have been entitled to some portion of the marital property and a portion of Michael's property under equitable distribution rules. Because she did not receive any property in the aborted divorce, she should be able to take some portion of Michael's estate under intestacy.[22]

Courts do not have to be so formalistic in considering non-intestacy situations, however. In *Sullivan v. Burkin*, 460 N.E.2d 572 (Mass. 1984), the Massachusetts Supreme Court did not allow the widow to take an elective share of property the decedent husband had placed in trust in 1973 during the marriage. The husband died in 1981 after having been estranged from his wife for at least 20 years. But in the intestacy context, courts are more constrained to follow the strict mathematical percentages.

3. What about not-quite-married spouses. Engaged couples, even those who have lived together for a significant period of time and may have commingled assets, do not count as married for intestacy purposes. In *Olver v. Fowler*, 168 P.3d 348 (Wash. 2007), two persons in a long-term committed relationship, but whose marriage was not legally valid, died simultaneously in a car accident. All the property the couple had worked to acquire was in the man's name, as per their Vietnamese culture, and the woman's executor sought to have a portion of the property treated as hers under equitable principles. The court recognized her equitable claim to some of the property because she helped earn it, despite the presumption that property titled in one spouse's name belongs solely to that spouse, but notably the court did not recognize the unmarried partner's property rights as an application of intestacy laws.

Other cases recognize the rights of long-term intimate partners to a share in the property of the other if there is adequate evidence of joint partnership in the acquisition of the property.[23] Although courts have acknowledged that without a legal marriage, the surviving spouse does not take an intestate share, he or she can take an *equitable* share in the property or be entitled to widow's benefits under social security or other investments because those aren't governed by the strict intestacy laws.

Putative spouses are generally recognized as spouses for intestacy purposes unless precluded by statute. A putative spouse is one who believes he is married and has cohabitated with his spouse under the mistaken belief that his marriage is valid. Participating in a marriage ceremony is good evidence of a putative marriage, even if the ceremony is invalid because the legal formalities were not met. Determining the rights of a putative spouse are much more difficult, however, when more than one claimant exists. Where a second, third, or fourth marriage is bigamous the Restatement argues that the court should equitably apportion the decedent's property in a manner appropriate to the circumstances.[24] The Uniform Marriage and Divorce Act (1983) adopted the putative spouse doctrine.

4. Common law marriages. Common law marriages remain legal in thirteen states and the District of Columbia.[25] It can no longer be contract-

---

[22] See also Est. of McDaniel, 161 Cal.App.4th 458 (Cal.App. 3 Dist., 2008).

[23] See *In re Marriage of Lindsey*, 678 P.2d 328 (Wash. 1984); *Peffley–Warner v. Bowen*, 778 P.2d 1022 (Wash. 1989).

[24] See Restatement § 2.2 comment e.

[25] Alabama, Colorado, Georgia [only if entered into prior to 01–01–1997], Idaho [only if before 1–1–96], Iowa, Kansas, Montana, Ohio [only if before 10–10–91], Oklahoma, Pennsylvania [only if before 01–01–2005], Rhode Island, South Carolina, North Carolina and Texas.

ed in 26 states, and was never permitted in 11 states. Utah allows a statutory version of common law marriage, which is similar in most aspects to the traditional common law marriage, except that Utah never had the traditional variety. The requirements for a common law marriage generally include speaking words of present consent ("I marry you" not "I will marry you") and consummation of the marital relationship, often for a substantial period of time. The parties also have to hold themselves out as married. Case law on common law marriage rights tends to vary significantly depending on the claim of the petitioner. Where a surviving partner claims social security benefits or survivor's benefits from a deceased partner, courts tend to be lenient in recognizing the common law marriage. Where a petitioner claims a common law marriage in order to claim an equitable share of the partner's property in a dissolution action, however, the courts tend to be less lenient in recognizing the common law marriage.[26] Can you imagine why the differences?

5. Same sex marriages. Although same sex marriages are quite recent phenomena, the states that recognize same sex marriage allow for intestate succession by surviving same sex spouses. The more difficult questions arise when a married same sex couple moves from a state that recognizes same sex marriage to one that does not. In that situation, the survivor is not entitled to intestate property that is held or acquired in the new domiciliary. However, real property that is owned in a same sex marriage state will be probated according to the laws of that jurisdiction even if the marriage won't be recognized in the new domicile. Thus, a same sex couple that marries in Iowa and owns real property in Iowa, but moves to Florida, and purchases real property there as well, will find that the survivor has intestate rights to the Iowa property but not the Florida property.[27]

Even more difficult are the domestic partnership and civil union states. Some of these "marriage lite" states recognize registered domestic partners for intestacy purposes and others do not. [28] And some states recognize couples married or with registered domestic partnerships from other states who move to their state, but will not allow their own citizens to marry. And still others allow same sex couples to use contracts or "domestic partnership agreements" to effectuate some of the same rights as accorded married couples, including intestacy rights.[29] Should any two adults be able to enter into a contract whereby one gives to the other spousal intestacy rights? Although a will can essentially do the same thing, might a contract be more or less preferable?

Since the mid-nineteenth century, most states have been fairly uniform in recognizing the marriages, and divorces, of outsiders. And certainly after *Loving v. Virginia*, 388 U.S. 1, in 1967, a valid marriage in one state generally creates a status relationship that is recognized in all 50 states

---

[26] See, e.g., *In re Est. of Collier*, 2011 WL 2420989 (Tex.App. 2011) (finding a common law marriage for inheritance purposes); *Douple v. Wagner*, 2011 WL 945966 (Ohio App. 2 Dist. 2011) (finding no common law marriage for inheritance purposes); *In re Hyde*, 255 P.3d 411 (Okla., 2011) (finding a common law marriage for worker's compensation benefits).

[27] See, e.g. *Est. of Ranftle*, NYLJ 34 (Feb. 4, 2009) (N.Y. Surrogate's Court Decision).

[28] See Hillel Levin, *Resolving Interstate Conflicts Over Same-sex Non-Marriage*, 63 Fla. L. Rev. 47 (2011).

[29] Colorado Designated Beneficiary Agreements Act of 2009, Colo. Rev. Stat. Ann. § 15–22–101 (West 2009), Hawaii Reciprocal Beneficiaries Act, HAW. REV. STAT. § 572C (West 1997).

and carries with it the same spousal rights.[30] But the diversity of same-sex marriage laws has become a serious challenge to LGBTQ couples who want the legal benefits of marriage. And it's not just a problem for LGBTQ couples; couples married internationally who have property in the U.S. may find that different laws apply regarding marital status for intestate purposes between property held in the other country, and property held in the U.S.[31]

For a quick visual view of the diverse marriage laws in the 50 states, consider this map regarding same-sex marriage.

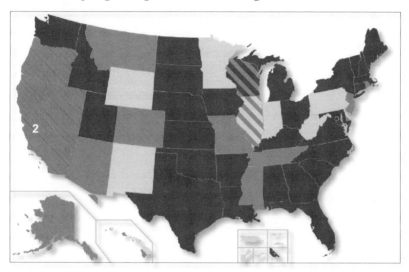

Laws Regarding Same-Sex Partnerships in the United States as of 5/21/2013[32]

Same-sex marriage recognized by law: *Maine, Maryland, Vermont, New Hampshire, New York, Iowa, Washington, Massachusetts, Connecticut, District of Columbia, Minnesota*

Domestic partnerships or civil unions recognized by law granting rights similar to marriage: *California, Oregon, Nevada, Illinois, Delaware*

States giving limited or enumerated rights to domestic partners or civil unions: *Colorado, New Jersey, Hawaii, Wisconsin*

Same-sex marriages not performed in the state, but such marriages that are legal where performed are recognized: *Rhode Island*

No specific prohibitions or recognition of same-sex marriages or civil unions: *New Mexico*

Statute bans same-sex marriage: *Wyoming, Indiana, West Virginia, Pennsylvania*

Constitution bans same-sex marriage: *Alaska, Montana, Arizona, Missouri, Tennessee, Mississippi*

Constitution bans same-sex marriage and other kinds of same-sex unions: *Florida, Alabama, Arkansas, Georgia, Louisiana, Texas, South Carolina, North Carolina, Virginia, Kentucky, Ohio, Michigan, Oklahoma, Nebraska, Kansas, South Dakota, North Dakota, Utah, Idaho*

---

[30] Loving v. Virginia declared unconstitutional state anti-miscegenation laws. Although other state prohibitions on marriage may lead to some discrepancies among states, the majority of significant barriers have been removed.

[31] See, e.g., *Est. of Salathe*, 703 So.2d 1167 (Fla.App. 2 Dist. 1997).

Practice Point: Same Sex Marriage and the Transgendered Client

Given the widespread variance among state laws, it's easy to see why careful planning becomes particularly important for clients in a same sex relationship. And, just like any other planning situation, the case takes on additional importance if the couple has children. But what about the transgendered client? How might these same laws affect her and her partner? Consider this example (which can be a fairly typical one for an adult who transitions from one gender to another later in life):

Debbie and her partner Liz want you to draft their wills. As you discuss their goals, you learn that Debbie was born Derek, a biological male. As Derek, he married a woman named Carol when he was in his twenties and they had one child together named Susan, who is now an adult. The marriage failed, however, and a few years after the divorce, Derek transitioned to Debbie. Although she has not had surgery, Debbie takes medication, including hormone replacement therapy, and holds herself out to the world as a woman. Years later, she married Liz and the two identify as a lesbian couple. You are interested to learn that, although your state law prohibits same sex marriage, Debbie and Liz have a Certificate of Marriage from your state. They explain that this occurred because Debbie's gender has never legally changed and she still had her birth certificate listing her as male, so they were married as Husband and Wife.

Two years ago, Debbie and Liz decided that they wanted to have a child together. Debbie stopped her hormone therapy for a while in an attempt to successfully harvest viable semen, but was ultimately unsuccessful. She and Liz decided instead to use a sperm donor and, at the time of your meeting, Liz is now pregnant.

Although we are still early into the discussions of the law of succession, can you already identify some of the issues that Debbie and Liz's plans need to address? Is this a traditional marriage or a same sex marriage? Should there be special planning considerations given to make sure that Debbie's adult daughter, Susan, is provided for, as well as their future children together? And there are seemingly easier questions that can puzzle a planner, as well, such as how to clarify names and relationships in the plan—as well as how to effectively use pronouns (particularly since Debbie is still legally considered to be a male).

As we continue delving deeper into the laws relating to wills, trusts and estates, many of the answers to these questions will become much more clear. For now, though, the ability to identify the issues and contemplate how you might think they could be addressed is the first step in becoming a planner in times where notions of marriage, gender and parentage are constantly changing.

C. SHARES OF CHILDREN AND OTHER DESCENDANTS

As with spouses, we often think we know who children are—they are the biological offspring of a man and a woman who are their parents, right? For centuries a child could not inherit from either parent if they were unmarried, and in many states in the nineteenth century a non-marital child could only inherit from its mother. In 1925 England amended its intestacy laws to allow a biological child to inherit from both parents, regardless of their marital status.[33] The same is now true in all the United States, by

---

[33] Administration of Estates Act, 1925 15 & 16 Geo. Part IV, c. 23, § 46(1)(b)(ii). (providing no mention of illegitimacy) (available at http://www.legislation.gov.uk/ukpga/Geo5/15–16/23/section/46/enacted). For cases recognizing a right of *illegitimate* children to inherit as "issue," *see, e.g.: Illinois:* Smith v. Garber, 286 Ill. 67, 121 N.E. 173 (1918), *Minnesota:* North-

virtue of the Constitutional prohibition against corruption of blood and recent equal protection cases stating that there is no rational state justification for treating legitimate and illegitimate children differently for inheritance purposes.[34]

The remainder of a decedent's intestate estate that does not pass to the surviving spouse, or all of it in the absence of a surviving spouse, will pass entirely to children of the decedent, and descendants of deceased children by representation. All states recognize the concept of *representation* to allow the descendants of a deceased child to take that child's portion. Thus, if a decedent died leaving 2 children (A and B) and two children of a deceased child (C), then A and B would each take one-third of the decedent's estate and the two grandchildren would split C's share to take one-sixth each. Representation is a very important concept in succession law. It not only comports with the intent of most decedents—i.e. that the children or grandchildren of a deceased beneficiary should be able to step into that beneficiary's shoes and share in the estate. Representation avoids disinheritance of lineal descendants and also limits the number of descendants entitled to take a share to those of the closest degree to the decedent. We will see the concept of representation arise in the context of wills and trusts and the application of the anti-lapse statutes that operate in every state. For purposes of intestacy, however, the rule is relatively straightforward. No person of a more remote degree of relationship will take a portion of an intestate share unless the closer relation predeceased the decedent.

It is important to remember that an *heir* is the person or persons who are entitled to an intestate share of a decedent's estate determined at the time of her death only. Thus, no one can be an heir of another until the latter actually dies; before that time they can be *heirs apparent* or *heirs presumptive*, but not *heirs*. Because a potential heir might die simultaneously with the decedent, we cannot know for sure who the actual heirs will be until the decedent truly dies. At that point, heirs are established, and their death shortly after the decedent will not affect their right to inherit from the decedent unless there is a survivorship requirement (as with the Uniform Simultaneous Death Act requiring survivorship by 120 hours before an heir is entitled to take from a decedent). Similarly, a new heir might be born or be *in utero* just before the death of the decedent who would be entitled to take a portion of the decedent's intestate estate.

The UPC provision for intestate distribution to descendants is similar to that of many states.

UPC § 2–103. Share of Heirs other than Surviving Spouse.

Any part of the intestate estate not passing to the decedent's surviving spouse under Section 2–102, or the entire intestate estate if there is no surviving spouse, passes in the following order to the individuals designated below who survive the decedent:

(1) to the decedent's descendants by representation; . . .

---

western Nat'l Bank v. Simons, 308 Minn. 243, 242 N.W.2d 78 (1976); *Mississippi:* Gadberry v. Swayze 140 Miss. 726, 106 So. 442 (1925).

[34] See *Trimble v. Gordon*, 430 U.S. 762 (1977); *Reed v. Campbell*, 476 U.S. 852 (1986). See also Martha Davis, *Male Coverture: Law and the Illegitimate Family*, 56 RUTGERS L. REV. 73 (2003).

Despite the simplicity of the foregoing provision, there are three different mathematical schemes for determining the percentages each descendant will be entitled to take. These are: *classic per stirpes, per capita by generation,* and *per capita with representation (*also called *modern per stirpes).* Although in many simple cases the distributional outcome will be the same under all three schemes, once multiple generations are included in the intestate distribution, the calculations for the different schemes can become quite complicated.

1.   CLASSIC PER STIRPES (CPS)

Classic *per stirpes* (meaning "by the stocks") follows the traditional English rule of dividing the estate with each line of descendants. This is the scheme most people are familiar with and prevails in about one-third of the states. If a decedent (X) has four children (A, B, C & D) and A, B, and C predecease X, leaving descendants, the estate will be divided into four initial shares. D will take her one-fourth share, and then A's descendants will divide her one-fourth share, B's descendants will divide his one-fourth share, and C's descendants will divide his one-fourth share.

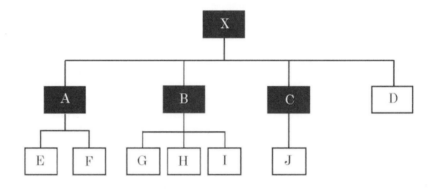

Illustration 1

(black boxes mean the person predeceased the decedent—the decedent is X)

In this example we get the following shares:

D	1/4
E & F	1/8 each
G, H, & I	1/12 each
J	1/4

This scheme is relatively simple because each person who takes by representation takes the share (or a portion of the share) that would have gone to her ancestor. As *each share* drops down to the next level, it is distributed equally among takers at that level. Also, if a potential heir has predeceased the decedent but does not leave surviving issue, that person's share is redistributed to the other takers at that level.

Thus, if C in Illustration 1 above predeceased X but did not leave issue, then D would take one-third, A's descendants would take her one-third share, and B's descendants would take his one-third share. Thus, we do each division of shares for the number of descendants at that level, including deceased descendants who have surviving issue. Deceased descendants with no issue are simply omitted. The arrangement would look like this:

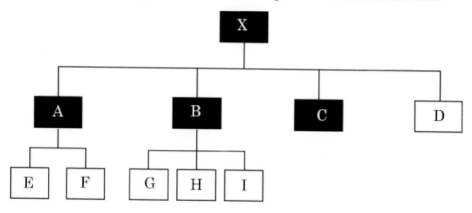

Illustration 2

Because we omit C's share since she predeceased X without leaving living issue, the distribution would be:

D	1/3
E & F	1/6 each
G, H, & I	1/9 each

If there are more than two generations of heirs, and a variety at each level have predeceased the decedent, the calculations can be quite complicated. Consider this example:

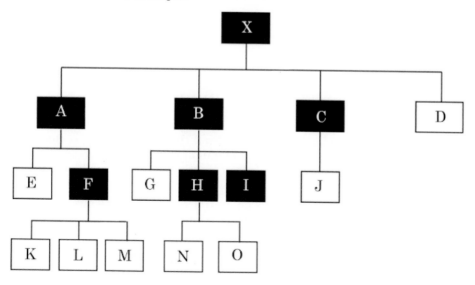

Illustration 3

In this example, we would do an initial division of X's estate into four shares and D would take her one-fourth. Then A's one-fourth share would be divided into two (i.e. 1/8th each) for E and F, but F's share would be further divided into three more shares so that K,L, & M would each take 1/24th of X's estate. B's one-fourth share would be divided into two shares (I's share is redistributed to G and H because I died without issue surviving) so G would take 1/8th and H's 1/8th share would be further divided between N and O (each taking 1/16th each). C's one-fourth share would pass directly to J. We can write this out to make sure we have the right percentages as follows:

D & J	1/4 each (or 1/2 total)
E & G	1/8 each (or 1/4 total)
K, L, & M	1/24 each (or 1/8 total)
N & O	1/16 each (or 1/8 total)

To check our fractions and make sure we've accounted for the entire estate, we can add up the shares to make sure we total one.

$$1/4 + 1/4 + 1/8 + 1/8 + 3/24 + 2/16 = 1.0$$

But what about spouses of deceased descendants? In Illustration 3, what if I had predeceased X but had left a spouse—would I's spouse be entitled to I's share? NO! I's spouse is not a descendant of X and is therefore not entitled to any of X's estate by intestacy. So what could I do to ensure that her spouse gets her share? She can't leave a will devising all of her share of X's estate to her spouse because intestacy doesn't allow any person who predeceased the decedent to take a share. Thus, I couldn't take a share to then pass on through her will to her spouse. Can I make her spouse count as her child? YES! Many states allow adult adoptions, even of a spouse.[35] I might have to divorce her spouse and then adopt him as her son in order for the spouse to take a share of X's estate. If I's 1/12th share of X's estate is worth it, a divorce and adult adoption might come in handy, especially if I's spouse could use the money for his end-of-life care. Upon I's death, I's spouse may lose his means of support and if X doesn't write a will providing for I's spouse, then I might be able to make appropriate arrangements for her spouse's future after her death as part of her estate planning.

2. PER CAPITA BY GENERATION (PCBG)

This scheme has been adopted in about twelve states and follows the model of the UPC. The basic principle behind the PCBG system is that the takers at each generation are treated equally and that no division is done at a generational level where there are no survivors. Consider Illustration 3 above.

In this instance we would do an initial division at the first level of children because D has survived. Thus, D takes ¼. But the remaining 3/4ths of X's estate is combined (A's, B's, and C's ¼ shares) and divided equally among the living grandchildren and predeceased grandchildren with issue surviving. Thus, the 3/4ths of the estate is divided into 5 shares

---

[35] Not all states allow adult adoptions, and some won't allow it in the absence of a true parent/child relationship. But many states do allow it, as you saw in Chapter 2.

for the 5 grandchildren (I does not take a share because she died without issue). Then, E, G, and J would each take an equal one-fifth share of the remaining 3/4ths of the estate, or 3/20ths each. The remaining two one-fifths shares of the 3/4ths (or 6/20ths) would be divided equally among the great-grandchildren (K, L, M, N & O) who would then take 6/100ths each.

We can write this out as follows:

D   1/4 (25%)

E,G, & J   3/20 each (9/20 total or 45%)

K, L, M, N, & O   6/100 each (3/10 total or 30%)

The important principle for PCBG is that descendants who take by representation take equal portions if they are of the same generation as others. Unlike the classic *per stirpes* scheme, where N & O take 1/16 shares and K, L, & M only take 1/24th shares, all descendants of the same generational level take the same share. This means that whatever is not distributed at any given level is combined and passed down to the next level to be divided equally by the number of living descendants and deceased descendants with surviving issue.

But what happens if D also predeceases X, as in Illustration 4?

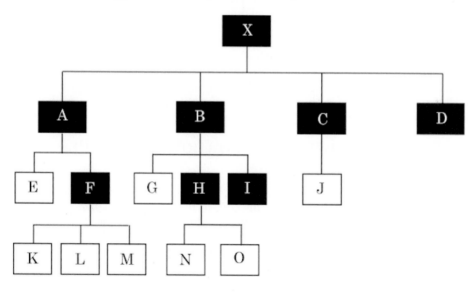

Illustration 4

Thus, if A, B, C, and D all predeceased X, we would do the initial distribution of shares at the grandchildren level—thus dividing the estate into 5 shares. E, G, and J would each take 1/5th, I takes nothing because I also predeceased without leaving surviving issue. The remaining 2/5ths of the estate (F's 1/5th share and H's 1/5th share) would be combined and divided into 5 parts for the great-grandchildren. Thus, under PCBR, the distribution would be:

E, G, & J   1/5 each (total of 3/5)

K, L, M, N, & O   2/25 each (total of 2/5)

A really good question you should be asking right now is, how does one know what distributional scheme a state adopts. Many states use the straightforward provision that "Descent shall be per stirpes, whether to descendants or to collateral heirs."[36] The UPC provides for *Per Capita* by Generation using the following provision:

UPC § 2–106

(a) . . .

(b) [Decedent's Descendants.] If, under Section 2–103(a)(1), a decedent's intestate estate or a part thereof passes "by representation" to the decedent's descendants, the estate or part thereof is divided into as many equal shares as there are (i) surviving descendants in the generation nearest to the decedent which contains one or more surviving descendants and (ii) deceased descendants in the same generation who left surviving descendants, if any. Each surviving descendant in the nearest generation is allocated one share. The remaining shares, if any, are combined and then divided in the same manner among the surviving descendants of the deceased descendants as if the surviving descendants who were allocated a share and their surviving descendants had predeceased the decedent.

Admittedly this is not the simplest language, but it is reasonably straightforward for reaching the UPC's goal of treating all descendants of the same relational level equally. Thus, all grandchildren take the same share, and all great-grandchildren take the same share. Although in the end some grandchildren may receive more or less than others, it is a result of some grandchildren not inheriting directly from their grandparent, but through their parent who was alive at the grandparent's death. Thus, in Illustration 4 above, D might have children who will eventually inherit D's ¼ share of X's estate. Or they might inherit nothing if D spends it all before she dies.

3. PER CAPITA WITH REPRESENTATION (MODERN PER STIRPES) (PCR OR MPS)

The *Per Capita with Representation*, which has been adopted in nearly half of the states, is a hybrid of the *classic per stirpes* and *per capita by generation* rules. Under PCR, the intial division is done at the first generation in which there is living issue. Thus, in Illustration 4 above, if D also predeceased X there would not be an initial division of 1/4th, but the entire estate would be divided at the grandchildren level into the number of living grandchildren and predeceased grandchildren with living issue. Thus, if A, B, C, & D all predeceased X, the estate would be initially divided into fifths, with E, G, & J each taking one-fifth each. However, once the initial distribution is done, we follow *per stirpes* for the successor generations. So F's 1/5th share would be divided three ways between K, L, and M who would therefore take 1/15th each. And H's 1/5th share would be divided two ways among N and O, who would take 1/10th each.

E, G, & J   1/5 each (total of 3/5)

K, L, & M   1/15 each (total of 1/5)

N & O   1/10 each (total of 1/5)

---

[36]   FLA. STAT. ANN. § 732.104 (West 2007).

PROBLEMS

To get a handle on the differences between the three schemes, work the following problems. Work each under all three schemes.

3.7. Using the family relationships of Illustration 4 above, work out the distribution if A, B, C & D all predeceased X, but all their children and grandchildren survived.

3.8. Using the family relationships of Illustration 4 above, work out the distribution if B, C, D, & H predeceased, but all the rest survived.

3.9. Using the family relationships of Illustration 4 above, work out the distribution if A, B, C, E, F, & H predeceased (but not I) and E has 4 surviving children (P, Q, R & S).

3.10. Using the family relationships of Illustration 4 above, work out the distribution if A, B, C, E, F, & H predeceased (but not I) and E has 4 surviving children (P, Q, R & S) and 2 surviving grandchildren (U & V) who are the children of T who also predeceased.

Problems with Children's Shares

Numerous problems arise in the context of determining who takes an intestate share as a child. These include adult adoptions, gay adoptions, virtual adoptions, the not-yet-completed adoption, and children conceived or born after the death of the decedent. Besides adoptions, questions about legal status for children conceived through artificial reproductive techniques, as discussed in Chapter 2, can be quite daunting. These become compounded when we consider adoptions and births of grandchildren and great-grandchildren after the death of their ancestors, but before the death of the decedent. And consider the case discussed in Chapter 2 of *In re Adoption of Holland*, 965 So.2d 1213 (Fla.App. 2007), where a grandfather adopted his adult grandson in order to obtain federal educational aid available to children, but not grandchildren, of disabled veterans. Now the grandson is to be treated as a legal son, and would presumably be able to inherit an intestate share from his grandfather, equal to the share his father will receive, even though his father may still be alive. Remember that under intestacy, a more remote descendant will not take a share if a less remote descendant is still alive. Normally, a grandchild would not take a share of a grandparent's estate if the grandchild's parent (the grandparent's child) is still alive. But under *Holland*, both would be entitled to take a share because the parent/child relationship between the grandson and the son has been terminated by virtue of the adoption. Now the biological son and grandson are adoptive brothers!

Consider the following cases:

Wingate v. Est. of Ryan

149 N.J. 227, 693 A.2d 457 (1997)

The Plaintiff, Joanne Wingate, grew up believing that her mother's husband, Willard Wingate, was her natural father. At the age of 32 she was informed by her mother that another man, John Ryan, was her father, just days before Ryan's death. When Joanne petitioned for an intestate share of

Ryan's estate, she was required to prove she was the natural daughter of the decedent. Once she proved to a 99.99% probability using DNA that she was Ryan's daughter, the executor and primary beneficiary of Ryan's estate moved to dismiss her action on the ground that it was not filed within 23 years of her birth, as required by the New Jersey Parentage Act. The Parentage Act requires only a preponderance of evidence standard for proof of parentage if the father is dead at the time paternity is sought. Under the New Jersey Probate Code, suit to prove parentage need only be brought within a reasonable time, but the standard of proof was clear and convincing, setting up both a substantive and procedural conflict between the two Acts. Although New Jersey eventually reconciled the standards of proof necessary to prove paternity (and under either standard Joanne had succeeded), the issue of the different statute of limitations periods had not been reconciled. Although the probate code was amended to reflect the more generous Parentage Act's substantive standard of evidence in 1991, the New Jersey Supreme Court concluded that its failure to adopt the Parentage Act limitations period was intentional, and that such a period would be illogical in light of the fact that fathers don't always die within 23 years of an illegitimate child's birth. Thus, Joanne received the benefit of the longer limitations period of the Probate Code, even though the Probate Code had adopted the substantive elements of the Parentage Act (and referred to it directly).

Query: Children far too numerous to count, and far more than anyone knows, have irregularities in their genetic lineage. Should these children be able to inherit from the persons who act as functional parents (Willard Wingate in this case) as well as from their gamete providers (John Ryan), and what should the courts do if Joanne is successful in her suit to inherit from Ryan, and she had already inherited from Wingate, or *vice versa*?[37]

Technology Trend: The Result of that DNA Test and How It Affects the Plan

When we think about adult children who might discover a genetic irregularity in their lineage, we typically think of those that find out that the man who raised them (and sometimes the man who was married to their mother) was not their biological father. Maybe this is because the mother is the person who actually gives birth and, therefore, parentage is established, unequivocally, at the time she gives birth. After all, we have all heard stories about birth certificates with incorrect names for fathers, but the mother's name is often taken as a given. Of course, real life shows us that this assumption can be quite misleading—and that sometimes children never really give that birth certificate much thought or attention.

In a rather famous edition of Rolling Stone Magazine in 1984, Nancy Collins questions actor Jack Nicholson about how he felt when, at 37 years old, he discovered that the woman he called "mother" his entire life was actually his grandmother and that the woman who he had grown up with and called "sister" was actually his mother. Unfortunately, at the time of this discovery, both women had already passed away, taking not only the ability for Jack to confront them but also taking

---

[37] If England's Prince William should die without issue, should Prince Harry have to prove his parentage before he can inherit? Speculations have been rampant that he is not the biological son of Prince Charles, but the legal presumption that he is the child of his mother's husband would prevail unless Prince Charles rejected the presumption.

the identity of Jack's biological father with them to the grave. When asked about his sister (who was actually his mother), Jack responded, "We both fought hard. It didn't do her any good not to tell me, but she didn't because you never know how I would have reacted when I was younger."[38]

In close family circumstances, like those in Jack Nicholson's case where the biological grandmother, mother, and child all live a family life together, does it make sense to allow the child to inherit from both parties as a son? Would it make a difference in your thinking if instead of fostering a lifelong relationship, Jack's sister moved away from home at the time of his birth, never to establish contact?

From an estate planning perspective, there is a flip side to consider as well. What about the parent who discovers that he is *not actually* the parent? In an age where DNA paternity testing is surprisingly easy to perform, some savvy adult children have taken matters into their own hands when they become absolutely convinced that "that man just cannot be my dad—especially when I look so much like my dad's best friend, Roger." And, before you know it, dad and Roger are having a sit down with the child, hearing the results of a DNA test, both suddenly understanding why their toothbrushes went missing last month.

As technology gets more and more advanced, it is becoming much harder for people to take their secrets to the grave with them. And, for the estate planner, that sometimes means that you will be the one to help deal with the discovery and prepare to clean up the mess.

Woodward v. Comm'r of Social Security

435 Mass. 536, 760 N.E.2d 257, 17 A.L.R.6th 851 (2002)

Surviving widow sought social security benefits for herself and her twin daughters born of sperm from her deceased husband who had died two years before their birth. The U.S. District Court certified the following question to the Massachusetts Supreme Court, which answered in the affirmative. "If a married man and woman arrange for sperm to be withdrawn from the husband for the purpose of artificially impregnating the wife, and the woman is impregnated with that sperm after the man, her husband, has died, will children resulting from such pregnancy enjoy the inheritance rights of natural children under Massachusetts' law of intestate succession?" Noting that the Massachusetts intestacy law does not define issue, or posthumous issue, and that there were competing policy issues, the court held that the children would be entitled to inherit if it is shown that the deceased affirmatively consented to the posthumous reproduction and affirmatively consented to support any resulting child. The competing policy issues the court identified were: *the best interests of children, the State's interest in the orderly administration of estates, and the reproductive rights of the genetic parent.* The court held that although the mother had come forward with conclusive proof of genetic paternity, she had not yet met the burden of showing that the *genetic father* should be treated as a *legal father* for intestacy purposes, but the case was remanded to allow her to put forward such proof. Noting that this was the second time the court had been confronted with the novel questions involving children born from artificial reproductive technologies, the court opined: *As these*

---

[38] Nancy Collins, *The Great Seducer Jack Nicholson*, ROLLING STONE MAGAZINE, Mar. 29, 1984.

technologies advance, the number of children they produce will continue to multiply. So, too, will the complex moral, legal, social, and ethical questions that surround their birth. The questions present in this case cry out for lengthy, careful examination outside the adversary process, which can only address the specific circumstances of each controversy that presents itself. They demand a comprehensive response reflecting the considered will of the people.

Query: How long should an estate remain open to allow for the possibility of posthumously-born children? And what kind of evidence of consent from the deceased parent should be sufficient? Should the mere fact that the mother or father had eggs or sperm cryo-preserved be enough? Should we limit the rights of people who preserve their genetic material by demanding that they set aside sufficient assets to support the children in case they are born? If so, what do we do with the property if they are not conceived?

Think back to the cases on equitable adoption and consider whether the law should be more liberal in recognizing equitable adoption in cases like *Bean v. Ford*, where the equitably adopted child has performed the duties of a child, and if the court denies the adoption the decedent's estate will pass to remote heirs (also called laughing heirs). Is there any reason to limit equitable adoption to intestacy cases, as in *Est. of Seader*, if the definition and identify of children are relevant for all sorts of inheritance rules and rights?

D. SHARES OF ANCESTORS AND COLLATERAL RELATIVES

If a decedent is not survived by a spouse or descendants, then her property will pass to her parents (which may implicate many of the issues just discussed about the parent/child relation) and/or collateral relatives. Collateral relatives are those who descend from ancestors (siblings, aunts and uncles, cousins, nieces and nephews, and other more remote relatives). The UPC provides that in the absence of a surviving spouse and descendants, the estate shall pass first to parents, then descendants of parents (siblings and their descendants), then to grand-parents, then to descendants of grand-parents (aunts and uncles and their descendants). Finally, if there is no living relative that is at least a descendant of a grand-parent, then the UPC provides that the estate shall descend to the descendants of the last surviving spouse (step-children) and, if none, the estate shall escheat to the state.

UPC § 2–103. Share of Heirs other than Surviving Spouse.

(a) Any part of the intestate estate not passing to a decedent's surviving spouse under Section 2–102, or the entire intestate estate if there is no surviving spouse, passes in the following order to the individuals who survive the decedent:

(1) to the decedent's descendants by representation;

(2) if there is no surviving descendant, to the decedent's parents equally if both survive, or to the surviving parent if only one survives;

(3) if there is no surviving descendant or parent, to the descendants of the decedent's parents or either of them by representation;

(4) if there is no surviving descendant, parent, or descendant of a parent, but the decedent is survived on both the paternal and maternal sides by one or more grandparents or descendants of grandparents:

(A) half to the decedent's paternal grandparents equally if both survive, to the surviving paternal grandparent if only one survives, or to the descendants of the decedent's paternal grandparents or either of them if both are deceased, the descendants taking by representation; and

(B) half to the decedent's maternal grandparents equally if both survive, to the surviving maternal grandparent if only one survives, or to the descendants of the decedent's maternal grandparents or either of them if both are deceased, the descendants taking by representation;

(5) if there is no surviving descendant, parent, or descendant of a parent, but the decedent is survived by one or more grandparents or descendants of grandparents on the paternal but not the maternal side, or on the maternal but not the paternal side, to the decedent's relatives on the side with one or more surviving members in the manner described in paragraph (4).

(b) If there is no taker under subsection (a), but the decedent has:

(1) one deceased spouse who has one or more descendants who survive the decedent, the estate or part thereof passes to that spouse's descendants by representation; or

(2) more than one deceased spouse who has one or more descendants who survive the decedent, an equal share of the estate or part thereof passes to each set of descendants by representation.

UPC § 2–105. No Taker.

If there is no taker under the provisions of this Article, the intestate estate passes to the [state].

There are two principal schemes for the descent of intestate property to collateral relatives: the *parentelic* and the *degree of relationship* scheme. The parentelic is the scheme used by the UPC, which refers up to certain ancestors and then down to their descendants. The degree of relationship scheme allows those relatives who are of the closest degree of relationship to inherit if there are no descendants, even if grand-nieces and first cousins who are the same degree of relationship are related through different ancestors. The following Table of Consanguinity (Illustration 5) shows all those difficult relationships and explains how second cousins are related to first cousins once removed.

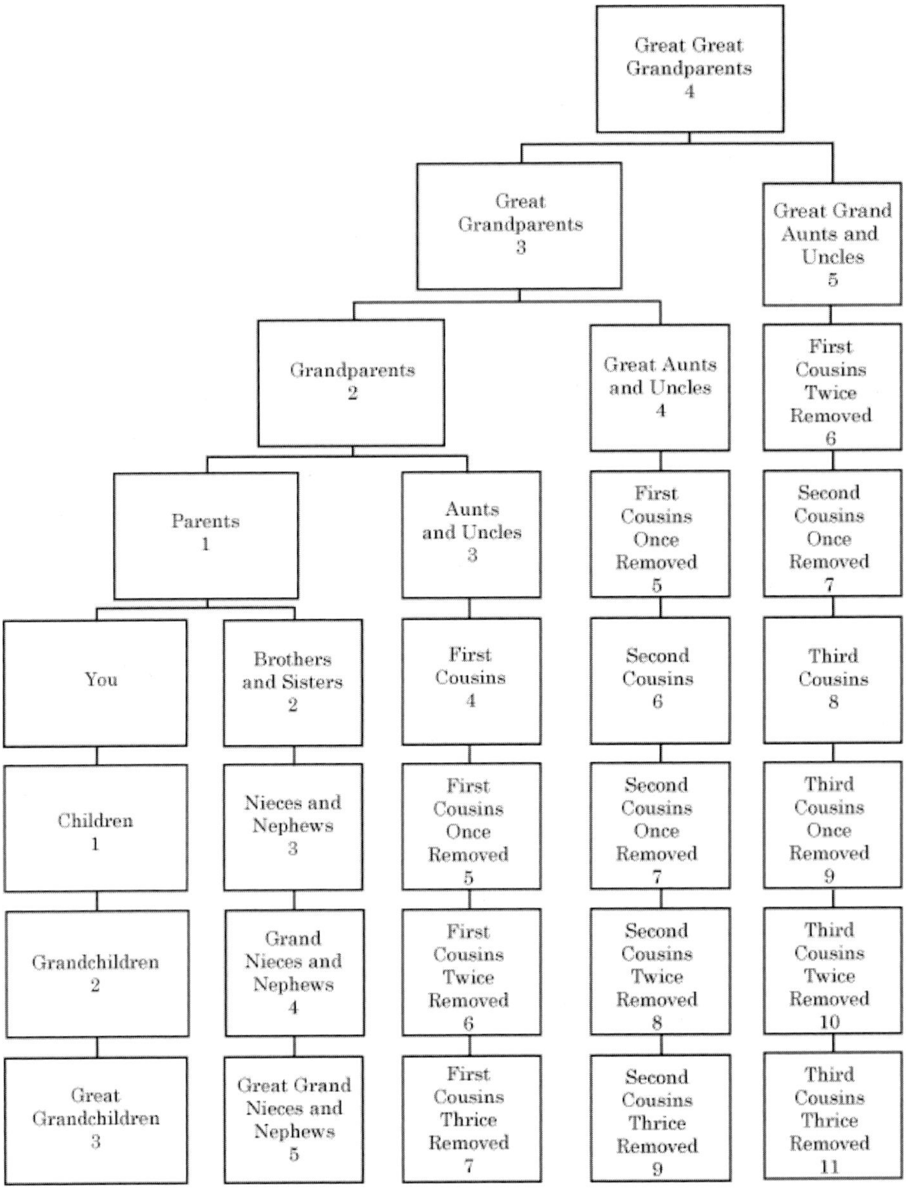

Illustration 5
Table of Consanguinity
Legal Heirs

PROBLEMS

Consider the family relationship below, but imagine that D is the decedent for the following problems.

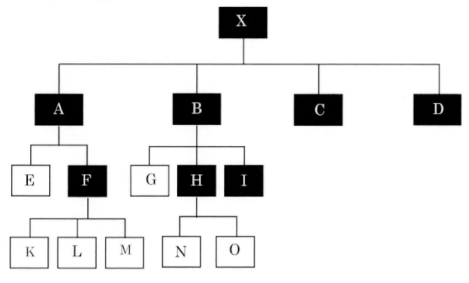

Illustration 6

3.11. Using the family relationships of Illustration 6 above, how would D's estate be distributed under all three intestacy schemes if D has no spouse, children, or parents living and X, A, B, C, F, H and I predeceased D?

3.12. Using the family relationships of Illustration 5 above, how would D's estate be distributed if D was survived by 1 parent, X?

3.13. Using the family relationships of Illustration 5 above, how would D's estate be distributed if no parent but one sibling, C, survived D and X, A, B, F, H and I predeceased?

3.14. Using the family relationships of Illustration 5 above, how would D's estate be distributed if A, B, C, E, F, & H predeceased (but not I) and E has 4 surviving children (P, Q, R & S) and 1 predeceased child T, and 2 surviving grandchildren (U & V) who are the children of T?

Problems with Collateral Heirs

Numerous difficulties can arise when intestate estates descend to remote collateral heirs. Most people know who their parents or brothers and sisters are, but many people die with no relative closer than a distant cousin. With the advent of DNA testing, it is now much easier to determine who is entitled to share in an estate like that of Ida Wood, the widow of a U.S. Congressman who, upon her marriage, made up a story about her past and took it to the grave with her. She claimed that she was born a Mayfield of New Orleans, but when she died intestate and over 1,100 persons claimed to be her next of kin (most of them Mayfields), the court determined that she was born Ellen Walsh in Ireland, and her estate went to some first cousins once removed that she had not seen for nearly all of her adult life.[39]

Consider some of the following difficulties:

- *Laughing heirs.* Laughing heirs are remote relatives who are entitled to take even though they have so little knowledge of the decedent's life and are so little upset by the decedent's death that they simply laugh all the way to the bank. Ida Wood's first cousins once removed are five degrees of relationship away from Ida and I'm sure they laughed their way to the bank with her $900,000 estate in 1932. Should the law of intestacy cut off the claims of more remote heirs even more than it already does, given the greater likelihood that second cousins will live at a distance and many people won't know relatives outside their immediate family? If so, should the law replace their rights with those of closer relatives by marriage, or preferred charities, or the government?

- *Sheer numbers of collateral relatives.* The number of possible collateral relatives is immense. Blackstone noted that if you go back 20 generations, one could have 1,048,576 ancestors (assuming people only had two children). Ida Wood had 1,103 potential heirs claiming her estate, but as the court settled on her husband's five closest relatives, that pre-empted the claims of 74 more distant relations.[40] Proving who are the closest relatives can be quite costly and time-consuming even with modern technological advances. An estate that will descend to remote relations is one very likely to be challenged by distant relations who will benefit if the claims of closer relatives can be defeated.

- *Half-bloods.* Although children and grandchildren either are or are not one's descendants, some siblings and other collateral relatives are more directly related than others. Half-bloods share just one ancestor. Thus, a half-sister to the decedent shares only one parent with other whole-blood siblings. Some states prohibit half-bloods from taking altogether, which follows from the English common law rule.[41] Others allow the half-blood to take a half share and a whole-blood relative to take an entire share (Florida and Texas follow this rule).[42] Other states allow half-bloods to inherit only if there are no whole-blood relatives of the same degree.[43] The UPC, however, treats whole-bloods and half-bloods equally, allowing all to share regardless of the legal origins of the property. See UPC § 2–107.

---

[39] See *In re Wood*, 299 N.Y.S. 195 (Surr. Ct. 1937) and JOSEPH A. COX, *The Recluse of Harold Square: The mystery of Ida E. Wood* (1964).

[40] *Id.*

[41] Before 1833 distant collateral relatives would inherit before nearer half-bloods. But this was changed by the Inheritance Act of 1833, 3 & 4 Will IV, c. 106 as amended by 22 & 23 Vict. c. 35, which now allows a half-blood to inherit.

[42] *See e.g.,* FLA. STAT. ANN. § 732.105 (West 1974), TEX.: Acts 2009, 81st Leg., ch. 680, § 1, eff. Jan. 1, 2014 (to be codified at V.T.C.A. § 201.057).

[43] The court in Davidson v. Brownlee (1917) 114 Miss 398, 75 So 140, construing a statute which provided that . . . that the kindred of the whole blood, in equal degree, should be preferred to the kindred of the half blood in the same degree. See also Jones v Stubbs (1983, Miss) 434 So 2d 1362, 47 ALR4th 555.

As if the fractional calculations aren't difficult enough, calculating half-blood shares means even more complicated division if they are to receive half of what their whole-blood relatives receive. The key is to count each whole-blood relative as 2 shares and each half-blood relative as 1 share. Thus, if A dies leaving 2 whole-blood siblings and 1 half-blood siblings (and no descendants or spouse or parents), A's estate will be divided into 5 shares, 2 for each of the whole-blood siblings and 1 for the half-blood sibling. And note that a half-blood isn't necessarily a biological relative. Your mother's adopted child could be your half-sibling if your father did not adopt your sibling. Moreover, with the growing prevalence of sperm and egg donation, you could have whole or half siblings living in hundreds of homes across the country.

**Practice Point: The Expanded Notion of Siblings
in the Technological Era**

With the growing popularity of sperm banks, sperm/egg donation, and donor embryos, our traditional notion of the 'family" has certainly expanded. We now find it commonplace to deal with situations our own parent's generation couldn't have dreamed of: that one person could biologically parent multiple children that s/he never meets or even knows about—and is not only relieved of the responsibility of supporting those children during life, but also able to prevent those children from inheriting at death (even via intestate succession).

And though these ideas might have seemed remarkable even a generation ago, society has certainly adapted its notions of what it means to be a "parent" far beyond biology. Just as in the cases of adopted children who desire to find their birth parents, there is a growing uptick in services which can "match up" children with the donors whose sperm was used to ultimately conceive them.[44] (This was one of the central plots in the 2010 movie *The Kids Are Alright*). And it was only a matter of time until half-siblings began contacting each other, as well. The process of connection is remarkably easy—all it takes is a donor number and a service that allows individuals to connect with others who share the same donor. You can even find blogs about parents who set up playdates or annual reunions to get half-siblings from the same donor together from all over the country with the goal that these children will develop lifelong relationships with each other. Just because donor-dad wants legal immunity doesn't mean donor siblings don't have legitimate reasons for connecting with each other. If you have a minute, Google "Donor Sibling" and see what questions come to mind from an estate planning perspective as you view the results.

Labs are now offering DNA tests for dating couples to determine that they are not inadvertently dating a half-sibling or cousin. Services like *23andme.com*, *familytreedna.com*, and even *Ancestry.com* offer "sibling tests" and keep registries of millions of genetic samples to assuage the modern fears of genetic defects that might come from the offspring of an incestuous union. The 1996 mystery film *Lone Star* may not be so far-fetched afterall.

One of the most compelling ideas relates to the notion of half-blooded siblings as discussed in this chapter, and its possible relation to the anti-lapse provisions discussed in Chapter 5. We will discuss the issues in more detail later, but at present, consider the effects that having a close-sibling-like relationship with a person

---

[44] See Rachel Lehmann-Haupt, *Are Sperm Donors Really Annonymous Anymore?*, SLATE MAGAZINE (March 2010).

who is related by blood—but not by law—might have on an estate plan. Take two women, both the biological child of the same sperm donor, but who grew up in separate homes with separate families. Assume that they met as children at yearly play dates and then kept up with each other over the years, eventually becoming close and calling each other "sister," even though they understood that they were not legally siblings. If one of the women dies and provides for the other in her will, what happens to that distribution if the other woman predeceases her but leaves children of her own? Does the gift lapse? Or would anti-lapse provisions save it? More on that to come.

PROBLEM

3.15. Calculate the distribution of the estate of D in Problems 3.13 and 3.14 above if B is a half-sibling of D and half-bloods get a half share and whole-bloods get a whole share using classic *per stirpes*. Note that *per capita* by generation or perhaps *per capita* with representation are incompatible with differential treatment of half-bloods because those schemes rely on equal treatment of relatives in the same generation.

———————

Besides the difficulties of keeping track of your nieces' and nephews' birthdays, as populations become more mobile it becomes even more difficult to keep track of more distant relatives. Even with the tightening of immigration laws and policies, the world's populations are more mobile than ever before in the history of human existence and your job (or maybe your paralegal's job) will be to find out who the closest heirs are who might have a claim on an estate. In the wildly popular *Downton Abbey*, the presumed heir of the title and the estates, Patrick Crawley, was listed as one of the drowned passengers on the doomed Titanic in the first episode. A year later, a badly burned Canadian army officer claiming to be Patrick showed up at Downton Abbey to throw the Granthams into a panic. Claiming to have suffered amnesia from the ordeal on the Titanic, he supposedly lived in Canada until a war-injury jogged his memory and he came looking for his nearest relatives. Skepticism abounded as the entire Grantham clan, including the successor heir apparent, Mathew Crawley, rethought their ambitions and relationships. Though *Downton Abbey* is fictional, the dilemma is certainly real. Finding long lost heirs before they show up and file a claim in your client's estate litigation makes sense, especially when distant relatives are looking for a get rich quick scheme and some simple estate planning can eliminate their claims (unless you are Lord Grantham and your estates are entailed).

Technology Trends: Everybody's Got a Cousin in Miami[45]

Jimmy Buffett knew whereof he spoke, or sang in this instance, for we've got cousins all over the world, and your job may very well be trying to locate them. Unless your life is like a John Grisham novel, you are not likely to be another Nate O'Riley, charged with journeying through the Brazilian rainforests of the Pantanal looking for the missionary beneficiary of a billionaire's will.[46] More likely, you will

---

[45] Jimmy Buffett and Michael Tschudin, *Everybody's Got a Cousin in Miami*, (MCA Records 1994).

[46] See John Grisham, *The Testament* (1999).

be stuck looking through old phone directories or public records at your computer, poring over utility bill read-outs and digging through grandma's 47 boxes of old correspondence trying to find the right John Smith or Li Chang. Once again, however, the internet has profoundly changed the way we practice law. There are dozens of internet search engines and sites that have come out of the endless curiosity of the genealogists and historians to aid in the search for all of grandpa's family. *www.USGenWeb*, *www.Ancestry.com*, and the Library of Congress, *www.lcweb.loc.gov/rr/genealogy*, are helpful sites. There are more specific sites like Afrigeneas and JewishGen and Mormon Church Family Search sites. Even Lexis–Nexis has a tracking system, P–Trak, that can be used to trace heirs.

Even direct internet searches through Yahoo People Search or Locateme.com aren't the only ways to trace heirs. Many national archives have put wills and property documents online, allowing searchers to access these documents from their laptops. And one of the most helpful is older census data that is gradually coming online. Government records can be another source if the records are available. Unfortunately, wars have had a devastating effect on families around the world who have lost touch with each other, sometimes forever. But more and more countries are diligently trying to maintain adequate databases of births and deaths. And the UN's High Commission for Refugees does its best to retain information about people's location and identity.

Hopefully, once you track down the right people you won't have to hike through the Pantanal to get the signature of a primary heir on a settlement agreement since they can sign electronically on their smart phones or satellite phones and you can even get 2-day express shipping to remote places like Antarctica and Mt. Kilimanjaro. Fortunately you can read the latest detective novel while surfing the web on your iPad without leaving your office.

Despite the same basic mechanical formula for distributing intestate estates among biological (consanguineous) relatives, there are some very interesting differences among intestacy rules in the different states when there are no collateral relatives able to take. For instance, in Arkansas (§ 28–9–214(7)), Illinois (755 ILCS § 5/2–1(f)), Maine (18A § 2–103(5)), Maryland (E & T § 3–104(d)), Missouri (§ 474.010(2)(d)), and New York (EPTL§ 4–1.1(a)(7)) if there are no grandparents or descendants of grandparents, the estate may pass to great-grandparents or their descendants. In Colorado if there are no descendants of grandparents the estate can pass to adopted-away children and if none to the natural (birth parents) of the decedent's adopted child (Colo.Stat. §§ 15–11–103(6) and (7)). Connecticut, New Jersey, Ohio, and South Carolina give an intestate estate to stepchildren and those who legally represent them if there are no collaterals within the required degree of relationship (Ct. Stat. § 45a–439(a)(4); NJ St. § 3B:5–4(f); Oh.St. § 2105.06(j); S.C.St. § 62–2–103(6)). And many states, following the UPC's lead, have added descendants of the last surviving spouse if there are no collateral relatives who are otherwise entitled to take. See Jeffrey Schoenblum, *2012 Multistate Guide to Estate Planning*, Table 7.

E. ESCHEAT

Finally, all states provide that if there are no qualified takers under the intestacy statute, the decedent's estate *escheats* to the state. But most states provide a substantial grace period for claimants to come forward and prove their rights to an escheated estate. Although the property is likely to be sold if no legal heir appears, the long lost claimant may be able to receive the cash value of the decedent's estate. For instance, Florida allows 10 years for a claimant to come forward, Fl.Stat. § 732.107(3); but California allows only the period of suit, which is any time at least two years after the decedent's death, during which the property is to be determined to be escheated and then sold, Cal. Civil Procedure Code § 1420–1424. Illinois, like many states, has adopted the Uniform Disposition of Unclaimed Property Act which outlines the procedures and rights associated with escheated property. 765 I.L.C.S. 1025 *et seq.* In that case, escheated property is determined to be abandoned after a period of from five to seven years, after which time the state may sell the property and put the proceeds into the state treasury, subject to a limited time for claimants to come forward and make a claim.

F. ADVANCEMENTS

What happens when a decedent makes a very large lifetime gift to a potential heir and the stated or unstated assumption is that the gift is to be treated as an *advancement* on the heir's inheritance? The traditional rule on advancements was that large lifetime gifts were to be treated as advancements on the inheritance and the heir had the duty to prove that the gift was not an advancement but rather an outright gift. Because of administration hassles, the presumption has shifted in most states, and under the UPC, such that lifetime gifts are not treated as advancements in the absence of evidence (usually written evidence) to the contrary. Lifetime gifts that qualify as advancements generally are not the $20.00 bill in the birthday card or the eighteen years of allowances. But advancements could easily include the money a parent spends sending a child to college, money for an extravagant wedding and honeymoon, or money to make a down payment on a house. Most siblings keep track of large gifts and feel slighted if mom and dad spend more on one child than on the others. But difficulties proving that a gift was not intended to be an advancement are significant, and today most parents spend large amounts on their adolescent and adult children without assuming they are advancements against an inheritance. Treating all of these gifts as advancements would be an accounting nightmare. The UPC and most states have switched the presumption with statutes like the following:

UPC § 2–109. Advancements.

(a) If an individual dies intestate as to all or a portion of his [or her] estate, property the decedent gave during the decedent's lifetime to an individual who, at the decedent's death, is an heir is treated as an advancement against the heir's intestate share only if (i) the decedent declared in a contemporaneous writing or the heir acknowledged in writing that the gift is an advancement or (ii) the decedent's contemporaneous writing or the heir's written acknowledgment otherwise indicates that the gift is to be taken into account in computing the division and distribution of the decedent's intestate estate.

(b) For purposes of subsection (a), property advanced is valued as of the time the heir came into possession or enjoyment of the property or as of the time of the decedent's death, whichever first occurs.

> (c) If the recipient of the property fails to survive the decedent, the property is not taken into account in computing the division and distribution of the decedent's intestate estate, unless the decedent's contemporaneous writing provides otherwise.

Calculating an intestate share when advancements are to be included is a process called *Hotchpot*. Two or more calculations may be required to successfully compute hotchpot. The first is to add together the decedent's net probate estate *plus* all lifetime gifts determined to be advancements. Then, divide the total value by the number of heirs and their percentages. That number will determine the total value of each person's inheritance. Any heir who received less than that amount will be entitled to a portion of the intestate estate to make up the difference. Any heir who already received more than that amount will be removed from the intestate calculation altogether, and a new calculation will be done minus that person.

For example, decedent X has four children A, B, C and D. During life, X gave A $50,000 for a house and gave B $70,000 for her college tuition. She made no substantial lifetime gifts to C and D. At her death, X's estate is worth $120,000. To calculate hotchpot we add the $50,000 given to A, the $70,000 given to B and the $120,000 of the intestate estate for a total of $240,000. Divided by four, the total for each child should be $60,000.

But B already received more than that amount. So we don't ask B to reimburse the estate the extra $10,000 that B received over and above her share of the inheritance. But, because she already received more than her share, we recalculate the total shares of her siblings, leaving her out. That means we start all over and add the $50,000 given to A with the $120,000 intestate estate for a total of $170,000 and divide by 3 for a share to each of the remaining three children (A, C and D) of $56,666.67. Since A already received $50,000, she will be entitled to $6,666.67 of her mother's intestate estate and C and D will each take $56,666.67 for a total of $120,000.

If any of X's children predeceased her, they would not have to pay back any of their advancements, and their descendants would still take what would have been their parent's share by representation as though their parent received nothing. Thus, if B predeceased X leaving issue surviving, they would take a share of their grandmother's estate even though their parent, B, already received an advancement on her inheritance. This is the result of UPC § 2–109(c).

PROBLEMS

3.16. Using the complicated problem of Illustration 7 below, calculate the dollar values of each person's inheritance if X made a lifetime gift to A of $50,000 for college tuition, a lifetime gift to B of $100,000 to purchase a home, a lifetime gift to D of $40,000 to start a business, a lifetime gift to E of $20,000 to take a trip around the world. Assuming X's net probate estate is valued at $180,000 and that the lifetime gifts are treated as advancements, what would each person be entitled to under Classic *Per Stirpes*, *Per Capita* by Generation, and *Per Capita* with Representation?

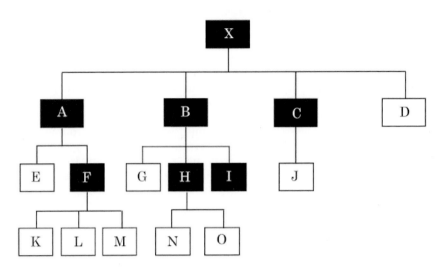

Illustration 7

3.17. Now work out the same problem but assume that X's net probate estate is only $70,000.

3.18. Now assume D also predeceased X.

G. CONCLUSION

Intestacy may seem like a complex distributional scheme, especially when one has to determine if a particular state is a *per capita* or *per stirpes* state, whether it follows *parentelic* or *degree of relationship*, and whether lifetime gifts are considered advancements. But there are probably more similarities among the various intestacy statutes than among testacy and trust rules. So as long as you understand the terminology and the different outcomes that can result from different rules, you should be able to advise clients when it is safe to rely on the intestacy rules and when they should avoid intestacy. It isn't always necessary to advise against intestacy, especially if the client has a small estate and the decedent would want the surviving spouse and/or descendants to be entitled to the whole property. But there are times when intestacy is not a good idea, either because clients don't like the outcomes under intestacy and would prefer a different distribution of their estate, there are complicated relationships that pose challenges to traditional intestacy rules (like a separated but not divorced spouse, minor children, children in the process of adoption, adult or other non-traditional adoptions, blended families, or step- or foster-children), or because remote heirs may challenge an estate plan. Intestacy is a perfectly sensible estate plan in many circumstances and the good lawyer should be able to tell when an estate can be administered smoothly and quickly under intestacy, without the expense of a will or a trust, and when the beneficiaries are easy to determine. While it is certainly not true that all the 50% or more of estates that are ultimately administered under intestate succession rules should be administered that way, it is true that the vast majority of intestate estates are administered quite efficiently and in a manner that corresponds to the wishes of most decedents.

On the flip side, intestacy is not a sensible estate plan for many estates of significant size, where there are complex family relationships, where there are minor children, and where there aren't close family relations who are the undisputed takers. For a person who does not like the intestate distribution scheme, or who has a complex estate, there are numerous other ways to cause a decedent's property to pass differently. In the next Chapter we take up a variety of different mechanisms to alter the default rules of intestacy.

THE ESTATE PLANNER'S TOOLBOX AND SALVAGE DOCTRINES

CHAPTER 4

A Brief Introduction to the Tools of Estate Planning

There are countless reasons why a decedent might not want to have her estate pass according to the default rules of intestate succession. A few of the most common reasons are:

- she might have a non-traditional family or wants to provide for non-blood relatives,
- she has few only distant relatives and would rather benefit friends or charities,
- she has sizable wealth and wants to spread her wealth to as many people as she reasonably can,
- she wants to minimize estate and inheritance taxes,
- she has minor children and wants to avoid the complexities of a guardianship for their property,
- she is newly married or newly divorced,
- she has recently changed domiciles or has property in multiple states,
- she inherited some of her property and wants it to pass back to the relations from whom she received it,
- she is separated but not divorced,
- she has a special needs child or other dependant,
- her children have different financial needs and she wants to deal with them differently,
- she is part-owner of a business,
- she has charitable ambitions,
- she wants to feel more in control of the disposition of her estate,
- she has family heirlooms she wants to dispose of to particular people,
- she is expecting to have large medical debts upon her death,
- any of a thousand other good reasons.

We all know that the most common way for people to control the disposition of their property is through a *will*—a testamentary document that spells out how the decedent wants her property to be distributed. We also know the countless horror stories of interminable and expensive will challenges, of sneaky beneficiaries who destroy the wills that disinherit them, of failed will executions because one witness wasn't in the room at the right time, of opportunistic caregivers who influence weak patients into leaving all their worldly possessions to them, of will bequests upset by crazy hypo-

theticals under the Rule Against Perpetuities, of endless probate procedures, and so on.

The will has been in existence for centuries as a legal device to control
the disposition of property after death. *Wills* were traditionally used to
convey real property and *Testaments* were traditionally used to convey personal property, but today a will can transfer all property, whether acquired
before or after will execution, although lawyers and form books still use the
term "Last Will and Testament." And most people think of the will when
they contemplate succession of their own property at death, despite the fact
that they probably all have at least one will substitute: a joint tenancy, a
trust, a POD or TOD account, life insurance, or they have split ownership
over time using a future interest. The rituals around will execution and
probate are also deeply embedded in our collective imagination, as are the
Sam Spades, Miss Marples, and Inspector Morses, who are familiar characters because of the real-life property implications of death. Yet many of the
complex will doctrines we will study here are slowly passing the way of the
springing executory interest, they are important in a relatively small set of
situations where wills get challenged and litigation follows. But wills are
becoming more and more simplified and most of the real work of succession
law is currently being done through trusts and other will substitutes.

As with intestate estates, testate estates (those involving wills) also
have to be probated as part of the court-supervised administration process
and many people are justifiably wary of anything involving courts, judges,
and lawyers. In 1965, Norman Dacey published his wildly popular book,
How to Avoid Probate, which fed on the fears of many people that their
estates, like that of the mythic Jarndyce and Jarndyce, would be entirely
consumed in legal fees and administrative costs, leaving nothing for their
beneficiaries.[1] Dacey recommended that people put all their property into
living trusts that would allow the successor trustee to simply distribute the
property according to an easily revocable and revisable trust document
without ever stepping foot in the courthouse.

Trusts are a lot like corporations; they are fictitious legal entities that
can own property. But, like corporations, they require planning, attention,
and maintenance to establish and benefit from financially. Like corporations, there are strict elements for creating and operating a trust which
Dacey didn't make as clear as he should have done when he extolled their
virtues. And unfortunately, too many people followed Dacey's advice without following through on all the requirements of trust administration. They
also did not realize that there were more strings attached to their property
now that it was in trust and they could not manage the property as easily
as when it was owned outright. They also got careless and acquired new
property without putting it in the trust, thus leaving property that still had
to be probated. (As will be discussed in the following section, in order to
avoid probate, a properly "funded" trust necessarily involves re-titling assets in the name of a trustee or re-aligning beneficiary designations in
accordance with the trust plan). And it turned out that for many people, the
cost of establishing the living trust was greater than the cost of probate.

While the book set off a frenzy of probate phobia, and it brought the
idea of the living trust into the average person's consciousness, it may have
done more harm than good by not encouraging people to think more holisti-
cally about their estate plans. And it is hard to write a book about the

---

[1]   *See,* Charles Dickens, *Bleak House.*

supposedly excessive costs of lawyers and courts to be avoided, while also suggesting that people seek out good estate planners to develop sensible individualized plans. The one-size-fits-all living trust was, and continues to be, simply bad legal advice.

This chapter will introduce you to the basic tools of estate planning, how to create wills, trusts, joint tenancies and a variety of other instruments and mechanisms for holding property, what they do, and what their strengths and weaknesses are. The most important thing to remember is that people are different—their circumstances and wishes are different, their assets and needs are different, and their families are different. No estate plan should come unchanged out of a form book. Even much of the boilerplate of a trust or will should be individualized if the situation warrants it. Professor Jeffrey Pennell admonishes estate planners to "identify and then to challenge [their] assumptions about what is appropriate or best for [their] clients, not in terms of the latest tax motivated changes, but rather based on the family or individual side of the endeavor."[2] This chapter gives you the tools, but you will need to learn when and why to use any particular one. More details on the internal structure and challenges of these tools are provided in later chapters.

A. WILLS

1. FORMS AND FORMALITIES

A will is a testamentary writing expressing the intent of the testator to have her property distributed according to the dispositive provisions of the document. Every state allows a person to make a will, but each state also requires that the will be executed with a certain amount of formality; a letter, an email, a death-bed utterance, and a post-it note attached to one's television identifying the proposed taker are usually insufficient to meet the statutory requirements in most states. Historically, contracts also had to be executed with a certain amount of formality; they had to be in writing and executed under seal. But most contract formalities have been dispensed with. Will formalities, however, have proven more resistant to change, perhaps because the uncertainties and fears of death make us take comfort in the familiarity of the will execution ritual and its surrounding mythology.

The UPC provisions for executing a valid will requires that the will be in writing, signed, witnessed, and that the testator be of sound mind and age.

UPC § 2–501. Who May Make Will.

An individual 18 or more years of age who is of sound mind may make a will.

---

² JEFFREY PENNELL, *It's Not Your Father's Buick, Anymore: Estate Planning for the Next Generation(s) of Clients*, Hecherling Institute on Estate Planning, 2009 at 13–5.

UPC § 2–502. Execution; Witnessed or Notarized Wills; Holographic Wills.

(a) [Witnessed or Notarized Wills.] Except as otherwise provided in subsection (b) and in §§ 2–503, 2–506, and 2–513, a will must be:

(1) in writing;

(2) signed by the testator or in the testator's name by some other individual in the testator's conscious presence and by the testator's direction; and

(3) either:

(A) signed by at least two individuals, each of whom signed within a reasonable time after the individual witnessed either the signing of the will as described in paragraph (2) or the testator's acknowledgment of that signature or acknowledgment of the will; or

(B) acknowledged by the testator before a notary public or other individual authorized by law to take acknowledgments.

(b) [Holographic Wills.] A will that does not comply with subsection (a) is valid as a holographic will, whether or not witnessed, if the signature and material portions of the document are in the testator's handwriting.

(c) [Extrinsic Evidence.] Intent that a document constitute the testator's will can be established by extrinsic evidence, including, for holographic wills, portions of the document that are not in the testator's handwriting.

As you can see, for a will to be valid it must be:

- in writing, **except** oral (*nuncupative*) wills are valid in a few states when reduced to writing by the witnesses shortly after the decedent's death,
- signed by the testator, **except** when the testator is unable to sign and directs a surrogate to sign for her,
- signed by at least two witnesses who saw the testator sign or affirm her signature, **except** where the state allows holographic wills (entirely in the testator's own handwriting) or if the state allows the witnesses to sign in the conscious presence of the testator (as perhaps after talking to the testator on the phone), or if the state allows the witness to sign weeks or months after witnessing the testator's signature,
- the witnesses must be credible witnesses and usually disinterested (i.e. not beneficiaries under the will and of a reasonable age—14 in some states), **except** where they can be beneficiaries (the UPC rule),
- the testator must be of sound mind (not under the undue influence of another, not suffer from lack of mental capacity or insane delusion or fraud),
- the testator must be 18 years of age or an emancipated minor, and
- the testator must intend the document to be her will.

Keeping track of the will elements, and exceptions, in light of evolving execution standards, can be daunting. The easiest solution is to strictly adhere to the statutory formalities and not cut corners. In light of its goal to rationalize and liberalize will rules to further testamentary intent, the UPC makes two important changes from earlier, more strict statutes—it does not require that the testator sign the will at the end of the document or that the testator actually sign in the presence of the witnesses. But even with these modest changes the UPC, and every state and territory, has a set of formal procedures for will execution that can easily trap the average person.

More importantly, once executed, a will generally cannot be changed without executing a new will or a *codicil* (amendment) to the will, though it can be revoked by destroying, defacing, or obliterating the document. These formalities, enshrined in every state's Statute of Wills, are slowly being eroded as we move into the digital age where documents can be easily changed, where video technology allows us to visualize the testator at the time of execution (perhaps making irrelevant the requirement of witnesses), and where well-laid estate plans can be ruined because the formalities set traps for the unwary. Unscrupulous beneficiaries who want to influence a will can easily insure that the formalities are followed. At the same time, an innocent testator can easily skip a step causing her will to be invalid and her entire estate to pass by intestacy, even when there is clear and convincing evidence that the testator wanted the document to be her will. The modern trend, therefore, is to ease up on the will formalities, but many states retain strict execution rules.

There are four generally-accepted reasons why we retain the will formalities:

1. they provide evidence of the testator's true intent (the *evidentiary* function);

2. they allow a will to move smoothly through the probate process (the *channeling* function);

3. they protect testators from fraud, undue influence, and mistake by requiring that the execution be in front of witnesses (the *protective* function); and

4. they impose on the testator's mind the seriousness of her actions so she gives proper consideration to their legal implications (the *ritualistic* function).

As you read about the will formalities in this section, reflect on whether any, and if so which, functions are supported by the various legal rules.

Despite two hundred years of carefully adhering to the ritual, there is a strong liberalizing trend these days to ease the requirements of the will formalities, especially where a harmless error, that does not undermine the testator's intent, would cause great upset to a testator's estate plan. This can easily happen in cases where husbands and wives execute joint reciprocal wills, each giving all to the other, and if the other has predeceased, to the same set of secondary beneficiaries. Despite careful attention to the details, husbands have signed their wives' wills, and vice versa, leaving courts with the strange situation of having to probate a will in which a testator leaves everything to himself.[3] Other problems can arise when the pages of a will get mixed up, or a page goes missing, or the staple comes off and the pages fall apart.[4] Such insignificant errors can cause a will to be

---

[3] *See, e.g., Snide v. Johnson,* 418 N.E.2d 656 (Ct.App. NY 1981); *In re Pavlinko's Est.,* 148 A.2d 528 (Pa. 1959).

[4] *See, e.g., Est. of Norton,* 330 N.C. 378, 410 S.E.2d 484 (N.C. 1991).

rejected, even though there is clear and convincing evidence that the testator wanted the document to be her will. Sometimes testators attach notes or draft copies of their wills to their formally-executed will, or they write on them thinking they will revise their will soon, and then die without executing a new will.[5] Simple changes on a will may cause it to be revoked or may be completely ignored even when testators clearly intended them to be effective.

There are four basic approaches that states have adopted for dealing with the will formalities. Some states require *strict compliance* with the formalities, including requirements that the will be signed at the end; that the witnesses sign in the presence of the testator, after the testator, and in the presence of each other; that the witnesses be disinterested; and that accidentally signing the self-proving affidavit (discussed below) instead of the will is not permissible. These strict compliance states have not passed legislation to allow witnesses to sign in the *conscious presence* rather than in the *actual presence* of the testator, or for courts to correct harmless errors. If you plan to practice in a strict compliance state you want to be sure you develop a fail-safe routine for will execution and that you check all the documents twice, or thrice, to make sure all the pages are in order. And for goodness' sake, don't let anyone leave the room until the entire will is fully executed. Pre-emptive bathroom breaks should be done before the ceremony begins.

Following the lead of Professor John Langbein, some states have adopted the *substantial compliance* doctrine which allows a will to be probated if the testator substantially complied with will formalities and there is sufficient evidence that the testator wanted the will to dispose of her property rather than have it pass by intestacy. The substantial compliance doctrine is mostly judge-made and is recommended by scholars in states where legislatures have not adopted a specific rule for easing the requirements of the formalities. The substantial compliance doctrine can save many wills that would otherwise fail because the lawyer did not stop the execution when one of the witnesses stepped outside of the room to take a phone call, or when the attestation clause and the self-proving affidavit were switched. But substantial compliance can be difficult to ascertain. If one witness signed in the address line and put her address on the signature line, the will is probably acceptable. But if the testator simply did not sign or could only find one witness, courts will have difficulty deciding just how "substantial" the compliance should be. Must a will be in writing? Must the testator be of age? Certainly the sound mind requirement cannot be waived, but perhaps the writing requirement could be. What if the will is merely a file on a computer? Is that substantial enough? As one court explained when it rejected a will for noncompliance with the formalities:

> *substantial compliance does not mean noncompliance, and the fact that the testator's and witnesses' signatures may be genuine does not obviate other express statutory requirements. Kirkeby v. Covenant House*, 970 P.2d 241 (Or.App. 1998).

Though fewer wills may be rejected under substantial compliance than strict compliance, the doctrine is often so indeterminate as to provide little guidance for lawyers except to try to follow the formalities as strictly as

---

[5]   *See, Clark v. Greenhalge*, 411 Mass. 410 (Mass. 1991).

possible and hope that breaches are slight and unimportant (and judges are understanding).[6]

A third approach, recommended by the UPC and the Restatement 3d of Property, is to allow a court the power to *dispense* with the formalities if there is *clear and convincing evidence* that the testator wanted the instrument to serve as her will. Under the UPC's *dispensing power*, a will can be probated even if there was no attempt to comply with the will formalities so long as there is ample evidence the instrument was intended to be a will. See UPC § 2–503.

UPC § 2–503. Harmless Error.

Although a document or writing added upon a document was not executed in compliance with Section 2–502, the document or writing is treated as if it had been executed in compliance with that section if the proponent of the document or writing establishes by clear and convincing evidence that the decedent intended the document or writing to constitute (i) the decedent's will, (ii) a partial or complete revocation of the will, (iii) an addition to or an alteration of the will, or (iv) a partial or complete revival of his [or her] formerly revoked will or of a formerly revoked portion of the will.

The evidentiary standard in most probate issues is a preponderance of the evidence. Thus, by elevating the standard to clear and convincing, the UPC is attempting to provide some protection against fraud or mistake while allowing many innocent mistakes to prove harmless. The dispensing power must be adopted by legislation, and some of the states that have adopted the UPC have included the dispensing power, but not all have done so.[7] So do not assume that a UPC state will have adopted the harmless error doctrine. And some states, through common law modification, might allow a witness to sign after the will execution ceremony, but still require they sign in the presence of the testator,[8] or a state might require the witnesses sign in the presence of the testator and not allow them to sign just the self-proving affidavit, yet will allow the self-proving affidavit to be signed after the execution.[9] The exact requirement of the will formalities in your state are likely to be on your bar exam and anyone planning to set up a wills practice should know thoroughly the requirements and exceptions. Most probate sections of the local bar associations have promulgated procedures for will execution compliance, so be sure to seek the assistance of others who have paved the way.

The dispensing power is particularly helpful when testators make changes to a validly executed will. For instance, a testator may strike out a particular gift or beneficiary and write in a different amount or a different taker. Under both strict and substantial compliance, these changes are not permissible because they were not made by an instrument in compliance

---

[6] *See, In re Will of Ranney*, 589 A.2d 1339 (N.J. 1991); John H. Langbein, *Excusing Harmless Errors in the Execution of Wills: A Report on Australia's Tranquil Revolution in Probate Law*, 87 Colum. L. Rev. 1 (1987); Lloyd Bonfield, *Reforming the Requirements for Due Execution of Wills: Some Guidance from the Past*, 70 Tul. L. Rev. 1893 (1996).

[7] A version of UPC § 2–503 has been adopted in California, Colorado, Hawaii, Michigan, Montana, New Jersey, South Dakota, Utah, and Virginia, but some of these are limited to minor errors in execution.

[8] *See, Wheat v. Wheat*, 244 A.2d 359 (Ct. 1968).

[9] *See, Keaner v. Archibald*, 533 N.E.2d 1268 (Ind.Ct.App. 1989); IND. STAT. § 29–1–5–3(b)(1)(B).

with the statutory formalities. In certain circumstances, the entire will might be voided; in others, only the additions will be voided. Of course, if a testator makes numerous handwritten changes, and then *re-executes* the document, the changes will be effective. But changes made after execution of the will are deemed invalid testamentary gifts if the formalities are not followed.

Testamentary changes in a strict or substantial compliance state should be made through a *codicil*, which is a separate, validly executed document that makes new testamentary dispositions and thus revokes any inconsistent dispositions in the original will, but a codicil leaves the rest of the will in effect. One commentator believes the dispensing power should be adopted universally.[10]

Finally, a fourth approach is that adopted by the Uniform Law Commission in its 2008 amendments to the UPC, which is to permit a *notarial will*. A notarial will is a written instrument, intended by the testator to be a will, but executed only by signing before a notary public. *See*, UPC § 2–502(a)(3)(B). Some states also allow what are called *statutory* wills, which are simple wills that follow a set statutory formula (usually fill in the blanks) and are valid if executed either according to the formalities or in front of a notary. California, Maine, Massachusetts, Michigan, New Mexico, and Wisconsin have adopted statutory will provisions. Although the notarial will and statutory will seem like good alternatives to the cumbersome formalities of regular wills, many of the states that have adopted them impose sometimes quite significant restrictions on their form.[11]

Perhaps the most important reason for requiring the will formalities is to draw a distinction between *inter vivos* gifts (that require delivery) and testamentary gifts that take effect at death (but require execution according to the will formalities). If we abolished the will formalities and allowed testators to simply write a note during life allegedly making a testamentary gift for the future, we would have a hard time knowing if the letter was a naked promise to make a gift, which is unenforceable, or a valid testamentary gift to be made in the future. The will formalities and the delivery requirement create a bright line between *inter vivos* and testamentary gifts, which is helpful if one must determine the value of the gift for tax purposes (i.e. is it valued at the time of delivery or at time of death? The answer depends on what type of gift it is). It is also helpful if testators change their minds and revoke their wills. One cannot take back an *inter vivos* gift if it is completed and the recipient doesn't want to give it back. Also, gift taxes can apply to certain *inter vivos* gifts precisely because the giver has relinquished the dominion and control we associate with ownership. Testamentary gifts, on the other hand, are not effective until the testator's death, thus allowing the testator full dominion and control until death. The will formalities help to maintain that line, even as many people try to blur the distinctions before death in order to gain the tax benefits of *inter vivos* gifts while retaining the power over the property of testamentary gifts.

---

[10] See, Stephanie Lester, *Admitting Defective Wills to Probate, Twenty Years Later: New Evidence for the Adoption of the Harmless Error Rule*, 42 REAL PROP., PROB. AND TR. J. 577 (2007). But the probate bar, like most lawyers, cling to time-tested doctrines.

[11] For instance, the Maine Statutory Wills Act (ME. REV. STAT.tit. 18–A, § 2–514) requires the signatures of two witnesses and you cannot change, delete, or add words to the face of the will. The Wisconsin Basic Wills statute requires that the testator sign in each box used to identify a gift of property or write "not used" in empty boxes. The will also requires two witnesses. See WIS. STAT. ANN. § 853.55.

Although much of this area of law is concerned with the complicated characteristics of property ownership and control, with very nuanced distinctions that can profoundly affect people's disposition of their property, the formalities usually appear to be easy. They are the formalistic requirements that should not take a lot of court time and attention. However, nothing in law is entirely simple. Consider these cases and whether you would allow these wills to stand because the formalities were or were not adequately followed:

Chester v. Smith

677 S.E.2d 128, 285 Ga. 401 (2009)

Decedent *Campell, who was in poor health, attempted to execute her Will while seated in the passenger seat of a car that was parked in a bank parking lot. The driver of the car in which Campbell was seated called a bank employee, Christina Evans, and asked Evans to come outside to the bank parking lot to assist Campbell in executing her Will. Evans agreed, exited the bank, and walked to the vehicle occupied by Campbell. Evans read the Will to Campbell, and Campbell signed it while still seated in the car. Evans then carried the Will inside the bank and asked two bank tellers, Betty Wilson and Kim Hulsey, to sign the Will as witnesses. Wilson and Hulsey signed the Will at their respective teller stations inside the bank. Although the Will contained an attestation clause that stated that the witnesses had signed the Will in Campbell's presence, affidavits from Evans, Wilson, and Hulsey established that Campbell could not have seen the witnesses sign the Will inside the bank based on Campbell's position in the parked car outside of the bank. Indeed, Campbell remained inside the vehicle when the witnesses signed the Will, and the structure of the bank directly prevented Campbell from seeing the witnesses sign her Will inside the bank. Because the undisputed evidence reveals that Campbell was unable to see the witnesses sign the Will if she had desired to do so, 'any presumption of proper execution arising from the will's attestation clause has been rebutted by clear proof that the will was not properly executed.'* Will not probated. Georgia follows the line of sight test.

Query: Of course you, as estates lawyers, would never allow this to happen. But how do we avoid these kinds of pitfalls by ordinary testators who don't use lawyers? Which is more important, the testator seeing the witnesses sign, or the witnesses seeing the testator sign? Why?

In re Est. of Pittson

2009 WL 1065384 (Ohio App. 5 Dist.)

During the hearing, the trial court heard the testimony of the following witnesses: 1) Decedent's son-in-law *testified that on December 14, 2000, at his home, he saw the decedent sign the will. He stated that, when the decedent signed the will, he was in the living room approximately two feet away from the decedent.* 2) Decedent's daughter-in-law *stated that she saw the decedent sign the document. On cross-examination, she stated that she was approximately ten feet away from the decedent when he signed the will.* 3) Decedent's son *testified that on December 14, 2000, at approximately 5:30 P.M., he [and 4 others] gathered in the living room of [decedent's son-in-law's] house. He stated that the will was prepared by Attorney Lori Mills. He stated that it was the decedent's intention to execute the will and leave him, (Dennis Jr.), everything. He testified that he sat next to the decedent on the couch when the will was signed.* 4) Decedent's friend *Anthony Zumbo testified that he met [the son] Dennis Pittson Jr. in high school through the all star bowling league and got to be friends with his family. He stated that on December 14, 2000, he saw* the decedent *sign the will and then he signed as a witness. He stated he was the only non-family member present. He stated the signing took place at a table in the dining room. He stated the decedent was seated at the table and he was standing next to the table. He stated the table was cluttered and there was only room for one person to sit. He stated no one else was present at the table when* the decedent *signed the will."* Only Zumbo's signature was on the will as a witness. The court denied probate because the *testimony did not prove by clear and convincing evidence that there were two people who witnessed* the decedent *sign and execute the will. The trial court found in its findings of fact and conclusions of law that the testimony of* the others *was "suspect." The court noted that* the son *is the sole beneficiary of the estate as set forth in the will, and his wife would therefore benefit monetarily as well.* The son-in-law *admitted that* his brother and sister-in-law *had helped him through the years, and he felt indebted to them.*

Query: Assuming many of the decedent's family were in fact present in the home at the time decedent signed, and perhaps even saw him sign, as did Zumbo the witness who actually signed as witness, why not allow the will to stand? What value is preserved in denying this will to probate, even if the family witnesses were "suspect?" Is it more important to sign as a witness and not actually see the testator sign, or see the testator sign and not ascribe your signature as a witness?

In re Est. of Miller

149 P.3d 840, 143 Idaho 565 (2006)

On January 14, 2000, Bruce Miller and his fiancé, Christine Spelius, went to a local bank where Spelius wrote out a will for him at his request. Miller told Spelius to make changes to the document, and so she rewrote the document. The handwritten will stated:

> *To Whom it may concern:*
>
> *I Bruce G. Miller Jr. of sound mind + body make my last will and testament.*
>
> *I want Christine Ann Spelius to inherit my entire estate including real estate, personal property and any money and my dog "Buddy." I also want her to be conservator of my estate.*

Miller signed the will, and both Spelius and a bank employee witnessed him do so. The bank employee then signed the will on a handwritten line designated "witness." He was also a notary public, and he affixed his notary seal to the will. Spelius did not sign the will as a witness at that time. After leaving the bank, Spelius kept possession of the will with Miller's consent.

On July 2, 2004, Miller died at the age of sixty-six years. After Miller died, Spelius contacted an attorney to probate Miller's will, and upon his advice she signed the will as a witness. On July 12, 2004, Spelius filed a petition for formal probate of Miller's will. In that petition, she informed the court that she did not sign the will as a witness until July 12, 2004. Will upheld as valid because Idaho law did not specify when a witness must sign the will.

Query: Why in the world would Spelius think she didn't need to sign the will? How many adults today participate in a will execution ceremony and then don't bother to actually sign? Does her failure to sign trigger any suspicions in your mind?

In re Est. of Speers

179 P.3d 1265 (Ok. 2008)

On June 15, 1982, Shirley Joyce Speers (testatrix) signed a "Last Will and Testament" (will/instrument). It named her husband, Ralph Speers (husband) as her executor and Doyle Wesley Fincher as her alternate executor. It also gave her daughter, Sherry Arlene Ross, her household furnishings and appliances, and her son, Daniel Eugene Speers, her livestock. Her husband was named the beneficiary of the rest of the estate, provided he paid the estate's expenses. If he failed to do so, his share was devised in equal parts to James Nelson Fincher and Jonathan Clyde Fincher, the testatrix's grandsons. The will expressly omitted LeeAnn Fincher, the testatrix's daughter. It was signed by Sadie B. Walton (Walton) and Walter Durbin (Durbin) as witnesses and notarized by Vicky Thomas (notary), but it was not stamped with a notary seal. The testatrix died on April 20, 1997, and the instrument was not probated at the time of her death.

At some point after his wife's death, the husband married Ann Speers (appellee). The husband died some time before June of 2005, and upon searching his records, his second wife discovered the will. She filed her petition on June 2, 2005, seeking to admit it to probate. The instrument submitted by the appellee contained several handwritten strikeouts and interlineations. On June 7, 2005, the testatrix's children, Danny Speers, LeeAnn Fincher, and Sherry Ross (collectively, contestants) filed an objection to the petition for probate of the will and contest of the will, arguing that instrument was invalid because the original will was destroyed, thereby invalidating any copies. Court refused to probate will because without notary seal the will was not self-proved, thus requiring the testimony of witnesses. Only one witness testified and the only evidence about the status of the second witness was a question to the first as to whether he had heard the other witness was deceased. He said yes. Without sufficient evidence of the death of the second witness the will was not adequately proved by two witnesses as required by law.

Query: Why did the second wife try to probate the first wife's will? Do you think the court was more interested in upholding the will formalities and ensuring that the witnesses truly prove the will, or was it more interested in protecting settled expectations of children against a step-mother who wanted property of her husband's first wife?

In re Est. of Wiltfong

148 P.3d 465 (Colo.App. 2006)

Randall Rex (proponent) and Ronald Wiltfong (decedent) *were domestic partners for twenty years until decedent's death. They lived together and intermingled most of their finances. On proponent's birthday in 2003, proponent and decedent celebrated with two friends. In the presence of the friends, decedent gave proponent a birthday card containing a typed letter decedent had signed. The letter expressed decedent's wish that if anything should ever happen to him, everything he owned should go to proponent. The letter also stated that proponent, their pets, and an aunt were his only family, and "everyone else is dead to me." Decedent told proponent and the friends the letter represented his wishes.* Decedent died from a heart attack a year later. *The trial court ruled the letter was not a will because it did not meet the* statutory formalities. The appeals court remanded to determine if the defects in the letter were technical drafting mistakes that would constitute harmless error in light of decedent's intent to create a will or whether his intent was not to create a will at all.

Query: Do you think the decedent intended the letter to be his will? Should it matter if he knew it would not have legal effect, so long as it accurately reflected his intentions as to the disposition of his property?

―――――――――

There are two important formalities issues that generally face courts. The first is whether a document that doesn't really look like a will (a letter, a list) should be given testamentary effect as a will because the decedent wanted it to control the disposition of her property, even though she probably knew it wasn't a true will. The second is whether a document intended by the testator to be a will was executed in conformity with the statutory formalities and can be proved and therefore probated. The first issue, as in the *Wiltfong* case, asks a court to dispense with will formalities altogether to give legal effect to a document that identifies how the decedent wanted her property to pass. These kinds of cases are far easier in states that allow holographic wills (discussed below). The second issue, as in *Chester, Speers,* and *Miller,* concern the adequacy of the proof of proper execution. The case of *Pittson* is the most troubling because it appears that the decedent did execute a will, he did do so in front of at least one witness, and presumably wanted the document to serve as his will. But the irregularities were so glaring, and the evidence of lying by beneficiaries was sufficient, to make the court deny the will. Wills with greater errors have been probated, but when the court smells a rat, it is likely to rely on the will formalities to base its decision not to probate the will, which is what seems to have happened in both *Speers* and *Pittson.*

The lesson to be learned is to follow the will formalities religiously, to check everything twice, and figure courts will bend the rules only in cases where the equities appear to demand it. Santa Claus only has to check his lists twice; a good estate lawyer should check things multiple times, and then revisit her clients' wills periodically to see if circumstances have changed, and codicils, new documents, or additional plans should be made. You don't want to be the estate lawyer submitting a client's will to probate that is covered with notes, strike-outs, interlineations, or changes that you did not know about because you hadn't bothered to check in with your client for years. Of course, even if you are in regular contact and recommend regular check-ups for your client's estate plans, you may be submitting the same difficult will; at least in that instance it's not your fault that the estate plan is likely to be a litigator's nightmare.

Practice Point: The Dreaded Duplicate Original Will

Consider the following set of facts, once common in many jurisdictions, and still present in a few: Upon the death of your firm's client, the named Executor brings to you the decedent's original, signed will that had been drafted years ago by a now retired partner in your firm. On the will, you notice, much to your dismay, several pages containing hand-written notes. Further, there are two paragraphs which have been crossed out all-together. In your own file, however, you find that you have a properly signed and witnessed version of the will, dated consistently with the will containing the markings. It is not a photocopy, nor does it have a stamp or other marking indicating that it is a copy. What should you do? Do you actually have two original wills, or does one version "trump" the other? When the client wrote on her will, did she actually revoke it? And, if so, did she also revoke the version that you have in your file?

This situation has caused many problems over the years for both attorneys and clients. Why would an attorney ever want to execute two duplicate original wills? Some felt that it made clients feel more secure knowing that if their version could not be found at their death, that the attorney could easily produce one and move the estate forward. But this highlights a big problem, doesn't it? What if the client just changed her mind and revoked her will without telling the attorney? This practice makes it extremely difficult for a client to revoke her own will (and she is the only one who has the power to do so, anyway) because, obviously, the attorney has that other original on file.

Let's assume for a moment that the marked-up version of the will was the only version in existence, and that the markings did not convey a clear attempt by the testator to revoke the will. At that point, the document could perhaps still be probated and, depending on the jurisdiction, the untouched provisions may still stand as valid. However, in this scenario of duplicate original wills, that's not the case at all. Are both documents equally valid? The Georgia Supreme Court in *Horton v. Burch*, 267 Ga. 1 (1996), in addressing a situation inolving duplicate original wills, held that only the first instrument signed by the testator and the witnesses can legally constitute a valid will and that all other executed or signed copies may only be admitted upon evidence that the original will was lost or destroyed—but not revoked.

So, practically speaking, in our example, you might find the resolution only plays out in court, with your crafty arguments hopefully demonstrating that the testator did not intend to revoke her version of the will by writing on it. The biggest lesson we can learn, however, is to be proactive in our own planning for clients: execute only *one* will at the signing ceremony to steer clear of this problem. Photocopies can be used for back-up protection, but only one original should be lurking around.

The law on duplicate original wills is that either version can be probated, so it is tempting to have a client execute two, or maybe more originals, especially if you worry your client is prone to losing things, lives in a hurricane zone, or has sneaky and unscrupulous kids known to prowl through their mom's safe or filing cabinets. But duplicate originals create nothing but headaches in many cases. The client cannot easily modify or revoke her will without physically controlling all copies (in which case, what's the point of having additional versions?) and if changes are made to one version and not the other, courts have to wade through the evidence to determine testamentary intent or, more likely, will simply ignore any changes regardless of testamentary intent. We discuss revocation and modification in more detail in Chapter 10. For now keep in mind that one of the most important benefits of a will is the ability to change one's mind until death—for no testamentary gifts are effective until the donor actually dies. Duplicate originals significantly limit the flexibility of testamentary gifts by making it cumbersome to modify or revoke will provisions. This may be good if grandma is like most modern politicians, quick to change their minds with whatever direction the political winds are blowing. But even if grandma is susceptible to the influences of televangelists, cable television advertisers, and door-to-door salesmen, and it might be wise to erect a few road-blocks to grandma's compliant personality, duplicate originals is unlikely to be the best method of doing so.

Technology Trends: Smart phones, Facebook, and Microsoft Outlook

I find it really creepy that someone can send me an email about setting up a phone meeting and my computer magically reads my email, logs the date and time of the meeting on my outlook calendar, and beeps me a reminder when the time is nearing. I realize the sender had to do something on his end to register the meeting on my calendar (I'm not entirely sure what), but it's a little like someone snooping through my wallet—there are no secrets anymore. With modern computer technology we can easily imagine being able to simply speak into our smart phone an order to remove a particular paragraph from our will, which will stay constantly updated with our changing whims and intentions each time we turn it on. Or, I could post my will signing video onto Facebook and all my friends, who watched me sign, could "like" it and record themselves as witnesses. Or, I could sign my name on my will with my finger on the screen of my iPhone the same way I sign for credit card charges at my local hair salon, never once touching a pen or a piece of paper.

Does it make sense with electronic discovery and e-filing in most court systems to type up a will on the computer, print off a hard copy for paper execution following all the proper statutory formalities, and then scan it back for safe-keeping and submission to the court? It is only a matter of time before all of this will be done digitally and then how does a client make changes, revoke the will, or prevent its going viral on the internet? If it does go viral how do we know which is the original? Many law firms are going paperless and, like many other aspects of succession law, the probate bar is loath to come into the twentieth century, much less the twenty-first century. Our laws, as you can already see, are based on paper technology to memorialize and make effective our estate plans. Yet paper is tremendously ephemeral. It could be destroyed easily by natural disasters or unscrupulous relatives. But prior to copy machines it was easy to tell which piece of paper was the original and handwriting experts could make a living testifying to writing styles on estate documents. Today, with laser printers and e-signatures, where testamentary documents can reflect testamentary intent in real time, the will formalities may be going the way of the dinosaurs. What, if any, protections need to be put into place if the paper-based will formalities are going to be dispensed with?

PROBLEMS

4.1. Charlie executed a valid will in 2010, leaving his entire estate to his four children, equally. In 2011, Charlie sent an email to his attorney, as follows:

It is my intention that my estate now be divided into two shares. Half goes equally among my children and the other half shall pass to Carol, my fiancée. Please make the changes and get it legal.

The attorney drafts a new will for Charlie with the revised distribution pattern but, before it is executed, receives news that Charlie died in a car accident, apparently just after his fiancée, Carol, ended their relationship. Who inherits the estate? And, what effects could UPC § 2–503 have in this case?

4.2. A new client brings a handwritten will to you for some "easy legal advice." He has asked that your office merely type it, as is, and make sure that it is properly executed and witnessed as a valid will in your state. He, being very laid back and understanding, even says that you do not need to put your name, or even your firm's name, on the will (assume that this part of the scenario does comply with the law in your jurisdiction). He stresses that he has a very limited income and can't afford to pay you for further advice and only expects typed versions of the will he brought to you. What are some of your concerns? And you may be surprised how often this scenario will actually happen to you in practice. The client may feel like he knows what he wants and has done all the work and you are simply a scrivener, adding a few legal terms of art and pasting in the proper attestation language.

2. HOLOGRAPHIC WILLS

Holographic wills are the only common exception to the will formalities, and are permitted in 29 states.[12] The term comes from two Greek words, meaning "whole" and "written," and states that allow them generally require that they be entirely in the handwriting of the testator.[13] Holographic wills must be signed but do not need witnesses, on the assumption that a document entirely in the testator's handwriting is hard to forge and a testator who bothered to write the entire will out by hand is unlikely to be under duress. New York, for instance, allows holographic wills but only for members of the armed services.[14] Many states will permit holographic wills if they were validly executed in another state by a domiciliary of that state who later moves to a non-holograph state.[15] But some states, like Florida, not only do not permit holographic wills to be valid in the state, but will not accept holographic wills to be imported even if they were valid where executed.[16] Acceptance of holographic wills tends to cluster in Southern and Western states. Most states in the Northeast prohibit the use of holographic wills. The Midwest, as with most things, is a mixed bag.

Consider Gary Coleman's holographic will, filed in Utah by his former wife, Shannon Price.[17] Even if they hadn't divorced, which would normally revoke such a will, would you give this will effect? If not, what do you want to know about the execution of the will and what, if anything, triggers any suspicions you might have about the will?

---

[12] *See,* Schoenblum, 2012 Multistate Guide to Estate Planning, Table 1.

[13] *See,* R.H. Helmholz, *The Origin of Holographic Wills into English Law,* 15 Leg. Hist. 97 (1994).

[14] *See,* N.Y. EST., POWERS, & TRUST. LAW § 3–2.2.

[15] *See, e.g.,* N.M. STAT. ANN. § 45–2–506.

[16] *See,* FLA. STAT. § 732.502(2).

[17] http://tmz.vo.llnwd.net/o28/newsdesk/tmz_documents/0610_coleman_3.pdf.

ept. 4, 2007

Addendum to All Wills & Trusts

All wills and trusts are to remain in force and to not be broken, ignored, changed or rewritten. The exceptions are the heirs and issue per stirpes. Shannon Michelle Price, also may or may have been known as Shannon Michelle Coleman, is the sole heir of all and any monies, properties, bank accounts, earnings, model trains, vehicles, cars, toys, games, electronics, homes, other inheritances if any, all things physical and/or intellectual shall be forth, upon Gary Wayne Coleman's death, be Shannon Michelle Price's physical and intellectual properties, monies, earnings, collections, holdings and goods. I made this change of free will and was not coerced in any way. This I have done because of my personal selfishness and weakness and I Love her with all my heart.

Sept. 4, 2007 11:44pm mst

What about this one?[18]

All Tai-Kin Wong's → Xi Zhao. my best half

12-31-92

FILED

FILMED

130221

PR 130221   Exh # 1

Identification ☒ Admitted
Estate of Wong
Date NOV 1 2 1993   Clerk JOE VELA

---

[18] Zhao v. Wong, 40 Cal.App.4th 1198 (Cal.App. 1st Dist. 1995).

Or this one?

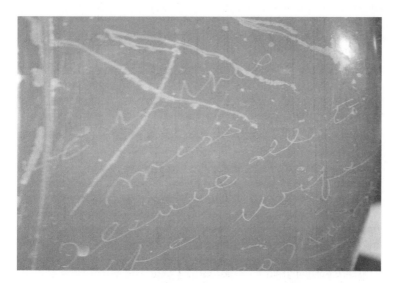

This third will was written by a farmer, George Cecil Harris, who was trapped under his tractor for 12 hours. It was etched into the fender and reads: "In case I die in this mess, I leave all to the wife. Cecil Geo Harris." The fender was taken off the tractor and filed for probate in the Kerroburt Courthouse, in Saskatchewan, Canada.[19]

Holographic wills are often the subject of humor and ridicule, but they do serve an important function in the lives of ordinary people facing imminent death. Charles Kuralt wrote the following letter to his mistress of many years:

June 18, 1997

Dear Pat—

Something is terribly wrong with me and they can't figure out what. After cat-scans and a variety of cardiograms, they agree it's not lung cancer or heart trouble or blood clot. So they're putting me in the hospital today to concentrate on infectious diseases. I am getting worse, barely able to get out of bed, but still have high hopes for recovery . . . if only I can get a diagnosis! Curiouser and curiouser! I'll keep you informed. I'll have the lawyer visit the hospital to be sure you <u>inherit</u> the rest of the place in MT. if it comes to that.

I send love to you & Shannon. Hope things are better there!

Love,

C.

Kuralt died shortly after writing this letter and never having met with his lawyers. In lengthy litigation, the Montana Supreme Court upheld the letter itself as a valid holographic codicil to Kuralt's formal will executed in New York, which left everything to his wife, Petie, and their two children.[20]

The law on holographic wills has changed over the years, from the early twentieth century when courts hesitated to probate a will that was not *entirely* written in the testator's handwriting, and was signed and fully

---

[19] http://news.usask.ca/archived_ocn/09–jan–23/see_what_we_found.php.

[20] *In re* Est. of Kuralt, 15 P.3d 931 (Mt. 2000).

dated by the testator. With the 1990 UPC, however, only *material* portions of the holographic will must be in the testator's handwriting, and it must be signed, but other portions of the will, like the introductory wording or other boilerplate, can be printed.[21] The UPC allows extrinsic evidence to be used as to testamentary intent, which means the document, eggshell, petticoat, or post-it note need not even state explicitly that it was meant to be a will.[22]

States allowing holographic wills do so, most often, on the policy of facilitating the donative freedom of ordinary people who might not feel comfortable, or be able to afford, hiring a lawyer to draft a formal will. But certainly documents like the letter in Kuralt should give one pause. Clearly Kuralt did not intend the letter to be a will, though he just as clearly intended his mistress to get the property. Should we completely abolish the requirement that a testator intend the document to be a will in our rush to facilitate a testator's dispositive intent? If so, the post-it note on the TV should be sufficient. Where and how should courts draw the line?

3. Proving a Will

The laws of most states only require that the witnesses see the testator sign her will and then affix their signatures as witnesses. Then, when a will is admitted to probate, the witnesses are called and examined as to the totality of the circumstances surrounding the execution of the will. They are asked things like whether they saw the testator sign, whether they saw each other sign, whether they knew it was a will, and whether the testator appeared to be of sound mind, age, and evidenced the intent that the instrument be her will. Two simple provisions can help avoid having to locate perhaps long-lost or deceased witnesses and drag them into court. The first is the *attestation* clause. An attestation clause states that the testator freely signed the document as her will and that she requested the witnesses affix their signatures to the instrument. A typical attestation clause reads something like this:

> *We, witness A and witness B, attest that the testator declared this to be her last will and testament, that she signed and executed this instrument in our presence, willingly, was under no constraint or duress, and that she requested that we affix our signatures as witnesses hereto.*

The most important purpose of the witnesses is to affirm that it was indeed the testator who signed the will, and not someone forging the testator's signature. If the testator already signed the will so the witnesses aren't going to see her affix her signature, then the witnesses need to see the testator acknowledge that the signature they see on the page is indeed the testator's and not someone else's. And the witnesses can speak to whether someone held a gun to the testator's head to get her to sign, was standing over her threatening to drop her favorite poodle out the 10th floor window, or whether the testator was drunk, high, incompetent, or asleep. The attestation clause speaks primarily to the issue of the testator's signa-

---

[21] *See,* UPC § 2–502(b).

[22] A quick internet search reveals a variety of unusual holographic wills. *See,* http://law professors.typepad.com/trusts_estates_prof/2007/09/unusual–hologra.html for details of a holographic will on the inside flaps of a cardboard box and some paper plates and napkins; http://jenaragon.blogspot.com/2012/03/holographic–wills.html#!/2012/03/holographic– wills.html for details of holographic wills written on the bottom of a drawer and the sides of a purse. *See also* Bruce Mann, *Self-Proving Affidavits and Formalism in Wills Adjudication,* 63 Wash. U. L. Q. 39, 50 (1985).

ture. An attestation clause is not necessary. It is presumed that the two signatures of witnesses following the testator's signature identify the people who indeed saw the testator sign. But sometimes people witness the testator's signing without signing themselves, and sometimes people sign as witnesses who did not actually see the testator sign, as we saw in the cases described earlier in this chapter. Bank tellers take the word of their supervisor that the signature on the document is that of the woman sitting in the car out in the teller lane and girlfriends and sisters-in-law see the testator but don't sign for all kinds of reasons.

But knowing that the testator actually signed the will is only one piece of important information that a court requires to determine if a will was validly executed. For instance, the witness signatures don't tell us whether the witnesses signed in the presence of each other, that each witness actually signed in the presence of the testator, or that either even knew whether the document was a will and that they were being asked to witness its execution. Hence, even if we are confident that the signature is the testator's, a will that is merely signed and witnessed must still be proved in court by bringing the witnesses in to provide testimony about the entire execution process.

To avoid having to locate witnesses perhaps decades later when a will is finally probated, the law in most states provides for a process that affirms that the entire ritualistic process was properly completed. Thus, a *self-proving affidavit* can be affixed to the end of the will to affirm that all the statutory requirements of will execution were scrupulously followed, not just that the testator actually signed the last page. Because a self-proving affidavit is a legal affidavit, a notary must also sign, meaning you will need two witnesses and a notary in most cases. Therefore, most wills today are signed twice by the testator and twice by the witnesses, once following the attestation clause and once on the self-proving affidavit, allowing for all kinds of mishaps if the drafter is careless. The UPC provides typical language for a self-proving affidavit.

We, _____, _____, and _____, the testator and the witnesses, respectively, whose names are signed to the attached or foregoing instrument, being first duly sworn, do hereby declare to the undersigned authority that the testator signed and executed the instrument as the testator's will *and that (he) (she) had signed willingly (or willingly directed another to sign for (him) (her)), and that (he) (she) executed it as (his) (her) free and voluntary act for the purposes therein expressed, and that each of the witnesses, in the presence and hearing of the testator, and of each other, signed the will as witness and that to the best of (his) (her) knowledge the testator was at that time [18] years of age or older, of sound mind, and under no constraint or undue influence.*

_____Testator   _____Witness   _____Witness

[Notarization follows] [23]

We have italicized above the parts of the self-proving affidavit that are not implied by the mere witness signatures or the attestation clause, so you can see how the self-proving affidavit makes the necessity of witness testimony in the probate proceedings unnecessary. Some states allow the self-proving affidavit and attestation clause to be merged to allow for a single

---

[23]   UPC § 2–504.

signature on the instrument.[24] The UPC provides a step-by-step process and separate attestation clause and self-proving affidavit that will meet the formality requirements of all 50 states. Yet even with a self-proving affidavit, there is no guarantee the will won't be challenged on formalities grounds, as in *In re Est. of Pittson.*

Problems often arise when only the self-proving affidavit is executed, usually because the lawyer forgot to include the signature line and attestation clause for the witnesses. In this case, some states allow the self-proving affidavit to be *integrated* into the will to become a part of it, thus allowing the signature on the affidavit to validate the will. But strict compliance states generally do not allow this. Indiana does not allow the integration of the affidavit into the will,[25] but Idaho and Hawaii allow it by statute.[26] It seems that Florida might validate a will if the witnesses signed the affidavit and not the will itself, but not if the testator did the same.[27] The District of Columbia, however, does not provide for a self-proving affidavit, though an attestation clause may serve the same purpose.[28]

Two general rules have arisen regarding whether witnesses have to actually see the testator sign or can merely be aware that she is signing. These are referred to as the *conscious presence test* and the *line of sight test.* These two tests were first outlined in the famous case of *Cunningham v. Cunningham*, 83 N.W. 58 (Minn. 1900), in which an ill testator signed his will sitting on the edge of his bed. His two witnesses, physicians that he requested serve as witnesses, took the will to a table in an adjoining room to sign. When the will was challenged, the Minnesota Supreme Court explained these two tests and upheld the will under the conscious presence test. It was not necessary that the testator actually see, or presumably even be able to see had he opened his eyes or shifted in his bed. It was enough that he knew they were signing his will as witnesses. But states that follow the line-of-sight test require that the testator actually see, or could have seen had she looked at the witnesses. *Chester v. Smith* shows that Georgia is such a state. In a line-of-sight state a witness who puts her hand up at the top of the paper to hold the pages may inadvertently block the testator's view and cause the will to be voided.

Go back and consider whether the wills described above in part 1 would be approved if the states had followed the conscious presence test, or the line-of-sight test. And consider whether the following wills should qualify as having been executed properly according to the requirements of the formalities:

In re Est. of Peters

526 A.2d 1005 (N.J. 1987)

In December 1983, the testator, Conrad Peters, was in the hospital for treatment following a stroke. While Peters was hospitalized, a will was prepared for his signature by Sophia M. Gall, Peters' sister-in-law.... On December 30, 1983, Sophia Gall came to the testator's hospital room with

---

[24]   *See, e.g.,* Ariz. Rev. Stat. Ann. § 14–2504; N.J. Stat. Ann. § 3–:3–4; Mont. Code Ann. § 72–2–524.

[25]   Keener v. Archibald, 533 N.E.2d 1268 (Ct.App. 1989).

[26]   Idaho Code Ann. § 15–2–504(1); Haw.Rev. Stat. § 560:2–504(c).

[27]   In *re* Est. of Charry, 359 So.2d 544 (Dist. Ct.App. 1978).

[28]   *See,* D.C. Code § 20–312(b).

her husband and Marie Peters [the testator's wife]. *Ms. Gall read the provisions of the will to Mr. Peters; he then assented to it, and signed it. Although Ms. Gall, her husband, and Mrs. Peters were present at the time, none of these individuals signed the will as witnesses. It was the apparent intention of Ms. Gall, who was an insurance agent and notary, to wait for the arrival of two employees from her office, who were to serve as witnesses. When those two employees, Mary Elizabeth Gall and Kristen Spock, arrived at the hospital, Sophia Gall reviewed the will briefly with the testator, who, in the presence of the two women, again indicated his approval, and acknowledged his signature. Ms. Gall then signed the will as a notary, but neither of the two intended witnesses placed her signature on the will. Ms. Gall folded the will and handed it to Mrs. Peters. Conrad Peters died fifteen months later, on March 28, 1985. At the time of his death the will was still not signed by either of the witnesses.*

At the Probate Court proceeding, Ms. Gall testified as to why the two intended witnesses never signed the will:

> *As I say, just because of the emotional aspect of the whole situation, my sister-in-law was there, my husband, her brother was there, myself and the two girls. There were six of us. The other patients had visitors. It got to be kind of—I don't know how to explain it, just the situation, and the girls were in a hurry to get back to the office, because they had to leave the office.*

> *I honestly think in their minds, when they saw me sign the will, they thought that is why they were there. And we folded up the will, gave it [to] my sister-in-law. It was just that type of situation.*

The trial court found that the proffered instrument "was properly executed" because it was signed by the testator in the presence of two individuals [Ms. Gall and Marie Peters, the testator's wife], who were in his presence and that of each other. It further found that in such circumstances, the notary could be considered a subscribing witness and the probate action handled just as if one of two witnesses had died and the instrument were being proved by the testimony of the one surviving witness. According to the court, the failure of the intended witnesses to subscribe the instrument could be ignored as a mere "quirk," which should not be allowed to frustrate the obvious testamentary intent of the decedent.

On appeal, however, the New Jersey Supreme Court reversed, finding:

The narrow issue in this case is whether the statute authorizes a person who has witnessed the testator's execution or acknowledgement of the will to sign the will as a witness after the testator has died; the broader issue is whether the statute places any limits on how long after the testator's execution or acknowledgement of the will a witness may affix his or her signature.

It cannot be overemphasized that the Legislature, in reforming the Wills statute [to adopt the UPC substantial compliance doctrine], did not dispense with the requirement that the execution of a will be witnessed.Indeed, it is arguable that as the number of formalities have been reduced, those retained by the Legislature have assumed even greater importance, and demand at least the degree of scrupulous adherence required under the former statute. The court then required that subscription by witnesses must occur within a *reasonable* time after witnessing the testator's signature, and the 18 months in this case was deemed too long, though there may be instances when signing after the testator's death would comply with the statute.

Query: How important should it be that the witnesses actually *sign* the will so long as they *see* the testator sign? What are they supposed to be witnessing anyway? Why is it important for the testator to see the witnesses sign? Could the witnesses have signed back in the office?

In re Burke's Est.

613 P.2d 481 (Okl.App. 1979)

Early on the date of November 3, 1978, Lillian Burke telephoned her cousin, Jack Laughlin, and asked him to have a will drawn up for her to provide as she instructed him on the telephone. Pursuant thereto, Jack Laughlin had his attorney to draw the subject will for Lillian Burke, and Jack Laughlin took the will to where he met Lillian Burke at about 1:00 o'clock that date in Cushing, Oklahoma. The reading and signing took place in and at the pickup truck of Jack Laughlin. In this regard, the transcript of hearing reflects the following:

COURT: *I'm still not clear. No one else wants to ask the questions so I will. Let me get this full picture. You were in your pickup, I assume?*

A [Jack Laughlin]: *Yes, sir.*

COURT: *And Mrs. Burke was in the pickup with you?*

A: *Yes, sir.*

COURT: *All right. And you didn't sign it at the lawyer's office?*

A: *No, sir.*

COURT: *All right, So you came down to the pickup and you went over. When did you go over the will with her, before the witnesses got there or after?*

A: *While the witnesses were there, sir.*

COURT: *Now, we have got Mickey Berlowitz and A. J. Laughlin. Who is A. J. Laughlin?*

A: *That is my son.*

COURT: *All right. Now, and then the Notary was Phyllis Berlowitz?*

A: *Yes, sir.*

COURT: *All right. So we got the pickup here and we have got Mickey Berlowitz and A. J. Laughlin standing beside the drivers side?*

A: *Yes, sir.*

COURT: *Where was the Notary?*

A: *The Notary was standing there by them, sir.*

COURT: *She was standing there with them?*

A: *Yes, sir.*

COURT: *All right. What did you say to Mrs. Burke and what did she say to you and the witnesses?*

A: *All right. She got in the pickup, I helped her in and she said, "Did you get the will drawn up?" And I said, "Yes." And she said, "Do you have it?" And I said, "Yes." And she said, "Did you put in it what I asked you to?" And I said, "Well, as far as I know." I said, "I'll read it to you." I said, "Do you want to read it." And she said, "No, you read it to me." So I started out read-*

ing it to her. I got down where it said a nephew instead of a cousin and she stopped me. She said, "You mean you didn't know that we are cousins?" And I said, "Yes, I knew it." But, I said, "I don't know why they typed it like that." We finished reading it and I asked her, "If there were any more questions." And she said, "That she did. It was put in there to take care of Cleo." And I said, "Yes." And I said, "I'll reread it to you again." And I did. I handed it to her to sign.

COURT: Now, where were the witnesses all of this time?

A: Standing right there by the driver's side.

COURT: And who had gotten the witnesses?

A: I had.

COURT: And you had lined up the witnesses?

A: Yes, sir.

COURT: All right. And you handed her the will to be signed?

A: Yes, sir.

COURT: And she signed it?

A: Yes, sir.

COURT: And then who did she hand it to or did you hand it to?

A: She handed it back to me and I handed it to the witnesses.

COURT: Which witness did you hand it to?

A: I handed it to A. J. Laughlin.

COURT: Okay. And then did the Notary take it?

A: After the two signed it.

"We conclude from the evidence and the four corners of the will, that Lillian Burke signed it with testamentary intent.

The remaining question is whether there was sufficient compliance with paragraphs 2, 3 and 4 of Section 55, supra [the State's Wills Act].

While Jack Laughlin and Lillian Burke were seated in the pickup truck, with Jack on the left, the left window was down and the witnesses and notary public whose names appear thereon, were standing by said left open window. Jack had asked the witnesses and notary public to come there for the occasion. Within the hearing of all, Jack read the will to Lillian, and at her request, he read the will to her a second time. Thereupon, Lillian Burke affixed her signature to the will in the pickup truck. Jack then handed the will to A. J. Laughlin, who together with the other witness, affixed their signature thereto while the will lay on the hood of the pickup within the vision of Lillian Burke. Although Lillian Burke said nothing to the witnesses about witnessing her signature, they knew why they were there and what they were doing by virtue of what Jack Laughlin had said to them and by virtue of the conversation to which they had listened between Jack Laughlin and Lillian Burke about the will. Will admitted to probate.

Query: If the witnesses and notary signed on the hood of the truck, and the testator signed inside the truck, do you think anyone actually saw the others sign? Did this court follow the line-of-sight or conscious presence test?

In re Daly's Will

402 N.Y.S.2d 747 (N.Y. Sur. 1978)

The first witness, Ronald B. Witkowski, testified that he was employed by decedent at the latter's funeral parlor; that some time in the middle of December, 1976 decedent called him into his office and asked him to sign a document; that he did not know what he was signing; that he thought it might be a stock transfer; that he was never told it was decedent's will; that decedent did not sign the document in his presence; that the document was handed to him by decedent folded in such a fashion that he could not tell whether there were any other signatures upon it; and that he does not know whether decedent's signature was on the document when he signed it.

Shortly thereafter, decedent called into his office the second witness, Leo H. Hodge, also his employee. This witness testified that decedent asked him to witness a document; that he insisted upon knowing what it was that he was to sign; that thereupon decedent showed him the front side of the document which indicated that it was decedent's last will and testament; that the witness then affixed his signature thereto; that the document was folded in such a fashion when it was handed to him that he could only see witness Witkowski's signature but he was not sure whether decedent's signature was on the document or not. The court explained:

The pertinent statute *mandates that the testator's signature be made in the presence of each of the subscribing witnesses, or be acknowledged by him to have been so made. The testator may either sign in their presence or acknowledge his signature to each attesting witness separately. Two facts are essential[sic.] that the testator sign his name, and that the witnesses see him sign or that he acknowledges his signature to them. It is not required that the signing or acknowledgment be in the presence of both witnesses at the same time. . . .*

In summarizing a series of *precedents, it can be stated that where the witnesses cannot recollect the circumstances surrounding the execution of the instrument, the document may be admitted to probate. . . .   Where however there is no question that the testator did not sign his name in the presence of the witness and further failed to acknowledge his signature, then in such a case a motion for Summary Judgment would indeed be appropriate. . . .*

Finally, this Court must note how this proceeding once again points up the disastrous results which can occur when a lay person takes it upon himself to do his own will. In this case, decedent was a young and intelligent person who was knowledgeable in death and estate matters due to his professional status as a funeral director. Nevertheless, his do-it-yourself will did not meet the requirements of law, with the unfortunate result that his intentions as expressed in the purported will were thwarted. The Court cannot ignore this opportunity to warn others to seek professional legal advice and guidance before they execute such a vitally important document as their Last Will and Testament.

Query: Should the will formalities require that the witnesses know the testator is signing his *will*, or should it be enough to know the testator is signing his *name* to a document? Shouldn't a testator be able to say, "I am signing an important document and I want you to witness that this is my signature"? How effective is the court's warning?

Flagle v. Martinelli

172 Ind.App. 588 (1977)

After the death of Quintin C. Nelson on October 19, 1972, her sister-in-law Florence E. Flagle presented an instrument dated August 30, 1970, intended to be the last will and testament of the decedent to the Elkhart Superior Court for probate. A hearing was held in which Flagle testified that she received a telephone call from the decedent to the effect that she was sending a document over via her husband Dr. Charles Nelson to be signed. Upon receiving the instrument Flagle signed her name below the previously subscribed signature of the decedent. She then passed the paper to Dr. Nelson who signed the document in a separate room. The trial court, on consideration of this evidence, ruled that the purported will of 1970 was not entitled to probate and the court of appeals affirmed.

Query: The court in *Daly's Will* indicated that it was enough for the witnesses to know the testator signed; they did not necessarily have to see him sign. Why wasn't that enough in this case? The Indiana court stated that it has adopted the substantial compliance doctrine but that this will did not meet even that lower standard. What all went wrong?

Smith v. Neikirk

548 S.W.2d 156 (Ky.App. 1977)

The testator signed his will while a patient of the VA hospital in the presence of two witnesses and a notary. *The record of testimony indicates that witness Runk was within the presence of the testator and the other witnesses at all times. The fact that she may have had her back turned at the moment of execution does not disqualify her as a witness. All that is required to be proved by the subscribing witness is the identification of the signature. It has been repeatedly held that substantial rather that a literal compliance with the statute (KY REV. STAT. ANN. § 394.040) will suffice. This Court has also indicated that where the technical requirements for execution of wills have been substantially complied with, the will should be probated.* Will held to be validly executed.

Query: Of all the possible things that can go wrong, and all the possible opportunities for fraud and undue influence to enter into the will-execution process, do you believe the formalities rules strike the right balance in promoting donative freedom?

As an interesting experiment, next time you have 3 other people together, ask them to witness your signature and sign their names and addresses below. Then watch to see what each person does as he or she is signing. Do some people put their hands up, or do they bend down close to the paper and obscure their writing? Do the bystanders look away while they are waiting to sign or after they have signed, or do they look at the person signing and not the signature? Do others start to sign before the first people are finished? With the advent of computer passwords, ATMs, and PIN numbers at the grocery store check-out lane, we tend to avert our eyes when others are engaged in writing checks or signing credit card receipts, unless we are secret agents or identity thieves. Are these will formality rules merely traps for the unwary, or do they offer any kind of substantial protections?

This small sample of cases reflect a substantial subset of the will formalities problems—reflecting the fact that while the testator usually signs, the will is usually in writing, and the testator is usually of age, the traps lie in the role of the witnesses and the smooth completion of the execution ceremony. Considering the four functions outlined earlier, which are served by the witness presence rules and how confident are you that the witnesses are a valuable addition to the will execution and validation process? Should we move to notarial wills, where testators need merely sign in the presence of a notary? That is how they do it in many countries which don't seem to have excessive problems with fraud or undue influence.

The witness requirement played its hand in the very public cases determining the ultimate distribution of the estate of Stieg Larsson, the Swedish author of *The Girl with the Dragon Tattoo*. After his sudden death in 2004, a will from 1977 was discovered which would have left his (now sizable) estate to the Socialist Party. Swedish witnessing requirements, however, were not met in the will's execution, and Larsson's estate instead passed to his brother and father under intestacy laws. His partner of more than 30 years was not considered a beneficiary of the estate since he never married her, named her in a valid will, nor was she an intestate heir under Swedish law. What if Larsson's will had been properly witnessed? Would it make good policy sense to assume that a will drafted more than three decades ago would trump his desire to provide for his legal heirs or for a partner he subsequently met and remained with for the rest of his life?

PROBLEMS

4.3. Colonel Mustard had his lawyer draft a will for him, which he intended to execute that night during a dinner party. After dinner, while sipping his cognac, Colonel Mustard asked three of his guests, Professor Plum, Miss Scarlett, and Mrs. Peacock, to join him in the library and witness the execution of his will. They all walked into the library behind Colonel Mustard. While he was retrieving the folded will from the pocket of his jacket, that was lying on the back of the sofa, Miss Scarlett slipped arsenic into the Colonel's glass of cognac. Professor Plum and Mrs. Peacock saw her dastardly deed but said nothing. The will left everything to his three best friends: Professor Plum, Miss Scarlett, and Mrs. Peacock equally. This new will changed his customary distribution scheme which was to give all five of his best friends equal shares of his estate, thus including the housekeeper Mrs. White, and the rogue Mr. Green. The Colonel signed his name at the table while all three witnesses watched, then he picked up his glass and toasted his best friends. All three of the witnesses watched Colonel Mustard finish off the cognac in a single gulp and then they turned to the will. Miss Scarlett was the first to sign her name and address and the other two witnesses observed her signature. Mrs. Peacock was the second to sign, but while signing her name, Miss Scarlett had moved to the sofa with her drink and was chatting with Colonel Mustard and could not see the surface of the table. Professor Plum kept glancing back and forth between Colonel Mustard and Miss Scarlett and did not realize Mrs. Peacock was finished signing until she too moved to sit down next to Colonel Mustard on the sofa. Just as Professor Plum picked up his pen to sign, the Colonel began to choke and cough. The Professor was just able to sign his name, but not his address, when the Colonel dropped to the floor, dead. Consider whether this will was validly executed in any state, under the variety of doctrines discussed in this section. Would it be valid in your state?

4.4. What if the Colonel had dropped to the floor dead before Professor Plum signed his name, but the Professor went ahead and signed after the Colonel had died?

4.5. What if Colonel Mustard sat on the sofa immediately after signing his will and had a heart attack that killed him immediately, but no one noticed until after the signing ceremony was complete because they were all still standing around the table watching each other sign?

We will come back to the question of what happens when will beneficiaries are guilty in procuring the death of the testator in Chapter 10. But you might want to ask yourself now whether the courts should strictly enforce the formalities requirements in circumstances like this where the witnesses are arguably up to no good. Should Mrs. Peacock and Professor Plum lose their inheritances just because they stood by and said nothing, assuming they could not have prevented the poisoning or Colonel Mustard's ingestion of it?

4. INTERESTED WITNESSES AND PURGING STATUTES

In the past, witnesses who were named as beneficiaries under a will generally were not permitted to testify in court and therefore could not serve as valid witnesses to the execution of a will. It was deemed self-serving for an interested party to witness a will. But, as the above cases illustrate, many witnesses are not privy to the contents of the will and might not even know they are named as beneficiaries. Moreover, in many instances, close family members might serve as witnesses and be beneficiaries under the will without a hint of undue influence or fraud, because they are closest companions and are diligently watching out for the testator's interests. As a result, most states have adopted *purging statutes* to deal with the interested witness in one of three ways.

The first is the common law rule that would disqualify any interested witness, rendering the will invalid if there were not a sufficient number of disinterested witnesses. Under the traditional rule, a will that has three witnesses, one of whom is a beneficiary under the will, is valid so long as the other two are disinterested and the state's statute only requires two witnesses. But if two of the three witnesses are interested, even if one is given only a token gift, the will would be entirely invalid because the witnesses are tainted. Moreover, a beneficiary generally may not save the will by disclaiming the gift because the disclaimer is not effective until the death of the testator when the gift becomes vested. But by that time, the will ceremony is long past and the supposed harm has already occurred.[29] Fortunately, voiding of the entire will because of an interested witness has been abolished in every state.

The majority approach, adopted by 30 states, is to allow the will to stand but to void the gift to the interested witness. This is generally fine if the beneficiary/witness stands to receive only a small gift, but where the witness is the primary beneficiary, she may prefer the will fail and she

---

[29]   *In re* Est. of Parsons, 103 Cal.App. 2d 384 (Cal. Ct. App. 1st Dist. 1980).

receive an intestate share, than to give up her gift under the will while the rest of the will is allowed to stand.[30]

Imagine that mom wrote a will leaving her house (which was her most valuable asset) to her unmarried daughter who took care of her in her declining years, and she left the residue of her estate to her two sons equally. The daughter signed the will as a witness because the lawyer's paralegal was out sick the day of the execution ceremony. Under the standard purging statute, the daughter loses the gift of the house which then lapses and falls into the residuary, thus passing to her two brothers, along with the rest of mom's estate. She takes nothing at all despite being the person mom intended to benefit most. She would certainly prefer the old rule that voided the will altogether, so each of the three children would take one-third of their mother's estate by intestacy. She might have to sell the house, but she would at least get a third of mom's estate.

Recognizing the perverse incentives on the part of interested witnesses to challenge the will completely, perhaps by claiming the testator lacked capacity, some states have modified their rules by voiding only the gift that is in excess of what the beneficiary would have received under intestacy.[31] Thus, in the above example, the daughter would receive all testamentary gifts up to the value of her intestate share (which would be one-third of the total estate in this case). The rest of her gift would lapse and pass into the residue to be distributed to the brothers, thus obtaining the same result as intestacy in this example. But what if the will instead gave the daughter the house, the two sons received mom's securities accounts, and the residue, which included a valuable farm and a vacation home on the beach, was to go to a charity. In this case, if the house is worth less than one-third of mom's total estate, the daughter can keep it and the rest of the will stands, including the gifts to the charities. But now all three children might wish to challenge mom's will in order to defeat the gifts to the charities, which they would not need to do under the old rule holding that wills with interested witnesses were entirely void. And on the other side, the charities would be advocating that no purging is necessary and that mom was completely sound in her intentions.

A third approach, advocated by the UPC, is that witnesses do not need to be disinterested at all and can take whatever bequest is made to them in the will. See UPC § 2–505(b). The remaining 20 states generally follow this rule. The comments to the UPC note that allowing interested witnesses to take does not undermine the integrity of the wills process. It allows for the use of family members as witnesses on home-drawn wills without penalty, while still acknowledging that interested witnesses may imply suspicious circumstances that can be better addressed through the doctrines of undue influence or fraud.

Ideally, however, interested witnesses should not be used. Also, persons who are younger than the testator and easily found, if necessary, make the best witnesses.

---

[30] *See, e.g.*, Mass. Gen. Laws ch. 191, § 2.

[31] *See, e.g.*, NY. Est. Powers & Trusts Law § 3–3.2(a)(1) and Schoenblum, 2012 Multistate Guide to Estate Planning, Table 1 for a state-by-state breakdown.

Practice Point: The Terminally Ill Client and the Witness Dilemma

As a practitioner, you will undoubtedly receive messages from hospital bound clients, wanting to ensure that their health care documents and wills are up to date. Sometimes all they need is for you to look over their existing plan and discuss it with them in order to give them the peace of mind they seek. Those facing death, however, sometimes have a change of heart in their planning decisions and may ask you to draft a codicil or an entirely new will in order to accomplish their newly discovered goals. Quickly.

What does this mean for you, as attorney? When executing a will in a hospital setting, particularly if the changes in any way disrupt what otherwise might be a "normal" property distribution pattern (i.e. your client decides to disinherit a child, or leave her entire estate to charity instead of her descendants), you will need to make sure to choose your witnesses wisely. Because part of good planning involves covering your bases in the event of a will contest, it is crucial that the witnesses be disinterested, of course. But other concerns surface as well—such as determining the mental capacity of your client who is, say, taking large amounts of morphine to ease her pain.

In these instances, it is certainly worthwhile to consider using hospital nurses or practitioners as witnesses. Along with the self-proving affidavit, the hospital caregiver provides a witness to the patient's alertness (sound mind), which may actually be something that "comes and goes." Of course, you want to get that will signed after it has come and before it goes, so the caregiver's knowledge of medication schedules and ability to communicate can provide proactive planning if a will contest might be suspected. It is true that hospitals vary in their willingness to perform these services, but those that are flexible can provide some extra protection in your client's end of life plan.

Once again, remember, it is always easier to redo the execution ceremony than to litigate the will after the testator's death. Unless the testator is literally on her deathbed, it should be possible to find disinterested witnesses and lock everyone in the room until the execution is over. For the homemade will, executed at home and witnessed by family, the UPC takes the sensible position that the will should stand unless there is some separate evidence of impropriety. But there is absolutely no excuse for any deviation from strict compliance when an estates attorney is overseeing the will execution language and process. Missing attestation clauses, switched pages, or the wrong name mistakenly missed by the *find and replace* function are inexcusable errors that could lead to malpractice claims.

Even if you do everything right, however, unexpected disasters can happen. Imagine driving home from the execution ceremony with the client's documents in your briefcase and, while you are stopping at a rest area, your car is stolen. Ideally you re-execute the documents. But what if the documents were stolen out of your office, after the death of your client? Well that's okay, because one can always prove the contents under the "lost documents" doctrine. But consider this recent Florida case.

Smith v. DeParry

86 So.3d 1228 (Fla.App. 2 Dist. 2012)

The decedent, Scott P. Smith, owned two fox red Labrador Retriever dogs. . . . Mr. Allen was a longtime attorney for the decedent. On Oct-ober 19, 2007, Mr. Allen traveled from his office in Orlando to the decedent's residence in St. Petersburg where [Smith's] last will and testament was formally executed. At that time, the decedent, at the age of 77, was in failing health. Simultaneously with the presentation of the will, and for reasons that were unclear, Mr. Allen presented to the decedent the first codicil to the will. The codicil established a $40,000 trust fund through which Lance Smith, the other Co-Personal Representative, would care for the decedent's dogs. Upon presentation of the codicil to the decedent, Mr. Allen learned that a dog's name had been misspelled. Thus Mr. Allen returned to his office, corrected the codicil, and then went back to the decedent's home on October 24, 2007. . . . Following execution of the codicil, Mr. Allen retained possession of it and returned to his office in Orlando. There the document was misplaced, and it has never been found. The decedent eventually passed away on March 30, 2008. Scott D. Smith, III, a minor, is the decedent's grandson and a beneficiary. Astrid DeParry is the guardian ad litem (the GAL) for the minor. The GAL contested the Co-Personal Representatives' petition to establish the lost codicil on behalf of the minor beneficiary.

The Applicable Law:

Section 733.207 outlines the procedure for establishing a lost or destroyed will:

> Any interested person may establish the full and precise terms of a lost or destroyed will and offer the will for probate. The specific content of the will must be proved by the testimony of two disinterested witnesses, or, if a correct copy is provided, it shall be proved by one disinterested witness.

The term "will," as used in the statute, includes a codicil. [Two issues were thus before the court: 1) whether a computer copy printed off Lawyer Allen's hard drive constituted a "correct copy," and 2) whether either of the co-personal representatives were disinterested witnesses. The probate judge ruled against the petitioners on both issues. On appeal, the court of appeals reversed both determinations, but upheld the probate judge's order under the tipsy coachman doctrine.[32] Regarding the computer copy, the court explained:]

> The Co-Personal Representatives proffered at the final hearing a copy of the codicil that they generated from the hard drive of the computer in Mr. Allen's office that was used to prepare the original document. The probate court ruled that the computer copy was a "draft" that did not qualify as a "correct copy" within the meaning of section 733.207. Tracking the language of the supreme court's decision in *Parker II*, the probate court stated that " '[c]orrect copy' means a copy conforming to an approved or conventional standard [and] this requires an identical copy such as a carbon or photo static copy."

---

[32] The tipsy coachman doctrine provides that a higher court will not overturn the decision of a lower court so long as the conclusion was correct, even if the reasoning was not. *See* Lee v. Porter, 63 Ga. 345, 346 (1879).

For three reasons, we think the probate court misread the supreme court's holding in *Parker II*. First, in the *Parker* litigation, the "copy" of the alleged lost will produced for probate was a handwritten, preliminary draft of a later typewritten version of the original lost will. In other words, the draft at issue in the *Parker* litigation differed substantially from the lost original will . . .

Second, the probate court misconstrued the portion of the supreme court's holding in *Parker II* referring to the requirement of "an identical copy such as a carbon or photostatic copy." Both the probate court and the GAL read this language as exclusive. In their view, the only type of copy that can be used to prove the content of a lost will or codicil under the statute is a carbon copy or a photocopy. Such an interpretation would preclude the use of a computer-generated copy. . . .   [T]he carbon copy and the photocopy are not the only kind of copy that can qualify as an identical copy of an original document. Unquestionably, a copy of a document generated on a computer can be identical to—and indistinguishable from—the original.

Third, the supreme court decided the *Parker II* case in 1980. Although some personal computers were sold in the late 1970s, the personal computer did not come into general use in law offices and other businesses until the 1980s, after *Parker II* was decided. We do not think that the supreme court's reference in 1980 to carbon copies and photostatic copies as examples of "an identical copy" was intended to limit for all time the types of copies that could be used to establish the contents of a lost instrument, regardless of future technological developments. Indeed, the legal profession in Florida is now reported to be on the brink of a transition to the paperless office and the paperless courthouse. As we face this transition, it would be an anachronism to adopt a rule that a copy of a lost will or codicil retrieved from the hard drive of a computer or from a cloud database[33] cannot be a "correct copy" within the meaning of section 733.207. [The court held that a computer copy can satisfy the statute's requirement of a "correct copy."

In discussing the question of whether either or both of the co-personal representatives were disinterested, the court explained:] The general definitions section of the Florida Probate Code defines the term "interested person," in pertinent part, as follows:

> "Interested person" means any person who may reasonably be expected to be affected by the outcome of the particular proceeding involved. *In any proceeding affecting the estate or the rights of a beneficiary in the estate, the personal representative of the estate shall be deemed to be an interested person.* § 731.201(23) (emphasis added).

The probate court concluded that the Co-Personal Representatives could not qualify as "disinterested witnesses" under section 733.207 because each of them was deemed an "interested person" under the Probate Code. Once again, we disagree. There is a significant distinction between the concept of an "interested person" under section 731.201(23) and the concept of "disinterested witnesses" as used in section 733.207. Under the

---

[33] "A cloud database is a database that typically runs on a Cloud Computing platform, such as Amazon EC2, GoGrid and Rackspace." Cloud database (Jan. 11, 2012, 7:00 p.m.), http://en.wikipedia.org/w/index.php?title=Cloud_database&oldid=470836337. "Cloud computing is the delivery of computing as a service rather than a product, whereby shared resources, software, and information are provided to computers and other devices as a metered service over a network (typically the Internet)." Cloud computing (Feb. 6, 2012, 4:38 a.m.), http://en. wikipedia.org/w/index. php?title=Cloud_ computing&oldid=475340599.

Probate Code, the term "interested person" refers to a person's or entity's standing, i.e., the right to notice and an opportunity to be heard in a particular proceeding pending in a probate or guardianship matter.

On the other hand, a person may be described as "disinterested" when he or she is "[f]ree from bias, prejudice, or partiality; not having a pecuniary interest." *Black's Law Dictionary* 536 (9th ed. 2009). It follows that a "disinterested witness"—as the term is used in section 733.207—refers to a person "who has no private interest in the matter at issue." *Black's Law Dictionary* 1740 (9th ed. 2009). To put it differently, a "disinterested witness" has no stake in the outcome of the matter in which he or she offers evidence. The probate court's ruling erroneously assumed that an "interested person" under the Probate Code could not simultaneously be a "disinterested witness."

The personal representative of an estate is an interested person in virtually every proceeding affecting the administration of an estate. Describing the personal representative as an interested person is another way of saying that he or she is entitled to notice and an opportunity to be heard before the matter under consideration is determined. A personal representative can be an interested person in a proceeding while remaining disinterested in the result of the proceeding. . . . In reaching its ruling in this case, the probate court overlooked this significant distinction.

Nevertheless, the probate court reached the correct result in the matter before it. Although the Co-Personal Representatives were not legally disqualified from establishing the content of the lost codicil by virtue of their fiduciary roles, they were disqualified because they were both interested in fact. Mr. Smith and Mr. Allen each had a substantial private interest in the outcome of the proceeding to establish the lost codicil. [The parties did not offer Mr. Smith, the future trustee of the pet trust as a disinterested witness, but they did offer Mr. Allen, the lawyer, as a disinterested witness. The court disagreed, explaining:]

Mr. Allen's personal interest in the outcome derives from at least two factors. First, Mr. Allen was directly responsible for the loss or destruction of the codicil from which Mr. Smith was to benefit. An adverse ruling on the petition might result in a claim by Mr. Smith against Mr. Allen for damages. [citing precedent that third party beneficiaries of testamentary documents have standing in legal malpractice cases if they are able to show 'that the testator's intent as expressed in the will is frustrated by the negligence of the testator's attorney *and that an action may be brought* by beneficiaries under a lost will against an attorney for alleged negligence in failing to produce the will or a copy of the will after the decedent's death.] Second, if Mr. Smith failed to return the $40,000 to the estate with interest, the beneficiaries might make a claim against Mr. Allen, as Co-Personal Representative, predicated on the default of his fellow fiduciary. Thus Mr. Allen, like Mr. Smith, did not qualify as a disinterested witness because of his direct stake in the outcome of the pending proceeding.

Query: This was a case not about interested witnesses to the will execution, but the role of witnesses in the probate proceedings. Witnesses do more than simply watch a testator sign. Do you understand the difference between a disinterested witness and an interested party? Assuming the codicil cannot be proved, the trust fails. If you were the attorney in this case, would you have ever imagined that the possibility of being sued for malpractice, which exists in every case, would disqualify you as a disinterested witness? Wow! Now what happens to the fox red Labrador Retrievers?

PROBLEMS

4.6. Revisit the case of *In re Burkes Estate*, covered in this chapter. What considerations would you voice to a client who has you draft a (really great, in your opinion) will, only to find that, on signing day, he tells you that he is just picking it up and intends to sign and have it witnessed later, perhaps in the cab of a pick-up truck or in the drive-thru lane of the local bank. Practically speaking, in order to comply with this, you would likely have to change and reprint several pages, if not all of the document, leaving the witness and attestation sections with blank lines instead of printed names and contact information. What would you do? And why in the world would anyone ask for such a thing, after paying you not only to draft but also ensure proper execution?

4.7. Herman comes to your office to execute his will, which makes three provisions for local charities to receive outright gifts of $10,000 each and the remainder is to be split one-third to his wife Wila, and one-third to each of their two children, Seth and Doris. He asks you to come by his house to execute the will because you are a notary and because he is wheel-chair bound and it is hard for him to travel. You gladly comply and drop by at the appointed time, only to learn that Wila and Seth are the only other adults nearby and that he desperately wants the will executed right now. You realize that you can be one of the two necessary witnesses, as well as the notary on the self-proving affidavit, but you really want at least one other disinterested witness. Just then, the postman drops by and you ask him in to quickly witness the will. He and Wila then serve as witnesses and you serve as the notary. At probate of Herman's will, it comes out that you are on the board of one of the charities that Herman provided for. What is the likely outcome in a state that voids all gifts to interested witnesses, and in a state that voids only the gifts greater than the witness would receive under intestacy? What if Seth had been the witness rather than Wila (use the UPC or your state's intestacy statute to determine how the estate would be distributed and which gifts, if any, will be purged)? From working out the answer to this question, can you see whether, if you are over a barrel, it is better to choose the wife or the son to serve as witness?

5.   INTEGRATION

One of the first questions any executor or court has to resolve is just what exactly is the will. Of course, this is a simple question when someone has a nice, neatly typed document, labeled "MY LAST WILL AND TESTAMENT" stapled to a nifty report cover. It is even better when the pages are in order, each page is initialed, and all the pages are of the same font, same color ink, and on the same paper. But life is rarely as simple as office supply stores would have us believe. With the advent of computers and printers, people can execute their wills, then redo a page when they want to make changes, assuming either that no one will notice or that the changes are valid. Or, pages fall out, draft copies are accidentally stapled into the document, people make changes on the face of their will and hope they are valid, or they staple lists or pages of instructions to the back. Under most state's rules, these changes are not valid because post-execution changes must comply with the will formalities. That is the purpose of a codicil.

What if a testator has a nice neat will folded in an envelope labeled as her will, and then tucks an executed deed to her home into the envelope, assuming the deed will become effective at her death when the deed is discovered and the will is offered for probate? If the will purports to give "all the rest and residue of my property" to her son, but the deed grants the house to her daughter, who should take the house? The answer, as with most legal questions, is that "it depends." If the deed is *integrated* into the will, i.e. if it is treated as a part of the will, then it is a special bequest that takes priority over the residuary bequest and the daughter takes the house. But if the deed is not integrated, then it is void and the son takes everything because the deed cannot be a valid *inter vivos* gift if there was no delivery during the testator's life, and it cannot be a valid testamentary gift because it was not executed with the will formalities.[34] While the principles of law are quite clear (*inter vivos* gifts require delivery and testamentary gifts require the formalities), people's lives, wishes, and actions are far from clear.

On the other hand, people may include a variety of different writings and papers into their wills. It is not necessary that everything be typed into a single document. For instance, one could include a copy of an old deed in the will to provide the detailed description of a parcel of land without having to retype the description. Alternatively, one could write a cover page that says "I give all of my property listed herein to the people whose names are adjacent to the property." Then there could be stapled to the cover page 15 pages listing different property and the recipients. But, to be valid, there must be a final signature page that meets the appropriate statutory will formalities. The 15 pages of lists, however, could have been drafted at any time as long as they were in existence at the time the will was executed and intended to be part of the will. They will be deemed *integrated* into the will and therefore a part of the will. But obviously, one cannot integrate documents that were not in existence when the will was executed, even if one had the intent that certain property was to go to a certain recipient. The doctrine of integration, therefore, requires that documents in *writing* (required by the statute of frauds) and in *existence* at the time the will is executed can be integrated as part of the will if the testator has the requisite *intent*.

Although there are some wonderful wills cases raising all sorts of technical questions about what documents were intended to be part of the will and whether later changes could be considered holographic codicils or are ineffective partial revocations, most people understand that there is a document called a will, and that there are other documents that are clearly not their wills but which they hope will have testamentary effect. Thus, the deed in the will envelope the testator surely knows is not part of her will, but she hopes and intends that it can be given legal effect at her death. Likewise, the envelope of war bonds with a son's name on it in the safety deposit box, the list of family heirlooms with the names of intended recipients tucked into the drawer of important papers, and the yellowed letter to a beloved child "giving" her the family china are not wills, but people want them to have legal effect.

Consider the case of Charles Kuralt mentioned above. In 1989 he wrote a holographic will devising his Montana property to his mistress,

---

[34] Even though a deed for real estate usually requires witnesses and similar formalities as for the execution of a will, there is no testamentary intent that the deed actually be a will. Of course, if a letter can be a will why not a deed? But that is a different question.

Patricia Shannon. In 1994 he executed a formal will in New York leaving everything to his wife and their children, with no mention of the Montana property or his mistress. Two weeks before his death in 1997 he wrote a letter to Shannon telling her he was terribly sick. He said he would call his lawyer to visit him in the hospital to see to it that she would inherit the Montana property. Kuralt apparently realized that the 1994 formal will revoked the 1989 holographic will and that Shannon was not entitled to the Montana property unless he did something "will-like." Certainly his 1997 letter is not incorporated into the 1994 formal will, since it did not exist then, but it does represent a very common human event—a change of mind. In this case Kuralt was over a barrel. If he provided for Shannon in his formal will, his wife would discover their affair. If he didn't provide for Shannon in the formal will, he ran the risk of her not getting anything at his death. While it was clear that Kuralt wanted Shannon to get the Montana property on his death, the court had to stretch a bit to find the 1997 letter, stating that he would call his lawyer to fix it so Shannon would get the property, to be a holographic codicil. The letter itself is clearly not a will but the Montana Supreme Court gave it testamentary effect because he clearly intended that outcome and his sudden death cut short his ability to follow through on those intentions.

But death always cuts short our ability to complete many transactions. When should we give testamentary effect to efforts that fall short of full and valid execution of a clearly coherent document called a will? Consider the following integration cases and whether you would have found these actions and writings to be valid:

Keener v. Archibald

533 N.E.2d 1268 (Ind.App. 1989)

After Ed Archibald died January 16, 1987, Phyllis Felton found four sheets of paper stapled together underneath his television set. The first page was a preprinted form will titled "Last Will and Testament"—"Unmarried Individual with Two or More Beneficiaries." The first page was signed by Ed Archibald, three witnesses and dated February 21, 1986. The second page was a preprinted form will affidavit signed by three witnesses and notarized February 21, 1986. The last two pages of the document consisted of a devisee list with names and addresses in the left column, phone numbers in the middle column and dollar amounts in the right column. The last page is signed by Edward Archibald and notarized October 17, 1985.

The four pages were offered for probate. . . . The trial court found that the last two pages of the document were not incorporated by reference into the form will and the will was improperly executed. . . . Appellant argues that the trial court should have integrated the form will and the devisee list. Appellant contends that the form will and the list of devisees were connected internally by the meaning of words and attached physically by staple. The form will has the words "equal shares" crossed out and leaves blank the line for an executor and the space for devisees. The last two pages name Burl Keener administrator and list devisees. Appellant claims that the decedent had the last two pages present when the form will was signed. . . . Indiana has not adopted the doctrine of integration by case law or statute. In Indiana, there is no such thing as a substantially correctly executed will. Either the will meets the legislative requirements or it is void. Since the last two pages were not incorporated, the preprinted form will devises nothing. The trial court correctly ruled that the decedent died intestate.

Query: Would the Indiana court have affirmed the will if the last two pages had been stapled between the first page and the second page with the affidavit? Should it have?

Est. of Rigsby

843 P.2d 856 (Okla.App. 1992)

Don Rigsby, the surviving spouse of Jessaline Pasquali Rigsby, found the purported will of the decedent consisting of two pages *folded together in a ledger, but not otherwise fastened to each other. Both pages are written in the hand of the Decedent, and are initialled and dated at the top of each page with the same date. One page was signed at the bottom of the writing, leaving approximately two and one-half inches below it blank. This page, the parties agree, exhibits testamentary intent, beginning: "Inasmuch as I do not have a will, I would like to make the following arrangements in the event of my death." The second page, just as the other, is not numbered and does not refer to the first in any way. This page is a simple list of personal property, with each item followed by the name of an individual. Although this page is initialled at the top, it is not signed.* There were inconsistencies between the bequests in the first page and the second page. The court ruled that only the first page consisted of the will and was entitled to probate.

Query: When we get to the incorporation by reference doctrine, you will see one reason why the list was not included as part of the will. But do you think the testator intended the list to be part of her will? Would the result have been different if the two pages had been stapled together? What if the second page had a pre-printed title that said "List of Property-Beneficiaries"? Would the substantial compliance or dispensing power help? How is this list different from the list in *Keener v. Archibald*?

Est. of Beale

15 Wis.2d 546, 113 N.W.2d 380 (1962)

Howard Beale, a history professor at the University of Wisconsin, planning to take a trip to Russia, dictated the document [the 1959 will] on either June 16 or June 17, 1959, to his part-time secretary, Mrs. Jessica Burleigh. This dictation took place in the Rathskeller of the Wisconsin Union late in the evening. Mrs. Burleigh typed the will, 14 pages in all, with three complete carbon copies, and gave them, original and copies, to Beale on June 20, 1959, in his Bascom Hall office. Beale then left for New York with his two eldest sons on his way to Moscow. On June 21, 1959, Beale attended a party in New York given in his honor at the apartment of a friend who was a history professor at Columbia University. During the festivities he asked three of his friends, all professors at various eastern colleges, one being his host, to witness his will. The four people went into an adjoining room where Beale placed some papers in a 'pile' on the table, declaring this was his will. Two of the witnesses testified that they saw Beale sign the last page of the will, while the third remembered only that Beale's signature was on the document when the witness signed. All three testified that they signed the document at the usual attestation clause in the presence of the testator, in the presence of each other and at the testator's request. None of the witnesses were able to identify at the trial any of the pages except the page they had signed. Beale then picked up all the papers and replaced them in his briefcase. Although the will is dated June 22nd it is undisputed that it was executed June 21st. By letter dated June 21, 1959, Beale sent Mrs. Burleigh pages 12 and 13 of the will, asking her to make certain changes and corrections. The only change affecting the meaning was the substitution of 'my friend, Alexander H. McLeod' for 'wife, Georgia Robison Beale' as co-executor. The others were corrections of grammar and punctuation. Mrs. Burleigh made the corrections on the original and sent the pages to Beale in Moscow. The envelope inclosing the letter to her and the two will pages has not been found and there is no positive proof of when or where it was mailed. At different times Mrs. Burleigh testified it was mailed to her from New York and at another she testified that she received the two pages in an envelope from Beale in London. A sealed envelope, postmarked September 7, 1959, from London, was later found among Beale's possessions at his death. The envelope was self-addressed to Beale and contained pages 12 and 13 of a copy of the 1959 will. These pages, along with all other pages of the 1959 will, contained the initials 'H.K.B.' in the left hand margin. After returning from Russia, Beale asked Mrs. Burleigh to re-type the entire two pages but she testified that she did not do this until after Beale's death and then did it at the later request of Beale's son, Henry. These pages also had the initials 'H.K.B.' on them. After Beale's death all the will pages except page 1 were found in his office at the Wisconsin Library. The pages were in looseleaf form and located under other papers on his desk. Underneath these pages was a carbon copy of all the will pages, including a copy of the missing page 1. Then under these copy pages was a 1954 will and a 1958 codicil. The pages of the 1954 will and codicil were stapled together. The missing first page of the 1959 will was located several months later in Beale's Bascom Hall office among some American History notes. The court upheld the version of the will that existed when it was executed, the version Mrs. Burleigh first typed, though it remarked on the following odd set of facts:

A few days before Christmas, 1959, Beale, who had returned to Madison, directed Mrs. Burleigh to re-type the altered pages 12 and 13 on the same typewriter she had used when she first typed the will. We may guess that Beale wanted pages which did not show they had been tampered with, as was apparent on the two original sheets now showing erasures and re-typed corrections. We may guess, further, that Beale intended to insert in the will without discovery the new pages without republication and re-execution of the will. This is no more than guesswork and is of no consequence. Before Mrs. Burleigh typed the two new sheets Beale's death intervened on December 27, 1959. Whatever his purpose, nefarious or not, he did not accomplish it. Mrs. Burleigh had not begun this final typing when she was told that Professor Beale had died. She then typed the two pages as Professor Beale directed and gave them to Beale's son, Henry. There were then no marginal initials on them. These pages are in evidence and, although Professor Beale never in his life had them or saw them, his initials are now on the margin of each of these pages and, as Mrs. Burleigh testified, are in his handwriting. We began with a consideration of the unnatural. At the end we are confronted by the supernatural. We consider ourselves fortunate that this weird addition to the facts turns out to be immaterial.

Query: Since both sets of later-typed pages were rejected, and only the pages as they existed at the time of execution were deemed integrated into the will, do you feel confident that the document reflected the testator's true intent? If not, does it matter?

DeGraaf v. Owen

598 So.2d 892 (Ala 1992)

The undisputed evidence reveals that on October 1, 1988, approximately a month before his death, the decedent [Clarence G. Owen] *executed four documents, each purporting to be a "Last Will and Testament." In each of the documents, which were actually forms taken from a "will kit," the decedent made specific devises of his real property and bequests of his personal property. In one document, the decedent stated that he was leaving to his sister, Minnie Marie deGraaf, and to John Owen, "my love," stating, "they have more than I did." In another document, the decedent left to his nephew Edward Owen a 1982 model pickup truck and a house and lot that Edward Owen was already purchasing from the decedent. In a third document, the decedent divided several items, consisting mainly of rings and insurance policies, between William Glen Owen and Artie Ray Owen. In the fourth document, the decedent divided certain other items of personal property among three of his nieces and Jack deGraaf. In the three documents in which devises and bequests were made, the decedent appointed Jack deGraaf as executor and William G. Owen as alternative executor. In the document containing only a statement of his love for Minnie Marie deGraaf and for John Owen, the decedent left blank the provision concerning the appointment of an executor and alternative executor.* The documents were found, as per the decedent's instructions, in a metal box, folded together in an envelope. The trial court ruled that the documents were invalid as the testator's will, and the Supreme Court of Alabama reversed, citing an ALR article: *Where two or more testamentary documents are proffered as the last will and testament of the testator, and they are not wholly inconsistent with each other in the testator's scheme of distribution of his estate, all the documents will ordinarily be admitted to probate as one will, no matter in what order they were executed. . . .   And the same rule has been applied not only where the documents in question appeared to have been executed as a will and codicil, but also where they did not appear to be related to each other in any manner.*

Query: Would it make more sense to treat the first document as a will and the remainder as codicils, rather than as a single integrated will? Does it matter?

Walsh v. St. Joseph's Home for the Aged

303 A2d 691 (Del. 1973)

Decedent, James Dugan, left a will containing the following clause: *"All United States Savings Bonds in safety deposit box #559 (sic) Farmers Bank 10th (sic) and Market Sts. Wilmington Del. to be given to the people and places as marked."* The decedent's will was found after his death in the safety deposit box mentioned in that clause. There were also found in the box a number of envelopes containing United States Savings Bonds, and a handwritten list of the names of various individuals and organizations, each of which name is followed by serial numbers, dates and face amounts *corresponding to specific bonds. The list was addressed to three persons designated 'executors,' although none are named in the will itself. There were on each of the envelopes handwritten notations obviously designating the intended recipients of the bonds contained in the envelope. Small slips of paper on which were written further specific notations were secured by rubber bands around each bond or group of bonds intended for a given recipient. All of the individuals and organizations designated are engaged in religious, educational, community or charitable work.* Denying integration of the envelopes, the court explained:

> *It is obvious that neither the list, the envelopes nor the small slips of paper, whether taken singly or together, satisfy the statute. They are not signed by the decedent and they are not witnessed. But the defendant charities argue that these writings might yet be effective to invoke the testator's intent under either the doctrine of integration or the doctrine of incorporation by reference. . . .   None of the dispositive writings at issue here can be shown to have been in existence at the time the will was executed. It is plain that the list of instructions was not, because it refers to bonds issued long after the will was executed. The writing on the envelopes is either undated or dated well after the date of execution. The small slips of paper bear no dates, and even though they are in some cases affixed to bonds which were clearly in existence as of the date the will was executed, there is simply no evidence of when the slips might have been written and placed on the bonds. The defendants argue that at least those bonds which were in existence as of the date of the will ought to effectively pass. But the bonds on their face and alone do not constitute any sort of dispositive writing. The writings containing the instructions are the crucial papers, and they cannot be shown to have been in existence at the time the will was executed.*

Query: What should courts do when testators take steps to indicate their intentions that certain people will take their property upon their death, but they fail to follow the strict rules requiring formal execution to effectuate testamentary gifts?

Technology Trends: .Pdfs, Attachments, and the Cloud

Howard Beale's case has some interesting implications when viewed in light of current technology. Clearly Beale wanted to make some changes to his will, both before execution and afterwards, that would have been far simpler with WordPerfect or Microsoft Word. He needn't have sent the actual pages from London back to his secretary for retyping, although think how important that carbon copy turned out to be. One obvious issue to think about is how to deal with documents that can be changed on the computer (like pdfs) if one has the proper program. Does the ease of making changes suggest that you should not supply your client with digital copies of their estate documents? Of course, everyone has a scanner now, so the digital copy is just a button push away. Do you think that your client should have the right to a digital, unsigned draft of the will that you prepare for her? What about a .pdf of the will, properly executed? Many will request both and some clients will try to change their will after execution despite the fact that you told them they could not do so.

Also think about a simple email attachment or hyperlink. Future integration issues may not be about physical lists and pages actually stapled together, but whether a pre-existing list on the computer was properly attached to a will document to be considered integrated. Should a court be more or less willing to consider attached documents as part of a will if they are stored on the cloud, on the lawyer's, or on the testator's own computer? What if the documents are all in a file folder on the computer labeled "My Will" but as separate documents? How far does the UPC's dispensing power get us toward resolving some of these looming issues?

PROBLEMS

4.8. Gary Coleman, whose holographic will is reproduced above, had executed two wills prior to his marriage to Shannon Price in 2007 and the execution of the holographic codicil reproduced above. The first, executed in 1999, was relatively short and appointed his business manager, Dion Mial, as executor, poured all of his property into a trust executed the same day, and directed that his remains be cremated and a wake planned that would be attended only by people who "had no financial ties to me and can look each other in the eyes and say they really cared personally for Gary Coleman." No members of the press were to be allowed at the wake or funeral.

In February, 2005, Coleman executed a complex 23-page will that revoked all prior wills and codicils, stated that he is unmarried and has no children or issue of deceased children, stated that he wanted to be cremated and there be no funeral service, appointed Anna Gray as executor and conservator of his person and estate, and gave all items of personal property, free of trust, to Anna Gray. The rest of his property he gave to charities or poured into his trust. This will was executed in California and stated that California law was to be applied. Anna Gray was a friend, caretaker, and CEO of a business he started in 2001.

A few months after executing this will, Coleman met Shannon Price on the set of the film *Church Ball*, where she was working as an extra. Shortly thereafter, Price moved into Coleman's Los Angeles home with Gray, and Gray moved out. Near the end of 2005, Price and Coleman moved from Los Angeles to Santaquin, a small town south of Salt Lake City, Utah.

In 2005, after moving to Santaquin, a new will was drawn up that closely resembled the 2005 Gray will in complexity. This new will added a provision noting that he had established the Gary Coleman Living Trust, deleted the funeral provision from the 2005 will, named Shannon Price as executor and conservator of his person and estate, poured all his property over into the Gary Coleman Living Trust, and stated that Utah law was to be applied. This second 2005 will was neither signed nor witnessed.

In early 2007, Coleman married Shannon Price. A few days later he wrote a single page holographic will in which he left all prior wills and trusts in force, but bequeathed everything to Shannon Price outright, free of trust. He also noted that he "was not coerced in any way." This will was stapled to the unexecuted 2005 will.

Assuming you are the lawyer for Shannon Price, how would you argue for the validity of the unexecuted second 2005 will that was stapled to the holographic will? How would you argue that it is not valid?

4.9. Wila is Howard Smith's second wife, whom he married late in life. She has little property of her own and devotes ten years of her life to nursing him through his final illness. Shortly before his death, Herman wrote a will leaving "all my property, real and personal, to my wife Wila, but if she fails to survive me by 120 hours, then all my property, real and personal, is to pass to my two children, Seth and Doris, by my first marriage." Wila lives for 30 years after Howard's death, never remarries, and is on good terms with Seth and Doris. Not wanting to be out the expense of a lawyer, Wila drafts her own will by taking the original page from Howard's will that made the provision to her and the kids, crosses out all other language on the page except the sentence cited above. She then writes a first page stating: "I leave all of my property as follows:" and on the third page she signs the will and has it witnessed. She staples the three pages together and feels confident that all the property she acquired from Herman will now pass back to his children, and not to her remote cousin, a gambler from Vegas. Is she right?

What if, instead, she simply wrote as her will, "I leave all of my property, real and personal, to the beneficiaries of my husband's will"? Which is better?

Although integration seems like it should be a fairly straightforward salvage doctrine, it cannot resolve all of the different ways people try to memorialize their wishes about how their property is to be distributed at their death. When integration can't answer the relevant question, courts turn to three important doctrines that allow other documents to have dispositive effect, even though they are not part of an executed will.

6. INCORPORATION BY REFERENCE, SEPARATE WRITING, AND (F)ACTS OF INDEPENDENT SIGNIFICANCE

Integration addresses the question of what sheets of paper constitute the will itself. Thus, if a formal will is found in the same envelope with a draft of the will, is the draft considered part of the will? Or, if one page is out of order and is located after the signature page, should it be considered part of the will? *Incorporation by Reference, Separate Writing,* and *(F)acts of Independent Significance* are doctrines that allow **other**, non-integrated documents or actions to have dispositive effect. This does not mean that they are considered part of the will itself; rather, they are non-will documents that get special treatment by being allowed to guide the disposition of a decedent's property. The three doctrines often overlap, but the essential character of each is as follows:

- *Incorporation by Reference* is a doctrine that allows a separate writing, that was in existence at the time the will was executed, to be given dispositive effect IF the separate writing is identified in the will (i.e. referred to in the will) and it was the intent of the testator to have that document control certain dispositions. This doctrine is usually a codification of a traditional common law rule that allowed writings beyond the will itself to have effect, which was especially useful in a time when wills were often oral death-bed utterances. Nearly every state allows Incorporation by Reference, though Georgia, Louisiana, Nevada, New York, and Wyoming do not and the law in Vermont is hazy.[35] The UPC provision is typical.

---

[35] See Schoenblum, Table 5.02.

> **UPC § 2–510 Incorporation by Reference**
>
> A writing in existence when a will is executed may be incorporated by reference if the language of the will manifests this intent and describes the writing sufficiently to permit its identification.

- *Separate Writing* is a newly created (usually statutory) doctrine allowing separate writings to be given dispositive effect even if they are created or changed after the will was executed so long as they are signed by the testator, referenced in the will, and the testator has the intent to have that document control dispositions, BUT the doctrine is limited to dispositions of tangible personal property. It generally is not necessary that this separate writing be entirely in the testator's handwriting. This doctrine is less universal than Incorporation by Reference, having been adopted by statute in only 28 states.[36] The statutes vary somewhat by state, but the idea that a separate writing, if signed, can be amended after the will is executed, is an important change from the traditional common law limitations of incorporation by reference. Consider the UPC provision on separate writing.

> **UPC § 2–513 Separate Writing Identifying Devise of Certain Types of Tangible Personal Property**
>
> Whether or not the provisions relating to holographic wills apply, a will may refer to a written statement or list to dispose of items of tangible personal property not otherwise specifically disposed of by the will, other than money. To be admissible under this section as evidence of the intended disposition, the writing must be signed by the testator and must describe the items and the devisees with reasonable certainty. The writing may be referred to as one to be in existence at the time of the testator's death; it may be prepared before or after the execution of the will; it may be altered by the testator after its preparation; and it may be a writing that has no significance apart from its effect on the dispositions made by the will.

- *(F)acts of Independent Significance* is a doctrine that allows a testator to provide that certain dispositions will be guided not by a written document, but by acts or events that have independent significance beyond disposing of the testator's property. Independent significance means that the acts or events have a purpose of their own. For instance, a testator could write a will that says "I give $5 million to the five graduates of my high school with the highest GPA" or "I give $50 to the authors of the first 10 books listed in the local card catalogue of my public library." These will be valid because my high school's graduates and the card catalogue have independent significance apart from disposing of my property. More likely, the doctrine will be used to validate a will that says "I give the residue of my estate to whoever my husband (father) (daughter) (sister) names in his/her will (or trust) if he/she survives me." This doctrine is even less common than the other two and, where states have not adopted it by statute, there may be case law endorsing the idea. Roughly half the states and the District of Columbia do not

---

[36] See Schoenblum, Table 5.01.

have a case or statute on point, though that does not mean they would not adopt it if presented with the right case.[37]

UPC § 2–512 Events of Independent Significance

A will may dispose of property by reference to acts and events that have significance apart from their effect upon the dispositions made by the will, whether they occur before or after the execution of the will or before or after the testator's death. The execution or revocation of another individual's will is such an event.

These doctrines arose to deal with a number of common human actions. One of those is the *LIST*. Many people do not want to list every single item of property in their wills, but want a general statement of who gets what, often with a more specific list of family heirlooms or other items of personal property that is to be treated differently from the general dispositions. Thus, one might make a will that states that all personal property passes to my husband, except those specific items listed in the notebook or memorandum to be found in my top desk drawer. Rather than list each item itself in the will, it is easier to provide a list of those items that the testator wants to pass differently than primary bequests or residuary bequests in a will. But, people have a tendency to make changes to those lists, or to add new items when they are acquired, without thinking they need to re-execute their wills. The *Incorporation by Reference* doctrine goes a long way to incorporate many of these lists, but it doesn't address the needs of the testator who wants to make small changes after the will is executed or wants to control where newly-acquired property goes. Hence, the doctrine of *Separate Writing* was enacted to allow people to continue the practice of making lists without having to re-execute their wills every single time they made a change. But the Separate Writing requires a signature (and preferably a date too), it is limited to devises of tangible personal property only (no real property, money, or intangible property), and the writing must be clearly referred to in the will in some way.

A second common human action is to want some other *will-like* document to actually control dispositions. Thus, the *pour-over will* (discussed more fully below in the section on Trusts) simply provides that all of the testator's property not already in the trust is to pass into her revocable living trust to be disposed of according to the trust provisions. Or, she might want her probate property to pass according to her husband's will, or her husband's trust. Because these other documents are not executed *by the testator* with the will formalities, they generally would not be given effect, and the vessel receiving property from the pour-over will would fail, leaving the estate to pass by intestacy, if there were not some way to validate the dispositive provisions of these other documents. Of course, the testator's husband's will would have been executed with the will formalities, but for it to control the testator's property she needed to have executed it. Incorporation by Reference can be used to save the testator's dispositions if the other document was in existence when the testator executed her will, so long as the other document is not changed afterwards, and only so long as it is clearly referenced in her will, and she had the requisite intent. But think how easy it is to mess up one or other of these elements.

Acts of Independent Significance also can save this disposition if the other document has an independent purpose besides disposing of the testa-

---

[37] *Id.* at Table 5.02.

tor's property. Another person's will would certainly have an independent purpose, but the testator's own revocable living trust might not, especially if the bulk of the testator's property was not in the trust before her death. In that case the dispositive provisions of the trust were really intended to dispose of the decedent's probate estate and so the trust would not have independent significance.

Two problems often arose in the early days of the living trust and pour-over will. The first was when the trust was unfunded and therefore did not have a separate existence until the testator died and her property poured into the trust. The UPC and all states have dealt with this problem by passing specific legislation allowing a pour-over into an unfunded trust (thus getting around the Acts of Independent Significance problem of requiring an independent non-dispositive purpose). The UPC provision on pour-over wills provides that:

UPC § 2–511 Testamentary Additions to Trusts

(a) A will may validly devise property to the trustee of a trust established or to be established (i) during the testator's lifetime by the testator, by the testator and some other person, or by some other person, including a funded or unfunded life insurance trust, although the settlor has reserved any or all rights of ownership of the insurance contracts, or (ii) at the testator's death by the testator's devise to the trustee, if the trust is identified in the testator's will and its terms are set forth in a written instrument, other than a will, executed before, concurrently with, or after the execution of the testator's will or in another individual's will if that other individual has predeceased the testator, regardless of the existence, size, or character of the corpus of the trust. The devise is not invalid because the trust is amendable or revocable, or because the trust was amended after the execution of the will or the testator's death.

(b) Unless the testator's will provides otherwise, property devised to a trust described in subsection (a) is not held under a testamentary trust of the testator, but it becomes a part of the trust to which it is devised, and must be administered and disposed of in accordance with the provisions of the governing instrument setting forth the terms of the trust, including any amendments thereto made before or after the testator's death.

(c) Unless the testator's will provides otherwise, a revocation or termination of the trust before the testator's death causes the devise to lapse.

You can see from the UPC language that the limitations of the Incorporation, Acts of Independent Significance, and the Separate Writing doctrines are explicitly overcome in the narrow case of the pour-over into the unfunded trust. Although we haven't discussed trusts yet, one of the most important requirements for a valid trust is that it have property in it—i.e. that it be funded. Without property, it is a mere shell with no legal existence. Of course, the best advice is that anyone who is using a pour-over will into a trust should fund the trust with enough property to give it independent significance. But that isn't always possible, as when a house is the only thing to be poured over into the trust, or property that one hasn't yet acquired is to fund the trust.

A second problem with the pour-over will is determining whether the trust provisions, especially those set to take effect at the settlor's death, should really be considered testamentary gifts since the settlor usually retains significant control over the property until her death. Because trusts designed to dispose of all the testator's property at death could be executed (and changed) without the will formalities, a trust established at the time the will is executed could look an awful lot like an attempt to make a will. Trust gifts at death sure look like testamentary gifts, and we all know that testamentary gifts must be made according to the will formalities. If the trust provisions don't meet the will formalities, then the gifts in the trust need to be *inter vivos* gifts, which require delivery. States approached this problem in two ways. Some states, using rather contorted logic, held that placing property into a revocable trust in which the settlor retains a life estate and the power to remove the property from the trust and consume it, but with a remainder in a beneficiary constituted an *inter vivos* gift. *See Farkas v. Williams*, 125 N.E.2d 600 (Ill. 1965). This method relies on a legal fiction that a present transfer of a contingent property interest was given to the beneficiary (i.e. the right to get the trust property IF the trust is not revoked).

The other way many states have dealt with the discomfort of the easily revoked trust and the will formalities, is to require that dispositive provisions of trusts be executed with the same formalities as that used for wills. Only two states have adopted this (Florida and New York), but we may see more do so as the typical estate plan becomes one with multiple interrelated documents only one of which was traditionally required to be executed with the formalities.

Fla. Stat. § 736.0403(2)(b)

The testamentary aspects of a revocable trust, executed by a settlor who is a domiciliary of this state at the time of execution, are invalid unless the trust instrument is executed by the settlor with the formalities required for the execution of a will in this state. For purposes of this subsection, the term "testamentary aspects" means those provisions of the trust instrument that dispose of the trust property on or after the death of the settlor other than to the settlor's estate.

Requiring that testamentary provisions of trusts be executed with the will formalities means that settlors cannot change trust terms easily, which defeats some of the benefits of the trust over a will, but has the benefit of insuring that trust provisions will not be voided because they are deemed by a court to be testamentary rather than *inter vivos* transfers. By treating the testamentary aspects of trusts and wills alike, the law harmonizes the two otherwise disparate sets of rules and reinforces for testators that their wills and their trusts should work together in a harmonious estate plan.

You will see that many states have followed the Uniform Trust Code's (UTC) lead in harmonizing wills and trusts doctrines. Thus, typical wills rules, like those covered here, might be included in various forms in trust codes as well. Additionally, anti-lapse, simultaneous death, revocation by operation of law, and a variety of other wills rules have been expanded to apply to trusts, although they often are not identical rules, as you will see in the next chapter when we discuss anti-lapse.

Despite the modern changes to these will doctrines, it often can be difficult to decide which doctrine to apply to a given circumstance. Consider the following case.

Clark v. Greenhalge

582 N.E.2d 949 (Mass. 1991)

■ *NOLAN, J.*

The testatrix, Helen Nesmith, duly executed a will in 1977, which named her cousin, Frederic T. Greenhalge, II, as executor of her estate. The will further identified Greenhalge as the principal beneficiary of the estate, entitling him to receive all of Helen Nesmith's tangible personal property upon her death except those items which she "designate[d] by a memorandum left by [her] and known to [Greenhalge], or in accordance with [her] known wishes," to be given to others living at the time of her death. Among Helen Nesmith's possessions was a large oil painting of a farm scene signed by T.H. Muckley and dated 1833. The value of the painting, as assessed for estate tax purposes, was $1,800.00.

In 1972, Greenhalge assisted Helen Nesmith in drafting a document entitled "MEMORANDUM" and identified as "a list of items of personal property prepared with Miss Helen Nesmith upon September 5, 1972, for the guidance of myself in the distribution of personal tangible property." This list consisted of forty-nine specific bequests of Ms. Nesmith's tangible personal property. In 1976, Helen Nesmith modified the 1972 list by interlineations, additions and deletions. Neither edition of the list involved a bequest of the farm scene painting.

Ms. Nesmith kept a plastic-covered notebook in the drawer of a desk in her study. She periodically made entries in this notebook, which bore the title "List to be given Helen Nesmith 1979." One such entry read: "Ginny Clark farm picture hanging over fireplace. Ma's room." Imogene Conway and Joan Dragoumanos, Ms. Nesmith's private home care nurses, knew of the existence of the notebook and had observed Helen Nesmith write in it. On several occasions, Helen Nesmith orally expressed to these nurses her intentions regarding the disposition of particular pieces of her property upon her death, including the farm scene painting. Helen Nesmith told Conway and Dragoumanos that the farm scene painting was to be given to Virginia Clark, upon Helen Nesmith's death.

Ms. Nesmith executed two codicils to her 1977 will: one on May 30, 1980, and a second on October 23, 1980. The codicils amended certain bequests and deleted others, while ratifying the will in all other respects.

Greenhalge received Helen Nesmith's notebook on or shortly after January 28, 1986, the date of Ms. Nesmith's death. Thereafter, Greenhalge, as executor, distributed Ms. Nesmith's property in accordance with the will as amended, the 1972 memorandum as amended in 1976, and certain of the provisions contained in the notebook. Greenhalge refused, however, to deliver the farm scene painting to Virginia Clark because the painting interested him and he wanted to keep it. Mr. Greenhalge claimed that he was not bound to give effect to the expressions of Helen Nesmith's wishes and intentions stated in the notebook, particularly as to the disposition of the farm scene painting. Notwithstanding this opinion, Greenhalge distributed to himself all of the property bequeathed to him in the notebook. Ms. Clark thereafter commenced an action against Mr. Greenhalge seeking to compel him to deliver the farm scene painting to her.

The probate judge found that Helen Nesmith wanted Ms. Clark to have the farm scene painting. The judge concluded that Helen Nesmith's notebook qualified as a "memorandum" of her known wishes with respect to the distribution of her tangible personal property, within the meaning of Article Fifth of Helen Nesmith's will.[5] The judge further found that the notebook was in existence at the time of the execution of the 1980 codicils, which ratified the language of Article Fifth in its entirety. Based on these findings, the judge ruled that the notebook was incorporated by reference into the terms of the will. The judge awarded the painting to Ms. Clark.

The Appeals Court affirmed the probate judge's decision.[6] We allowed the appellee's petition for further appellate review and now hold that the probate judge correctly awarded the painting to Ms. Clark.

A properly executed will may incorporate by reference into its provisions any "document or paper not so executed and witnessed, whether the paper referred to be in the form of . . . a mere list or memorandum, . . . if it was in existence at the time of the execution of the will, and is identified by clear and satisfactory proof as the paper referred to therein." The parties agree that the document entitled "memorandum," dated 1972 and amended in 1976, was in existence as of the date of the execution of Helen Nesmith's will. The parties further agree that this document is a memorandum regarding the distribution of certain items of Helen Nesmith's tangible personal property upon her death, as identified in Article Fifth of her will. There is no dispute, therefore, that the 1972 memorandum was incorporated by reference into the terms of the will.

The parties do not agree, however, as to whether the documentation contained in the notebook, dated 1979, similarly was incorporated into the will through the language of Article Fifth. Greenhalge advances several arguments to support his contention that the purported bequest of the farm scene painting written in the notebook was not incorporated into the will and thus fails as a testamentary devise. The points raised by Greenhalge in this regard are not persuasive. First, Greenhalge contends that the judge wrongly concluded that the notebook could be considered a "memorandum" within the meaning of Article Fifth, because it is not specifically identified as a "memorandum." Such a literal interpretation of the language and meaning of Article Fifth is not appropriate.

"The 'cardinal rule in the interpretation of wills, to which all other rules must bend, is that the intention of the testator shall prevail, provided it is consistent with the rules of law.' " The intent of the testator is ascertained through consideration of "the language which [the testatrix] has used to express [her] testamentary designs," as well as the circumstances existing at the time of the execution of the will. . . .   The circumstances existing at the time of the execution of a codicil to a will are equally relevant, because the codicil serves to ratify the language in the will which has not been altered or affected by the terms of the codicil.

From application of these principles in the present case, it appears clear that Helen Nesmith intended by the language used in Article Fifth of

---

[5]   Article Fifth of Helen Nesmith's will reads, in pertinent part, as follows: "that [Greenhalge] distribute such of the tangible property to and among such persons *as I may designate by a memorandum left by me and known to him, or in accordance with my known wishes,* provided that said persons are living at the time of my decease" (emphasis added).

[6]   The Appeals Court rejected the appellant's additional argument that the appellee should have been prevented from proceeding at trial on the theory of incorporation by reference, since she allegedly did not specifically raise or argue this theory in any pretrial pleading. *Gallant* v. *Worcester,* 383 Mass. 707, 709–710 (1981). The record demonstrates that the appellant had sufficient notice of the theory of testamentary bequest as a possible ground for this action. We conclude therefore that this argument is without merit.

her will to retain the right to alter and amend the bequests of tangible personal property in her will, without having to amend formally the will. The text of Article Fifth provides a mechanism by which Helen Nesmith could accomplish the result she desired; i.e., by expressing her wishes "in a memorandum." The statements in the notebook unquestionably reflect Helen Nesmith's exercise of her retained right to restructure the distribution of her tangible personal property upon her death. That the notebook is not entitled "memorandum" is of no consequence, since its apparent purpose is consistent with that of a memorandum under Article Fifth: It is a written instrument which is intended to guide Greenhalge in "distribut[ing] such of [Helen Nesmith's] tangible personal property to and among . . . persons [who] are living at the time of her decease." In this connection, the distinction between the notebook and "a memorandum" is illusory.

The appellant acknowledges that the subject documentation in the notebook establishes that Helen Nesmith wanted Virginia Clark to receive the farm scene painting upon Ms. Nesmith's death. The appellant argues, however, that the notebook cannot take effect as a testamentary instrument under Article Fifth, because the language of Article Fifth limits its application to "a" memorandum, or the 1972 memorandum. We reject this strict construction of Article Fifth. The language of Article Fifth does not preclude the existence of more than one memorandum which serves the intended purpose of that article. As previously suggested, the phrase "a memorandum" in Article Fifth appears as an expression of the manner in which Helen Nesmith could exercise her right to alter her will after its execution, but it does not denote a requirement that she do so within a particular format. To construe narrowly Article Fifth and to exclude the possibility that Helen Nesmith drafted the notebook contents as "a memorandum" under that Article, would undermine our long-standing policy of interpreting wills in a manner which best carries out the known wishes of the testatrix. The evidence supports the conclusion that Helen Nesmith intended that the bequests in her notebook be accorded the same power and effect as those contained in the 1972 memorandum under Article Fifth. We conclude, therefore, that the judge properly accepted the notebook as a memorandum of Helen Nesmith's known wishes as referenced in Article Fifth of her will.

The appellant also contends that the judge erred in finding that Helen Nesmith intended to incorporate the notebook into her will, since the evidence established, at most, that she intended to bequeath the painting to Clark, and not that she intended to incorporate the notebook into her will. Our review of the judge's findings on this point, . . . proves the appellant's argument to be without merit. The judge found that Helen Nesmith drafted the notebook contents with the expectation that Greenhalge would distribute the property accordingly. The judge further found that the notebook was in existence on the dates Helen Nesmith executed the codicils to her will, which affirmed the language of Article Fifth, and that it thereby was incorporated into the will pursuant to the language and spirit of Article Fifth. It is clear that the judge fairly construed the evidence in reaching the determination that Helen Nesmith intended the notebook to serve as a memorandum of her wishes as contemplated under Article Fifth of her will.

Lastly, the appellant complains that the notebook fails to meet the specific requirements of a memorandum under Article Fifth of the will, because it was not "known to him" until after Helen Nesmith's death. For this reason, Greenhalge states that the judge improperly ruled that the notebook was incorporated into the will. One of Helen Nesmith's nurses testified, however, that Greenhalge was aware of the notebook and its contents, and that he at no time made an effort to determine the validity of the bequest of the farm scene painting to Virginia Clark as stated therein. There is ample support in the record, therefore, to support the judge's conclusion that the notebook met the criteria set forth in Article Fifth regarding memoranda.

We note, as did the Appeals Court, that "one who seeks equity must do equity and that a court will not permit its equitable powers to be employed to accomplish an injustice." To this point, we remark that Greenhalge's conduct in handling this controversy fell short of the standard imposed by common social norms, not to mention the standard of conduct attending his fiduciary responsibility as executor, particularly with respect to his selective distribution of Helen Nesmith's assets. We can discern no reason in the record as to why this matter had to proceed along the protracted and costly route that it did.

Judgment affirmed.

———————

This case is particularly instructive because it raises numerous issues regarding integration, incorporation, separate writing, and republication (discussed in the next section below). Like many people, Ms. Nesmith did what she was told to do by her lawyer, which was to keep a list, titled a *memorandum*, of certain items of personal property that she didn't want to bother listing individually in her will. But like many people, she made changes after her will was executed, started a new list in a different notebook, and probably didn't realize that had she not executed the codicils, the new entries would not have been valid. She was lucky that the court was willing to liberalize the rules on Incorporation by Reference and not require that the memorandum be correctly titled or that the reference to a single memorandum would limit her to only one incorporated document. Massachusetts does not have a statute or a case allowing for a separate writing that could be amended after the will was executed, but even if it had, Ms. Nesmith would have had to sign her notebook with each new entry.

Ms. Nesmith's bequest of the painting to Ginny Clark was saved, however, by the doctrine of republication by codicil which we take up in the next Section. But before we do so, consider some of these other cases and which doctrine, if any, you would argue should apply to save the gift.

Est. of Richardson

50 P.3d 584 (Okla.Civ.App. Div. 1, 2002)

A.E. Richadson, *Decedent, executed his Last will and Testament June 22, 1998 (Will). The Will provided that after debts, funeral expenses, and taxes were paid, the residue of the estate would pour over into The A.E. Richardson Trust, dated September 25, 1992 (1992 Trust). The Will appointed the Bank as Executor of Decedent's estate. The Will did not refer to his son, James E. Richardson [Son] by name or by class. Also on June 22, 1998, Decedent executed a First Amendment to the Declaration of Trust of A.E. Richardson (1998 Amendment). The 1998 Amendment amended the 1992 Trust in its entirety [and] provided that if any beneficiary of the trust contests the 1992 Trust or the Will, or seeks any adjudication that the trust or Will is in any way void, then that person will be treated as if he prede-ceased Decedent. That provision also specifically stated "The Settlor's son, John R. Richardson, is not named in this trust document as a beneficiary, as he has been assisted and provided for during the Settlor's lifetime." Dece-dent's son James was not mentioned at all in the will or the 1998 Trust Amendment. The trust provided that all proceeds would go to a Charitable Foundation.*

Decedent executed the Second Amendment to the Declaration of Trust of A.E. Richardson March 9, 1999 (1999 Amendment). The 1999 Amendment indicated that it changed the 1998 Amendment only by adding Article 3(B)(6) [which states]:

> *6.   Intentional Omissions: The omission in this Trust Declaration of any provision for the Settlor's sons, JOHN RICHARDSON and JAMES RICHARDSON, or any other relative or person is not due to oversight or neglect, but is based upon the Settlor's considered desire to omit such person and to benefit only the beneficiaries designated herein. Notwith-standing any and all of the other provisions of this trust instrument, if any beneficiary or potential beneficiary shall object to this trust instru-ment, any provisions hereof or any part of the trust estate hereunder, then he or she shall be deemed to have predeceased the Settlor for the purposes of this Trust and any provisions herein contained.*

Decedent died April 17, 1999. The trial court admitted to probate Decedent's Last Will and Testament executed June 22, 1998, found that Decedent's survivors included a wife and his two adult sons, and appointed Bank as Executor.

Executor argued that the Will specifically incorporates the 1992 Trust and pours all the estate assets into the trust,[38] and the 1992 Trust expressly omits Son from receiving any distribution. Executor argued that the incor-porated Trust, as amended, satisfied the requirements for an intentional omission of a legal heir.[39] . . .

The trial court granted summary judgment to Executor. Son does not dispute the material facts. Rather, the parties dispute the legal effect of whether the Will and pour-over trust accomplished the result of intentional-ly omitting Son from inheriting from Decedent. . . . The Oklahoma Supreme Court has held that the intent to omit a child from inheriting must appear on the face of the will in "strong and convincing language." Additionally, extrinsic evidence may be admitted to show an heir was unintentionally

---

[38]   9 Article III of the Will provides, in part: "I give all the rest and residue of my proper-ty, not already in trust, of every kind and description, real personal, and mixed, . . . including any lapsed or void bequest or devise, to the Trustee of the A.E. Richardson Trust, dated Sep-tember 25, 1992, as may be amended, to be administered and distributed in accordance with the provisions of that Trust, which is incorporated by reference in this Will." And it states: "If for any reason the disposition referred to above is not operative or is invalid, . . . then I give the residue of my estate, . . . to the Trustee named in the present provisions of said Declara-tion of Trust to act upon my death, to be administered . . . as provided in . . . said Declaration of Trust, which for this purpose I incorporate by reference in this Will."

[39]   84 O.S. § 132. Provision for Children Unintentionally Omitted, provides: "When any testator omits to provide in his will for any of his children, or for the issue of any deceased child *unless it appears that such omission was intentional,* such child, or the issue of such child, must have the same share in the estate of the testator, as if he had died intestate, and succeeds thereto as provided in the preceding section."

The preceding section, 84 O.S.1991 § 131, provides that children born after the execution of a will, for whom no provision is made in the will, succeed to that portion of the estate that they would have received had the testator died intestate.

omitted, but extrinsic evidence is not admissible to show intent to omit *a natural heir. In addition, simply leaving the entire estate to others is not alone sufficient to show intent to omit a child.*

The issue then, is what constitutes the "face of the will." [R]elevant in determining what constitutes the "face of the will" is the doctrine of incorporation by reference. There are two factors required to successfully incorporate another document into a will by reference: first, the other document must be in existence when the will is executed; second, the other document must be referred to in the will so as to reasonably identify the other document. The court held *that a document which is successfully incorporated by reference may constitute part of the "face of the will" for purposes of finding intent to omit a natural heir on the face of the will.*

The undisputed evidence in the instant case shows that the 1992 Trust and 1998 Amendment were in existence at the time the Will was executed and that the Will expressly provides for Decedent's intent that the trust be incorporated into the Will. Indeed, Article III of the Will states that the 1992 Trust (as amended) is incorporated by reference. However, the intent to omit Son was first mentioned in the 1999 Amendment to the trust, which was made well after the Will was executed. Nothing in the record indicates that the 1999 Amendment to the trust was executed with testamentary formalities. Thus, the issue is whether a later amendment may be considered as part of "the face of the will. . . . " The court said no, explaining:

In the instant case, the face of the will contains no "strong and convincing language" indicating intent to omit Decedent's children. Additionally, the document which does indicate intent to omit Son, the 1999 Amendment, was not in existence at the time the Will was executed and therefore may not be included in the terms of the Will as incorporated by reference. The Will admitted to probate in the instant case, including the incorporated trust as it existed at the time the Will was executed, fails to mention Son by name or class. Therefore, Son is a pretermitted heir—a forgotten child. As such, Son shall take the share of Decedent's estate to which he would be entitled had decedent died intestate, according to the Oklahoma pretermitted heir statute.

Query: Wow—how's that for donative freedom? Note how the common wills rule on omitted heirs was probably written at a time when revocable trusts were rare. The statute envisions the testator explaining in the *will* why he is omitting a provision for his child, and doesn't speak to whether the same provision in a trust should have the same effect. Without applying the will rule to the trust, the Executor has to try to use incorporation by reference to validate the testator's intent. Is there anything else the Executor should have argued? If no, what should the testator's lawyer have done to prevent the suit? Obviously something came up that led them to execute the second trust amendment, but they botched it. How?

In re Tipler

10 S.W.3d 244 (Tenn.Ct.App. 1998)

Mrs. Gladys S. Tipler ("Testatrix") executed a formal will on April 2, 1982. This will left the bulk of her estate to her husband, James Tipler ("Husband"), upon the contingency that he survive her. Two days later, Testatrix executed a holographic codicil to the formal will. The codicil read:

> *Should my husband predecesse [sic] me I hereby declair [sic] that his last Will and testament upon his death is our agreement here to four [sic] made between us in Section III of my Will. With the exception Mr. Tipler or myself can elect to make any changes as we desire depending upon which one predeceasest [sic] the other. If no changes are made by either of us this will be our last will and testament.*

At the time the codicil was executed, Husband had not yet executed a will. Husband died in 1990. His will, executed six months prior to his death, created a trust for Testatrix, and directed that upon her death the property be distributed to his relatives. Testatrix died in 1994.

The beneficiaries under Husband's will sought enforcement of Testatrix's codicil. This action was challenged by Testatrix' heirs, who would otherwise take under the Tennessee intestacy statute. The Testratix' heirs asserted that the holographic codicil should not be enforced because it referred to a document not yet in existence, i.e. Husband's will. They argued that Tennessee law requires that for a holographic will to be enforceable, "all its material provisions must be in the handwriting of the testator. . . ." Since Testatrix' holograph referred to Husband's will, Testatrix' heirs maintained that material provisions were not in Testatrix' handwriting.

At the trial, the beneficiaries under Husband's will introduced evidence regarding Testatrix' intent. The testimony indicated that Testatrix was not close to her family. One witness stated that Testatrix described her sisters as "greedy," indicating that "if anything happened to her [Testatrix]," her sisters would be like "a bunch of vultures" or "a bunch of barracudas. . . ." Evidence indicated that Testatrix "thought of Mr. Tipler's family as her family." Witnesses testified that Testatrix loved her husband dearly and frequently said, "whatever Tippy [Husband] wants is what I want."

The trial court found that the issue of incorporation by reference was not applicable because Husband's will was not in existence at the time Testatrix' codicil was written and that the relevant inquiry is whether the doctrine of facts of independent significance applies. The trial court then found that the Husband's will had independent significance. On appeal, the court noted that prior precedents involving facts of independent significance did not involve holographs, which require that the material portions of the will be in the testator's handwriting. To resolve the case, the court of appeal needed to determine if all material portions of the will were in the testator's handwriting. The court explained:

> *In determining whether this codicil contained "all material provisions" in Testatrix' handwriting, we must note that the identity of the beneficiaries is obviously an important item in a will. In this case, the witnesses' testimony does not indicate that Testatrix wanted her estate to be distributed to particular members of Husband's family. Rather, it indicates that Testatrix wanted her estate to be distributed to whomever Husband wished. Under these circumstances, a holograph which bequeaths her estate to persons named as beneficiaries under Husband's will would contain all material provisions in Testatrix' handwriting, and therefore would be valid, even though the specific identity of the beneficiaries is contained in another document not in Testatrix' handwriting.*

> *In sum, then, the doctrine of facts of independent significance is applicable in this case to permit Testatrix' codicil to refer to Husband's will, provided the document is a valid holographic codicil. To determine whether the holograph contains all material provisions in Testatrix' handwriting,*

the trial court properly considered Testatrix' intent. Evidence preponderates in favor of the trial court's finding that Testatrix was estranged from her family and wanted her estate to go to Husband's family. Since Testatrix wanted her estate to go to whomever Husband wished, the codicil contained all material provisions in Testatrix' handwriting, even though it stated only that her estate should go to the beneficiaries under Husband's will and did not specifically name beneficiaries. Therefore, the trial court did not err in distributing Testatrix' estate to the beneficiaries under Husband's will.

Query: Did you notice that had Mrs. Tipler's intent been to benefit the actual people named in her husband's will, then the holographic codicil would have failed? Do you see why?

PROBLEMS

4.10. The doctrines of Incorporation by Reference and Separate Writing both serve to allow testators to more easily detail who will receive their tangible personal property after their deaths. But what about the client who only knows that he wants his children to have everything but doesn't want to bother with more details? What are your thoughts about including a provision similar to the following in a client's will directing that tangible personal property shall be distributed:

> in substantially equal shares to my then living children, as they shall agree among themselves. In the event that my then living children shall fail to agree on the distribution of any item(s), I direct my executor to sell said item(s) and distribute the proceeds equally among my then living children.

How could this work to eliminate disputes? Are there circumstances you could imagine where such a provision could cause disputes?

4.11. In many states, stepchildren can receive the same beneficial tax treatment for inheritance tax purposes as natural/adopted children. When considering jurisdictions such as that in *Estate of Richardson*, where the courts tend to adhere to the "face of the will" doctrine, how might you draft protections for a client who expresses to you that his marriage is shaky (let's assume for this scenario that his spouse has separate legal counsel) but that he wishes to always treat his step-children as equal beneficiaries along with his other children in his estate? Or, what if he indicated that if the marriage failed, he wanted the step-children to receive nothing?

4.12. Go back and revisit question 4.9 above and see if your answer to that question has changed now that you have studied Incorporation by Reference and (F)acts of Independent Significance. How would you advise Wila if she simply wants all of her property to pass to the same people Herman passed his property to, but she doesn't want the bother of spelling it all out in her will?

4.13. Carmen drafts her own home-made will in which she leaves all her property to her three children in equal shares. It is properly executed with the required formalities. But a year afterwards, she decides that she wants her oldest daughter, Maria, to get a new painting that she just acquired and which she knows Maria loves. So she sits down and writes a letter to Maria telling her that she wants her to have the painting at her death, and Carmen sends copies of the letter to all of her children, with a note that says: I just want you all to know about this and honor it." Who will get the painting on Carmen's death and why?

4.14. Can an unfunded trust ever guide the disposition of property from a pour-over will in the absence of a pour-over statute?

———————

As you can see, codicils very often play important roles in validating separate documents or testamentary dispositions that were changed after the original will was executed. So let's examine the notion of publication.

7. Publication, Republication, and Codicils

When a testator executes a will, the term we use to describe the act is *publication*. Now this does not mean that the testator hires out a publishing firm and mass produces her will for public consumption. Rather, publishing refers to the act of giving legal effect by making something public. In the case of a will, the term comes from the Roman law requirement that a testator hold up the document and ask the witnesses to bear witness that the document is the testator's will. Today, however, most states do not require that the testator tell the witnesses that it is a will she is signing, though some states require the testator identify the document itself as a will.[40] Hopefully the testator will know that she is signing her will, otherwise she may not have the appropriate testamentary intent. But the witnesses don't need to know it is a will they are witnessing, unless they are also executing a self-proving affidavit which attests that the will formalities are being followed, though it is always a good idea if they are told it's a will in case they need to be called to give evidence about the execution.

Ideally, no case should turn on whether the testator actually identified to the witnesses that the document was a will, because people should be forthcoming about the fact that they are executing a will and not, for example, ordering lunch.[41] And there certainly is no requirement that the testator explain the contents of the will to the witnesses. It generally isn't even required that the witnesses see the entire set of pages of the will; the testator can keep the majority of the will in a folder or in his coat pocket and merely provide the signature pages for the witnesses to see, though as you saw in *Estate of Beale*, the witnesses may be needed to help identify what pages actually are integrated into the will. In any event, so long as the testator knows she is signing her will, and that the witnesses know they are witnessing the testator's signature, the formalities are technically satisfied.

The date when the will is executed is the date it is published, though it has no legal effect until the death of the testator. Until then the will has no effect on the property rights of the testator or the beneficiaries under the will, and it can be revoked freely without consequence. But, as you saw in *Clark v. Greenhalge*, changes to the will or to incorporated writings after the date of the will are ineffective unless the will is re-executed or a codicil is executed that *republishes* the will. A *codicil* is a document used to amend or modify a will. It usually identifies itself as a codicil to a particular will,

———————

[40] *See* N.Y. Est. Powers & Trusts Law § 3–2.1(a)(3), (4).

[41] See, e.g. Est. of Bearbower, 426 N.W.2d 392 (Iowa, 1988); Faith v. Singleton, 692 S.W.2d 239 (Ark. 1985); Matter of Est. of Burke, 613 P.2d 481 (Okl.App. 1979).

identifies the portion of the will to be changed, and sets forth the new testamentary provision. Sometimes, however, it is difficult to determine whether something should be treated as an entirely new will or as a codicil.

New wills have the effect of revoking prior wills. Thus, if a new will revokes a prior will but does not dispose of all the testator's property, that undisposed portion would pass by intestacy. But, if the new will is treated as a codicil instead, then it merely revokes the inconsistent portions of the prior will, and leaves everything else intact. Thus, if the first will disposes of all of a testator's property to her daughter, and a second writing disposes of everything but her house to her son, treating the second as a codicil allows the house to pass to the daughter under the first will because it is not inconsistent with the codicil. Look back at Gary Coleman's holographic document above. Is this a will or a codicil?

More important for incorporation purposes is that a codicil is deemed to *republish* a will at the time the codicil is executed. Thus, any changes made on a will (names omitted, bequests changed) can be given effect if a codicil is executed after the changes are made. In most circumstances, the codicil should refer to the will that it is republishing or reaffirming, though that is not always necessary. The republication doctrine originated in the common law when a will could not dispose of land that was acquired after the will was executed, though it could dispose of after-acquired personal property. Though the law was changed in England in 1837 by the Statute of Wills, many states still treat codicils as republishing prior wills in order to include after-acquired property. The Restatement 3d of Property (Wills) at § 3.6, Comment D, notes that codicils republish wills such that the latter will be deemed to have been executed at the later date the codicil was executed and therefore can validly dispose of newly acquired property.

Codicils do not need to change property dispositions, however. Codicils can be used to change personal representatives, to identify newly-acquired property, make new provisions for guardians or trustees, or change burial instructions.

One important aspect of republication by codicil is that a validly executed codicil *may* save an improperly executed will. In other words, if a will was not properly executed and was therefore invalid, the proper execution of a codicil republishing the will can breathe new life into the will. The circumstances under which this can occur, however, vary by state. If a will is invalid because the testator lacked mental capacity, it is unclear whether a valid codicil should validate the will if the testator had capacity when the codicil is executed. While the testator may have had a temporary break in capacity we probably should allow a later document to revitalize an earlier one if that is the testator's intention. But should a holographic codicil, like Gary Coleman's, republish a will that was never executed? Note how both republication by codicil and integration could be argued to validate his unexecuted 23-page will.

Republication is a very important doctrine, as there can be significant consequences to moving forward in time the effects of proper will execution. Consider the following cases to that effect:

In re Est. of Hendler

316 S.W.3d 703 (Tex.App. 2010)

Charles Hendler left a valid will dated April 30, 1990. At the time he made the will, he was married to Melissa McCormick and had no children. In the 1990 will, Charles left all of his property to [his brother] *Richard or Richard's children; he left nothing to McCormick. He and McCormick later divorced, and he married Virginia. Charles and Virginia had two children: Austen, who was born in 1995, and Katherine, who was born in 1997. Charles and Virginia were divorced on March 12, 1999. At the bottom of the signature page of the 1990 will is a handwritten note that reads as follows:*

> *9/9/99 I am now divorced from Melissa McCormick & Virginia Dillon. The same will and testament exists now as on 4/30/99 Charles Hendler*

The trial court granted summary judgment that the note was a valid holographic codicil that republished the will. The court further ruled that Charles's two children, who were born between the execution of the will and the writing of the note, were not pretermitted children entitled to shares of his estate under the probate code. On appeal, the court reversed in part, and affirmed in part, stating: *We begin with the language of the note itself, and we conclude that the language does not conclusively demonstrate or negate testamentary intent. The note is both brief and cryptic. The note could be reasonably read merely to state facts—that the testator was twice divorced, and that he had not revoked whatever will existed on April 30, 1999. On this reading, the note demonstrates no testamentary intent. On the other hand, a reasonable reader could infer from the language that Charles was acting with testamentary intent. A reader could conclude that Charles had reviewed his will with his two divorces in mind, decided that his will still correctly stated his testamentary wishes, and intended to republish his will by writing that his same will still "exists." Both readings are reasonable, so the language of the note standing alone furnishes no basis for summary judgment.*

The court then explained that if the codicil expressed testamentary intent, then both children were not pretermitted; they were expressly omitted and are entitled to nothing. If the codicil merely expressed the fact of the will being in existence, then the two children were pretermitted and entitled to an intestate share if the testator did not otherwise provide for the children. The court then found that because Austen was a contingent beneficiary on a life insurance policy, naming Virginia the primary beneficiary, that Austen was otherwise provided for and could not take a pretermitted child's share, but that Katherine could if it was determined that the note did not express testatmentary intent.

Query: Do you think Charles intended to fully disinherit both his children? What should the law do when testators don't seem to fully comprehend the complex effects of competing statutes? Where does Charles' estate ultimately go?

In re Est. of Wells

983 P.2d 279 (Kan. App. 1999)

On January 12, 1996, Emery Wells executed his Last Will and Testament. Sharon Wells (from whom Emery was divorced) executed a valid consent, waiving her statutory rights. They remarried later that same day. In April 1996, Emery adopted Sharon's daughter, Trisha Gerber. On July 2, 1996, Emery executed the "First Codicil of Emery G. Wells, Jr. to Last Will and Testament of Emery G. Wells dated January 12, 1996" (First Codicil). This codicil left Sharon additional vehicles and real estate, and added Sharon to the residuary legatees. The First Codicil contained the following provision: "As modified by the foregoing provisions in this my FIRST CODICIL . . . I confirm and republish my LAST WILL AND TESTAMENT DATED JANUARY 12, 1996 in all respects except as the same is modified by this my FIRST CODICIL thereto." This codicil met with all of the necessary testamentary formalities, and again Sharon executed a consent, waiving her statutory rights as a surviving spouse.

On July 16, 1996, Emery executed the "Second Codicil to Last Will and Testament of Emery G. Wells, Jr. dated January 12, 1996" (Second Codicil). The Second Codicil was executed to correct typographical errors and was essentially identical to the First Codicil in all material respects. It too contained a clause confirming and republishing the "Last Will and Testament dated January 12, 1996." Still again, Sharon executed a consent waiving her statutory rights as a surviving spouse.

Emery died 2 days after execution of the Second Codicil. A petition was filed to admit to probate Emery's will of January 12, 1996, as amended by the Second Codicil of July 16, 1996. Pursuant to the will, Emery's son Eric was proposed as executor. The petition also requested the court to determine Sharon's consents to be valid. Sharon filed a voluntary entry of appearance and waiver of notice. On September 3, 1996, an order was entered by the district magistrate judge admitting the will to probate, appointing Eric as executor, and determining the consents to be valid.

On October 23, 1996, in apparent response to a motion pertaining to Wells' testamentary trust, Sharon, through her attorney, filed an "answer," asserting the invalidity of Emery's Last Will and Testament of January 12, 1996. She alleged their subsequent marriage and Emery's adoption of her daughter revoked the will, pursuant to K.S.A. 59–610, and that Emery died intestate. K.S.A. 59–610 provides, in pertinent part: "If after making a will the testator marries and has a child, by birth or adoption, the will is thereby revoked." She requested a denial of the will to probate.

A hearing was held before the district magistrate judge on the same day her "answer" was filed. No evidence was offered. Sharon's attorney, with her present, argued Emery's will was void by operation of law and that it should not be admitted to probate. Eric argued Emery had republished his will subsequent to remarriage and adoption by his codicils. Eric pointed out the will had been admitted to probate and that Sharon had not objected. He also argued Sharon had consented to the will and both codicils. . . .

Kansas has long recognized the right of a testator to revive a prior will despite previous explicit revocation. Should a reasonable person, properly informed or advised, conclude a testator cannot revive a will after statutory revocation as provided in K.S.A. 59–610? Admittedly, there are no Kansas cases directly addressing whether republication by a subsequent codicil revives a will after statutory revocation, pursuant to K.S.A. 59–610. But the "substantial likelihood of success" analysis should not end there. There appear to be no decisions from any jurisdiction which suggest a prohibition of such a revival. The author of Annot., 33 A.L.R.2d 922, 924 states:

> *"It is clear that a revoked will or codicil which is in existence can be revived by a subsequent codicil, executed with the formalities required by the particular jurisdiction, and no case has been found categorically holding that this cannot be accomplished. . . .*
>
> *"Whether or not a given will or codicil which has been revoked is revived by a subsequent codicil most frequently resolves itself into a question as to the intention of the testator, or identification of the instrument to which the codicil purports to be a codicil." (Emphasis added.)*

While there appears to be no authority to the contrary, there are ample authorities supporting such a revival. A will revoked pursuant to K.S.A. 59–610 by marriage and subsequent birth or adoption of a child may be revived by republication through a codicil or other instrument which meets the necessary testamentary formalities. The substance of Sharon's attack was contrary to this universally recognized principle of probate law. Court rejected Sharon's attack on the validity of the codicil.

Query: This will also included an *in terrorem* clause, one that prohibited a beneficiary from taking a bequest if he or she challenged the legality of the will. The court applied the clause to Sharon, thus voiding the bequests in the will that Emery had given her. The court also affirmed the validity of her contractual waivers of statutory rights, in effect completely disinheriting her. What should Sharon have done in this case? Is there anything Emery's attorney could have done to avoid this outcome?

Practice Point: Planning for the Client Who Really Wants to Disinherit

As illustrated by numerous cases in this chapter, lawyers must ensure that they use extreme care in drafting wills to effectuate their client's wishes. Often, this process actually involves thinking "outside the will" in order to make sure that all relevant areas are covered. When a client chooses to disinherit a child, for example, not only must the attorney use clear language, consistent with state laws to express the clear intention to disinherit, but it is also critical for the lawyer to look at the client's estate as a whole to make sure that everything is properly aligned. For example, what happens to life insurance policies and retirement plans that generally pass not according to the provisions of the will but instead according to the beneficiary designation on the contract? Sometimes these contracts do not even enter the client's mind as being part of the estate plan (and might have been completed a decade or more ago when a designation of "equally to my then living children" might have seemed like a good idea) but they will certainly come into play after the client's death. Moreover, the will doctrines we just examined apply to wills, not necessarily to other mechanisms like trusts, life insurance, or POD contracts. So, part of your job as an estate planning attorney is to ask LOTS of questions and gather/examine those ancillary documents to ensure that they also are flowing according to plan. The following sections of this chapter deal with these types of contracts in more detail.

An important part of republication by codicil is that the date of the original will moves forward in time to the date of the codicil. Thus, if a child is born, adopted, or the testator marries or divorces, between the date of the original will and the date of the codicil, courts will look to the later date. This has the effect, as in *Est. of Hendler*, of potentially disinheriting his children based on a will he drafted before he had children. Moreover, in *Est. of Richardson*, the trust amendments were not deemed to be codicils and thus did not have the effect of republishing the decedent's will as of the later date of the trust amendment. In that case, clear references of disinheritance were not given effect because they occurred after the will was drafted and in a written document that could not be incorporated into the will. A codicil would have saved the day in that case, as it did in *Greenhalge*.

The lesson for you as potential estate-planning attorneys is to keep up with the changing circumstances of your clients and draft entirely new wills if necessary, realizing that most of the doctrines we just covered are *salvage* doctrines. They are designed to fix problems when testamentary intent is being frustrated by literal reading of the documents or straightforward application of the will formalities rules. They should not be relied on to guide testamentary dispositions.

8. PROS AND CONS OF WILLS

There are numerous benefits and disadvantages of wills, many of which can be gleaned from the discussion above. People know what a will is—it is a part of our general consciousness—and they accept the mythology and ritual of will execution. We have seen that the formalities, irrespective of how well they accomplish this, are designed to help avoid fraud and duress. Wills can be revoked at any time before the testator's death, meaning they give the testator full, unfettered control over her property up until her last moment. She never needs to worry about having to rely on the kindness of family to whom she has already made *inter vivos* gifts of all her property if she suddenly becomes needy. One of the greatest fears of many elderly people is that they won't have enough property to support themselves in their last years and that they will become dependent on family or friends. The will allows people to keep control over all their property until they truly do not need it anymore. Wills are also portable and can be given legal effect if the testator moves from the state in which she executed her will to a new state, so long as the will was valid in the state of execution (with the exception of holographic wills in some states).

But wills are quintessentially public documents. They require probate to validate the will before the property can be transferred to the beneficiaries, and they can become quite long if one intends to spell out every single item of property. They are cumbersome in terms of execution and can be disregarded if the formalities are not carefully followed. The formalities can prove traps for the unwary who seek to dispense with the advice and assistance of lawyers, who can be costly. Wills probably are not flexible enough for people who change their minds a lot, who acquire and transfer property frequently, and who have multiple beneficiaries whose interests might change with each new acquisition. Also, by retaining full ownership and control up until death, many testators hamper effective property management during a period of incapacity prior to death. Thus, property might be neglected or lost because only the testator can manage it. Wills can be easily lost or destroyed since they are usually kept by the testator. And some states make it a crime, as does the District of Columbia,[42] to knowingly destroy a will of another, which may be tempting for a disinherited beneficiary who has access to the decedent's will. Wills themselves are

---

[42] See D.C. Code § 18–112.

susceptible to being lost, destroyed accidentally, or overlooked by beneficiaries. Will challenges are also very public events, allowing the airing of a family's dirty laundry.

One should know the family history, the identity of heirs and other relations, and how well they all get along when advising a client on the use of a will. Certain provisions may leave lasting emotional scars on surviving family members, and you can be sure that will contest litigation does little for sibling rivalries. Wills, by their very nature, are public documents. Or at least become public after the testator's death. For many families, the probate process runs smoothly, without snags or contests. But, what about family situations which are, even at the time of planning, ripe for contest? Some families just have that one litigious member who is always suing someone for something. Should this raise a red flag if he is a potential beneficiary under a will that you are drafting? And, perhaps more importantly, what if he is NOT a named beneficiary in the will? Sometimes a more private plan, like a revocable living trust, for example, could mitigate the effects of a potential contest by a disgruntled family member. Similarly, planning for same-sex couples and non-traditional families may involve using tools which provide the greatest privacy and strength against a possible contest from family members who disapprove of the relationship. The more you know about the family situation, the better position you will be in to help advise your clients.

Once you are familiar with what you can do with a will and what the pitfalls are, you can turn to other mechanisms for treating property at death. Will substitutes are exactly what the name implies, documents or legal mechanisms with testamentary powers that dispose of property through means other than a will. The most common are the trust and the joint tenancy, but others discussed below are equally important.

B. Trusts

1. Origins of the Trust

A trust is a legal fiction; it is a mechanism for holding property whereby title is split between the legal owner (the trustee) and the equitable owner (the beneficiary). The trust originated in the medieval *use*, which was a device to avoid the incidents of military tenure. Most landholders in England held their land in *socage*, which meant that at the owner's death the land would descend to the eldest son automatically unless the son was underage (under age 14) in which case it would go into a court-supervised guardianship until the son reached 14. But land held in *military tenure* (a special form of landholding for the aristocracy) would escheat[43] if the landowner's eldest son was under age 21. If the landowner had no sons, the land would descend equally to all daughters, and if any heirs were minors their land would be held in *wardship*. By establishing that aristocratic land would escheat rather than pass into a guardianship, the crown developed a way to assess significant fees (we can call them *estate taxes*) upon the descent of large landed estates. When the owner of land held in military tenure died with an underage heir, the lord from whom he held the land (usually the king by the 16th century) had the legal right to take possession of all of the minor child's land, he could take all the income from the land

---

[43] Land that escheats returns to the lord from whom the tenant holds the land. In modern parlance, escheat refers to ownerless property that passes to the government.

until the child reached 21, and he could take physical custody of the child himself which gave him the right to control who the child would marry.[44]

The English referred to the state in which land descended to a minor child as *wardship*. Although wardship entailed control and custody of the minor child himself, most people hated wardship because it gave the king three things: a) the right to all the income and profits from the ward's land during the period of wardship (including timber and mineral rights), b) the right to determine the marriage of the ward which made it possible to sell the marriage rights to someone willing to pay handsomely to have the child married into his own family, thus bringing with him all of the child's wealth, and c) the right to demand that when the ward reached 21 he had to pay a sum of money (usually a value set at two years' worth of income on all the land) to redeem it and regain possession. The sale of marriages on the open market and the hardships the sale caused to families was a source of much criticism during the English Civil War. Ultimately, the ruination of men's families and estates spurred passage of a law abolishing landholding in military tenure and wardship in 1646.[45]

Having an estate fall into wardship could be disastrous. The king could pillage the property until the heir came of age, sell the heir's marriage rights, and then demand the heir pay a hefty ransom to redeem it. Making matters worse, the heir often had to borrow the ransom money because he did not have the income from the property. Due to the potentially dire consequences of having an estate fall into wardship, landowners came up with a variety of ways to avoid it. The only completely effective way was to make sure that the landowner never died owning property held in military tenure. Of course, if we all were omniscient and knew when we would die, we could arrange to give our property away the day before and it would never descend by intestacy. But sadly we aren't omniscient. And if we try to play the odds we either give it away too soon, like King Lear, or we wait too late and don't get it done. So, for all of us fallible human beings, the common lawyers devised different mechanisms to solve the wardship problem.

One way was to make an *inter vivos* transfer of a remainder and retain a mere life estate. When the life tenant died, the land passed by virtue of the remainder and not by the laws of descent. Therefore, wardship would not attach. But the life estate and remainder arrangement had some real problems, especially when the remainderman predeceased the life tenant or the life tenant needed to mortgage the property and the remainderman did not consent. As with all *inter vivos* gifts, a gift of a remainder is irrevocable. Property becomes much more difficult to manage when two owners have to agree on things. Even worse, if the remainderman was underage when the life tenant died, you'd have wardship all over again. So although the usual pattern was for a landowner to transfer the remainder in his land to his son upon his son's marriage and retain for himself and his wife the life estate, this didn't work if the landowner died before the son reached an age to marry. There are other problems with life estates and remainders which make them a risky mechanism, especially with real property, and we discuss them below in Chapter 8.

The most effective way to avoid wardship would be to transfer ownership of the land to an entity that could not die. By transferring ownership

---

[44] *See,* JOHN BAKER, AN INTRODUCTION TO ENGLISH LEGAL HISTORY 223–243 (London: Butterworths, 4th ed. 2002).

[45] Abolition of Military Tenures Act, 12 Car. 2, ch. 24. (1660).

to a monastery or other corporate owner with a promise that the landowner and his family could continue to reside on the land, the landowner could avoid wardship. However, this transfer could not guarantee that the monks would not decide to move into the manor house and kick the transferor's family out. And the common law courts of Kings Bench and Common Pleas would not look behind the simple legal fact of who had title. If the monastery had title, then the monks were entitled to occupancy. Any promise made to hold the land for the benefit of the original landowner's family was unenforceable if the legal title resided with the monastery. But if a landowner could not get relief in a law court, he could always go to the *Chancery* court, the court of equity, where the court's motto was to do what was right and just. If the monastery tried to kick the family out, they could sue for an injunction in equity and require the monastery to either do the right thing (i.e. continue to hold the land for the benefit of the family) or transfer the land back to the family so they could find a different holder who would honor the obligation. This is the origin of the medieval *use* whereby a landowner would transfer land "to A for the use of B," where A is a corporate owner (called the *enfeofee to uses*) and B is the landowner and his family (called the *cestui que use*).

There were numerous variations on the use that could be adopted. One was to have A be a group of people, perhaps a handful of lawyers, who would deed another person into the group whenever one died. By rotating living people in, and establishing that ownership was held in joint tenancy with rights of survivorship, the group merely had to keep the ranks filled with healthy bodies so that the land never was in the state where the legal owner(s) were all dead.[46] Another, as mentioned above, was to find a corporate entity to hold the property since corporations didn't die.

Of course, in the 13th century the corporation as we know it did not exist; rather, religious orders or municipal organizations served this function. The problem with a corporate owner, however, was that over time the details of the terms of the use and the nature and extent of the property could be forgotten. Additionally, there were often tensions between the church and the crown. But in 1536, Lord Dacre's Case was decided, which held that a will instructing the *enfeofees to use* to transfer property upon the *cestui que use's* death was invalid because it defrauded the King of his feudal revenues.

Members of Parliament were horrified at the idea that the wills they had been using were invalid, resulting in the enfeofees to use getting to keep the property. Consequently, they agreed to passage of the *Statute of Uses*, which destroyed nearly all the uses that had been established by medieval land lawyers. The Statute of Uses essentially held that all land held "to A for the use of B," would now be held unequivocally in fee simple absolute by B. That way the beneficiaries did not lose the land they were living on to the *enfeofees to use*, especially when they were the Church, and the King was busily disbanding the monasteries and taking over their lands. But, as a consequence, the land owners suddenly found themselves subject to wardship again, which was Henry's plan, and he and his Master of the Wards resumed extracting the profits and marriage revenues from land in which the owner died with underage heirs. This upset years of estate planning and led Parliament to demand that, in exchange for the Statute of Uses, Henry agree to the Statute of Wills.

---

[46] All the joint tenants had to be men, of course, because women who married lost their property to their husbands under the law of coverture.

The Statute of Wills allowed landowners to exempt from the effect of wardship two-thirds of land held in military tenure, and all of land held in socage tenure, by allowing it to pass according to a will. Remember, prior to 1540, land could not be legally devised by will; it had to pass by intestate descent so the king had the opportunity to claim wardship. The remaining one-third of land held in military tenure was required to pass by descent, thus allowing the Crown its feudal revenues through wardship on the remainder.[47] A hundred years and one civil war later, however, wardship was entirely abolished, and the crown's benefit in having land descend solely by intestacy disappeared. From 1646 on, therefore, the Crown had to look to other forms of revenue, like estate taxes and fees to make up for the lost wardship revenue.

But back to the use. The use was a tremendously ingenious mechanism. By splitting legal and equitable title, and having the legal title holder function to prevent the land from descending, while the equitable title holders got all the benefit of continuing to live on and enjoy possession of the land itself, the *trust* was born. Although the Statute of Uses abolished uses in 1536, the lawyers just simply recreated the use in a slightly different form, and called it something different: a trust. The Statute of Uses had provided one exception to the otherwise complete abolition of uses. A use was allowed to continue in operation so long as the legal title holder had some sort of affirmative duties or obligations to perform toward the land or the beneficiaries. This was held to be an *active use*, as opposed to a *passive use*, and active uses were allowed to continue in existence after 1536 because there was a purpose for the use besides merely avoiding the incidents of wardship. As the common law of trusts emerged out of the Tudor land policies, therefore, one of the most important aspects of the trust was that the trustee (the legal title holder) must have *active responsibilities* toward the property and the beneficiaries. In today's terms, the trustee became a *fiduciary*.[48]

The trust is essentially a renamed use. For many centuries the trust was still only enforced in the equity courts because legal title in the trustee was deemed proof positive that the land was *owned* by the trustee. As the trust became ubiquitous, however, all 50 states have legislated the trust as

---

[47] You might wonder why King Henry VIII would agree to reduce his wardship rights from all land held in military tenure to only one-third of it. Here is the back story; medieval lawyers did such a good job concealing wardships, and because uses had been used for so long to shelter them, that inquisitions had to be formed to determine if a particular piece of land really was held in military tenure or was held in socage tenure, which did not carry with it the onerous feudal dues. This meant going back to the Domesday Books of the eleventh century and tracing land titles down to the present in an era of no land recording offices. The cost of the inquisitions was high, and a landowner who lost could expect little sympathy from the Master of the Wards when it was discovered that he had been trying to evade the king's rights to wardship. Consequently, Henry put the landowners to the test: accept his offer and get two-thirds of their land free and clear in exchange for the Crown's more secure rights on one-third, or continue to fight and risk having the entire estate vulnerable to the Crown's claims. It turned out to be a win–win situation for both the landowners and the Crown and the one-third/two-thirds ratio has continued to operate throughout many of our property and succession laws ever since.

[48] *See,* All Saints Parish Waccamaw v. Protestant Episcopal Church in Diocese of South Carolina, 685 S.E.2d 163 (S.C. 2009) involving title to land originally given in 1745 to trustees for the benefit of the parish. Two-hundred fifty years later, when the congregation split over religious matters, the court had to decide who owned the land on which the church was located. The trial court ruled it was owned by the heirs to the original 1745 trustees. The South Carolina Supreme Court reversed, holding that because the trustees had no active duties, no true trust was created, and the Statute of Uses executed the trust, giving the legal title to the beneficiaries.

a form and mechanism of holding property, and they are now enforceable in law as well as in equity. Even though law courts will enforce the rights of beneficiaries under a trust, we still refer to the trustee as the *legal* title holder and the beneficiary as the *equitable* title holder.[49] The trust is such a frequently used legal form that many of its common law characteristics have been modified by statute. But the most important still remain, including the active duty rule. A beneficiary cannot waive the trustee's fiduciary obligations.

In most conveyances of property, there are two parties, the transferor (the owner) and the transferee who takes all the property sticks of the transferor when the deed or conveyance is executed. In a trust, however, there are three parties, the transferor who generally owns full legal title to the property about to be transferred in trust,[50] the transferee, and the beneficiary. The transferor is usually referred to as the *settlor* or *trustor*, the transferee of the legal title is the *trustee*, and the transferee of the equitable title is the *beneficiary* (also called the *cestui que trust* or *cestui que use*). Although there are three parties, or three hats to be worn, a single person can wear all three hats. Thus, a person can own property as the settlor, place it in trust with himself as the trustee and hold it for himself as the beneficiary. The only limitation is that there must be one other person in the mix who can keep an eye on this transaction and insure that the active duties are performed. That person can either be a co-trustee or a co-beneficiary with a remainder interest in the property in the trust. This requirement is a hold-over from the medieval use.

There are also complex and diverse rules on trust duration and limitations on alienability that we discuss later in Chapter 8. Suffice it for now to understand that, for hundreds of years, the trust form was deemed to be a somewhat temporary way of managing property to accomplish some limited goals: avoidance of the incidents of wardship, providing for the uncertainties of the next one or two generations, and insuring that the family estate remained intact from the predations of spendthrift beneficiaries and greedy monarchs. Once the property came out of trust, it could be re-established in a new trust to start the perpetuities period all over again. But the coming out allowed for taxes to be incurred, which gave the government some chance to collect on the property as it changed hands, although currently it is without the stringent rules of forced descent and primogeniture. And even though the Internal Revenue Service has devised a number of taxes to equalize the effects of intestate descent with *inter vivos* or testamentary gifting, so the initial tax avoidance reasons for the trust are basically gone, there are other tax reasons for using the trust format. We discuss those in Chapter 9.

Additionally, there remain significant estate planning reasons for the trust, especially when settlors want to provide for future generations without using cumbersome future interests that can hamper the marketability and management of land. The active duties requirement is also important because it imposes fiduciary obligations on trustees so the property is not

---

[49] Some American states were suspicious of equity courts which they believed followed arbitrary rules and ignored legal precedents. Consequently, in Massachusetts for instance, equity courts were not created until the mid-nineteenth century, which meant that typical trust laws were late in developing. *See,* Phyllis Maloney Johnson, "No Adequate Remedy at Law: Equity in Massachusetts 1692–1877," *Yale Student Legal History Papers.* Paper 2. http://digitalcommons.law.yale.edu/student_legal_history_papers/2.

[50] The settlor can place lesser interests in trusts, like contract rights, life estates, mortgages and security interests. If it is property it can be held in trust.

squandered or mishandled by an improvident owner. This allows for a tremendous accumulation of wealth that can almost guarantee the support of generations of descendants in perpetuity if the trust is not terminated by the Rule Against Perpetuities and the property returned to outright full legal ownership. Whether trusts serve valid public purposes or lead to a decline in incentives to labor and productivity is a question that no one can answer. Whether society would be better off had the trust been completely abolished in 1536 is another question we cannot answer. The trust is here to stay. Our job is to decide when the benefits of splitting legal and equitable title outweigh the expenses and fiduciary burdens and make the establishment of a trust a sensible estate planning tool. And to that end we must study the creation, limitations, and requirements of the trust.

PROBLEMS

Identify the Settlor, Trustee, Successor Trustee, Beneficiary and Contingent Beneficiary in the following:

4.15. I, Mary Lenny, hereby give, devise and bequeath all of my property, wheresover located, to Lorie Lenny, as Trustee, for the benefit Carol Troy. In the event that Carol Troy shall predecease me, her share shall pass instead to Terrance Troy. In the event that Lorie Lenny shall fail or cease to serve, I appoint Bob Starks to so serve in her stead and place.

4.16. We, Sam and Margaret Keller, hereby direct that upon the death of the last of us to die, all of our remaining property be delivered to Seasons Bank, as Trustee, to be held in trust for the benefit of our then living children. In the event that any of our children shall predecease us, their share shall instead pass to their issue, *per stirpes*". (Assume that Sam and Margaret have two children: Anne, who has three children of her own, and Tommy, who has two children).

4.17. I, Bill Gates, hereby declare the formation of the Bill Gates Revocable Living Trust. I appoint to myself the power to manage the property in the trust and to make all decisions relevant thereto. I also declare that I hold this property for the benefit of myself alone. If, however, at my death I have not revoked this trust, then the property therein is to pass to John Ford, the trustee of the Bill and Melinda Gates Charitable Trust.

2. CREATION OF TRUSTS—FORMS AND FORMALITIES

A trust is created when one person transfers property to another *on condition* that the latter will use and manage the property for the benefit of the beneficiary. The trustee has either explicitly or implicitly promised to comply with the conditions in exchange for the transfer. In return, the trustee may collect a fee for her services, but a breach of the promise/conditions can result in either the imposition of penalties on the trustee or the transfer being deemed void. The settlor *trusts* the trustee to honor the condition and is entitled to rescind the transfer if a breach occurs. Because of this promise element, this form of holding property was named a *trust*. Trusts, therefore, are *property* transfers made pursuant to a *contract*. This gives rise to both property-based and contract-based remedies. Most important, the settlor trusts the trustee to use the property not for her own benefit, which would be permissible in an outright gift or transfer to the trustee, but for the benefit of the beneficiaries. Beneficiaries, on the other hand, are usually not parties to the transfer and may not revoke the trust if the trustee misbehaves, although they are entitled to damages under third party beneficiary doctrines.

Trusts are created in two general ways: by *deed* and by *declaration*. A deed is used to transfer ownership of property from one individual or entity to another or, in this case, from the settlor to the trustee. A deed of trust is therefore the appropriate document to use when the settlor and the trustee are different persons. A deed of trust must be in writing but generally need not be enacted with the formalities of the Wills Act, even though the trust documents may dispose of property at the settlor's death. Deeds involving real property, however, must comply with the Statute of Frauds, which in most states requires that it be in writing and witnessed.[51]

A declaration of trust is used when the settlor and the trustee are the same person, i.e. when a settlor declares herself to be the trustee of certain property, held for the benefit of herself and/or someone else. A declaration of trust must be in writing if it involves real property pursuant to the Statute of Frauds, but need not be in writing if it involves only tangible personal property.

Creation of a trust involves a transfer of property from the settlor to the trustee. Therefore, in addition to the trust documents spelling out the disposition of the property, all appropriate title documents must be executed to transfer the property into the trust. Thus, if Herman wants to establish a revocable living trust for himself, with his children as successor beneficiaries, he can *declare* himself trustee for the tangible personal property and is not required to re-title the property (like the sofa, the television, and the beer in the refrigerator). But if he wants to put the house in the trust, he will need to execute a deed transferring the house from himself—as an individual, to himself—as trustee of the Herman Smith Revocable Living Trust. Since the trust will hold real property, the trust declaration needs to be in writing as well, pursuant to the Statute of Frauds. So, Herman will need to execute a Declaration of Trust document by which he declares himself trustee, he identifies either his successor trustee or successor beneficiaries, and he identifies the conditions under which the property is being held. Remember, the trust needs active duties, so Herman will need to identify what he plans to do with the property.

Practice Point: Why Does the Trust Cost So Much More Than a Will?

When you are in practice, you are likely to encounter the cost-wary client, the client who can't imagine why it costs thousands of dollars to establish a trust that supposedly won't change the way she controls her property. From her perspective, nothing much is changing except that there is a lot of paperwork, she gets the benefit of avoiding probate for her estate, and you seem to be getting rich. First off, to do a proper estate plan, you need to know your client's total assets. You will also need to **see** all the documentation on their retirement plans, their life insurance, their bank accounts and their prior wills or trusts, for inevitably they will tell you that they have updated their beneficiary designations or paid the property taxes on their house when they haven't. What you will discover is that the car your client wants

---

[51] There are all variety of cases on whether a writing is necessary for a trust, and even though the Statute of Frauds requires a writing for a transfer of real property, there are cases validating oral trusts of land. These usually entail the court focusing on some element unrelated to the trust creation itself, like misrepresentation or fraud. *See,* Savage v. Walker, 969 A.2d 121 (Vt. 2009); Heible v. Heible, 316 A.2d 777 (Conn. 1972); Pappas v. Pappas, 320 A.2d 809 (Conn. 1973); and Goodman v. Goodman, 907 P.2d 290 (Wash. 1995).

put in the trust is actually titled in the name of your client and her husband, or the bank account she claims is hers still has her mother's name on it. All of these forms of property will need to be re-titled in the name of the trustee if the probate avoidance benefit is to be achieved. Countless lawyers, however, have sent their clients away with a nifty folder full of instructions for re-titling the car, the bank accounts, the house, the securities, the life insurance, the house, and everything else, only to find the folder, unopened, in the bottom of the client's desk drawer at her death.

A large part of the cost of establishing a trust comes from the requirement that the client must fund the trust with the property she wants to be protected, and that means filling out the dreaded paperwork and sending it in, and following up when the company has questions or needs additional information. A settlor can stand in the middle of a room and proclaim to a hundred people that she is going to be the trustee for her car, but if the car is not re-titled through the state's motor vehicle department, the car isn't in the trust and her proclamations are in vain.

Moreover, many clients feel they are perfectly capable of filing the paperwork and don't want to pay you, the lawyer, to do mindless administrative work. But, as the lawyer, you have an obligation to ensure that the trust is properly established, funded, and managed. So how do you get your clients to accept the indisputable reality that they will procrastinate and not get the property fully re-titled?

One option to consider is to make the funding of the trust part of the process—that is, instead of giving the client blank, generic instructions for trust funding, actually complete funding letters on behalf of your clients for the banks and other institutions (complete with account numbers), along with a short form of the trust, which will certainly be necessary for the clients to successfully transfer title. You also will be drafting new deeds for real estate in your jurisdiction which is to be titled in the trustee's name, so you can simply make attendance at the "funding meeting" which involves signing the new deeds and specific funding letters part of the trust process. Your engagement letter with your client should certainly spell out what you will be doing and that it is the responsibility of the client to deliver the letters. Some firms actually complete all of the funding and track the asset re-titling, but, as you can imagine, the fees generally increase significantly for this work as it can involve a great deal of time.

And how do you know if it all has been done? And what if your client sells his house next year and buys another but forgets to take it titled in the name of the trust? Consider scheduling review meetings every couple of years for your trust clients. You may decide not to charge for these sessions unless work needs to be done or assets are outside of the trust that need to be put in, but the upside is that, on the back-end, administration can be much smoother.

Trust instruments have two important sets of provisions: dispositive provisions to beneficiaries (which we discuss at length throughout the book) and administrative provisions dealing primarily with the fiduciary and accounting obligations of the trustee (which are usually covered in a course on fiduciary administration). When the trust provisions are set to take effect at the decedent's death, the trust itself begins to look an awful lot like a will. In fact, that is the point—it is a *will substitute*. But in most cases trusts do not have to be executed with the formalities of a will because they are treated as *inter vivos* transfers (from the settlor to the trustee and the settlor to the beneficiaries).

But what happens when the settlor and the trustee are the same person, the trust is revocable by the settlor during her life, and it becomes irrevocable only at her death when the successor trustee is to distribute the property to a variety of beneficiaries? The change in form from ownership by the settlor to ownership by the same person as trustee can look illusory and the trust begins to closely resemble a will. To maintain the distinction, some courts focus on the *present transfer* of property rights into the trust to validate its *inter vivos* character. See *Farkas v. Williams* and discussion below in this Chapter. But when the main purpose of the trust is to dispose of the decedent's property on death, some states have held these trust instruments to be testamentary trusts, and voided them if they were not executed with the formalities necessary for wills.[52] The more the trust acts like a will, the more courts are justified in demanding that it be executed with the appropriate formalities. The more independent *inter vivos* purpose it has and the less it looks like a will, the more appropriate it is for trusts to have their own distinct set of rules that may differ significantly from corresponding will rules. This tension is highlighted in the next case, *Clymer v. Mayo,* set forth below.

As noted earlier, a few states have determined that the best way to deal with the tension between *inter vivos* and testamentary gifts in the context of a trust is to require that trusts that make testamentary dispositions be executed with the formalities of a will or deed (deeds for real property also require two witnesses and often a notary). New York and Florida have adopted such rules.[53] The New York rule provides:

N.Y. Est. Powers & Trust Law § 7–1.17 Execution, Amendment and Revocation of Lifetime Trusts

(a) Every lifetime trust shall be in writing and shall be executed and acknowledged by the initial creator and, unless such creator is the sole trustee, by at least one trustee thereof, in the manner required by the laws of this state for the recording of a conveyance of real property or, in lieu thereof, executed in the presence of two witnesses who shall affix their signatures to the trust instrument.

(b) Any amendment or revocation authorized by the trust shall be in writing and executed by the person authorized to amend or revoke the trust, and except as otherwise provided in the governing instrument, shall be acknowledged or witnessed in the manner required by paragraph (a) of this section, and shall take effect as of the date of such execution. Written notice of such amendment or revocation shall be delivered to at least one other trustee within a reasonable time if the person executing such amendment or revocation is not the sole trustee, but failure to give such notice shall not affect the validity of the amendment or revocation or the date upon which same shall take effect. No trustee shall be liable for any act reasonably taken in reliance on an existing trust instrument prior to actual receipt of notice of amendment or revocation thereof.

Query: Do you think requiring the formalities for executing testamentary aspects of trusts defeats the purpose of using trusts? Does it serve the protective, ritual, channeling and evidentiary functions that the will formalities serve? Or should we dispense with formalities altogether, both for wills and trusts, which seems to be the direction of the UPC?

---

[52] *See, e.g.,* Palozie v. Palozie, 927 A.2d 903 (Conn. 2007).

[53] *See,* N.Y. Est. Powers & Trust Law § 7–1.17; FLA. STAT. § 737.111.

3. TRUST ELEMENTS

The Uniform TrustCode (UTC) provides for the validity of a trust in § 402, which reads:

UTC § 402.   REQUIREMENTS FOR CREATION

(a) A trust is created only if:

(1) the settlor has capacity to create a trust;

(2) the settlor indicates an intention to create the trust;

(3) the trust has a definite beneficiary or is:

(A) a charitable trust;

(B) a trust for the care of an animal, as provided in Section 408; or

(C) a trust for a noncharitable purpose, as provided in Section 409;

(4) the trustee has duties to perform; and

(5) the same person is not the sole trustee and sole beneficiary.

(b) A beneficiary is definite if the beneficiary can be ascertained now or in the future, subject to any applicable rule against perpetuities.

(c) A power in a trustee to select a beneficiary from an indefinite class is valid. If the power is not exercised within a reasonable time, the power fails and the property subject to the power passes to the persons who would have taken the property had the power not been conferred.

From reviewing this provision, you should be able to see that formation of a valid private requires:

- a settlor who has capacity and owns property,
- a trustee with active duties to perform,
- ascertainable beneficiaries (trusts for animals and charities have different rules that we discuss later),
- a trust res (i.e., the trust property),
- and intent to impose a trust.

The UTC, as we discussed in the Introduction, was promulgated in 2000 to unify trust laws between states and to bring many trust doctrines into correspondence with will doctrines. Trust law across the states continues to be quiet diverse. This is mainly due to the lack of well-developed trust rules in some states as a result of their resistance to equity courts and the fact that trust law was primarily judge-made law. With the adoption of the UTC in at least 25 states and territories, and more underway, the goal of harmonizing state trust laws has been significantly furthered. But as with the UPC, states made changes that make each state's code unique. In the absence of a comprehensive trust code, you may find that some states have amended certain of their will provisions to include trusts, and others continue to rely entirely on common-law rules with extensive guidance from the Restatements. The Uniform Law Commission, on its website, has posted a state-by-state, section-by-section comparison of the UTC as it has been adopted in the various states.[54] This is a good resource for learning the unique differences of your state.

As we go through the various elements of a valid trust, be sure to refer back to UTC § 402 to see how the current statutes are treating the issue. You will find that further provisions of the UTC have amended long-standing common-law rules, but you should still be careful. Trusts created prior to the adoption of the UTC are usually going to be governed by the earlier laws. This is an area of law that is currently in flux and you will do well to understand both the old and the new rules.

a.   The Trust Res

Trusts very often consist of money that is invested by the settlor or the trustee, the income from which is payable to the beneficiaries. The money might be used to purchase stocks, bonds, or mutual funds, or it might be used to invest in a business. Or the money might just sit in the bank accruing interest. Or the trust might hold land, either the family home or investment properties like rental houses, farms, and commercial buildings. There might be no income payable from the trust, but the use of the home or an automobile for a period of time would constitute the beneficial interest. A trust might hold a business. There is really no limit to the kind of property that can be held in a trust, and the nature of the property will dictate, to a large extent, the duties of the trustee. Very often when a group of children or grandchildren inherit jointly a large piece of real estate, perhaps a ranch or family farm, they might establish a trust to own and manage the property. Most large trusts consist of a variety of property. But all trusts, to exist, must contain some property. Courts have held that until there is a trust *res*, the trust is an empty shell with no legal existence.

I like to think of a trust as a cookie jar. If I have a plate of cookies that I just baked, I can eat them all right away (which I have unfortunately done and soon regretted doing) or I can put most of them in a cookie jar. Once protected in thae cookie jar, the cookies are kept safe from roaming children and retain their freshness. If I have full control over the cookie jar, I can reach inside and take out a cookie anytime I want one. It's a little more work than just picking one up from the plate, but not much. If I am on a diet, however, and I want to ration my consumption of cookies, I can give the jar to a neighbor and tell her to only give me one a day, no matter how much I beg or rationalize why I need to eat 10 of them with my morning coffee. I can also tell my neighbor that if I die before I eat all the cookies, she should either give the whole jar to my children where they can take them out and put them in their own jars or eat them all, or ration out the cookies to my children. If I eat them all before I die and there aren't any left for my children, well they can't complain since I made them. Afterall, they were my cookies and it's my cookie jar.

The trust is the cookie jar. Without the cookies, the jar doesn't do anything. Without the jar, the cookies just lie around in random places where I can easily eat them all when I need a midnight snack. Putting them in the jar takes some effort and, depending on who has control over the jar (myself or my neighbor), the contents are more or less easily consumed. One of the best benefits, besides keeping the cookies fresh, is that the jar and the cookies in the jar stay safe until they are taken out and eaten. Although one transfer occurs when I put the cookies in the jar, and that transfer is poten-

---

[54]   *See,* http://www.uniformlaws.org/Act.aspx?title=Trust Code for the comparison charts.

tially taxable, there are no further transfers when my beneficiaries take their cookies out. Thus, if I don't put the cookies in the jar and some are left at my death, the cookies pass to my heirs or will beneficiaries, and if they don't eat all the cookies, they will pass to their heirs or beneficiaries. Each of these transfers is potentially taxable. But by putting the cookies into the jar, I only make one transfer and all subsequent raids on the jar are tax free.

The other cool thing about this particular cookie jar is that when there are cookies in the jar, they often reproduce themselves, generating more cookies. So if I can be happy eating just the number of cookies that are reproduced each year, then when I die the jar will still be full and my successor beneficiaries can enjoy a seemingly endless supply of cookies. This pattern will continue repeating so long as the successor beneficiaries don't get greedy and take all the cookies out of the jar as soon as they have access to it. Thus, who put the cookies in the jar, who has control over the jar, what rules exist to limit the settlor's trips to the jar, what rules guide access to the jar both before and after the settlor's death, and who gets the jar next are the important elements that must be established to create a valid trust. Cookie jars function best when there are limits on the number of trips to the jar, but they also need cookies.

Therefore, without property, no trust can exist. Thus, when a stock speculator decided to declare himself the trustee of the proceeds he would earn on his stock investments for the upcoming year, for the benefit of his wife, mother and minor children (who were in a lower income tax bracket than he was), the court held there was no trust. The court reasoned that there was no way of knowing whether there would even be any earnings.[55] The trust could not come into being until the property came into being. Once the property came into being, and only then, the settlor could transfer the property into the trust. Of course, the income tax benefits would be lost if he had to own the profits before they were transferred into the trust. What could Brainard have done? According to the court, he should have put the money he was investing into the trust, then any profits on those investments would accrue to the trust and not to Brainard personally. That is how he could avoid the tax liabilities. However, if the initial funds were placed into the trust, Brainard would not be free to speculate as freely as he could if he held the money personally because his fiduciary obligations to the beneficiaries would have limited his full exercise of control over the funds. He could invest, but perhaps not speculate wantonly. So he had a choice—retain full control and pay the taxes, or lessen the tax burden but become subject to fiduciary duties in the management and expenditure of his property.

But not all speculative property is as inchoate as stock profits; the right to royalties can be the *res* of a trust. In *Speelman v. Pascal*, 178 N.E.2d 723 (N.Y.App. 1961) the court upheld a trust in which the settlor had given to his loyal secretary 5% shares in the profits from the stage play that would eventually be *My Fair Lady*. The settlor had the English and American rights to produce a musical play based on George Bernard Shaw's *Pygmalion*. Even though he had not even managed to have the script written before his death, the court upheld the secretary's rights to the profits on the grounds that the settlor could assign a portion of his rights to anticipated earnings.

---

[55] *Brainard v. Commissioner*, 91 F.2d 880 (7th Cir. 1937).

Though some have found it difficult to reconcile *Brainard* and *Speelman*, there are some important distinctions between the cases. One is that in *Brainard* the profits were purely speculative while in *Speelman* the settlor had the exclusive rights to produce a musical play from the Shaw estate. This meant that although a play might not ever be written and produced, there was no risk that some stranger would beat them to it. The second is that the purpose of the trust in *Brainard* was to avoid taxes, a purpose that is against public policy and would not likely prompt a court to rule liberally on the *res* issue. In *Speelman*, there was no public policy against the trust. Third, the hypothetical profits in *Brainard* are not readily identified as property rights that are currently bought and sold, while legal rights to future Broadway plays are readily identified as currency in the marketplace. Without the enforceability of those rights investors would be hesitant to put on a large Broadway production.

Consider whether you think the following should or should not constitute the *res* of a trust.

- The next foal born to my racehorse sired by Secretariat.

- The royalties from my next casebook

- My right to purchase next season's football tickets. *See, Kully v. Goldman*, 305 N.W.2d 800 (Neb. 1981).

- Proceeds of a life insurance policy. *See, Clemens v. Sandee Manuf. Corp.*, 252 N.E.2d 897 (Ill.App. 1969).

- A letter of intent to form a partnership to develop land. *See, Maykus v. First City Realty and Financial Corp.*, 518 S.W.2d 887 (Tx.Civ.App. 1975)

- The profits from all the tomatoes I sell at next year's farmer's market.

- My undivided beneficial interest in a pre-existing trust. *See, North Carolina Nat. Bank v. Goode*, 259 S.E.2d 288 (N.C. 1979).

- My share of the earnings from my stock investment club. *See, Bank of California v. Connolly*, 36 Cal.App.3d 350 (Cal.App. 1975)

- One-third share of any damages award I receive in my slip and fall case against the local grocery store. *See, Vittands v. Sidduth*, 730 N.E.2d 325 (Mass.Ct.App. 2000).

- Anything I inherit from my father's estate. *See, Succession of Burgess*, 359 So.2d 1006 (La.App. 1978)

- The development rights for my oceanfront land in Louisiana. *See, Hoyle v. Dickinson*, 746 P.2d 18 (Az.App. 1987).

- Any natural gas or oil that may underlie my land. *See, Schaneman v. Wright,* 470 N.W.2d 566 (Neb. 1991).

- The profits from any meteorite that falls to earth and embeds itself on my land.

- Dividends from my real estate investment trust. *See, Bridges v. Autozone Properties, Inc.*, 900 So.2d 784 (La. 2005).

- Post-mortem publicity rights. *See, Shaw Family Archives v. CMG Worldwide*, 486 F.Supp.2d 309 (S.D. N.Y. 2007).

- Title II Firearms, like silencers, machine guns, and the proverbial AK–47. *See*, Margaret Littman, Florida Lawyer Fashions Gun Trust (And Niche Practice), ABA Journal, (Feb. 1, 2011) at http://www.abajournal.com/magazine/article/in_goldman_guns_trust/.

You should already have a sense of what property is too speculative or contingent to place in a trust, and what property, in the form of legally enforceable and recognized rights, are the common currency of property transactions. Intangible property and contract rights, like insurance proceeds or mortgages, can certainly be the *res* of a trust. But it is always safer, as we learned in *Brainard*, to put Secretariat or the business or my tomato farm in the trust before they produce foals, widgets, income, or tomatoes.

Technology Trend: Apple, Bruce Willis, and the Cloud

Just days after Apple won a stunning victory over Samsung about proprietary rights in the rounded corners and general layout of the iPad and iPhone,[56] Bruce Willis quipped that it's unfair Apple can own its round corners but he can't own, and therefore pass on at death, the music in his iTunes library.[57] Since the license we receive when we download from Amazon or iTunes is only good during our lifetimes, we cannot likely pass those rights on at our death. This is true even though we could pass on the music if we bought the actual CD and cluttered up our libraries with thousands of plastic boxes. Although Willis is denying rumors that he intends to sue Apple, the point is much larger. If we don't own the music stored in the cloud, but do have a right to use it during our lives, we can put our iTunes library into an *inter vivos* trust during our lives. Licensing rights of music in the cloud should be similar to the license to stage *My Fair Lady*. But presumably in the case of music in the cloud, at our death the trust res will disappear, because it was only a life interest even though the music is more real at the time it was placed in the trust than the right to stage a play that isn't even written yet. This makes a certain amount of sense (even if we don't particularly like the fact) when it comes to licensing of games and music. But what if we store original content on the cloud, like the manuscript of our next novel, our next world symphony, or the next edition of our casebook?

The Standby Trust

Today, many people have what are called *pour-over* wills. These are wills that simply devise all the decedent's probate property into a pre-existing *standby trust*. As we discussed in the section on Incorporation by Reference and Acts of Independent Significance, that works fine if the trust is already in existence (i.e. already funded with a trust *res*), no changes are made to the dispositive provisions, and/or the trust has an independent purpose besides making the dispositions of the property in the estate. But the requirement that a trust have property before it can come into existence caused many standby trusts to fail, or at least to be deemed testamentary trusts rather than *inter vivos* trusts.[58] And why did that matter? If the trust documents are executed with the will formalities, then

---

[56] Apple, Inc. v. Samsung Electronics Co., Ltd., C11–1846 & C12–0630 (N.D. Calif., 9/2/2012).

[57] *See,* Jess Collen, *Apple, Bruce Willis, and Internet Immortality*, FORBES, Sept. 5, 2012 at http://www.forbes.com/sites/jesscollen/2012/09/05/apple–bruce–willis–and–internet–immortality/.

[58] *See, In re Estate of Daniels*, 665 P.2d 594 (Colo. 1983).

there is no problem treating the unfunded trust as a shell waiting to be funded from the property in the will. But most trusts aren't executed with the will formalities and, therefore, unless they are funded, would be treated as invalid testamentary trusts. They can't be *inter vivos* trusts with independent significance because they haven't been funded, and they can't be testamentary trusts because they are not formally executed. The following case illustrates the potential problems and statutory solutions with pour-over wills and standby trusts, made complicated by a divorce.

Clymer v. Mayo

473 N.E.2d 1084 (Mass. 1985)

■ HENNESSEY, CHIEF JUSTICE.

At the time of her death in November, 1981, the decedent [Professor Clara Mayo], then fifty years of age, was employed by Boston University as a professor of psychology. She was married to James P. Mayo, Jr. (Mayo), from 1953 to 1978. The couple had no children. The decedent was an only child and her sole heirs at law are her parents, Joseph A. and Maria Weiss.

[Clara and James had reciprocal wills making each the principal beneficiary of the other, pouring the residue of each will into a revocable trust established the same day the wills were executed, and Clara named her trust the principal beneficiary of her life insurance and retirement annuities.]

In the event that Mayo survived the decedent, the trust estate was to be divided into two parts. Trust A, the marital deduction trust, was to be funded with an amount "equal to fifty (50%) per cent of the value of the Donor's 'adjusted gross estate,' . . . Mayo was the income beneficiary of Trust A and was entitled to reach the principal at his request or in the trustee's discretion. The trust instrument also gave Mayo a general power of appointment over the assets in Trust A.

The balance of the decedent's estate, excluding personal property passing to Mayo by will, or the entire estate if Mayo did not survive her, composed Trust B. Trust B provided for the payment of five initial specific bequests totaling $45,000. After those gifts were satisfied, the remaining trust assets were to be held for the benefit of Mayo for life. Upon Mayo's death, the assets in Trust B were to be held for "the benefit of the nephews and nieces of the Donor" living at the time of her death. The trustee was given discretion to spend so much of the income and principal as necessary for their comfort, support, and education. When all of these nephews and nieces reached the age of thirty, the trust was to terminate and its remaining assets were to be divided equally between Clark University and Boston University to assist in graduate education of women. . . .

At the time of its creation in 1973, the trust was not funded. Its future assets were to consist solely of the proceeds of the [insurance and retirement] policies and the property which would pour over under the will's residuary clause. . . .

Mayo moved out of the marital home in 1975 [and the parties divorced in 1978; in the divorce settlement] Mayo waived any "right, title or interest" in the decedent's "securities, savings accounts, savings certificates, and retirement fund," as well as her "furniture, furnishings and art." Mayo remarried on August 28, 1978, and later executed a new will in favor of his new wife. The decedent died on November 21, 1981. Her will was allowed on November 18, 1982, and the court appointed John H. Clymer as administrator with the will annexed.

What is primarily at issue in these actions is the effect of the Mayos' divorce upon dispositions provided in the decedent's will and indenture of trust. . . .

2. Validity of "Pour-over" Trust.

The Weisses claim that the judge erred in ruling that the decedent's trust was validly created despite the fact that it was not funded until her death. They rely on the common law rule that a trust can be created only when a trust res exists. Arguing that the trust never came into existence, the Weisses claim they are entitled to the decedent's entire estate as her sole heirs at law [by intestacy].

In upholding the validity of the decedent's pour-over trust, the judge cited the relevant provisions of G.L. c. 203, § 3B, inserted by St.1963, c. 418, § 1, the Commonwealth's version of the Uniform Testamentary Additions to Trusts Act.

> A devise or bequest, the validity of which is determinable by the laws of the commonwealth, may be made to the trustee or trustees of a trust established or to be established by the testator . . . including a funded or unfunded life insurance trust, although the trustor has reserved any or all rights of ownership of the insurance contracts, if the trust is identified in the will and the terms of the trust are set forth in a written instrument executed before or concurrently with the execution of the testator's will . . . regardless of the existence, size or character of the corpus of the trust (emphasis added).

The decedent's trust instrument, which was executed in Massachusetts and states that it is to be governed by the laws of the Commonwealth, satisfies these statutory conditions. The trust is identified in the residuary clause of her will and the terms of the trust are set out in a written instrument executed contemporaneously with the will. However, the Weisses claim that G.L. c. 203, § 3B, was not intended to change the common law with respect to the necessity for a trust corpus despite the clear language validating pour-over trusts, "regardless of the existence, size or character of the corpus." The Weisses make no showing of legislative intent that would contradict the plain meaning of these words. It is well established that "the statutory language is the principal source of insight into legislative purpose." Moreover, the development of the common law of this Commonwealth with regard to pour-over trusts demonstrates that G.L. c. 203, § 3B, takes on practical meaning only if the Legislature meant exactly what the statute says concerning the need for a trust corpus.

This court was one of the first courts to validate pour-over devises to a living trust. In *Second Bank–State St. Trust Co. v. Pinion*, 341 Mass. 366, 371, 170 N.E.2d 350 (1960), decided prior to the adoption of G.L. c. 203, § 3B, we upheld a testamentary gift to a revocable and amendable inter vivos trust established by the testator before the execution of his will and which he amended after the will's execution. . . .

However, in Pinion, we were not presented with an unfunded pour-over trust. Nor, prior to G.L. c. 203, § 3B, did other authority exist in this Commonwealth for recognizing testamentary transfers to unfunded trusts. The doctrine of independent significance, upon which we relied in Pinion, assumes that "property was included in the purported inter vivos trust, prior to the testator's death." Restatement (Second) of Trusts § 54, comment f (1959). That is why commentators have recognized that G.L. c. 203, § 3B, "[m]akes some . . . modification of the Pinion doctrine. The act does not require that the trust res be more than nominal or even existent."

By denying that the statute effected such a change in the existing law, the Weisses render its enactment meaningless. "An intention to enact a barren and ineffective provision is not lightly to be imputed to the Legislature." . . .

For the foregoing reasons we conclude, in accordance with G.L. c. 203, § 3B, that the decedent established a valid inter vivos trust in 1973 and that its trustee may properly receive the residue of her estate. We affirm the judge's ruling on this issue. . . .

4. Termination of Trust A.

The judge terminated Trust A upon finding that its purpose—to qualify the trust for an estate tax marital deduction—became impossible to achieve after the Mayos' divorce. Mayo appeals this ruling. It is well established that the Probate Courts are empowered to terminate or reform a trust in whole or in part where its purposes have become impossible to achieve and the settlor did not contemplate continuation of the trust under the new circumstances.

The language the decedent employed in her indenture of trust makes it clear that by setting off Trusts A and B she intended to reduce estate tax liability in compliance with then existing provisions of the Internal Revenue Code. Therefore we have no disagreement with the judge's reasoning. However, we add that our reasoning below—that by operation of G.L. c. 191, § 9, Mayo has no beneficial interest in the trust—clearly disposes of Mayo's claim to Trust A.

5. Mayo's Interest in Trust B.

The judge's decision to uphold Mayo's beneficial interest in Trust B was appealed by the Weisses, as well as by Boston University and Clark University. The judge reasoned that the decedent intended to create a life interest in Mayo when she established Trust B and failed either to revoke or to amend the trust after the couple's divorce. The appellants argue that we should extend the reach of G.L. c. 191, § 9, to revoke all Mayo's interests under the trust.[4] General Laws c. 191, § 9, as amended through St.1977, c. 76, § 2, provides in relevant part:

> If, after executing a will, the testator shall be divorced or his marriage shall be annulled, the divorce or annulment shall revoke any disposition or appointment of property made by the will to the former spouse, any provision conferring a general or special power of appointment on the former spouse, and any nomination of the former spouse, as executor, trustee, conservator or guardian, unless the will shall expressly provide otherwise. Property prevented from passing to a former spouse because of revocation by divorce shall pass as if a former spouse had failed to survive the decedent, and other provisions conferring a power of office on the former spouse shall be interpreted as if the spouse had failed to survive the decedent.

The judge ruled that Mayo's interest in Trust B is unaffected by G.L. c. 191, § 9, because his interest in that trust is not derived from a "disposition

---

[4]   None of the parties contests the judge's ruling that G.L. c. 191, § 9, revokes those provisions in the decedent's will which benefited Mayo.

. . . made by the will" but rather from the execution of an inter vivos trust with independent legal significance. We disagree, but in fairness we add that the judge here confronted a question of first impression in this Commonwealth.

General Laws c. 191, § 9, was amended by the Legislature in 1976 to provide in the event of divorce for the revocation of testamentary dispositions which benefit the testator's former spouse. The statute automatically causes such revocations unless the testator expresses a contrary intent. In this case we must determine what effect, if any, G.L. c. 191, § 9, has on the former spouse's interest in the testator's pour-over trust.

While, by virtue of G.L. c. 203, § 3B, the decedent's trust bore independent significance at the time of its creation in 1973, the trust had no practical significance until her death in 1981. The decedent executed both her will and indenture of trust on February 2, 1973. She transferred no property or funds to the trust at that time. The trust was to receive its funding at the decedent's death, in part through her life insurance policy and retirement benefits, and in part through a pour-over from the will's residuary clause. Mayo, the proposed executor and sole legatee under the will, was also made the primary beneficiary of the trust with power, as to Trust A only, to reach both income and principal.

During her lifetime, the decedent retained power to amend or revoke the trust. Since the trust was unfunded, her co-trustee was subject to no duties or obligations until her death. Similarly, it was only as a result of the decedent's death that Mayo could claim any right to the trust assets. It is evident from the time and manner in which the trust was created and funded, that the decedent's will and trust were integrally related components of a single testamentary scheme. For all practical purposes the trust, like the will, "spoke" only at the decedent's death. For this reason Mayo's interest in the trust was revoked by operation of G.L. c. 191, § 9, at the same time his interest under the decedent's will was revoked.

It has reasonably been contended that in enacting G.L. c. 191, § 9, the Legislature "intended to bring the law into line with the expectations of most people. . . .   Divorce usually represents a stormy parting, where the last thing one of the parties wishes is to have an earlier will carried out giving everything to the former spouse." To carry out the testator's implied intent, the law revokes "any disposition or appointment of property made by the will to the former spouse." It is indisputable that if the decedent's trust was either testamentary or incorporated by reference into her will, Mayo's beneficial interest in the trust would be revoked by operation of the statute. However, the judge stopped short of mandating the same result in this case because here the trust had "independent significance" by virtue of c. 203, § 3B. While correct, this characterization of the trust does not end our analysis. For example, in *Sullivan v. Burkin*, 390 Mass. 864, 867, 460 N.E.2d 572 (1984), we ruled prospectively that the assets of a revocable trust will be considered part of the "estate of the decedent" in determining the surviving spouse's statutory share.

Treating the components of the decedent's estate plan separately, and not as parts of an interrelated whole, brings about inconsistent results. Applying c. 191, § 9, the judge correctly revoked the will provisions benefiting Mayo. As a result, the decedent's personal property—originally left to Mayo—fell into the will's residuary clause and passed to the trust. The judge then appropriately terminated Trust A for impossibility of purpose thereby denying Mayo his beneficial interest under Trust A. Yet, by upholding Mayo's interest under Trust B, the judge returned to Mayo a life interest in the same assets that composed the corpus of Trust A—both property passing by way of the decedent's will and the proceeds of her TIAA/CREF annuity contracts. . . .

We do not agree that reference to an existing trust in a will's pour-over clause is sufficient to incorporate that trust by reference without evidence that the testator intended such a result. However, it is not necessary for us to indulge in such reasoning, because we have concluded that the legislative intent under G.L. c. 191, § 9, is that a divorced spouse should not take under a trust executed in these circumstances. In the absence of an expressed contrary intent, that statute implies an intent on the part of a testator to revoke will provisions favoring a former spouse. It is incongruous then to ignore that same intent with regard to a trust funded in part through her will's pour-over at the decedent's death. As one law review commentator has noted, "[t]ransferors use will substitutes to avoid probate, not to avoid the subsidiary law of wills. The subsidiary rules are the product of centuries of legal experience in attempting to discern transferors' wishes and suppress litigation. These rules should be treated as presumptively correct for will substitutes as well as for wills." Langbien, The Nonprobate Revolution and the Future of the Law of Succession, 97 Harv.L.Rev. 1108, 1136–1137 (1984).

Restricting our holding to the particular facts of this case—specifically the existence of a revocable pour-over trust funded entirely at the time of the decedent's death—we conclude that G.L. c. 191, § 9, revokes Mayo's interest under Trust B.[7]

[The court also held that bequests to decedent's nieces and nephews in her will and trust documents were valid even though she had no blood relatives, and the only nieces and nephews she had were related to her through her former husband. The court determined that although the law revoked the gifts to her former husband upon their divorce, it would not revoke gifts to relatives of the husband.]

The court in *Clymer* relied on the Massachusetts version of the Uniform Testamentary Additions to Trusts Act (UTATA) to save Clara Mayo's trust. The UTATA was promulgated by the Uniform Law Commission in 1960 and has subsequently been adopted in nearly every state.[59] The UTATA explicitly permits a trust shell to be valid when the only property in the trust is the property to be poured over from a will. You might reasonably be thinking "so what? The trust is funded at death when the estate's property is poured into it, and so what if the trust documents were created before (sometimes years before) the trust itself is funded? Why do we need a special statute to do what seems rather obvious?" Let's unpack the issue a bit.

---

[7]   As an alternative ground the appellants argue that the terms of the Mayos' divorce settlement, in which Mayo waived "any right, title or interest" in the assets that later funded the decedent's trust, amount to a disclaimer of his trust interest. We decline to base our holding on such reasoning because a disclaimer of rights "must be clear and unequivocal." *Second Bank–State St. Trust Co. v. Yale Univ. Alumni Fund,* 338 Mass. 520, 524, 156 N.E.2d 57 (1959), and we find no such disclaimer in the Mayos' divorce agreement.

[59]   *See,* Statutory Note to Restatement 3d of Property, § 3.8.

The UTATA of 1991 provides:

Uniform Testamentary Additions to Trusts Act, § 1.

(a) A will may validly devise or bequeath property to the trustee of a trust established or to be established (i) during the testator's lifetime by the testator, by the testator and some other person, or by some other person including a funded or unfunded life insurance trust, although the trustor has reserved any or all rights of ownership of the insurance contracts, or (ii) at the testator's death by the testator's devise to the trustee, if the trust is identified in the testator's will and its terms are set forth in a written instrument, other than a will, executed before, concurrently with, or after the execution of the testator's will or in another individual's will if that other individual has predeceased the testator, regardless of the existence, size, or character of the corpus of the trust. The devise or bequest is not invalid because the trust is amendable or revocable, or because the trust was amended after the execution of the will or the testator's death.

(b) Unless the testator's will provides otherwise, property devised or bequeathed to a trust described in subsection (a) is not held under a testamentary trust of the testator but it becomes a part of the trust to which it is devised or bequeathed, and must be administered and disposed of in accordance with the provisions of the governing instrument setting forth the terms of the trust, including any amendments thereto made before or after the testator's death.

(c) Unless the testator's will provides otherwise, a revocation or termination of the trust before the testator's death causes the devise or bequest to lapse.

The ultimate question is whether the beneficiaries of the trust are receiving *inter vivos* or testamentary gifts. If they were receiving a bequest directly from the will, the gifts would be testamentary and therefore, to be valid, they must be executed with the will formalities. Assuming the trust document is created and executed at the same time as the will, the trust document can make dispositive provisions through the doctrine of Incorporation by Reference. However, the gifts would still be considered testamentary, just like a separate list in the will. But isn't the point of a trust that it is easily amended, without the requirement of witnesses and doesn't this scenario miss the point? For example, if the settlor executes both the will and trust on the same day, but later wants to amend the trust provisions after the will is executed, the changes won't be given effect because Incorporation by Reference does not permit post-will-execution changes to the separate document. If the trust is not funded, it has no independent significance and therefore cannot guide distribution.

Remember, the key here is to pinpoint what document assigns and identifies the gifts and recipients—if it is a document that is not executed with the will formalities, or is not incorporated with one of the three will doctrines discussed earlier, it cannot be given effect IF the gifts are to be deemed testamentary. You should see now why New York and Florida took the simple road, which was to require that dispositive provisions of *inter vivos* trusts be executed with the will formalities. However, that extra requirement makes amending trusts much more difficult and eliminates at least one of the benefits of a trust over a will.

In the rest of the states, to avoid the will formalities requirement, the trust somehow needs to make *inter vivos* gifts, not testamentary gifts, to the beneficiaries. But how can it do that if the trust doesn't become valid until the death of the testator and the testator's property is poured into the trust from the will? If the trust is funded and has independent significance, then one can easily say the dispositive provisions of the trust are not testamentary. But if the trust is unfunded and easily revocable and amendable, it is very difficult to legitimately say that an *inter vivos* gift was made to the trust beneficiaries when that gift could be revoked at any time and the trust might never actually be funded (let's say the will is voided for lack of mental capacity). This legal bind motivated the Uniform Law Commission to recognize that a statutory solution was best—it was simply too difficult to say that the beneficiaries received *inter vivos* gifts from an *unfunded* standby trust.

What the UTATA does, therefore, is permit an unfunded trust, executed before or after the will, to dispose of a settlor's property, even though the trust is revocable (therefore no vested interest passes to the beneficiary until the settlor dies without revoking), **so long as the trust is appropriately referenced in the will**. Note how the UTATA retains the requirement that the trust be identified in the will, as is required for Incorporation by Reference or (F)acts of Independent Significance. The UTATA states that property devised to such a trust *"is not held under a testamentary trust,"* thus allowing the trust to be valid without being executed with the formalities.

Also, it must be noted that while the standby trust with the pour-over will may permit the testator to make effective changes after the will is executed, the trust mechanism does not avoid probate. Only property within the trust prior to the testator's death can pass outside probate. The property disposed of by the pour-over will must be probated before it is placed in the trust and disposed of according to the trust's provisions; the only benefit of the pour-over is that dispositive changes can be made after the will is executed by simply amending the trust.

Few people today opt for purely empty standby trusts because they don't get the probate avoidance benefits if the trust is entirely unfunded. Rather, the lawyer will send the client home with a revocable trust that is partially funded (usually with real estate or other non-liquid assets) and a pour-over will that will channel whatever remaining property (or newly acquired property) into the trust for orderly management and disposition at death. This means that it is important to re-title assets in the name of the trust. Not only does it give the trust independent significance, but all property already in the trust at the settlor's death can pass outside the probate process.

Clymer v. Mayo also raises some additional issues regarding incorporation by reference, revocation, ambiguities, reformation of trusts, and the applicability of will rules to will substitutes. Although we discuss more fully the effect of divorce on estate documents in Chapter 10, and the prevalence of statutes revoking gifts to ex-spouses, the Massachusetts court was faced with an even bigger problem in this case than the unfunded standby trust. If it treated the trust and the will together as part of a holistic estate plan, so that divorce knocked the husband out of both the will and the trust, then perhaps the court should have demanded that the trust also be executed with the will formalities since it was primarily established to make testamentary dispositions. If the court instead treated them differently, and recognized the trust as an *inter vivos* instrument that did not need the will formalities, then was it appropriate to apply a will rule on revocation to a non-*testamentary* instrument? The revocation of the trust provision to Mayo really tests the boundaries of the *inter vivos*/testamentary gift distinctions that characterizes many of the legal issues involving trust validity.

Tax Tip: Taxes and the Cookie Jar

As we have already discussed, taxes may be assessed on certain gratuitous transfers of property. So let's think about the cookie jar analogy a bit more. Let's say I have 20 cookies and I eat 5 of them and give the rest to my son. Then my son eats 5 and gives the remaining 10 to his son. Then my grandson eats 5 of those and gives the remaining 5 to his son. Then my great-grandson eats the last 5. In that case, there have been three potentially taxable transfers: 15 cookies from me to my son, 10 cookies from my son to my grandson, and 5 cookies from my grandson to my great-grandson. That means that taxes may be due from the transfer of 30 cookies, when I only had 20 to start with.

So one obvious thing to do is for me to only give my son 5 cookies, and then give my grandson 5 cookies, and my great-grandson 5 cookies. I still have three taxable transfers, but at least taxes only are assessed on the transfer of 15 cookies instead of 30. But what if I don't know how many cookies my son, grandson, and great-grandson are going to need, I don't even know if I am going to have a great-grandson, so I can't give him any cookies during my life, and I want all my beneficiaries to have the option of taking more cookies if they need them, but I don't want to give them the cookies if they are going to be squandered or go stale. The obvious answer is that I put my extra 15 cookies in the cookie jar and I give each of my three beneficiaries the right to take only as many cookies as they want or need. The cookie jar is the trust.

Now remember that we don't tax the recipients of gratuitous gifts, only the donor. Thus, my transfer of the 15 cookies into the trust is a potentially taxable transfer, but the withdrawing of the cookies by my beneficiaries is not taxable. They received their rights to the property in the trust when I established it. Putting the cookies into the trust, therefore, may seem tax neutral when compared to just giving each beneficiary 5 cookies each, although it does have the added benefit of allowing the beneficiaries to take more or fewer cookies depending on their needs, which I might not properly be able to plan for if I simply give each one 5 cookies outright. If my son only needs 4 cookies and has one left at his death to pass to his son, there's another possible taxable transfer.

But the trust has another added benefit; it can discount the value of the cookies for transfer tax purposes. How much would you pay to buy a plate of 20 cookies that you can eat anytime, anywhere, and do with as you please? Would you pay the same price for those 20 cookies if they were kept locked up in a cookie jar under the control of your very disapproving second-grade babysitter? The mere existence of the trust may result in the discounting of the value of the cookies so that when I put the 15 cookies into the trust, I will pay less transfer tax than if I gave the 15 cookies away outright to my beneficiaries.

Furthermore, while the cookies are in the jar uneaten they are likely to generate more cookies (income) or increase in value (appreciate). My son, grandson, and great-grandson may ultimately be able to take 7 cookies each out of the jar simply because I structured the gift to stagger the recipient's acquisition of the property and benefit from its careful management. Controlling who has access to the cookie jar, and under what conditions, therefore, can help the donor structure a trust to minimize tax consequences while keeping the cookies safe and sound for that mid-night snack emergency.

b. The Trustee and Fiduciary Obligations

Every trust requires a trustee, "but no trust will fail for lack of a trustee." This rather cryptic sentence means that although a trustee must exist for there to be a valid trust, the court will simply appoint a trustee to serve if the trustee designated by the settlor is unable or unwilling to serve (or the settlor fails to appoint one). Being a trustee is not always an easy job, however. Trustees manage the property and they owe fiduciary obligations to *both* the property itself and the beneficiaries. Trustees cannot act toward the property just like owners do, who can squander and waste their own property if they choose. Remember *Brainard v. Commissioner* about the plaintiff who wanted to establish a trust, naming himself as trustee, for the profits he hoped to make speculating on the stock market. If the funds used to invest were held in trust, he would not be able to act in quite as reckless a manner as he could as an outright owner. That is a good thing if one is interested in preserving money or generating a steady income stream; it is not so good if you want to take risks in the hopes of making it big.

Besides being a fiduciary, the trustee must provide accountings to the beneficiaries and/or the court and must comply with whatever administrative provisions are established by the trust instrument and state trust laws. Remember too that for a trust to be valid, there must be active duties for the trustee. Thus, a trust instrument that gives the trustee complete, unfettered discretion to do as she chooses with the property, even to invade the trust corpus and spend it on herself, and for which she has no obligations to pay out the income to anyone at any time would probably be held invalid by either statute or case law.[60]

And although a trust will not fail for lack of a trustee, many people establish trusts with a particular person in mind to serve as trustee (a child who is an attorney, or the one stable niece who seems to get along with everyone). If that person cannot serve, or chooses not to serve, is it better to appoint another family member, or a stranger? Even the most saintly and patient family member may become overwhelmed if family tensions escalate and that person, at least, might be relieved to pay the trustee fees to a professional.

Practice Point: Subsequent Marriages as a Factor in Trustee Selection

In *Clymer*, the court revoked gifts made to a prior spouse but upheld gifts made to relatives of the spouse. The idea that divorce fundamentally changes the relationship between spouses but not necessarily that between other family members plays an interesting role in the trust *planning* process, and family dynamics should be considered when clients in certain family situations are selecting their trustees. For example, one of the benefits of a revocable living trust is that a disability trustee can be named, whose duty will be to continue to manage the trust property for the benefit of the settlors in the event that they can't do it for themselves. Often, settlors want to name their adult children as disability trustees. But what about complex family situations where the settlors have each had several marriages and whose adult children are not particularly pleased with the current

---

[60] *See, e.g.*, N.Y. EST. POWERS & TRUST LAW §§ 7–1.1, 7–1.2; *Est. of Gagliardi*, 55 N.Y.2d 109, 432 N.E.2d 774 (1984).

marriage? Each of the settlor's own children may find it easy to serve as trustee for their natural parent, but what about their parent's new spouse? Can they be fair-minded? And, what about a situation where they could be serving as a co-trustee along with the other settlor's child(ren)? Under these circumstances, and depending on state law and the level to which the settlors have co-mingled their property, separate trusts, rather than joint trusts, may make more sense, since they would each only manage the property owned by each settlor. In any case, the trust plan should be designed to work *with* the family structure and flow with all of the complexities that follow.

The most common scenario facing the trustee, however, is balancing the interests and concerns of multiple beneficiaries. Where a trustee has the power to invade the principle for the benefit of the life tenant, should she do so when she knows that it will reduce the final payout to the remaindermen? What if the trustee is a successor beneficiary and paying mom's extra bingo charges at the nursing home will reduce the trustee's remainder interest? The following case illustrates just a few of the difficulties facing trustees, as well as the personal liability they face if they fail. These obligations also fall on the trustee of the self-settled trust when the settlor, trustee, and beneficiary are the same person. Think how hard it would be to have a fiduciary duty to yourself!

Marsman v. Nasca

30 Mass.App.Ct. 789, 573 N.E.2d 1025 (1991)

■ DREBEN, JUSTICE.

This appeal raises the following questions: Does a trustee, holding a discretionary power to pay principal for the "comfortable support and maintenance" of a beneficiary, have a duty to inquire into the financial resources of that beneficiary so as to recognize his needs? If so, what is the remedy for such failure? A Probate Court judge held that the will involved in this case imposed a duty of inquiry upon the trustee. We agree with this conclusion but disagree with the remedy imposed and accordingly vacate the judgment and remand for further proceedings.

1.   Facts. Sara Wirt Marsman died in September, 1971, survived by her second husband, T. Frederik Marsman (Cappy), and her daughter by her first marriage, Sally Marsman Marlette. Mr. James F. Farr, her lawyer for many years, drew her will and was the trustee thereunder. Article IIA of Sara's will provided in relevant part:

> "It is my desire that my husband, T. Fred Marsman, be provided with reasonable maintenance, comfort and support after my death. Accordingly, if my said husband is living at the time of my death, I give to my trustees, who shall set the same aside as a separate trust fund, one-third (1/3) of the rest, residue and remainder of my estate . . . ; they shall pay the net income therefrom to my said husband at least quarterly during his life; and after **having considered the various available sources of support for him**, my trustees shall, if they deem it necessary or desirable from time to time, in their sole and un-controlled discretion, pay over to him, or use, apply and/or expend for his direct or indirect benefit such amount or amounts of the principal thereof as they shall deem advisable for his **comfortable support and maintenance**." (Emphasis supplied).

Article IIB provided:

> "Whatever remains of said separate trust fund, including any accumulated income thereon on the death of my husband, shall be added to the trust fund established under Article IIC. . . . "

Article IIC established a trust for the benefit of Sally and her family. Sally was given the right to withdraw principal and, on her death, the trust was to continue for the benefit of her issue and surviving husband.

The will also contained the following exculpatory clause:

> "No trustee hereunder shall ever be liable except for his own willful neglect or default."

[During their marriage, Sara and Cappy lived comfortably. They owned their home in Wellesley as joint tenants and Cappy took sole ownership at Sara's death. After Sara's death, the trust for Cappy was valued at about $65,600, more than twice the value of the Wellesly home. After Sara's death Cappy remained in the home but his standard of living dropped. A year later he met and married his second wife, Margaret, and took out a $4000 mortgage to pay expenses. Attorney Farr knew of this mortgage but never inquired as to Cappy's financial needs. In 1973 Cappy had Farr write him a new will leaving all to Margaret. Once, in 1974, Cappy asked Farr for some funds from the trust and Farr sent him $300 after asking Cappy to explain in writing why he needed the support. The trial judge found that Farr, by his actions, discouraged Cappy from making any more requests. No further distributions of principal were made until1983 when Cappy entered a nursing home. In the fall of 1974, Cappy's financial needs had intensified to the point that he agreed with Sally and her husband that they would take over the mortgage payments, the real estate taxes, insurance, and major repairs on the Wellesley house and, in return, Sally would get the house upon Cappy's death. Farr prepared the documents to effectuate the transfer, communicating solely with Sally. No writing set forth Sally's obligations to Cappy, but Farr did prepare a deed transferring the house to Sally and her husband, reserving a life estate in Cappy. The trial judge found Cappy understood the financial transactions and that Margaret would have no interest in the house upon his death.]

Although Farr had read Sara's will to Cappy and had written to him that the will was "broad enough to permit a distribution of principal," the judge found that Farr failed to advise Cappy that the principal of his trust could be used for the expenses of the Wellesley home. The parsimonious distribution of $300 and Farr's knowledge that the purpose of the conveyance to Sally was to enable Cappy to remain in the house, provide support for this finding. After executing the deed, Cappy expressed to Farr that he was pleased and most appreciative. Margaret testified that Cappy thought Farr was "great" and that he considered him his lawyer.

Sally and Marlette complied with their obligations under the agreement. Sally died in 1983, and Marlette became the sole owner of the property subject to Cappy's life estate. Although Margaret knew before Cappy's death that she did not have any interest in the Wellesley property, she believed that Sally would have allowed her to live in the house because of their friendship. After Cappy's death in 1987, Marlette inquired as to Margaret's plans, and, subsequently, through Farr, sent Margaret a notice to vacate the premises. Margaret brought this action in the Probate Court.

After a two-day trial, the judge held that the trustee was in breach of his duty to Cappy when he neglected to inquire as to the latter's finances.

She concluded that, had Farr fulfilled his fiduciary duties, Cappy would not have conveyed the residence owned by him to Sally and Marlette. The judge ordered Marlette to convey the house to Margaret and also ordered Farr to reimburse Marlette from the remaining portion of Cappy's trust for the expenses paid by him and Sally for the upkeep of the property. If Cappy's trust proved insufficient to make such payments, Farr was to be personally liable for such expenses. Both Farr and Marlette appealed from the judgment, from the denial of their motions to amend the findings, and from their motions for a new trial. Margaret appealed from the denial of her motion for attorney's fees. As indicated earlier, we agree with the judge that Sara's will imposed a duty of inquiry on the trustee, but we disagree with the remedy and, therefore, remand for further proceedings.

2. Breach of trust by the trustee.

Contrary to Farr's contention that it was not incumbent upon him to become familiar with Cappy's finances, Article IIA of Sara's will clearly placed such a duty upon him. In his brief, Farr claims that the will gave Cappy the right to request principal "in extraordinary circumstances" and that the trustee, "was charged by Sara to be wary should Cappy request money beyond that which he quarterly received." Nothing in the will or the record supports this narrow construction. To the contrary, the direction to the trustees was to pay Cappy such amounts "as they shall deem advisable for his comfortable support and maintenance." This language has been interpreted to set an ascertainable standard, namely to maintain the life beneficiary "in accordance with the standard of living which was normal for him before he became a beneficiary of the trust."

Even where the only direction to the trustee is that he shall "in his discretion" pay such portion of the principal as he shall "deem advisable," the discretion is not absolute. "Prudence and reasonableness, not caprice or careless good nature, much less a desire on the part of the trustee to be relieved from trouble . . . furnish the standard of conduct."

That there is a duty of inquiry into the needs of the beneficiary follows from the requirement that the trustee's power "must be exercised with that soundness of judgment which follows from a due appreciation of trust responsibility." . . .

Farr, in our view, did not meet his responsibilities either of inquiry or of distribution under the trust. The conclusion of the trial judge that, had he exercised "sound judgment," he would have made such payments to Cappy "as to allow him to continue to live in the home he had occupied for many years with the settlor" was warranted.

3. Remedy against Marlette.

The judge, concluding that, had Farr not been in breach of trust, "[C]appy would have died owning the house and thus able to devise it to his widow, the plaintiff," ordered Marlette to convey the house to Margaret. This was an inappropriate remedy in view of the judge's findings. She found that, although the relationship between Cappy and Sally was "close and loving," there was "no fiduciary relation between them" and that Sally and Marlette "were not unjustly enriched by the conveyance." She also found that "Sally and Richard Marlette expended significant monies over a long period of time in maintaining their agreement with [C]appy."

Because the conveyance was supported by sufficient consideration (the agreement to pay the house expenses) and because Sally and Marlette had no notice of a breach of trust and were not themselves guilty of a breach of fiduciary duty, they cannot be charged as constructive trustees of the property. That portion of the judgment which orders Marlette to convey the property is vacated.

4. Remainder of Cappy's trust.

The amounts that should have been expended for Cappy's benefit are, however, in a different category. More than $80,000 remained in the trust for Cappy at the time of his death. As we have indicated, the trial judge properly concluded that payments of principal should have been made to Cappy from that fund in sufficient amount to enable him to keep the Wellesley property. There is no reason for the beneficiaries of the trust under Article IIC to obtain funds which they would not have received had Farr followed the testatrix's direction. The remedy in such circumstances is to impress a constructive trust on the amounts which should have been distributed to Cappy but were not because of the error of the trustee. Even in cases where beneficiaries have already been paid funds by mistake, the amounts may be collected from them unless the recipients were bona fide purchasers or unless they, without notice of the improper payments, had so changed their position that it would be inequitable to make them repay. Here, the remainder of Cappy's trust has not yet been distributed, and there is no reason to depart from the usual rule of impressing a constructive trust in favor of Cappy's estate on the amounts wrongfully withheld. There is also no problem as to the statute of limitations. The period of limitations with respect to those we hold to be constructive trustees (the beneficiaries of the trust under Article IIC) has not run as, at the earliest, their entitlement to funds occurred at Cappy's death in 1987.

That Cappy assented to the accounts is also no bar to recovery by his estate. The judge found that he was in the dark as to his rights to receive principal for the upkeep of the home. An assent may be withdrawn by a judge "if it is deemed improvident or not conducive to justice." The accounts were not allowed, and we need not consider the effect of G.L. c. 206, § 24, which permits the impeachment of an account after a final decree has been entered only for "fraud or manifest error."

The amounts to be paid to Cappy's estate have not been determined. On remand, the Probate Court judge is to hold such hearings as are necessary to determine the amounts which should have been paid to Cappy to enable him to retain possession of the house.

5. Personal liability of the trustee.

Farr raises a number of defenses against the imposition of personal liability, including the statute of limitations, the exculpatory clause in the will, and the fact that Cappy assented to the accounts of the trustee. The judge found that Farr's breach of his fiduciary duty to inquire as to Cappy's needs and his other actions in response to Cappy's request for principal, including the involvement of Sally in distributions of principal despite Sara's provision that Cappy's trust be administered separately, led Cappy to be unaware of his right to receive principal for house expenses. The breach may also be viewed as a continuing one. In these circumstances we do not consider Cappy's assent, or the statute of limitations to be a bar. The judge also found that Margaret learned of Cappy's right to principal for house expenses only when she sought other counsel after his death.

The more difficult question is the effect of the exculpatory clause. As indicated in part 3 of this opinion, we consider the order to Marlette to reconvey the property an inappropriate remedy. In view of the judge's finding that, but for the trustee's breach, Cappy would have retained ownership of the house, the liability of the trustee could be considerable.

Although exculpatory clauses are not looked upon with favor and are strictly construed, such "provisions inserted in the trust instrument without any overreaching or abuse by the trustee of any fiduciary or confidential relationship to the settlor are generally held effective except as to breaches of trust 'committed in bad faith or intentionally or with reckless indifference to the interest of the beneficiary.' " The actions of Farr were not of this ilk and also do not fall within the meaning of the term used in the will, "willful neglect or default."

Farr testified that he discussed the exculpatory clause with Sara and that she wanted it included. Nevertheless, the judge, without finding that there was an overreaching or abuse of Farr's fiduciary relation with Sara, held the clause ineffective. Relying on the fact that Farr was Sara's attorney, she stated: "One cannot know at this point in time whether or not Farr specifically called this provision to Sara's attention. Given the total failure of Farr to use his judgment as to [C]appy's needs, it would be unjust and unreasonable to hold him harmless by reason of the exculpatory provisions he himself drafted and inserted in this instrument."

Assuming that the judge disbelieved Farr's testimony that he and Sara discussed the clause, although such disbelief on her part is by no means clear, the conclusion that it "would be unjust and unreasonable to hold [Farr] harmless" is not sufficient to find the overreaching or abuse of a fiduciary relation which is required to hold the provision ineffective. See Restatement (Second) of Trusts § 222, comment d (1959).[10] We note that the judge found that Sara managed all the finances of the couple, and from all that appears, was competent in financial matters.

There was no evidence about the preparation and execution of Sara's will except for the questions concerning the exculpatory clause addressed to Farr by his own counsel. No claim was made that the clause was the result of an abuse of confidence.

The fact that the trustee drew the instrument and suggested the insertion of the exculpatory clause does not necessarily make the provision ineffective. No rule of law requires that an exculpatory clause drawn by a prospective trustee be held ineffective unless the client is advised independently.

The judge used an incorrect legal standard in invalidating the clause. While recognizing the sensitivity of such clauses, we hold that, since there was no evidence that the insertion of the clause was an abuse of Farr's fiduciary relationship with Sara at the time of the drawing of her will, the clause is effective. . . .

---

[10] The Restatement lists six factors which may be considered in determining whether a provision relieving the trustee from liability is ineffective on the ground that it was inserted in the trust instrument as a result of an abuse of a fiduciary relationship at the time of the trust's creation. The six factors are: "(1) whether the trustee prior to the creation of the trust had been in a fiduciary relationship to the settlor, as where the trustee had been guardian of the settlor; (2) whether the trust instrument was drawn by the trustee or by a person acting wholly or partially on his behalf; (3) whether the settlor has taken independent advice as to the provisions of the trust instrument; (4) whether the settlor is a person of experience and judgment or is a person who is unfamiliar with business affairs or is not a person of much judgment or understanding; (5) whether the insertion of the provision was due to undue influence or other improper conduct on the part of the trustee; (6) the extent and reasonableness of the provision."

The judgment is vacated, and the matter is remanded to the Probate Court for further proceedings to determine the amounts which, if paid, would have enabled Cappy to retain ownership of the residence. Such amounts shall be paid to Cappy's estate from the trust for his benefit prior to distributing the balance thereof to the trust under Article IIC of Sara's will.

———————

As Clara Mayo's executor learned, establishing a trust doesn't necessarily avoid the likelihood of an expensive lawsuit. And as Cappy's executor learned, full discretion on the part of the trustee doesn't mean a trustee can ignore some beneficiaries in order to help others. A trustee who does so risks a lawsuit against the estate and the trust. Who are the real parties in interest in these two cases and who do you think is ultimately paying the bills for this litigation?

Mandatory and Discretionary Powers in the Trustee

Attorney Farr was given discretion in whether or not to invade the principal of the trust for Cappy's benefit. But what about the income? Go back and look at the trust provisions and see if you think Farr had to pay Cappy the income every period, or could withhold it at his discretion. If a trustee may not choose whom to pay or how much to pay them, then the trust is mandatory and the trustee is merely an agent, following through on the settlor's instructions. But if the trustee has the ability to pay more or less, or to choose among a group of beneficiaries, then the trustee has discretionary powers that, as you will learn later, can be very useful.

The typical trust consists of property held for the benefit of one or more individuals, for the duration of their lives, then, maybe, for some others for their lives, and eventually to pay the remainder to one or more remainder beneficiaries. A common example would be:

> I hereby place $1 million in trust for the benefit of my widow for the duration of her life, then for the benefit of my three children for their lives, and then to pay the principal to my grandchildren, or issue of deceased grandchildren at the death of my last surviving child.

Without more, this trust is *mandatory*. The trustee *must* pay the income on the $1 million to the spouse for her life, then the trustee *must* pay the income to the three children for their lives, and finally, at the death of the last child, the trustee *must* distribute the principal to the grandchildren in equal shares regardless of their needs.[61] The important point is that the trustee has no discretion to withhold income to any of the life beneficiaries, nor to place the principal in a further trust if, for instance, one of the grandchildren happens to be underage or incapacitated.

Mandatory trusts simply require the payment of income and principal to the designated beneficiaries regardless of whether they are incapacitated, won the lottery and don't need the money, or are currently going through bankruptcy and the payout from the trust will be immediately

---

[61] The only real question in this case is what happens to the income when the first child dies—does it get distributed to the other two children (like a joint tenancy with right of survivorship) and then all to the final surviving child, or should the trustee distribute the income to the issue of the first child to die, then the income of the second child to her issue, and then when the last child dies distribute all the principal? This raises the question of what a trustee should do when a trust document is less than clear about distributions of principal and distributions of income.

attached by creditors. Trustees generally like these kinds of trusts because they are easy. Unlike Lawyer Farr in *Marsman*, trustees of mandatory trusts don't need to inquire into the other means of support of the trust beneficiaries, nor do they need to set up protections for incapacitated or special needs beneficiaries. But not building some level of discretion into a trust is almost malpractice, unless there are special reasons for making the trust entirely mandatory. Flexibility should be the estate planner's mantra unless there are compelling tax reasons, or other special reasons, for limiting a trustee's flexibility. *Discretionary* powers given to the trustee can allow the trustee to balance the needs of multiple beneficiaries and take account of future changes in circumstances.

Note that discretion doesn't mean the trustee may act arbitrarily and capriciously. Even when a trust instrument gives a trustee *discretion* to make payments to the beneficiaries, that discretion is not unlimited. The Restatement 3d of Trusts (2003) provides:

Restatement 3d of Trusts, § 50

(1) A discretionary power conferred upon the trustee to determine the benefits of a trust beneficiary is subject to judicial control only to prevent misinterpretation or abuse of the discretion by the trustee.

(2) The benefits to which a beneficiary of a discretionary interest is entitled, and what may constitute an abuse of discretion by the trustee, depend on the terms of the discretion, including the proper construction of any accompanying standards, and on the settlor's purposes in granting the discretionary power and in creating the trust.

Comment c elaborates:

It is contrary to sound policy, and a contradiction in terms, to permit the settlor to relieve a "trustee" of all accountability. Once it is determined that the authority over trust distributions is held in the role of trustee (contrast non fiduciary powers mentioned in Comment a) words such as "absolute" or "unlimited" or "sole and uncontrolled" are not interpreted literally. Even under the broadest grant of fiduciary discretion, a trustee must act honestly and in a state of mind contemplated by the settlor. Thus, a court will not permit the trustee to act in bad faith or for some purpose or motive other than to accomplish the purposes of the discretionary power. Except as the power is for the trustee's personal benefit, the court will also prevent the trustee from failing to act, either arbitrarily or from a misunderstanding of the trustee's duty or authority.

Do you think Attorney Farr violated the letter or the spirit of the Restatement? Is it good public policy to allow attorneys to draft exculpatory clauses? Why do you think exculpatory clauses might make sense?

The most common form of discretion given to a trustee is to pay income or principal for the *Health, Education, Maintenance, or Support (HEMS)* of a beneficiary. This type of discretion establishes some parameters for guiding the trustee without tying her hands too closely. But the HEMS standard is not always straightforward. Support is likely to mean maintenance in the style to which the beneficiary is accustomed, but it can have both an upward and downward element. Maintenance usually means the payment of necessaries, although maintenance and support both are terms that have been heavily litigated. Even education can be broad, meaning the solo round-the-world yachting excursion just as much as the tuition to Harvard. It can include room and board, and perhaps the bar tab from the frat party at the end of finals. Health seems straightforward, but if my insurance won't pay for experimental drugs or non-traditional medicine, should my trust?

To avoid the indeterminacy of the HEMS standard, some settlors simply give the trustee complete and unfettered discretion. But, as discussed above in *Marsman v. Nasca*, even that discretion does not extend to acting unreasonably. We explore specific reasons for building discretion into trusts later, especially in the context of creditor rights. At this point, I want you to be sensitive to the language necessary to create discretion on the part of the trustee, and some of the possible reasons why discretion is an important element.

PROBLEMS

Consider the following language and decide whether it creates mandatory or discretionary powers in the trustee with regard to income or principal or both:

4.18. Settler hereby conveys Blackacre to T, in trust, for the following purpose: I want my spouse to live in Blackacre for the rest of her life, but if she remarries I want the house sold and the proceeds retained in trust to pay the income to my children for their lives, and at the death of my last child my Trustee is to distribute the principal to my surviving grandchildren. If my wife does not remarry and continues to reside in Blackacre until her death, at that time my trustee may maintain Blackacre in trust if any child chooses to reside there; otherwise she is to sell Blackacre and distribute the proceeds to my living children.

4.19. Settlor gives the residue of my estate to the First National Bank, in trust, to distribute the income to my spouse for her life, and at her death to distribute the remainder in any proportion, to my then living children, as my trustee sees fit. My spouse is to have the right to make withdrawals from principal up to a maximum of 10% per year.

4.20. Settlor includes this provision in his will: "I give the rest and residue of my estate, real and personal, to my surviving wife, in trust, to liquidate the property and invest the proceeds in income-producing stocks, and to pay the income to my children, at least quarterly, for their support and maintenance, and to distribute the principal to them when they reach 25."

4.21. What about this one? "I give the rest and residue of my estate to my three children, for the benefit of my three children. My trustee may pay the income directly to them or on their behalf. At the death of each of my children, my trustee is to pay that child's share of the principal to a charity selected by that child. If my child does not select a charity, my trustee may select the charity."

None of these trust provisions is discretionary. Do you see why? Can you rewrite them to make them discretionary?

Practice Point: The Attorney–Trustee

As revocable living trusts began to catch on, many law practices (particularly those of solo practitioners who often had personal, long-standing relationships with their client base) had a common practice of naming the drafting attorney as Successor Trustee of the trust at the death of the Settlors, with the idea that the attorney could help facilitate the easy administration of the trust estate (a similar practice as naming the attorney as Executor under a will). What lessons can attorneys glean from *Marsman* as they consider the wisdom of accepting such appointments? They certainly must thoroughly examine state laws and conflict considerations, of course. But, barring any such problems, the attorney must remember that she would be serving in a fiduciary capacity, managing property for the beneficiaries. And she will be held to a very high standard. If the property is to be immediately divided and distributed at death, then such an appointment may be relatively simple. If, however, the trust terms dictate that the Trustee manage property for the beneficiary over a number of years, the duties and potential liabilities might exceed the convenience or peace of mind the settlors had in naming the attorney.

Consider the following Arizona Ethics Opinion:

96–07: Conflict of Interest; Lawyer as Trustee; Wills; Estates 03/1996

<u>Question Presented:</u> Is it ethically proper for an attorney who drafts a revocable living trust with a pour-over will on behalf of a client who is both the trustor and testator (testatrix) to be named as a successor trustee and personal representative in such documents and ultimately to serve in such capacity?

<u>Facts:</u> The inquiring attorney represents a client who has requested that the attorney draft a revocable living trust with a will that pours over into the trust. The client has requested that the attorney be named as the personal representative of the will and as successor trustee under the trust. The attorney has advised the client that the attorney would prefer that the client name a family member, a trusted friend or a corporate fiduciary such as a bank as personal representative and successor trustee. The client has rejected the option of a corporate fiduciary and the only family member the client would trust to serve in such a capacity has declined.

<u>Opinion:</u>

ER 1.8(c) provides:

> A lawyer shall not prepare an instrument giving the lawyer or a person related to the lawyer as parent, child, sibling, or spouse, a substantial gift from a client, including a testamentary gift, except where the client is related to the donee.

This provision was considered in South Carolina in Opinion 91–07 (4/91) and it was held that a lawyer could draft a will or trust agreement naming himself as personal representative or trustee at the client's request. Similarly, in Opinion 91–1, the Formal Advisory Opinion Board of the State Bar of Georgia held that a lawyer who drafts a will or trust instrument for a client may also be named as executor or trustee provided that the lawyer does not promote himself or exert undue influence over the client's choice of executor or trustee, the lawyer obtains the client's consent in writing and the lawyer charges a reasonable fee for his services. Although this opinion was decided under the Model Code rather than the Model Rules, the standard set forth in the Georgia decision will remain equally applicable. This decision stated that the lawyer should disclose at a minimum the following: 1) other potential choices for executor and trustee and their relative abilities and fees; 2) the role of the lawyer as fiduciary and as counsel and his fees; 3) the possibility, if permitted under local law, that the lawyer may retain his own firm to represent the estate or trust and the fee anticipated for this representation; and 4) the lawyer should advise the client concerning the desirability of independent counsel for the client in making this decision.

The Committee agrees with the South Carolina and Georgia opinions and is of the opinion that ER 1.8(c) does not prohibit an attorney from writing a will or trust naming the attorney as successor trustee, executor, or even initial trustee. Moreover, such appointments would not constitute a gift under ER 1.8(c). The Committee notes, however, that the fees received as successor trustee may not be in addition to legal fees charged for the same work. Attorneys serving in such capacities should be cognizant of the possible conflicts in such a position if litigation ensues.

Another ethical rule involved is ER 2.1, which requires that a lawyer "exercise independent, professional judgment and render candid advice." The lawyer must decide in each circumstance whether the lawyer could exercise her independent, professional judgment and render candid advice if the lawyer or her law firm was acting both as executor/trustee and lawyer for the trust or estate.

Conclusion: An attorney may draft a revocable living trust with a pour-over will for a client and be named as trustee and/or personal representative. Such an arrangement does not constitute a gift under ER 1.8, but the lawyer may not recover trustee fees in addition to legal fees for the same work. The lawyer must be able to exercise independent professional judgment when acting as both trustee and counsel to the estate. [ERs 1.8, 2.1]

Query: Did Farr violate the ethics rules discussed in the Arizona ethics opinion?

The choice of a trustee is one of the most important decisions a settlor must make. My aunt recently died, leaving a revocable living trust that named her three children successor, co-trustees and naming them as equal beneficiaries. Obviously, she wanted them all to feel that she was treating them equally and loved them the same. But the first thing we had to do was execute a trustee power delegation agreement to allow one trustee to act individually in closing accounts and paying final bills. Otherwise, every single transaction would have required all three signatures, and they lived in three different states. Arizona's trust code does not have a provision that allowed, as some trust codes do, that a single co-trustee may act individually unless instructed otherwise by the co-trustees. Besides, why would a settlor want to prove her equal love to her children by making the CPA daughter and the ballet dancer son both have to do all the trustee work? The learning curve just to understand the terminology and legal import of the trust may not be worth the benefit of having your children feel that you have treated them absolutely equally. Some family members are simply better suited to the task than others and a settlor should be encouraged to recognize that fact.

At the same time, you might want to caution people about accepting trustee appointments. Even if the filing of a bond is not required, being a trustee is an onerous task that requires meticulous attention to details, the obligation to understand and inquire about the needs of beneficiaries, and the business savvy to manage the property in a prudent manner.[62] Many of the cases in Chapter 8, *Planning for the Future*, involved trustees who were unsure how to proceed and brought declaratory actions for guidance on interpretation and distribution rules. The litigation cost associated with these suits cost the trusts a lot of money. There are benefits to corporate trustees and there are benefits to family friends as trustees. Each client's situation is different and you must engage your client in a lengthy conversation to discover who, if anyone, will be the best trustee.

c. *Ascertainable Beneficiaries*

Trusts also require *ascertainable beneficiaries*, i.e., persons who can be determined to meet the qualifications established in the trust and who can enforce the provisions of the trust against the trustee. A trust to give "$500 to all the *nice* people who help old ladies across cross-walks" would not qualify. A trust to distribute "all of my property to my friends and family" also will not qualify. Does the settlor mean all family members, regardless of how remote their relationship might be? And how close does a friend have to be to qualify? Even trusts to give property to "my children" can be difficult to determine if the settlor intended step-children, adopted children, foster children, or adopted-out children to qualify. Some courts have even held that grandchildren can qualify as children if there is evidence the settlor wished that outcome.[63]

Trust beneficiaries do not have to be immediately ascertainable, however, so long as they are ascertainable within the relevant rule against perpetuities period. Thus, a provision giving the principal of a trust to "my then living grandchildren, or issue of deceased grandchildren" is permissible so long as the date of distribution occurs within the perpetuities period. Section 44 of the Restatement 3d of Trusts provides:

Restatement (3d) of Trusts § 44

A trust is not created, or if created will not continue, unless the terms of the trust provide a beneficiary who is ascertainable at the time or who may later become ascertainable within the period and terms of the rule against perpetuities.

There are a number of common problems that arise in the context of identifying the beneficiaries of a trust. One is the trust to benefit an ill-defined group of people, like *friends* or *relatives*.[64] Some courts may try to validate a trust for the benefit of "family" or "relatives" by reference to the

---

[62] The Uniform Prudent Investor Act governs the actions of Trustees who are required to pursue investment strategies that balance risk and return. It has been adopted in all but a small handful of states.

[63] *See* Cox v. Forristall, 640 P.2d 878 (Kan.Ct.App. 1982) and further discussion of this subject in Chapter 8.

[64] *See, Clark v. Campbell*, 82 N.H. 281 (1926); and *In re Wylie's Estate*, 342 So.2d 996 (1997).

state's intestacy statute, but others do not.[65] Section 45 of the Restatement 3d of Trusts provides:

Restatement (3d) of Trusts § 45.

The members of a definite class of persons can be the beneficiaries of a trust.

Comment d explains:

d. "Relatives." Whether the term "relatives" is a definite class depends on the settlor's intended meaning in using the term.

If it is shown that, in using the word "relatives," the settlor intended to create a trust for all individuals who are related to the designated person, the intended class is not sufficiently ascertainable to sustain a trust, because a person has an indefinite number of close and remote relatives. Thus, an intended trust to divide the trust property equally among all relatives of a designated person fails under the rule stated in the Section.

On the other hand, under the preferred construction, an intended trust for "relatives" is to be interpreted not to mean all relatives (supra) but to mean some definite group of near relatives or some other ascertainable group of relatives. Absent evidence of the settlor's actual intention (or a power of selection, see below and Comment c), the term will be construed to refer to the heirs of the designated person. Under any such construction, the class is definite within the rule stated in this Section.

d(1). Selected "relatives." A trust for the benefit of "relatives" of the settlor or other designated person does not fail if the trustee has power to select who among the relatives shall take and in what portions. See Comment b. In such a case, the trustee may select any person or persons who reasonably fit within the meaning of the term, whether or not they would be heirs of the designated person.[66]

     According to the Restatement, the members of a definite class can be beneficiaries, but members of an indefinite class may not be beneficiaries. An indefinite class like friends, colleagues, club members, Democrats, or right-handed people will not suffice either because the class is simply too large, or the definition is not sufficiently distinct for the trustee to know for sure who is in and who is out. Even a definite class, like children or descendants, might be presumptively permissible but may become ambiguous if evidence shows that the settlor intended a particularly broad or narrow definition. A class like relatives may be too narrow if interpreted only to mean the settlor's legal heirs but too broad if interpreted to mean every person related by blood, no matter how remote. A large, definite class may

---

[65] See, *Binns v. Vick,* 260 Ark. 111 (1976).

[66] The Reporter's Notes to Comment d provide: "*On the term "relatives" or its equivalent, See, Estate of Lawrence,* 104 N.H. 457, 189 A.2d 491 (1963), 5 A.L.R.3d 709, *and Lundie v. Walker,* 126 N.J.Eq. 497, 9 A.2d 783 (1939)*; but see, Binns v. Vick,* 260 Ark. 111, 538 S.W.2d 283 (1976). "The term 'relatives' is construed to mean heirs in order to avoid uncertainty. The trustee can select a relative who is not an heir, but if the trustee fails to make a selection, the property passes to the heirs in the proportions established by law." WILLIAM M. MCGOVERN, JR., SHELDON F. KURTZ & JAN ELLEN REIN, WILLS, TRUSTS, AND ESTATES § 8.5 (Hornbook 1988).

    On the term "family," see, Garner v. Andreasen, 96 Idaho 306, 527 P.2d 1264 (1974)*; McLendon v. Priest,* 259 Ga. 59, 376 S.E.2d 679 (1989)*;* LEWIS B. SIMES & ALLEN F. SMITH, THE LAW OF FUTURE INTERESTS § 726 (2d ed. 1956); M. Minow, "*Redefining Families: Who's In and Who's Out?,*" 62 Colorado L. Rev. 269 (1991); and Note, 154 A.L.R. 1411 (1945)."

be permissible if the trustee has discretion to choose freely among members, so long as the trustee can tell who the permissible members are and who are not permissible members. Thus, two things can save a questionable class: either discretion in the trustee to choose among a broad but distinct class or reference to some independent criteria, like the state's intestacy statute or 401(c)(3) charitable status.

A second common problem arises when the settlor tells the trustee orally who she wants to be benefitted by the trust, but does not identify the people in the trust instrument. This type of *semi-secret* trust will often fail if there is not clear and convincing evidence of the identity of the beneficiaries. This way, the benefiticaries know and the trustee knows who the settlor intends to benefit. *See, Olliffe v. Wells*, 130 Mass. 221 (1881) (decedent left a will giving everything to the Rev. Eleazer M.P. Wells "to distribdistribute the same in such manner as in his discretion shall appear best calculated to carry out wishes which I have expressed to him or may express to him" and the court voided the gift to Wells because it was clear that a trust was intended, not an outright gift to Wells, but that without guidance on the beneficiaries the trust had to fail.) The trustee and the court need to know the identity of the beneficiaries so they can know who has standing to enforce the trust provisions.

Sometimes a settlor gives a trustee broad discretion to benefit a variety of people and courts will uphold the trust because the trustee's discretion is so broad as to include doing nothing, in which case the property passes by default outside the trust to intestate heirs or other beneficiaries. For instance, Marilyn Monroe gave her trustee sole discretion to distribute her personal effects and clothing "among my friends, colleagues and those to whom I am devoted." There was no claim that the trustee had been told in secret who the beneficiaries should be; rather, the trustee was to simply exercise his discretion.[67] If the trustee failed to distribute the items accordingly, they would pass back into the residue of her estate. Most importantly, no friend or colleague could complain if the trustee did not distribute the clothing to him or her. So long as it could be determined that anyone who received personal effects or clothing qualified as a colleague or friend, the trustee had not breached his trust.

A third common problem arises when the settlor establishes a trust for a specific purpose but with no particular beneficiaries at all, or beneficiaries who are dead. Leona Helmsley, the famous billionaire hotelier, left $3 million in trust so the trustees could acid wash and steam clean the Helmsley Mausoleum, that held her husband's and her remains. There are no ascertainable beneficiaries but courts, following the Restatement 1st and 2nd of Trusts, have found these *honorary* trusts to be valid if the purpose is clearly identifiable. The UTC provides for honorary trusts in limited circumstances.[68]

---

[67] *See*, Alyssa A. DiRusso, *He Says, She Asks: Gender, Language, and the Law of Precatory Words in Wills*, 22 Wisc. Women's L.J. 1, 1–3 (2007). DiRusso argues that because women tend to speak in terms that are more likely to be interpreted as precatory, courts should rethink their distinction between conditions and precatory language.

[68] *See also*, Statutory Note to Restatement 3d of Property, § 3.8.

UTC § 409. Noncharitable Trust without Ascertainable Beneficiary.

Except as otherwise provided in Section 408 or by another statute, the following rules apply:

(1) A trust may be created for a noncharitable purpose without a definite or definitely ascertainable beneficiary or for a noncharitable but otherwise valid purpose to be selected by the trustee. The trust may not be enforced for more than [21] years.

(2) A trust authorized by this section may be enforced by a person appointed in the terms of the trust or, if no person is so appointed, by a person appointed by the court.

(3) Property of a trust authorized by this section may be applied only to its intended use, except to the extent the court determines that the value of the trust property exceeds the amount required for the intended use. Except as otherwise provided in the terms of the trust, property not required for the intended use must be distributed to the settlor, if then living, otherwise to the settlor's successors in interest.

Honorary trusts have become more common as courts have recognized that valuable activities can be performed if they ease up on the strict requirement of ascertainable beneficiaries. Most notably, people often want to make provisions that don't qualify as full-blown charitable trusts, but which have beneficial outcomes. For instance, a bequest to an executor to use $500 to plant a tree in the local town park, or to place a bench on a favored overlook is not a charitable trust.[69] But because the beneficiaries are the general public, and there is no way to ascertain who should be able to enforce the trust, a court may determine that there is no trust. On the other hand, it is quite simple to determine whether the trustee has actually complied with the request. Thus, many states have codified common law rules on honorary trusts that permit them to stand subject to two limitations: 1) they can only survive for 21 years (the minimum period under the rule against perpetuities), and 2) so long as the purpose is valid and the trustee agrees to undertake the commission. A trust to acid-wash one's mausoleum is somewhat beneficial (it employs people and keeps mausoleums and cemeteries tidy), it is relatively easy to determine if the trust has been carried out and, after 21 years, the trust must end.

One important subset of honorary trusts, and a fourth common problem, is when a settlor leaves money in trust for their pets. Since animals cannot enforce the terms of a trust, they cannot be deemed ascertainable beneficiaries. Further, since the people who are providing the care are being reimbursed, they are simply providing a service for valuable consideration and are not the direct beneficiaries. An early case on pet trusts, *In re Searights's Estate*,[70] dealt with a trust of $1,000 given to the decedent's executor to pay his neighbor, Florence Hand, $.75 per day for the care of his dog Trixie. The court held that because the purpose of the trust was definite and neither illegal nor capricious, the trust would be deemed valid as an *honorary trust* that could be sustained so long as the trustee was willing to carry out the duties. The court then went on to discuss the applicability of the Rule Against Perpetuities to this trust and held that

---

[69]   We discuss charitable trusts in greater detail in Chapter 9. Charitable gifts are strictly construed and unless trusts serve clear educational, religious, charitable, or humane purposes they won't count as charitable trusts.

[70]   95 N.E.2d 779 (Ohio Ct.App. 1950).

although many honorary trusts might be invalid under the RAP because there is no definite ending date, this trust could stand because the trust itself would run out of funds at the rate of $.75 per day before the perpetuities period ended.

Besides wanting her mausoleum acid washed, Leona Helmsley also left a whopping $12 million in trust for the benefit of her Maltese poodle, Trouble. It turns out, however, that the income from the trust was far more than necessary to cover Trouble's expenses, including the maintenance on his New York penthouse and the salary of his caretakers. It also more than covered the security costs needed when Trouble started getting death threats from people outraged at the bequest.[71] The Trouble Trust was held to be valid, but $10 million was returned to Helmsley's estate because it wasn't needed to provide for the dog, even in its very lavish lifestyle.

Most states, following the lead of the Restatement 1st and 2nd of Trusts, validate trusts for pets as honorary trusts, or have enacted statutes that permit a trust for a pet animal. The UTC provides for pet trusts but with some limitations.

UTC § 408. Trust for Care of Animal

(a) A trust may be created to provide for the care of an animal alive during the settlor's lifetime. The trust terminates upon the death of the animal or, if the trust was created to provide for the care of more than one animal alive during the settlor's lifetime, upon the death of the last surviving animal.

(b) A trust authorized by this section may be enforced by a person appointed in the terms of the trust or, if no person is so appointed, by a person appointed by the court. A person having an interest in the welfare of the animal may request the court to appoint a person to enforce the trust or to remove a person appointed.

(c) Property of a trust authorized by this section may be applied only to its intended use, except to the extent the court determines that the value of the trust property exceeds the amount required for the intended use. Except as otherwise provided in the terms of the trust, property not required for the intended use must be distributed to the settlor, if then living, otherwise to the settlor's successors in interest.

So does the UPC.

UPC § 2–907. Honorary Trusts; Trusts for Pets.

(a) [Honorary Trust.] Subject to subsection (c), if (i) a trust is for a specific lawful noncharitable purpose or for lawful noncharitable purposes to be selected by the trustee and (ii) there is no definite or definitely ascertainable beneficiary designated, the trust may be performed by the trustee for [21] years but no longer, whether or not the terms of the trust contemplate a longer duration.

(b) [Trust for Pets.] Subject to this subsection and subsection (c), a trust for the care of a designated domestic or pet animal is valid. The trust terminates when no living animal is covered by the trust. A governing instrument must be liberally construed to bring the transfer within this subsection, to presume against the merely precato-

---

[71]   *See,* Jeffrey Toobin, *Rich Bitch: The Legal Battle Over Trust Funds for Pets,* New Yorker, Sept. 29, 2008, at 38. *See also,* Adam J. Hirsch, *Trusts for Purposes: Policy, Ambiguity, and Anomaly in the Uniform Laws,* 26 Fla.St.U.L. Rev. 93 (1999).

ry or honorary nature of the disposition, and to carry out the general intent of the transferor. Extrinsic evidence is admissible in determining the transferor's intent.

(c) [Additional Provisions Applicable to Honorary Trusts and Trusts for Pets.] In addition to the provisions of subsection (a) or (b), a trust covered by either of those subsections is subject to the following provisions:

(1) Except as expressly provided otherwise in the trust instrument, no portion of the principal or income may be converted to the use of the trustee or to any use other than for the trust's purposes or for the benefit of a covered animal.

(2) Upon termination, the trustee shall transfer the unexpended trust property in the following order:

(i) as directed in the trust instrument;

(ii) if the trust was created in a nonresiduary clause in the transferor's will or in a codicil to the transferor's will, under the residuary clause in the transferor's will; and

(iii) if no taker is produced by the application of subparagraph (i) or (ii), to the transferor's heirs under Section 2–711.

(3) For the purposes of Section 2–707, the residuary clause is treated as creating a future interest under the terms of a trust.

(4) The intended use of the principal or income can be enforced by an individual designated for that purpose in the trust instrument or, if none, by an individual appointed by a court upon application to it by an individual.

(5) Except as ordered by the Court or required by the trust instrument, no filing, report, registration, periodic accounting, separate maintenance of funds, appointment, or fee is required by reason of the existence of the fiduciary relationship of the trustee.

(6) A Court may reduce the amount of the property transferred, if it determines that that amount substantially exceeds the amount required for the intended use. The amount of the reduction, if any, passes as unexpended trust property under subsection (c)(2).

(7) If no trustee is designated or no designated trustee is willing or able to serve, a Court shall name a trustee. A Court may order the transfer of the property to another trustee, if required to assure that the intended use is carried out and if no successor trustee is designated in the trust instrument or if no designated successor trustee agrees to serve or is able to serve. A Court may also make such other orders and determinations as shall be advisable to carry out the intent of the transferor and the purpose of this section.]

How do the UPC and UTC pet trust provisions deal with the possibility that some animals, like parrots and tortoises, live as long as, or longer than, humans? Which is the better approach? As you can imagine, many animal lovers would like to use pet trusts to provide for endangered animals, preservation of animal habitats, and other environmental purposes. But pet trusts are not the appropriate mechanism; the better method is a charitable trust, discussed later in Chapter 9. Can you see why the pet trust is unlikely to accomplish the grand purposes that animal lovers might have?

RAP Trap: The Pet Trust

As the Court in *Searight's Estate* noted, some animals can live longer than 21 years which, as you should remember from your first-year Property class, is the default period during which contingent future interests are allowed to remain un-vested in the absence of measuring lives. Since Fido and Boots can't be measuring lives, trusts established for the care of animals must either terminate within 21 years or the remainder interest will be void. You might be thinking, "so what, so long as the present interest in the trustee is valid, the trust should be able to exist until the pet's death, leaving a reversion in the settlor's estate?" A gift of Blackacre "to A so long as my dog Rover is alive, remainder to my surviving issue" violates the RAP, but it's the remainder interest to the surviving issue that causes the problem, not the indefiniteness of the interest based on Rover's life. Why isn't the same thing true of pet trusts? The problem lies in the nature of a trust. Because trusts split legal and equitable title, and impose strict fiduciary limitations on the property, the entire trust may be deemed void if the remainder violates the RAP. We must know for sure that the trust will end within the perpetuities period for the trust to be valid at all. Thus, a remainder interest that violates the RAP will cause the entire trust to fail, even though that would not happen in the case of a legal interest based on Rover's life. And even though few dogs and cats have ever lived beyond age 21, the possibility remains, like the fertile octogenarian, that an animal could outlive the perpetuities period. Consequently, states have generally had to legislate to allow pet trusts at all. On the other hand, all pets will die, just like all people, so we could treat the remainder as an indefeasibly vested remainder that is not subject to the RAP at all. But if we did that, then we might be headed down the slippery slope of basing the longevity of a trust on the lifetime of a sequoia or a fruit fly.

Courts have every incentive to validate trusts that are ambiguous as to benefi-ciaries if the alternative is intestacy or an escheat to the state. But, the important lesson about these trust requirements is that drafters must be as clear as possible, without being so near-sighted as to lose sight of possible non-traditional takers. Thus, step-children, posthumously born children, or descendants of pre-deceased children should not be excluded in a trust for *children* if the settlor would have wanted to include a wider class of beneficiaries. Your job is to anticipate the whole panoply of possible beneficiaries and carefully draft your client's trust to include all those she would want to include and exclude those she wants to exclude, leaving open the possibility of new members of the group while minimizing the likelihood of litigation from those who feel unjustly excluded.

Query: Do you think it is a good policy to allow a private express trust without an ascertainable beneficiary to be enforced? Do you think that the ultimate goal of the trust is important in making this decision? What should courts do about questionable trusts, or bequests, that don't have valuable public benefits?

In December, 2011, Georgia Lee Dvorak died, leaving her $1.3 million estate to a number of animal charities. In her will, however, she directed that any cat she owned at her death be euthanized. Do the Trustees have any say in whether or not they must see that Georgia's cat is actually eu-thanized? Consider this article from the Chicago Tribune:

"Though there was a will, Fifth Third found a way to save Boots"[72]

Boots, an 11-year-old stray cat adopted by the testatrix, Georgia Lee Dvorak, was to be painlessly euthanized, according to Dvorak's will. But a public administrator for Cook County, in charge of administering estates for people who die with no next of kin, contacted Fifth Third Bank, Dvorak's trustee, and encouraged the Bank to seek an alternative disposition of Boots. Fifth Third's director of personal trust, Jeffrey Schmidt, who has written about pet trusts, went to court to petition the probate judge for an order allowing Boots to be placed in a no-kill shelter and Judge Susan Coleman agreed. Boots was to be placed in the *Cats are Purrsons Too* shelter, but only on condition that the shelter be endowed $2000 to pay for Boots' care. Judge Coleman agreed to apply $1000 of Dvorak's nearly $1.4 million estate for the endowment on condition that Fifth Third donate the other $1000 from its trustee fees.

Lawyers for Fifth Third from Spain, Spain & Varnet pled that "It would violate public policy to euthanize a healthy housecat where an appropriate shelter has been identified." They also identified precedent in Pennsylvania refusing to comply with a will directing that any dog the decedent had at his death be destroyed, and a Vermont precedent refusing to honor a bequest that a testator's horses be "shot by the Royal Canadian Mounted Police and then burned."

PROBLEMS

Consider the following situations. Do you see any potential problems in the beneficiary designations? If so, how could the language be clarified?

4.22. "A trust to be equally distributed to all of the people who have Friended me on Facebook at my death."

4.23. "A trust to be equally distributed to my siblings, except those who say nasty things about me at my funeral."

4.24. "5% of the annual trust income to be distributed to my pets, for their comfort, upkeep, care and housing."

4.25. "10% of the annual trust income to be used to host a party each year to celebrate our lives."

d. Intent

As with wills, trusts are not valid if the settlor does not *intend* to create a trust. Now, most people who want to create a trust know to go to a lawyer and they expect to come home with a neatly executed document titled "John Smith's Living Trust." Even better, they will fund the trust by re-titling property in the name of the trustee and refer to their trust in other documents. They will also keep it in a safe deposit box or, other safe place, and they won't just jot down notes or changes. Instead, they will execute amendments to the trust, when necessary, following all the usual formalities.

---

[72] Becky Yerak, Chicago Tribune (April 04, 2012), *available at*: http://articles.chicago tribune.com/2012–04–04/business/chi–cat–survives–death–sentence–in–owners–will–after– fifth–third–bank–intervenes–20120404_1_fifth–third–bank

But as you will quickly learn, there are always clients who do things differently. Obviously, a court will not find a trust if there was no intent to create a trust. But what expression of intent is sufficient?

Consider whether you think a trust was intended in the following cases and, if so, whether other infirmities should void the gift or whether the intent to create a trust should prevail despite problems with certain aspects of the gift (think too about whether the UTC or Restatement provisions would change the outcome in any of these cases):

Colton v. Colton

127 U.S. 300 (1888)

Decedent, David Colton, left a will stating: I give and bequeath to my said wife, Ellen M. Colton, all of the estate, real and personal, of which I shall die seized or possessed or entitled to. I recommend to her the care and protection of my mother and sister, and request her to make such gift and provision for them as in her judgment will be best. When Ellen Colton refused to make any provision for her sister-in-law and mother-in-law, they sued, arguing that they were entitled to some property under the decedent's will. The Court agreed, finding that a trust was intended and ordering Ellen to make a permanent provision for them that was suitable and sufficient for their care and protection. The Court further noted that the use of the term "request" did not defeat the evidence of a trust; that an expression of desire or wish will often be equivalent to a positive direction, where that is the evident purpose and meaning of the testator.

Query: Even if Colton intended to impose a mandatory trust on his wife, can a court reasonably enforce it without knowing what property, or how much, to subject to the trust? Why do you think the U.S. Supreme Court was involved in this case? Do you think the case would have come out the same way in 2012? The Court also distinguished between a peremptory command in a will that would create a trust, and precatory language that would not. Which do you think was the testator's intent?

Clark v. Campbell

133 A. 166 (N.H. 1926)

Decedent, Charles Cummings, left a will stating: *I therefore give and bequeath to my trustees all my property . . . aforesaid in trust to make disposal by the way of a memento from myself, of such articles to such of my friends as they, my trustees, shall select.* The court struck down the trust for lack of ascertainable beneficiaries. Although it was clear the decedent intended to create a trust, the class of "friends" was too undefined for the trustees to be properly restrained.

Query: Could the court have held this to be a general power of appointment? Could the court have allowed this as an honorary trust? How would the outcomes differ under the various alternative resolutions?

Moss v. Axford

246 Mich. 288 (Mich. 1929)

Decedent, Caroline Girard, left a will stating: *I give, devise, and bequeath all the rest, residue and remainder of my property to Henry W. Axford with the instruction to pay the same to the person who has given me the best care in my declining years and who in his opinion is the most worthy of my said property.* The court upheld the trust because the decedent had *prescribed a rule whereby his beneficiary could be identified with certainty.* Furthermore, any trustee could perform the trust by determining the limited class of people who cared for the decedent in her final years.

Query: Why does this language create a trust? If the executor is told to distribute property to one named beneficiary and one unnamed beneficiary, what's the difference between the two? Is it plausible to suppose the trustee can determine who gave the "best care"?

Spicer v. Wright

211 S.E.2d 79 (Va. 1975)

Decedent, Leila Wilson Spicer, left a will stating: *My estate of every kind and description, personal, real estate, etc., I give to my sister, Anne Beecher Wilson to be disposed of as already agreed between us.* The court found no trust to have been created because of the indefiniteness of the purpose and beneficiaries. Then the court had to decide whether the decedent intended a trust, that then failed, resulting in intestacy, or whether the decedent intended an outright gift to her sister. The court determined: *that the language Mrs. Spicer employed is precatory, that the extrinsic evidence is insufficient to render that language imperative or to establish a testamentary intent to impose a legal obligation to make a particular disposition of property, that no express trust was intended or created, and that the language constitutes an absolute testamentary grant to Miss Wilson.*

Query: Why did the court let the sister keep the property instead of having the gift fail? Note that without the imposition of the trust, the sister can do what she wants with the property. The principal reason courts can't validate semi-secret trusts is that they cannot know for sure if the trustee has acted according to the settlor's commands, since the latter are secret. And trusts require that element of enforceability. If the court can't find the beneficiaries who can enforce the trust? Is it better to let the trustee keep the property and hope he or she acts honorably and fulfills whatever secret agreement the parties had, or have the gift fail and pass to someone entirely different (like an intestate heir) who has no obligation, moral or otherwise, to use the property as the testator wished and for whom the gift is essentially a windfall?

Goodman v. Goodman

907 P.2d 290 (Wash. 1995)

The decedent, Clive Goodman, transferred his major asset, Ozzie's East Tavern, to his mother, Gladys Goodman a year before he died. Almost immediately, Gladys sold the tavern and deposited the proceeds of the sale in her bank account. Clive had 4 minor children at the time of his death. Eight years after Clive's death, his children requested money from their grandmother out of the sale of the tavern but she refused. They then brought suit alleging that Clive had intended that Gladys hold the property in trust for the benefit of his children, and a jury agreed. The court found that an express trust was intended and that although the exact terms of the trust were unstated, Gladys had a duty to use the property for the benefit of her grandchildren, and not herself.

Query: Would this case have come out the same way if the decedent had transferred the tavern to his wife instead of his mother and the wife refused to use the property for the benefit of the children? What about the statute of frauds in this case? There was no written agreement about the transfer of the real estate; thus, pursuant to the statute of frauds no trust can be established. How do you think the court got around that issue?

In re Est. of Bolinger

943 P.2d 981 (Mont. 1997)

Decedent, Harry Albert Bolinger, III, left a will giving everything to his father, or if his father predeceased him, to his father's wife, his stepmother. In his will, he explained: *I intentionally give nothing to my three children, . . . for the reason that I feel confident that any property which either my father or my step-mother . . . receive from my estate will be used in the best interests of my said children as my said beneficiaries may determine in their exclusive discretion.* The trial court found an express trust was created for the benefit of decedent's children. The Montana Supreme Court reversed, finding that the decedent left an outright gift to his father and stepmother. The court explained: *there was not the sort of "unmistakable," "clear," "convincing," "explicit," "unequivocal" and "practically free from doubt" evidence that would support a legal conclusion that Decedent clearly and directly expressed his intention to create an express trust in favor of the children through his use of precatory language in the Fifth paragraph of his will.* The dissent argued that the language that the property be used in the best interests of the children was "peremptory" and not "precatory."

Query: The decedent's father predeceased him and thus his entire estate passed to his step-mother who refused to honor the trust language, thereby entirely disinheriting his three children. It was argued by the children that he had intended to impose a trust on the property because the children were minors and he was trying to avoid having his ex-wife, the children's mother, have control over the property. Was this a botched will, did he simply not judge his step-mother's character correctly, or did the court make the right decision?

Dunnewind v. Cook

697 N.E.2d 485 (Ind.App. 1998)

Decedent, Florence Cook, learning that she had only a few months to live, placed all of her property in trust (family home, all household goods, and personal property) for the benefit for her husband for life, remainder to her children by a previous marriage. The decedent had been married nearly 25 years at her death to her second husband. The sole purpose for creating the trust was to prevent her husband from exercising his rights to an elective share in his wife's estate, and to guarantee that all the real and personal property would ultimately pass to her children. When the husband sued to set aside the trust and to determine the assets of his wife's estate for purposes of determining his elective share, the trial court ruled that the trust assets would be available for the husband's elective share. On appeal, the court affirmed, noting that although the elective share can only be taken against property that passes by descent or devise, and not against property in a valid *inter vivos* irrevocable trust, there are exceptions to that rule: namely, when the sole purpose is to deny a surviving spouse an elective share. The court noted that this is especially true where, as in this case, the trust itself was administered to allow the settlor to enjoy the full benefits of the property and thus was administered to take effect upon the settlor's death (like a testamentary trust) and did not seem to constrain the settlor during life (like an *inter vivos* trust would).

Query: Here the testator clearly intended to create an express *inter vivos* trust, and she did so, re-titling all her property in the name of the trust. The court revoked the trust on a portion of the property, however, because her intent in creating the trust was to avoid a legal obligation to provide for her husband. The court found the trust to be fraudulent and therefore voided it with regard to the property the husband was legally entitled to take. Although we haven't discussed the elective share yet, many states have elective share statutes that allow a surviving spouse access to property held in an *inter vivos* trust so that spouses cannot use trusts to disinherit their spouses. Other states, like Indiana, will look behind the intent of the settlor to determine if the trust is fraudulent or illusory. Which is the better rule do you think?

Foster v. Foster

682 S.E.2d 312 (S.C. App. 2009)

Harvey Foster, age 83, executed a deed for his home transferring it to his daughter, Jean Burbage, *as trustee*, while reserving a life estate for himself. He also gave Burbage a power of attorney to handle his financial affairs. After Foster moved out of an assisted living facility that he had resided in temporarily, and in with his new wife, he had a change of heart and sued to void the deed and regain $78,000 his daughter had transferred out of his various accounts. The trial court, finding no trust existed, voided the deed. On appeal, Foster's children claimed that the signed deed and Foster's will, which left his home to his children, were enough evidence to prove a trust was created. The Court of Appeals disagreed, however, and affirmed the trial court explaining: *To prove the existence of a trust, the following elements must be shown: (1) a declaration creating the trust, (2) a trust res, and (3) designated beneficiaries. Furthermore, the trust declaration must be in writing when the trust property includes realty. The Appellants have not produced a written declaration creating a trust, and Burbage testified she was not aware of any trust Foster created. Moreover, while the Appellants contend they are the beneficiaries of the trust, they failed to present a trust document or any other evidence to support their position. Because no written trust document was presented to the court, we do not believe a trust existed. Therefore, Burbage was not a trustee. Without a trustee, the deed is void because it designates a grantee that does not exist.*

Query: Do you think the testator had the requisite intent at the time he executed the deed transferring the home to his daughter? If his change of heart occurred after he got out of the nursing home and found a new wife, should he be able to revoke the deed? What would a lawyer have done had Foster gone to a lawyer when he initially transferred the house to his daughter? What would a lawyer have done when he changed his mind? Is the court using the statute of frauds to give Foster his home back because, had he done things right, it should have been held in a revocable trust and he could have revoked the transfer anyway?

This last case shows the problem of trying to avoid probate by making an *inter vivos* transfer to a trust without complying with all the legal requirements for trust creation. Do-it-yourself quickie trusts aren't really trusts; they can be set aside if the trust settlor or others with an interest in the property change their minds. Should the court have voided this trust or used the will and deed to imply a trust for the benefit of Foster and his children? Should the court have been more probing on questions of undue influence, by both Foster's children and his new wife? Are you suspicious of the motives of any of the parties in this case? What should a court do when people don't go to lawyers and do things right?

These cases illustrate a number of important trust rules that you need to master before drafting trusts for clients. **First**, the settlor must truly intend to impose a trust obligation on the trustee—mere precatory language or a desire that the recipient use the property in a particular way will not give rise to a legally-binding trust obligation. **Second**, even if the settlor intends to create a trust, doing so for illegal or fraudulent reasons, like avoiding a spouse's elective share, will be likely to lead a court to void the trust. **Third**, once a trust is created, the trustee has obligations and limitations on her ability to manage the property, and if the settlor of a self-settled trust does not take seriously the trustee duties, the court may void the trust and whatever benefits the settlor sought will be lost. **Fourth**, if a court voids a trust, it then has to decide what to do with the purported gift—should it find that the grantor made an irrevocable outright gift? Or should it find that the gift was void and lapses, usually to pass by intestacy?

The use of resulting or constructive trusts, which are equitable remedies courts use to fix some of the problems grantors create for themselves, are explained at the end of this section. Remember that any gift to "A for a particular purpose" may be interpreted to be an outright gift to A, it may be deemed a transfer into trust to A as trustee obligated to comply with the purpose, or it may be deemed an ineffective transfer into trust and therefore void, resulting in no transfer at all to A. In the latter case the property will transfer to someone else, like a residual beneficiary or an intestate heir for whom the transfer may be a windfall. Complying with the trust formalities and understanding the requisite elements of a trust, therefore, are crucial for avoiding the problem of ineffective transfers.

4. REVOCABILITY—THE PRESENT TRANSFER TEST

What happens when a settlor establishes a trust for the benefit of himself for life and other, successor beneficiaries after his death, names himself the trustee, and retains the power to completely revoke the trust? In the absence of a statute, in order to qualify as an *inter vivos* trust there must be a present transfer of a property interest to a beneficiary. When no property interest passes during the life of the settlor, the trust is testamentary and must be executed with the will formalities. But what is this property interest that must pass during the life of the settlor? It is an equitable contingent remainder that can be defeated simply by the trustee revoking the trust. In other words, the settlor has declared himself trustee over his own property for his benefit during his lifetime, and IF he doesn't revoke the trust, which he can do at any time, the property will pass to the holder of the equitable contingent remainder interest upon the settlor's death. Boy that sure sounds like a testamentary transfer. If the trust can be revoked at any time, it looks an awful lot like a will, and beneficiaries have no recognizable property interests in property devised by a will until the death of the testator precisely because the will is revocable at any time. To validate the revocable trust, therefore, the property interest passing to the beneficiary must be greater than the mere expectancy of a will bequest.

Exactly how big must the property stick be (will a mere toothpick count) in the case of a revocable *inter vivos* trust to impose sufficient restrictions on the trustee to give the trustee the active duties required to form a trust? That is the fundamental question that had to be resolved if the revocable *inter vivos* trust was going to be given legal effect. The case of *Farkas v. Williams* is one of the most important early cases recognizing the validity of such trusts based on the *present transfer* to a beneficiary of a small sliver of property whose interest could be revoked at any time, and which the beneficiary didn't even know existed. Since the 1970s, the revocable, or *living* trust has become ubiquitous, usually through legislation allowing it to be given legal effect.

Farkas v. Williams

5 Ill.2d 417 (Ill. 1955)

■ Hershey, Justice.

Albert B. Farkas died intestate at the age of sixty-seven years, a resident of Chicago, leaving as his only heirs-at-law brothers, sisters, a nephew and a niece. Although retired at the time of his death, he had for many years practiced veterinary medicine and operated a veterinarian establishment in Chicago. During a considerable portion of that time, he employed the defendant [Richard] Williams, who was not related to him.

On four occasions (December 8, 1948; February 7, 1949; February 14, 1950; and March 1, 1950) Farkas purchased stock of Investors Mutual, Inc. At the time of each purchase he executed a written application to Investors Mutual, Inc., instructing them to issue the stock in his name 'as trustee for Richard J. Williams.' Investors Mutual, Inc., by its agent, accepted each of these applications in writing by signature on the face of the application. Coincident with the execution of these applications, Farkas signed separate declarations of trust, all of which were identical except as to dates. The terms of said trust instruments are as follows:

'Declaration of Trust—Revocable. I, the undersigned, having purchased or declared my intention to purchase certain shares of capital stock of Investors Mutual, Inc. (the Company), and having directed that the certificate for said stock be issued in my name as trustee for Richard J. Williams as beneficiary, under this Declaration of Trust Do

Hereby Declare that the terms and conditions upon which I shall hold said stock in trust and any additional stock resulting from reinvestments of cash dividends upon such original or additional shares are as follows:

'(1) During my lifetime all cash dividends are to be paid to me individually for my own personal account and use; . . .

'(2) Upon my death the title to any stock subject hereto and the right to any subsequent payments or distributions shall be vested absolutely in the beneficiary. . . .

'(3) During my lifetime I reserve the right, as trustee, to vote, sell, redeem, exchange or otherwise deal in or with the stock subject hereto, but upon any sale or redemption of said stock or any part thereof, the trust hereby declared shall terminate as to the stock sold or redeemed, and I shall be entitled to retain the proceeds of sale or redemption for my own personal account and use.

'(4) I reserve the right at any time to change the beneficiary or revoke this trust, but it is understood that no change of beneficiary and no revocation of this trust except by death of the beneficiary, shall be effective as to the Company for any purpose unless and until written notice thereof in such form as the Company shall prescribe is delivered to the Company at Minneapolis, Minnesota. The decease of the beneficiary before my death shall operate as a revocation of this trust.

'(5) In the event this trust shall be revoked or otherwise terminated, said stock and all rights and privileges thereunder shall belong to and be exercised by me in my individual capacity. . . .

The applications and declarations of trust were delivered to Investors Mutual, Inc., and held by the company until Farkas's death. The stock certificates were issued in the name of Farkas as 'trustee for Richard J. Williams' and were discovered in a safety-deposit box of Farkas after his death, along with other securities, some of which were in the name of Williams alone.

The sole question presented on this appeal is whether the instruments entitled 'Declaration of Trust—Revocable' and executed by Farkas created valid inter vivos trusts of the stock of Investors Mutual, Inc. The plaintiffs [executors of Farkas' estate] contend that said stock is free and clear from any trust or beneficial interest in the defendant Williams, for the reason that said purported trust instruments were attempted testamentary dispositions and invalid for want of compliance with the statute on wills. The defendants, on the other hand, insist that said instruments created valid inter vivos trusts and were not testamentary in character.

It is conceded that the instruments were not executed in such a way as to satisfy the requirements of the statute on wills; hence, our inquiry is limited to whether said trust instruments created valid inter vivos trusts effective to give the purported beneficiary, Williams, title to the stock in question after the death of the settlor–trustee, Farkas. To make this determination we must consider: (1) whether upon execution of the so-called trust instruments defendant Williams acquired an interest in the subject matter of the trusts, the stock of defendant Investors Mutual, Inc., (2) whether Farkas, as settlor–trustee, retained such control over the subject matter of the trusts as to render said trust instruments attempted testamentary dispositions.

First, upon execution of these trust instruments did defendant Williams presently acquire an interest in the subject matter of the intended trusts? If no interest passed to Williams before the death of Farkas, the intended trusts are testamentary and hence invalid for failure to comply with the statute on wills. But considering the terms of these instruments we believe Farkas did intend to presently give Williams an interest in the property referred to. For it may be said, at the very least, that upon his executing one of these instruments, he showed an intention to presently part with some of the incidents of ownership in the stock. Immediately after the execution of each of these instruments, he could not deal with the stock therein referred to the same as if he owned the property absolutely, but only in accordance with the terms of the instrument. He purported to set himself up as trustee of the stock for the benefit of Williams, and the stock was registered in his name as trustee for Williams. Thus assuming to act as trustee, he is held to have intended to take on those obligations which are expressly set out in the instrument, as well as those fiduciary obligations implied by law. In addition, he manifested an intention to bind himself to having this property pass upon his death to Williams, unless he changed the beneficiary or revoked the trust, and then such change of beneficiary or revocation was not to be effective as to Investors Mutual, Inc., unless and until written notice thereof in such form as the company prescribed was delivered to them at Minneapolis, Minnesota. An absolute owner can dispose of his property, either in his lifetime or by will, in any way he sees fit without notifying or securing approval from anyone and without being held to the duties of a fiduciary in so doing.

It seems to follow that what incidents of ownership Farkas intended to relinquish, in a sense he intended Williams to acquire. That is, Williams was to be the beneficiary to whom Farkas was to be obligated, and unless Farkas revoked the instrument in the manner therein set out or the instrument was otherwise terminated in a manner therein provided for, upon Farkas's death Williams was to become absolute owner of the trust property. It is difficult to name this interest of Williams, nor is there any reason for so doing so long as it passed to him immediately upon the creation of the trust. As stated in 4 Powell, The Law of Real Property, at page 87: 'Interests of beneficiaries of private express trusts run the gamut from valuable substantialities to evanescent hopes. Such a beneficiary may have any one of an almost infinite variety of the possible aggregates of rights, privileges, powers and immunities.'

[The court then noted that the provision revoking the beneficiary designation if Williams predeceased Farkas was not enough to turn the trust interest into a mere expectancy like that under a will. It was simply another contingency, like the settlor's power to revoke, that did not reduce the property right to nothing.

The court then went on to discuss whether the settlor retained such power over the property as to render the transfer illusory. Noting the settlor's power to revoke as well as to benefit from the property during life, the court explained:]

It is well established that the retention by the settlor of the power to revoke, even when coupled with the reservation of a life interest in the trust property, does not render the trust inoperative for want of execution as a will. Only when it is thought that there are additional reservations present of such a substantial nature as to amount to the retention of full ownership is a court likely to invalidate an inter vivos trust by reason of its not being executed as a will. . . .   We conclude therefore, in accordance with the great weight of authority, said powers which Farkas reserved to himself as settlor were not such as to render the intended trusts invalid as attempted testamentary dispositions.

A more difficult problem is posed, however, by the fact that Farkas is also trustee, and as such, is empowered to vote, sell, redeem, exchange and otherwise deal in and with the subject matter of the trusts.

That a settlor may create a trust of personal property whereby he names himself as trustee and acts as such for the beneficiary is clear. . . .   In the instant case the plaintiffs contend that Farkas, as settlor–trustee, retained complete control and dominion over the securities for his own benefit during his lifetime. It is argued that he had the power to deal with the property as he liked so long as he lived and owed no enforceable duties of any kind to Williams as beneficiary. . . .

That the retention of the power by Farkas as trustee to sell or redeem the stock and keep the proceeds for his own use should not render these trust instruments testamentary in character becomes more evident upon analyzing the real import and significance of the powers to revoke and to amend the trust, the reservation of which the courts uniformly hold does not invalidate an inter vivos trust.

It is obvious that a settlor with the power to revoke and to amend the trust at any time is, for all practical purpose, in a position to exert considerable control over the trustee regarding the administration of the trust. For anything believed to be inimicable to his best interests can be thwarted or prevented by simply revoking the trust or amending it in such a way as to conform to his wishes. . . .   Even though no actual termination of the trust is effectuated, however, it could hardly be questioned but that the mere existence of this power in the settlor is sufficient to enable his influence to be felt in a practical way in the administration of the trust. . . .

In the case at bar, the power of Farkas to vote, sell, redeem, exchange or otherwise deal in the stock was reserved to him as trustee, and it was only upon sale or redemption that he was entitled to keep the proceeds for his own use. Thus, the control reserved is not as great as in those cases where said power is reserved to the owner as settlor. For as trustee he must so conduct himself in accordance with standards applicable to trustees generally. It is not a valid objection to this to say that Williams would never question Farkas' conduct, inasmuch as Farkas could then revoke the trust and destroy what interest Williams has. Such a possibility exists in any case where the settlor has the power of revocation. Still, Williams has rights the same as any beneficiary, although it may not be feasible for him to exercise them. Moreover, it is entirely possible that he might in certain situations have a right to hold Farkas' estate liable for breaches of trust committed by Farkas during his lifetime. In this regard, consider what would happen if, without having revoked the trust, Farkas as trustee had given the stock away without receiving any consideration therefor, had pledged the stock improperly for his own personal debt and allowed it to be lost by foreclosure or had exchanged the stock for another security or other worthless property in such manner as to constitute gross impropriety and gross negligence. In such instances, it would seem in accordance with the terms of these instruments that Williams would have had an enforceable claim against Farkas' estate for whatever damage had been suffered. Contrast this with the rights of a legatee or devisee under a will. The testator could waste the property or do anything with it he wished during his lifetime without incurring any liability to those designated by the will to inherit the property. In any event, if Farkas as settlor could reserve the power to sell or otherwise deal with the property and retain the proceeds, which the cases indicate he could, then it necessarily follows that he should have the right to sell or otherwise deal with the property as trustee and retain the proceeds from a sale or redemption without having the instruments rendered invalid as testamentary dispositions.

[The court added that the formality of the documents further supported Farkas' intent to create an enforceable trust and that he was free of fraud and duress.] For the reasons stated, we conclude that these trust declarations executed by Farkas constituted valid inter vivos trusts and were not attempted testamentary dispositions. It must be conceded that they have, in the words of Mr. Justice Holmes in Bromley v. Mitchell, 155 Mass. 509, 30 N.E. 83, a 'Testamentary look.' Moreover, it must be admitted that the line should be drawn somewhere, but after a study of this case we do not believe that point has here been reached.

Reversed and remanded, with directions.

––––––––––

Because of the legal stretching needed to find a present transfer in order to validate revocable trusts, all states have enacted legislation independently validating revocable trusts. As a result, the revocable *inter vivos* trust has become ubiquitous. But despite statutory provisions allowing revocable *inter vivos* trusts to exist, estate planners should be careful to understand that the present transfer test and active fiduciary duties are the underlying legal bases for validating all trusts. If planners move too far away from the basic trust elements they risk having the trust voided if a compelling contestant appears.

The UTC provides explicitly for revocable trusts as follows:

UTC § 601. Capacity of Settlor of Revocable Trust.

The capacity required to create, amend, revoke, or add property to a revocable trust, or to direct the actions of the trustee of a revocable trust, is the same as that required to make a will.

UTC § 602. Revocation or Amendment of Revocable Trust.

(a) Unless the terms of a trust expressly provide that the trust is irrevocable, the settlor may revoke or amend the trust. This subsection does not apply to a trust created under an instrument executed before [the effective date of this [Code]].

(b) If a revocable trust is created or funded by more than one settlor:

(1) to the extent the trust consists of community property, the trust may be revoked by either spouse acting alone but may be amended only by joint action of both spouses;

(2) to the extent the trust consists of property other than community property, each settlor may revoke or amend the trust with regard the portion of the trust property attributable to that settlor's contribution; and

(3) upon the revocation or amendment of the trust by fewer than all of the settlors, the trustee shall promptly notify the other settlors of the revocation or amendment.

(c) The settlor may revoke or amend a revocable trust:

(1) by substantial compliance with a method provided in the terms of the trust; or

(2) if the terms of the trust do not provide a method or the method provided in the terms is not expressly made exclusive, by:

(A) a later will or codicil that expressly refers to the trust or specifically devises property that would otherwise have passed according to the terms of the trust; or

(B) any other method manifesting clear and convincing evidence of the settlor's intent.

(d) Upon revocation of a revocable trust, the trustee shall deliver the trust property as the settlor directs.

(e) A settlor's powers with respect to revocation, amendment, or distribution of trust property may be exercised by an agent under a power of attorney only to the extent expressly authorized by the terms of the trust or the power.

(f) A [conservator] of the settlor or, if no [conservator] has been appointed, a [guardian] of the settlor may exercise a settlor's powers with respect to revocation, amendment, or distribution of trust property only with the approval of the court supervising the [conservatorship] or [guardianship].

(g) A trustee who does not know that a trust has been revoked or amended is not liable to the settlor or settlor's successors in interest for distributions made and other actions taken on the assumption that the trust had not been amended or revoked.

UTC § 603. Settlor's Powers; Powers of Withdrawal.

(a) While a trust is revocable [and the settlor has capacity to revoke the trust], rights of the beneficiaries are subject to the control of, and the duties of the trustee are owed exclusively to, the settlor.

(b) During the period the power may be exercised, the holder of a power of withdrawal has the rights of a settlor of a revocable trust under this section to the extent of the property subject to the power.

PROBLEM

4.26. Tom and Linda create a revocable living trust, naming themselves as Settlors, Trustees and Beneficiaries during their lifetime. In the event that Tom or Linda fail to serve as Trustee while they are both alive (upon disability, for example), their trust names their two beloved daughters, Tina and Jessica to serve as Co-Trustees along with their other parent to manage all trust property for the benefit of Tom and Linda. According to the trust, at the death of both Tom and Linda, all of the remaining property in the trust passes outright to Tina and Jessica, equally.

As Tom and Linda age, Tina and Jessica begin to worry that their future inheritance is being eaten up by their mom and dad's expenses in caring for their sizable house. When confronted, Tom and Linda state that they have no intention of downsizing their home and that they may well spend all of their existing savings on a trip around the world they are planning together. Alarmed, Tina and Jessica decide to sue their parents in order to force conservation of their inheritance since the trust names them as beneficiaries upon their parents' death. What result?

5.   Managing the Property: To Trust or Not to Trust?

In the case of revocable *inter vivos* trusts, settlor/trustees often act as though the property remains fully within their control. But problems can also arise if trust settlors of self-settled revocable trusts are not reasonably careful about maintaining the distinction between trust property and non-trust property. Consider the following case.

Heaps v. Heaps
124 Cal.App.4th 286, (Ct. of App. Ca. 2004)

This case illustrates the sort of unexpected complications that can arise from the so-called "living trusts" which are hawked so aggressively these days. The bottom line here is that the casual use of a living trust as a quickie estate planning device meant that a husband was worth a lot less than his second wife thought he was worth when she married him. Unbeknownst to her, the husband's erstwhile assets had already been tied up for the first wife's children because of an overly broad clause involving how the trust would hold title. As we explain below, the import of that clause is that it meant that removing an asset from the trust required something—anything really—more than just taking title in one's own name. We will therefore affirm a judgment which requires the second wife to pay over assets that she thought were the husband's, and later thought were hers, to the first wife's children.

In 1985, during the course of a long marriage, George and Barbara Heaps—the husband's first wife—executed a revocable living trust with both spouses acting as their own trustees. The trust would, however, become irrevocable with the death of one of the original trustors. Upon that death, the trust was to be split into two trusts: a "family" trust consisting of the maximum amount of assets that would pass to the "estate of the Trustor" free of estate tax and a "marital" trust for the remainder. George and Barbara's son William Heaps and son-in-law Frank Ciotti would join the survivor as co-trustees of the family trust, but the surviving spouse would remain sole trustee of the marital trust. . . .

This case concerns the only important asset put into that trust, a residence on Circle Haven owned by George and Barbara at the time the trust agreement was made. [Title was transferred by quitclaim deed to the trust, though the deed was never recorded, and then the property subsequently sold for $320,000 for which George and Barbara got back a note and a deed of trust, title to which was taken as joint tenants.]

[O]n Barbara's death the trust became irrevocable. The question on which this case turns is . . . whether the proceeds from the sale of the Circle Haven property were still in the trust as of Barbara's death in 1994.

If those proceeds were property of George and Barbara individually, then the actions of George and his second wife Mary Ann, whom he married a few months after Barbara's death in February, were perfectly legitimate. Those actions were these: In 1996, George and his second wife Mary Ann created their own family trust, and executed a quitclaim deed to transfer any interest in the Circle Haven property and in the all-inclusive trust deed received in return for that property to that new trust. What's more, after George died in 2002—in fact, during the pendency of this very case—Mary Ann transferred all the assets from the 1996 trust to her own revocable trust.

However, if the proceeds were still in the 1985 trust, the 1996 and 2002 transfers were, in effect, conversions of property not belonging to George or Mary Ann. For what it is worth, there is no evidence in the record that George himself ever treated the 1985 trust as having any force or validity after Barbara's death.

Two clauses in particular bear on the question of whether, by taking title as joint tenants, George and Barbara took the proceeds of the Circle Haven property out of the trust. We now quote them verbatim.

First is the portion of the trust agreement involving amendment:

> "Section 1.06 Amendment and Revocation

> "At any time during the joint lives of the Trustors, jointly as to Community Property and individually as to his or her own separate property, Trustors may, by a duly executed instrument,

> "a) Amend this trust agreement (including its technical provisions) in any manner and/or

> "b) Revoke this trust agreement in part or in whole, in which latter event any and all trust properties shall forthwith revert to such Trustor free of trust. Such instrument of amendment or revocation shall be effective immediately upon its proper execution by Trustor(s), but until a copy has been received by a trustee, that Trustee shall not incur any liability or responsibility either (i) for failing to act in accordance with such instrument or (ii) for acting in accordance with the provisions of this trust agreement without regard to such instrument." (Emphasis added.)

Second is the portion of the trust agreement concerning holding title:

> "Section 5.06 Manner of Holding Title

> "The Trustee may hold securities or other property held by Trustee in trust pursuant to this Declaration in Trustee's name as Trustee under this Declaration, in *Trustee's own name without a designation showing it to be Trustee under this Declaration*, in the name of Trustee's nominee, or the Trustee may hold such securities unregistered in such condition that ownership will pay by delivery." (Emphasis added.)

The basic rule governing the interpretation of these clauses is exceedingly simple: "The whole of a contract is to be taken together, so as to give effect to every part, if reasonably practicable, each clause helping to interpret the other." (Civ.Code, § 1641, emphasis added.)

At oral argument, counsel for Mary Ann eloquently argued that pulling assets out of living trusts should not be difficult for people who are both the trustees and beneficiaries of such a trust. And that idea certainly makes sense in the abstract, and dovetails nicely with her central legal theory, which is that merely by taking title to the proceeds as joint tenants, George and first wife Barbara were exercising the power they necessarily had to pull assets out of the trust.

But the theory fails because the only way we can "give effect to every part" is to interpret the trust agreement to require, when assets are being withdrawn from the trust, something—anything in fact—in addition to merely taking title in a form that would be in some name other than the trust's.

The first clause, section 1.06, is fairly prosaic. A "duly executed instrument" was needed to amend the trust. Since George and Barbara were their own trustees, presumably a signed memo to themselves purporting to amend the trust would have been sufficient.[73]

But the second clause, section 5.06, is a landmine, ostensibly buried in the trust agreement to make it easy and convenient for the trust to hold property—but in the end, too easy and convenient. By saying that title to trust property could be held in any way, it necessarily meant that selling an asset and taking title in a name other than that of the trust's would not, by itself, take the property out of the trust. The whole point of section 5.06 is that title could be taken in the name of the trustors as distinct from the trust itself and the property would still be in the trust.

By the same token, the fact that after Barbara's death George simply ignored the 1985 trust he had entered into with Barbara could not take the Circle Haven proceeds out of the trust. After all, section 5.06 was obviously put in the trust so that it would be easy to ignore the existence of the trust and still maintain assets in it. But there is a price to be paid for such convenience. In computerese, section 5.06 made "remain in trust" the default setting. Some affirmative action beyond merely a change in form of title on the part of the trustors was required to click off that default.

Having determined that the placement of assets within the trust became irrevocable with Barbara's death in 1994, it follows that George and Mary Ann's attempt to place those assets in another trust in 1996, and Mary Ann's subsequent attempt to further place those assets in yet a third trust in 2002, constituted conversion of the assets of the original trust. Conversion exists if there is substantial interference or "an exertion of wrongful dominion over the personal property of another in denial of or inconsistent with his rights therein.

[The court denied Mary Ann's Laches claim and further denied her claim for contributions she supposedly made to the trust. The court did explain, however, that because George acted as though the trust didn't exist, as though it was a true fiction, he didn't do any affirmative act that was necessary to revoke the trust.]

———————

Query: Given the likely objectives of probate avoidance and protection for the children that motivated the first trust, can you think of ways to draft the trust to achieve these purposes while maximizing the flexibility that George Heaps apparently sought?

———————

[73] The provision for delivery to the trustee was probably a result of taking a more conventional trust and not editing it so as to adapt it for cases where the trustors are their own trustees—editing, as journalists say, "with a shovel." The provision, of course, has its comic aspect: George and Barbara could have made a modification of their trust by signing a memo to themselves, which would have been effective at the moment of signing but George and Barbara would suffer no liability to themselves as trustees if they didn't deliver it to themselves! Delivery, for what it is worth, is not an issue in this case. The dispositive thing here is that there was nothing at all, delivered or undelivered, to indicate that by selling Circle Haven the proceeds were to be taken out of the trust.

Of course, if you step back and look at the record in broader terms George's inertness makes a certain kind of sense: One can reasonably infer that George did not want to acknowledge to Mary Ann that assets she thought were his were really tied up in an earlier trust made for the benefit of the children of first wife. For George to have formally revoked his one-half interest in the trust, or formally requested the 5 percent principal distributions or general income distributions, would have been to acknowledge that those assets weren't really his.

How reasonable is it for spouses to use trusts or will contracts to tie their spouse's hands after their own death? The George and Barbara Heaps trust became irrevocable at the death of the first spouse to die, thus ensuring that the survivor could not remove the property from the trust and, as George tried to do, give that property to a second spouse to the exclusion of the children. Is that a sensible estate plan? We have seen numerous cases of second marriages pitting the surviving spouse against the children of a prior marriage. Given the statutory set-asides and elective shares that prioritize the rights of the surviving spouse; how should testators and their lawyers balance the interests of surviving spouses, who want to start a new life, maybe a new family, and control the joint assets accumulated during their first marriage, against the interests of prior marriages' children who feel entitled to a portion of their deceased parent's property which the survivor is now spending on a step-parent?

The California court in *Heaps* was far from subtle in criticizing the sloppiness of lawyers drafting boilerplate trusts by making wholesale use of their computer's cut and paste functions. The court was also quite critical about the prevalence of these trusts, especially when the estates are relatively small and consist, as most do, of the principal residence. While Barbara Heaps may be quite satisfied that Mary Ann doesn't get the house to the exclusion of her two children, the inefficiency of using these trust mechanisms, executing all of these trust documents, and still having to go through litigation should make you wonder if everyone needs a trust, as Norman Dacey suggested. One main reason for the revocable trust is to avoid probate. But in the case of the Heaps, it also helps guarantee an inheritance for children in the event the surviving spouse remarries. Can you think of ways to achieve both of these goals (probate avoidance and protected inheritance) that aren't as complex as the revocable trust or as inflexible?

Notice how the opposing parties consist of the children by a first marriage and a surviving step-parent. Had George Heaps outlived Mary Ann, it's quite likely that he would have left the remainder of his property to his two children (perhaps to the exclusion of Mary Ann's children by a prior marriage) and there would have been no problems from them. But he would likely have inherited some of Mary Ann's property as well and would be likely to devise that property to his children and not hers, setting up the reciprocal problem if she had children who expected to inherit not only from their mother, but perhaps also the property their mother inherited from their father. As you can imagine, children are likely to hold very bitter feelings toward a step-parent who walks off with their entire inheritance. Building protections into an estate plan so that at least the property of the first parent can pass to the children, subject perhaps to a life estate in the surviving parent, makes sense. That's why the Heaps' revocable trust became irrevocable upon the death of the first settlor.

Practice Point: Merge with Caution

Technology abounds in the area of estate planning. Just Google *Revocable Living Trusts* with your state's name and you will certainly find sample trusts, just waiting for you to admire. Sometimes kind benefactors even post blank, draft documents, ready for completion. As lawyers we know, of course, that there is much more involved in completing the trust than simply filling in a form—the particular words used to draft gifts and dispositions, the proper naming of fiduciaries, the decision to distribute *per stirpes* or not, the proper funding formula to use in a joint trust, etc. are all simple examples of complex issues that make good use of your legal education.

But, what about draft documents that might accompany your professional membership in an estate planning association with other lawyers? Most competitive organizations now offer their own software packages, many of which include "easy" formation of a whole range of complex trusts.

In all of your excitement to access this technological goldmine and chat with fellow estate planners in the process, the first rule is to proceed with caution. When your software magically cranks out a trust document in excess of 120 pages, you should definitely take the time to become VERY familiar with every little nook and cranny it contains. This will take a lot of work on the front-end, and you will likely make many changes that align the document consistently in your comfort area. After all, YOU will be on the hook for whether the plan works or not, so the very least of your duties is to make sure that the document you present to your client is your own.

---

6. Pros and Cons of Trusts

There are certainly advantages to a well-drafted trust. But for many people, the complexities of a trust may simply not be worth the effort. The irony is that George Heaps didn't learn the lesson the first time. Instead, he and Mary Ann went with the same trust process for their estate plans despite not having properly managed the trust he had with Barbara. Trusts certainly have their probate avoidance aspects. Specifically, they enable property to be passed to others at the death of the settlor with relatively little administrative cost. They are also more private than wills; they don't require probate and the terms remain confidential in the hands of the trustee. Of course, if they are challenged, many of the trust documents will become public. So if confidentiality is important, you want to insure that the trust documents are clear and carefully followed.

In addition, trusts, in those states that have significantly lengthened or abolished the rule against perpetuities, can continue in existence for a very long time. This avoids the problems of disbursing trust principal to minors, to unexpected beneficiaries, or to those who don't want the tax burdens of forced principal distributions. As a general rule, it's never a good time to end a trust and disburse principal. For the wealthy, decedents with complex estate plans, and those with charitable purposes, a trust is probably the best way to go. But for many average decedents, the trust may be more trouble than it is worth.

There are sometimes quite extensive fees to establish a trust, often more than required to draft a will. Property has to be placed into the trust and managed under fiduciary duties throughout the lifetime of the trust. Property must be carefully managed and kept distinct from non-trust property. If the trust generates income, a tax return has to be filed every year and accountings may be required, in addition to individual tax returns, (only after the Settlor's death in the case of a revocable living trust). Trustees often have to post a bond, which may be costly. Further, the trustee is entitled to annual fees. This cost may be avoided if the settlor serves as the trustee, but may kick in if the settlor becomes incapacitated or dies and a successor trustee becomes necessary. Trusts can also be inflexible if the trustee is not given significant discretion. Conversely, discretionary trusts may be too flexible for the average settlor. If trusts do not require active duties and provide some constraints on trustees, they may lose certain of their tax benefits. Even simple things, like naming successor trustees, may become too rigid if those successors are unable or unwilling to serve and a corporate trustee becomes necessary. Finally, all the ease and flexibility of a revocable trust may disappear when corporate trustees take over management of the trust property. While management of a stock portfolio might be within the competence of a corporate trustee, management of real estate (the family home), personal property, or business interests may be less easily managed in the form of a trust.

We deal with many of the more specific advantages and disadvantages of particular types of trusts in the remaining chapters as we work through different types of estate problems and goals. Keep in mind, however, that although certain types of trusts are very advantageous, and have been validated by statute, the basic elements of a trust *res*, ascertainable beneficiaries, active duties, and intent cannot be brushed aside. In addition, trusts to avoid income taxes, a surviving spouse's elective share, or to secretly defraud legitimate claimants will likely be declared invalid. But trusts can be incredibly powerful tools to achieve important estate planning goals. Just be sure you and your client understand that trusts require more attention, maintenance, and careful planning than any of the other tools we have in our toolbox.

7. RESULTING AND CONSTRUCTIVE TRUSTS

A last note should be made about resulting and constructive trusts. Although you have no doubt heard of both, resulting and constructive trusts should not be confused with express trusts of the type we have been discussing in this chapter. Constructive and resulting trusts are *equitable remedies* courts use when property, usually the legal title, has somehow wound up in the wrong person's hands. When a person has defrauded another and acquired title to property that should have gone to someone else, a court will impose a *constructive* trust to force the transfer of the property from the wrongful to the rightful owner. Constructive trusts are used to prevent unjust enrichment and don't usually last very long. They often exist just long enough to cause the transfer of title to the proper owner.

A secret trust created by a will may result in a constructive trust. A testator who leaves everything to her caretaker, with no language indicating her intent to create a trust, may have done so on representations by her caretaker that the latter will distribute the property as the testator wishes. If there is sufficient evidence of the true intended beneficiaries' identities, the court might impose a constructive trust rather than allow the caretaker to take it all outright. A constructive trust can also be used when an improper trustee receives property that should have gone to a different trustrustee.

Consider what happens when a testator leaves property to a distant cousin on the promise that the cousin will use the property to care for the testator's mistress, unbeknownst to the testator's spouse. If there is evidence that the distant cousin was not intended to be the recipient of the property outright, and that a trust was intended, but a court feels uncomfortable naming the cousin as trustee, a constructive trust may be used to prevent the unjust enrichment of the cousin and a court can name a corporate trustee to manage the property for the care of the testator's mistress. Once the constructive trust remedy has been used, the property itself will then reside in an express trust according to the terms outlined by the settlor.

When a court is unsure about who the rightful owner is, as with many secret trusts for instance, a *resulting* trust is used to return the property to the original settlor/grantor. Thus, where a testator leaves her residuary estate to her "lawyer, in trust, knowing that he will distribute it to the charities I most value," the express trust fails for lack of identifiable beneficiaries. However, legal title has technically shifted to the testator's lawyer, which was not her intention. A resulting trust would be used to return the residuary estate back to the testator to pass via intestacy to her heirs. On the other hand, a testator who writes a will leaving everything to her daughter, but is unduly influenced by her son and revokes the will, and who dies intestate does not truly intend for the son to share in her estate. When her estate is administered, a court might impose a constructive trust on the son's share to require he transfer it to his sister according to the intent of his mother.

The term resulting trust is a variant on the term *reversion*, where the property reverts to the transferor or the transferor's estate. Neither constructive nor resulting trusts are something drafters and estate planners should rely on. They are salvage doctrines to fix a drafting error that would otherwise result in unjust enrichment or violate the intent of the testator. But despite our best efforts, both are frequently resorted to in litigation because of badly worded wills, trusts, and other conveyances.

C. Powers of Appointment

In 1938, Professor W. Barton Leach, proclaimed that the "power of appointment is the most efficient dispositive device that the ingenuity of Anglo-American lawyers has ever worked out."[74] I agree wholeheartedly that powers of appointment are incredibly flexible. Notwithstanding their flexibility, and due in part to the proliferation of trusts as an estate planning device, they are underutilized in modern estate planning. Many estate planners feel they must provide a trust or the client will feel that her estate plan is not important enough. But powers are making a comeback in both modest and substantial estates.

A power of appointment is precisely that—a **power** to **appoint** property owned by one person to someone else. Thus, an owner (called the *donor* when we are talking about powers) may give the power to another (the *donee*) to appoint the property among a group of beneficiaries (called the

---

[74] W. Barton Leach, *Powers of Appointment*, 24 A.B.A. J. 807 (1938).

objects of the power). For instance, a donor with small children may decide that if she dies before the children reach majority, she would like to give her husband the power to decide how to distribute her assets to the children when the children reach an appropriate age. When the children grow up, her husband may decide that the majority of his deceased wife's property should go to one child and not be distributed equally because that child has special needs. When he appoints the property, now or in the future, to a permissible object of the power, the person receiving the property becomes the *appointee*. The value of powers is that they postpone into the future the decision-making about distributions when more is known of the needs and circumstances of the beneficiaries.

A donor of a power has no way to guarantee that the donee will actually exercise the power; the donee may die suddenly or may choose not to exercise the power at all. Because there is no legally binding obligation to do anything with the power, unlike a trustee's duty to manage trust property, the donor should always provide an alternative disposition in case the power is not exercised. The recipients of this alternate gift are called the *takers in default*. Thus, a donor could establish a power as follows: "I hereby give to my daughter a power to appoint the residue of my estate among any of my grandchildren, but if she fails to exercise the power, then my estate is to pass to my lineal descendants by representation." The donee is the daughter, the objects are the grandchildren, and the takers in default are the lineal descendants of the donor.

There are two types of powers, *general* powers and *special* powers (or *non-general* powers). General powers are those in which the donee of the power is also a permissible object of the power. General powers also include those in which the donee's estate, creditors, or creditors of his estate are permissible objects of the power of appointment. Thus, if grandpa gives his granddaughter a power to appoint his estate among all of his descendants, the power is general because the granddaughter can appoint the property entirely to herself or she can distribute it entirely to others. She cannot, however, appoint the property to a non-object, e.g. a charity or a cousin who is not a descendant of the donor. Special powers may not be used to distribute property to a donee or for the benefit of a donee. Thus, a trustee who has the ability to distribute principal at her discretion to any of the beneficiaries holds a special power (assuming the trustee is not a beneficiary). The term *special* powers is used in the estate planning world and *non-general* powers in the tax world, and although they have similar meanings there are a few differences.[75] We use the term special powers here as that is consistent with the terminology of the Restatements and the Uniform Probate Code.

Powers can also be exercised at two different times: during life and via a will or other testamentary instrument. Thus, there are *inter vivos (or lifetime)* and *testamentary* general powers and *inter vivos (or lifetime)* and *testamentary* special powers. An *inter vivos* power can usually be exercised at any time by the donee (presently exercisable), though sometimes it is postponed until a certain event (like when the donee reaches a certain age,

---

[75] These differences generally have to do with the size of the class of permissible objects. The Restatement (First) of Property § 320 provided that the class of permissible objects could not be "unreasonably large," while the Internal Revenue Code does not limit the class of permissible objects of special powers. The Restatement 3d of Property has come in line with the tax code. (§ 17.3, cmt b).

marries, or some other circumstance). Testamentary powers can only be exercised by the donee at her death.

One might wonder why a donor would give a donee a testamentary general power of appointment if the donee cannot appoint the property to herself until her death. The usual reason is to postpone until the donee's death the time at which dispositive decisions have to be made. This keeps the property intact through the donee's lifetime. The donee can then use the power to capture the property and add it to her estate, thus passing it to her testamentary beneficiaries, or she can appoint the property in her will to others.

Powers serve two important purposes: they postpone decision-making until more information is available about the needs and interests of beneficiaries and they can help minimize tax implications of large estates by allowing gifts to be made to persons who were not alive at the donor's death. One of the most important aspects of a power of appointment is the *relation-back doctrine*. Let's imagine that a 90 year old donor, Frank, wants his property to go to his great-grandchildren. However, he isn't sure whether they are all born yet, the living great-grandchildren are minors, and the great-grandchildren won't need the property until they go away to college. So, he gives his granddaughter, Shirley, an *inter vivos* special power to appoint the property among any or all of his great-grandchildren. At his death, Frank has 3 great-grandchildren who qualify as objects of the power. Twenty years later, he has 14 great-grandchildren who are approaching college-age. Shirley decides to give 1/14th of her grandfather's estate to each great-grandchild when he/she finishes college. She gives out seven portions to the seven great-grandchildren who have already graduated from college, and hangs onto the rest to distribute it as each finishes. When those first seven receive their shares, the law treats the gift as coming directly from Frank (certainly not taxable to Shirley's estate) and date it back to be effective as of the date of Frank's death. As each successive child receives her share, it is treated as coming directly from Frank.

But what if one child wins the lottery and Shirley decides that he doesn't need any of Frank's property? As a result, she redistributes that child's share to the remaining 13 great-grandchildren. This is perfectly fine—there is no obligation on Shirley's part to distribute it equally and she can consider the economic circumstances of each permissible appointee at the time she makes appointments.

If Shirley dies before all the great-grandchildren graduate from college, she may exercise the power in favor of the remaining beneficiaries in her will either by establishing a trust to distribute each grandchild's share at the appropriate time, or she can exercise the power of appointment in her will to take effect immediately, even if they haven't graduated. If she forgets to exercise the power in her will, then the remainder of the unappointed property will pass to the entire class of permissible objects as default takers. If a power is not exercised, or is partially exercised, the remaining property will pass according to the donor's instructions to the *takers in default*. If there are no takers in default, the property passes back to the donor's estate to be distributed either under the residuary clause or through intestacy.

Another advantage of a power of appointment is that the donee is not a fiduciary and can make decisions without considering the welfare of the beneficiaries. This means that the decisions made by a donee are generally not reviewable by a court.

Compare this process to a trust. There is no need for a separate document like a deed of trust when creating a power of appointment. The executor of Frank's estate will hold the property in trust until Shirley exercises the power. But the trustee doesn't have to do very much except safeguard the property. No distributions have to be made unless Shirley exercises the power. Had Frank established a testamentary trust in his will to benefit his great-grandchildren, there would have been trustee fees and the trustee would have had to distribute the property equally unless Frank specified otherwise. The trustee would not have the discretion to withhold property from the child that won the lottery. If the trustee did have the discretion, then the trustee essentially has a power of appointment. All the rules of trust administration would apply, and each great-grandchild would take a vested remainder subject to open that could be taxable to that beneficiary's estate, even if the beneficiary died before coming into possession.[76] In other words, unless you structure the trust very flexibly, unforeseen events may cause Frank's estate, or the estates of beneficiaries, to pass in rigid formulas or to pay higher taxes. The discretion one builds into a trust is essentially a power of appointment, but powers can be free-standing as well.

The advantage of a trust over powers of appointment is their durability. Powers are personal and will die with the donee. A trust, on the other hand, will continue to exist even if the trustee dies; a court will simply appoint a successor trustee if one is not identified in the trust documents. But successor trustees will often agree to serve only if they are compensated. Donees of a power are not fiduciaries, usually have no duties whatsoever to the property, and the exercise of the power can be quite simple. "Here, I'm giving you grandma's china collection." Thus, donees usually are not compensated. Even if structured flexibly, the trust generally is not as flexible as the power of appointment.

Powers are still subject to the Rule Against Perpetuities and other legal constraints, but usually no more than are trusts.[77] A discretionary trust, which is a power coupled with a trust, may only serve to give a corporate trustee discretion that it chooses not to exercise precisely because the trustee is not familiar with the family's needs and circumstances. A well-placed power is almost always given to a close relative who shares the donor's preferences about how the property is to be distributed and to someone who the donor does not want to saddle with the fiduciary and accounting duties of a trustee.

Of course, a donee need not accept the power (Shirley could disclaim it or release it, in which case the property would pass immediately to the default takers[78]) and if she does accept it she need not exercise it (again, the property will pass to the default takers). Powers can be very powerful tools if structured to take advantage of the benefits they give to the donor and the donee, and if the donee is up to exercising the power. They are more flexible than the trust in many ways and avoid the retitling, fees, and

---

[76] This assumes that the trust established mandatory percentages for each great-grandchild. If not, it would be a discretionary trust and the trustee would have a power of appointment.

[77] In those states that have modified their Rule Against Perpetuities to extend or abolish its operation in the context of trusts, powers are still subject to the Rule unless they are powers of a beneficiary or a trustee to appoint trust property (i.e., power in a trust).

[78] There may be tax consequences to a disclaimer unless the donee complies with § 2518, but that is not the focus here.

fiduciary obligations of trustees. Because they are less formal, however, they only work well among people who trust one another.

You are probably thinking "wait a minute"—isn't this the same thing as when grandpa dies and your mom and uncle Bob are going through grandpa's house and ask you if you want the ugly painting of Aunt Marge or grandpa's new table saw? Technically, no, it isn't the same thing. In the typical example, grandpa dies and your mom and her brother inherit all of grandpa's personal property. It is theirs immediately upon his death and if they choose to keep it themselves (which they will likely do with grandpa's bank accounts or the house), give it to you (which they will often do with personal property that is well suited to a particular family member), or donate it to charity (which they will often do with grandpa's outdated ties and size 14 bowling shoes), the transfer of the property is coming from them, not from grandpa. But if grandpa instead writes a will and gives mom and uncle Bob a presently-exercisable power of appointment, and they give you the table saw and the painting of Aunt Marge, the gift is coming directly from grandpa. Thus, there is only one transfer of property rights in the second example where there were two transfers in the first example. And your tax radar should be going off right now. If that ugly painting of Aunt Marge just happened to be painted by Pablo Picasso and is worth $18 million, one transfer makes far more sense than two.

However, problems can arise when the donee dies before exercising the power because powers are personal. When a donor gives a donee a general power of appointment hoping the donee will exercise the power by spraying the property among a large class of beneficiaries in accordance with each one's special circumstances, and the donee dies before exercising the power, the donee may inadvertently *capture* the property and pass it to her beneficiaries instead. For instance, if grandpa gave mom a presently-exercisable general power of appointment over his estate, she dies shortly after he does, and her will contains a general capture clause, she may capture all of grandpa's property and pass it, through her will, to her beneficiaries. This can easily happen if grandpa gave mom a general power, which means she can appoint the property to herself or to her estate. Thus, mom's will might state: "I give the rest and residue of my property, *including any property over which I have a power of appointment*, to my only daughter." At the time the will was executed, mom might not know she was going to receive a power. But this boilerplate language is put into most wills and can cause all of the donor's property to pass to the donee's estate for distribution according to the donee's will. If your tax radar is working this could entail double estate taxation if the transfers are large enough and double administration of the estate. There is a transfer when mom captures the property and then again when she devises it to her daughter.

It may very often be the case with free-standing powers that the donee might not want to exercise the power in favor of her testamentary beneficiaries, especially if some of them are not specified objects of the power. But because the donee is an object, the law treats the donee as capturing the property, making it hers, and then passing it to whomever she chooses in her will. And although the donor gave a general power to the donee, knowing that the donee could take it all herself, most donors don't imagine that the donee will capture *all* the property and pass it to non-permissible appointees without even enjoying the benefit of the property herself. Thus, powers can be very useful estate planning devices, but they require some care in establishing, and drafters of wills should use caution before inserting general capture clauses in the wills of donees.

There also are some important differences between special powers and general powers when it comes to creditors of the donee being able to reach the donor's property. Thus, a spouse may be entitled to an elective share in property over which a donee holds a general power of appointment, even if the donee does not exercise the power or chooses to exercise it in her will in favor of others.[79] A donor should think carefully about the implications of creating general and special powers. Further, mom isn't likely to appoint the Picasso to a child with huge gambling debts or a drug problem, but her careful protection of the property is for naught if she dies with a will that captures the property and passes it to her children equally. Creditors of permissible appointees cannot force an exercise of the power, but creditors of the donee can in certain instances if the power is general.

Two other concepts are also important to understand in the context of powers. The first is *exclusivity*. An *exclusive* power is one that can be exercised in a way that completely excludes some permissible appointees. Thus, a special power to a child to appoint the property to any or all of her children is exclusive if the donor intended to give the donee the power to appoint all the property to one appointee to the complete exclusion of the other permissible appointees. A power is *non-exclusive* if the donee must give at least some amount to every permissible appointee. Whether a power is exclusive or non-exclusive depends on the intent of the donor but, in the absence of clear guidance, the majority of states take the position that powers are exclusive.

The second concept is that of powers *coupled with an interest*. If the donee of a power has another interest in the property, like a life estate or the donee is also the trustee of a trust holding the property, then the donee has a *power in gross*. If the donee has no other interest in the appointive property other than the power itself, it is a *collateral power*. Collateral powers are less likely to result in the appointive property being valued as part of the donee's estate for elective share purposes, or for attachment by creditors, but there are some large caveats to the general rule that we will discuss further in this section.

When deciding whether or not to use a power of appointment in an estate plan, one should analyze the power from the perspective of the donor and from the donee, and it may be that while the donor would benefit greatly, the donee would not, or vice versa. So to analyze the pros and cons of powers, we will begin by studying them through both sets of eyes.

1. THE DONOR

In most instances, the donor who establishes a power of appointment in her will doesn't really care whether she uses a power or a trust. She can feel confident that after her death the donee or the trustee will take care of following through on her wishes. But she may want to give the most flexibility to her agent without saddling that person with the fiduciary duties and accounting obligations of a trustee. If the donor knows someone personally who she believes is a good judge of character and will make better decisions than she herself could make, a power of appointment is the easi-

---

[79] *See, e.g.*, UPC § 2–205(1)(A); Fl. Stat. § 732.2035(c)(2).

est way to do this. Perhaps the easiest way would be to just give the property to the donee outright. This may not be optimal if the donee doesn't need the property, might have taxation issues with her own estate, or the donee's creditors might be lining up to get a crack at the donor's property. However, a special power of appointment eliminates the possibility that the donor's property will be joined to the donee's property for tax or creditor liabilities.[80] A special power of appointment, therefore, can give the donee the most flexibility to act as an agent for the donor without the donee having to worry about tax issues herself.

Unlike a trust, where beneficiaries can enforce trustee obligations against the trustee who is shirking her duty, permissible appointees cannot demand that the donee exercise the power. They can beg, cajole, and reason with the donee, but the donee is free to ignore the power altogether. However, if the donee chooses to exercise the power, she must act within the scope of the power in distributing the donor's property. Thus, a well-crafted power MUST include default provisions and takers in case the donee fails to act.

From the donor's perspective, the biggest concern is the donee who predeceases her or who just chooses not to exercise the power. Failure to exercise can leave the donor's property in limbo for years as the donee sits on it. But this problem can be easily solved by instructing the donee to act within a certain period of time with an instruction that failure to act results in the property passing according to default rules established by the donor. Even without a time limit, the donor should always provide reasonably clear instructions as to who will take the property if the donee fails to act. Consider the following case of a donee who only partially acted and the many lawsuits that were spawned by a less-than-clear will.

Loring v. Marshall

484 N.E.2d 1315 (Mass. 1985)

This complaint, here on a reservation and report by a single justice of this court, seeks instructions as to the disposition of the remainder of a trust created under the will of Marian Hovey.[3] In *Massachusetts Inst. of Technology* v. *Loring,* 327 Mass. 553 (1951), this court held that the President and Fellows of Harvard College, the Boston Museum of Fine Arts, and Massachusetts Institute of Technology (the charities) would not be entitled to the remainder of the trust on its termination. The court, however, did not decide, as we now must, what ultimate disposition should be made of the trust principal.

Marian Hovey died in 1898, survived by a brother, Henry S. Hovey, a sister, Fanny H. Morse, and two nephews, John Torrey Morse, Third, and Cabot Jackson Morse. By her will, Marian Hovey left the residue of her estate in trust, the income payable in equal shares to her brother and sister during their lives. Upon her brother's death in 1900, his share of the income passed to her sister, and, upon her sister's death in 1922, the income was paid in equal shares to her two nephews. John Torrey Morse, Third,

---

[80] More on the tax and creditor issues *infra* at Section 2.

[3] Questions involving the wills of Marian Hovey and her nephew, Cabot Jackson Morse, have been before this court on four prior occasions. *See, Welch* v. *Morse,* 323 Mass. 233 (1948); *Massachusetts Inst. of Technology* v. *Loring,* 327 Mass. 553 (1951); *Frye* v. *Loring,* 330 Mass. 389 (1953); *Loring* v. *Morse,* 332 Mass. 57 (1954).

died in 1928, unmarried and without issue. His share of the income then passed to his brother, Cabot Jackson Morse, who remained the sole income beneficiary until his death in 1946.

At that point, the death of the last surviving income beneficiary, Marian Hovey's will provided for the treatment of the trust assets in the following language:

> At the death of the last survivor of my said brother and sister and my two said nephews, or at my death, if none of them be then living, the trustees shall divide the trust fund in their hands into two equal parts, and shall transfer and pay over one of such parts to the use of the wife and issue of each of my said nephews as he may by will have appointed; provided, that if his wife was living at my death he shall appoint to her no larger interest in the property possessed by me than a right to the income during her life, and if she was living at the death of my father, he shall appoint to her no larger interest in the property over which I have a power of disposition under the will of my father than a right to the income during her life; and the same limitations shall apply to the appointment of income as aforesaid. If either of my said nephews shall leave no such appointees then living, the whole of the trust fund shall be paid to the appointees of his said brother as aforesaid. If neither of my said nephews leave such appointees then living the whole trust fund shall be paid over and transferred in in [sic] equal shares to the Boston Museum of Fine Arts, the Massachusetts Institute of Technology, and the President and Fellows of Harvard College for the benefit of the Medical School; provided, that if the said Medical School shall not then admit women to instruction on an equal footing with men, the said President and Fellows shall not receive any part of the trust property, but it shall be divided equally between the Boston Museum of Fine Arts and the Massachusetts Institute of Technology."[4]

The will thus gave Cabot Jackson Morse, the surviving nephew, a special power to appoint the trust principal to his "wife and issue" with the limitation that only income could be appointed to a widow who was living at Marian Hovey's death.[5] Cabot Jackson Morse was survived by his wife, Anna Braden Morse, who was living at Marian Hovey's death, and by his only child, Cabot Jackson Morse, Jr., a child of an earlier marriage, who died in 1948, two years after his father. Cabot Jackson Morse left a will which contained the following provisions:

> *Second*: I give to my son, Cabot Jackson Morse, Jr., the sum of one dollar ($1.00), as he is otherwise amply provided for.

> *Third*: The power of appointment which I have under the wills of my aunt, Marian Hovey, and my uncle, Henry S. Hovey, both late of Gloucester, Massachusetts, I exercise as follows: I appoint to my wife, Anna Braden Morse, the right to the income during her lifetime of all of the property to which my power of appointment applies under the will of Marian Hovey, and I appoint to my wife the right during her

---

[4]   The parties have stipulated that at the relevant time the Harvard Medical School admitted women to instruction on an equal footing with men.

[5]   We are concerned here only with "property possessed" by the testatrix at her death and not property over which she had "a power of disposition under the will of [her] father." That property was given outright to his widow under the residuary clause of the will of Cabot Jackson Morse. See *Frye* v. *Loring*, 330 Mass. at 396. *See also, Loring* v. *Morse,* 332 Mass. at 64.

widowhood to the income to which I would be entitled under the will of Henry S. Hovey if I were living.

Fourth: All the rest, residue and remainder of my estate, where ever situated, real or personal, in trust or otherwise, I leave outright and in fee simple to my wife, Anna Braden Morse.

In *Welch v. Morse,* 323 Mass. 233 (1948), we held that the appointment of a life interest to Anna Braden Morse was valid, notwithstanding Cabot Jackson Morse's failure fully to exercise the power by appointing the trust prin-principal. Consequently, the trust income following Cabot Jackson Morse's death was paid to Anna Braden Morse until her death in 1983, when the principal became distributable. The trustees thereupon brought this complaint for instructions.

The complaint alleges that the trustees

are uncertain as to who is entitled to the remainder of the Marian Hovey Trust now that the trust is distributable and specifically whether the trust principal should be paid in any one of the following manners: (a) to the estate of Cabot Jackson Morse, Jr. as the only permissible appointee of the remainder of the trust living at the death of Cabot Jackson Morse; (b) in equal shares to the estates of Cabot Jackson Morse, Jr. and Anna Braden Morse as the only permissible appointees living at the death of Cabot Jackson Morse; (c) to the estate of Anna Braden Morse as the only actual appointee living at the death of Cabot Jackson Morse; (d) to the intestate takers of Marian Hovey's estate on the basis that Marian Hovey failed to make a complete disposition of her property by her will; (e) to Massachusetts Institute of Technology, Museum of Fine Arts and the President and Fellows of Harvard College in equal shares as remaindermen of the trust; or (f) some other disposition.

Before us each named potential taker claims to be entitled to trust principal.

In our 1951 opinion, *Massachusetts Inst. of Technology* v. *Loring,* 327 Mass. at 555–556, we explained why in the circumstances the charities had no interest in the trust:

The rights of the petitioning charities as remaindermen depend upon the proposition that Cabot J. Morse, Senior, did not leave an 'appointee' although he appointed his wife Anna Braden Morse to receive the income during her life. The time when, if at all, the 'whole trust fund' was to be paid over and transferred to the petitioning charities is the time of the death of Cabot J. Morse, Senior. At that time the whole trust fund could not be paid over and transferred to the petitioning charities, because Anna Braden Morse still retained the income for her life. We think that the phrase no 'such appointees then living' is not the equivalent of an express gift in default of appointment, a phrase used by the testatrix in the preceding paragraph.

In *Frye v. Loring*, 330 Mass. 389, 393 (1953), the court reiterated that the charities had no interest in the trust fund.

It is apparent that Marian Hovey knew how to refer to a disposition in default of appointment from her use of the terms elsewhere in her will. She did not use those words in describing the potential gift to the charities. A fair reading of the will's crucial language may rightly be that the charities were not to take the principal unless no class member who could receive principal was then living (i.e., if no possible appointee of principal was living at the death of the surviving donee). Regardless of how the words "no such appointees then living" are construed, the express circumstances under which the charities were to take did not occur. The question is what disposition should be made of the principal in the absence of any explicit direction in the will.

Although in its 1951 opinion this court disavowed making a determination of the "ultimate destination of the trust fund," the opinion cited the Restatement of Property § 367(2) (1940), and 1 A. Scott, Trusts § 27.1 (1st ed. 1939)[6] to the effect that, when a special power of appointment is not exercised and absent specific language indicating an express gift in default of appointment, the property not appointed goes in equal shares to the members of the class to whom the property could have been appointed. Restatement (2d) of Property § 24.2 (Tent. Draft No. 7, 1984).[7]

Applying this rule of law, we find no specific language in the will which indicates a gift in default of appointment in the event Cabot Jackson Morse should fail to appoint the principal. The charities argue that the will's reference to them suggests that in default of appointment Marian Hovey intended them to take. On the other hand, in *Welch* v. *Morse,* 323 Mass. at 238, we commented that Marian Hovey's "will discloses an intent to keep her property in the family." The interests Marian Hovey gave to her sister and brother were life interests, as were the interests given to her nephews. The share of any nephew who died unmarried and without issue, as did one, was added to the share of the other nephew. Each nephew was limited to exercising his power of appointment only in favor of his issue and his widow. We think the apparent intent to keep the assets within the family is sufficiently strong to overcome any claim that Marian Hovey's will "expressly" or "in specific language" provides for a gift to the charities in default of appointment.[9]

---

[6]   In Restatement: Property, § 367 (2), it is said, with certain immaterial exceptions, that 'where there is a special power and no gift in default of appointment in specific language, property not effectively appointed passes to those living objects to whom the donee could have appointed at the time of expiration of the power, unless the donor has manifested an intent that the objects shall receive the property only so far as the donee elects to appoint it to them.' In Scott, Trusts, § 27.1, the author says, 'Where there is no express gift over in default of appointment the inference is that the donor intended the members of the class to take even though the donee should fail to exercise the power. The inference is that he did not intend that they should take only if the donee should choose to exercise the power. . . .   The cases are numerous in which it has been held that the members of the class are entitled to the property in equal shares where the donee of a power to appoint among them fails to exercise the power.' *See,* Farwell, Powers (3d ed. 1916) 528; Kales, Estates Future Interests (1920) § 616." 327 Mass. at 556.

[7]   Section 24.4, concerning the disposition of unappointed property under a non-general power of appointment, states: "To the extent the donor of a non-general power has not specified in the instrument creating the power who is to take unappointed property, the unappointed property passes (1) In default of appointment to the objects of the power (including those who are substituted objects under an antilapse statute) living at the time of the expiration of the power as though they had been specified in the instrument creating the power to take unappointed property, if—(a) the objects are a defined limited class and (b) the donor has not manifested an intent that the objects shall receive the appointive property only so far as the donee elects to appoint it to them; or (2) To the donor or the donor's estate, if subsection (1) is not applicable."

[9]   The nominal distribution made to his son in the donee's will provides no proper guide to the resolution of the issues in this case. We are concerned here with the intention of Marian Hovey, the donor of the special power of appointment. The intentions of the donee of the power of appointment are irrelevant in construing the donor's intent. Similarly, those who rely on language in *Frye* v. *Loring,* 330 Mass. 389 (1953), as instructive in resolving questions in this

If we were to depart from the view taken thirty-four years ago in *Massachusetts Inst. of Technology* v. *Loring,* 327 Mass. 553 (1951), and now were to conclude that under the terms of Marian Hovey's will the charities were to receive the trust principal, we would face the problem that, under normal principles of res judicata, our earlier decision against the charities is binding on them. [We choose not to do so now.] . . . The same arguments made by the charities and the Attorney General in this case were considered and rejected in 1951. Surely in a case such as this, at least in the absence of a statute to the contrary, the public interest in protecting the charities' rights was fully accommodated by the Justices of this court in its prior decision. . . .

What we have said disposes of the claim that the trust principal should pass to Marian Hovey's heirs as intestate property, a result generally disfavored in the interpretation of testamentary dispositions. . . . The claim of the executors of the estate of Anna Braden Morse that her estate should take as the class, or at least as a member of the class, must fail because Marian Hovey's will specifically limits such a widow's potential stake to a life interest.

A judgment shall be entered instructing the trustees under the will of Marian Hovey to distribute the trust principal to the executors of the estate of Cabot Jackson Morse, Jr. The allowance of counsel fees, costs, and expenses from the principal of the trust is to be in the discretion of the single justice.

So ordered.

■ O'CONNOR, J. (dissenting, with whom HENNESSEY, C.J. joins).

As the Attorney General argues, the event specified in Marian Hovey's will as triggering the charities' right to the trust principal occurred—Marian Hovey's nephews died without leaving living appointees of the trust principal. Therefore, contrary to the court's holding, the trustees should not be instructed to pay the principal to the executors of Cabot Jackson Morse, Jr.'s, estate. Rather, they should be instructed that "the whole trust fund shall be paid over and transferred in equal shares to the Boston Museum of Fine Arts, the Massachusetts Institute of Technology, and the President and Fellows of Harvard College for the benefit of the Medical School." . . .

Even if normal principles of res judicata are to be applied so as to bar the charities' claims, they do not bar the Attorney General's claim that the charities are entitled to the remainder of the trust fund. The Attorney General, the representative of the public, was not a party in the *Massachusetts Inst. of Technology* v. *Loring* case. Even if the decision in that case be deemed binding on the charities, it does not follow that the Attorney General is also bound. . . .

Whenever possible, a will ought to be construed as providing a rational plan for the disposition of the testator's property. . . . As I will demonstrate, the relevant language in Marian Hovey's will is reasonably susceptible of only one construction consistent with a reasoned method of accomplishing her manifest over-all objective, and that construction should be adopted by this court.

---

case miss the point that Cabot Jackson Morse's intention with regard to his exercise of the power of appointment is irrelevant in determining his aunt's intention concerning the consequences of his partial failure to exercise that power.

Marian Hovey's will clearly expresses her intent to dispose of the entire residue of her estate, in trust, for the benefit of several classes in accordance with expressed priorities; first, for the benefit of her brother, sister, and nephews; second, for the benefit of her nephews' wives (income only) and her nephews' issue to the extent the nephews, in their discretion, might determine; and, third, for the benefit of the charities to the extent that the trust fund is not exhausted for the benefit of the nephews' wives and issue. The provision that if neither nephew leaves "such appointees then living" the whole fund is to go to the charities obviously was designed to give to the charities those trust funds not appointed to issue who were living at the expected time of distribution. . . . The will, construed in any other manner even remotely justified by its language, fails to express a cohesive rational plan to dispose of Marian Hovey's property. . . .

The doctrine of res judicata does not require that the court follow *Massachusetts Inst. of Technology* v. *Loring,* and, because the values in overruling that decision outweigh the values underlying stare decisis, I would overrule it, and I would instruct the plaintiff trustees to distribute the remainder of the trust fund in equal shares to the Massachusetts Institute of Technology, the Boston Museum of Fine Arts, and the President and Fellows of Harvard College.

———————

Query: What do you think the testator's intentions were with regard to this power of appointment? Would she have preferred the trust corpus pass to the estate of her nephew's son or to the charities she named? Does it bother you that the child who was essentially disinherited by his father ended up inheriting the trust corpus years after he too had died? Would it matter if Cabot Jr's estate passed to his mother, Anna Braden Morse, who Marian Hovey did not want to have take the trust principal?

———————

The Restatement 3d of Property § 19.23 provides that where a donee of a special power of appointment fails to exercise her rights to appoint the property, and where default takers are not specified, there is an implied gift in default to the potential appointees. Does this rule make sense? If a donor gave a donee a special power of appointment to distribute donor's property to a particular group of charities without providing for default takers, and the donee failed to exercise her power, should the property pass equally to the charities or should there be a resulting trust for the benefit of donor's estate or intestate takers? What if the permissible appointees were the donor's *lineal descendants*?

The main issues that donors face with powers of appointment are:

- whether the donee will exercise the power faithfully, i.e. in the manner the donor would have wished or according to the specific instructions of the donor,
- whether the donee exercises the power at all, and
- whether the donor has adequately specified what should happen if the donee predeceases the donor or fails to exercise the power fully.

As you can see from *Loring v. Marshall*, even a fairly well-drafted power can lead to litigation if EVERY possibility is not accounted for explicitly.

2. The Donee

Powers of appointment are usually far more problematic from the perspective of the donee. This is especially true for general powers. Because the donee of a general power has the ability to capture all the property for herself, the Internal Revenue Code treats property over which the donee has a general power of appointment as taxable to the donee, even if the donee exercises the power to give it to another. Prior to 1942 appointive property was not taxed to the donee until the power was actually exercised for the benefit of the donee. Since 1942, however, powers are treated like ownership interests for some tax purposes.[81] A presently exercisable general power of appointment certainly looks like ownership, since the only thing the donee has to do is exercise the power by signing a paper or taking title. A testamentary general power of appointment seems a bit different, though, since the donee cannot capture the property and enjoy it during her life. Nevertheless, the IRS treats the property as part of the donee's estate even if she makes a will giving the property to others. Creditors of the donee may also be able to reach property over which the donee has a general testamentary power of appointment by suing to have the executor of the donee's estate exercise the testamentary power of appointment in favor of her estate or her creditors.[82]

A confounding problem is that the IRS may treat the exercise of a general power of appointment in favor of another as a gift from the donee. Rather than relying on the relation-back doctrine and treating the donee as an agent who simply decided which permissible appointee was to receive the donor's property, the IRS treats the appointment as though the donee captured the property for herself and then made a gift of it to the appointee.[83] From a property perspective this makes a certain amount of sense. A donee with a general power of appointment is as close to an owner as one can get without being an actual owner of the appointive property, and when the donee chooses to exercise the power on behalf of a beneficiary, that act has all the markers of ownership that the law values: dominion, control, and alienability. But such a rule undermines some of the beauty of the power of appointment (hence the change in the tax code) which is that it made the donee a mere agent, and not an owner for tax purposes. With such a rule, are powers of appointment still useful? Absolutely.

First, special powers avoid all the tax problems of general powers, though they do not allow the donee to benefit directly from the appointive property. We discuss the tax implications of powers in Chapter 9 but it is good to reiterate here that the vast majority of estate, more than 99%, don't face any tax issues at all. Second, powers avoid the fiduciary obligations of trusts to allow the donee far more flexibility to deal with the property without fear of a lawsuit from the potential beneficiaries. Even a trustee with discretion to distribute principal remains a fiduciary and cannot act completely without concern for the welfare of beneficiaries. Third, powers still give the advantage of delayed decision-making, postponing gifts until bene-

---

[81]   I.R.C. § 678 and § 2702.

[82]   State laws vary on the rights of creditors to attach property over which a donee has a power of appointment. *See, Univ. Nat. Bank v. Rhoadarmer,* 827 P.2d 561 (Colo.App. 1991) and Restatement, 2d, of Property (Donative Transfers) § 13.2. However, New York allows creditors to attach such property. *See,* N.Y. Est. Powers & Trust Law § 10–7.2.

[83]   *See,* I.R.C. § 2041 and § 2702.

ficiaries have identifiable needs or until more information is available. Consider the following case:

Holzbach v. United Virginia Bank

216 Va. 482, 219 S.E.2d 868 (Va. 1975)

■ POFF, JUSTICE.

By will admitted to probate on October 9, 1964, Arthur Ray Hall (donor) established a 'marital trust' with a corpus equal to 'so much of my property . . . which will avail my estate of the full marital deduction permitted by the Federal Estate Tax Law which is applicable at the date of my death.' The income from the corpus of the marital trust was to be paid to his wife for life. With respect to disposition of the corpus, the will provided:

> My wife, Julia H. Hall, is hereby given as to the corpus of the marital trust existing at her death, a general power of appointment, by specific reference to the powers granted herein, in her will, in favor of her estate, or, at her election, in favor of any other party. Should she fail to so appoint as to all or any portion of such corpus, then, upon her death such unappointed corpus, shall become a part of the Residual Trust to be administered as herein after provided.

Donor's will then established a 'Residual Trust' under which the corpus remaining upon the death of the Cestui que trust was to be distributed, Per capita, among the 'issue' of donor's two brothers.

The will of Julia Henry Hall (donee) was admitted to probate on August 17, 1972. Article II provided:

> I give and bequeath unto my beloved sister, HAZEL H. HOLZBACH, provided she survives me, all of my estate, be it real, personal or mixed, or in which I may have a power of appointment of whatsoever nature, kind or description, and wheresoever the same may be located, in fee simple and absolutely.

The chancellor heard the cause of the pleadings, the two wills, and an affidavit filed by the scrivener of donee's will. The affidavit stated that donee 'was fully familiar with the fact that she had power of appointment under the will of her husband and we discussed this at the time her will was prepared'.

By final decree entered November 11, 1974, incorporating a letter opinion dated September 13, 1974, the chancellor held 'that the general power of appointment created by the will of Arthur Ray Hall has not been exercised by the will of Julia Henry Hall' and ordered 'that the corpus of the marital trust . . . be distributed as a part of the Residuary Estate of Arthur Ray Hall. [On appeal, the court explained:]

A power of appointment is a unique legal creature. It is created, never by implication or by operation of law, but only by deliberate act. The law calls its creator the 'donor', its owner the 'donee', and its beneficiary the 'appointee'. A power of appointment concerns property but is not, itself, 'an absolute right of property'. Title to the property concerned remains with the donor until the power has been effectively exercised by the donee, at which time title passes through the donee as a conduit to the appointee.

The general rule is that a donor may impose particular conditions and requirements upon the power and the manner in which it must be exercised. Holzbach contends that the general rule has been modified by Code

§ 64.1–50 (Repl.Vol.1973),[3] and that under that statute, noncompliance with the particular requirement donor imposed here cannot serve to defeat the exercise of the power. We do not agree. In paraphrase, the statute provides that if an exercise of a power of appointment by will is to be effective, the donee must execute his will with all of the formalities required by law, and if he complies with those formalities, the appointment will be effective even though he failed to comply with 'some additional or other form of execution or solemnity' required by the donor. We hold that a donor's requirement that his donee make 'specific reference' to the power is not within the intendment of Code § 64.1–50, and that noncompliance with such a requirement defeats the exercise of the power.

Holzbach argues that the residuary clause in donee's will effectively exercised the power. The statute provides that, by operation of law, a general testamentary power of appointment will be exercised by a general residuary clause in the donee's will, unless the donee's will manifests a contrary intent. As we construe the statute, it has no application where, as here, the donor has expressly imposed upon the exercise of the general power a special requirement of specific reference to the power created in the donor's will.

Having determined that noncompliance with donor's requirement defeats the appointment, we consider whether the language in donee's will constitutes compliance.

Holzbach insists that donee's intent controls this question. Pointing to donee's general reference to All powers and to the affidavit which indicates that she was aware of the particular power in question, Holzbach says that 'it is clear that the donee intended to exercise the power of appointment in favor of her sister.'

Holzbach applies the wrong test of compliance. The test is not whether donee intended to appoint but rather whether donee Manifested her intent in the manner prescribed by donor, I.e., by making specific reference 'in her will' to the power granted by donor's will. "Powers are to be construed in accordance with the intention of the donor. . . . "

Donor's will, read against the background of death tax laws, indicates that his purpose was to provide for his wife during her lifetime and, thereafter, for the remaindermen he named. For the benefit of both, he wanted to avail has estate of the maximum marital deduction permitted by federal estate tax laws and regulations. To accomplish this, it was necessary to couple his wife's life estate with a general power of appointment. Int. Rev. Code § 2056(b)(5). To validate the deduction, the power of appointment must be tailored to fit the rules prescribed by the tax regulations. A donor's requirement that the power must be exercised 'by specific reference to the power' does not defeat the deduction. Treas. Reg. § 20.2056(b)–5(g)(4). Donor adopted this requirement and then designated the beneficiaries to whom his property would pass in the event his wife failed to exercise the power in the manner required.

---

[3] § 64.1–50. When execution of appointment by will valid.–No appointment made by will, in exercise of any power, shall be valid unless the same be so executed that it would be valid for the disposition of the property to which the power applies, if it belonged to the testator; and every will so executed shall be a valid execution of a power of appointment by will, notwithstanding the instrument creating the power expressly require that a will made in execution of such power shall be executed with some additional or other form of execution or solemnity.

On brief, the parties speculate as to donor's motives in requiring donee to manifest her intent in the manner he prescribed. Appellees say that donor's motive was simply to protect his estate and the natural objects of his bounty against an 'inadvertent' exercise of the power by a nonspecific residuary clause. Appellant suggests that donor's motive was to qualify his estate for the tax deduction but, at the same time, to 'lay a trap for an unwary donee', hoping that, for want of a 'specific reference . . . in her will', donee's attempt to appoint would fail and his estate would pass to beneficiaries of his choice rather than to donee's appointee.

It is not necessary to our decision to guess which of these motives prompted donor. Indeed, one is not exclusive of the other. The requirement imposed is not unlawful; it does not offend public policy; and it does not entail 'some additional or other form of execution' within the intendment of Code § 64.1–50. When a donor imposes such a requirement, a donee, who enjoys no title to donor's property, can make no valid appointment affecting that property unless he complies with donor's requirement.

Pursuing his right to dispose of his property as he saw fit, donor created a power of appointment and selected the conduit through which it should pass. Upon the exercise of that power, he imposed a lawful requirement that his donee manifest on the face of her will an intent to exercise the power by making specific reference to the power created in his will. While donee's will makes general reference to powers of appointment, it makes no specific reference to donor, to his will, or to the power created by his will. We hold that donee's will failed to comply with donor's requirement and, therefore, failed to make an effective appointment of donor's property.

The chancellor's decree is Affirmed.

■ HARRISON and COCHRAN, JUSTICES (dissenting).

We dissent. It can be safely said that the primary motive of the great majority who avail themselves of the marital deduction is to qualify their estates for the tax deductions and benefits that flow therefrom. However, to reap these benefits, a wife for whom a marital trust is created, must be given a general power of appointment.

The Treasury regulation, which permits a donor to require that a power of appointment must be exercised by specific reference to the power, is not designed to provide the donor with an escape valve, or a technical tool, to deprive the donee of the use of the power. Its purpose is to provide a donor with the means of assuring himself that any power of appointment given will be Consciously and Knowingly, not inadvertently, exercised by the donee. That is all that he has a right to expect from or demand of the donee.

Arthur R. Hall created a marital trust and gave his wife, Julia H. Hall, as to the corpus, 'a general power of appointment, by specific reference to the powers granted herein, in her will, in favor of her estate, or, at her election in favor of any other party'. The husband did not specify the manner in which the specific reference was to be made. However, the will of Julia H. Hall was specific, and in it she made specific reference to the power of appointment she had been given. She devised to her sister, Hazel H. Holzbach, All of her estate. She particularized by adding 'be it real, personal or mixed, Or in which I may have a power of appointment . . .'. (Emphasis supplied) By the use of this language she made a distinction between her property and the property which she could devise as donee.

This wording also indicates a deliberate, conscious and knowing disposition of (1) her own property, and (2) the property over which she had a power of appointment.

All that Arthur R. Hall required of his wife was a 'specific reference' in her will to the 'powers' which he had granted her by his will, not a reference to his will or any specific clause thereof. What he granted was a power of appointment, and this is what the wife 'had'. In Julia H. Hall's will she referred to the power of appointment 'I may have.' This language constituted a 'specific reference' to the powers granted her. It indicated her considered intention to exercise the power.

The only reason for a reference in the wife's will to the power of appointment she had was to manifest her intent to appoint in the manner prescribed by her husband. But for the requirement imposed by his will there would have been no occasion for any reference to the power. See Code § 64.1–67.

A power of appointment must be executed in the manner prescribed by the donor. Thus, a power to appoint by will may not be exercised by deed. Nevertheless, under Code § 64.1–50, a validly executed will exercising a power shall be deemed to be a valid execution of a power of appointment by will, even though the will creating the power may 'expressly require' that the will exercising the power 'shall be executed with some additional or other form of execution or solemnity'. Thus, the donee is not always required to adhere strictly to the donor's directions in exercising a testamentary power of appointment. It is apparent from this statute and from the cases that powers of appointment are favored in Virginia. Where a donee undertakes to exercise a testamentary power of appointment by a validly executed will substantial compliance with the donor's requirements should suffice. Indeed, substantial compliance by deed has been held to be sufficient. To hold that the donor's directions in the present case can only be fulfilled by a detailed reference in the wife's will to the power of appointment created by her husband's will, when she has carefully disposed of all property over which she has a power of appointment, is to adopt an unduly strained, technical and artificial construction.

When Hall elected to establish the marital deduction trust, with its attendant tax benefits, he voluntarily accepted the risk that his wife, as donee of the testamentary power, might appoint beneficiaries other than those preferred by her husband in his will. Aside from tax advantages, the flexibility of a power of appointment makes it especially attractive as a means of meeting unanticipated changes in circumstances. Its use should be encouraged rather than frustrated by rigid formalism. Here, the intent of the donee to exercise the power of appointment pursuant to the donor's requirements is clear. We would hold that the power was validly exercised and reverse the decree of the trial court.

Query: Do you think Julia Hall intended to exercise the power given by her husband? If so, was the dissent correct that the majority was using strict formalism to allow the donor to get the tax benefits of the marital deduction trust AND still control the property's ultimate distribution? How would you do things differently if you were the lawyer for Arthur or the lawyer for Julia? Does the donor's intent matter if the donee knew about the power and intended to exercise it?

Consider this case as well:

In re Tognotti's Estate

128 Ill.App.2d 120, 262 N.E.2d 803 (Ill.App. 1970)

Zaverio Tognotti died testate on June 20, 1935, and was survived by his wife, Catherine, no children having been born to or adopted by them. His Last Will and Testament provided that after payment of his debts all his property was to pass to his wife, Catherine, to have hold, use and enjoy for and during the time of her natural life, with the right to sell, mortgage, pledge, invest expend, give away, and otherwise dispose of and deal with the same, or the proceeds thereof; and after her death, if there be anything left, I give, devise and bequeath the same in equal shares to be held in trust and given to his grand-nephews and grand-nieces when the youngest reaches 21. After Zaverio's death, Catherine caused many of her husband's stock shares to be cancelled and certificates issued in her name, without reference to her life estate. After Catherine's death, her executor and sole beneficiary retained the stock, and Zaverio's trustee claimed the stock was not properly appointed by Catherine and therefore should pass to the trust. The trial court agreed with the trustee, and the court of appeals affirmed, stating: A life estate in personal property has long been recognized in Illinois. A life estate may include, as this one did, a power to dispose of the subject of the estate which if exercised will defeat the interest of the remaindermen. It is clear from the terms of the will that it was Zaverio's intention that his wife, Catherine, have a life estate in the securities. He explicitly provided how and to whom any which remained at her death were to be distributed. To provide for Catherine's support, Zaverio gave her the power to dispose of all the shares in her lifetime. She could have sold them, or under the terms of the will, even given them away. However, we do not think that her causing the shares to be registered in her individual name without designation as a life tenant was a disposition of the stock. . . .   Catherine Tognotti still held control over the property at the time of her death. She had not disposed of it. The language of Zaverio's Will is unmistakable. His denial of a power of testamentary disposition is explicit because it states 'if there be anything left' it is to go to a named trustee. Every phrase and word of a Will must be given effect, and none may be rejected as surplusage. The words 'if there be anything left,' must be given their natural meaning, that is, all property which Catherine received from Zaverio and which she still owned at the time of her death passed to the trustee under Zaverio's Will, and not, under Catherine's Will. The property, therefore, was not a part of her estate, but passes under her husband's will.

Query: What kind of power of appointment did Zaverio give to Catherine? Do you think Catherine understood that she had a life estate with a power to consume/dispose and do you think that when she took title to any property solely in her own name she thought that she was exercising the power in her own behalf? Catherine lived for 32 years after Zaverio. Does it seem reasonable to have the property pass according to Zaverio's will when he died more than 30 years earlier and the default takers he designated may very well have predeceased Catherine by many years? What is the power to consume or dispose if not the power to take title?

The *Tognotti* case raises the issue of the life estate coupled with the power to consume or to dispose of the property. For those of you who remember your estates and future interests from first-year property, you know that a life tenant cannot waste the property during life and cannot dispose of the property at death, for the remaindermen already have a property interest that cannot be destroyed. But there is no reason a donor cannot give to a donee a life estate coupled with a power, which simply turns that vested remainder into a contingent remainder in the takers following the life tenant. Thus, rather than a grant of Blackacre "to A for life, then to B" (which gives B an absolutely vested remainder), C could instead give Blackacre "to A for life, then to whoever A designates in her will, and if A fails to designate a successor, then to B." Clearly B now has a contingent remainder; it is contingent on A NOT exercising her testamentary power to appoint the property to someone else. But where is that other alternate contingent remainder, the one that will allow the property to pass to whoever A designates? It remains in O until A either designates herself the successor, designates another as the successor, or fails to designate anyone, in which case Blackacre passes to B.

The life estate coupled with a power, especially a general presently-exercisable power, looks a heck of a lot like outright fee ownership. That's probably why Catherine Tognotti figured she could retitle her husband's stock certificates. But as you will see in Chapter 8, the takers in default of a power of appointment have a contingent remainder in the property that cannot be destroyed except by compliance with the condition placed on that interest. Thus, in a case in which a life tenant had the power to devise real estate and he sold the property at a below-market value to one of the default takers, the other default takers complained. They claimed that as a life tenant the donee had a duty to all the default takers who were the contingent remaindermen to only dispose of the property at a full and fair market value. The court, however, disagreed, stating three important rules:

1. A life tenant with power to dispose of real property devised to him for life with remainder to certain designated persons owes a duty [to] the remaindermen to act honorably and in good conscience in the exercise of that power.

2. A life tenant of real estate coupled with a power of disposal is not empowered to dispose of the fee by way of gift.

3. The power of disposal possessed by a life tenant of real estate is not limited to providing for himself the bare necessities of life, but comprehends any *bona fide* sale, the proceeds from which are used to promote his legitimate purposes or to benefit his interests.[84]

In other words, the court held that the life tenant could not give away the property because that would defeat the remaindermen's contingent interests in the property and go against the spirit of the donor's intent. A life tenant also cannot waste the property, even if the life tenant has a power to consume or dispose of the property, because the life tenant must act in good faith.

---

[84] *See, Stump v. Flint*, 195 Kan. 2, 402 P.2d 794 (Kan. 1965).

Access to Property by Creditors of the Donee

As noted earlier, conflicts often arise when creditors of a donee of a general power of appointment try to legally force the donee to exercise the power on the creditors' behalf. The common law rule is that until the power is actually exercised, a creditor of the donee has no access to the donor's property. Under the common law, if the donee exercises the power on behalf of someone else, creditors cannot complain. But creditors did complain and the trend has been to allow certain privileged creditors access to property over which a donee/debtor has a general power of appointment. Obviously, creditors have no claims if the donee merely holds a special power. But when the donee holds a general power, many state legislatures became sympathetic to children, ex-spouses, and tort claimants who feel that if the IRS considers the property to belong to the donee, they also should have access to it. We will see the same issue arise in the context of spendthrift trusts as well. Consider the following case and the Restatement's new rule and rationale. Also consider whether it should matter if the debtor is the donee of a self-settled power, is the donee of a general power of appointment, or is a permissible appointee of a non-exclusive power.

Irwin Union Bank & Trust Co. v. Long

312 N.E.2d 908 (Ind.App. 1974)

Appellee, Victoria Long, obtained a judgment in the amount of $15,000 against her ex-husband, Philip Long, in 1957 and she now seeks to satisfy that judgment against funds that Philip's mother, Laura Long, placed into trust but which allowed Phillip to withdraw 4% of the principal every year. The trial court allowed Victoria to access the 4% but on appeal, the court reversed, explaining: *Appellee . . . argues that Philip has absolute control and use of the 4% of the corpus and that the bank does not have control over that portion of the corpus if Philip decides to exercise his right of withdrawal. Appellee argues that the intention of Laura Long was to give Philip not only an income interest in the trust but a fixed amount of corpus which he could use as he saw fit. Thus, Philip Long would have a right to the present enjoyment of 4% of the trust corpus. A summation of appellee's argument, as stated in her brief, is as follows: "So it is with Philip—he can get it if he desires it, so why cannot Victoria get it even if Philip does not desire it?". . . .*

Contrary to the contention of appellee, it is our opinion that Philip Long has no control over the trust corpus until he exercises his power of appointment and gives notice to the trustee that he wishes to receive his 4% of the trust corpus. Until such an exercise is made, the trustee has the absolute control and benefit of the trust corpus within the terms of the trust instrument.

Philip Long has never exercised his power of appointment under the trust. Such a situation is discussed in II Scott on Trusts, § 147.3 as follows:

. . . Where the power is a special power, a power to appoint only among a group of persons, the power is not beneficial to the donee and cannot, of course, be reached by his creditors. Where the power is a general power, that is, a power to appoint to anyone including the donee himself or his estate, the power is beneficial to the donee. If the donee exercises the power by appointing to a volunteer, the property appointed can be reached by his creditors if his other assets are insufficient for the payment of his debts. But where the donee of a general power created by

> *some person other than himself fails to exercise the power, his creditors*
> *cannot acquire the power or compel its exercise, nor can they reach the*
> *property covered by the power, unless it is otherwise provided by stat-*
> *ute. . . .*

Indiana has no statute which would authorize a creditor to reach property
covered by a power of appointment which is unexercised.

Query: With *inter vivos* gifts, a donee's choice is to accept or reject the gift. If it
is rejected, ownership remains with the donor and the donor may offer the gift
to another. If it is accepted, the donee is the absolute owner and may choose to
keep it or pass it to someone else. But a general power exercised on behalf of
another is somewhat in between these two options: the donee accepts for purposes of deciding who will be the final recipient and for cutting off the donor's
power, but without taking ownership and therefore not becoming an owner for
tax or property purposes. Because of the relation-back doctrine, the property
passes directly from the donor to the appointee. Should a donee of a general
power be able to avoid the claims of creditors by merely refusing to exercise the
power? In other words, are the fancy legal machinations justifiable under public policy reasons when one major use of the power is to limit access to
creditors?

The Restatement 2d of Property supported the rule of *Irwin* that, until
the power is exercised, creditors of the donee could not reach the property.
But the Restatement 3d of Trusts[85] and the Restatement 3d Property (Wills
and other Donative Transfers) have shifted positions entirely.

**Restatement 3d Property, § 22.3 Creditors of the Donee—General Power
Created By Someone Other Than The Donee**

(a) To the extent that the property owned by the donee is insufficient to satisfy the
claims of the donee's creditors, property subject to a presently exercisable general
power of appointment that was created by someone other than the donee is subject
to those claims to the same extent that it would be subject to those claims if the
property were owned by the donee.

(b) Upon the death of the donee, to the extent that the donee's estate is insufficient
to satisfy the claims of creditors of the donee's estate, property subject to a general
power of appointment that was created by someone other than the donee and that
was exercisable by the donee's will is subject to those claims and expenses to the
same extent that it would be subject to those claims and expenses if the property
had been owned by the donee.

Comment a. A presently exercisable general power of appointment is an ownership-
equivalent power . . . "The power to become the owner at will is in essence ownership. . . .   The general power presently exercisable is the practical equivalent of
ownership, since it gives to the donee the power to acquire ownership at any time by
appointing to himself."

---

[85]   U.T.C § 505(b)(1).

Numerous states have legislated that creditors can reach the donor's property,[86] and the Bankruptcy Code has followed suit.[87] Many states, following the UPC, also allow a surviving spouse to reach appointive property as part of the elective share, which we discuss further in Chapter 7.[88] Those privileged creditors tend to be the government (for tax debts or Medicaid claims), children (for child support claims), spouses, and tort creditors, generally in that order of priority. Not all states that allow privileged creditors access to a donee's appointive property allow all of these creditors to compel a donee's exercise.

PROBLEMS

4.27. Tonya's holographic will leaves all of her property to "Bob for the duration of his life, with the full power to dispose of the property however he may wish, and at his death, the remaining property shall pass to my siblings, equally." What interest does Bob have at Tonya's death?

4.28. Aunt Susan's will leaves her entire estate to her oldest, most responsible niece, Harriet, with the power to appoint the property to herself or anyone else she desires during her lifetime or at her death. After Aunt Susan died, Harriet spent the entire estate on a glorious trip around the world for herself and her husband. Fuming, Harriet's youngest sister, Clara, brings suit, claiming that Aunt Susan told her at last Thanksgiving dinner that she was leaving everything to Harriet because Harriet was "the only one who would know how to divvy up the property to your crazy siblings in any way that made sense." Did Harriet have a duty to distribute property to her siblings?

3. SELF-SETTLED POWERS

What happens when the donor and the donee are the same person, the so-called *self-settled power*? If the power is a *general* power, then it only makes sense that creditors of the donor can reach the appointive property. The Restatement 3d of Property agrees.[89] But a self-settled *special* power may be protected from the donee's creditors. In *Ahern v. Thomas*, 733 A.2d 756 (Conn. 1999) the court did not make trust principal available to the settlor for purposes of qualification for Medicaid when the settlor/trustee held a special testamentary power. Under a property theory this makes sense. The donor has already taken herself out of the property loop when she creates a special power and names permissible appointees and default takers. Either way, some third person will receive the property regardless of whether the donee exercises the appointment or not. In addition, once a donee of a self-settled general power has exercised the power in favor of a third party, creditors may not revoke the exercise or in any way reach the appointed property unless it was a fraudulent conveyance.[90]

---

[86] *See e.g.*, N.Y. EST. POWER & TRUST LAW § 10–7.2; Cal Prob. Code § 682.

[87] 11 U.S.C. § 541(b)(1).

[88] *See*, U.P.C § 2–205.

[89] Restatement 2d of Property § 22.2. *See also*, *U.S. v. Ritter*, 558 F.2d 1165 (4th Cir. 1977).

[90] Restatement 3d of Property (Wills and Donative Transfers) § 22.2, cmt c.

The property analysis is clear with a power of appointment, just as it is with a trust. Once a donor transfers property into trust, or creates a power of appointment over it, the donor's ability to deal freely with the property has been curtailed. A property rights stick has transferred *inter vivos*. Although a trust settlor of a revocable trust may be able to get the stick back, through complying with certain trust procedures, the important point is that the stick has been transferred and, if the settler does nothing, the property will pass according to the settlor's original terms. The same is true with a power. Once the power to appoint has been given to another, or the power to alienate the property has been narrowed to a small class of beneficiaries, the donor of a power no longer has the same control over the property as she had before she created the power even if she is the donee as well.

The real question, therefore, is whether we should allow people to give property away to others (as gifts!) knowing that their creditors will not be able to satisfy their claims with the donor's remaining property. To the extent the law allows someone to give away all her property before a tort judgment is issued against her, the same policies should govern whether we would allow a donor or trust settlor to put property in revocable trusts or create self-settled powers with the similar result of placing that property out of the reach of creditors. Not surprisingly, the government (particularly the federal government) is not supportive of these kinds of transfers, especially if the settlor/donor retains the functional benefit of enjoying the property during life. Thus, tax debts and health care debts often receive favorable priority by courts when property owners have attempted to shield their assets through trusts and powers. The claims of children, to receive back child support, also receive sympathetic treatment by courts. Further, legislatures often pass laws prohibiting transfers into homestead, into trust, or *inter vivos* with the intention of defrauding creditors. If anything is constant, however, it is that the laws will continue to respond to the creativeness of humans who use legal mechanisms to escape paying taxes. Long before Henry VIII abolished the use, the crown was fighting property owners who used the technical tricks of the land conveyancers to shield family wealth.

4. Creation of a Power of Appointment

The rules governing creation of a power of appointment are generally the same as for transferring any property. Creating a power in real property must conform to the statute of frauds; it must be in writing and witnessed according to state law. The mental capacity for creating a power is usually the same as for writing a will. Remember that this is a lower standard than for making *inter vivos* gifts.[91] But it is the same standard for other testamentary actions.

Certain formalities may also have to be followed when creating a power. Obviously, a donor creating a power of appointment in her will must follow the will formalities. But the creation of a power by deed need only follow the same requirements as are necessary for *inter vivos* gifts

The acts necessary for exercise of a power are basically the same as for creating a power. A donee of a testamentary power must exercise it through a testamentary document executed with the requisite formalities. A donee

---

[91] We discuss mental capacity later, in Chapter 11. At this point it is important to know that the level of capacity is the same as for other testamentary instruments.

of a presently exercisable power need follow only the formalities necessary for making *inter vivos* gifts unless the donor has established specific requirements. *See*, Restatement 3d of Property (Wills and Donative Transfers), § 19.9.

But what happens if a donee of a testamentary power attempts to exercise the power in her will, but the will fails for lack of the appropriate number of witnesses or fails some other formal requirement? Some courts will allow the invalid will to exercise the power, even though it is not a valid testamentary document, on the grounds that the statute of wills imposing the will formalities does not impose the same formalities on the exercise of powers. *See*, *Est. of McNeill*, 463 A.2d 782 (Me. 1983). The court in *McNeil* followed an equitable exception that allowed the appointment to be effective if "it approximates the manner of appointment prescribed by the donor and the appointee is a natural object of the donee's affection."

Some states have adopted substantial compliance doctrines when the donor specifies how the power is to be executed and the donee tries, but doesn't quite get it right.[92]

5.   EXERCISE OF A POWER OF APPOINTMENT

The most common difficulty with powers of appointment is determining whether an appointment has actually been made when the donee does not explicitly state that she is exercising the power. Thus, should a donee of a special power of appointment be deemed to have exercised the power if, in her will, she gives the "rest and residue of my estate, including property over which I have a power of appointment, to X?" If X is not a permissible appointee, then the exercise cannot be effective. But if X is a permissible appointee, do we assume that the donee intended to exercise the particular power if she didn't explicitly refer to it? What if she received the power after she wrote her will that contained the generic capture clause?

Obviously, the best way to exercise a power would be to state "I hereby exercise the power of appointment I have in the property of my father, given to me in his will dated _____ on behalf of my two children, X and Y." And the donee should draft this document in accord with the will formalities if it is a testamentary power, or in accord with the statute of frauds if it is an *inter vivos* gift, and should describe the property, the beneficiaries, and the document creating the power with enough specificity to avoid any confusion. But if you have learned anything so far, it is that people, even lawyers, often fail to be as precise and thorough as we would hope.

Consequently, the states have adopted a variety of rules and presumptions for determining what type of statement is necessary to exercise a power. So here are the basic rules and options.

If the donee has a general testamentary power of appointment, the following scenarios might play out:

1.   The donee makes no reference in her will whatsoever to the power, but gives all the "rest and residue of my property to X." Should this disposition be deemed to have captured the property so as to make it the donee's so she can pass it to X? The majority rule is that this is not enough to capture the property and so it passes to the default takers. The Restatement 3d of Property takes a more

---

[92] *See*, Cal. Prob. Code § 631; W. Va. Code § 41–1–4; *Motes/Henes Trust v. Motes*, 761 S.W.2d 938 (Ark. 1988).

nuanced approach, though, and would allow this general residuary clause to capture the donor's property IF there are no takers in default or the default clause is ineffective. *See,* Restatement 3d Property § 19.4.

2. The donee uses a general residuary clause with a general capture provision that gives all the "rest and residue of my property, including any property over which I have a power of appointment, to X." The majority rule is that this language will capture the appointive property for the benefit of the donee and it will be included in the donee's estate for estate tax purposes and will pass to X. The Restatement 3d of Property, again, takes a more nuanced approach. If the donor named takers in default AND the donee's exercise is ineffective to pass the property to others, then the Restatement would not have this general blending clause capture the property for the benefit of the donee's estate. Because these blending clauses are more likely the result of boilerplate form language than a concerted effort by the donee to exercise the power, the Restatement cautions against having even this language capture the property. *See*, Restatement 3d of Property, § 19.21.

3. The donee uses the general residuary clause language of #2 above, but the donor required that the donee exercise the power by explicit reference to the power. The majority rule is that the general capture clause is not enough to capture the property and, as a result, it passes to the default takers, but a few states allow this language to suffice under certain circumstances.

4. The donor gave donee a general testamentary power of appointment in Blackacre, and donee devises Blackacre to her daughter, X. In this case, although donee has not mentioned the power, she has implicitly exercised it by acting like Blackacre is hers to devise. *See*, Restatement 3d of Property § 19.3.

5. The donor gave donee a general testamentary power of appointment in $500,000 and donee devised $550,000 to X, with no mention of the power or the property. If donee only owned property worth $100,000 at her death, the court will interpret the gift to X as exercising the power. *See*, Restatement 3d of Property § 19.5.

If the donee has a special testamentary power of appointment, the following scenarios might play out:

1. The donee makes no reference in her will whatsoever to the power, but gives all the "rest and residue of my property to X" and X is a permissible appointee. Again, the majority rule is that this is not adequate to exercise the power, especially if the donor has named default takers.

2. The donee uses a general residuary clause with a capture provision that gives all the "rest and residue of my property, including any property over which I have a power of appointment, to X" and X is a permissible appointee. The majority rule is that this is sufficient to exercise the power in favor of X unless the donor has listed more specific requirements.

3. The donee uses a general residuary clause with a capture provision that gives all the "rest and residue of my property, including any property over which I have a power of appointment, to X" and X is

not a permissible appointee. This is clearly an invalid exercise because it is to a person who is not a permissible appointee.

4. The donee uses a general residuary clause with a capture provision that gives all the "rest and residue of my property, including any property over which I have a power of appointment, to X, Y and Z" and X is a permissible appointee but Y and Z are not. In this case, courts will try to approximate the donee's intentions. Where the donee has treated X, Y, and Z equally, but the appointive property is greater than the donee's, then it would be apparent the donee did not intend to exercise the power because X would get far more than Y and Z. But if the donor's property is one-third or less of the total property, then the court will allocate the donor's property to X, and the donee's own property to Y and Z in ways that treat them equally.

Most states have statutes or case law giving presumptions for interpreting general blending clauses with regard to the exercise of powers. But all bets are off if the donor established specific rules for the donee's exercise of the power. How many of the scenarios listed above are addressed by the UPC?

UPC § 2–608. Exercise of Power of Appointment.

In the absence of a requirement that a power of appointment be exercised by a reference, or by an express or specific reference, to the power, a general residuary clause in a will, or a will making general disposition of all of the testator's property, expresses an intention to exercise a power of appointment held by the testator only if (i) the power is a general power and the creating instrument does not contain a gift if the power is not exercised or (ii) the testator's will manifests an intention to include the property subject to the power.

Certainly the most litigated question involving powers has to do with whether an exercise was valid, since default takers and permissible appointees often are on opposite sides of the answer. Consider the following cases:

Estate of Hamilton

593 N.Y.S.2d 372 (New York App. Div. 1993)

This case involves the widow/donee of a general testamentary power of appointment in the donor's 1982 will that the donor explicitly limited to be *exercisable only by specific reference to said power in [donee's] last Will and Testament*. The donee died 15 days after the donor, leaving a last will and testament dated 1967. Paragraph second of donee's will provided as follows:

*By this paragraph of my Last Will and Testament, I do specifically exercise the power of appointment given to me by paragraph "Sixth" of the Last Will and Testament of my husband * * * dated the 26th day of August, 1966, in favor of my son, JOHN HENRY RICKETSON * * * or to his issue him surviving, to the extent of seven-eighths (7/8ths) of the fund over which I have the power of appointment, and I give, devise and bequeath to SUE M. RICKETSON, wife of my son, one-eighth (1/8th) of the fund over which I have the power of appointment under the said Last Will and Testament of my husband * * *. By these provisions, I do specifically exercise the power of appointment given to me by the Will of my said husband (emphasis supplied).*

Because the donee's reference to the power was to a power created by the donor's 1966 will, and not his subsequent 1982 will, the courts held that the power was not exercised and the property would pass to the donor's takers in default. The court explained: *EPTL 10–6.1 sets forth the rules governing the exercise of a power of appointment and provides, in pertinent part, that "[i]f the donor has expressly directed that no instrument shall be effective to exercise the power unless it contains a specific reference to the power, an instrument not containing such reference does not validly exercise the power" (EPTL 10–6.1 [b]). . . . Here, in order to effectively exercise the power of appointment granted her in decedent's 1982 will, Hamilton had to make "specific reference to said power" in her last will and testament. This she did not do. The only power referenced by Hamilton in her will was the power of appointment granted her under decedent's 1966 will which, as noted previously, had been revoked by decedent's subsequent execution of a new will in 1975 and again in 1982, in which decedent clearly manifested his intent to revoke all prior wills and codicils. Thus, Hamilton's sole reference was to a power that had ceased to exist.*

Query: Is it possible to exercise a power that is created after the donee purports to exercise it, if the donor put in place specific reference requirements? Although specific reference requirements help prevent inadvertent exercise, they can also prevent the intentional exercise if some sort of substantial compliance or equitable doctrine is not used to salvage it. Would you resolve this case the same way if the only difference between the 1966 will and the 1982 will was the appointment of a different personal representative and there were no differences in property dispositions?

Hargrove v. Rich

604 S.E.2d 475 (Ga. 2004)

In her last will and testament, Cecil H. Rich, the mother of Frances Rich and appellee Jack Rich, granted a power of appointment over one-fourth of her estate to Frances by providing in Item III(B):

> *[Frances] shall have the power at any time and from time to time, by instrument in writing signed by her and delivered to the Trustees, or at death by her Last Will and Testament, making express reference to this power, to direct the Trustees to turn over any part or all of the property in this Trust to her brothers or sisters or her nieces and nephews, or descendants of deceased nieces and nephews, and in such manner, in Trust or otherwise, as [Frances Rich] may in such instrument direct or appoint, provided that she shall have no power to appoint such property to herself, to her estate, to her creditors or the creditors of her estate.*

In her will Frances exercised the power of appointment in favor of her niece, appellant Hargrove, to the exclusion of other nieces and nephews. Frances's will specifically referred to the power of appointment in Item III(B) of her mother's will as follows:

> *It is specifically my intent to exercise that certain power of appointment granted to me pursuant to Item III(B)(4) of the Last Will and Testament of Cecil H. Rich in favor of Frances Ann Hargrove.*

The trial court found that the language in Frances's will was ineffective to exercise the power of appointment to Hargrove because (1) it did not follow the specific requirements of Cecil H. Rich's will requiring Frances to direct the trustees to turn over any part or all of the property in this trust, and (2) it improperly excluded all other nieces and nephews contrary to the express intention of Cecil H. Rich. The Georgia Supreme Court affirmed in part, stating:

> *Under Georgia law, a power of appointment can be exercised only in the manner specified by the donor. At the same time, the donee of a power may execute it without expressly referring to it, or taking any notice of it, provided that it is apparent from the whole instrument that it was intended as an execution of the power. The execution of the power, however, must show that it was intended to be such execution; for if it is uncertain whether the act was intended to be an execution of the power, it will not be construed as an execution. The intention to execute a power will sufficiently appear—(1) when there is some reference to the power in the instrument of execution; (2) where there is a reference to the property which is the subject matter on which execution of the power is to operate; and (3) where the instrument of execution would have no operation, but would be utterly insensible and absurd, if it was not the execution of a power. Applying the above principles, we find that pursuant to the unambiguous language of Cecil H. Rich's will, Frances was authorized to exercise the power of appointment granted to her either during her life by instrument signed by her and delivered to the trustees or upon her death, by including in her will language making express reference to the power.*
>
> *Although we hold that the language of Frances's will was sufficient to exercise the power of appointment, we nevertheless agree with the trial court that Frances did not have the authority to exercise the power of appointment in favor of only one niece. . . . Under the plain language of Item III(B) Frances had only limited authority to exercise the power in favor of "her brothers or sisters or her nieces and nephews, or descendants of deceased nieces and nephews." The donor's use of the conjunctive "and" in the phrase "nieces and nephews" indicates her intent to limit the power of appointment to preclude Frances from exercising the power in favor of one niece to the exclusion of other nieces and nephews. This intent is further evident when looking at the document as a whole. In an almost identical provision granting a power of appointment to her son R.L. Rich, Jr., Cecil H. Rich granted him the express power to exercise the power "to or among such of his children. . . . " The absence of such language in Item III(B) demonstrates the donor's intent to place additional limitations on the permissible beneficiaries under that provision. Inasmuch as the donee of a power can do only what she is empowered to do, Frances was without authority to exercise the power of appointment solely in favor of Hargrove.*

Query: Do you think the donor's intent was to create a non-exclusive power of appointment such that the property had to be appointed to all the permissible appointees of the nieces and nephews? Assuming the court is right, how much should Frances have been required to give each niece and nephew other than Hargrave? One dollar? One hundred dollars? An equal share? Assuming the exercise was ineffective, what happens now? The power is deemed unexercised and the property will pass to the takers in default, if any. If there aren't any takers in default, the property will pass equally to the class of permissible appointees (brother, sister, nieces, nephews, and their lineal descendants by representation). What is the best outcome? Do you think the use of the conjunctive in Frances' power was intentional, or simply language created by the lawyer with no real thought to the issue of exclusivity?

Illinois State Trust Co. v. S. Illinois Nat'l Bank

329 N.E.2d 805 (Ill.App. 1975)

In his will, Martin F. Oehmke established a trust. Under the trust Oehmke's wife, Jane W. Oehmke, was to receive all of the income from such trust and she could withdraw up to $10,000 of the principal of such trust each year. The trust specified that upon the death of Jane W. Oehmke, the principal and undistributed income of the trust assets should be 'distributed to or for the benefit of such person or persons, or the estate of my wife in such amount and proportions as my wife shall appoint by her will.' Such trust further provided in default of the exercise of such power of appointment or 'insofar as such appointment shall not extend to or take effect,' the trustee should.

' * * * pay any and all inheritance and Federal estate taxes that may be assessed in any way by reason of her death, her funeral expenses and the expenses of her last illness, and the balance, if any, shall be distributed unto Shriners Hospital for Crippled Children, a corporation, to be used exclusively for the benefit of the hospital located in the City of St. Louis, Missouri, owned, operated and maintained by said corporation.'

The will of Jane W. Oehmke, dated February 8, 1965, provided for specific bequests of $50,500 and for, "All the rest, residue and remainder of my Estate of every name and nature, and whatsoever situate, of which I shall die seized or possessed, I give, devise and bequeath as follows: One-third each to three individuals. The issue before the court is whether the general residuary clause was adequate to exercise the general testamentary power of appointment the testator had. Holding in the affirmative, the court explained:

It is well settled that the question of whether a testamentary power of appointment has been exercised depends upon the intention of the donee of such power. It is equally well settled that the burden of proof rests upon the party claiming the exercise of the power of appointment. The donee's intention to exercise a power of appointment, however, need not be manifested in any given way. Technical language is not necessary to the exercise of a power of appointment nor is it necessary that the intention to execute the power appear by express terms or recitals. In other words, 'Reference to the power is not essential, and the instrument need not take the slightest notice of it, provided the intent to exercise the same appears.' Such intention may be sufficiently manifested by the circumstances surrounding the transaction . . . . .

Finally, we find sufficient evidence in the record to sustain the trial court's finding that the testator, Jane Oehmke, intended to exercise her testamentary power of appointment by her will dated February 8, 1965. It is undisputed that prior to such date Jane Oehmke was advised orally and in writing of her right to exercise such power. There was sufficient evidence to establish that absent the exercise of such power, the personal assets of Jane Oehmke, as of February 8, 1965, would have been insufficient to satisfy the specific bequests, much less, the residuary legacies, contained in her will. There was also substantial evidence presented to establish that the residuary legatees were the primary objects of Jane Oehmke's bounty. This conclusion is supported not only by the testimony of several witnesses, but by the undisputed fact that Jane Oehmke made substantial gifts to each of the residuary legatees during her lifetime. More significant, however, from the standpoint of the instant case, was the testimony of several witnesses that

Jane Oehmke disapproved of her husband's bequest to the Shriners' Hospital and her alleged statements that she did not want Shriners to receive her money.

When these circumstances are evaluated in light of the fact that, 'The lodestar of will construction is to ascertain and effectuate the intention of the testator, provided such is not contrary to the law and the fact that 'the intention of the testator supercedes the formal requirements with respect to the exercise of a power of appointment, no error can be found in the trial court's order finding that the residuary clause of Jane Oehmke's will was sufficient to exercise the testamentary power of appointment conferred upon her by the trust provisions of her late husband's will.

Query: Certainly you would not draft a will in which your client intended to exercise a power of appointment without at least mentioning the power. Should the court have found an exercise here simply from evidence that the donee disliked the takers in default and the donee purported to give away more property than she owned without the appointive property? Do you think the donor would have wanted the donee to capture the property and pass it to her favored beneficiaries rather than his taker in default? Whose intention matters?

———————

Estate of Hamilton, above, raises an important issue in the law of powers; that is, whether a donee can attempt to exercise a power before it is created. Certainly, a donee's attempt to exercise a power of appointment will fail if the donee has no such power. Just because I know my father is going to leave me a general presently-exercisable power in his will doesn't mean I can exercise the power in my behalf before my father has died and the power comes into being.

But just as a testator can execute a will devising property she will acquire in the future, a testator can execute a will purporting to exercise any powers she may now have or may later acquire, so long as the power comes into effect before the testator dies and her will exercising the power becomes effective. The fly in the ointment of this rule, however, comes when donors impose stringent requirements on the exercise of the power which the donee obviously doesn't know about at the time the donee is executing her will.

Other complications can arise if a donee attempts to exercise her power on behalf of persons who predecease the donee, and whether the state's anti-lapse statute should allow lineal descendants of the predeceased appointee to take in his stead. Complications regarding the lapse of powers are taken up in Chapter 5. At this point, you should know that most state statutes are silent as to whether laws primarily aimed at lapses in wills, or revocation and pretermission in relation to wills, also apply to powers.

Practice Point: Considering the Power of Appointment in the Family with Children at Staggered Ages

Without question, the power of appointment can be an extraordinarily powerful, and sometimes simple, way for a donor to pass along her property. Although they may not be familiar with the term "power of appointment," many clients actually request a plan involving such a power during the planning phase. For example, when asked about how mom and dad want their property to be distributed at death, a first response is sometimes something like "Oh, let's just give it all to Carol, our oldest. She will know what to do with it and make sure that the young ones get what they need to finish college." Simple enough, right?

At *this* particular moment, however, you, as the attorney should have some alarm bells ringing. Of course, the power that mom and dad are referring to is a general power of appointment to Carol. But they also are expressing a desire that their youngest children have the ability (and presumably, the assets) to go to college. And, it may be true that Carol might actually have the moral wherewithal to always make sure that her young siblings are cared for and finish school. But, as attorney, you also know that Carol would have no legal responsibility to do so if she holds a general power of appointment. So, in talking through the possible outcomes in greater depth, sometimes mom and dad have a change of heart. Maybe a special power of appointment with the young ones as permissible appointees would be better here for a portion of the property? Possibly, but what if one of the young siblings falls out of Carol's favor and she just decides to exclude him as an appointee? Is that what mom and dad would want?

The answer, of course, can only come from mom and dad. Maybe the above scenario IS exactly what they desire. Or, maybe another planning solution altogether would better fit their needs. Maneuvering through the counseling phase often involves these sorts of mental gymnastics—until a good balance between family goals, property disposition and tax issues can be reached. Would a trust be a better mechanism to provide for younger siblings in a case like this?

6. Objects of the Power and Takers in Default

In many cases, donors provide that the takers in default are the same class as the objects, but the use of the power allows the donee to distribute the property unequally to some or just one of the objects if the donee feels that an equal distribution is not ideal. Not surprisingly, permissible appointees who are not actually appointed any property are often disappointed, and may challenge a donee's exercise to a single appointee, as in *Hargrove v. Rich*, above. Takers in default may complain if a donee's exercise of the power in favor of permissible appointees doesn't strictly comply with the donor's instructions, as in *Illinois State Trust v. S. Illinois State Bank*, above.

Two rules generally prevail in interpreting whether a donee has adequately exercised a power. The first is a presumption in favor of exercise if that is a reasonable interpretation. This presumption relies on the fact that the donor apparently preferred the class of permissible appointees over the default takers, the latter being alternate beneficiaries and not primary beneficiaries. Thus, if a donee exercises the power in favor of a permissible appointee, courts will assume the donor would have preferred that outcome to a failure to exercise and the property passing to the default takers.

But that preference is not quite so clear in every case. For example, where there is a general testamentary power of appointment and there are questions about whether the donee intended to exercise the power in favor of herself, so as to capture the property and pass it to strangers to the donor as in *Illinois State Trust v. S. Illinois State Bank*, rather than have the property pass to the default takers (the charities preferred by the donor). When it comes to special powers and limitations placed by the donor, the ultimate issue is usually the donor's intent. But when the donor has created a general power of appointment, the question is usually whether the *donee* intended to capture the property for herself in order to pass it to the donee's beneficiaries or leave it to pass to the default takers.

The second rule, as adopted by the Restatement and that reflected in *Loring v. Marshall*, is that if no default takers are named, and the donee fails, or partially fails, to exercise the power, the property will pass to the permissible appointees rather than lapse and revert to the donor to pass by intestacy. This rule assumes that the donor would rather have the property pass equally to the permissible appointees (as default takers) rather than by intestacy. This rule follows from the general presumption against intestacy.

Permissible appointees and takers in default are likely to cry foul, too, if the donee exercises the power in favor of a non-object, or in a way designed to benefit a non-object. Trying to prevent a *fraud on a power*, the courts frown on donees of special powers appointing the property to a permissible appointee, for instance, in exchange for a promise to transfer the property to a non-object. In the famous case of *Will of Carroll*, 8 N.E.2d 864 (N.Y. 1937), the donor gave his daughter a special power to dispose of his property "to and among her children or any other kindred who shall survive her." Elsa, the donee, who had no children or other descendants, left $5,000 to her brother, and $250,000 to a remote cousin in her will. The attorney who drafted Elsa's will testified that he told her she could not lawfully make her husband a beneficiary of any part of her father's estate, and that her prior will leaving her father's property to her brother with the request that he pay her husband $10,000 per year was unenforceable. Determined to benefit her husband, Elsa convinced her cousin that if he agreed to give $100,000 to Elsa's husband, he could keep the remaining $150,000 of a total appointment of $250,000. The Cousin agreed to put this in writing, and Elsa's attorney drafted a letter reflecting this agreement. At the will contest, the Court of Appeals ultimately denied the cousin the entire $250,000 because voiding just the $100,000 that constituted a gift intended to pass to a non-object would not punish the cousin for his participation in the attempted fraud.

Of course, fraud isn't generally an issue when the power is general, because the donee can always capture the property for herself and then pass it to anyone she likes. But special powers are far more restricted. At the same time, special powers, because of their restrictions, are not subject to forced exercise by the donee's creditors and property subject to a special power is not considered part of the donee's estate for elective share or estate tax purposes. Thus, there are advantages in both types of powers, and it depends on the donor's estate planning goals as to which type of power should be used.

And just to throw just one more teeny little wrench into the mix, what happens when the donor and the donee are domiciliaries of different states, with different rules about capture, exercise, and creditor rights in powers? Consider this case:

Will of Block

598 N.Y.S.2d 668 (N.Y. Surr. 1993)

Decedent, Dina W. Block, died in 1981, a domiciliary of New York. Her will established a trust of one half of her residuary estate for the benefit of her son Paul, Jr. and his twin sons, Allan and John. The trust terminated upon Paul Jr.'s death and he was given a limited power to appoint the trust principal by will "unto and among" these two sons in whatever proportion he chose. The twins' older half-brother Cyrus was not a permissible appointee. In default of the exercise of the power, the trust fund was to be divided into separate trusts for the life income benefit of Allan and John.

Paul, Jr. died an Ohio domiciliary in 1987. His will, which was executed more than a year after his mother's death, did not refer to his power of appointment under her will. It left his entire residuary estate to a revocable inter-vivos trust he had created in 1974. Under the 1974 trust, after certain payments to his wife (not relevant here), there are separate subtrusts for all three of Paul's sons: 35% each to Allan and John, and 30% to Cyrus. Noting that Cyrus was not a permissible appointee, the court determined that under Ohio law the general residuary clause of Paul Jr.'s will exercised the power. It then concluded that the appointive property could be marshaled to pass to Allan and John, and a greater proportion of Paul's own property would then pass to Cyrus. The court explained:

Having deemed the power exercised, it is now necessary to determine the extent of its exercise. It is undisputed that the power could not be exercised in favor of Cyrus. The question is what becomes of the 30% share invalidly allocated to him by Paul, Jr.'s will. Was the power of appointment exercised with respect to 70 percent only or the entire appointive property? Here the court's task is to further the valid portions of the testator's plan where to do so does not disturb his fundamental intention.

There is nothing in the pertinent instruments or in the applicable statutes which warrants the conclusion that the power of appointment was executed only partially. The provisions of Paul's will and trust dispose of property of much greater value than the appointive assets. The court determines that Paul, Jr.'s bequests of 35 percent each of the residuary estate to Allan and John demonstrate that his testamentary scheme was to benefit his twin sons equally. Consequently, the court concludes that the entire appointive property is to be disposed of for their primary benefit, in equal shares.

Query: What would the court have done had Paul Jr.'s property comprised, let's say, 50% of the total assets in the trust, and the appointive property comprised the other 50%?

PROBLEMS

4.29. Scott dies holding a general power of appointment over a sizable piece of property he received from his father's estate. Scott's will makes no specific reference to the power, but instead distributes all of his property via a residuary clause leaving "the rest, residue and remainder of my property to St. Luke's Elementary School." No contingent beneficiaries are named under the will. The school claims that Scott's will validly exercised the power of appointment via the residuary clause. What result?

4.30. Angus has a special testamentary power of appointment, with permissible appointees being any of his living siblings. Angus has three siblings: Scott, Mary, and Tom. In 2007, Scott died. In 2009, Angus married Scott's widow, Claire. Subsequently, Angus drafted a new will containing the following residuary clause: "the rest and residue of my estate, including the property over which I have a special power of appointment shall be distributed to Mary, Tom, and Claire (since she was married to Scott at the time of his death and was the beneficiary of his estate), equally." What is Claire entitled to receive?

7. CONTRACTS AND RELEASES OF POWERS

As you saw in the *Carroll* case, contracts to exercise powers, especially contracts to exercise testamentary powers, may be deemed void. The general rule is that contracts involving powers that are not presently exercisable are void. But a promise to exercise in the future a *presently-exercisable* power is valid (enforceable by the promisee) so long as neither the contract nor the promised appointment confers a benefit upon a non-object. But most donees, rather than make a contract to exercise the power in the future, simply exercise it if there is some financial or practical reason to do so. Thus, if a husband in a divorce action has a presently-exercisable general power of appointment from his mother's will, he may exercise it immediately as part of a property settlement, he may exercise it immediately on behalf of his children if that is a condition of the property settlement, or he may contract to make a will exercising it for the benefit of his children in the future. But he may not make a contract regarding the power if it is not presently-exercisable.

The more common approach is to *release* the power—that is, to execute a document that states the donee will not exercise the power on behalf of certain permissible appointees, thus reducing the class of permissible appointees. A donee of a special testamentary power of appointment that may be exercised in favor of her children or lineal descendants may release the power as it relates to two of her three children and their issue, thus limiting the class of permissible appointees to the first child and his or her issue. The donee can release the power as it relates to all but one appointee. This doesn't mean the donee must exercise the power, however, for she can refuse to exercise it at all and the property will pass to the default takers. But the release will be binding IF she exercises the power at all by preventing her from exercising it to benefit anyone for whom she has agreed to release the power.

Many critics have pointed out that most people can use a release to get almost the same result as a contract to exercise a power. But the law continues to adhere to the arcane distinction. This is because a contract to exercise a power in favor of a single appointee, in essence, forecloses the other permissible appointees AND the takers in default AND compels an exercise, which is contrary to the nature of a power. Powers, by their very nature, are optional, very much unlike the duties of a trustee. A donee simply doesn't have to do anything with respect to the power. A release in favor of a single permissible appointee, however, only forecloses the other permissible appointees, not the takers in default and there is no compulsion to exercise the power even after the release.

Where releases can be very handy, though, is when the donee of a general power agrees to release the power as it relates to herself, thus turning it into a special power that cannot be attached by creditors.

PROBLEM

4.31. Tom and Janet, who have three children, get divorced. Tom received a general power of appointment from his mother, which he may exercise during life or at death over a stock portfolio currently worth $500,000. Can Tom include a portion of the stock portfolio in the property settlement upon dissolution of the marriage?

8. Pros and Cons of Powers

As you can see, powers of appointment are a wonderfully flexible tool for the estate planner. But they must be used carefully. They are flexible to the extent they allow the donee to exercise unfettered discretion about whether to exercise the power and for which beneficiaries. They also allow the donee, usually, to appoint the property into trust or to grant another power, thus extending the time for final decision making. This is discussed further in Chapter 8. But powers are subject to the Rule Against Perpetuities, so they do have limitations. Special powers have very advantageous tax benefits but, like self-settled revocable trusts, the general power will often be treated as outright ownership in the donee. And although donees do not have the fiduciary or accounting duties of trustees, they have been known to attempt fraudulent transfers that must be reviewed by a court. The costs of establishing a power, unlike a trust, are quite minimal, but powers are personal to the donee. If the donee predeceases the creation of the power, the power lapses. And the donee may not bequeath the power to another. Powers are quite useful in smaller estates where the bulk of the property will be passing to family members anyway. Limited powers are certainly important in the context of trusts, like giving certain beneficiaries the power to invade the corpus (which is a general power of appointment) or the trustee the discretion to pay income or principal to beneficiaries (which is a special power in the trustee). But powers are probably best utilized when the benefits of delaying decision making about final bequests can be safely trusted to a close family member or friend.

There are also a number of important rules about releasing powers or entering into contracts to appoint in a particular way that are necessary before one can utilize a power in an estate plan. We discuss many of these rules in later chapters as we encounter particular goals and challenges to an estate plan.

The rest of this chapter will be devoted to a variety of different will substitutes, including joint tenancies, multi-party accounts, accounts with POD and TOD designations, retirement accounts, life insurance, and family limited partnerships. Many of these subjects could use an entire chapter on their own, if not an entire book. And many of these are also covered in more detail in other courses. Consequently, we provide here a simple overview as to how many of these different ways of holding and managing property fit into the estate planner's toolbox.

As you review these tools, be sure to think about the constraints we have learned so far, such as the requirement of testamentary formalities or fiduciary constraints on trusts. Remember too what goals could be achieved through the use of wills, trusts, and powers. Probate avoidance, life-time control, ease of management and revocation, tax minimization, and post-poned decision making until future beneficiaries are known are all important aspects of a good estate plan. Most likely, any client you have will already have one or more of these in place, or will at least have opinions about which they want. Generally just a few of these will suffice for a modest estate plan where a single asset, like the family home, is the only item of significant value. Yet even the complex estate plan for the very wealthy will include a wide variety of these mechanisms as well.

D. JOINT TENANCIES

As you should recall from your first-year Property class, property held as *Joint Tenancy with Right of Survivorship* passes automatically to the other joint tenant(s) upon the death of the first tenant. A joint tenancy is created by a deed specifying that property is held in joint tenancy and it historically required the four unities of time, title, interest, and possession. Joint tenancy is commonly used to avoid having real property pass through the probate estate because, upon the death of the first joint tenant, the property vests entirely and automatically in the surviving tenants.

Tenancy by the entirety, in those states that still allow it, is similar to a joint tenancy, though it is limited to married couples.[93] The tenancy by the entirety is a bit more robust in that it cannot be defeated by unilateral action of one tenant, but it has the same probate avoidance effect as a joint tenancy. For purposes of our discussion here, we use the term joint tenancy to refer to both a joint tenancy and tenancy by the entirety, unless otherwise specified. But there are both tax and property attribution differences between the two that should be understood. Joint tenancies are also commonly used with bank accounts, but bank accounts have more flexibility in the structure and effects of the tenancy than joint tenancies of real property.

Because joint tenancies and tenancies by the entirety are routinely covered in first-year property classes, we won't discuss the basic elements here. Just a few points are important.

First, if the tenancy is in real property, the unities of time, title, interest, and possession generally must be met. This means that the interests of all tenants must be created at the same time, through the same instrument, giving each tenant equal interests, and all tenants must have co-equal rights to possession of the whole. Although the Restatement allows for relaxation of the unities requirement, not all states have dispensed with them. Joint tenancies in land require the consent of all joint tenants when making management or other important decisions. When a single grantor adds a joint tenant to his deed, it cannot be revoked by the grantor; a present interest in the property will have passed to the other tenant and her consent is necessary to alter the tenancy. Joint tenancies in personal property are somewhat more flexible, as discussed below.

Second, fractional shares of property held in joint tenancy cannot be devised by will because they pass directly to the surviving joint tenants by operation of law. Thus, the transfer happens outside of probate. If a joint tenant wishes to pass her share by will, she must convert the joint tenancy to a tenancy in common. The unilateral action of a single joint tenant can change the joint tenancy into a tenancy in common, usually accomplished by executing a deed conveying the joint tenant's interest and thereby destroying the unities. The tenancy by the entirety can be changed to a tenancy in common only with the consent of both spouses, or by operation of law if the parties divorce.

Third, creditors of joint tenancies usually must attach a joint tenant's interest prior to the tenant's death, because after the tenant's death there

---

[93] As of 2010, 26 states plus the District of Columbia permit tenancies by the entirety, and possibly Alabama. See Schoenblum, Table 5.1.

is no interest to attach.[94] A joint tenancy, however, can be seized by creditors, where one person's share of a tenancy by the entirety generally cannot be seized or attached by creditors. See *Sawada v. Endo*, 561 P.2d 1291 (Haw. 1977) which summarizes the various types of tenancies by the entirety recognized in the different states.[95]

Fourth, most joint tenancies are treated by the Internal Revenue Service as being owned by the person who contributed the funds. Thus, if father put ¼ and son put ¾ of the funds into a joint bank account, the IRS will treat the interest income as attributable to each in the same proportion as their contribution. The same is true if two or more people buy real property and hold it in joint tenancy. The presumption is that ownership is allocated according to financial contribution, but that presumption can be shifted if the parties intend a different allocation. Thus, son may make a gift of ¼ of the bank account to his father in order for them both to own ½ interests, or one person may acquire greater ownership interests in real property by doing physical work on the land or paying more for it. The IRC's treatment of ownership for tax purposes clearly contradicts the historic property understanding of the four unities necessary for a joint tenancy, namely that each tenant holds equal interests. The IRC treats joint tenancies like tenancies in common, in part because many people don't always intend to make a gift when they put another person's name on a piece of property or a bank account, and in part because the intentions of many people is not to create a joint tenancy with right of survivorship, despite the terms of the title documents. Often people want either sole ownership and control but with a right of survivorship, or they want a tenancy in common with different fractional shares but also with a right of survivorship, but they have to use the joint tenancy because state law requires it.

The exception to the rule on ownership being tied to contribution is in the case of husbands and wives, where the presumption is that a gift was made of half the account or half the property from the contributing, to the non-contributing spouse. Because of the unlimited marital tax deduction, the IRS doesn't expect people to keep track of gifts or other property that passes back and forth between spouses. No gift tax return would be required if a spouse makes a gift larger than $14,000 to her spouse.[96] This is one more example of the way in which marriage is given special treatment, ironically not because of the historically gendered law of coverture and married women's legal incapacities to hold property, but because of the administrative difficulties of keeping track of marital property and marital decision making. Because many view marriage as a partnership, many

---

[94] *See* Hurlbert v. Shackleton, 560 So. 2d 1276 (Fla. Dist. Ct. App. 1st Dist. 1990) holding that Judgment creditor's lien on physician's undivided one-half interest in corporate stocks and bonds held with his wife as joint tenants with right of survivorship was no longer viable after physician's death and Perrott v. Frankie, 605 So. 2d 118 (Fla. Dist. Ct. App. 2d Dist. 1992) providing that a judgment creditor did not have claim on property where judgment was entered after debtor's death and where judgment creditor did not file certified copy of judgment in official records of county until after death of debtor.

[95] *See generally* Beal Bank, SSB v. Almand & Assocs., 780 So. 2d 45 (Fla. 2001) and Xayavong v. Sunny Gifts, Inc., App. 5 Dist., 891 So.2d 1075 (2004) providing that if property is held as a joint tenancy with right of survivorship, a creditor of one of the co-owners may attach the joint tenant's portion of the property in order to satisfy that joint tenant's individual debt.

[96] $14,000 is the current annual exemption for *inter vivos* gifts, allowing a donor to give property or cash valued up to $14,000 to another without it counting against the donor's lifetime exemption for gift tax purposes or necessitating the filing of a gift tax return. For more on the annual exemption, see Chapter 9.

states, and the federal government in this situation, view joint tenancies as true equal shares if between spouses.

It can be confusing to keep track of whether a joint tenancy should be treated as co-equal interests or treated differently based on the contributions of each joint tenant. So let's break down the issue a bit more. Thus, if Larry owns Blackacre outright in his own name, and decides to deed it to himself and his partner John in joint tenancy with right of survivorship, and John did not contribute to the purchase of Blackacre, the law of property will treat the transfer as making a present gift to John from Larry of half the value of Blackacre. Then, if John survives Larry and receives Larry's half interest at his death through his right to survivorship, he receives a gift at that time of the second half interest in Blackacre. If Larry survives John, then Larry receives back the half interest in Blackacre that he gave to John when he executed the deed.

Everything you have learned about present transfers, *inter vivos* gifts, revocability, and property law support the idea that when a person adds someone else's name to the title of property (real or personal), a gift of half the sticks is made at the time the second person's name is added. This is because the second person can now withdraw funds from the account or manage her half of the real estate. She has a co-equal right to possession and, at least to the rest of the world, appears to be a half owner with a future interest in the contingency of becoming the full owner if she survives the donor. A joint tenancy is very similar to joint life estates with alternate contingent remainders. Regardless of how Larry and John might think of the property, the rest of the world will view them each as equal partners with equal property rights in Blackacre. If Larry and John were married, the tax code would consider them as co-equal owners, regardless of who originally purchased Blackacre.

Assuming Larry and John are not married,[97] and that a planning goal is to use joint tenancies as a probate avoidance mechanism without intending to make an *inter vivos* gift of a half interest to their co-tenants, the I.R.C. will treat Larry and John's interests for tax purposes as corresponding to their contributions. Thus, income on the property will be taxed entirely against Larry because he contributed the full amount of the purchase price for Blackacre. If Larry does not want this result, he should file a gift tax return noting that he has actually made a gift to John of a half interest in Blackacre, and he should indicate the value of that half interest. If he does that, then the IRS will split the tax liability for income taxes equally.

The I.R.C. recognizes that many people use joint tenancies, especially in the context of bank accounts, without intending to make *inter vivos* gifts to their joint tenant(s). This corresponds to another important property rule that, in many instances, the presumption of equal interest in joint tenancies can be rebutted with sufficient evidence that the parties did not intend to make *inter vivos* gifts to their joint tenants. Thus, when grandpa puts his caretaker's name on his bank account to help him pay bills, and the only box on the bank's information card is "joint tenancy," grandpa can go to court to defeat the caretaker's claim to half of the funds in his account

---

[97] As of the writing of this chapter, the federal DOMA remains intact, which prohibits the federal recognition of a legal same-sex marriage. It is likely, however, that not long after the publication of this book, DOMA will be repealed or struck down, in which case, if Larry and John are legally married in their state of residence, the I.R.C. will treat their joint interests the same as it would opposite sex married partners.

when she takes off on a cruise around the world with his money. Under the common law, the presumption is equal ownership interests regardless of the contributions of each joint tenant, with the right to rebut the joint tenancy label with evidence of contrary intent. Under the I.R.C., the presumption is ownership interests based on contribution, regardless of the label, with the requirement of evidence of a completed gift if an *inter vivos* gift is intended. The I.R.C.'s rule is modified in the case of married spouses to the common law rule of equal interests.

Moreover, defeating the default rule is difficult. Thus, although many owners of real property think they can put someone else's name on the deed as joint tenants and avoid probate in the future while retaining full dominion and control over the property, they are likely to be mistaken. The legal effect of the present transfer of a half interest in Blackacre is irrevocable and potentially taxable, depending on the value of the interest. In the event of wrongdoing, equitable remedies, like constructive trusts can be ordered if there is sufficiently clear evidence of fraud, undue influence, mistake, or lack of true intent on the donor's part to provide some relief. To plan effectively, however, lawyers should not rely on salvage doctrines. If you are going to advise your clients to use joint tenancies, then you should apprise the contributing client that he or she is making a gift of a half interest at the time the deed is executed and file the appropriate gift tax returns or reduce the donor's gifting intentions to writing.

This is obviously not a problem with joint tenants who purchase the property together, each contributing an equal share. In that case there is no gift from one to the other of a half interest. For tenancies by the entirety, even if one spouse owned the property before the marriage and retitled it in both names, there are no tax implications because of the unlimited marital deduction. The unlimited marital deduction doesn't mean that a gift was not made. In fact, a gift is made if the property was owned entirely by one person, who subsequently conveyed an interest to a spouse in tenancy by the entirety or joint tenancy. And elective share statutes will look at the value of property when it was originally titled in both names, and then again when the right of survivorship caused the entire interest to vest in the survivor for calculating the elective estate.

As you recall, marital property acquired in community property states are held as *community property* which is essentially a tenancy in common of equal undivided shares. Increasingly a number of community property states are now allowing spouses to take title to property as *community property with rights of survivorship*, thus giving each other the probate avoidance benefits of joint tenancies while maintaining the equal shares rule of community property.[98]

Note that joint tenancies in real property can be used to defeat some elective share statutes and some homestead protections. Consider the following case:

---

[98] Whitney Savage, Comment, *Texas and California's Option of Community Property with Survivorship Rights: Triumphs, Struggles, and Potential Improvements*, 3 EST. PLAN. & COMMUNITY PROP. L.J. 343 (2011) citing Act of August 28, 1989, ch. 297, 1987 Tex. Laws 715 (providing that "spouses may agree between themselves that all or part of their community property, then existing or to be acquired, becomes property of the surviving spouse on the death of a spouse."); the Act became effective on August 31, 1987 and is codified as Tex. Probate Ann. Code § 439 (Vernon 2003) and CAL. CIV. CODE § 682.1 (West 2001) (establishing right of survivorship on or after July 1, 2001).

Ostyn v. Olympic

455 So.2d 1137 (Florida District Court of Appeal, 1984)

In 1971 Steve Olympic, a single man at that time, executed a deed conveying the property in question to himself and three other persons as joint tenants with right of survivorship. Two of these other persons were Steve Olympic's sister and brother-in-law. The third person was his sister's daughter, Steve Olympic's niece, and the plaintiff in this suit. Steve Olympic's sister and brother-in-law died, and then Steve Olympic died on August 22, 1982. The defendant had married Steve Olympic on September 12, 1975, and they resided on the property as their marital home. The defendant is currently in possession of the premises.

The plaintiff brought this suit to establish her ownership of the property as sole surviving joint tenant. On the plaintiff's motion for summary judgment, the trial judge entered an order adjudging that the defendant's "homestead right" as Steve Olympic's surviving spouse attached to the marital home acquired by her husband prior to their marriage and that right intervened with the rights of the plaintiff as surviving joint owner of the property. The court then declared that the plaintiff's rights as surviving joint tenant vested upon the death of Steve Olympic but subject to a life estate in the defendant as Steve Olympic's surviving spouse.

We can discern no basis for the trial judge's ruling in this case. While it is not necessary that the entire estate in property be vested in one occupying land as a homestead before it may be impressed as homestead in character, the homestead exemption applies only to the beneficial interest owned by the head of a family. Our supreme court early held that where a marital residence is owned by spouses as tenants by the entireties, it becomes upon the death of one spouse the sole property of the remaining spouse to the exclusion of the heirs of the decedent, even though occupied during the lifetime of both parties as a homestead. The court said: "The homestead provisions of the Constitution adopted for the benefit of heirs of the head of a family to take effect upon his demise do not apply to such property and it may be disposed of by tenants by the entireties as may any other property not exclusively owned by the head of a family and occupied by him as a homestead." Denham v. Sexton, 48 So.2d 416 (Fla.1950). The same reasoning applies, in our view, to a marital home jointly owned by the head of a family and a person other than his or her spouse.

Query: You might find it interesting to learn that although a joint tenancy can defeat the spouse and children's *homestead* rights, it cannot defeat the spouse's *elective share* in Florida. In 2001, the Florida legislature modified the state's elective share statute to allow a surviving spouse to include in the decedent's estate for elective share purposes, the decedent spouse's share of property held as joint tenancy. At the time of this case, however, Steve Olympic's surviving spouse not only did not receive the homestead, she received no interest from the house as part of her elective share because it passed outside probate. Do you think Steve Olympic intended to deny his spouse her homestead and her elective share in the house? After he created the joint tenancy, what could Olympic have done to protect a homestead right in his wife? Anything?

Tax Tip: Income Shifting with Joint Tenancies

Imagine that your elderly and very wealthy client owns oodles of stock and is in a very high income tax bracket. The stock is producing good dividends that she doesn't really need, but might need later, down the road, when she is fully retired. She wants to shift the income now, so that it is attributed to someone in a lower income tax bracket, but have it shift back to her after she is retired and her income has decreased. At her death, she wants the property to pass automatically to one of her three children outside probate, all of whom are currently in college and unemployed. If she creates a joint tenancy in the stock, one-third with herself and each child, she can shift the income to her children, who are in lower income tax brackets and reduce the total income tax liability. Later, when she retires, and her children are in good jobs with high earnings, they can shift the income back to her and she can claim the income and pay the taxes based on her, now lower, tax bracket.

Will the IRS allow joint tenants to split the income tax liability between co-owners to suit themselves? Yes, so long as both co-owners have undivided co-equal interests in the property, they can agree to distribute the income from the jointly owned property how they will. However, if the joint ownership arrangement is not a true joint tenancy, but is an agency account or a POD, the income cannot be shifted because the beneficiary or co-owner does not have presently possessory property rights. So although PODs and agency accounts have other benefits, they do not provide the income-shifting benefit of true joint tenancies.

There is something else to pay attention to when planning to use joint tenancies for income shifting. Banks, stock accounts, and other entities that pay interest on accounts report that interest to the IRS on a form 1099. That form only has a single box to provide a single social security number for the taxpayer who will be liable for the tax on that income. If the wrong joint tenant's number is listed by the bank or securities agent, you almost have to move heaven and earth to get the IRS to credit the income to the other person. However, when it is time to shift the income to the other joint tenant, you can simply change the tax I.D. number with the bank so it is attributed to the other tenant on the 1099 that is reported to the IRS. So making sure that your clients understand the tax implications of joint tenancies and decide up front who will be claiming the income and using that person's social security number as the primary owner can go a long way toward unifying the property and tax aspects of joint tenancies.

Under traditional common law rules, the quintessential use of the joint tenancy was for real estate and, to this day, joint tenancy interests in real estate are the least susceptible to judicial interpretation as TODs or testamentary gifts. Bank accounts lie on the other extreme, however, where people have had all sorts of reasons for adding another person's name to their accounts and courts have been willing to look behind the title documents to determine if there was a different intent than giving a half interest. Personal property, especially items of tangible personal property that do not have title documents (like clothes, jewelry, and furniture) lie somewhere in between. But just because I don't have a particular title deed to my television doesn't mean I can't own my television in joint tenancy with right of survivorship. But my joint tenant will need to show evidence of the joint tenancy if, at my death, my administrator wants to include the television in my estate, especially if my administrator can show that I paid for the tv and it was in my house where I lived alone. Hopefully you won't have to litigate ownership of the tv or the bowling shoes, but you might very well have to litigate the joint bank account. If the owner of a bank account adds another person to the account, but does not give up possession of the checkbook or the passbook, what should we conclude about the donor's intent to make an *inter vivos* gift? Fortunately, the law on bank accounts has undergone tremendous clarification in the past fifty years, although litigation remains needlessly commonplace in many states.

1. MULTI-PARTY ACCOUNTS

Joint tenancies in personal property, particularly bank and other financial intermediary accounts, have rules that are more flexible than the joint tenancy with right of survivorship typically used in real estate transfers. These rules shield the financial institutions from liability while attempting to promote the intentions of most grantors to avoid probate. Because many people put another's name on a bank account for the sole purpose of making a gift upon death, but without wanting to make a present transfer of a half interest, a bank account can be held as a *payable on death* account or *Totten Trust* account. Other people put a second person's name on a bank account to assist in paying bills but without any intention that the person retain whatever remains in the account upon the death of the primary account holder; this is called an *agency* account. Other times, an account holder may put another's name on the account in order to give that person both control during life to use the money in the account and to take the remainder upon death; this is a true *joint tenancy* account. Cohabiting partners often use a true joint tenancy, with each having complete control over the account.

But banks often don't give depositors a choice of a joint tenancy, an agency, or a POD account, which can lead to litigation between surviving joint tenants and the executors of estates. As a result of the promulgation and adoption of the Uniform Multiple Person Accounts Act in a minority of states,[99] and revision by other states of their banking codes along similar lines, many states are now requiring that financial institutions have the principal account holder designate the type of account she is establishing when she adds a co-tenant's name. Even without the possibility of checking a box as to which type of account a depositor intends, courts will often look through the joint tenancy label to distinguish a depositor's most likely intent. The chart below helps identify the critical aspects of each type of account, assuming the account was entirely funded by a single owner and was not funded by both account holders.

---

[99] The Uniform Multiple Party Account Act, first promulgated in 1989, has been adopted in Alabama, Arizona, District of Columbia, Florida, Massachusetts, Montana, Nebraska, U.S. Virgin Islands. The 1969 Uniform Probate Code had similar provisions. Consequently, a state may have enacted some law resembling this UMPAA in its probate code.

Type of Account	Present transfer of ½ interest during life to co-tenant (*inter vivos* gift)	Present transfer of only the right to manage the account for the benefit of primary account holder (no gift intended)	Present transfer of the right to survivorship (future interest to take the contents upon the death of the principal)
True Joint Tenancy	Yes	No	Yes
POD Account (Totten Trust)	No	No	Yes
Agency Account	No	Yes	No

Most state banking laws limit the liability of financial institutions if they distribute money from an account to any co-tenant, treating all joint bank accounts as true joint tenancies. When the non-contributing joint tenant withdraws money from an account, either before or after the primary account holder's death, the primary account holder, or his personal administrator, generally cannot hold the bank liable for releasing the funds to a co-tenant whose name was added, even if it was added for a very limited purpose. If grandpa's caretaker goes off on a trip to Vegas with grandpa's money, he can't sue the bank for wrongfully disbursing the money in his joint bank account unless it is held as a POD account. Grandpa's sole recourse is to sue to recover the money from his sure-to-be ex-caretaker. This has resulted in hundreds of cases between joint tenants, or the surviving joint tenant and the estate of the deceased joint tenant, litigating the question of whether the intent in adding a joint tenant's name was to create a true joint tenancy or a POD, totten trust, or agency account. Even though the bank is free of liability, however, there is no joint tenancy if the primary account holder's intention was not to make an *inter vivos* gift of the funds in the account. Thus, this litigation focuses on the property questions of intent for making a valid gift and delivery of the appropriate indicia of control as between the two joint tenants, not vis-à-vis the bank or the outside world. Consider the following cases:

Sandler v. Jaffe

913 So.2d 1205 (Fla. Dist. Ct. App. 4th Dist. 2005)

Mildred Jaffe ("Mildred"), the decedent, had two adult children, Ellen Sandler ("Ellen") and Michael Jaffe ("Michael"). The record is undisputed that Mildred placed Ellen's name on all of her bank accounts, including the Unibank savings account that is the subject of this appeal; that the account was jointly titled with a right of survivorship; and that she fully funded the account. As of May 1999, the account had a balance of approximately $90,000. On June 1, 1999, Ellen withdrew $84,000 from the account, and simultaneously opened a separate account with Unibank, titled "Ellen Sandler, ITF Mildred Jaffe." Ellen later transferred the funds to an account in the name of her husband and daughter and withdrew $27,000 for her personal use. Thereafter, Mildred filed suit against Ellen seeking re-

turn of the money and alleging that she intended only an agency account. Mildred died 2 days later and her son, Michael, as personal representative of Mildred's estate, was substituted in the lawsuit. The trial judge imposed an order freezing the account and entered judgment imposing a constructive trust for the benefit of Mildred's estate. On appeal, the court affirmed in part and reversed and remanded in part, explaining:

> At trial, appellant improperly relied on section 655.78(1), Florida Statutes (2003), to advance her position that as a joint owner of the account she was entitled to withdraw the funds. Section 655.78(1) provides as follows:

>> Unless otherwise expressly provided in a contract, agreement or signature card executed in connection with the opening or maintenance of an account, including a certificate of deposit, a deposit account in the names of two or more persons may be paid to, or on the order of, either or any of such person or to, or on the order of, the guardian of the property of any such person who is incompetent, whether the other or others are competent. The check or other order for payment to any such person or guardian is a valid and sufficient release and discharge of the obligation of the institution for funds transferred thereby.

> The intent of section 655.78(1) is to protect a financial institution from liability for distributing funds from a multiple-party account to any of thendividual account holders. However, the relationship between a banking institution and the holders of a joint account does not in any manner shape the relationship between the account holders themselves. As such, while Ellen was authorized to withdraw the funds, she was not authorized to use the funds for her personal benefit.

> Appellant's argument that, as a title holder on a joint account with right of survivorship, she was entitled to the funds upon her mother's death is without merit as the withdrawal occurred prior to her mother's death. In addition, appellant's argument that the funds were a gift is also without merit as the withdrawal occurred prior to her mother's death and despite demands, the funds were not returned.

> The trial court found that appellant breached her fiduciary duty to her mother when she withdrew the $84,000 from the account and imposed a constructive trust on the Greenpoint bank account, which contained slightly over $59,000, for the benefit of the Estate. Appellee argues on cross-appeal that the trial court neglected to grant relief for the difference between the $84,000, which Ellen withdrew, and the $59,000, which was all that remained in the Greenpoint account. The trial court should have, consistent with its finding that Ellen improperly removed $84,000, have entered a judgment against Ellen for the balance.

Query: In this case, Mildred seemed to be using the joint tenancy form to effectuate a testamentary transfer without following the will formalities. By not recognizing Ellen's rights to access the money in the account, either during life or after her mother's death, the court was supporting Mildred's attempt to avoid probate and the will formalities by allowing her to revoke the gift. Is there a valid policy reason for doing so? Why is Mildred entitled to demand return of the money? Was it a gift?

Lebitz-Freeman v. Lebitz

803 A.2d 156, (N.J. Super A.D. 2002)

This case involves a claim by plaintiff Ellen Lebitz-Freeman to certain securities which her father, Alexander Lebitz, held in a brokerage account at the time of his death. Defendant is the executor of decedent's estate, Mary Elizabeth Lebitz, who is plaintiff's sister. The facts are that the decedent opened a joint brokerage account at Dean Witter in his and plaintiff's names because he was concerned about her and wanted the securities in the account to pass to her at her death. The account documents stated that either joint tenant could buy or sell securities or receive distributions equally without notice to the other. The decedent maintained sole control over the joint account, he *was the only one who communicated with Dean Witter, he received the income from the account and paid the taxes, and the monthly statements were sent to his residence.* After discord developed between them, the decedent transferred the securities to a joint account at Merrill Lynch, and then to an individual account solely in his name a month later, forging his daughter's signature on both the Dean Witter and Merrill Lynch transfer forms. Neither company was required by law to obtain both signatures but did so as company policy. The decedent died two years later leaving a will which bequeathed most of the securities in the Merrill Lynch account to two of his other daughters.

Plaintiff subsequently brought this action against her father's estate, alleging that the transfer of the Dean Witter joint account to Merrill Lynch and the subsequent transfer of the securities in the account into an individual account in decedent's name constituted a "conversion by false pretenses." Plaintiff sought to set aside the transfers and also sought compensatory and punitive damages.

The trial court dismissed Plaintiff's complaint after a bench trial. On appeal, the court affirmed, explaining:

Plaintiff's essential argument is that by creating a joint account, with a right of survivorship, decedent made an irrevocable gift to her of a joint interest in the securities, which he converted by forging her name on the forms transferring the account from Dean Witter to Merrill Lynch and then into his individual name.

However, the creation of a joint account, with a right of survivorship, in a bank or other financial institution does not, by itself, constitute an inter vivos gift by the party depositing assets into the account to the other named party. Instead, our case law recognizes that such accounts are often used as a means of testamentary disposition, commonly referred to as a "poor man's will."[1] If a joint account, with a right of survivorship, is established for this purpose, the assets in the account remain the sole property of the depositor during his or her lifetime. Moreover, if the depositor's intent is to make a testamentary disposition of the assets in the account, he may countermand that testamentary instruction by will. Thus, the determination of ownership of the assets in a joint account turns on whether the depositor's intent in creating the account was to make an inter vivos gift or solely to establish a vehicle for testamentary disposition.

---

[1]   Such joint accounts are also sometimes created as "convenience accounts" to enable the other named party to pay the depositor's bills and manage his or her finances. When a joint account is created for this purpose, the assets in the account do not pass to the other named party upon the depositor's death. There is no suggestion that decedent's intent in opening a joint brokerage account with plaintiff was to create such a convenience account.

"The requisite elements of a valid inter vivos gift are . . . (1) an unequivocal donative intent on the part of the donor; (2) an actual or symbolical delivery of the subject matter of the gift; and (3) an absolute and irrevocable relinquishment by the donor of ownership and dominion over the subject matter of the gift, at least to the extent practicable or possible, considering the nature of the articles to be given." Proof of each of these elements of an inter vivos gift must be "clear, cogent, and persuasive." Proof of the delivery element may pose conceptual problems when the subject matter is intangible property such as an account in a financial institution. However, there is no need to explore what evidence would be required for a purported recipient of a joint interest in a brokerage account to satisfy this element, because plaintiff failed to prove the other elements of a valid inter vivos gift.

Decedent did not "relinquish ownership and dominion" over the securities in the account. The Dean Witter form that decedent and plaintiff executed to create the joint account would have allowed decedent to sell all the securities in the account and direct Dean Witter to distribute the proceeds to him in cash. Furthermore, decedent in fact exercised sole control over the account. He continued to receive all the income from the securities he had deposited in the account and to pay the taxes on that income. He also was the only one who communicated with the brokerage firm, and the monthly account statements were sent to his residence.

Moreover, the evidence would not support a finding that decedent "intended to make a [present] gift" when he created the joint account. Although plaintiff testified that "my father wanted me to be taken care of . . . wanted me to have this money[,]" she did not indicate that decedent ever expressed an intent to give her any interest in his securities while he was still alive, and she never took any steps to assert an interest in those securities until his death. Therefore, even disregarding the other evidence that decedent always viewed the securities in the joint account as his own, plaintiff's testimony could not support a finding that decedent intended to make an inter vivos gift to her of those securities.

Because decedent did not make an inter vivos gift when he created the joint brokerage account and thus continued to be the sole owner of the securities in the account, the trial court correctly concluded that decedent's forgery of plaintiff's name on the forms required to transfer the securities from Dean Witter to Merrill Lynch and then into his individual name was "immaterial." Even if decedent had continued to maintain the joint account at Dean Witter until his death, the disposition of the securities in the account would have been governed by his will rather than by his designation of plaintiff as the joint owner of the account.

Affirmed.

Query: Is it reasonable to allow someone who puts another's name on a joint tenancy account to revoke the right of survivorship, either before death or by will? Or should the father in this case have to reconvert the joint tenancy to sole ownership with his daughter's permission before being able to dispose of the property by will? Remember in *Heaps v. Heaps* that the trust settlors were not allowed to simply retitle the house and revoke the trust on it without following the trust's rules. Should dad be able to revoke the joint tenancy designation simply by forging his co-tenant's name, even if he never intended to create a true joint tenancy?

In both of these cases the courts found that a true joint tenancy was not intended. The *Lebitz-Freeman* court even found that the purpose of the joint account was only to create a right of survivorship in the decedent's daughter which could be defeated by a will! The account wasn't any of the three (joint tenancy, PoD, or Agency account). Is that going a bit far in giving a joint tenant free rein to create any kind of property rights in a joint account that are completely revocable by will but allow the owner to avoid probate and the will formalities if he doesn't change his mind? Although many courts find against the non-contributing joint tenant, courts often will find that *inter vivos* gifts were intended in the cases of spouses and even romantic partners. See *Varela v. Bernachea*, 917 So.2d 295 (Fla. Dist. Ct.App. 3d Dist. 2005) where the court validated the non-contributing joint tenant's withdrawal of $280,000 from a cash management account with Merrill Lynch where the owner of the account added his mistress' name and gave her free use of a visa card and check-writing privileges during their relationship. Following a heart attack, during which the mistress withdrew the funds, the donor attempted to retrieve the money. Even though the donor was alive to testify about his intentions at the time he added his mistress' name to the account, the court ruled in favor of the donee because the donor was an attorney who had been explicitly instructed that in putting the donee's name on the account he was making a present gift to her of the funds in the account.

Practice Point: Parent–Child Relationships in Consideration of Joint Tenancies

Both *Sandler* and *Lebitz-Freeman* offer bleak illustrations of what can happen to a parent–child relationship when money is involved. We can all think about families that look nice from the outside but which are really housing children with latent time-bombs of anger and resentment towards mom and dad or other family members, just waiting to explode. Or, sometimes, certain members are just money-hungry and will stop short of nothing (even bankrupting mom, for example) in order to get their hands on some cash. Therefore, when mom decides that maybe it is a good idea to "just add the kids' names" to her bank account, or real estate, because it seems like an easy way to pass the property along and avoid probate, your job as attorney will be to have a candid conversation about what joint tenancy actually involves. And, let's face it, even if a court might actually rule in your mom's favor if her child grabs her life savings, there may still be a high emotional cost to her by having to sue her own daughter in order to recover her assets. Like so many of the tools discussed in this chapter, your client's goals and personal situation will have just as great an effect on her plan as do her property and tax goals.

If you think bank accounts are the problem and real estate transactions are straightforward, consider this case of a joint tenancy deed.

Bernard v. U.S. Department of Interior

674 F.3d 904, (8th Cir. 2012)

Maynard Bernard, a member of the Sisseton Wahpeton Indian Tribe in South Dakota, owned 45.5 acres of land held in trust by the United States for his benefit. He and his cousin, Grady Renville, decided to develop some of the land and, in discussions with a realty officer of the Bureau of Indiana Affairs (BIA), Carol Jordan, agreed to execute a deed transferring the land to himself and Renville as joint tenants with rights of survivorship. Bernard thought the document he executed was a mortgage to help protect Renville's rights since Renville was footing most of the cash for the development. The BIA then approved the deed. When the development failed, and the cousins' relationship soured, Renville refused to reconvey his joint interest to Bernard. Bernard then requested that the BIA rescind the deed, but the BIA refused, stating that BIA procedures had been properly followed. On appeal, the BIA's refusal was upheld. The Bernards then brought suit in federal district court against the Dept. of the Interior (which houses the BIA) claiming that the BIA violated its fiduciary duty in not explaining fully the effect of the deed to Bernard. The district court ordered mediation and Bernard and Renville agreed to split the proceeds of the sale of 17 acres, and Renville returned the rest of the land to Bernard. The district court then denied the claims against the BIA and dismissed the case. Bernard then sought to have the case transferred to the Court of Federal Claims (CFC) for money damages against the BIA for breach of fiduciary duty, a claim that he had dropped earlier in his suit against the BIA because he wanted to focus on rescinding the deed. The district court denied his motion to transfer to the CFC, and this appeal ensued.

Noting the procedural conflicts and Bernard's failure to retain his Tucker Act claim for damages, the 8th Circuit affirmed the district court's denial of his motion to transfer, stating:

> We recognize that the facts of this case are troubling. Apparently on her own initiative, the BIA realty officer advised Bernard to sign a gift deed conveying half of his interest in his entire property to Renville in a joint tenancy with the right of survivorship. In addition she told Bernard that this would be only a "temporary" arrangement based on Renville's alleged oral assurances, and she permitted Bernard to waive appraisal of his land before the transfer. She also allowed Renville to fill out the gift deed application, apparently because Bernard's eyesight was so bad he could not do it himself.

> The Bernards do not challenge the district court's decision on the merits of their APA claim, however, and they were not left completely without a remedy. Through a settlement with Renville, they received half of the proceeds from the sale of the property originally intended for the joint venture and Renville deeded back the remaining acres.

> We conclude that the district court did not abuse its discretion by denying the motion to alter the judgment to transfer the money damages claim to the CFC since the Bernards had withdrawn that claim several years before final judgment was entered. Accordingly, the judgment of the district court is affirmed.

Query: The Bernards got neither rescission of the joint tenancy deed nor damages. They were forced to drop their damages claim during an early phase of the litigation when the government asserted that the district court did not have jurisdiction to hear their case for both rescission and damages and moved to transfer. Not wanting to transfer the case, they dropped the claim for damages but they ended up in forced mediation that did not result in rescission of the deed. Do you think the BIA officer breached her fiduciary duty by allowing the joint tenancy deed to be executed? Were the Bernards between a rock and hard place? They wanted the deed rescinded, which would be done by the district court, but if not, then they wanted damages, which required bringing suit in the CFC. Do you think they would have had a better chance dropping the rescission suit and going for damages all along?

2.   Pros and Cons of Joint Tenancies

The obvious benefit of a joint tenancy is that the property passes to the survivor outside of probate, automatically, by operation of law. The disadvantage of joint tenancies is that the property passes automatically in cases where the donor may not have intended to make a gift and a lawsuit might be necessary to get possession back. The joint tenancy may be used to defeat elective shares and homestead, which can be good and bad, depending on the circumstances. Although most people will have a joint bank account at some time during their lives, and ultimately no lawsuit will be necessary because both parties will know the expectations and legal rights of the other, the ease of creating the joint tenancy can lead many people into unintended situations.

As the cases above noted, banks are generally free of liability if they release funds to a joint tenant. Still, financial institutions do not want to be caught up in lawsuits either, which is why Dean Witter and Merrill Lynch in *Lebitz* required the signatures of both joint tenants, even though the court acknowledged that the owner's forgery of the co-tenant's signature was irrelevant. Requiring the signatures of both co-tenants helps ensure that neither party acts without the other's knowledge. But you can imagine why a co-tenant would chafe at having to get his co-tenant's signature when it's his money and he only put his co-tenant on the account to give her survivorship rights.

Furthermore, despite the potential for litigation, most states have not adopted laws requiring that banks give tenants an option of what kind of joint account they would like to create. This requires that donors be explicit about their intent at the time of creation when they don't have appropriate paperwork in front of them. Even with a set of explicit options, however, there continues to be quite a lot of litigation over the simple question of whether an *inter vivos*, testamentary, or no gift was intended when a joint tenant's name is added to a financial account.

The IRS generally attributes income in financial accounts to the person who contributed the basis, unless an *inter vivos* gift was intended, and a gift tax return filed where necessary. See discussion of joint tenancies and contribution rules in Chapter 9. Thus, many donors find themselves between a rock and a hard place when they use joint tenancies to get favorable tax benefits (as by attributing half the income to a joint tenant who has a lower income tax rate), while retaining full control and dominion. Donors generally don't get to have it both ways; either they must give up dominion and control for better tax savings, or they may retain full control and have the property treated as a POD account, but then they have to pay all the income taxes at their own rate. Some courts may be sympathetic to the use of joint tenancies to avoid probate, lessen taxes, dispense with the will formalities, and yet still retain full control over the property, but any estate lawyer who advises a client that she can have her cake and eat it too with a joint tenancy is giving very risky advice. There are many benefits that can be achieved with the use of a joint tenancy, but the donor must be willing to part with some control, or a court may be reluctant to recognize the joint tenant's claim that he should be able to revoke the gift. As with a trust, donors must give up some control to be confident in gaining the beneficial effects of the joint tenancy with right of survivorship. But unlike a trust, a joint tenancy is generally non-revocable. So one should use it with caution and understand the laws of the state regarding donative intent. Remember, if it is a true joint tenancy, it is an *inter vivos* gift that is non-revocable, as Mr. Bernard learned to his dismay, which may have some very advantageous tax or elective share benefits, but may be too risky for some donors.

PROBLEMS

4.32. Ann and Tyler, brother and sister, own the family farm together as joint tenants with rights of survivorship. Ann recently adopted two children and wishes for her portion of the farm to pass to those children upon her death. Accordingly, Ann requested that her attorney draft a codicil to her will to effectuate this desire. Tyler says that he is fine with this and gives Ann the "green light" to make the change. Will the codicil accomplish Ann and Tyler's goals?

4.33. Meg and Sue legally married in 2009. They owned their home as tenants by the entirety. In 2011, Meg and Sue divorced; however, they neglected to record a deed to change the ownership of their real estate. In 2012, Meg died. Her will left her entire estate to her brother as Trustee for a trust share established for Meg's children. Who receives Meg's interest in the home?

4.34. In 2005, John purchased a parcel of land, nicely situated in the mountains, where he intended to build his dream home. He built that home in 2007 and, in 2009, he deeded the property to himself and his longtime girlfriend, Sarah, as joint tenants with rights of survivorship. In 2010, John was involved in a car accident that resulted in the death of the other driver and a judgment for $2 million was entered against him. Unable to pay, John filed for bankruptcy, but the day after he filed, John died. His creditors filed a claim against his estate, the sole asset of which is his interest in the home. What is the result?

E. PAYABLE ON DEATH, TRANSFERABLE ON DEATH DESIGNATIONS

Payable on death (POD) and transferable on death (TOD) provisions are often placed into contracts of investment to permit the property to pass automatically from the account holder to the beneficiary upon the death of the former, outside of probate. You can designate a beneficiary to your bank account, stock brokerage account, the proceeds from your investment club account, your business partnership, your life insurance and retirement accounts, the promissory note from your brother-in-law, and a variety of other accounts and arrangements created pursuant to contract. Traditionally, such a designation was deemed void to pass the property at death if the arrangement was not executed with the proper will formalities because such a designation looked an awful lot like a testamentary gift.

But something as straightforward as life insurance would be entirely ineffectual if a beneficiary could not be designated. The whole point of life insurance was to pay a sum of money to someone else at the death of the insured. Life insurance was the first type of POD designation to be recognized and it was validated on the basis of *contract* law, not gift law or property law. Life insurance isn't technically a testamentary gift because the money being paid to the beneficiary is not the donor's money, kept separate in a bank account, but is an obligation the company undertook in exchange for periodic premiums. Life insurance essentially consists of a contractual agreement whereby the insured pays small sums of money periodically to the insurer, and the latter pays the designated beneficiary if the insured dies during the term of the policy. It is easy to see that although the insured pays a premium every month, the beneficiary is not getting the actual money that was the property of the insured. Rather, the insured and the insurer had an agreement that, in exchange for premiums, the insurer would pay out of its general fund a particular amount if a particular event occurred. It was easy to distinguish this contract from a testamentary gift because a gift entails the transfer of the transferor's own property to the beneficiary. We discuss life insurance in more detail below in Section G.

On the other hand, it was not so obvious that a beneficiary designation on a bank account or stock brokerage account was not a testamentary gift. The owner of the account retained full control during life and could change the beneficiary whenever she wanted, just as she could with her will beneficiaries, she could consume the property without injury to the beneficiary, and she could make changes to the beneficiary designation without executing the changes according to the will formalities. Such a designation appeared a clear and obvious attempt to defeat the will formalities and effect a testamentary gift. And for exactly that reason, courts traditionally ruled that POD designations void as ineffectual testamentary gifts.[100] Yet the distinction between the bank account and the life insurance was not so obvious as to justify allowing the latter and preventing the former from operating. Bank accounts are opened by depositing money, as a result of that deposit the bank gives you more money (interest) and safeguards the money you deposited, and when you withdraw it they give you the *value* of your deposit back but not the exact same bills that you deposited. Hence the distinction between a bailment and a deposit. With a bailment, you get the same property back from the bailee; with a deposit you get back goods of the same value but not the exact same goods. Stock accounts are a cross between a bailment, that is governed by traditional property rules, and insurance, that is governed by contract.

Because of the contractual basis for deposits, life insurance, and other kinds of similar financial arrangements, courts began to view the beneficiary designation of *Payable on Death* as just one of many contract terms that was part of the larger agreement for which there was a meeting of the minds and adequate consideration. The beneficiary designation was not, therefore, a purported testamentary gift, but rather a completion of the terms of the contract between the depositor and the bank that covered the management and disposition of money or other usually intangible property. The beneficiary's right to receive the property upon the death of the depositor was covered under third-party beneficiary doctrines and was an obligation by the bank for which it had been compensated. This contractual way of looking at the beneficiary designation made it seem less like an attempt to avoid probate and make a testamentary gift without the will formalities, and more like a small piece in a larger transaction that was adequately governed by contract doctrines. If the bank provided a service,

---

[100] *See, e.g.,* Truax v. Southwestern College, 522 P.2d 412 (Kan. 1974); *In re* Will of Collier, 381 So. 2d 1338 (Miss. 1980); Blais v. Colebrook Guar. Sav. Bank, 220 A.2d 763 (N.H. 1966); Waitman v. Waitman, 505 P.2d 171 (Okla. 1972); Brown's Estate, 22 A.2d 821 (Pa. 1941); Northwestern Nat'l Bank v. Daniel, 127 N.W.2d 714 (S.D. 1964); Tucker v. Simrow, 21 N.W.2d 252 (Wis. 1946).

and one piece of that service was to transfer the funds to the person the depositor designated, then the entire transaction resembled insurance far more than a testamentary gift where the testator designates a beneficiary in a formally-executed will to receive a particular item of property.

An early case dealing with a beneficiary designation in an investment club account was *Est. of Hillowitz*, 238 N.E.2d 723, 725 (Ct.App. N.Y. 1968), in which the court affirmed a designation to pay the decedent's interest in the account, at his death, to his surviving widow. The court explained:

> A partnership agreement which provides that, upon the death of one partner, his interest shall pass to the surviving partner or partners, resting as it does in contract, is unquestionably valid and may not be defeated by labeling it a testamentary disposition. We are unable to perceive a difference in principle between an agreement of this character and one, such as that before us, providing for a deceased partner's widow, rather than a surviving partner, to succeed to the decedent's interest in the partnership. These partnership undertakings are, in effect, nothing more or less than third-party beneficiary contracts, performable at death. Like many similar instruments, contractual in nature, which provide for the disposition of property after death, they need not conform to the requirements of the statute of wills. In short, members of a partnership may provide, without fear of running afoul of our statute of wills, that, upon the death of a partner, his widow shall be entitled to his interest in the firm. This type of third-party beneficiary contract is not invalid as an attempted testamentary disposition.

The contractual basis, and contractual remedies, that underlay arrangements like partnerships, life insurance, and deposit accounts provided a suitable justification for POD designations because they were just one small part of a larger arrangement between the investor and the investment company. But over time, people naturally saw POD designations as a convenient way to avoid probate, effect testamentary gifts outside of wills, and retain full control over the property until death. As they were with revocable living trusts, the courts were skeptical at first. In *Est. of Atkinson*, 175 N.E.2d 548 (Ohio P. Ct. 1961), the court refused to validate POD designations on certificates of deposit with a bank, stating: "[t]he daughters contend that there is no difference between the certificates of deposit marked 'P.O.D' and bank accounts or securities which are listed in the names of two persons or the survivor, which have been held effective to pass title to the survivor upon the death of a co-owner, even though they were not executed with the necessary formalities to make a testamentary disposition . . . [A]n examination of the cases leads inevitably to the conclusion that the contention of the daughters cannot stand, but that the registration of the certificates of deposit in this case is an ineffectual attempt at a testamentary disposition of the deposits involved." The decedent's surviving spouse was therefore permitted to include the value of the CDs in the estate for purposes of taking her elective share and the CDs did not pass to the daughters by operation of the POD designation.

One reason for the distinction between these two cases is that in the first there was consideration for the agreed-upon terms of the investment club and the club account had an independent significance besides merely making a testamentary disposition. In the second, the POD designation was a principal goal of holding the property in that form and the recipient of the CDs were true donees; i.e. in the case of *Atkinson* the CDs were gifts to the daughters; in the case of *Hillowitz* the funds were simply returned to the surviving spouse when the decedent was unable to use them. But the difference between gifts and contracts can't always explain the cases that tended not to permit pure POD designations. Some beneficiaries tried to rely on a present transfer theory, that the decedent had made a present transfer of a revocable future interest to the beneficiary of the POD designation, which was the theory used to validate revocable trusts, but the present transfer test more often failed in the context of these POD designations. As Yale Law Professor John Langbein explained:

> The odor of legal fiction hangs heavily over the present-interest test. We see courts training to reach right results for wrong reasons and insisting that will-like transfers possess gift-like incidents. Courts have used such doctrinal ruses to validate not only the revocable *inter vivos* trust, but the other will substitutes as well. . . .   Similarly, the joint bank account created merely as a probate avoidance device has been treated as a true joint tenancy, despite the depositor's power to exercise total lifetime dominion over the account. Of the pure will substitutes, only the transparently labeled P.O.D. account has persistently failed the present-interest test and has had to depend for the most part upon statutory validation.[101]

The statutory validation of POD designations began rather slowly, but has taken hold in nearly every state. The UPC provision on PODs allows such designations in a wide variety of accounts and arrangements, including mortgages, promissory notes, trusts, conveyances, and deeds of gift. Note, however, that even the statutory provisions go back to the contractual origins of these arrangements in validating designations in *agreements* or other *written instruments of a similar nature*. For the most part, these are not mere gifts.

UPC § 6–101. Nonprobate Transfers on Death.

A provision for a nonprobate transfer on death in an insurance policy, contract of employment, bond, mortgage, promissory note, certificated or uncertificated security, account agreement, custodial agreement, deposit agreement, compensation plan, pension plan, individual retirement plan, employee benefit plan, trust, conveyance, deed of gift, marital property agreement, or other written instrument of a similar nature is nontestamentary. This subsection includes a written provision that:

(1) money or other benefits due to, controlled by, or owned by a decedent before death must be paid after the decedent's death to a person whom the decedent designates either in the instrument or in a separate writing, including a will, executed either before or at the same time as the instrument, or later;

(2) money due or to become due under the instrument ceases to be payable in the event of death of the promisee or the promisor before payment or demand; or

(3) any property controlled by or owned by the decedent before death which is the subject of the instrument passes to a person the decedent designates either in the instrument or in a separate writing, including a will, executed either before or at the same time as the instrument, or later.

---

[101] John Langbein, The Nonprobate Revolution and the Future of the Law of Succession, 97 HAR. L. REV. 1108, 1128 (1984).

The POD designation (meaning payable on) is commonly used for bank accounts, life insurance, retirement funds, promissory notes, or contractual *rights to receive money*. The acronym TOD (*transfer on death*) is used for those accounts where the account itself is to be transferred or the property in the account is to be transferred to the beneficiary. Thus, stock brokerage accounts in which the stock will need to be retitled in the name of the beneficiary upon the death of the account owner is usually a TOD account. The entire account is simply transferred to the beneficiary upon proof of death. Use of the term TOD characterizes an account that does not have to be sold and converted to cash in order to pay out to the beneficiary, but can simply be transferred. On the other hand, imagine the case of real property. Should I be able to hold title to my house in a TOD form; i.e. "to X, transfer on death of X to Y?" If X dies, should the house pass to Y according to the deed or to X's estate to pass according to X's will?

As you can imagine, we've come a long way from the life insurance and the POD designation in the investment club to having actual items of intangible and tangible property, and not just money, be held with a TOD designation. It is one thing to enter into a contract with a life insurance company whereby the insured will pay premiums and the company will pay out a sum of money on the occurrence of the event. It's quite another when a property owner can hold title to a car in his own name, but with a TOD designation that upon his death the car shall belong to his son, and the Dept. of Motor Vehicles is to retitle the car in the son's name solely upon proof of death without compliance with the will formalities. The TOD designation sure looks an awful lot like a testamentary gift, especially since one is not contracting with the DMV to provide a series of services that are appropriately covered by contract law. The case of real property, therefore, is at the furthest extreme from the insurance and investment club arrangement because there is no pretense of contractual obligations to justify use of different legal rules. Thus, the TOD designation, for real or tangible property, is remarkably close to a testamentary gift. Where allowed, however, TODs are always used in contexts where property is retained by another entity, like a bank or stock account, or property that requires institutional action to transfer the property, as with cars and land where the property owner needs another entity to act in order to effectuate the transfer in title.

Some states have adopted the TOD form to allow real property or other tangible personal property to pass outside of probate and outside of a will, simply by the use of a TOD deed recorded prior to the death of the owner. Not all states have applied their TOD statutes to conveyances of real property or have recognized the form by judicial decree.[102] The Uniform Real Property Transfer on Death Act was promulgated by the Uniform Law Commission in 2009, which explicitly permits TOD designations in deeds of real property. It is decidedly a minority position.[103] In reading through this case, ask yourself whether it is good public policy to allow TOD designations in real estate deeds, or whether real estate should continue to require compliance with the will formalities.

---

[102] See Schoenblum, Table 5.1

[103] Thirteen states had adopted the TOD designation in deeds for real estate prior to the promulgation of the Uniform Act in 2009. They were Missouri (1989), Kansas (1997), Ohio (2000), New Mexico (2001), Arizona (2002), Nevada (2003), Colorado (2004), Arkansas (2005), Wisconsin (2006), Montana (2007), Oklahoma (2008), Minnesota (2008), and Indiana (2009). Since then, five additional states have adopted the Uniform Act (Hawaii, Illinois, Nebraska, North Dakota, and Oregon). It is pending in Alaska and the District of Columbia.

In re Est. of Roloff

36 Kan.App.2d 684, 143 P.3d 406 (2006)

Charles A. Schletzbaum was a grantee beneficiary of real estate under a transfer-on-death (TOD) deed. Schletzbaum appeals from the trial court's judgment that the growing crops on that real estate were personal property and belonged to the grantor's estate. The TOD deed was devoid of any language reserving the growing crops. The ultimate question is whether the trial court properly determined that the growing crops on the real estate in question were personal property under K.S.A. 59–1206 and, therefore, belonged to the grantor's estate rather than to Schletzbaum. . . .

In the spring of 2004, Henry M. Roloff planted wheat, corn, and soybeans on his farmland in Atchison County, Kansas. On June 26, 2004, Roloff named Schletzbaum, a long-time employee, as a grantee beneficiary under a TOD deed of certain farmland located in Atchison, Kansas. Roloff did not include a reservation of the corn and soybeans growing on the real estate in the TOD deed. Roloff recorded the TOD deed with the Atchison County Register of Deeds on June 28, 2004. Roloff died intestate on July 24, 2004.

Commerce Trust Company (Commerce), a division of Commerce Bank, N.A., was appointed as administrator of Roloff's estate. Commerce told Schletzbaum that the growing crops at the time of Roloff's death did not pass to Schletzbaum with the deeded farmland and demanded an accounting of the proceeds received from the sales of the crops. . . .

The trial court determined that the growing crops should be considered personal property and that the proceeds should go to Roloff's estate rather than to Schletzbaum. The trial court ordered that the net proceeds from the sales of the crops, $67,424.65, plus interest be paid to Commerce. . . .

Schletzbaum points out in his brief that an interest of a grantor to be conveyed by a deed is controlled by statute:

> [E]very conveyance of real estate shall pass all the estate of the grantor therein, unless the intent to pass a less estate shall expressly appear or be necessarily implied in the terms of the grant. (Emphasis added.) K.S.A. 58–2202.

Schletzbaum further notes that our Supreme Court has interpreted the statute to mean that *all* of a grantor's interest in the real estate is conveyed:

> It is established that the word 'estate' used in [K.S.A. 58–2202] means 'interest', so the statute is to be read as though it were phrased: '. . . [E]very conveyance of real estate shall pass all the interest of the grantor therein, unless the intent to pass a lesser interest shall expressly appear or be necessarily implied in the terms of the grant.'

Furthermore, our Supreme Court has specifically held that growing crops are conveyed with the real estate unless expressly reserved by the grantor. . . . As a result, under Kansas statutory law and common law, as between grantor and grantee, a deed conveys the grantor's entire interest, including growing crops, unless the deed contains a reservation of such crops.

TOD Deed

Under K.S.A. 59–3501 to K.S.A. 59–3507, the Kansas Legislature created a method to allow a nonprobate transfer of an interest in real estate. K.S.A. 59–3501 states:

(a) An interest in real estate may be titled in transfer-on-death, TOD, form by recording a deed signed by the record owner of such interest, designating a grantee beneficiary or beneficiaries of the interest. *Such deed shall transfer ownership of such interest upon the death of the owner.* A transfer-on-death deed need not be supported by consideration. (Emphasis added.)

The TOD deed need not be supported by consideration.

Further, K.S.A. 59–3504 states:

(a) Title to the interest in real estate recorded in transfer-on-death form shall vest in the designated grantee beneficiary or beneficiaries on the death of the record owner.

(b) Grantee beneficiaries of a transfer-on-death deed *take the record owner's interest in the real estate at death,* subject to all conveyances, assignments, contracts, mortgages, liens and security pledges made by the record owner or to which the record owner was subject during the record owner's lifetime including, but not limited to, any executory contract of sale, option to purchase, lease, license, easement, mortgage, deed of trust or lien, claims of the state of Kansas for medical assistance, as defined in K.S.A. 39–702, and amendments thereto, pursuant to subsection (g)(2) of K.S.A. 39–709, and amendments thereto, and to any interest conveyed by the record owner that is less than all of the record owner's interest in the property. (Emphasis added.)

In adopting K.S.A. 59–3504(b), the legislature used the phrase "record owner's interest." As noted by Schletzbaum in his brief, this phrase under Kansas law means all interests of the grantor in the real estate. Schletzbaum further points out that the term "deed," as used and construed in Kansas statutes, "is applied to an instrument conveying lands." The terms "land," "real estate," and "real property," as used and construed in Kansas statutes, "include lands, tenements and hereditaments, and all rights to them and interest in them, equitable as well as legal."

We could find no Kansas case that has dealt with our specific question in this case. Nevertheless, we believe that when the legislature enacted the transfer-on-death, TOD, real estate ownership provisions, the legislature did not abrogate the well-established law that as between grantor and grantee, a deed conveys the growing crops with the title to the land, unless the deed expressly reserves the growing crops. In holding that the legislature has been specific when it has intended to abrogate the common law in this state, this court stated: "There is no merit to appellant's contention that the Kansas Probate Code abrogates the common law in this state. We find no indication that the legislature intended such a result. When that body has so intended they have not hesitated to pass specific legislation to such effect. . . . "

The TOD deed form, K.S.A. 59–3502, created by the legislature is comparable to other deed forms used to convey an interest in real estate. . . .

The major exception, however, is that under a TOD deed, a grantee beneficiary's interest vests only after the grantor's death. Before the legislature enacted K.S.A. 59–3507, this form of conveyance would have been considered a testamentary disposition. Nevertheless, under K.S.A. 59–3507, the legislature has specifically stated that a TOD deed is not testamentary and is not invalid due to nonconformity with the probate code.

Turning our attention to the above-mentioned deeds authorized by the legislature, we note that a warranty deed, quitclaim deed, sheriff's deed, executor's deed, and an administrator's deed all convey an interest in land. See K.S.A. 58–2202. There is little doubt that if a grantor were to fail to reserve growing crops in the above-mentioned deed forms, the growing crops would pass with the title to the land. . . .

Yet, in drafting the TOD deed statutes, the legislature understood the well-established law in Kansas that as between grantor and grantee, a deed transfers growing crops, unless there is a reservation of such crops. . . .

Kansas common law and statutory law state that a deed conveys all of the grantor's interest in real estate, including growing crops, if not reserved by the grantor. Consequently, a TOD deed is subject to that established law. Therefore, we determine that because Roloff did not reserve the growing crops in the TOD deed, the growing crops passed with the title to the land.

TOD Interest Similar to Joint Tenancy with Right of Survivorship

Moreover, as pointed out by Schletzbaum, a TOD deed creates basically the same interest that is created by the survivorship attribute of a joint tenancy deed—an interest with the right of survivorship . . .

A TOD deed has many of the same survivorship characteristics as a joint tenancy deed. These characteristics are as follows: (a) that the record owner's interest automatically transfers to the grantee beneficiary upon the death of the record owner; (b) that no other action or procedure is required to transfer full title to the grantee beneficiary; (c) that any attempt by the record owner to revoke or convey the record owner's interest in real estate subject to a TOD deed by the record owner's will is invalid; (d) that because title in the real estate vests immediately in the grantee beneficiary upon the death of the record owner, the real estate is not included in the record owner's probate estate; and (e) that the transfer of the real estate by a TOD deed is not testamentary in nature, and is not subject to the provisions of the probate code.

When a joint tenant dies, title to the property under the joint tenancy deed immediately vests in fee simple to the surviving joint tenants. The deceased joint owner does not die seized of any heritable interest in the property under the joint tenancy deed that could be distributed under the terms of the deceased joint tenant's will. Upon the death of a joint tenant, no title passes to such joint tenant's heirs. Instead, fee simple title vests in the surviving joint tenants under the deed. As a result, a court does not have authority to distribute the joint tenancy property. The same result occurs with a TOD deed. A grantor of a TOD deed does not die seized of any heritable interest in the real estate that could be distributed under the terms of the grantor's will. Moreover, no title to the real estate passes to the grantor's heirs; fee simple title vests in the grantee beneficiary upon the record owner's death, and a court has no authority to distribute the real estate.

As a result, the growing crops on the real estate transferred by the TOD deed passed to Schletzbaum, as the grantee beneficiary, because the

TOD deed did not contain a reservation of the growing crops, the same as if Roloff and Schletzbaum had owned the property in joint tenancy with right of survivorship. The survivorship attribute for both forms of deeds is a contractual relationship which causes title in such property to vest immediately upon either the record owner's or the joint tenant's death.

Reversed.

Query: It appears that states are lining up to follow Kansas and the handful of others in permitting TOD deeds for real estate. Does this mean that by statute we are creating a new estate in land, an estate that is a non-inheritable fee simple? Is it possible to create a right of survivorship in real estate that is revocable by the present estate holder and in which there is no present transfer of a future interest? Should we allow real property holders to create survivorship rights through TOD designations that do not conform to the will formalities?

Remember that, until the last decades of the twentieth century, TODs were deemed ineffective testamentary gifts if not executed with the will formalities. In the states where TODs have been validated, it was done only because of the contractual basis of the arrangement. By analogy to life insurance, TOD and POD contracts are usually not about transferring actual items of property at death, yet this is precisely what the Kansas statute permits. Are states that follow Kansas' lead completely forswearing their reliance on the will formalities and accepting blatant efforts to avoid probate? Or are TOD designations in real estate simply an effort to do with real property what we've already done with bank accounts—recognize that the joint tenancy with right to survivorship is often used to achieve a TOD effect and it is more sensible to provide an explicit mechanism to allow testators to retain control during life than to have to fall back on the kinds of litigation that routinely follows when testators use joint tenancies to obtain TOD effects?

The Uniform Probate Code provides a series of provisions dealing with POD and TOD accounts and designations. Here are some of the more important provisions, but we have excised sections of each, so for complete provisions, refer to the full UPC.

UPC § 6–203. Types of Account; Existing Accounts.

(a) An account may be for a single party or multiple parties. A multiple-party account may be with or without a right of survivorship between the parties. Subject to Section 6–212(c), either a single-party account or a multiple-party account may have a POD designation, an agency designation, or both. . . .

UPC § 6–204. Forms.

(a) A contract of deposit that contains provisions in substantially the following form establishes the type of account provided, and the account is governed by the provisions of this part applicable to an account of that type:

UNIFORM SINGLE- OR MULTIPLE-PARTY ACCOUNT FORM

PARTIES [Name One or More Parties]: _____

OWNERSHIP [Select One and Initial]: _____

_____ SINGLE-PARTY ACCOUNT

_____ MULTIPLE-PARTY ACCOUNT

Parties own account in proportion to net contributions unless there is clear and convincing evidence of a different intent.

RIGHTS AT DEATH [Select One and Initial]:

_____ SINGLE-PARTY ACCOUNT

At death of party, ownership passes as part of party's estate.

_____ SINGLE-PARTY ACCOUNT WITH POD (PAY ON DEATH) DESIGNATION

[Name One Or More Beneficiaries]: _____

At death of party, ownership passes to POD beneficiaries and is not part of party's estate.

_____ MULTIPLE-PARTY ACCOUNT WITH RIGHT OF SURVIVORSHIP

At death of party, ownership passes to surviving parties.

_____ MULTIPLE-PARTY ACCOUNT WITH RIGHT OF SURVIVORSHIP AND POD (PAY ON DEATH) DESIGNATION

[Name One Or More Beneficiaries]: _____

At death of last surviving party, ownership passes to POD beneficiaries and is not part of last surviving party's estate.

_____ MULTIPLE-PARTY ACCOUNT WITHOUT RIGHT OF SURVIVORSHIP

At death of party, deceased party's ownership passes as part of deceased party's estate.

AGENCY (POWER OF ATTORNEY) DESIGNATION [Optional]

Agents may make account transactions for parties but have no ownership or rights at death unless named as POD beneficiaries.

[To Add Agency Designation To Account, Name One Or More Agents]:

_____

[Select One And Initial]:

_____ AGENCY DESIGNATION SURVIVES DISABILITY OR INCAPACITY OF PARTIES

_____ AGENCY DESIGNATION TERMINATES ON DISABILITY OR INCAPACITY OF PARTIES

(b) A contract of deposit that does not contain provisions in substantially the form provided in subsection (a) is governed by the provisions of this part applicable to the type of account that most nearly conforms to the depositor's intent.

UPC § 6–211. Ownership during Lifetime.

(a) In this section, "net contribution" of a party means the sum of all deposits to an account made by or for the party, . . .

(b) During the lifetime of all parties, an account belongs to the parties in proportion to the net contribution of each to the sums on deposit, unless there is clear and convincing evidence of a different intent. As between parties married to each other, in the absence of proof otherwise, the net contribution of each is presumed to be an equal amount.

(c) A beneficiary in an account having a POD designation has no right to sums on deposit during the lifetime of any party.

(d) An agent in an account with an agency designation has no beneficial right to sums on deposit.

UPC § 6–212. Rights at Death.

(a) Except as otherwise provided in this part, on death of a party sums on deposit in a multiple-party account belong to the surviving party or parties. If two or more parties survive and one is the surviving spouse of the decedent, the amount to which the decedent, immediately before death, was beneficially entitled under Section 6–211 belongs to the surviving spouse. If two or more parties survive and none is the surviving spouse of the decedent, the amount to which the decedent, immediately before death, was beneficially entitled under Section 6–211 belongs to the surviving parties in equal shares, and augments the proportion to which each survivor, immediately before the decedent's death, was beneficially entitled under Section 6–211, and the right of survivorship continues between the surviving parties.

(b) In an account with a POD designation:

(1) On death of one of two or more parties, the rights in sums on deposit are governed by subsection (a).

(2) On death of the sole party or the last survivor of two or more parties, sums on deposit belong to the surviving beneficiary or beneficiaries. If two or more beneficiaries survive, sums on deposit belong to them in equal and undivided shares, and there is no right of survivorship in the event of death of a beneficiary thereafter. If no beneficiary survives, sums on deposit belong to the estate of the last surviving party.

(c) Sums on deposit in a single-party account without a POD designation, or in a multiple-party account that, by the terms of the account, is without right of survivorship, are not affected by death of a party, but the amount to which the decedent, immediately before death, was beneficially entitled under Section 6–211 is transferred as part of the decedent's estate. A POD designation in a multiple-party account without right of survivorship is ineffective. For purposes of this section, designation of an account as a tenancy in common establishes that the account is without right of survivorship.

(d) The ownership right of a surviving party or beneficiary, or of the decedent's estate, in sums on deposit is subject to requests for payment made by a party before the party's death, whether paid by the financial institution before or after death, or unpaid. The surviving party or beneficiary, or the decedent's estate, is liable to the payee of an unpaid request for payment. The liability is limited to a proportionate share of the amount transferred under this section, to the extent necessary to discharge the request for payment.

UPC § 6–213. Alteration of Rights.

(a) Rights at death of a party under Section 6–212 are determined by the terms of the account at the death of the party. . . .

(b) A right of survivorship arising from the express terms of the account, Section 6–212, or a POD designation, may not be altered by will.

UPC § 6–214. Accounts and Transfers Nontestamentary.

Except as provided in Part 2 of Article II (elective share of surviving spouse) or as a consequence of, and to the extent directed by, Section 6–215, a transfer resulting from the application of Section 6–212 is effective by reason of the terms of the account involved and this part and is not testamentary or subject to Articles I through IV (estate administration).

UPC § 6–216. Community Property and Tenancy By The Entireties.

(a) A deposit of community property in an account does not alter the community character of the property or community rights in the property, but a right of survivorship between parties married to each other arising from the express terms of the account or Section 6–212 may not be altered by will.

(b) This part does not affect the law governing tenancy by the entireties.

UPC § 6–221. Authority of Financial Institution.

A financial institution may enter into a contract of deposit for a multiple-party account to the same extent it may enter into a contract of deposit for a single-party account, and may provide for a POD designation and an agency designation in either a single-party account or a multiple-party account. A financial institution need not inquire as to the source of a deposit to an account or as to the proposed application of a payment from an account.

UPC § 6–302. Registration in Beneficiary Form; Sole or Joint Tenancy Ownership.

Only individuals whose registration of a security shows sole ownership by one individual or multiple ownership by two or more with right of survivorship, rather than as tenants in common, may obtain registration in beneficiary form. Multiple owners of a security registered in beneficiary form hold as joint tenants with right of survivorship, as tenants by the entireties, or as owners of community property held in survivorship form, and not as tenants in common.

UPC § 6–306. Effect of Registration in Beneficiary Form.

The designation of a TOD beneficiary on a registration in beneficiary form has no effect on ownership until the owner's death. A registration of a security in beneficiary form may be canceled or changed at any time by the sole owner or all then surviving owners without the consent of the beneficiary.

UPC § 6–307. Ownership on Death of Owner.

On death of a sole owner or the last to die of all multiple owners, ownership of securities registered in beneficiary form passes to the beneficiary or beneficiaries who survive all owners. On proof of death of all owners and compliance with any applicable requirements of the registering entity, a security registered in beneficiary form may be reregistered in the name of the beneficiary or beneficiaries who survive the death of all owners. Until division of the security after the death of all owners, multiple beneficiaries surviving the death of all owners hold their interests as tenants in common. If no beneficiary survives the death of all owners, the security belongs to the estate of the deceased sole owner or the estate of the last to die of all multiple owners.

UPC § 6–309. Nontestamentary Transfer on Death.

A transfer on death resulting from a registration in beneficiary form is effective by reason of the contract regarding the registration between the owner and the registering entity and this Act and is not testamentary.

The effect of all of these complex new statutes is to permit POD and TOD designations on a variety of accounts and to change any common law rules that had prohibited these designations when they did not conform to the state's wills act. Despite these nifty rules, however, many banking institutions will steer investors toward the true joint tenancy account which gives all the owners an equal right to consume the funds in the account and to take any funds in the account at death of the co-owner. Despite the probate avoidance advantages of POD and TOD accounts, these type of accounts allow the owner to have complete unfettered control during life, with the power to revoke the beneficiary designation, and yet have the assets transfer directly upon death. However, just as the law has become more liberal in validating these kinds of non-probate transfers, the law will prevent transferors from using them to defraud spouses or other creditors who in the past have been limited to the probate estate for determining their interests. Just as decedents have more complicated estate plans, with property held in a variety of different mechanisms, the law has responded by giving many surviving spouses elective share or homestead rights in property held in a POD or TOD account.

Technology Trend: Who Gets Grandma's Blog?

We have mentioned earlier in this book potential legal issues with regard to disposing of digital property, such as one's music collection on iTunes, that may be located on the cloud or even encrypted on a decedent's home computer. Digital media and licensing rights are the kinds of intangible personal property that would be quite suitable to POD and TOD designations. But the biggest issue may be simply identifying all of one's digital accounts, and appointing a digital executor who can comply with each company's requirements as well as the decedent's wishes. For instance, a typical decedent may have one or more email accounts, a Facebook or Twitter account, may have eBay or Paypal accounts, may have photos stored on Flickr or Shutterfly, may have a LinkedIn profile, and may have online subscriptions to the New York Times and the Wall Street Journal. She may even have her own website with a paid domain name. For some of these accounts, a decedent might want her wall or basic information to stay on the web and be accessible to viewers. Other accounts, like Paypal, will need to be deactivated. And what about those credit card, mortgage, and utility payments that are being paid automatically from the decedent's checking account? I have no fewer than 75 different online accounts with passwords and usernames, some with numbers and punction and some without. Many will just become dormant at my death, but others certainly require attention if I were to die. But as you all know, some accounts make you change your password every few months, or if you haven't accessed the account in a while. And you certainly aren't supposed to write all these passwords down in a notebook in your desk drawer. No, strong passwords are to be committed to memory. How are we going to manage our digital accounts as we age and die?

Most of these online companies don't have very detailed death policies, so you as an estates attorney need to be proactive in getting your client to think about her digital property and what should happen to it when she passes away. Where companies have the equivalent of a TOD designation, you should probably take advantage of it. Account holders should not only have a list of all their digital accounts, but should identify someone who can manage the account upon their deaths and, except for highly sensitive or encrypted data, pass those accounts on to others. Most digital companies don't yet have POD or TOD capabilities, but some are beginning to provide online services for storing documents dealing with one's estate (like the account user names and passwords) and actually triggering certain actions upon notification of the account holder's death.

Pros and Cons of PODs and TODs

The POD and TOD account, like the multi-party bank account or the joint tenancy stock brokerage account, provide for convenient ways to transfer money or stocks directly, without having to transfer the account to the decedent's personal administrator for administration and probate. In all of these accounts, the beneficiary or joint tenant usually needs merely to provide a copy of a death certificate and the financial institution will rename the account or pay out the funds to the beneficiary. Property in these accounts is not deemed to be part of the probate estate and therefore is not subject to the creditors of the estate or, in some states, the surviving spouse's elective share.

Many other states, following the lead of the UPC, have recognized that POD and TOD accounts remain the property of the decedent up until death, and may include property in those accounts for valuing the elective share or homestead. And certainly the IRS will view the transfer of property under a POD or TOD designation as occurring at the decedent's death. Property in a POD or TOD is part of the testator's gross estate for estate tax purposes. So while the decedent can avoid the will formalities (in essence because the financial institution's rules and procedures help protect account holders from fraud) and avoid probate, the transfers are deemed testamentary and consequently there are no estate tax benefits from using them. Unlike a true joint tenancy, however, the POD and TOD do allow the donor complete, unfettered control during life. Thus, many bank accounts will be deemed to be POD accounts and not true joint tenancies if the donor retains sole access to the funds or the passbook and formed no intent to make an *inter vivos* gift.

As you will see in Chapter 9, however, there may be sensible reasons for making *inter vivos* gifts rather than testamentary gifts. The states that have strong homestead protections for surviving spouses have not yet adopted the TOD real estate deed, so it remains an open question whether such a deed could be used to defeat homestead. Under the reasoning of *Olympic*, the donor should have to give up some significant ownership interests before the TOD deed would be able to defeat homestead. But consider whether states that are jumping on the TOD bandwagon are ultimately rendering their wills statutes irrelevant and perhaps opening donors up to fraud and undue influence, or are they simply providing well-regulated mechanisms for doing what donors will do anyway?

PROBLEMS

4.35. Under the Uniform Multiple Persons Account Act, Steve added his friend Tim to his account in an agency capacity. When Tim fell into financial trouble, his creditors attempted to attach to Steve's account. Should they be successful?

4.36. In *Sandler v. Jaffe*, the court found that although a bank might be protected if it releases funds from a Joint Tenancy with Rights of Survivorship account to another, that the intent of the parties still controls whether a gift was ultimately made. What would happen if instead of a bank account, Mildred had left her cash in a suitcase with a note saying "The contents herein shall be owned by myself and my daughter Ellen as joint tenants with rights of survivorship?"

F. RETIREMENT ACCOUNTS

Many people today will die with at least one retirement account, besides social security: either an individual retirement account (IRA), a 401(k) plan, a 403(b) plan or any of a large number of specialized retirement accounts that they have paid into over their working years. Others may have pension plans or annuities from various employers that will pay out certain benefits during life, and even upon death. Many of these plans are typical POD or TOD accounts, but they may have specialized tax rules. If the funds used to purchase the investments were pre-tax (no income tax was paid on them at the time of purchase), then the retiree and her beneficiaries will have to pay taxes on them as they are withdrawn. And there are limits to how long money can remain in these funds without being withdrawn by both the retiree and once they are inherited by beneficiaries. These rules are far too complex to go into very much detail here.[104]

To make things more complex, retirement plans are generally subject to any variety of federal and state regulations, most likely the Employee Retirement Income Security Act of 1974 (ERISA), that itself is over 200 pages long. Other tax provisions of the Internal Revenue Code and various state laws govern private pension plans as well. Moreover, despite the doom and gloom reports of some forecasters, social security is likely to be

---

[104] See Natalie B. Choate, Life and Death Planning for Retirement Benefits, (7th ed. 2011).

around well into the second half of the twenty-first century but the regulations governing it are likely to continue getting more and more complex. All retirement accounts, pension plans. and beneficiary benefits under social security are important to consider in estate planning, primarily for support of the primary owner, but also as to which accounts transfer on death to successors or provide death benefits to survivors. If a retiree's retirement account pays out to survivors, those benefits are considered testamentary gifts.

Most people of even modest estates are likely to have some kind of retirement account that may come into play in estate planning, especially if there was a divorce and second marriage involving dissolution, property settlement agreements, and/or prenuptial agreements. Some estate planning, as well as divorce or prenuptial agreements, may be affected by ERISA. The tax consequences of retirement plans often can require specialized financial and legal advice. At this point, just be aware that ERISA preemption can nullify a variety of estate planning elements as well as reliance on traditional probate and property rules. Consider the following Supreme Court case on beneficiary designations in ERISA-covered plans.

Egelhoff v. Egelhoff

532 U.S. 141 (2001)

■ JUSTICE THOMAS delivered the opinion of the Court.

A Washington statute provides that the designation of a spouse as the beneficiary of a nonprobate asset is revoked automatically upon divorce. We are asked to decide whether the Employee Retirement Income Security Act of 1974 (ERISA), 88 Stat. 832, 29 U.S.C. § 1001 *et seq.*, pre-empts that statute to the extent it applies to ERISA plans. We hold that it does.

Petitioner Donna Rae Egelhoff was married to David A. Egelhoff. Mr. Egelhoff was employed by the Boeing Company, which provided him with a life insurance policy and a pension plan. Both plans were governed by ERISA, and Mr. Egelhoff designated his wife as the beneficiary under both. In April 1994, the Egelhoffs divorced. Just over two months later, Mr. Egelhoff died intestate following an automobile accident. At that time, Mrs. Egelhoff remained the listed beneficiary under both the life insurance policy and the pension plan. The life insurance proceeds, totaling $46,000, were paid to her.

Respondents Samantha and David Egelhoff, Mr. Egelhoff's children by a previous marriage, are his statutory heirs under state law. They sued petitioner in Washington state court to recover the life insurance proceeds. Respondents relied on a Washington statute that provides:

> "If a marriage is dissolved or invalidated, a provision made prior to that event that relates to the payment or transfer at death of the decedent's interest in a nonprobate asset in favor of or granting an interest or power to the decedent's former spouse is revoked. A provision affected by this section must be interpreted, and the nonprobate asset affected passes, as if the former spouse failed to survive the decedent, having died at the time of entry of the decree of dissolution or declaration of invalidity." Wash. Rev.Code § 11.07.010(2)(a) (1994).

That statute applies to "all nonprobate assets, wherever situated, held at the time of entry by a superior court of this state of a decree of dissolution of marriage or a declaration of invalidity." It defines "nonprobate asset" to include "a life insurance policy, employee benefit plan, annuity or similar contract, or individual retirement account."

Respondents argued that they were entitled to the life insurance proceeds because the Washington statute disqualified Mrs. Egelhoff as a beneficiary, and in the absence of a qualified named beneficiary, the proceeds would pass to them as Mr. Egelhoff's heirs. In a separate action, respondents also sued to recover the pension plan benefits. Respondents again argued that the Washington statute disqualified Mrs. Egelhoff as a beneficiary and they were thus entitled to the benefits under the plan.

The trial courts, concluding that both the insurance policy and the pension plan "should be administered in accordance" with ERISA, granted summary judgment to petitioner in both cases. The Washington Court of Appeals consolidated the cases and reversed. It concluded that the Washington statute was not pre-empted by ERISA. Applying the statute, it held that respondents were entitled to the proceeds of both the insurance policy and the pension plan.

The Supreme Court of Washington affirmed. It held that the state statute, although applicable to "employee benefit plan[s]," does not "refe[r] to" ERISA plans to an extent that would require pre-emption, because it "does not apply immediately and exclusively to an ERISA plan, nor is the existence of such a plan essential to operation of the statute." It also held that the statute lacks a "connection with" an ERISA plan that would compel pre-emption. It emphasized that the statute "does not alter the nature of the plan itself, the administrator's fiduciary duties, or the requirements for plan administration." Nor, the court concluded, does the statute conflict with any specific provision of ERISA, including the antialienation provision, 29 U.S.C. § 1056(d)(1), because it "does not operate to divert benefit plan proceeds from distribution under terms of the plan documents," but merely alters "the underlying circumstances to which the distribution scheme of [the] plan must be applied."

Courts have disagreed about whether statutes like that of Washington are pre-empted by ERISA.

II

Petitioner argues that the Washington statute falls within the terms of ERISA's express pre-emption provision and that it is pre-empted by ERISA under traditional principles of conflict pre-emption. Because we conclude that the statute is expressly pre-empted by ERISA, we address only the first argument.

ERISA's pre-emption section, 29 U.S.C. § 1144(a), states that ERISA "shall supersede any and all State laws insofar as they may now or hereafter relate to any employee benefit plan" covered by ERISA. We have observed repeatedly that this broadly worded provision is "clearly expansive." But at the same time, we have recognized that the term "relate to" cannot be taken "to extend to the furthest stretch of its indeterminacy," or else "for all practical purposes pre-emption would never run its course."

We have held that a state law relates to an ERISA plan "if it has a connection with or reference to such a plan." Petitioner focuses on the "connection with" part of this inquiry. Acknowledging that "connection with" is scarcely more restrictive than "relate to," we have cautioned against an "uncritical literalism" that would make pre-emption turn on "infinite connections." Instead, "to determine whether a state law has the forbidden connection, we look both to 'the objectives of the ERISA statute as a guide to the scope of the state law that Congress understood would survive,' as well as to the nature of the effect of the state law on ERISA plans."

Applying this framework, petitioner argues that the Washington statute has an impermissible connection with ERISA plans. We agree. The statute binds ERISA plan administrators to a particular choice of rules for determining beneficiary status. The administrators must pay benefits to the beneficiaries chosen by state law, rather than to those identified in the plan documents. The statute thus implicates an area of core ERISA concern. In particular, it runs counter to ERISA's commands that a plan shall "specify the basis on which payments are made to and from the plan," and that the fiduciary shall administer the plan "in accordance with the documents and instruments governing the plan," making payments to a "beneficiary" who is "designated by a participant, or by the terms of [the] plan." In other words, unlike generally applicable laws regulating "areas where ERISA has nothing to say," which we have upheld notwithstanding their incidental effect on ERISA plans, this statute governs the payment of benefits, a central matter of plan administration.

The Washington statute also has a prohibited connection with ERISA plans because it interferes with nationally uniform plan administration. One of the principal goals of ERISA is to enable employers "to establish a uniform administrative scheme, which provides a set of standard procedures to guide processing of claims and disbursement of benefits." Uniformity is impossible, however, if plans are subject to different legal obligations in different States.

The Washington statute at issue here poses precisely that threat. Plan administrators cannot make payments simply by identifying the beneficiary specified by the plan documents.[2] Instead they must familiarize themselves with state statutes so that they can determine whether the named beneficiary's status has been "revoked" by operation of law. And in this context the burden is exacerbated by the choice-of-law problems that may confront an administrator when the employer is located in one State, the plan participant lives in another, and the participant's former spouse lives in a third. In such a situation, administrators might find that plan payments are subject to conflicting legal obligations.

To be sure, the Washington statute protects administrators from liability for making payments to the named beneficiary unless they have "actual knowledge of the dissolution or other invalidation of marriage," and it permits administrators to refuse to make payments until any dispute among putative beneficiaries is resolved. But if administrators do pay benefits, they will face the risk that a court might later find that they had "actual knowledge" of a divorce. If they instead decide to await the results of litiga-

---

[2] Respondents argue that in this case, the disposition dictated by the Washington statute is consistent with that specified in the plan documents. Because Mr. Egelhoff designated "Donna R. Egelhoff wife" as the beneficiary of the life insurance policy, they contend that once the Egelhoffs divorced, "there was no such person as 'Donna R. Egelhoff *wife*'; the designated person had definitionally ceased to exist." In effect, respondents ask us to infer that what Mr. Egelhoff meant when he filled out the form was not "Donna R. Egelhoff, who is my wife," but rather "a new legal person—'Donna as spouse,'" They do not mention, however, that below the "Beneficiary" line on the form, the printed text reads, "First Name [space] Middle Initial [space] Last Name [space] Relationship." Rather than impute to Mr. Egelhoff the unnatural (and indeed absurd) literalism suggested by respondents, we conclude that he simply provided all of the information requested by the form. The happenstance that "Relationship" was on the same line as the beneficiary's name does not, we think, evince an intent to designate "a new legal person."

tion before paying benefits, they will simply transfer to the beneficiaries the costs of delay and uncertainty. Requiring ERISA administrators to master the relevant laws of 50 States and to contend with litigation would undermine the congressional goal of "minimiz[ing] the administrative and financial burden[s]" on plan administrators—burdens ultimately borne by the beneficiaries.

We recognize that all state laws create some potential for a lack of uniformity. But differing state regulations affecting an ERISA plan's "system for processing claims and paying benefits" impose "precisely the burden that ERISA pre-emption was intended to avoid." And as we have noted, the statute at issue here directly conflicts with ERISA's requirements that plans be administered, and benefits be paid, in accordance with plan documents. We conclude that the Washington statute has a "connection with" ERISA plans and is therefore pre-empted.

III

Respondents suggest several reasons why ordinary ERISA pre-emption analysis should not apply here. . . .

Second, respondents emphasize that the Washington statute involves both family law and probate law, areas of traditional state regulation. There is indeed a presumption against pre-emption in areas of traditional state regulation such as family law. But that presumption can be overcome where, as here, Congress has made clear its desire for pre-emption. Accordingly, we have not hesitated to find state family law pre-empted when it conflicts with ERISA or relates to ERISA plans. See, *e.g., Boggs v. Boggs,* 520 U.S. 833, 117 S.Ct. 1754, 138 L.Ed.2d 45 (1997) (holding that ERISA pre-empts a state community property law permitting the testamentary transfer of an interest in a spouse's pension plan benefits).

Finally, respondents argue that if ERISA pre-empts this statute, then it also must pre-empt the various state statutes providing that a murdering heir is not entitled to receive property as a result of the killing. In the ERISA context, these "slayer" statutes could revoke the beneficiary status of someone who murdered a plan participant. Those statutes are not before us, so we do not decide the issue. We note, however, that the principle underlying the statutes—which have been adopted by nearly every State—is well established in the law and has a long historical pedigree predating ERISA. And because the statutes are more or less uniform nationwide, their interference with the aims of ERISA is at least debatable.

The judgment of the Supreme Court of Washington is reversed, and the case is remanded for further proceedings not inconsistent with this opinion.

Opinions by Justice Scalia, with whom Justice Ginsburg joins, concurring and by Justice Breyer, with whom Justice Stevens joins, dissenting are omitted.

———————

Query: One of the problems that Justice Breyer raised in his dissent is that Donna Egelhoff received significant amounts of property in the property settlement at the dissolution of the marriage. In exchange, David Egelhoff received all the funds in the pension plan. Now that the Court has invalidated the effect of Donna's waiver in the property settlement, Donna Egelhoff will receive an additional $80,000 that would have passed to the decedent's children by a prior marriage under state law. Of course, the answer is that the lawyers drafting the settlement agreement must be aware of the effects of ERISA's preemption and draft settlement agreements accordingly. They should also direct their clients to amend their beneficiary designations immediately. Should David Egelhoff's children have a cause of action against David's lawyer for not dealing with the beneficiary designation promptly? After *Egelhoff*, should a lawyer who doesn't draft a change to a beneficiary designation upon divorce or acknowledge the effects of ERISA preemption on retirement plan property, be subject to liability?

You could take an entire course on ERISA and probably still not understand all of its inner workings and the inconsistent interpretations given to it by the district and circuit courts. But there are at least four ways in which ERISA can change or defeat estate planning instruments.

1. ERISA's preemption clause defeats state laws governing beneficiary designations in ERISA-covered plans, even though ERISA contains no substantive provisions bearing on the topic. See Egelhoff v. Egelhoff, 532 U.S. 141 (2001). There are scholarly articles on this problem, which argue that the case is wrong, but that if preemption is applied, then federal common law should be developed, patterned on the provisions of the Restatement (Third) of Property: Wills and Donative Transfers, or the UPC/UTC.

2. ERISA preemption has a similar effect on divorce and other marital property agreements. See Kennedy v. Plan Administrator for DuPont Sav. & Inv. Plan, 129 S.Ct. 865 (2009).

3. ERISA contains provisions that prevent or interfere with spousal agreements regarding pension property. These are discussed in John H. Langbein et al., Pension and Employee Benefit Law (Foundation, 5th ed, 2010), at 289–90 (premarital waiver); and 290–91 (marital waivers).

4. ERISA disregards state community property law. See Boggs v. Boggs, 521 U.S. 1138 (1997).[105]

Just understanding that retirement and pension plan wealth can be quite substantial, and that any estate planner should understand the tax and ERISA implications of this form of wealth transferral before doing any estate plan involving retirement or pension plans, is enough at this point. For further reading, see John H. Langbein et al., Pension and Employee Benefit Law (Foundation, 5th ed, 2010)

G. Life Insurance

Life insurance is an important part of many estate plans, and there are countless insurance agents ready to sell you the latest new policy that will put your mind at ease in case you die unexpectedly. But of course, we all will die eventually, so unlike car insurance or flood insurance, many life insurance schemes work differently than other types of insurance; they are ponzi schemes, of which social security is the most prominent. That means

----

[105] I am indebted to John Langbein for his helpful comments in this area and his patient explanations to me of the interface between ERISA and traditional trusts and probate rules.

life insurance companies, in order to make a profit, have to collect more than they pay out. How do they do that?

There are two types of life insurance: *whole* life and *term* life. Term life insurance is a lot like your car insurance. An insured takes out a policy and pays premiums for a set term (10, 15, 20, 30 years), and if she dies during the term of the policy, the insurance company pays out the contracted-for benefit. If she doesn't die during the term of the policy, the policy ends and the company gets to keep all the money that was paid in premiums. Insurance companies hire people to make complex calculations based on actuarial tables as to the odds that any given person of a particular age, gender, health status, smoking habits, and penchant for sky-diving are going to die within the term of the policy. As long as most people don't die during the term of their policies, the company will have enough money to pay out for those who do. Because the company doesn't have to pay out benefits on term life insurance policies unless the insured actually dies during the term of the policy, companies can charge lower premiums than if they had to pay out for every insured.

Of course, if I'm 85 and want to take out a 20 year term life insurance policy, you can bet I'm going to have to pay very high premiums. In fact, if my risk factors indicate that I'm likely to die within 5 years, the premiums for a $100,000 policy will probably be in the neighborhood of $20,000 per year. At that point, I'm better off just keeping my money. But if I am 20 and have low risk factors, my premiums will be quite inexpensive for a lot of valuable insurance if I happen to die early.

Whole life insurance, on the other hand, is a combination of life insurance and an investment account. With whole life policies, the insured pays premiums regularly and the insurance company invests the premiums and hopefully earns enough money to pay out a defined amount at the insured's death, regardless of when that occurs. Normally, a whole life policy will require that premiums be paid for a certain period of time (say 20 years), and then if the insured dies during the 20 years, the company pays out the full contracted-for benefit. If the insured lives for 50 more years, she stops paying premiums after 20 years, the money accrues and is invested by the company, and whenever she dies the company pays out the policy amount or an amount based on the investment value of the account, but not necessarily the entire amount that the premiums have increased in value. How else would the insurance company make money to pay its agents and administrators?

Whole life is essentially a savings account with a built-in term life insurance policy in case the insured dies before the entire amount of premiums are paid in. But once the premiums are all paid, there is a guaranteed pay-out at death, whenever it occurs. If the insured dies after the term of the premiums, the policy functions like a POD.

Life insurance is taxable property in a decedent's estate, though it is not taxable as income to the beneficiaries, nor is it part of the probate estate (provided that the policy pays to named beneficiaries rather than the decedent's estate). So in terms of avoiding estate taxes, life insurance is not the mechanism, though there are ways to shift some of the tax burdens that we discuss below. Life insurance, however, has some very valuable benefits, the most important of which are these four:

1. Life insurance is income replacement for people who are still working, especially those with minor children. Thus, a young couple

with minor children should probably have some life insurance to replace the earnings of either or both parent in case they die while the children are still young. For this type of benefit, term life is probably the most sensible because it is relatively inexpensive, and provides very valuable benefits in the unlikely event of an early death by the principal wage-earner in the family. Most experts suggest that life insurance should be purchased at roughly 6–10 times the value of the insured's annual income. Thus, a wage earner making $75,000 per year would want to purchase a term life insurance policy for 10 or 20 years (long enough to get the minor children through college) in an amount of somewhere between $400,000 and $750,000. Assuming the proceeds of the insurance are invested and pay out between 6–10%, the beneficiary can expect to receive somewhere between $25,000 and $75,000 per year in replacement income.

2. Life insurance can also be used to pay a surviving spouse's tax debt or provide for dependants when the second spouse dies. These are called *second-to-die policies*, and are usually purchased by a married couple. When the first spouse dies, all of his property usually is passed to his surviving spouse free of estate tax liability because of the unlimited marital deduction. When the second spouse dies, her estate may be subject to estate taxes because it now includes the combined wealth of both spouses. In that case, it might make sense to purchase insurance to cover the tax debt of the surviving spouse. The indirect beneficiaries of these policies are the children or other takers of the couple's estate who don't lose their inheritances because of estate tax liability. This is especially important if the primary asset is a business, or a large family farm, that would require liquidation if the beneficiaries or the estate don't have the liquid assets to pay the estate taxes.

3. Life insurance can also be used as an investment strategy for those who aren't very good about putting that 10% of their paycheck into the savings account. Whole life policies are a type of forced savings plan and, if your client isn't reliable at saving, a whole life policy may give her the benefits of a savings plan with the added benefit of some life insurance in case she dies early. Whole life premiums are usually higher than term life premiums for the same benefit though, of course, the premiums aren't lost if the insured outlives the term of the policy. However, most studies show that people who regularly invest the same amount on their own, rather than in a whole life policy, will make more over their predicted lifetime; unless of course they win the lottery and die early. Only with life insurance is it good to die early.

4. Life insurance is also a very effective way to cover a surviving spouse's elective share. Thus, a second spouse can be the recipient of life insurance of a sufficient amount to cover the one-third or one-half of the decedent spouse's estate that would be available as an elective share, thus leaving the entire estate to pass according to the decedent's well-drafted estate plan. A surviving spouse who receives adequate amounts of life insurance usually may not elect against a decedent spouse's estate.

Tax Tip: Life Insurance and Trusts Go Hand-in-Hand

Now that you are beginning to think about many of the different products that are out there to buttress a client's financial security, you should also be thinking about how they might affect the taxable estate. Many people buy life insurance to help protect their loved ones in case they die unexpectedly, or simply to leave a nice nest egg for their survivors. Life insurance is great because the proceeds are not taxable to the recipient. So what's not to like? Life insurance that is payable to the individual or his estate will pass outside probate, but the benefits of the insurance will be included in the gross estate for federal tax purposes. Life insurance that is payable to someone else but is purchased by the deceased is also included in the deceased's estate for determining federal estate tax liability. Only if the policy is transferred to another at least three years before the decedent's death will it not count as part of the deceased's gross taxable estate.

Imagine an average client with a house worth $500,000; retirement funds and accounts worth $1,000,000; personal property and other real estate worth $500,000; and a share of a business worth $2,000,000. The client is planning a trip overseas and decides to buy a big life insurance policy in case something happens on the trip. He buys a $3,000,000 policy for a small $100 first-time premium. Sure enough, he is killed on the trip. Now his gross taxable estate has nearly doubled, from the $4 million in assets he owned, to $7 million because of his foresight in buying life insurance.

Regardless of whether the life insurance pays out to others, or to his estate, he is now looking at having to pay estate taxes. Fortunately, he's got an extra $3 million from which to pay the taxes, right? Wrong. If the insurance is payable to beneficiaries, the rest of his estate will have to pick up the taxes, thus potentially forcing the sale of the house, the business, or the securities.

Enter the *life insurance trust*. Life insurance can be purchased by a trust from money placed in the trust by the decedent. As a separate legal entity, the trust itself purchases the insurance, pays taxes on any income in the trust, and designates the beneficiaries of the life insurance. Because the trust owns the policy, and not the decedent, the benefits will not be included in the decedent's taxable estate. This type of trust is created solely to avoid estate taxes while still allowing life insurance proceeds to be payable to beneficiaries. It is important that this type of trust be irrevocable in order to get the proceeds out of the decedent's estate, although the decedent may serve as trustee of the trust.[106]

A second way in which trusts and life insurance go hand in hand is when a decedent uses life insurance to help pay any potential estate tax liability, especially in the case of a married couple when the estate tax isn't due until the death of the survivor, but the insurance is payable upon the death of the first spouse. By naming a standby trust as the beneficiary of the life insurance, the proceeds can be held in the trust, managed by the surviving spouse until the latter's death, and then used to pay any estate tax liability accruing upon the death of the survivor. This way the proceeds of the insurance is not part of the survivor's gross estate for tax purposes because it is now owned by the trust.

---

[106] There may be issues with these trusts involving whether the trust qualifies as an interested party and may legally purchase life insurance on an individual, but that is a debate for another day.

Life insurance is one of the oldest and most well-established will substitutes, and it plays an important role in many estate plans. Many people, however, may not even know the life insurance policies they have, nor are they likely to update their beneficiary information very often. Many employers provide term life insurance for employees up to a percentage of a year's annual salary. It was also common in the middle of the twentieth century for grandparents or aunts and uncles to purchase small whole life insurance policies on grandchildren, payable at a nickel or a quarter per week. These whole life policies may be completely paid up and the persons on whose life the policies are based may not even know they exist. Some credit cards provide life insurance for people in case they die on international travel, and many people purchase life insurance from the little kiosks in the airports to pay out if their plane crashes. Many of these policies are hard to keep track of (the insurance companies are counting on that!) and a good estate planner should encourage her clients to keep documents like these in a safe, secure place where survivors can easily find them. In the end, though, it is always a good idea to be worth more alive than dead.

H. FAMILY LIMITED PARTNERSHIPS AND MISCELLANEOUS OTHER WILL SUBSTITUTES

The Family Limited Partnership (FLiP) is a relatively new mechanism for transferring wealth from one generation to the next by a device that has been in use for years in the business world. A FLiP is well suited to wealth consolidated in a family-run business or farm where the value of the assets would normally be enough to trigger sizable estate taxes and the only assets to pay the taxes are the farm or business itself. Studies suggest that 90% of family-run farms and businesses fail in the second generation. A FLiP can help prevent that. But don't even think of establishing a FLiP unless you understand the mechanisms of partnership law and taxation of partnerships. However, a well-formed FLiP may mean the difference between selling the family farm or keeping it intact for generations. Since this isn't a course in partnership law, we will only briefly touch on the basic mechanism so you know what to look for when you are doing estate planning involving business or farming entities.

Let's say Mr. and Mrs. Smith own a large family farm worth $10 million in land, farming machinery and equipment, and crops. They have four children and eight grandchildren, but only one child, Dorothy, is interested in continuing the farm. The rest all live out of state and have jobs that prevent their moving back to Kansas to help Dorothy on the farm. Mr. and Mrs. Smith have a number of options—a trust, a joint tenancy, a power of appointment, a life insurance trust—but the key issue they face is avoiding their administrators being forced to sell the farm, or mortgage it to the hilt, just to pay the estate taxes, or their children wanting to force a partition and sale in order to get their share of the inheritance immediately.

In this scenario, Mr. and Mrs. Smith could establish a FLiP for the farm, which would then hold the $10 million in assets, with themselves as general partners. General partners have full management control over the business and make all decisions regarding use and investment of the assets. They would then transfer 99% of the assets to their children and grandchildren as limited partners. These transfers would constitute *inter vivos* gifts and would be subject to gift tax rules. But because the children and grandchildren are limited partners, they have no control over the assets; only the general partners can control the property. Because they have no control, the value of the assets to the children and grandchildren is less than full fair market value. The value of their partnership interests would therefore be reduced by some factor, let's say 30%, to account for the lack of control over the property. The assets transferred are now worth only $7 million, which can be passed by Mr. and Mrs. Smith free of estate taxes. Upon the death of Mr. and Mrs. Smith, Dorothy or another child can be named general partners with management control, and that partner can transfer her prexisting interest in the partnership to other family members as limited partners so that the cycle can repeat itself. Obviously, salaries to the general partners and all expenses will be deducted against income for the partnership, so that only the profit passes on to the general and limited partners as income, subject to regular income tax rates. Income will always be taxed against some partner. But the beauty of the FLiP is that the big $10 million chunk of property is divided into partnership shares that are then each valued at less than the estate tax exemption minimum.

Once the initial partnership is established, and shares are divided among a variety of limited partners who will receive income based on the partnership agreement, the estate tax consequences can be significantly reduced. Moreover, because no limited partner, who would be a beneficiary under a will if the farm or business passed outright to the heirs, would be able to force a sale or partition. Limited partners could only sell their partnership interests, and usually only to other family members. The assets remain whole, thus reducing the likelihood that the family business will fail as the next generation battles to either perpetuate the business or partition it and take out their shares. In addition, the property won't have to be sold to pay for the estate taxes, which is what causes so many family businesses to fail in the second generation. This is probably the most valuable benefit of the FLiP. Because the assets remain intact, and only shares of the partnership are transferred from generation to generation, the business remains viable and the greater and greater fractionation of the legal property interests that normally comes with descent to successive generations is avoided.

FLiPs have taken off in the past decade, and it is likely that tax rules may change as they become too common or people begin abusing the mechanism. But even with tax changes that might decrease the tax benefit, the FLiP is a very sensible way to manage the descent of large ongoing businesses that can't easily liquidate 50% of their value to pay for estate taxes or can't survive a partition action as the ownership passes to multiple beneficiaries. Most large business operations are already in some form of corporate or partnership ownership, but the family farm or small sole proprietorship are ideal for a FLiP. And although one can put any property into a FLiP, including a stock portfolio or the family's Palm Beach mansion,[107] there may be equally beneficial ways of passing this property that might not trigger an audit and an expensive lawsuit.

Family Limited Liability Corporations (LLCs) have a number of similar estate tax savings benefits as FLiPs, and of course there are off-shore trusts or other ways to hold the property in a form that does not make it vulnerable to partition by beneficiaries. If you are going to represent clients

---

[107] IRS is particularly skeptical of FLiPs used to shelter passive or liquid assets. See IRS publication, Edelstein, *Appeals Coordinated Issue Settlement Guidelines*, at http://www.irs. gov/pub/irs–utl/asg_penalties_family_limited_pships_finalredacted10_20_06.pdf

who have these kinds of assets, you want to familiarize yourself with partnership, corporate, and trust law.

I. CONCLUSION

There are a variety of will substitutes, specialty trusts, and tax shelters that may appeal to wealthy estate holders. But many of these mechanisms can be used by people in all wealth levels, and a sound estate plan will probably include a variety of them. FLiPs should only be created by experts in partnership tax who know what they are doing. Joint tenancies, however, can be created by anyone with relative ease. The trust form has become the predominant mechanism for most estate planners looking for ways to avoid probate and perhaps minimize taxes. As a result, there are hundreds of types of specialty trusts, from Totten Trusts, to Crummey Trusts, to QTIP Trusts, to Asset Protection Trusts, to Spendthrift Trusts, to Special Needs Trusts, to Credit Shelter Trusts, to Charitable Trusts, to Charitable Remainder Trusts, to Grantor Retained Income Trusts and a host of others. Every year there is a fashionable new trust that estates lawyers tout as the trust to end all trusts. And every year, the Internal Revenue Service comes out with a new regulation disallowing certain favorable tax benefits of many of the new trust forms.

We have all become far more sophisticated than Henry VIII and his Master of the Wards in seeking, and avoiding, tax liabilities. In the end, however, a good estate planner does not lose sight of the fundamental characteristics of these different mechanisms for making donative transfers, and she should always keep in mind the human needs of her clients. Very few of us will have to worry about estate taxes, but we all will die, and we all want to provide for those we care about. That is the most important job of the estate planning lawyer. And with a well-equipped toolbox, estate planning attorneys can fashion individual plans to meet virtually any set of circumstances. No longer is it acceptable to cut and paste a form revocable trust out of an online database. As we move on to study the different applications of these different tools, remember that almost every problem you face can be handled with multiple resources. Your job is to understand what the different implications are and to ask the right questions to ascertain which mechanism will best further your client's needs.

CHAPTER 5

WRENCHES AND OTHER GLITCHES: LAPSE, ADEMPTION, ABATEMENT, DISCLAIMER

Even the best well-laid estate plan can get fouled up if things beyond the testator's control go wrong. Although most of us expect to outlive our children, many people die unexpectedly, and if the testator's plan depended on the exercise of a power of appointment by a trusted child who predeceases the testator, the plan might not work so well. The law has created certain default outcomes, most of which can be overridden by explicit instructions to the contrary. So it is important to understand how these default outcomes work and how they can be used to further your client's plan. In general, problems arise because the beneficiaries change (especially because there is often a time lag between execution of testamentary documents and death), the property changes, or the legal or familial circumstances change that had motivated a particular plan. We will talk about these in order, though you should understand that any or all of these things might happen in any given estate, even one of your most successful plans.

A. LAPSE

Remember that under the law of intestate succession, a descendant who predeceased the decedent "dropped out" and their descendants (if any) would take by representation their deceased ancestor's share. Thus, if the decedent (Martha) had three children, Agnes, Bob, and Charlie, and each of those children had two children, the grandchildren would not take if their parents were alive. But if Agnes predeceased her mother, Agnes' two children would take her share, and Bob and Charlie would each take the other two shares. The reason for this is that persons who predecease the decedent cannot take a share under intestacy. Imagine how difficult it would be if, instead of having descendants take by representation their predeceased ancestor's share, we instead had to track down the executors of the estates of all the descendants who predeceased the decedent and reopen their estates to have the share they would have inherited administered to pass to their beneficiaries. For obvious reasons, the law requires that in order to take a share by intestacy the beneficiary must be alive.

The same is almost always true for beneficiaries who would take under a will, trust, or other testamentary document. Where Martha has instead made a will leaving one-third of her estate to each of her three children Agnes, Bob, and Charlie, and Agnes predeceases Martha, the law treats the gift to Agnes as having *lapsed*. Dead people cannot take delivery of a gift. Hence, the one-third to Agnes that is ineffective must pass some other way. There are a number of different ways it could pass:

1. It could pass to Agnes' estate and thus be distributed to her designated beneficiaries. This is what happens if someone owns a vested remainder following a life estate but fails to survive the life tenant. Agnes could have devised her estate to her surviving spouse, her children, or to the Red Cross.

2. It could lapse and pass according to Martha's will to other (alternate or residuary) beneficiaries. If Martha provided that all of her real property was to pass in one-third shares to Agnes, Bob, and Charlie, and the residue of her estate was to pass to the Red Cross, then Agnes' share would fall into the residue and pass to the Red Cross.

3. The devise to Agnes could be deemed ineffective for purposes of her one-third share and thus it would pass by intestacy to Martha's descendants (Agnes' two children, Bob, and Charlie). For instance, if she left the residue to Agnes, Bob, and Charlie in equal shares and Agnes' gift lapsed, it would drop out and pass by intestacy to all of Martha's intestate heirs.

4. A substitute gift could be made in Agnes' children who would take by representation the share Agnes would have taken.

As you can see, most of these outcomes could be explicitly provided for if Martha thought in advance about the possibility that Agnes would not survive to take her share. She could write in her will:

> I give the rest and residue of my property to my three children, Agnes, Bob, and Charlie, but if any child predeceases me, then I want that child's share to pass to
>
> a) the beneficiaries of that child's estate,
> b) to my surviving child or children, if any,
> c) to my intestate heirs, or
> d) to that child's living issue.

But many people don't think about every possible scenario of who might predecease whom and what option for each they desire, so a common law rule developed for what to do with lapsed gifts that seemed sensible and predictable.

- If the gift was a specific or general devise and the testator had provided for alternate takers, the alternate takers would take the gift.

- If the gift was a specific or general devise and no alternate taker was provided, the gift lapsed and passed to the residuary beneficiaries.

- If the gift was part of a class gift (e.g., *to my children*), the lapsed gift was redistributed to surviving members of the class.

- If the gift was part of the residuary clause, the gift lapsed and fell outside the will to pass by intestacy (*no residue of a residue rule*).

What the common law did not do was either the first or the fourth option above, i.e., allow the gift to pass to the predeceased beneficiary's estate (which would entail reopening Agnes' estate and having the gift pass to whoever Agnes designated in her will) or to the descendants of the beneficiary (Agnes' two children by representation). And ironically, these are most likely to be the outcomes the testator would most have wished for had the testator thought about the problems of lapse.

Most testators devise the principal portion of their estates through their residuary clause. Thus, if Martha had made a few small bequests to friends or charities, and then left the residue to her three children equally, under the common law rules the outcome would have been far from equal if Agnes predeceased Martha. Because of the *no residue of a residue rule*, Agnes' one-third share would drop out and pass by intestacy to *all* of Martha's intestate takers. Thus, Bob and Charlie would each take their one-third share of Martha's estate from her will PLUS one-third each of Agnes' share (for a total together of 8/9ths of the estate), and Agnes' two children would only share the remaining 1/9th. The other alternative was to treat the gift like a class gift, which would mean that Agnes' children take nothing and Bob and Charlie each take half as the surviving class members. (We discuss class gifts in more depth in Chapter 8). Neither of these outcomes would seem to further the testator's most likely intent, which would be that Agnes' children would take her share if she predeceased Martha because the testator would want to treat not only her children similarly, but would want to provide for her grandchildren if her child is unable to do so. But the common law couldn't get to an outcome by which a lapsed gift would pass to the intestate heirs of the predeceased beneficiary instead of the intestate heirs of the testator without a little help from the legislature.

Hence, every state has adopted what are called *anti-lapse* statutes that attempt to better approximate the testator's most desired outcome for lapsed gifts where no alternative gift is provided for in the will. And not surprisingly, there is great deviation among the statutes. All anti-lapse statutes provide that a substitute gift is created in the issue of the beneficiary, who will take the lapsed gift in place of the predeceased beneficiary (our option 4 above). However, some statutes will apply only to gifts made to beneficiaries who are related to the testator by some certain degree of relationship. Other statutes allow any beneficiary, regardless of any relationship to the testator, to have the benefit of the statute. In the latter states, a gift in a will to a caretaker of the testator will pass to the caretaker's children if the caretaker predeceases the testator even though the testator might never have met the caretaker's children. In the former states, the most common degree of relationship is the same as that used for intestate succession. Thus, if the testator devises property to a child, grandchild, parent, sibling, cousin, aunt or uncle, or grandparent, and that beneficiary predeceases the testator, the anti-lapse statute will create a substitute gift in the issue of that beneficiary.

Some anti-lapse statutes apply only to gifts to beneficiaries who are descendants of the testator and won't apply it to beneficiaries who are siblings, ancestors, or collateral relatives.[1] Other statutes apply to gifts to all relatives of the testator regardless of the remoteness of the relation.[2] The UPC applies the statute to any gift to a beneficiary who is issue of the testator or issue of grandparents of the testator. (UPC § 2–603).

---

[1] ARK. CODE ANN. § 28–26–104(2) (West 2005) (providing that Arkansas's antilapse provisions apply only to descendants of the testator. Collateral heirs, ancestors, and surviving spouses are not covered by the antilapse statute). See also MISS. CODE ANN. § 91–5–7 (West 1972) (directing that when the beneficiary is a child of the testator, and such child predeceases the testator, the bequest does not lapse, but rather passes as if the beneficiary had survived the testator and then died intestate).

[2] OHIO REV. CODE ANN. § 2107.52 (West 2011).

Most statutes apply only if the qualified beneficiary has *issue*, but Maryland, for instance, allows a substitute gift in a qualified beneficiary to pass to that person's *intestate* or *testate* heirs![3] This means that if Agnes predeceased Martha, the gift would pass to whoever Agnes left the residue of her estate to in her will, or to her intestate takers if she didn't make a will. Notably, Agnes' intestate heir could be her surviving spouse who clearly would not be a qualified substitute taker under the UPC and the majority of anti-lapse statutes because they create substitute gifts only in the *issue* of a beneficiary. Some states include gifts to spouses, so that stepchildren may benefit if the spouse predeceases the testator.[4]

As you can see, it can be difficult to determine if the anti-lapse statute even applies, and, if it does, who gets the substitute gift. In the simple case of Martha and Agnes, most statutes would create a substitute gift in Agnes' two children, but some statutes might create a substitute gift in the intestate heir of Agnes (who could be her surviving spouse, parent, sibling, children, or collateral relatives) or possibly in the testate takers of Agnes' estate (option 1 above).

The UPC provides that testamentary gifts to any descendant of the testator's grandparent or to a stepchild will be saved and passed to that beneficiary's lineal descendants (UPC §2–603). If the gift is not saved by anti-lapse, it fails and passes according to UPC §2–604.

UPC § 2–603. Antilapse; Deceased Devisee; Class Gifts.

(a) [Definitions.] [omitted] . . .

(b) [Substitute Gift.] If a devisee fails to survive the testator and is a grandparent, a descendant of a grandparent, or a stepchild of either the testator or the donor of a power of appointment exercised by the testator's will, the following apply:

(1) Except as provided in paragraph (4), if the devise is not in the form of a class gift and the deceased devisee leaves surviving descendants, a substitute gift is created in the devisee's surviving descendants. They take by representation the property to which the devisee would have been entitled had the devisee survived the testator.

(2) Except as provided in paragraph (4), if the devise is in the form of a class gift, other than a devise to "issue," "descendants," "heirs of the body," "heirs," "next to kin," "relatives," or "family," or a class described by language of similar import, a substitute gift is created in the surviving descendants of any deceased devisee. The property to which the devisees would have been entitled had all of them survived the testator passes to the surviving devisees and the surviving descendants of the deceased devisees. Each surviving devisee takes the share to which he [or she] would have been entitled had the deceased devisees survived the testator. Each deceased devisee's surviving descendants who are substituted for the deceased devi-

---

[3] MD. CODE ANN. EST. & TRUSTS § 4–403 (West 1974).

[4] *In re* Schroeder's Estate, 293 N.W. 492, 228 Iowa 1198 (1940) ("where testator's wife was sole devisee under testator's will, and wife died before testator, wife's heirs inherited property devised to wife, unless from terms of will a contrary intent was manifest."). Compare with *In re* Estate of Baxter, 798 P.2d 644, 647–48 (Okla. Ct. App. 1990) citing *In re* Prather's Estate, 527 P.2d 211 (Okla. App. 1974) (holding the term "other relation" as used in Oklahoma's antilapse statute included only blood relatives of the testator and excluded the spouse of testator, thus causing a devise to wife from testator, where testator died with no issue, leaving the entirety of his estate to his wife under the bequeath "to have and to hold unto her and her heirs forever" to result in a failure of testamentary disposition when wife predeceased him leaving issue).

see take by representation the share to which the deceased devisee would have been entitled had the deceased devisee survived the testator. For the purposes of this paragraph, "deceased devisee" means a class member who failed to survive the testator and left one or more surviving descendants.

(3) For the purposes of Section 2–601, words of survivorship, such as in a devise to an individual "if he survives me," or in a devise to "my surviving children," are not, in the absence of additional evidence, a sufficient indication of an intent contrary to the application of this section.

(4) If the will creates an alternative devise with respect to a devise for which a substitute gift is created by paragraph (1) or (2), the substitute gift is superseded by the alternative devise if:

> (A) the alternative devise is in the form of a class gift and one or more members of the class is entitled to take under the will; or

> (B) the alternative devise is not in the form of a class gift and the expressly designated devisee of the alternative devise is entitled to take under the will.

(5) Unless the language creating a power of appointment expressly excludes the substitution of the descendants of an appointee for the appointee, a surviving descendant of a deceased appointee of a power of appointment can be substituted for the appointee under this section, whether or not the descendant is an object of the power.

(c) [More Than One Substitute Gift; Which One Takes.] If, under subsection (b), substitute gifts are created and not superseded with respect to more than one devise and the devises are alternative devises, one to the other, the determination of which of the substitute gifts takes effect is resolved as follows:

(1) Except as provided in paragraph (2), the devised property passes under the primary substitute gift.

(2) If there is a younger-generation devise, the devised property passes under the younger-generation substitute gift and not under the primary substitute gift.

(3) In this subsection:

(A) "Primary devise" means the devise that would have taken effect had all the deceased devisees of the alternative devises who left surviving descendants survived the testator.

(B) "Primary substitute gift" means the substitute gift created with respect to the primary devise.

(C) "Younger-generation devise" means a devise that (i) is to a descendant of a devisee of the primary devise, (ii) is an alternative devise with respect to the primary devise, (iii) is a devise for which a substitute gift is created, and (iv) would have taken effect had all the deceased devisees who left surviving descendants survived the testator except the deceased devisee or devisees of the primary devise.

(D) "Younger-generation substitute gift" means the substitute gift created with respect to the younger-generation devise.

UPC § 2–604. Failure of Testamentary Provision.

(a) Except as provided in Section 2–603, a devise, other than a residuary devise, that fails for any reason becomes a part of the residue.

(b) Except as provided in Section 2–603, if the residue is devised to two or more persons, the share of a residuary devisee that fails for any reason passes to the other residuary devisee, or to other residuary devisees in proportion to the interest of each in the remaining part of the residue.

Compare the UPC anti-lapse provisions to those of Maryland and the District of Columbia.

Md. Code, Estates and Trusts, § 4–401. Death of legatee

A legatee, other than his spouse, who fails to survive the testator by 30 full days is considered to have predeceased the testator, unless the will of the testator expressly creates a presumption that the legatee is considered to survive the testator or requires that the legatee survives the testator for a stated period in order to take under the will and the legatee survives for the stated period.

Md. Code, Estates and Trusts, § 4–403. Lapse or failure of legacy

(a) Unless a contrary intent is expressly indicated in the will, a legacy may not lapse or fail because of the death of a legatee after the execution of the will but prior to the death of the testator if the legatee is:

(1) Actually and specifically named as legatee;

(2) Described or in any manner referred to, designated, or identified as legatee in the will; or

(3) A member of a class in whose favor a legacy is made.

(b) A legacy described in subsection (a) shall have the same effect and operation in law to direct the distribution of the property directly from the estate of the person who owned the property to those persons who would have taken the property if the legatee had died, testate or intestate, owning the property.

(c) Creditors of the deceased legatee shall have no interest in the property, whether the claim is based on contract, tort, tax obligations, or any other item.

D.C. Code § 18–308. Death of devisee or legatee; lapsed or void devises or bequests.

Unless a different disposition is made or required by the will, if a devisee or legatee dies before the testator, leaving issue who survive the testator, the issue shall take the estate devised or bequeathed as the devisee or legatee would have done if he had survived the testator. Unless a contrary intention appears by the will, the property comprised in a devise or bequest in a will that fails or is void or is otherwise incapable of taking effect, shall be deemed included in the residuary devise or bequest, if any, contained in the will.

What would be the result of Martha's lapsed gift to Agnes under the UPC, Maryland, or the DC Code? Which of the three rules makes the most sense in your mind? Which do you think most testators would want?

In determining the applicability of an anti-lapse statute we should also remember that these statutes are default rules that can be defeated by evidence of contrary intent on the part of the testator. Thus, if the testator provides for an alternate gift if a beneficiary predeceases, then clearly that alternate gift should prevail over application of the anti-lapse statute. Hence, if Martha had devised "all the rest and residue of my estate to my three children, Agnes, Bob, and Charlie in equal parts, *or to their children by representation if any predeceases me*," then Agnes' share would pass to the alternate takers under Martha's will. But what would happen if both Agnes and one of Agnes' children, David, predeceased Martha? In that case both the primary taker (Agnes) and one of the alternate takers (David) predeceased. How would Agnes' share be distributed if David had two children surviving him (Frank and Greta) and his sister, Ethel?

The answer to that question depends, of course, on the anti-lapse statute. A well-crafted anti-lapse statute like the UPC has a complicated provision for younger generation devises that actually simplifies the determination of who takes. Under the UPC, if the alternate beneficiaries under Martha's will (Agnes' issue) are a younger generation of the primary beneficiary (in this case Agnes), then the substitute takers of the alternates take rather than the substitute takers of the primary. Let's look at this carefully and identify the relevant parties.

First remember again what the devise was: "all the rest and residue of my estate to my three children, Agnes, Bob, and Charlie in equal parts, *or to their children by representation if any predeceases me*." Bob and Charlie survive Martha, but Agnes does not. Agnes had two children, David and Ethel, but David also predeceased Martha leaving 2 children surviving him, Frank and Greta.

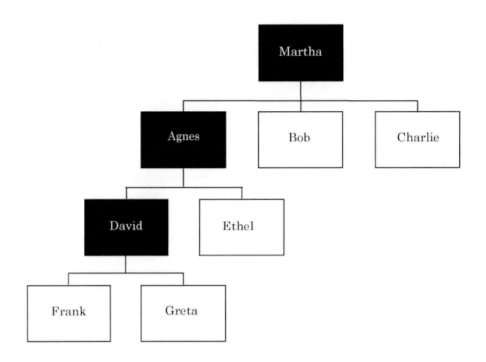

Illustration 8

Illustration 8

- Primary Beneficiary = Agnes

- Alternate Beneficiaries = David and Ethel

- Substitute Takers of the Primary Beneficiary = David and Ethel

- Substitute Takers of the Alternate Beneficiaries = Frank and Greta

  (David's substitutes) and Ethel's children (if any)

In our example above, Bob and Charlie each take their 1/3rd share but the primary beneficiary of the last 1/3rd share (Agnes) predeceased the testator, so we then look to the alternate beneficiaries named in the will. The alternates are David and Ethel, Agnes' two children. Under the alternate gift, Ethel will take half of Agnes' share (or 1/6th of Martha's estate) as a surviving beneficiary of the alternate gift.

Bob	1/3rd of total estate
Charlie	1/3rd of total estate
Ethel	1/6th of total estate (half of Agnes' 1/3rd share)
???	1/6th of total estate (David's half of Agnes' 1/3rd share)

But what happens to David's half? Because both the primary and alternate gift lapsed, it can either pass via the anti-lapse statute to the substitute takers of the primary beneficiary (David and Ethel) or the substitute takers of the alternate beneficiaries (Frank and Greta). Most anti-lapse statutes do not specify what would happen if both the primary and alternate beneficiaries predeceased the testator. The presumption is that the substitutes of the primary take under the anti-lapse statute. This is done on the theory that the primary was the testator's most important beneficiary and the testator would prefer that if the alternates can't take, that the gift passes to the primary's substitutes. But a quick example shows why the UPC adopted the rule that the substitutes of the alternate beneficiary takes under the anti-lapse statute.

If David's half passes to the substitutes of the *primary* beneficiaries, Martha's estate would be distributed as follows:

Bob	1/3rd of total estate
Charlie	1/3rd of total estate
Ethel	1/6th of total estate (half of Agnes' 1/3rd share)
Ethel	1/12th of total estate (half of David's 1/6th share)
Frank	1/24th of total estate (1/4th of David's 1/6th share)
Greta	1/24th of total estate (1/4th of David's 1/6th share)

If David's half passes to the substitutes of the *alternate* beneficiaries, Martha's estate would be distributed as follows:

Bob	1/3rd of total estate
Charlie	1/3rd of total estate
Ethel	1/6th of total estate (half of Agnes' 1/3rd share)
Frank	1/12th of total estate (1/2 of David's 1/6th share)
Greta	1/12th of total estate (1/2 of David's 1/6th share)

Under the UPC, the second outcome would be the result of application of UPC§ 2–603(c)(2), and it more closely approximates the result that would be achieved under intestacy. The UPC provides that when the alternates are a younger generation of the primary beneficiary (which they are here because David and Ethel are a younger generation than Agnes), a gift that lapses because of failure of *both* the primary and the alternate takers passes to the substitutes of the alternate beneficiaries and not the substitutes of the primary beneficiary. Thus, Ethel would take her half under the alternate gift, and the other half would pass to Frank and Greta as the substitute takers for David (the alternate).

One of the times anti-lapse can get really complex is when a beneficiary has numerous intestate heirs who would take under an anti-lapse statute, but the testator has provided for only a small group of her issue or relatives to take. For instance, what if Agnes had a third child, Walter, who was excluded from Martha's will altogether, and what if Walter had predeceased Martha leaving three children? The substitute takers of the primary beneficiary would include Walter's three children, as well as Ethel, Frank, and Greta. Thus, Martha could have devised all her property to my "three children, Agnes, Bob, and Charlie, or in case Agnes predeceases me, to her two youngest children, David and Ethel, and not Walter because he won the lottery and doesn't need the money." Even though Martha has provided that Walter would not take a share if Agnes predeceased, his children could take a share under the anti-lapse statute as substitutes for Agnes.

Another complication is the *void* devise. What if Agnes not only predeceased her mother, but had died prior to the execution of her mother's will, and yet the will purported to give one-third of Martha's estate to Agnes? This was called a *void* gift; it was a gift that was void at its inception because there was no donee at the time the will was made. At common law it generally did not matter if a gift was void or lapsed, though if you think about it, a testator might want a different outcome. For instance, if the decedent knew her daughter Agnes had predeceased her and yet she included her in the will, it might be that the decedent wanted Agnes' estate to share in the gift and she just didn't know how to express it. Most anti-lapse statutes apply to both lapsed and void gifts, but one should be certain to read the statutes carefully.

Consider the scenario where the testator left the residue of her estate to all her "nieces and nephews." At her death, the testator had 5 nieces and nephews. A sixth niece, Sylvia, had died 35 years before the testator as an infant. For obvious reasons the common law would completely exclude Sylvia, or her estate, from taking. But some anti-lapse statutes, like the one in Maryland, might give Sylvia's share to her intestate or testate takers. In the case of an infant, Sylvia's parents would most likely be her intestate takers (the testator's brother or sister). Of course, if they too predeceased the testator, then the surviving nieces and nephews might be Sylvia's heirs. If that were the case we would get to the same outcome through a series of complicated calculations. Quite logically, therefore, the common law assumes that anyone who dies prior to the execution of the testator's will should not take any share of a bequest.

Now consider if Sylvia died two days prior to the execution of the will, and the testator died 2 days after executing her will. Family members might not have wanted to tell the testator about Sylvia's death because the testator herself was in failing health and they saw no reason to upset her. Additionally, what would be the result if Sylvia left three minor children? Should the children be entitled to take Sylvia's share under the anti-lapse provision even though the bequest was technically void rather than merely lapsed? Most states would say yes and we can feel confident this is what the testator would have wanted.

As you can imagine, accounting for long dead relations makes little sense, but accounting for recently deceased beneficiaries might be a different story. What if Sylvia died many years ago but left 3 minor children who are now adults and in college? Does it make sense to apply the anti-lapse statute to save Sylvia's share because there are descendants that the testator would probably want to provide for? If you say yes, what happens if the testator had already made a specific devise to Sylvia's three children, and then left the residue of her estate to her nieces and nephews? Should Sylvia's children take their individual bequest and also take Sylvia's share of the residue? There are no easy answers, and no statute is going to be able to provide the best results for all possible circumstances. Consequently, a well-drafted will or trust should indicate whether predeceased class members should be included, and they should provide for alternative gifts if some or all of the beneficiaries predecease the testator. And just to be on the safe side, it's not a bad idea to make a final alternative bequest to a charity or another entity that isn't likely to predecease the testator in case the primary and alternate beneficiaries' gifts lapse.

Another difficulty with anti-lapse statutes is deciding whether they should apply to other testamentary documents besides wills. The UPC has adopted additional provisions giving anti-lapse effects to interests in trusts and powers (UPC § 2–707(b) and § 2–603(b)(5)), but many states have not amended their probate codes to apply traditional will doctrines to any will substitutes. Thus, one could easily find that a substitute gift is created for a predeceased beneficiary under a will, but no substitute gift is created for the same beneficiary in a trust created as part of a comprehensive estate plan.

And a final particularly thorny problem arises in determining *contrary intent*. The UPC provides that the anti-lapse statute applies unless the testator expresses a contrary intent (UPC § 2–601). What does that contrary intent look like? Certainly, as noted above, an alternate provision shows contrary intent. The more difficult question is whether survivorship language (as "to Agnes if she survives me") is enough to show contrary intent in the absence of an alternate gift. The majority rule is that survivorship language **is** sufficient to defeat application of the statute, thus causing the lapsed gift to fail entirely and perhaps result in the beneficiary's descendants being completely disinherited. Because the survivorship language is often boilerplate in many wills, the UPC takes the position that the survivorship language alone is **not** enough to defeat application of the anti-lapse statute.

UPC § 2–603(b)(3)

For the purposes of Section 2–601, words of survivorship, such as in a devise to an individual "if he survives me," or in a devise to "my surviving children," are not, in the absence of additional evidence, a sufficient indication of an intent contrary to the application of this section.

Ideally, the will drafter should be explicit about whether substitute gifts should be created in descendants of beneficiaries. For instance, a simple statement in the will that reads, "I expect all devisees under my will to survive me, and if they fail to survive me by 120 hours I do not want any of their gifts to pass to their descendants by operation of the anti-lapse statute" is sure to do the trick. Or, "I expect all devisees under my will to survive me, and if they fail to survive me by 120 hours I want their issue to take their gift, regardless of whether they are related to me by any degree." Most importantly, alternate gift language draws the testator's attention to the possibility of lapse.

Consider the following case.

In re Est. of Murphy

6 N.Y.S.3d 36, 843 N.E.2d 140 (2005)

In 1924, the testator, Mildred B. Murphy, gave birth to a son, Arthur. Arthur went to live with Jim E. and Mae Manning and was known throughout his childhood as Clair Willard Manning. The Mannings officially adopted him in 1944, when he was 19. Mildred had no other children. Clair and his birth mother reestablished their relationship some time after World War II.

In 1998, Mildred executed the will that is the subject of this suit. In the will, Mildred left her Keuka Lake cottage to Clair, along with $8,000 and half of the residuary estate. In addition to her bequests to Clair, she willed cash gifts to two of Clair's children. The will also provided that the remaining half of the residuary estate go to her sister-in-law, Evelyn Beckman. Clair died on March 4, 2001, survived by four children. Mildred died 11 months later, on February 14, 2002.

After the will was admitted to probate, the executors brought this construction proceeding to determine the fate of the bequests to Clair. Beckman asserts that the bequests lapsed and should become part of the residuary estate. She argues that Domestic Relations Law § 117(2) mandates that adopted-out children be treated as strangers for the purpose of construing the will of a birth relative and that the bequests were not saved by EPTL 3–3.3. The Surrogate agreed, ruling that the gifts to Clair lapsed in their entirety and passed to Beckman with the whole of the residuary estate. The Appellate Division affirmed the decree. We granted leave and now reverse.

The appeal before us involves the interplay of EPTL 3–3.3 and Domestic Relations Law § 117(2). EPTL 3–3.3, the antilapse statute, provides that when a bequest is made to the issue or siblings of the testator, and the beneficiary predeceases the testator, the gift does not lapse but vests in the beneficiary's surviving issue. The anti-lapse statute was designed "to abrogate . . . the common-law rule that a devise or legacy to [a predeceased child] lapsed and to substitute the children of the deceased child for the primary object of the testator's bounty." The harshness of that common-law rule, more often than not, defeated the testator's intention. We must determine whether the testator's adopted-out child, expressly named in her will, qualifies as her issue within the meaning of EPTL 3–3.3. In simplest terms, the issue is "issue."

In 1986, the Legislature revised subdivision (b) of EPTL 3–3.3, along with Domestic Relations Law § 117, defining "issue"—for the purpose of triggering the anti-lapse provision—to "include adopted children and their issue to the extent they would be included in a disposition to 'issue' " under EPTL 2–1.3 and Domestic Relations Law § 117(2). Domestic Relations Law § 117(2)(a) provides:

> Except as hereinafter stated, after the making of an order of adoption, adopted children and their issue thereafter are strangers to any birth relatives for the purpose of the interpretation or construction of a disposition in any instrument, whether executed before or after the order of adoption, which does not express a contrary intention or *does not ex-*

pressly include the individual by name or by some classification not based on a parent–child or family relationship. (Emphasis added.)

The Manning children contend that by naming their father—the adopted-out child—as a beneficiary under her will, Mildred altered his status from "stranger" to "issue" for the purposes of the anti-lapse statute with respect to that gift. Because much of Domestic Relations Law § 117(2)(a) would lose meaning if we were to rule otherwise, we agree with this contention and reverse the Appellate Division order.

Until 1985, when we decided *Matter of Best,* 66 N.Y.2d 151, 495 N.Y.S.2d 345, 485 N.E.2d 1010 [1985], it was not clear that adoption had any effect on the rights of adopted-out children to take under the testamentary instruments of their birth relatives, though the Legislature had limited the rights of such children in intestacy.[2] In *Best,* we held that an adopted-out child will not take in a class gift from a birth relative unless that child is "specifically named in a biological ancestor's will, or the gift is expressly made to issue including those adopted out of the family."

The Legislature has amended section 117 several times since. In 1986, it adopted a modified version of the *Best* rule. Among the modifications, it allowed children adopted by certain other relatives within the birth family to take through class gifts under both lines. The Law Revision Commission had recommended that, where these intrafamily adoption rules did not apply, adopted-out children should be excluded from membership in "a class of persons based upon natural relationship . . . unless the will or instrument expresses a contrary intention." The Legislature employed this language and expanded upon it by providing that such children are strangers to a birth relative's will if it "does not express a contrary intention or does not include the individual by name." The 1987 revision added a parallel provision to section 117(1) for intrafamily adoption in intestacy situations, although, of course, without provision for the contrary intention of the decedent.

We based our decision in *Best* on three major policy considerations. We emphasized the importance of maintaining the confidentiality of adoption records, preserving the stability of real property titles and assimilating the adopted child into the adoptive family. These concerns are no less substantial today than they were 20 years ago, but we note that none of them is implicated in this case. We rely here on statutory construction.

Beckman argues, and the dissent agrees, that the language of section 117 supports her position. Because section 117 specifically states that "adopted children *and their issue*" are strangers to the will unless one of the conditions is met, the "individual" to be included by name (her argument goes) is any person claiming a right under the will as issue. Beckman contends that, because Clair (although named) had died, his children may not take because *they* are not individually named.

---

[2] Adoption did not exist at common law, and New York did not authorize it by statute until 1873 (L. 1873, ch. 830). That first adoption statute explicitly excluded inheritance from among the rights acquired or lost through adoptive relationships. Fourteen years later, the Legislature amended the statute to allow adopted children to inherit through both birth and adoptive lines (L. 1887, ch. 703). The matter stood that way through the enactment of the Domestic Relations Law and several versions of what, in 1961, became Domestic Relations Law § 117 (L. 1961, ch. 147). It was not until 1963 that section 117 was amended to preclude adopted-out children from inheriting through their birth relationships, except in cases of adoption by a stepparent. A further amendment in 1966 clarified section 117's scope by expressly limiting the inheritance preclusion to intestate descent and distribution.

This argument would be plausible only if we read section 117 in isolation, devoid of its relationship to EPTL 3–3.3. Indeed, as the Manning children argue, if we were to read the section as Beckman and the dissent advocate, the testator's expressed contrary intention or naming of the adopted-out child would have no practical or legal effect other than to allow the named individual to take the bequest. The named adopted-out child would then be in the same position as any other named nonrelative in any will. Surely the Legislature did not enact section 117(2)(a) merely to state the obvious: that someone named in a will may inherit.

Moreover, the provisions in section 117(1) and section 117(2) are parallel insofar as possible, considering the inevitable differences between intestate distribution and probate of a will. This was a primary consideration in the 1987 revision, which added provisions for intestacy similar to those promulgated the year before for testamentary instruments In *Matter of Seaman* we held, concerning the treatment of intrafamily adoptions in section 117(1):

> The issue's right to inherit from the natural family was severed, however, in 1963 when the Legislature severed the adopted child's right to so inherit. From this, it follows that when the Legislature restored the right of the adopted-out child to inherit from the natural family under the circumstances specified in Domestic Relations Law § 117(1)(e), it also restored the right of the adopted-out child's issue to do so.

As a result, we concluded that it was unnecessary for the Legislature to refer expressly to the adopted-out child's "issue" when enacting section 117(1)(e). The statute implicitly restored inheritance rights to the issue of the adopted-out child when it restored them to the child.

The dissenting opinion reads EPTL 3–3.3's reference to section 117(2) as a broad reference to the classes of intrafamily adoptions that preserve birth inheritance rights, rather than as a reference to section 117(2)(a) (dissenting op. at 48, 809 N.Y.S.2d at 508, 843 N.E.2d at 148). That interpretation is untenable because section 117(2) is the subdivision of section 117 that covers adopted-out children in the testacy context. A will remains a prerequisite for anti-lapse, and section 117(2) is the only subdivision of section 117 to which the anti-lapse statute could be referring. Our dissenting colleague contends that, by allowing testators to invoke the anti-lapse statute for their adopted-out children, our reading "does not treat the issue of adopted-out children comparably under the laws of intestacy and testacy" (dissenting op. at 47, 809 N.Y.S.2d at 508, 843 N.E.2d at 147). The dissenter's argument, however, fails to note that section 117(2)(a) is the very provision that marks the necessary differences between the two contexts. If there could be a perfect parallel, there would be no need for separate subdivisions.

The question before us is analogous to the one answered in *Seaman,* and it is *not* one of the few instances that section 117 requires us to treat differently between testacy and intestacy. To follow the legislative parallel between testamentary law and the law of intestacy as much as the necessary differences allow, we must treat the restoration of Clair's status as issue as the restoration of that status to his children as well.

We therefore conclude that, under Domestic Relations Law § 117(2)(a), adopted children and their issue are ordinarily "strangers" to their birth relatives, and thus are excluded from class gifts. They are not "strangers" when the bequest is to a named adopted-out child—here, to Clair Manning. If "stranger" or the three "nonstranger" conditions of section 117(2) are to have any meaning, it must mean that biological children who are not "strangers" are "issue" under the anti-lapse statute. We therefore conclude that when Mildred Murphy named her adopted-out son Clair as a beneficiary of her will, she triggered the condition in section 117(2) that made him a nonstranger, and thus her issue, with respect to the relevant bequest. His children, therefore, are entitled to the benefit of the anti-lapse statute.

■ READ, J. (dissenting).

While the majority's interpretation of the "interplay" between Domestic Relations Law § 117(2)(a) and EPTL 3–3.3 is certainly not fanciful, it strikes me as implausible in light of relevant statutory language and history. Accordingly, I respectfully dissent. [The dissent then explains at great length the history of Subdivision 2 of Section 117 of the Domestic Relations Law, including bills that were not passed, and deals struck by the legislature and the Law Revision Committee and the Estates and Trusts section of the Bar Association, which indicates that the 1986 revisions were not meant to make substantive changes to the inheritance rights of adopted out children. The dissent explains:]

There is nothing in the legislative history of chapter 408 to suggest that the Legislature intended the addition of the refashioned subdivision (2)(a) to accomplish anything other than what the State Bar Committee envisioned; namely, a technical, not a substantive change to the original bill. There is certainly no basis for concluding that this technical change caused EPTL 3–3.3, the anti-lapse statute, to bear on Domestic Relations Law § 117(2) in the way advocated by Clair Manning's children and adopted by the majority. Under the majority's interpretation, however, by making a bequest to an adopted-out child by name, a testator restores the adopted-out child to his preadoption rights of inheritance as biological kindred with respect to that bequest. Thus, the child adopted out by strangers, merely by being named in a will, achieves inheritance rights on a par with the child adopted out by close kindred. A testator will have to express the contrary intention in order to avoid this result whenever making a bequest to an adopted-out child by name. This cuts against the grain of chapter 408, which presumes that the average testator would likely only intend for the issue of a child adopted out by specified close kindred to qualify as substituted takers under the anti-lapse statute.

Nor does section 117(2)(a) lack meaning and effect unless interpreted in conjunction with EPTL 3–3.3 in the way suggested by the majority. It is under subdivision (2)(a) that the bequests to two of Clair Manning's four children pass. Under section 117(2)(a), as issue of an adopted-out child they were made strangers to their birth grandmother for purposes of interpreting the dispositions in her will. Subdivision (2)(a), then, simply makes clear that notwithstanding this, these two grandchildren may take by name as would any other stranger. Further, testator could have, for example, provided in her will that she intended to make her bequests to "My child, Clair Manning, as though he had never been adopted"; or she could have directed that the adoption of Clair Manning was to be disregarded for purposes of construing the dispositions in her will. In either event, she would have "express[ed] a contrary intention" under subdivision (2)(a), thus contradicting the legislative presumption that adopted-out children and their issue are strangers to their biological relatives for purposes of inheritance, except as specified in subdivision (2)(b). But, of course, she did not do this. Finally, subdivision (2)(a) also preserves bequests to an adopted-out child as a member of some classification not based on the parent–child or family relationship; for example, testator might have made a bequest to the members of her Saturday afternoon bridge club. Assuming that Clair Manning was a member of this classification, the majority's interpretation creates some odd results. Presumably, this gift to him would not lapse if EPTL 3–3.3, in fact, saves gifts to an adopted-out child taking a bequest under the terms of Domestic Relations Law § 117(2)(a). If the testator had made the bequest to "Clair Manning, John Doe and Jane Roe, with whom I have enjoyed playing bridge on Saturday afternoon for 25 years," and both Clair Manning and John Doe predeceased her, the bequest to Clair Manning clearly would not lapse under the majority's interpretation (because Clair Manning was named and because he was biological issue), but the bequest to John Doe would.

Additionally, the majority's interpretation of Domestic Relations Law § 117(2)(a) ignores some of its language. Section 117(2)(a), as relevant in this case, applies to "adopted children *and their issue*" unless "*the individual*" is included by name (emphasis added). The phrase "and their issue" is superfluous under the majority's reading of section 117(2)(a), for the majority reads the word "individual" as synonymous with the phrase "adopted child [ ]." The majority's reading of section 117(2)(a) also does not treat the issue of adopted-out children comparably under the laws of intestacy and testacy, the Legislature's avowed purpose when it amended Domestic Relations Law § 117(1) in 1987.

Finally, although this appeal turns on statutory interpretation, nothing on the face of testator's will indicates any intention to favor Clair Manning's four children over her Beckman relatives. In the will's "Ninth" paragraph decedent makes 16 separate bequests to 13 named individuals and three churches, charities or societies. Only two of Clair Manning's four children are included in any of the 13 bequests to named individuals, one for $5,000 and the other for $3,000; at least four of these 13 bequests (and perhaps more-it is not apparent from the face of the will or otherwise from the record) are made to Beckman relatives, two for $10,000, the most of any of the individual bequests, and two for $5,000. The will's executors are Beckman relatives.

In sum, statutory language and legislative history belie the notion that Domestic Relations Law § 117(2)(a) is dependent on EPTL 3–3.3 for its meaning and effect. Clair Manning's children should not take under section 117(2)(a) except to the extent that two of them are the named beneficiaries of specific bequests; they should not take under EPTL 3–3.3 because their father was not adopted by any of the limited categories of close kindred specified in Domestic Relations Law § 117(2)(b). Accordingly, I would affirm the order of the Appellate Division.

Query: The dissent's argument is based on the idea that merely naming an adopted out child in a will should not return the child, *and all his issue*, to the status of biological child with all the inheritance rights pertaining to that status. But is it likely that a testator will include an adopted out child in a will, even if she did play bridge with him for 25 years, and think of that child like other non-relatives to whom she may be devising property? In other words, did Mildred Murphy include Clair Manning in her will because she thought of him like a son, or did she include him because she had gotten to know him and thought he was a nice young man who she wanted to benefit? If it is more likely that testators who include adopted out children in their wills want to provide for them, in part, because they feel badly about having rejected them at birth, and want to atone for their sins in some sense, should the legislation create a presumption that the child is re-established as a relative unless contrary intention appears, or *vice versa*?

Practice Point: The Importance of Careful Drafting

In *Murphy*, the dissenting opinion takes care to discuss the ways that Mildred might have drafted her will which might have avoided the messy contest and litigation over whether or not she wished to have Clair viewed as though he had not been adopted out. But, did Mildred actually draft the will herself? Isn't it more likely that her attorney simply made a mistake in drafting, or neglected to ask her what her intentions were? This point seems obvious enough when taken in the context of case studies where our purpose is to examine not only the law but how to practice the law. But, we can bring this one step closer: when observed under the theory that your actions as an estate planning attorney will actually be viewed by the court, surviving family members and, sometimes, the public at large as reflecting the wishes of the testator, it becomes a much heavier responsibility. Taking time in planning meetings to not only understand *who* the named beneficiaries are but also their *relationship and personal importance* to the testator therefore become crucial parts of a well-executed plan.

Lapse is not particularly difficult once you know whether the anti-lapse statute is going to apply or not. Although, as you should realize by now, the simple cases are not the ones that get litigated. Equitably adopted children, testators who don't understand the technical meaning of will and trust terms, and even beneficiaries who try to position themselves to take greater percentages of a bequest all can throw a wrench into an otherwise clear estate plan. Consider these cases:

Lorenzo v. Medina

47 So.3d 927 (Fla. 3d DCA 2010)

Cecilia Lorenzo passed away on October 20, 2008, *with an estate consisting of a parcel of residential property in Hialeah. The Testator's will provided for a bequest of the entire estate as follows:*

> [T]o my brother, JOSE R. MEDINA and to my brother in law, JESUS LORENZO, in equal shares. If either of them do not survive me, the share of the deceased shall be given to their surviving spouse, JUANA R. MEDINA or MARIA LORENZO respectively.

Without question, the operation of the will provides for a minimum fifty percent share of the Testator's estate to the Testator's brother-in-law, Jesus Lorenzo ("the brother-in-law"), who survived the Testator. The issue in this appeal is who is entitled to the remaining fifty percent of the Testator's estate since the intended recipients, the Testator's brother, Jose R. Medina, and his wife, Juana R. Medina, both predeceased the Testator. The trial court's order awarded this disputed portion of the Testator's bequest to the appellees, *Isabel Medina and Jose Antonio Medina ("the niece and neph-ew"), who are the surviving children of Jose R. Medina and Juana R. Medina.*

As a matter of common law, when a will provides for a bequest to a per-son who predeceases the testator, the gift lapses. The potentially harsh effects of this common law rule are ameliorated to an extent by the operation of statute. When the predeceased devisee is a descendant of the testator's grandparents, section 732.603 will "save" the lapsed gift by creating a sub-stitute gift in the devisee's descendants. Because section 732.603 is in derogation of the common law, we must strictly construe its provisions.

In this case, the operation of the Testator's will prevents any recovery by the niece and nephew. At the moment of the Testator's death, her will pro-vided for a bequest of fifty percent of the Testator's estate to Jose R. Medina. Jose R. Medina, however, predeceased the Testator. The will also provided that in the event that Jose R. Medina predeceased the Testator, Jose R. Me-dina's share would pass to his wife, Juana R. Medina. Thus, upon the death of the Testator, the named devisee was Juana R. Medina. Juana R. Medina, however, also predeceased the Testator.

Pursuant to the common law rule outlined above, the bequest lapsed. And because Juana R. Medina is not a descendant of the Testator's grand-parents, the niece and nephew cannot invoke the operation of section 732.603(1) to "save" the bequest and provide them with a substitute gift. Thus, we conclude that the niece and nephew are not entitled to the Testa-tor's lapsed bequest. Accordingly, we reverse the order under review.

Query: Assuming Cecilia never expected both her brother and his wife to pre-decease her, shouldn't the anti-lapse statute apply to the lapsed gift to the brother (he is of the required degree of relationship) after the alternate gift to the sister-in-law lapsed as well? What is the benefit of passing all of the proper-ty to a brother-in-law (non-relative) and avoiding the relatives (nieces and nephews) just because the alternate gift was to a non-relative?

This case illustrates how typical will statutes do not recognize spouses as heirs. Cecilia's sister-in-law is not her heir even though she is Cecilia's broth-er's heir. Gifts to spouses are generally excluded from most anti-lapse statutes, like the UPC, which limits the applicability to relations by blood or adoption only.

Larson v. Security Nat'l Bank of Sioux City

791 N.W.2d 710 (Iowa Ct. App. 2010)

Esther Ruth Myrtue Larson died on September 11, 2009. *Esther's will made a specific bequest of certain assets to her husband, "Howard V. Lar-son, per stirpes." Howard Larson predeceased Esther. Howard was survived by four children from a previous marriage. Esther's will provided that the residue of her estate pass to Security National Bank of South Dakota as trustee of the Esther Ruth Myrtue Larson Trust for the benefit* of four unre-lated individuals. In a suit between the children of her predeceased husband and the beneficiaries of the residuary trust, the question was whether, under Iowa's anti-lapse statute, the testator's intent was clear that the statute should apply. The Iowa anti-lapse statute provides:

The devise to a spouse of the testator, where the spouse does not survive the testator, shall lapse notwithstanding the provisions of [the antilapse statute], unless from the terms of the will, the intent is clear and explicit to the contrary. § 633.274.

Both the husband's children and the residuary beneficiaries argued that the will was clear: the children argued that the *per stirpes* language clearly meant Esther intended an alternate gift in her husband's children, and the residuary beneficiaries argued that the will was quite clear that no intent existed. Ruling in favor of the residuary beneficiaries, the court explained: *Because the phrase "per stirpes" only operates to direct how a bequest should be distributed among a designated class, it is meaningless if there is no class designated to which the bequest is to be distributed. Here, Esther failed to designate such a class; thus, the use of the phrase "per stirpes" is meaningless. On its own, the phrase does not operate to demonstrate an intent that the bequest pass to Howard's children because they were not an identified class. Esther's will made a specific bequest to Howard with no provision as to what would happen if Howard predeceased her. Esther's use of the phrase "per stirpes" alone does not demonstrate a clear and explicit intent that the bequest to Howard not lapse if he predeceased her.*

Query: What in the world was Esther thinking when she made a bequest to her husband, an individual, followed by the term *per stirpes*? Was this likely to mean she wanted the property to be distributed to his issue *per stirpes* if he failed to survive her, or was it likely to mean she didn't want it to be distributed to his issue? Or did it likely mean she didn't know what she was doing? If the latter, should the court just flip a coin? The point of anti-lapse statutes is to create presumptions in favor of substitute gifts for certain takers the legislature thinks would fit an average testator's likely intent? Should spouses be included in the group that gets such special treatment, along with blood relatives?

Most states do not apply the anti-lapse statute to save bequests to a spouse who predeceases the testator. Why? The most common reason is that the issue of the spouse are also likely to be the issue of the testator and the testator's issue are probably provided for separately in the will already. Or, if the issue of the spouse are not the issue of the testator, then most states assume a testator would not want the spouse's share to pass to the step-children to the exclusion of the testator's own children. How would you draft an anti-lapse statute to deal with bequests to a spouse who predeceases the testator? How would you draft a will to deal with the bequest?

Keck v. Walker

922 N.E.2d 94 (Ind. Ct. App. 2010)

Edith M. Dawdy ("Dawdy") executed her Last Will and Testament ("the Will") on April 13, 1994. The Will included a residuary clause which provided that Luella Keck ("Luella"), who was Dawdy's first cousin and the mother of the Plaintiffs, would receive a share of the residue of the Estate:

> *I give, bequeath and devise all the rest and residue of my property to Luella Keck, Edith Zimmer, Jean Frazier, Bill Frazier and Margaret Ruger in equal shares, share and share alike.*

On July 8, 1995, Luella died. Less than six months later, on December 26, 1995, Dawdy executed a Codicil to her Will. This first Codicil amended the residuary clause to include Mary Ann Walker as a beneficiary but still listed the now-deceased Luella. On February 6, 2001, over five years after Luella died, Dawdy executed another Codicil to her Will. This second Codicil amended the residuary clause yet again, but still included Luella as a beneficiary. Dawdy died on April 28, 2006, almost five years after executing the Second Codicil.

Acknowledging that Luella's bequest is not saved because the Indiana anti-lapse statute applies only to gifts to descendants of the testator, Luella's children argued that the testator's actions and continued inclusion of her deceased cousin in her codicils indicated an intent to benefit Luella's issue. The court disagreed, stating: *Here, we acknowledge that it is not entirely clear why Dawdy continued to include Luella in the codicils to her will even after Luella's death. However, the general rule is that a bequest to a beneficiary who predeceases the testatrix lapses. And if Dawdy had truly intended that the Plaintiffs take the share that would have gone to their mother Luella, Dawdy could have clearly so provided simply by including the phrase "or her heirs" after Luella's name or otherwise provided for a substitution. But she did not. Using the rules for the construction and interpretation of wills, Dawdy's Will and Codicils are not ambiguous, and we need not consider any extrinsic evidence.*

Because the court determined Dawdy's will was unambiguous, it refused to consider extrinsic evidence made by affidavit, which averred that: *Dawdy had sent flowers to Luella's funeral and personally attended the services; that Dawdy had sent the Plaintiffs $50 to help pay for the expense of Luella's funeral; and that after Luella died, Dawdy repeatedly told [the affiant] that [the plaintiffs] would be taken care of in Dawdy's will by receiving Luella's share of the estate.*

Query: Indiana has a particularly parsimonious anti-lapse statute, applying only to bequests to a testator's descendants. Should the fact that the testator kept including as beneficiary a person she knew to be dead trigger some finding of ambiguity that would allow a court to look beyond the four corners of the will itself? Should the lack of the term "or her heirs" be decisive? Does this will show "contrary intent" to have the anti-lapse statute not apply? If so, how?

In re Est. of Harper

975 A.2d 1155 (Pa. Super. Ct. 2009)

In this case the decedent, Samuel Harper, died leaving a will which provided that the residue of his estate should be distributed to his two sons, "share and share alike." One son predeceased him, leaving one adult child who claimed his father's share under the anti-lapse statute. The other residuary devisee objected, claiming that the term share and share alike indicated clear intent not to apply the anti-lapse statute, and that he should take the entire proceeds of the residuary estate. In the alternative, the surviving devisee claimed that the half share lapses and passes by intestacy (half to himself and half to his nephew) so that he receives a total of ¾ of the estate. The court disagreed, however, citing Missouri precedent that: *Here, Testator never used the terms 'per capita' or 'per stirpes' in his will; he simply directed that named beneficiaries were to 'share and share alike.' While it is true that terms of equality, such as 'share and share alike,' whether referring to specifically named individuals or to a class of individuals, have been interpreted to cause an equal division of the property [on a] per capita and not per stirpes basis, it is equally true that terms such as these have application in determining the mode of **distribution** among a class and **not in establishing the members** of that class.*

Query: How does a testator indicate that he does not want an anti-lapse statute to apply, and how does he indicate that he does? The court held that this testator did not evidence intent to reject application of the anti-lapse statute. If the deceased son had had three children instead of one, so the distribution would be ½ to the surviving son, and 1/6th to each of the grandchildren, would the *share and share alike* argument have been more compelling?

In re Est. of Snapp

233 S.W.3d. 288 (Tenn. Ct. App. 2007)

Cleo Snapp died leaving a will that provided for her three sisters as follows:

ITEM VII.   I give, devise and bequeath to my three sisters, VIOLA SWINGLE, ANNE E. FOWLER and LENA MAE HARTSELL, my 1/4 interest in and to the Juanita Farm. PROVIDED, HOWEVER, if any sister should predecease me, then, in that event, the surviving sister(s) shall take the deceased sister's share.

ITEM VIII.   The rest and residue of my estate, including all property, real, personal or mixed, tangible and intangible, of whatsoever kind and wheresoever situated, I give, devise and bequeath in equal shares unto my three sisters, VIOLA SWINGLE, ANNE E. FOWLER and LENA MAE HARTSELL. PROVIDED, HOWEVER, if any sister should predecease me, then, in that event, the surviving sister(s) shall take the deceased sister's share.

All three of Cleo's sisters predeceased her, but only two (Lena and Viola) left issue. Lena was the last to die of the three sisters. Lena's issue argued that they should take the entire disputed property as the beneficiaries of Lena's will, Lena taking all by right of survivorship. The trial court ruled that Lena and Viola's issue share the property by virtue of the anti-lapse statute, but that Ann's share lapsed and passed to the other two sisters. Cleo's intestate heirs argued that anti-lapse should not apply because Cleo evidenced adequate intent that it not apply by requiring that at least one sister survive her. The Court of Appeals reversed, holding that the survivorship language precluded application of the anti-lapse statute, and that therefore the entire residuary bequest lapsed and passed by the laws of intestacy.

Query: Should use of the term "surviving sister" refer to surviving the testator or survival among the three sisters? And why would the testator refer to survivorship, when all beneficiaries have to survive the testator in order to take?

Isn't the term surplusage? If so, do you think testators know enough about anti-lapse statutes to realize that reference to survivorship may very well cause a bequest to lapse and not be saved by the anti-lapse statute for the descendants of the donee?

Practice Point: Questions, More Questions and the Remote Contingency Pattern

As clients seek counsel regarding the planning of their estate, many will insist from the outset that the plan is "simple" (and will often ask you for a "simple" fee to go hand in hand). And, sometimes, certainly, a properly executed plan may really be pretty simple. For example, if a married couple wishes to leave everything to each other at the first death and, when both spouses are gone, then everything to their one adult child with no issue, or if she has died then to a named charity—that might actually be a simple plan to draft. But, often life and family situations are not so clear-cut. When a client enters your office, for example, with a long list of specific devises she wishes for you to draft into her will, be prepared to let her know that you will need a little time to ask her some questions because, as the prior cases illustrate, you will want to make sure that the testator's wishes are carried out even if some of her named beneficiaries might die before she does. This is often an issue with single clients who have substantial collections they wish to pass on, or to un-married couples who desire to keep all of their property, even household items, separate during life and death. So, ask, ask, ask. And, then take care to draft as clearly as possible what the testator intends (this is also a time to consider why Incorporation by Reference, discussed previously, may not be such a good idea in plans which involve a substantial number of specific bequests). The more specific you are as a drafter, the less likely it is that problems of lapse or abatement (covered in the next section) will surface at the testator's death. It is also a widely-used practice to draft not only a residuary clause into the plan, but also a remote contingency clause, which would apply only in circumstances where there is absolutely no residuary beneficiary living at the time of the testator's death. Unlikely? Yes. But truth often is stranger than fiction. A typical remote contingency pattern for a married testator might be to split the estate equally between each spouse's heirs at law under the state's intestacy scheme or to name a longstanding charity to receive. In either instance, planning ahead is much better than litigating later.

Go back and look again at UPC § 2–603(b)(3) dealing with survivorship language and anti-lapse. Many courts have had to grapple with the question of whether the survivorship language in the following devise should preclude application of the statute to the primary but not the alternate's substitute takers if both the primary and alternate devisee predecease the testator.

> *I hereby devise the residue of my estate to my daughter Agnes if she survives me. If she fails to survive me then I devise the residue to my son, Bob.*

If both Agnes and Bob predecease the testator, should the survivorship language attached to Agnes' gift preclude application of the anti-lapse statute altogether? Or should it preclude application only to Agnes' gift, allowing Bob's substitute takers to inherit? Or should it not preclude either, thus allowing Agnes' issue to take in her place? The UPC would go ahead and apply the anti-lapse statute to Agnes' gift regardless of the survivorship language without additional evidence of testamentary intent.

Usually, gift over language of an alternate taker, in conjunction with the survivorship language, is enough to preclude application of the anti-lapse statute to Agnes' gift. But we are back at square one if *both* Bob and Agnes predecease the testator and we have a choice of Agnes' substitute takers, Bob's substitute takers, or neither.

For a comprehensive state by state analysis of anti-lapse statutes see the Restatement (3d) of Property, § 5.5. Remember, however, that anti-lapse statutes apply if the beneficiary fails to survive the testator, because lapse is a *will* doctrine. Whether a trust beneficiary or life insurance beneficiary has to survive the settlor is a completely different question. The UPC has provided a similar anti-lapse provision for trusts, life insurance, PODs, and TODs, but they have not been adopted yet in a majority of states. In most states, the issue is unclear.[5] And as you learned about ERISA pre-emption, it is unlikely that even if your state had an anti-lapse statute applying to a POD designation in a retirement account, for instance, it would be controlling. The UTC has no anti-lapse provision whatsoever, although some states have added the UPC's anti-lapse provision for trusts in their trust codes. The UPC's trust anti-lapse provision (§ 2–707) does more than deal with predeceasing the settlor, but completely upends the law of future interests, as you will see when we cover it in greater detail in Chapter 8.

It can be argued that in the case of a trust, even a revocable *inter vivos* trust, the beneficiary has already received a contingent future interest when the trust is established and funded. Therefore, because of the present transfer of a future interest in the remainder of the trust, the beneficiary does not need to survive the settlor. That is the reasoning of many courts, including the court of appeals in *In re Estate of Button*, 79 Wn.2d 849, 490 P.2d 731 (1971).

Under the present transfer theory, the death of the beneficiary before the death of the settlor simply means that the property will pass through the beneficiary's estate to that person's testate or intestate heirs.

On appeal in *Button*, however, the Washington Supreme Court held that the anti-lapse statute should be extended to apply to trusts as well as wills. That court stated: "there being no conflicting statutory provision, a statute covering gifts by will which would lapse in the absence of the statute, applies to gifts provided in a trust."[6] Applying the anti-lapse statute to trusts because of the overriding public policy to avoid the lapse of gifts in wills is the minority position, but it is the position of the Restatement 3d Trusts.[7] In *Button*, therefore, the trust remainder passed to the living descendants of the remainder beneficiary under the anti-lapse statute, rather than to those the remainder beneficiary designated in her will.

Even if your state has anti-lapse statutes dealing with the variety of will-substitutes, you will want to make certain that your clients' beneficiary designations consist of primary and alternate beneficiaries. In the absence of living beneficiaries who can take, property like life insurance proceeds or retirement accounts will lapse and pass to the decedent's estate, where it will be probated and distributed according to a will or by intestacy, depending on the decedent's estate plan. Your client will lose all of her probate

---

[5]   See UPC §§ 2–702, 2–706, and 2–707.

[6]   *In re* Est. of Button, 490 P.2d 731, 734 (1971).

[7]   See Restatement 3d Trusts, § 25 comment e.

avoidance benefits if this happens. Thus, it is vital to list primary **and** alternate beneficiaries in all beneficiary designations, just as one should do in a will.

Tax Tip: The Taxable Transmissible Remainder Problem

The important distinction in *Est. of Button* between the Court of Appeal's decision and the Washington Supreme Court's decision has to do with the taxable transmissible remainder. Under the Court of Appeals' reasoning, a property stick transferred to the remainder beneficiary upon the establishment of the trust so that her death prior to taking possession of the remainder was irrelevant. The remainder interest in the trust was her property and it passed to her devisees in her will. "Yippee," her devisees were thinking. Let's imagine that the value of that trust interest was a mere $10 million. By including the value of the remainder in her estate, it is added to her own property and, if her total estate is over the estate tax exemption, her estate will have to pay transfer taxes on that remainder interest, even though she never enjoyed the benefit of the money. Her beneficiaries will take smaller devises because a big chunk will have been eaten up by taxes. On the other hand, if the anti-lapse statute is applied, the remainder passes directly to her issue without passing through her estate and without being subject to transfer taxes. By requiring that the trust beneficiary survive to distribution, the UPC § 2–707 avoids taxing remainders that simply pass through a deceased beneficiary's estate.

You can see why the Court of Appeals adopted the present transfer of a property right theory, however, since that is how most revocable *inter vivos* trusts were allowed to stand since they fail to satisfy the will formalities. Such is the reasoning of *Farkas v. Williams*, in Chapter 4. But stretching the state's will-based anti-lapse statute to apply in the context of a revocable trust, the Washington Supreme Court was able to avoid the potential of double taxation. Would you call that unjustifiable judicial activism, public policy pragmatism, or furthering testamentary intent? Assuming her will beneficiaries are the same as her intestate takers, so the final recipients are the same, wouldn't you be glad the Supreme Court fixed on a rule that saved you millions of dollars in taxes? Of course, if the beneficiaries are different, I suspect that the will beneficiaries would gladly pay double taxes in order to receive some quantity of the trust principal.

PROBLEMS

To help familiarize yourself with the working of anti-lapse statutes, work the following problems under each of the statutes listed above (UPC, Maryland, the District of Columbia, and the anti-lapse statute of your state):

5.1. Testator devises her residue to Harold and Wilma, close neighbors who helped care for her in her final years. Harold predeceased the testator.

5.2. Harold and Wilma both predeceased the testator.

5.3. Testator devises her residue to Harold and Wilma, or to their issue if either or both predeceases her, and Harold predeceased the testator leaving issue.

5.4. Testator devises her residue to her two children and her niece in equal shares. The niece predeceased the testator leaving three children.

5.5. Testator devises her residue to her two children and her niece in equal shares, but if any predeceases her, then that person's share is to pass to the Red Cross. The niece predeceased the testator leaving three children.

5.6. Testator devises the residue of her estate to her sister Carol and her surviving nieces and nephews. Carol survives the testator and has two children, but two nephews predeceased the testator leaving three grand nieces.

5.7. Testator devises the residue of her estate to her issue. Testator had one child, John, who died in infancy, another child, Sally, who predeceased the testator leaving one living child, and one grandchild who predeceased the testator leaving two children.

B. ADEMPTION

What happens if all the named beneficiaries survive the testator but the property devised to some of them is missing from the estate? For instance, the testator bequeaths her diamond ring to her daughter, her Ford car to her son, and her 20 shares of XYZ stock to her spouse. At testator's death her estate contains no diamond ring, a toyota car, and 10 shares of ABC stock. There are two doctrines that apply here. The first is *ademption* (by extinction or satisfaction) and the second is the *change in form* doctrine. Ademption, from the latin *adimere*, meaning to take away, occurs when devised property is not in the estate at death. This might be because the testator decided to make an *inter vivos* gift of the property to the designated beneficiary before she died. Thus, even though the testator bequeathed her diamond ring in her will to her daughter, she may have decided to go ahead and give the ring to her daughter before she died. In that case, we call the item *adeemed by satisfaction*. The bequest has already been made through an *inter vivos* gift and the beneficiary is certainly not entitled to some sort of replacement property just because she did not get the ring through the will. She got the ring.

More likely, the ring is not in the estate because the testator gave it to someone else or sold it. In that case, the daughter receives nothing and the gift is held to have been *adeemed by extinction*. Ademption by extinction is easy when a testator bequeaths the Picasso painting of *Guernica* hanging over his fireplace to his son and the painting simply is not in the estate at the testator's death. There is only one Picasso *Guernica* and it is either in the estate or not. Ademption is much more difficult, however, when more common items are involved. The testator bequeaths her jewelry to her daughter and her library to her son. If certain items of jewelry or certain books that the beneficiaries were hoping to receive are not in the jewelry box or library shelves, they are out of luck. They get the books and the jewelry that are in the estate at the testator's death and nothing more.

But a bequest as generic as *jewelry* or *books* will include property acquired after the execution of the will. For a time, the common law would not allow a will to dispose of property acquired after its execution because it was not contemplated at the time of execution. That doctrine has been abolished and after-acquired property, if adequately described, can be disposed of by a will written prior to acquisition of the property. But then what happens if property is sold or exchanged for new property?

Consider a testator who gives her Ford car to her son, and at her death she doesn't own a Ford, but does own a Toyota. Should the son receive the

Toyota? Under the *identity* theory, the answer would be no, a Toyota is not a Ford. But under the *intent* theory a court would look at whether the testator would have intended the son to receive whatever car she happened to own at death. Of course, if the testator had simply devised *"my car"* to her son the problem would have been avoided, unless of course she sold everything she owned to purchase an Indy race car or James Bond's Aston Martin DB5 from the movie *Goldfinger* because she is a collector of rare automobiles. Because people are constantly acquiring and divesting themselves of property, the good estate planner must walk a fine line between being too descriptive and running into ademption problems or too generic and possibly including property that the testator would not have intended to pass to particular beneficiaries.

Ademption can cause problems with many items of property, including homes, cars, stocks and bonds, bank accounts, and the like. As a general rule, however, only *specific devises* are adeemed if they are not in the estate at death.

A *specific devise* is a devise of a particular item of property, like my wedding ring, my toyota car, or my home located at 123 Main Street.

A *general devise* is a devise of money which, if not in a bank account or under the mattress, might require liquidation of certain assets. Thus, a gift of $10,000 to my daughter doesn't run into ademption problems because the representative can sell the estate's assets to come up with the cash for the bequest. This does not mean there might not be other problems, like the estate might not have the assets to liquidate. This is a problem of *abatement*, which we cover in the next section. But general devises are not subject to ademption.

A *demonstrative devise* is a cross between a specific and a general devise and, like specific devises, may run into ademption problems. A devise of "$10,000 payable from the proceeds of the sale of my yacht" is a demonstrative devise. If there is no yacht, there can be no proceeds from the sale of the yacht. Sometimes, however, demonstrative devises are not adeemed. So a gift of "$10,000 payable from the proceeds of my stocks and bonds portfolio" may be satisfied by the sale of other items if the portfolio does not include stocks and bonds of sufficient value. For instance, the bequest of $6,000 from life insurance failed when there was no life insurance in the estate.[8] But a bequest of $500,000 to numerous named individuals payable from a stock fund was held not adeemed when the fund contained stock worth only $46,000.[9] The executor had to liquidate other assets of the estate to make up the missing $454,000.

Because ademption by extinction often turns on whether the devise is identified as a specific, a demonstrative, or a general devise, many states have ameliorated the inconsistent results by adopting a non-ademption provision for certain common specific devises. The UPC § 2–606 is the model.

---

[8] *In re* Norwood Estate, 178 Mich. App. 345, 443 N.W.2d 798 (1989).
[9] *In re* Estate of Lung, 692 A.2d 1349 (D.C. 1997).

UPC § 2–606. Nonademption of Specific Devises; Unpaid Proceeds of Sale, Condemnation, or Insurance; Sale by Conservator or Agent.

(a) A specific devisee has a right to specifically devised property in the testator's estate at the testator's death and to:

(1) any balance of the purchase price, together with any security agreement, owed by a purchaser at the testator's death by reason of sale of the property;

(2) any amount of a condemnation award for the taking of the property unpaid at death;

(3) any proceeds unpaid at death on fire or casualty insurance on or other recovery for injury to the property;

(4) any property owned by the testator at death and acquired as a result of foreclosure, or obtained in lieu of foreclosure, of the security interest for a specifically devised obligation;

(5) any real property or tangible personal property owned by the testator at death which the testator acquired as a replacement for specifically devised real property or tangible personal property; and

(6) if not covered by paragraphs (1) through (5), a pecuniary devise equal to the value as of its date of disposition of other specifically devised property disposed of during the testator's lifetime but only to the extent it is established that ademption would be inconsistent with the testator's manifested plan of distribution or that at the time the will was made, the date of disposition or otherwise, the testator did not intend ademption of the devise.

(b) If specifically devised property is sold or mortgaged by a conservator or by an agent acting within the authority of a durable power of attorney for an incapacitated principal or a condemnation award, insurance proceeds, or recovery for injury to the property is paid to a conservator or to an agent acting within the authority of a durable power of attorney for an incapacitated principal the specific devisee has the right to a general pecuniary devise equal to the net sale price, the amount of the unpaid loan, the condemnation award, the insurance proceeds, or the recovery.

(c) The right of a specific devisee under subsection (b) is reduced by any right the devisee has under subsection (a).

(d) For the purposes of the references in subsection (b) to a conservator, subsection (b) does not apply if after the sale, mortgage, condemnation, casualty, or recovery, it was adjudicated that the testator's incapacity ceased and the testator survived the adjudication for at least one year.

(e) For the purposes of the references in subsection (b) to an agent acting within the authority of a durable power of attorney an incapacitated principal, (i) "incapacitated principal" means a principal who is an incapacitated person, (ii) no adjudication of incapacity before death is necessary, and (iii) the acts of an agent within the authority of a durable power of attorney are presumed to be for an incapacitated principal.

Note how UPC § 2–606 uses the *change of form* doctrine to validate bequests when the actual item of property has been changed by the testator, or others, to something different, but was not intentionally disposed of. Clearly, if the house is condemned or burns to the ground two days before the testator's death, the devisee should receive the proceeds of the insurance or condemnation award. UPC § 2–606 provides that money or certain other property that resulted from the sale or foreclosure of the property will pass to the devisee. And § 2–606(a)(5) provides that replacement property will pass to the devisee even if the originally devised item of property is no longer in the estate. This covers the Toyota car that replaced the testator's Ford car.

But what happens when a testator devises her diamond ring to her daughter, then gives her daughter $10,000 for a down payment on a house, telling the daughter that it's a loan against the ring she will be inheriting? The testator tells the daughter that she has to repay the loan to get the ring. What if the daughter doesn't repay the money and the ring is only worth $5,000? Does the daughter get the ring in addition to the lifetime gift? UPC § 2–609 deals with property that is given in full or partial satisfaction of a specific bequest.

UPC § 2–609. Ademption by Satisfaction.

(a) Property a testator gave in his [or her] lifetime to a person is treated as a satisfaction of a devise in whole or in part, only if (i) the will provides for deduction of the gift, (ii) the testator declared in a contemporaneous writing that the gift is in satisfaction of the devise or that its value is to be deducted from the value of the devise, or (iii) the devisee acknowledged in writing that the gift is in satisfaction of the devise or that its value is to be deducted from the value of the devise.

(b) For purposes of partial satisfaction, property given during lifetime is valued as of the time the devisee came into possession or enjoyment of the property or at the testator's death, whichever occurs first.

(c) If the devisee fails to survive the testator, the gift is treated as a full or partial satisfaction of the devise, as appropriate, in applying Sections 2–603 and 2–604, unless the testator's contemporaneous writing provides otherwise.

If the testator devised his library to his grandson, but he had given ten of his most valuable books to the grandson during life, the grandson would not be entitled to the value of those ten books plus the rest of the library at his grandfather's death. He has already received the books and they would be considered adeemed by satisfaction. But if the testator gave the books to the local library instead, the grandson would argue that he should receive the remaining books plus cash equal in value to the cost of the missing books. Would he be successful? No. Since the testator gave the books away himself (not a conservator, guardian, or executor), and since he did not receive any compensation for the books, they would be held adeemed by extinction. If grandpa sold the books, however, and received either money or other valuable property, his grandson could argue that he should be entitled to the replacement property. But the issue would turn on grandpa's intention—was the new property meant to *replace* the books or was grandpa simply selling a few books to buy himself a golf cart to get to the club house. If the latter, the grandson would be out of luck.

As you can see, the key is in determining the testator's intentions. If someone else, like the government, a guardian, or the stock company takes the property, sells it, or replaces it with stock in a newly formed company, it seems reasonable to allow the devisee of specific property to ask for the proceeds or replacement items. But if grandpa decides it is easier to just sell the library or the diamond ring and spend the money rather than write a new will when he decides to change a devise, that is certainly an option that will be valid. That's the point of writing a will—it can be revoked at any time, either by revoking the will or by disposing of the property covered by the will. But a lot of property changes form over time, especially intangible property. Thus, most states have adopted special statutes for dealing with stock and other securities. UPC § 2–605 is the model in many states.

UPC § 2–605. Increase in Securities; Accessions.

(a) If a testator executes a will that devises securities and the testator then owned securities that meet the description in the will, the devise includes additional securities owned by the testator at death to the extent the additional securities were acquired by the testator after the will was executed as a result of the testator's ownership of the described securities and are securities of any of the following types:

(1) securities of the same organization acquired by reason of action initiated by the organization or any successor, related, or acquiring organization, excluding any acquired by exercise of purchase options;

(2) securities of another organization acquired as a result of a merger, consolidation, reorganization, or other distribution by the organization or any successor, related, or acquiring organization; or

(3) securities of the same organization acquired as a result of a plan of reinvestment.

(b) Distributions in cash before death with respect to a described security are not part of the devise.

Ademption seems relatively straightforward but, as usual, the devil is in the details. Consider a devise of:

- my diamond ring to A,
- my Ford car to B,
- my stock in the Wireless Widget Company to C,
- and the $5,000 in my local Smalltown Bank account to D."

The diamond ring is easy—it is a specific devise that is either in the estate or not. If the testator sold the diamond ring to buy a new car, the gift to A is extinguished because it is no longer in the estate. And if the testator gave the ring to A in advance of death, it is adeemed by satisfaction. Ademption by satisfaction is therefore quite similar to advancements, which we saw in the context of intestacy. But what if the testator pawned the ring for $5,000 and has the money in the bank? Should A get the proceeds of the ring? Or should D get the money if these were the only four items that the testator owned at death? According to UPC § 2–606(a)(1), A would get the money if the testator pawned the ring or sold it, and A would get the insurance proceeds if the ring was stolen. But under the traditional common law rule, A would get nothing if the ring was pawned or sold.

The Ford car is less easy. Obviously, if the Ford car is in the estate B gets it. But what if the Ford car was sold and the testator bought a different Ford car? What if the testator bought a Toyota instead? What if the testator sold the car and bought a yearly bus pass? What if the car was totaled in a collision and the testator spent the insurance money on a cruise, but while on the cruise won big-time on the slots and invested her winnings in the bank? What if she invested the winnings in her stock brokerage account? What if she gave B $10,000 from her winnings before she died so B could purchase a car? What if the Ford car turned out to be the very car that Bonnie and Clyde were driving when they were ambushed by a Texas posse and killed? What if the car is actually worth $5 million? Although the UPC provides that property purchased to replace property no longer in an estate will pass to the designated beneficiary, the testator may have decided to replace the Ford car rather than the diamond ring because the testator wanted to adeem the gift to B and not the gift to A. If a testator does not want to go to all the trouble of writing a new will when her gifting plan changes, she can certainly revoke some testamentary gifts simply by getting rid of the property.

The gift of stocks should be straightforward, but they too can get quite complicated. If the WWC was bought out by AT & T, C should get the AT & T stock. But should C get the stock in the WWC that was owned by the testator as well as that portion of the testator's mutual funds that she purchased with her slot winnings that were also held in WWC stock? What if at the time of execution of the will, testator had 50 shares of WWC stock and 500 shares of AT & T stock, but after AT & T bought out the WWC, she sold all of her tech stock and bought U.S. Government bonds? What if the WWC stock split? What if the WWC stock was worth $5.00 per share at the execution of her will, but because of a new patent for wireless toaster ovens was worth $500.00 per share at testator's death? If the diamond ring, the Ford car, and the WWC stock were all worth roughly $5,000 each at the time of execution, should C benefit when the price of diamonds and Ford cars goes down and WWC stock goes up? Should the administrator of testator's estate have to purchase some shares of WWC if none was owned by the testator at death?

What about D's gift of $5,000? If there is no cash in any bank account and no other property but the ring, the car, and the stock, should D's gift be extinguished altogether? What if there was only $4,000 in the bank account? What if there was $10,000 in the bank account? What if the testator closed the bank account and put the $5,000 into a money market account with her stock broker? What if she bought a second car with the $5,000? What if the testator had a brief episode of dementia and the conservator who was appointed to manage her property loaned the money to testator's son-in-law in exchange for a promissory note, but when the testator recovered she voided the promissory note?

The UPC and most state ademption statutes help us answer many of the questions above but, as with all statutes, they cannot address every possible scenario that might arise. And even if the statute applies, some of the provisions may be defeated if there is clear and convincing evidence of contrary intent. If the statute does not apply, then the common law rules will operate and two theories have been adopted by state courts for dealing with ademption problems. As described in our earlier discussion about the Ford, the first is the *identity* theory, which provides that if a specifically identified item is no longer in the estate, then the bequest is extinguished. The second is the *intent* theory, which provides that other property, or replacement property, should be used to satisfy a bequest if it was the *intent* of the testator that a bequest not be extinguished. Some courts use the *change of form* doctrine to avoid ademption if a bequest can be traced to other property in the estate and the testator would not have wanted the bequest to be extinguished. Change of form doctrine is often used in the situation of stocks and bonds, where a testator may buy and sell stock on a regular basis and likely wanted the beneficiary to have whatever stock she owned at the time of her death.

The *identity* theory is strict and does not allow replacement property to substitute for specifically devised property. Under the *intent* theory, devisees need to offer evidence that a testator intended substitute property to pass to the devisee in place of the missing specifically devised property. The *change of form* doctrine applies when property, like securities, change their form but not their substance, as when Wells Fargo Bank buys out the local Smalltown Bank and afterwards the testator's description of her bank account becomes inaccurate, even though the account never actually changed.

Consider the following cases and whether you would have found that the gift was adeemed or not:

Est. of Donovan

162 N.H. 1, 20 A.3d 989 (2011)

The decedent, Timothy M. Donovan, died in June 2009. His will provided, in pertinent part: "All my intangible personal property, including but not limited to bank accounts, stocks, mutual funds, and the like, **but excluding shares in Optimum Manufacturing,** *I devise and bequeath to* Cathy Carter." The will also provided: *All the rest, residue and remainder of my estate, of every kind and description, and wheresoever situated, including but not limited to my* **shares of stock and/or other interests in Optimum Manufacturing Corporation,** *and the Optimum Real Estate, I give, devise and bequeath to . . . the Timothy M. Donovan Revocable Trust of 2001.* The Revocable Trust provided that the Optimum Manufacturing stock was to be sold and the proceeds distributed to Donovan's family members upon his death. In August 2008, before he died, decedent sold his Optimum Manufacturing stock for $15 million.

The trial court ruled that the stock was adeemed and that Cathy Carter took the entire $15 million proceeds as intangible personal property under the will. The trust beneficiaries appealed and the New Hampshire Supreme Court affirmed, explaining: *any bequest of the decedent's Optimum Manufacturing stock was adeemed when he sold the stock before he died. Ademption applies when a decedent no longer owns property specifically devised at the time of death, or when the character of that property has so changed as to be no longer identifiable.* "A mere change in the form of the gift is not an ademption, but a complete change in nature and character is." *It is well-settled that if, after a testator has executed his will in which he makes a specific bequest of corporate stock, the testator sells the stock and does not acquire other stock, an ademption occurs, and a legatee has no valid claim on the proceeds of the sale. In arguing for a contrary result, the Donovan Family relies upon the distribution set forth in Article 4(E) of the Third Amended Appendix to Trust. The Donovan Family contends that because the will incorporated the trust by reference, it is necessary to review the trust's terms, and that under the Third Amended Appendix to Trust, the proceeds from the sale of Optimum Manufacturing must be distributed to the family according to the schedule set forth therein. For the purposes of this discussion, we will assume, without deciding, that the trust documents are incorporated by reference into the will. . . . Viewing the plain meaning of the trust, when examined as a whole, we conclude that the distribution to which Article 4(E) of the Third Amended Appendix to Trust refers applies only if, when he died, the decedent still owned shares of Optimum Manufacturing stock. Article 4(E) is part of Article 4, which specifically concerns the disposition of assets after the decedent's death. . . . In context, then, the distribution set forth in Article 4(E) applies to the sale of stock that Article 4(D) authorized the trustee to make after the decedent's death. The plain meaning of these provisions evince the decedent's intent that the distribution of the proceeds from the sale of stock set forth in Article 4(E) applies only to a post-death sale of stock authorized by Article 4(D), and does not apply to the proceeds from any sale of stock that occurred before the decedent's death.*

Query: Which theory did the court use to resolve this case—the intent theory or the identity theory? Since the decedent took such care to exclude the Optimum Manufacturing stock from the will bequests to Carter, and since the trust evidenced decedent's intent to sell the stock for the benefit of the trust beneficiaries, was the court correct in its determination? Would your assumptions about the decedent's intent change if you knew that Cathy Carter was his caretaker and nurse? What if she was his second wife? What if she was an adopted daughter? Why do you think the decedent sold his stock? Did he intend to defeat the trust gift to his family, or was he selling it early because the price was unusually high? If the latter, what should he have done to ensure the proceeds would go to his family?

Spiegel v. KLRU Endowment Fund

228 S.W.3d 237 (Tex. App. Austin 2007)

Decedent, Martha Speigel, was married to Robert Spiegel for 30 years, from their marriage in 1970 until Robert filed for a divorce in 2000. The court ordered Robert and Martha to attend mediation and they signed a mediated settlement agreement giving Martha the home that they had lived in (the Plum Creek residence), and Robert another home they owned some miles away. Martha died the day before the hearing scheduled to enter the final divorce decree. Martha's will, written in 1999, gave Robert "our homestead and my car." The court first found that the mediated settlement agreement was binding immediately upon execution.

Regarding Robert's claim for the homestead property, the court explained: *Robert argues that because at the time Martha wrote her will in 1999, her use of the phrase "our homestead" referred to the Plum Creek residence where she lived with Robert, her intent can only be effectuated by declaring that the Plum Creek residence should pass to Robert under her will. We find that this contention lacks merit because Robert lived in a separate residence that he established as his tax homestead at the time of Martha's death and because he agreed that Martha would keep the Plum Creek residence as her separate property. A will speaks at the time of the testator's death. In construing a will, the court's focus is on the testator's intent, which must be ascertained from the language within the four corners of the will. Ademption describes the extinction of a specific devise because of the disappearance of the subject matter of the devise. Robert contends that*

*because the Plum Creek residence still physically existed and had not been
sold at the time of Martha's death, the doctrine of ademption cannot apply
to the devise. Robert would be correct if Martha had left the Plum Creek
residence to him in her will; however, Martha devised "our homestead" to
Robert, and no property could be identified by that phrase at the time of
Martha's death, which is when her will speaks. . . . Although the phrase
"our homestead" may have accurately identified the Plum Creek residence
when Martha authored her will in 1999, the evidence presented in this case
conclusively proves that Robert had abandoned the Plum Creek residence as
his homestead by the time of Martha's death. Consequently, the devise of
"our homestead" to Robert adeemed, and the Plum Creek residence became
part of Martha's residuary estate.*

Query: This case would have been avoided if Robert and Martha had completed their divorce. Why? Did the court have to stretch the ademption doctrine in
order to deny Robert's claim to property under his soon-to-be ex-wife's will?

In re Est. of Greenamyre

219 S.W.3d 877, (Tenn. Ct. App. 2005)

Dr. Greenamyre, a sociology and philosophy professor at Tennessee
Technological University, drafted his own will leaving everything to his
wife, but if she predeceased him, then he devised assorted items of personal
property to colleagues and friends, including all personal property not specifically devised to others to Dr. Stanger and all of Dr. Greenamyre's
framed pictures, hanging artwork, pottery, a woman's Rolex watch, and two
men's Rolex watches to Dr. Dixon. In 1998 Dr. Greenamyre was placed in a
nursing home and a conservator was appointed for him by the court. The
petition filed by the nursing home asked that Kelly Tayes of the Office of
the Public Guardian for the Upper Cumberland Development District be
appointed as Dr. Greenamyre's conservator. *Dr. Stanger also sought to be
named conservator. Following a hearing on May 1, 1998, the trial court
appointed Ms. Tayes as the conservator for Dr. Greenamyre's person and
property. On June 25, 1998, Ms. Tayes filed a petition seeking permission to
sell Dr. Greenamyre's personal property at auction. She stated that he
owned household goods and furnishings, two automobiles, and other personal property that he would not need in the future. She supported this
petition with the affidavit of Dr. Greenamyre's physician stating that Dr.
Greenamyre would never be able to return home. The trial court entered an
order on July 6, 1998 authorizing the public auction. Dr. Greenamyre's personal property was sold at public auction on August 11, 1998. Among the
items sold were a 1.8 carat diamond ring, a ruby ring, a woman's Rolex
watch, two men's Rolex watches, and two automobiles. The auction grossed
$61,692.00 and netted $50,993.30. Ms. Tayes deposited the auction proceeds
in Dr. Greenamyre's checking account at Union Planters Bank. The trial
court confirmed the sale on August 28, 1998.*

Dr. Greenamyre died on December 5, 2000 at the age of seventy. On
January 23, 2001, a petition was filed in the trial court to probate Dr.
Greenamyre's April 12, 1994 will. On August 20, 2001, an inventory valuing
Dr. Greenamyre's estate at $592,594.11 was filed. Thereafter, questions
arose regarding the fate of Dr. Greenamyre's bequests to Dr. Stanger and the
Dixons. There were also questions about Dr. Greenamyre's instructions re-

garding his funeral and burial expenses, the safe-keeping of his six cats, and a $25,000 contribution to the Twin Cities Buddhist Association. Dr. Stanger insisted that she was entitled to receive an amount equal to the balance in Dr. Greenamyre's Union Planters Bank account on May 4, 1998 when the conservatorship was created, as well as the proceeds from the sale of the personal property she would have received under Dr. Greenamyre's will. The Dixons insisted that they were entitled to receive an amount equal to the proceeds from the sale of Dr. Greenamyre's art and the three Rolex watches. Relying on In re Estate of Hume, *984 S.W.2d 602 (Tenn.1999), the trial court concluded that the sale worked an ademption by extinction of the specific bequests of personal property to Dr. Stanger and the Dixons. Accordingly, the trial court determined that Dr. Stanger was only entitled to the $8,474.68 balance in Dr. Greenamyre's Union Planters Bank account at the time of his death and that the Dixons were entitled to nothing.*

On appeal, Dr. Stanger disagreed with the trial court on a number of grounds. First, she claimed that reliance on *Est. of Hume's* identity theory was incorrect as *Hume* should be limited to its facts. She also argued that the UPC's rejection of the identity theory in the case of property sold by a guardian or conservator was not inconsistent with Tennessee law. Finally, she argued that the Tennessee General Assembly's adoption of the UPC's § 2–606 in 2004 showed that Tennessee was aligned with the intent theory states. The Court of Appeals, however, rejected all of her arguments and found that it was bound by the holding of *Est. of Hume* and application of the identity theory. As a result, the court agreed *that the bequest to Dr. Stanger was a specific bequest and, therefore, was subject to ademption by extinction. Based on the law as it stood in December 2000 when Dr. Greenamyre died, we have also concluded that the auction sale of Dr. Greenamyre's personal property in 1998 amounted to an ademption by extinction of the personal property bequeathed to Dr. Stanger. The subjects of these specific bequests no longer exist. Accordingly, she is not entitled to the net proceeds of the sale of this property.* The court explained that *Ademption by extinction results because of 'the doing of some act with regard to the subject-matter which interferes with the operation of the will.' In these cases: the rule [of ademption by extinction] prevails without regard to the intention of the testator or the hardship of the case, and is predicated upon the principle that the subject of the gift is annihilated or its condition so altered that nothing remains to which the terms of the bequest can apply. In other words, it only matters that the subject of the specific bequest no longer exists because of 'the doing of some act;' it is irrelevant who or what initiates 'the doing.'*

Query: Should conservators and guardians be allowed to dispose of property during the life-time of the decedent if that property is going to be judged adeemed under a state's application of the identity theory? Should conservators be personally liable if they dispose of property in ways that unreasonably interferes with a devisee's bequest?

––––––––––

The modern tendency is to treat property as not adeemed if there is a plausible argument that the testator would have wanted the beneficiary to take replacement property, or wanted the beneficiary to have the value of the bequest even if the specific item of property isn't in the estate at death.

But if the situation doesn't fit nicely into one of the categories carved out in your state's statute, you could find yourself arguing traditional common law ademption, which relies heavily on the identity theory. In this world of disposable property, corporate reorganizations, potentially lengthy conservatorships, and fluctuating markets, however, the UPC and the intent theory would seem to promote testamentary intent better than the identity theory.

Practice Point: Avoiding Ademption Problems with the Client Who Has Collections

Consider the client who possesses an extensive collection of rugs and other woven materials, some of which are quite valuable. He has very clear ideas on which of his friends should receive which pieces (although his descriptions make it difficult for you to distinguish the pieces from one another). He also tells you that he is constantly buying and selling rugs as part of his international travel.

How do you best describe and identify the pieces in the will, especially if they are changing frequently? You might actually need to take a trip out to the client's home or have photographs emailed to you in which you can properly see and therefore describe the property. A second issue should be brewing in your mind, as well: if your client happens to sell the items described in his will, won't you have an ademption problem? Recognizing the problem before it arises can allow you to plan for the potential glitches. For example, instead of leaving certain pieces to specific beneficiaries, what about instructing an executor to distribute all pieces to a group of named individuals as they shall agree among themselves (giving the executor the power to sell items that cannot be agreed upon and distribute the proceeds instead)? Or, you might specify that all pieces of certain dimensions go to certain individuals? Or, all new rugs could go to X and old rugs to Y, or an ongoing list could be maintained under separate writing doctrines. Or, the testator could give rugs up to a certain value to each particular devisee. What kind of devise would this latter be? How did Dr. Greenamyre deal with all of his artwork?

Assuming that not everyone knows the difference between a Bidjar and a Tabriz, or a Navaho and an Afghan rug, should the testator integrate photographs into his will? If he changes property frequently, the photographs may cause a bequest of an 8' x 10' Bidjar rug to be adeemed, even though the testator replaced it with a different 8' x 10' Bidjar rug since the patterns in the photograph will show that the new rug is different from the old one the testator had when he executed his will. What do you think is the best way to manage gifts of valuable collections?

PROBLEMS

5.8. Consider the following specific bequest:

> Because I know that my sons will always love to ride, I hereby give, devise and bequeath my Paul Smart Sport Classic Ducati (a motorcycle) to my son, Julian. My son Paulo may have the choice of any motorcycle I own at my death.

Paulo and Julian happen to enjoy a testy and contentious lifelong relationship as siblings. Guess what motorcycle Paulo, also the named Executor, chooses for himself, even though their father owned 5 other motorcycles at the time of his death? The Paul Smart Sport Classic, of course. Under the common law, the

UPC, or the ademption statute of your state, 1) Did Paulo have the right under the will to take the bike which was bequeathed to Julian: and 2) If so, does Julian still get a motorcycle?

5.9. Identify the ademption problems in the following specific bequests under the UPC and under the ademption statute of your state:

    a.   "All of my books and music, tangible and electronic, to Shauna . . . and the remainder of the estate passes to Shantel." Stashed in the pages of the books was over $5,000. Who gets the money?

    b.   "$3,000 each to Tom and Jim, payable from the sale of my truck. The residue of my estate is to go to Sally." At the time of death, the testator is in a nursing home, having sold her only vehicle, the truck, 3 years prior to her death.

Technology Trend: Abatement and Really Intangible Property

In the past few decades, one of the growing forms of wealth, as we know in the case of Bill Gates and Steve Jobs, is the employee stock option; i.e. the right to purchase shares of stock at a set price and then resell them if the share price is high enough to net a tidy profit. It is a way to encourage employees to invest their energies in making the company profitable for the long haul but keep the cash in the company and defer large amounts of compensation rather than paying it out in bonuses and salaries. But what happens to the stock option when the employee dies and the executor seeks to liquidate all the decedent's assets for distribution? A stock option is certainly a form of property and is part of a decedent's estate, except that some options may be forfeited upon the death of the employee if they have not vested. Others may have an accelerated vesting date or will expire within a certain period. What do you do, however, to protect the value of the stock options during a financial downturn if you are the executor of an employee's estate? If the option is exercised by the employee before death, should the stocks pass to the devisees who were given the options in the employee's will?

In general, the stock option itself will give you limited choices at death depending on the type of option and the company's policies. But do you have any flexibility? Your devisee will be very unhappy if you devise vast amounts of stock options to a favorite grandchild and it turns out the options all terminate at the testator's death. If the options are reduced at death, should the estate have to compensate for the loss of the gift? Besides knowing the specifics of each option, you as the lawyer need to know what can be done and how the value of the options may fluctuate with market changes and with the death of the employee so that you don't run into ademption problems, or have a devisee challenging a will on the grounds that grandpa would have wanted her to have the actual stock he bought three days before his death using the options.

C. ABATEMENT

We now know what happens when specifically devised property is not in the estate at the decedent's death, but what happens when generally devised property, such as cash, is in the estate but is not sufficient to pay all of the decedent's debts and bequests? If the estate doesn't have the assets, the various bequests have to *abate*, that is, each bequest of a particular kind will be reduced, *pro rata*, along with all other similar bequests, until the shortfall is taken care of. But bequests don't all abate at once. Remember, homestead, exempt property, and family allowance set-asides come off the top before the decedent's debts. So if there is only enough property to pay those, then case closed. After the set-asides and the debts (including administration fees and lawyer fees), then the representative can think about whether the estate is large enough to pay the decedent's bequests.

Historically, land was treated differently from personal property. At death, the land passed automatically to the legal heir or devisee, while the personal property passed to the personal representative for administration of the estate. As a result, land could not be used to satisfy the decedent's debts. Some states continue to treat land and personal property differently, allowing the personal property to abate before the real property. The UPC eliminates the distinction, but doing so can frequently require that land be sold if the liquid assets of the estate are insufficient to pay the debts and other bequests. This would have been a perfect opportunity for some life insurance to infuse cash into the estate.

Some states also treat certain devisees differently than others—thus, relatives might receive preferential treatment over friends, charities, or others. In such a case, a residuary bequest to the testator's two nieces and her best friend in equal shares could result in the friend's share abating first.[10]

Under the common law, the first property to abate was property not disposed of by a will (i.e., intestate property); the second to abate was usually the residuary property, followed by general and then specific devises. Thus, if a decedent left a will giving her diamond ring to A, her Ford car to B, her stocks and bonds to C, $5,000 to D, and the residue to E, the representative will honor the specific bequests first, then the demonstrative and general bequests, and then the residuary bequest. If there is nothing left in the residue, then E is out of luck. A, B, C, and D are also out of luck if the decedent's estate is not large enough to pay the set-asides and debts. In that case, all of the property will be sold and used to satisfy the set-asides or debts.

The UPC continues the general common law order of asset abatement, but it allows for a different order of abatement if the typical order would defeat an express or implied purpose of the devise. For instance, if a testator sets out a general devise to a surviving spouse designed to take advantage of a particular tax exemption, and abating that property along with the rest will result in greater tax liability, a court may accept evidence that the will expresses an intent to minimize taxes and therefore the usual abatement pattern should be changed.

UPC § 3–902. Distribution; Order in Which Assets Appropriated; Abatement.

(a) Except as provided in subsection (b) and except as provided in connection with the share of the surviving spouse who elects to take an elective share, shares of distributees abate, without any preference or priority as between real and personal property, in the following order:

---

[10] 20 PA. CONS. STAT. § 3541 (2012).

(1) property not disposed of by the will;

(2) residuary devises;

(3) general devises;

(4) specific devises.

For purposes of abatement, a general devise charged on any specific property or fund is a specific devise to the extent of the value of the property on which it is charged, and upon the failure or insufficiency of the property on which it is charged, a general devise to the extent of the failure or insufficiency. Abatement within each classification is in proportion to the amounts of property each of the beneficiaries would have received if full distribution of the property had been made in accordance with the terms of the will.

(b) If the will expresses an order of abatement, or if the testamentary plan or the express or implied purpose of the devise would be defeated by the order of abatement stated in subsection (a), the shares of the distributees abate as may be found necessary to give effect to the intention of the testator.

(c) If the subject of a preferred devise is sold or used incident to administration, abatement shall be achieved by appropriate adjustments in, or contribution from, other interests in the remaining assets.

This order of abatement also can be problematic for the typical testator who makes small bequests to a variety of friends, distant relatives, and charities, and then leaves the residue to the primary beneficiary. If a large tort claim or expensive medical bills for end of life care suddenly eats into a modest estate, the testator might have preferred to forego the specific bequests in order to give the entire estate to the primary residuary beneficiary. But under the common law rules and the UPC that won't happen unless the testator explicitly provides an order of abatement in the will itself, thus lengthening and complicating what should be an otherwise relatively simple document.

Another difficulty arises because of the common use of trusts and other probate avoidance mechanisms, like joint tenancies, life insurance, and beneficiary designations in POD and TOD accounts. In most states, all of the decedent's debts are chargeable against the probate estate, and not against property passing outside probate through other means. Estate taxes are also usually chargeable against the probate estate first, though many states have separate statutes for dealing with the payment of estate taxes. Assuming a testator knows that debts will be charged against the probate estate and not the trust, joint tenancy, or other property, the testator can plan accordingly. But many testators don't think that the debts will eat up their estates, or that property just won't be there. The testator who planned on having his stock in his 8-track tape manufacturing company sold to pay his generous bequests might be surprised to discover that the stock is no longer worth anywhere near the value he imagined it might have. The same is often true of jewelry, artwork, or other personal possessions that the owner thinks are more valuable than the rest of the world seems to appreciate.

Consider the following cases:

Hayes v. Est. of Hayes

479 So.2d 304 (Fla. 2d DCA 1985)

Appellant (surviving spouse) and Frank C. Hayes (testator) entered into a prenuptial agreement on November 17, 1977, which provided that each relinquished all claims of any kind to the other's estate or property under any law. At testator's death in 1983, his will provided the following specific bequests:

> a) $5,000 (Five Thousand and no/100) Dollars to my wife, DELLA A. HAYES. I am making no other provision for my said wife, DELLA A. HAYES, not out of lack of love or affection, but because we have entered into a Pre-Nuptial Agreement dated November 17, 1977, setting forth terms and conditions relating to each others alternate estates.

> b) Testator made four more specific bequests, one to a stepson and three to his sons, which totalled $13,000.00.

> The will also provided that eight grandchildren were the residual beneficiaries and it affirmed the pre-nuptial agreement. It was silent on abatement priorities.

At testator's death, the final accounting revealed only $4,004.90 in assets available for distribution to the beneficiaries. Accordingly, the personal representative filed a plan giving the wife 5/18ths of the estate and dividing the remainder 4 ways for the sons and step-son, leaving nothing for the grandchildren. The surviving spouse objected to the plan of distribution, claiming that under Fla. Stat. § 733.805(2), she was entitled to the entire remaining distributable estate because surviving spouses are granted preferential treatment when applying rules of abatement where the available distributable assets are insufficient to satisfy all the bequests to members of a class of specific devisees. The statute provides in pertinent part: "Devises to the decedent's surviving spouse, *given in satisfaction of, or instead of, the surviving spouse's statutory rights in the estate,* shall not abate until other devises of the same class are exhausted. [Emphasis added.]" The court explained that: *in order for appellant's devise to come under the protection of the statute, it would have to have been given "in satisfaction of, or instead of" her statutory rights in her deceased husband's estate. A review of the will reveals a contrary intent.*

Testator gave appellant a specific bequest of $5,000.00. He made no other provision for appellant, his wife, "because we have entered into a Pre-Nuptial Agreement dated November 17, 1977, setting forth terms and conditions relating to each others alternate estates." It is clear from the will that testator did not intend to revoke or to have the will supersede the terms of the prenuptial agreement by which appellant and testator relinquished all statutory claims to each other's estates. It is also clear that while testator wanted to give appellant a part of his estate, he did not want her to have the bulk of it or a share that one commonly leaves to a spouse.

Accordingly, because appellant entered into a prenuptial agreement by which she relinquished all claims to testator's estate and because testator's will did not repudiate the terms of the prenuptial agreement, we hold that appellant's devise was not given "in satisfaction of, or instead of," her statutory rights in her deceased husband's estate; therefore, her devise does not come within the purview of § 733.805(2) but instead abates ratably along with the other specific devises.

Query: Do you think the parties anticipated that the effect of the pre-nuptial agreement would be to reverse the surviving spousal preference in the abatement statute?

Norton-Children's Hospitals, Inc. v. First Kentucky Trust Co.

557 S.W.2d 895 (Ky. Ct. App. 1977)

Mrs. Lily Moorman left a will explaining that *"My stepmother, Marion S. D. Belknap, died on or about May 6, 1966, and under the provisions of her will dated February 10, 1960 I became entitled to receive one-half of the residue of her estate. It is this particular portion of my estate, which has been devised to me under the will of my said stepmother which I am disposing of in this item of my will."* Moorman then devised, in pertinent part, (Item IV) $5,000 to a friend, $225,000 in trust to the University of the South, and $200,000 to Berea College *"to be paid out of said fund* [her stepmother's estate]." The residue of her estate (Item VII), including anything left from her step-mother's estate, was to be paid to Berea College and the Children's Hospital of Louisville, Kentucky.

Although Moorman had made $430,000 in legacies traceable to her step-mother's estate, the estate only netted her $377,000. The court had to determine if the legacies were specific, general, or demonstrative. If specific, then the legacies of the fund's money would abate; if demonstrative, then the residue would abate and the total amount of the legacies would be paid. The court held them to be demonstrative, giving the following reasons:

> *The primary consideration in determining whether the bequests contained in Item IV of Mrs. Moorman's will are demonstrative or specific is the intention of Mrs. Moorman as determined from an examination of the entire will. However, it is clear that the law favors demonstrative legacies over specific legacies and that a legacy is presumed to be demonstrative rather than specific. It has been stated that a legacy will not be construed as specific unless the testator clearly intended it to be specific. The legal presumption in favor of demonstrative legacies is based on the factual presumption that a testator's or testatrix' expressed affection for a beneficiary is not so ephemeral as to be contingent upon the value of the property remaining unchanged. It is therefore the opinion of this Court that the residuary estate disposed of in Item VII of Mrs. Moorman's will must be used to provide the deficiency necessary in order to satisfy the bequests contained in Item IV.*

Query: From what you understand of specific, general, and demonstrative bequests, do you think the bequests in Item IV of Mrs. Moorman's will are demonstrative?

In re Est. of Goldman

215 Ariz. 169, 158 P.3d 892 (Ariz. Ct. App. 2007)

Elliot Goldman died in 1995, leaving a will that provided that all expenses were to be paid from the residue, then in Article IV of the will he created trusts for his two children up to $900,000 each, and he made several specific bequests, including $250,000 and the marital residence to his wife, $25,000 to his cousin, $20,000 to his business manager, and $300,000 to his brother Jay Goldman, who was also named personal administrator of his estate. In Article V, Elliot made devises to several charitable organizations, including $50,000 to the Jewish Community Foundation of Southern Arizona. The residue of the estate was then to go into the children's trusts. At the date of Elliot's death, the estate's total value was $2,732,733 which, after reduction of expenses, debts, and taxes, left a total of $2,023,853 for distribution to all the devisees. Article V also provided that if there weren't enough assets to pay all the bequests, the Article IV bequests were to take priority. Jay Goldman therefore abated the Article IV bequests ratably and paid none of the charitable bequests of Article V.

In 2003, however, real property remaining in the estate was reappraised, and an increase in its value resulted in an estate balance of nearly $2,000,000. Jay then made payments to all the Article V devisees except the Foundation because he was concerned the Foundation could not accomplish the goals Elliot had set out of endowing an annual trip to Israel. The Foundation brought suit for an accounting and payment of the devise, and the trial court ordered payment, with interest, ruling that the law governing abatement applied to the value of the estate at the time of distribution, not to the value determined at death. On appeal, Jay claims that the Article V claims were entirely abated and that "[a]ny post death appreciation would benefit the creditors and the unabated beneficiaries," and "[t]here is no legal basis for claiming an abated beneficiary interest is somehow resurrected because probate assets later appreciate in value." The case is one of first impression nationally, and the Arizona Court of Appeals affirmed the trial court, relying on the Arizona probate code provisions that define an *estate* in ways that appear to contemplate its existence over time, that includes newly discovered property, and that discuss applying relevant rules to the time of "distribution," not "death." The court rejected the argument that because a devisee's interests in an estate vest at death, it must be valued at death.

Raising various policy concerns, Jay also argues that, "[i]n order to facilitate the orderly administration of the estate," to lend certainty and predictability to the PR's role, and to eliminate "the unavoidable conflicts that will certainly emerge between abated and unabated beneficiaries where abatement decisions are made at the time future distributions are made," "the law should require that date of death values be used to determine abatement." And, Jay further contends, "[u]se of a date certain [to value the estate for abatement purposes] eliminates the need to speculate about future values." Jay argued that PRs would be in a conflict between their obligation to manage and close the estate expeditiously and the possibility that, over time, the estate would appreciate in value enough to pay all otherwise abated devises. The court rejected Jay's arguments, explaining:

We are not persuaded by these arguments. First, it is not clear that a date-of-death valuation rule would be more easily applied, or more likely to avoid the conundrum Jay postulates, than would a rule by which abatement is determined based on the value of estate assets at the time of distribution. If assets were to be valued for abatement purposes as of the testator's date of death but, as in this case, the estate assets appreciate in value during administration of the estate, the question of what to do with the excess value would remain. The PR could not simply allocate that excess to the unabated beneficiaries absent legal authority or a will provision to that effect. Nor could the PR disregard the order of abatement prescribed in § 14–3902(A), unless the will expressly provided a different order of abatement or the statutory scheme would defeat "the testamentary plan or the express or implied purpose of the devise." . . . In sum, Jay's policy arguments do not clearly militate in favor of adopting a date-of-death valuation rule for abatement purposes. Rather, in our view, a rule requiring date-of-distribution values to be used in determining abatement will encourage PRs "to settle and distribute the estate . . . as expeditiously and efficiently as is consistent with the best interests of the estate."

Query: Do you agree with Jay's concern that a PR could not feel confident about abating any bequest until the estate is finally and completely distributed? Jay did choose to fulfill the other Article V bequests and denied only the Foundation's. Do you think the court adopted a date of distribution rule because it was uncomfortable with Jay's discretion in deciding to pay certain of the abated bequests and not others? If so, is this still the best rule?

Practice Point: The Race to Open an Estate

Given the rules of abatement, can you see from where the unsavory description of lawyers "racing to the courthouse" to open an estate arises? Assuming that there is enough property to satisfy homestead/exempt assets, lawyers opening the estate can generally feel confident that they will be paid from the estate, as part of the debts, fees and expenses of the estate—even if that means that there is little to nothing left for beneficiaries. This is good for lawyers, but what about the beneficiaries? And who pays the attorney who represents a beneficiary in a will contest? The answer on this varies from state to state and, often, on whether the will contest is successful or not. But, the estate fees are generally considered to be safely within the pre-residuary abatement order. Would you set a different order?

PROBLEMS

Determine how the following estates would abate under the UPC's § 3–902 and the abatement statute of your state.

5.10. In her will, testator made the following bequests: "I hereby give my house at 123 Main Street to my daughter, Agnes; I give my personal property and all money standing in my name in any financial accounts, including my stock brokerage account at Merrill Lynch, up to the value of $150,000 to my son Ben; and I give the rest and residue of my estate, to the Red Cross." At her death, testator's net probate estate consisted of her house at 123 Main Street, $100,000 in personal property and $50,000 in financial accounts. She also had $50,000 in credit card debt and she had just been assessed $25,000 by the City for sewer upgrades for her house.

5.11. In her will, testator made the following bequests: "I hereby give my house at 123 Main Street to my daughter, Agnes; I give my personal property and all money standing in my name in any financial accounts, including my stock brokerage account at Merrill Lynch, up to the value of $150,000 to my son Ben; and I give the rest and residue of my estate, to the Red Cross." At her death, testator's net probate estate consisted of $100,000 in personal property and $50,000 in financial accounts. She also had $50,000 in credit card debt. And she had a legal judgment in an inverse condemnation action for the value of $150,000 against the City which had condemned her house to tear it down and build a shopping mall.

5.12. In her will, testator made the following bequests: "I hereby give my house at 123 Main Street to my daughter, Agnes; I give my personal property and all money standing in my name in any financial accounts, including my stock brokerage account at Merrill Lynch, up to the value of $150,000 to my son Ben; and I give the rest and residue of my estate, to the Red Cross." At her death, testator's net probate estate consisted of her house at 123 Main Street, $100,000 in personal property and $50,000 in financial accounts. She also had $50,000 in credit card debt. In her will, testator had specified that if her estate was insufficient to pay all bequests, all bequests would abate ratably without consideration for type or form of bequest.

5.13. In her will, testator made the following bequests: "I hereby give my house at 123 Main Street to my daughter, Agnes; I give my personal property and all money standing in my name in any financial accounts, including my stock brokerage account at Merrill Lynch, up to the value of $150,000 to my son Ben; and I give the rest and residue of my estate, to the Red Cross." At her death, testator's net probate estate consisted of her house at 123 Main Street, $100,000 in personal property and $50,000 in financial accounts. She also had $20,000 in credit card debt and a mortgage of $50,000 on her house. In order to pay her debts, her personal administrator sold the house for $175,000 to the City because it was offering 90% of fair market value in order to purchase lands for a shopping mall and the housing market was down and the administrator didn't think she would find a better offer for a long time, if ever.

D. EXONERATION

The two liabilities that are most likely to foul up an estate plan are the decedent's debts, which can include mortgages on real property in the estate, end-of-life medical expenses, unexpected business losses or tort claims, and estate taxes. We cover the problem of estate taxes in the next section on *Apportionment*. First let's consider who should pay the decedent's debts and from what property the debts should be paid. When a testator leaves real property, let's say the vacation house, to his son, and the family house to his daughter, do they take the property free and clear of any mortgages and, if so, where does the money to pay the mortgages come from? Under the common law, the presumption was that mortgages on any property specifically bequeathed to a beneficiary were to be paid out of the general funds of the estate. However, heirs at law, under intestacy rules, took real property subject to the mortgage; i.e. they took only the equity in the property. This is just one of many differences between testate and intestate distribution rules. The UPC has reversed the common law presumption, by requiring specific directions to pay mortgages on any specifically devised real property.

UPC § 2–607. Nonexoneration.

A specific devise passes subject to any mortgage interest existing at the date of death, without right of exoneration, regardless of a general directive in the will to pay debts.

The UPC only speaks of *mortgage* debts, and it is unclear whether it would apply to a car loan or promissory note on personal property. UPC § 2–403 on Exempt Property allows the beneficiary to claim up to $15,000 of exempt property in excess of *security interests*. The use of the term *security interest* in the Exempt Property section dealing with personal property, and *mortgage interest* in the Exoneration section implies that only mortgages on real property are covered by § 2–607. Limiting nonexoneration to real property means the estate has to pay off the car loan or other security interests on personal property before they are distributed. Furthermore, attributing mortgage debts to particular items of real property might seem relatively straightforward. However, with increased advertisements suggesting the use of home equity loans to help pay for a second honeymoon or to send a child to college, devisees of mortgaged real property may complain if their bequest is saddled with a debt that was used to send a sibling to college. Just because mom and dad wanted to gain the tax benefits of a home equity loan rather than student loans doesn't mean they want the child who is to inherit the home to be hit with the college tuition debt.

Also, general provisions to "pay all my just debts" or to "distribute after the payment of my debts" can get one in trouble if the decedent died owing money on a car loan, a credit card, or the purchase price on stock that can be traced to specific property. At what point must an executor trace a debt to a particular item of property? Real estate mortgages are easy, but parsing through the credit card bills to determine whether the recipient of the tv, the testator's new bedroom slippers, or the donee of grandma's unopened box of oatmeal should take that property saddled with the appropriate debt would be an administrative nightmare. Traditionally, people didn't have a lot of debt on personal property, and even mortgages were not as common or as high as they currently are. When the common law rule on exoneration evolved, debts were only acquired for large acquisitions or to pay unexpected medical bills. But with average credit card debts in the neighborhood of $15,000,[11] and many homes under water, a personal administrator can have a very difficult job deciding how to allocate debts if the estate is not particularly solvent.

Consider the following cases and whether you think the testamentary directive regarding exoneration was clear enough or not:

In re Est. of Mathews

409 Ill.App. 3d 780, 948 N.E.2d 187, 350 Ill.Dec. 118 (Ill. App. Ct. 1st Dist. 2011)

Testator died in October, 2007, bequeathing $20,000 and real estate in Sarasota, Florida to the Respondent, Kenneth Radamacker, and the residue of his estate to Cheryl Herbeck. His will also provided as follows: "I give my Executor or Successor–Executor the following powers and discretions, in each case to be exerciseable without court order: . . .

---

[11] Tim Chen, Bad News: Credit Card Debt is Down, FORBES (May 30, 2012) available at http://www.forbes.com/sites/moneybuilder/2012/05/30/bad–news–credit–card–debt–is–down/

(e) To pay all governmental charges, taxes or liens imposed upon my estate or upon the interest of any and all beneficiaries hereunder by any law of any state, foreign state or federal government, relating to the transfer of property by descent or devise, and I do further direct that all such charges, taxes and liens be considered and treated as expenses and costs of administering my estate and be paid out of the same before distribution thereof.

The respondent paid delinquent real estate taxes for the Sarasota real estate for 2006 amounting to $12,702.30; $12,056.01 in delinquent real estate taxes for 2007; and $10,918.75 in delinquent real estate taxes for 2008; and he advanced $1,782 for the 2009 fiscal year. Accordingly, he sought to recover $37,459.06 that he had paid to satisfy the property's real estate tax obligations from decedent's estate. After the trial court ruled that the estate was liable for the real estate taxes, the court of appeals reversed, stating: *The decedent's reference to the taxes imposed on his estate concerns the payment of estate and inheritance taxes, not real estate taxes. Real estate taxes are not imposed on a decedent's estate or upon a beneficiary; rather, they are assessed and imposed against real property and constitute an encumbrance on the property upon which they are assessed. Because real estate taxes are imposed against the property itself and not against the estate or a beneficiary named in the will, the provision in decedent's will merely directing the payment of all charges 'imposed upon [his] estate or upon the interest of any and all beneficiaries . . . relating to the transfer of property by descent or devise' is not sufficient to shift the real estate tax obligation to the estate.*

Query: If the testator died in 2007, who should be responsible for taxes from 2007 onwards? Should the estate have to pay, or the devisee, if probate takes 2 or 3 years before the property is finally transferred to the devisee? Who should have to pay penalties for late taxes? Consider this in light of the distribution rule established in *Est. of Goldman*, on the issue of abatement, discussed above.

Bond v. Est. of Pylant

63 So.3d 638 (Ala. Civ. App. 2010)

Testator and his wife had purchased, as joint tenants with right of survivorship, a number of parcels of real estate in Alabama, taking mortgages totaling more than $700,000. In 2001 the testator wrote his will, providing the usual boilerplate language that: "*I desire that all my just debts, including the expense of my last illness, be paid by my Executor, hereinafter named, as soon after my death as may be practicable.*" In 2004, he and his wife executed an agreement that provided, in pertinent part, that "*it is agreed that if either spouse dies, all mortgages and debts of both parties will be paid in full by the estate of the deceased spouse and become the property of the surviving spouse.*" They each signed that agreement in the presence of a single witness. In 2005, testator was killed in a motorcycle accident. The court held that there was no exoneration, stating that: *in the case now before us, Pylant's general directive in his will to pay his debts did not entitle Kim to exoneration. Kim argues that the agreement she and Pylant signed on December 16, 2004, in which they agreed "that if either spouse dies, all mortgages and debts of both parties will be paid in full by*

*the estate of the deceased spouse and become the property of the surviving
spouse" should be considered as parol evidence explaining Pylant's intent
with respect to exoneration. However, Pylant's general directive in the will to
pay his debts is not ambiguous—it unambiguously omits any provision for
exoneration. 'We must take the terms which the testator used in the will and
parol evidence is never admissible to show terms the testator intended to use
and did not use.'*

Query: Because the agreement was not included in or referenced in the will, it
was inadmissible to give the surviving spouse any interest in the property itself, or to prove her right to exoneration. What should they have done?
Assuming the surviving spouse may not have a right under the will, would she
have a cause of action for breach of contract against the estate? Would the UPC
have solved this problem?

Gibbon v. Est. of Gibbon

829 N.E.2d 27 (Ind. Ct. App. 2005)

Testator died leaving a will devising his 2001 Lincoln automobile to
his son, Mark Gibbon, that was subject to a $12,000 lien. The son paid the
lien and sought reimbursement from his father's estate, which was denied
by the personal representative. The court held that no exoneration was due
even though the will had the following provision: it directed the personal
representative *"to pay out of my residuary estate, the following: Section 1.
The expenses of my last illness, administration expenses, and all legally
enforceable creditor claims."* The court held that the will provision was not
specific enough to overcome the statutory presumption against exoneration.

Query: The Indiana statute, unlike the UPC, specified that personal property
subject to a lien will be taken subject to the lien unless the will provides "expressly or by necessary implication" that the lien is to be paid.[12] How specific
does a testator need to be that he wants ALL debts paid? And if personal property debts are not to be paid, how is the administrator to attribute credit card
debt for the new television or the Sears bill for the new refrigerator to the appropriate beneficiary?

While it might be understandable that a testator would not want to
see his estate completely wiped out in order to pay large mortgages on real
property, do most testators distinguish between the payment of the credit
card debts that may have paid for last week's groceries, and the payment of
the car loan? With the increasing use of credit cards used to purchase personal property on credit, should there be a difference between the credit
card debt for the 60″ plasma TV and the Ford Fiesta car? For a brief history
of the exoneration doctrine see, Thomas E. Clary III, *Property—In re Estate
of Vincent: The Tennessee Supreme Court Declines to Extend the Common
Law Doctrine of Exoneration to Survivorship Property,* 34 U. MEM. L.REV.
695, 697–98 (2004). Even where exoneration might apply to specifically
devised property, should it also apply to property passing outside of pro-

----

[12]   IND. CODE ANN. § 29–1–17–9 (West 1953).

bate, like joint tenancy property or trust property? Most courts have refused to extend the exoneration doctrine to non-probate property, preferpreferring to limit the doctrine more and more. But even if an estate can avoid payment of certain liens and debts on property owned by the decedent at death, thus passing the debts onto the devisees, it cannot escape the payment of estate taxes, which will be explored next.

PROBLEM

5.14. Agnes drafts a will at a very happy time in her life. She owns her home outright and has no other debts. In her will, she specifically bequeaths the following to her daughter, Bella:

> my home, in fee simple, which is located at 444 Main Street. The residuary of the estate shall pass to my son, George.

The value of her home at this time was $150,000 and the value of the remainder of her estate was $150,000. The will contained boilerplate debt language which contained a general directive that the executor pay "all debts and encumbrances." Five years later, Agnes takes out a $100,000 mortgage on her home and dies shortly thereafter. How would UPC § 2–607 apply in this case? What if she had added: "It is my specific intention to treat my two children as equally as possible"?

E. APPORTIONMENT

When estates are large enough to be facing estate taxes ($5,250,000 under the federal revenue code for 2013, and varying amounts under state estate tax codes[13]), the estate pays the taxes before distributions to beneficiaries. In that sense, the estate tax is simply another debt against the estate. But unlike most of the decedent's debts, that are entirely paid out of the probate estate unless the testator indicates otherwise, the Uniform Estate Tax Apportionment Act (UETAA) apportions the tax burden across all the property that is included in the gross taxable estate if the decedent does not specify a different apportionment scheme. Thus, if property passing by joint tenancy, and therefore outside of probate, is included in the taxable estate, it must pay its fair share of the estate tax. The UPC's §§ 3–9A–101 to 115 is modeled on the UETAA. Instead of placing all the liability for the estate tax on the residuary estate, the UPC apportions estate taxes to all recipients of taxable property. This means that ALL property is reduced pro rata, regardless of whether it is in a revocable trust, held as a joint tenancy, is in a securities account with a POD, is a specific bequest for the testator's 8-track tape collection in the will, or is the residuary devise of the will. The Restatement 3d of Property § 1.1, comment g, prorates estate tax liability across all non-probate property, but assesses the estate tax liability for probate property solely against the residue unless the decedent provided otherwise. That protects the 8-track tape collection and other specific and general devises in the will, but not the residuary and non-probate property. Not all states have adopted the UPC or the UETAA, however, and

---

[13] In 2011, seventeen states plus the District of Columbia collect state level estate taxes. They are: Connecticut, Delaware, Hawaii, Illinois, Maine, Maryland, Massachusetts, Minnesota, New Jersey, New York, North Carolina, Ohio, Oregon, Rhode Island, Tennessee, Vermont, and Washington.

complications can arise when an estate owes estate taxes and property passing outside of probate is exempt from paying its share.

Most of the fewer than 1% of decedents who will face estate taxes have lawyers draft their estate plans, and of these lawyers most will include an apportionment clause. As noted earlier, the decedent might have purchased life insurance to help pay his tax liability. Others may have a life insurance trust to pay the taxes. Some decedents might want all estate taxes paid out of a particular asset (like a securities account), while others might choose to defer estate taxes until the death of their surviving spouse by taking advantage of the unlimited marital deduction. They can pass the maximum allowable to third parties and then pass the residue of their estate to their spouses, with an instruction to pay the estate taxes out of the residuary. Because there won't be estate taxes, the instruction is really boilerplate. But, life and death don't always go as the big expensive lawyers plan.

Consider the following well-known case (among estate planners that is):

Est. of Kuralt

315 Mont. 177, 68 P.3d 662, 2003 MT 92 (2003)

Appellants, Susan Bowers and Lisa Bowers White (Bowers and White), the daughters of Charles Kuralt and personal representatives of the Estate of Charles Kuralt (the Estate), appeal from the decision of the Fifth Judicial District Court, Madison County, ordering that all estate taxes due as a result of the administration of the estate of Charles Kuralt be imposed on the residual estate. We affirm.

We address the following issue on appeal:

Did the District Court correctly apply New York law to the Kuralt codicil when it ordered that the taxes on the property conveyed therein shall be imposed on the residual estate?

Charles Kuralt died testate in a hospital in New York City on July 4, 1997. While the bulk of his estate was in New York, he also owned property in Madison County, Montana, on the Big Hole River. Mr. Kuralt's widow, Suzanna "Petie" Baird Kuralt, thereafter filed a petition in a New York state court seeking to probate the estate. On September 15, 1997, Petie, as the Domiciliary Foreign Personal Representative of the Estate of Charles Kuralt, through Montana counsel, filed a Proof of Authority seeking to probate the real property owned by Kuralt in Madison County.

On September 30, 1997, Kuralt's long-time and intimate companion, Patricia Elizabeth Shannon, filed a Petition for Ancillary Probate of Will, challenging the application of Kuralt's New York will to the Madison County property based, in part, on a letter which she had received from Mr. Kuralt shortly before his death a letter that this Court, in *Kuralt II,* determined to be a valid holographic codicil conveying the Madison County property to Shannon.

Mr. Kuralt's wife, Petie, was initially appointed as the personal representative of the Estate in both New York and Montana. She died in October 1999, . . . Bowers and White were appointed as successor personal representatives of the Kuralt Estate in New York and, on August 21, 2000, petitioned the Montana District Court to appoint them successor personal representatives of the Estate in Montana. The District Court denied their request, and we reversed in *Kuralt III*.

Left undetermined in the previous cases was the question of whether the Estate or Shannon was responsible for the estate taxes associated with the bequest to Shannon of the Big Hole River property in Madison County. As a consequence of this Court's decision in *Kuralt II* concluding that Kuralt's 1997 letter was a valid holographic codicil conveying the Big Hole River property to Shannon, there exists a federal estate tax obligation in regard to the property.

On January 4, 2001, Shannon filed and served a "Demand upon Estate of Suzanna Baird Kuralt for Payment of Taxes" demanding that the co-personal representatives, Bowers and White, pay from the residuary of the Estate all federal, state and gift taxes due as a result of the bequest of the Big Hole River property to Shannon.

Bowers and White opposed Shannon's demand for payment out of the residuary of the Estate and argued that, under both New York and Montana law, estate taxes should be apportioned under the New York apportionment statutes, notwithstanding language to the contrary in Kuralt's 1994 will. They contended that the conveyance of the property to Shannon created adverse tax consequences against the Estate, contrary to the "dominant purpose or plan of distribution" of the 1994 will to take full advantage of the marital deduction and to protect Mrs. Kuralt from burdensome taxation.

Shannon responded that, under the applicable New York statutory and case law as well as Montana law, where the language of the will makes it clear that there is to be no apportionment of estate taxes according to state statute, the courts of both states will abide by the explicit language in the will.

The District Court agreed with Shannon and concluded that, under substantially similar laws of New York and Montana, the court must adhere and give effect to the testator's plan if such plan can be ascertained. The District Court further concluded that, under Article Twelve of Kuralt's 1994 will, wherein it states that all death taxes "shall be paid without apportionment," all taxes are to be paid by the residual estate and thus ordered that the taxes generated from the bequest of the Big Hole River property to Shannon be paid accordingly.

Bowers and White now appeal the District Court's decision.

DISCUSSION

Initially we note that Charles Kuralt was domiciled in New York at the time of his death and that his 1994 will was executed in New York and was admitted to probate there. This Court determined in *Kuralt II* that Kuralt's 1997 letter to Shannon was a valid holographic codicil to the 1994 will, and thus, a part of the 1994 will. Under these circumstances, Bowers, White and Shannon agree and have stipulated that New York law applies to the construction of the will as well as the codicil. Furthermore, Montana law is essentially the same on the points at issue in this case.

On appeal, Bowers and White argue that the District Court should be reversed because its decision that the estate taxes attributable to the Big Hole River property is chargeable against the residuary is contrary to Kuralt's "purpose or plan" as expressed in his 1994 will and contrary to the well established New York statutory law and public policy.

The applicable New York statute provides:

> Unless otherwise provided in the will or non-testamentary instrument, and subject to paragraph (d–1) of this section: (1) The tax shall be apportioned among the persons benefited in the proportion that the value of the property or interest received by each person benefited bears to the total value of the property and interest received by all persons benefited. . . .   EPTL § 2–1.8(c).

When interpreting the earliest version of this statute, the Court of Appeals of New York stated that the statute "requires apportionment of Federal and State estate taxes among the legatees and devisees 'in the proportion that the value of the property or interest received by each such person' . . . *except where the testator 'otherwise directs in his will.' "* . . .

Bowers and White contend that the rule in *Dewar* [that instructions as to apportionment in a will shall be extended to new devises in a codicil] is inapplicable to the current case because Kuralt's 1994 will did contain a "manifest intent to the contrary," that intent being Kuralt's intent to take full advantage of the marital deduction, thus ensuring that Mrs. Kuralt's share would be tax free. They argue that the Surrogate's conclusion, and the Court of Appeal's affirmation in *Dewar,* was not only consistent with the anti-apportionment clause in the will, but was also consistent with the undisputed intention of the testatrix in *Dewar* to opt out of the apportionment statute.

Bowers and White contend that, in the instant case, it is likewise undisputed that Kuralt's "dominant purpose or plan of distribution" was to insure that Mrs. Kuralt's share would be tax free, and that this dominant purpose is inconsistent with the tax burden now generated by the bequest in the codicil of the Big Hole River property to Shannon. They contend that this inconsistency generates an ambiguity such that there is no clear and unambiguous direction that the taxes generated from the Big Hole Property should not be apportioned to its recipient, and that such taxes should, therefore, be paid by Shannon, notwithstanding the language in Article Twelve of Kuralt's 1994 will. Article Twelve provides:

> A.   All estate, inheritance . . . and other death taxes . . . which shall be imposed by reason of my death . . . *shall be paid without apportionment* in the following manner:
>
> (a) first, out of that portion, if any, of the balance of my residuary estate disposed of under Paragraph B of Article FIVE of this Will with respect to which my wife shall have made a qualified disclaimer;
>
> (b) second, out of the fractional share, if any, of my residuary estate disposed of under Paragraph A of Article FIVE of this Will; and
>
> (c) third, out of (the balance of) my residuary estate disposed of under . . . Article FIVE of this Will . . .

While Bowers and White agree that Article Twelve presents a clear and unambiguous direction that taxes should not be apportioned among the recipients of the Estate, thus opting out of the default apportionment provision of EPTL § 2–1.8(c), they also contend that, where a reading of the entire will reveals a "dominant purpose or plan of distribution," the individual parts must be interpreted in light of that purpose, and be given effect accordingly, despite the fact that a literal reading might yield an inconsistent meaning. In other words, they argue that Kuralt's holographic codicil renders ambiguous the otherwise clear language of the will, and that, in light of this ambiguity, there exists a conflict between the dominant purpose of the will and the anti-apportionment language of Article Twelve.

Thus, they argue that the alleged ambiguity created by the holographic codicil requires this Court to look to the overall scheme of the will, and that, pursuant to *Matter of Pepper* (1954), 307 N.Y. 242, 251, 120 N.E.2d 807, 811, and given the strong policy in favor of statutory apportionment, any ambiguity in the testator's intent must be resolved in favor of the EPTL apportionment scheme, thus requiring Shannon to pay the estate taxes generated by the Big Hole River property.

In *Matter of Pepper,* the testator's will first directed that all bequests and trusts in the will be set up free of tax and then directed that the trusts be created out of the residuary estate. However, the will went on to direct that all taxes be paid from the same residuary estate out of which the trusts were to be created, thus placing a tax on the trusts. *Matter of Pepper,* 307 N.Y. at 249–50, 120 N.E.2d at 810–11.

> If the latter direction be followed, viz., that the taxes be paid out of the residuary estate, the result is that the trusts created are not set up freed of taxes as he directed in the opening portion of paragraph Third, but are set up each having borne a share of the taxes. If the early direction be followed, viz., that the trusts be set up freed from all deduction for inheritance, transfer, estate or any other tax, then the direction that the taxes be paid out of the residuary estate is meaningless for the property going into the trusts comprises the entire residuary estate and after the trusts are set up freed from taxes no residuary remains from which taxes can be paid. The first clause directing the trusts to be set up free of tax and the last clause directing all taxes to be paid out of the residuary estate cancel out or neutralize each other. *The net result is that this will does not contain a direction against statutory apportionment.*

Absent a clear and unambiguous direction against statutory apportionment, combined with a strong policy favoring apportionment with the burden of proof being on the party contending against apportionment, the *Pepper* Court concluded that, "[i]n case of doubt as to what the will means on the subject of taxes the statutory direction to apportion is absolute."

Shannon argues that *Matter of Pepper* is not applicable to Kuralt's will, as *Matter of Pepper* involved the interpretation of an internal conflict within the will and did not involve a later codicil. Shannon also notes that *Dewar* was decided after *Matter of Pepper,* and that the *Dewar* Court, in fact, cited to *Matter of Pepper* yet held that, where anti-apportionment language of the will is unequivocal, it must be faithfully followed by the courts and that a codicil must be construed in conformance with the will unless the codicil contains a clear contrary direction. Shannon argues that the instant case is identical or nearly identical to *Dewar* because the Kuralt will contains an unambiguous directive against apportionment of estate taxes, and like *Dewar,* involves a codicil that did not direct otherwise.

We thus conclude that *Matter of Pepper* [does not] resolve the current dispute.

34 N.Y. EPTL § 1–2.1 provides:

> A codicil is a supplement to a will, either by adding to, taking from or altering its provisions or confirming it in whole or in part by republication, but not totally revoking such will.

"A review of the relevant statutes discloses that EPTL § 1–2.18(b) provides that 'Unless the context otherwise requires, the term "will" includes a "codicil" ' . . . . If probate is decreed, the will and the codicil become one instrument constituting the last will of decedent. The law clearly provides that a will includes any and all codicils."

We disagree with Bowers and White that *Dewar* is distinguishable by virtue of the fact that the codicil in *Dewar* specifically "ratified and confirmed" the provisions of the decedent's previous will. Under New York law, a valid codicil, by definition, alters and supplements or adds and subtracts from an already existing will, whether or not the codicil contains specific language to that effect. A codicil that is silent on method of payment of estate taxes, therefore, does not add or subtract from clear and unambiguous language in the original will specifically directing how estate taxes should be paid, even if the bequest in the codicil generates a tax burden not previously existing under the original will. Similar to *Dewar,* in the instant case there is no question but that the direction to avoid apportionment against specific devisees in Kuralt's 1994 will is both clear and unambiguous, and that this, indeed, was Kuralt's intention.

While there is a strong public policy in favor of statutory apportionment under New York law, we hold that the District Court correctly concluded that Shannon satisfied the burden of proving that Kuralt's will directs, clearly and unambiguously, in Article Twelve, against statutory apportionment, and that all estate taxes are to be paid by the residual Estate, including those generated by the bequest of the Big Hole River property to Shannon.

The decision of the District Court is affirmed accordingly.

Query: Even assuming Kuralt intended the letter to Shannon to be a holographic codicil, do you think he intended, or even thought about, the apportionment issue in his will, or how it would apply to the property covered by the codicil?

The history of the *Kuralt* case, as the court indicated here, was extremely complicated and quite upsetting for Kuralt's family. Apparently, Kuralt had been carrying on an affair with Patricia Shannon in Montana for over 30 years, unbeknownst to his wife and children living in New York. He purchased Montana property with the idea that Patricia would inherit it after his death. He even wrote a codicil to leave the property to her. But thereafter he wrote a new will in 1994 in New York, failing to mention the Montana property and Patricia, leaving everything to his wife Petie and his children. That will revoked the earlier codicil in favor of Patricia. The will also took advantage of the unlimited marital deduction by leaving a substantial portion of property to his wife that would pass tax-free in the residuary clause. But Kuralt's lawyer included probably boilerplate language that the tax liability would be paid from the residuary estate, figuring that there would be no tax liability because all property over and above the taxable limit was passing tax-free to Petie.[14]

When he was suddenly taken ill, Kuralt wrote Patricia a letter from his New York hospital room, stating that he was going to call in a lawyer to draft a new codicil to make sure she got the Montana property. But he died before he could do that. When Patricia showed up with the letter from Kuralt claiming that she was entitled to the Montana property, Kuralt's wife and children opposed her claim. The family argued that the letter stating that Kuralt was going to draft appropriate documents so Patricia could get the property was not a holographic codicil because it clearly anticipated the future execution of a testamentary document. The Montana Supreme Court disagreed and held that the letter itself was a holographic codicil. This ruling allowed Patricia Shannon to receive the Montana property, as Kuralt had apparently intended. To add insult to injury, Patricia refused to pay her share of the estate taxes for the value of the Montana property. The Montana Supreme Court again sided with the mistress and against Kuralt's wife. Thus, the estate taxes for the Montana property came out of the wife's share of the residuary estate and reduced the amount of the estate that passed tax-free, increasing the estate tax liability. Had the tax liability been apportioned against the non-exempt property, a larger share of Kuralt's estate would have passed tax free, and the taxes that ultimately accrued would not have been added to his taxable estate thereby increasing his tax liability.

Surely this was not how Kuralt intended things to transpire. Certainly had his lawyer known of the Montana mistress and her claim to the Montana property, the lawyer might have drafted the non-apportionment clause of the will differently. It would have been so easy for Kuralt to have placed the Montana property into a revocable living trust, naming himself as trustee and Patricia as successor trustee and beneficiary. And although the property would still be part of his taxable estate, he could have provided in the trust for payment of estate taxes, or, better yet, given Patricia a life interest in the trust property with a remainder over to a charity to avoid estate taxes altogether. Suffice it to say that keeping one's mistress secret from one's wife can be emotionally costly to the surviving family, but keeping the mistress secret from one's lawyer can be economically quite costly. It may just be that boilerplate language apportioning tax liability to the residuary beneficiary constitutes malpractice. But then, could the law-

---

[14] To understand the details of why this blunder was so expensive, assume Kuralt's estate was worth $30 million and he can pass $5 million to his children or other beneficiaries without tax. The remaining $25 million he passes to his spouse tax-free, thus avoiding all tax liability at his death. Now, assume that the Montana property is worth $3 million and, rather than passing to his wife free of tax liability, it is passing to Pat Shannon, and is now included in his taxable estate, bringing that to $8 million. For mathematical ease, let's assume that he pays 50% estate tax on all amounts over $5 million, so he now has a tax liability of $1.5 million that also has to come out of the residuary bequest to his wife, reducing the share of property that is passing under the marital deduction. But what is worse, the $1.5 million in taxes is now part of his taxable estate, so it's not $8 million, but rather $9.5 million, so he has another $.75 million to pay, which is also deducted from the spousal bequest. And this gets compounded so that his spouse takes only $19 million, his non-exempt beneficiaries take their $8 million, and the federal government gets $3 million. At a 50% tax rate the government gets a dollar in tax for every dollar over the $5 million exemption because of the compounding! For a fuller discussion of the compounding of federal estate taxes, see Chapter 9.

yers have anticipated that Kuralt's letter to Patricia would be deemed a valid holographic codicil?

Another issue that we don't have the time or space to explore in any detail are the conflicts between state apportionment statutes, some of which allow apportionment instructions in trusts to operate on will bequests, and others of which don't. Thus, an apportionment instruction in a trust may not be given effect if the state's statute allows estate tax instructions only in a will, as does the Tennessee Code.[15] The New York statute at issue in *Kuralt* allows a testator to opt out of the statutory apportionment by a clause in either a "will or non-testamentary instrument."[16] Since many people who are likely to be hit with estate taxes are likely to have sizable non-probate transfers, either during life or at death, the state's apportionment statute could have significant limitations on the desirability of using non-probate transfers to non-exempt beneficiaries.

PROBLEMS

5.15.Luther dies in 2010. Under his will, all property passes equally to his two children, Teena and Sven. Luther also owns a family farm as a joint tenant with rights of survivorship with his brother, Thorn. During Luther's estate administration, a $1M estate tax liability exists. Under the UETAA and the UPC, how would the taxes be apportioned on the farm?

5.16.Bridget died in 2012 leaving a will (dated 2009) that directed that any estate tax liability shall be paid out of the residue of her estate. In 2010, she decided to place the bulk of her property into a revocable living trust and instructed the trustee to pay any estate tax liability out of the trust so that her relatively small but very important specific devises in her will would not suffer. In 2011, however, she executed a codicil that reaffirmed her will but changed the person she wanted to appoint as personal administrator of her estate. At her death, her residuary clause would devise $50,000 worth of property, she has $50,000 in specific bequests in her will, and her revocable trust has $10 million in securities. Under the UETAA or the UPC, how would the estate taxes be apportioned?

F. DISCLAIMER

So far we have talked about things that can go wrong with an estate plan if the drafter is not paying attention to the infinite variety of events that can happen between the execution of the will or other estate documents and the testator's death. In this time lapse, beneficiaries may die, causing their gifts to lapse. The value of property may decrease or the testator may acquire new property or new debts. Property bequeathed in a will may also be sold or given away. It's not very often that a year like 2010 will come around, when the federal estate tax will be zero. Rather, it is far more likely that the laws will change, tax rates will increase, or family circumstances will suddenly change so that a rational estate plan will no longer seem quite so rational. But when the grim reaper finally decides to visit, even when nothing changes with regard to the testator, changes affecting beneficiaries may also affect an estate plan. One of the most likely

---

[15] TENN. CODE ANN. § 30–2–614 (West 1943).

[16] N.Y. Est. Powers & Trusts Law § 2–1.8(c) (McKinney 2000).

changes is that a beneficiary will choose to renounce or *disclaim* a bequest, causing it to lapse or pass to other beneficiaries in ways that might profoundly affect an estate plan. Why, you might ask, would anyone choose to reject a gift, especially a gift of money?

One obvious reason is that the beneficiary doesn't need the money. If you were Bill Gates, you probably wouldn't want to be bothered inheriting a house, a car, or a stack of old records. But even if you aren't as rich as Bill Gates, you might not need the money, especially if you are advanced in years, have good health insurance, and relatively few expenses. In that case, why take the inheritance, only to have to devise it to your own beneficiaries in a few years, which causes the property to be probated twice, with all the cost and bother of double administration and possibly double taxation. The most common reason people disclaim is to avoid increased estate tax liability. But there are some very important limitations on the power to disclaim and other reasons to do it.

For one, an individual can't decide to disclaim and have property pass to others after the individual has enjoyed the property. The law does allow a beneficiary to take a reasonable amount of time to consult financial planners or estate attorneys to decide whether to make a disclaimer or not. If the property is disclaimed, it does not pass to designees of the disclaimant. Instead the disclaimed property passes to the donor's alternate beneficiaries, residuary legatees, or intestate heirs depending on the original donor's intentions. Consider the following hypothetical:

Herman writes a will leaving everything to his wife Wila, but if she predeceases him, he wants all of his property to pass to his two children, Seth and Doris. A week after Herman dies, Wila's long lost uncle dies, leaving her $5 million. With her uncle's money, her own money, and now Herman's money, she will very likely have to pay some significant estate taxes on her death. But if she disclaims Herman's bequest, at least that property will be treated as though she predeceased him, and thus will pass directly to Seth and Doris. Now Herman's property won't be part of Wila's estate when she dies.

But what about the fact that Wila didn't know she was going to inherit her uncle's estate until after Herman died and after the property had supposedly passed to her? Remember, property rights vest at the donor's death. As long as Wila didn't take possession of Herman's property or voluntarily transfer, pledge, assign, or convey it, she can take however long she needs to decide whether to accept or disclaim the inheritance. She can therefore wait to see if her uncle is really going to leave her everything, or if she is going to win the lottery, or her stock investments are going to pay off. So long as she hasn't accepted any *benefit* from Herman's estate, she can disclaim it and the property she disclaims will pass according to Herman's will to his alternate beneficiaries. But what if she waits nine months before disclaiming it and then, when she does so, it has now appreciated in value? Who owned it during the interim when she was making up her mind and who gets the increased value?

The executor of Herman's estate was acting as a trustee and directly managing the property during the interim, but once Wila disclaims the property, courts may use the *relation back doctrine* to treat the property as though it passed immediately upon Herman's death directly to Seth and Doris. The relation back doctrine can't go back hundreds of years, but it can be a very useful device for stalling the transfer of property just long enough to figure out how other events might transpire and then using the legal fiction that the property actually transferred back when the original transaction occurred to avoid certain liabilities. If that sounds like the law is letting you manipulate the tax liabilities until you know more and can plan better, you are exactly right. Consequently, you have to be very careful to follow the disclaimer requirements precisely or risk double transfers.

The UPC's exhaustive disclaimer provision, based on the Uniform Disclaimer of Property Interests Act, §§ 2–1101 to 1117, is the most comprehensive disclaimer statute written. It also makes some important changes to earlier disclaimer statutes, ones that might still be in effect in many states. It eliminates the nine-month rule for disclaiming an interest, a time-period governed by the Internal Revenue Code for tax-qualified disclaimers, but not necessarily relevant to disclaimers of other kinds of property. By eliminating the time period, therefore, the practitioner must be very careful to consult other statutes affecting the consequences of disclaimers to determine if the disclaimer will have the appropriate effects. It also does away with the relation back doctrine and instead spells out when a disclaimer will become effective, thus recognizing that interests in joint property, revocable trusts, and other forms might not function under the relation back doctrine the same way as property interests passing via a will.

UNIFORM DISCLAIMER OF PROPERTY INTERESTS ACT
(1999)

---

§ 2–1103. Scope.

This Part applies to disclaimers of any interest in or power over property, whenever created.

---

§ 2–1105. Power to Disclaim; General Requirements; When Irrevocable.

(a) A person may disclaim, in whole or part, any interest in or power over property, including a power of appointment. A person may disclaim the interest or power even if its creator imposed a spendthrift provision or similar restriction on transfer or a restriction or limitation on the right to disclaim.

* * *

(c) To be effective, a disclaimer must be in a writing or other record, declare the disclaimer, describe the interest or power disclaimed, be signed by the person making the disclaimer, and be delivered or filed in the manner provided in Section 2–1112. * * *

(d) A partial disclaimer may be expressed as a fraction, percentage, monetary amount, term of years, limitation of a power, or any other interest or estate in the property.

(e) A disclaimer becomes irrevocable when it is delivered or filed pursuant to Section 2–1112 or when it becomes effective as provided in Sections 2–1106 through 2–1111, whichever occurs later.

(f) A disclaimer made under this Part is not a transfer, assignment, or release.

§ 2–1106. Disclaimer of Interest in Property.

(a) In this section:

(1) "Future interest" means an interest that takes effect in possession or enjoyment, if at all, later than the time of its creation.

(2) "Time of distribution" means the time when a disclaimed interest would have taken effect in possession or enjoyment.

(b) Except for a disclaimer governed by Section 7 or 8, the following rules apply to a disclaimer of an interest in property:

(1) The disclaimer takes effect as of the time the instrument creating the interest becomes irrevocable, or, if the interest arose under the law of intestate succession, as of the time of the intestate's death.

(2) The disclaimed interest passes according to any provision in the instrument creating the interest providing for the disposition of the interest, should it be disclaimed, or of disclaimed interests in general.

(3) If the instrument does not contain a provision described in paragraph (2), the following rules apply:

(A) If the disclaimant is not an individual, the disclaimed interest passes as if the disclaimant did not exist.

(B) If the disclaimant is an individual, except as otherwise provided in subparagraphs (C) and (D), the disclaimed interest passes as if the disclaimant had died immediately before the time of distribution.

(C) If by law or under the instrument, the descendants of the disclaimant would share in the disclaimed interest by any method of representation had the disclaimant died before the time of distribution, the disclaimed interest passes only to the descendants of the disclaimant who survive the time of distribution.

(D) If the disclaimed interest would pass to the disclaimant's estate had the disclaimant died before the time of distribution, the disclaimed interest instead passes by representation to the descendants of the disclaimant who survive the time of distribution. If no descendant of the disclaimant survives the time of distribution, the disclaimed interest passes to those persons, including the state but excluding the disclaimant, and in such shares as would succeed to the transferor's intestate estate under the intestate succession law of the transferor's domicile had the transferor died at the time of distribution. However, if the transferor's surviving spouse is living but is remarried at the time of distribution, the transferor is deemed to have died unmarried at the time of distribution.

(4) Upon the disclaimer of a preceding interest, a future interest held by a person other than the disclaimant takes effect as if the disclaimant had died or ceased to exist immediately before the time of distribution, but a future interest held by the disclaimant is not accelerated in possession or enjoyment.

§ 2–1107. Disclaimer of Rights of Survivorship in Jointly Held Property.

(a) Upon the death of a holder of jointly held property, a surviving holder may disclaim, in whole or part, the greater of:

(1) a fractional share of the property determined by dividing the number one by the number of joint holders alive immediately before the death of the holder to whose death the disclaimer relates; or

(2) all of the property except that part of the value of the entire interest attributable to the contribution furnished by the disclaimant.

(b) A disclaimer under subsection (a) takes effect as of the death of the holder of jointly held property to whose death the disclaimer relates.

(c) An interest in jointly held property disclaimed by a surviving holder of the property passes as if the disclaimant predeceased the holder to whose death the disclaimer relates.

§ 2–1109. Disclaimer of Power of Appointment or Other Power Not Held in Fiduciary Capacity.

If a holder disclaims a power of appointment or other power not held in a fiduciary capacity, the following rules apply:

(1) If the holder has not exercised the power, the disclaimer takes effect as of the time the instrument creating the power becomes irrevocable.

(2) If the holder has exercised the power and the disclaimer is of a power other than a presently exercisable general power of appointment, the disclaimer takes effect immediately after the last exercise of the power.

(3) The instrument creating the power is construed as if the power expired when the disclaimer became effective.

§ 2–1110. Disclaimer By Appointee, Object, or Taker In of Exercise of Power of Appointment.

(a) A disclaimer of an interest in property by an appointee of a power of appointment takes effect as of the time the instrument by which the holder exercises the power becomes irrevocable.

(b) A disclaimer of an interest in property by an object or taker in default of an exercise of a power of appointment takes effect as of the time the instrument creating the power becomes irrevocable.

§ 2–1113. When Disclaimer Barred or Limited.

(a) A disclaimer is barred by a written waiver of the right to disclaim.

(b) A disclaimer of an interest in property is barred if any of the following events occur before the disclaimer becomes effective:

(1) the disclaimant accepts the interest sought to be disclaimed;

(2) the disclaimant voluntarily assigns, conveys, encumbers, pledges, or transfers the interest sought to be disclaimed or contracts to do so; or

(3) a judicial sale of the interest sought to be disclaimed occurs.

* * *

Disclaimers are primarily used to avoid double administration or double taxation when the donee[17] of the property simply doesn't need the property and doesn't want to have to mess with managing it or transferring it. By disclaiming the property it passes directly to the alternate recipients without passing through the donee's hands at all. Disclaimers are also used effectively to limit the access of the recipient's creditors to property that may become available to a debtor after the debt arose. Thus, if I killed a pedestrian with my car on the way to my mother's funeral, and I am going to inherit a fortune from my mom only to lose it to the victim's family in a tort judgment, I could disclaim the interest and it will pass to my mother's alternate beneficiaries as though I predeceased my mother. That leaves my tort claimants only able to attach my property, not my mom's property. Disclaimers can also be used effectively to speed up possession of future interests. If I am the life income beneficiary of a trust, and my children are the remainder beneficiaries, I can disclaim the life interest and the trust corpus will pass directly to my children, despite the fact that the grantor intended my children to take the principal only upon my death.

The most important aspect of disclaimers is that upon an effective disclaimer the property simply bypasses the intended recipient and goes instead directly to the donor's alternate beneficiaries. However, if the donee of the property uses it for a while and then decides to relinquish it to the donor's alternate takers, it is treated as a subsequent transfer. For instance, if I am given a life estate in my mother's trust, with a remainder to my children, and I disclaim my interest *before* I benefit from the property at all, then it passes directly to my children. But if I receive the income for ten years and then win the lottery and decide to renounce my interest in the trust to accelerate possession to my children, I do so by *transferring* to them my remaining life estate which merges with their remainder interest. The value of my life estate should be less after I've accepted it for ten years, and so the financial consequences of the transaction may be relatively inconsequential. But because I have benefitted from the income interest for ten years (or one hour) I may not disclaim the interest and thereby avoid the double transfer issue.

We will revisit specific aspects of disclaimers in Chapter 7 on planning for the future and in Chapter 9 on tax minimization. Disclaimers are also very effective ways to limit the rights of creditors who are quite thrilled when a debtor is about to inherit a bundle of money. In that regard, consider the following case:

Est. of Baird

131 Wash.2d 514, 933 P.2d 1031 (1997)

The question presented is whether an anticipatory disclaimer of an expectancy interest in an intestate estate is valid and effective under RCW 11.86. We hold the plain language of the statute does not authorize an anticipatory disclaimer of an expectancy interest created by intestacy, and affirm the order of the probate court declaring this disclaimer invalid.

---

[17] We are using the term donee here simply to indicate a recipient of property, not a recipient of a power of appointment.

Facts

Phyllis Baird died intestate on December 29, 1994. She was survived by two children, James Thomas Baird and Julie A. Breckenridge. James Baird has two children, Jayme Baird and Hunter Baird, from his first marriage to Cheryl Kern. [In 1988 Susan (Saulsbury) Baird was appointed guardian for Phyllis, and she and James Baird married four years later, in 1992. In February, 1993, James Baird assaulted Susan Baird, permanently disfiguring her and causing her to suffer permanent cognitive defects. He was convicted of first degree assault in March, 1994 and was given a sentence of 20 years in prison. Susan filed a personal injury action against her husband for the injuries suffered shortly after the assault, but before the conviction. The day of his conviction, James] executed an instrument purporting to disclaim "any and all interest" he "may have" in his mother's estate. This instrument was filed in his mother's guardianship proceeding that same day. On October 19, 1994, Susan Baird was awarded a judgment of $2.75 million in her personal injury action against James Baird. One week later, on October 26, 1994, James Baird filed a petition for Chapter 7 bankruptcy. Susan Baird's judgment constitutes approximately 95 percent of the outstanding creditor claims in the bankruptcy proceeding.

As previously stated, Phyllis Baird died intestate on December 29, 1994. Her estate is valued in excess of $500,000. James Baird's share of his mother's estate represents approximately 60 percent of his potential assets available in the bankruptcy proceeding.

[James' two children petitioned the probate court for an order declaring the disclaimer valid. The bankruptcy trustee opposed the petition. Susan intervened in the probate proceeding and the bankruptcy court held off determining the issue of validity of the disclaimer until the probate court ruled on its validity. The probate court allowed Susan to intervene and ruled the disclaimer invalid without an explanation. On appeal by James' children, the court affirmed, explaining:]

Disclaimers

Disclaimers[4] are defined in RCW 11.86 as "any writing which declines, refuses, renounces, or disclaims any interest that would otherwise be taken by a beneficiary." RCW 11.86.011(4). Statutory disclaimers have their roots in the common law principle that a beneficiary under a will has the right to disclaim or renounce a testamentary gift. This rule was based on the theory that no one could be forced to accept a gift. However, at common law an interest passing via intestacy could not be disclaimed. . . .

At common law and under our current statute, a properly executed and delivered disclaimer passes the disclaimed interest as if the disclaimant "died immediately prior to the date of the transfer of the interest." RCW 11.86.041(1). So long as a disclaimer is properly executed and timely delivered, the legal fiction of "relation back" treats the interest as having never passed to the intended beneficiary or heir at law.

In this case, Jayme and Hunter Baird argue that this legal fiction applies and prevents James Baird's interest in his mother's estate from

---

[4] The terms "disclaimer" and "renunciation" are used interchangeably in case law to express what in common law terms is the means to reject a testamentary gift in such a way that it passes to the renouncer's heirs as if he or she had predeceased the testator. *See* Mark Reutlinger & William C. Oltman, *Washington Law of Wills and Intestate Succession* 163–64 (1985). Washington statutes uniformly use the term "disclaimer," as will this opinion.

becoming an asset of his bankruptcy estate.[6] They argue the instrument executed on March 8, 1994 by James Baird met all of RCW 11.86.031(1)'s content requirements and was properly delivered according to RCW 11.86.031(2) by being filed in Phyllis Baird's ongoing guardianship proceeding or, alternatively, in the probate proceeding following Phyllis Baird's death. Thus, Jayme and Hunter Baird assert the disclaimer was valid and effective as of the date their father executed the instrument.

We disagree. The result of adopting the children's argument in this case would be to extend the legal fiction of "relation back" at the potential expense of the bankruptcy estate and Susan Baird. That we will not do. "The doctrine of relation 'is a legal fiction invented to promote the ends of justice. . . . It is never allowed to defeat the collateral rights of third persons, lawfully acquired.'

Our disclaimer statute provides: "A beneficiary may disclaim an interest in whole or in part . . . in the manner provided in RCW 11.86.031." RCW 11.86.021(1). "Interests" that may be disclaimed include:

> the whole of any property, real or personal, legal or equitable, or any fractional part . . . thereof, any vested or contingent interest in any such property. . . . 'Interest' includes but is not limited to, an interest created . . . [b]y intestate succession.

RCW 11.86.011(2)(a). An intestate interest is created only upon the death of the creator of the interest, i.e., the death of the intestate. Thus, at the time James Baird executed the instrument at issue, he did not yet have an "interest" in his mother's estate to disclaim. . . . As stated above, an intestate interest is not created until the death of the creator/transferor. Thus, James Baird could not have met the statutory delivery requirement on the date the instrument was executed, or, for that matter, at any time prior to his mother's death, because the "interest" had yet to be created.

Additionally, James Baird was not a "beneficiary" under RCW 11.86 when he executed the disclaimer. The statute defines a "beneficiary" as "the person entitled, but for the person's disclaimer, to take an interest." RCW 11.86.011(1). James Baird was not entitled to take any interest in his mother's estate prior to her death; see RCW 11.04.250 and RCW 11.04.290 (heirs have legal interests only upon the death of the creator).

We hold that as a matter of law the instrument executed by James Baird on March 8, 1994 is invalid under RCW 11.86 because at that time he did not have an "interest," nor was he a "beneficiary." In sum, RCW 11.86 does not authorize anticipatory disclaimers of expectancy interests.

---

[6] Under federal bankruptcy law, a bankruptcy estate includes any interest in property that would have been property of the estate if such interest had been an interest of the debtor on the date of the filing of the petition, and that the debtor acquires or becomes entitled to acquire within 180 days after such date by bequest, devise, or inheritance. 11 U.S.C.A. § 541(a)(5). Applying this definition, James Baird's potential share of his mother's estate would be an asset of the bankruptcy estate. However, if a bankrupt validly executes and delivers a disclaimer prior to the filing of the bankruptcy petition, then the testamentary gift at issue is not part of the bankruptcy estate and descends according to state law. *See In re Atchison*, 925 F.2d 209 (7th Cir.1991); Stephen E. Parker, *Can Debtors Disclaim Inheritances to the Detriment of Their Creditors?*, 25 LOY. U. CHI. L.J. 31, 39 (1993).

Query: Knowing that the property James Baird tried to disclaim was originally acquired and owned by another, in this case his mother, do you think it is fair to allow disclaimers so the property will pass to other family members and not be lost to creditors? Or are there certain types of creditors (children for whom child support orders have been made, tort victims, the Department of the Treasury, nursing homes that provide end-of-life care) who should be able to prevent a disclaimer? If so, where would you draw the line?

Consider also this case which had a variety of motives behind the disclaimer:

Will of Hall

318 S.C. 188, 456 S.E.2d 439 (S.C. Ct. App. 1995)

Mary Lightsey Hall (the Testatrix) died testate April 4, 1992. Her children, Mary Hall McCallum, Wilton E. Hall, Jr., Perry D. Hall, and Sarah Hall Hayes, survived her. Item III of the Testatrix's will provides as follows:

> *I give and devise my home and 2-story garage and storage room located at 229 South Boulevard, Anderson, South Carolina to my daughter, SARAH HALL HAYES, for her lifetime. At her death, or if she has not survived me, I give and devise the said real property to the children of SARAH HALL HAYES, to share and share alike, per stirpes. If no children of my said daughter then survives, such property shall be divided so as to provide a share of equal value for each child of mine surviving me and for the descendants of each deceased child of mine, per stirpes. In the event of such a distribution to several beneficiaries and they do not agree as to the division of such property, my Executors shall make such division among them in the manner my Executors determine, and the decisions of my Executors shall be in all respects binding upon the beneficiaries.*

The probate court followed the established rule that property cannot be disclaimed after the donee has exercised dominion and control over it. The court found because Hayes had accepted the benefits of her life estate, she could not make a qualified disclaimer under federal law.[1] The court found Hayes took the following actions, which evidenced she had exercised power over the property before she executed the purported disclaimer:

> 1. *executing a deed of distribution to herself in December 1992 as a co-executor or personal representative of the estate;*
>
> 2. *executing a receipt and release on December 9, 1992, in which she acknowledged receipt of a life estate in the property;*
>
> 3. *procuring insurance on the property in December 1992 or January 1993; and*

---

[1]   Federal law may be used to construe state law under § 62–2–801 of the South Carolina Probate Code. Subsection (f) reads:

It is the intent of the legislature of the State of South Carolina by this provision to clarify the laws of this State with respect to the subject matter hereof in order to ensure the ability of persons to disclaim interests in property without the imposition of federal and state estate, inheritance, gift, and transfer taxes. This provision is to be interpreted and construed in accordance with, and in furtherance of, that intent. S.C. CODE ANN. § 62–2–801(f) (1987).

4. *listing the property for sale with Remax in early January 1993.*

On appeal, the court of appeals affirmed the lower court's holding that if an attempted disclaimer does not comply with S.C. § 62–2–801, it is not otherwise effective to disclaim an interest in property devised under a will.

Hayes and her children next argue the lower court erred by characterizing the remainder interests to Hayes's children in Hall's will as contingent.

The lower court properly held the will must be considered in light of Hall's intent. . . . In order to characterize the remainder, words used to determine vesting must relate to one of three dates: (1) the date of the will; (2) the date of the testator's death; or (3) the date of the death of the life tenant. Here the words of survivorship, "If no children of my said daughter then survives," relate to the date of distribution, which is the death of the life tenant. Hayes's children's interest cannot vest until she dies, for until that time, it is impossible to know which, if any, of her children will be living at her death. Moreover, the will provided for a contingent disposition of the property if none of Hayes's children were living at Hayes's death. If words of survivorship relate to the period of distribution, or, here, the death of the life tenant, the remainder must be characterized as contingent because who will take the remainder is uncertain until the life tenant's death.

Query: Do you think Sarah really did accept the benefits of the property interest? And even if the disclaimer was not a qualified disclaimer under the Internal Revenue Code, should Sarah have been able to renounce her interest anyway and have possession pass immediately to her children under state property law? Would her disclaimer have been valid under the Uniform Disclaimer of Property Interests Act? What should Sarah's mother's lawyer have done to prevent this problem? What should Sarah's lawyer have done?

Sarah Hall had a number of possible reasons for wanting to disclaim her interest. Her mother had created a legal life estate and a bunch of contingent remainders in real property, which is generally a bad idea. The life tenant cannot sell the property, mortgage it, or manage it efficiently. So Sarah decided to disclaim the interest and have the remainder vest immediately in possession in her children, who then would have interests in tenancy in common and would be able to sell the house. Because a disclaimer operates as though the disclaimant *predeceased* the donor, Sarah's disclaimer would accelerate the contingent remainders of her children, thereby cutting off the alternate contingent remainders in her siblings.

And that is precisely what would have happened if she had merely transferred her life estate to her children prior to 1536. But after 1536, contingent remainders generally could not be destroyed by these kinds of transfers. And all states but Florida have abolished the *destructibility of contingent remainders* rule, making it harder to cut off the interests of the siblings in a case like this. Hence, by interpreting the remainder in Sarah's children as a contingent remainder, that would not vest until the death of Sarah, the court kept alive the alternate contingency in Sarah's siblings. Had the disclaimer been valid, the acceleration of the remainder in Sarah's children would have terminated the sibling's remainder because disclaimer statutes override the non-destructibility of contingent remainders rule.

Do you see why Sarah needed to disclaim her life estate and could not simply transfer her interest to her children? The mere transfer, which she could do at anytime during her life, operates to *merge* the present estate and future interests, but cannot destroy the alternate contingent remainders that could vest if she survives her children. By disclaiming, however, she would speed up the remainders, thus causing them to vest immediately. Since vesting is what terminates Sarah's siblings' remainders, they would be effectively terminated, even though they would not be terminated if her interest merely merged.

Don't worry if this explanation isn't entirely crystal clear yet. It will become more so after Chapter 8. Suffice it to say that disclaimers of legal life interests are very common, often because the life tenant doesn't need the property, and because by disclaiming she can accelerate the remainder. Some life income beneficiaries can even disclaim an interest in a trust in order to accelerate distribution of principal, although not always.

Tax Tip: The Countdown Begins—Watch the Clock

The IRC provides that disclaimers of inherited property are effective if made within 9 months of the decedent's death. But think about how quickly that time passes. It takes at least two weeks to hold a funeral and locate the will. Then the survivors have to decide on a lawyer and who will file the will for probate. The banks and credit cards have to be notified of the death, and the initial accounting has to be filed. Oh, and the court has to set a hearing, or at the very least it will take time to issue the Letters Testamentary before the personal administrator can begin to manage the property. Then it's the holidays and everyone goes on vacation for a month. Next thing you know, the 9 months within which to make a qualified disclaimer is quickly approaching or, worse, has passed. Beneficiaries might not even know they are going to inherit anything and the time will have slipped away. In the case of Sarah Hall, she probably wasn't even thinking about the possibility of a disclaimer until after she had been managing the property and purportedly benefitted from it. This is another reason why it is important to get legal advice right away before doing too much with grandma's property.

But many states have extended the time for making disclaimers, as South Carolina has. Why? Disclaimers can also protect the property from the creditors of the beneficiary. Thus, if Sarah Hall had large debts that she didn't want to pay off with her inheritance, she could disclaim the property and have it pass to the alternate or residuary beneficiaries. Many estates lawyers have tripped up by looking only to the date indicated in the state statute, which may be unlimited, and missed the 9 month deadline for *qualified* disclaimers under the IRC. So if you are managing an estate you will want to watch that 9-month clock very closely. It might constitute malpractice to recommend a disclaimer to a client to avoid creditors, but then miss the deadline and subject the beneficiary's estate to additional taxes.

As you can see, two principal reasons for disclaiming a bequest or inheritance are to reduce possible estate taxes and shield the property from creditors. Another is to terminate unwieldy life estates that are difficult to manage efficiently if they are not in trusts where the trustee can prudently manage the real property itself. And while these seem like very modern, and very crass, concerns, basic property rules that require acceptance before any gift is valid are at the heart of the doctrine. I can refuse to accept the hideous portrait of Great Aunt Gertrude because it's ugly and I don't like it, or because I don't want to subject my estate to greater taxes when I die because the portrait happened to be painted by Picasso. The law generally does not look to the motives of individuals who choose not to accept a gift.

A similar conflict arises in the context of powers. If James Baird held a general power of appointment over his mother's estate, could he be forced by certain creditors to exercise that power for their behalf? A disclaimer can be used to avoid giving property you have been given to your creditors, allowing it to pass to alternate beneficiaries. And the creditors can try to invalidate the disclaimer, as Susan successfully did in *Est. of Baird*. Creditors can also try to force the exercise of a general power of appointment in order to reach assets to pay the donee's debts. But forcing someone to exercise a power is more difficult than preventing him from disclaiming. In both situations, the creditor is trying to get the debtor to take ownership over property that is available to him. In one the creditor is asking the debtor to take control and in the other the creditor is asking the debtor not to relinquish control. If you were writing your will and wanted to make sure that your estate isn't eaten up by your son's creditors, would you use a power or hope your son disclaims?

You are likely to learn a lot more about disclaimers if you take advanced courses in estate planning and tax. Just remember, however, that estate plans should not rely on beneficiaries disclaiming their interests in order to keep the property in the family. If James Baird's mother wanted to ensure that her property did not go to any of her beneficiaries' creditors, what should she have done? She should probably have set up a discretionary spendthrift trust, a device we will cover in Chapter 8.

Moreover, disclaimers can cause an estate to pass in a dramatically different way than the testator planned. Consider a decedent who writes a will leaving everything in trust to his two children for their life, then to his two named grandchildren for their lives, remainder outright to any great-grandchildren. Both the decedent's children disclaim their life interests in the trust (but not in their father's estate by intestacy), as do the two living grandchildren, and the great-grandchildren through a guardian.[18] Because there are no trust beneficiaries, the trust fails and the estate passes by intestacy, perhaps to a surviving spouse, remainder outright to the children. The grandchildren take nothing.

Another nifty device is the *disclaimer trust*, by which a surviving spouse can disclaim all of a decedent spouse's estate and it can pass into a disclaimer trust established by the decedent spouse's will. The surviving spouse can have limited access to the trust principal for health, education, maintenance, and support, plus a lifetime income interest in the trust, but the principal will pass at the survivor's death without being considered part of the surviving spouse's estate. To take advantage of a disclaimer trust, each spouse must establish that upon a disclaimer by the surviving spouse, any property disclaimed is to pass into the trust, subject to whatever particular limitations are necessary, with the principal to pass to their children or other third parties upon the death of the surviving spouse.

---

[18] I.R.S Priv. Ltr. Rul. 9638014 (Sept. 20, 1996).

> ### Tax Tip: Disclaimers and Alternative Valuation Dates
>
> The relation back doctrine can be a very valuable mechanism for dealing with property that might fluctuate greatly in value. Some property goes down upon the death of the person holding it, and some goes up. Stock in a self-created company often goes down with the death of the founder. Apple stock decreased in value from the announcement of founder Steve Jobs' illness, and took another dip upon his death.[19] Other property increases in value, such as paintings by a known artist. Jobs' stock in Apple and Andy Warhol's cookie jars fluctuated in value simply by virtue of the owner's death. When the death effect kicks in, or when other unrelated circumstances affect the value of property, the IRC provides for an alternative valuation date of six months after the date of death to determine the value of property for estate tax purposes. Knowing that you can look six months out to settle on the value of property, and have nine months to make a disclaimer, beneficiaries of volatile property can pick and choose which date to use while still relying on the relation back doctrine to reduce possible estate tax liabilities and benefit from the step up in basis that comes with inherited property.
>
> The details of how one does this are best left to a course in advanced estate planning or estate administration. For now, be aware that volatile property may require some special handling.

PROBLEMS

5.17. Lyle dies at age 81. His will leaves his entire probate estate to his son, Karl. The sole asset of the estate is a beachfront home, with a date of death value of $700,000. During the estate administration, Karl files for divorce from his wife, Mary. As part of the property settlement, Mary seeks distribution of the beach front real estate where she and Karl lived for the last six months of their marriage (a time which was entirely within the estate administration period of Karl's father's estate). Karl proceeds to file a disclaimer in his father's estate. Is the disclaimer allowable?

5.18. Sally's father makes a specific bequest of a grandson of Secretariat to her in his will. The horse is about to run in the Kentucky Derby but the odds are only 40 to 1 that he'll win. Sally and her four siblings are the residuary beneficiaries of her father's will. And Sally has three children. If the horse wins he'll be worth millions and Sally would like her siblings to share in their good fortune. If the horse loses, he'll be retired and will make a modest income for them in stud fees. In the meantime, the publicity about the offspring of Secretariat got her an interview on Jay Leno for which she was paid $500.00 to cover her travel costs. What should she do?

G. SIMULTANEOUS DEATH

In this age of mass transportation, global terrorism, climate change, and other common disasters, it is not unthinkable that a testator and her beneficiary will die simultaneously, or there will be no evidence that either survived the other. In the case of simultaneous death, the logical solution is to treat each person as having predeceased the other. Thus, if a husband

---

[19] Dan Burrows, Apple's Stock Dips upon Death of Steve Jobs, MoneyWatch, CBS News (Oct. 6, 2011), available at: http://www.cbsnews.com/8301–505123_162–49042941/apples–stock–dips–after–death–of–steve–jobs/

and wife die simultaneously, we would administer the husband's estate as though he survived his wife, and administer the wife's estate as though she survived him. But the increase in mass disasters has also come during an age of profound medical advancement by which we can easily keep people alive for days or even years. It is not uncommon to keep one spouse alive on life support until the family can assemble and say their final goodbyes, while the other spouse may be kept off of life support because an advanced health care directive stated that she didn't want to be kept alive artificially. In such a situation, where one spouse is kept alive longer than the other, that spouse may likely be deemed to have survived the other and would therefore become the beneficiary of the first spouse's entire estate. If the spouses are in their second marriage and both have children from a previous marriage, one set of children could easily inherit most or all of the couple's property, leading to family friction and a likely lawsuit.

The Uniform Simultaneous Death Act (USDA) of 1940 provided that persons would be deemed to have died simultaneously if "there is no sufficient evidence" of survivorship. This led to complex, expert-witness driven litigation about the differences between neurological death and cardio-pulmonary death, and graphic speculation about how long people could survive with life-threatening injuries.[20] The USDA was revised in 1993 to provide that in order to be deemed to have survived the decedent, the beneficiary must survive by at least 120 hours. The 1993 USDA applies to all forms of property, whether acquired by intestacy, by devise, in a trust, by a right of survivorship, in life insurance, as a power of appointment, and so on. But the presumption of simultaneous death can be defeated if the donor of the property provides alternative disposition if she and the beneficiary die simultaneously. The Uniform Simultaneous Death Act has been adopted in twelve states, plus the District of Columbia and the Virgin Islands, and provides:

USDA § 2. REQUIREMENT OF SURVIVAL BY 120 HOURS UNDER PROBATE CODE.

Except as provided in Section 6, if the title to property, the devolution of property, the right to elect an interest in property, or the right to exempt property, homestead or family allowance depends upon an individual's survivorship of the death of another individual, an individual who is not established by clear and convincing evidence to have survived the other individual by 120 hours is deemed to have predeceased the other individual. This section does not apply if its application would result in a taking of intestate estate by the state.

Simultaneous death cases can be very difficult, especially if there are wrongful death claims or life insurance proceeds to deal with and the decedent and beneficiary die simultaneously. Although every state's wrongful death statutes govern who can bring claims for wrongful death, when persons who would have wrongful death actions both die simultaneously, there may be competing claims by spouses, parents, children, or other relatives. And the courts are likely to be involved in messy litigation no matter how

---

[20] One example that drove the ULC in its amendments was Matter of Bucci, 57 Misc.2d 1001 (N.Y. Surr. Ct. 1968), where a husband and wife both died in a small plane crash but the wife was deemed the survivor because there was evidence of carbon monoxide in her blood that was not in the husband's blood.

simple the estate once the attorneys for the insurance companies are brought in.

Although we don't generally know when or how we are going to die, nor when or how our primary beneficiaries are going to die, we can still take steps to simplify administration of our estates if we specify certain survivorship conditions and alternate beneficiaries. By now you should also be realizing why wills are no longer short, 1 page documents, but run 20 or 30 pages of possible contingencies. Consider what, if anything, these decedents could have done to avoid litigation in the following cases:

Est. of Lensch

177 Cal.App. 4th 667 (Cal. App. 1st Dist. 2009)

On March 12, 2008, at 2:30 a.m. Gladys Lensch died in a San Mateo County nursing home. She was 98 years old. She left the following three-sentence holographic will:

> *I Gladys Lensch do hereby declare, being of sound mind, that my estate be equally divided between my daughter Claudia and my son Jay. Claudia being married has 2 daughters, and my son by a previous marriage has 2 sons. They will provide for the well being of my grandchildren in the event of my death or serious incapacity due to lengthy illness. God Bless the Family. Gladys Clausen Lensch May 10, 1993.*

Eleven hours after Gladys died, Jay, Gladys's son, was found dead in his home in Trinity County. He had shot himself with a 12-gauge shotgun. The time of death on Jay's death certificate was recorded as the time his body was found: 1:15 p.m. on March 12, 2008. Jay's body was cremated without an autopsy and his remains were buried five days later.

In a 10-page handwritten will, with a four-page addendum, Jay made small cash gifts to friends, and left another friend an undeveloped parcel of land. The residue of his estate was left in equal shares to the Unitarian Universalist Service Committee and Direct Relief International. He left nothing in his will to his two sons, appellants Jason and Ean Lensch.

Jay Lensch's sons filed a "Petition to Determine Survival and to Determine Persons Entitled to Distribution." The trial court denied the petition determining that Jay Lensch's death certificate was the only reliable evidence of time of death; all other evidence was hearsay. Because Jay survived his mother, he was entitled to take the bequest and devise it to the two charities and not to his sons. Had Jay predeceased his mother, the state's anti-lapse statute would have created a substitute gift in Jay's sons because the mother's will did not indicate a contrary intent. On appeal, the 1st District Court of Appeal reversed and remanded for an evidentiary hearing on survivorship, noting that the party whose claim depends on survivorship (the beneficiaries under Jay's will—the charities) has the burden of proof.

Query: It was possible that Jay had died anytime from two days before his mother (when someone last spoke to him) until a few hours after her. Who would have benefitted from a 120-hour survivorship requirement as under the USDA? Jay indicated in his will that he was not leaving anything to his two children because he disapproved of their treatment of him. Would your analysis of the case change if you knew that Gladys knew of Jays' feelings and agreed with him?

In re Est. of Miller

840 So.2d 703 (Miss. 2003)

This appeal involves the tragic murder/suicide of a husband and wife where the order of death cannot be determined. On October 30, 1999, Byron Keith Miller shot his wife Martha Jeanette Page Miller. Byron then shot himself shortly thereafter. Byron and Martha died from their gunshot wounds, but the order of their deaths could not be determined. They had no children together, but Byron had a six-year-old son, Hunter Keith Miller, by his ex-wife Ann Miller. The court appointed Byron's father administrator of his estate and Martha's mother administrator of her estate. Martha's mother petitioned to take a share of Byron's estate by application of the state's slayer statute. *Under the Mississippi slayer's statute, a slayer cannot inherit from the victim and is deemed to have predeceased his victim for succession purposes:*

> *If any person wilfully cause or procure the death of another in any way, he shall not inherit the property, real or personal, of each other; but the same shall descend as if the person so causing or procuring the death had predeceased the person whose death he perpetrated.* Miss.Code Ann. § 91–1–25.

Martha's mother argued *that since Byron is deemed to have predeceased Martha under Miss.Code Ann. § 91–1–25, the order of death was established for purposes of distributing Byron's estate by intestate succession. As a result, Martha's estate would be entitled to a child's share allowed to a widow under Miss.Code Ann. § 91–1–7 (1994).*

The court explained that: *we have held that one who wilfully causes the death of another is barred from participating in the victim's estate. We have not, however, addressed the question of whether a victim's estate can participate in his slayer's estate. Slayer's statutes are strictly construed and narrow in purpose: . . . The sole purpose of a "slayer statute" is to prevent the slayer from benefitting from the death of the victim or profiting from the wrongdoing.* The Mississippi Supreme Court rejected the application of the slayer statute to this case to override the application of the simultaneous death act which treated each as predeceasing the other and therefore not entitled to a share of the other's estate. As a result, Byron's estate passed to his son, Hunter, and Martha's estate passed by intestacy to her parents.

Query: What if there was evidence that the wife was shot in the chest and the husband in the head? See *Est. of Hughes*, 735 S.W.2d 787 (Mo.App. S.D. 1987) (finding that there was sufficient evidence that wife survived because experts testified about the instant fatality of the husband's wound to the head and the wife's son testified that his mother breathed for a few minutes before dying). In most murder/suicides would you assume that the murder victim died first because he/she was the first to be injured?

Practice Point: Considering Simultaneous Death in Drafting Guardian Provisions

The appointment of a guardian for minor children is one of the biggest decisions that parents make as they go about drafting their wills (and is discussed in more detail in the following chapters). During the planning process, many couples have already given this matter great thought and will have a clearly defined "pecking order" of those people whom they would wish to raise their children in their place if they were to die while their children still needed a caregiver. Occasionally, however, each parent will have *their own* pecking order. That is, the issue (often highly emotional) is a point of contention between the couple and they just can't both agree on who to choose. (For some reason, each usually thinks that the best choices exist on their side of the family tree). So, you may be asked to just draft separate guardian choices in each spouse's will to solve the problem and move the will process along. Easy enough, right? But does this makes sense? Perhaps it does, if you are assuming that the spouses will politely stagger their deaths out so that there is clearly a surviving spouse caring for the children for a number of years before dying and setting into motion his or her guardianship preferences. But what happens in the case of simultaneous deaths? Does it make any sense that the children's guardians would be selected from a list which was generated just because one spouse was presumed to predecease the other? Explaining this very possibility to clients can sometimes be all that is necessary for them to begin to agree on a compromise. Suddenly, Aunt Susan, who lives on the horse farm in the country can start to look like a much more appealing choice.

Janus v. Tarasewicz

135 Ill.App.3d 936, 482 N.E.2d 418, 90 Ill.Dec. 599 (Ill. Ct. App. 1985)

The facts of this case are particularly poignant and complex. Stanley and Theresa Janus had recently returned from their honeymoon when, on the evening of September 29, 1982, they gathered with other family members to mourn the death of Stanley's brother, Adam Janus, who had died earlier that day from what was later determined to be cyanide-laced Tylenol capsules. While the family was at Adam's home, Stanley and Theresa Janus unknowingly took some of the contaminated Tylenol. Soon afterwards, Stanley collapsed on the kitchen floor.

Theresa was still standing when Diane O'Sullivan, a registered nurse and a neighbor of Adam Janus, was called to the scene. Stanley's pulse was weak so she began cardiopulmonary resuscitation (CPR) on him. Within minutes, Theresa Janus began having seizures. After parmedic teams began arriving, Ms. O'Sullivan went into the living room to assist with Theresa. While she was working on Theresa, Ms. O'Sullivan could hear Stanley's "heavy and labored breathing." She believed that both Stanley and Theresa died before they were taken to the ambulance, but she could not tell who died first.

Ronald Mahon, a paramedic for the Arlington Heights Fire Department, arrived at approximately 5:45 p.m. He saw Theresa faint and go into a seizure. Her pupils did not respond to light but she was breathing on her own during the time that he worked on her. Mahon also assisted with Stanley, giving him drugs to stimulate heart contractions. Mahon later prepared the paramedic's report on Stanley. One entry in the report shows that at 18:00 hours Stanley had "zero blood pressure, zero pulse, and zero respira-

tion." However, Mahon stated that the times in the report were merely approximations. He was able to say that Stanley was in the ambulance en route to the hospital when his vital signs disappeared.

When paramedic Robert Lockhart arrived at 5:55 p.m., both victims were unconscious with non-reactive pupils. Theresa's seizures had ceased but she was in a decerebrate posture in which her arms and legs were rigidly extended and her arms were rotated inward toward her body, thus, indicating severe neurological dysfunction. At that time, she was breathing only four or five times a minute and, shortly thereafter, she stopped breathing on her own altogether. Lockhart intubated them both by placing tubes down their tracheae to keep their air passages open. Prior to being taken to the ambulance, they were put on "ambu-bags" which is a form of artificial respiration whereby the paramedic respirates the patient by squeezing a bag. Neither Stanley nor Theresa showed any signs of being able to breathe on their own while they were being transported to Northwest Community Hospital in Arlington Heights, Illinois. However, Lockhart stated that when Theresa was turned over to the hospital personnel, she had a palpable pulse and blood pressure.

The medical director of the intensive care unit at the hospital, Dr. Thomas Kim, examined them when they arrived in the emergency room at approximately 6:30 p.m. Stanley had no blood pressure or pulse. An electrocardiogram detected electrical activity in Stanley Janus' heart but there was no synchronization between his heart's electrical activity and its pumping activity. A temporary pacemaker was inserted in an unsuccessful attempt to resuscitate him. Because he never developed spontaneous blood pressure, pulse or signs of respiration, Stanley Janus was pronounced dead at 8:15 p.m. on September 29, 1982.

Like Stanley, Theresa Janus showed no visible vital signs when she was admitted to the emergency room. However, hospital personnel were able to get her heart beating on its own again, so they did not insert a pacemaker. They were also able to establish a measurable, though unsatisfactory, blood pressure. Theresa was taken off the "ambu-bag" and put on a mechanical respirator. In Dr. Kim's opinion, Theresa was in a deep coma with "very unstable vital signs" when she was moved to the intensive care unit at 9:30 p.m. on September 29, 1982.

While Theresa was in the intensive care unit, numerous entries in her hospital records indicated that she had fixed and dialated pupils. However, one entry made at 2:32 a.m. on September 30, 1982, indicated that a nurse apparently detected a minimal reaction to light in Theresa's right pupil but not in her left pupil.

On September 30, 1982, various tests were performed in order to assess Theresa's brain function. These tests included an electroencephalogram (EEG) to measure electrical activity in her brain and a cerebral blood flow test to determine whether there was any blood circulating in her brain. In addition, Theresa exhibited no gag or cord reflexes, no response to pain or other external stimuli. As a result of these tests, Theresa Janus was diagnosed as having sustained total brain death, her life support systems then were terminated, and she was pronounced dead at 1:15 p.m. on October 1, 1982.

Death certificates were issued for Stanley and Theresa Janus more than three weeks later by a medical examiner's physician who never exam-

ined them. The certificates listed Stanley Janus' date of death as September 29, 1982, and Theresa Janus' date of death as October 1, 1982. Concluding that Theresa survived Stanley, the Metropolitan Life Insurance Company paid the proceeds of Stanley's life insurance policy to the administrator of Theresa's estate.

In affirming the trial court's conclusion that Theresa survived Stanley, the appeals court explained: *In conclusion, we believe that the record clearly established that the treating physicians' diagnoses of death with respect to Stanley and Theresa Janus were made in accordance with "the usual and customary standards of medical practice." Stanley Janus was diagnosed as having sustained irreversible cessation of circulatory and respiratory functions on September 29, 1982. These same physicians concluded that Theresa Janus' condition on that date did not warrant a diagnosis of death and, therefore, they continued their efforts to preserve her life. Their conclusion that Theresa Janus did not die until October 1, 1982, was based on various factors including the restoration of certain of her vital signs as well as other neurological evidence. The trial court found that these facts and circumstances constituted sufficient evidence that Theresa Janus survived her husband. It was not necessary to determine the exact moment at which Theresa died or by how long she survived him, and the trial court properly declined to do so. Viewing the record in its entirety, we cannot say that the trial court's finding of sufficient evidence of Theresa's survivorship was against the manifest weight of the evidence.*

Query: This case was an important spur to the Uniform Law Commission to add the 120 hour survivorship requirement to the USDA and to the UPC. But does it make sense for Theresa's estate to inherit Stanley's property even if she survived 5 days if she was never conscious enough to enjoy it? Should there be a longer requirement, like 6 months or a year? What happens to Stanley and Theresa's life insurance and intestate property as a result of the finding that Theresa survived Stanley? Consider things like homestead, exempt property, and elective share as well.

———————————

Some commentators are critical of the USDA's requirement of clear and convincing proof for survivorship, because the failure to meet that standard may cause bequests and transfers to one's spouse to lapse, which may have a negative tax effect. "They may lose the opportunity to use both spouses' unified credits for estate tax purposes." See Gary, Borison, Cahn, Monopoli, *Contemporary Approaches to Trusts and Estates*, p. 572. However, it seems to me that since fewer than 1% of estates will even need to worry about estate taxes, and that the odds of spouses in that wealth category dying simultaneously are as low as any other spouses, the criticism is misplaced.[21] For the one in 5 million couples who might face this problem,

———————————

[21] It's difficult to identify a particular statistic about how many estates pay estate taxes. In 2008, for instance, 2.4 million people died and only 1 in 166 had to pay estate taxes. But if the basic exclusion amount decreases from $5 million to $1 million, which it will do in 2013 if Congress fails to act, far more people may be subject to estate taxes. In 2011 it is estimated that there will be only 3.3 thousand taxable estates. Assuming the same death rate of 2.4 million people, that will be only .14% of estates that will face any tax liability. See Tax Policy Center Briefing Book at: http://www.taxpolicycenter.org/briefing–book/key–elements/estate/how–many.cfm.

there are dozens of other people for whom the presumption of simultaneous death will lead to a fairer distribution of their estates and greater sense of equity and peace for the living.

Technology Trend: Advanced Life Support Technologies and the Legal Process of Dying

Not surprisingly, law has not kept up with medical advances in life-saving technology. Eighty percent of the roughly 2.4 million people who die each year will die in a hospital setting, many in the Intensive Care Unit where they are closely monitored and provided with life saving technologies. Ever since the first reported case of using CPR to revive a dying patient in the 1700s, doctors and nurses have been developing life saving technologies ranging from mechanical ventilators to defibrillators to feeding tubes to intraaortic balloon pumps. What the next new technology will be we can only guess. Statistics suggest that most of us will receive some kind of life-saving technology before we finally reach the end of the dying process, despite DNR orders and advance directives. As we begin to think more philosophically about the process of dying, and as many people reject some of the superhuman efforts to keep them alive, we must be aware of the legal implications of controlling the dying process. When we humans can time someone's death with the flip of a switch, it would seem time for the law to begin to address the effects of that decision on different estate beneficiaries. Just as we have amended the UPC to acknowledge that guardians, the government, conservators, and trustees can dispose of a decedent's property in ways that might create abatement problems, the timing of death can create similar problems. Should inheritances depend on whether someone was hooked to a mechanical ventilator or not? Until the laws figure out a way to honor testamentary intent, despite the interventions of modern medicine, we lawyers will need to draft estate plans with this technology in mind.[22]

PROBLEMS

5.19. Anne and Tim owned all their assets as tenants by the entirety. In 2007, they executed reciprocal wills, identical except that Anne's will contained the following provision (and Tim's reflected the same simultaneous death language):

> Simultaneous Death. In the event that my husband and I shall die simultaneously or that the order of our deaths cannot be ascertained, it shall be assumed for purposes of this will that I predeceased my husband.

Anne drives, drunk, with Tim as a passenger. She fails to stop at a stop sign and hits a car driven by Shawn. Anne, Tim and Shawn all are killed immediately. How does the survivorship language affect the disposition of Anne and Tim's property? What if Shawn's estate sues Anne?

5.20. Over a three-day period, professional wrestler Chris Benoit strangled his wife, his son, and then hanged himself, leaving two other children from a prior marriage alive. It is unclear whether his wife or his son died first. How would the two estates pass if the wife survived, or if the son survived? Under the law of most states, the person who kills another may not benefit from the victim's

---

[22] Annette Browning, "Life Support Technology and the Dying Experience: Implications for Critical-Care Nursing Practice," 29(5) Dimensions of Critical Care Nursing 230–237 (2010).

estate (slayer statutes). In the case of Benoit, however, it was later determined from autopsies that he suffered an advanced form of dementia, similar to Alzheimers, and that his brain resembled that of an 85-year old Alzheimer's patient. Assuming this was the case, should Chris's estate be able to inherit from his wife or his son because he was not criminally liable? Would any of the answers change if Chris and his family lived in a state that followed the USDA's 120 hour survivorship requirement, but owned real property in a state that did not?

H. CONCLUSION

As you can see, all manner of things can go wrong to upset an inflexible estate plan, from beneficiaries predeceasing the testator to the property decreasing in value. Beneficiaries may die simultaneously with the testator, or they may get into financial trouble. Building flexibility into an estate plan means thinking about all the things that can go wrong, providing alternative dispositions, having a realistic understanding of one's assets, and building in protections so that those who are still alive can channel assets into productive uses when greater information is known about the life situations and characteristics of the beneficiaries. Corporate trustees don't die, hence their attractiveness as trustees or donees of powers of appointment who can take care of distributing property to those still living after the decedent's death. But corporate trustees cost money, quite a bit more than the trusty friend. Counting on the trusty friend to distribute property is all well and good if we can lock her up in some safe house where nothing bad can happen to her. On the other hand, the odds that a decedent and ALL of her beneficiaries will die simultaneously are pretty remote. Some simple precautions can cover most situations.

As you review the material from this chapter, think back over the cases and ask yourself what the decedents could have done differently, from using joint tenancies or powers of appointment, or merely consulting an attorney, to avoid the litigation. As we've said before, it is always easier to add a sentence to a will, or re-execute it, than to litigate it afterwards. And beneficiaries are always happier if their inheritances are not eaten up in lawyer fees and administrative costs. Wrenches happen, but most don't need to lead to litigation if you understand your client's situation and clearly plan for the worst.

PRINCIPLES AND PRACTICES OF ESTATE PLANNING

CHAPTER 6

PROTECTING THE CLIENT: PLANNING FOR INCAPACITY AND DEATH

If you ask most young people what their greatest fear is about aging, it is usually growing to look, sound, and act like their parents. If you ask parents that question, their answer is usually becoming dependent on their children. Aging is wonderful when you are strong, healthy, and capable, especially when you get your first driver's license or can walk into a bar with your very own ID and order a drink. It is very insulting when it involves incontinence, weakness, bad breath, and dementia. For most of us, the gradual slide into old age is terrifying, and we fight it in all sorts of ways, from bungee jumping on our 80th birthday to buying a 1964 Ford Mustang to reminiscing over our old home videos. But unless we are lucky enough to drop dead at 103 after running a marathon, we all face the very real prospect of becoming incapacitated and needing physical, legal, and financial assistance. Aging is not only terrifying for those going through it, but for those loved ones who can often only stand by and watch. Dylan Thomas's famous poem speaks to both.

Do Not Go Gentle Into That Good Night[1]

Do not go gentle into that good night,
Old age should burn and rave at close of day;
Rage, rage against the dying of the light.

Though wise men at their end know dark is right,
Because their words had forked no lightning they
Do not go gentle into that good night.

Good men, the last wave by, crying how bright
Their frail deeds might have danced in a green bay,
Rage, rage against the dying of the light.

Wild men who caught and sang the sun in flight,
And learn, too late, they grieved it on its way,
Do not go gentle into that good night.

Grave men, near death, who see with blinding sight
Blind eyes could blaze like meteors and be gay,
Rage, rage against the dying of the light.

---

[1]   By Dylan Thomas, from THE POEMS OF DYLAN THOMAS, copyright ©1952 by Dylan Thomas. Reprinted by permission of New Directions Publishing Corp.

> And you, my father, there on the sad height,
> Curse, bless, me now with your fierce tears, I pray.
>
> Do not go gentle into that good night.
> Rage, rage against the dying of the light.

Many people refuse to write a will because doing so admits to themselves their own mortality. How do you, as a lawyer, get a client to understand that good planning is probably the best gift she can leave her surviving family? How do you counsel her to plan for her health and physical needs while also protecting her estate for her successors? Some elderly clients will fight tooth and nail against becoming dependent on their children and consequently deplete their savings or make bad financial decisions, especially if they do not tell their family what is going on down at the bingo hall or why they gave their credit card information to that nice young man who came to the door last week. Others will neglect their own health and happiness in order to save as much as possible for their children's inheritances, depriving themselves of medical care that could improve their quality of life. Some are annoyingly secretive about their property, leaving children to search through the mattresses, attics, and under the chicken coop to find all the relevant documents to administer their estates. Others make copies of every piece of paper, in quintuplicate, giving copies to every child to ensure that all feel they are equally loved and in the loop. Balancing the needs of this generation with that of the next generation is not easy, and no simple formula can replace talking to your clients and getting to know their fears and their ambitions.

In this chapter we begin our study of estate planning by focusing on the client herself. What should she do to protect herself and her estate from her own slide into incapacity and her escalating medical expenses? Because medical expenses for end-of-life care can easily swallow a life-time's worth of savings,[2] estate planning for the elderly or disabled usually focuses primarily on managing health care costs while protecting enough wealth to provide for surviving spouses or children. Besides documents like powers of attorney, health care proxies, living wills, advance directives, and organ donation cards, the elderly need to think about their retirement plan, government benefits like social security and Medicare, how they want their body disposed of, and even who is going to take care of their surviving pets. Without a sensible plan for managing their property before they die, they are unlikely to have much property left over to pass on to their loved ones.

Elder Law, as a subject, comprises a vast array of legal fields, including estate planning, health care law, government benefits, retirement and annuity accounts, insurance, and housing and age discrimination. For our purposes, we are going to focus on three basic subjects: 1) estate planning, retirement, and wealth preservation, 2) health care, advance directives, and living wills, and 3) funeral plans and disposition of one's body. Issues like nursing home care, age discrimination, and the best retirement accounts to supplement social security are best covered in a specialized course on Elder Law, as are health insurance, supplemental insurance for Medicare, long-term care insurance, and the details of specific health care

---

[2] Yuval Rosenberg, *Out-of-Pocket Medical Costs Threaten Seniors*, The Fiscal Times, (Sept. 10, 2012), http://www.thefiscaltimes.com/Articles/2012/09/10/Out–of–Pocket–Medical–Costs–Threaten–Seniors.aspx#page1.

needs. At this point we have time to focus only on the basics of planning for one's own declining years and eventual death. However, while there are many professionals who can offer excellent advice on insurance, medical care, and retirement planning, most clients look to their estate planning lawyers to advise them on most aspects of aging, dying, and succession of property. So you need to know the basics of what resources are available and how they fit together.

A. THE GOLDEN YEARS: A COMFORTABLE RETIREMENT, ASSET PROTECTION, AND A GOOD SUCCESSION PLAN

Since this is a book primarily on estate planning, we should discuss the *estate* first. In order to have an estate at death, one must accumulate wealth and assets during life, which most of us do by working and saving. We will use most of our earnings for the support of ourselves and children, and to enjoy life during our working years. The last few years before retirement when the kids are finally on their own are usually peak earning years, so people need to think about ways to manage income taxes. This is often accomplished by deferring the taxes until they have fully retired and are in a lower tax bracket. During these peak earning years, people should be focused on the final pieces of the nest egg they will need for a comfortable retirement. Although experts say you should start saving for retirement when you get your first job delivering newspapers, most of us don't get serious about it until the kids are taking their SAT exams and we realize we can't retire at 65 and send the daughter to Bennington College.

Once a person retires, whether it happens gradually or quickly, she will start to consume her savings or, if she is lucky, she will have enough savings that she can live off the income of her investments without dipping into the principal. During retirement, health care costs are likely to escalate despite Medicare insurance coverage, so she will need to think about insurance costs and lifetime caps for medical care in most insurance plans. Inflation is likely to mean that living expenses will increase over time. A healthy, active woman may need to plan for 30 or more years of support, while an unhealthy or disabled man may only have a life expectancy of less than 10 years. Gender, race, class and lifestyle all dramatically affect life expectancy and you need to be able to help your clients plan their declining years sensibly.[3]

Depending on the size of the estate, a client may quickly begin eating into her savings, leaving her vulnerable to impoverishment as she gets older. Other clients may find that their investments are growing more than they need to cover their living expenses. These latter clients may want to start thinking about lifetime giving before they die to take advantage of certain tax rates or other benefits. Others may want to retain complete control of their assets until death.

Most people also are likely to face a period of incapacity as they reach the end of their lives.[4] If we are lucky, the period will be short and a guardian or conservator will not be required. But others will languish in nursing homes or assisted living facilities for years, some with dementia and others

---

[3]   National Institute on Aging, *Growing Older in America: The Health and Retirement Study,* Washington, DC, National Institutes of Health, 22–26 (2007), http://hrsonline.isr. umich.edu/sitedocs/databook/HRS_Text_WEB_Ch1.pdf.

[4]   *Id.* at 85, see figure 4.7, *available at* http://hrsonline.isr.umich.edu/sitedocs/databook/ HRS_Text_WEB_Ch4.pdf.

with physical ailments that will prevent their being able to manage their basic financial affairs. Planning for this period of incapacity is terribly important. Without proper planning, an estate can easily become prey to unscrupulous friends or relatives, and going to court to have a guardian appointed can be expensive, time consuming, and emotionally scarring for loved ones.

At death, what's left of a person's estate then must be administered. Some clients will want to provide for a surviving spouse; others might want to leave an inheritance for their children and grandchildren; others might want to benefit their favorite charities. A well planned estate plan can smooth this last step as well. Survivors who are emotionally upset at the loss of a loved one are usually comforted when they can focus their grief and their energies on following explicit instructions from their dearly departed. That assumes, of course, that grandpa doesn't leave everything to his secret mistress, like Charles Kuralt did.

You may find it difficult to get clients to think about the decline into old age and incapacity. And you may also find that clients will have received a wide variety of recommendations and information from friends, relatives, and financial planners eager to help them "manage" their wealth. You need to tread carefully in steering them away from Cousin Vinny's get rich quick investment in tomato peelers or in naming Uncle Al to be their trustee just because he always played Santa Claus at the family reunions. You may not be an expert in financial planning—so don't venture into retirement planning or investment management unless you have appropriate training and licensing. As an estate planning attorney, your primary job is to plan for the control, management, and succession of your client's property. But you will often be the only person who has a clear picture of your client's entire situation, from the diversity of their family members to the contents of their investment portfolio. Therefore, you are their first line of defense in establishing the mechanisms for a smooth succession.

Some of the material we cover in this section will be brief and other material more detailed, depending on how central it is to the overall subject of succession planning. But even if something is only briefly mentioned, try to think about how it factors into the total project at hand.

1. RETIREMENT PLANNING

Most people work for many years in order to have a comfortable retirement. They scrimp and save so they will not have to rely on the kindness of strangers, or their ungrateful children, in their later years. So how do they best protect themselves with a suitable income when they are unable to just go out and find a job to pay the bills? The first thing is to have an adequate retirement plan. This should include a variety of savings and investments to supplement social security. I had always hoped that I could stay in school and defer my student loans until I retired, at which time I could use my social security to pay back my student loans. But the federal government is so unreasonable that it makes you work a minimum of 40 quarters (that's 10 years!!!) before you are even *vested* in social security and entitled to benefits. So I got a job as a law professor, which was the next best thing to staying in school.

Seriously though, in order for most people to have a comfortable retirement, they will need investments to supplement social security. Social security only pays about 40% of one's pre-retirement income. Yet experts say one needs 70–85% of one's pre-retirement income to have a comfortable retirement. In many cases the most recent projections indicate closer to 90% to deal with inflation and increasing health care costs.[5] That means one needs investments in addition to social security, as well as finding the optimum date to start collecting social security. If one retires at the earliest date to start collecting benefits (age 62 for most people), social security payments will be as much as 25% lower than if one retires at age 67. If your client can wait until age 70, and keep working and contributing to her social security until that time, her benefits will be even greater.

Any financial planner can offer advice on various investment products, from stock accounts, bonds, mutual funds, and Individual Retirement Accounts (IRAs) to real estate investments and reverse mortgages to whole life insurance policies and annuities. There is a wealth of options available for growing one's savings and then providing ways to slowly cash out the funds. Some plans create annuities, whereby a guaranteed income stream can be established. Others put the risk on the retiree not to cash out all of one's accounts, making sure to leave some for a rainy day. Many tax-deferred retirement funds, like 401(k)s, 403(b)s, and IRAs, impose a penalty if the owner does not start taking withdrawals by a certain age. They also impose a penalty if the owner starts taking withdrawals too early. Other investments use after-tax dollars, and therefore can be spent at any time.

Most securities accounts, like IRAs and mutual fund plans, can be passed on to a beneficiary at the account-holder's death, but the federal regulations on passing on tax-deferred investments are quite complex.[6] Thus, if the holder dies shortly after retiring, the unused funds become part of the decedent's estate or most likely pass according to POD or TOD designations. Other retirement plans like social security and most government and some employer sponsored pension plans, simply terminate upon the individual's death, though there may be spouse or dependent beneficiary benefits provided for a limited time. Making a decision about whether to invest in a *defined-benefit* pension plan, that may disappear if the covered individual dies early, or to invest in a *defined contribution* plan that survives death and can be passed on to survivors is something that is usually worked out with a financial planner, who takes into account the likely existence of survivors who would be entitled to benefits and the likely life expectancy of the covered individual. There are risks involved in both. If you die early, you want to have most of your money in a defined-contribution plan; if you die late, you get more benefits through a defined-benefit plan. And if we knew which it was going to be, we could probably win the lottery too and wouldn't need a retirement plan.

Most experts talk about retirement planning as being composed of three basic elements: 1) social security, 2) private savings, and 3) employer-sponsored pension plans. Employees have little choice about paying into social security during their working years; their only real choice is when to start withdrawing from it. Retirement planning should therefore include social security, but recognize that it is only one support, it is not very flexible, and it doesn't require much managing.

---

[5]   Patrick J. Purcell, *Income Replacement Ratios in the Health and Retirement Study,* Social Security Bulletin, Vol. 72 No. 3 (2012), http://www.ssa.gov/policy/docs/ssb/v72n3/v72 n3p37.html#mt15.

[6]   NATALIE CHOATE, LIFE AND DEATH PLANNING FOR RETIREMENT BENEFITS (Ataxplan Publication, 7th ed. 2011).

Employer pension plans, the second pillar, may be generous or bare-bones, may require some oversight and management, and may be flexible enough to require planning and constant supervision. Others, however, are quite inflexible. Teachers, police, and firefighters often have government-sponsored pension funds that provide a set array of benefits once the employee is vested. Back in the good old days when workers stayed with a company for their entire lives and became vested in the company's pension plan after a certain number of years, they could count on a monthly stream of income upon retirement. Vested employees often could continue to be covered under the employer's health insurance plan until the employees' death or the pension plan went belly-up. There was nothing to do but keep working until the employee was vested. These defined benefit pension plans, however, have proven far more expensive than employers originally thought when they were established, resulting in complex bankruptcies and renegotiating of pension plan contracts in many industries. Some people have lost their entire pension plans while others have seen their benefits dramatically reduced in exchange for government guarantees of minimum benefits.

Today, with the more mobile work force and the escalating costs of defined benefit pension plans, traditional defined benefit plans are often unavailable. Instead many employees may have an opportunity to invest in various tax-deferred retirement accounts, like IRAs, 401(k)s, or 403(b)s, and their employer may also invest in the plans on their behalf. These are called *defined contribution* plans. They are heavily regulated by ERISA, so an employee can't decide to invest his retirement dollars in his sister's eBay trading business, but they do allow employees to take their retirement accounts with them if they change jobs and, the big draw, pass on their unused value to survivors. These plans require some attention and planning. These accounts can be quite beneficial if well managed; but if employees don't pay into them or don't keep an eye on them, they may not grow enough to provide sufficient income. With many local governments and large employers facing bankruptcy, and considering the peaks and valleys of the stock market, all pension plans carry some risk. For instance, employee managed retirement accounts can be extremely advantageous if the money is invested well, but disastrous if the investments go south.

Finally, the third pillar is private savings—which usually includes savings accounts, certificates of deposit, equity in one's home, and perhaps the Van Gogh above the fireplace. People amass all kinds of interesting items of property throughout their lives, and some of it is even done with an eye to investing for the future. Thus, there are the usual savings forms, like investing in stocks, bonds, mutual funds, or real estate that can be sold when one's income levels drop. But one might also invest in expensive artwork that will appreciate in value and be marketable when one needs an infusion of cash. Others invest in batman paraphernalia, comic book collections, salt and pepper shakers, antique blenders, race horses, model cars, jewelry, tools, boats, RVs, or any variety of personal tangible property that is meant to retain or appreciate in value and which the owner thinks can be liquidated when money is needed.

The internet and eBay have revolutionized the way we think about savings and investing, perhaps for the good and perhaps not. Great Aunt Edna may think her salt and pepper shaker collection will fund her comfortable retirement because she saw some Louis XVth candlesticks bring a fortune on *Antiques Roadshow*. But she could be wrong, and that unopened

Kiss-Me-Kate Barbie Doll from 1943 may be worth only $10.00. One of your jobs will be to candidly assist your client in managing the unlimited variety of property she will have acquired and to recommend ways to hold it that best serve the client's long term needs. Whether your client squirrels all her money away in the mattress or invests in a time-share in Des Moines, you can advise her on which property to have in relatively liquid forms (i.e. in cash or an easily accessible money market account) and which property should be set aside for emergencies only.

Technology Trends

Secrets of the eBay Millionaires by Greg Holden isn't just a book about how to make money in the glorified digital garage sale of eBay. It's about how to tap into the most revolutionary technology of the twentieth century. PowerSellers on eBay get to put the prestigious icon next to their user ID if they have more than $1000 per month in gross sales. At the top of the list, some PowerSellers are able to leverage their brand with their unique product lines to earn hundreds of thousands of dollars per year. They do this by understanding how to present their products on the internet, how to locate buyers, and how to keep products available, because eventually those garage sales dry up. When a frosted flake shaped like Elvis' head sells for $6.50 you might think that a $3.95 box of cereal is a goldmine. But converting the products into cash, paying taxes, and building a business that can sustain a family, especially during an economic slump, are not easy. See http://digital journal.com/article/37214. Think about how you would advise a client about planning for her retirement if she is an eBay PowerSeller.

---

2.   ASSET PROTECTION AND PLANNING FOR DISABILITY

Once your client has an appropriate amount of savings and investments to provide adequate retirement income and is traveling the globe playing golf, touring the wineries of Europe, or hanging out at the country club, it is necessary to plan for the next phase of senior living—incapacity and death. Your clients will need to think about 1) paying for their escalating health care (i.e. health insurance, disability insurance, and other savings plans) without running out of money before they die; 2) nominating others to manage their property if they are incapacitated; and 3) nominating others to make medical decisions for them, including termination of life support, if they become physically or mentally unable to make decisions on their own. We take up #3 later in the Chapter. Here we focus on the asset management necessary to cover medical costs beyond insurance, nominating others to manage the estate if the client becomes incapacitated, and planning for the smooth transmission of property at death.

But what blend of PODs, insurance, or joint tenancies makes sense? And does a client need a revocable living trust, a power of appointment, or a FLiP? Invariably, anyone with even a modest amount of property will hold some of it in one or other of the multiple forms we talked about in Chapter 4. So to begin applying what we have learned let's revisit the tools in the toolbox with an eye toward different types of property, and how it can best be used for your client's needs and the needs of her family or preferred beneficiaries.

a.   *Putting the Tools to Work*

We have covered a variety of tools that have multiple effects. Some are probate avoiding, some have beneficial tax implications, and others retain donor control for as long as possible. The job of the estate planner with regard to the client's estate is two-fold: to establish any lifetime asset protection mechanisms necessary to ensure adequate funds last up until death, and to plan for the smooth transmission of any left-over wealth at the client's death. For large estates, this may entail setting up life insurance trusts to pay estate taxes or irrevocable trusts for asset protection during life, and drafting the appropriate wills and testamentary instruments for passing the residue at death. And unless your client is supernaturally prescient, you are likely to be somewhat risk averse and will want to make sure that adequate resources are available for end-of-life expenses and not tied up or already given away.

At the same time as you balance lifetime giving with mechanisms that make the property more or less difficult to access, your client will want to get the maximum benefit out of will-substitutes in order to avoid the expense and hassle of probate, and that means finding the appropriate balance of easily accessible assets (liquid wealth) with long-term investments and strategic use of lifetime gifts and trusts. The most important thing, however, will be building enough flexibility into the plan so that your client has access to what she needs throughout her life and can control the succession of what is left with a minimum amount of expense and administration for her surviving beneficiaries. So a refresher on the variety of techniques and wealth-holding mechanisms available in the estate planner's toolbox is in order here.

- Wills—The will can dispose of recently-acquired property and any other property titled in the decedent's name at death that is completely within the decedent's dominion and control. For ease of use, money for next week's groceries and the personal property the decedent uses everyday will most likely be titled solely in the decedent's name and will succeed according to the terms of the client's will. This property is included in the decedent's probate estate and may require court-supervised probate to effectuate transfer of the property to successors.

- Revocable Living Trust (RLT)—Property in the RLT is subject to the terms of the trust and is not subject to a will, thus passing outside probate. Until the death of the settlor, this property is fairly easily available to the settlor's control depending on the trust terms, and any property in the RLT is part of the decedent's gross estate for federal estate tax purposes and available for many state's elective shares. Trust property generally has to be managed more carefully in compliance with fiduciary obligations and a successor trustee can take over management upon the death or incapacity of the settlor.

- Irrevocable Inter-vivos Trust (IIT)—Property in the IIT is not easily available to the settlor (if at all) and is most likely not included in the decedent's gross estate for federal estate tax purposes or elective shares, and the beneficiaries have strong property rights to control the trustee during the settlor's lifetime. For all intents and purposes, this property is already substantially given away, even if the settlor retains limited rights to income or to invade the principal. IITs have important tax benefits as well as avoiding probate.

- Testamentary Trust (TT)—Property in a TT does not become subject to the trust terms until the death of the settlor, thus allowing a settlor to direct the use of the property after death while retaining full and complete control during life. A TT is a good way to provide for minor children in the unlikely event the settlor dies before her children reach adulthood, but she retains complete control over the property until her death and can choose to spend it all or not fund the trust at anytime. This property will most likely pass through probate before being placed in the TT so the probate avoidance benefits are lost.[7]

- General Power of Appointment (GPA)—A GPA is the next best thing to having absolute ownership of property but without the need to provide for where it will go at the donee's death. Thus, a self-settled power gives the donor/donee the power to use the property for any purpose, but dictates where it will go after the donor/donee's death if it is not otherwise appointed. Property subject to a GPA can avoid probate if it is either appointed to a permissible appointee during the donee's life, or is set to pass to default takers at the donee's death. Only if the GPA is exercised in the donee's will does the property have to be probated. Powers are usually created within the context of a will or a trust, but they don't have to be. Free-standing *inter vivos* powers can operate much like a will yet allow for probate avoidance.

- Special Power of Appointment (SPA)—An SPA is very good at getting property out of the donee's estate for tax or probate purposes, but the donee does not have the power to appoint it to herself, thus making the property inaccessible for the donee. Unless the decedent is a permissible appointee of the SPA, that property will no longer be available for the use or control of the decedent.

- Joint Bank Accounts—Joint Bank Accounts can be held in a variety of forms, from an agency account to a true joint tenancy to a POD type account, all of which give the depositor free control over the funds in the accounts but, depending on the form, may require probate at the depositor's death, or may give joint tenants enough control to take over the property to the exclusion of the depositor. All or a portion of the funds in a joint bank account will be part of the decedent's gross estate for federal estate tax purposes or for some state's elective share, but the funds in the account will pass outside probate.

- Joint Tenancy with Right of Survivorship (JTRS)—A JTRS can be used for real property, personal property, bank accounts, securities, or any other tangible or intangible property. Depending on the source of the property, it can be easily changed to a tenancy in common which would give the decedent only a fractional share of the total and may result in gift tax consequences.[8] But JTRS prop-

---

[7]   POD or life insurance benefits can pay directly into a testamentary trust without going through probate, but any property titled solely in the decedent's name will have to be probated before it can be placed into the trust.

[8]   See discussion of gift tax liabilities in Chapter 9.

erty passes entirely outside probate and can be used to defeat certain elective share rights or homestead rights.

- PODs and TODs—Usually used in the context of securities or bank accounts, they can also be used for real estate deeds in some states. The POD or TOD form gives the owner complete control over the property during life, including the power to change the beneficiary designation, but allows the property to pass at death to the named beneficiaries without passing through probate. POD and TOD property is part of the decedent's gross estate for federal estate tax purposes and for some state's elective share.

- Life Insurance—A special form of POD contract, life insurance provides an infusion of cash to beneficiaries or the estate upon the death of the insured but the proceeds may be part of the decedent's gross estate for federal estate tax purposes or for the elective share depending on who owns the policy and who benefits from it.

- FLiPs and other business/partnership interests—Shares in a partnership or business can be structured to pass directly to successors without going through probate, and they may have valuable tax minimization effects. But property held in these forms is usually not easily liquidated and there is usually little flexibility in managing these interests and passing them to the next generation. If keeping the business or farm intact is the goal, you will want to establish strict controls on alienation and descent of these property interests.

As you can see, you have learned already about many mechanisms for holding property, some of which maximize control powers during life, some of which minimize administration at death, and some of which can have powerful tax savings effects. For a small estate, probably only two or three of these mechanisms will be necessary to give the client adequate control during life with the minimum hassle at death for the survivors. For larger estates, however, many more of these mechanisms are likely to be useful, and how to apportion assets between them will depend on the individual circumstances of your client. If your client is wealthy but has minor children, you will almost certainly be looking at a testamentary trust. But depending on the wealth, you may also be looking at some RLTs, JTRSs, PODs and TODs, and some life insurance. If your client is super wealthy you should already be thinking about IITs, charitable gifts, specialized trusts, or partnership forms.

Ironically, the most common trust form used for modest estates today is the Revocable Living Trust, whose primary goal is to avoid probate and provide a mechanism for managing property during a period of incapacity. Property is placed in the trust and it can be removed and used by the settlor at any time, giving the settlor virtually unlimited flexibility during life. But at the settlor's death the trust becomes irrevocable and the property passes outside probate according to the terms of the trust. As you saw in *Heaps v. Heaps*, in Chapter 4, trusts can have drawbacks if they are not properly managed. Newly acquired property needs to be taken in the name of the trustee, not the settlor individually, and property in the trust needs to be managed according to the terms of the trust. Beneficiaries can sometimes enforce trust terms even if the settlor is still alive.[9] Trusts can be

---

[9]   C.J.S. Trusts § 719 citing Burrows v. Palmer, 5 Ill. 2d 434, 125 N.E.2d 484 (1955); Kelly v. Womack, 153 Tex. 371, 268 S.W.2d 903 (1954).

somewhat expensive to establish and may not be worth the bother for a modest estate.

Are there other mechanisms that are easier to manage during life, cost less to establish, and provide the same or even greater benefits than a revocable living trust? Yes, stand-alone general powers of appointment can provide some of the same probate avoidance benefits if properly established while giving greater flexibility to manage and control during life. Joint tenancies with right of survivorship are much easier to establish than a trust if the client is sure that the joint tenant will not withdraw the funds or sever the joint tenancy. Joint tenancies are sensible if a decedent has no spouse and a single child who is going to inherit all the property anyway. POD and TOD designations are absolutely essential for most intangible property accounts that can be simply transferred to the successor beneficiary at death. However, large POD and TOD accounts may run into tax issues, and may best be handled through a trust. And regardless of the complex machinations of lawyers, everyone will die owning at least some personal property outright for which a will, even a simple will, is important, especially if the default intestacy rules don't fit the client's wishes or non-traditional family.

Practice Point: When to Call In the Team

How's this for a good day at the office? You've just finished an initial conference with a potential client, age 67, whose net worth is somewhere in excess of $7 million (she is not exactly sure how much she is worth), children from 3 marriages and a new husband on the way. Better yet, for you at least, she has no existing wills or trusts. She likes you and wants you to do her planning. You are not exactly sure what the plan will include yet, so you wisely schedule the next meeting and tell her that you can begin discussing details and fees at that time.

As she leaves, you kick up your feet and begin to celebrate—for a solo or small firm practitioner, a client with this net worth can be extremely important; not only will the fees for a more complex plan be, most likely, considerably larger than normal, but the future business and referrals from such a client can be a true game changer. Things are looking up.

And, then, a reality hits. What sort of plan does she need? Will it involve charitable foundations, more complicated tax structuring and utilization of all of those trusts with 4 letter abbreviations? If so, your next step should be to very carefully examine your experience, education and abilities to successfully guide this client through the planning process. If you have an advanced degree in taxation, for example, and experience drafting the necessary documentation, you may be on solid ground. But if not, remember that it is ALWAYS a wiser move to call in a team of advisors (for the client and yourself) than to venture alone into perilous territory because that large fee may be beckoning.

Of course, if you need help right away and don't know any qualified professionals, you can always seek referrals from other trusted sources; but we must admit that this leaves you a bit vulnerable to their good intentions. We all find out, one way or the other, that sometimes the people we trust to help us may not have our best interests at heart. The best solution here is a bit of prevention. When you open your practice, begin making calls to accountants, tax experts and financial planners. Go to lunch with them. Get to know them over time and complete your due diligence well in advance of needing it. That way, when the big client comes along, you will be set to gather the team around you and proceed with confidence.

PROBLEMS

Consider the following situations and types of property and suggest which type of property is likely to be the best form for providing access to sufficient funds until death with relative ease of administration at death:

6.1. Your client is Bill Gates, who is outrageously rich. He has a wife, threeinor children, and he is still relatively young and healthy. Most of his net worth is in stock options for Microsoft, but he has tangible and intangible property worth over $500 million.

6.2. Your client is Justice Ruth Bader Ginsburg, widowed, with two grown children and grandchildren. She is 79 years old, has a modest estate totaling $4 million, which includes a home in Washington DC and some investments.

6.3. Your client is Tom Cruise who is currently in the process of being divorced by his third wife, Katie Holmes. He has two children he adopted with his second wife, Nicole Kidman, who are 20 and 17, and a third child born to Katie Holmes who is 6. He is worth roughly $300 million and belongs to the Church of Scientology, which believes that humans are aliens who live multiple lives, and are merely living one of their lives as humans on earth. The Church would love to have access to some of his money.

6.4. Your client is Jerry Sandusky, the assistant football coach at Penn State University, who is going to jail for sexually assaulting minor boys. He is unlikely to survive any jail sentence. He is 67 years old, married, with 6 adult adopted children. He has a modest estate of $10 million in real estate and investments, but he is looking at catastrophic debts if any of the assaulted individuals sue him for damages.

6.5. Your client is Theodore Kaczynski, the Unabomber, who is 70 years old and owns only a shack, without electricity or running water, in rural Montana. He is unmarried and currently resides in the federal penitentiary in Florence, Colorado. He continues to write extensively and retains the royalties to his Unabomber Manifesto and subsequent books valued at more than $2 million.

6.6. Your client is Representative Barney Frank, whose net worth is $650,000. He is 72 years old, is retiring from Congress in 2013, and is set to marry his current partner, Jim Ready. Frank has no children, and his closest family member is a sister.

Now go back and consider what would happen to all of these clients' estates if the client became incapacitated three years prior to death. Not only must the estate planning attorney plan for adequate resources to satisfy a client's lifetime needs, but must also plan for a period of incapacity. Besides the mechanisms listed above, there is one more important instrument in the estate planner's toolbox: the ubiquitous *Durable Power of Attorney*.

b.   *The Durable Power of Attorney*

The most common mechanism for allowing someone else to manage one's property is the *Power of Attorney*. This instrument, executed by the property holder (the principal), grants to another the power to act on the property holder's behalf, as an agent. The actual instrument can be drafted to give an agent power to act in respect to a single item of property, a single type of transaction, or for a specified period of time. Or, it can be broad, giving the agent power to undertake any and all reasonable transactions related to the owner's property subject to the general law of Agency, which imposes fiduciary duties of loyalty, care, and obedience on the actions of the agent. Notably, powers of attorney have one fatal flaw—they terminate upon the incapacity of the principal.

Hence the creation of the *Durable Power of Attorney*. The Durable Power of Attorney is designed to survive the incapacity of the principal. The durable power of attorney is governed by UPC §§ 5–501 to 5–505 and by statutes in every state which provide that the power of attorney is not to terminate upon the incapacity of the principal. As a result, the durable power of attorney has become quite common when mom or dad is beginning to have difficulty managing affairs. Often a trusted child, family member or friend is asked to take over paying bills and depositing the social security checks.

Most people think of the durable power of attorney as a short-term fix to an immediate need. They can download a copy off the internet or photo-copy the form from the statute books, get grandma's signature and, in the wink of an eye, the agent can act to keep the lights on. Few people, however, plan to use the durable power of attorney for long-term management.

The agent is, in many respects, a pseudo-trustee with regard to the principal's property. The agent may not benefit herself by transferring all of mom's money into her own personal checking account. And she usually cannot use a durable power of attorney to modify grandma's will. Although the agent does have important fiduciary duties, there are some important differences and limitations between an agent and a trustee.

For instance, the durable power of attorney terminates upon the *death* of the principal, thus resulting in all the property returning to the decedent's estate for probate. Trusts, however, survive the death of the settlor. Trustees can also be given the power to amend the terms of the trust as the estate is being administered; agents may not alter the terms of the power of attorney, although they may be able to establish a trust. And if a trustee dies before the settlor, the trust can designate successor trustees, or one can be appointed by a court. A power of attorney will terminate upon the death of the agent. A new power must be created by the principal. If the principal is then incapacitated, a court-supervised conservatorship or guardianship must be established. Another distinction is that trustees own the trust property and can therefore fully manage, sell and reinvest the property if necessary. An agent, on the other hand, only has the specific powers spelled out by the instrument, and courts interpret such powers narrowly. Moreover, many financial institutions do not like the power of attorney, deeming it too transient and subject to abuse. They will often require an agent prove that the Power has not been revoked before they will follow the agent's instructions. If property is titled in the trust's name, there is little question that a trust exists.

Most states have adopted the Uniform Power of Attorney Act (UPAA), or its predecessor the Uniform Durable Power of Attorney Act (UDPAA). Both shift the presumption of powers of attorney by making the instrument durable unless the principal indicates otherwise. In the following UPAA, only death terminates the power. In the prior UDPAA, there was a box to check if the principal did not want the power to continue after incapacity.

STATUTORY FORM POWER OF ATTORNEY: IMPORTANT INFORMATION This power of attorney authorizes another person (your agent) to make decisions concerning your property for you (the principal). Your agent will be able to make decisions and act with respect to your property (including your money) whether or not you are able to act for yourself. The meaning of authority over subjects listed on this form is explained in the Uniform Power of Attorney Act [insert citation].

This power of attorney does not authorize the agent to make health-care decisions for you.

You should select someone you trust to serve as your agent. Unless you specify otherwise, generally the agent's authority will continue until you die or revoke the power of attorney or the agent resigns or is unable to act for you.

Your agent is entitled to reasonable compensation unless you state otherwise in the Special Instructions.

This form provides for designation of one agent. If you wish to name more than one agent you may name a coagent in the Special Instructions. Coagents are not required to act together unless you include that requirement in the Special Instructions.

If your agent is unable or unwilling to act for you, your power of attorney will end unless you have named a successor agent. You may also name a second successor agent.

This power of attorney becomes effective immediately unless you state otherwise in the Special Instructions.

If you have questions about the power of attorney or the authority you are granting to your agent, you should seek legal advice before signing this form.

DESIGNATION OF AGENT

I, _____ , name the following person as my agent:

(Name of Principal)

GRANT OF GENERAL AUTHORITY

I grant my agent and any successor agent general authority to act for me with respect to the following subjects as defined in the Uniform Power of Attorney Act [insert citation]:

(INITIAL each subject you want to include in the agent's general authority. If you wish to grant general authority over all of the subjects you may initial "All Preceding Subjects" instead of initialing each subject.)

(___)	Real Property	(___)	Retirement Plans
(___)	Tangible Personal Property	(___)	Claims and Litigation
(___)	Stocks and Bonds	(___)	Personal and Family Maintenance
(___)	Commodities and Options	(___)	Taxes
(___)	Banks and Other Financial Institutions	(___)	Estates, Trusts, and Other Beneficial Interests
(___)	Operation of Entity or Business	(___)	Benefits from Governmental Programs or Civil or Military Service
(___)	Insurance and Annuities	(___)	All Preceding Subjects

GRANT OF SPECIFIC AUTHORITY (OPTIONAL)

My agent MAY NOT do any of the following specific acts for me UNLESS I have INITIALED the specific authority listed below:

(CAUTION: Granting any of the following will give your agent the authority to take actions that could significantly reduce your property or change how your property is distributed at your death. INITIAL ONLY the specific authority you WANT to give your agent.)

(___)   Create, amend, revoke, or terminate an inter vivos trust

(___)   Make a gift, subject to the limitations of the Uniform Power of Attorney Act [insert citation to Section 217 of the act] and any special instructions in this power of attorney

(___)   Create or change rights of survivorship

(___)   Create or change a beneficiary designation

(___)   Authorize another person to exercise the authority granted under this power of attorney

(___)   Waive the principal's right to be a beneficiary of a joint and survivor annuity, including a survivor benefit under a retirement plan

(___)   Exercise fiduciary powers that the principal has authority to delegate

[(___)   Disclaim or refuse an interest in property, including a power of appointment]

LIMITATION ON AGENT'S AUTHORITY

An agent that is not my ancestor, spouse, or descendant MAY NOT use my property to benefit the agent or a person to whom the agent owes an obligation of support unless I have included that authority in the Special Instructions.

SPECIAL INSTRUCTIONS (OPTIONAL)

You may give special instructions on the following lines:

_____

_____

_____

_____

EFFECTIVE DATE

This power of attorney is effective immediately unless I have stated otherwise in the Special Instructions.

NOMINATION OF [CONSERVATOR OR GUARDIAN] (OPTIONAL)

If it becomes necessary for a court to appoint a [conservator or guardian] of my estate or [guardian] of my person, I nominate the following person(s) for appointment:

* * * *

RELIANCE ON THIS POWER OF ATTORNEY

Any person, including my agent, may rely upon the validity of this power of attorney or a copy of it unless that person knows it has terminated or is invalid.

SIGNATURE AND ACKNOWLEDGMENT

* * * *

IMPORTANT INFORMATION FOR AGENT

Agent's Duties

When you accept the authority granted under this power of attorney, a special legal relationship is created between you and the principal. This relationship imposes upon you legal duties that continue until you resign or the power of attorney is terminated or revoked. You must:

(1) do what you know the principal reasonably expects you to do with the principal's property or, if you do not know the principal's expectations, act in the principal's best interest;

(2) act in good faith;

(3) do nothing beyond the authority granted in this power of attorney; and

(4) disclose your identity as an agent whenever you act for the principal by writing or printing the name of the principal and signing your own name as "agent" in the following manner:

(Principal's Name) by (Your Signature) as Agent

Unless the Special Instructions in this power of attorney state otherwise, you must also:

(1) act loyally for the principal's benefit;

(2) avoid conflicts that would impair your ability to act in the principal's best interest;

(3) act with care, competence, and diligence;

(4) keep a record of all receipts, disbursements, and transactions made on behalf of the principal;

(5) cooperate with any person that has authority to make health-care decisions for the principal to do what you know the principal reasonably expects or, if you do not know the principal's expectations, to act in the principal's best interest; and

(6) attempt to preserve the principal's estate plan if you know the plan and preserving the plan is consistent with the principal's best interest.

Termination of Agent's Authority

You must stop acting on behalf of the principal if you learn of any event that terminates this power of attorney or your authority under this power of attorney. Events that terminate a power of attorney or your authority to act under a power of attorney include:

(1) death of the principal;

(2) the principal's revocation of the power of attorney or your authority;

(3) the occurrence of a termination event stated in the power of attorney;

(4) the purpose of the power of attorney is fully accomplished; or

(5) if you are married to the principal, a legal action is filed with a court to end your marriage, or for your legal separation, unless the Special Instructions in this power of attorney state that such an action will not terminate your authority.

Liability of Agent

The meaning of the authority granted to you is defined in the Uniform Power of Attorney Act [insert citation]. If you violate the Uniform Power of Attorney Act [insert citation] or act outside the authority granted, you may be liable for any damages caused by your violation.

If there is anything about this document or your duties that you do not understand, you should seek legal advice.

As you can see, the power of attorney gives the agent broad or narrow powers, depending on which boxes are checked, and it persists beyond incapacity unless indicated in the special instructions section.

The durable power of attorney can be an effective device, especially if the agent is given broad powers to make *inter vivos* gifts of the principal's property, modify trust or will provisions and beneficiaries, change beneficiary designations on POD or TOD accounts, remove co-tenants from joint tenancies, or do other estate planning that might seem to deviate from the principal's intentions. But active agents are likely to be in for some strenuous opposition that could have been stanched had the decedent provided clearer instructions about her ultimate estate plan. Because powers of attorney are often used as emergency measures when better planning failed to happen, an active agent may be in for litigation if she does more than simply pay the bills and deposit the checks, even if she is following grandma's verbal instructions.

Countless cases have litigated whether an agent may, for instance, sell the principal's house and use part of the proceeds to pay for end of life care. If by doing so the agent receives a greater inheritance, then whoever was entitled to the house under the principal's will is going to complain.[10] Conversely, the sale of the house might reduce the agent's inheritance if he or she does not know the contents of a will. If the agent knows that she is going to inherit certain property from grandma's will and acts to preserve that property and not property that would be inherited by her cousins, has she acted inappropriately? On the other hand, if she doesn't know the contents of grandma's will and acts in ways that reduce her inheritance, should she be entitled to replacement property or compensation from the principal's other property?

There are no easy answers to these questions and there are few acts by the agent that won't be challenged by someone else who felt the agent was self-dealing. If the agent modifies the will and estate plan so that all the potential beneficiaries pay ratably for grandma's unexpected end of life medical expenses, those whose shares are reduced will complain. If the agent, trying to keep harmony in the family and avoid litigation, pays the unexpected expenses out of the property that she would have inherited, then she is likely to feel bitter and less inclined to serve as an agent in the future. Unless the principal has a single heir and beneficiary, and names that person her agent, conflicts are likely to arise. The solution in many cases is a revocable trust, one in which the settlor acts as trustee during life, but a successor trustee is named to act at the settlor's death or incapacity. If the trustee is a stranger, then hard feelings can be avoided when difficult decisions must be made about which properties to liquidate to pay grandma's unexpected expenses.

If the principal is likely to have a lengthy period of incapacity, has significant wealth, has numerous beneficiaries, complex property, or has minor children, the durable power of attorney is likely to be insufficient to meet her needs. A revocable or irrevocable trust is another common mechanism for dealing with incapacity because it helps make a smooth transition from incapacity to death as well as avoiding probate. The durable power of attorney does neither. With a trust, the property remains in the hands of the trustee to be administered according to the trust terms

---

[10] *See, e.g., In re* Est. of Hegel, 668 N.E.2d 474 (Ohio 1996); Crosby v. Luehrs, 669 N.W.2d 635 (Neb. 2003).

after the death of the settlor. More importantly, the trust will survive the death of a trustee, while a power of attorney will not survive the death of the agent.

Powers of appointment, PODs and TODs, and joint tenancies can also be used during a period of incapacity if the property doesn't require much attention. If a testator doesn't want to use a trust, a well-drafted power of attorney, in conjunction with adequate will-substitutes may suffice. But remember, someone has to pay the utility and credit card bills, make sure insurance payments are up to date, and pay the property taxes if grandma or grandpa is unable to do so. Without some legal mechanism for enabling a surrogate to make those decisions, a court-ordered custodianship may be required.

Consider the situations facing these families and whether a different mechanism would have avoided some or all of the problems:

In re Estate of Curtis

83 A.D.3d 1182, 923 N.Y.S.2d 734 (3d Dep't 2011)

Martha Curtis suffered a series of strokes in 2002 and moved in with one of her daughters, Gail Akins, and her husband. Gail was given a power of attorney executed by Curtis allowing her, among other powers, to make gifts to Curtis' children and grandchildren. At the time Curtis moved in with the Akins, she purportedly agreed to pay $2500 per month for her room and board. In the following two years before Curtis' death, Gail sold her mom's mobile home, naming herself as a mortgagee for the buyer, transferred an investment account into her name, and helped herself to $2500 each month from her mother's checking account. At her death in 2004, Curtis' will gave all of her estate equally to Gail, another daughter Patricia, and the children of a deceased daughter. At the time of her death, however, there wasn't much property left, and Patricia sued for an accounting and then to rescind Gail's actions on the grounds that they were fraudulent, self-dealing, and in violation of her fiduciary duty. The court determined that all of Gail's actions were done with her mother's consent and that Gail need reimburse the estate only for $1,268.73, a credit from room and board expenses paid in advance during Curtis' last month.

On appeal, Patricia disputed the court's finding that Curtis' mental capacity was not diminished and therefore actively participated in the management of her assets. Noting that a presumption of self-dealing arises where an attorney in fact acts in ways to benefit herself, the court on appeal found that because the *power of attorney specifically authorized respondent to make gifts to decedent's children, which would include respondent,* no self-dealing had occurred. *Furthermore, the court credited respondent's testimony that the investment account was transferred in decedent's presence, and that decedent was also present at the closing when her mobile home was sold and respondent was named as a co-mortgagee. Under these circumstances, we agree with Surrogate's Court that respondent established that the challenged actions were taken with decedent's knowledge and at her direction.*

Query: What should Gail have done to prevent her sister filing suit accusing her of stealing from their mother? What should Patricia have done? How could Curtis have done a better job avoiding the litigation that undoubtedly ate up a large chunk of what was left of her daughters' inheritances?

Burchfield v. McMillian-Ferguson

Slip Copy, 2011 WL 2112414 (Ohio App. 10 Dist., 2011)

John McMillian had seven children, including Steve, Brenda, and Inez. Inez prepared a Power of Attorney in early 2006 for her father, naming herself Attorney in Fact. The same day, Inez prepared a survivorship deed that deeded her father's interest in his house to him and Inez jointly. Ten months later, Inez prepared a quit-claim deed transferring her father's share of the house to her brother Steve. She then prepared another quit-claim deed transferring the property back from Steve to her father, and then another from her father to herself shortly before his death. Inez signed her father's name on the last deed without indicating that she was signing as his attorney. It's unclear whether she signed any of the other deeds for her father. She also cashed a check for $189.50 her father had received after his death and kept the proceeds. The administrator of her father's estate filed a complaint against Inez for concealing assets and the trial court ordered Inez to return her father's house to the estate and the $189.50, and pay attorney fees for the costs of the suit.

On appeal, Inez disputed the claims of self-dealing and conflict of interest but the court disagreed, stating: *The law is zealous in guarding against abuse in a fiduciary-principal relationship. Any transfer of property from a principal to his attorney-in-fact is viewed with some suspicion. Self-dealing transactions by a fiduciary are presumptively invalid.* Inez not only failed to indicate that she was signing the deed as POA, but her sister Brenda testified that her witness signature on the deed was not her own. Even though Inez undertook to maintain her father's house and pay all the bills on it, the suspicious circumstances of the multiple quit-claim deeds was held to be sufficient to justify the trial's court's finding of conflict of interest. The trial court had also struck the 2006 survivorship deed creating the joint tenancy between her father and Inez. On appeal the court affirmed, stating that the trial judge was the best judge of the conflicting evidence as to whether her father signed that deed under undue influence or duress. The trial court also had refused to admit affidavits from the notary who notarized the survivorship deed and the POA, her father's doctor who stated that her father was under no duress when he signed the POA and the survivorship deed and was of sound mind and had excellent judgment, and her father's financial planner who affirmed that she had discussed with McMillian having Inez' name added to the property. The court of appeal refused to reverse the trial judge's findings in the absence of evidence that the judge abused his discretion or the decision was *unreasonable, arbitrary, or unconscionable, and not merely an error of law or judgment.* Noting that Inez had not explained why she hadn't provided the three witnesses in person to allow cross-examination, the court of appeals affirmed the trial court's denial of the affidavits. The court then affirmed that Inez would have to pay the costs of the conflict of interest litigation out of her share of the inheritance.

Query: What went wrong in this suit? Is it likely that Inez was closest to her father and that he supported transferring to her the title to the house in joint tenancy? Or do you think she breached her fiduciary duty to her principal? Assuming she has no fiduciary duty to her siblings, who is harmed now that her father is dead? Do you think that had she produced the notary public, the doctor, and the financial planner she would have prevailed? If so, did she actually breach her fiduciary duty or simply hire a lousy attorney to litigate the challenge? Is this a case of self-dealing or mismanagement by an agent who simply failed to understand how to undertake her responsibilities? Would you feel differently if you knew Inez was a lawyer, or if she was a concert violinist?

———————

These two cases illustrate typical problems with powers of attorney and management of the incapacitated person's financial affairs. In *Curtis*, the decedent had suffered a series of strokes and required constant in-home care. Assuming she didn't have long-term care insurance, she was likely to be best cared for in the home of one of her daughters. Is it unreasonable to assume that an elderly parent who dreaded being a burden on any of her children would offer to compensate the child who cares for her in her declining years? Would Gail have felt slighted if her mother had insisted that every penny be split equally between Gail, her sister Patricia, and the children of her deceased sister if she, Gail, was footing the bill to provide for her mother, driving her to all of her doctor appointments, and providing emotional care and support as well? There are no easy answers. Certainly, siblings can squabble over a parent's inheritances and accuse the one who gets more of exercising undue influence or self-dealing. At the same time, isn't it likely that the child who is providing the day-by-day care for mom would not argue when mom insists that she receive a larger share of mom's estate? Short of shunting mom back and forth between children so that all take on a proportionate share of the care-giving expenses, how do you help your client avoid the sibling rivalries and the last-minute financial shenanigans that often accompany the last few years of life?

Do we know anything about the mental state of either of these decedents? Both clearly had medical problems in their last two years of life, but there is nothing to indicate that either was so mentally impaired as to require a guardianship or custodianship. Do we just assume that the elderly are more susceptible to the pressures of the child who is providing the primary care, or is it likely that the elderly parent is driving most of these financial decisions? Of course, we cannot know after the fact. What we can do, however, is work with our clients well in advance to provide mechanisms to protect their testamentary plans if they become incapacitated, but also provide flexibility when end-of-life medical situations require adjustments to the plans. One of the most common devices estates lawyers use today is the self-settled revocable living trust.

c.   *Self-Settled Trusts and Powers—The Revocable Living Trust*

Besides simply owning the property outright and having it pass according to a will, even a modest estate can benefit from an instrument establishing a self-settled trust or a self-settled power. Remember, these are forms of holding property by which the settlor (donor) gives to the trustee (donee) the power to use the property for a beneficiary (permissible appointee). When the client is both the settlor and the beneficiary, the client can insure that the property will be used for her benefit AND that it will pass to successor beneficiaries at her death outside of probate. The revocable living trust serves this purpose quite well, although more specialized self-settled trusts have become popular in the last decade. These include GRATs, GRITs, DAPTs and Medicaid Trusts which we discuss in the next section.

In 2009, the American College of Trusts and Estates Counsel (ACTEC), a prestigious group of leading trusts and estates practitioners, sent out a survey on the use of revocable trusts nationwide. Totaling over 1500 pages, the survey results give detailed information about the trust law of each state. The summary, however, is a readable 31 pages, and provides a wealth of information about why practitioners in most states continue to use the revocable trust as the cornerstone of most estate plans.[11] Numerous reasons were given about the value of the revocable trust, and some disadvantages. They include:

Advantages:

- Immediate access to assets upon the death of the settlor, which is not true with probate assets.
- Avoid time delays, costs, and irregular supervision of probate.
- Privacy—most states do not require filing of revocable trusts (New York and Louisiana provide some exceptions).
- Planning for new spouses and/or avoidance of elective share (some states).
- Planning for incapacity, including an agent to amend or revoke the trust terms (wills cannot be amended or revoked by an agent) and avoiding a conservatorship.
- Banks prefer working with trustees over agents and persons with a power of attorney.
- Much easier to manage out-of-state property and to avoid ancillary probate than outright ownership or durable powers of attorney.
- Often have less court supervision than a testamentary trust or a probate estate.
- In at least two states (North Dakota and Rhode Island) creditors of the settlor cannot reach trust assets in a revocable trust once the settlor dies.
- Eleven states protect revocable trust property from the elective share.
- Inheritance tax benefits (for instance, life insurance benefits payable to a revocable trust are not subject to inheritance taxes where benefits payable to the estate are in Nebraska and Ohio).
- Can be used to hold separate property in a community property state to maintain its distinct character or vice versa.
- May reduce the likelihood of a challenge if the trust has been in existence for a long time, more so than a will or a power of attorney.

---

[11] Ira Mark Bloom, *Summary of Actec Survey on Revocable Trusts,* http://www.actec.org/public/Documents/Studies/Bloom_Revocable_Trust_Survey_3_09.pdf.

Disadvantages:

- In some states probate is very quick and inexpensive (Pennsylvania) and often is cheaper than setting up a trust.
- Statute of Limitations for will contests is shorter than for challenges to a trust.
- Incomplete funding and failure to retitle assets in the trust's name leads to probate anyway.
- Double retitling is necessary (once at trust creation and again at distribution), and corresponding liability for possible deed taxes.
- Title Insurance and Homeowners insurance companies may have issues with properties held in trust—may lose insurance upon retitling in the name of the trust and have to pay to get a rider or new policy.
- In some states holding property in a revocable trust may limit homestead protections.
- Creation and operation costs are higher than with wills.
- Some states (New York and Virginia) either don't allow motor vehicles to be titled in the trust or designate them business vehicles if they are.
- Other property protections, like tax rebates for low income property owners or protection from increases in property taxes (Prop 13 in California) may be lost when property is transferred to a trust.
- Can lose protections and bring the property under consideration for Medicaid in certain states.
- Property subject to a mortgage may require the mortgage company's approval or the entire amount due may be accelerated upon the transfer.
- Some states require a trustee to register acceptance of the trust and failure to do so voids the trust.
- Creditors of the settlor can reach trust assets at any time prior to the death of the settlor.

As you can see, there are some pretty important benefits to be gained by the use of a revocable trust, one of the most important of which is management of the property during a period of the settlor's incapacity (usually preceding death). The trust avoids the need for a conservatorship or guardianship which is heavily supervised by the courts. There are the obvious probate avoidance benefits as well. There are some pretty important drawbacks too, including the general tendency of trust settlors not to manage their trusts well (failure to fund and retitle, failure to notify mortgage companies or title insurance companies), and the shorter statute of limitations on will challenges may be particularly attractive for certain clients.

Another important consideration is UTC § 112, which provides that "The rules of construction of the jurisdiction applicable to the interpretation of and disposition of property by wills is to apply to the interpretation of the terms of the trust in the disposition of the trust property." In those states that have adopted UTC § 112, all the rules you learned about (or will learn about) revocation of provisions to spouses upon divorce, or anti-lapse, slayer disqualification, or constructional rules for future interests, to name just a few, are applicable to trusts as well. In many other states the rules are not applicable and, as a general rule, twice as many states do not have synchronicity of wills and trusts rules as do.[12]

PROBLEM

Go through the disadvantages listed above and see if there are other tools in our toolbox that might avoid some or all of those consequences.

In particular, consider how often a stand-alone self-settled power might avoid some of the disadvantages listed above, either as a general or a special power of appointment. All revocable trusts give the settlor the power to revoke the trust with regard to particular items of property, which is essentially a trust coupled with a general power of appointment. Where the trustee is not the settlor, and the trustee has the power to appoint trust assets on behalf of the settlor or anyone the settlor directs, the trustee has a special power of appointment. These are common and important discretionary powers that build flexibility into any trust. In addition, what about stand-alone powers? Do they avoid any of the disadvantages of the revocable trust? Think too about joint tenancies and agency accounts.

The revocable living trust is a very effective way to avoid court-supervised guardianships or custodianships for clients who become incapacitated and are unable to manage their financial affairs, and for this reason alone they may be advisable, even if the costs and technical administration are more intensive. Providing for a successor trustee to take over upon incapacity allows a settlor to manage her property as trustee on her own and feel confident that the person she has appointed as successor will take over either on her death or on becoming incapacitated. Furthermore, unlike with a durable power of attorney, if the successor trustee predeceases the settlor, she can name (or a court can name) an alternate trustee so the trust will not fail. Powers of attorney and powers of appointment are personal, however, and if the donee of the power or the agent predeceases the donor/principal, the power will fail. This is a good thing if the donor/principal is relying on the personal knowledge of the donee/agent and trusts that person's judgment. Some mechanisms don't depend on anyone else making decisions, like joint tenancies and PODs. The property merely passes as established. But powers and trusts depend on the judgment of others; so choosing a trustee or agent should not be taken lightly.

d. Asset Protection—Irrevocable Trusts

Imagine you are sitting down with your mother and father, both in their 70s, and they are fretting about whether their escalating health care costs are going to eat up their entire life's savings, leaving you and your sister with an ugly painting of Great Aunt Edna (not the one painted by Picasso) as your entire inheritance. Dad may have to go into a nursing home or Mom needs expensive surgery and, although your parents are comfortable, they are not rich. They own their house in full, which is valued at about $300,000. They have some stocks and other securities worth about $200,000 and a modest assortment of furniture including artwork, clothes,

---

[12] See *Id.* at 28–29.

and cars. They can easily pay their bills now, but they do not qualify for long-term care insurance or disability insurance that would cover expensive nursing home or in-home care. They are thinking that Medicaid, the government funded health-care for the indigent, will cover their nursing home, but they've heard that Medicaid won't pay a cent until they have expended virtually all of their assets first. They perk up when you mention the term *asset protection trust*—afterall, what's not to like about protecting one's assets?

Asset Protection Trusts are a special type of self-settled trust designed to protect assets from creditors, especially upon threat of divorce or bankruptcy, or to protect assets in order to qualify for Medicaid. They do not conceal assets from taxation and these kinds of trusts won't be allowed if they are set up with the intent to defraud legitimate creditors. Many states don't even allow them at all. But in those states that do allow them, if set up properly as irrevocable trusts with only the income payable to the settlor, the trust corpus **may** be deemed out of reach of certain creditors. Due to attempts to shield assets from creditors, very strict rules have been established on trusts set up with the sole aim of protecting the corpus from claimants. Many states disallow these trusts altogether as fraudulent and, unless the trust is set up in time, it may not help avoid the pay-down required to qualify for Medicaid. Of course, the devil is in the details, and we don't have the time or space to discuss all of the details. But there are three general types of trusts that you should be aware of: Medicaid Trusts, Special Needs Trusts, and Domestic Asset Protection Trusts (DAPTs).

i.   Medicaid Trusts

Medicaid is the government sponsored health care program for low income persons and persons with disabilities. Unlike Medicare, which is a federal insurance program for all seniors, Medicaid is a federal/state partnership where federal funds are given to the states to use for providing health care for target populations. Every state has a different Medicaid program, making it difficult to speak universally about planning for Medicaid coverage. However, as a general rule, Medicaid will cover some long-term care in a nursing home and will cover medical expenses for persons who are unable to pay or are without insurance. But Medicaid has a number of limitations. First, the patient must be indigent in order to qualify for Medicaid.[13] Second, the types of facilities and types of care that are covered are generally not as extensive as those provided for under regular insurance or on a private pay plan. Third, because the states administer their own Medicaid programs, the specific rules and financial thresholds may differ across state lines. With that in mind, how does a Medicaid trust work?

Assuming that mom and dad are still fairly healthy and have adequate resources, they can place most of their property into an irrevocable trust with an unrelated trustee (not a spouse or other close relative), give themselves the income only and, if the trust was established more than 5 years before they require Medicaid care, the property in the trust will not be considered as theirs for Medicaid eligibility purposes. The rationale is that the

---

[13] Not all assets must be liquidated in order to qualify, however. Certain properties are exempt, like homestead. But putting the home into a revocable trust could mean that the settlor has to sue to make sure that the home isn't treated as non-exempt just because it was put into a trust. See Pfautz v. Ohio Dept. of Job and Family Svcs., 2007 WL 4225502 (Ohio. App. 2007).

property now belongs to someone else; the trustee and the remainder bene-ficiaries. So if mom and dad get moving early, they can place most of their property in trust to avoid having it qualify as assets for determining Medi-caid eligibility.

Sounds great—but is it? First, the trust must be *irrevocable* which means, like King Lear, mom and dad must give the property away during life and they cannot retain the right to receive even discretionary payments of principal. This is simply giving one's property away during life, before one needs it, in the hopes that if the need arises either the government or the recipients of the property will step in. In the current political situation that may be a big IF. Once the trust is made irrevocable, mom and dad cannot have any legal entitlement to control or benefit from the property. Second, they cannot appoint themselves or their spouses as trustees, be-cause, as you can imagine, using the very family members who are seeking to protect the assets makes the whole thing rather fishy. Mom and dad cannot have any discretionary rights to invade principal, although the set-tlor can retain the right to appoint trust property to others (i.e. a special power of appointment). They can also retain the right to change the trus-tee. Most importantly, mom and dad can have no right to principal if the trust is going to work. If they have a right to income from the trust assets, that income will be directed toward health care bills, leaving Medicaid to pick up the remainder. Furthermore, the trust must be established **5 years** before the need for Medicaid arises. If the 5 year threshold is not met, Med-icaid guidelines require looking back at 60 months worth of property transactions to ensure that the applicant did not do precisely what mom and dad are doing, giving all their property away in order to qualify for government benefits.[14]

For many people, this might sound like a great deal. But think about it. If mom and dad give away all their property during life so they can qual-ify for government benefits, they actually have to give it away. That means that if their remote cousin, the trustee, decides not to use any of the trust property to pay for the extra cable television for their room in the nursing home, and instead lets his kids spend it on a cruise to the Bahamas, then mom and dad don't get any of the benefit of their property. Even though it is their property and they worked hard all their lives to accumulate it, once they place it in the irrevocable trust they no longer have any control over it. Rather, mom and dad can only hope that the trust beneficiaries will actual-ly use some of the money to benefit them. If the beneficiaries show such chivalry, doing so would be a gift from the beneficiary to mom or dad, and could be taxable unless the gift amount is less than $14,000 per year. Mom and dad can't even demand that the trust beneficiaries send a birthday card to them every year from the trust funds.

Moreover, the beneficiaries of the Medicaid trust will only get the med-ical care that Medicaid will cover—which will likely fall short of the benefits that most people would want. Medicaid doesn't cover private rooms, physical therapy, cable TV, or a lot of amenities that are deemed luxuries to the government that is footing the bill. They may look like ne-cessities to people who have lived fairly comfortably during their lives, but asking the government to pay for their medical bills so they can watch ca-ble TV may stretch the tax-payer's generosity.

---

[14] *See* Est. of Gonwa v. Wisc. Dept. of Health & Family Servs., 668 N.W.2d 122, (Wis. Ct. App. 2003); Ahern v. Thomas, 248 Conn. 708 (Conn. 1999).

Finally, the current Medicaid laws provide that the government will look back 60 months to see if people were disposing of assets in order to look poor. The more this is done, the more likely Medicaid will increase the look-back period or disallow the trust altogether. Of course, if the irrevocable trust is set up for a legitimate reason, like a charitable remainder trust or a special needs trust for a dependent child, the situation is different. In such cases, there are reasons beyond qualifying for Medicaid which legitimize the transfer and, assuming those reasons make sense, the government isn't likely to complain. For instance, if 30 years before mom and dad became eligible for Medicaid they gratuitously paid for their children's college educations, surely there is no reason to punish them for their generosity upon applying for Medicaid. Rather, the goal is to dissuade people from giving their property away with the sole motive of impoverishing themselves in order to qualify for tax-payer funded governmental benefits. It's a risk, as King Lear well learned, but it certainly can be done if done early enough and if mom and dad live in the right state.

For more information on Medicaid Trusts see: *Boruch v. Neb. HHS*, 11 Neb. App. 713, 717 (Neb. Ct. App. 2003) (explaining the "trust gap" whereby the use of irrevocable trusts permitted persons "to have their cake and eat it too," by using the trusts to indirectly retain access to assets for personal benefit while receiving Medicaid assistance, when such assets would otherwise have precluded eligibility for such public assistance); *Thorson v. Neb. HHS*, 274 Neb. 322, 327–328 (Neb. 2007) (discussing the Congressional amendment of 1986 codified at § 1396a(k), thereafter repealed and replaced in 1993 by § 1396p(d) which expanded the types of trusts counted in determining an applicant's Medicaid eligibility, commonly known as Medicaid qualifying trusts, so as to close the loophole whereby persons could no longer use irrevocable trusts to shield assets that would otherwise be counted in determining Medicaid eligibility). For related matters see also Lee R. Russ, *Eligibility for welfare benefits, under maximum-assets limitations, as affected by expenditures or disposal of assets*, 19 A.L.R.4th 146 (2012) (reviewing the effect on Medicaid eligibility upon occurrence of particular property transfers); Lee R. Russ, *Validity of statutes or regulations denying welfare benefits to claimants who transfer property for less than its full value*, 24 A.L.R.4th 215 (2009); and Lee R. Russ, *Eligibility for Welfare Benefits as Affected by Claimant's Status as Trust Beneficiary*, 21 A.L.R.4th 729 (2010).

ii.   Supplemental Needs Trusts for the Disabled

The federal Medicaid law, 42 U.S.C. § 1396(d), allows for three types of self-settled trusts to benefit a Medicaid recipient without disqualifying her for benefits. The first two, however, can only benefit disabled individuals who are under age 65. Only the third can help mom and dad if they are already over that age.

The first, the D–4A trust, allows for the placement of the settlors' property into an irrevocable trust, with income payable to the settlor and the right to invade principal on behalf of the settlor and, upon her death, the principal repays the government for its health care expenditures on behalf of the settlor. But there are strict limitations on this kind of trust. The beneficiary must be disabled, the trust must be established by a parent, grandparent, guardian or the court, using the disabled individual's own property, it must be established before the beneficiary is 65 years old and, upon the death of the beneficiary, the trust principal will be used to compensate the government for the medical expenses expended on the beneficiary. Only if there is anything left in the trust can it pay to a beneficiary of the disabled trust settlor. The D–4A trust is commonly used when a minor or young adult is injured and is given a large settlement to provide for future medical and living care because that person is no longer able to care for herself. The disabled settlor can still receive government medical benefits without depleting the principal of the trust but the benefits are essentially a loan, to be paid back after the disabled settlor's death.

A second type of trust is available in those states that have an income cap for Medicaid patients. If a disabled individual requiring long-term health care receives income from, say, a trust or a pension plan, and that income might place the person over the limit for Medicaid eligibility, the income from the trust or pension can be set to pay into a separate trust. Then, the income from the new trust can be used to pay for non-covered health care, and the remainder of the trust corpus will be used to repay Medicaid for expenditures upon the death of the settlor. This kind of trust avoids the hassle of going on and off Medicaid each year for the recipient whose income fluctuates around the threshold limit. For example, if John is the beneficiary of a trust set up by his deceased mother, which pays him $30,000 once a year on January 1st, and the cut off of assets for Medicaid benefits is $15,000, John would have to go off Medicaid each year on January 1st, and then reapply when he had used up half of the trust income that was paid to him. Then, the next year he would have to go off Medicaid again until he had spent down his assets to the appropriate eligibility level. Instead, by depositing the entire $30,000 into a separate trust, which gives him the income for his life, he can count on a regular (albeit smaller) income stream from the new trust to pay for incidental medical needs, and he can dip into the principal for medical expenses as well. At his death, the principal reimburses the government for its expenditures on John. If the trust corpus is larger than his expenses, the remainder can pay to John's beneficiaries.

A third type of self-settled trust is a *non-profit pooled income trust*. This type of trust is established and managed by a non-profit organization solely for this purpose. An account within the larger trust is established for the disabled beneficiary, and upon that person's death the corpus is retained by the non-profit to be used for medical care for indigent persons or is used to repay Medicaid.[15]

The benefit of these three types of trusts is to allow a person of modest means to preserve assets in order to use them during end-of-life incapacity to pay for expenses not typically covered by Medicaid. Rather than spend down all of one's assets before becoming eligible for Medicaid benefits, a disabled person can set the assets aside, use what she needs during her life to augment Medicaid, and then what is left at her death will reimburse Medicaid for expenses paid on behalf of the individual. If it turns out that not all of the trust assets are needed to reimburse Medicaid, then that property passes according to the trust terms to secondary beneficiaries.

Let's go back to mom and dad, who are in their 70s already. It's too late to use the first type of trust—the D–4A trust. Assuming that they want to protect their house, especially if only one spouse requires Medicaid assistance and the other does not want to become indigent, they can establish a Medicaid trust as discussed in section i. Let's say they put all of their major

---

[15] *See* In re Pooled Advocate Trust, 813 N.W.2d 130 (S.D. 2012).

assets, their house and securities, into the trust, and it amounts to $500,000. If dad doesn't need Medicaid assistance for three years, then his expenses for the next two years will need to come out of the trust, but no more after that. Thus, if dad needs $6000 per month to pay for his nursing home, the two years' of expenses will amount to $144,000. After the trust pays out for dad's care for the two years, the remainder of the trust assets, or $356,000 will be protected. Income can be used to benefit mom after dad dies and, if she needs expensive surgery after the 5 years, the remaining trust assets won't be included in her estate for determining her Medicaid eligibility.

What if mom and dad don't bother to establish a Medicaid trust and dad goes into a nursing home for his last year of life. They spend $72,000 on his care and mom has $428,000 left in her name. Now she is looking at expensive surgery and possible nursing home care herself. By placing her assets into a non-profit pooled income trust, she can receive the income to augment Medicaid benefits, and any property left over at her death repays Medicaid for its expenses. That might make sense if she calculates that she is likely to live long enough to get back in benefits more than what she puts into the trust. But if she wants to leave something more than Great Aunt Edna's portrait to her children, it may just make more sense to use her assets for her own medical care. If she doesn't survive the surgery, there is likely to be something left for her kids. If she survives the surgery but doesn't live very long, she can still pay down her assets and likely not use them all up, leaving some for the kids. Only if she lives four or more years after going in the nursing home is she likely to use up all of her assets. At that point maybe a pooled income trust would have been sensible, but it's obviously hard to predict.

Because younger disabled individuals may live a very long time in assisted living facilities and require very expensive medical care, these supplemental needs trusts make sense. But for many people who only need nursing home care in the last year or two of life, it may be simpler and cheaper to simply pay down assets. The biggest worry, however, concerns married couples when the first is looking at expensive medical bills and the second doesn't want to live out her widowhood in poverty because she spent every penny of their savings on her husband's care. For that reason, Medicaid does not require that a married couple sell the house if the surviving spouse can remain living in it.[16]

With the escalation in medical costs for end-of-life care, experts have estimated that a 65 year old couple will need to have saved nearly $250,000 just to pay for the medical expenses, insurance, drugs, and other related health care costs for the rest of their lifetimes.[17] It is also predicted that health care costs will consume between 25% and 50% of a retiree's net income.[18] That leaves little to pay the rent, keep the lights on, buy food, pay for car insurance, and still have something to pass on to the kids. Despite the pleas and promises of politicians, the health care situation in this country is unlikely to get better in the short term. For the person of modest

---

[16] 42 *U.S.C.A.* § 1396p(a)(2)(A); Matter of Labis, 314 N.J. Super. 140, 145 (App. Div. 1998) (providing that "there is also no Medicaid lien or claim upon the marital home as long as the community spouse" continues to reside in the residence).

[17] Report of the Social Security Advisory Board, *The Unsustainable Cost of Healthcare*, 8, (Sept. 2009), http://www.ssab.gov/documents/TheUnsustainableCostofHealthCare_graphics. pdf.

[18] *Id.* at 6.

wealth, planning for end-of-life health care may be the most important element of their estate plan.

iii.   Domestic Asset Protection Trusts (DAPTs)

Medical expenses may not be the most pressing concern for certain clients, like those with sizable estates, those facing other debts, and those who simply want a steady income stream but don't want to manage their property and worry about it while they are off on safari or sipping Mai Tais at the country club. DAPTs allow a trust settlor to place property in an *irrevocable inter vivos* trust, name a third party trustee, nominate himself and others as beneficiaries, and impose a spendthrift provision to prohibit alienation and attachment by creditors.[19] So long as the trustee has discretion not to pay out of the trust to the settlor or for his benefit, the settlor's creditors cannot reach the trust assets. If that sounds like a free lunch, that's what it purports to be. And since there are no free lunches, you should be wary of internet claims or client expectations to be able to shield their property, benefit from it during life, and pass it on to their children free of claims of creditors.

Of the 14 or so states that permit DAPTs, and the half dozen others that allow certain limited creditor protections to these irrevocable trusts, all refuse to shield property placed in the trust with the intent of defrauding creditors. In fact many states refuse to shield property from privileged creditors like former spouses or children who have alimony or support claims against a trust beneficiary.[20] Like the Medicaid trust, the states that allow DAPTs require that a certain amount of time go by before the trust is creditor-proof. Alaska, for instance, requires four years, after which creditors of the settlor may not gain access to trust assets.[21]

Alaska, Delaware, Nevada, and South Dakota are generally believed to be the best states for allowing DAPTs, but a 2011 case in Alaska involving a bankruptcy may call into question the viability of the DAPT. In *Battley v. Mortensen*, 2011 WL 5025249 (Bankruptcy, D. Alaska, 2011), a trust that was safe from creditors under the state's 4 year look back period was made available to creditors in bankruptcy proceedings. The 2005 amendments to the bankruptcy code allow for a 10-year look back period, which brought the trust into the debtor's estate for bankruptcy purposes. Some experts think this is not the end of DAPTs, but the law is still quite undeveloped on whether certain privileged creditors will be given access to self-settled asset protection trusts.

If your client isn't trying to escape future debts with a DAPT, however, many kinds of irrevocable *inter vivos* trusts, like lifetime gifts, can serve other quite valid purposes. An IIT can have valuable tax benefits by making lifetime gifts of the principal to remainder beneficiaries. So long as the trust is irrevocable, the gift of a future interest is completed and the property will be valued as of the date the trust was established. If the point is to move assets out of one's estate before death, and to retain the right to bene-

---

[19] We discuss spendthrift provisions in more detail in the next Chapter. For now, understand that a spendthrift provision prohibits the attachment of any part of the trust by the creditors of a beneficiary.

[20] For more state-by-state information on DAPTs, see *Actec Comparison of the Domestic Asset Protection Trust Statutes*, updated through December 2011, available at: http://www.actec.org/public/Documents/Studies/Shaftel_DAPT_CHART_12_2011.pdf.

[21] ALASKA STAT. ANN. 34.40.110(d)(1)(A), (2) (West 2012).

fit from or use the property during life, an IIT can help reduce estate tax liability.

There are numerous types of irrevocable self-settled trusts that give the settlor certain lifetime benefits, like *grantor retained annuity trusts* (GRATs), *grantor retained income trusts* (GRITs), and *grantor retained unit trusts* (GRUTs). These types of trusts have lifetime asset protection as one of their benefits, but they are usually aimed more at reducing tax liabilities related to the transfer of the remainder of the trust to beneficiaries than protecting assets from the settlor's creditors. Thus, we will briefly take up those in Chapter 9.

For obvious reasons, there are numerous policy concerns about allowing a property owner to retain the benefit of assets during life, transfer those assets to beneficiaries, and escape liabilities to creditors. The Medicaid trusts and Supplemental Needs Trusts are heavily regulated and exist to deal with the very serious problem of escalating health care costs and the needs of surviving spouses. DAPTs and other asset protection devices that are meant to escape credit card debts or tort judgment creditors don't have corresponding policy benefits to justify their use and support under state trust laws. While the few states that have allowed DAPTs do so to attract trust business to their state, the fall-out of public perceptions of unfairness may ultimately lead to judicial restrictions on their application or legislative changes. The law is extremely unsettled at this time in regards to DAPTs and anyone who uses them should be comfortable with a certain amount of risk.

Fiorello LaGuardia and Milton Freedman can feel vindicated that there is no free lunch, or if there is it's not likely to stay open for long. As you think about powers of attorney, revocable trusts, and some of these limited irrevocable trusts, you will want to be sensitive to the stability of the law in these areas. An estate plan based on a DAPT may be a disaster, and open you up to malpractice, if the laws are struck down or bypassed by judges concerned with protecting taxpayers or sympathetic creditors. As you think about different mechanisms to protect your client's financial autonomy and health at the end of life, be sure you have a full understanding of the variety of options facing seniors as they prepare for their journey into that good night. Planning for what happens to your client's *estate* after death is the topic of the next three chapters.

B. HEALTH CARE PLANNING, ADVANCE DIRECTIVES, AND LIVING WILLS

Besides adequately providing for a client's financial needs, both during life and at death, the estate planning attorney often provides basic health care instruments that enable a surrogate to make health care decisions if the principal is incapacitated, including the right to withdraw life-support and ultimately terminate the client's life. The default rules on who can make health care decisions for an incapacitated patient are often set out in state statutes, usually prioritizing the spouse or guardian of the patient, adult children, parents, siblings, close friends, and then the guardian of the estate if no one else is able or willing to serve.[22] This statutory order may

---

[22] 42 C.F.R. § 483.10(a)(3) (providing that "in the case of a resident adjudged incompetent under the laws of a State by a court of competent jurisdiction, the rights of the resident are exercised by the person appointed under State law to act on the resident's behalf"); See, for example 755 ILL. COMP. STAT. ANN. § 40/25(a) (West 2009); ARK. CODE ANN. § 20–17–214(a)

work fine for patients in traditional families, but can be quite contrary to the wishes of lesbian and gay patients, patients in blended families, and many elderly persons whose family members live far away. Since the Supreme Court's decision in 1990 in *Cruzan v. Director, Mo. Dept. of Health*, 497 U.S. 261, which recognized a constitutional right to make health care decisions, including the right to refuse medical treatment, all states have implemented laws permitting patients to execute a variety of instruments to govern in case they are incapacitated or unable to make their own health care decisions. In addition, since 2000 the federal Health Care Decisions Law (Stats. 1999, ch. 658) gives competent adults sweeping powers to direct their own health care. The two most important instruments are the *Health Care Proxy* and the *Living Will*.

The *Health Care Proxy* (or *Durable Power of Attorney for Health Care*) designates an agent to make health care decisions for a patient whenever the patient cannot make his or her own decisions, including things like the use of artificial feeding tubes or respirators or even blood transfusions, flu shots, or antibiotics. The *Living Will* (or *Advance Directive*) is often a separate instrument stating how aggressively a patient wants to be treated at the end of life, whether to use feeding tubes, ventilators, or other life-prolonging devices or to "pull the plug" if the patient is in a persistent vegetative state. The Living Will might include a direction not to resuscitate a patient (a DNR direction). All of these powers can be combined in a single document that not only expresses the patient's preferences for certain types of treatments, but also designates an agent to make other health care decisions, including the decision to terminate life support.

The nuances of the law on health care decision-making are too complex for a thorough discussion here. There are lengthy federal and state laws, including the Patient Self-Determination Act (104 Stat. 1388), that permit patients to provide advance directives on their health care. In the absence of such directives, costly litigation may ensue. And if you are particularly unlucky, you might get the Governor of Florida, the U.S. House of Representatives, the Florida Supreme Court, and the President involved, as happened in the case of Terri Schiavo. Terri Schiavo suffered extensive brain damage as a result of sudden cardiac arrest and never regained consciousness after her collapse in February, 1990. Because she had no advance medical directives on file, her husband, Michael Schiavo made medical decisions for her, including taking her to San Francisco for experimental nerve treatments. By 1993, however, in consultation with her doctors he had concluded that there was no hope for Terri and he instituted a *Do Not Resuscitate* order in her file. When Michael Schiavo finally requested removal of Terri's feeding tube in 1998 the legal battles began, which lasted for the next 7 years and involved 14 appeals, 5 suits in federal district court, Florida state legislation that was stuck down by the Florida Supreme Court, Congressional legislation, the denial of 4 writs of certiorari by the U.S. Supreme Court, and the involvement of President George W. Bush. By her death, Terri had required constant medical treatment for fifteen years, treatment that cost upwards of $80,000 per year. Her husband had obtained a $750,000 payment in a medical malpractice suit that was placed into a supplemental needs trust, but Medicaid paid most of Ter-

---

(West 2005); DEL. CODE ANN. tit 16 § 2507(b)(2) (West 2004); KY REV. STAT. ANN. § 311.631(1) (West 2004).

ri's medical bills. In 2005 when Michael finally won the right to remove Terri's feeding tube, she died 13 days later.

No family should ever have to go through the trauma experienced by Michael Schiavo and Terri's parents and siblings. Terri's name became a household word as political parties used her tragedy for their own benefit. Despite the media frenzy surrounding Terri's final months, however, and the publicity surrounding the political maneuverings on both sides of the aisle, the majority of Americans do not have either a health care proxy or a living will. And despite the reams of legislation encouraging advance directives, the 2010 Affordable Care Act did not reauthorize that portion of the Patient Determination Act that would reimburse health care providers for counseling patients regarding advance directives because of the furor over political claims about death panels. Regardless of whether your client wants minimal intervention or for superhuman efforts to be used to try to keep her alive, a health care proxy is the best way to achieve that end. It is simply assumed that a parent will make medical decisions for minors, but until recently there has been little attention to the legal issues of having a surrogate make medical decisions for an adult.

The Uniform Law Commission promulgated the Uniform Health Care Decisions Act in 1993, which has been adopted by six states, and which reflects the rules already in place in a majority of states. The relevant part of the Act provides:

---

§ 2. ADVANCE HEALTH-CARE DIRECTIVES.

(a) An adult or emancipated minor may give an individual instruction. The instruction may be oral or written. The instruction may be limited to take effect only if a specified condition arises.

(b) An adult or emancipated minor may execute a power of attorney for health care, which may authorize the agent to make any health-care decision the principal could have made while having capacity. The power must be in writing and signed by the principal. The power remains in effect notwithstanding the principal's later incapacity and may include individual instructions. Unless related to the principal by blood, marriage, or adoption, an agent may not be an owner, operator, or employee of [a residential long-term health-care institution] at which the principal is receiving care.

(c) Unless otherwise specified in a power of attorney for health care, the authority of an agent becomes effective only upon a determination that the principal lacks capacity, and ceases to be effective upon a determination that the principal has recovered capacity.

(d) Unless otherwise specified in a written advance health-care directive, a determination that an individual lacks or has recovered capacity, or that another condition exists that affects an individual instruction or the authority of an agent, must be made by the primary physician.

(e) An agent shall make a health-care decision in accordance with the principal's individual instructions, if any, and other wishes to the extent known to the agent. Otherwise, the agent shall make the decision in accordance with the agent's determination of the principal's best interest. In determining the principal's best interest, the agent shall consider the principal's personal values to the extent known to the agent.

> (f) A health-care decision made by an agent for a principal is effective without judicial approval.
>
> (g) A written advance health-care directive may include the individual's nomination of a guardian of the person.
>
> (h) An advance health-care directive is valid for purposes of this [Act] if it complies with this [Act], regardless of when or where executed or communicated.

There are many questions and issues that arise in the context of health care advance directives. Some advocates would give relatively little weight to advance directives that are executed when the patient is young and healthy, without a firm understanding of the feelings and effects of a debilitating illness.[23] Others worry about overreaching by agents who might benefit from the early termination of a patient's life, or about the nomination of health care providers, like nursing home doctors or administrators, who have a financial stake in prolonging or terminating health care.[24] Access to private medical records, protected by HIPAA, the Health Insurance Portability and Accountability Act of 1996, can be difficult even if an agent has a validly executed health care proxy unless the principal has explicitly given the agent authorization to receive medical information. Of course, without that information, an agent cannot act intelligently and compassionately. Also, states that have not passed advance directive legislation treat living wills as requests, not directives, thus allowing health care providers and agents to ignore a patient's wishes. In such states, advocates for the patient may have to seek judicial intervention to ensure that the patient's stated wishes are carried out. There is always room for an advocate to claim that the particular circumstance in which the patient's directives are being either followed or ignored were not circumstances previously considered by the patient and for which separate evidence should be required.

Consider the following cases involving health care directives and analyze whether or not you think the lawyers could have done more to prevent the litigation that ensued.

Cruzan v. Director, Missouri Dept. of Health

497 U.S. 261 (1990)

After an automobile accident, Nancy Cruzan was in a persistent vegetative state requiring a respirator and a feeding tube. Her parents requested that the life support be withdrawn, in accordance with Nancy's right to refuse medical treatment under state law doctrines of informed consent and Constitutional privacy rights, but the employees of the hospital refused. Nancy's parents sued to force the hospital to withdraw the treatment and the trial court agreed that Nancy would not have wanted to remain kept alive under such circumstances. The only evidence supporting what Nancy would have wanted was testimony of a friend who Nancy allegedly told she would want to be allowed to die if she were ever in such a situation. The Missouri Supreme Court reversed, however, holding that any decision to withdraw life support must be based on clear and convinc-

---

[23] See Ray Madoff, *Autonomy and End-of-Life Decision Making: Reflections of a Lawyer and a Daughter*, 53 BUFF. L. REV. 963 (2005).

[24] See generally 63 AM. JUR. Decisionmaking at the End of Life, 1 § 19 (1997).

ing evidence that the patient would have wanted the life support withdrawn. On appeal to the U.S. Supreme Court, the Missouri requirement of heightened clear and convincing evidence was sustained.

Justice Rehnquist, writing for the majority, explained: *But in the context presented here, a State has more particular interests at stake. The choice between life and death is a deeply personal decision of obvious and overwhelming finality. We believe Missouri may legitimately seek to safeguard the personal element of this choice through the imposition of heightened evidentiary requirements. It cannot be disputed that the Due Process Clause protects an interest in life as well as an interest in refusing life-sustaining medical treatment. Not all incompetent patients will have loved ones available to serve as surrogate decisionmakers. And even where family members are present, "[t]here will, of course, be some unfortunate situations in which family members will not act to protect a patient." A State is entitled to guard against potential abuses in such situations. Similarly, a State is entitled to consider that a judicial proceeding to make a determination regarding an incompetent's wishes may very well not be an adversarial one, with the added guarantee of accurate factfinding that the adversary process brings with it. Finally, we think a State may properly decline to make judgments about the "quality" of life that a particular individual may enjoy, and simply assert an unqualified interest in the preservation of human life to be weighed against the constitutionally protected interests of the individual.*

The court affirmed a patient's liberty interests in being able to decide to reject life-saving medical treatment, but ultimately rejected Nancy Cruzan's parents' claim that in the absence of clear evidence of Nancy's intent, a court should accept the "substituted judgment" of close family members. Conjuring images of death panels and greedy heirs, the Court explained: *No doubt is engendered by anything in this record but that Nancy Cruzan's mother and father are loving and caring parents. If the State were required by the United States Constitution to repose a right of "substituted judgment" with anyone, the Cruzans would surely qualify. But we do not think the Due Process Clause requires the State to repose judgment on these matters with anyone but the patient herself. Close family members may have a strong feeling—a feeling not at all ignoble or unworthy, but not entirely disinterested either—that they do not wish to witness the continuation of the life of a loved one which they regard as hopeless, meaningless, and even degrading. But there is no automatic assurance that the view of close family members will necessarily be the same as the patient's would have been had she been confronted with the prospect of her situation while competent. All of the reasons previously discussed for allowing Missouri to require clear and convincing evidence of the patient's wishes lead us to conclude that the State may choose to defer only to those wishes, rather than confide the decision to close family members.*

Query: After *Cruzan*, a patient cannot rely on the oral statements of family and friends about her intent; she must take her own health care treatment into her own hands and, ideally, put into writing as many details as possible about her wishes. But is that realistic? Should a state be required to adopt the substituted judgment doctrine in order to protect a patient's liberty interest in directing her health care treatment?

Bouvia v. Superior Court

225 Cal. Rptr. 297 (Cal. Ct. App. 1986)

Elizabeth Bouvia was a 28-year-old who suffered from severe cerebral palsy, quadriplegia, and arthritis. She was mentally alert but could only move the fingers of one hand and had some slight facial and head movements. She was otherwise entirely immobilized and in extensive pain. She dictated to her lawyers instructions that she was to be allowed to die, and signed an X with a pen in her mouth. The City of Los Angeles, that operated the health care facility in which she resided, refused to deny her treatment and inserted a feeding tube against her will. She sued to have the treatment stopped and that she be allowed to starve to death, but the state court denied her request, asserting that her actions were tantamount to committing suicide, and the state would not participate in such an act. On appeal, the trial court was reversed, holding that none of the state's four purported policy interests were applicable. The state had asserted four interests: *(1) preserving life, (2) preventing suicide, (3) protecting innocent third parties, and (4) maintaining the ethical standards of the medical profession, including the right of physicians to effectively render necessary and appropriate medical service and to refuse treatment to an uncooperative and disruptive patient.* In denying the state's interests, the court explained: *Here Elizabeth Bouvia's decision to forego medical treatment or life-support through a mechanical means belongs to her. It is not a medical decision for her physicians to make. Neither is it a legal question whose soundness is to be resolved by lawyers or judges. It is not a conditional right subject to approval by ethics committees or courts of law. It is a moral and philosophical decision that, being a competent adult, is her's alone. . . . Moreover, the trial court seriously erred by basing its decision on the "motives" behind Elizabeth Bouvia's decision to exercise her rights. If a right exists, it matters not what "motivates" its exercise. We find nothing in the law to suggest the right to refuse medical treatment may be exercised only if the patient's motives meet someone else's approval. It certainly is not illegal or immoral to prefer a natural, albeit sooner, death than a drugged life attached to a mechanical device.* Justice Compton's concurring opinion noted that the penal code, which punishes anyone who aids and abets a suicide, would be inhumane if applied to health care personnel faced with a patient in extreme suffering who chooses to end her life. He explained: *If there is ever a time when we ought to be able to get the 'government off our backs' it is when we face death—either by choice or otherwise.*

Query: Are we splitting hairs when we recognize a patient's right to refuse medical treatment but won't allow anyone to assist in that refusal under threat of penal sanctions for aiding a suicide? At what point down the slippery slope to incapacity do we tell a patient, "you are now too far incapacitated (physically or mentally) to do what we would let you do on your own. But because you now require assistance in carrying out your desire to refuse medical treatment, we can't recognize your privacy rights"? Are we condoning assisting suicide? If not, is the privacy right meaningful? What else could Elizabeth Bouvia's lawyers have done?

Scheible v. Joseph L. Morse Geriatric Center, Inc.

988 So.2d 1130 (Fla. 4th DCA 2008)

Madeline Neumann, a resident of the Morse Geriatric Center, suffered from senile dementia and a seizure disorder. Upon her admission, Neumann's granddaughter, Linda Scheible, presented the Center with a Living Will and other health care documents, signed by Neumann, stating there was to be no life-prolonging medical treatments or life support if she had a terminal condition or was in the process of dying. Nearly three years after she entered the Center, Neumann was found unresponsive in her bed. Paramedics were called, she was intubated, administered drugs, and taken to the hospital. In the ambulance she tried to remove the tubes and her arms and hands were restrained. She died in the hospital a few days later and her granddaughter, as administrator of Neumann's estate, sued the Center for willful disregard of advance health care directive under chapter 765, Florida Statutes (1995), willful disregard of the federal patient self-determination act, common law intentional battery, violation of the Nursing Home Resident's Rights Act (section 400.022(1), Florida Statutes (1995)) (NHRRA), breach of contract, and negligence. The Center succeeded in getting summary judgment granted as to the health care advance directive count and the violation of the federal patient self-determination act count on the grounds that no private cause of action existed under those statutes. The trial court also granted the Center summary judgment on the violation of the NHRRA claim because the Act allowed a personal representative to bring suit for violation of the Act only if the patient died as a result of the violation. Because Neumann did not die as a result of the violation of her Living Will, the Act was held inapplicable and its violation was deemed irrelevant. In a jury trial on the breach of contract and negligence issues, the granddaughter was awarded damages for the breach of contract claim, but not negligence.

On appeal, Scheible argued that summary judgment was inappropriate for the NHRRA claim, because although the legislation expressly states that a personal administrator may recover only if the resident dies as a result of the violation, reading the statute literally undermines the patient's rights to health care decision making. The Court of Appeals disagreed, however, limiting the granddaughter to her breach of contract claim. The Court stated: *Despite appellant's argument, the holding of this court in Knowles [v. Beverly Ent.-Fla. Inc], and the supreme court's opinion affirming it, is that deprivation of the right to refuse health care cannot constitute a legal cause of death for which a plaintiff may sue. In affirming this court's opinion in Knowles, the supreme court made very clear its agreement that "the plain meaning of the language used in the statute indicates that only personal representatives of the estate of a deceased resident whose death resulted from the deprivation or infringement of the decedent's rights may bring an action for damages under the statutory rights scheme." 898 So.2d at 6 (emphasis in original). As already noted, appellant attempts to fit her claim into the holding of Knowles by characterizing the nursing home's violation of the patient's bill of rights as the supervening cause of a different kind of death than Mrs. Neumann otherwise would have experienced. We hold this characterization to be incorrect.*

Query: Just how viable is a patient's right to refuse medical treatment if there is no private right of action? If you were the nursing home, what would you advise your staff? Abide by the Living Will, allow the patient to die, and risk being sued because you didn't intervene in what, with hindsight, might turn out not to have been a terminal condition, or intervene against the patient's wishes, prolonging life perhaps for a few hours, days, or even years and risk a breach of contract suit? In which suit are the damages likely to be lower? Should Neumann's estate be able to sue for "wrongful life?"

Est. of Maxey v. Darden

124 Nev. 447 (2008)

Avis Maxey, aged 72, ingested over 200 prescription pills in an attempted suicide attempt. At the time, she was living with her ex-husband, Theodore, who discovered her unconscious. He waited several hours before calling Avis's daughter-in-law, explaining that he wanted to honor Avis's desire to kill herself. Paramedics were called, however, and Avis was taken to the emergency room. Theodore told the paramedics that he had "power of attorney" and did not want them to attempt to resuscitate Avis, but the paramedics determined that the suicide attempt cancelled out the power of attorney and they began efforts to resuscitate her. In the emergency room, the doctor intubated Avis, but withdrew the tubes and placed her on oxygen when Theodore filled out hospital forms stating that Avis did not want life-prolonging treatment. Shortly thereafter the oxygen mask was removed and the attending doctor and nurse indicated that it was "per husband's instructions." Because it was determined that Avis would not survive, she was placed on morphine as a palliative measure only. She died a half hour later.

Nevada's Act on the Rights of the Terminally Ill permits the withholding or withdrawing of life-sustaining treatment only on the patient's firsthand declaration (a living will), consent from the patient's designee (designated through a durable health care power of attorney) or consent from the patient's family members (so-called surrogate consent). This case turned on whether Theodore's statements and execution of hospital forms constituted surrogate consent. To be effective, the surrogate consent had to be 1) in writing and attested by two witnesses, 2) the attending physician had to determine that the patient is in a terminal condition, and 3) the patient must not already have an effective declaration concerning life-sustaining treatment. The trial court entered summary judgment in favor of the hospital and attending physicians and Avis' two sons appealed.

The Nevada Supreme Court determined that the emergency room doctor was the attending physician, not the patient's regular physician, at the time emergency medical treatment was being administered. The Court also determined that the attestation requirement of the surrogate consent requires the witnesses have personal knowledge that the surrogate is providing consent to the withdrawal of medical treatment, although the statute does not require the witnesses actually sign the surrogate's consenting document. The court remanded to determine if the nurse, who wrote in Avis's chart that life-support was being withdrawn "per the husband's order," had personal knowledge that Theodore had given consent or had merely written the instruction from the doctor's information. The court also remanded to determine if the emergency room doctor had adequate evidence to conclude that Avis' condition was terminal.

Notably, Avis's sons did not dispute Theodore's rights to act as a surrogate, despite the fact that they were no longer married.

Query: If you were an emergency room doctor, how effective do you think the Nevada legislation is on surrogate consent? Does this decision make it easier or harder to withhold medical treatment? As a lawyer, what do you think should have happened in this case? As a doctor, what do you think should have happened? As Avis's sons, what do you think should have happened?

Knowing that life rarely conforms to expectations, and regardless of how well-written legislation is, situations arise that aren't provided for. What do you think is the best approach to these difficult decisions? Should the law make it easier or harder for surrogates to make these decisions? If the law required a living will in all cases, do you think more people would execute them? And even if more people did execute living wills, do you think outcomes would conform to patient intentions more often? How do we strike the best balance between client/patient autonomy and public policy concerns?

If a patient's husband and children, in consultation with the doctors, decide to withdraw life-prolonging treatment, do you think the doctor should put them on hold to look in the files to see if there is a Living Will? Should the doctor follow it if the instructions in the Living Will differ from the decision being made by the family? If the instructions in the Living Will are to discontinue life-prolonging treatment, should the doctor be liable if she never consulted the Living Will and simply went with the family's instructions? If there isn't time to consult the Living Will and medical personnel have to make medical decisions in a hurry, should they have to stop their work or unplug the patient if, later on, the Living Will is brought to their attention? Can you see why a 1997 study of the Journal of the American Medical Association found a high incidence of doctors failing to follow patient's living wills?[25]

Practice Point: Facing Doctors in the Worst of Times

One of the great advantages in being an estate planning attorney is the opportunity to have a close professional relationship with many of your clients. If the clients trust you enough to discuss their financial affairs, their health care needs, and many of their deepest family secrets (i.e. the adult child with drug addictions; or the existence of an unsupported child born outside of marriage), then don't be surprised if you are the one your clients choose to call at times of their greatest crisis. For some, these will be true legal matters, like a call from jail (by the way, always have a good list of criminal attorneys ready to go); but for others, the call may come from the hospital, particularly in end of life situations.

One of my dear clients called me in the presence of the physicians who had just diagnosed her husband with advanced, invasive brain cancer. She needed reassurance before any treatment began that his health care directions and living will were up to date and able to protect him if needed. On another occasion, a client who had been through the planning process but not yet signed documents fell critically ill and requested that I bring her documents to the hospital for execution. She was in isolation and had only brief moments of lucidity between the administration of pain medication, so the biggest initial hurdle to overcome was finding a medical

---

[25] Nina Garas, M.D. & Steven Z. Pantilat, M.D., *Advance Planning For End-of-Life Care*, http://www.ahrq.gov/clinic/ptsafety/chap49.htm.

team member willing to witness the documents. On other occasions, clients have called me to just sit with them in hospice. Not for legal advice, but for companionship. But once I am there, I always make sure that their living will and heath care documents have been entered into the system. A lawyer has to be a lawyer, afterall.

The benefit of having health care directives in place is, of course, that in the event that they are needed, the client can rely on them. Yet, don't be surprised if you discover that some critical care doctors really just would rather not know about them—they will instead prefer to discuss matters with the family and try to proceed according to *the family's* wishes. This might be seen as a way to avoid malpractice litigation, but we have to remember that this method of communication by family vote (such as, is everyone in agreement that we should take mom off of life support) is precisely what your client has attempted to avoid when executing her living will. We also have to remember that most statutes give clients the choice of end of life options. Most choose the one which allows life support to be discontinued in end of life situations, but others specifically state the opposite—that the client wishes to continue the administration of life support even if he is terminally ill, in the process of dying, and physicians agree that he cannot recover. And, if a client chooses that route, it is his legal right, not the right of family members. And, of course, the opposite is true as well.

One critical care pulmonologist went so far as to tell me that in his experience, the medical community does not read the living will at all, nor the health care directives past the point of determining who is the appointed surrogate. He added cryptically that any other language which a practitioner may add to further protect a client's wishes may serve no real purpose at all. To this, I replied that perhaps the status quo may be at work in many cases, but the documents can certainly be enforced in a court of law, birthing our extraordinary collection of law school case book decisions which each seem to arise from circumstances where the doctors and the lawyers seem to be talking past one another and our clients are caught in the middle. We both agreed, however, that more work needs to be done on the disconnect between the legal rights of clients and their understanding and effectiveness within the medical community.

As part of the planning process, therefore, you will have the opportunity to discuss not only the legal implications of your clients' plans, but also the practical ones. We can now use technology to our benefit and easily create digital versions of the health care documents that they can carry with them to the hospital. If they haven't done so already, it is also a good idea for them to discuss their wishes with their family members, so that they can start to identify potential problems ahead of time. Remember, though, that no matter how secure your plan seems to be, you will likely be receiving some late night calls from your clients in crisis. So, keep your files close and be ready to start making some calls of your own.

It is certainly true that I can choose to forego invasive radiation therapy or chemotherapy when suffering from terminal cancer. I can then go home, the cancer can progress, and I will die from it. If the right to refuse medical treatment allows me to make decisions that, in the long run, will hasten my death, is it any different to request a nurse unplug my respirator or feeding tube when doing so will certainly end my life within a week? These questions, of course, are best left to philosophy and bio-ethics courses or specialized courses on health care law. The lesson for the estate planner, however, is that even if, as a society, we cannot seem to settle on whether the decisions are the patient's, the doctor's, the lawyer's, the family's, or the politician's to make, as lawyers we can do our best to maximize our client's likelihood of being able to control not only their own lives, but their own deaths. If Terri Schiavo or Nancy Cruzan had had a living will, it is certain their deaths would have been attended with less turmoil and pain for the living. They certainly would have required less, if any, litigation. But their actual deaths would have changed very little. What is the ultimate goal? How do we balance the interests of the survivors with the needs of the dying?

C. Funeral Directives and Disposition of the Body at Death

Although most of us, both as clients and as lawyers, are accustomed to the traditional language in most wills directing disposition of the decedent's body, that it be cremated, or a funeral conducted with only close family members for example, the law does not give the decedent power to control the disposition of her body. The body is not property of either the decedent or the decedent's legal heirs, and therefore directions regarding the body are ineffective at law. Where a countervailing public interest exists, as when the decedent is a victim of a violent crime and an autopsy is necessary, the decedent's wishes and the family's wishes are irrelevant. However, in the vast majority of situations, the state has no particular interest in how a body is disposed of or whether ashes are strewn over the ocean or off the Statute of Liberty so long as all applicable health and safety laws are complied with. Thus, for most people, those funeral directions will be complied with, even if they are only precatory. Afterall, now that grandma is dead, people tend to be more likely to do what she wants.

But if everyone's ashes were thrown off the top of the Empire State Building, or over the Grand Canyon, there also would be health issues related to the accumulation of too much ash. On the other hand, if only a few people per year are seeking to dispose of grandpa's ashes at the top of Mt. Ranier, and the state has authorized the cremation, then family members are free to follow the decedent's wishes, or not. If no one in the family wants to brave the heights of Mt. Ranier, grandpa's ashes may be laid to rest in a local mausoleum, left on his daughter's mantel, or buried in the back yard.

Notwithstanding the fact that there are no private property rights in the body, every state has laws on the books regulating the proper treatment of dead bodies and providing for tort relief against funeral homes, medical facilities, or intermediaries for mishandling the body of a loved one. Damages for emotional distress can be assessed against hospitals that remove a decedent's organs without obtaining proper consent. You may recall the horrors of the Tri-State Crematory in Northwest Georgia where more than a hundred corpses were found piled up, dumped in sheds, or sealed in vaults, which is not supposed to happen in our modern regulatory world. Although the state doesn't display the heads of executed criminals on pikes or bury their bodies in crossroads, state regulation and normalized cultures of embalming and respectful treatment of the body are not always effective in preventing the mishandling of human remains. No matter how well we plan for our own death, we can't always control fraud, incompetency, or neglect of our wishes.

1. FUNERAL INSTRUCTIONS

The most common planning issues occur in the context of funeral instructions and organ donations. In the absence of a delegation of authority to make burial decisions by the decedent, a decedent's spouse has the legal right to determine where and how the body will be disposed of. That can mean controversy, as when Rosemary Perez brought suit to prevent her daughter's soon-to-be ex-husband from burying her in Florida rather than in Illinois with the rest of her family, or when Andy Meadows found out his father was being exhumed and moved at the behest of his second wife, Gretchen Meadows.[26] There are already plenty of opportunities for conflict between second spouses and children of a first spouse without adding disputes about disposition of dad's body. Thus, if a client has specific wishes regarding disposition, those wishes should be made known to all.

Because the instructions in the will won't be validated until the will is proved, and the will won't be validated until filed with a court, a client who has firm notions of how she wants her body disposed of, or a client with family members who are likely to disagree, can execute an *Authorization for Disposition of Remains*, nominating a survivor to have the final say on how the body will be disposed of. So long as the method of disposition complies with state law and there are no supervening public policies against the method, the Authorization should control.

Although the Authorization cannot insist that one's body be disposed of in violation of state law, it can authorize an individual to make final decisions, and adjustments, if the preferred method of disposition is illegal or impracticable. It is also a nice way to provide instructions for everyone about what kind of service (if any) the client wants, whether to be cremated or embalmed, whether she wants her remains to reside in a mausoleum, a grave, or be spread out to sea. Gary Coleman, feeling abandoned by true friends, left this instruction in one of his wills. His will provided that only "those who have no financial ties to me and who can look each other in the eyes and say they really cared personally for Gary Coleman" were permitted to attend the funeral.[27] He also directed that no members of the press were to be present at his wake or funeral. As you can imagine, such a provision is unenforceable. How would one know if the attendees really cared personally for Coleman? And what would happen if a member of the press snuck into the memorial? Would Coleman's estate have a cause of action for trespass? No. These kinds of instructions serve only to influence the survivors' memories of the deceased.

Many people have religious beliefs involving the disposition of their bodies, including prohibitions against autopsies and cremation. Unfortunately, even with an Authorization, the decedent cannot prohibit an autopsy if the state demands one, and the person given the Authorization may be forced to choose cremation because of pressing unexpected circumstances. Where permitted, an Authorization is a good idea. If not, it makes sense to leave instructions in a will, with the understanding, however, that the directions are merely precatory. One would hope that survivors would honor and respect the instructions of a decedent, whether in a will or in

---

[26] Justin Sacharoff, *Quarrels Over Where Loved Ones are Buried Brings Attention to Burial Rights in Florida*, Florida Times Union, Mar. 17, 2011.

[27] Ken Lee, *Gary Coleman Leaves Bittersweet Instructions for Funeral*, PEOPLE MAGAZINE (June 6, 2010), available at: http://www.people.com/people/article/0,,20392290,00.html.

pre-arranged agreements with a funeral home. Although none of these are legally binding, there is always one way to try to head off the family spat when people can't agree on burying Grandpa in the family cemetery in West Virginia or spreading his ashes off Mt. Ranier. Grandpa can leave instructions in his will, or preferably in a separate document, and then condition all gifts made in his will to not contesting or interfering with the disposition instructions. I might strongly feel that grandpa should not be laid to rest in West Virginia, but if I am going to lose a large bequest by insisting that we take his remains to Mt. Ranier, I am likely to hold my tongue.

Consider the following will of Ingrid Newkirk, the director of PETA, the animal rights advocacy group.

DIRECTIONS FOR THE DISPOSITION OF THE REMAINS OF INGRID NEWKIRK[28]

As someone who has dedicated a part of my life to the alleviation of animal suffering in various parts of the world, it is my wish that upon my death, my body be used to further that same goal. It is with this purpose in mind that I make the following directions and designations relating to the disposition of my final remains. I make these directions and designations after thorough consideration and pursuant to my firm belief in the purposes for which they are made.

1. Upon my death, it is my wish that my body be used in a manner that draws attention to needless animal suffering and exploitation. To accomplish this, I direct that my body be donated to People for the Ethical Treatment of Animals (PETA), 501 Front Street, Norfolk, Virginia 23510, to be used in whatever manner it chooses in order to accomplish the specified purpose, with the hope that most of my body will be put to use in the United States, with parts also dispatched to awaken the public consciousness of governments and citizens in the United Kingdom, where I was born, in India, my beloved childhood home, and in Canada, Germany, and France.

2. While the final decision as to the use of my body remains with PETA, I make the following suggested directions:

a. That the "meat" of my body, or a portion thereof, be used for a human barbecue, to remind the world that the meat of a corpse is all flesh, regardless of whether it comes from a human being or another animal, and that flesh foods are not needed;

b. That my skin, or a portion thereof, be removed and made into leather products, such as purses, to remind the world that human skin and the skin of other animals is the same and that neither is "fabric" nor needed, and that some skin be tacked up outside the Indian Leather Fair each year to serve as a reminder of the government's need to abate the suffering of Indian bullocks who, after a life of extreme and involuntary servitude, as I have seen firsthand, are exported all over the world in this form;

c. That in remembrance of the elephant-foot umbrella stands and tiger rugs I saw, as a child, offered for sale by merchants at Connaught Place in Delhi, my feet be removed and umbrella stands or other ornamentation be made from them, as a

---

[28] Available at http://www.peta.org/features/ingrid–newkirks–unique–will.aspx. Reproduced courtesy of Ingrid Newkirk, PETA, www.peta.org.

reminder of the depravity of killing innocent animals, such as elephants, in order that we might use their body parts for household items and decorations;

d. That one of my eyes be removed, mounted, and delivered to the administrator of the U.S. Environmental Protection Agency as a reminder that PETA will continue to be watching the agency until it stops poisoning and torturing animals in useless and cruel experiments; that the other is to be used as PETA sees fit;

e. That my pointing finger be delivered to Kenneth Feld, owner of Ringling Bros. and Barnum & Bailey Circus, or to a circus museum to stand as the "Greatest Accusation on Earth" on behalf of the countless elephants, lions, tigers, bears, and other animals who have been kidnapped from their families and removed from their homelands in India, Thailand, Africa, and South America and deprived of all that is natural and pleasant to them, abused, and forced into involuntary servitude for the sake of cheap entertainment;

f. That my liver be vacuum-packed and shipped, in whole or in part, to France, to there be used in a public appeal to persuade shoppers not to support the vile practice of force-feeding geese and ducks for foie gras;

g. That one of my ears be removed, mounted, and sent to the Canadian Parliament to assist them in hearing, for the first time perhaps, the screams of the seals, bears, raccoons, foxes, and minks bludgeoned, trapped, and sometimes skinned alive for their pelts; that the other ear be removed, preserved, and displayed outside the Deonar abattoir in Mumbai to remind all who do business there that the screams of the cattle who are slaughtered within its walls are heard around the world;

h. That one of my thumbs be removed, mounted upwards on a plaque, and sent to the person or institution that, in the year of my death or thereabouts, PETA decides has done the most to promote alternatives to the use and abuse of animals in any area of their exploitation;

i. That one of my thumbs be mounted in a downward position and sent to the person or institution that, in the year of my death or thereabouts, has gone against the changing tide of societal opinion and frightened and hurt animals in some egregious manner;

j. That a little part of my heart be buried near the racetrack at Hockenheim, preferably near the Ferrari pits, where Michael Shumacher raced in and won the German Grand Prix;

k. That anything else be done with my body that PETA believes will serve to draw attention to and so abate the plight of exploited animals.

3. As a resident of Virginia, and pursuant to Virginia law, including § 54.1–2825 of the Virginia Code, I designate PETA as the "person" who shall make arrangements for carrying out the directions contained in this document for the disposition of my remains upon my death. If, at any time, PETA is unable or unwilling to carry out these directions, I designate, in the alternative, Daniel Mathews as the individual who shall make arrangements for carrying out the directions contained in this document for the disposition of my remains upon my death. If Daniel Mathews is unable or unwilling to carry out these directions as required, I authorize either of the two listed "persons" in this paragraph to designate a third party to make arrangements for carrying out the directions contained in this document for the disposition of my remains upon my death.

4. While I prefer that my directions be first executed in the United States, I also direct that parts of my body be transported to the United Kingdom, of which I also am a citizen, and to India, my beloved spiritual home, to be executed there. If my directions cannot be executed in any of these countries, I authorize the transport of my remains to any location where my disposition directions, in whole or in part, may be lawfully executed.

5. I authorize the person carrying out these directions to deviate from them in any manner he or she deems appropriate to further the purpose expressed herein. If any provision or provisions of this document shall be held to be invalid, illegal, unenforceable, or in conflict with the law of any jurisdiction, the validity, legality, and enforceability of the remaining provisions shall not in any way be affected or impaired thereby.

Are any of these provisions likely to be enforceable?

PROBLEMS

Assume that you are the lawyer for Ingrid Newkirk and she has personally charged you with trying to effectuate as many of these provisions as possible. What would you do?

Assume that you are the lawyer for People for the Ethical Treatment of Animals (PETA) and you want to make sure that Newkirk's will is widely promulgated and discussed in order to bring public awareness to the plight of animals. What would you do?

Assume you are the lawyer for members of Newkirk's family who strongly oppose this will and want to hush it up as quickly as possible. What would you do?

Assume you are the attorney general for the state in which Newkirk is domiciled at her death and her executor files this will for probate. What would you do?

What do you do with the client who has unorthodox views about funerals, disposition of remains, or other aspects of death and dying? Consider the following practice point.

Practice Point: The Client with the Unusual Beliefs

As mentioned earlier, you may very likely find yourself facing the client who wants her skull dried and bleached for mounting on the hood of her boyfriend's car. If he plays in a heavy metal band it might not seem so weird. But how do you convince your client that putting such an instruction in a will can actually open the will up to challenges on the basis of mental capacity? Clients with very strong religious, moral, ethical or merely whimsical beliefs about the disposition of their body can put their entire estate plan into jeopardy if they insist on having things done their way.

What would you recommend to your client if he came to you wishing to put the following epitaph on his father's gravestone?

Donald Robertson born, 14th January 1785,
died 4th June 1848, aged 63 years.
He was a peaceable, quiet man and to all appearance a sincere Christian.

His death was much regretted which was caused by
the stupidity of Laurence Tulloch in Clothister (Sullom)
who sold him nitre instead of Epsom salts by which
he was killed in the space of 5 hours after taking a dose of it.[29]

Would you risk a libel suit, even if you could follow it with a wrongful death action?

2. ORGAN DONATION

The need for donated organs in this country is tremendous. But there is no mandatory program that requires decedents or family members to allow organs to be harvested to save the lives of others. In 1968, the Uniform Anatomical Gift Act was promulgated to permit individuals to designate that a gift *can be* made of any or all of their salvageable organs. The donative authorization either had to be in a will, signed and witnessed (by now you should see the problem with that), or in a separate card, signed and witnessed by 2 persons. It's bad enough getting people to follow the will formalities for wills; do you think they are going to do so for organ donation? The Act was revised in 1987 to abolish the witness requirements and allow for a single card, signed by the decedent, either carried separately or attached to the back of a driver's license. Despite the Act, only about 30% of persons dying have organ donation instructions.[30]

Even with the simplicity of making organ donations, the extreme shortage has led to numerous calls to switch the presumption in favor of organ donation, by requiring a signed card or other instrument if someone wishes to *opt out*. But policymakers in this country have hesitated at such a dramatic change in the current law, even though countries that have adopted the presumption, like most European countries, have very few people opt out. See Cass R. Sunstein & Richard H. Thaler, *Libertarian Paternalism is Not an Oxymoron*, 70 U. CHI. L. REV. 1159, 1192 (2003). It is believed that over 85% of Americans favor organ donation, but few follow through and sign organ donor cards. And when pressure is put on family members by hospitals and doctors, it's usually too late to get a thoughtful, unemotional response. When family members are facing the death of a loved one, they are usually too caught up in their own grief to think rationally about organ donation.

Technology Trend: Cryopreservation and Human Cloning

It's not just in *Star Trek* and *Harry Potter* that we can imagine running a wand over someone's broken body and rebuilding muscle and bone tissue. With the advancements of modern medicine, and recent laws on human cloning in many states, the possibility of building a new body in a laboratory to replace a failing one is not that far off. Although bills have been introduced to prohibit human cloning in Congress, it is only a matter of time before the technology forces Congress to take a decisive stand, though how long that stand will last is anyone's guess. We may even see federal funding of research on human cloning within our own lifetimes. If not, a laboratory will be built in the Grand Caymans or Switzerland where people with enough money can do almost anything they wish with their bodies. Shouldn't I be

---

[29] Found on a gravestone in the Cross Kirk graveyard, in Eshaness, Shetland.

[30] See organdonor.gov/about/data.html, noting that only 100 million people in the U.S. are signed up to be a donor.

able to donate my body to a laboratory with the express understanding that it will be used to try to replicate me? Approximately 250 people are currently kept in a state of cryopreservation, and a new facility is being built in Australia to tend to the wishes of the wealthy in the southern hemisphere.

Both human cloning and cryopreservation may be a century off, but think for a few minutes about the succession law implications of both. I certainly would want to retain my estate in a trust if my body were being preserved for future thawing. Would that mean the trust would never end because there is always the possibility that I would be revived? But what if I accidentally thawed, as happened with nine bodies preserved by the Cryonics Society of California? Then the trust would become impossible. Would beneficiaries be unable to take a share of the trust so long as the settlor was still frozen, even if scientific evidence suggested that successful reanimation was virtually impossible given the physiological damage of being preserved in liquid nitrogen? And what would happen with the rule against perpetuities if I could simply clone myself every time I reached age 50? The term *lives in being* would take on a new meaning.

D. CONCLUSION

The first step in planning for retirement and incapacity is to get your client to face the fact that she will die at some point. Most of us just can't be bothered—we are so busy raising children, working, or even enjoying our retirement to write a health care power of attorney or sit down and draft a comprehensive estate plan. We are healthy and enjoying life. Getting our clients to face the fact that eventually they won't be healthy and probably won't be enjoying life is difficult. And once they aren't healthy and are facing death, they often won't feel like going through the bother of locating their insurance policies, confirming their beneficiary designations, and thinking about setting up a trust. Illness usually makes us grumpy.

I would be willing to bet that most of your professors don't have a will, much less your fellow students. Most people begin to think about wills only after the kids are grown, they are facing retirement, a parent or loved one dies, or perhaps when they have their first health scare. But if you have learned anything, it is that few of us can plan our deaths, and we have very little control over whether we will be incapacitated for years, or will drop dead at 103 after running that marathon. The key, however, is to be prepared for almost anything. More importantly, being prepared means modifying your client's estate plan as her situation changes. The plan a working client with minor children might need is quite different from one she will need as a widow in her final years facing a nursing home and possible Medicaid assistance. One of the most important things you give a client is the peace-of-mind in knowing that her plan is in place in case something happens to her.

If your client is like most people, however, she is not going to call you to revisit her estate plan every time something changes in her life. Many clients think they'll forego that $500 lawyer fee needed to revise their wills just before they take that trip to the South Pole. They will simply hope nothing goes wrong as they fly over the Amazon rain forest where a plane could disappear and never be found. And most likely, nothing will go wrong. But you can have an open door policy that encourages your client to make revisions as her life situations change. Consider how your own billing practice can influence a client's likeliness of making timely revisions and updates to her estate plan. If you bill a flat fee that covers periodic updates and modifications, your client is far more likely to call and ask you to include a new grandchild or write a joint tenancy deed when her situation changes. If the client needs more comprehensive changes, then a new fee can be charged. But something as simple as your billing practice can dramatically affect the smooth succession of a client's estate.

CHAPTER 7

PROTECTING THE LIVING

Most clients, when asked who they want to have benefit most from their estate plans, say they want to benefit their spouses and minor children, people they know and with whom they have a relationship. Only after taking care of their own needs and those of their spouses and dependent children, do they think about adult children, grand-children, more remote relatives, or a favored cause. Many of the complex trusts designed to spread wealth across broad groups aren't of interest to many people of modest wealth who have simple goals; they just don't want their property to be eaten up by their own end-of-life care or administration costs, potentially leaving their spouses penniless. It may be argued that people would stop working to accumulate property if they could not pass it on to their loved ones. And average people tend to feel that their first and foremost obligation is to their close family members. After accumulating this property, most people are risk averse and therefore don't give away all their property during their lifetimes in case they need it later. In the same vein, most also want to leave property still owned at death to their close family members and will use a variety of mechanisms to maximize these gifts.

As discussed in Chapters 2 and 3, the law provides a number of protections for spouses and dependent children in the form of homestead, family allowance, exempt property, and intestate priorities. In the context of testate estates, the most important protection/limitation is the *elective* (or *forced*) spousal share. All but one common law state allows a surviving spouse to renounce what is given to her under a will, and instead take a statutorily-defined amount of property from a deceased spouse's estate. Elective share laws mean that although a testator may devise all of his property outside his immediate family, his spouse may void a portion of those devises and take the property for herself.

What you will realize quickly in practice is that this restraint on testamentary freedom is often irrelevant in happy marriages, or in marriages of long duration, because most spouses usually want to leave most or all of their estates to their life-time partners, especially if the partner helped earn the property, raise the children, or helped contribute to a happy life together. More complex are second or third marriages, especially those of short duration and those with children by earlier marriages, where the elective share often becomes a thorn in everyone's side. Unhappy marriages, where the spouses don't want to get a divorce (probably thinking that they'll lose even more property under equitable distribution rules at divorce) or where they are hoping to outlive each other, require very careful estate planning around the elective share statutes. Some testators have been known to physically move just to settle in a state that has stingy elective share provisions so they can cut their spouses out of as much property as possible

In some states, the elective share is as large as 50% of a decedent spouse's estate,[1] in others it is as low as 25%,[2] in Georgia the spouse re-

---

[1] COLO. REV. STAT. ANN. § 15–11–201(1) (West 1994); 755 ILL. COMP. STAT. § 5/2–8(a) (West 1976); MINN. STAT. ANN. § 524.2–202(a) (West 1994).

ceives only a year's worth of income,[3] and in Rhode Island the spouse receives a life estate in all real estate owned in fee simple by the decedent at death but no personal property.[4] Thus you can see how state law becomes relevant to settling the elective share awarded in the estate.

Usually, because of gender norms, differential earning capacities, and life-expectancies, the battles will be between the children and the stepmother. The elective share is the most significant limitation on testamentary freedom embedded in our probate laws, and it is strictly tied to marriage. Consequently, many couples choose not to marry in order to avoid elective share rights, and same-sex couples that do not have the choice to marry do not have the protections against disinheritance that underlie these laws. Many same-sex partners would like to have the option of an elective share, and opposite-sex unmarried partners sometimes even claim elective share rights under common-law marriage doctrines. Notably, those states that have domestic partnership or civil unions have not been entirely uniform in granting elective share rights to couples whose unions don't meet the strict legal definition of marriage, even though the partners function as married persons. Thus, simply finding out if your client is married will not always resolve elective share issues.

The community property states do not have elective share statutes *per se*, because all marital property is held as community property, which entails undivided co-ownership in equal shares. Yet some community property states provide for an elective share in separate marital property that was brought into the state and would have been community property had it been acquired in the community property state.[5] Thus, the couple that moves from Illinois to Idaho in their retirement years, bringing large amounts of investments and personal property acquired during their marriage, will find that the property still titled individually is considered *quasi-community property* and will be subject to the surviving spouse's elective share. Not all of the community property states have elective share provisions for quasi-community property, however, so the same surviving spouse may receive very little if the couple moved to Arizona instead of Idaho.

One big caveat to an elective share, however, is that the surviving spouse may not elect against a will if the decedent devised to the survivor property of value equal to or greater than that to which the survivor would be entitled under the elective share statute. Therefore, providing adequately for a surviving spouse, as with life insurance, can prevent an election that could otherwise result in a spouse taking a portion of property intended to go to others. Moreover, a spouse who is devised very little does not have to elect a larger share if she does not want or need the property. Many spouses choose not to elect at all. Surviving spouses may disclaim property devised to them and may also waive their elective share rights through a pre-nuptial or post-nuptial contract. Nonetheless, we will discuss how guardians of surviving spouses may be required by law to elect, even when doing so could upset an estate plan that both spouses agreed upon. Also, although a surviving spouse may not be entitled to pick and choose the property he wants to take from a decedent spouse's estate, the spouse is

---

[2] OR. REV. STAT. ANN. § 114.105(1) (West 2011).

[3] GA. CODE ANN. § 53–3–1 (West 1996).

[4] R.I. Gen. Laws Ann. § 33–25–2(a) (West 1978).

[5] These states are California, Idaho, New Mexico, and Wisconsin. The others do not (Arizona, Louisiana, Nevada, Texas, and Washington).

entitled to a share, perhaps as much as 50% of the *value* of the estate. This means that the decedent is simply unable to exercise testamentary control over that portion of her estate. But the testator is not entirely hamstrung. Just because the survivor wants the yacht doesn't mean he gets it if the decedent gave the yacht to someone else. However, if the decedent instructed his administrator to liquidate his estate and give cash to all of his bene-beneficiaries, each bequest will abate ratably to pay the elective share.

In Louisiana, a dependent or minor child is also entitled to a mandatory share of a deceased parent's estate and a testator is prohibited from devising such property away to others.[6] Forced heirship is the law in most countries, leading to messy choice of law problems for people who own property abroad. Most states also have *pretermission* statutes that allow spouses and/or children to take a share of an estate if they were excluded from a will because the decedent executed the will before the marriage or before the birth or adoption of the child. This ability to take a share of a decedent's estate reflects, in a majority of cases, the presumed wishes and expectations of most testators and, therefore, is not generally seen as a burdensome infringement on testamentary freedom. On the other hand, a well-crafted estate plan can go very wrong if a survivor's elective or pre-termitted share is not adequately provided for in the plan.

In this chapter we begin with the statutory rights of spouses: elective share, community property rights, pretermission. Then we discuss trusts and powers that have particular mechanisms to benefit surviving spouses. We also discuss prenuptial agreements—contracts by which one spouse waives rights to a share of his spouse's estate. Prenuptial contracts can waive rights to homestead, exempt property, family allowance, intestate shares and elective shares. Then we turn to children, and their rights, including guardianships and custodianships, pretermission rights, and trusts for minors and dependents with special needs.

In earlier chapters, we discussed some of these concepts in more general terms. Let's delve in deeper so that you can get a better feel for how they can work together in practice to protect the living.

A. SPOUSAL PROTECTIONS: THE ELECTIVE SHARE

One could probably write an entire treatise on the elective share, including subtle differences among states and different countries, as well as the choice of law problems that arise when property is located in different states. What property is available to satisfy a spouse's elective share is also a hugely important subject. Even the simple question of whether a devise in trust for a surviving spouse can be elected against has no easy answer. Part of the problem is that there are two somewhat conflicting theories behind the elective share (I bet that is surprising news to you!).

The first theory is the *support* theory, and it originated in the common law obligation of a husband to support his wife. The gender aspect was eventually eliminated under equal protection doctrines, but the elective share still remains based in the obligation to support one's surviving spouse both before and after one's death. Trusts that provide lifetime in-

---

[6]   See LA. CIV. CODE ANN. art. 1495 (1996), setting the *Legitime* at one-half if there are two or more children, or one-quarter if there is only one child. The French Civil Code of 1804 set fixed shares for descendants in order to prevent the reinstitution of primogeniture that was associated with aristocracy.

come to a surviving spouse are generally sufficient to satisfy elective share obligations in states that base their statutes on the duty of support.

The second theory is the *partnership* theory, which treats an elective share as property the survivor is entitled to by virtue of his or her contribution to the joint accumulation of wealth that was possible because of the mutual collaboration, or partnership, of the parties. Trusts that provide lifetime income generally are not sufficient to satisfy an elective share in states that have adopted the partnership theory of marital wealth. Most states initially adopted elective share statutes with the support idea in mind, and only recently have some of them moved, some more and some less, toward the partnership theory.

To understand the elective share, one must realize that it, like all laws, are dynamic. This means that it is constantly evolving, from its early origins in dower and curtesy under the law of coverture, then changing as it passed through periods of recession and economic hardship where creditor's rights against family property were curtailed, then changing once again under the influence of the feminist revolution and the rise in married women's own employment and property control, then now responding to the effects of the probate revolution and the rise of perpetual trusts. Views on the surviving spouse's rights run the gamut from the indisputable right of the survivor to property he helped amass, to creating an impediment to complex wealth management and the asset building possibilities of dynasty trusts. Elective shares are important, and they must be understood well in order to best manage a client's estate.

1. HISTORY OF THE ELECTIVE SHARE: DOWER AND CURTESY

For centuries, and across the globe, complex laws have existed for the governance of marital property; namely, how is the property that comes into a marriage managed, who has best title to property earned or acquired during the marriage, and how is the property allocated at death to reflect the fact that two separate individuals worked together to acquire it? In some countries, property the wife brought to the marriage remains linked to her family, and property the husband brought to the marriage remains linked to his family, so that if the spouses die without issue, their property passes back to their collateral relatives. Of course, if they have issue, the property then becomes commingled in character as it passes to the children but, upon the children's marriages, property they acquire from their parents now becomes identified with its maternal or paternal origins. So a couple's property that passes to a son may be commingled in the sense that the aunts and uncles have lost their claim on it, but upon the son's marriage, that property is linked to his family (including his brothers and sisters) in case he dies without issue. In such a case, the property would not pass to his wife's family but would pass to the son's collateral heirs. We have certainly retained some aspects of the identity of property with consanguineous relations in the collateral heir provisions of intestacy.[7] Although we don't parse out the property based on its prior origins, in many states people who die without a spouse, issue, parents, or siblings, have their property pass half to their collateral relatives on their grandmother's side and half to those on their grandfather's side, in recognition of

---

[7] You saw this argument being made in Matter of Brewington's Estate, 173 Mont. 458, 568 P.2d 133 (Mont. 1977) back in Chapter 2.

kinship claims upon property that may have come from grandparents or aunts and uncles.

In many East Asian countries, like India, Pakistan, and others, the property fathers give as dowry upon the marriage of their daughters is commingled into the family of the groom's father, and is not owned by the groom himself. If the groom dies without issue, the family has to give back the dowry. Understandably, the reluctance to do so led India to pass laws restricting the rights of widows to remarry, because remarriage meant the widows could take the property that was given by their family upon their marriage out of their first husband's family. This relegated many young girls to a life of celibate widowhood trapped in the homes of their deceased husband's brothers.

In England, which is the source of marital property laws in all the common law states, coverture gave husbands near total control over property a wife brought to marriage or earned during marriage, in exchange for the wife's absolute right to be supported. The law of coverture provided that, upon marriage, all of a woman's personal property would be deemed to be owned entirely by her husband for the duration of the marriage, and all real property would be controlled and managed by him during his life. If she died before him and a child had been born, he continued to own all her personal property as well as all personal property acquired during the marriage and he was entitled to a life estate in all real property she brought to the marriage. If he died before she did, she received a life estate in all personal property owned by her husband at death (which included personal property she had owned outright before her marriage) and a life estate in one-third of all real property her husband had owned at any time during his life.

William Blackstone explained coverture by reference to the unity of person doctrine that underlay the religious view of marriage as a sacrament. "By marriage, the husband and wife are one person in law: that is, the very being or legal existence of the woman is suspended during the marriage, or at least is incorporated and consolidated into that of the husband: under whose wing, protection, and cover, she performs everything; and is therefore called in our law–french a *feme–covert*; is said to be *covert–baron*, or under the protection and influence of her husband, her baron, or lord; and her condition during her marriage is called her *coverture*."[8] The law of coverture was quite unusual in the pre-Modern world for cutting off the wife's family's claims to property and giving the husband virtually unlimited control over property owned by his wife before marriage. During the heyday of coverture, it was transferred to the various colonies England claimed and controlled, including the American colonies.

By contrast, the marital property laws of Spain and France allowed wives to retain ownership of property brought to their marriages, and for community ownership and management of property acquired during the marriage. Widows' rights were therefore greater in the Civil Law countries, and Louisiana and the western states that derived their marital laws from French and Spanish codes recognized a wife's separate property during the term of her marriage as well as her rights to half of all property earned during the marriage.

The effects of coverture in the United Kingdom and the common law portions of the United States were so harsh that William Blackstone could

---

[8]   William Blackstone, Commentaries on the Law of England, Bk I, Ch. 15.

rationalize the marital property law of coverture only by reference to the wife's absolute right (in law if not in practice) to support by her husband during their marriage. The wife could pledge his credit for necessaries and could, though it was rarely done, seek protection of marital property through the equity courts if he squandered the family's wealth. She could sue him for support if he neglected to provide for her, though the level of support ordered by courts often did not correspond to her status in life. Most importantly, she could not control, manage, or dispose of any property she brought to the marriage or property acquired during the marriage unless it was carefully held in a separate trust for her benefit, controlled by male trustees. Because wives could not own property, make a will, or sue in their own names, they simply could not legally exercise control over property that was once theirs, property given to them by their family, or property they helped to earn. Even their wages were deemed the property of their husbands. In exchange for giving up all property rights, wives received the right to support during their husband's life and at his death.

Dower was the widow's primary form of support after her husband died, and it consisted of a life estate in one-third of real property owned by a husband at any time during the marriage and a life estate in all of the personal property owned at her husband's death. This meant that the widow could live on the property in which she had dower rights (the proverbial *dower house*) if there were multiple properties, or she was entitled to one-third of the income produced from all real property owned by her husband during marriage. If the husband owned no real property, there was little a widow could receive. But if the husband did own real property, the widow's dower right was a significant cloud on his ability to alienate the property during his lifetime.[9]

In response to the constraints dower placed on their ability sell and buy land, many husbands asked their wives, at marriage, to waive their dower rights in exchange for a guaranteed annuity or a life interest in a particular piece of land through the use of what was called a *strict settlement*.[10] Though we don't use strict settlements today, a prenuptial agreement serves much the same purpose. The parties agree to forego their statutory shares as surviving spouses in exchange for some known quantity of property. They replace the risk of not knowing whether they will die penniless, with the assurances of a settled income; but at the same time they give up the possibility of added income if their husbands are successful and acquire more wealth during their lifetimes. Security now in exchange for possibly greater income later is a trade-off that many spouses are asked to take when they sign a prenuptial contract.

Because dower truly did hamper the alienation of land, landowners came up with numerous devices to defeat dower, including the medieval use (the forerunner of the trust), the strict settlement, or a collusive lawsuit called a *fine and recovery*.[11] In the absence of one of these techniques, a

---

[9] Dower has the same root as the verb endow, which of course is used in marriage ceremonies when referring to endowing a spouse with one's worldly possessions. It is entirely gender-based in origin, meaning a gift from the groom to the bride.

[10] For an excellent analysis of how the strict settlement further eroded wives' property rights, see Eileen Spring, Law, Land and Family: Aristocratic Inheritance in England, 1300–1800 (Chapel Hill: UNC Press, 1993).

[11] After passage of the 1833 Fines and Recoveries Act, husbands were able by deed or by will to cut off their wives from dower. But most elite families in England had been using strict settlements for centuries, which had entailed the cutting off of dower rights far earlier than 1833.

husband seeking to sell his property had to get his wife's signature releasing her dower interest. Many deeds to real property used well into the twentieth century in the United States include a wife's release of her dower interest, even after dower was legally abolished in many states. Ohio still retains dower and both spouses must therefore sign a deed to transfer any real property acquired during the marriage by either spouse, regardless of whose name was on the deed. Dower rights attach as a lien on the real property of all married individuals.

Dower must be distinguished from *Curtesy*, which was the husband's right to a life estate in all of his deceased wife's real property. Remember, he already owned all of the personal property she brought to the marriage as well as all personal property acquired during the marriage. Curtesy therefore gave him a life estate in *all* of his wife's real property as well (real property that was settled on her or which she owned in her own name prior to her marriage). Curtesy only arose, however, if a child was born of the marriage, even if the child did not survive. A husband was called a *tenant in curtesy* when he was in possession of his wife's real property after her death. A husband, too, could relinquish his curtesy rights at the time of marriage, though that was rarely done, since he had the job, nominally at least, of managing all the property.

In the United States, both dower and curtesy were common rights recognized in the laws of all states after the revolution. Dower was the interest that most hampered the alienation of land because husbands, who had full management and control over all real property of the couple, might alienate their land without getting wives to release dower and the latter could sue the grantees for recovery. Husbands who sold their wives' land, however, gave up their curtesy interests automatically when they transferred the property. Thus, because of the gender disparities in the manner in which property was held and managed during life, and because of the fundamental differences between dower and curtesy, dower was essentially a form of support for a surviving widow while curtesy was simply the continued control after death that a husband had had over his wife's property during her life. It was dower, not curtesy, that hampered the alienation of estates and, therefore, its avoidance was the target of estate planners.

Where challenged, many states ruled that differential treatment of dower and curtesy rights for husbands and wives violate either state or federal equal protection guarantees. Then, in 1974, in *Kahn v. Shevin*, 416 U.S. 351, the Supreme Court upheld a Florida law giving widows a property tax exemption denied to widowers. The Court held that the social and economic barriers to widows' job opportunities and quality of life justified differential treatment. It is unlikely the Court today would rule the same way. Since then all states have adopted equal treatment for widows and widowers in inheritance rights, even if, as in Ohio, they still call it dower.

Dower and curtesy were abolished in most states during the twentieth century to be replaced by a gender-neutral elective share in a portion of the property the decedent spouse owned at death. Even when still called dower, the right more closely resembles the modern elective share rather than the pre-modern dower of England. As the differential laws were crumbling, every state had the option of giving husbands the equivalent of dower (a 1/3d interest for life) or giving wives the equivalent of curtesy (control over the decedent's entire property). Not surprisingly, they all chose the dower model. Thus, 40 states have enacted statutes giving a surviving spouse (regardless of gender) an interest in a decedent spouse's estate, now called an *elective* share or a *forced* share because the spouse can *elect* to reject what the decedent left her in his will, or because she can *force* a share that will be given to her.

As the twentieth century came to a close, however, following profound shifts in married women's employment and the feminist revolution, some states rejected the support basis of the elective share, and amended their laws to give the surviving spouse an outright ownership share based on that spouse's contribution to the acquisition of the decedent spouse's wealth. Although none give the entire estate to the survivor if the decedent made a will, changes in intestacy laws giving the surviving spouse 100% of the intestate estate, and limitations on the use of trusts to satisfy the elective share, marked a recognition that the surviving spouse had more than a support claim on the decedent's estate. Thus, rather than assume that a decedent is supposed merely to support his surviving spouse, these revised elective share statutes grant the survivor a share of the decedent's estate because she helped earn it. Using this partnership theory of marriage, which was the hallmark of the 1969 UPC, states have tried to move closer to the values of community property states that recognize a spouse's absolute right to control half of all property acquired at any time during the marriage. Wisconsin has gone so far down the road of the partnership theory that it adopted the Uniform Marital Property Act which treats marital property essentially like community property. Wisconsin has no elective share statute because half of all marital property is owned by the surviving spouse. Other states, however, have resisted the equalizing trend of the elective share and Georgia only gives a surviving spouse merely a year's income off the decedent's estate, presumably enough to get out of mourning, find a job, or get remarried.

PROBLEMS

7.1. Clyde and Helga marry in 2007. In 2009, Helga surprises Clyde by purchasing a waterfront home in fee simple, into which they happily settle. In 2011, after the birth of their twins, the couple decides to move to a bigger home. Helga is surprised to learn that Clyde's signature is required before she can sell the waterfront home, which is titled in her name alone. Explain why this is the case.

7.2. Let's step back in time for a moment. Franklin is a tenant in curtesy, as his wife, Angelica, died just hours after giving birth to their only child, Franklin Jr., who also only lived a few hours. At the time of Angelica's death, they lived on a family farm that was given to Angelica by her now deceased father years before her marriage. Is Franklin entitled to the home? Can he sell it?

2.   THE MODERN ELECTIVE SHARE

The elective share statutes of the 40[12] common law states generally fall into 1 of 3 different types, laid over with a variety of rules that are either based on the support theory or the partnership theory, resulting in roughly six different types of regimes. The three types differ based on the amount of property that is included in the decedent's estate for elective share purposes. Then the two variables (support-based or partnership-based) generally affect the kinds of property rights a decedent can give to a

---

[12]   This omits Georgia, which gives a surviving spouse merely 1 year's support.

surviving spouse that will prevent an election. So let's begin with the first variable—the property that makes up the elective estate.

All states originally gave a surviving spouse an elective share in a portion of the decedent's *net probate estate*—that is, the property the decedent owned at death. However with the probate revolution and the rise of will substitutes, many states amended their elective share statutes to allow the surviving spouse to take a share of property the decedent had placed in numerous non-probate forms (revocable trusts, joint tenancies, retirement accounts, and the like), as well as property in her net probate estate. Catching all of this probate and non-probate property into what is called the *augmented estate* was the brainchild of the drafters of the 1969 UPC. The Uniform Law Commissioners had found that many spouses were being intentionally and sometimes unintentionally disinherited through the use of these probate-avoidance mechanisms when decedent spouses really may not have intended to disinherit their spouses, or intended to but should not be allowed to get away with it. If the only property against which a spouse could take an elective share was the net probate estate, a decedent spouse could put everything into a revocable trust and avoid the elective share altogether. The augmented estate fixed that problem, although there continues to be disputes over whether life insurance payable to others should be included in the elective estate with life insurance companies lobbying strongly against inclusion. They don't want to pay out on a claim to a beneficiary, only to be sued by the surviving spouse claiming a percentage of the life insurance payment.

The UPC also adopted the partnership theory by giving a surviving spouse half of all property outright in the decedent's elective estate. Moreover, the UPC took into account the wealth of the surviving spouse. Thus, if a surviving spouse owned the lion's share of the couple's wealth, it made no sense for that spouse to also retain an elective share in the less wealthy deceased spouse's estate. To account for disparities in individual wealth, the UPC combined the augmented estates of BOTH the deceased and the surviving spouse, and then credited back a portion of the surviving spouse's property. The complex calculation resulted in an elective share of $0 if the surviving spouse had more property in her augmented estate than her deceased spouse. To elaborate—under the partnership theory it is assumed that roughly half of the husband's property titled in his name equitably belongs to the wife and half of the wife's property titled in her name equitably belongs to the husband. If the wife dies first and the husband takes his half out of her estate he should also have to contribute half of his property to her. The UPC therefore offsets the husband's elective share against the wife's share of his property to try to replicate a community property distribution.

In 1991, the Uniform Law Commission amended the UPC once again to deal with the common phenomenon of the second marriage by two persons previously married, who each had wealth in their own name. The augmented estate didn't recognize that a surviving spouse of a very short marriage had not contributed as much to the couple's accumulated wealth as the spouse of a longer marriage. Using an accrual method, the UPC adopted a graduated scale of elective share percentages so that for a short marriage of a single year the surviving spouse would be entitled to only 3% of the deceased spouse's estate while a surviving spouse of a 15-year marriage would be entitled to 50%.

Because the UPC had two complex calculations (the inclusion and crediting back of the surviving spouse's wealth and the graduated percentage based on length of marriage), many states backed away and simply adopted a straightforward augmented estate that gives surviving spouses a flat percentage (usually less than half) of the deceased spouse's augmented estate. They tackled the non-probate property problem but left the wealth disparity and length of marriage problems. This model may be simpler, though not as simple as the net probate estate method. In addition, it can be quite inflexible and lead to unfair results. Consequently, an estate planner needs to think about how to arrange the plan to address these other issues under a simple augmented estate regime. The UPC's complex calculations better reflect expectations, but they require keeping track of a large amount of property.

The current UPC, adopting what we will refer to as the *graduated-super-augmented estate*, is a comprehensive elective share regime that takes into account the surviving spouse's wealth (to prevent a wealthier spouse from taking a share of a less wealthy spouse's estate), the length of marriage (to gradually ratchet up the percentage share a surviving spouse would take based on length of marriage), and the growing use of non-probate and lifetime transfers.

And because the graduated-super-augmented estate wasn't complicated enough, the Uniform Law Commission then amended the 1991 UPC to better reflect its commitment to the partnership theory of marriage in 2008. Fortunately the amendments actually have virtually no effect on the outcome of an elective share calculation. So you don't need to know Calculus, although Algebra doesn't hurt. To get a sense of the elective share, let's look at some examples of all three models, from the simplest to the most complex:

- The Net Probate Estate;
- The Augmented Estate; and
- The Graduated Super Augmented Estate.

a.   *The Net Probate Estate*

Under this model, a surviving spouse is entitled to a percentage of the decedent spouse's net probate estate. Now remember, the net probate estate consists of all property titled in the decedent spouse's name at death, usually after funeral expenses, administrative expenses, homestead, exempt property, family allowance, and debts have been taken out. A typical example of this is the Illinois Code, which provides:

---

755 ILCS § 5/2–8. Renunciation of will by spouse.

(a) If a will is renounced by the testator's surviving spouse, whether or not the will contains any provision for the benefit of the surviving spouse, the surviving spouse is entitled to the following share of the testator's estate after payment of all just claims: 1/3 of the entire estate if the testator leaves a descendant or 1/2 of the entire estate if the testator leaves no descendant. . . .

The District of Columbia has added domestic partners to its election provision and spells out the typical process for renouncing provisions made in a will.

D.C. Ord. § 19–113. Renunciation of devises and bequests; election; time limitations; renunciation or election by guardian or fiduciary; maximum rights; effect of no devise or bequest or if nothing passes under either; antenuptial or postnuptial agreements.

(a) Subject to section 19–114, a surviving spouse or surviving domestic partner is, by a devise or bequest specified in section 19–112, barred on any statutory rights or interest he has in the real and personal estate of the deceased spouse or deceased domestic partner unless, within 6 months after the will of the deceased spouse or deceased domestic partner is admitted to probate, he files in the Probate Court a written renunciation to the following effect: "I, A B, surviving spouse or surviving domestic partner of ___ late of ___, deceased, renounce and quit all claim to any devise or bequest made to me by the last will of my spouse or domestic partner exhibited and proved according to law; and *I elect to take in lieu thereof my legal share of the real and personal estate of my deceased spouse or deceased domestic partner.*

. . .

(d) Where a decedent has not made a devise or bequest to the spouse or domestic partner, or nothing passes by a purported devise or bequest, the surviving spouse or surviving domestic partner is entitled to his legal share of the real and personal estate of the deceased spouse or deceased domestic partner without filing a written renunciation.

(e) The legal share of a surviving spouse or surviving domestic partner under subsection (a) or (d) of this section is such share or interest in the real or personal property of the deceased spouse or deceased domestic partner as he would have taken if the deceased spouse or deceased domestic partner had died intestate, **not to exceed one-half of the net estate bequeathed and devised by the will**.

(f) A valid antenuptial or postnuptial agreement entered into by the spouses or domestic partners determines the rights of the surviving spouse or the surviving domestic partner in the real and personal estate of the deceased spouse or deceased domestic partner and the administration thereof, but a spouse or domestic partner may accept the benefits of a devise or bequest made to him by the deceased spouse or deceased domestic partner.

As you can see, section (e) provides that the elective share is equal to a surviving spouse's intestate share, "which is not to exceed one-half of the net estate bequeathed and devised by the will."

Mississippi, apparently not eager to make comprehensive amendments to its gender-specific election statute, enacted a rather interesting update to treat surviving husbands the same as surviving wives. The legislature merely added the last sentence.

Miss. Code § 91–5–25. Right of spouse to renounce will; form ofrenunciation; right to intestate share.

When a husband makes his last will and testament and does not make satisfactory provision therein for his wife, she may, at any time within ninety (90) days after the probate of the will, file in the office where probated a renunciation to the following effect, viz.: "I, A B, the widow of C D, hereby renounce the provision made for me by the will of my deceased husband, and elect to take in lieu thereof my legal share of his estate." Thereupon she shall be entitled to such part of his estate, real and personal, as she would have been entitled to if he had died intestate, except that, even if the husband left no child nor descendant of such, the widow, upon renouncing, shall be entitled to only one-half (1/2) of the real and personal estate of her deceased husband. The husband may renounce the will of his deceased wife under the same circumstances, in the same time and manner, and with the same effect upon his right to share in her estate as herein provided for the widow.

Roughly 17 states, plus the District of Columbia, have elective share statutes that are based primarily on the right to take against the net probate estate. A few states, like Indiana, Kentucky, South Carolina, and Vermont, include some non-probate trust property or other property if it was put in that form by a desire to avoid the spousal share. Indiana also takes into account the number of children to modify the percentage the surviving spouse takes, as well as whether the marriage is a second or subsequent one.[13] And some states, like Michigan, Missouri, and Oregon, factor into the elective share calculation property that passes to the surviving spouse outside probate, to reduce the elective share against the estate.

There are also a few unique states, like Georgia, that gives the surviving spouse only a year's worth of support[14] and Rhode Island, that gives the surviving spouse only a life estate in all real estate owned in fee simple by the decedent at death and no interest in personal property.[15] The usual percentage is between half and one-third, and a few states vary the percentage depending on length of marriage or number of children. Oregon only gives one-quarter, and some states do as they do with intestacy, which is to give the surviving spouse the first $25,000 or $50,000 of the decedent's estate, and then a percentage above that.[16]

As you study the different types of elective share statutes, consider the two primary motivations behind them—support for the surviving spouse and recognition and compensation for the spouse's contribution to the couple's wealth. A mere life estate, like that provided for under Rhode Island law, is clearly premised on the theory of support. On the same basis, some states permit a decedent spouse to provide for his surviving spouse through a life interest in a trust of property whose value is equal to the elective share amount. Such provisions allow the decedent to ultimately control the final disposition of all of his property, rather than having one-third or one-half ultimately pass according to the surviving spouse's estate plan, perhaps to non-relatives. Moreover, providing for a spouse by giving him a life estate in property up to the value of the elective share will prevent the spouse from making an election and upsetting the rest of the decedent's estate plan. Other states allow a trust to satisfy the elective share only if it is valued at the amount of the elective share. Thus, if a surviving spouse is entitled to an elective share of $100,000, some states allow the decedent spouse to establish a trust giving the surviving spouse a life income in

---

[13] IND. CODE ANN. § 29–1–3–1 (West 1982).

[14] GA. CODE ANN. § 53–3–1 (West 1996).

[15] R.I. Gen. Laws Ann. § 33–25–2(a) (West 1978).

[16] MASS. GEN. LAWS ANN. ch. 191, § 15 (West 1956); N.Y. Right of election by surviving spouse § 5–1.1–A(a)(2) (McKinney 2011); S.D. CODIFIED LAWS § 29A–2–202(a) & (b) (1995).

$100,000,[17] others require the value of the life estate itself to be at least $100,000,[18] and others have a different calculation.[19]

One common way that some states dealt with the problem of property passing through the survivor's estate, especially to non-family members, was to revoke dower and elective share rights if the survivor remarried. Decedents often revoke a surviving spouse's shares in trusts or other property if the survivor remarries. Commentators have explored the very gendered origins of the support theory of marriage and have noted that revocation upon remarriage is far more often placed on gifts to surviving wives than surviving husbands, despite the fact that surviving husbands are more likely to remarry than surviving wives.[20]

The partnership theory of marriage, that would mandate the survivor receive an absolute, outright share of a portion of the marital property, avoids the gendered aspect of the support provisions, but also has its own complications. Where the wealthier spouse is the survivor, it makes little sense to allow that spouse to also take a share of the decedent spouse's estate, especially when the marriage was short-lived and the survivor's contributions had little to do with acquisition of the decedent's wealth.

To the extent a single statutory scheme cannot satisfy all the competing social values behind the elective share, it makes sense to at least build some flexibility into the plan. Unfortunately, the states that adopted the augmented estate model without accounting for length of marriage or the surviving spouse's wealth went a bit too far the other way when trying to account only for the explosion in non-probate transfers that characterized the last half of the twentieth century.

b.   *The Augmented Estate*

In 1969, the Uniform Law Commission developed a proposed model elective share statute that would take into account all property that passed outside probate as a result of death. Thus, where a decedent spouse held property in a joint tenancy with right of survivorship, the surviving spouse had been unable to include that property in the elective estate under the net probate estate model because only property the testator actually owned at death was available. The 1969 UPC, therefore, allowed a surviving spouse to take an elective share in a decedent spouse's net probate estate, as well as most property passing by will substitute. The combined estate, or elective estate, was called the *augmented estate*. In the decades after 1969, a majority of the common law states adopted some version of the UPC rule.

Delaware, Florida, New York, New Jersey, North Carolina, Pennsylvania, Tennessee, and Virginia still retain an elective share provision that relies heavily on the 1969 UPC's augmented estate but fail to account for

---

[17] For instance, North Carolina bases the value of the trust on mortuary and annuity tables, with very conservative values attributed to the trust for the spouse. See N.C. GEN. STAT. ANN. §§ 8–46 and 8–47 (West 1997).

[18] Rhode Island gives a life estate in one-third of real property owned by the decedent at death. See R.I. Gen. Laws Ann. § 33–25–2(a) (West 1978).

[19] For instance, Florida and New Jersey allow a decedent to place 60% or 66%, respectively, (twice the elective share percentage) of his estate in a trust with the income only to his spouse to satisfy the elective share requirement. Thus, either 30% outright or 60% in trust is the rule of thumb in Florida. See FLA. STAT. ANN. § 732.2095(2)(a) & (b) (West 2001); N.J. STAT. ANN. § 3B:8–17 (West 2006).

[20] See Pennell, Jeffrey N., *The Joseph Trachtman Lecture—Estate Planning For The Next Generation(s) Of Clients: It's Not your Father's Buick Anymore,* 34 ACTEC J. 2, 8–9 (2008).

the surviving spouse's own wealth. By giving all spouses, regardless of individual wealth or length of marriage, a sizable percentage of the deceased spouse's augmented estate, these laws are quite inflexible and in many respects counter to most notions of fairness and equity. For illustration's sake, and because it has such a unique homestead law, the Florida statute is a good example. Florida allows a surviving spouse to elect to take 30% of a decedent spouse's *elective* estate, which comprises the following property:

Fla. Stat. § 732.2035—Property entering into elective estate

Except as provided in § 732.2045, the elective estate consists of the sum of the values as determined under § 732.2055 of the following property interests:

(1) The decedent's probate estate.

(2) The decedent's ownership interest in accounts or securities registered in "Pay On Death," "Transfer On Death," "In Trust For," or coownership with right of survivorship form. . . .

(3) The decedent's fractional interest in property . . . held by the decedent in joint tenancy with right of survivorship or in tenancy by the entirety. . . .

(4) That portion of property . . . transferred by the decedent to the extent that at the time of the decedent's death the transfer was revocable by the decedent alone or in conjunction with any other person. . . .

(5)(a) That portion of property . . . transferred by the decedent to the extent that at the time of the decedent's death:

1.   The decedent possessed the right to, or in fact enjoyed the possession or use of, the income or principal of the property; or

2.   The principal of the property could, in the discretion of any person other than the spouse of the decedent, be distributed or appointed to or for the benefit of the decedent.

(b) . . .

(c) . . .[21]

(6) The decedent's beneficial interest in the net cash surrender value immediately before death of any policy of insurance on the decedent's life.

(7) The value of amounts payable to or for the benefit of any person by reason of surviving the decedent under any public or private pension, retirement, or deferred compensation plan, or any similar arrangement, other than benefits payable under the federal Railroad Retirement Act or the federal Social Security System. . . .

---

[21] This subsection does not apply to any property if the decedent's only interests in the property are that:

1. The property could be distributed to or for the benefit of the decedent only with the consent of all persons having a beneficial interest in the property; or

2. The income or principal of the property could be distributed to or for the benefit of the decedent only through the exercise or in default of an exercise of a general power of appointment held by any person other than the decedent; or

3. The income or principal of the property is or could be distributed in satisfaction of the decedent's obligation of support; or

4. The decedent had a contingent right to receive principal, other than at the discretion of any person, which contingency was beyond the control of the decedent and which had not in fact occurred at the decedent's death.

(8) Property that was transferred during the 1-year period preceding the decedent's death as a result of a transfer by the decedent if the transfer was either of the following types:

(a) Any property transferred as a result of the termination of a right or interest in, or power over, property that would have been included in the elective estate under subsection (4) or subsection (5) if the right, interest, or power had not terminated until the decedent's death.

(b) Any transfer of property to the extent not otherwise included in the elective estate, made to or for the benefit of any person, except: [Exceptions omitted]

(9) Property transferred in satisfaction of the elective share.

Fla. Stat. § 732.2065—Amount of the elective share.

The elective share is an amount equal to 30 percent of the elective estate.

The point of the augmented estate was to capture, as fully as possible, all property over which the decedent spouse had dominion and control shortly before her death and make a portion of that property available to the surviving spouse. The augmented estate even includes certain lifetime gifts made in the one or two years preceding the testator's death. The principle behind the augmented estate was to protect the surviving spouse's interest in property that the decedent spouse had placed in revocable trusts, joint tenancies, or other forms designed to avoid probate, but not necessarily done with the motive of avoiding the elective share. Thus, some spouses may have placed 90% of their wealth in will substitute forms, leaving only 10% to pass by will or intestacy, and under the net probate estate statutes the surviving spouse was only entitled to a fractional share of that remaining 10%. Under the augmented estate, all of the decedent spouse's wealth could be included and the surviving spouse would take his proportionate share. These augmented estate regimes make it very difficult to avoid the elective share, for valid or invalid reasons.

This complex Florida statute is based in large part on the UPC's augmented estate which, unfortunately, tries to capture all the property that would be included in the decedent's gross estate for federal estate tax purposes, using Revenue Code definitions and not state property law definitions. I say unfortunately because two things have happened. Many states, when adopting the UPC provision, tinkered with specific details regarding certain property. For instance, Florida doesn't attribute the full value of life insurance proceeds into the elective estate; rather, it attributes only the cash surrender value. So one has to be very careful to parse the state's elective share statute to see what property is included, what is excluded, and where the elective estate may differ from the gross estate for federal estate tax purposes.

Second, the internal revenue code changes on a fairly regular basis. So spelling out the property in great detail in the probate code means that the state legislature must either amend the statute every time the tax code changes, or accountants have to make two complex calculations to determine the elective estate and the gross estate for tax purposes.

Delaware wisely defined its elective estate as the decedent's gross estate for federal estate tax purposes, regardless of whether an estate tax return must be filed.[22] By tying the elective share to the federal tax code, the probate code can be much simpler, and probate attorneys don't have to worry whether the elective share statute includes or excludes some form of property that is included in the decedent's gross estate as defined by the Internal Revenue Code.

PROBLEM

7.3. To illustrate the kinds of calculations necessary to determine an elective share, let's take a relatively simple estate and calculate the elective share under both the net probate model and the augmented estate model. Consider the following situation if Harry, the decedent husband, has the following property at death. Remember that the net probate estate is calculated *after* funeral expenses, debts, homestead, exempt property, and family allowance have been paid.

Net Probate Estate which Harry devises by will to his children	$100,000
Property Harry put in a Revocable Trust payable to his children	$500,000
Term Life insurance Harry bought, payable to his spouse, Wilma	$300,000
Farm Harry bought entirely but held in a joint tenancy with right of survivorship with his brother	$200,000
Property from Harry's mother's estate over which he has a general testamentary power of appointment and which he appoints to his children	$300,000
Retirement Account with POD designation benefitting his children	$600,000
Total wealth at death	$2,000,000

Under a net probate estate regime like that of Mississippi, Wilma would be entitled to one-half of the net probate estate—$50,000. She would also receive the life insurance of $300,000, for a total entitlement of $350,000. The property in the revocable trust, the joint tenancy, the power of appointment over his mother's estate, and his retirement accounts would all pass to the designated beneficiaries. Wilma would therefore receive, at most, 17.5% of her husband's total estate.

If Harry had made the life insurance payable to his children as well, Wilma would receive only $50,000, or 2.5% of Harry's estate! On the other hand, if Wilma was the beneficiary on the revocable trust, the life insurance, the joint tenancy, and the retirement account, she would take $1,600,000 outside probate and still be entitled to elect against the will for an additional $50,000 from the property that Harry had devised to his children, for a total of $1,650,000, or 82.5% of Harry's total estate.

As you can see, widespread use of will substitutes to avoid probate could intentionally, or unintentionally, disinherit a surviving spouse, or it could result in

---

[22] DEL. CODE ANN., tit. 12, § 902 (West 2007).

the spouse taking a disproportionate share if the testator used his net probate estate to provide for others. The augmented estate solved that problem.

7.4. Now let's look at the elective estate under an augmented estate regime. With the property identified above, Wilma would be entitled, under Florida's elective share law for example, to property amounting to 30% of the total augmented estate. The augmented estate would consist of three categories of property:

1.   Harry's Net Probate Estate (NPE)

2.   Harry's non-probate transfers to others (NPTO)

3.   Harry's non-probate transfers to his surviving spouse (NPTSS)

In our example, Harry's NPE consists of $100,000. His NPTO consist of the revocable trust ($500,000), the joint tenancy property ($200,000), his mother's property ($300,000), and his retirement account ($600,000), for a total of $1,600.000. Harry's NPTSS consist only of the life insurance ($300,000). However, in Florida, term life insurance policies payable to anyone are not included in calculating the elective share. Only the cash-surrender value of whole life policies are included.[23] Thus, the $300,000 life insurance policy would not be included in calculating Wilma's elective share. Harry's augmented estate, therefore, is $1,700,000 and Wilma's elective share is 30% of that, or $510,000.

Once we know the amount of the elective share, we next need to determine whether or not Wilma can elect against Harry's estate. She can elect only if she is not given at least $510,000 through either probate or non-probate transfers. If Harry has not adequately provided for Wilma, there can be potential abatement problems (as we discussed in Chapter 5). With this larger pool of property comprising the elective estate, there needs to be some priority for deciding which property will be used to pay the elective share and, possibly, which will-substitute gifts will be voided, if the spouse has not been adequately provided for. The Florida statute (in greatly simplified form) provides:

Fla. Stat. § 732.2075—Sources from which elective share payable; abatement.—

(1) Unless otherwise provided in the decedent's will or, in the absence of a provision in the decedent's will, in a trust referred to in the decedent's will, the following are applied first to satisfy the elective share:

(a) Property interests included in the elective estate that pass or have passed to or for the benefit of the surviving spouse, . . .

(b) To the extent paid to or for the benefit of the surviving spouse, amounts payable under any plan or arrangement described in s. 732.2035(7). [pension or retirement benefits.]

(c) To the extent paid to or for the benefit of the surviving spouse, the decedent's one-half of any property described in s. 732.2045(1)(f). [decedent's half of community property.]

(d) To the extent paid to or for the benefit of the surviving spouse, the proceeds of any term or other policy of insurance on the decedent's life if, at the time of decedent's death, the policy was owned by any person other than the surviving spouse.

---

[23]   FLA. STAT. ANN. § 732.2035(6) (West 2007).

(e) Property held for the benefit of the surviving spouse in a qualifying special needs trust.

(f) Property interests that would have satisfied the elective share under any preceding paragraph of this subsection but were disclaimed.

(2) If, after the application of subsection (1), the elective share is not fully satisfied, the unsatisfied balance shall be allocated entirely to one class of direct recipients of the remaining elective estate and apportioned among those recipients, and if the elective share amount is not fully satisfied, to the next class of direct recipients, in the following order of priority, until the elective share amount is satisfied:

(a) Class 1.—The decedent's probate estate and revocable trusts.

(b) Class 2.—Recipients of property interests, other than protected charitable interests, included in the elective estate under s. 732.2035(2), (3), or (6) and, to the extent the decedent had at the time of death the power to designate the recipient of the property, property interests, other than protected charitable interests, included under s. 732.2035(5) and (7).

(c) Class 3.—Recipients of all other property interests, other than protected charitable interests, included in the elective estate.

. . .

(5) The contribution required of the decedent's probate estate and revocable trusts may be made in cash or in kind. . . .

With this very complex code provision to guide us, we start with the property already passing to Wilma outside probate (the NPTSS). In Florida, term life insurance purchased by the decedent and payable to the surviving spouse is included in calculating the spouse's actual share.[24] So the first thing we credit against the elective share of $510,000 is the $300,000 life insurance. This leaves $210,000 remaining that Wilma is entitled to out of Harry's estate.

Fla.Stat. § 732.2075(2)(a) tells us to look next to the Class 1 property, the net probate estate and property in a revocable trust, to satisfy the elective share. Harry has $100,000 in his NPE and $500,000 in his revocable trust. Thus, Wilma is entitled to take $210,000 out of this combined $600,000, pro rata. She will get 35% of his NPE (35,000) and 35% of the property in his revocable trust ($175,000). If Harry's NPE and revocable trust did not have sufficient property to satisfy the remainder of Wilma's elective share, we would abate the Class 2 property next. Note that the $300,000 from Harry's mother's estate is not included in the NPE even though he disposed of it in his will; rather, it is Class 2 property. The donee of a power of appointment does not own the property over which he has the power.

Looking carefully at the statute, you can tell that certain property is more protected from the elective share than other property. Hence, as an estate planner you would need to make sure that you apportion the testator's estate to rationally allocate the expenses of the elective share. Using Harry's estate as

---

[24]   FLA. STAT. ANN. § 732.2075(1)(d) (West 2009).

an example under the Florida statute, the property to be used to pay the elective share is deducted in the following order:

1. Life Insurance—NPTSS

2. NPE and the revocable trust (class 1 property)

3. Retirement account, joint tenancy property, cash surrender value of life insurance, and property over which the decedent has a general power of appointment (class 2 property)

4. All other property, other than protected charitable interests, included in the elective estate (class 3 property)

Harry has no class 3 property in this example, and it is unlikely that a decedent will hold more than 70% of his estate in class 3 property. But if he does, then the surviving spouse would be entitled to invade that category of property to make up the remainder of her elective share.

In a state like Florida that does not include term life insurance policies in calculating the elective estate, but does use it for calculating the NPTSS, we can see that life insurance can easily protect an estate plan from any ademption for the elective share. If Harry had had a life insurance policy payable to Wilma for $500,000, she would have been able to claim only $10,000 more from Harry's NPE and revocable trust, leaving the rest of his estate plan intact.

7.5. Now work out Wilma's elective share using the elective share statute of your state, and if the state uses the augmented estate determine the order in which the property abates to pay Wilma's share.

7.6. Let's change the facts a bit just to see what would happen to the elective share calculation under the augmented estate model. What if Harry's mother had given him only a *special* power of appointment to appoint the property among his lineal descendants, so now that portion of his devised property would not be part of the elective estate?[25]

And what if, instead, the farm held in joint tenancy with Harry's brother was the family home held as tenancy by the entirety? In that case we would add half of the value of the joint tenancy property ($100,000) to the elective estate. Remember, Wilma already owns half, so we are talking only about Harry's half. The elective estate would consist of Harry's NPE ($100,000), his NPTO (trust—$500,000, retirement account—$600,000), and his NPTSS (tenancy by the entirety property—$100,000, life insurance—$300,000). Assuming Harry held only a special power of appointment over his mother's property, the elective estate would be $1,300,000 and Wilma's elective share would be 30% or $390,000. With the life insurance and the tenancy by the entirety property, Wilma is already receiving $400,000 (her NPTSS), which is greater than her statutory entitlement, and she would therefore not be able to elect against Harry's estate.

You should immediately be thinking about potential problems and potential solutions. What if most of the property was held in joint tenancy with right of survivorship and the surviving spouse is entitled to void some of that property? It's one thing to take money out of the revocable trust, but quite another to override the joint tenancy deed. What if most of Harry's wealth was in a private retirement plan with a POD designation? Would the state's elective share stat-

---

[25] Remember that special powers give the donee the ability to appoint property to limited objects, but not to the donee herself, her estate, her creditors, or creditors of her estate.

ute override the beneficiary designation, or would it be preempted under ERISA? If pre-empted, then the elective share must come from other sources, meaning that they will pay more than their fair share. In a state that has adopted a relatively inflexible augmented estate, an estate planner must be extremely careful to make sure that the spouse's elective share does not upset the overall estate plan, by voiding property transfers that could cause all sorts of tax or administration nightmares. Even Harry's mother should be thinking about the elective share when she gives Harry the power of appointment because property over which the donee has a general power is usually included in the elective estate.

Of course, a surviving spouse is not entitled to take an elective share if the decedent spouse provides adequately for the survivor. Thus, in a net probate estate regime, so long as the testator devises the relevant percentage of his probate property to his surviving spouse, she cannot elect against the will and the testator can pass all sorts of property outside probate free of the spouse's claims.[26] Similarly, in an augmented estate regime, so long as a decedent provides adequate life insurance, tenancy by the entirety, or POD designations for a sufficient amount of property, a surviving spouse may not elect against the estate.

It is important to note, however, that in an augmented estate regime, a decedent spouse has virtually no wiggle room to lessen the impact of the elective share, regardless of whether the surviving spouse has more wealth than the decedent and regardless of whether the marriage was of very short or very long duration. The survivor is entitled to a minimum of a fixed percentage of the decedent spouse's total wealth, and the only way to maintain any flexibility in the estate plan is to make significant provisions for the surviving spouse. The moral: LIFE INSURANCE! By purchasing adequate amounts of life insurance payable to the surviving spouse, the decedent is then free to have the rest of his wealth pass by any of the probate or probate-avoidance mechanisms to anyone he chooses, including his children by a prior marriage, his mistress, his favorite charity, or his future lineal descendants.

A Side Note on the Elective Share

The elective share is a very complex and controversial issue. Especially today when women have supposedly equal job opportunities and may control equal or greater shares of wealth, many people feel that spouses should not be able to elect against a decedent spouse's estate. In cases where the surviving spouse is elderly, may even be in a nursing home or under a guardianship, and has a very short life expectancy, guardians are generally required by law to elect against a deceased spouse's estate. This is true even though the surviving spouse may not directly benefit from the additional property to which she is entitled. But failing to elect may disqualify the survivor for government benefits.[27] There are many circum-

---

[26] One must be careful not to use non-probate mechanisms to defraud the spouse of an elective share. Most states will void non-probate transfers if they were solely motivated with the desire to deny a spouse an elective share.

[27] And although electing may disqualify the surviving spouse from government benefits as well, once the estate is consumed, the government benefits can resume, whereas failure to elect may disqualify the surviving spouse permanently.

stances in which a surviving spouse may choose to disclaim property devised to her, or may choose not to elect against her deceased spouse's will, but the mandatory obligation of guardians or trustees to elect may in fact go against both spouse's estate plans.

Some even think the elective share is unconstitutional because it takes property from one individual and gives it to another.[28] On that reasoning however, under a partnership theory of marriage state laws that still adhere to a title-based marital property regime may also be unconstitutional. There are no easy answers to these questions. From an international perspective, most U.S. laws are very liberal in allowing a decedent spouse to drastically limit the survivor's property rights. This amount of testamentary freedom was unknown historically. And there are good public policy reasons for not permitting a decedent spouse to pass extensive property to others while leaving a penniless spouse who will be in need of public aid, especially since spouses have the legal obligation to support each other.

At the same time, subsequent marriages, the claims of non-marital children, and the vast amount of divorce that occurs in western societies make the traditional models of spousal protections less relevant. The elective share should serve both to provide suitable support for a surviving spouse as well as acknowledge the surviving spouse's contribution to the acquisition of a deceased spouse's wealth under the partnership theory of marriage. Nevertheless, some spouses might not need or want the full amount of their elective share and an estate planner who does not deal intelligently with the spouse's property rights may cause significant tax costs to both estates, emotional scars to surviving family members, and administrative headaches for all.

Only about 8 states retain, or have recently adopted, the augmented estate in the relatively inflexible form illustrated by the Florida code. Delaware, Florida, New Jersey, New York, North Carolina, Pennsylvania, Tennessee, and Virginia have elective share statutes that take into account all, or most, of the decedent's non-probate property, and do not also factor in the survivor's own property or the length of marriage. North Carolina's elective share statute does, however, reduce the percentage based on number of children, to try to reduce the shares that second or third spouses will take if the couple has not had children together

Although the UPC addressed the situation of the surviving spouse having more wealth than the deceased spouse in its 1969 version, and even though most states did not adopt that part of the UPC's elective share model statute, it had not addressed the other situation that was leading to extensive litigation, the relatively short second and third marriage. In 1990 the UPC turned its attention to how best to equitably address the claims of surviving spouses of relatively short duration while protecting the claims of surviving spouses of longer marriages. To achieve that, the UPC developed a complex formula to account for the surviving spouse's wealth as well as the length of marriage.

---

[28] See *In re* Estate of Magee, 988 So. 2d 1 (Fla. 2d DCA 2007) where the probate court rejected the assertion that the elective share statutes are unconstitutional under the Florida and United States Constitutions; and determined that the spouse was entitled to an elective share under §§ 732.201 to 732.2155 of the Florida Statutes.

c.   The UPC's Graduated Super Augmented Estate

In addition to capturing a deceased spouse's non-probate property for purposes of determining the elective estate, the UPC also includes the surviving spouse's augmented estate into the total wealth calculation, and it pro-rates the percentage that a surviving spouse can take based on length of marriage. Thus, for a couple married 15 years or more, the surviving spouse is entitled to a 50% share of the total combined wealth of both spouses. So, if the surviving spouse owns 80% of the total wealth, she cannot elect to take half of her deceased spouse's estate, because that would result in her taking 90% of the couple's total wealth. On the other hand, if the surviving spouse only owns 20% of the couple's combined wealth, and she is entitled to an elective share of half, then she can take 37.5% of her deceased spouse's estate.

How does this work? Let's assume the decedent husband owns an augmented estate worth $800,000 at his death, and his wife owns an augmented estate worth $200,000. The wife's augmented estate consists of the same categories of property that would consist of her augmented estate if she were the decedent. We can see that the combined wealth of the couple is $1,000,000 and a surviving spouse of 15 years would be entitled to half, or $500,000. Because the surviving spouse already owns $200,000 in her own right, she would be entitled to $300,000 of her deceased husband's $800,000 estate, which is 37.5% of his augmented estate ($300,000 ÷ $800,000).

Unfortunately, the UPC's elective share statute is not nearly as simple as my example would suggest. Consider the UPC's introductory comments to the elective share:

UPC Part 2—Introduction

The general effect of implementing the partnership theory in elective-share law is to increase the entitlement of a surviving spouse in a long-term marriage in cases in which the marital assets were disproportionately titled in the decedent's name; and to decrease or even eliminate the entitlement of a surviving spouse in a long-term marriage in cases in which the marital assets were more or less equally titled or disproportionately titled in the surviving spouse's name. A further general effect is to decrease or even eliminate the entitlement of a surviving spouse in a short-term, later-in-life marriage (typically a post-widowhood remarriage) in which neither spouse contributed much, if anything, to the acquisition of the other's wealth, except that a special supplemental elective-share amount is provided in cases in which the surviving spouse would otherwise be left without sufficient funds for support.

You can imagine that the statutory details and mathematical calculations to account for all of these variables, from the surviving spouse's wealth, to all relevant non-probate property of both spouses, to length of marriage, makes for a very complex analysis.

Let's begin with the elective share percentage. To recognize the partnership-theory of marriage, the UPC gives the surviving spouse a 50% share of the (a) *marital property portion* of the (b) *augmented estate*.

UPC § 2–202. Elective Share.

(a) [Elective-Share Amount.] The surviving spouse of a decedent who dies domi-ciled in this State has a right of election, under the limitations and conditions stated in this Part, to take an elective-share amount equal to 50 percent of the val-ue of the marital-property portion of the augmented estate.

(b) [Supplemental Elective-Share Amount.] If the sum of the amounts de-scribed in Sections 2–207, 2–209(a)(1), and that part of the elective-share amount payable from the decedent's net probate estate and nonprobate transfers to others under Section 2–209(c) and (d) is less than [$75,000], the surviving spouse is enti-tled to a supplemental elective-share amount equal to [$75,000], minus the sum of the amounts described in those sections. The supplemental elective-share amount is payable from the decedent's net probate estate and from recipients of the decedent's nonprobate transfers to others in the order of priority set forth in Section 2–209(c) and (d).[29]

(c) [Effect of Election on Statutory Benefits.] If the right of election is exer-cised by or on behalf of the surviving spouse, the surviving spouse's homestead allowance, exempt property, and family allowance, if any, are not charged against but are in addition to the elective-share and supplemental elective-share amounts. . . . [30]

The marital property portion of the *super-augmented estate* consists of essentially the same property we calculated in section 2(b) above. There-fore, we are not going to repeat all the statutory language here regarding the decedent's NPE, the decedent's NPTO, and the decedent's NPTSS. Note that also included is the surviving spouse's property (SSP) and the surviv-ing spouse's nonprobate transfers to others (SSNPTO). We can think of this as a *super-augmented estate* because it includes the surviving spouse's total wealth (assets and entitlements) as well as the decedent spouse's total wealth. It is all of the wealth that both parties own or have legal control over at the death of the first spouse to die.

Notwithstanding the foregoing, not all of that property was necessarily acquired during the marriage, or should be attributed to the joint efforts of the parties. For such situations the UPC multiplies the super augmented estate by a percentage to roughly approximate the amount of total wealth that can be considered *marital property*. The *marital property portion* rang-es anywhere from 100% for a marriage of 15 years or longer to 3% for a marriage of less than one year.

UPC § 2–203. Composition of the Augmented Estate; Marital-Property Por-tion.

(a) . . . the value of the augmented estate, . . . consists of the sum of the values of all property, whether real or personal, movable or immovable, tangible or intangible, wherever situated, that constitute:

(1) the **decedent's net probate estate**;

(2) the **decedent's nonprobate transfers to others**;

---

[29] This provision gives the surviving spouse a supplemental amount of $75,000 if the surviving spouse's assets and other entitlements are less than $75,000.

[30] Note, the UPC gives the surviving spouse elective share benefits in addition to home-stead, family allowance, and exempt property.

(3) the **decedent's nonprobate transfers to the surviving spouse**; and

(4) the **surviving spouse's property and nonprobate transfers to others**.

(b) The value of the marital-property portion of the augmented estate consists of the sum of the values of the four components of the augmented estate as determined under subsection (a) multiplied by the following percentage:

If the decedent and the spouse were married to each other:	The percentage is:
Less than 1 year	3%
1 year but less than 2 years	6%
2 years but less than 3 years	12%
3 years but less than 4 years	18%
4 years but less than 5 years	24%
5 years but less than 6 years	30%
6 years but less than 7 years	36%
7 years but less than 8 years	42%
8 years but less than 9 years	48%
9 years but less than 10 years	54%
10 years but less than 11 years	60%
11 years but less than 12 years	68%
12 years but less than 13 years	76%
13 years but less than 14 years	84%
14 years but less than 15 years	92%
15 years or more	100%

The specific details of what property makes up the super augmented estate are detailed in UPC Sections 2–204 (Decedent's Net Probate Estate), 2–205 (Decedent's Nonprobate Transfers to Others), 2–206 (Decedent's Nonprobate Transfers to the Surviving Spouse), and 2–207 (Surviving Spouse's Property and Nonprobate Transfers to Others). The UPC also requires that the surviving spouse be living at the time of election to reduce the disarray of allowing a spouse's executor to elect for the surviving spouse's estate when the surviving spouse will not benefit personally from the property. If a guardian or conservator makes such election on behalf of an incapacitated spouse, the property must be placed in a custodial trust for the benefit of the surviving spouse, with a remainder over to the decedent spouse's residuary beneficiaries (this is the general idea though it's much more complicated than this). See UPC § 2–212.

For example, assume that Herman and Wilma were married 10 years and had a super augmented estate (combined total wealth) of $500,000. The marital portion of the elective estate would be 60% of their total wealth, or $300,000. Wilma would then be entitled to half of that as her elective share, or $150,000. Now that we know how much her elective share would be, our next step is to determine if she is entitled to elect. She can only elect if she has not received an equivalent amount through probate and non-probate transfers to her, and only if she does not already own more than half of the couple's combined wealth. We will get to that determination in a moment.

Not all states that have adopted some version of the UPC's graduated super augmented estate have adopted all of the elements. Some elective share statutes, like Alabama's, take into account the surviving spouse's wealth, but allow the survivor to take a flat share, regardless of length of marriage. Alabama also has a much less complicated statute for identifying the property that goes into the elective estate, which makes it easier to calculate. Colorado, Hawaii, Kansas, Minnesota, Montana, South Dakota, Tennessee and West Virginia, however, adjust the percentage for length of marriage.[31] Other states have adjustments depending on the existence of issue and/or parents of the decedent spouse.

Consider the Alabama Code provision and compare it to the UPC's super-augmented estate.

Alabama Code § 43–8–70

(a) If a married person domiciled in this state dies, the surviving spouse has a right of election to take an elective share of the estate. The elective share shall be the lesser of:

(1) All of the estate of the deceased reduced by the value of the surviving spouse's separate estate; or

(2) One-third of the estate of the deceased.

(b) The "separate estate" of the surviving spouse shall include:

(1) All property which immediately after the death of the decedent is owned by the spouse outright or in fee simple absolute;

(2) All legal and equitable interests in property the possession or enjoyment of which are acquired only by surviving the decedent; and

(3) All income and other beneficial interests:

a.   Under a trust;

b.   In proceeds of insurance on the life of the decedent; and

c.   Under any broad-based nondiscriminatory pension, profit-sharing, stock bonus, deferred compensation, disability, death benefit or other such plan established by an employer.

(c) If a married person not domiciled in this state dies, the right, if any, of the surviving spouse to take an elective share in property in this state is governed by the law of the decedent's domicile at death.

Is property held in a POD or TOD securities account covered in Alabama's elective share law? What about property over which the deceased spouse had a general power of appointment?

Whether the elective estate is the augmented estate or the graduated super augmented estate, to the extent it differs from the decedent's gross estate for federal estate tax purposes, there exists a gap that can be exploited by clever decedents to limit the elective share. Roughly 13 states have adopted some form of the super augmented estate, or have graduated amounts for length of marriage, or account for both variables, like the UPC.

---

[31] See, e.g. COLO. REV. STAT. ANN. § 15–11–201(1) (West 2010); HAW. REV. STAT. § 560:2–202 (West 1997).

PROBLEM

7.7. Take the estate we considered above, and let's add a few more complications, like Wilma's wealth, and length of marriage to the equation.

Net Probate Estate which Harry devises by will to his children	100,000
Property Harry put in a Revocable Trust payable to his children	500,000
Term Life insurance Harry bought, payable to his spouse, Wilma	300,000
Farm Harry bought entirely but held in a joint tenancy with right of survivorship with his brother[32]	200,000
Property from Harry's mother's estate over which he has a general testamentary power of appointment and which he appoints to his children	300,000
Retirement Account with POD designation benefitting his children	600,000
Personal and Real property owned in her sole name by Wilma, the surviving spouse	300,000
Life insurance purchased by Wilma on Harry's life, payable to Wilma	500,000
Property held in tenancy by entirety by Harry and Wilma (total value)[33]	500,000
Wilma's retirement account with POD designation benefitting Harry	300,000
Total Wealth at death of Harry	2,250,000
Total Wealth of Wilma at Harry's death	1,350,000
Total Wealth of Couple	3,600,000

If Harry and Wilma had been married for 10 years, we first have to calculate the marital property portion of the augmented estate. According to the UPC, § 2–203, the marital property portion would be 60% of the total wealth of the couple. Thus, 60% of $3,600,000 would be $2,160,000. Then, the elective share would consist of 50% of the marital property portion, or $1,080,000.

Once we have calculated the value of the elective share, we then have to decide if Wilma is even entitled to elect against the will—i.e., was the amount she received through probate and non-probate transfers, in addition to a portion of her own property, greater than the elective share? To determine this, we must first figure out how much of her own property gets credited back against her share. Remember, it is important under the partnership theory to give

---

[32] The joint tenancy property is valued at the amount of the deceased husband's contribution to the property.

[33] Half of tenancy by the entirety property is credited to the husband's estate and half to the wife's.

Wilma her proportionate share of Harry's estate as her elective share, but we also need to offset her claims by recognizing that Harry is entitled to his proportionate share of her property. If Harry's share of her property is greater than her share of his property, she is not entitled to elect at all, regardless of whether Harry gave her any property at his death. Look at UPC § 2–209(a)(2) and (b).

UPC § 2–209. Sources from Which Elective Share Payable.

(a) **[Elective-Share Amount Only.]** In a proceeding for an elective share, the following are applied first to satisfy the elective-share amount and to reduce or eliminate any contributions due from the decedent's probate estate and recipients of the decedent's nonprobate transfers to others:

(1) amounts included in the augmented estate under Section 2–204 which pass or have passed to the surviving spouse by testate or intestate succession and amounts included in the augmented estate under Section 2–206; and

(2) the marital-property portion of amounts included in the augmented estate under Section 2–207.

(b) **[Marital Property Portion.]** The marital-property portion under subsection (a)(2) is computed by multiplying the value of the amounts included in the augmented estate under Section 2–207 by the percentage of the augmented estate set forth in the schedule in Section 2–203(b) appropriate to the length of time the spouse and the decedent were married to each other.

(c) **[Unsatisfied Balance of Elective-Share Amount; Supplemental Elective-Share Amount.]** If, after the application of subsection (a), the elective-share amount is not fully satisfied, or the surviving spouse is entitled to a supplemental elective-share amount, amounts included in the decedent's net probate estate, other than assets passing to the surviving spouse by testate or intestate succession, and in the decedent's nonprobate transfers to others under Section 2–205(1), (2), and (3)(B) are applied first to satisfy the unsatisfied balance of the elective-share amount or the supplemental elective-share amount. The decedent's net probate estate and that portion of the decedent's nonprobate transfers to others are so applied that liability for the unsatisfied balance of the elective-share amount or for the supplemental elective-share amount is apportioned among the recipients of the decedent's net probate estate and of that portion of the decedent's nonprobate transfers to others in proportion to the value of their interests therein.

(d) **[Unsatisfied Balance of Elective-Share and Supplemental Elective-Share Amount.]** If, after the application of subsections (a) and (c), the elective-share or supplemental elective-share amount is not fully satisfied, the remaining portion of the decedent's nonprobate transfers to others is so applied that liability for the unsatisfied balance of the elective-share or supplemental elective-share amount is apportioned among the recipients of the remaining portion of the decedent's nonprobate transfers to others in proportion to the value of their interests therein.

(e) **[Unsatisfied Balance Treated as General Pecuniary Devise.]** The unsatisfied balance of the elective-share or supplemental elective-share amount as determined under subsection (c) or (d) is treated as a general pecuniary devise for purposes of Section 3–904.

Thus, Wilma's individual wealth was $1,350,000. To calculate the portion of her estate that is to be credited against her elective share, we multiply her estate by 60%, for a total of $810,000 (§ 2–209(a)(2)). This represents, in essence, Harry's portion of Wilma's property. Her elective share in the total wealth of the couple is $1,080,000, but we credit against her share $810,000, leaving a total of $270,000 to be made up by first looking to property the decedent gave to her or that passed to her by probate or non-probate transfers (§ 2–209(a)(1)): the $300,000 life insurance and $250,000 in the tenancy by the entirety property (the husband's share). Because the wife is already receiving $550,000, which is in addition to her own property of $810,000, she is above the amount entitled to elect. Therefore, the estate will pass exactly as planned and Wilma may not elect.

Alternatively consider what would result if the couple had been married for 15 years or more, so that the marital property portion of the estate is 100% of the total combined wealth, or $3,600,000? In that case, Wilma is entitled to an elective share of 50%, or $1,800,000. Now, 100% of her own property of $1,350,000 is credited back against her elective share, leaving $450,000 to be made up from Harry's estate. Then again, because she is already receiving $550,000 in nonprobate transfers from her deceased husband, she received more than her statutory entitlement and therefore cannot elect against the estate.

What if Harry's life insurance was payable to his children instead of Wilma? She would then be $200,000 short. To determine where the spouse takes the property, we look to UPC § 2–209(c) which provides that:

> amounts included in the decedent's net probate estate, other than assets passing to the surviving spouse by testate or intestate succession, and in the decedent's nonprobate transfers to others under Section 2–205(1), (2), and (3)(B) are applied first to satisfy the unsatisfied balance of the elective-share amount.

Thus, Wilma would be entitled to deduct a percentage from the NPE, the revocable trust, the joint tenancy property, a portion of the mother's estate, and the retirement account to make up her $200,000.

The UPC provides that property will be used to pay the elective share in the following order:

1. Property passing to the spouse by will or by intestacy and NPTSS (§ 2–209(a)(1)).

2. The marital portion of the surviving spouse's property that is credited back against him (§ 2–209(a)(2)—this is equal to the surviving spouse's augmented estate multiplied by the same value as is used to determine the marital portion of the augmented estate (§ 2–209(b)).

3. Property passing in the NPE to others and certain NPTO (revocable trust property, property over which the decedent held a general power of appointment, joint tenancy property, PoD and ToD property, and life insurance proceeds—all property covered in UPC § 2–205(1), (2), and (3)(B)) (§ 2–209(c))

4. Remaining NPTO property.

Notice that if the probate and non-probate transfers to the surviving spouse and the surviving spouse's own marital property are not enough to satisfy the elective share, most of the decedent spouse's probate and non-probate transfers to others are abated ratably. Florida abated the NPE and revocable trust property first before turning to joint tenancy property or property over which the decedent had a power of appointment. The UPC abates them all, meaning that joint tenancy property may have to be sold, or portions of appointed property may have to be voided to cover the elective share.

Now switch the facts, and consider what would happen if Wilma predeceased Harry, with the same property, except the two life insurance policies are on Wima's life, not Harry's life. In that case, Harry's total wealth is greater than Wilma's, and therefore he could never elect against the estate, regardless of whether his wife left him any property at all. This is because whatever percentage of his estate that is credited back against the elective share under § 2–209(a)(2) will always be greater than his portion of the elective share because he owns more than half of the couple's total wealth. This is a vital part of the UPC elective share calculation, so be sure you understand how it works.

To summarize the UPC's graduated super augmented estate, here's what you need to do:

1. Calculate the total wealth of both spouses (all probate and non-probate property, including recent lifetime gifts, life insurance, PODs, and the like) to determine the *(Super) Augmented Estate*.

2. Multiply the total wealth by the relevant percentage for length of marriage to determine the *Marital Portion of the Augmented Estate*.

3. Divide in half to determine the *Elective Share*.

4. Multiply the surviving spouse's augmented estate by the same percentage used to calculate the marital portion to determine the amount of the surviving spouse's own property credited back against the elective share.

5. If the amount in #4 is greater than that in #3, the surviving spouse *may not elect*.

6. If the amount in #4 is less than in #3, deduct 4 from 3 to determine how much property the surviving spouse is entitled to from the decedent spouse's estate.

7. Next calculate how much property is given to the surviving spouse through probate and non-probate transfers. If that amount exceeds the difference determined by the calculation in #6, then the surviving spouse also *may not elect*.

8. If the amount in #6 exceeds the amount of property given to the surviving spouse from probate and non-probate transfers, then look to the abatement priorities to satisfy the remainder of the surviving spouse's elective share.

7.8. For more practice on the elective share, consider this estate:

Harry and Wilma have been married 2 years. Harry has 2 children by a prior marriage; Wilma has 3 children by a prior marriage. They have no children by each other. The following assets are owned by each. In the column headed "Type" you should write in which part of the super augmented estate this property comes under, i.e. decedent's net probate estate (NPE), decedent's nonprobate transfers to others (NPTO), decedent's nonprobate transfers to the surviving spouse (NPTSS), or the surviving spouse's property (SSP).

In general, you should attribute half of all jointly held property to each spouse's estate unless one or the other paid for the entire property. In the latter case, if Harry paid for all the property which Wilma receives at his death, the property is valued at its full value as a NPTSS. However if Wilma paid for all the property, and Harry dies first, she retains full ownership and the property is considered entirely part of her surviving spouse's estate. Where each contributed half, then we attribute half to each spouse's estate.

Type	Property	Value
_____	House titled only in Harry's name worth	$500,000
_____	Bank accounts titled in Harry's name only	$50,000
_____	Bank accounts titled in both Harry and Wilma's names[34]	$50,000
_____	Bank accounts titled in only Wilma's name	$50,000
_____	Harry's car titled in his name	$25,000
_____	Wilma's car titled in her name only	$20,000
_____	Yacht Harry bought so they could travel in their retirement titled in both names—paid entirely by Harry	$100,000
_____	Harry's stock portfolio PoD his daughter and son	$500,000
_____	Wilma's stock portfolio PoD her three children	$250,000
_____	Harry's daughter's house in JT w/ RS with Harry—he contributed the full value	$250,000
_____	Term Life insurance bought by Harry payable to Wilma	$1,000,000
_____	Term Life insurance bought by Harry payable to Daughter and Son	$500,000
_____	Term Life insurance on Harry's life bought by Wilma and payable to Wilma	$500,000
_____	Property in revocable trust est. by Harry in 2006 giving him a life interest and his daughter and son the remainder interest	$1,000,000
_____	Property in Harry's mother's estate over which Harry has a general power of appointment	$500,000
_____	Gift Harry made to a niece 6 months before his death	$50,000
_____	Gifts to Wilma made by Harry in the year before his death—jewelry	$100,000

---

[34] When valuing marital property, the presumption is that each partner contributed equal amounts so half of all joint property should be credited to each person's estate.

_____	Personal property of Harry	$100,000
_____	Personal property of Wilma	$50,000
_____	Harry's share of business (this is his share of a business held in tenancy in common)	$500,000
_____	RV Wilma bought just after their marriage titled in both names as joint tenants with rights of survivorship	$100,000
_____	Condo in New York City they bought just after their marriage titled in both names as joint tenants with rights of survivorship (each paid half)	<u>$500,000</u>
	Total property	$6,695,000

To calculate the elective shares, do the analysis under 1) a net probate estate regime, 2) a regular augmented estate regime, and 3) the 2008 UPC. Also, don't forget to deduct the relevant homestead, exempt property, and family allowance provisions from the estate. Note that other states may use different percentages or include slightly different property, and some allow homestead in lieu of an elective share. These are just examples. Assume also that the decedent died with $5,000 in funeral expenses and $95,000 in debts. The lengthy answer using the code for the District of Columbia, Florida, and the UPC is in the back of the book. There are a number of additional issues raised by going through the problem carefully, plus some hypothetical changes that profoundly affect the disposition. As you work through the problem, you will see the importance of identifing the different types of property (e.g. NPE, NPTO, NPTSS, SSP) and the importance of applying the different jurisdiction's homestead, exempt property, and family allowance provisions.

After you have worked through this problem carefully, you can take comfort in the fact that few attorneys actually have to do all of the complex valuations and calculations we've done here. But attorneys must know what property is included in which category in order to advise the CPA or accountants where to put each item of property and how to divide up the allocations. This exercise should give you a good sense of how to structure an estate plan to make sure the spouse receives enough so he or she cannot elect against the decedent's will and estate plan. The last thing you want is for every nonprobate beneficiary to have to give back 5% of their gifts because the spouse's elective share wasn't properly dealt with.

Moreover, regardless of the planning and agreements between the spouses that may have led up to a particular estate plan, a surviving spouse may go against a verbal agreement not to elect, or a guardian or conservator of a disabled surviving spouse may be required to elect, even if you planned otherwise. So making sure that a surviving spouse is appropriately provided for is one of the most important aspects of a sound estate plan. Either that, or have the spouse sign a waiver (a pre-nup or post-nuptial agreement).

Tax Tip: Why Would You File a $0 Gift Tax Return?

Although we haven't discussed in any great detail the filing of gift tax returns, this exercise on the elective share should give you some idea of why it might be advantageous to file a gift tax return even if no taxes are due at the time of filing. In particular, think about joint tenancy property. In the case of the farm that Harry purchased in its entirety but held as a joint tenant with his brother, only half would be included in the elective share calculation if Harry made a completed gift of the other half to his brother more than two years before his death.[35] By filing a gift tax return and subsequently treating the property as a joint tenancy (i.e. giving up co-equal rights to possession and sharing the income tax liabilities), Harry could reduce the value of the farm that would be included in his elective estate. If Harry had simply added his brother's name on his own farm with the idea that the right of survivorship would serve as a TOD if Harry predeceased his brother, then the entire value of the farm could be included in calculating the elective estate. The gift tax return is not necessarily proof positive of a completed gift, and certainly the failure to file a gift tax return won't defeat a completed gift. But it is further evidence of a completed *inter vivos* gift and it has a nifty side benefit as well.

Filing the gift tax return starts the 7 year statute of limitations with the IRS. After 7 years the IRS cannot question the fact of the gift or the value of the gift as reported on the return unless the Service had raised the issue within the statutory period. And what is the likelihood of that happening when the return shows that no taxes are due?

Joint tenancies can be troublesome in calculating the elective estate. Assume the decedent spouse entirely funded a bank account with money she owned before her marriage. Then after her marriage she puts her new husband's name on the account. The question is whether the decedent spouse made a lifetime gift of half at the time she added the surviving spouse's name to her bank accounts, or whether she intended the joint tenancy as a TOD account. If the latter, the entire value of the account could be included in the decedent's elective estate if the state includes non-probate property in the elective share.

In states that follow the simple augmented estate, the presumption that joint tenancies between spouses are attributed 50% to each spouse can actually reduce the elective share in some instances and increase it in others. If the surviving spouse is entitled to an elective share of 50% of the decedent spouse's augmented estate, the survivor might be entitled to the half he received when his name was originally added, plus half of the decedent's half as elective share, for a total of 75% of the value of the property. This could be reduced if the state elective share credits lifetime gifts, in which case the surviving spouse would take none of the decedent's share of the bank account, but would only be entitled to the half he received at the time his name was added. In a state that takes into account non-probate transfers to the surviving spouse, the 50% he already received could disqualify him from receiving any further amount as elective share. Thus, understanding which property is included in the elective share and whether lifetime gifts are credited against the elective share is important not only

---

[35] Different states look back different periods of time to catch any *inter vivos* transfers that may have been made to defraud a spouse of the elective share or which unwittingly would reduce the elective share.

for calculating the elective share, but for managing jointly held property to maximize or minimize the amount included in the elective estate.

Of course, we can't really talk about each individual piece of property and assume a surviving spouse will receive a proportionate share of each. Rather, the smaller the augmented estate, the smaller the elective share; and the larger the non-probate transfers to the surviving spouse, the less has to be taken from other sources. Making irrevocable lifetime gifts prior to death not only can lessen tax liabilities, but can dramatically affect the elective share.

Consider the following cases, which tend to focus simply whether a spouse is entitled to the elective share or not. All legally married spouses are entitled to an elective share unless they waived their rights through a pre- or post-nuptial agreement. And, as stated before, even if they are incapacitated and unlikely to benefit directly from the property, most conservators are required by law to elect unless a valid agreement was executed waiving elective share rights. Consider also whether you think domestic partners or those in civil unions, either opposite-sex or same-sex, should be entitled to elective shares. And should states build flexibility into their elective share statutes to treat the non-traditional couple, the unusual estate plan, or the possibilities of inequitable distributions?

In re Est. of Cross

664 N.E.2d 905 (Ohio, 1996)

On August 23, 1992, Carroll R. Cross died testate leaving his entire estate to his son, Ray G. Cross, who was not a child of the surviving spouse. At the time of his death, Beulah Cross, the surviving spouse, was close to eighty years old, suffering from Alzheimer's disease, and was living in a nursing home paid by Medicaid. Due to Mrs. Cross's incompetency, she was unable to make an election against her husband's will. Therefore, the probate court appointed a commissioner, who investigated the matter and determined that the court elect for Mrs. Cross to take her intestate share against the will. As a result of this election, Mrs. Cross would receive twenty-five thousand dollars in spousal allowance and one-half of the net estate, which was approximately nine thousand dollars.

Decedent's son appealed the probate court's decision. While the appeal was pending, Mrs. Cross died. The court of appeals, with one judge dissenting, reversed, finding that the election to take against the will was against Mrs. Cross's best interest and was not necessary to provide her adequate support, since the cost of her nursing home care was already covered by Medicaid. On appeal by the administrator of the wife's estate, the Supreme Court of Ohio reversed the Court of Appeals, stating:

Ohio R.C. 2106.08 provides that the court may elect for the surviving spouse to take against the will and under R.C. 2105.06 "only if it finds, after taking into consideration the other available resources and the age, probable life expectancy, physical and mental condition, and present and reasonably anticipated future needs of the surviving spouse, that the election to take under 2105.06 of the Revised Code is necessary to provide adequate support for the surviving spouse during his life expectancy."

Prior to the amendment of R.C. 2106.08 (effective December 17, 1986), the probate court made its determination of whether to elect to take under the will or against the will based upon which provision was "better for such spouse." In essence, the court based its decision on which provision was more mathematically advantageous to the surviving spouse. However, in passing R.C. 2106.08, the General Assembly moved away from a simple mathematical calculation, taking into consideration such factors as other available resources, age, life expectancy, physical and mental condition, and the surviving spouse's present and future needs. In either case, the probate court must ascertain what the surviving spouse would have done for her financial benefit had she been competent to make the decision herself.

In this case, the court of appeals determined that had Mrs. Cross been competent she would [not] have elected to take under the will, since her nursing home expenses were covered by Medicaid. However, in reaching this conclusion and in striking down the election made by Judge Corrigan for Mrs. Cross to take against the will, we believe that the court of appeals ignored Medicaid eligibility requirements. [E]ligibility for Medicaid benefits is dependent upon a recipient's income or available resources. The term "resources" includes "property owned separately by the person, his share of family property, and property deemed to him from a parent or spouse." This also encompasses "those resources in which an applicant/recipient has a legal interest and the legal ability to use or dispose of * * *."

Mrs. Cross clearly had a legal interest in and the ability to use or dispose of her intestate share under her right to take against the will. Thus, she had available to her a potential resource for Medicaid eligibility purposes. This is critical to the facts presented, since the Medicaid rules specifically state that the nonutilization of available income renders a Medicaid applicant or recipient ineligible for benefits. . . . Such nonutilization of income available upon request constitutes ineligibility. * * * "

As applied to this case, in order to maintain Mrs. Cross's Medicaid eligibility and to continue to have her nursing home expenses provided for by public assistance, Judge Corrigan was required to elect for Mrs. Cross to take against the will and to receive her intestate share.

Query: Despite Ohio moving from a strict mathematical calculation as to the surviving spouse's best interests to a consideration of all factors relevant to an election, it continues to base decisions about election on the surviving spouse's need for support. Does that factor weigh in favor of Beulah Cross' election or against it under the support theory or the partnership theory of marriage?

In re Est. of Cooper

592 N.Y.S.2d 797, 187 A.D.2d 128 (App. Div. 1993)

The question to be resolved on this appeal is whether the survivor of a homosexual relationship, alleged to be a "spousal relationship", is entitled to a right of election against the decedent's will, pursuant to EPTL 5–1.1. In our view, the question must be answered in the negative. The petitioner's claim was based on the following argument: "I met William Cooper in 1984. From approximately the middle of 1984 until his sudden death from a congenital heart condition in February 1988, I lived with him in Apartment 1, 183 Wyckoff Street, Brooklyn, New York in a spousal-type situation. Except for the fact that we were of the same sex, our lives were identical to that of a husband and wife. We kept a common home; we shared expenses; our friends recognized us as spouses; we had a physical relationship. Of course, we could not obtain a marriage license because no marriage license clerk in

New York will issue such a document to two people of the same sex. . . . The only reason Mr. Cooper and I were not legally married is because marriage license clerks in New York State will not issue licenses to persons of the same sex. . . . However unconstitutional the denial of the right to a marriage license to Mr. Cooper and myself may have been, the Court cannot undo that now that Mr. Cooper is deceased. Since the Court, however, also is an instrument of the State . . . it cannot compound this unconstitutionality by saying that because we could not obtain a State-issued marriage license, I cannot be recognized as a spouse by State Court for the purpose of claiming spousal rights. . . . I ask this Court simply to declare that if I can establish that Mr. Cooper and I, at the time of his death, were living in a spousal-type relationship, I am entitled to spousal rights, and the State-imposed unconstitutional impediment of making it impossible for two people of the same sex to obtain a marriage license does not alter this.

The court rejected the petitioner's argument, stating: *Generally, in the construction of statutes, the intention of the Legislature is first to be sought from a literal reading of the act itself or of all the statutes relating to the same general subject-matter"* The Legislature has expressly defined a *"surviving spouse" in EPTL 5–1.2, as follows:*

*"(a) A husband or wife is a surviving spouse within the meaning, and for the purposes of * * * 5–1.1". (Emphasis added.)*

Indeed, even in the absence of any express definition of the term "surviving spouse", an interpretation of the statute to the same effect would be warranted. It is well settled that "the language of a statute is generally construed according to its natural and most obvious sense . . . in accordance with its ordinary and accepted meaning, unless the Legislature by definition or from the rest of the context of the statute provides a special meaning." The court then went through the constitutional equal protection analysis and found no merit in the claim that same-sex marriage is a right that was denied to the parties. Therefore, the probate court was not required to extend surviving spouse benefits to a same-sex partner.

Query: Now that New York recognizes same-sex marriages, will there be pressure on probate courts to recognize elective share rights for cohabiting couples who do not marry?

Lovett v. Lovett

329 S.C. 426, 494 S.E.2d 823 (S.C. Ct. App., 1997)

Thomas Henry Lovett died in October, 1994, leaving a will that provided: *I hereby give, devise, and bequeath unto my wife, VIOLET MAE KIMBLE LOVETT, my home located on Hardscrabble Road, near Columbia, South Carolina, for the term of her natural life, a life estate, provided however, that she (1) continues to occupy the home; (2) that this provision is null and void should she remarry; (3) that this provision is null and void should we divorce or be separated at the time of my death; and (4) provided that she and she alone occupies the home.*

The remainder of his estate he left to his three children, one of whom was appointed personal representative and who later refused to pay Violet either her life estate or an elective share. The son brought suit seeking to declare the marriage between Violet and his father invalid because she had been married eight times previously and, *although her second through fourth marriages ended in either divorce or annulment, there is no record of a divorce or an annulment for her first, fifth, sixth, seventh, or eighth marriage.*

The probate judge denied Violet her life estate, ruling that the clear intent of Henry's will was to provide for Violet only if she were his wife. The judge also found Violet was not entitled to an elective share because the marriage was invalid. On appeal, the court agreed that Violet was not legally married and therefore not entitled to her elective share under the putative spouse doctrine. The court explained that Violet did not argue the putative spouse doctrine at trial, but even if she had it would have been ineffective because the spouse has to believe in good faith in the validity of her marriage. The court explained, however, that *given the number of her previous marriages and their largely unresolved status, the issue of her good faith would certainly be an unresolved question of fact for determination by the probate judge. Because Appellant failed to request such a finding, we decline to address the issue on appeal.*

The court reversed, however, on whether Henry intended Violet to have the life estate. Quoting Page on the Law of Wills, the Court explained: *If a gift is made to one who is named or otherwise identified, and who is also described in the will as the husband or wife of a given person, and such beneficiary is the ostensible, but not the legal husband or wife of such a designated person, the validity of the gift depends on the intention of testator in adding such description of relationship. If it is added by way of further description, which is usually the case, the beneficiary will take.... If the designation of relationship is added to indicate the character or capacity in which the beneficiary can take, the gift fails.... Most courts assume that, as a matter of construction, the designation of the relationship is a mere matter of description, and they then proceed to inquire whether the mistake as to the relationship or any fraud of the beneficiary defeats the gift.*

The court upheld her bequest of the life estate, explaining: *The cases appear to support the conclusion that under a testamentary gift to the "husband," "wife," or "widow" of a designated person, one who, although he or she went through the ceremony of a marriage with the person in question, is actually not the latter's lawful spouse or relict because the attempted marriage was illegal as being bigamous, . . . is nevertheless entitled to take the gift, in the absence of any indication of a contrary intention on the part of the testator.*

Query: Was the court correct in its interpretation of either Henry's will or the elective share statutes? Would Violet have been entitled to take under Henry's will if they had been divorced and he still used the term "wife" in describing her? Thinking back to the class and race implications of equitable adoption rules that strictly require contracts, do you think strict interpretation of elective share statutes might also disadvantage the working classes who might not have the resources to obtain a legal divorce? Should there be some greater flexibility in the elective share laws?

In another case, *Shaw v. Shaw*, 337 Ark. 530, 989 S.W.2d 919 (1999), the Supreme Court of Arkansas denied an elective share to a wife who had married the same husband four times. The first three ended in divorce, but the fourth ended in the death of the husband. However, the fourth marriage lasted only 13 days, and Arkansas law grants an elective share to a surviving spouse of a marriage only if the marriage lasts longer than one year. The court refused to tack her earlier marriage periods, noting that with each divorce her elective share or dower rights were fully extinguished. This case, and *Lovett* and *Cooper* and many others, show how courts can be strict in interpreting elective share rights to apply only to heterosexual couples with valid marriage licenses. Common law spouses, unmarried partners, persons who have had multiple marriages, and same-sex couples are not likely to benefit from elective share laws.

In re Wurcel

196 Misc. 2d 796, 763 N.Y.S.2d 902 (Sur. Ct. New York County 2003)

Paul Wurcel died in 1998, followed a year later by the death of his wife, Esther Wurcel, who had been living in a nursing home since 1993 because of her severe dementia and Alzheimers. Paul's nephew, Arkadiy Sherer, who was a beneficiary was also appointed executor under Paul's will when he finally filed it for probate in 2000, two years after Paul's death. At that time, Esther's executor, Jeannie Possick, filed for an elective share, which was denied because an executor may not claim an elective share for a surviving spouse after the surviving spouse's death. No guardian had been appointed for Esther and no attempt had been made to elect her statutory share during her life. Possick alleges that Sherer delayed filing Paul's estate for probate in order to prevent Esther from claiming her elective share. Noting that 1992 amendments to the New York elective share law moved it from being support-based to partnership-based, the court also noted that the post-death election limitation had not been removed. The court upheld the probate judge's denial of Esther's election rights. However, the court did permit Possick to move forward on her claim of fraud, explaining: *Nonetheless, the court also cannot disregard allegations of fraudulent conduct on the part of a conflicted fiduciary. Esther's estate is not without a possible remedy here. To hold otherwise would be putting a premium on ignoring the rights of unrepresented and incompetent surviving spouses by persons whose interests conflict with them. Here, Sherer, as a beneficiary under decedent's will, stood to lose a portion of what he would take as legatee if the surviving spouse elected. If he did so deliberately, he will not be permitted to benefit at the expense of an unrepresented incompetent.*

Query: If, as the court explained, the *duty to probate a will is moral, not legal*, should Possick have a cause of action at all? Shouldn't the surviving spouse's representative be responsible for making sure that her husband's estate is probated in a timely manner? The court noted that a constructive trust could be placed on the property that should have been Esther's, for the benefit of her intestate heirs or, more likely, to repay Medicaid. Should there be a policy priority of facilitating elections to help reduce taxpayer-funded health care costs? Should Possick have to prove fraud if the elective share statute aims to protect the surviving spouse's partnership interest in marital property?

There are thousands of elective share cases, often pitting second spouses against children of a prior marriage, or guardians of incapacitated spouses against other beneficiaries. And although many probate judges have been ruthless in not allowing testators to use non-probate mechanisms to avoid their spousal support obligations, others turn a blind eye on efforts to disinherit spouses. And judges are not consistent in interpreting elective share rights in conformity with partnership theories of marriage. As in *Possick*, if Esther and Paul had worked for 50 years accumulating the joint marital wealth, but most of it was titled in Paul's name, shouldn't Esther be able to benefit from her share? Most likely the property was jointly titled, but once Esther went into a nursing home her name probably came off of the joint bank accounts and the house in order to qualify her for Medicaid. Does it seem reasonable to prevent an election after the death of the surviving spouse under either a support or partnership theory, especially if the surviving spouse has creditors who provided services in her final year of life?

Another important area of litigation concerns whether limited rights over a decedent's property, such as a life interest in a trust or a life estate in real property, is sufficient to satisfy a decedent spouse's obligation to provide for a surviving spouse. In Florida, for instance, the elective share constitutes 30% of the decedent spouse's augmented estate which is given outright to the surviving spouse to be disposed of according to the survivor's will. But, if the decedent spouse really wishes to control the final disposition of his entire estate, he can place 60% of his augmented estate into trust with a life income for his surviving spouse, and a remainder to others.[36] In that way, final disposition of the property remains with the decedent spouse. In other states, however, a life estate in trust, no matter how large, is not sufficient.[37]

Additional litigation often occurs over the right of a surviving spouse to pick and choose the property he will take, either by renouncing or disclaiming certain property devised under the will (like the hideous portrait of great aunt Edna) and taking cash instead, or by requesting certain items of property. Although the latter is generally not permitted, spouses who have partial interests in certain property, as when a husband and wife own property as tenants in common, the court may allow the survivor to take the other half of the co-tenancy property in partial satisfaction of the elective share, leaving the devisee of that property to take a cash equivalent. The details of picking and choosing which property to take (the 1000 shares of Apple or the 1000 shares of Facebook), and the effects of disclaimer and election are beyond the scope of this book. Just understand that one must be very competent in understanding the full parameters of one's elective share laws in order to advise a surviving spouse; and most importantly, a lawyer who drafts the decedent's will should not be giving advice to the surviving spouse as to elections. Doing so creates a conflict under the Model Rules of Professional Responsibility.

Finally, the tax consequences of election are also important to understand. When a decedent spouse's estate may be hit with estate taxes, a

---

[36]   FLA. STAT. ANN. § 732.2095(2) (West 2001).

[37]   VT. STAT. ANN. tit. 14, § 461 (West 2009); N.Y. EST., POWERS & TRUST LAW, Right of election by surviving spouse § 5–1.1–A(b)(1)(F) (McKinney 2011).

surviving spouse's election may reduce the estate tax liability by siphoning off assets tax free. On the other hand, where the surviving spouse's estate is sufficiently large to incur estate taxes, disclaiming or not electing will help keep the survivor's estate from paying extra taxes. Decisions about electing should always be made by competent estate lawyers with the advice of accountants, and should not turn on whether the surviving spouse doesn't want to upset the decedent's plan, or whether the heirs of the survivor want as much as they can get from the decedent's estate. Electing to take against an estate will almost always leave hard feelings among the other estate beneficiaries. Thus, it is always advisable to provide adequately for the surviving spouse and not leave the final distribution up to chance.

PROBLEM

7.9. To practice elective share problems, go back and calculate Wilma's elective share from problem 7.8 above under the UPC after removing Herman's joint tenancy property with his daughter, his revocable trust property, his mother's estate, and the business and see if she would still be entitled to elect if they had been married 15 years or longer.

3. COMMUNITY PROPERTY

A spouse's interest in a deceased spouse's estate can be much simpler in community property states where the survivor has already received a one-half undivided interest in all community property acquired during the marriage. Usually, each spouse may freely devise his or her share of the community property to others, without regard for a surviving spouse's interest. Similarly, a spouse may not create a revocable trust for himself, payable to his children for instance, with community property unless the other spouse agrees. Just as I cannot devise away property my spouse owns, I cannot transfer *inter vivos* my spouse's share of the community property. Community property states also recognize separate or individual property (usually property acquired before marriage and property acquired during marriage by gift or inheritance) and quasi-community property (marital property transferred into a community property state), and some give elective share rights in some or all of this property. For instance, California allows a surviving spouse to elect one-half of the quasi-community property of a decedent spouse.[38]

Under intestacy law, most community property states give to the surviving spouse an intestate share of the decedent's community property, sometimes as much as 100%, but usually 50% if there is issue. For states such as Wisconsin, which has passed the Uniform Marital Property Act in order to treat property acquired during marriage as though it were community property, there are complex rules for dealing with property at death. For instance, marital property is deemed to be owned 50–50 by each spouse. This allows a decedent to dispose of her share of the marital property by will, or will substitute, as she chooses.[39] If the decedent dies without a will, however, her spouse will inherit half or all of the decedent's community property under the Wisconsin intestacy law.[40] But for property acquired prior to the adoption of the Uniform Marital Property Act, or

---

[38] CAL. Quasi-community property PROB. § 101 (West 1991).

[39] WIS. STAT. ANN. § 861.01 (West 1986).

[40] WIS. STAT. ANN. § 852.01(1)(a) (West).

property not defined as marital property, a surviving spouse is entitled to an elective share of 50%.[41] Thus, Wisconsin has community property for some property acquired during the marriage, but also recognizes separate and deferred marital property that is subject to different rules.

One development in a few states is to allow married couples to hold their community property with a right of survivorship. Upon the death of the first spouse, the surviving spouse takes undivided ownership of all community property. This format shifts community property from being a tenancy in common (which is freely inheritable and freely devisable by each tenant) to a joint tenancy (in which the survivor takes the undivided total share in the whole).[42]

While the elective share is relatively inconsequential in community property states, serious complications can arise with the migratory couple—the couple who moves from a common law to a community property state, or *vice versa*. Most community property states do not provide protections against disinheritance if most of the property was acquired in a common law state and is titled in the decedent spouse's name, but the decedent dies domiciled in a community property state. As we discussed in Chapter two, four states, California, Idaho, Washington, and Wisconsin, provide limited protection for these spouses. California and Washington give the surviving spouse an automatic half interest in the *quasi-community property* of the decedent spouse as well as in any community property acquired during the marriage after relocation to the community property state. Quasi-community property is defined as property acquired by a decedent outside a community property state that, had the decedent been domiciled in California or Washington, would have been deemed community property and therefore would be half owned by the spouse. Idaho and Wisconsin give an elective share to the surviving spouse in the quasi-community property (Idaho's is based on the UPC's augmented estate and Wisconsin is a 50% share in *deferred marital property*).

Couples going the other way, from a community property to a common law state, face different issues. Although community property retains its community character, common law states tend to be unfamiliar with community property characteristics and leave it to the surviving spouse to trace community property origins in property that gets retitled or commingled in the common law state. Fourteen states[43] have adopted the Uniform Disposition of Community Property Rights at Death Act (UCPRDA), which creates a rebuttable presumption that property acquired in a community property state was acquired as community property and retains its character after relocation to a common law state. Upon the death of the first spouse to die, half of the property subject to the UCPRDA is deemed to be held as tenancy in common by the surviving spouse and is therefore nonalienable by the decedent at death. The other half may be alienated by the decedent spouse as she chooses. Moreover, the decedent spouse's half of the property subject to the UCPRDA is not included in the elective estate for elective share purposes.

For states that have not adopted the UCPRDA, a surviving spouse may have a difficult time proving her community rights and instead must

---

[41] WIS. STAT. ANN. § 861.02 (West 1986).

[42] CAL. Community property of husband and wife; subject to express declaration in transfer documents; application and operation of section CIV. Code § 682.1. (West 2001).

[43] Alaska, Arkansas, Colorado, Connecticut, Florida, Hawaii, Kentucky, Michigan, Montana, New York, North Carolina, Oregon, Virginia and Wyoming.

rely on her elective share. Although community property laws more closely replicate the partnership theory of marriage and thus do not include elective share provisions, the fact that the majority of states are common law states and are not familiar with the details of community property rights means that migrating couples have to be careful how they manage property across state lines. Even though community property states do not have elective share provisions vis-à-vis community property, they may have elective share protections for quasi-community property that is brought into the state. Such protections often give to the surviving spouse the lion's share of the community property if the decedent spouse dies intestate. Thus, in a common law state that gives a surviving spouse a 50% share of the decedent's intestate estate or a 30–50% share of the decedent spouse's probate estate as an elective share, the surviving spouse will take substantially similar amounts under either intestacy or testacy. In a community property state, however, a surviving spouse retains her half of the community property and may take 50%–100% of a decedent spouse's half of the community property if he dies intestate, but may take nothing if the decedent dies testate and leaves his half of the community property to others. Thus, while the surviving spouse's shares may differ by a factor of 10% or 20% in a common law state between intestacy and testacy, especially if the elective estate is the net probate estate, the differences between testacy and intestacy may differ significantly in a community property state. Understanding the nuances of your state, as well as the overall differences between common law and community property regimes is vital to effective estate planning for migratory, as well as stationary couples.

4. SAME SEX MARRIAGE PROTECTIONS FOR SURVIVING SPOUSES/PARTNERS

In those states that have adopted same-sex marriage, same-sex spouses are entitled to all of the elective share and intestacy rights of opposite-sex spouses. Same sex couples who migrate from common law to community property states face the same issues that affect heterosexual spouses. The problems compound, however, in those states that have various forms of registered domestic partnership or civil unions, i.e. are "marriage lite states."[44] For example, in the District of Columbia, a registered domestic partner has all the same rights as a spouse for intestacy, elective share, and inheritance purposes. In California, however, registered domestic partners may opt to acquire property as community property, whereas domestic partners are not entitled to full intestacy rights or elective share of quasi-community property. Nor are they entitled to homestead, exempt property, and family allowance. Thus, while California has added domestic partnership to its laws, and has amended portions of the probate code to give domestic partners certain intestate inheritance rights and rights to preferential appointment as administrators, the state hasn't updated all of its code provisions to give domestic partners full equal rights as surviving spouses.

The only good way to know what rights domestic partners have in their states of domicile, or in new states to which they might relocate, is to study the probate code very carefully, being sensitive to the way in which marital status influences everything from lapse to intestacy to statutory

---

[44] See Hillel Levin, Resolving Interstate Conflicts over Same-sex Marriage, 63 FLA. L. REV. 47 (2011).

revocation. Many states give preferences against abatement for spousal bequests, for instance, or other priorities in the administration of an estate. However when considering the states that recognize domestic partners, very few have fully aligned all the benefits of domestic partners to those that spouses receive.

Practice Point: The Power of Divorce

By now, we can clearly see that the law favors the institution of marriage. So, if my spouse forgets about me in his will, or tries to disinherit me, I can choose to elect against the estate and recover at least some of what I think I am owed. Or, in a community property state, I would already be the owner of half of the marital property. But, if I have lived with my partner for 30 years in a separate property state and never married, either because I couldn't or didn't want to, the law won't come to my rescue if my partner did not provide for me in an estate plan. The famous case of Steig Larsson and his girlfriend of three decades who was unable to claim a share of his estate is still recent enough to illustrate this point.

In a political environment where the definition of marriage is still hotly contested, we can see that being deemed a *spouse* under the law bestows undeniable rights—both during life and at death. In the same vein, consideration should be given to couples who can't marry. These persons may include same sex couples living in states which do not allow same sex marriage/domestic partnerships, or heterosexual couples who just don't want to get married, but who want to provide for their partner *as if* they were married.

From an estate planning perspective, you can certainly assist all of your clients by drafting plans that effectuate their desires at death, to the extent allowed by law. For example, you can draft reciprocal wills for a gay couple that leave all, or a portion of the testator's estate, to the surviving partner. Planners should also provide good counsel by asking the clients if it is their intentions that they give each other at least the minimum protections in their plan that a legal spouse would be entitled to through intestacy.

Once those plans are in place, you might feel great. After all, helping provide peace of mind to your clients is one of the best side effects of estate planning. Still, it is critical to realize that the moment that the unmarried couple leaves your office with a good plan, they are in a much more precarious position than the married couple who leaves your office with a good plan. Can you think of why this might be?

Enter the power of divorce. As we have already discussed, when a marriage ends, the law assumes that a provision in a will providing for the former spouse becomes void by operation of law. Why? Well, for one, because countless cases have demonstrated to the courts that sometimes we just forget to change our wills after we divorce and that, by and large, most people don't want to still give their property to their Ex after that nasty divorce.

What about the non-married couple, whose plans treat each other like spouses by giving all or a significant portion of their estate to one another at death? What happens when they split up?

Of course, nothing happens. They split up and go about their lives. And although the law might be of some help to them in division of property upon the split-up if they have previously entered into an enforceable agreement with consideration (something other than sexual services), few couples, whether same-sex or opposite-sex, have the foresight to do that.[45]

Can you imagine what these clients might face, however, if THEY forget to change their wills and one dies? Do you think the distribution to a former partner would be void by operation of law just like in a divorce situation? Don't count on it. As we discussed, the law greatly favors donative freedom and the most prudent advice you can give your clients (in their Engagement Letter, most likely) is that they should regularly review their plans and that if the relationship ends, their plan may no longer work to effectuate their wishes. Therefore, it is worthwhile to explain these possible outcomes in detail to your clients ahead of time, and document them in writing, even if it casts a shadow over their otherwise happy execution.

5. TRUSTS AND POWERS PROTECTING THE SURVIVING SPOUSE

There are a number of trust structures that can be used to provide for a surviving spouse, some of which are motivated by the elective share, some by a desire to provide well for a spouse if he or she is unable to directly manage the property in later years, some by tax motivations, and by other reasons. Some decedents use trusts to limit a surviving spouse's control over property, very often in cases where the decedent fears the survivor will remarry and devise the property to the new spouse rather than the decedent's issue. Some use trusts, where available, to avoid giving a spouse outright control over the property covered by the elective share. Where available, an *elective share trust* gives a surviving spouse the lifetime income from the elective share property, but ultimately leaves final dispository power in the decedent, who can appoint the remainder of the trust property as he sees fit, rather than allowing his surviving spouse to dispose of it according to her will or estate plan. Certain trusts exist to take advantage of portability aspects of the estate tax exemption or the unlimited marital deduction. These very specific tax related trusts are covered in a bit more detail in Chapter 9, after you have been introduced to the transfer tax rules. For now, considering that fewer than 1% of estates are likely to be subject to the estate tax means that a sound estate planner should be looking to family planning, support, and asset protection more often than tax minimization. Fortunately some trusts may do almost everything. And many of us are such optimists that even though we can barely pay our bills, we think we might someday win the lottery or inherit a bunch of loot and we too will be in that 1% that has to plan seriously around potential estate tax liabilities.

By now we all know that the law greatly favors and protects the institution of marriage. For instance, the tax code goes above and beyond to ensure that the death of the first spouse doesn't have to trigger any transfer taxes. Under the Internal Revenue Code § 2056, an unlimited federal estate tax marital deduction is granted for certain qualifying dispositions of property to the surviving spouse at the death of the first spouse. So, if I die and leave to my spouse, outright, my entire estate, it will pass to my spouse free of estate and inheritance taxes, end of story. This is true even if I hap-

---

[45] See *Property Division Issues in NonMarital Relationships*, by Mary Bonauto, Michele Granda and Karen Loewy for a state by state case analysis, available at: http://www.glad.org/uploads/docs/publications/property–division–index.pdf.

pen to be extraordinarily wealthy and leave my spouse a whopping $1.2 billion at my death. As long as it passes directly to him and he has control over it, it would qualify for the Unlimited Marital Deduction for Federal Estate Tax purposes and a tax bill of exactly $0 would ensue.

This result could leave some us of scratching our heads and wondering why this would be possible? And, if it is true that spouses can receive unlimited amounts of property free of tax, why should we mess around with all of these marital trusts at all and instead just leave everything outright to our spouses? Suffice to say, that the IRS is one step ahead of us here. Although everything *could* pass free of the Federal Estate Tax at the first death via the marital deduction, the IRS will wait patiently until the second spouse dies, at which point the entire estate (property belonging to *both* spouses) is subject to the tax, but now we only have one spouse's exemption to use—that of the second spouse to die—because the first spouse never used her exemption if everything just passed to the second spouse outright via the unlimited marital deduction.

Tax Tip: Estate Taxes, Emergency Fiscal Planning, and Portability

As you no doubt realize by now, Congress and the Presidents bicker over tax reform with every new administration. When they leave everyone up in the air about the size of the estate tax exemption, going from $600,000 to $5 million and back to $1 million in a little over a decade, estate planners get nervous. One of the important provisions of the Tax Relief, Unemployment Insurance Reauthorization, and Job Creation Act of 2010 was to make the estate tax exemption *portable* between spouses. Remember, each individual is allowed to transfer a certain amount of property exempt from estate taxes to anyone, and they can also transfer unlimited amounts of property to spouses and/or qualified charities. So if a husband and wife can each transfer $5 million[46] tax free to their children and grandchildren, with proper planning they can transfer a total of $10 million. *Portability* allows for any unused exemption amount of the first spouse to be transferred to the second spouse. For example, let's say grandpa dies first with an estate worth $7 million. He gives half to his children and half to grandma. The $3.5 million to his children uses up 70% of his $5 million exemption, and the remaining $3.5 million passes to grandma tax free pursuant to the unlimited marital deduction. Now let's say grandma has her own $7 million, which is now $10.5 million because of grandpa's property that she acquired. Upon her death, she passes it all to her children, but her estate has to pay taxes on $5.5 million (the amount over her $5 million exemption). Prior to portability, their estate planners would have set up some complex credit shelter and QTIP trusts (and they will probably still do so even after portability because they serve additional purposes beyond taking full advantage of each spouse's exemption amount).

But now, with portability, grandma only has to pay taxes on $4 million because grandpa's unused $1.5 million exemption can be transferred to her and used at her death IF grandpa's executor checks the right box. Portability allows the executor of the first spouse to die to file an estate tax return, check a box stating that he wants to transfer grandpa's estate tax exemption amount to grandma (or whatever was left of his exemption), and the surviving spouse will be entitled to add the unused portion of the first spouse's exemption to her own. In January, 2013,

---

[46] Although the amount is $5.25 million for 2013, and will rise with inflation each year thereafter, I use $5 million here in this example just for simplicity's sake.

Congress made portability permanent as between married couples for gift and estate taxes, but not for the GST tax, a matter we address in greater detail in Chapter 9.

Although we delve into the tax issues in much more detail in Chapter 9, for now it's helpful to know that one of the benefits that trusts can provide between spouses is that both spouses can fully utilize their exemption amounts while coordinating the plan with the unlimited marital deduction. If the trust is drafted carefully, the first spouse to die can even allow the surviving spouse to receive varying benefits from the exempted property, while directing that the remainder pass to other beneficiaries (like children from a prior marriage, for example), with a result that at the first death, the Federal Estate Tax Bill could still be $0.

If we think about spousal trusts and why a decedent would want to use a trust rather than give his property outright to his surviving spouse, we generally get one or more of four possible answers.

1. The decedent spouse wants to give a surviving spouse as much property as he needs, but ultimately wants to control the final disposition of whatever property is left at the survivor's death and therefore doesn't want to give the property outright.

2. The decedent spouse wants to make sure property is well-managed in case the surviving spouse becomes incapacitated.

3. The decedent spouse detests his wife and her family and wants to give her the absolute minimum required by law and knows that he will pay less if he manages the estate plan effectively than if he gets a divorce, especially if he moves to Georgia. So even if he doesn't outlive his spouse, he can get his final revenge.

4. The decedent spouse wants to minimize tax liabilities by taking full advantage of both spouse's estate tax exemption amounts.

Most spousal trusts can accomplish more than one of these goals, although some are obviously contradictory. All trusts should provide for the surviving spouse's possible incapacity and, if there is a relevant concern, could be established to allow the surviving spouse to qualify for government health benefits like Medicaid. A Medicaid trust for a surviving spouse is essentially like one for the settlor so we won't repeat what we have already covered on planning for incapacity.

Furthermore, any trust providing life income to a spouse with the discretion to invade principal for the spouse's benefit can accomplish the first goal of having the remainder of the property pass according to the decedent's wishes and not through the surviving spouse's estate. The probate avoidance mechanism of trusts functions just as effectively when trying to keep the property out of the spouse's estate as out of the decedent's estate. Trusts have the added benefit of ensuring that a decedent spouse's estate ultimately passes to his issue and not to his second or third spouse's issue or new husband. Thus, they are highly recommended for blended and non-traditional families. In this sense spousal trusts are no different than trusts for other beneficiaries—probate avoidance, dispositive control, planning for incapacity, and disposing of property differently than the default rules of intestacy all adhere in spousal trusts.

Noteworthy are two aspects of marriage (and marital rights and duties) that make certain spousal trusts unique: the elective share and the unlimited marital tax deduction. Thus, spousal trusts can have particular effects if certain conditions apply and certain elements are built into the trust.

a. Elective Share Trusts

In some marital situations, a person may seek to have her trust operate in a way that will provide the minimum that her spouse would be legally entitled to, so that the rest can pass to others (usually this would be children from a prior marriage). To effectuate those goals, a trust can be drafted so that the surviving spouse receives his share in a separate trust which would be funded only with the amount of property he would have been entitled to elect against the estate under the state's elective share statute. A decedent may choose an elective share trust because she can't stand her husband and doesn't want to get a divorce, because she knows her husband already has plenty of wealth of his own but wants to be sure he has some benefit from his elective share property without saddling his estate with additional property, because she wants to set up the trust with a charitable remainder to minimize tax liabilities, because she knows her husband is easy prey to unscrupulous conartists and might lose the property if he has it outright, because she can't stand the thought that if he remarries his new spouse might have control over the property, and for an infinite number of other reasons.

Importantly, however, not all states will permit an elective share trust. Some states, especially those following the partnership theory of marriage, require that the surviving spouse be given a portion of the deceased spouse's estate outright in fee simple. But in those states that permit an interest in a trust to satisfy the elective share, it may make sense to set up an elective share trust to receive all property required under the state's elective share statute, provide for remainder beneficiaries to take upon the death of the surviving spouse, provide for successor trustees upon the incapacity of the surviving spouse, and perhaps give the surviving spouse (or trustee) discretion to invade the trust corpus for certain stated purposes, but not to be squandered on a new spouse. Be aware, however, that a trust interest in property is not the equivalent in value of being given the same property outright. Thus, if a spouse is entitled to an elective share of $500,000, the trust may have to be funded with up to twice that amount to be *valued* at the elective share amount.

We have already discussed one way to avoid the elective share in states that use only the net probate estate to determine its value: put everything into a revocable trust. For states that include non-probate property in the elective estate, few ways are available to minimize the effects of the elective share if a decedent wants her property to pass primarily to her children or favorite charity, even if the surviving spouse is independently wealthy and doesn't need an elective share. An elective share trust may just be the ticket, especially for providing for surviving spouses who are in a nursing home or dependent on Medicaid. A well-built special needs trust can keep a surviving spouse qualified for Medicaid, ensure that the remainder is transferred to the children, and still satisfy the elective share.

b.   *Credit Shelter and QTIP Trusts (the so-called AB Trust Regime)*

As mentioned above, a principal reason for using various spousal trusts is to minimize tax liability. While the extension of portability may resolve this issue to some extent, these trusts are still important for married couples who want to take advantage of the unlimited marital tax deduction. Remember, in order to fully take advantage of both spouse's estate tax exemption amounts ($5.25 million each in 2013) the first spouse will generally give his first $5.25 million to non-exempt beneficiaries (children and other friends and family) and the rest of his property to his spouse. Then upon the death of the second spouse, her estate will pay taxes on her wealth plus whatever she received from her deceased spouse if her estate exceeds $5.25 million. This can easily be accomplished by simply having the first spouse (Henry) give his $5.25 million directly to his children, and what's left he gives outright to his surviving spouse Wilma. (Note of course that Wilma has to receive at least as much as her elective share amount although she might want to waive it if she has adequate property and they are doing joint estate planning to minimize tax liabilities.) Let's say Henry wants to make sure Wilma has free access to property, including access to the $5.25 million he wants to give directly to his children, but he doesn't want it to be included in her estate for tax purposes. Henry also would really like it if some portion of that $5.25 million he is putting in the trust can count as Wilma's elective share. Proper planning will include a trust that gives her plenty of control but is still treated as a gift from him to his children so it's not included in her estate for tax purposes. Essentially, the trust will be designed to give Wilma the closest thing to ownership without the property actually passing into her estate. We can call this the "I want her to have it, but I don't want it to look like she has it" trust.

At the same time, Henry may be worried that Wilma will remarry or will decide to devise her entire estate to the First Church of Billy Bob, including the property he gave to her that utilized his unlimited marital deduction. He can't really do much about her own property, but he might want to place restrictions on the property he gives to her so that she can't fully dispose of it while simultaneously ensuring the property is included in Wilma's estate for tax purposes. The I.R.C. allows for certain gifts of limited interests to count as a transfer even though there are some fairly significant limitations. This is the "I don't want to give it to her, but I want it to look like I did" trust.

To effectuate this complex purpose, estate planners have devised a two-trust regime utilizing a credit shelter trust and a QTIP Trust that work together to have the decedent spouse control the disposition of property in both trusts, property that he supposedly gave to his spouse, and property he supposedly didn't give to his spouse. These trusts are designed to allow the decedent spouse to control ultimate disposition of the trust property and to take advantage of the various tax exemptions.

i.   The Credit Shelter Trust

The first trust is established and funded with an amount equal to the first spouse's federal estate tax exemption. This trust, the *credit shelter trust*, gives the surviving spouse a life interest in the income and *may* give the spouse the flexibility to withdraw principal if needed, but at the second spouse's death the remainder passes to children or other beneficiaries free of estate tax. By funding the first trust with the full amount allowed under the federal estate tax exemption, the total principal will pass without tax liabilities to the remainder beneficiaries. The point of the credit shelter trust is to give the surviving spouse as much access as possible to the property and significant benefits without having the property be deemed a transfer to the spouse and therefore be included in the second spouse's estate.

The great benefit of the credit shelter trust is that it can provide the surviving spouse with all the income, as well as distributions of principal for the surviving spouse's health, education, maintenance and support, while passing the remainder at the death of the second spouse, to the couple's children. The spouse can even be provided with a limited power to appoint principal of the credit shelter trust among the named beneficiaries, so that the plan can stay consistent with the family's goals. After all, if one of the children develops a drug problem, the surviving spouse may want the freedom to specify how and what that child should receive from the credit shelter trust at the second spouse's death. In order for this trust to utilize the first spouse's full estate tax exemption, it cannot give the surviving spouse *unfettered* discretion to invade principal or a general power of appointment. But the spouse can be given the next best thing: income for life, the right to invade principal for limited reasons, and a special power to appoint the remainder.

All of this can occur without triggering any Federal Estate Tax, either at the first death (because the trust share is funded using the estate tax exemption amount of the first spouse to die) or at the second death (because it was never part of the surviving spouse's estate due to the limited income interest). Depending on the terms of the trust, a credit shelter trust share may be distributed outright to the children at the death of the second spouse, or continue on in trust for the benefit of the children. By imposing a few strings and limitations, the first spouse can provide for his surviving spouse and still control final disposition of the property, have the property be deemed a transfer from him to the remainder beneficiaries, and utilize his estate tax exemption. Hence, he can give it to her without it looking like he did.

ii.   The Marital Deduction Trust or QTIP

Then, a second trust is established and funded with the remainder of the first spouse's property. This trust, to receive the full benefit of the marital deduction, must give the surviving spouse more control over the property than merely the life income. In a marital deduction trust, the spouse must have not only a life income, but the right to withdraw principal for any reason (i.e. have a general power of appointment). At the death of the second spouse the value of the trust corpus will be included in the surviving spouse's estate for estate tax purposes even though the first spouse dictated the final disposition of the remainder of the property. If the second spouse's combined estate and the trust corpus of this marital trust don't equal the amount of the second spouse's estate tax exemption, then no taxes will be due on the trust corpus. If the second spouse's estate is over the exemption, then taxes will have to be paid at the death of the second spouse, but they are postponed and possibly reduced if the second spouse actually spent some of the trust corpus or made lifetime gifts, in which case the gift tax might apply. Thus a generous *marital deduction* trust combined with a generous credit shelter trust can give the surviving spouse plenty of access to the trust property, including the lifetime income off both, while taking advantage of both spouse's estate tax exemptions.

On the other hand, what if the first spouse wants to take advantage of the unlimited marital tax deduction but doesn't want his surviving spouse to have access to the principal, especially if she is going to squander it on a new beaux, is likely to have huge debts, or might even let it sit and appreciate in value so more taxes will have to be paid? What if she is in a nursing home and won't benefit from it anyway? The marital deduction trust can also be more restrictive if it is set up to take advantage of the *Qualified Terminable Interest Property* (QTIP) rules of IRC § 2056. Prior to 1981, § 2056 of the Internal Revenue Code, which contains the marital deduction statute, only granted the marital deduction for absolute dispositions to a spouse. If I had wanted to limit what my spouse received in any way, I would be free to do so, but the transfer would not qualify for the marital deduction. In 1981, however, the Section was amended to allow for the possibility that certain *qualified terminable interest property* could qualify for the marital deduction.

Section 2056(b)(7) of the I.R.C. provides that a life estate for a surviving spouse qualifies as a QTIP so long as the "surviving spouse is entitled to all the income from the property, payable at least annually," "no person has a power to appoint any part of the property to any person other than the surviving spouse," and a timely election is made by the first spouse's executor to treat the property as a QTIP. To qualify as a QTIP trust and still count as part of the surviving spouse's estate at her death, therefore, she must be entitled to the full income from the property, and there can be no power to reduce the trust corpus by giving it to anyone other than the surviving spouse. The trust also has to be designated a QTIP trust by the executor of the first spouse to die and the election is irrevocable. The trust will be deemed part of the second spouse's estate even if she wins the lottery and now has to pay estate taxes at a higher rate than her deceased spouse.

The QTIP Trust is a great planning tool for use in estates where the ultimate transfer tax situation may be unclear at the time the trust is drafted, or when a settlor wishes to make full use of the marital deduction but also wants to limit a surviving spouse's access to trust assets. Since the decision of whether or not to make the "QTIP election" for federal estate tax purposes does not occur until after the first spouse's death, an executor has great flexibility in determining how the QTIP property should be properly taxed.

Why would a spouse want to limit the survivor's control over trust property at the survivor's death? Usually, this scenario arises in blended families and in situations where the couple knows that the survivor will not need to rely on assets within the QTIP trust to continue living at his or her accustomed standard. The surviving spouse can also be granted distributions of principal for her health, education and maintenance as well as given a right to withdraw the greater of 5% or $5,000 from the trust each year, for any reason. This specific power, described further in the tax section, is called a "Five and Five Power" (5/5 Power). The 5/5 Power can be an added layer of protection for a surviving spouse, in that this amount will be available for any reason, even those that fall outside of the ascertainable standards for health, education, maintenance and support. So, if the surviving spouse wants to use the 5/5 Power to invade the principal so that she can have money to paint the house, buy a new dog, or go on a trip around the world, she is free to do so.

At the death of the second spouse, the remainder of the QTIP Trust will pass to the beneficiaries designated by the first spouse to die. Usually, these would include children of the first spouse to die instead of the children of the surviving spouse, (or worse yet, to the survivor's new spouse! which might happen if the spouse were given the property outright), although the second spouse to die can be given some limited powers of appointment over this trust share, as well as over property in the credit shelter trust. The full value of the QTIP trust property, however, would be included in the estate of the second spouse to die.

As you can see, the credit shelter trust can be set up to give the surviving spouse very little access to the property (no problem since it's deemed a gift to the remainder beneficiaries anyway and uses up the first spouse's estate tax exemption amount) or a fairly significant right of access (this is the dicey part—giving the surviving spouse plenty of access without the trust being deemed a transfer to the spouse). On a continuum of stingy to generous with regard to the credit shelter trust, it's as we move toward the generous end of the scale that we start pushing the boundaries of property law principles. You can't give the property to the surviving spouse and have it not count as a gift unless you tie it up with at least a few strings. An unfettered discretion to invade principal or a general power of appointment over the trust corpus is too much freedom in the surviving spouse and will cause the trust to be deemed a transfer to the survivor.

At the same time, marital deduction trusts can be set up to give the surviving spouse lots of access (no problem since it is deemed a gift to the spouse and the property is included in her estate) or very little access (this is the dicey part here—giving the surviving spouse very little control but still calling it a gift). Thus, on the stingy/generous continuum it's when the trust is stingy that you run up against the property principles. As a general rule, you won't be setting up the trusts to be generous in the first and stingy in the second, although you might want to be stingy in the first and generous in the second. More often the first spouse will want to be stingy in both or generous in both, so you should be pushing the envelope only with one of these trusts. Which way you go, however, depends on multiple factors that will be unique with your clients. Understanding why you want to be stingy with one or generous with the other, however, requires a much better understanding of the transfer tax regime than we can provide here.

Furthermore, even in the vast majority of estates that won't face estate tax liabilities, a spousal trust that provides for incapacity, support, and final disposition to the first spouse's beneficiaries may be a must for blended families, non-traditional families, second and third marriages, or other unusual family situations. The key to understanding marital trusts, however, is deciding whether you want the trust to count as a gift to the spouse even though you have tied the property up with lots of strings, or have it count as a gift to others even though you have given the spouse fairly free rein to benefit from it. And that can only be determined after lengthy counsel with your clients and a firm understanding of their entire family situation.

A Social Policy Footnote

As I'm sure you have noticed, we try to alternate between using *he* or *she* throughout this book to refer to testators or spouses in an effort to be gender neutral, but there really is no way to be truly neutral. In fact, the law of succession is one of the most gendered areas of law you will encounter. Because of the history of coverture, employment and education limitations, and gender role expectations, married women are starting far behind married men in their ability to amass wealth and control it. Historically, however, women often did regain significant wealth in their later years, because while all the laws disfavored women, biology gave them longer lives. Thus, they were far more likely to outlive their husbands, assuming they survived childbirth, and could ultimately control much of a couple's wealth.

But where the widow actually possessed her first husband's property, she became prey to fortune hunters, which gave rise to the common stereotype that widows should be closely guarded. At least the U.S. and the U.K. didn't enact laws prohibiting widows from remarrying, as was the policy until the twentieth century in India. History, however, repeats itself, because just as the common lawyers of the eighteenth century worked diligently to separate a widow from her husband's property through the use of strict settlements, thus making sure the property didn't transfer from her first husband's family to her second husband's family, the estates lawyers of today make a living ensuring that the surviving widow has the bare minimum of control over the *husband's* wealth after his death, often just enough to take advantage of *her* estate tax exemption. What gets glossed over, of course, is the fact that under coverture some of the husband's property had originally belonged to the wife before marriage, and most wives certainly contributed to the acquisition of property during marriage.

The QTIP trust is one more mechanism in the long history of restricting a widow's rights to property that may have actually been hers at one time, or is arguably a product of her labor and investment. There is a sizable literature on the sexist attitudes behind the QTIP—because it is very often the product of the husband's estate plan, and not the wife's. Jeffrey Pennell has opined that estate planning has not changed much since he learned it 35 years ago, and yet the demographics of the clients have changed dramatically. Baby boomers have more debt, fewer children, more marriages, more pensions, and married later than the generation before them. Generation X-ers are more likely to have pre-marital children, don't expect to have social security, and invest more heavily in mutual funds than the boomers. Widows are less likely to get remarried than widowers and yet the traditional estate plan includes a QTIP with strict limitations on surviving wives and there are very few QTIPs in the estate plans of women. This is because, as Pennell suggests, the fear of a wife remarrying and disinheriting the children of the first marriage. This is the bogeyman of the pre-Boomer generation. A 1989 study reported by Lawrence Waggoner showed that only 8% of surviving widows remarry, and they wait an average of 8 years, while over 20% of widowers remarry, and they do so within 4 years.[47] Yet "most estate planners will confirm that surviving remarried widows seldom engage in disinheritance planning, whereas surviving remarried widowers do so with much greater frequency."[48]

---

[47] Lawrence W. Waggoner, *Marital Property Rights in Transition*, 59 MO. L. REV. 21, 49 (1994).

[48] Jeffrey Pennell, *It's Not Your Father's Buick Anymore: Estate Planning for the Next Generation(s) of Clients*, Heckerling Inst. on Est. Planning, 13–1, 13–18 (2009).

> The QTIP trust is a product of marital distrust that may not actually exist and it is certainly used in gendered ways to disempower wives, just as the eighteenth century strict settlement did. And ironically, the QTIP trust has come of age during a time of unprecedented female employment, a historically high number of female-headed households, and when women's education levels are beginning to outpace that of men. You will be in the forefront of twenty-first century estate planning and will need to think seriously about the assumptions and stereotypes implicit in the planning tools that were developed by those of a very different generation.

PROBLEMS

7.10. Harry and Winifred have been married for 55 years, have three grown children, and have both worked to amass a joint estate of $10 million. The vast majority of the property, however, is titled in Harry's name; only her car, a bank account, and a small retirement account are in Winifred's name. Harry has just inherited an additional $2 million from his mother and they have come to you for some estate planning. They trust each other implicitly and want the survivor to have as much access to the joint property as he/she needs, but upon the death of the survivor they want it all to pass to their three children. What would you recommend?

7.11. Sally and Joan have been cohabiting partners for 55 years, have three grown children (Sally is the biological mom and Joan adopted all three), and have both worked to amass a joint estate of $10 million. The majority of the property is titled jointly, or is equally split between Sally and Joan individually. Sally has just inherited an additional $2 million from her mother and they have come to you for some estate planning. They trust each other implicitly and want the survivor to have as much access to the joint property as he/she needs, but upon the death of the survivor they want it all to pass to their three children. What would you recommend?

6. PRE-NUPTIAL AGREEMENTS WAIVING SPOUSAL PROTECTIONS

Historically, in an age of coverture and reliance on the unity of person doctrine (which viewed husband and wife to be one in law), spouses could not enter into legally binding contracts with each other, either before or after marriage. After marriage they couldn't enter into contracts because that was seen as making a contract with oneself. Before marriage they could enter into a contract, but once the marriage occurred, there was no enforcement mechanism, again because it would be like enforcing a breach of contract action against oneself. Husbands had to be the parties filing suit. Even if a woman wrote a will before she married, then married and was widowed, the will would be deemed revoked by the marriage and not revived because the period of coverture essentially wiped the slate clean. For that reason, all pre-marital settlements, agreements, and contracts were entered into by the husband and the wife's father, brother, or uncle, i.e., two independent legal agents.

Today, however, husbands and wives can enter into contracts with each other, both before and during marriage, thanks to the passage of Married Women's Property Acts in all states. These statutes allow married women to have a separate legal identity for holding property which they can then manage as they choose. The idea that a spouse, historically a wife, would agree in advance of marriage to waive her statutory dower rights has a long pedigree. Because dower was such a strong encumbrance to free alienation of property, strict settlements became common during the Tudor/Stuart period to facilitate land transfers. The strict settlement, that replaced dower, was a contract between a bride's father and her future husband, and sometimes her father-in-law, by which each father agreed to settle property on the couple, the bride waived her dower rights, and in exchange she was to be guaranteed an annuity, which was a set income for life if her husband predeceased her. How many young brides actually understood that they were waiving real property rights in exchange for a relatively modest income is something we will never know. Fortunately, unlike the early modern courts, judges today cast a protective eye over pre-nuptial agreements to ensure that both parties fully understand what they are giving up.

Most pre-nuptial agreements (also called ante-nuptial agreements) are executed by couples entering into second or later marriages where they have children from a prior relationship. And most agreements consist of, either, each spouse waiving all statutory rights in the other's estate, or the less wealthy spouse waiving all statutory rights in exchange for a guaranteed amount. This guaranteed amount can be either a life interest in a trust, some kind of annuity, or particular items of property. Similar to a strict settlement, it provides a guaranteed pay out in exchange for the uncertainty of a percentage of the decedent spouse's estate. Even if I marry Donald Trump tomorrow and feel confident that a 30% share of his estate will make me richer than I could ever imagine, all that wealth could be lost after the marriage and I will get very little if the Donald goes bankrupt. Let's hope Bernie Madoff's wife married for love and not money?

Despite their long pedigree, however, pre-nuptial agreements have been looked at with some disfavor by courts, especially when it turns out that the decedent had concealed significant assets from his soon-to-be bride. She will be justifiably miffed when she discovers that her husband was sheltering billions of dollars in off-shore assets or owned a couple of mansions in Palm Beach that he never told her about. Thus, as with all contracts, fraud, misrepresentation, or mistake can void the agreement. She (and it is usually a she, though not always) needs to know what she is giving up before she can make an informed decision whether to waive her statutory rights to a share of her spouse's estate.

Because spouses are in a *de facto* confidential relationship, the common law, and later statutes, have come to require fair and reasonable disclosure on the part of both spouses and no overreaching or duress. But how realistic is that? Given the current demographics, wives tend to be younger than their husbands, have less wealth going into a second or third marriage, and less likely to have their own legal counsel. It is common knowledge among high-powered family lawyers that you don't broach the subject of a pre-nuptial agreement until after the wedding invitations are sent out. What bride wants to have the wedding postponed while the lawyers work out the messy property details? How would that reflect on her character? Consider how gender, class, race, and sexuality differences might play out in the application of the Uniform Premarital Agreement Act.[49]

---

[49] The UPAA has been adopted in 24 states: Arizona, Arkansas, California, Connecticut, Delaware, Florida, Hawaii, Idaho, Illinois, Indiana, Kansas, Maine, Montana, Nebraska,

Uniform Premarital Agreement Act (1983)

§ 2. Formalities. A premarital agreement must be in writing and signed by both parties. It is enforceable without consideration.

§ 3. Content.

(a) Parties to a premarital agreement may contract with respect to:

(1) the rights and obligations of each of the parties in any of the property of either or both of them whenever and wherever acquired or located;

(2) the right to buy, sell, use, transfer, exchange, abandon, lease, consume, expend, assign, create a security interest in, mortgage, encumber, dispose of, or otherwise manage and control property;

(3) the disposition of property upon separation, marital dissolution, death, or the occurrence or nonoccurrence of any other event;

(4) the modification or elimination of spousal support;

(5) the making of a will, trust, or other arrangement to carry out the provisions of the agreement;

(6) the ownership rights in and disposition of the death benefit from a life insurance policy;

(7) the choice of law governing the construction of the agreement; and

(8) any other matter, including their personal rights and obligations, not in violation of public policy or a statute imposing a criminal penalty.

(b) The right of a child to support may not be adversely affected by a premarital agreement.

§4. Effect of Marriage. A premarital agreement becomes effective upon marriage.

§ 6. Enforcement.

(a) A premarital agreement is not enforceable if the party against whom enforcement is sought proves that:

(1) that party did not execute the agreement voluntarily; or

(2) the agreement was unconscionable when it was executed and, before execution of the agreement, that party:

(i) was not provided a fair and reasonable disclosure of the property or financial obligations of the other party;

(ii) did not voluntarily and expressly waive, in writing, any right to disclosure of the property or financial obligations of the other party beyond the disclosure provided; and

(iii) did not have, or reasonably could not have had, an adequate knowledge of the property or financial obligations of the other party.

(b) If a provision of a premarital agreement modifies or eliminates spousal support and that modification or elimination causes one party to the agreement to be eligible for support under a program of public assistance at the time of separation or

---

Nevada, New Mexico, North Carolina, North Dakota, Oregon, Rhode Island, South Dakota, Texas, Utah, Virginia, and the District of Columbia. It has been introduced in 2012 in West Virginia.

marital dissolution, a court, notwithstanding the terms of the agreement, may require the other party to provide support to the extent necessary to avoid that eligi-eligibility.

(c) An issue of unconscionability of a premarital agreement shall be decided by the court as a matter of law.

The UPC also provides for pre-nuptial agreements.

UPC § 2–213. Waiver of Right to Elect and of Other Rights.

(a) The right of election of a surviving spouse and the rights of the surviving spouse to homestead allowance, exempt property, and family allowance, or any of them, may be waived, wholly or partially, before or after marriage, by a written contract, agreement, or waiver signed by the surviving spouse.

(b) A surviving spouse's waiver is not enforceable if the surviving spouse proves that:

(1) he [or she] did not execute the waiver voluntarily; or

(2) the waiver was unconscionable when it was executed and, before execution of the waiver, he [or she

(A) was not provided a fair and reasonable disclosure of the property or financial obligations of the decedent,

(B) did not voluntarily and expressly waive, in writing, any right to disclosure of the property or financial obligations of the decedent beyond the disclosure provided;

(C) did not have, or reasonably could not have had, an adequate knowledge of the property or financial obligations of the decedent.

(c) An issue of unconscionability of a waiver is for decision by the court as a matter of law.

(d) Unless it provides to the contrary, a waiver of "all rights," or equivalent language, in the property or estate of a present or prospective spouse or a complete property settlement entered into after or in anticipation of separation or divorce is a waiver of all rights of elective share, homestead allowance, exempt property, and family allowance by each spouse in the property of the other and a renunciation by each of all benefits that would otherwise pass to him [or her] from the other by intestate succession or by virtue of any will executed before the waiver or property settlement.

A spouse can waive any or all of his statutory property rights, including rights to homestead, family allowance, exempt property, intestate shares, elective shares, pretermitted spousal shares, and the like. But spousal contracts don't often cover the more remote ways in which marriage provides benefits, as in anti-lapse statutes, or preferences against abatement. A premarital agreement can also be made regarding life insurance, retirement beneficiary designations, and pension rights. Furthermore it can contain a catch-all provision that waives all legal claims on behalf of a spouse, like the right to recover for the wrongful death of a spouse. A typical provision might read:

each party hereby waives and releases to the other party and to the other party's heirs, executor, administrators and assigns any and all rights and causes of action which may arise by reason of the marriage between the parties . . . with respect to any property, real or personal, tangible or intangible . . . now owned or hereafter acquired."[50]

The effect of pre-nuptial agreements on rights covered by ERISA is also somewhat complicated. ERISA has a provision allowing spouses to waive their rights but the waiver is invalid unless:

1. The spouse consents in writing,
2. The election designates a beneficiary (or a form of benefits) which may not be changed without spousal consent, and
3. The spouse's consent acknowledges the effect of such election and is witnessed by a plan representative or notary public.[51]

The typical catchall provision cited above was held to be invalid for waiving ERISA rights because it did not designate a beneficiary or include the spouse's consent.[52]

As a general matter, pre-nuptial agreements are governed by standard contract doctrines of consideration, disclosure, and reasonableness. But where a statute has been enacted, the specific requirements of the statute must necessarily be met.

As you can see, there are extensive spousal protections provided by the probate codes of all the states, and testators can certainly give the surviving spouse all or most of their estate at death. Careful manipulation of spousal rights arises most often in cases involving second or later marriages, where there are children by different spouses, and, unfortunately, some tension or strife exists between the couple. While good planning before marriage is important, most estate planning happens after the marriage. For instance, it is difficult to convince a client that she cannot disinherit her husband just because he a) has more wealth than she does, b) orally agreed that he didn't marry her for her money and doesn't want anything but fond memories of her after she dies, c) had an affair and wants a divorce, d) is a jerk, or e) all of the above. But proper planning can help both preserve wealth and reduce the emotional scars that so often plague married life.

B. PROTECTIONS FOR CHILDREN

Probably one of the most important reasons people amass wealth during their lifetimes is to leave something for their children, so that they can have a head start in the race of life. We all know that until they reach the age of majority, children are not capable of managing property, nor may they make a will unless they are emancipated minors. The *Law of Infants,* as it used to be called, prohibited minors from entering into contracts, being sued, managing property, serving as trustees, or obtaining credit. These age-related constraints continue, although at least the child of today is not going to be removed from his home by his parents' lord, nor is his or her marriage going to become a commodity on the open market if dad dies before his son reaches age 21. The child can come into his inheritance without

---

[50]   Hurwitz v. Sher, 982 F.2d 778, 781 (2d. Cir. 1992).

[51]   See 29 U.S.C. § 1055(c)(2)(A).

[52]   *See Hurwitz v. Sher,* 982 F.2d 788 (2nd Cir. 1992).

having to pay one or two-year's income to acquire his father's estates, and she doesn't have to pay a high penalty if she rejects the marriage partner proposed for her by her guardian.[53] Note that this doesn't mean that there are no legal consequences to children inheriting property. Because children cannot manage property, some sort of arrangement must be made for them, both for their persons and their property. Guardianships, custodianships, and trusts all provide mechanisms for taking care of children when their parents are unable to do so.

Perhaps the most important aspect of planning for surviving dependent children is to first provide adequately for their basic needs until they reach adulthood and, only after that, to provide additional support for college, buying a house, setting up in a business, or making other gifts. There are default legal mechanisms for dealing with children who inherit property but, not surprisingly, the default guardianship is cumbersome and inflexible. Trusts and powers provide greater flexibility beyond merely providing for basic support and can be established to take effect only upon the death of the parents. We will discuss a number of these mechanisms, including trusts for dependents who have special needs, in the following sections. Currently it is important to realize that the basic tools we have already discussed are usually better than the default options, even if they aren't adapted for the special needs of dependent minors.

1. GUARDIANSHIPS AND CUSTODIANSHIPS

Originally, a guardianship was the only *legal* way to deal with property passing to minors, usually upon the death of their father. A trust could be created in equity, but for children without resources, guardianship was the only solution. With a guardianship, both the person and the property had to be provided for, and courts were jealous supervisors of guardianships. Originating in the ecclesiastical courts, guardianships could serve three different functions and three different people might be assigned the different roles: the care and upbringing of the minor child's person, the care and management of the child's property generally, and control for the limited purpose of managing lawsuits (the modern-day *guardian ad litem*).

For hundreds of years, there were no legal consequences to a child if the mother died. But if the father died, even if the mother still lived, the child was considered an orphan and his estate and person were subject to guardianships. Prior to 1660, the ecclesiastical courts would appoint a family member to take care of the child's person, usually the mother, although to avoid potential conflicts it was never a person who could benefit from the death of the child. The late medieval and early-modern law was quite practical in that regard. With the exception of heirs to large properties who might find themselves in wardship to their lord upon the death of their fathers, most orphans went to live with family members, and their fates were probably no worse than the fates of any children during an age of plagues, pestilence, war, and primitive sanitation. Another family member, and often it was the mother, would be appointed guardian of the child's estate. The mother was actually the preferred guardian because she was not a legal heir to her child and, therefore, could manage the property and child's person together without the taint of self-interest. Children who were to inherit sizable estates, however, would usually find themselves with two guardians, one for their person and one for their estates, and it was not

---

[53] See discussion of feudal wardship, *infra* at Chapter 7A below.

unusual for there to be disagreements about how the child should be raised and whether adequate sums were provided from the estate to the caretaker to cover the cost of the child's education and upbringing.

After 1660 a father could appoint a guardian in his will for either the person or estate of his minor children, and the guardian of the person, if appointed, would take precedence over the child's mother. The testamentary guardian might choose to allow the child to remain with his mother, or he could remove the child from his mother's care at any time. This led to over two centuries of legal conflicts between mothers and testamentary guardians. Slowly the litigation pushed the courts to develop rules that the guardianship of the person as well as of the estate was a *trust*, that it had to be exercised for the *benefit* of the child, and that the courts had ultimate power to intervene and *remove* a guardian, despite the father's testamentary appointment, if the guardian was failing in his fiduciary duties. In the nineteenth century mothers were given the right to also make testamentary appointments of guardians who would serve with guardians of the father. Mothers, however, could not make testamentary appointments of guardians to serve with the father because they could not make a will while their husbands were still alive. It wasn't until the 20th century that mothers acquired equal rights to make educational, religious, and medical decisions for their children, and to be deemed the guardian of the children if the father died while they were still minors.

Today we think of orphans as only those children who have lost both parents, for while two parents are better than one, one is certainly better than none. However, one parent today is legally sufficient to prevent the need for guardianship. But if both parents die, an adult must be appointed guardian for the person of the minor. This is done pursuant to the state's guardianship laws. Although a parent can name a guardian for her children in her will, a court is not bound to appoint that person guardian if the court is not convinced doing so would be in the child's best interests. Persons who are appointed as guardians are often given control over the child's property and inheritances, which is usually why there might be a long line of people lining up to offer themselves as guardians for the children of wealthy celebrities, like Michael Jackson and Anna Nicole Smith. But in many instances a guardian is not necessarily given the power over the child's estate. This is especially true if the property remains in a trust until the child comes of age. While the courts will usually honor a testamentary appointment of a guardian for either the child's person or estate, they will still undertake a thorough investigation of the child's best interests. Generally, however, a trustee of property will not be questioned unless an interested party challenges the trustee's actions. So even if a decedent parent cannot avoid judicial oversight in the appointment of her child's physical custodian, she can avoid judicial oversight in the appointment of the trustee over her child's estate.

There are important distinctions between guardians and parents (natural or adoptive). Guardians of the person generally do not have the full range of parental rights that go with adoption although they can make day-to-day decisions about what schools to attend, where the children will spend their vacations, and whether they have to write those darned thank-you notes before they can play with their new toys. Most importantly, a child does not inherit from his guardian and a guardian does not inherit from his ward. A legal adoption by the guardian may be necessary to fully round out the parental rights over a non-biological child.

This class is focused on the property of the child, from the $3.00 left by the tooth fairy[54] to the $20.00 birthday check, to the earnings and inheritances of millionaire models, child actors, and celebrity orphans. Therefore, we are not concerned with the procedures and rules regarding guardianship of the person here. These issues are usually covered in family law classes. The property aspects are complex enough. Because children, even while their parents are still alive, may not manage and control any property they might acquire, some adult has to be legally responsible for their property. Legal parents are the *de jure* and *de facto* guardians of their children's property but they can be, and have been, removed if they breach their fiduciary obligations. Your child, or his guardian *ad litem*, probably won't sue you for throwing out the box of broken model airplane parts, but they have been known to sue parents for mismanaging their earnings or for self-dealing. LeAnn Rimes, Drew Barrymore, McCauley Culkin, and Gary Coleman are in the small class of celebrity children who sued their own parents for mismanaging their fortunes. Fortunately, however, most of us won't be sued by our children, although it is not unusual for children to harbor strong resentment against a parent who abuses the child's property. Once they come of age, the children have also sued to recover property that their parents inappropriately disposed of.[55]

Probably the simplest way to deal with small gifts to minors, such as $200 for the college savings account, perhaps a car when the child reaches 16, or investments of stock in a child's name, are the Uniform Gifts to Minors Act (UGMA) and the Uniform Transfers to Minors Act (UTMA) promulgated by the Uniform Law Commission in 1956 and 1983 respectively. The UGMA was promulgated to deal with gifts of cash and securities to minors and was adopted in all states and jurisdictions in the United States in some form or other.[56] It provided that certain banks and financial institutions could serve as depositories of custodial funds, and amendments in 1965 and 1966 broadened the types of financial institutions that could serve as depositories while expanding the property subject to the Act to life insurance policies and annuity contracts. While most states amended their UGMA after 1966, at least 11 did not, and many more added additional types of property that could be the subject of a gift under their versions of the Act. As a result, there was a tremendous lack of uniformity in the law among the various states.

Since one of the points of the Uniform Law Commission's recommended Uniform Acts is to avoid conflict of laws issues between the states, the Uniform Law Commission promulgated the UTMA in 1983 to broaden the scope of the UGMA to reflect many of the more inclusive versions of state laws while bringing the states back to some semblance of uniformity. The UTMA also dramatically expanded the possible property that could be held pursuant to the act. It permits any kind of property, real or personal, tan-

---

[54] Yes, inflation has even affected the tooth fairy, who now brings, on average, $3.00 per tooth. See Sadie Whitelocks, *Tooth Fairy falls victim to inflation as children receive average $3 a tooth*, MAIL ONLINE (Sept. 4, 2012), http://www.dailymail.co.uk/femail/article–2198362/Tooth–Fairy–immune–inflation–children–receive–3–milk–teeth.html.

[55] Jimenez v. Lee, 274 Or. 457, 547 P.2d 126 (1976); *see also* Jodi Wilgoren & Geraldine Fabrikant, *Knives Drawn for a $15 Billion Family Pie*, N.Y. TIMES (Dec. 11, 2002) and Mark Maremont, *Pritzkers Settle Family Lawsuit; Cost: A Fortune*, WALL ST. J. (Jan. 7, 2005), (where Hyatt heir Robert Pritzker was sued by his daughter Liesel Pritzker, for misappropriation of trust funds which resulted in each of Pritzker's children, Liesel and Matthew, receiving approximately $450 million in settlement).

[56] Revisions in 1965 and 1966.

gible or intangible, to be made the subject of a transfer to a *custodian* for the benefit of a minor. It includes transfers outright, but also transfers from trusts, estates, and guardianships, and from third parties indebted to a minor, such as tort claim debtors.

Although entitled a *custodianship* under the Act, the adult who manages the property closely resembles a guardian. Property is registered or transferred as follows: O to _____ "as custodian for _____ (name of minor) under the [state's] Uniform Transfers to Minors Act". However, unlike a trust, a custodianship is not a separate legal entity; the property is indefeasibly vested in the minor and therefore taxable income is attributable to and reportable by the minor. The custodianship also terminates, automatically, at age 21 and may not be extended except by placing the property into a trust. Moreover, the custodian is not a trustee with the full panoply of fiduciary duties; rather, the custodian must "observe the standard of care that would be observed by a prudent person dealing with property of another."[57]

If property is not placed into a custodianship under the UTMA, which requires an intentional transfer to the designated custodian using the appropriate terminology, then the court will have to order a traditional guardianship for the property. A guardianship is far less flexible than a custodianship, and both are less flexible than a trust. Guardians typically must file a bond, provide periodic accountings to a court, seek court approval for sales, investment or distribution of property, and the guardianship ends when the child reaches 18. Both because guardianships end before many children are ready to manage large quantities of property, and because they require extensive court supervision, anyone who is giving property to a child should consider doing so through a trust if the property requires management or supervision. Although a custodianship under the UTMA is fine for small bank accounts, it is probably not adequate for real property or large sums of money that need to be invested carefully. Additionally, although courts treat guardians like trustees, who must manage the child's property for the benefit of the child, trustees can be given more flexibility by the settlor, and the trust can be set up to last longer than the child's reaching majority. Most importantly, the custodian/guardian/trustee of the property need not be the guardian of the child's person.

In situations where a child inherits property unexpectedly, or is the recipient of a large tort judgment for instance, and a trust was infeasible, a court-supervised guardianship will be necessary. Because courts don't want to supervise guardians very closely, however, they are likely to approve placing the property into a trust, like a supplemental needs trust, that doesn't require constant court supervision.

You already know the basics about trusts, which are no doubt the best tool for dealing with substantial wealth that devolves on a minor (like Anna Nicole Smith's daughter or Michael Jackson's children). One good thing about a trust is that it can be established to end only on certain conditions, like when the child is mature enough to handle the money or when the trustee believes the child is responsible, thus avoiding the Paris Hilton problem. It doesn't have to automatically end at age 18, like a guardianship, or age 21, like a custodianship. Clients with minor children, therefore, might consider creating a testamentary trust in their wills in the unlikely event they do not survive until their children reach majority. And trusts for

---

[57] UTMA § 12(a)(3).

minors will likely want to take advantage of certain flexible elements to maximize their efficacy.

2. TRUSTS AND POWERS FOR MINORS

As with trusts for spouses, trusts and powers for minors are often premised on two sometimes conflicting policies: estate planning (support, maintenance, and family planning) and tax minimization. In wealthy estates, planning entails considering both. But in the vast majority of estates, estate tax concerns are non-existent. That doesn't mean, however, that some of the tax-motivated mechanisms might not also serve well in the context of a modest-sized estate. As you remember from Chapter 4, there are two basic types of trusts: mandatory and discretionary. When it comes to children, there are many good reasons to use discretionary trusts. Why pay out if a child is going to squander the money on trips to Disney Land, a pile of Legos, the newest iPhone 48, or a sports car? On the other hand, certain tax benefits accrue only if the trust is irrevocable or the beneficiary has the power to withdraw. Balancing powers requires having a good sense for the child's responsibility level and the overall needs of the estate.

a. Basic Mandatory or Discretionary Trust

A basic mandatory trust can be established via a will, or *inter vivos*, to provide income for a child until he or she reaches a certain age, and then the trust will pay out the principal to the child at age 25, or 30, or some other appropriate time. The trust can also pay out in sequence: one-third at age 25, one-third at age 30, and one-third at age 35, for example. The trust could also impose certain conditions on pay-out: graduate from college, marry, have a child, buy a house, win a Nobel Prize. If these conditions do not occur, the trust must specify where the trust corpus will go upon failure of the conditions. In most states, as long as the trust will terminate during the lifetime of a known child, there are no perpetuities problems, and as long as the conditions and terms are reasonably ascertainable, the trust can be performed as planned.

But life often doesn't go as planned. What if, after the trust settlor's death, the child is injured and permanently disabled and requires extensive medical aid to survive? The mandatory pay-out of the trust may disrupt government health benefits, and may result in the trust corpus being used up before insurance or other benefits kick in. What if the child becomes addicted to drugs and wants to spend the trust income and principal on her cocaine habit? What if the child doesn't want to go to college, and instead becomes a Pulitzer Prize winning author and stable mother of three children, but can't reach the trust corpus because the condition of college was mandatory? What if the child wants to live in a 1973 VW micro-bus with her boyfriend or girlfriend while she surfs all year? What if your child is a delightful, generous person, who has some very abusive friends?

These kinds of uncertainties lead many parents to build some kind of discretion into trusts for their children, especially if they aren't alive to help guide their children through those difficult adolescent years. If a co-parent is still alive, a nuclear family probably doesn't need a testamentary trust unless there are other issues, like questions of remarriage or estate taxes. If these issues do arise, then the co-parent can serve as trustee, and be given the discretion to support the child who wants to travel the European museums in preparation for her studies as an art historian, but not the child who wants to surf the waves of the Philippines and taste-test every beer ever made. There is also the uncertainty of the co-parent dying simultaneously with the parent, or shortly thereafter, leaving the trusteeship either to remote relatives who may not share the same parenting values, or to corporate trustees who are very good at diversifying the trust portfolio but not very good at judging between ballet lessons and trips to the ball game.

Unfortunately, there are no easy formulas for this particular problem. Clients should be counseled to carefully consider who should serve as trustee and/or guardian of their children and whether certain requirements, like a child must go to college, should be built into the trust, or left to the trustee's discretion. We think we might have a good sense of our children's most likely futures, but something as simple and terrible as 9–11 or Hurricane Katrina can change a family's future forever.

In certain situations, it might make more sense to use a stand-alone power rather than a trust. If one parent dies and the other is still alive caring for the children, the decedent parent can give the other parent a special power of appointment over her estate to use the property for the benefit of the children. There is no trust, therefore no trust obligations, and the surviving parent has broad discretion to use the property for the children's benefit, but there is no transfer of the property from the deceased to the surviving parent, and thus no tax liabilities at the death of the surviving spouse.

It is almost always better to give discretion to the trustee if you feel confident that the trustee not only will make good decisions, but will be immune to pressure from cranky teenagers to make distributions whenever their credit card balances get too high.

b. Support Trusts

Support trusts are often used for both children and surviving spouses, and give the trustee discretion to distribute income and/or principal for the *support* of the beneficiaries. Support trusts are set up to require that the funds be used for the *support* of the beneficiary, and not for frivolous flings or luxuries. And certainly using the funds for food, housing, utilities, tuition, and medical expenses counts as support. But support trusts raise an additional set of questions about the level of support (basic physical needs or support in the manner to which the beneficiaries have been accustomed) and whether the trust should pay out even if the beneficiary has adequate income to provide support. As a general rule, the trustee of a support trust must pay income, and principal if the trust allows invasion of the trust corpus, to support the beneficiary, at a minimum, in the manner to which he is accustomed, regardless of whether the beneficiary already has an adequate income to support him. Thus, the beneficiary should be able to turn to the trust to pay bills and other support expenses, and use his lottery winnings or salary on discretionary items.

That said, support trusts can be limiting if a beneficiary needs money for some unusual expense, like setting herself up in business, which in the long run might help alleviate the beneficiary's need for support. Furthermore, if the trust is a mandatory income trust, the trustee must pay the income regardless of whether the beneficiary is using the money wisely for support purposes. Most support trusts, therefore, are discretionary, both with regard to income and principal, and that requires a trustee who is paying close attention to the needs and lifestyle of the beneficiary. Remember the lawyer–trustee who got in trouble in *Marsman v. Nasca*, 573 N.E.2d 1025, 1030–1031 (Mass. Ct. App. 1991), for failing to pay out income or principal when Cappy's expenses caused him to lose his house? Trustees are not immune from lawsuits by beneficiaries who think the trustee should be paying out more than the trustee is choosing to pay. Using up trust assets in litigation is certainly not what most trust settlors want; thus, giving the trustee complete discretion may be beneficial and it may be counter-productive depending on the trustee's and the beneficiary's needs and personalities.

Settlors should indicate priorities among beneficiaries if there is more than one. For instance, even a support trust for one's children, with the principal payable when they reach age 30, can cause problems if a trustee has distributed more to one child than another. Should the trustee then calculate the greater benefits paid to the one child when distributing the principal? This is even harder when the income beneficiaries and remaindermen are different people, usually the typical case of a life income to a surviving spouse followed by a remainder to one's children. If the trustee exercises discretion and distributes principal to the spouse, will the children complain when the trust corpus is thereby reduced? If they complain, will they have a cause of action? The case of *Marsman v. Nasca* clarifies this issue as well. A trustee has a duty to both, and a responsible trustee should balance the needs and interests of both sets of beneficiaries. But a good settlor can help in setting priorities by explicitly stating that "my first priority is to provide comfortably for my spouse and children while they are under twenty-one. The interests of others are subordinate to these." Or, "so long as my spouse has adequate income to maintain him, my primary goal is to preserve trust assets to benefit my children. Thus principal should be invaded only in extreme circumstances."

Practice Points: Choosing Your Trustee Wisely—Trusts Can Be Powerful!

Although we are just touching on the basics of trust shares established for children, we can already see the incredible power and protection that trusts can offer a family in the event that both parents die prematurely. If the parents want to use the full power allowed under trusts, they can actually give their children powerful tools like asset protection and remarriage protection that the children could never provide for themselves. But, who should they name as Trustee? Since a trust generally operates in a much less formal manner than wills, does it even matter?

There is no trick in that question, is there? Of course it matters. It is actually one of the most important questions that a parent can answer in planning, after those relating to the choice of guardians for their minor or incapacitated children, because the selection of trustee will have drastic results to the beneficiaries, not just in terms of ease of distribution (as in, Aunt Carol is always in touch with what the kids are doing at school and might be better able to understand when they are in need of extra money, whereas Uncle Jamie is always grumpy and saying No to everything) but also in terms of the amount of protection the trust will ultimately provide the beneficiary in the event that the child marries, divorces, or declares bankruptcy.

We discuss these topics in greater detail in other sections, but some simple fact scenarios can illustrate the power that different trustees can give to a trust. For example, if a trust share is set up to benefit Sally, age 35, and the provisions of the trust allow discretionary distributions of principal and income, what would be the effect if Sally, alone, is named Trustee of that share? No big surprise here—since Sally is the sole trustee and can distribute to herself at will, she is deemed to have control over the whole trust corpus. So, if American Express sues her to recover that $25,000 credit card debt she defaulted on, a judgment could attach to her trust share even if she doesn't want to make a distribution (and it's more than likely that she doesn't).

Consider if Sally was the sole beneficiary and a completely independent entity, like a bank, served as Trustee of her discretionary trust? Generally speaking, if Sally can't demand access to distributions, then neither can her creditors. This is one reason, by the way, that some settlors now steer away from the once common mandatory distribution schemes of 1/3 of the trust as the child attains 3 different ages, because as soon as that beneficiary has access to the distribution, so do her creditors. Why not just establish a trust with discretionary distributions over her lifetime for her health, education and maintenance with an independent trustee?

Hybrid solutions, which give the beneficiary the power to remove and appoint trustees can offer the beneficiary some of the same protections, but give them a little bit more control if they want to remove a trustee who is difficult to work with, for example. It is essential that if mom and dad wanted to give some asset protection as well, that the trust stipulate that Sally cannot appoint herself as Trustee and must replace a named trustee she wishes to remove with another independent trustee (often a bank or CPA).

As you can imagine, the cases get a bit murkier when we name Aunt Carol as Trustee, particularly if she is just there "for show" and it's really Sally alone who is calling the shots. There will be more on this to come. For now, it is important to understand why the discussion of who to select as trustee is every bit as important during that planning meeting as discussing how property should pass at death.

Consider the actions of trustees in these cases and whether you think they acted either beyond the terms of the trust or in an unreasonable manner:

Austin v. U.S. Bank of Washington

869 P.2d 404 (Wash. Ct. App. 1994)

James Wade devised his entire estate to the Old National Bank of Washington, in trust, to pay $100.00 per month to his sister for her life, plus additional sums "for any emergency or need, in the sole discretion of my trustee," and then to pay the remainder of the income for the use and benefit of his daughter and three grandchildren, *"as may be deemed advisable by my trustee for the maintenance and support of such persons. I expressly direct that such distribution shall be made to such persons only when they are in actual need of income for their maintenance, support and medical expenses and that the trustee shall take into consideration other income available to them, particular[l]y income from the ELOUISE D. WADE trust. . . . "* Upon the death of his daughter, the trust was to terminate and the principal was to be paid to the three grandchildren.

At some point during the life of the sister, the trustee received a letter from the sister's attorney asking that the trust pay $500 per month rather than $100 per month, attaching a letter from her doctor stating that she had severe arthritis, diverticulitis and a hernia. The doctor's letter concluded that she needed household help and that living alone required that she hire someone. The bank responded that it needed to know the sister's other sources of income and the sister's lawyer complied, sending a letter spelling out her various sources of income and expenses, showing that she could not pay her expenses on her income. In reliance on the letter, the bank's Trust Administrative Committee approved the additional $400 monthly increase and, given the sister's age of 76 and medical problems, made no provision for further review of the payment.

Seven years later the sister's lawyer again wrote, asking for an increase to $1000 per month, citing the sister's hospitalization and again including a doctor's letter. Relying on these letters the trust company agreed to the increase. Two of the grandchildren complained to the bank at this time, but a few months later their mother died and the trust was to be divided into equal shares and distributed to the grandchildren. However, because the sister was still alive, the bank requested more information on the sister's assets to determine if an annuity should be established to pay the sister's bequest for the rest of her life.

The grandchildren filed suit alleging the bank breached its fiduciary duty it owned them and alleging negligence in increasing the sister's monthly payments. The trial court agreed with the grandchildren and charged the bank $57,000 plus interest for its payments to the sister above the $100.00 provided for in the the will. The court found for the grandchildren in large part because the sister had over $300,000 in securities that generated between $2000 and $5000 in income each year. The bank had determined financial need by an analysis of income and expenses, without considering the sister's actual assets. Citing *Scott on Trusts* and the *Restatement*, the Court of Appeals affirmed. *"A trustee may be guilty of an abuse of discretion where he pays the beneficiary more than could reasonably be thought necessary for his support." W. Scott, Law of Trusts, § 187.2 (4th ed. W. Fratcher, 1988) and "In determining the question whether the trustee is guilty of an abuse of discretion in exercising or failing to exercise a power, the following circumstances may be relevant: (1) the extent of the discretion conferred upon the trustee by the terms of the trust; (2) the purposes of the trust; (3) the nature of the power; (4) the existence or nonexistence, the definiteness or indefiniteness, of an external standard by which the reasonableness of the trustee's conduct can be judged; (5) the motives of the trustee in exercising or refraining from exercising the power; (6) the existence or nonexistence of an interest in the trustee conflicting with that of the beneficiaries." Restatement (Second) of Trusts § 187, Comment d.*

More specifically, the court held that *U.S. Bank could have sent a very simple form to Lawrence's attorney in 1988 requesting disclosure of her "Sources of Income". Instead, it elected to rely on the statement of a third person, Lawrence's attorney, who may not have been fully aware of her financial situation. Having failed to make adequate inquiries or investigation, U.S. Bank cannot claim to have met an "external standard of reasonableness."*

We also agree with the trial court that a trustee should not increase trust payments based upon "need" or "emergency" where the beneficiary has accumulated assets that are generating a low level of interest income, or no income at all. In our judgment a trustee, in determining a beneficiary's "need" or "emergency", has a duty to consider undisclosed assets which are not reasonably required to sustain the beneficiary's standard of living or which are producing income (e.g. stocks and certificates of deposit).

Query: If, as the bank argued, it still would have made the payments to the sister even if it had done a more substantial inquiry, should the grandchildren have still won? What would have happened had the testator's daughter been the trustee and she agreed to the higher payments simply because she kept in touch with her aunt and had heard numerous complaints about bill collectors? Was this case the result of a corporate trustee being held to a higher level of due diligence than a personal trustee likely would be?

Finch v. Wachovia Bank & Trust Co.

577 S.E.2d 306 (N.C. Ct. App. 2003)

Harry Browne Finch died in 1988 leaving the bulk of his property in a marital trust for the benefit of his wife, Helen Finch, for life, remainder to his three children. His will did not specify the exact terms of the trust and so his testamentary intent was incorporated into a Family Settlement Agreement approved by the Superior Court in 1990. The marital trust provided that Helen would receive the entire net income, and further provided:

> *If, in the judgment of the Trustee, the income payable to Helen in accordance with the provision of paragraph 3) above, supplemented by income (other than corporate gains) from other sources to her, shall not be sufficient to meet the reasonable needs of Helen in her station in life—as to all of which the judgment of the Trustee shall be conclusive—then, and in that event, the Trustee will be authorized to pay or apply for the benefit of Helen so much of the principal of this trust as the Trustee, in its sole discretion, shall from time to time deem requisite or desirable to meet the reasonable needs of Helen—even to the full extent of the entire principal of this Trust.*

Wachovia adjusted Helen's living expenses off the trust periodically throughout the 1990s in response to requests by Helen. In April, 2000, Helen requested another increase that included $28,000 per year to be given away to her family, church, and charities. Wachovia refused to give her any funds for gifting, claiming that *"[w]e do not believe [the statement] 'meet the reasonable needs of Mrs. Finch' is broad enough to allow us to distribute trust assets to her to make gifts.'"*

Upon denial of her request for funds to make gifts, Helen Finch sued Wachovia for an interpretation of paragraph 5 of the Marital Trust. The trial court found that Wachovia had abused its discretion by failing to allow her to make reasonable gifts and ordered Wachovia to determine a reasonable amount to give Helen that would allow her to make gifts. Upon appeal, the court affirmed the determination that the trustee had abused its discretion, stating:

> *The trustee of a discretionary trust must exercise its discretion and its judgment in considering the proper way to administer the trust. Failure to exercise judgment is one way a trustee can abuse its discretion. Plaintiff argues and the trial court found that Wachovia failed to exercise any judgment by asserting the position that they lacked the authority to consider plaintiff's gift requests in determining her reasonable needs. We agree.*

> *We hold that the trial court's conclusion of law that Wachovia abused its discretion is based upon the trial court's findings of fact which are supported by competent evidence, particularly Wachovia's letter of 6 July 2000 to plaintiff. The letter states that Wachovia does "not believe [its] discretionary authority is broad enough to permit [it] to invade principal of the trust*

to enable Mrs. Finch to make gifts." Given the broad discretion allowed by the trust in determining plaintiff's "reasonable needs" and the lack of an express prohibition, we hold that Wachovia failed to exercise judgment and abused its discretion in failing to consider plaintiff's request.

Finally, the court reversed the trial court's order that the trustee was to determine a reasonable amount to give Helen, instead stating that the court should not substitute its judgment for that of the Trustee who was chosen by the Testator. The order to determine a reasonable amount was held to conflict *with the trust language which states that the Trustee's decision to determine plaintiff's "reasonable needs" shall be "conclusive". Enforcing the trial court's order would strip discretion from the trustee and replace it with the judgment of the court. Wachovia has the authority, but cannot be forced, to pay over any sums out of the corpus to satisfy the gifting desires of plaintiff.*

Query: What's the point in finding that a trustee abused its discretion if the court is going to then tell the trustee that its determination of an amount to distribute is conclusive? Can the trustee choose to distribute $1.00 to Helen from which she can make gifts? Will the trustee, after this case, feel comfortable with distributing any amount? Isn't the trustee between a rock and hard place—if it doesn't distribute anything it is charged with abusing its discretion by the life tenant; if it does distribute principal for a goal the remaindermen think is frivolous, they may sue for abuse of discretion? What protections, if any, does a trustee have? Was this a case of the trustee "failing" to exercise its discretion or a trustee exercising it in a way that the primary beneficiary disapproved of?

Both of these cases raise the question of whether it is better to have a corporate trustee or a personal friend or family member serve as trustee. As you can see, corporate trustees have certain procedures in place for collecting information, distributing accountings, and making decisions about distributions. Some even go so far as to call a meeting of trust officers or a trustee board to make final decisions. Others, however, are very likely to put the trust in the drawer, set up the computer to make requisite income payments, and forget about it until time to file yearly tax returns or collect on their trustee fees. Only if someone writes a letter or contacts them about trust distributions do they bother to see if a beneficiary's income levels have changed or their status makes them less or more needy. Corporate trustees, for obvious reasons, prefer trusts that are straightforward to administer and don't entail pesty beneficiaries constantly calling for additional distributions.

A personal trustee, like a trusted friend or child, may be more knowledgeable about each beneficiary's financial needs, but that person may also be more inclined to hand out checks if Cousin Joan or Uncle Paul whine enough on the phone about the bills piling up. It's much harder to pressure corporate trustees to be generous with trust dollars, especially if their trustee fees are affected by the size of the trust corpus.

What these cases also show is that someone is likely to be unhappy no matter how much or how little discretion a trustee is given. The trustee can't seem to get anything right—simply asking for an accounting of income and expenses is not enough if the beneficiary has other assets that could be sold for her support. At the same time, trustees must act reasonably, and that includes understanding the beneficiary's accustomed standard of living and not paying out whenever the beneficiary finds she's overspent her line of credit. If Helen Finch was used to being able to put $20.00 each week into the Church plate every time it passed around, a trustee should continue to make her able to do that, even if it annoys the remainder beneficiaries who might think she is squandering their property. But notice how giving ultimate discretion means the trustee may be able to choose not to distribute anything to a beneficiary, even if a court has determined that the trustee has abused its discretion. Is that what a testator would have wanted? Can you try to draft trust instructions for the trustees in *Finch* and *Austin* that would have avoided the lawsuits and satisfied the testators and beneficiaries?

PROBLEMS

7.12. You represent the First National Bank of the State of Sunshine and are the trust officer for the Seamus Finley Trust. This trust was established by the settlor, Seamus Finley, as a Credit Shelter Trust giving his spouse, Irene, the income for life plus a special power of appointment, plus the right to invade principal for Irene's health, education, maintenance, and support. After Seamus' death, Irene moved to Arizona to escape the cold and remarried a Gulf War veteran, Lionel, who has extensive injuries from his army days. Irene uses all of hers and Lionel's social security to pay for Lionel's health care costs, and the limited income off their few securities goes to pay the rent. Irene would like to receive not only the income but 1% of the principal per month from Seamus' trust to pay for their additional expenses, like food and utilities. Lionel is the trustee/beneficiary of a discretionary trust established by his mother, but they don't want to invade that trust because they both like the remainder beneficiaries of Lionel's trust better than those of Seamus' trust. Seamus left the remainder of his credit shelter trust to his obnoxious brother and spoiled nieces and nephews. What obligations do you have as trustee to investigate the assets of Irene and Lionel and should you invade the principal to satisfy Irene's requests?

7.13. You are the trustee of your mother's trust, which left her entire estate to you and your two siblings, because you are the most responsible of the three. Your sister, Junie, is married to an incompetent braggart who is convinced he is going to get rich with some new scheme selling used fence posts on eBay. Your brother, Jason, is very responsible but is married to a wife who spends her days at the spa, the country club, or ordering Louis Vuitton accessories for every outfit. Your mom's trust has support provisions allowing for invasion of principal for the health, education, maintenance, or support of yourself and your siblings. You live next door to Junie and her husband and frequently bear the brunt of their wild schemes, and you have had to lie to bill collectors and do their grocery shopping when they were broke just so their kids would have something to eat. You decide to secretly pay some of their debts from the trust so they will have enough credit to buy Christmas presents for their kids. Meanwhile, Jason and his wife have moved to New York City and you only hear from them once a year when you get a holiday card from them. This year you find out that Jason lost his job in June and his wife has had to cancel her country club membership. You figure that if they needed money they would have let you know and so you do nothing. Have you abused your discretion in either instance?

3. SPENDTHRIFT TRUSTS

What is a parent or other settlor to do about the child or grandchild whose eye, and pocketbook, is drawn to every new gizmo and gadget invented to separate a person from his money? The child who must have the best and the newest of everything can run through the income and principal of a trust fund faster than you can say "Porsche 911." The obvious first step is to place any property for that child into a trust rather than giving it outright. And giving discretion to the trustee to distribute income and principal for the support of the beneficiary only, or to pay creditors directly who have provided necessary goods and services, will hopefully limit the uses of the trust funds to those acceptable to the settlor. But once funds have been released to a beneficiary, that person may use the money to pay rent, go bungee jumping in Brazil, or add to his collection of batman memorabilia. And trust settlors are generally OK with the idea that once the money is in the hands of the beneficiary, the settlor can only offer advice on how it should be spent. What many settlors find more upsetting than beneficiaries who squander their income payments, however, are trust beneficiaries who borrow against their trust funds, or who sell their rights to receive benefits from the trust fund for cash right now.

The poet Percy Bysshe Shelley was expelled from Oxford University in 1811, and then eloped to Scotland with the daughter of a tavern keeper, Harriet Westbrooke, when he was 19. When his father, who was a baronet, discovered Percy's over-hasty indiscretion, he cut off Percy's allowance and left the newly-weds penniless in Scotland until they came to their senses. Percy was not the type to easily conform to his Tory father's bourgeois ways, so he borrowed enough money from friends to return to London, where he then raised *post-obit* bonds on his grandfather's estates. His grandfather was still alive but held his land as a life tenancy, with a remainder in Percy. Thus, upon reaching 21, Percy could alienate his remainder interests for a fraction of their total value, thus casting off his father's disapproving iron grip. Of course, if Percy had not been on the outs with his family, and his father had continued to provide an allowance, Percy would not need to have sold his remainder interests at a discounted value and ultimately, had he lived, he would have come into possession of his grandfather's estates.

Percy Shelley's post-obit bonds of early nineteenth-century England were the functional equivalent of selling one's future interest in a trust for a discounted value. Many trust settlors frown, however, on their beneficiaries selling their interests in a trust in order to accelerate possession, especially if it entails discounting the true value of the trust interest. Thus, many settlors include a *spendthrift* provision in the trust. The spendthrift provision does not prevent a trust beneficiary from squandering the funds she receives, once a payment is made from the trust. The provision does, however, prevent a beneficiary from alienating her interest in the trust before it becomes possessory. A settlor need merely add language like "any attempt by a beneficiary to alienate his or her interest in this trust will result in forfeiture of that beneficiary's interest." This kind of language prohibits the *voluntary* alienation of a trust interest.

But what should be done if a trust beneficiary has run up excessive credit card debts and Citibank wants to attach the beneficiary's interest in a trust? Should a restraint on alienation also apply to creditors who want to seize a beneficiary's property interests in a trust against the wishes of the beneficiary or the trust settlor? This kind of *involuntary* alienation can also be guarded against with the proper language. Typical language is:

> No interest of any beneficiary in the income or principal of this trust shall be assignable in anticipation of payment or be liable in any way for the beneficiary's debts or obligations and shall not be subject to attachment.[58]

Moral dilemmas have been recognized by numerous judges and commentators, however, who feel that creditors should not be stuck with a bad debt and no remedy while trust-fund recipients live in the lap of luxury. Why shouldn't creditors be able to attach a debtor's trust fund interests before they are paid into the hands of the spendthrift, just as they can attach most other property interests? There is nothing special about equitable interests in trusts that should give rise to a different rule from the common law rule that restraints on alienation are against public policy.

On the other hand, the money in most trusts came from the settlor, not the beneficiary, and so long as it's mom's money, it seems reasonable to allow her to limit the trust fund not to pay her child's debts, especially if she disapproves of them. During life mom could choose to pay her child's rent, or college tuition, but not an excessive credit card bill; why not allow her to set up a trust with the same discretion?

In England, spendthrift provisions (both voluntary and involuntary restraints on alienation) were void, regardless of whether they were attached to legal or equitable interests.[59] But by the late nineteenth century, certain American courts were validating spendthrift restraints on the grounds that settlors should be able to impose the same conditions on trusts that they could use to guide their own personal giving. Other courts considered the fate of the poor creditors who relied on the appearance of wealth that the beneficiary displayed because of the trust. The Massachusetts Supreme Court explained:

> It is argued that investing a man with apparent value tends to mislead creditors, and to induce them to give him credit. The answer is, that creditors have no right to rely upon property thus held, and to give him credit upon the basis of an estate which, by the instrument creating it, is declared to be inalienable by him, and not liable for his debts. By the exercise of proper diligence they can ascertain the nature and extent of his estate, especially in this Commonwealth, where all wills and most deeds are spread upon the public record.[60]

In this sense, the property rights in the trust are no different from other forms of property that are exempt from attachment, like homestead—certain forms of property should not be used as the basis for extending credit because they are unattachable, and any creditor who extends credit on the basis of that property does so at his peril.

The history of the gradual acceptance of the spendthrift provision is lengthy and complex. New York, for instance, passed a statute in 1828 that prohibited the alienation of trust interests except in very limited circumstances.[61] Massachusetts validated the spendthrift provision by common

---

[58] Gregory Alexander, *Waggoner, Alexander, Fellows and Gallanis' Family Property Law Cases and Materials on Wills, Trust and Future Interests*, 840 (4th ed. 2006).

[59] Brandon v. Robinson, 18 Ves. 429 (1811).

[60] Broadway Nat'l Bank v. Adams, 133 Mass 170, 174 (1882).

[61] N.Y., EST. POWERS & TRUST LAW, When trust interest inalienable; exception § 7–1.5 (McKinney 1966).

law, and then later the legislature affirmed and slightly modified the power by statute.[62] The majority rule today is that spendthrift provisions are valid, and only a few states prohibit them outright (Kentucky, New Hampshire, Rhode Island). But the differences among the states that have allowed them are extensive. Some states, like Nevada and Texas, allow for broad restraints on the alienability of trust shares, while others, like Alabama, limit spendthrift protections only in trust gifts to children or blood relatives.[63] A state-by-state analysis is given in Scott on Trusts, § 152.1. The Restatement 3d of Trusts § 58 and the Uniform Trust Code both approve spendthrift provisions.

The most controversial question tends to be whether certain creditors should be given privileged status to defeat a spendthrift provision: namely government creditors, children or spouses with support or maintenance orders, tort judgment claimants, creditors of necessary medical or support provisions, and the like.[64]

As an exercise in policy considerations, analyze the following cases and the courts' reasoning for upholding or refusing to uphold the spendthrift provisions in the narrow circumstances given and whether breach of contract can provide an adequate alternative remedy:

In re Est. of Vought

250 N.E.2d 343 (N.Y. 1969)

Chance Vought left his estate in trust with a life interest payable to his parents, his wife, and his two sons. Upon the death of the last of his parents and his wife, the remainder was to indefeasibly vest in half shares in his two sons. One son, Chance Jr., had assigned his remainder interest in the trust, valued at $1.86 million, prior to his own death, which preceded that of his mother by a year and half. On the mother's death, the assignees of the trust sued for payment of the trust principal directly to them. The court held that the father's undisputed intent was to make the trust inalienable by using the following language: *'the principal shall not be assignable, nor can the income or principal of said Trust funds become attached by garnishment or other legal proceedings while in the hands of the Trustees, except to the extent permitted by law.'* The trial court held the inalienability provision valid and that the trust corpus passed to Chance Jr.'s estate. The court could find no policy reason for invalidating the trust provision since the property itself was freely alienable by the trustee. The New York Court of Appeals gave a lengthy analysis of the common law on the issue of inalienability provisions in trusts and concluded that worries about *reviving feudal tenures, mortmain, or of reversing historic trends that wrought their demise* did not justify nullifying a settlor's inalienability provision. The court further explained that: *In the instant case, the issue is*

---

[62] Generally, although Massachusetts recognizes the validity of spendthrift trusts, such trust is ineffective against creditors if the settlor creates a trust for the settlor's own benefit and retains the power to amend, revoke or invade the principal of the trust. 226 B.R. 507 citing 179 B.R. at 389. *See also Merchants Nat'l Bank v. Morrissey, 329 Mass. 601, 605, 109 N.E.2d 821 (1953)* (providing that "The established policy of this commonwealth long has been that a settlor cannot place property in trust for his own benefit and keep it beyond the reach of creditors."). Massachusetts adopted the Uniform Trust Code in 2012, so now spendthrift provisions are generally valid. MASS. GEN. LAW ANN. § 203E–502.

[63] NEV. REV. STAT. ANN. §§ 166.010–166.160; TEX. PROP. CODE ANN. § 112.035 (West 2007); ALA. CODE § 19–3–1 (2007).

[64] For a detailed analysis, see Scott on Trusts, § 152.1.

whether generally a creator may post-pone for a limited period the beneficiary's control of material wealth until a time when the beneficiary is believed to be more able to manage it more wisely. Such a desire is not unnatural in a creator of trusts, nor does it work an undue hardship on those who extend aid to the beneficiary, provided they extend aid with the knowledge that they will not be reimbursed out of the principal against the creator's wishes.

The creditors then asked that even if the assignment is not going to be deemed valid during the lifetime of the trust, they should at least be able to go against the trust principal now that it is being distributed to the remainder beneficiaries. The court held against them, stating: *Such a result, however, would render meaningless any provision providing for inalienability of the principal for, indeed, the beneficial owner has no present interest to be protected but the right to receive the principal at a later date. If by an assignment during the life of the trust he is deemed to have transferred this sole right of later possession he has transferred virtually all his interest. Moreover, the creator's wishes would be completely frustrated, the beneficiary not only getting the funds the creator had intended be delayed, but the beneficiary receiving a fraction, after discount, of what was eventually intended.*

Query: Assuming the son received some value for the assignments of his remainder interest in the trusts, do the assignees have any remedy now that the court has held the assignments to be entirely null and void? Here the court held that the trust principal was to pass to Chance Jr.'s estate for distribution to his devisees, but now the principal will be subject to estate taxes in Jr.'s estate. Does the spendthrift provision prevent a trust beneficiary from making a lifetime gift of the future trust principal in order to minimize taxes? Assuming Chance Sr. was of the same mind as Sir Timothy Shelley, that his son was too young and irresponsible to be able to alienate his trust interests prior to his mother's death, should there not be some way to manage a remainder interest subject to a spendthrift provision so as to avoid double administration and possible double taxation? What if Chance Jr. had disclaimed his interest in exchange for a loan from his brother, who would receive the trust principal upon Jr.'s disclaimer?

Sligh v. First Nat'l Bank of Holmes County

704 So.2d 1020 (Miss. 1997)

On January 30, 1993, William Sligh was involved in an automobile accident with Gene Lorance, an uninsured motorist who was driving while intoxicated. Sligh suffered extensive injuries, including paralysis from the waist down. In a tort suit against Lorance, Sligh and his wife received a $5,000,000 judgment. Lorance has no assets other than beneficiary interests in two trusts established by his mother with spendthrift provisions. The Slighs filed writs of garnishment against First National Bank, as trustee, but the Bank moved for a dismissal on the grounds that the spendthrift provision prevented their payment of the trust interest to the Slighs. In the court proceedings the Slighs argued that: *Lorance's mother, Edith Lorance, had actual knowledge of the following facts: her son was an habitual drunkard who had been unsuccessfully treated for alcoholism; he was mentally deficient and had been previously committed to mental institutions; he had impaired facilities due to his alcoholism and mental disorders; he regu-*

larly operated motor vehicles while intoxicated; he was a reckless driver who had been involved in numerous automobile accidents; and he had been arrested and convicted on numerous occasions for driving under the influence. The complaint alleged that despite her actual knowledge of these facts, Mrs. Lorance established the two trusts as part of her intentional plan and design to enable her son to continue to lead his intemperate, debauched, wanton and depraved lifestyle while at the same time shielding his beneficial interest in the trusts from the claims of his involuntary tort creditors. They claimed it was against public policy for courts to protect trust interests from involuntary tort claimants. The trial court ruled against the Slighs.

On appeal, the Mississippi Supreme Court reversed, explaining that spendthrift provisions were not valid in the case of self-settled trusts, and the precedents in which they had been recognized were limited to cases of creditors who extended credit to the trust beneficiary without determining the source of the debtor's income. Looking to the Restatement (2d) of Trusts, that reflects exceptions to spendthrift protections for privileged creditors like children and wives, for creditors who supply necessary services, for services provided to preserve the interest of the beneficiary, and for claims by the United States or a State, the Mississippi Court felt claims by involuntary tort creditors fell in the same category as those identified by the Restatement. Moreover, according to the Court, none of the three reasons for enforcing spendthrift provisions applied in this case. They are: *(1) the right of donors to dispose of their property as they wish; (2) the public interest in protecting spendthrift individuals from personal pauperism, so that they do not become public burdens; and (3) the responsibility of creditors to make themselves aware of their debtors' spendthrift trust protections.*

Query: Should legislatures be the ones who should narrow the applicability of spendthrift provisions to protect tort creditors? Are legislatures likely to do so? The Mississippi Legislature passed legislation rejecting any exception for tort liability in 1998. Miss. Code Ann. § 91–9–503. Who do you think has the better argument, the Legislature or the majority of the Court?

───────────

Spendthrift provisions are pretty well established in most states, and a trust settlor who imposes a spendthrift provision on a beneficiary's interest can feel confident that the property won't go to the beneficiary's creditors. Although many states do allow privileged creditors access to trust interests, like children claiming child support payments or ex-spouses claiming spousal maintenance, the federal and state governments, and lawyers who provide services to maintain the beneficiary's interest. What happens when a beneficiary files for bankruptcy? Generally the bankruptcy court will only reach the same assets that could be reached under state law. Thus, if spendthrift interests in trusts are protected assets under state law, they will be protected in bankruptcy as well. All bets are off, however, if the spendthrift provision is in a self-settled trust, even an irrevocable domestic asset protection trust.

PROBLEMS

Using the spendthrift trust provision of your state, determine if there are any privileged creditors, then decide how you would best provide for your client's beneficiaries in the following circumstances:

7.14. Your client is Wilma, who is estranged from her husband Harry, but who doesn't want to divorce him because she is worried that she will have to take on half of his debts. Harry has a gambling problem and spends way too much time watching the shopping channel. When he isn't ordering ginzu knives, he is buying fake rolex watches and exercise equipment that never gets used. She knows she has to provide him an elective share, but her state permits her to place the amount of property she would be required to give him under the elective share statute into a trust with income for life so long as he has the right to invade principal up to $5,000 per year or 5% of the trust corpus or for his health, education, maintenance, and support. Can Wilma use a spendthrift provision and, if so, can she effectively limit his ability to invade the principal?

7.15. Your client, Walter, is widowed, with three grown children. Two are responsible, but one, Jackson, is intemperate, drives aggressively, is a social drug user, and is on his third relationship. Jackson has wonderful kids by his first two relationships but he doesn't provide adequate child support for them and he has never married. Walter would like to make sure that Jackson's children are taken care of but that he is not encouraged in any of his bad habits, including his habit of producing non-marital children. What tools can Walter use to provide for Jackson and his grandchildren?

C. PRETERMISSION

Most states have what are called *pretermitted,* or *omitted heir,* statutes that apply to both spouses and children. These statutes generally give a surviving spouse or child an intestate share of a decedent's estate if the decedent made a will prior to marriage or the birth or adoption of the child and did not provide for the spouse or child. Historically, a subsequent marriage voided a will in its entirety, but no state today completely voids a premarital will. Instead, they give the surviving spouse an intestate share of the decedent's estate unless the premarital will indicates that the omission was intentional and/or the decedent provides through other mechanisms for the survivor.

Typically, the omitted spouse is a second spouse who claims a right to take an intestate share of her deceased husband's estate which he devised to his children by a prior marriage. The typical omitted child is one who was born shortly before the testator's death, often after a testator has made provisions for his other children. One thing to keep in mind, however, is that these statutes generally give the spouse or child only an *intestate* share in the decedent's net probate estate. Thus, a spouse who is omitted from a premarital will may forego her rights under the pretermitted spouse statute and instead opt for an elective share if the elective estate is in the augmented estate. Also, many pretermitted child statutes give the omitted child an intestate share, regardless of whether his pre-existing siblings received anything under the testator's will. Consider the UPC statutes on pretermitted spouses and children.

UPC § 2–301. Entitlement of Spouse; Premarital Will.

(a) If a testator's surviving spouse married the testator after the testator executed his [or her] will, the surviving spouse is entitled to receive, as an intestate share, no less than the value of the share of the estate he [or she] would have received if the testator had died intestate as to that portion of the testator's estate, if any, that neither is devised to a child of the testator who was born before the testator married the surviving spouse and who is not a child of the surviving spouse nor is devised to a descendant of such a child or passes under Sections 2–603 or 2–604 to such a child or to a descendant of such a child, unless:

(1) it appears from the will or other evidence that the will was made in contemplation of the testator's marriage to the surviving spouse;

(2) the will expresses the intention that it is to be effective notwithstanding any subsequent marriage; or

(3) the testator provided for the spouse by transfer outside the will and the intent that the transfer be in lieu of a testamentary provision is shown by the testator's statements or is reasonably inferred from the amount of the transfer or other evidence.

(b) In satisfying the share provided by this section, devises made by the will to the testator's surviving spouse, if any, are applied first, and other devises, other than a devise to a child of the testator who was born before the testator married the surviving spouse and who is not a child of the surviving spouse or a devise or substitute gift under Section 2–603 or 2–604 to a descendant of such a child, abate as provided in Section 3–902.

Although the statute envisions the possibility that a testator may draft a will, intentionally omitting a future spouse (which is often done in the context of second marriages when individuals do their estate plans shortly before they remarry), the spouse is only prevented from taking his pretermitted spousal share if the omission was intentional. Writing a will intentionally omitting a future spouse cannot preclude the spouse from taking an elective share, which is always an option if the decedent spouse dies testate and the surviving spouse is not adequately provided for. Thus, the only way to prevent both an omitted spousal share under a premarital will AND the elective share is through the use of a pre-nuptial agreement. If the testator drafts a will after the marriage, however, then the omitted spousal share is precluded but not the elective share.

UPC § 2–302. Omitted Children.

(a) Except as provided in subsection (b), if a testator fails to provide in his [or her] will for any of his [or her] children born or adopted after the execution of the will, the omitted after-born or after-adopted child receives a share in the estate as follows:

(1) If the testator had no child living when he [or she] executed the will, an omitted after-born or after-adopted child receives a share in the estate equal in value to that which the child would have received had the testator died intestate, unless the will devised all or substantially all of the estate to the other parent of the omitted child and that other parent survives the testator and is entitled to take under the will.

(2) If the testator had one or more children living when he [or she] executed the will, and the will devised property or an interest in property to one or more of the then-living children, an omitted after-born or after-adopted child is entitled to share in the testator's estate as follows:

(i) The portion of the testator's estate in which the omitted after-born or after-adopted child is entitled to share is limited to devises made to the testator's then-living children under the will.

(ii) The omitted after-born or after-adopted child is entitled to receive the share of the testator's estate, as limited in subparagraph (i), that the child would have received had the testator included all omitted after-born and after-adopted children with the children to whom devises were made under the will and had given an equal share of the estate to each child.

(iii) To the extent feasible, the interest granted an omitted after-born or after-adopted child under this section must be of the same character, whether equitable or legal, present or future, as that devised to the testator's then-living children under the will.

(iv) In satisfying a share provided by this paragraph, devises to the testator's children who were living when the will was executed abate ratably. In abating the devises of the then-living children, the court shall preserve to the maximum extent possible the character of the testamentary plan adopted by the testator.

(b) Neither subsection (a)(1) nor subsection (a)(2) applies if:

(1) it appears from the will that the omission was intentional; or

(2) the testator provided for the omitted after-born or after-adopted child by transfer outside the will and the intent that the transfer be in lieu of a testamentary provision is shown by the testator's statements or is reasonably inferred from the amount of the transfer or other evidence.

(c) If at the time of execution of the will the testator fails to provide in his [or her] will for a living child solely because he [or she] believes the child to be dead, the child is entitled to share in the estate as if the child were an omitted after-born or after-adopted child.

(d) In satisfying a share provided by subsection (a)(1), devises made by the will abate under Section 3–902.

Note how the UPC omitted child statute attempts to treat all children equally by giving the omitted child a share based only on the property given to other children included in the will. This is a deviation from most pretermitted child statutes which simply give an omitted child an intestate share. Thus, if a testator devises $500,000 to his spouse and others, and only $50,000 cumulatively to his three children, a fourth omitted child is only able to take a share of the $50,000 given to her siblings, not the $68,750 that might have been her share had the decedent truly died intestate.[65] This is especially important if the other siblings have to settle for the share devised to them and cannot opt for a larger intestate share like their omitted sibling.

Also, some states permit an omitted child to claim a share, even if the will was written after the child's birth or adoption, in certain limited cases. The California statute allows this:

---

[65] This assumes that the spouse would take half of the total estate valued at $550,000, and the four children would divide the remaining half four ways for $68,750 each.

> **Cal. Prob. Code § 21622**
>
> If, at the time of the execution of all of decedent's testamentary instruments effective at the time of decedent's death, the decedent failed to provide for a living child solely because the decedent believed the child to be dead or was unaware of the birth of the child, the child shall receive a share in the estate equal in value to that which the child would have received if the decedent had died without having executed any testamentary instruments.

Under the California code, an omitted child gets a full intestate share regardless of the provisions, if any, for other children, even if the decedent was unaware of the birth of the child. You can surely imagine the surprises that are in store for surviving family members from the appearance of the pre-marital love child born from that one-night stand when the decedent was first in college.

Pretermitted spouse and child claims often arise in cases where an omitted spouse feels unfairly left out of an estate, or where unknown children pop up to claim a share of a parent's estate. As you can see from the following cases, courts are hesitant to recognize such claims, especially where the testator appears to have known about the spouse or child and simply chose not to make additional provisions. Also, think about the role a codicil can play in knocking out pretermission claims. A simple codicil changing the executor, for example, if executed after the marriage or birth of a child, re-executes the will as of the date of the codicil, often precluding claims of pretermission. A spouse, on the other hand, is usually not going to be disinherited because he or she can always claim an elective share even if a pretermitted spousal share is unavailable (unless, of course, the spouse has renounced or waived an elective share by a prenuptial contract). A child may be out of luck, however, unless she lives in Louisiana which prohibits the disinheritance of minor or dependent children.

Consider the following cases:

In re Est. of Tollefsen

2009 WL 3470401 (Cal. Ct. App. Oct. 28, 2009)

Linda Lowney, a California estates and trusts attorney, drafted a will and living trust for Thor Tollefsen in 2002, naming Tollefsen's sister and niece as beneficiaries. For the next three years, Lowney and Tollefsen maintained a social relationship and Tollefsen gave Lowney two checks for roughly $10,000 each. With the first check, Lowney asked an attorney friend if it was permissible to keep the check, telling the friend that Tollefsen was her boyfriend. She did not tell the friend that Tollefsen was her client. Over the next few years, Lowney helped amend the trust documents to reallocate assets that had been going to Tollefsen's relatives. In January, 2006, a "License and Certificate of Confidential Marriage" between Lowney and Tollefsen was filed in San Francisco. A year later Tollefsen died. The court noted that Tollefsen was *an elderly person in poor health, suffering from cancer, using a walker and a wheelchair; and, when he slept at home, he used a hospital bed.* A few days after Tollefsen's death, Lowney filed a spousal property petition alleging that she was the surviving spouse and asking for her omitted spousal share of decedent's estate. Tollefsen's relatives objected, claiming that the marriage was void, that Lowney had misrepresented potential future tax consequences to his trust, and that she had induced him to give her access to Tollefsen's fund accounts totaling more than $350,000. The trial court denied Lowney's claim for a spousal share and for breach of fiduciary duty against the trustees of Tollefsen's trust for failing to keep her informed of trustee actions.

On appeal, the California Appeals Court affirmed, stating: *California law permits two different types of marriage: A traditional "public" marriage and the less common "confidential" marriage . . . In the present case, appellant concedes her marriage was not authenticated by a witness. Thus, the marriage does not qualify as a valid public marriage. . . . The primary purpose of the confidential marriage statutes is to "shield the parties and their children, if any, from the publicity of a marriage recorded in the ordinary manner, and thereby to encourage unmarried persons who have been living together as man and wife to legalize their relationship. Interpreting the term "living together" to mean actually residing in the same dwelling is consistent with this statutory purpose. In the present case, it is undisputed that decedent and appellant did not live together at any time prior to their marriage.* Citing precedent, the court explained further: *Living in the same dwelling is the most significant characteristic of daily life that creates the impression that a couple is married. It is unmarried couples who have lived together and held themselves out as husband and wife, and any children of that relationship, who are most likely to be embarrassed and stigmatized by revealing in a nonconfidential marriage that they were not previously married, that their representations to others that they were married were a sham and that children born of that relationship were illegitimate. [S]ection 500 seeks to encourage this group to legalize their marriages with the inducement that the fact that they were not previously married will not be revealed." . . . In sum, we have no difficulty in concluding that a confidential marriage license obtained based on a willful misrepresentation that the parties lived together renders the resulting marriage invalid from its inception.*

Because the marriage was deemed void, Lowney was not entitled to an omitted spouse share, and the court further commented: *We find the circumstances of this case to be troubling. In particular, an inference may be drawn that appellant, a licensed attorney, knowingly made a false representation on a recorded instrument in an attempt to take advantage of a client in order to secure a portion of his estate for herself. This case also raises implications regarding the laws that pertain to the financial abuse of elders. Accordingly, we are forwarding a copy of this opinion to the California State Bar so that it may evaluate whether a disciplinary investigation of appellant is warranted.*

Query: In this case Lowney amended the trust to make herself a beneficiary, and then she claimed an omitted spousal share after supposedly marrying her client. Did she overreach? Do you think she didn't encourage Tollefsen to execute a new will because then she would not be able to take advantage of the omitted spouse statute? Because most state pretermitted spouse statutes don't take into account property passing to the surviving spouse by non-probate transfers, while most elective share statutes do, it may be more advantageous to claim an omitted spousal share and take 50% of the intestate estate, as well as non-probate gifts, rather than the elective share. Was Lowney a very good estates and trusts attorney in the way she handled Tollefsen's estate plans?

In re Est. of Will

88 Cal.Rptr.3d 502 (Cal. App. 2d Dist. 2009)

On April 13, 1980, Ted Will executed a will and trust, declaring that he was divorced and had five children, including respondent Lori Tinsley. Many years later, Ted became reacquainted with his high school classmate, Gertrude Fochs, a widow with five adult children. Ted and Gertrude later lived together in his Ventura home. Ted had acquired substantial real properties in Ventura and elsewhere. Gertrude assisted him with accountings of income from his real properties and stock holdings. Ted, then 81 years old, and Gertrude, then 80 years old, decided to marry. Gertrude suffered from lung cancer, and Ted intended to obtain medical insurance and treatment for her. They contemplated that she would not survive Ted due to her illness.

On October 1, 2003, Ted and Gertrude visited Grover Howe, Ted's long-time attorney. Ted presented Gertrude with a prenuptial agreement drafted by another attorney. The agreement provided that Ted and Gertrude waived their respective community property interests and inheritance rights in each other's property. It also provided that the separate property of each party would pass to his or her children, but that Gertrude could live in Ted's home for five years rent-free after his death. The agreement contained schedules listing the assets of each party. Gertrude later described the prenuptial agreement as "he keeps his assets, I keep mine."

The following day, Ted and Gertrude married. During the marriage, the parties filed separate income tax returns, maintained their separate properties, and did not acquire any community property or hold joint bank accounts.

The uncertainty of human expectations became apparent when, two years after the marriage, Ted died, leaving Gertrude the survivor. He had not amended his 1980 will and trust nor had he executed another will and trust after his marriage to Gertrude.

Gertrude later filed a petition in the probate of Ted's estate contending that she is an omitted spouse. She sought a one-third statutory interest in Ted's trust and estate pursuant to section 21610, subdivision (c). Gertrude asserted that the prenuptial agreement is unenforceable because it did not comply with the specific requirements of Family Code section 1615 concerning advice of independent counsel, seven days' advance notice of the agreement, and a separate written explanation of property rights relinquished.[66] Lori, the administrator of Ted's estate, conceded that circumstances surrounding execution of the prenuptial agreement did not meet the specific requirements of Family Code section 1615, subdivision (c).

The probate court determined that the prenuptial agreement was independently enforceable pursuant to Probate Code. It also found that the agreement represented the parties' mutual intentions, it was fair and reasonable, Gertrude knew the extent and nature of Ted's financial affairs at the time, and it would be inequitable not to honor the waiver. The probate court then concluded that Gertrude was not entitled to a statutory share of Ted's trust or estate.

---

[66] The court found, however, that *Howe read and explained each provision of the prenuptial agreement to Ted and Gertrude and answered their questions. He also informed Gertrude that he was Ted's attorney and was not representing her. Howe offered to obtain independent counsel at Ted's expense for Gertrude. She declined the offer and stated that she had read the agreement. Ted and Gertrude executed the document after leaving Howe's office.*

The court of appeals affirmed, stating that although the prenuptial agreement did not meet the requirements of the Family Code, it met the requirements of the probate code for relinquishment of spousal inheritance rights, which only *requires a waiver of inheritance rights to be in writing and signed by the surviving spouse. . . . [and makes] a fair and reasonable disposition of the rights of the surviving spouse, or that the surviving spouse had adequate knowledge of the property of the decedent, and the decedent did not violate any fiduciary duty to the spouse.* Allowing that the probate code's less specific requirements override the Family Code's more strict requirements, the court explained: *Each scheme primarily concerns fair and reasonable disclosure of property at the time the premarital agreement or inheritance waiver was executed. The statutory framework of the Family Code and the Probate Code concerning inheritance waivers seeks to safeguard the rights of surviving spouses by similar disclosures and protections.*

Query: Was the court more interested in resolving a conflict between the Family Code and the Probate Code regarding the enforceability of a prenuptial agreement, or in denying the surviving spouse her pretermitted spousal share since she died shortly after her husband? Should her death matter? And what is California thinking—it has one set of requirements to validate a prenuptial agreement under the family law code (applicable to property division at divorce) and a different standard under the probate code (applicable to property division at death). That would seem to be a disaster waiting to happen.

Bailey v. Warren

319 S.W.3d 185 (Tex. App. Tyler 2010)

The testator's will left everything to his wife if she survived him. Otherwise, his property was to go to his heirs at law. The testator's only two children, Keith Lee Bailey Hodges and Christian Matthew Warren, were nonmarital children. They claim to be pretermitted children and therefore entitled to an intestate share of their father's estate. In the trial court, both sides moved for summary judgment. The trial court granted summary judgment for the children, virtually revoking the testator's will.

Appellee Keith Hodges ("Hodges") was born to Barbara Hodges on August 9, 1984. Barbara Hodges was unmarried. After Hodges's birth, Kevin Ray Bailey, the decedent, married Beth Carroll Bailey ("Beth"). On or about April 27, 1993, Kevin Ray Bailey underwent a genetic blood test that indicated a 99.9% likelihood that Hodges was his son.

On July 29, 1996, Kevin Ray Bailey executed his will. The will left his entire estate to his wife, Beth Carroll Bailey, if she survived him. If she did not survive him, then he directed that all of his property "shall go and be distributed to my heirs-at-law."

Shortly after the execution of the will, Hodges's mother filed suit seeking child support and submitting the results of the 1993 DNA test to establish that Kevin Ray Bailey was Hodges's father. In 1997, the 173rd Judicial District Court of Henderson County rendered an order establishing a parent–child relationship, declaring Hodges to be the son of Kevin Ray Bailey, ordering the payment of back child support, and changing Hodges's name to Keith Lee Bailey Hodges.

Although he remained married to Beth Carroll Bailey, Kevin Ray Bailey spent 2002 living in Louisiana with Lisa Kay Warren. On July 15, 2003, Lisa Kay Warren gave birth to Christian Matthew Warren.

On November 19, 2006, Kevin Ray Bailey died in Dallas, Texas. On January 22, 2007, his will was admitted to probate and, as directed in the will, the court appointed Appellant Beth Carroll Bailey independent executrix of his estate.

Both Hodges and Warren filed motions for summary judgment that they were Bailey's pretermitted children. The trial court granted both Hodges and Warren's motions and decreed that each takes one-half of the decedent's one-half of the community estate, and one-third of his separate property subject to Beth's life estate. In reversing, the Court of Appeals, explained (citing precedent): *"The object of the pretermission statute is to guard against testamentary thoughtlessness; it is not a limitation on a testator's power to dispose of his estate."* For the statute to apply, it must *"appear from the will[,] interpreted in the light of all the circumstances [,] that the failure to provide for the child or descendant was accidental, due to inadvertence or oversight."* If the pretermitted child is provided for in the will, the value of that provision is of no consequence to the court. *"The gift of a nominal sum, a contingent interest, or a future interest, however slight, will be sufficient to avoid the application of the statute."*

Regarding Hodges, the older son, the court explained: *A pretermitted child is one who is born or adopted after the testator's execution of the will. Hodges was born in 1984, twelve years before Kevin Ray Bailey executed his will in 1996. It is also undisputed that Hodges is the biological child of Kevin Ray Bailey, and that Hodges was never formally adopted by him.*

Hodges argues that the definition of "child" in the probate code "does not include a child with no presumed father." As a nonmarital child, Hodges had no presumed father. However, probate code section 42(b) provides a list of exclusive methods for a nonmarital child to establish paternity for inheritance purposes. One such method is for the child to be adjudicated the child of the father by court decree as provided by Chapter 160, Family Code. . . . " Id. Hodges argues that he was not a "child" of Kevin Ray Bailey or "born," as that term is used in the probate code section 3(b) definition, until he was adjudicated to be so by court order in 1997. Since Bailey executed his will the year before in 1996, Hodges maintains that he is a pretermitted child, one "constructively born" after the execution of the will. Since Hodges was not a "child" or "born" when Kevin Ray Bailey made his will, he argues, he "was not a 'child' and thus not an 'heir'. . . . " Therefore, in Hodges's view, Bailey's direction that his estate go to his "heirs at law" was not a provision for either Hodges or Christian.

Hodges cites no authority for his argument that he was not "born" for the purposes of the pretermitted heir statute until he was adjudicated a child in 1997, one year after Bailey made his will.

The supreme court has addressed a will case involving a child born without a presumed father. See Garza v. Cavazos, 148 Tex. 138, 141, 221 S.W.2d 549, 551 (1949). In Garza, the court held that, if the father married the mother and recognized the child, a nonmarital child is treated as having been a living child of the testator from the time of the child's birth.

Otherwise a child actually born before the making of the will but legitimated after the will was executed would be treated as an after-born child, with the result that a "constructive birth" would have the effect of partially revoking the will under § 67 if no children presumed the testator's were in existence at the time of the will. Such authority as exists from other states is opposed to this result.

Based upon the holding in Garza, we reject the proposition urged by Hodges that, for purposes of the pretermission statute, he was not "born" until he was adjudicated Bailey's child in 1997. Once adjudicated to be Bailey's child, he is to be treated as having been Bailey's living child from the date of his actual birth. Hodges is not a pretermitted child.

As regards Christian Warren, the court explained: *It is undisputed that Christian is a pretermitted child. When a testator has one or more children living when he executes his last will, a pretermitted child's intestate share is limited to the disposition made to those children under the will. This rule applies only if provision is made "therein" for one or more of the living children.*

In concluding, the court explained its logic thus: *There is no question that both Hodges and Warren are "heirs-at-law" of Kevin Ray Bailey. . . . If the testator's wife had predeceased the testator, Hodges concedes that he would have taken under the will as an heir at law. There no longer exists any statutory provision preventing nonmarital children from inheriting from their father. That neither Hodges nor Christian were born of a lawful marriage would not affect their legal status as Kevin Ray Bailey's heirs at law.*

Hodges, born thirteen years before Bailey executed his will, is not a pretermitted child. Therefore, he is not entitled to invoke the Texas pretermission statute. He may not seek a partial revocation of the will to obtain an intestate share of Bailey's estate. Christian, on the other hand, is indisputably an after-born or pretermitted child. But, under the statute, he may succeed to an intestate share in his father's estate only if he is not mentioned or provided for in the will or "otherwise provided for by the testator." Although pretermitted, Christian is also a member of a class, "heirs-at-law," designated by Bailey to receive his entire estate if his wife predeceased him. Our review of the case law from Texas and other jurisdictions leads us to the conclusion that Bailey's direction in his will that his estate go to his "heirs at law" if his wife failed to survive him constituted a provision in the will for Christian. Consequently, Christian is also barred from succeeding to an intestate share in Bailey's estate.

However, even assuming the provision for "my heirs-at-law" is not a provision for the after-born or pretermitted child, the result is the same. Hodges was living when his father executed his will. Bailey was unquestionably aware that Hodges was his son and potential heir. Bailey had undergone genetic testing three years before he made his will. The test results showed that he was Hodges's father. After he learned the results of the test, Bailey provided informal support for Hodges and established a social relationship with him. Under the circumstances, it strains credulity to believe that when he included the contingent provision in his will three years after the test, he was unaware that Hodges was his son and potentially his heir. Bailey plainly provided for Hodges in his will by directing that, if his wife predeceased him, all his property should go to his heirs at law.

Since Bailey provided for a child living when the will was made, the share of the pretermitted child is limited to the disposition to children under the will. The contingency upon which any disposition to "my heirs-at-law" depended, the prior death of his wife, did not come to pass. Therefore, Hodg-

es is entitled to no disposition from the estate. Christian is limited to an equal share in the disposition made to Hodges in the will. Since Hodges receives nothing, Christian receives nothing, even if we assume that he was unmentioned and unprovided for in the will.

Query: Note how the court denied Hodges a share because he was "otherwise provided for in the will" as a living child, and then limited Warren's share to the same thing Hodges received, which was merely a contingent interest in case Bailey's spouse predeceased him. If Texas gave a pretermitted child an intestate share, regardless of the shares given to other living children (as does California), Warren would have been entitled to something. Which is the better rule, to treat all children the same, or treat them differently if the testator has explicitly disinherited one pre-existing child, but not said or done anything about an afterborn child?

PROBLEM

7.16. George drafts a will in 2004, leaving everything to his spouse, Karen, and if she predeceases him, then to his 2 children, Gloria and Kaley, in equal shares. In 2008, Karen died. In 2009, George began dating Ellen, who delivered their first child, Caleb, nine months later. By 2012, Ellen and George have married and have given birth to another child, Joe, when George dies unexpectedly. His 2004 will is admitted to probate.

　　a.　Under UPC § 2–301, would Ellen be entitled to a pretermitted spousal share? If so, in what amount?

　　b.　Under UPC § 2–302, what rights do Caleb and Joe have?

D. CONCLUSION

This chapter has introduced you to additional legal protections for spouses beyond the homestead, family allowance, and exempt property that we encountered in Chapter 2; they include the incredibly powerful elective share and the pretermitted spouse statutes as well as a variety of marital trusts. We have also talked about trusts and powers to benefit surviving children. Once a client's own needs are taken care of, these protections for surviving spouses and children are the bread and butter of the estate planning attorney. Especially for estates that don't need to worry about taxes, planning for the surviving spouse's end-of-life care and getting the minor children through college may be the most important concerns facing most clients. Once the first spouse dies, the surviving spouse may be looking at remarriage and all the complications that go with blended families, or may be nearing the end of life himself and looking at extensive financial costs for end-of-life care that will easily eat up the couple's entire remaining assets. Whether your client is young or old, married or unmarried, straight or gay, rich or poor, the issues covered in this chapter are critical. Even an unmarried, childless client needs to think about elective share claims that could affect potential beneficiaries, or how her property will be managed if any of her devisees are underage. Because most of us amass wealth to provide for our loved ones, and hope that at least something will be left to our children or nieces and nephews to remember us by, planning with these beneficiaries in mind usually forms the heart of any estate plan.

It is usually only after the close primary beneficiaries are provided for that people begin to think about longer term estate planning, like providing for grandchildren and great-grandchildren or making large charitable gifts. As the estate grows in size, people also begin to think more strategically about long-term planning for multiple generations, family legacies, and minimizing tax liability. For the most part, planning for the living is much easier than planning for future generations because the client will usually know the identity of her living beneficiaries and will have some sense of their personal needs and quirks. But she is unlikely to know if her 13th great-grandchild is going to be a piano virtuoso or a kleptomaniac (or both!). Not only does the planner have to be thinking about giving trustees much more flexibility for longer-term trusts, the planner has to keep in mind the limitations on trust duration that may exist under the state's Rule Against Perpertuties. Balancing trust limitations with trust benefits for future generations is often tricky and requires a fluency in future interests beyond what you probably got in your first year Property course. The next chapter moves us beyond the living to the future unborn and unascertained beneficiaries of succession law. This is where we think about how to draft future interests so your client's estate doesn't wind up in Property or Trusts and Estates casebooks.

CHAPTER 8

PLANNING FOR FUTURE GENERATIONS

In your first year Property class, you probably learned about those pesky estates and future interests, things like the fee tail, life estates, and springing executory interests. You may have even learned the Rule Against Perpetuities (RAP), and while that probably wasn't the first time you thought about dropping out of law school, it was one of the moments when you thought maybe being a taxi driver was a better career option after all. But you stuck it out and here you are, thinking about drafting a will or a trust and all those horrible memories of first year are flooding back. You wonder "why can't the law just abolish those contingent remainders and the RAP and make all of our lives easier?" And states certainly could do that, but I promise you that it won't make our lives easier. In fact, it was not having the possibility of creating these future interests, or the possibility of writing a will, that led to the creation of the interests in the first place. People have a very strong desire to provide for their children, their grandchildren, and more distant future generations in the hopes that, with each generation, life will get a little bit better, a little bit easier, and certainly more comfortable because of the possibility of transferring wealth. It seems to be a natural human emotion to want to provide your children a better life than you had. Providing wisely and generously (which don't always go together) for future generations is both sensible and humane.

In Jane Austen's novel *Sense and Sensibility*, Mr. Dashwood leaves his entire estate to his son John through an oral declaration on his deathbed, but in doing so he elicits a promise that John will provide comfortably for his step mother and his three half sisters, Elinor, Marianne, and Margaret. In the flush of his new wealth, John thinks he should settle £1000 on each of his sisters. But as soon as John mentions it to his wife, Fanny, she convinces him, through impeccable logic, that Mr. Dashwood certainly didn't intend that John would actually *give* his half-sisters any money; surely all the money he inherited was necessary to provide comfortably for their own son Harry. Rather, John would be doing his father's bidding by helping them move to a small house, sending some fish and game when the season is right, and perhaps making a little present of furniture now and then. With his wife's help, John Dashwood saved himself £3000 per year and any guilt from failing to honor his father's deathbed wishes. As Fanny explained,

> Altogether, they will have five hundred a year amongst them, and what on earth can four women want for more than that?—They will live so cheap! Their house-keeping will be nothing at all. They will have no carriage, no horses, and hardly any servants; they will keep no company, and can have no expenses of any kind! Only conceive how comfortable they will be! Five hundred a year! I am sure I cannot imagine how they will spend half of it; and as to your giving them more,

it is quite absurd to think of it. They will be much more able to give you something.[1]

Fanny convinces her husband that they are doing the girls a favor by giving them nothing; it keeps expectations low and then they will be quite ecstatic with the neighborly gifts of game that Fanny and John Dashwood can spare from their own table. Afterall, they had their own son's inheritance to think of.

Unfortunately for the girls, Mr. Dashwood hadn't made a will, trusting instead to a deathbed oral promise, and the next scene shows the widow and her three girls walking out the gates of the only home they had known for their new life of poverty while John, Fanny, and Harry prepare to move into the family estate. With today's mortgage crisis, high unemployment, and the growing gap between the haves and the have-nots, estate planning for the future is important at all levels of wealth. But, as discussed earlier, the dead hand, if too controlling, can severely hamper the interests of the living. Estates can be tied up into inflexible trusts or future interests that result in high administrative costs, high taxes, or the distribution of wealth to minors or those unable to manage it. How do we balance the desire to provide for one's future descendants and give them the resources to make their own decisions yet ensure that they will not squander their inherited wealth or become the next trust fund baby to grace the cover of *The National Enquirer*?

Some of the most nightmarish property cases involve wills and trusts with pages and pages of provisions for future generations to take if they marry, if they survive, and if they have issue, but not if their great Aunt Edna remarries, in which case the money goes to the local church, but if not used for church purposes then to their step-siblings *per stirpes*, and only on condition that they change their names and never drink alcohol, and if they do then to a trust for education that can only be used to attend Harvard, and what do they do if they can only get into Yale? In this chapter we will focus on the use of future interests, primarily in trusts, and how to build flexibility into instruments that have an intended life span of more than one generation. As times change, the trustees need flexibility to adapt to changing circumstances and changing laws. Sir Edward Coke probably never imagined that his stable world of future interests would be more in flux than during the Elizabethan reign, but the post-modern legal world of the dot.coms and baby boomers is profoundly changing the deeply entrenched property rules developed by the landed elite of seventeenth-century England.

A. ESTATES AND FUTURE INTERESTS

In a world in which a landowner could not transfer real property by will to avoid the effects of primogeniture, future interests and uses (the precursor to the modern trust) were invaluable. Also, in a world in which the majority of children would lose at least one parent before they reached majority, the likelihood that a large landowner would die leaving an under-age heir was almost a given. And in a world in which the surviving spouse was entitled to strict dower and curtesy rights, *inter vivos* transfers of land in fee simple absolute could be difficult. How to provide for all of one's children, not just the eldest son, how to defeat the widow's dower rights

---

[1] Jane Austen, *Sense and Sensibility*, Chapter 2.

through *inter vivos* transfers, and how to prevent one's estate from falling into wardship drove common lawyers to devise the complex rules of estates in land and future interests that you learned in Property. And although today testators can devise real property by will, most children will reach majority with at least one parent still alive, primogeniture has been abolished, and estate taxes hit only the wealthiest of decedents, future interests are still invaluable for providing for future generations of descendants while maintaining the property intact. Thus, although many of the spurs that drove the early modern testator may have disappeared, the near-universal desire to provide for future generations remains a driving factor in nearly all testamentary instruments.

To begin our study of future interests, think back to the bundle of sticks that make up the most complete and perfect ownership we recognize today—the fee simple absolute. Because the fee simple absolute is of *infinite duration*, and because it is *inheritable* (i.e. transmissible both during life and at death), the current owner has the ability to determine who will own it next (i.e. can determine the transferees of the property), and because it doesn't terminate upon the owner's death, it is descendible to the owner's intestate heirs or devisable to his testamentary devisees. All property, real or personal, can be owned in fee simple absolute, and all owners of a fee simple absolute interest can transfer it *inter vivos*, transfer it by will, or have it transfer by intestate succession in fee simple absolute. Or they can break up the bundle of sticks and transfer portions of ownership to different successive owners. The ability to break up the bundle and transfer consecutive ownership interests for the duration of one person's life to a spouse, then to a child for a period of years, then to another child upon certain conditions, then to a grandchild for the duration of her life, and then to a great grandchild is an attribute of ownership that is unknown in most of the rest of the world. The power arose out of the unique circumstances of late medieval English feudalism, but remains one of the most powerful attributes of dead hand control recognized in the Anglo-American common law. And today it is absolutely critical in the drafting of trusts for future generations.

To begin to understand how future interests work, you must keep four things in mind. **First**, at any given time there is just one *present estate* (the estate held by the person who has the present ownership and possession) but there can be many *future interests* (vested or contingent rights to receive future ownership and possession if certain conditions occur or fail to occur). So if I transfer Blackacre to my spouse for life, then to my children if they marry in the Buddhist faith, but if they don't, then to my grandchildren, I have created a single present estate in my spouse, and a bunch of contingent possible future interests in my children and my grandchildren. If we think of ownership in terms of a pie chart, the future interests, together with the present estate, should make up the whole pie. But some pieces are definitely going to be bigger than others. Sometimes the biggest will be the present estate; at other times the biggest pieces will be the future interests.

Second, there are only six[2] present estates and ten future interests recognized in the common law, so all legal ownership interests must conform to one of these. The *rule against the creation of new estates* prohibits the creation of springing executory life estates or other hybrids. Once you

---

[2]   There are technically seven but the fee tail has been abolished in most states and redefined in the others so that it is almost always interpreted to be one of the other interests.

know these 16 interests, and how they fit together, you will be well on your way to mastering this arcane subject.

Third, and perhaps most importantly, the categories and labels of these estates and future interests came AFTER people started dividing ownership and possession over time, not before. Thus, no medieval land lawyer sat down and said "I'm going to create a schematic structure and then we'll allow people to divide their bundle of sticks into these particular pieces." Instead, people started making crazy, complex devises with all sorts of conditions and limitations and the lawyers had to come in afterwards and try to classify the interests in order to determine how the law should treat each one. As a result, the categories (and their labels) try to capture the important characteristics of a transferor's intentions, but with the limitation on the number of categories that can be created, certain testator's intentions simply wouldn't fit within certain categories. You may often find yourself having to hammer a trapezoidal peg into either a round hole or a square hole because those are the closest to the perceived intent of the transferor.

A very common example of having to make the intentions fit the categories are wills that do the following:

> *I devise the residue of my estate to my wife, for her absolute use and enjoyment, but anything left over at my wife's death, I devise to my two children.*

The testator's intention here is clear. He wants his wife to have everything if she needs or uses it but, at her death, he wants anything left over to pass according to his own will and not his wife's. What he is devising to her is a life estate with the power to convert her life interest into absolute ownership for any property she decides to consume, but any property she doesn't exercise absolute ownership over will terminate with her death and pass automatically to his two children. But the power to exercise absolute ownership over the property is inconsistent with the limitations of a life estate.[3] Yet we have to hammer this interest into one of our holes. Thus, a court might say that the most important part of the testator's intent here was to give the wife the freedom to control the property absolutely, in which case a court would interpret the interest to be a fee simple absolute in the wife, leaving nothing for the children. Or, a court might say that the most important part of the testator's intent was to make sure that any left-over property passed to the children and not by virtue of the wife's will. In that case a court would interpret the wife's estate to be a mere life estate. A court might even interpret it to be a fee simple subject to an executory limitation with a shifting executory interest in the children. None of these interpretations truly fits what the testator wanted, which was to give his wife more than a life estate but less than a fee simple absolute, but there is no legal interest that falls between these two.

Now you should already be thinking creatively—if there are no *legal* categories that fit the testator's intention, could we accomplish the testa-

---

[3] We will come back to this, but it is possible to create a life estate with a power to consume (i.e. a general power of appointment) the property, which accomplishes this purpose. But one should note that the exercise of the power must be done according to the donor's instructions, and that if one gives the donee the life estate and the absolute power to appoint the property to herself at anytime in any way, a court may very well interpret the interest to be a fee simple absolute in the donee. This combination of property rights explains why the tax code treats certain interests as property even though common law property doctrines might not.

tor's intent if we used a trust? And the answer is yes! The rule against the creation of new estates applies only to legal interests in property, not to equitable interests. Thus, the husband in our example should have devised his property to X, in trust, for the benefit of his wife for her life, with the wife to have the power to consume absolutely any of the trust property, but if she fails to consume, then any trust corpus present at his wife's death is to pass absolutely to his two children. This would be an equitable life estate coupled with a general power of appointment. See how the existence of powers can fundamentally change the limited character and effects of the life estate! That is one reason why powers are so important.

This leads to the **fourth** point, that the sixteen categories we are going to discuss are limitations on *legal* interests but not necessarily on *equitable* interests. Thus, if the testator's intent seems not to fit nicely into the categories, you should be thinking of other ways to accomplish the testator's intent, rather than searching for a bigger hammer. But remember, once an interest is characterized a particular way, certain legal consequences will flow from that characterization. A life tenant may not devise the property, no matter the testator's intent. So learning the legal effects of each category of present estate and future interest is critical to figuring out how to divide up the pie. And since most testators are more interested in the legal effects than the labels, you must understand how the puzzle pieces work together to make a coherent estate plan. Don't forget, you would much rather spend the time getting the interests right the first time, than litigating later and trying to convince a judge that a testator wanted to give your client an absolute ownership interest when the document was badly drafted by someone who just took the trust language out of a form book.

1. THE FEE SIMPLE ESTATE

The basics of future interests can be understood if you simply ask a series of questions about each interest when you are analyzing a particular devise or conveyance. So let's begin with a fairly simple bequest:

> I give the residue of my estate to my wife, Wila, on condition that she not remarry, but if she does remarry, then I want the residue of my estate to pass to my two children, Seth and Doris, if they have reached age 21. If one or both have not yet reached age 21, then I want my executor to divide the property into two shares, one for Seth and one for Doris, and retain each share until each has reached age 21, at which time my executor shall transfer the share absolutely to each child. If either or both children fail to reach age 21, but leave issue surviving, I want my executor to establish a trust for that child's share on behalf of his or her issue immediately, which will pay to those issue when they reach 18. But if either or both children fail to reach age 21 and do not leave issue surviving, then I want that child's share to pass to the Red Cross.

Notice how what began as a very simple bequest got far more complicated as soon as we started to provide alternate bequests in the unlikely event that Seth or Doris did not reach age 21 by the time Wila remarries. Simply adding that provision "if they have reached age 21" meant adding the remaining three sentences, all to avoid a guardianship or custodianship if the children were underage at the wife's death. And we also provided what would happen if a bequest lapsed or a child failed to reach age 21, which is better than relying on the state's anti-lapse statute.

The first thing we want to do, therefore, is figure out how many people have interests in this property and see if any conditions or limitations are attached to any of them. Certainly, the wife Wila, and the children Seth and Doris have property interests. But their surviving issue also have a contingent interest, as does the Red Cross. With regard to each person's interest, we need to ask a series of questions and the questions will enable us to identify each person's interest.

First, *who has the* **present estate**? That is the person who has the present possession and ownership. Assuming that the testator has died and the will has been proved, Wila the wife has the present estate because she is the person in current possession of the property. Second, *is there a condition on the present estate*? If the answer is no, the present estate is a fee simple absolute. If the answer is yes, we need to find out what kind of condition. In the estates and future interests world there are two things that are absolutely certain to occur: death and the passage of time. Consequently, the types of conditions and limitations that one can create differ based on whether they are absolutely going to occur (definite), or are not certain to occur (indefinite).

Question 1	NO	YES
Is there a condition or limitation on the present estate?	***Fee Simple Absolute***	Go to the next question

Question 2	Definite	Indefinite
Is the condition definite (time or death) or indefinite (may occur and may not occur)?	***Life estate*** (death) ***Term of Years*** (time)	Defeasible Fee Simple

For Wila's present estate above, the condition that will cause her to lose her present estate is if she remarries. This may or may not occur—it is indefinite. So she has some kind of defeasible fee simple estate. *Defeasible* simply means that the fee simple estate may be defeated or terminated, but until it is terminated it acts like a fee simple—it is freely alienable, devisable, and inheritable. But there are three different kinds of defeasible fee interests, depending on the identity of the future interest holder. So to identify what kind of defeasible fee interest we must ask some more questions.

Question 3	Grantor	Third Party
Is the future interest in the grantor or in some third party?	***Fee Simple Determinable*** or ***Fee Simple Subject to Condition Subsequent***	***Fee Simple Subject to an Executory Limitation***

If the future interest is in the grantor, the interest is either a *fee simple determinable* or a *fee simple subject to a condition subsequent*. The fee simple determinable is an interest that terminates automatically upon the occurrence of the condition, and the future interest that follows it is a *possibility of reverter*. It is a *possibility* because it follows an estate that is subject to an indefinite condition (Wila might remarry and she might not) and it is a *reverter* because the future interest is in the grantor/testator.

A *fee simple subject to a condition subsequent* will terminate only if the grantor exercises a power to terminate the interest, which is called either a *power of termination* or a *right of re-entry*—they are the same thing. The point is that there is a condition on the grantor's reclaiming the property; he must assert his power or right to retake, and failure to do so will result in the property remaining with the present estate holder. If the grantor waits too long to exercise her right to re-enter, it will be barred, thus terminating the condition and allowing the present estate holder to transfer a fee simple absolute. The fee simple determinable, on the other hand, terminates automatically, and the property immediately vests in the grantor if the divesting event occurs.

If the future interest is in a third party, the present estate, subject to an indefinite condition, is called a *fee simple subject to an executory limitation*.[4] And the cool thing is that there are two kinds of executory interests that follow the fee simple subject to an executory limitation. The first is a *shifting executory interest* which is a future interest that vests automatically upon the occurrence of the condition (similar to the possibility of reverter). The second is a *springing executory interest* which is a future interest that vests only upon the occurrence of some condition on the future interest (similar to the power of termination).[5]

So to identify which of our defeasible fee interests Wila has, we must look to the future interest that immediately follows the present estate, and we can ask our next question.

Question 4	Terminates automatically	A Condition Precedent must occur before the future interest vests.
If the future interest is in the *grantor*, does the present estate terminate automatically or must the grantor terminate or re-enter to reclaim the property?	***Fee Simple Determinable***	***Fee Simple Subject to Condition Subsequent*** (Grantor must exercise power of termination)

---

[4]   Some authorities call this a fee simple determinable subject to an executory interest because the executory interest, like the possibility of reverter, divests the prior estate. But that simply makes the term too long and rests on an arcane distinction that is losing much of its cogency.

[5]   Classic textbooks on future interests explain that the shifting executory interest divests the transferee (or possessory estate) and the springing executory interest follows a gap in seisin whereby the estate transfers back to the grantor and thus divests the grantor's interest. Modern (20th century) future interests nomenclature is very bound up in the gritty distinctions between remainders and executory interests that prevailed before 1536, and their evolving similarities afterwards. Much of the technical difference rests in understanding the difference between conditions subsequent and special limitations, distinctions that in modern day usage seem to have very little effect. Consequently, I am trying to give a basic structure that will help make sense of this arcane subject. If you would like to delve deeper into the quagmire, see Bergin and Haskell, *Preface to Estates in Land and Future Interests*, 2d ed. (1984), pp. 113–117.

Question 5	Terminates automatically	Some condition must occur before third party's rights vest
If the future interest is in a third party, does the present estate terminate automatically or is there some condition on the future interest holder before her right to take the property will vest?	***Fee Simple Subject to an Executory Limitation followed by a Shifting Executory Interest***	***Fee Simple Subject to an Executory Limitation followed by a Springing Executory Interest***

Now, what interest does Wila have? There is a condition that if she remarries she loses the property, it is indefinite, the future interest is in a third party (Seth and Doris), not the grantor, and Seth and Doris have to do something before their interest vests in possession. They have to reach age 21 (let's assume they have not done so yet). So what interests do they have?

Wila has a *Fee Simple Subject to an Executory Limitation*, and

Seth and Doris have *Springing Executory Interests in fee simple absolute*.

Ironically, these are some of the hardest interests to identify, and yet they arose out of a remarkably simple testamentary intent.

PROBLEMS

For practice, see if you can categorize the present estates in the following devises:

8.1. I give the residue of my estate to my wife Wila, on condition that she has insufficient property of her own, but if she ever earns more than $100,000 per year or is entitled to that income, then the estate is to pass to my children Seth and Doris immediately.

8.2. I give the residue of my estate to my wife Wila, on condition that she reside in our family home, and if she fails to reside in our family home, then all the property is to pass to my executor, in trust, to distribute according to the terms of my testamentary trust established in paragraph 6 of this will.

8.3. I give the residue of my estate to my wife Wila, so long as she lives in the family home, but if she fails to reside there, then the trustee of my revocable living trust may retake the home, sell the property, and distribute the proceeds according to paragraph 5 of my will.

8.4. I give the residue of my estate to my wife Wila, so long as she is unmarried, but if she ever remarries then my estate is to pass to my heirs at law.

8.5. I give the residue of my estate to my wife Wila, so long as she remains unmarried.

8.6. I give the residue of my estate to my wife Wila, so long as she remains unmarried, but if she remarries the estate is to pass to my two children Seth and Doris so long as they have reached age 21.

Side Note: The Magic of Certain Terms

Under traditional estates and future interests doctrines, especially the rules learned by Sir Edward Coke and William Blackstone, certain terms automatically indicated certain interests. Thus, the phrases "upon condition that," or "provided that," or "but if" usually indicated that the interest was a fee simple subject to a condition subsequent. And the phrases "so long as," "while," or "during" indicated a fee simple determinable. Students were thus taught to look for these particular magical terms, and if they appeared, their problems were solved. Fortunately or unfortunately, courts today have pretty much dispensed with reliance on the magic words, and instead look more carefully at what the testator's likely intent was. There are lovely explanations for why these terms indicated different interests and what the difference between a condition and a limitation is (*condition* subsequent v. executory *limitation*). But for an introductory class we have chosen to focus on the practical and substantive differences, and not on the formalistic terminology that has fallen into disuse. Though you may often see courts today cite to the relevant language as supporting a particular categorization of a future interest, they generally do so only as additional support for an interpretation that focuses primarily on the testator's intent. Thus, you need to know the effects of classifying an interest as a fee simple determinable or a fee simple subject to a condition subsequent in order to know how best to label them. But if you want the details, a delightful romp through late medieval property law is provided by Bergin and Haskell's, *Preface to Estates in Land and Future Interests* (1984). A cautionary note, however, is that the book has not been updated since 1984, and so all the (relatively) modern materials are woefully out of date. But the historical explanations are quite helpful.

In general, the primary use of the defeasible fee simple estate is for land granted for a particular purpose (church purposes, hospital purposes, residential purposes) and to require the land be returned to the grantor if it is no longer used for those purposes. Thus, when we talk about charitable giving in Chapter 9, we will come back to this kind of interest. Because not all defeasible fee interests are charitable and these restrictions and conditions can hamper the marketability of land, however, many states have adopted a variety of statutes to limit or destroy possibilities of reverter, powers of termination, and executory interests in legal interests in land. Thus, Marketable Title Acts and Stale Uses and Reversions Statutes (laws terminating reversionary interests) will permit these interests to remain alive primarily only in the context of charitable gifts of land. Other reversionary interests of unlimited duration in private transfers are terminated either by the RAP (executory interests) or these Marketable Title or Stale Reversions Acts. Once the future interest is terminated, the present estate becomes freed of the restriction and can be transferred in fee simple absolute.

In the context of trusts, however, defeasible fee interests are alive and well. Although the RAP applies to certain future interests in both legal and equitable interests in real and personal property, the Marketable Title Acts and Stale Reversions Acts generally apply only to *legal* interests in land. Trust interests that vest or fail upon the happening of an indefinite event, like surviving the life tenant, reaching age 21, graduating, marrying or remarrying, having children, or any other uncertain event, are commonly used in planning for future generations.

Now think back to our example bequest at the beginning of this Chapter, "to Wila so long as she does not remarry." What happens if Wila does not remarry, and then dies? Up until her death, Wila could always remarry, and so her fee interest is defeasible. But once she dies, Wila can't get married. Does her present estate terminate and pass to her children, or does it vest in her absolutely? It vests in her absolutely. Once the condition becomes impossible, then the condition is removed and we treat her interest as a fee simple absolute. So another important point to remember is that, over time, the interests can change. We begin by classifying the interest at the time it becomes effective (if it's in a deed it becomes effective upon delivery, if in a will it becomes effective upon the testator's death). But certain unknowns may become known in a fairly short time and we have to revisit our categories if circumstances change that affect any conditions imposed on the interests.

But what if the bequest had been "to Wila, for life, or until her remarriage, whichever first occurs"? In that case, once Wila dies without having remarried, the estate ends, because the most she ever had was a life estate. It would end at the earliest of her death or her remarriage. Either way, it was going to end. So technically what Wila has in this instance is a *defeasible life estate*. Her failure to remarry, however, cannot extend the ultimate duration of her underlying present estate, which was only a life estate and not a fee. Here are two fairly complex cases to get your heads around the defeasible fee situation.

Evans v. Abney

396 U.S. 435 (1970)

■ MR. JUSTICE BLACK delivered the opinion of the Court.

[In 1911 Senator A. O. Bacon of Georgia executed a will that conveyed real property to his wife and daughter for their lives, and the remainder in trust to the City of Macon for the creation of a public park for the exclusive use of white people of that city. The park was to be under the control of a Board of Managers of seven persons. The City controlled the park land and eventually allowed the park to be used by non-white persons because it was unable to legally operate the park in a segregated manner. Individual members of the Board of Managers brought suit to change trustees in order to keep it desegregated but, on appeal to the U.S. Supreme Court, the park was ordered desegregated because it had acquired a public character that brought it under the Fourteenth Amendment's equal protection guarantee. On remand, the Georgia courts, including the Georgia Supreme Court, ruled that the parkland must revert to the heirs of Senator Bacon because the restrictive condition of operating the park in a segregated manner had been broken. On appeal to the U.S. Supreme Court on claims that the Georgia courts had violated the Fourteenth Amendment rights of the black citizens of Macon by causing the park to revert, the Court had to consider the following questions:

1. whether the Georgia Supreme Court's order the the trust failed and the park land was to revert because the City could no longer enforce the restrictive condition violated the equal protection guarantees of the Constitution;

2. whether the refusal to apply the *cy pres* doctrine to reform the trust to prevent it from failing violated the equal protection guarantees of the Constitution;

3. and whether the enforcement of the restrictive condition constituted state action under *Shelley v. Kraemer.* In ruling against the petitioners on all three counts, the Supreme Court explained:]

We are of the opinion that in ruling as they did the Georgia courts did no more than apply well-settled general principles of Georgia law to determine the meaning and effect of a Georgia will. At the time Senator Bacon made his will Georgia cities and towns were, and they still are, authorized to accept devises of property for the establishment and preservation of 'parks and pleasure grounds' and to hold the property thus received in charitable trust for the exclusive benefit of the class of persons named by the testator. Ga.Code Ann., c. 69–5 (1967); Ga.Code Ann. ss 108–203, 108–207 (1959). These provisions of the Georgia Code explicitly authorized the testator to include, if he should choose, racial restrictions such as those found in Senator Bacon's will. The city accepted the trust with these restrictions in it. When this Court in *Evans v. Newton, supra,* held that the continued operation of Baconsfield as a segregated park was unconstitutional, the particular purpose of the Baconsfield trust as stated in the will failed under Georgia law. The question then properly before the Georgia Supreme Court was whether as a matter of state law the doctrine of *cy pres* should be applied to prevent the trust itself from failing. [The Court then affirmed the Georgia Supreme Court's refusal to apply *cy pres* to reform the trust to allow an integrated park on the evidence that Senator Bacon was so adamant that the races not commingle that he would have preferred the trust fail than be reformed and the park operated on non-racial grounds.[6]]

Since racial separation was found to be an inseparable part of the testator's intent, the Georgia courts held that the State's *cy pres* doctrine could not be used to alter the will to permit racial integration. The Baconsfield trust was therefore held to have failed, and, under Georgia law, '(w)here a trust is expressly created, but (its) uses * * * fail from any cause, a resulting trust is implied for the benefit of the grantor, or testator, or his heirs.' Ga.Code Ann. s 108–106(4) (1959).[2] The Georgia courts concluded, in effect,

---

[6] The Court explained: "In this case, Senator Bacon provided an unusual amount of information in his will from which the Georgia courts could determine the limits of his charitable purpose. Immediately after specifying that the park should be for 'the sole, perpetual and unending, use, benefit and enjoyment of the white women, white girls, white boys and white children of the City of Macon,' the Senator stated that 'the said property under no circumstances * * * (is) to be * * * at any time for any reason devoted to any other purpose or use excepting so far as herein specifically authorized.' And the Senator continued:

'I take occasion to say that in limiting the use and enjoyment of this property perpetually to white people, I am not influenced by any unkindness of feeling or want of consideration for the Negroes, or colored people. On the contrary I have for them the kindest feeling, and for many of them esteem and regard, while for some of them I have sincere personal affection.

'I am, however, without hesitation in the opinion that in their social relations the two races * * * should be forever separate and that they should not have pleasure or recreation grounds to be used or enjoyed, together and in common.' "

[2] Although Senator Bacon's will did not contain an express provision granting a reverter to any party should the trust fail, s 108–106(4) of the Georgia Code quoted in the text makes such an omission irrelevant under state law. At one point in the Senator's will he did grant 'all remainders and reversions' to the city of Macon, but the Supreme Court of Georgia showed in its opinion that this language did not relate in any way to what should happen upon a failure of the trust but was relevant only to the initial vesting of the property in the city. The Georgia court said: 'Senator Bacon devised a life estate in the trust property to his wife and two daughters, and the language pointed out by the intervenors appears in the following provision of the will: 'When my wife, Virginia Lamar Bacon and my two daughters, Mary Louise Bacon Sparks and Augusta Lamar Bacon Curry, shall all have departed this life, and immediately upon the death of the last survivor of them, it is my will that all right, title and interest in and to said

that Senator Bacon would have rather had the whole trust fail than have Baconsfield integrated. . . .   [Here] the action of the Georgia Supreme Court declaring the Baconsfield trust terminated presents no violation of constitutionally protected rights, and any harshness that may have result- ed from the state court's decision can be attributed solely to its intention to effectuate as nearly as possible the explicit terms of Senator Bacon's will. [The Court then rejected the petitioners' arguments that closing the park was a penalty for having to comply with a constitutional mandate of deseg- regation, and that the Georgia judges were motivated by racial animus.]

Petitioners also contend that since Senator Bacon did not expressly provide for a reverter in the event that the racial restrictions of the trust failed, no one can know with absolute certainty that the Senator would have preferred termination of the park rather than its integration, and the decision of the Georgia court therefore involved a matter of choice. It might be difficult to argue with these assertions if they stood alone, but then peti- tioners conclude: 'Its (the court's) choice, the anti-Negro choice, violates the Fourteenth Amendment, whether it be called a 'guess,' an item in 'social philosophy,' or anything else at all.' We do not understand petitioners to be contending here that the Georgia judges were motivated either consciously or unconsciously by a desire to discriminate against Negroes. In any case, there is, as noted above, absolutely nothing before this Court to support a finding of such motivation. What remains of petitioners' argument is the idea that the Georgia courts had a constitutional obligation in this case to resolve any doubt about the testator's intent in favor of preserving the trust. Thus stated, we see no merit in the argument. The only choice the Georgia courts either had or exercised in this regard was their judicial judgment in construing Bacon's will to determine his intent, and the Con- stitution imposes no requirement upon the Georgia courts to approach Bacon's will any differently than they would approach any will creating any charitable trust of any kind. Surely the Fourteenth Amendment is not vio- lated where, as here, a state court operating in its judicial capacity fairly applies its normal principles of construction to determine the testator's true intent in establishing a charitable trust and then reaches a conclusion with regard to that intent which, because of the operation of neutral and nondis- criminatory state trust laws, effectively denies everyone, whites as well as Negroes, the benefits of the trust.

Another argument made by petitioners is that the decision of the Georgia courts holding that the Baconsfield trust had 'failed' must rest logically on the unspoken premise that the presence or proximity of Ne- groes in Baconsfield would destroy the desirability of the park for whites. This argument reflects a rather fundamental misunderstanding of Georgia law. The Baconsfield trust 'failed' under that law not because of any belief on the part of any living person that whites and Negroes might not enjoy being together but, rather, because Senator Bacon who died many years ago intended that the park remain forever for the exclusive use of white people. . . .

---

property hereinbefore described and bounded, both legal and equitable, including all remain- ders and reversions and every estate in the same of whatsoever kind, shall thereupon vest in and belong to the Mayor and Council of the City of Macon, and to their successors forever, in trust etc.' This language concerned remainders and reversions prior to the vesting of the legal title in the City of Macon, as trustee, and not to remainders and reversions occurring because of a failure of the trust, which Senator Bacon apparently did not contemplate, and for which he made no provision.'

In their lengthy and learned briefs, the petitioners and the Solicitor General as amicus curiae have advanced several arguments which we have not here discussed. We have carefully examined each of these arguments, however, and find all to be without merit.

The judgment is Affirmed.

■ MR. JUSTICE DOUGLAS, dissenting.

Bacon's will did not leave any remainder or reversion in 'Baconsfield' to his heirs. He left 'all remainders and reversions and every estate in the same of whatsoever kind' to the City of Macon. He further provided that the property 'under no circumstances, or by any authority whatsoever' should 'be sold or alienated or disposed of, or at any time for any reason' be 'devoted to any other purpose or use excepting so far as herein specifically authorized.'

Giving the property to the heirs, rather than reserving it for some municipal use, does therefore as much violence to Bacon's purpose as would a conversion of an 'all-white' park into an 'all-Negro' park.

No municipal use is of course possible where the beneficiaries are members of one race only. That was true in 1911 when Bacon made his will. *Plessy v. Ferguson*, decided in 1896, had held that while 'separate' facilities could be supplied each race, those facilities had to be 'equal.' The concept of 'equal' in this setting meant not just another park for Negroes but one equal in quality and service to that municipal facility which is furnished the whites. It is apparent that Bacon's will projected a municipal use which at the time was not constitutionally permissible unless like accommodations were made for the Negro race.

So far as this record reveals, the day the present park was opened to whites it may, constitutionally speaking, also have been available to Negroes.

The Supreme Court of Georgia stated that the sole purpose for which the trust was created had become impossible. But it was impossible in those absolute terms even under the regime of Plessy v. Ferguson, 163 U.S. 537, 16 S.Ct. 1138, 41 L.Ed. 256. . . .

The purpose of the will was to dedicate the land for some municipal use. That is still possible. Whatever that use, Negroes will of course be admitted, for such is the constitutional command. But whites will also be admitted. Letting both races share the facility is closer to a realization of Bacon's desire than a complete destruction of the will and the abandonment of Bacon's desire that the property be used for some municipal purpose. . . .

Bacon's basic desire can be realized only by the repeal of the Fourteenth Amendment. So the fact is that in the vicissitudes of time there is no constitutional way to assure that this property will not serve the needs of Negroes.

The Georgia decision, which we today approve, can only be a gesture toward a state-sanctioned segregated way of life, now passe. It therefore should fail as the imposition of a penalty for obedience to a principle of national supremacy.

■ MR. JUSTICE BRENNAN, dissenting.

[Justice Brennan issued a strenuous dissent, arguing that public money had been invested in the park and that state action infused all aspects of its development and operation. He also noted that the State of Georgia's probate laws, that permitted the discriminatory condition, constituted state action.]

In 1911, only six years after the enactment of §§ 69–504 and 69–505, Senator Bacon, a lawyer, wrote his will. When he wrote the provision creating Baconsfield as a public park open only to the white race, he was not merely expressing his own testamentary intent, but was taking advantage of the special power Georgia had conferred by §§ 69–504 and 69–505 on testators seeking to establish racially segregated public parks. As Mr. Justice White concluded in Evans v. Newton, "the State through its regulations has become involved to such a significant extent' in bringing about the discriminatory provision in Senator Bacon's trust that the racial restriction 'must be held to reflect * * * state policy and therefore to violate the Fourteenth Amendment." 382 U.S., at 311. This state-encouraged testamentary provision is the sole basis for the Georgia courts' holding that Baconsfield must revert to Senator Bacon's heirs. The Court's finding that it is not the State of Georgia but 'a private party which is injecting the racially discriminatory motivation' inexcusably disregards the State's role in enacting the statute without which Senator Bacon could not have written the discriminatory provision.

This, then, is not a case of private discrimination. It is rather discrimination in which the State of Georgia is 'significantly involved,' and enforcement of the reverter is therefore unconstitutional.

I would reverse the judgment of the Supreme Court of Georgia.

––––––––––

Query: Many scholars then, and today, believe this case was wrongly decided, and the heirs of Senator Bacon received a windfall when they suddenly found themselves the owners of a priceless city park. The key to this case, however, is the Georgia court's finding that Senator Bacon created a fee simple determinable, and not a fee simple subject to a condition subsequent. Do you see what the difference is and why it mattered so much? And what about that reversion? Why is it relevant that Senator Bacon had not included a reversion in case the trust failed?

––––––––––

We omitted much of the discussion about the application of the *cy pres* doctrine to charitable trusts, because we take that up later in Chapter 9. At this point, it is important to realize that transfers of land for charitable purposes receive a variety of legal benefits, from tax immunity to exemption from the Rule Against Perpetuities and stale conditions acts to eligibility for *cy pres* reformation under certain circumstances. Charitable trusts also do not require ascertainable beneficiaries. Transfers of land for private (non-charitable) purposes with use restrictions are much less favored in the law, and these conditions can often be defeated (terminated) quite easily. But the following case, also involving a charitable gift, illustrates the extent to which conditions and the dead hand can hamper efficient uses of land.

Cathedral of the Incarnation in the Diocese of Long Island, Inc. v. Garden City Co.

697 N.Y.S.2d 56 (App. Div. 1999)

In an action pursuant to RPAPL 1955[7] to modify or extinguish restrictions on the use of land held for charitable purposes, the defendant Garden City Company appeals from an order and judgment of the Supreme Court, Nassau County, entered August 20, 1997, which, upon granting the

---

[7]   Real Property Actions and Proceedings § 1955. *Modification or extinguishment of certain restrictions on the use of land held for charitable purposes.* 1. Where land is held, whether or not in trust, for benevolent, charitable, educational, public or religious purposes and the use of such land is restricted to such purpose or to a particular application of or means of carrying out such purpose by a special limitation or condition subsequent created in the conveyance or devise under which the land is so held, or by an agreement to convey, reconvey or surrender the land or the estate so held upon a contingency relating to its use, an action may be brought in the supreme court to obtain relief from such restriction as provided in this section.

2. No action for the relief provided in this section shall be commenced until the expiration of two years from the creation of the special limitation or condition subsequent, or the making of the agreement. The attorney-general shall be a party to such action.

3. In determining whether relief shall be granted, and the nature of such relief, the court shall consider and shall make findings with respect to the following:

(a) whether the primary purpose of the special limitation, condition subsequent or agreement to convey, reconvey or surrender was to restrict the use of the land;

(b) whether the purpose of the restriction was to ensure that the substantial value of the land or of the estate subject to the special limitation, condition subsequent or agreement, rather than the land itself, or such estate itself, be devoted to and employed for a benevolent, charitable, educational, public or religious purpose.

If the findings with respect to (a) and (b) are such as to make the following matters relevant or appropriate for consideration, the court shall also consider and make findings with respect to the following:

(c) whether the existence of the restriction is substantially impeding the owner of the land, or of the estate subject to the special limitation, condition subsequent or agreement, in the furtherance of the benevolent, charitable, educational, public or religious purposes for which the land is held;

(d) whether the person or persons who would have a right of entry, possessory estate resulting from the occurrence of a reverter, or right to conveyance, reconveyance or surrender of the land or estate in the event of breach of the restriction at the time of the action will suffer substantial damage by reason of extinguishment or modification of the restriction, and, in such event, whether damages or restitution of the land, or its value, in whole or in part, should be awarded to such person or persons.

4. The judgment of the court may include, in the discretion of the court, an adjudication (a) that the restriction is discharged in whole or in part, or that its tenor is modified as provided in the judgment;

(b) that the holder of the land or estate therein subject to the restriction be authorized or directed to convey, lease, mortgage or otherwise dispose of the land or estate therein free of the restriction and that the purchaser under such disposition shall take free of the restriction; (c) directing the use to which the avails of any such disposition shall be put; (d) declaring the interests that the owners of the possibility of reverter or right of entry, or persons having an interest pursuant to the agreement, shall have in any property paid for in whole or in part with the proceeds of the disposition; (e) awarding damages for such injury as a party to the action may sustain by reason of extinguishment or modification of the restriction. The judgment may include such other provisions as will in the opinion of the court further the benevolent, charitable, educational, public or religious purposes for which the land is held and such other provisions as equity may require.

5. This section shall apply to a special limitation or condition subsequent created or agreement made either before or after September 1, 1958, except that it shall not apply (a) where a right of entry or right to a conveyance, reconveyance or surrender of the property has accrued or a reverter has occurred prior to that date, or (b) where the conveyance creating the restriction was made by or the agreement creating the restriction was made with the United States, the state of New York or any governmental unit, subdivision or agency of the United States or the state of New York.

plaintiff's motion for summary judgment on the complaint, is in favor of the plaintiff and against, among others, the defendant Garden City Company, and, *inter alia,* extinguished the challenged deed restrictions. . . .

By deed dated November 20, 1891, the heirs of Cornelia Stewart (hereinafter the Stewart heirs) sold to the Cathedral of the Incarnation in the Diocese of Long Island, Inc. (hereinafter the Cathedral), for the sum of $43,247.50, two parcels of real property in Garden City. Pursuant to a restriction contained in the deed, the premises were conveyed to the Cathedral "and its successors forever for the use of the Protestant Episcopal Church in the Diocese of Long Island but without any power, right, or authority to grant, convey, or mortgage the same or any part thereof in any way or manner whatsoever." The deed also contained the further restriction that the premises were not to be "used or occupied for any other use or purposes than as sites or grounds for buildings or institutions connected with said Cathedral and devoted to its religious uses or educational purposes".

In 1893 the Stewart heirs conveyed to the predecessor of the defendant Garden City Company (hereinafter the Company) certain other property in Garden City which Cornelia Stewart had also owned, inclusive of "[a]ll the right, title, property and interest of the [Stewart heirs], or any of them in and to any reversion or remainder in all or any of the lands conveyed to the said The Cathedral of the Incarnation in the Diocese of Long Island". The Cathedral continued to own and occupy the demised premises in accordance with the restrictions contained in the deed from the time of the conveyance in 1891 until the commencement of this action.

In 1993 the Cathedral, which was in severe financial distress, filed a voluntary petition in bankruptcy pursuant to Chapter 11. The United States Bankruptcy Court for the Eastern District of New York, by stipulation and order dated October 28, 1993, directed that certain properties owned by the Cathedral be sold. In addition, the Cathedral entered into a contract to sell other portions of the property.

The Cathedral thereafter commenced this action pursuant to RPAPL 1955 to modify or extinguish the restrictions and for authorization to dispose of the land pursuant to the contracts of sale. In a verified answer with counterclaim, the Company asserted, *inter alia,* that it was the successor to all the rights, title, interest, and claims that belonged to the Stewart heirs, that the deed from the Stewart heirs to the Cathedral conveyed less than a full fee title so that the Company had the right thereunder to assert ownership of the property upon its cessation of use for religious purposes by the Cathedral, that the restrictions in the deed created either a condition subsequent or a conditional limitation, and that RPAPL 1955 as applied to extinguish the Company's interests was unconstitutional. The Cathedral subsequently moved for summary judgment.

By decision dated July 1, 1997, the Supreme Court, Nassau County, found that the Cathedral was entitled to summary judgment. The court observed that although a right of reentry (now known as a right of reacquisition) arose from the Cathedral's deed, the Company, as an assignee, could not enforce it since, when the deeds were made, the right of reacquisition was not assignable, devisable, or descendible. The court then noted that the circumstances of the case fell within the scope of RPAPL 1955, and that the Cathedral's application to extinguish the restrictions should therefore be granted. The court found that "to require the [Cathedral] to hold the land in perpetuity is unconscionable". Moreover, the court stated that the Company had failed to establish its entitlement to any damages. The court also noted that the Company's attack on the constitutionality of the statute was wholly conclusory, and that the Company had failed to meet its burden of proof on its contention. An order and judgment was thereupon entered granting summary judgment in favor of the Cathedral. We affirm.

The insistence by the Company that, for the purposes of applying RPAPL 1955, the court merely had to find that some kind of reversionary interest existed, without determining the specific reversionary interest created by the deed, is unpersuasive. Notably, the Company, in arguing that the court erred in finding that a possibility of reverter did not exist, appears to concede that the deed created either a possibility of reverter or a right of reentry. The Company, however, fails to cite any case law or language in the deed to support its claim that the deed created a possibility of reverter in the grantors rather than a mere right of reentry. Thus, contrary to the Company's position, absent any language in the deed itself providing for the automatic termination of the Cathedral's estate if the land were no longer used for church purposes, the court properly concluded that the deed created a right of reentry. Under the common law at the time the Stewart heirs made the deed to the Cathedral in 1891 and the deed to the Company in 1893, the right of reentry was not assignable or devisable Therefore, any right of reentry would be rendered void by any attempt by the Stewart heirs to assign it to the Company.

Moreover, with respect to the contention by the Company that in interpreting a deed, the intent of the grantors should prevail, there is nothing in the language of the deed nor in the record as a whole to support the conclusion that the Stewart heirs intended the Cathedral's estate to terminate automatically if the land were used for other than church purposes.

The Company's challenge to the court's application of RPAPL 1955 to extinguish the restrictions must also fail. RPAPL 1955 (3) provides that the Supreme Court, in determining whether to grant relief from certain restrictions upon the use of land held for charitable purposes, must consider and make findings with respect to various factors as set forth in the statute.

Although the Cathedral concedes that the restriction required that the land itself rather than the substantial value of the land be used for church purposes (see, RPAPL 1955 [3] [b]), as the Supreme Court observed, that factor alone is not determinative. Under the statutory framework, the inquiry then turns to whether the existence of the restriction substantially impedes the owner of the property in the furtherance of the purpose for which the land is held (RPAPL 1955 [3] [c]). Contrary to the suggestion of the Company, the approval by the Bankruptcy Court of the sale as part of a Chapter 11 reorganization plan, and the deposition testimony of Frederick Reuss, the Chancellor of the Cathedral, provided sufficient evidence that continued ownership of the properties is a burden and a drain on financial resources that could otherwise be used to provide programs and services to the community. The Company failed to present any evidence to the contrary, and its conclusory assertion that both a trial and expert testimony are needed to determine whether the restrictions substantially impede the Cathedral in the furtherance of the purpose for which the land is held must be rejected.

Moreover, the Company has not demonstrated its entitlement to damages under RPAPL 1955(4)(e), which provides that the court, in its discretion, may award damages "for such injury as a party to the action may sustain by reason of extinguishment or modification of the restriction".

Notably, although Morton Kassover, a Vice President of the Company, testified at his deposition that construction of "smaller" homes could have a negative impact on the Company's commercial properties, there is nothing in the record to substantiate such speculation. Moreover, Kassover's conclusory assertions were insufficient to raise any factual issue as to how the Company would be damaged by the extinguishment of the restrictions.

Equally without merit is the Company's attack on the constitutionality of RPAPL 1955 as applied to it. In the first place, the Company's discussion assumes that it does have a constitutionally-protected property interest arising from the 1891 deed. However, as the Supreme Court correctly held, that deed created a right of reentry in the grantors that was not assignable, and any such right is now therefore void and nonexistent. It is well settled that where there is no legitimate claim of entitlement to the property interest affected by a governmental decision, the requirements of procedural due process do not apply (*see, Board of Regents v Roth,* 408 US 564).

The Company's remaining contentions are without merit.

———————————

Query: This case introduces you to a number of important issues: the differences between a fee simple determinable and a fee simple subject to a condition subsequent, the non-transferability of reversionary interests rule, the role of stale conditions statutes, and the importance of removing conditions to improve alienability of property. Why did it matter that the court construed the grant to be a fee simple subject to a condition subsequent, and do you think the court was correct in doing so?

———————————

Note how the courts in these two cases interpreted these two conveyances to be a fee simple determinable in *Evans v. Abney* and a fee simple subject to a condition subsequent in *The Cathedral of the Incarnation* case. Can you give a principled explanation for the difference? How, if at all, did the language of the two bequests differ? And how, if at all, did the statutory regimes of Georgia and New York differ?

If Senator Bacon or the Stewart heirs came to you today asking for help in disposing of these properties, what would you recommend? What would you want to know about the law, the family members, and the donors' beliefs before you drafted these various documents?

PROBLEMS

Identify what kind of present estate and future interests were created in the following provisions:

8.7. O conveys a lot of land (the Rock House Lot) to buyer with the following provision: "[i]n the event that Buyer does not comply with the provisions in this paragraph, title to the Rock House Lot shall automatically revert to Seller in fee simple." Also, "[i]f no plat has been recorded creating a subdivided lot for the Rock House lot at the time of the event triggering the automatic reverter, then title to the property described as Tract No. 10 on the survey of the Grant Dedman Estate dated January 9, 1979 . . . shall automatically revert to Seller in fee simple." *See Lasater v. Hawkins,* 2011 WL 4790971.

8.8. Testator makes the following devise of his real property. "I give and devise to my surviving issue, if they shall survive me, any interest which I own at the time of my death in the house . . . , with the further understanding that my Personal Representative shall retain in trust the share of my son Ashley Brunson for a period not to exceed ten (10) years from the date of my death, after which period, if my son Ashley Brunson shall not appear or make his whereabouts known to my Personal Representative, then Ashley Brunson's share shall be distributed equally to my then surviving issue." *See Scott v. Brunson*, 351 S.C. 313 (S.C.App. 2002).

8.9. Testator makes the following devise of her property. "After the death of my two sisters, the trust shall terminate; and I give, devise, and bequeath all of the property, real, personal, and mixed, still in the hands of the Trustee, to Texas A & M University, of College Station, Texas, but to be used by it as an experimental farm for a period of 50 years from the date of the death of my last sister. This gift is made in memory of my father and mother, J.L. Kelley and Alice Kelley." See *Crowell v. Texas A. & M. University System*, 1995 WL 316833 (Tex.App. 1995).

8.10. Testator makes a devise of real property with the following limitation: "to have and to hold the above granted and bargained premises with the privileges and appurtenances thereof unto the said The City of Bridgeport and their successors as and for a Public Park to be designated and known as Beardsley Park with the unlimited and perpetual rights in said City to use and improve the same for that purpose. But it is hereby provided that if said City shall at any future time attempt to devote said premises or any part of the same to any other use than that of a Public Park designated as aforesaid or shall attempt to deliver or convey the same or any part thereof said City shall thereupon forfeit all right and title to said premises and the absolute title to same shall revert in the Grantor his heirs and assigns. See *Blumenthal v. White*, 1995 WL 225489 (Conn.Super 1995).

2. LIFE ESTATES, TERMS OF YEARS, AND REMAINDERS

In the context of private trusts and estate planning for the average client, the far more likely estates and future interests you will need to create are going to be life estates and remainders, so let's tackle those. Let's change the bequest from p. 561 to the following:

> I give the residue of my estate to my wife, Wila, for life and on condition that she not remarry, but if she does remarry or at her death, then the residue of my estate shall pass to my two children, Seth and Doris, if they have reached age 21. If one or both has not yet reached age 21, then I want my executor to divide the property into two shares, one for Seth and one for Doris, and retain each share until each has reached age 21, at which time my executor shall transfer the share absolutely to each child. If either or both children fail to reach age 21, but leave issue surviving, I want my executor to establish a trust for that child's share on behalf of his or her issue immediately, which will pay to those issue when they reach 18. But if either or both children fail to reach age 21 and do not leave issue surviving, then I want that child's share to pass to the Red Cross.

As mentioned earlier, Wila has a *defeasible* life estate. This means that Seth and Doris have a far better chance of getting the property than they did in the earlier version, because even if Wila doesn't remarry, she will certainly die. The only thing to prevent them from getting possession of the property in this grant is if they die before they reach age 21. But failing to reach age 21 is a condition on *their* interest, not on Wila's.

That is another key element here: identifying which conditions go with which interests and whether they are *conditions precedent* (pronounced prec<u>ee</u>dent—as in to *precede*) or *conditions subsequent*. Generally speaking, *conditions precedent* are conditions that must occur in order for an interest to vest (like reaching age 21) and *conditions subsequent* are conditions that, upon their occurrence, cause an interest or estate to terminate. Hence, Wila's remarriage is a condition *subsequent* on her present estate, while reaching age 21 is a condition *precedent* on Seth and Doris' interests. The former *divests* the present estate and the latter *vests* the future interest.

Another Side Note

We should also talk for a minute about vesting. Vestedness is defined as *an immediate, secured right to present or future enjoyment*. For our purposes, a present estate is always vested because it is currently being enjoyed by the present estate holder. But subsequent future interests become vested only when they are certain to become possessory, either now or in the future. Thus, a grant like the following,

> *to Wila for life, then to Seth*

is vested in Seth immediately because we know that Seth will become entitled to possession, with certainty, in the future at Wila's death (an event we know will occur). There is no condition precedent on Seth's future interest becoming possessory. The only thing that has to happen is the prior estate has to terminate, which we know it will do. Thus, when this bequest became effective, Seth's future interest became *vested in interest*. It will then become *vested in possession* when Wila dies and Seth succeeds to actual possession and ownership of the property. For most purposes, we aren't too concerned with the actual date an interest becomes vested in possession; we are very concerned with when it becomes vested in interest. When it is vested in interest, we can answer the big three questions: who? what? and when? We will know who (Seth), what (fee simple absolute), and when (at Wila's death). Once we can answer these questions, and we know that all conditions are definitely going to occur, or have been satisfied, or have failed, we know that Seth will be absolutely vested in his future interest. But what if we change the gift to read,

> *to Wila for life, then to Seth but only if he reaches age 21 by Wila's death.*

In this case Seth's future interest is not vested. Do you see why? Because we won't know until Wila's death whether Seth will survive her or not, so we don't know if his interest will ultimately become possessory. In that case, his interest is not vested in interest, it is *contingent*. It is contingent because, in addition to Wila's life estate terminating, there is a condition precedent on Seth's future interest (that he reach age 21 by Wila's death).

Now let's talk about the future interests that follow life estates and let's pick up our questions where we left off. First, we answered the question about the present estate and found that it was a life estate or term of years (i.e.—it was subject to a definite condition). To determine the future interests that follow life estates we ask the same questions we asked in the defeasible fee context: i.e., is the future interest in the grantor or a third party, and is there a condition precedent or a condition subsequent on the future interest.

Question 1	Definite	Indefinite
Is the condition on the present estate definite or indefinite?	***Life Estate* or *Term of Years***	***Defeasible Fee Interest***

Question 2	Life/Death	Period of Time
Is the definite condition based on someone's life/death or on a period of time?	***Life Estate***	***Term of Years***

Question 3	Grantor	Third Party
Is the future interest in the grantor or in a third party?	***Reversion***	***Remainder***

For both life estates and terms of years, the future interests that follow are either reversions (if they are in the grantor) or remainders (if they are in third parties). If they are reversions in the grantor, then the property will revert back to the grantor upon the termination of the present life estate or term of years. Regardless of whether there is a condition precedent or condition subsequent on the reversion, it is still called a *reversion*. So that means that even if there is a condition precedent on the reversion that makes it uncertain to return to the grantor, we call it a *reversion* and not a *possibility of reverter* because the latter only follow fees simple determinable. The possibility of reverter is a term of art referring only to the future interest that follows the fee simple determinable.

If the future interest is in a third person, there may be conditions precedent or subsequent on that future interest that will change the category of the remainder. There are five different types of remainder.

Question 4	No	Yes
Is there a condition precedent on the vesting of the Remainder (and no condition subsequent)?	***Absolutely Vested Remainder (AVR)***	***Contingent Remainder***

Question 5	Event	Ascertaining Persons
Is the condition precedent on the vesting of the remainder dependent on an event or ascertaining persons?	*Contingent Remainder on a Conditional Event (CRCE)*	*Contingent Remainder on Unascertained Persons (CRUP)* or *Vested Remainder Subject to Open (or Subject to Partial Divestment) (VRSO)*

Question 6	No	Yes
Is there a condition subsequent that will divest the remainder (and no condition precedent)?	*Absolutely Vested Remainder (AVR)*	*Vested Remainder Subject to Divestment (VRSD)*

This last set of questions can be confusing, but when you study it further, you realize that it closely parallels the future interests that follow defeasible fees. That is, just as we asked whether the future interest was in a third party or the grantor following a defeasible fee, we ask the same question when it follows life estates and terms of years.

Regarding remainders, we ask whether there is a condition precedent on the vesting of that remainder. If the answer is no, the remainder is vested (either absolutely or subject to divestment) and if the answer is yes, the remainder is contingent (either on an event or on ascertaining a person).

One confusing remainder is the *vested remainder subject to open* (or *subject to partial divestment*) because this identifies a remainder interest in a class of people in which some members are known (and therefore their interests are partially vested) and some are not yet in being (and therefore contingent). Because the full identity of the class is not yet known, we can't answer the *what* question because we don't know what percentage each member of the class will take. Until we close the class, we don't know if the current members will take all or just a part of the property. If there are five members of the class at the time the interest is created, but three more are born before the interest becomes possessory, then the property will be divided into eight shares instead of five shares, thus divesting each of the original five members of a portion of their share to make up the shares of the three new members.

This kind of interest would be expressed as follows:

to my wife Wila for life, then to my grandchildren.

Assuming Seth and Doris are still alive and able to have children after the testator dies but before Wila dies, the class will be in flux until the death of Wila, the life tenant.

Now that you have been introduced to all six present estates and all ten future interests, let's map them on a flow chart (and count them).

Present Estate	Conditions/ Limitations	Future Interest in Grantor	Future Interest in Third Party
Fee Simple Absolute (FSA) **(#1)**	None	None	None
Fee Simple Determinable (FSD) **(#2)**	Indefinite	Possibility of Reverter (PR)(automatic) **(#1)**	None
Fee Simple Subject to a Condition Subsequent (FSCS) **(#3)**	Indefinite	Power of Termination (PT) or Right of Re-Entry (RRE) (condition precedent) **(#2)**	None
Fee Simple Subject to an Executory Limitation (FSEL) **(#4)**	Indefinite	None	1) Shifting Executory Interest (SHEI) (no condition precedent) **(#3)** *or* 2) Springing Executory Interest (SPEI) (with condition precedent) **(#4)**
Life Estate or Term of Years (LE or TY) **(#5 & #6)**	Definite	Reversion (REV)**(#5)**	1) Vested Remainder (a) absolutely (AVR) **(#6)** (b) subject to divestment (VRSD) **(#7)** (c) subject to open (VRSO) **(#8)** *or* 2) Contingent Remainder on (a) conditional event (CRCE) **(#9)** (b) unascertained persons (CRUP) **(#10)**
Fee Tail (FT) **(#7)**	Indefinite	Reversion (REV) **(#5)**	

This chart simply shows the first level of estates and future interests that can be created. Not surprisingly, additional layers of conditions and limitations can be added on top of the first level. Thus, a grantor might make the following *inter vivos* grant:

I give Blackacre to my son so long as he remains unmarried, but if he marries then the property is to return back to me. If I have died before my son remarries, however, then Blackacre is to pass to the Red Cross. But if the Red Cross shall have gone out of business, or shall ever go out of business, then Blackacre is to pass to my heirs at law.

By imposing conditions on the future interests (like the survivorship requirement for the possibility of reverter and the condition subsequent on the Red Cross' interest), you have executory interests piled on top of the various first level future interests. To determine what those second level future interests are, you generally ask what the prior future interest will become when it vests in possession. Thus, in the above example, you would have the following:

- The son has a fee simple determinable in Blackacre.

- The grantor has a possibility of reverter that is subject to an executory limitation if the grantor fails to survive the son's state of non-marriage.

- The Red Cross has a shifting executory interest dependent on the termination of the grantor's prior possibility of reverter.

- The heirs at law have a shifting executory interest dependent on the Red Cross going out of business. If the Red Cross eventually gets possession of Blackacre, they could lose it if they go out of business. So when it becomes possessory in the Red Cross, they will have a fee simple subject to an executory limitation with a shifting executory interest in the heirs.

So how do we know that the Red Cross has an executory interest and not a contingent remainder? Each future interest is defined by reference to the present estate that precedes it, and to know what that is we have to determine what the preceding future interest will become when/if it becomes possessory. Thus, the most accurate analysis is to identify what present estate the future interest is *in*. Looking at the grant above, we can write the interests as follows:

- The son has a fee simple determinable in Blackacre.

- The grantor has a possibility of reverter *in a fee simple absolute* that is subject to an executory limitation if the grantor fails to survive the son's state of non-marriage.

- The Red Cross has a shifting executory interest *in a fee simple subject to an executory limitation* dependent on the termination of the grantor's prior possibility of reverter.

- The heirs at law have a shifting executory interest *in a fee simple absolute* dependent on the Red Cross going out of business. If the Red Cross eventually gets possession of Blackacre, they could lose it if they go out of business. So when it becomes possessory in the Red Cross, they will have a fee simple subject to an executory limitation with a shifting executory interest in the heirs.

What this additional information tells us is that there is no condition subsequent on the grantor's possibility of reverter or the interest of the heirs at law. That means that if their interests do become possessory, that's the end of the line; they will have fee simple absolute. But if the Red Cross gets it, it may lose Blackacre if the Red Cross goes out of business. Thus, the Red Cross's future interest is in a fee simple subject to an executory limitation.

A Side Note on the Fee Tail

A fee tail is described as an inheritable estate that MUST pass to the *lineal descendants* of the present estate holder and may not pass to collateral heirs. It was intended to ensure that property stayed in a family line, and was created through a grant: *to A and the heirs of his body* (or the male heirs of his body, or the female heirs of his body). In essence, the fee tail lops off the right of collateral heirs to inherit if the present owner has no lineal descendants, and replaces it with a reversion in the original grantor. And a fee tail traditionally could not be alienated, because the transferee would take only the grantee's fee tail. Thus, if O granted Blackacre to A and the heirs of his body, and A sold Blackacre to B, B would take A's fee tail, which would pass automatically to A's issue at A's death.

For obvious reasons, B wouldn't want to pay very much for what would turn out to be merely a life estate in the life of A, and so the common lawyers came up with a collusive lawsuit, called the *common recovery*, which operated to terminate the heirs' interests in the fee tail, just like it cut off dower rights. Through the use of some complex transfers to straw men, with a collusive lawsuit and a default judgment, a fee tail holder could transfer a fee simple absolute because the rights of the heirs to get it back would be cut off.

So the state of the law at the Revolution was that a fee tail could be created, and it would cut off the rights of collateral heirs to inherit in the absence of issue, but the common recovery would allow the fee tail holder to alienate a fee simple absolute, keeping the property marketable. But if the fee tail holder died in possession, his issue would take the fee tail automatically, but subject to the same conditions. It could be transformed into a fee simple absolute but, if not transferred *inter vivos*, it passed automatically to lineal heirs. It was not devisable by will and, in the absence of primogeniture, could lead to extreme fractionation of the interest through the generations. For that reason it was more popular in England and not particularly so in the U.S.

All states since 1776 have adopted fee tail statutes to convert them into a variety of more conventional forms: a fee simple absolute, a life estate in the present holder with a remainder in the life tenant's issue, a defeasible fee simple, a fee tail for one generation with an absolutely vested remainder in the next, or states might prohibit the fee tail altogether but allow a remainder over to take effect if the tenant dies without issue.

The important point to understand about the fee tail is that it could not be devisable by will; it functioned like a life estate but could be transferred *inter vivos* by the fee tail holder. The future interest holders were a limited class of legal heirs (not those determined by intestacy laws, but those lineal descendants only who were identified in the original grant) that excluded collateral heirs unless they were lineal descendants of the first fee tail holder. Also, the grantor (or his heirs) always retained a reversion in case the fee tail holder's lineal descendants failed.

A totally cool case that gives a great explanation of fee tails involves Robin's Island, New York, that was held in a fee tail during the Revolution, was confiscated under an Act of Attainder because the owner was a British sympathizer, was ordered returned by the Treaty of Peace of 1783, but was sold by New York in 1784 after New York abolished fees tail. A group trying to preserve the island from development obtained quit-claim deeds and releases from the potential heirs of the original holder in the 1980s and argued the state had only sold the life estate of the fee tail holder, not the remainder interest, to buyers in 1784, whose successors now wanted to develop the island. The New York statute abolishing fees tail purportedly converted them into fees simple absolute. The preservation group lost because their argument about the fee tail was wrong even though the State had clearly violated its own laws when it sold Robins Island in 1784 in violation of the Treaty of Peace. See *Robins Island Preservation Fund, Inc. v. Southold Devel. Corp.*, 959 F.2d 409 (2d Cir. 1992).

And for those of you addicted to Masterpiece Classic's *Downton Abbey*, remember that Lord Grantham had to marry the wealthy American, Cora, to get sufficient money to retain ownership of their vast estates, but they are entailed in tail male and he has only daughters. Thus, to keep the estates in the direct family, Mary is supposed to marry her cousin Matthew so their children will inherit. The entire first two seasons centered on whether Mary and Matthew would actually get together. But the fee tail will be abolished in England in 1925—do you think Sir Julian Fellowes has factored that into the plot? And why didn't Lord Grantham use a common recovery to alienate a fee simple and thus destroy cousin Matthew's interest? After Season 3, the fee tail problem looks to be solved with the birth of a son, but that only shows how Hollywood can avoid the vagaries of real life.

With that detour, let's think about the language necessary for creating a life estate or a term of years. A term of years is less frequently used today—you will probably learn that it is a common law leasehold (i.e. a tenancy for a specified period of time), but modern leaseholds are so heavily regulated by statute that they are hardly recognizable from the common law term of years. Rather, for our purposes it is best to think of a term of years as present ownership for a specified period of time. For instance, a settlor might establish a trust with the life income to his children until they reach age 35, at which time they are entitled to the principal. In that case, the children's interest in the life income is a term of years—it terminates upon a specific date, not at the end of a particular life. The term of years we are talking about here, therefore, is the functional equivalent to a life estate, and is not the leasehold that is commonly transferred in the landlord/tenant arrangement.[8]

PROBLEMS

See if you can identify the present estates and future interests in these simple grants.

8.11. I give the residue of my estate to my wife Wila, for her life, and at her death, the estate is to pass to the Red Cross.

8.12. I give the residue of my estate to my wife Wila, for her life, or until she remarries, and at either event, the estate is to pass to the Red Cross.

8.13. I give the residue of my estate to my wife Wila, until my children Seth and Doris reach age 21, and at the end of that time, it is to pass to my children.

8.14. I give the residue of my estate to my wife Wila for her life, and at her death it is to pass to my grandchildren.

---

[8] There is a very complex history of how the term of years transformed from the predecessor of the modern leasehold into its fairly rare form today, while the modern lease was formed almost from scratch through contract law. For a better discussion of the feudal and modern constructions of the term of years, see Bergin and Haskell, Preface to Estates in Land and Future Interests (1984), pp. 38–42 and subsequent discussions of reversions and seisin.

8.15. I give the residue of my estate to my wife Wila for her life, and at her death it is to pass to my children Seth and Doris, but if either of my children get a divorce from their current spouse, then that child's share is to pass in trust to my grandchildren.

Now, it would be wonderful if testators would use clear language like, "I convey to my wife a life estate in Blackacre," or "I give Blackacre to my wife, for her life only." As noted above, many people give property "absolutely," but with a remainder over to successors at the death of the first grantee. Is that a life estate or not? Consider the following cases and the rules of construction for determining whether a life estate was intended or not:

Cain v. Finnie

785 N.E.2d 1039 (Ill. App. 2003)

In 1949, C.E. Spurlock died. His will, as admitted to probate, provided in its entirety as follows: "I, C.E. Spurlock, leave all my property and holdings to Blanche Spurlock so long as she remains my widow." Blanche Spurlock never remarried and died as the widow of C.E. Spurlock in 1986. Barbara Finnie (defendant) is the daughter of Blanche and C.E. Spurlock. Rae Cain, Sue Jones, Grattena Ponce, and Erma Farley (plaintiffs) are the grandchildren of C.E. Spurlock from his first marriage. They are not heirs of Blanche Spurlock. The real property at stake consists of approximately 200 acres in Saline County.

The Court of Appeals held that a life estate was created, and not a fee simple determinable that ripened into a fee simple absolute when Blanche died having never remarried, because: *The critical phrase in C.E.'s will is "so long as she remains my widow." At first glance, one would believe that C.E. devised to Blanche a life estate in the property on the condition she never remarry. The ambiguity arises because there is no gift-over to others of the remainder interest upon the death of Blanche. Normally, when only a life estate is intended, a gift-over provision is included. Some courts have concluded that when no gift-over provision exists, the devise created a fee simple determinable or determinable fee simple. A fee simple determinable is a fee simple estate that has a condition or contingency attached thereto and that must be determined whenever the condition or contingency annexed to it is at an end, being a fee for the reason that it may last forever if the contingency does not happen but it could terminate because its duration depends upon collateral circumstances which qualify or debase it. The condition or contingency upon which the fee simple estate would terminate in this instance, Blanche remarrying, never occurred, because she remained C.E.'s widow for the remainder of her lifetime, and it can never occur, because Blanche is now deceased. The language of C.E.'s will clearly supports both interpretations. We therefore turn to extrinsic evidence, and this is where defendant loses.*

Defendant offered absolutely no evidence to show the circumstances under which the will was made or the relationship of the family members, particularly the offspring from C.E.'s first marriage. Plaintiffs, on the other hand, specifically alleged in their complaint that Blanche in her will, which was dated October 13, 1961, and was admitted to probate in 1986, acknowl-

edged that she only held a life estate to the property, with the remainder interest being left to all of the children equally. . . .   Given that Blanche herself considered her interest in the property to be only a life estate, we cannot say, under such circumstances, that the court erred in similarly interpreting the intent of the will and in granting a summary judgment in favor of plaintiffs.

Query: How would you have interpreted the simple language of Spurlock's devise to his wife? Why did the court interpret it to be a life estate given the fact that there is no mention of the term *life*? Do you think he intended a fee simple absolute, a fee simple determinable, or a life estate? And who gets the property upon Blanche's death? Does it go to Blanche's estate, C.E.'s estate, or somewhere else? Note, too, how the use of the magic term "so long as" is ignored here.

Dunkel v. Hilyard

766 N.E.2d 603 (Ohio App. 2001)

Leland Dunkel died testate in 1952. He had no children, but was survived by his wife, Eloise Dunkel. Leland's will provided in relevant part:

> *SECOND. I give, devise and bequeath to my wife, Elosie [sic.] Dunkel, all my property of which I may die seized, to be hers absolutely and in fee simple, subject only to the provision and condition that, if any of said property so devised and bequeathed to my said wife, remain, at the time of her death, unused and unexpended by her and identifiable as property passing and descending to her by this, my last will and testament, then and in such event, such unused and unexpended portion shall, at the death of my said wife, pass and descend under the provision of item Fourth of this my last will and testament.*
>
> * * *
>
> *FOURTH. * * * In the event however that my said wife should die subsequent to my decease, leaving no such child or children her surviving, then and in such event, at her death, I give, devise and bequeath all such unused and unexpended portion of my estate, remaining after her death, as above referred to, to my brother, H. Miller Dunkel, to be his absolutely and in fee simple; in the event that he should precede my said wife in death, she surviving me and he leaving any child or children him surviving, but my wife leaving no child or children her surviving, then such above referred to unused and unexpended portion of my estate, I give, devise and bequeath to such surviving child or children of my said brother, share and share alike, absolutely and in fee simple * * *.*

The trial court found that Leland conveyed all his property to Eloise in fee simple, and that Eloise expended the property, rendering it no longer identifiable.

On appeal, the court explained the four rules it used to find that the will devised a fee simple absolute to Eloise. *1. In the construction of a will, the sole purpose of the court should be to ascertain and carry out the intention of the testator. 2. Such intention must be ascertained from the words contained in the will. 3. The words contained in the will, if technical, must be taken in their technical sense, and if not technical, in their ordinary sense, unless it appear[s] from the context that they were used by the testator in some secondary sense. 4. All the parts of the will must be considered to-gether, and effect, if possible, given to every word contained in it."*

In applying these rules, the Court stated: *The first devise must contain some language indicating that a life estate or trust was intended; the mere existence of a remainder provision does not suffice to prove the testator's intent to devise less than the prima facie fee simple absolute.*

Query: In this case the court held that the use of the term "absolutely and in fee simple" governed the interpretation of the will, rendering all that followed surplusage. Another interpretation, derivable from the totality of the language, was a life estate with a power to consume. What did this lawyer do wrong (it was clearly written by a lawyer)?

Cooley v. Williams

31 S.W.3d 810 (Tex.App. 2000)

Decedent left the following holographic will:

> *If I die all my possions [sic] go to my husband Paul Odis McKee and when he dies everything goes to Rhobbin LaVern Jabbia [sic]. Written by Lillian E. McKee (wife).*

She was survived by her husband and two daughters, Margaret Elkund (Cooley's mother) and Marilyn Williams, both of whom are still alive. Decedent's husband died intestate fewer than two weeks after decedent's death. Cooley filed an application to probate decedent's will and to be appointed independent administrator. Williams contested it. After a hearing, the trial judge admitted the will to probate as a muniment of title, construed it to convey decedent's estate in fee simple absolute to decedent's husband with no "remainder" interest to Cooley, and ordered the estate's assets delivered to the administrator of decedent's husband's estate. Cooley appeals.

In construing the interests that passed under this will, the court explained the possible alternatives as: 1) *A "fee simple absolute" is an estate over which the owner has unlimited power of disposition in perpetuity without condition or limitation. 2) An "executory limitation" is an event which, if it occurs, automatically divests one of devised property. 3) A fee simple estate subject to an executory limitation is called a "determinable fee simple estate." This is a fee simple interest in every respect, except that it passes to another if the contingency happens. The recipient upon the contingency's happening has an "executory interest." 4) A life estate is created by words showing intent to give the right to possess, use, and enjoy the property during life. Additionally, the life tenant may expressly be given unlimited power to dispose of the property during his lifetime; if such power is exercised, it defeats the remainderman's interest in the disposed-of property. However, the life tenant may not devise any of that property that remains at her death. No particular language is required to make a life estate.*

We hold the will created a determinable fee simple in decedent's husband with an executory interest in Cooley. The first half of the sentence gave decedent's husband a fee simple estate. The second half of the sentence, however, also clearly gave "everything" after the husband's death to Cooley. To read the two halves together—without nullifying the second half and while preserving the greatest estate possible in the first devisee—is to construe decedent's husband's devise as a determinable fee simple.

Query: The court held the will to convey a fee simple subject to an executory limitation rather than a life estate with a power to consume. What is the difference, if any? What do you think was intended? What is the best interpretation given the language of the grant?

Guilliams v. Koonsman

279 S.W.2d 579 (Tx. 1955)

The will of J. J. Koonsman, deceased, reads as follows:

> 'I give and devise to my son, Alvin Koonsman, all of my undivided interest in all of the remainder of my real property situated in Scurry County, Texas, which I may own at the time of my death, and to his child or children if any survive him, and in the event of Alvin's death without issue surviving him, then to my son and daughter, Jesse J. Koonsman and Mrs. Cora Guilliams, share and share alike, and to their heirs and assigns forever.'

> *The trial court held that the paragraph devised to Alvin Koonsman 'an estate in fee, defeasible, however, upon his death without issue surviving him,' with a gift over to Jesse J. Koonsman and Mrs. Cora Guilliams. The Court of Civil Appeals affirmed.*

The question raised was whether the devise to "Alvin ... and to his child or children if any survive him" created a life estate with a remainder, a co-tenancy, a fee simple absolute, or a defeasible fee of some sort. The court explained: *If the devise in the fourth paragraph had been to Alvin Koonsman in fee, without other qualifying language, and with the added limitation 'and in the event of Alvin's death without issue surviving him, then to my son and daughter, Jesse J. Koonsman and Mrs. Cora Guilliams, share and share alike, and to their heirs and assigns forever', it clearly would . . . create in Alvin Koonsman a defeasible fee. Petitioner so admits in her brief.*

> *On the other hand, if the devise had been to Alvin Koonsman 'and to his child or children', without other qualifying or limiting language, and at the effective date of the will there was a child or children of Alvin Koonsman in esse, the great majority of the courts of this country, following the Second Resolution of Wild's case (6 Coke 16b, 77 Eng.Rep. 277), would treat it as vesting the fee title in Alvin Koonsman and his child or children in being at the effective date of the will as joint tenants or tenants in common. The will before us differs from both examples in that it combines the features there emphasized and adds to the words quoted in the second example—'and to his child or children'—the significant words, 'if any survive him'.*

> *The only evidence in the record before us, other than the will itself and the probate proceedings in connection therewith, is the testimony of Alvin Koonsman that J. J. Koonsman, the testator, died March 6, 1942, and that he (Alvin) has only one child, John Billy Koonsman, born October 15, 1942. From this testimony it appears that John Billy was in esse for the purpose of taking under the will on the date it became effective, that is, the date of J. J. Koonsman's death. . . .*

> *What is the meaning of the words 'and to his child or children if any survive him' following the devise to Alvin? We have been cited to and have found no case squarely in point. If the words 'if any survive him' had been omitted and we were to follow the weight of authority, heretofore noted, we would be compelled to hold that Alvin and his son, John Billy, took the first*

*estate created as cotenants. But those words were not omitted, and we as-
cribe to them a two-fold effect: first they limited the interest of Alvin
Koonsman to a life estate, and secondly, they operated to make the remainder to be taken by the child or children of Alvin contingent rather than
vested. . . .*

*The words 'if any survive him', qualifying the devise to the children of
Alvin, clearly indicate that his children were not to take as cotenants with
Alvin but were to take in succession to him, with the result that the devise to
Alvin is limited to a life estate. No particular form of words is necessary to
the creation of a life estate. 'It has been said that where the construction of a
will devising property to one and his children is doubtful, the courts lean
toward giving the parent a life estate, and that even a slight indication of an
intention that the children shall not take jointly with the parent will give a
life estate to the parent with a remainder to the children.'*

*The conclusion that the remainder in the child or children is contingent
rather than vested is also impelled by the words 'if any survive him.' Survival is made a condition precedent to the vesting of the remainder rather
than a condition of defeasance. While it has been said that 'The law favors
the vesting of estates at the earliest possible period, and will not construe a
remainder as contingent where it can reasonably be taken as vested', nevertheless, when the will makes survival a condition precedent to the vesting of
the remainder, it must be held to be contingent. . . .   The rule for determining whether a remainder is vested or contingent is thus stated by Gray in his
work on The Rule Against Perpetuities: 'If the conditional element is incorporated into the description of, or into the gift to the remainder-man, then
the remainder is contingent; but if, after words giving a vested interest, a
clause is added divesting it, the remainder is vested'. 3d Ed., s 108(3), page
85. Here the condition of survival is incorporated into the gift to Alvin
Koonsman's child or children.*

*There remains to be determined the nature of the estate devised to Jesse
J. Koonsman and Mrs. Cora Guilliams by the fourth paragraph of the will.
They are to take the fee 'in the event of Alvin's death without issue surviving
him.' Their estate must be held to be a contingent remainder also. It is to
take effect upon Alvin's death, but only if he dies 'without issue surviving
him'. It is an alternative contingent remainder. In 33 Am.Jur. 542 it is said:
'More than one estate in remainder may be limited after a single particular
estate if the limitation is in the alternative so that one may take effect if the
other does not.'. . . .*

*The judgments of the trial court and Court of Civil Appeals are re-
formed to define the word 'issue' as used in the fourth paragraph of J. J.
Koonsman's will to mean child or children, and to decree that the true
meaning and effect of the fourth paragraph of the will is that the plaintiff,
Alvin Koonsman, is therein and thereby given an estate for life in the property therein described, with a remainder in fee to the child or children of Alvin
Koonsman, conditioned upon their surviving him, and an alternative remainder in fee to Jesse J. Koonsman and Mrs. Cora Guilliams, or their
heirs and assigns, conditioned on the death of Alvin Koonsman without a
child or children surviving him, and as so reformed the judgments of those
courts are affirmed.*

Query: Are you convinced that J.J. Koonsman intended a life estate for his son Alvin, with a contingent remainder in Alvin's children, or do you think he likely intended a fee simple absolute, with an alternate gift to the children if Alvin predeceased the testator? Thus, was the intention to create a life estate with a future interest or a primary and an alternate gift to preclude application of the anti-lapse statute?

As courts have routinely stated, it is not necessary to use the terms "life estate" or "for life" when creating a life estate. If a grantor intends to devise only a life estate AND that is a plausible interpretation of otherwise ambiguous language, courts are likely to find a life estate is all that passed. But the cases above, when read together, show that there is no magic language or clear rule, although there are some general principles we can extract:

1. Use of terms "for life" or "life estate" are terms of art, like "fee simple" and "absolutely" that are likely to prevail. Clear terms in the granting language usually renders additional language and limitations to be deemed surplusage unless the limitation or condition is consistent with the estate devised in the granting clause.

2. Presence of gift-over language is likely to indicate a defeasible fee or a life estate.

3. A life estate is consistent with both a restraint on alienation and a power to consume—although a trust is usually a better mechanism for accomplishing both. Of course, life estates in trusts with restraints (spendthrift provisions) and powers (as with the QTIP trust) are quite common.

4. Other principles mostly applicable to grants of land are the presumption against forfeitures, and the presumption that the grantor transferred all interests that the grantor had to transfer unless there is clear language indicating an intent to retain an interest.

5. All conditions subsequent should be interpreted strictly and narrowly to prevent forfeitures.

These rules create a preference for a fee simple absolute if that is a plausible interpretation of an ambiguous grant of land because of the rules against restraints on alienation and the policy of promoting marketability of land. These don't operate as strictly in the context of wills and trusts, where a donor's likely intent may very well be to create multiple life estates and various conditions in order to spread wealth among more of his descendants and exercise that dead hand control in family relationships. But we would cut them off more readily in the non-familial marketplace in land. So keep in mind that the facts may very well determine which rules get applied to an ambiguous conveyance.

The life estate cases reproduced above illustrate common problems with contemporary future interests jurisprudence. Well-drafted estate plans don't get litigated over the question of what present estate or future interest was intended, although as you will see below there are much more complicated issues surrounding survivorship conditions and class gifts that even a well-drafted plan can run into. There is absolutely no reason for a lawyer-drafted will to mess up the issue of whether a fee simple or a life estate was intended. But obviously not everyone has a lawyer-drafted will.

Thus, it is up to courts and lawyers and executors to figure out which present estate and which future interests best represent the testator's inten-intentions while doing the least injustice to the actual language used. When faced with ambiguous grants, courts rely less and less on magical terms and more on effectuating the grantor's intent or, in some cases, finding an outcome that maximizes fairness and minimizes conflict between the survivors. Unfortunately, bad lawyering at both the drafting stage and the litigation stage can lead to results that are quite contrary to the grantor's intentions. This is especially true if the lawyers don't think outside the life estate/fee simple boxes to include defeasible fee interests and life estates coupled with powers, either of which may more accurately reflect what a grantor wanted.

PROBLEMS

To practice spotting drafting traps and thinking of options, go through the four cases above and:

8.16. Determine which interpretation seems most likely given just the language of the grant and explain why.

8.17. Determine what other interpretations seems reasonably possible given the ambiguous language and other facts of the case.

8.18. Determine who would get the estate based on the different possible interpretations.

3. CONTINGENT AND VESTED REMAINDERS: CONFUSION COMPOUNDED

Now that you have a better grasp of how to draft language to create the appropriate present estates, we can turn to the hard part—those rascally remainders and executory interests. As you learned earlier, there are five different types of remainders and two types of executory interests (i.e. future interests in third parties, not the grantor). Remember, the basic distinction that often trips up students is that:

- executory interests follow fee interests subject to indefinite conditions, and
- remainders follow present estates subject to definite conditions (life estates and terms of years)

All executory interests are contingent because they follow present estates subject to a condition subsequent that are not certain to occur. If they are subject to an additional condition precedent they are *springing* executory interests and if there is no additional condition other than the termination of the prior interest they are *shifting* executory interests. Some remainders, however, are immediately vested because they follow life estates or terms of years that are definitely going to terminate. But if there is an additional condition precedent on the remainder that is uncertain, that makes it become contingent.

You might think that it should be relatively easy to distinguish between a vested and a contingent remainder, but you would be very much mistaken. One of the most difficult classifications is between the *vested remainder subject to divestment* and the *contingent remainder on a conditional event*. The confusion arises because the language used to create them is remarkably similar but the legal effects of each can be quite different—

leading to litigation and much dispute over which was intended. The following is a clear example, and a not-so-clear example. The clear example of a *vested remainder subject to divestment* would be:

> *to A for life, then to B, but if B ever uses the land for non-residential purposes, then to C.*

This is clear because there is no condition precedent on B's vesting of the remainder, although B might lose the property if the condition subsequent of using it for non-residential purposes occurs. Grammatically and logically, B's interest is vested subject to being lost if B ever uses it for non-residential purposes. The condition on B's interest does not kick in until B acquires possession, and the onus is on B (and B's heirs and assigns) to not use it for non-residential purposes. There is no limitation on C's use of the property or on A's. The limiting condition is therefore a clear example of a condition subsequent that serves to divest B's interest.

We would write the interests of A, B, and C as follows:

- A has a life estate
- B has a vested remainder subject to divestment in a fee simple subject to an executory limitation, and
- C has a shifting executory interest in a fee simple absolute.

On the other end of the spectrum, a clear example of a *contingent remainder on a conditional event* would be:

> *to A for life, then if B has graduated from college at A's death, then to B, and if B hasn't graduated from college at A's death, then to C.*

This is clear because B must graduate from college by the time A dies in order for B's interest to vest. It may vest before A dies by B graduating college during A's life, at which time B's contingent remainder would become an absolutely vested remainder. But until B graduates from college, his interest remains contingent. Thus, the condition on B's interest is a condition precedent, not a condition subsequent, because it must be satisfied before B's interest vests. Grammatically and logically, the condition of graduating from college by the time A dies precedes and is attached to B's interest. We would write the interests of this grant as:

- A has a life estate
- B has a contingent remainder on a conditional event in a fee simple absolute
- C has an alternate contingent remainder on a conditional event in a fee simple absolute

Now a not-so-clear example:

> *to A for life, then to B, but if B fails to survive A, then to C.*

Grammatically B's interest looks like the vested remainder, but logically the condition resembles the condition precedent of the contingent remainder. So what is it? Here is another not-so-clear example:

> *to A for life, then to B but only if B is married.*

What if B is married when the interest is created but then gets a divorce during A's life, but then gets remarried before A dies? Is being married a condition precedent, or is getting divorced a condition subsequent?

The answers to these questions are all: *it depends*. It depends on the testator's intent, a variety of rules of construction adopted by courts, and public policy. In some cases grammar is used to resolve the question; in others it is the logic of who is responsible for satisfying or violating the condition; in others it may seem like a coin toss. But which it is can matter hugely in terms of outcome.

The most important rule of construction is the *preference for early vesting* (also known as the *early vesting rule*); i.e. if the language can be interpreted reasonably as either a vested remainder or a contingent remainder, courts prefer to classify the interest as a vested remainder because early vesting helps settle property interests.[9] Early vesting also helps avoid violations of the rule against perpetuities (which we discuss later). Other rules include the presumption that the grantor conveyed all property interests she had if there is no clear language retaining a reversionary interest. Because the grantor would retain a reversion if she only creates a contingent remainder, the presumption that she gave up that reversion if not explicitly retained may also work in favor of interpreting an ambiguous remainder as vested. Courts also look to the grantor's intent and administrative ease and certainty when interpreting ambiguous language. Generally these rules work in favor of interpreting an interest to be vested; however, sometimes they result in contrary interpretations.

Probably the most difficult condition to interpret (and one of the most commonly used) is survivorship to some point in the future. Thus, a grant may be made:

To A for life, then to A's surviving children

Is the interest in A's children contingent, vesting only in the children who are alive at A's death, or is the interest vested subject to divestment upon failure to survive A? Or does the interest in A's children vest if/when they survive the grantor? Of course, without further information about what happens to the interests of children who fail to survive A or O, it may be a distinction without a difference. But it can matter if the remainder in A's children is running up against a Rule Against Perpetuities time limit, or if an alternate gift is created. Consider these two cases that came to opposite conclusions for what, superficially, appear to be relatively clear expressions of the same testamentary intent.

Webb v. Underhill

882 P.2d 127 (Or.App. 1994)

Ernest Webb, owner of the Buck Hollow Ranch, died in 1972. His will devises all of his property to his wife Agnes for life, or until she remarries, with the remainder of the property to be divided equally among four of Ernest's six children upon Agnes' death or remarriage. If any one of the four named children is deceased at that time, that one-quarter share will go to his or her lineal descendants, if any.[10]

---

[9] For reasons we discuss below, the issue of early vesting is less important with extensions in the perpetuities period and/or adoption of statutes mandating survivorship until distribution to avoid the transmissible remainder problem.

[10] Specifically, the will provides: "For her use, benefit and enjoyment, for such period of her natural life as she shall remain unmarried, I give to my beloved wife, Agnes Webb, all of my property of every kind and nature, with the provision, however, that if my said wife shall remarry, that said property shall *at the date of the marriage* revert as follows: One Dollar ($1.00) each to Irene Barton and to Vivian Morse [two of Ernest's six children]. The remainder shall be divided equally between [the other four children]: Delbert Webb, Delores Rhodig, La Velle Underhill, Wayne L. Webb. But if one or more of these shall be dead, their share shall go to their lineal descendants, if any. If one or more of the four who live in Oregon and are last mentioned, shall be dead leaving no lineal descendants, the share of the deceased one, dead

After Ernest's death, his son Delbert died. Delbert is survived by his wife Carol, who subleases a portion of the ranch, and their three adult children (the grandchildren).

Plaintiffs, who seek to sell the ranch as a single parcel and distribute the proceeds according to their respective interests, are Ernest's wife Agnes, two of Ernest's children (Wayne and Delores), Delbert's wife Carol and the grandchildren. Defendant is Ernest's daughter La Velle.

To maintain an action to partition property, a plaintiff must be a tenant in common, with a vested remainder in the property. Agnes, as the sole life estate holder, is not a tenant in common, and Carol is a mere lessee. Therefore, neither of those parties fits within the requirements of the partition statute. Below, plaintiffs argued that the grandchildren's interests vested indefeasibly at the time of Delbert's death. They conceded below that the children's interests are contingent, but, on appeal, their reply brief may be viewed as an attempt to withdraw that concession. Defendant argued that all of the remainder interests are contingent, in that the children or their lineal descendants must survive Agnes' death or remarriage to take under the will.

The trial court ruled that both the children's and grandchildren's interests are contingent and conditioned upon surviving to the date of Agnes' death or remarriage. Having concluded that none of the plaintiffs holds a vested remainder, the court held that they could not maintain this partition action. Accordingly, it granted defendant's motion for summary judgment and dismissed the case.

The issues on appeal are whether the children's and grandchildren's interests in the property are vested, and whether resolution of that question involves a factual determination that precludes summary judgment. Holding that whether a remainder interest is vested or contingent is a purely legal one, the court went on to analyze the language of the will.

We turn to trial court's legal conclusions, beginning with an analysis of the future interests of Ernest's four named children. Plaintiffs acknowledge that the will contains a survivorship requirement that the children must meet, in order for them to personally take, but contend that the children's interests are most aptly described as "vested remainders subject to divestment" should they fail to survive the life tenant. That is incorrect. The devise in this case created alternative remainder interests in both the children and the grandchildren.[5] When a life estate is followed by two alternative re-

---

without lineal descendants, shall go to the survivors of the four who live in Oregon (last mentioned) or to their lineal descendants. The said four being Delbert Webb, Delores Rhodig, La Velle Underhill, and Wayne L. Webb."

"*At the death of my said wife,* if she shall yet be in the use and enjoyment of said property, such as remains shall be divided as follows: One Dollar ($1.00) each to Irene Barton and to Vivian Morse. The remainder shall be divided equally between: Delbert Webb, Delores Rhodig, La Velle Underhill, Wayne L. Webb. But if one or more of these shall be dead, their share shall go to their lineal descendants, if any. If one or more of the four who live in Oregon and are last mentioned, shall be dead leaving no lineal descendants, the share of the deceased one, dead without lineal descendants, shall go to the survivors of the four who live in Oregon (last mentioned) or to their lineal descendants. The said four being Delbert Webb, Delores Rhodig, La Velle Underhill, and Wayne L. Webb." (Emphasis supplied.)

[5]   There is support in the *Restatement* for plaintiffs' position that a remainder interest can be vested yet subject to a survivorship requirement, *i.e.,* a survivorship requirement does not necessarily mean that the remainder interest is contingent. However, *Love v. Lindstedt, supra,* supports the view that a devise "to A for life, remainder to B, but if B predeceases A, then to C" creates alternative remainder interests in B and C. Paulus, J., "Future Interests in

mainder interests, and "the vesting of the second depends upon the failure of the first, and the same contingency decides which one of the two alternative remainders shall take effect in possession," both interests are alternative contingent remainders. Here, surviving the death or remarriage of the life tenant is the contingency that decides whether and which of the alternative remainder interests will vest indefeasibly. If one of the children dies before the triggering event, his or her estate—and, accordingly, his or her spouse, if any—will take nothing under the will.[6] Until the triggering event takes place, it cannot be known who will be entitled to take under Ernest's will.

Plaintiffs contend that the only contingency that conditioned the present three grandchildren's interests was to survive their father's death. They argue that, once Delbert died, his interest in the property indefeasibly vested in his children. It is true that, if Delbert's lineal descendants were taking by devise or by intestate succession from Delbert, those heirs would be determined at the moment of his death. However, the future interests of Delbert's children, if any, flow directly from their grandfather Ernest's will, not Delbert's. Their interests stem only from their membership in a class described as "lineal descendants." When a will includes a gift to a class of persons, the devise takes effect in favor of those who constitute the class at the death of the testator, unless the will shows a contrary intent. As noted above, Ernest's will unambiguously expresses a contrary intent. It states that upon Agnes' remarriage or death, Ernest's property is to be divided among his four named children or their lineal descendants. That language fixed Agnes' death or remarriage as the date on which a determination of the members of the "lineal descendants" class is to be made.[8] There may or may not be any lineal descendants of Delbert living at the date of Agnes' death or remarriage. If none are living, Delbert's share will be divided among his named siblings who live in Oregon or their lineal descendants.

Furthermore, before the life tenancy ends and the class closes, it will be impossible to determine the entire membership of the class of lineal descendants. Plaintiffs argue that once Delbert died, he could have no more lineal descendants and that, as a consequence, his portion of the class closed with Delbert's three children as its only members. That is incorrect. The term "lineal descendants" encompasses more than just children. The term includes all those who proceed from the body of the person named to the remotest degree, including grandchildren and great-grandchildren. In sum, until Agnes' death or remarriage, all of the future interests in this case will remain contingent. There is presently no party who may maintain a partition action.

Oregon," 15 Will L Rev 151, 159 (1979). Under the facts of this case, "B and C" would represent Ernest's named children and their lineal descendants. [Arguably the court here misstates the grant in the *Love* case. eds.]

6   This is to be distinguished from a vested remainder interest that, although subject to a life estate, will become possessory at the termination of that estate; in such cases, the remainderman's estate will be entitled to take even if the remainderman has died.

8   The *Restatement (Second) of Property,* "Donative Transfers," § 28.2 (1988), states that when a gift is made to a class described as the "descendants" of a named person, or by another multigenerational term, "[a] class member must survive to the *date of distribution* in order to share in the gift." (Emphasis supplied). Under Oregon law, the "primary incidents of 'class gifts' * * * are survivorship and the admission of afterborn members." *Jorgensen v. Pioneer Trust Co.,* 198 Or. 579, 592, 258 P.2d 140 (1953).

Query: Do you think Ernest, or his lawyer, understood the difference between contingent remainders and vested remainders subject to divestment as they applied to a survivorship requirement? Besides being able to partition the property, are there other reasons the law might favor a vested remainder interpretation?[11]

Est. of Krooss

99 N.E.2d 222 (N.Y. 1951)

Herman Krooss died in 1932. He was survived by his wife Eliese and his two children, a son, John Krooss, and a married daughter, Florence Maue. By his will, he gave his residuary estate, real and personal, to his wife, 'to have and to hold the same for and during the term of her natural life,' when the power to use any part of it for her support and maintenance that she deemed necessary; no trust was created. The will further provided:

> *Upon the death of my beloved wife, Eliese Krooss, I then give, devise and bequeath all the rest, residue and remainder of my estate, as well real as personal, and wheresoever situate, to my beloved children, John H. Krooss and Florence Maue, nee Krooss, share and share alike, to and for their own use absolutely and forever.*

> *In the event that either of my children aforesaid should die prior to the death of my beloved wife, Eliese Krooss, leaving descendants, then it is my wish and I so direct that such descendants shall take the share their parent would have taken if then living, share and share alike, to and for their own use absolutely and forever.*

Florence Maue died, without having had descendants, in 1947, three years before the life beneficiary Eliese. Some months after Eliese's death, Florence's husband, as executor of his wife's estate, instituted the present proceeding in the Surrogate's Court of Bronx County to compel John Kroos, as executor under Eliese's will and as administrator c. t. a. of Herman Krooss' estate, to render and settle his respective accounts. In order to determine whether the executors of Florence's estate had status to prosecute the proceeding, the surrogate was required, initially, to construe Herman's will. He decided that the interest given to Florence was vested at the testator's death, subject to be divested only in the event of her predeceasing her mother leaving descendants, that it passed under her will, and that her husband, as executor, was entitled to bring the action. The Appellate Division modified that determination. Disagreeing with the surrogate's interpretation, the Appellate Division construed the will as imposing upon each of the remaindermen a condition that he or she survive the life beneficiary; Florence having died without children before Eliese, that condition was not met, and, concluded the court, as to Florence's share in the remainder, Krooss died intestate.

The law has long favored a construction of language in deed and will that accomplishes the vesting of estates; such a result is preferred because, among other things, it enables property to be freely transferred at the earliest possible date. Accordingly, the courts are intent upon restricting defeating events to the exact circumstances specified.

---

[11] Arguably the court could have focused on the definition of vested remainder from the partition statute and interpreted it to require that to sustain a partition action a person needed an indefeasibly vested remainder. How, if at all, would that have changed the outcome of this case?

The will under consideration is simple in language and simple in plan. The testator gave his widow a life estate and a power to use the principal if it proved necessary for her maintenance and support. What remained after her death he gave 'absolutely and forever' in equal shares to his two children, Florence and John. Had the will stopped at that point, there would be no question that the remainders were vested. And, since that is so, additional language will not be read as qualifying or cutting down the estate unless that language is as clear and decisive as that which created the vested remainder. The further language used by the testator in this case demonstrates, not that he was rendering the vesting of the estates in his children conditional upon survival of the life beneficiary, but that he was willing to have those estates divested only upon the combined occurrences of two further events. He explicitly provided, if either of his children died before his wife, 'leaving descendants,' then 'such descendants shall take the share the parent would have taken if then living'. If the words used mean what they say, then, divestiture of the remainder estates depended upon the happening of two plainly expressed and stipulated conditions: (1) the child, Florence or John, must die before the life beneficiary, and (2) the child so dying must leave descendants. Only if both of those conditions came to pass was the remainder by apt and unequivocal language already vested in Florence and John to be divested and bestowed instead upon the descendants of him or her who might have died.

When a will contains language that has acquired, through judicial decision, a definite and established significance, the testator is taken to have employed that language in that sense and with that meaning in mind. . . .   Over the years, the courts have uniformly held that language such as that used by the testator here, or language substantially identical, creates a vested remainder in fee subject to be divested by the remainderman's failing to survive the life beneficiary, if, but only if, such remainderman leaves issue or descendants surviving.

Turning to the will before us, we find that, at the expiration of the wife's life estate, the testator 'then' gave the remainder to his children 'absolutely and forever.' The use of the word 'then' as an 'adverb of time' must be, as it long has been, construed to relate solely 'to the time of enjoyment of the estate, and not to the time of its vesting in interest.' Hence, the sole combination of events which could divest the 'absolute' gift to the daughter Florence was her death before her mother, 'leaving descendants'. Only one of the specified conditions was fulfilled; although Florence did predecease her mother, she did not leave descendants. Consequently, her absolute gift remained vested and was not defeated. Not only the language employed, but the omission of any 'words of survivorship', to indicate an intent that Florence's brother was to take if Florence died without children, illumines the testator's design to give his daughter a vested remainder.

The court affirmed the decree of the Surrogate's Court and found that Florence received a vested remainder subject to divestment that was not divested because she did not predecease her mother AND leave descendants; thus, her husband, as executor of her estate, had standing to intervene.

Query: Is there any logical, functional difference between the language or the intent of the testator in this case and in the preceding case of *Webb v. Underhill*? I believe the court was right in both of these cases, even though one concluded the remainder interests were contingent remainders and the other were vested remainders. Do you see the important difference?

As you no doubt know by now, the lodestar of succession law is the donor's intent. Can you guess what Ernest Webb and Herman Krooss's intentions were? Do you think one intentionally intended to create a contingent remainder or the other a vested remainder? How, as a laywer drafting a will, can you best express your client's intent? Clearly, to do that, you must first *ascertain* that intent in your mind by asking all the relevant questions about what should happen to the property under all variety of scenarios.

Survivorship is one of the most common conditions grantors impose on remainder interests for the obvious reason that it is inefficient to reopen the estate of a vested remainderman to administer the remainder once the life tenant dies. This not only exposes the estate to additional administration fees, but additional taxes if the remainderman's estate is sufficiently large. And it is particularly inefficient if the remainderman never got to enjoy possession of the property. We will discuss below statutory efforts to deal with what has come to be called the *transmissible remainder* problem. But survivorship isn't the only limiting language that can cause confusion between vested and contingent remainders. Any kind of ongoing status can make it hard to interpret whether a condition precedent (and therefore a contingent remainder) or a condition subsequent (and therefore a vested remainder subject to divestment) was intended.

PROBLEMS

Consider the following grants and rewrite to make them clear vested remainders and clear contingent remainders.

8.19. To A for life, remainder to my married children.

8.20. To A for life, remainder to B so long as a fence is maintained between my house and B's house.

8.21. To A for life, remainder to B if B is unmarried.

8.22. To A for life, remainder to my nieces and nephews who reach age 21.

8.23. To A for life, then so long as my portrait hangs over the mantel, then to B and his heirs.

8.24. To A for life, then to the children of B who agree to live on the farm.

Now that you have a good sense of the difference between vested and contingent remainders, and how to draft the remainder to create an unambiguous condition precedent or condition subsequent, do the same thing with executory interests. Remember, executory interests are very like remainders, only they follow defeasible fee interests (FSELs), not life estates or terms of years. So repeat the exercise in the above six questions by transforming the present estate into a fee simple subject to an executory limitation, and then rewrite the ambiguous future interests to be unambiguous *shifting* executory interests and unambiguous *springing* executory interests.

4. SURVIVORSHIP

I know we have already seen how survivorship language complicates the interpretation of remainders, but we need to explore in more detail what exactly it is about survivorship that makes it so difficult. The main difficulty arises because a phrase like "to my surviving children" can mean:

1. "to my children who survive me, the testator,"
2. "to whichever of my children survives the rest,"
3. "to whoever survives to the time of distribution," or
4. "to whoever survives to some other important point (like reaching a certain age)."

These four options can lead to tremendous litigation, especially if the shares of children who do not survive are not provided for (which takes us back to the simple conveyance we began with, the interest in Wila, with the remainder (or executory interest) in Seth and Doris. Note: there is no problem if all the relevant beneficiaries actually survive to the time of distribution. Usually there is also no problem if a named beneficiary fails to survive the testator because of anti-lapse statutes. But most states have no protection for the interests of beneficiaries who survive the testator but not to the time of distribution. And they also don't have a way to give the surviving issue of a predeceasing beneficiary their ancestor's share if the ancestor fails to survive to some relevant point established by the testator. Remember, anti-lapse statutes apply only to gifts to beneficiaries who fail to survive the testator, not those who survive the testator but fail to survive to some other important point, like the death of the intervening life tenant.

Imagine a bequest: "to my spouse for life, remainder to my three children, Alice, Bob, and Carol." If Alice predeceases the testator leaving issue, the state's anti-lapse statute will usually create a substitute gift in Alice's issue so they would share the remainder with Bob and Carol. And what happens if Bob dies after the testator but before the spouse? Bob's absolutely vested remainder would simply pass through his estate to his testate or intestate takers. The same would be true if a child of Alice also survived the testator but predeceased the surviving spouse—the child's estate would take the child's share because the remainder interest had vested upon the testator's death.

Now imagine the grant instead reads: "to my spouse for life, remainder to my surviving children, Alice, Bob, and Carol." The survivorship language could knock Alice out altogether, so that Bob and Carol would take the remainder at the testator's death and Alice's issue take nothing because anti-lapse won't apply when the testator expressly indicates a time in the future until when they must survive. Alice, Bob and Carol's interests here are typically interpreted to be contingent remainders. Furthermore, if Bob survived the testator but not the surviving spouse and left issue, anti-lapse statutes can do nothing to save Bob's share for his issue. Assuming a court interprets the survivorship language to apply to the death of A, neither Bob's estate nor his issue are entitled to a share. That may be what the testator intended, or, more likely, the survivorship language was put in there by a lawyer who didn't follow through and draft the appropriate alternate gifts in case a named beneficiary failed to survive. Usually, the intent would be to have Bob's issue take his share by making his remainder contingent on surviving the life tenant, and then creating an alternate gift in Bob's lineal descendants if he fails to survive the life tenant. Doing so avoids the transmissible remainder issue of vested remainders, as well as the possibility that Bob might devise his share to strangers. And as you know by now, being explicit is always better than relying on salvage doctrines to effectuate the purpose of a badly-worded will or trust.

Consider the cost, litigation nightmare, and emotional impact of this case involving a will drafted by some of the best Philadelphia estates lawyers of the day. (It is such an interesting case with such a good discussion of the differences between vested and contingent remainders that we included most of the opinion. Plus, it's very complicated and therefore quite fun.)

Est. of Houston

201 A.2d 592 (Pa. 1964)

This appeal involves the important questions—was testator's gift of principal contingent or vested, and if vested, when vested and who took thereunder?

Henry H. Houston died a resident of Philadelphia County on June 21, 1895. His will was executed on February 2, 1962. At that time he had a wife, Sallie S. Houston; a married son, Samuel F. Houston; a married daughter, Sallie Houston Henry; and an unmarried daughter, Gertrude Houston, who married and became Gertrude Houston Woodward on October 9, 1894. All of these children survived the testator.[1] At the time of testator's death he had six living grandchildren; six other grandchildren were born after his death.

Testator executed a lengthy will, including a lengthy trust. The will contains 64 items and covers 25 printed pages. Testator provided in 'Item Fifty-ninth: All the rest residue and remainder of my estate real and personal wheresoever the same may be I give devise and bequeath to the Executors hereinafter named in trust to pay over the *net income* arising therefrom in the manner following.' There then follow five separate gifts of a specified amount to be paid annually to five of testator's cousins '*during her [or his] life.*' these are followed by 11 directions to pay out of the said income the sum of specified dollar amounts annually to named individuals *during their respective lives, and at the death of each*, he provided: 'I direct to be paid out of the principal of the residuary estate the sum of [specified] Dollars in equal shares *to each of his children who may be living at the time of his decease*, the children of any deceased child taking however their deceased parents share.' There then followed three additional gifts to a Church, and an annual gift to a sister-in-law during her life upon certain conditions.

We come then to Paragraph *Twenty-second* of Item Fifty-ninth which, relevantly, is the most important part of the will, and reads:

Twenty-second: All the rest, residue, and remainder of the *net income* of my estate including herein such income as may fall into and become

---

[1]   Mr. Houston had had three other children, who predeceased him, unmarried and without issue: Gertrude Bonnell Houston (who died in 1857); Eleanor Anne Houston (who died in 1875); and Henry H. Houston, Jr. (who died in 1879).

a part of the residue by reason of the death of any of the beneficiaries hereinbefore mentioned, I direct shall be paid and distributed one fourth thereof to my believe [sic.] wife Sallie S. Houston *during her life*. One fourth thereof to my daughter Sallie H. Henry *during her life*, one fourth thereof to my son Samuel F. Houston *during his life* and one fourth thereof to my daughter Gertrude Houston *during her life*. On the death of my said wife I direct that the one fourth of the income payable to her shall thereafter be payable to my said children in equal shares *during their lives* (sic) and should any of my said children be dead *leaving children* at the time of the death of their mother I direct that the said income be *paid to the children* of such deceased child until the death of my last surviving child. On the death of any one of my said children *without leaving lawful issue him or her surviving* I direct that the income heretofore payable to such deceased child shall be paid to my wife and *surviving children* in equal shares and if either of the said children shall *then be dead leaving issue*, such issue shall take the deceased parents share. On the death of any one of my said *children* leaving *lawful issue him or her surviving*, I direct that the *income* to which such deceased child would have been entitled if living, shall be paid in equal shares to and among his or her children and the issue of deceased children, *if any there be*, such issue taking their deceased parents share, until the death of my last surviving child. **On the death of my last surviving child** I direct that **the whole of the principal** of the trust estate shall be distributed **in equal portions to and among my grand-children**, the children of **any deceased grandchild taking their deceased parents share.'**[12]

Both appellants and appellees also point out, although each draw a different conclusion therefrom, that testator specifically provided for the spouse of each of his then married children. . . .

Sallie S. Houston, testator's widow, died intestate on November 13, 1913; his daughter, Sallie Houston Henry,[13] died on July 6, 1938; his son, Samuel F. Houston,[14] died May 2, 1952; and testator's *last surviving child*, his daughter, Gertrude Houston Woodward,[15] died on October 2, 1961. . . .

If the remainders for testator's *grandchildren* were vested at testator's death, or became vested on birth after testator's death, subject in both cases to being *divested in favor of their children* if any such grandchild predeceased testator's last surviving child, the principal of the residuary trust (which is carried at over $25,000,000., but is allegedly worth approximately $145,000.000.) will be divided into 12 *equal parts*—eight of such parts being for testator's eight living grandchildren; three of such parts for

---

12 Emphasis added.

13 Sallie Houston Henry (testator's daughter) had two children (daughters) who survived testator's last living child. She also had a son, T. Charlton Henry, who predeceased his mother, leaving a wife and two daughters who are still living. Charlton willed his entire estate to his wife.

14 Samuel F. Houston (testator's son) had four children, three of whom still survive. The fourth, Henry H. Houston II, born April 5, 1895, was killed in action in World War I, on October 18, 1918. His father, Samuel F. Houston, was his sole heir.

15 Gertrude Houston Woodward (testator's daughter) had three children who survived her and two who predeceased her. Her son, H. H. Houston Woodward, was born February 27, 1896, and was killed in action in World War I on April 1, 1918. Another child of Mrs. Woodward, Gertrude Houston Woodward, *Jr.*, who was born April 21, 1909, died March 6, 1934. Each of these children died intestate and unmarried. The sole heirs of each of these deceased children were their parents, Gertrude H. Woodward and Dr. George Woodward.

the heirs (or personal representatives) of testator's three grandchildren who died after testator's death but before the death of testator's last surviving child (Mrs. Woodward), intestate and unmarried; and one such part for the two (living) daughters of testator's deceased grandson, T. Charlton Henry.

If, however, the remainders were contingent upon testator's grandchildren or their children living at the death of testator's last surviving child (Mrs. Woodward), testator's remainder estate would be divided into and distributed in nine *equal* parts—eight such parts to testator's eight living grandchildren, and the ninth part to the two living daughters *per stirpes* of testator's deceased grandchild, T. Charlton Henry.

The Orphans' Court unanimously held (in scholarly opinions) that testator gave a vested interest in the principal of his residuary trust estate in equal portions to his grandchildren who (a) survived him, or (b) were born after his death, the children of any deceased grandchild taking their deceased parent's share-and consequently divided (and awarded) the principal into 12 equal parts.

We first place ourselves in the armchair of the testator and remember that the intention of the testator is the polestar in the construction of every will. . . .

"It is now hornbook law (1) that the testator's intent is the polestar and must prevail; and (2) that his intent must be gathered from a consideration of (a) all the language contained in the four corners of his will and (b) his scheme of distribution and (c) the circumstances surrounding him at the time he made his will and (d) the existing facts; and (3) that technical rules or canons of construction should be resorted to only if the language of the will is ambiguous or conflicting or the testator's intent is for any reason uncertain." . . .

Appellants' Contentions

Appellants vigorously contend—and this is their principal contention—that the testator intended to give the remainder (principal) of his trust estate to, and *only to living* persons, and that he demonstrated this intent *impliedly* in his gift of this remainder (principal) and very many times *expressly* throughout his entire will, and particularly in other gifts in this *Twenty-second* paragraph. Numerous times throughout the prior provisions of this will, testator made absolute gifts to then living persons *or to those surviving* a life beneficiary, *or to the living* members of a class, after the death of a named life beneficiary. Moreover, in this very *Twenty-second* paragraph of Item Fifty-ninth, as well as in other paragraphs of Item Fifty-ninth of his will, testator gave the income from a particular trust *only to living persons*. From a consideration of his *entire* will, and particularly from his gift of *income* only to *living* persons in this Twenty-second paragraph, appellants argue that testator must have meant and intended to give the *principal* of this large trust estate to his *then living* descendants, namely, to such of his grandchildren and the children *per stirpes* of his deceased grandchildren as were living at the death of his (testator's) last surviving child. Appellants further contend (1) that this construction is fortified by testator's evidence [sic] intent to keep this residuary trust estate in his family blood line, since (a) he made no provision therein for a spouse of a deceased grandchild, nor (b) did he give a deceased grandchild a power of appointment, and (2) that this construction would obviously have the desirable result of a colossal tax saving for his descendants. This reasoning is plausible and appealing but unfortunately has three serious weaknesses.

First and most important, appellants' interpretation glosses over or ignores the clear language of testator's gift of the principal *in equal portions to his grandchildren per capita*, which at first blush certainly creates in the grandchildren a *vested* interest. Moreover, this language—at least prima facie—shows a different intent from testator's *gift of income to his grandchildren per stirpes.* Secondly, in *11* paragraphs in his very *Fifty-ninth Item* of his will, as well as in many prior items in his will, testator made gifts conditional upon survivorship, *thus clearly demonstrating that he knew how to make a contingent gift, i. e., conditional upon survivorship when that was his intention.* The third weakness of appellants' contentions is the oft repeated statement that testator demonstrated in the language of his entire will that he wished to leave his property *only to living* persons. This is substantially but not entirely correct.

All of this indicates, sometimes clearly and at other times very remotely, that the testator did not in every instance make his gifts conditional upon survivorship or living, and therefore it cannot be accurately said that testator demonstrated in the income provisions of this *Twenty-second* paragraph that he always wished to leave his income *only* to living persons.

Appellees' Contentions

Appellees' basic contentions are twofold: (1) Testator gave the *principal* of his trust estate *clearly* and *unquestionably* to his *grandchildren per capita*, and this is in striking contrast with his gift of *income* to his grandchildren *per stirpes*; and (2) All the canons of construction require that the gift of principal be construed to be *vested* in testator's grandchildren, subject to subsequent divesting upon the happening of one particular event.

Analysis of Testator's Language

When we read and reread and very carefully analyze all of testator's will from its four corners, and of course particularly the language of the *Twenty-second* paragraph of the Fifty-ninth item—we believe that he gave and intended to give the whole of the principal of his residuary trust estate (after the death of his last surviving child) to his *grandchildren per capita*, or if any grandchild was at that time dead and had left children, such children should take their deceased parent's share. In order to adopt appellants' interpretation and that of the dissenting opinion, we would have to change and rewrite the testator's gift of principal by *interpolating* the words 'then living,' so that the testator's gift of principal *as changed* would read: 'On the death of my last surviving child, I direct that the whole of the principal of the trust estate shall be distributed in equal portions to and among my *'then living'* grandchildren, the *'then living'* children of any deceased grandchild taking their deceased parent's share.'

Expressing the same thought in more technical language, we believe testator gave and intended to give a *vested* interest in this *principal per capita* (a) to those of his grandchildren who were living at the time of his death and (b) those subsequently born—such gifts to *vest in possession* at the death of testator's last surviving child, *subject to being divested* in one instance *only*, viz., *if any such grandchild was deceased leaving children*. In that particular event, the children of any such deceased grandchild were given their parent's interest (or share) per stirpes.

We are impressed by the fact that in this meticulously drawn will—in spite of the fact that throughout his entire will and throughout this very

Twenty-second paragraph, testator had repeatedly demonstrated that he knew how to make a gift, contingent upon survival-testator was careful not to say that he gave this principal in equal shares to his grandchildren *who were living at the death* of testator's last surviving child, with a substitutionary gift to the *then living children* of any deceased grandchild per stirpes. The gift of principal to his *grandchildren per capita* was express and absolute; no prior condition or limitation or contingency of survivorship was attached thereto. This clearly expressed gift of principal to his grandchildren per capita was subject only to one condition, a condition subsequent, viz., that if a grandchild was deceased at the death of testator's last surviving child leaving children, such deceased grandchild's children should take their deceased parent's share. Testator's grandchildren were his designated legatees, and if any grandchild was deceased at the termination of the last life estate, leaving children, the deceased grandchild was the source and fountainhead of the interest of his children.

This gift of principal to testator's grandchildren *per capita*, we repeat once more, is in striking contrast to his gift of *income* to his grandchildren *per stirpes*. While a contingent interest can be created either expressly or by implication, the thought keeps recurring: If testator in this skillfully drawn will intended to give the principal of his remainder estate *to and only to* his grandchildren who *survived* his last living child, and to the children of his deceased grandchildren who were *then living*, why didn't he say so, when he had so often and so clearly created contingent interests in this very residuary trust as well as in other items throughout his will? It is both clear and certain that there was no express contingent gift of principal; moreover, considering the will in this particular paragraph and as a whole, we believe there was no contingent gift of principal by implication.

PART II

Our interpretation of testator's intention as expressed in and by his will, is further *supported* by the canons of construction respecting vested and contingent interests.

Vested or Contingent Interests

Whether a gift is contingent, or vested, or vested subject to be divested, has perplexed or vexed the Courts for centuries. Where a testator's language is ambiguous, or for any reason his intent is uncertain, Courts are aided in their discovery of his intent, by a consideration of whether the gift is vested or contingent. The rules as to vesting are (with but a few minor exceptions) well settled, although (as we shall see) they are at times difficult of application and the cases are not always consistent or harmonious in their application of the rules or indeed in the language setting forth the rules.

In Gray, The Rule Against Perpetuities, 4th Ed., the law is well stated:

'§ 101.   Vested and Contingent Remainders. Since contingent remainders have been recognized, the line between them and vested remainders is drawn as follows: A remainder is vested in A., when throughout its continuance, A., or A. and his heirs, have the right to the immediate possession, whenever and however the preceding freehold estates may determine. A remainder is contingent if, in order for it to come into possession, the fulfilment of some condition precedent other than the determination of the preceding freehold estates is necessary.

'§ 102.   A remainder is none the less vested because it may terminate before the remainder-man comes into possession; thus if land be given to A. for life, remainder to B. for life, B. may die before A., yet the remainder is vested, for during its continuance, namely the life of B., it is ready to come into possession whenever and however A.'s estate determines. This result is not affected by the fact that the termination of the remainder is contingent; that is, that it is subject to a condition subsequent. *For instance, if land is devised to A. for life, remainder to B. and his heirs, but if B. dies unmarried then to C. and his heirs, B.'s remainder is vested, although it is possible that he may die unmarried in A.'s lifetime.*

* * *

'§ 108.   Common Law Rule * * * Whether a remainder is vested or contingent depends upon the language employed. If the conditional element is incorporated into the description of, or into the gift to, the remainderman, then the remainder is contingent; *but if, after words giving a vested interest, a clause is added divesting it, the remainder is vested*. Thus on a devise to A. for life, remainder to his children, but if any child dies in the lifetime of A. his share to go to those who survive, *the share of each child is vested*, subject to be divested by its death. But on a devise to A. for life, remainder to such of his children as survive him, the remainder is contingent.' See further to the same effect, Gray, The Rule Against Perpetuities, § 110.

In Newlin's Estate, 367 Pa. 527, pages 532, 533, 534, 80 A.2d 819, pages 823–824, the Court stated at length the pertinent principles which previously had been severally iterated:

If a bequest is to a class who take at the death of a life tenant, the fact that the members of the class are unknown or even not in being at the death of the testator, or that their interest is subject to be increased or decreased or divested by subsequent events, will not render the gift contingent or violate the rule against perpetuities. . . .

Where an estate is given to a life tenant, with remainder to the children of the life tenant, the estate vests at once upon the birth of each child, subject to open and let in after–born children, * * * without regard to the question of whether or not a child survives the life tenant'. In re Edwards' Estate, 255 Pa. 358, 361, 99 A. 1010, 1011; In re Edwards' Estate, 360 Pa. 504, 508, 62 A.2d 763.

Where a bequest is to a class, the vesting is not postponed because of uncertainty as to who, if any, may be the constituents of the class at the time fixed for the enjoyment of it. If there is a present right to a future possession, though that right may be defeated by some future event, contingent or certain, there is nevertheless a vested estate. In re McCauley's Estate, 257 Pa. 377, 382, 101 A. 827, 829; In re Reed's Estate, 307 Pa. 482, 484, 161 A. 729.

The law leans to vested rather than to contingent estate, and the presumption is that a legacy is vested. [In re] Carstensen's Estate, 196 Pa. 325, 46 A. 495; and 'the presumption that a legacy was intended to be vested applies with far greater force where a testator is making provision for a child or a grandchild, than where the gift is to a stranger or to a collateral relative.' Wengerd's Estate, 143 Pa. 615, 22 Atl. 869, 13 L.R.A. 360.

The intention of a testator or settlor to create a contingent interest must appear clearly and plainly,[8] otherwise the interest will be construed to be vested, or vested subject to be divested.

A myriad cases state, we repeat, that a Court is to place itself in the armchair of a testator and determine his intent from his language and the circumstances surrounding him at the time he made his will. 'However, where a testator uses words which have a legal or technical meaning, "they are to be so interpreted according to the law in effect at the testator's death unless the will contains a clearly expressed intention to the contrary'.

There can be no doubt that when Mr. Houston's will was written and at the time of his death, and for a century prior thereto, his gifts of the principal or remainder of his trust estate created a vested interest in his grandchildren, and since the will itself evidences the hand of an expert will-draftsman it is persuasive that testator intended this gift to be vested rather than contingent. . . .

We reach this construction of the will with regret because (a) it gives a share of the principal to descendants long dead, and (b) it would permit strangers to testator's blood (a deceased grandchild's spouse, or his legatees, or his heirs under the intestate laws) to receive a substantial portion of his estate without any express gift and (c) it greatly depletes, by colossal unforeseeable taxation, the property which the testator desired and intended to go to his descendants. However, such sentiments or results are not legally sufficient to allow us to ignore or distort testator's language, or rewrite his will. It is not what the Court thinks testator might or should or would have said if he could have foreseen the existing circumstances and conditions, but what he actually did say.

Notwithstanding the very able argument of counsel for the appellants, the Decree must be affirmed.

■ ROBERTS, JUSTICE (dissenting).

My reading and study of decedent's will and our past decisions preclude me from joining the majority. In my view, the majority have incorrectly construed testator's gift of residuary principal.

Although almost three-quarters of a century span the years between decedent's will and its present construction, his intention, as expressed in his will and reflected by the circumstances surrounding his armchair, must prevail.

All must agree that the best evidence of decedent's intention is his language.

'And, while the words employed in a will necessarily constitute the gauge of the testator's intent (Ludwick's Estate, 269 Pa. 365, 371, 112 A. 543), a construction that would lead to a highly improbable result is to be avoided, if at all possible; and a meaning conformable to the tes-

---

[8] Several cases state that an interest will not be construed to be contingent unless it is *impossible* to construe it as vested. The word 'impossible' is an unfortunate expression, as many people believe that nothing is impossible. Several other cases use the expression 'clear, plain and manifest' while others use 'clear, plain and indisputably' or 'indisputable.' However, we believe that it is fair and correct to say that an analysis of these authorities discloses an intention in each of the prior cases to express the same meaning, albeit in different language. The variety of language used to express this test has caused such confusion that we deem it wise to herein use and apply the test hereinabove set forth in this opinion, since it appears to be the fairest and most correct test.

tator's plausible intent should be ascribed to his words if agreeable to reason.

In seeking to ascertain the intention and meaning of decedent's language, this Court has said:

> 'The proper course of procedure for the interpreter of a testamentary writing is not to apply rules of construction until all reasonable effort to deduce a meaning from the writing itself has been exhausted with no understandable and sensible result.' Buzby's Estate, 386 Pa. 1, 8, 123 A.2d 723, 726 (1956).

In reality, this controversy is governed by that portion of decedent's will which provides:

> 'On the death of my last surviving child I direct that the whole of the principal of the trust estate shall be distributed in equal portions to and among my grand-children, the children of any deceased grandchild taking deceased parents share.'

This language, testator's meaning and his intention are clear. I agree with the majority that canons of construction should be resorted to only if the language of the will is ambiguous or testator's intent is uncertain. Yet the majority's conclusion appears to be based upon (rather than supported by) rules of construction despite the clarity of testator's words and intention.

Furthermore, proper construction of this gift does not require the application of the presumption that an interest is vested rather than contingent. Basically, this presumption, even though a very ancient one, is itself merely a rule of construction. To counterbalance the absoluteness of the presumption of vesting the 'pay and divide rule' was developed over many years. With the proper abolition of the 'pay and divide rule' by Mr. Justice, now Chief Justice Bell, speaking for a unanimous Court, in Dickson's Estate, 396 Pa. 371, 152 A.2d 680 (1959), this counter-balancing effect was destroyed. Thus, we must now avoid routine use of the presumption of vesting as an absolute rule but must apply it as it was originally intended, as a helpful rule of construction. Application of the presumption here requires the reopening of estates long closes with all the attending legal and practical difficulties. I fear this presumption may have unduly influenced the majority in its determination, thereby achieving the 'highly improbable result' to be avoided under Fahey's Estate, supra.

As the testator in his armchair contemplated the future and reflected upon the objects of his bounty, particularly the members of his immediate family, he was keenly aware from tragic personal experience that children may and unfortunately do predecease their parents. In his lifetime, he and his wife endured three such unfortunate losses. While he undoubtedly, hoped and prayed that his children, as parents, would be spared such tragedies, he could not and did not ignore the teachings of his own experience.

In view of testator's personal experiences, it is difficult and almost impossible to conclude that his gift to 'my grandchildren, the children of any deceased grandchild taking deceased parents share' is an expression of intention that his estate eventually pass to deceased grandchildren. I can find no indication anywhere in his will or in the revelant [sic.] attending circumstances to suggest that this alert, well-informed and well-advised testator, who created trust for many years in the future for many persons, and whose obvious and primary purpose was to benefit his descendants, intended to or did direct that the ultimate distribution of trust principal devolve through short-term, intermittent estates of deceased grandchildren. This is precisely what testator sought to avoid. His constant reference throughout his will to living persons announced and repeated that he was thinking, writing and providing for living persons only.

If, as the majority concludes, testator's gift was to grandchildren without reference to survival at the time of distribution and irrespective of whether deceased grandchildren were survived by children, he could have achieved that gift by ending with the phrase 'in equal portions to and among my grandchildren.' However, by adding 'the children of any deceased grand-child taking deceased parents share,' he sought to, and did, make clear that his gifts were to living persons and not to deceased grandchildren who left no children. In the case of a deceased grandchild who left children, he specifically provided a gift for such children. However, as to other deceased grandchildren—those leaving no children—the will is entirely silent. If, as the majority holds, testator intended them as beneficiaries also, is it likely that he would have said nothing about them? It is more likely that deceased grandchildren dying without children are not mentioned because testator did not intend them to benefit if they predeceased his last surviving child. Similarly, testator would not have awarded to such deceased grandchildren the same freedom to pass (by will or intestacy) the trust property as he granted to living grandchildren, a privilege not granted to deceased grandchildren leaving issue.

It seems clear to me that testator intended and his will provided that at the death of his last child, the principal should be distributed equally to his then living grandchildren, and if there were deceased grandchildren who left children, they (great-grandchildren) would take the share their parents would have taken.

In providing only for living grandchildren and the living children of deceased grandchildren, testator was carrying out his considered scheme of distribution and avoiding the incidents and consequences of almost immediate successive devolutions through estates of deceased persons. 'The exclusion of estates of deceased persons is the ordinary intention of a testator.' McCrea's Estate, 78 PaDist. & Co.R. 145, 151 (O. C. Philadelphia County, 1951).

The majority reaches its conclusion with three expressed regrets:

' * * * (a) it gives a share of the principal to descendants long dead, and (b) it would permit strangers to testator's blood (a deceased grandchild's spouse, or his legatees, or his heirs under the intestate laws) to receive a substantial portion of his estate without any express gift, and (c) it greatly depletes, by colossal unforeseeable taxation, the property which the testator desired and intended to go to his descendants.'

In my view, the first two majority regrets (a and b) are more than expressions of regret. I deem each to be a very persuasive factor in revealing testator's intention. Together they very strongly support the conclusion that testator created contingent and not vested gifts for his grandchildren. Each justifies and certainly both require a result contrary to that reached by the majority.

I regard the majority's tax regret as simply a regret, since it deals with tax circumstances and consequences unknown to this nineteenth century testator. However, in lieu of the majority's tax regret, it is suggested that the pyramiding of estate administration costs and expenses and the resulting diminution of assets occasioned by early and almost immediate successive administrations constitute a proper indication of testator's intention. These circumstances lend added support to the conclusion that testator's gifts of principal were to living grandchildren.

I dissent and would direct that the trust corpus be divided into nine equal shares.

Query: The problem in this case is that the testator used survivorship language quite effectively in dealing with the life interests in his children, but then he used a narrow class (grandchildren) without any survivorship qualification, or alternate gift over if class members were deceased without issue. Do you think he wasn't thinking as clearly about all the possible permutations of survivorship when he got to the distribution of principal because it was so far removed from the time he executed his will or did his lawyers just get sloppy? Would the case have been resolved easily if his lawyers had used the term "issue" instead of grandchildren? Do we always presume, perhaps to our clients' detriment, that there are only two options: survive and take, or predecease and the issue take? Imagine how much more complicated this case could have been were it decided in the twenty-first century, where blended and other nontraditional family structures could easily lead to additional litigation over who is a grandchild.

The problem with this case was not the survivorship language in the gift to the children. In fact, the grant was quite clear as to what was to happen if a child a) survived, b) predeceased leaving issue, or c) predeceased leaving no issue. But the contrast between the three options for the children and only two options for the grandchildren tied the court's hands. Without expressly identifying what would happen to the interests of grandchildren who predeceased without issue, the court applied the early vesting rule to give the three predeceased grandchildren's estates their share, thus opening their estates to additional tax and administration fees.

Assuming that the lawyers in *Houston* used the survivorship language to avoid the transmissible remainder problem, should courts simply adopt a rule that all remainders are contingent if a survivorship provision is used anywhere, on the assumption that the failure to use it was an oversight? Or should courts assume, as in *Houston*, that the failure to use it in certain instances is intentional?

The *Houston* case made such legal news that the Uniform Law Commission got busy thinking about how to resolve the transmissible remainder problem, although the fix wasn't finally adopted until 1990.[16] The problem in *Houston* was that if the three grandchildren who had predeceased the last life tenant held vested remainders, then their share of the trust principal would pass outside the family to their devisees (spouses or lovers) or intestate takers, which required reopening their estates, and resulted in additional taxation which the settlor would have been able to avoid had the survivorship language omitted the predeceased grandchildren. The result was the adoption of UPC § 2–707.

---

[16] See comments to UPC § 2–707.

UPC § 2–707. Survivorship with Respect to Future Interests under Terms of Trust; Substitute Takers.

(a) [Definitions.] . . .

(b) [Survivorship Required; Substitute Gift.] A future interest under the terms of a trust is contingent on the beneficiary's surviving the distribution date. If a beneficiary of a future interest under the terms of a trust fails to survive the distribution date, the following apply:

(1) Except as provided in paragraph (4), if the future interest is not in the form of a class gift and the deceased beneficiary leaves surviving descendants, a substitute gift is created in the beneficiary's surviving descendants. They take by representation the property to which the beneficiary would have been entitled had the beneficiary survived the distribution date.

(2) Except as provided in paragraph (4), if the future interest is in the form of a class gift, other than a future interest to "issue," "descendants," "heirs of the body," "heirs," "next of kin," "relatives," or "family," or a class described by language of similar import, a substitute gift is created in the surviving descendants of any deceased beneficiary. The property to which the beneficiaries would have been entitled had all of them survived the distribution date passes to the surviving beneficiaries and the surviving descendants of the deceased beneficiaries. Each surviving beneficiary takes the share to which he [or she] would have been entitled had the deceased beneficiaries survived the distribution date. Each deceased beneficiary's surviving descendants who are substituted for the deceased beneficiary take by representation the share to which the deceased beneficiary would have been entitled had the deceased beneficiary survived the distribution date. For the purposes of this paragraph, "deceased beneficiary" means a class member who failed to survive the distribution date and left one or more surviving descendants.

(3) For the purposes of Section 2–701, words of survivorship attached to a future interest are not, in the absence of additional evidence, a sufficient indication of an intent contrary to the application of this section. Words of survivorship include words of survivorship that relate to the distribution date or to an earlier or an unspecified time, whether those words of survivorship are expressed in condition-precedent, condition-subsequent, or any other form.

(4) If the governing instrument creates an alternative future interest with respect to a future interest for which a substitute gift is created by paragraph (1) or (2), the substitute gift is superseded by the alternative future interest if:

(A) the alternative future interest is in the form of a class gift and one or more members of the class is entitled to take in possession or enjoyment; or

(B) the alternative future interest is not in the form of a class gift and the expressly designated beneficiary of the alternative future interest is entitled to take in possession or enjoyment.

(c) [More Than One Substitute Gift; Which One Takes.] [anti-lapse with younger generation provision similar to UPC § 2–603]

(d) [If No Other Takers, Property Passes Under Residuary Clause or to Transferor's Heirs.] Except as provided in subsection (e), if, after the application of subsections (b) and (c), there is no surviving taker, the property passes in the following order:

> (1) if the trust was created in a nonresiduary devise in the transferor's will or in a codicil to the transferor's will, the property passes under the residuary clause in the transferor's will; for purposes of this section, the residuary clause is treated as creating a future interest under the terms of a trust.
>
> (2) if no taker is produced by the application of paragraph (1), the property passes to the transferor's heirs under Section 2–711.
>
> **(e) [If No Other Takers and If Future Interest Created by Exercise of Power of Appointment.]** If, after the application of subsections (b) and (c), there is no surviving taker and if the future interest was created by the exercise of a power of appointment:
>
> (1) the property passes under the donor's gift-in-default clause, if any, which clause is treated as creating a future interest under the terms of a trust; and
>
> (2) if no taker is produced by the application of paragraph (1), the property passes as provided in subsection (d). For purposes of subsection (d), "transferor" means the donor if the power was a nongeneral power and means the donee if the power was a general power.

Let's understand what this provision does to future interests in trusts (not legal future interests). Take a typical life estate followed by a remainder.

> *O grants Blackacre to A for life, remainder to B.*

In this case, A has a life estate in Blackacre and B has an absolutely vested remainder. The statute makes no change to this interest. But now let's place it in trust.

> *O grants Blackacre to T as trustee for the benefit of A for life, remainder to B.*

Under the common law rules we just learned, A has an equitable life estate in Blackacre, and B has an absolutely vested remainder.

But now let's look at what UPC § 2–707(b) does. Because the interest is in a trust, B has to survive A (the time of distribution) in order to take his remainder. If B predeceases A, leaving issue, a remainder is created in B's issue, but they are identified only at the time of possession, so a child of B who also predeceases A will not take a share. Remember, we are avoiding the taxable transmissible remainder problem.[17] If B predeceases A without leaving issue, Blackacre reverts back to O. Thus, we can write the interests as follows:

> A has an equitable life estate in Blackacre
>
> B has an equitable contingent remainder, based on a conditional event (surviving A)
>
> B's issue has an equitable contingent remainder, based on ascertaining B's issue and surviving A
>
> O has a reversion

Our tidy life estate in A, absolutely vested remainder in B, has now generated 2 additional contingent future interests simply by requiring that B survive A.

---

[17] We are, however, walking into a GST tax problem. See Chapter 9, *infra*.

In addition, the UPC provides that survivorship language is not enough to evidence contrary intent not to apply the statute (just as it does with the Anti-Lapse Statute—UPC § 2–603). Thus, an explicit provision like:

> *O grants Blackacre to T as trustee for the benefit of A for life, remainder to B but only if B survives A*

gets changed under the UPC. Note that O has required that B survive A, and if B has not survived A then the gift would normally lapse. But because of the survivorship provision of the UPC, rather than lapsing and reverting back to O, the anti-lapse provision of § 2–707 creates a substitute gift in B's issue. The only way for O to avoid the substitute gift is to explicitly state that upon B's failure to survive A, Blackacre must revert or pass to some alternate taker.

Not all states have adopted this future interest provision, but about a third have done so, either in their probate codes or their separate trust codes.[18] See Iowa Code § 633A.4701 & Fla.Stat. § 736.1106. Anyone setting up a trust needs to think about the implications of making trust interests contingent, in terms of the Rule Against Perpetuities, the use of disclaimers to terminate contingent remainders (remember *Est. of Hall?*), and of failing to state explicitly if they are not subject to survivorship requirements.

Furthermore, the scholarship on this provision is quite vocal on both sides, as you can see from the mere titles of some of these articles. David Becker, Uniform Probate Code Section 2–707 and the Experienced Estate Planner: Unexpected Disasters and How to Avoid Them, 47 U.C.L.A. L. Rev. 339 (1999); Jesse Dukeminier, The Uniform Probate Code Upends the Law of Remainders, 94 Mich. L. Rev. 148 (1995); and Lawrence W. Waggoner, The Uniform Probate Code Extends Antilapse-Type Protection to Poorly Drafted Trusts, 94 Mich. L. Rev. 2309 (1996).

PROBLEMS

8.25. In one paragraph of her will, Testator devises her house to her daughter, with the provision that if her daughter predeceases her, the daughter's surviving issue should take her share. She also devises other, roughly equal property, to her son. In her residuary clause she states that the rest and residue of her estate should be distributed equally to her daughter and son, and if they cannot agree, then the personal representative is to have sole discretion to distribute the property as equally as possible. Testator then sold the house after she wrote the will and used the proceeds to pay her end-of-life medical expenses. Then testator's daughter died, one month before the testator died. Is the daughter's son entitled to any property?

8.26. Testator devised his funeral home to his wife and daughter, with the following provision: "In the event my wife, [Bessie], or my daughter, [Sylvia], should predecease the other in death, then the survivor shall inherit the whole." Bessie and Sylvia operated the funeral home together for 20 years after the testator's death. Sylvia died testate leaving all of her property to her three children. Bessie died 5 years later leaving all of her property to her foster son. Who takes the funeral home interest?

---

[18] Alaska, Arizona, Colorado, Florida, Hawaii, Illinois, Iowa, Massachusetts, Michigan, Montana, New Mexico, North Dakota, Pennsylvania, South Dakota, Tennessee, and Utah.

5. CLASS GIFTS

After survivorship, class gifts are probably the next most confusing element of future interests. A class gift is a gift made to a group of people who a) share common characteristics and b) who are intended to get equal shares of property. As you should have noticed when reading the anti-lapse statutes, certain class gifts get different legal treatment than other class gifts. To understand why, we must realize that there are two different types of class:

> Type 1—Classes that both open and close physiologically, i.e. classes to a defined group like children, grandchildren, nieces and nephews, brothers and sisters, and the like. Often these are single-generation classes, but they don't have to be. The class of children opens when the first child is born, and closes naturally when the relevant parent dies. Similarly, the class of grandchildren opens when the first grandchild is born, and closes at the death of the last child. Future interests to type 1 classes are usually classified as *vested remainders subject to open*.[19]

> Type 2—Classes that usually open and close simultaneously to take in all members who meet the relevant definition at a particular time, or classes that are not guaranteed to close naturally. These classes are often multi-generational groups, like *heirs, issue, descendants, relatives, heirs of my body, next of kin*, or the like. Because these classes might never close naturally, we often interpret gifts to a type 2 class to be contingent upon surviving to distribution, at which point it opens and closes immediately, to include whoever the issue, kin, or heirs are at a definable moment. People who die before distribution take no share, and those born after distribution take no share. Future interests to type 2 classes are usually interpreted as *contingent remainders on unascertained persons*.

Class gifts focus on three important issues:

1. Identifying the members of the class (are adopted children, or stepchildren included, or can grandchildren count as children for purposes of the class?)

2. Determining when the class opens and closes so that people who come into the class have a vested interest even if they die before the interest becomes possessory or those who come later, after distribution, take nothing. That is, are the interests vested subject to open or contingent upon surviving to distribution?

3. Can we close a class early, before it closes physiologically, if it becomes possessory for at least one member of the class? This is the class closing rule, or the rule of convenience.

We will discuss each of these three issues in turn, and look at how the different type of classes (type 1 or type 2) may result in different outcomes.

a. *Identifying the Class Members*

Often the point of using a class gift designation (to my "grandchildren" rather than "to my grandchildren, G1, G2, G3 & G4") is to accommodate

---

[19] If there are no members of the class yet in being, the remainder would be a contingent remainder on unascertained persons; if at least one member is in being but the class is open to take in other class members, the remainder would be a vested remainder subject to open; and if the class has members but is physiologically closed it would usually be a fully vested remainder.

after-born members who meet the definition of the class but were not born when the interest was first created. Of course, an immediate gift to "my grandchildren" in a will is immediately possessory by the grandchildren and they will take their relative share immediately without waiting to see if more grandchildren happen to be born. If there are no grandchildren born at the testator's death, the gift will lapse.

This leads to the first important rule—if the gift is immediately possessory, the class members are identified at the time the gift is made and class members who are born after the gift is made take nothing. Also, the interests of class members who died before the gift was made lapse and get redistributed to other members of the class, unless they are subject to the state's antilapse statute. So an immediate gift in a will to "my grandchildren" will be distributed to all living grandchildren at the testator's death, plus to the issue of deceased grandchildren as substitute gifts under the state's antilapse statute.[20] But a grandchild who predeceased the testator and left no issue would take nothing, and afterborn grandchildren also take nothing.

Most state antilapse statutes treat immediate gifts to Type 2 classes differently, however. Thus, a gift to my "son's lineal descendants" or my "son's heirs" will include only those descendants or heirs who are living at the time of the gift. No antilapse statute will save the gift for predeceased descendants or heirs because the gift itself provides for the gift passing directly to that predeceased descendant's issue. You don't need antilapse protections because the issue of predeceased class members should be entitled to take in their own right.

But what happens when a gift of a future interest is made to a class? If the class is a type 1 class, like "to A for life, remainder to A's children," then the regular antilapse statute plays no role because A's children don't have to have been in existence at the testator's death because it's not an immediately possessory gift. Rather, the issue is whether they must survive A; that is, do they have to survive to distribution to be included in the class and take their share? There's no explicit or implicit requirement that a class member must survive to distribution in order to take a share of the remainder and so all people who satisfy the definition of being a child of A will be entitled to a share, whether they predeceased A or were born after the testator's death. Once born, their interests vest.

In the case of A and A's children, since A can't have children after her death,[21] we don't need to worry about children being born *after* the interest becomes possessory, but we do need to worry about what happens to the shares of children who die before A, leaving issue. Where there is no gift over or alternate gift provision for dealing with the interests of children who predeceased A, some courts have interpreted the term "children" to include "grandchildren" or "issue" as well.

The Restatement 3d of Property § 14.1 states that "unless the language or circumstances establish that the transferor had a different intention . . . the term 'children,' in a class gift to 'children,' means descendants in the first generation, and does not include grandchildren or

---

[20] A gift to "my best friend's grandchildren," however, will pass to the living grandchildren, but not to the issue of deceased grandchildren under an antilapse statute that applies only to save gifts to relatives of the testator.

[21] At this point we aren't concerned about posthumous conception since most probate codes do not allow for it, and those that do have explicitly provided for it.

more remote descendants." But courts have not followed such a narrow interpretation if including grandchildren or issue furthers the testator's overall dispositive plan. For instance, in *Cox v. Forristall*, 640 P.2d 878 (Kan.Ct.App. 1982) the court interpreted the phrase "my children then living" to include living children and living issue of deceased children. There are instances of other courts making similar constructions, but there are many more cases where courts refuse to interpret a gift to children to include grandchildren or other issue.[22]

So what happens to that predeceased child's share? If a substitute gift is not created in the child's issue, then it goes to that child's estate, perhaps to pass to his issue, but perhaps to pass to his spouse, his creditors, or his favorite charity. UPC § 2–707 prevents it going to the estate of the predeceased class member and instead creates a substitute gift in the class member's issue, if any, or treats the gift as reverting back to the testator if there are no issue (and no other class members or alternate takers), just as the regular antilapse statute does.

Another important aspect of identifying the class members is dealing with adopted or equitably adopted children, step-children, foster children, and the like. Most state probate codes today treat the adopted child as a biological child for class gift purposes, but in doing so they have legislatively rejected the *stranger to the adoption* rule that precluded adopted children from counting in class gifts made by relatives who were not the principal parties to the adoption. For a time, adopted children did not count as "heirs" or "lineal descendants" when class gifts were made by grandparents or collateral relatives. Thus, some statutes exclude adopted children from class gifts to heirs or similar multi-generational classes in reliance on the stranger to the adoption doctrine, while including adopted children in gifts by the adoptive parents. You will need to check your adoption statute carefully to determine how your state has dealt with the stranger to the adoption rule.

b. *Determining When the Class Opens and When It Closes*

This is probably the hardest determination to make, and once again we have different rules for the different types of classes. Thus, as a general rule, unless a contrary intent is indicated, a type 1 class opens when the first member is born and closes at the earlier date of either when the interest becomes possessory or when the class closes physiologically. Thus, a gift "to A for life, remainder to A's children" is a life estate in A, followed by a remainder in A's children. The class of A's children opens with the birth of the first of A's children, and closes naturally upon A's death, when A can no longer have any children. At the time the interest is created, the remainder is a contingent remainder on unascertained persons if no child of A is yet born; it is a vested remainder subject to open if at least one child has been born but A is still alive and could have more children; and the remainder is vested absolutely if there is at least one child of A and A has died and the class is physiologically closed. Assuming that at least one member of the class exists, that person's interest is vested immediately. That means that if a child of A predeceases A, that vested remainder is part of that child's estate and would not lapse and be redistributed to other class members or pass to that child's issue unless there was an antilapse statute applicable to future interests.

---

[22] See, e.g. Est. of Gustafson, 547 N.E.2d 1152 (N.Y. 1989).

With type 1 classes, the class is usually open for a sufficient period of time to take in all members who meet the relevant criteria, including after-born members. The most controversial issue with these types of class gifts is, as you saw in *Est. of Houston*, what happens to the gifts to class members who meet the definition (grandchildren) but who die before they are able to take their share of the gift. Should their gift lapse and be redistributed to other class members, as the 9 surviving grandchildren argued; should a substitute gift be created in their issue, as an antilapse statute would provide; or should the gift be deemed vested and pass to the deceased class member's estate and subject it to possible administration costs, as the court ruled in that case?

Type 2 classes function quite differently, however. Because they, by definition, are multi-generational, class members who don't survive to distribution simply don't take a share and that person's issue, if any, will take her share in their own right as members of the class. Thus, a gift "to A for life, remainder to A's *heirs*,"[23] means that we take a snapshot of the class of "A's heirs" at the moment of A's death and afterborn members don't take a share, nor do predeceased class members. Furthermore, we don't need an antilapse provision to create a substitute gift in a predeceased class member's issue because the issue are members of the class and can take in their own right.

The key to type 2 classes is that we treat the right to take a share, and we calculate the proportions of each member, the same way we do under the state's intestacy laws unless the testator indicates a contrary intent. Younger class members stand in the shoes of their predeceased ancestors by representation and distributions will be *per stirpes* or *per capita*, depending on either the state's intestacy statute or the testator's instructions.

To distinguish between type 1 and type 2 classes, and to identify the likely future interests, we can view this on a grid as follows (assume a gift was "to A for life, remainder to the class" where the class is:)

	Future Interest	**Disposition of interest of class members who die before distribution**	**Inclusion of after-born members?**
Type 1 Class— children, grandchildren, employees, Nobel Prize winners, etc.	Vested Remainder Subject to Open	Passes through the class member's estate	Afterborn members are added during the tenant's life, but no after-born members are added after distribution
Type 2 Class— heirs, issue, lineal descendants, etc.	Contingent Remainder on Unascertained Persons	No interest—it dies with the class member	No after-born members are added after distribution

---

[23] Ignore the potential Rule in Shelley's case problem here. The Rule in Shelley's case has been abolished in most states and is better left to advanced courses on future interests.

With the type 2 class, we take a snapshot at the moment of distribution and distribute the remainder to all members who are "issue" or "heirs" at the moment of distribution. Later born issue take nothing, and members of the class who died prior to distribution also take nothing. Moreover, we determine class members at the time of distribution even if the class might be different if it were determined at a different time. For instance, a gift "to A for life, remainder to B's heirs" could result in two different classes—the people who are B's actual heirs, calculated at B's death, or the people who would be B's heirs had B died at the time A dies when the remainder is distributed. Thus, if B is still alive when A dies we would determine B's heirs to be the people would take under the intestacy statute if B died at the same time as A. If B is already dead, perhaps for 30 years, before A dies, we calculate B's heirs at the later time so as not to run into the transmissible remainder problem. The membership of the class of B's heirs is likely to be far different at A's death than 30 years earlier at B's actual death and we don't want to reopen estates of heirs who predeceased A.

What throws a big wrench into this analysis, however, is the application of antilapse statutes like UPC § 2–707, which can turn that vested remainder into a contingent one with a substitute gift in the issue of the deceased class member, and/or the presence of survivorship language that might indicate that the testator wanted to require that the class members survive (either each other or the intervening life tenant). Now that you understand some of the important distinctions between type 1 and type 2 classes, go back and consider how UPC § 2–707 might change the classification of many of the future interests we've been discussing in this Chapter. To see how this might work, consider the following cases:

Central Trust Co. of Northern Ohio, N.A. v. Smith

553 N.E.2d 265 (Ohio 1990)

Loretta A. Smith (the "testatrix") executed her last will and testament on December 20, 1960, and a codicil to the will on June 16, 1964. The testatrix died testate on September 22, 1964. The will of the testatrix established a trust of which appellee, the Central Trust Company of Northern Ohio, has been trustee since October 9, 1967. Under the terms of the trust, the residuary estate was divided into three equal shares by the following language:

> The trust estate shall be treated as composed of three (3) equal shares to be used as follows:

> One share shall be for the benefit of the children of Ralph J. Smith, Jr., whether now living or born hereafter, equally, and shall be retained by the trustees, and the income therefrom, and such part of the principal as in the sole discretion of the trustees shall be necessary, shall be used for the college education of such children. In the event that any of the children of the said Ralph J. Smith, Jr. do not desire a college education, the said trustees are authorized to expend such child's share of the income or principal, to enroll him or her in a mechanical or trade school or such other course of learning in which said child may be interested. The trustees are also authorized to expend a child's share of the income or principal to help such child start or engage in a business for which such child is particulary [sic] adapted. It is my wish that my said trustees counsel with the children of said Ralph J. Smith, Jr. and give them the benefit of their experience and

knowledge. The said trustees are further empowered to use such part of the income or principal as they deem necessary for the support and maintenance of the children of said Ralph J. Smith, Jr. in the event an emergency arises and the parents of such children are unable to meet the emergency. The said trustees shall be the sole judges as to whether or not such an emergency exists. Each of the Children of the said Ralph J. Smith, Jr. upon attaining the age of twenty-five (25) years shall receive one-half (1/2) of the share due to him or her under this provision. Upon attaining the age of thirty (30) years each child shall receive the balance due to him or her. * * *

One share shall be for the benefit of the children of Margaret Smith Keller, whether now living or born hereafter, equally, and shall be retained by the trustees * * *.

In the event that, at the time of my decease, my daughter, Rosemary Smith, is single, or if married has no children, one of such shares shall be paid to her outright by said trustees. If Rosemary Smith has a child or children at the time of my decease, the said trustees shall retain such share * * *.

For the children of Margaret and Rosemary, provisions for the use of income and principal for education and for distribution of principal were similar to the quoted provisions for the first share.

At the time of the testatrix's death, her son, Ralph J. Smith, Jr., was alive and had five children. Thereafter, Ralph divorced and remarried twice, and subsequently adopted the appellant Bryan Smith, who had been born on August 28, 1961 and had resided in the home of Ralph J. Smith, Jr. and his third wife since 1967. The final decree of Bryan's adoption was issued by the Erie County Probate Court on July 15, 1975, when he was thirteen years old.

At the time of the testatrix's death, the oldest child of Ralph J. Smith, Jr. was nine years old. No distributions of income or principal were made from the trust to any beneficiaries until August 1972 when Ralph J. Smith, Jr.'s oldest child, Mary Jo Smith, reached the age of seventeen, and began college. At that time, the trustee exercised its discretion and distributed to Mary Jo Smith $4,063.50 to enable her to purchase an automobile. This distribution was accounted for on the trustee's books as a distribution of income from the share for the benefit of Ralph's children. Subsequent distributions to Mary Jo Smith during 1973, 1974 and 1975 were also accounted for on the trustee's books as distributions from the income of this share.

The first distribution of the one-half share of the principal to one of the children of Ralph J. Smith, Jr. was presumably made by the trustee soon after January 1980, when Mary Jo attained the age of twenty-five years. Sometime thereafter, the appellant, Bryan Smith, wrote to the trustee, claiming to be a beneficiary of the trust. The trustee responded that Bryan was not entitled to any benefits from the trust. After further exchanges with Bryan and his counsel, the trustee filed a declaratory judgment action on February 6, 1985, seeking a determination as to whether Bryan Smith was entitled to share in the trust.

The Probate Court of Erie County held that due to the language contained within Item VII of the testatrix's will, quoted above, the class composed of the children of Ralph J. Smith, Jr. closed on September 22,

1964, the date of Loretta A. Smith's death. The reasoning of the court was premised upon the following conclusions of law:

> 2. Bryan Smith was not one of the 'children of Ralph J. Smith, Jr.' as of September 22, 1964, the date of death of the testatrix, Loretta A. Smith.
>
> 3. Since Item VII of the testatrix's Will provides that 'The trust estate shall be treated as composed of three equal shares to be used as follows: One share shall be for the benefit of the children of Ralph J. Smith, Jr., whether now living or born hereafter, equally' and since the trustee was 'authorized to expend such child's share of the income or principal' for the purposes specified in the trust, the language of Item VII of the Last Will and Testament of Loretta A. Smith requires that separate shares be established as of the death of the testatrix.
>
> 4. Such a required division into shares as of the testatrix's date of death can only be accomplished if the maximum number of class members is known at the time of such division; therefore the bequest in trust must be restricted to those persons who are members of the class of beneficiaries at the time of the testatrix's date of death. . . .

The court of appeals affirmed, quoting " * * * the law favors the vesting of any and all interest in the testator's estate in the devisee or legatee at the earliest possible time, upon the death of the testator, unless an intention to the contrary clearly appears in the will." The appellate court further concluded that "[n]o contrary intention appears in the will in question." "Given the plain meaning of the language contained in item VII of the Will, wherein the phrase, ' * * * to expend such child's share * * * ' (emphasis added) is used, we can come to no other conclusion but that the testatrix intended her class to close upon her demise."

The court's function in construing a will, including its trust provisions, is to determine and apply the testator's intent as expressed in the language of the whole will, and read in light of the applicable law, and circumstances surrounding the will's execution. [The court first determined that Bryan was not precluded simply by being adopted. The court explained:] For all purposes under the laws of this state, including without limitation all laws and wills governing inheritance of and succession to real or personal property and the taxation of such inheritance and succession, a legally adopted child shall have the same status and rights, and shall bear the same legal relationship to the adopting parents as if born to them in lawful wedlock and not born to the natural parents. . . .

Having determined that the appellant Bryan Smith was eligible to be a member of the class consisting of the children of Ralph J. Smith, Jr., we must decide whether this class closed, and all property rights "vested," at the death of the testatrix, before the appellant was adopted. As in other facets of the interpretation of a will, in determining the time when a named class of beneficiaries closes, and the time when a distribution of the trust property will be made, a reviewing court must reasonably ascertain the intent of the testator from a practical application of the language of the whole instrument.

Both the probate court and the court of appeals agreed that the testamentary trust divided the residuary estate into three equal shares: one to be held in trust for the benefit of the children of her son, Ralph J. Smith,

Jr.; one to be held in trust for the children of her daughter Margaret Smith Keller; and one either to be held in trust for the children of Rosemary Smith if she had any children at the time of the death of the testatrix, or to be distributed to Rosemary herself.

Under the language of the trust, each share is a separate gift *per stirpes* to the beneficiaries of that class. In essence, each of these shares is a subtrust. This division of shares clearly indicates that the testatrix was thinking of each subtrust's beneficiaries as a class composed of the children of one of her children, from which a reasonable inference may be made that the testatrix had allowed for possible fluctuations in the membership of each group.

A "class gift" is a gift of an aggregate sum to be divided among a group of persons, uncertain in number and specific identification at the time of the gift, but which can be ascertained at a future time, the amount of each share depending on the ultimate number of persons included in the class.

If a testamentary gift to a class is in general terms, with no time specified for distribution, the death of the testator will, as a general rule, fix the time for distribution, and close the class at the time of death of the testator. However, if the gift is a present bequest to be distributed at a later determinable date, the class members who are in being at the testator's death take a vested interest in the fund then, subject to the addition of members of the class who are born after the testator's death but before the time provided for distribution.[4]

Although it is desirable, where a reasonable interpretation of the instrument would permit it, to close the beneficiary class early to allow the total vesting of the interests, we must also consider the testator's interest in holding the class open as long as reasonably possible, at least until the first member of the class is entitled to demand distribution of the principal.

In the present case, the testatrix made a gift in trust of the aggregate amount of one-third of her residuary estate, to be shared equally by the children of her son, Ralph J. Smith, Jr., whether living at her death or born thereafter. The trustee was given discretion to distribute income only for certain specific purposes, and could invade principal only if necessary at its sole discretion. The subtrust for the benefit of Ralph's children was handled as one trust fund for investment purposes, but was divided into five accounts setting forth the distribution of income and principal to each beneficiary. The appellees did not show that this subtrust lacked sufficient income earned and accumulated by the trust to satisfy all of the discretionary distributions made to these five original beneficiaries from 1972

---

[4]   Thus, the rules of construction that apply should make a reasonable choice between what might be said to be the initial desire of a donor, who describes beneficiaries by a class gift term, to include all who come within the described group at any time, and the public interest in promoting the early full utilization of property by closing the class at the time a class member is entitled to a possessory interest in the property. When the rule that is adopted closes the class at the time a class member is entitled to a possessory interest, it has been referred to as 'the rule of convenience.' "3 Restatement of the Law 2d, Property (1988) 132, Introductory Note.

The rule of convenience does not require a class to close when a class gift involves payments of income because no inconvenience is experienced by admitting new members to the class after this type of discretionary distribution has begun. The amount of each interest fluctuates with the addition of class members, until the class finally closes upon a required distribution of principal. Only when principal must be distributed does it become inconvenient and unfair to admit additional class members. Restatement of the Law of Property (1940) 1590–1591, Section 295, Comment *i;* Simes & Smith, *supra,* at 88–89, Section 643.

through 1975. Appellant Bryan Smith was legally adopted by Ralph J. Smith, Jr. on July 15, 1975, and we conclude that he thereupon became a member of the class, entitled to the same rights to the income and principal of the trust as the original five class members.

Here the language of the trust does not evidence the desire of the testator that immediately upon her death, each class of beneficiaries be closed, and that each of the three shares be divided into separate shares for each member of the class. Rather, the language of the trust provides that after three equal shares are established, the income and principal may be distributed to the beneficiaries for stated purposes by the trustee, when necessary in its discretion, but no distribution of a major interest in such shares was scheduled until future times, i.e., when each child in each class attained the ages of twenty-five and thirty.

The language of the trust provides that all members of the class shall share equally. Based upon this expressed desire of the testatrix, the probate court and the court of appeals determined that separate shares must be established for each of the children of the class as of the death of the testatrix.

In light of the totality of the will and the reasonable intent of the testatrix, we find that it was not necessary to close the class in order to establish separate shares for the beneficiaries of each class, even though we conclude that the number of the class could be increased. Appropriate accounting could establish the interests of the five children living at the date of the death of the testatrix. The separate accounting for this class, or subtrust, established by the will, could later reflect the increase in the number of members of this class through the adoption of Bryan, and show that originally each beneficiary had a one-fifth interest in the principal, but after the adoption, each member had a one-sixth interest.

Upon the testatrix's death, each of Ralph J. Smith, Jr.'s children took a vested interest in the trust subject to adjustment upon the birth (or adoption) of another class member prior to the first mandatory distribution, when the oldest child attained the age of twenty-five. The vesting of rights in class members upon the death of the testatrix cannot deny the rights of subsequent class members. If a sixth child had been naturally born to Ralph J. Smith, Jr. during the year following the testatrix's death, the rights of the class members immediately would have become one-sixth rather than one-fifth. Each child's interest was vested, but subject to fluctuation in size with the addition of class members, until the class finally closed, either upon the death of Ralph J. Smith, Jr., or upon the first mandatory distribution of principal. Distribution of principal from the trust was not required, and the class did not close, until the oldest child attained the age of twenty-five in January 1980. The testatrix's plan was to include in the three classes all of the children of her son Ralph J. Smith, Jr., and her daughters Margaret and Rosemary. This plan can be reasonably accomplished by determining the final number of members of each class either at the death of each of her children of when the oldest child of each of her children attained the age of twenty-five years, whichever first occurred.

For all the reasons as set forth hereinbefore, the judgment of the court of appeals is reversed, and we remand the cause to the probate court for further proceedings consistent with this opinion.

■ CACIOPPO, JUDGE, dissenting.

I must respectfully dissent from the majority decision. The majority states the well-established law that the court's function in a will construction case is to determine and apply the testatrix's intention, as expressed in the language of the whole will, and read in light of the circumstances surrounding the will's execution. The majority then construes the testamentary trust language as creating a per stirpes gift as to each share, for a class of beneficiaries identified as the children of one of the testatrix's children. I believe that construction is not based upon testatrix's intention as expressed, nor as read in light of the circumstances surrounding the will's execution.

Item VII of the will includes the instruction that "[t]he trust estate shall be treated as composed of three (3) equal shares * * *." Continuing, Item VII identifies the trust beneficiaries, provides for discretionary distributions from both trust income and principal, and provides for final distribution. Testatrix manifests her intent to correlate trust benefits to equal treatment among her three children, through the selected language and document conception. This prevalence of treating testatrix's children equally reveals testatrix's design for trust beneficiaries.

Bryan Smith contends and the majority so found that testatrix made a gift in trust, where one-third of her residuary estate would be shared equally among Ralph J. Smith's children. Upon testatrix's death, each child took a vested interest in the trust subject to open upon the birth or adoption of another child. This contention relies upon rules of construction as the means to establish validity. If the testatrix established a trust where the class of beneficiaries remained open, only an event which closed the class would terminate the opportunity to increase the class membership.

"Rules of construction are designed to aid in the interpretation of wills. None should be permitted to thwart the desire and purpose of the testator when they may be ascertained from the language employed." McCulloch v. Yost (1947), 148 Ohio St. 675, 679, 36 O.O. 274, 276, 76 N.E.2d 707, 709.

This case does not present a need to invoke rules of construction. Construing all parts of the will together, I believe testatrix intended the trust beneficiaries to be determined at her decease. . . .

Testatrix's express language clearly establishes the intent to determine trust beneficiaries upon testatrix's death. . . . Testatrix executed her will with the knowledge that Ralph J. Smith, Jr. and Margaret Smith Keller each had children, and that each could have more children. Testatrix was equally cognizant that Rosemary Smith had no children, but could have children in the future.

Testatrix chose to treat each of her three children equally in expressly instructing that the trust be treated as composed of three equal shares. Testatrix did not instruct that three separate trusts or subtrusts be administered, or that trust benefits be distributed per stirpes. The trust beneficiaries took individual gifts through testatrix's children. Testatrix did not create a class gift.

A class gift requires beneficiaries to take a per capita share. Testatrix chose not to provide the beneficiaries a per capita share, because to create such a scheme would allow testatrix's children to receive unequal benefits. The child having the most children would receive the most benefit. Testatrix also provided an express instruction which addressed the situation of a beneficiary's death occurring before final distribution. That instruction defeats any per capita distribution scheme. The majority chooses to ignore the instructive language in Item VII, which states:

> * * * In the event of the death of any of the children herein provided for before final distribution is made to such child, his or her share shall vest, at the time he or she would have attained the age of thirty (30) years, in such persons as shall then constitute the next of kin of such child according to the laws and statutes of the State of Ohio relating to descent and distribution then in force and effect.

The express distribution scheme for trust benefits defeats a per stirpes or per capita distribution.

Testatrix chose to describe the trust's individual beneficiaries rather than name those individuals. As is apparent from the trust provision for Rosemary Smith's children, testatrix did not know at the time of her will's execution who would be the beneficiaries. However, the express language which testatrix chose identifies the individual beneficiaries.

It is reasonable to infer from the express terms of the will that testatrix intended the trust benefits to accrue and be distributed to those grandchildren that she knew, as opposed to the trustee relying upon case law, a combination of distribution schemes, and rules of construction in order to determine those beneficiaries. For the foregoing reasons, the judgment of the court of appeals should be affirmed.

Query: What aspects of the trust language made the dissent so insistent that no class gift was intended or created here? If there was no class gift, then the gifts to the grandchildren had to close at the testator's death, precluding afterborn members. If it was intended to be a class gift, then it would be kept open until distribution to allow afterborn members. Which do you think best approximates the donor's intentions?

Est. of Houston, discussed earlier, raises the question of what happens to the interests of class members who die before distribution. If the court interprets the remainder interests to be vested subject to open, you have the transmissible remainder problem illustrated by that case,[24] as the interests of the three predeceased grandchildren, without issue, pass to their estates for further administration, probate, and taxation. Had the court interpreted the interests to be contingent (as would occur with a type 2 class), there would have been an implied survivorship requirement to distribution and the remainder would have been divided into only 9 shares for the 8 surviving grandchildren and the issue of the predeceased 9th grandchild who left issue. But what happens when the date of distribution does not correspond to the date the class physiologically closes?

c.   Can We Close the Class Early?

Our third issue concerns the *class closing rule*, or *rule of convenience*, that allows for the closing of a class early, before it closes physiologically, if

---

[24] Of course, the transmissible remainder problem can be avoided with a survivorship requirement in the form of a divesting condition subsequent, but the key here is to understand the risks of different types of conditions and classes.

it becomes possessory for at least one member of the class. Again, however, the application of the rule is dependent on testator's intent. The famous case of *Lux v. Lux*, 288 A.2d 701 (R.I. 1972), dealt with a trust, where the remainder was to pass to the decedent's grandchildren when the youngest reached 21. Because the decedent's son was still alive, and indicated an interest in having more children, the executor of the estate brought suit to determine when the class would close. The decedent had five grandchildren at the time of her death. Normally a trust provides for distribution, as in *Smith* above, when the *oldest* child reaches a certain age. Once the child reaches that age, the class closes and the first distribution of principal is made. Afterborn children are thus excluded from membership in the class because you can't make a distribution if you don't know the exact number of shares to divide the trust into. But in *Lux*, the gift was to vest in possession when the *youngest* reached 21, a time that could be extended if every 20 years the son had another child who then qualified as being the *youngest*. The son advocated for an interpretation that the class could not be closed and distributed until his own death, when it would be impossible for new class members to be born. Rejecting that view, the court closed the class when the youngest "at any time in being" was 21. Hence, if the youngest was 20, and the son had another child, the trust would continue. But once the youngest in being at any given time reached 21, the class would close and be distributed, and an afterborn member would be out of luck.

Another rule has been created, by the following case, that afterborn members can be included even after a distribution is made, so long as the addition of the new member does not alter the size of the gift made to the pre-existing members. Can you see why that would also be a valuable rule? If you were a class member you would want distribution to be as early as possible; but if you were an afterborn class member you would also want to be able to take a share. So how do we best balance the desire to close the class early under early vesting doctrines with the desire to keep it open as long as possible to take in as many qualified class members as possible? Taking in afterborn members is usually consistent with the donor's intent and is why she used class gift terminology in the first place. How you actually structure the trust can tip the balance one way or the other, as the following case demonstrates.

In re Earle's Estate

369 Pa. 52, 85 A.2d 90 (Pa. 1951)

George H. Earle, Jr., died February 19, 1928, leaving a will dated January 24, 1928. In that will he provided by the third paragraph of the Fifth Item of his will as follows: 'In the event that my estate, after the payment of taxes, shall at least amount to the net sum of Five Million ($5,000,000) Dollars or over, I give and bequeath to my Trustees in Trust for the benefit of each and every male child of my sons who shall by birth inherit and bear the name of Earle, the sum of One Hundred Thousand ($100,000) Dollars for each one of such male children. Said sum shall be held in Trust upon the same terms, conditions and uses as provided in Item Third in the trust for the benefit of my granddaughter Louise Dilworth Beggs, and in Item Fourth in trust for the benefit of my granddaughter Edith Earle Lee.'

The reference to the other items of the will makes clear that only the *income* not the principal is given to these grandsons.

The sole question before us on these appeals is whether Anthony Wayne Earle, who was born July 11, 1949, i. e., *after* the testator's death, is entitled to have a $100,000 trust set up for him in accordance with the paragraph quoted. . . .

It is well settled that the intention of a testator is the polar star in the construction of wills. Equally well settled is the corollary proposition that where the language used by the testator is plain and clearly discloses his intention, no rules of construction are necessary to arrive at an interpretation. And . . . it is the actual intent, as ascertained from the language of the will that must prevail in the light of the circumstances surrounding testator at the date of the execution of the will. Hence it is our first duty to examine the will and if possible ascertain its meaning *without* reference to canons of construction.

When we peruse the provision in question we see that the testator establishes a class composed of such of his grandsons as are born to his sons and defines the qualifications of members of that class explicitly by the words, 'I give and bequeath * * * for the benefit of *each* and *every male* child of my *sons*, who *shall* by birth inherit and bear the name of Earle,' etc. Analyzing this language it becomes clear that the phrase 'each and every' is an emphatic way of saying 'all' and can indicate only an intent that no son of his sons be excluded.

Next we note the testator adds to the phrase 'each and every male child' the words '*of my sons*,' which indicates *all* male progeny of *both* sons are intended to be included. The use of the plural becomes more important when we view the extraneous circumstances of the family situation from the testator's armchair. This we must do. The testator at the date of the will had two sons, George H. III, age 37 and married, who had three sons living at the date of the will and at the date of testator's death and one *en ventre sa mere* born thereafter on September 26, 1928, and Ralph Earle, 35 years of age, who though married had *no* children living at either the date of the will or of testator's death and none so far born since testator's death. Testator was on cordial terms with *both* of his sons for he designated both sons as co-trustees of the trust under his will. These circumstances confirm testator's intent to include any male offspring of both of his sons whenever born. Certainly it is unthinkable that he intended to cut off sons of Ralph, his younger son, just because he had no sons *then*.

Significant also is the future tense indicated by the word 'shall' in the phrase, 'who *shall* by birth inherit and bear the name of Earle.' To give effect to the future tense, it is reasonable to regard the testator's intent as including in the described class those born *after* his death as well as *before*.

It is equally clear that the motivating purpose that influenced these special bequests of income was pride in the family name and desire to have that name perpetuated by as many lineal male descendants of the *blood and name* as possible. To exclude grandsons that came within the described class merely because they happened to be born after the testator's death would do violence to the very purpose that actuated the gifts. To which may be added that normally if a testator has in mind individual members of a group he would describe them by name; therefore, when he uses a class designation he would seem to mean not only those known to him but all that may come into the class described unless there is some contrary intent manifested.

We have here then a clear case for the application of the principle referred to in Witman v. Webner, 1945, 351 Pa. 503, at page 507, where Mr. Justice Horace Stern said, 'It is well settled that if a person qualifies within the exact meaning of language describing a class he will be held to be a member of that class unless other language in the instrument expressly or by clear implication indicates a contrary intent.

We have examined the whole will to ascertain if there be any other language that impels such contrary intent and find nothing that compels a narrower construction of the testator's explicit language. In doing so we have been greatly assisted by the learned opinions of the three eminent judges of the court below and the excellent briefs of the able *guardians ad litem*.

Our respect for the learned judges below requires us to examine the reasons advanced in the adjudication and the opinion of the court en banc which led the court below to a different conclusion.

Judge Hunter in his adjudication begins by applying the general rule of construction known as 'the rule of convenience' which he states as follows: 'that in the case of an *immediate* gift to a class, the class closes as of the death of the testator.' . . .

However, the danger of such rules of construction is their tendency in the progress of time to become inflexible and in their application to circumstances where there is neither reason nor necessity until finally they become controlling. . . .

Therefore, we must be constantly alert to see that artificial rules of construction should be resorted to only where the intent of a testator as gleaned from his language is obscure, or where there is compelling practical necessity for their application; and when the reasons on which they are founded do not exist they ought not be applied. In this case the basic reason, which gave rise to the 'rule of convenience' is *not* present. There is here no gift of principal to any member of the class in question that vested at testator's death. Aside from a few minor legacies given outright to non-members of the family by Item Second only *income* is given. No distribution is made of the principal to any family beneficiary and the whole of it is withheld until the date of the termination of the trust as hereinafter noted. Indeed, the learned Auditing Judge admits the reason giving rise to the rule does not here exist and frankly says, 'If this testator intended that the executors pay $100,000 [income] legacies to grandsons living at his death, and that the trustees of residuary estate pay similar legacies to the afterborn, it must be admitted that there is no practical difficulty in so doing. The residuary trust will remain intact until 'the expiration of twenty-one (21) years after the death of my (the testator's) last surviving grandchild or great-grandchild living at the time of my decease.' Distribution at the termination of the residuary trust will not be delayed, because it does not seem possible that the trust can terminate before the death of testator's two sons, when the class of grandsons will be complete.' It therefore serves no purpose to restrict words of futurity of the gifts here made to the period between the date of the will and testator's death because when such restriction serves no purpose, words of futurity are not to be restricted to date of testator's *death* but are projected at least to the *date of distribution*. . . .

In justice to the learned Auditing Judge we should say it is evident from his adjudication that he does not rely with too much confidence on the rule of convenience for he concludes, 'Aside from the question of the testator's intent, I agree with the claimant in his contention that there is no reason for applying the rule of convenience, and that the class could remain open until the final termination of the residuary trust, without inconvenience to the estate.' . . .

In holding the real distribution date for the application of the rule to be the *distribution of principal* at the termination of the trust, we need not be concerned with the fancied disadvantages (recited in both the opinion and appellees' brief) that might arise if a later time than executors' audit were fixed for the fulfillment of the 5 million condition, e.g., such as the necessity of continuous reappraisement of the corpus, or the possibility of its future diminution below that figure and thereby exclude some after born child or reduce the income of the widow and children of the testator. All these speculations are unimportant in face of the facts that testator's net estate was approximately ten million at the time of the executors' audit and at the present time is still over eight million. . . .

The opinion finally suggests that in the first paragraph of the Ninth Item of his will the testator used the phrase, *either before my death or thereafter* and thereby demonstrated he know how to so specify when that was his intent. This is usually a persuasive argument but it loses its force when we observe testator did not use that phrase in the second paragraph nor in the fourth, fifth or sixth paragraphs of the same Item where it would have been equally appropriate; instead he seems to have relied on the plain implication of such words. So, too, it might also be answered by pointing out that in Item Fifth the testator had already used the all inclusive words, ' * * * each and every male child of my sons,' which coupled with the words of futurity, 'who *shall* by birth inherit and bear the name of Earle,' made the additional words redundant. Judge Bolger sets forth in his dissenting opinion other equally cogent reasons why the argument based on the omission of those words cannot prevail but which we find unnecessary to repeat.

To sum up our position briefly, we say that since the minor claimant here qualifies within the exact meaning of the language used in describing the class, he cannot be excluded by the application of a rule of construction which can only be invoked when it delays distribution beyond the time fixed in a will.

We conclude by saying that we have carefully read the entire will in the light of the learned opinions of the three judges of the court below and of the able arguments and briefs of the learned counsel and find nothing to shake the plain implication of the explicit words which bring the minor claimant within the class described by the testator. To hold otherwise would do violence not only to testator's unambiguous language but also to the clearly apparent motive, the sole reason for the gifts, namely, family pride and a desire to perpetuate an honored name.

We hold until the time fixed by the testator for the distribution of the corpus of his estate arrives, any son's male child born before that time who qualifies as a member of the class described in par. 3, of Item Fifth, cannot be excluded.

■ ALLEN M. STEARNE, JUSTICE (dissenting).

I am unable to join in this opinion. It is an ancient well established canon of will construction that where there is an immediate gift of a separate sum to each member of a class, the class closes as of the date of death of testator. This was precisely what happened here. By the will testator erected a $100,000 trust 'for the benefit of each and every male child of my sons who shall by birth inherit and bear the name of Earle.' This was followed by a gift of the residue, under which testator erected a trust, disposing of both income and principal which is to endure to the utmost limit of permissive remoteness-lives in being and twenty-one years thereafter. The beneficiaries under the residuary trust were the widow (since deceased) and each of testator's five named children and their issue.

Now the crux of this case is this: if the $100,000 trust now claimed by the afterborn child of George H. Earle III is taken from the residuary trust, such payment diminishes the shares of income and principal not only of George H. Earle III and his four other sons, and their issue, but also of testator's other children and their issue. In other words, the estate already given and bequeathed is necessarily cut down and diminished. To accomplish this effectively requires clear and unequivocal language. It must be conceded that testator used no *express language* directing that afterborn grandsons of the name of Earle should have their $100,000 trust funds paid out of the residuary trust. It is only by *necessary implication* that such an intent may be declared. The majority in their opinion seek to demonstrate such implied intent. To attempt to analyze and answer the many points submitted in substantiation of the claim of proof of implied intent, would result in entering a labyrinth of generalities and legal principles, most of which I freely concede, but which clearly have no application to this case. The inferences of testamentary intent which are so voluminously submitted become less convincing the more they are advanced. And strange as it may seem, apparently in an effort still further to strengthen their contentions, the majority not only conjecture what *testator* intended but venture to suggest what *counsel* regarded as testator's intent. In the opinion it is said: 'In passing we note that counsel for the accountant at that audit was Mr., later, Justice Barnes, who had been testator's personal counsel and witnessed his will. His acquiescence is somewhat indicative of the fact that afterborn children were intended to be include, otherwise he would no doubt have had a guardian or trustee ad litem appointed for that audit and the question *then* settled.'

In construing wills it is my opinion that there should be no straying from the solid and well defined highway of testamentary construction. We should refrain from entering the misty swamp of testamentary conjecture, following an illusory will-o'-the-wisp seeking to determine what we *surmise* was testator's true intent. It is axiomatic that in expounding a will it is not what the testator may have meant, but what is the meaning of his words. This principle is analogous to a provision of the Statutory Construction Act: 'The object of all interpretation and construction of laws is to ascertain and effectuate the intention of the Legislature. * * * the letter of [the statute] is not to be disregarded under the pretext of pursuing its spirit.' 46 P.S. § 551.

Judge Hunter's adjudication and Judge Klein's opinion in the court below comprehensively and accurately state the applicable authorities and reach the correct construction of this will. It would be unnecessarily repetitious for me to restate what they have so well said, and with which I thoroughly agree.

It is for these reasons I note my dissent.

Query: The dissent is certainly correct that any distribution, of income or principal, will diminish the shares of other class members. Is that a good reason to not allow a class to stay open to take in afterborn members? If not, when should this class have closed? Note that if the trust fund had not been so enormous, so that it could easily pay out the $100,000 shares to a large number of afterborn grandsons, would the court have decided the case the same way? And if we keep the class of grandsons open, what effect does that have on the separate residuary trust? Does a trustee's fiduciary duty to both the life tenant and the remaindermen compel a trustee to seek judicial advice on how to construe a class gift?

PROBLEMS

8.27. Uncle Al left a will that stated as follows: "I give the rest and residue of my estate, real and personal, to my beloved wife Angela, for her use during her life. At the death of my wife, the rest and residue of my estate I give to Angela's children, Alice, Bob, and Carol in equal parts." How is the estate distributed if Alice predeceased Al?

8.28. In his will, O devises his entire estate to his wife A for life, then to his 2 daughters B & C for their lives, then to B & C's husbands D & E for their lives if they survive their wives, then to his four grandchildren, B's 2 children (F and G) and C's two children, (H and I), "if they are alive at the time their devise vests in possession." O also specifies that any afterborn grandchildren shall take a share along with the named grandchildren. O also specifies that for any beneficiary who dies before his/her interest vests, that interest will be redistributed to the other beneficiaries of the same generation (i.e. if a child dies before vesting her interest goes to the other children and spouses, and if a grandchild dies before vesting her interest goes to the other granchildren).

    a.   B dies before O and no other grandchildren are born before O's death. What interests do each of the parties have at the time O dies?

    b.   During the duration of A's life estate, D & C both die, and C has had 2 additional children, J & K. What interests will the remaining parties have at A's death?

    c.   During the duration of E's life estate, F,G, and I die, leaving issue. What is the distribution at E's death?

8.29. In his will O devised Blackacre to A for life, remainder to the issue of A. When the will was written, A had 3 children (B,C, & D). Prior to O's death, A's child B died leaving issue (G). After O's death, A had 2 more children (E & F), but C died leaving issue (H & I). What future interests did O create and who takes what percentage of Blackacre at A's death?

8.30. O devises $100,000 in trust for A for life, remainder to B's children only on condition that they reach age 21. At O's death B has 2 children (C & D) who are both under age 21. During A's life, C reaches 21, then dies leaving a spouse (S) and issue (I & J). Also during A's life B has two more children (E & F) but E dies at birth. A then dies. One year after A's death B has another child (G) and the next year D reaches 21. On D's 23rd birthday, B has another child H. How is the remainder of the trust distributed?

6. CODA

There are many more issues that arise in the context of drafting future interests, besides getting survivorship and class gifts right. There is also the changing legal landscape of the UPC's § 2–707 that can profoundly change the characterization of future interests in trusts, especially in ways that can be negatively affected by the Rule Against Perpetuities. Because this is an introductory class, we don't have time to cover the details of the variety of future interests that can be created and all of the rules of construction that are applied when a testator or settlor is not excruciatingly clear about the interests she intends to create. The Rule in Shelley's Case, the Doctrine of Worthier Title, and the Destructibility of Contingent Remainders Rule can be important factors in your jurisdiction and you will need to master them before you start drafting your own trusts. The lesson at this point, however, is that planning for future generations MUST be flexible, to allow for adjustments when changed circumstances and unexpected events threaten to derail a good estate plan. Planning for future generations must also be undertaken with a thorough understanding of the rules, presumptions, and trends that will influence the construction of future interests and their consequent legal effects. The *presumption in favor of early vesting*, for instance, that was based on avoiding invalidity under the Rule Against Perpetuities, was offset by a corresponding rule, the *divide and pay over rule*. With the gradual demise of the divide and pay over rule, many courts dispute the need for the early vesting rule. These relative nuances can be important in drafting trust instruments in ways that will avoid litigation and best effectuate the testator's intentions. But let's turn now to the most common mechanisms used in planning for future generations.

B. THE RULE AGAINST PERPETUITIES

Although we can think of the Rule Against Perpetuities (RAP) as a mechanism for limiting the creation of contingent future interests in such a way as to deny a testator or settlor donative freedom, or as a statutory bar to certain testamentary gifts, you should think of it first and foremost as the boundary fence within which you must plan and draft your estate plan. A well-drafted future interest should not run afoul of the RAP and therefore should not be litigated or threaten to frustrate your client's plan. So even though many states are modifying their RAPs, and some have even dispensed with it altogether, you need to understand how it functions, what it can do, and how to avoid RAP traps to protect your client's estate plan.

The mere mention of the Rule Against Perpetuities is often enough to strike fear into the hearts of first year law students, and many practicing attorneys as well. But you should not let its reputation deter you from appreciating the many benefits of the Rule. If you thought the preceding future interests were difficult, then you should embrace the RAP as the limiting factor to creating crazy and complicated future interests.

There are actually four different rules relating to trusts and future interests that you need to recognize and keep straight. Unfortunately, courts that are faced with these questions don't keep them straight, and they are often combined, confused, partially modified by statute, completely ignored, or slavishly followed, depending on the state. These are:

1. The Rule Against Perpetuities, which is a rule against the remote vesting of contingent future interests.

2. Rules, if any, on the permissible duration of a trust.
3. The Rule Against Suspension of the Power of Alienation, which limits how long a trust can limit the power of the trustee to alienate the trust property.
4. Rules, if any, on how long a trust can accumulate income.

So how do these rules work? First, the RAP simply prohibits the creation of contingent future interests that are not sure to vest within the relevant perpetuities period. Why? A contingent future interest threatens to divest a present estate holder in possession. Thus, a grant "to A for residential use only, and if not so used, then to B and his heirs," places a big black cloud over A's ownership of the property. A can't sell the property as freely as she could without the limitation, and B has this shifting executory interest that is part of his estate that has some small value and which has to be kept track of over the generations as A and his successors continue to use the property for residential purposes. The RAP tells us that B's contingent executory interest must vest within the perpetuities period or it is void *ab initio*. Because there is no certainty that B's interest will vest anytime in the next millennium, B's remote future interest is void. Now this doesn't change A's present estate, which continues to be subject to the use limitation; rather, we replace B's interest with a possibility of reverter in the grantor. That brings us to the second rule.

In the context of legal interests, a grantor may impose a limitation, like the residential use limitation of the above example, and it can operate for a millennium with that possibility of reverter passing to the grantor's heirs or devisees virtually in perpetuity. Think about the heirs in *Evans v. Abney* who probably didn't even know they were entitled to the possibility of reverter in the park property. Because reversionary interests in the grantor are deemed vested from the start, the RAP does not terminate the grantor's possibility of reverter, and the big black cloud continues to hang over A's interest. This anomaly makes most people wonder what the point of the RAP was if it simply replaced one future interest with another and did nothing to make A's interest more marketable or put a time limit on that dead hand control. And those people who wonder such things are exactly right. So states have come up with a variety of other techniques for terminating that possibility of reverter which we will discuss below. But the important point is that it is not always the RAP that will blow away the big black cloud.

But in the context of trusts, the second rule has sometimes come into play to limit the actual duration of trusts. The RAP terminates futureinterests that might vest too far in the future, but it does nothing to a trust that could last into perpetuity. A settlor might give Blackacre "to X in trust for the benefit of A and his heirs so long as the property is used for residential purposes, and if not so used, then to the Red Cross." Because the interest in the Red Cross violates the RAP, it is terminated, but that leaves the trust for the benefit of A intact, simply followed by a possibility of reverter in the grantor. That was also the situation in *Evans v. Abney*, where the park was to be held in trust in perpetuity, with a possibility of reverter in the Senator's heirs. Since the RAP is only concerned with remote vesting, and not the actual duration of the present estate, many states have adopted rules limiting the actual duration of trusts, and most of those states adopted, as the relevant time period, the same period the state uses for the RAP. There is no point making things easy by adopting a clearly different rule (isn't that a surprise!).

Consequently, court decisions have often merged the effects of the two rules by indiscriminate use of the term "perpetuities," thereby ruling that a trust fails entirely if the remainder interests do not vest within the perpetuities period. This voids not only the contingent future interest under the RAP, but the present estate as well if it is of unlimited duration. But this latter effect is caused by the technical application of trust duration rules. Thus, certain trusts can survive and be modified by terminating the void contingent remainders and replacing them with a possibility of reverter in the settlor, but other trusts are perpetual and therefore may be entirely struck down because of their potential to last in perpetuity. Sometimes the decision to strike down a potentially unlimited trust is based on whether it is otherwise indestructible. Thus, if the trust has other ways to terminate it, especially through agreement by the beneficiaries, the trust may be allowed to stand. But if it is indestructible it is more likely to be voided.

There is no clear common law rule on the duration of trusts—some states have adopted rules that terminate trusts that don't have vested remainders, and others have allowed the trust to stand so long as there aren't other policy reasons against it. Because most dynasty trusts purport to give individual people successive life interests, at some point the RAP will do the work to cut off the potential takers and the trust will fail. But in other instances, like a trust to support a pet or a trust to accomplish a particular purpose, states often impose 21 year limits, as the UPC provision on honorary trusts. A trust to the City of Macon for a segregated park can stand in perpetuity because the RAP and rules on trust duration generally do not apply to charitable gifts. Thus, it is usually only in the context of a private trust with indefinite conditions (like the property being restricted to residential uses only) that we run into trust duration problems that aren't solved with the application of the RAP.

The majority rule on trust duration seems to be that there is no limit to the duration of a trust, but many states have not addressed the issue directly. Some states have also created specialized rules for certain elements of trust duration, like imposing durational limits on spendthrift trusts but not mandatory trusts, or allowing perpetual cemetery trusts but not dynasty trusts. But imagine the potential issues behind a trust of one's family farm that is to stand so long as the land is used to raise corn for ethanol.

With the recent modifications of the RAP, both by common law and by statute, many states have seen the basic foundations of trust law change, and they have not yet addressed many of the ancillary issues of trust duration or the continuation of reversionary interests. But the trend is toward not limiting trust duration so long as the future interests in the trust are valid under the RAP, even if they are contingent on remote events.

Third, several states have adopted rules limiting or invalidating trusts that suspend the power to alienate the trust property. One of the principal justifications for allowing trusts is that the property itself generally remains alienable by the trustee, even if the beneficiaries cannot manage or alienate the property themselves. Thus, assets that are depreciating in value can be sold and replaced to maintain the integrity of the trust without implicating the rule against restraints on alienation, while still allowing for extensive limitations on the beneficiaries' interests, including spendthrift provisions. But where the beneficiary and trustee of a spendthrift trust are the same person, such limitations can hamper the alienability of trust property. And many of the states that have lengthened the RAP period or abolished the RAP altogether have instituted statutory limitations on how long the power to alienate can be limited, most of which closely resemble the RAP period.[25] The point of these rules is to prevent the property from becoming static and out of the market for a lengthy period of time.

Fourth, although there was no common law rule prohibiting or limiting the accumulation of trust income originally, the leading English case of *Thellusson v. Woodford*[26] in 1798 held a trust valid that provided that all income was to be retained until the trust ended and the remainder vested in the final beneficiary. After that, Parliament enacted the Thellusson Act,[27] which restricted accumulations of income to a period generally shorter than the RAP period. Since the early days of the Republic, many states have enacted statutes limiting the period during which income can be accumulated, and some were even more restrictive than the English rule. But most today, if they have limitations, tie the limitations to the perpetuities period.[28] And most states do not have any limitation at all, either relying on the vague common law rule or permitting accumulations of income without limit. Where states did have limits, however, and have since modified their RAP, they are unlikely to have also dealt with the income accumulation problem at all—leaving the field quite uncertain at this time.

In many states, therefore, the RAP might be used to accomplish all of these goals; in other states the RAP might only apply to the vesting of contingent future interests while other rules might exist to deal with these additional questions about trust duration, limitations on alienation, or income accumulation. But the RAP is most often the cornerstone, and to master the field you must master the RAP.

So to begin, realize that the RAP is your friend! Embrace it. Enjoy it. Venerate it, because it does two important things: first, it forces the reaggregation of all the sticks in the property bundle back into fee simple absolute after they have been distributed through the creation of future interests so there aren't any "perpetuities," i.e. contingent property interests that can hang out there and threaten the present estate. Second, it indirectly compels the termination of private express trusts and the distribution of principal so that the trust limitations are removed from the property. Both of these goals are aimed at freeing property from the dead hand control that we have been talking about throughout the book and getting everything back to the good old fee simple absolute.

How the RAP does this, however, may seem counterintuitive, when it might have been simpler to just legislate that no private trust can last longer than 50 years, or 100 years. Or, the law simply could have required that future interests are terminated if they don't become possessory within a certain time frame. But such pragmatic solutions don't have the historical pedigree we have come to expect with the common law, so instead we have created a rule that relies on fertile octogenarians, bottomless gravel pits, unborn widows, and slothful executors. Like your family, you have to take them with all their quirks and flaws and lovable eccentricities. But also

---

[25] See Alaska Stat. § 34.27.100; S.D. Codified Laws § 43–5–1; Wis. Stat. Ann. § 700.16; Idaho Code Ann. § 55–111; N.J. Stat. Ann. § 46:2F–10.

[26] 4 Ves. 228 (1798), 11 Ves. 112 (1805).

[27] 39 & 40 Geo. 3., Ch. 98 (1800).

[28] See Cal. Civ. Proc. Prob. § 24:38; N.Y. EPTL § 9–2.1(b).

like your family, the RAP will be there when you really need it to do the important work of releasing the dead hand.

1. The Common Law Rule Against Perpetuities

The Rule was first expounded by the musings of Lord Chancellor Nottingham in the *Duke of Norfolk's Case*[29] when he pondered how long a contingency could be allowed to hang out and threaten a tenant in possession with forfeiture.[30] The Rule we have today looks very little like Lord Nottingham's musings. In the late nineteenth century, Professor John Chipman Gray explained the law as it had evolved in the following terms:

> *No [nonvested property] interest is good unless it must vest, if at all, not later than 21 years after some life in being at the creation of the interest.*

To understand its application, we should break the Rule down into its component parts. **First**, the Rule applies only to *nonvested* property interests that could, if they vest, result in forfeiture of the property and possession shifting to someone else. Thus, contingent remainders, executory interests, pre-emptive rights, options to purchase, and the vested remainder subject to open are all *nonvested (or partially non-vested) property interests*. The vested remainder subject to open is somewhat special because, although it is partially vested in the holders of the interest, the property is not fully vested because the shares class members will ultimately acquire can increase or decrease as new members are born or members die. The Rule applies to both legal and equitable interests in property, so future interests in trusts are subject to the Rule, just like legal future interests. Go back and review the discussion of vestedness in Section A above. The vesting of a contingent remainder and an executory interest are both dependent on a future event that is uncertain to occur. It is that uncertainty that concerns us. This Chart should help you first figure out if a future interest is even subject to the Rule.

Future Interests ALWAYS Subject to the RAP	Future Interests NEVER Subject to the RAP	Future Interests SOMETIMES Subject to the RAP
• Contingent Remainders (on a conditional event or on an unascertained person)	• Vested Remainders (absolutely or subject to divestment)	• Options to Purchase
• Executory Interests (shifting or springing)	• Possibilities of Reverter	• Pre-emptive Rights
• Vested Remainders Subject to Open	• Reversions	• Rights of First Refusal
	• Powers of Termination	

---

[29] 3 Ch.Cas. 1, 22 Eng. Rep. 932 (1682).

[30] He queried: "But what Time? And where are the Bounds of that Contingency? You may limit, it seems, upon a contingency to happen in a Life: What if it be limited, if such a one die without issue within twenty-one Years, or 100 Years, or while Westminster-Hall stands? Where will you stop, if you do not stop here? I will tell you where I will stop: I will stop wherever any visible Inconvenience doth appear;. . . ."

The **second** aspect of the Rule focuses on *when* the nonvested interest will vest. For the interest to be valid, there must be a time in the future when we will know for certain whether the interest will vest or fail. Consider this conveyance:

> *O conveys Blackacre to A so long as used for residential purposes, but if not so used, then to B.*

A has the present estate and present estates are always vested (that's one of the definitions of being vested—the interest holder has the *present right to possession*) so A's interest is fine. But what about B's interest? B's interest depends on an indefinite event (the use of Blackacre for nonresidential purposes). Because it is uncertain to occur, and is a future interest in a third party, B has a shifting executory interest (which is subject to the Rule). We now must ask if there is a point in time, in the future, when we will know for certain that B will either get Blackacre, or B's interest will fail (i.e. we will know for certain that the event will NEVER occur)? The answer is no. Thus, B's interest violates the Rule because we cannot say for certain that the interest will vest in B or that it will absolutely fail. Thus, B's executory interest is void *ab intio*, and so we delete it, replacing it with a possibility of reverter in O.

First Side Note

Future interests in the grantor (reversions, possibilities of reverter, and powers of termination) are deemed to be vested *ab initio* because the grantor was seised of the property in fee simple absolute at the time the grant was made, and the conveyance by the grantor to the grantee of the present estate does not divest the grantor of her retained future interest. It is a bit more complicated than this, but for our purposes now, realize that the Rule simply does not apply to reversionary future interests retained by the grantor.

Now consider this conveyance:

> *O conveys Blackacre to A for life, remainder to B but only if B has graduated from law school by A's death.*

Here the present estate for life is in A, and the remainder to B is contingent on B graduating from law school before A dies. This contingent remainder is subject to the Rule, so now we have to test B's interest to determine if it violates the Rule or not. B's nonvested interest will vest if B graduates before A dies, and it will fail if B has not graduated by A's death. Both of these events will take place within A's lifetime, so we will know whether B's interest vests or fails no later than at the death of A. We can say with certainty that at A's death we will know whether B graduated or not.

If B graduates after A dies, too bad. The conveyance required that B graduate before A's death. So A's death is the latest point at which we will know for certain whether B's interest will vest. Of course, if B graduates quickly, while A is still alive, B's contingent remainder will become an absolutely vested remainder.

This brings us to the **third** component of the rule: the time limit for the vesting or failure of the future interest (the *perpetuities period*). The interest must vest (or fail) within *21 years after the death of some life in being at the creation of the interest.* The life in being component is usually the hardest aspect of applying the Rule because it's not always clear whose life serves as the measuring or validating life by which we measure compliance with the Rule. But one rule of thumb is to ask whether the vesting or failure of the future interest depends either on someone's death, or must occur within a particular person's lifetime. In our example above, A's death is the event that will allow us to determine whether B's future interest vests or fails. So long as A was alive at the time the interest was created, then B's future interest is good.

Second Side Note

The rule talks about lives in being *at the creation of the interest.* Property interests can be created by a deed, an *inter vivos* gift, a will, a non probate instrument, or a power of appointment. When the interest is created is therefore important for telling us when the perpetuities period begins to run. This shouldn't be too difficult to determine, but you do have to pay attention to the instrument that creates the interest. Thus, a future interest created in a will is not effective upon execution of the will, but must wait until the death of the testator—for that is the event that causes the property rights to transfer out of the testator and to the beneficiaries. An *inter vivos* gift is immediate so long as there is delivery. But other interests are harder to determine. A remainder interest in a revocable trust is generally deemed not to transfer until the trust becomes irrevocable (usually by the death of the settlor). And property rights in property over which a donee has a power of appointment are created at different times, depending on the type of power. The following chart tells us when the future interest is created for purposes of the Rule.

Type of transfer or mechanism for creating interest	Time at which the future interest is created
Will	Death of Testator
Inter vivos gift	Delivery
Irrevocable trust	When the trust is funded
Revocable trust	When the trust becomes irrevocable
Special Power of Appointment or General Testamentary Power of Appointment[31]	When the power is created by the donor
Presently Exercisable General Power of Appointment	When the power is exercised by the donee

---

Back to our measuring life issue. If the interest will vest or fail within a particular person's lifetime (or class of people's lives), then we need merely determine if that person was a life in being when the interest was created. Thus, our example of the conveyance *to A for life, remainder to B if B has graduated from law school by A's death*, makes A the measuring life. So long as A was alive when the interest was created, then B's future interest does not violate the Rule. But what if the conveyance was instead:

O to A for life, remainder to B so long as B graduates from law school.

---

[31] Some courts treat the general testamentary power of appointment like the presently-exercisable power, but they are in the minority.

In this example, B doesn't have to graduate before A dies; B can graduate after A dies and the contingent remainder will vest or fail during B's lifetime. If B dies without graduating, then the interest will fail. Thus, it will either vest during B's lifetime or fail at his death, so we will know for certain whether it vests or fails no later than B's death. B is now the measurmeasuring life for B's own interest. So long as B was alive at the creation of the interest, then B's interest is not void. Thus, we have to find the person (or persons) whose life or death is relevant to whether the interest will vest or not; that person is the measuring life.

Now let's look at some slightly more complicated examples. Consider this one:

O conveys Blackacre to A for life, remainder to B's children.

The remainder to B's children can be either absolutely vested (B is dead and has left at last one living child); vested subject to open (B is alive but has at least one child); or contingent (B is alive and has no children). If it is absolutely vested, then the remainder in B's children is not subject to the Rule. But if B is still alive, B's children's interest is subject to the Rule. But does it violate the Rule? What we need to know in order to determine if the remainder will vest or fail is whether there will be any children of B and, if so, how many? When will we know that? Certainly no later than B's death. So long as B was alive at the creation of the interest, then the interest in B's children is valid.

But let's change the example to:

O conveys Blackacre to A for life, remainder to B's grandchildren.

The remainder in B's grandchildren is going to be void if B is still alive. Why? When will we know for sure whether B will have any grandchildren and how many there are? We will know that at the death of B's last child. Because B is still alive, B might have more children after the interest is created, and that child might end up being the last child alive. If that last child alive, whose death determines the vesting of the grandchildren's remainder, was not alive at the creation of the interest, the grandchildren's interest is void.

Now think back to the class closing rule we learned earlier in our discussion of class gifts. If there is at least one grandchild alive at A's death, we can apply the Rule of Convenience and close the class at the time of possession, thus saving the remainder interest. Voila! The class closing rule is often used to save gifts that would otherwise be void under the RAP. But the rule won't apply if there are no grandchildren alive at A's death, and we might need to wait and see if any are born if there aren't any alive at the creation of the instrument. So once again the difficulties of class gifts crop up.

Third Side Note

Students often get confused when the vesting or failure to vest depends on a class of people, like the open class of B's children and the open class of B's grandchildren. Assuming B is alive and has children at the time the interest is created, we know that the identity of the entire group of grandchildren will depend on actions by the children that have to happen during their lifetimes. (You can ignore frozen sperm and embryos at this point.) Assuming some of those grandchildren are already in being at the creation of the interest, it is tempting to assume that the class of grandchildren is certainly going to close within the lifetimes of all the living children and grandchildren. But the sticking point here is that the Rule requires certainty. That means that if it is possible, even if it is *extremely unlikely*, that the class of grandchildren won't close until the death of a person who was not a life in being (or 21 years later), then all the interests are void. What is most likely to happen is that B has children and grandchildren at the time the interest is created, and at B's death the class of children closes permanently. But most likely B won't have any more children if she already has grandchildren. In fact, then, the class of children doesn't change between the creation of the interest and the death of B. That means that all of B's children were lives in being at the creation of the interest and we should therefore be able to use the last surviving child as the measuring life for determining the identity of the class of grandchildren. But we can't. We can't because it is POSSIBLE, even though extremely unlikely, that B would have another child after the creation of the interest, that child could be the survivor among the class of children, and that child could then have a child (who would count as a grandchild) more than 21 years after the death of all the other children and all the grandchildren who were living at the creation of the interest. It is the unlikely possibility that causes the grandchildren's interest to fail. Because we cannot be certain that the grandchildren class will close within the lifetime of a person who was alive at the creation, the entire interest fails. But the possibility that all children and grandchildren of B will die simultaneously in a plane crash, and that B will then have another child after the creation of the interest, and that that child will have a child more than 21 years after the death of B is enough to void the interest, regardless of the unlikelihood of these events transpiring in this way.

So you have to pay attention to membership in the class and realize that often the validity of an interest will depend on ascertaining future interest holders at the death of the last surviving member of that class. We don't need to know immediately which of B's children will be the survivor; it is enough to know that at the death of the last of B's children the class of grandchildren will permanently close. And it is the possibility that that last surviving child won't have been a life in being that leads to the problem. If B is dead already, however, we know for certain that B can't have any more children, so the class of B's children is closed, and the survivor of them will serve as the validating life for the class of grandchildren.

This gets us to the **fourth** component of the Rule: the twenty-one years. The perpetuities period is *21 years* after the death of some life in being at the creation. The 21 year period serves a number of purposes. It originally gave the future interest holder time to come of age if that person was born immediately preceding the death of the measuring life. Becauseminors could not manage property, the Rule allowed a contingent future interest to remain contingent for a period amounting to a lifetime, plus an additional 21 years to allow the future interest holder to come of age. Courts then added a 9 month gestation period to capture potential future interest holders even if they were *in utero* at the death of the measuring life. Consider this example:

> *O conveys Blackacre to A for life, remainder to those of B's children who reach age 21, or if any child dies under age 21 survived by issue, then that child's share shall pass to that issue.*

The interest in B's children is contingent on being born and on reaching age 21. If they die before they reach 21, they take nothing. Their issue, if they have any, will take their parents' share. If they don't have issue and don't reach 21 their share is redistributed to the other class members. When will we know for certain who the takers are? We will know who B's children are at B's death (or 9 months later if a child of B has been conceived)—thus, we will know the maximum number of members of the class. But we won't necessarily know at B's death how many of B's children will in fact reach age 21, or whether those who don't will have issue. But we will know the total number of class members entitled to take 21 years and 9 months after the death of B. This was the classic use of the 21 year tack-on.

But sometimes future interests are made contingent on events that don't rely on a person's birth or death and thus aren't dependent on a measuring life. Consider this one:

> *O conveys Blackacre to A for 30 years, then to O's lineal descendants alive at the end of the term of years.*

Now we have a problem. O's lineal descendants include children, grandchildren, great-grandchildren, and so on. This class potentially never closes naturally, so we can't say that at the death of a particular person we will know for sure who the members of the class are. Without a measuring life to validate the future interest, we must look instead at the preceding present estate. It will terminate 30 years after the creation of the interest. The 30 years is not dependent on any person's life or death. A could die and her term of years will pass to her estate, or she could alienate it during life. So even though we will know who O's lineal descendants are after 30 years, their contingent remainder is void because without a measuring life, the perpetuities period is only 21 years. Thus, when the happening of the event does not depend on a particular life in being, we generally only have 21 years within which to determine if the future interest will vest or fail.

In addition to vesting events that are not dependent on a person's life or death, or events that will happen during a particular person's life (like B graduating from law school), the perpetuities period is also 21 years for interests in non-persons like corporations or interests that depend on a period not defined by a person's life. Thus, the following examples of future interests all receive only 21 years of uncertainty before the interest must vest or fail:

- O retains the present estate but conveys to A an option to purchase Blackacre.
- O conveys $5,000 in trust to support O's dog Trixie during Trixie's life, with a remainder to B's heirs.
- O conveys $5,000 in trust to pay for the acid washing of O's mausoleum every year in perpetuity, with a contingent remainder to B's heirs who are alive at the time the acid washing fails to occur.
- O conveys Blackacre to A so long as the giant oak tree on the corner of the property is still alive, after which Blackacre goes to B
- O conveys Blackacre to A's surviving lineal descendants upon the final closing of O's estate
- O conveys Blackacre to A's lineal descendants alive after all the gravel has been removed from the property by O's lessees.
- O conveys Blackacre to A so long as a Democrat is in the White House, and then to B when a Republican is in the White House.

First RAP Trap

Watch out for basing the vesting or failure of a future interest on an event that is not certain to occur. The *slothful executor* and the *bottomless gravel pit* are iconic examples of Rule violations in which the vesting of an interest in heirs or descendants (an unascertained group) was postponed until the occurrence of some event. The famous California case of *Lucas v. Hamm*, 364 P.2d 685 (Cal. 1961) involved the following provision in a will:

Paragraph Eighth of [decedent's will] 'transmitted' the residual estate in trust and provided that the 'trust shall cease and terminate at 12 o'clock noon on a day five years after the date upon which the order distributing the trust property to the trustee is made by the Court having jurisdiction over the probation of this will.'

Because it was possible that the executor of the estate would be slothful, and not obtain a final order distributing the trust property for 16 or more years, the remainder beneficiaries would not be ascertained within 21 years as required by the Rule. Note, they don't get 21 years after some life in being because the vesting event is not dependent on a person's life or death. The remainder interest in the trust was therefore determined to be void, and the intestate heirs of the testator took the property. When the trust beneficiaries sued the attorney for malpractice in drafting the trust in violation of the Rule, the California Supreme Court excused the lawyer on the argument that the Rule Against Perpetuities and the Rule Against Restraints on Alienation

> *have long perplexed the courts and the bar. Professor Gray, a leading authority in the field, stated: 'There is something in the subject which seems to facilitate error. Perhaps it is because the mode of reasoning is unlike that with which lawyers are most familiar. * * * A long list might be formed of the demonstrable blunders with regard to its questions made by eminent men, blunders which they themselves have been sometimes the first to acknowledge; and there are few lawyers of any practice in drawing wills and settlements who have not at some time either fallen into the net which the Rule spreads for the unwary, or at least shuddered to think how narrowly they have escaped it.' Gray,* The Rule Against Perpetuities *(4th ed. 1942) p. xi; see also Leach,* Perpetuities Legislation *(1954) 67 Harv.L.Rev. 1349 (describing the rule as a 'technicality-ridden legal nightmare' and a 'dangerous instrumentality in the hands of most members of the bar'). Of the California law on perpetuities and restraints it has been said that few, if any, areas of the law have been fraught with more confusion or concealed more traps for the unwary draftsman; that members of the bar, probate courts, and title insurance companies make errors in these matters; that the code provisions adopted in 1872 created a situation worse than if the matter had been left to the common law, and that the legislation adopted in 1951 (under which the will involved here was drawn), despite the best of intentions, added further complexities.*

> *In view of the state of the law relating to perpetuities and restraints on alienation and the nature of the error, if any, assertedly made by defendant in preparing the instrument, it would not be proper to hold that defendant failed to use such skill, prudence, and diligence as lawyers of ordinary skill and capacity commonly exercise.*

Lucas v. Hamm was soundly criticized by scholars who felt that, of all perpetuities errors, this one was pretty obvious and should not have been missed. Nonetheless, the mythology of the Rule as a trap for the unwary and a technicality-ridden legal nightmare remains quite alive.

The other situation where perpetuities questions often arise in the context of events not limited to a person's life or death, is the option to purchase, the right of first refusal, or other contractual rights that can result in the forfeiture or forced sale of land. In this class of cases the applicability of the Rule to these contract rights is generally applied more flexibly (unlike the applicability of the Rule to executory interests and contingent remainders, which is mandatory). Thus, options to purchase that are not limited to 21 years *may* be voided if they restrain alienation of property. However, options to purchase in leases, or options that mandate payment of fair market value, may be upheld, even if they persist for more than 21 years, if validating them furthers the interests of the Rule. Because the Rule is a tool to remove the dead hand and promote alienability and marketability of land by terminating stale future interests that could cut short current possession, the Rule is not inexorably applied to contractual rights that do not hamper land's marketability.

Second RAP Trap

The second perpetuities trap concerns consecutive interests in open classes. Certainly a future interest in a living person is fine so long as it is not subject to an indefinite contingency, and a future interest in an unascertained class is fine *if* the class will be closed and the interest fully vested in members ascertained during the lifetime of a living person. Consider these examples:

> *O conveys Blackacre to A for life, remainder B's issue.*

> *O conveys Blackacre to A for life, remainder to A's children for life, remainder to A's grandchildren.*

Do you see why the remainder interest in the first example is valid and the remainder in the second is not? In the first example, the open class of B's issue (open because B is still alive) will close at the death of A under the Rule of Convenience, even though B might have issue after A's death. *Issue* is a multi-generation class (a Type 2 Class) that potentially never closes (so long as B's issue don't die out altogether). Thus, it must be closed at some point, and that point is the time of distribution, which in the first example is at A's death. Assuming A is a life in being at the creation of the interest, the class of B's issue will close at A's death and the interest will therefore be valid.

But the second example has what I call an open class following upon an open class. Assuming A is alive at the creation of the interest, A's life estate is fine because it is the present estate. The future interest in the class of A's children is also fine because the class will close physiologically at A's death and we will know who A's children are at that time. But A could have a child after the interest was created who was not a life in being. The open class of grandchildren, therefore, will not close until the death of the last of A's children, and if that last child happens to be one born after the interest was created, the class of grandchildren is not certain to close within a life in being.

There also is no guarantee that the class of grandchildren will close within 21 years of all lives in being. This is where the Rule gets a bit tricky. Imagine that A has 2 children (B & C) alive when the interest was created. During A's life, however, A has another child, D, who was not alive when the interest was created. At A's death, B, C, & D will take their joint life estates, and presumably have children. But then B and C die young, leaving their own children who were not yet alive at the creation of the interest, and D who then lives for 40 more years and has children during that time. When D finally dies and the class of grandchildren closes, that event is not certain to have occurred less than 21 years after the deaths of B and C. Because the measuring life for the grandchildren's interest *might be* a child of A who was not a life in being at the creation, the interest in the grandchildren fails. And if you are worried that A might have a child at 80 (the fertile octogenarian), remember that adopted children count as children for such purposes.

Now look back at the second example above. If A were not alive, then the class of A's children would be closed when the interest is created, and therefore A's children would all be lives in being for purposes of validating the interest in the grandchildren. But because A is still alive, even if she is 95 and incapacitated, the Rule operates on certainties. It's possible, though extremely unlikely, that A might regain her mental faculties and adopt a child before she dies, who might be a person who was not alive when the interest was created. And that child might live for more than 21 years after the death of all the other children and grandchildren, and then she might adopt a child.

Class gifts can generate perpetuities traps in two different ways. First, the class might be open to new members indefinitely (Type 2 classes), which means that the class opens when the interest is created but will not close until the property becomes possessory. The ability to take in after-born members, or for members of the class to come into being because of after-born persons or events, means that such an interest won't vest until the time of possession. This is the ever-expanding class. The other trap involves the decreasing class. Although a class, like grandchildren, might be closed physiologically, if the future interests are to be distributed only to surviving grandchildren, or grandchildren who reach age 30, or grandchildren who stop smoking, the class membership may decrease. Thus, the contingency on the class members' interest opens the class to perpetuities problems.

Third RAP Trap

The third perpetuities trap involves gifts of future interests to unascertained and unnamed persons, usually by reference to their status—the proverbial unborn widow problem. Consider the following example:

> *O conveys Blackacre to A for life, then to A's surviving spouse for life, then to A's surviving grandchildren.*

Again, A's life estate is fine because it is vested, and A's surviving spouse's life estate is fine because we will know who A's surviving spouse is at A's death. But we won't know who A's *surviving* grandchildren are until the death of the spouse. Because we don't know who the surviving spouse might be (he or she is unnamed) it is possible that the spouse might not have been born when the interest was created, in which case the open class of grandchildren might not be completely ascertainable until the death of the spouse, which may be more than 21 years after the deaths of all other lives in being. Note that even if the gift were to A's surviving children, the interest would fail. Of course, A is the measuring life to the class of A's children, but although we might know the identity of all of A's children at A's death (the maximum members of the class), we won't know the actual takers of the remainder interest at A's death because some of A's children might predecease the spouse, thus decreasing the class. In other words, the survivorship requirement means that their interest is contingent until the time for possession.

> ### Fourth Side Note
>
> Here is where the difficult interpretation between vested remainders subject to divestment and contingent remainders on conditional events matters. If we interpret the interests in A's children as remainders contingent on surviving the spouse, their interests are void under the Rule. However, if we interpret them to be vested subject to divestment if they fail to survive the spouse, then their remainders are not subject to the Rule at all. Hence the constructional preference in favor of early vesting—it helps avoid perpetuities violations!
>
> Of course we avoid the RAP trap but in doing so may end up creating problems for the executory interest that follows the remainders. For what would happen if A had no surviving grandchildren? In that case, the estate would revert back to O. By deeming the remainders to be vested, we wait and see if there actually are takers before we risk terminating the remainder and sending the estate back to O. If we deem the remainders to be contingent immediately, the remainder fails, and a possibility of reverter is immediately created in O.

Fourth RAP Trap

The fourth perpetuities trap involves age requirements, especially if those requirements extend beyond 21 years. Consider this conveyance:

> *O conveys Blackacre to A for life, remainder to A's children who reach age 30.*

Because a child of A might be born after the creation of the interest, and might reach age 30 more than 21 years after the death of A (the measuring life), the remainder interest in the children is void. The one instance when courts are willing to apply *cy pres* doctrines to reform a will or trust provision seems to be when an age requirement can be decreased to 21 to avoid invalidity under the Rule. Despite the fact that most of us would probably not think a 21-year old is the ideal candidate to inherit a pot of money, and we would prefer to postpone the inheritance to age 30 or 40, the Rule originated at a time when 21 was the age of majority and few parents lived to see their children come of age. Thus, children at age 21 were almost middle-aged by comparison with today's youth.

It is not always true that an age requirement above 21 will violate the Rule, but if you see an age in excess of 21 you should pay special attention to the terms used to define the future interest. So long as the person who has to reach a particular age was a life in being, there are no problems. But when payment is to a class of people at a particular age, and membership of the class is still open, you will almost always find yourselves in a perpetuities trap.

Now that you know what the elements are, and where the traps lie, consider the following cases that all found a Rule violation. Can you identify the problem and suggest a way to fix it?

Walker v. Bogle

260 S.E.2d 338 (Ga. 1979)

Jeanette C. D. Bogle died testate in 1978, survived by two sons who have no children. Her will provided that her residuary estate be placed in trust and divided into Fund A and Fund B one fund for each son. The provisions for each fund are identical. The son is to receive the income for life.

At his death, the fund is to be divided into shares per stirpes for the son's then living lineal descendants. The descendants are entitled immediately to receive the income from their respective shares and to receive the principal when they reach age 30. The trustee has discretionary power to invade the principal for the beneficiary's support. If a trust beneficiary dies after the trust fund is divided into shares but before reaching age 30, his share is to be distributed to his lineal descendants, if any, and if none, the share is to be added to the shares of the other beneficiaries. If a son dies leaving no lineal descendants, the assets of his trust fund are to be added to the other son's fund and administered under its provisions. If no trust beneficiaries exist for both Funds A and B, the trust property is to be divided equally between the Nature Conservancy and Mount Holyoke College.

Dickerson v. Union Nat'l Bank of Little Rock

595 S.W.2d 677 (Ark. 1980)

Nina Martin Dickerson died on June 21, 1967, leaving a holographic will. *The testatrix named the appellee bank as executor and directed that at the close of the administration proceedings the bank transfer to itself as trustee all the assets of the estate. The terms of the trust [provided] as follows:*

> *VIII. This Trust shall continue until the death of both my sons and my son Martin's widow and until the youngest child of either son has reached the age of twenty-five years, then at that time, the Trust shall terminate and the Union National Bank Trustee shall distribute and pay over the entire balance of the Trust Fund in their hands to the bodily heirs of my son, Cecil H. Dickerson, and the bodily heirs of my son, William Martin Dickerson, in the same manner and in the same proportions as provided for by the general inheritance laws of Arkansas.*

Nelson v. Kring

592 P.2d 438 (Kan. 1979)

George M. Hoffman's wife predeceased him and he had no children. By will and codicil he set up the following testamentary trust:

> *SECOND: I will and direct that the sum of Sixty Thousand Dollars ($60,000.00) shall be set apart by my executor hereinafter named to be paid by him to and held in trust by a reliable and responsible Trust Company, the choice of which shall be subject to the approval of the Probate Court of Rice county, Kansas which approval, if questioned, shall be subject to final approval of the District Court of Rice county, Kansas. Said Trust Company shall keep and hold said fund in trust for the following purposes and subject to the following conditions the net income or interest from said fund shall be paid by said Trust Company at least once each year to the Board of Directors and Trustees of The George M. Hoffman Memorial Hospital of Little River, Kansas to be used by them for the benefit of and the maintenance of said The George M. Hoffman Memorial Hospital. Should said Hospital fail to be operated as a hospital for any reason whatever for one year then said entire fund, with any accumulated interest or income from the same shall go to and become the absolute property of my friend George Green of Little River, Kansas or if he be dead then to his legal heirs. . . . At no time and under no circumstances shall said Hospital or any of its Board or*

Trustees or other person representing it, receive the principal of said sum. This fund and gift, . . . being subject to the provisions of the NINTH provision or paragraph of my will. . . .

Kennewick Public Hospital Dist. v. Hawe

214 P.3d 163 (Wash.App. 2009)

Albert Luth executed a last will and testament in 1957. He devised his Benton County real property to the Kennewick Public Hospital District:

> *I now give, devise and bequeath all of my right, title and interest in and to any real property owned by me at the time of my death within the County of Benton, State of Washington, to the Kennewick Public Hospital District, a municipal corporation, to keep and maintain the same, to collect the rents, issues and profits therefrom and to expend the income therefrom in the up-keep, maintenance and improvement of the hospital building and grounds as in the judgment of the duly elected commissioners of said hospital district seems best. I now direct that the real property shall not be sold but shall be retained as an investment. This devise is in perpetuity, and the property shall at no time be transferred, incumbered [sic] or otherwise alienated from the purposes herein expressed and intended, and if the same or any part thereof, shall at any time be conveyed, transferred or incumbered [sic], by deed, mortgage or otherwise, then in such case I do devise all of the above mentioned real estate to the County of Benton, and in default thereof, to the State of Washington.*

Security Trust Co. v. Cooling

76 A.2d 1 (Del.Ch. 1950)

By the Ninth Item, the testator [Severson Cooling] bequeathed and devised the residue of his estate, both real and personal, to Security Trust Company, the plaintiff, in trust, however, to pay 'one-half of the net income derived therefrom' to each of his two sons, Samuel Cooling and Severson B. Cooling, Jr., during their respective lives. The same item further provided:

> ** * * and from and after the death of either and both of my said sons, leaving issue living, in further trust to pay over one-half of said net income, in equal shares, to the issue of each of my sons so dying, for and during their respective lives; and upon and after the death of such issue, respectively, to pay over an equal share of the one-half of said principal then remaining in the hands of my said Trustee, and one-half of the then accumulated income thereon, to the issue of any child or children of my respective sons, in equal shares, freed and discharged from any trusts. If any such issue of any child or children of my respective sons should die without leaving issue living, then to pay over his, her or their respective share of said principal, and any interest then accrued thereon, to the issue of the survivor or survivors of them, freed and discharged from any trusts. If either of my said sons should die during the continuance of the trusts herein provided, without leaving issue living, then in further trust to hold said principal and pay said net income to the survivor of my said sons, and his issue, and to pay said net income and distribute said principal to his and their issue, as hereinabove provided.*

Meduna v. Holder

2003 WL 22964270 (Tex.App. 2003)

The grantors of the deed in question were August Meduna, Sr. and Minnie Meduna. The grantees include their three children—Ruth Holder, August Meduna, Jr., and Gary Meduna—and various descendants of these children. The deed was signed on June 17, 1997, but there is no evidence in the record that the deed was ever delivered. The deed was discovered in 1998, after the death of August Sr. On November 6, 2001, Minnie was found to be an incapacitated person, and her daughter Ruth was appointed guardian of her person and her estate.

The original deed purported to divide a single piece of property into three tracts, and retained a life estate in all three tracts for August and Minnie, or the survivor of them. Upon the death of the last of the grantors, the deed conveyed a life estate in Tract I to Ruth, a life estate in Tract II to August Jr., and a life estate in Tract III to Gary. At the end of Ruth's life, Tract I passed in undivided interests to August Jr. and Gary for life, and then to Gary's children for life. At the end of August Jr.'s life, Tract II passed to Gary for life, then to Gary's children for life. Similarly, at Gary's death, Tract III passed to his children for life. At the end of the lives of Gary's children, all three tracts passed "in successive life estates until the perpetuities period expires," at which time all three tracts were to be distributed to Gary's living descendants.

Hagemann v. National Bank & Trust Co.

237 S.E.2d 388 (Va. 1977)

The will of Mildred Hart Woodward, executed January 15, 1971, was admitted to probate on March 16, 1971 and National Bank and Trust Company, the trustee named in the will, qualified as administrator, c. t. a. The testatrix was survived by her children, Anne Mutter Woodward Hagemann, Fletcher D. Woodward, Jr., and Malcolm P. Woodward, her sole heirs at law, all of whom were named as beneficiaries in her will.

Article Eight, the residuary clause of the will, creates two equal trust funds, one for Fletcher and his descendants and the other for Malcolm and his descendants. The clause contains eight paragraphs. Paragraph 1 provides that the son will receive the income so long as he lives and has living children under the age of 25 years and that, upon the son's death, the income shall be paid to his surviving wife and children for their "support, comfort and education"; paragraph 2 authorizes the trustee to invade the corpus for such purposes. Paragraph 3 provides:

> *When the youngest living child of such son of mine has reached age twenty-five years, that trust shall end and the fund shall be divided one-third to such son of mine and two-thirds equally to his then living descendants, per stirpes. Should such son of mine not then be living, the whole of the fund shall go to his then living descendants, per stirpes.*

. . . The provisions of paragraph 8, however, considered in context with those of paragraph 3, are of crucial relevance:

> *8.   Notwithstanding the foregoing, if any portion of my estate is in any contingency capable of being held in trust for a longer period than is permitted by the law of the state of my domicile, or if in any such contingency the vesting of any interest hereunder may occur after the*

expiration of such permissive period, then upon the happening of any such contingency such portion of my estate shall not be held in further trust, but shall rather be paid over absolutely to the person or persons to whom, and in the proportions in which, such portion would ultimately go under the provisions hereof.

Rogers v. Rooth

229 S.E.2d 445 (Ga. 1976)

Floy Rogers died on June 17, 1959 leaving a last will and testament which was probated in solemn form. Item Four of that will . . . reads as follows:

> *Upon the death of my said wife, Cleone B. Rogers, upon her remarriage, or upon her failing to make the premises described in Item Three her home for a continuous period of time exceeding Twelve (12) months, title to said property shall pass to my daughter, Dorothy R. Thompson, for and during her natural life. Upon the death of my said daughter, title to said premises shall pass to my son, Floy S. Rogers, for and during his natural life. Upon the death of my said son, title shall pass to and become the property of the child or children born or to be born unto my said son, for and during their natural life or lives, with remainder over, at the death or deaths of them, to their children, in fee simple. However, should the child or children of my said son, Floy S. Rogers, die without leaving a child or children, or descendents, then title to said property shall pass to the sons of my deceased brother, O. C. Rogers, to-wit: Joe Rogers, Casper Rogers, and Robert Rogers, share and share alike, or their heirs, if they should not be in life.*

PROBLEM

8.31. For each of the cases above, identify the present estates, the future interests, the relevant conditions, and the measuring and validating lives. Then identify what part of the dispositions causes the violation of the common law RAP.

What happens when a future interest is voided as a result of the RAP? The quick answer is that in the absence of a valid future interest, the law simply implies a reversion back to the grantor. Thus, if Blackacre is conveyed "to A for life, then to A's children for life, then to A's grandchildren," and the remainder in A's grandchildren is void under the RAP, then Blackacre reverts back to O after the death of the last of A's children. That is the point at which the last valid interest has terminated. Because reversions are deemed to be vested *ab initio*, the final interest in O is not affected by the Rule. The law will almost always assume a reversion in O in case the relevant future interests are voided by law (under the RAP or under other rules, like the rule against unreasonable restraints on alienation or unreasonable restraints on marriage) or if a grantor establishes certain conditions precedent on the taking of an estate and those conditions fail to occur. But there are two situations in which the answer is not a simple reversion in the grantor.

The first is when additional, otherwise valid interests, are also extinguished under what is called the doctrine of *infectious invalidity*. The second is when, for a variety of legal and policy reasons, the effect of voiding a future interest under the RAP is to entirely extinguish the limitation or condition on the present estate, converting it into a fee simple absolute rather than making it subject to a reversionary interest in the grantor. In this second situation, no reversion is created in O; rather, the present estate holder is allowed to have the limiting condition removed. This is not the place for a lengthy exposition of either of these situations, but a couple of examples should give you some sense of the circumstances in which these results can occur.

In the case of *Connecticut Bank & Trust Co. v. Brody*, 174 Conn. 616, 392 A.2d 445 (Ct. 1978), the doctrine of infectious invalidity was used to terminate not just the final remainder interest, but some valid intervening interests as well. In that case William Skinner, the testator, died in 1922 leaving a will that provided that one-third of his residuary estate would be placed in a trust for the benefit of his children for their lives, then his grandchildren for their lives, and then to pay out the remainder to his great-grandchildren upon the death of his last grandchild. The court held that the gifts to the grandchildren and great-grandchildren were both class gifts; as such they were vested subject to open and therefore subject to the RAP. The remainder to the great-grandchildren clearly violated the Rule and was voided. The court then faced the question of whether it should allow the valid life estates of the grandchildren to run out before terminating the trust, or terminate it immediately upon determining that the final remainder was invalid and the property would pass by intestacy to the testator's grandchildren and great-grandchildren anyway. The court terminated the trust early, explaining:

> *Having concluded that the remainder interest in the great-grandchildren is void under the rule, we must determine whether the life estate in the grandchildren is so inextricably intertwined with the void remainder that it too must fail. Such a determination can only be made by looking to the intent of the testator to ascertain the function of the life estate in the general testamentary scheme.*
>
> *Although, in general, an effort will be made to preserve a life estate even when it is followed by a void remainder; this can be accomplished only when the testator's primary intention "is not frustrated by cutting out the bad part." "If the leading and primary object was to accumulate a fund for illegal distribution; or if the trusts were strictly subservient or auxiliary to such a distribution so as to be themselves tainted with the illegality; or if they are so connected therewith that they cannot be separated and carried into effect without involving consequences substantially and materially different from what the testator intended, then they, too, must fall with the illegal distribution."[32]*
>
> *In the case before us, the provision for the benefit of the grandchildren appears to serve no function other than to preserve a portion of the testator's estate intact for ultimate distribution to his great-grandchildren. There is no indication that a primary purpose of the life estate in the grandchildren was to see that they were comfortably provided for during their lifetimes, as might be inferred were there a*

---

[32]   Citations omitted.

provision for invasion of the corpus of the trust. Nor is there evidence that an underlying purpose was to preclude the possibility that the spouse of a grandchild might gain control of a portion of the testator's estate. Thus, the only apparent purpose of the life estates to the grandchildren was to postpone the distribution to the great-grandchildren. Because we have found that the provision for postponed distribution to the great-grandchildren violates the rule against perpetuities, the provision for the grandchildren, which is clearly subservient or auxiliary to the disposition of the remainder, must fail as well.

As the court explained in *Brody*, if the only reason for interposing numerous life estates is to merely postpone the final payout to the last possible moment, and the remainder is void under the RAP, there is no reason to uphold the intervening life estates. If, on the other hand, the testator clearly wanted to benefit each of the life tenants, and indicated a personal interest in each one having income for life, then a valid reason would exist for keeping the trust intact through the end of the last valid life estate. Giving the trustee discretion to invade the trust corpus to benefit the grandchildren, or indicating a desire that the grandchildren use the property for a particular purpose would both indicate an intent on the part of the testator that the trust remain active as long as possible. But the mere rote and mandatory nature of the trust implied that the only purpose was to postpone the final payout. Once that became illegal, there was no reason to drag out the trust any longer. This concept should resonate again when we take up voluntary termination of trusts in Chapter 10.

The second instance in which the straightforward rule of replacing the void future interest with a simple reversion in the grantor occurred in the case of *Kennewick Public Hospital Dist. v. Hawe,* discussed above. In that case the testator had conveyed real estate to the Hospital District for use as a hospital, and if not so used then it was to pass to the County or to the State of Washington. When the executory interest was struck under the RAP, the court had a choice of replacing it with a possibility of reverter in the testator (his estate) or simply removing the limitation. The court chose the latter, explaining:

We consider first and foremost the testator's intent in construing Mr. Luth's will, and we look to the language of the will as the primary evidence of that intent. There is no language here indicating an intent to create a reverter. First, the will's language indicates the Mr. Luth intended to leave the land to the Hospital "in perpetuity." And if the Hospital "at any time . . . conveyed, transferred or incumbered [sic]" the property, the language clearly intends that the property go to the County or, in the alternative, to the State. That is not possible. Second, specific words creating the potential for defeasance are important. Unlike the conveyance addressed in Brandt[33] *there is no reverter language here. The* Brandt *conveyance used the words "reverts back." To the contrary, Mr. Luth's will provides that the property escheat to the County or the State. The language here then creates a fee simple subject to executory limitation when it created a future interest in the County and the State, not a fee simple determinable. And when the executory limitation was invalidated, the Hospital is left with fee simple absolute.*

---

[33] Wash. State Grange v. Brandt, 136 Wash.App. 138, 148 P.3d 1069 (2006).

The court also held that because the limitation posed an unreasonable restraint on alienation, the limitation was to be voided, leaving the Hospital with fee simple absolute, and not a fee simple determinable.

Of course, in *Evans v. Abney* there was no reversionary language that would indicate an intent by the testator that the park property revert if it could no longer be used in a segregated manner. Like the unreasonable restraint on alienation in *Hawes*, the illegal racial covenant in *Evans v. Abney* could have been stricken, leaving the City of Macon with fee simple absolute. The Georgia court did not take that approach. Can you think of a legal or policy reason why? The moral of both of these cases, however, is that it's not at all clear what the outcome will be if a future interest is voided under the RAP. That means that, unless the parties can agree, litigation is likely to be the result. Consequently, as the lawyers unsuccessfully tried to do in *Hagemann v. National Bank & Trust Co.*, a well placed savings clause can save the day. A simple provision like the following could have avoided the litigation in all of these cases:

> *Item XIV(a) Having in mind the rule against perpetuities, I direct that (notwithstanding anything contained to the contrary in this last will and testament) each trust created under this will (except such trusts as have heretofore vested in compliance with such rule or law) shall end, unless sooner terminated under other provisions of this will, twenty-one (21) years after the death of the last survivor of such of the beneficiaries hereunder as are living at the time of my death; and thereupon that the property held in trust shall be distributed free of all trust to the persons then entitled to receive the income and/or principal therefrom, in the proportion in which they are then entitled to receive such income.*[34]

Another approach would be to simply provide that any interest given under a will or trust that fails for any reason will pass to a specified beneficiary. This would ensure that if a future interest is voided under the RAP, the property would then pass to the designated beneficiary and not back to the testator or his estate. Savings clauses like this limit the standing of people who can challenge a testamentary provision because if only the alternative beneficiary can challenge a future interest, then hopefully conflicts of interest can be minimized.

C. MODERN MODIFICATIONS TO THE RULE AGAINST PERPETUITIES

As some of your colleagues may tell you, the RAP is on its way out, modern courts don't rely on unborn widows or fertile octogenarians, and the states have all adopted statutory rules that make the headaches go away. Don't be fooled! A few states have abolished the Rule, and some have extended its time period to a ridiculously high number (like 360 or 1000 years), but settlors are not going to benefit for long when Congress amends the GST tax to hit all property in trust every 25 or 30 years, or does as Henry VIII did when his wealthy landowners went too far in avoiding their feudal obligations. Reimplementing the Rule is going to be very difficult, if not impossible. So instead, I predict these states are going to enact some fancy legislation (along the lines of the graduated super-augmented estate for elective shares) to regain control over perpetual trusts and their nearly

---

[34] Last Will and Testament of Elvis A. Presley.

infinite future interests to improve alienability. Although the RAP technically only deals with indefinite vesting problems, many states still could impose limits on trust duration that would rein in some of the tax avoidance and inalienability of perpetuitual trusts.

The Rule is your friend. The Rule cuts off those pesky future interests that hamper alienation and marketability of property. Despite claims that trust property is fully alienable and marketable, it is simply not true. Trust property is subject to strict limitations under fiduciary investment standards, and the existence of generations of unborn beneficiaries is likely going to lead to extra litigation and trust administration fees that will soon have beneficiaries doing everything they can to get these perpetual trusts invalidated. And although their best weapon, the Rule, may be gone, something will likely replace it, especially when the Internal Revenue Code and the Bankruptcy Code are amended to abolish the tax and creditor protection benefits of dynasty trusts (discussed later in this Chapter).

But because of the race to attract big trust business, it is important that you know what the modern modifications to the Rule are and how they operate. There are four different modifications, though some states have adopted more than one.

1. *CY PRES*

Cy Pres (pronounced "see pray") is an equitable reformation doctrine that allows for the reformation of trust provisions when, because of circumstances not anticipated by the settlor, the trust might fail if the strict trust provisions are followed. It is usually used in the context of charitable trusts when the particular purpose of the trust has become impossible, illegal, or impracticable, but the settlor's general charitable intent would justify reforming the trust to achieve a similar charitable goal. Thus, a charitable trust to benefit a local college may have to be reformed if the college is taken over by the state university system, or a trust to provide a segregated public park may be reformed to allow for inclusion of all races when segregation is declared illegal.[35]

In the context of private trusts, the UTC allows a court to "modify the administrative or dispositive terms of a trust or terminate the trust if, because of circumstances not anticipated by the settlor, modification or termination will further the purposes of the trust." Since most settlors don't anticipate that they are drafting trust or will provisions that violate the RAP, courts have applied *cy pres* to modify the provisions to save them from invalidation.

In the last 25 years, many states have adopted some form of legislation dealing with the Rule, and many have included limited provisions for reformation. As a result of adopting this legislation, courts are now unlikely to apply general *cy pres* doctrines if the state has provided certain narrow grounds on which reformation is applicable. For example, the Uniform Statutory Rule Against Perpetuities (USRAP) allows for reformation as follows:

---

[35] Of course, reformation was not done in *Evans v. Abney* because the court concluded that the testator lacked a general charitable intent that could be separated from his specific charitable intent.

USRAP § 3. Reformation

Upon the petition of an interested person, a court shall reform a disposition in the manner that most closely approximates the transferor's manifested plan of distribution and is within the 90 years allowed by Section 1(a)(2), 1(b)(2), or 1(c)(2) if:

(1) a nonvested property interest or a power of appointment becomes invalid under Section 1 (statutory rule against perpetuities);

(2) a class gift is not but might become invalid under Section 1 (statutory rule against perpetuities) and the time has arrived when the share of any class member is to take effect in possession or enjoyment; or

(3) a nonvested property interest that is not validated by Section 1(a)(1) can vest but not within 90 years after its creation.

As with any such reformation doctrine, you don't want to rely on it. Learn the Rule well and you should not be in court asking for *cy pres*.

2. WAIT AND SEE

Many states have adopted a Wait and See approach by judicial construction. Wait and See occurred as a result of litigation of cases in which the crazy, unlikely event did not occur and, but for the Rule's strict requirement of certainty, the future interests would in fact have vested within lives in being. In some instances, the parties may not have realized there was a Rule violation, and the trustee managed the property during the life tenant's life, only to be informed some years later that the remainder interests violated the Rule. At that later date, however, the parties could determine that the unlikely event had not occurred and the future interests had vested in people who were in fact alive at the creation of the interest. In such a circumstance, it seemed harsh to invalidate the future interests because of a possible event that in fact did not occur. Consequently, courts used their equitable powers to not invalidate the interests by adopting *wait and see*, thus furthering the testator's intent, and allowing the trust interests to stand.

Once a court admitted the evidence of later events, it seemed unreasonable to invalidate future interests if the RAP violation were caught early, but not if the RAP violation was not discovered until after it could be shown that the interests did in fact vest. If future evidence could be used to save future interests in litigation where we already knew that the unlikely event did not occur, then it was a small step for courts to simply dismiss litigation brought right away until facts about those future events could be known. Thus, wait and see became an official doctrine that would prohibit declarations of invalidity at the start, when future events were not known.

But once wait and see was adopted, courts had two choices about how long they would be willing to wait: 1) they could wait until the end of the entire perpetuities period (21 years after the deaths of all relevant lives in being), or 2) they could wait only until the end of the first life tenancy, which would usually provide an answer to whether a surviving spouse was an unborn widow or whether an 80-year-old life tenant really did adopt a child. In states that adopted the 2nd approach, an interest might still violate the Rule even if future facts and events were unknown. The benefit of resolving property interests and settling expectations as soon as possible supports the adoption of the earlier cut off, but waiting the full perpetuities period promotes the likely intent of grantors who would rather see their testamentary plans succeed, even if interests are left in limbo for a longer period of time, rather than fail and revert.

3. THE UNIFORM STATUTORY RULE AGAINST PERPETUITIES (USRAP)

The USRAP was promulgated in 1986 and has been adopted in 29 states and the District of Columbia and the Virgin Islands. The USRAP still relies on the common law rule of lives in being plus 21 years (thus you still need to understand the basic Rule). But it provides for both reformation if a future interest violates the Rule (as noted above), and it also provides a 90 year wait and see period to determine if the unlikely events that would prohibit vesting actually occur.

The slightly amended USRAP provides as follows:

SECTION 1. STATUTORY RULE AGAINST PERPETUITIES.

(a) [Validity of Nonvested Property Interest.] A nonvested property interest is invalid unless:

(1) when the interest is created, it is certain to vest or terminate no later than 21 years after the death of an individual then alive; or

(2) the interest either vests or terminates within 90 years after its creation.

(b) [Validity of General Power of Appointment Subject to a Condition Precedent.] A general power of appointment not presently exercisable because of a condition precedent is invalid unless:

(1) when the power is created, the condition precedent is certain to be satisfied or becomes impossible to satisfy no later than 21 years after the death of an individual then alive; or

(2) the condition precedent either is satisfied or becomes impossible to satisfy within 90 years after its creation.

(c) [Validity of Nongeneral or Testamentary Power of Appointment.] A nongeneral power of appointment or a general testamentary power of appointment is invalid unless:

(1) when the power is created, it is certain to be irrevocably exercised or otherwise to terminate no later than 21 years after the death of an individual then alive; or

(2) the power is irrevocably exercised or otherwise terminates within 90 years after its creation.

(d) [Possibility of Post-death Child Disregarded.] In determining whether a nonvested property interest or a power of appointment is valid under subsection (a)(1), (b)(1), or (c)(1), the possibility that a child will be born to an individual after the individual's death is disregarded.

(e) [Effect of Certain "Later-of" Type Language.] If, in measuring a period from the creation of a trust or other property arrangement, language in a governing instrument (i) seeks to disallow the vesting or termination of any interest or trust beyond, (ii) seeks to postpone the vesting or termination of any interest or trust until, or (iii) seeks to operate in effect in any similar fashion upon, the later of (A) the expiration of a period of time not exceeding 21 years after the death of the survivor of specified lives in being at the creation of the trust or other property arrangement or (B) the expiration of a period of time that exceeds or might exceed 21 years after the death of the survivor of lives in being at the creation of the trust or other property arrangement, that language is inoperative to the extent it produces a period of time that exceeds 21 years after the death of the survivor of the specified lives.

Note how the USRAP covers nonvested future interests, general powers of appointment, non-general (special) powers, and the possibility of a post-death child. Extensive commentary covers unborn widows, bottomless gravel pits, and the other perpetuities traps.

4. EXTENDED OR ABOLISHED PERPETUITIES PERIODS FOR TRUSTS

A handful of states have extended the time period from 90 years to 360 years for interests in trusts (Florida),1000 years (Colorado; Utah; and Alaska for powers, an unlimited period for other interests), or set no time limit at all for certain trust interests only (Illinois, Maine, Maryland; Michigan; Missouri; Ohio; Virginia; and Washington). Nebraska and New Hampshire appear to allow a trust settlor to opt out of the Rule. And Delaware, Idaho, New Jersey, Pennsylvania, Rhode Island, and South Dakota have abolished the Rule altogether.[36]

It is tempting to feel relief if you are practicing in a state that has abolished the Rule because you won't be liable in malpractice for drafting a deed, will, or trust instrument that unknowingly violates the RAP. However, imagine the types of property and the public policies that governed legal decisions about property rights 360 years ago, in 1650. Consider what property rights will look like, and what public policies will prevail 360 years from now, in 2370. To allow dead hand control for 100 years (the rough equivalent of a generation plus 21 years) seems like a long time. It took about 300 years for the vast majority of land in England to be held in a medieval use, which tied it up and prevented the collection of estate taxes, when Henry VIII cut through the logjam with the Statute of Uses in 1536. Eventually, when too much wealth is no longer available for private investment and speculation, it is likely that legal changes will be made to break the iron grip of the dead hand.

5. RAP AS APPLIED TO POWERS

The RAP also applies to Powers of Appointment, just as it does to future interests in trusts for the same reason: the exercise of a power causes ownership of property to shift from one person to another. But different powers are treated differently under the Rule.

- A presently exercisable general power of appointment is valid if the power is *certain to become exercisable* during the perpetuities period.
- A special or testamentary general power of appointment is valid only if the power *must be exercised*, if at all, within the perpetuities period.[37]

---

[36] For details on the RAP in each state, see Jeffrey Schoenblum, *2012 Multistate Guide to Estate Planning*, Table 9.

[37] The power cannot remain exercisable beyond the period of the RAP.

To see the differences, let's look at a few examples.

> *O conveys Blackacre in trust for the benefit of A for life, then to A's children for life, and then to whoever A's last surviving child appoints the property to in her will.*

A's last surviving child has a general testamentary power of appointment. Because A is still alive, A's last surviving child might not be a life in being. That means the measuring life for the life estate of A's children is A. It is possible that A's last surviving child will live more than 21 years after A's death and have not been a life in being. That means the power won't be exercised until that last child's death which, according to the second rule above, violates the Rule. What about this one?

> *O conveys Blackacre in trust for the benefit of A for life, then to A's children for life, and then to whoever A's last surviving child appoints the property to at any time after she reaches age 20 years and 364 days.*

Now, the general power that is created will be *exercisable* within the perpetuities period because A's last surviving child will be able to exercise the power a day before she turns 21, which will be within 21 years of A's death. A is a life in being, and so the power will be exercisable within the perpetuities period. And because A's last surviving child may simply appoint the property immediately to herself, the inalienability problem is avoided. What about this one?

> *O conveys Blackacre in trust for the benefit of A for life, then to A's children for life, and then to whichever of O's descendants A's last surviving child appoints the property to at any time after she reaches age 21.*

This power is invalid because special powers must be exercised within the perpetuities period, and because A's last surviving child might not make the actual appointment until 21 years after the death of all lives in being. Therefore, the certainty of exercise or failure is not guaranteed. Moreover, the relation back doctrine will treat the actual exercise of a special power or a general testamentary power as though it occurred at the time the power was created. Thus, if a recipient of a special power appoints the property in further trust, the trust will be evaluated as though it was established at the time the donor created the special power, not at the time the power was exercised.

Now that you have mastered many of the issues involved with the RAP, here are a few problems to test your new skills.

PROBLEMS

8.32. Testator, who had 3 children, devised "all the rest, residue and remainder of my estate, both real and personal, of every nature, and wherever situate to my grandchildren, to be held in trust by my son, A, and my daughter-in-law, B, and used for the educational benefit of all of my grandchildren." Do any of the interests in this trust violate the RAP, why or why not and, if so, how should it be rewritten?

8.33. O devises his estate to his wife, A, for life, remainder to whoever A shall by deed or will appoint. In her will, A appoints the property in trust to B for life, remainder to the children of B. B was not alive at the testator's death, but was alive at A's death. Does A's appointment violate the RAP, why or why not, and how is the bequest rewritten if it does?

8.34. In his will, O devises his entire estate to his wife A for life, with a special testamentary power of appointment to appoint the principal of the estate to any "of my then living issue." At O's death, he had 3 children, B,C, & D. In her will, A appointed the property "in a discretionary trust to D, as trustee for the life of D, with the power to invade principal for the benefit of D or any of her children." At her death, D gave all the remaining undisbursed principal to M, her grandchild, who was not alive at O's death. What parts of this distribution, if any, violate the RAP and why? And if so, how is it rewritten to purge the offending devise?

D. GENERATION SKIPPING AND DYNASTY TRUSTS

Most people, after providing for themselves and their spouses, want to ensure that their children are properly cared for and are quite content leaving their estates to their children. But the vast majority of people will die at a relatively late age, leaving children who are most likely in their 40s or 50s, and grandchildren who are either in their twenties, or are still minors. If one's children are financially secure, why should parents give property to them, when they are in a high income tax bracket or might face significant debts? Moreover, parents certainly don't want to leave a large bequest directly to their children just in time for their child to get a divorce and the estranged spouse to take half. On the other hand, grandparents probably don't want to give property directly to their grandchildren either, especially if the grandchildren are young and irresponsible or might require a guardianship. This dilemma has plagued people for centuries: the children don't exactly need the assets and the grandchildren are too young for it. So what is the answer: a generation skipping trust with powers to invade for the children.

Back before 1976, Congress taxed large estates only when a significant amount of wealth was passed by *inter vivos* gift or at death (gift and estate taxes respectively). And any holder of wealth who died in possession of that property would be subject to these taxes. But just because a grandparent was subject to the tax didn't mean the children AND the grandchildren should all have to pay the tax as the property passed from grandparent to child to grandchild. By passing the property directly to one's grandchildren, the testator could avoid having the property be taxed in her child's estate. And so the idea came about of skipping a generation, to avoid the property being taxed in the estates of the skipped generation.

But Congress remedied that with the passage of the Generation Skipping Transfer Tax (GST—see discussion *infra* at Chapter 9). Yet even if the tax advantages have been closed, the generation skipping concept remains important in estate planning, especially if the skipped generation might have its own financial problems, like divorce or possible bankruptcy.

The GS Trust is based on the idea that we want to give the children of the settlor the maximum use and control over the trust without giving them so much control that the property will be deemed part of their estates at their death, thus requiring administration and possible estate taxes. Thus, the typical GS trust gives the children (1st generation beneficiaries) the income for life on the corpus, a right to invade for health, education, maintenance and support (HEMS), it gives an independent trustee the discretion to invade the corpus for other reasons, and it gives the beneficiary a special power of appointment to appoint the trust property, at any time, for the benefit of the beneficiary's lineal descendants. Probably, it should also have a spendthrift provision. The key is to make the trust property available to beneficiaries if needed, but not accessible to the claims of an elective share, creditors, or make the estate of the beneficiary liable to taxes. The point is for the beneficiary to be able to reach the property if he or she needs it or wants to spend it, but not give it to the beneficiary outright if it is simply going to be retained and then passed on at the beneficiary's death. This should remind you of the Credit Shelter Trust that was used for spouses. The same basic motivation guides the GS Trust—give it to the kids without having the property count in the kids' estates.

In states that still have the Rule Against Perpetuities (RAP) in fairly traditional form, private trusts can only exist for 2 to 3 generations. They are usually established by elderly settlors to provide for their spouse for life, their children for life, maybe their grandchildren for life, and with a final termination and distribution of the trust corpus to great-grandchildren (though probably not all of them because of class closing and RAP issues). Usually distribution will be to surviving grandchildren and great-grandchildren alive at the death of the last child or grandchild who was alive at the settlor's death.

The point, however, is that most private trusts have been established to take care of children and grandchildren, with great-grandchildren taking a share only if their parent predeceased the time for distribution. Recall the trust in *Estate of Houston*. But as my co-author, Professor Tritt, likes to remind me, there is never a good time to terminate a trust. In the *Houston* case, the trust corpus was paid out to a number of minor beneficiaries who ultimately needed guardians for the property. And in the case of children and grandchildren who predeceased the time for distribution, their estates had to be opened and estate taxes had to be paid. Paying out to deceased beneficiaries is expensive and inefficient. If the remainder beneficiaries are elderly, they may have little need for the property and it will merely be taxed again in their estates, or it may disqualify them from government benefits. If the remainder beneficiaries are middle-aged high income earners, they don't need the property. And if the remainder beneficiaries are young and impulsive, they might squander it. No settlor wants his property to be used to pay off a spouse during a divorce nor to pay a tort judgment assessed against a beneficiary. But with limits on the duration of private trusts, property will eventually pass out of trust to remainder beneficiaries in fee simple absolute and they can do with it as they choose, completely free of the dead hand of the settlor.

So if there is no good time to terminate a trust, one solution is to not use a trust. A testator can simply bequeath his property to his children and grandchildren directly and know that his beneficiaries can have full and complete control over the property immediately. Or, a settlor can structure the trust to allow for further appointments of the property into trust, thus perpetuating the trust benefits, through the use of powers of appointment. But to do that, the property ultimately has to come out of trust and be available to the new person who is going to return the property to a trust form, and if that person has creditors or is untrustworthy, the same problems can arise.

But knowing that the trust must end within 90 years or so, most trust settlors will need to create complex future interests in multiple generations, like in *Estate of Houston*, and must consider both the survivorship problems and the class gift problems discussed above. And although a power to reappoint the property into further trust may avoid payouts to minor children or to spendthrift beneficiaries, it will not avoid potential tax liabilities. For that, however, see Chapter 9.

In those states that have abolished or significantly lengthened the RAP, however, dynasty trusts have become quite attractive.[38] And the concept is quite simple. By placing a large amount of money into a trust, even if doing so requires paying estate taxes when it is placed in the trust, further estate taxes can be avoided by structuring the trust to pay income for life to successive generations of beneficiaries, with a final distribution of the principal to a charity only upon the death of all relevant beneficiaries. Thus, a settlor may establish an irrevocable trust to pay the income for life to the settlor, his spouse, his children, his grandchildren, his great-grandchildren, etc., until such time as there are no further descendants of the settlor, in which case the trust pays out to the Red Cross. Although no estate taxes are due because the trust corpus remains in the trust until the settlor's descendants die out and the remainder is paid to a charity, income taxes will be due. And with payouts to skipped generation beneficiaries, a GST tax may be due. But dynasty trusts can purchase homes or cars and allow beneficiaries to *use* them potentially free of gift and estate tax liability. As the home appreciates in value, the trust corpus increases as well. But no estate tax will be due because the home will remain in the trust in perpetuity until the settlor's line dies out and the principal is paid to a charity. And of course, no estate taxes are due if a gift is made to an accredited charity.

There are many benefits to dynasty trusts in terms of avoiding large pay-outs to spendthrift beneficiaries and avoiding estate taxation at every generation. But the dynasty trust has costs as well. First, to effectively take advantage of the trust benefits, it needs to be irrevocable with fairly strict distribution requirements. No beneficiary should have the power to invade the trust corpus without significant cost. And perhaps most importantly, with a guaranteed income stream provided to the settlor's children, grandchildren, great-grandchildren, and so on, the risk increases significantly that future descendants will become lazy and irresponsible and there will be no power by trustees or parents to channel the trust property to more deserving beneficiaries. Not only will the property be tied up, but it won't necessarily be available to be put to its most efficient use. And although I would love to have a guaranteed income stream so that I don't have to work during college, I am not sure I want a great-grandparent to put in place an income stream for my children that I cannot control.

Many scholars and commentators have strongly criticized dynasty trusts as creating a new aristocracy,[39] but estate planners and banks are thrilled that dynasty trusts can generate hundreds of years of trustee fees. And although dynasty trusts have not been in existence long enough to have generated enough litigation to guide drafters in avoiding complex survivorship and class gift problems, future interests are likely to re-emerge from the dusty closet of legal antiquities where they are often rele-

---

[38] Alaska, Arizona, Colorado, Delaware, Florida, Idaho, Illinois, Maine, Maryland, Missouri, New Jersey, Ohio, Rhode Island, South Dakota, Wisconsin and Virginia have all made some revisions to their RAP.

[39] See Ray Madoff, America Builds a New Aristocracy, Op-Ed, The New York Times (July 11, 2010); Robert Sitkoff and Max Schanzenbach, *Jurisdictional Competition for Trust Funds: An Empirical Analysis of Perpetuities and Taxes*, 115 YALE L. J. 356 (2005); Joel Dobris, *Undoing Repeal of the Rule Against Perpetuities: Federal and State Tools for Breaking Dynasty Trusts*, 27 CARDOZO L. REV. 2537 (2006); Verner F. Chaffin, *Georgia's Proposed Dynasty Trust: Giving The Dead Too Much Control*, 35 GA. L. REV. 1 (2000).

gated by property professors and impatient law students. To gain the tax benefits of dynasty trusts the settler must put the trust corpus pretty much out of control of the beneficiaries and establish complex and relatively inflexible multi-generational future interests. This should give estate planners an incentive to very carefully draft the future interests to avoid disastrous estate tax problems like that of *Est. of Houston*.

E. CONCLUSION

Although you need to understand the complex law surrounding the federal transfer tax regime, and the complex nuances of the RAP, before you begin drafting GS or dynasty trusts, you should be starting to recognize many of the complexities that arise in planning for unborn generations. Building flexibility into any plan is usually a good idea, although some flexibility may defeat a settlor's ultimate plan, like the desire to establish a dynasty trust, which has to be somewhat inflexible. Regardless of the type of estate planning or estate litigation you ultimately end up doing, understanding future interests is crucial.

You have covered a dizzying amount of material in this chapter very quickly. The law on future interests developed over hundreds of years to deal with a variety of complex estate planning issues and we were only able to cover the basic rules in this Chapter. The Rule Against Perpetuities has also evolved over a long period of time and has been modified in various ways in different states that we could only hint at. We didn't have time to cover such classic rules as the Doctrine of Worthier Title or the Rule in Shelley's Case. And we didn't have time to cover the nuances of Marketable Title Acts or Stales Uses and Reversions Acts. An advanced course in Future Interests, or in drafting trusts, is advisable if you are planning on practicing in this area. But with a couple of good supplements and some time reading treatises, you can master this arcane subject and thus be at the center of stimulating conversations at dinner parties and bar meetings. Future interests may seem arcane and counter-intuitive; but once you realize that they are the tools by which property owners can provide for their children, grandchildren, and later generations, you will realize that this area of law is critical for promoting your clients' interests.

And for most of your clients, whose estates are not in the millions or billions of dollars, relatively simple future interests can help them to benefit not just themselves and their surviving spouse, but their children and grandchildren too. You don't need to be looking at dynasty trusts to benefit from sensible uses of future interests. And with the ubiquitous revocable living trust, future interests and the RAP could play a large role in the estate plans of millions of Americans.

CHAPTER 9

PLANNING FOR TAX MINIMIZATION: THE TAX CONSEQUENCES OF DONATIVE TRANSFERS

If you have gotten this far through the book you have already encountered numerous references to the bogeyman lurking above everything: the *death tax*! Of course, the term death tax is a misnomer. No one is actually taxed for dying. Rather, the federal government imposes a tax on the transmission of wealth during life and at death, if the donor's total transfers are sufficiently large and the transfers are not exempted from taxation because of the purpose of the transfer, the size of the transfer, or the relationship of the donor to the donee. Whew—the complexity of that sentence should clue you in that this is not the most straightforward material in the book. As with most things concerning the federal government, the complexities and loopholes make the entire tax system seem like confusion compounded. But most of the rules and technicalities were added because some enterprising tax lawyers found gaps between the tax definitions of property transfers and state property law definitions, gaps that could be exploited to avoid or at least minimize certain taxes. So the first thing you are likely to notice is that the Internal Revenue Code seeks to identify more things as property and tax more transactions that resemble property transfers, even if they might not be considered property or transfers under state property law. Thus, the tax umbrella is likely to be much larger than the probate or elective share umbrellas we have been discussing so far in this book.

Because most trusts and estates courses don't have time to focus heavily on the tax consequences of donative transfers, there are special courses you can take to study the transfer tax system and various tax strategies for minimizing both federal and state tax liabilities. Consequently, we will cover only the basic outline of the federal tax regime involving donative transfers, just enough to give you a sense of the different tax issues and mechanisms you will need to consider in order to minimize a client's tax liabilities. And, as we've mentioned before, less than 1% of estates will even face the possibility of estate taxes. Thus, the considerations you will study here are generally for the exceptional estate and not the average one, and won't be factors in most of your estate planning careers. But even if you don't represent Bill Gates or Donald Trump, you need to understand the basic blueprint of the transfer tax regime so you can competently negotiate the minefields and safe harbors to protect your client's interests.

Taxes have been around at least since the Roman times, and Robin Hood was not the only hero in history who thrived on obstructing the tax man. But as much as we may fuss about writing that check on April 14th, we also realize that governments need money to provide roads, sewers, courthouses, police, armies, fire fighters, schools, hospitals, interplanetary rovers, innovative research and even the insurance to protect our bank accounts. There are four principal types of taxes and fees a government can collect to fund itself:

1. Taxes on increases in wealth (taxes on individual incomes, corporate profits, capital gains, including social entitlement taxes like social security, payroll taxes, and Medicare/Medicaid taxes)

2. Property taxes (taxes on real or personal property, intangibles, or business property)

3. Excise taxes (sales taxes, gift, estate, or inheritance taxes, and impost or customs taxes)

4. Fees for services (fishing licenses, drivers license fees, motor vehicle tags, and filing fees for court documents)

Taxes can also be broken down into different categories, like taxes based on the value of a particular good or service, which are called *ad valorem* taxes. These include sales, estate and gift, and many property taxes. Some taxes, like property taxes, are assessed every year, whether or not the owner transfers the property or the value of the property changes. Other taxes are based solely on increases in value. Other taxes are assessed only when property is sold or transferred, like capital gains, sales, and gift and estate taxes. Some taxes are assessed on the increase in value of goods when they are transferred, like capital gains taxes; and others are assessed on wages to help fund social entitlements like social security, Medicare, Medicaid, and unemployment insurance. Some taxes are intermittent, like special assessments to improve sewer services or build new schools. Others are recurring, like income taxes, while sales taxes and estate taxes are assessed only when the relevant transaction occurs.

Some taxes are progressive and others are regressive, meaning that they increase or decrease as income or wealth increases or decreases, while others are directly proportional to the wealth or value of the item or transfer. Sales taxes are usually proportional, consisting of a flat percentage of the value of the transfer being taxed. Income tax is progressive because the rate decreases as the income goes down and increases as income goes up, thus hitting the highest income earners with the highest rates. Social security taxes, however, are regressive, because they are assessed on all wages up to a certain level, and then stop for wages above that threshold, thereby imposing a heavier burden on low earners than on high earners.

As you can imagine, understanding the entire range of tax issues that might face a particular estate can be overwhelming. There are taxes on the income of trusts, capital gains taxes on the increased value of property that is sold, as well as transfer taxes on the value of gifts made during life and at death that must all be considered in drafting an estate plan. However, for our purposes here we are going to focus exclusively on the federal transfer tax regime that is most directly central to estate planning.

Gift and *estate* taxes are assessed on the *gratuitous* transfer of property from one individual to another. Thus, if an owner sells property, a sales tax may be assessed, and if an owner gives the property away, there may be a corresponding *gift* or *estate tax*. The federal government does not tax inheritances by beneficiaries as income, so if you inherit Aunt Edna's doily collection you can rest well knowing that you don't have to pay any taxes on the gift. Some states, however, do tax inheritances, treating them essentially like income (though of course they are taxed at different rates and aren't subject to the variety of taxes that wages are subject to). They figure, why should you pay a tax on the interest earned in your savings account and not on your new acquisition of grandpa's valuable art collection? The federal gift and estate taxes, and state gift and estate taxes, are assessed on the *donor's transfer* of property (hence on the donor, or the donor's estate), whether the transfer was *inter vivos* (gift tax) or testamentary (estate tax). Inheritance taxes are assessed on the *receipt* of property and will be paid by the donee of the gift, just like income taxes are paid by the earner of the income.

Estate and gift taxes are progressive in that the rates increase with the increasing size of the estate. For relatively small estates, there is no estate or gift tax. But transfers over $5.25 million are taxed at a flat 40% rate.[1]

A. HISTORY OF THE GOVERNMENT'S SHARE

Think back to the history of estates and future interests that we discussed in Chapter 8. Under feudalism, landholders held their land from their lord, and in exchange for uninterrupted possession, the tenant pledged an oath of fealty and agreed to pay certain rents for the land. If the land was held in socage tenure, the rent was a fixed amount of cash, but if the land was held in military tenure, the services owed could be quite onerous. A tenant in military tenure might owe his lord a knight or two, and he would have to supply funds if his lord was captured or his lord's son needed to be outfitted as a knight. And sometimes he owed his lord personal duties, like providing personal services (serving at his lord's table, holding his head on sea passages, or helping with military obligations). Not just any person could provide these personal services. Daughters could not serve, and some sons were just too unreliable to provide the services or even to manage the lands well enough to earn the money owed each year to the lord. As a result, the lord had the option, at the death of each tenant, to regain the land and give it to someone else if the deceased tenant left only daughters or minor children.

But what tenant would spend a lot of time, money, and energy improving land or adding onto buildings if the lord was just going to reclaim the land upon the tenant's death and give it to someone else? This led tenants and lords to negotiate for a form of landholding that included the automatic right to have the land descend to the tenant's eldest son, so long as the son was of age to take over the services. Remember that magic language: to A *and his heirs*. The "and his heirs" provision indicated that the estate was *inheritable*, meaning the lord could not just reclaim the estate upon the tenant's death so long as he had a legal heir. The problem arose, of course, if he had a legal heir but that heir was underage. In that case, the lord

---

[1] Actually, the gift and estate tax rates are determined by a complicated calculation in which transfers over $14,000 are taxed at variably increasing rates, beginning at 18% for transfers over $10,000 and culminating in 40% for transfers over $5.25 million. But, each person receives a credit, called the *unified credit*, for whatever the tax would have been for any amount up to $2,100,000 in tax, thus allowing for the tax free transfer of any amount up to $5.25 million. So why should we care about the increasing rate changes up to 40% if everyone receives a credit for whatever the taxes would have been over $5.25 million? The answer has to do with calculating the rate (and keeping it low) for transfers under the maximum amount, so that a decedent can transfer his remaining unused credit to his spouse. More on that issue below. See I.R.C. § 2001(c)(1) as amended by section 302(a)(2) of the Tax Relief, Unemployment Insurance Reauthorization, and Job Creation Act of 2010.

could temporarily reclaim the land during the heir's minority, strip it of valuable timber or minerals, rent it out and keep the income, and charge a hefty fee to the heir when he came of age and sought to reclaim it. Land held in wardship easily could be lost to a family when life spans were short and plagues and wars were common.

Over time, the effects of various land statutes and the creation of the office of Master of the Wards under Henry VII led to a consistent policy of asserting the Crown's rights to financial compensation when land would pass to minor heirs. The Master of the Wards and the Court of Wards were, in large part, the early agencies of the Crown's estate tax collection laws. Wardship was finally abolished in 1660 and all land was deemed to be held in socage tenure, which did not give rise to the devastating incidents of wardship. Still, something had to be done to replace the income that the Crown was receiving from the sale of wardships. Parliament agreed to give the King an allowance, a stipend that was to help defray certain costs of the court and the executive branch, which was to supplement the income the King received from Crown lands. But as you can imagine, very few monarchs were able to live within their means, and more revenue creating means were devised, including impost and customs taxes, stamp taxes, and the sale of public offices. In the nineteenth century, England finally abolished the sale (and inheritance) of offices, and put in place a meritocratic system in which government officials were paid a salary and the fees they had traditionally collected for their services were paid into the central treasury. England dramatically reformed its tax system in the nineteenth and again in the twentieth centuries to keep up with the escalating costs of the burgeoning welfare state.

The idea that heirs have to pay a portion of their inheritance to the Crown, or the state, when they come into their inheritances has a long pedigree. But even in seventeenth century England it made little sense to require that underage heirs pay a whole lot and adult heirs pay relatively little. The dramatic difference in effect was certainly inequitable—estates passing smoothly to adult heirs faced little or no economic consequence, and estates passing to underage heirs could sometimes lose more than half their value. Avoiding those inequities kept most of the estate planners busy. And although we have a very different system of taxation, those early laws taxing estates or inheritances led to many of the property mechanisms we still use today: trusts, future interests, and powers of appointment.

The Americans were perhaps even less enthusiastic about paying taxes than the British, especially when the money went overseas to the Crown, and they even grumbled about fees payable to the early federal government. Prior to 1862, the U.S. government survived primarily on tariffs from imported goods and, at varying times, from taxes on distilled spirits, carriages, sugar, slaves, and property sold at auction. But with the high costs of the Civil War, a temporary income tax was instituted with a tax rate beginning at 3% of annual income, and increasing gradually as the person's income increased.[2]

The Act of 1862 also created the office of the Commissioner of Internal Revenue with the power to assess, levy, and collect taxes, a power granted to Congress in the Constitution.[3] In 1868, Congress again taxed tobacco

---

[2] Revenue Act of August 5, 1861, Chap. XLV, 12 Stat. 292.

[3] See U.S. Constitution, Article I, § 8.

and distilled spirits, and in 1872 it eliminated the income tax. After short revivals in 1894 and 1895 of the income tax, it was ruled unconstitutional in 1895.[4] In 1913, the 16th Amendment to the Constitution was ratified, making the income tax permissible both on individual and corporate income. Beginning in 1981, significant income tax reform began to occur, almost yearly, with major reform in 1986 and 2001. Currently, the highest income tax rate for individuals and corporations is 39.4%, down from its highest level of 94% for individuals in 1944 and 53% for corporations in 1968.[5]

Like medieval wardship, the gift and estate taxes that comprise the bulk of the federal transfer tax regime have a much longer pedigree than the income tax. The estate tax was first assessed in 1797 as a stamp tax on wills admitted to probate to help pay debts from the war with France. To finance the Civil War, an estate tax was instituted in 1862. It was repealed in 1870, and then reenacted in 1916 to help fund World War I. Much of the questions around the taxing power, however, have dealt primarily with which kind of tax—sales taxes, income taxes, wealth transfer taxes, or fees—are included in the Constitutional authorization to "lay and collect taxes."[6] Although many still debate the nuances regarding the types of taxes that could be collected under the early Constitution and the 16th amendment, most agree that taxes may be legally imposed on the transfer of property, whether it is a gratuitous transfer or a sale.

Current debates regarding transfer taxes usually focus on their use as a way of leveling inherited wealth; they arguably prevent the large accumulations of wealth that created an aristocratic class in medieval and modern Europe. However, a historical look at these taxes reveals that they were typically only used as a revenue-generating device in times of exigency and war.[7] Our modern estate tax, originally enacted in 1916 to raise revenue for World War I, continued to exist on its own until 1924 when Congress first introduced the gift tax as a complement to the estate tax which, at the time, could be avoided by simply making gifts during one's life. The gift tax was repealed in 1926, but reenacted in 1932, with lower rates than the estate tax. This lower rate encourage the wealthy to make lifetime gifts to avoid the estate taxes, thus raising quick revenue during the Great Depression. Of course, that came at the expense of future reve-

---

[4]   Pollock v. Farmers' Loan & Trust Co., 157 U.S. 429 (1895).

[5]   These are marginal rates, and very few people or corporations pay the full percentage on the dollar figures earned at the top of the scale. There are credits, deductions, and exemptions to bring taxable income down, and the given tax rates are only on the dollars earned above a certain amount. Thus, when we factor in the lower rate on a large portion of the income earned at the lower levels, the actual taxes paid are significantly less than the rates would indicate. Consider the corporation earning $10 million that is faced with a 53% tax rate on all income earned over $1 million. It only pays tax at 20% for the first $1 million. Thus, it simply has to split the business into 10 separate corporations that each earns $1 million to keep its total tax rate at 20%. Individuals can do much the same thing with the use of trusts, partnerships, or other legal entities.

[6]   A fee is not a tax, but it is a form of revenue. Taxes benefit society at large and fees often benefit only the party paying the fee. See 84 C.J.S. Taxation §3.

[7]   The estate tax had been implemented periodically, from as early as 1797 through 1916, to temporarily fund war measures. The first tax was to fund the formation of the Navy, and enacted in 1862 to help defray costs of the Civil War. A War Revenue Act of 1898 imposed an inheritance tax to fund the Spanish-American War. The gift tax of 1932 was enacted to raise immediate cash during the Great Depression. Though today lawmakers talk about the estate tax and its relation to job creation or leveling inherited wealth, even the 2012 ATRA was passed under the shadow of a looming fiscal debt crisis.

664   PLANNING FOR TAX MINIMIZATION: THE TAX CONSEQUENCES OF

    DONATIVE TRANSFERS   CHAPTER 9

nue collections, which lead to gradually increasing of the gift and estate tax rates.

Throughout the middle part of the twentieth century, different tax rates between gift and estate taxes, and the right to separate exemptions from both, caused many wealthy, and even middle-class, Americans to begin making strategic estate plans aimed at minimizing the taxes that would be due at their death. When the estate tax rate was at 77% for estates over $10 million, and the gift tax rate was only 58% for those same years, there was quite an incentive to do some fancy planning. Thus was born the first large crop of estate planners who built tax minimization into the estate plans of the growing middle class.

After 1976, when Congress linked the gift and estate taxes, creating a shared rate table and creating a *unified credit* in lieu of separate exemptions, the two taxes have been generally in line with each other.[8] We can now speak of the tax system as a *transfer tax*, a tax on the transmission of wealth from one person to another, regardless of whether it is through an *inter vivos* gift or occurs at death. And if you thought that you could avoid at least one level of tax by gifting property to your grandchildren or great-grandchildren, thus avoiding the payment of estate taxes by your children, you underestimate Congress' ability to close gaps in the transfer tax system. In 1976, and revised in 1986, Congress enacted a generation skipping transfer tax (the GST tax) to make sure large gifts were taxed with every passing generation if devises to grandchildren or great-grandchildren were used to avoid paying estate or gift taxes.

Further extensive reforms were passed in 1986 and again in 2001 as the political parties argued about whether rates should increase or decrease progressively with the size of the estate, and whether a larger amount of property should be allowed to pass tax-exempt. Before the last round of amendments, the highest gift and estate tax rates were 55% and the exclusion was $675,000.[9] This meant that the unified credit only covered transfers up to the first $675,000, leaving many people in the middle class facing the possibility of a significant estate tax liability.

The current estate tax rates were set in a complex, graduated scheme in the Economic Growth and Tax Relief Reconciliation Act of 2001 (EGTRA), which gradually reduced the highest estate tax rates of 55% in 2001, to the 2012 rate of 35%. And the amount exempt from estate taxes increased from $675,000 in 2000 to $2 million in 2008 to $3.5 million in 2009.[10] The estate tax was effectively repealed entirely for 2010. In 2011,

---

[8] There are a few very important differences, however, which still make it important to consider certain benefits of lifetime giving. See discussion at Section C—The Estate Tax section and principally Section E(1) concerning Effective Estate Planning—Tax Benefits of Making Lifetime Gifts.

[9] These were the rates for 1997.

[10] For estates formed after 1976, an Internal Revenue Code (IRC) Section 2010 credit may in most cases reduce or even eliminate estate tax liability. [DALE S. ADAMS & ROBERT B. SMITH, FEDERAL ESTATE & GIFT TAXATION § 3.02 (2012) (hereinafter FEGT WGL]. "This credit is statutorily referred to as an "applicable exclusion amount," which is converted to an "applicable credit amount." [FEGT WGL, 3.02].

The credit is authorized by IRC Section 2010(a) which provides: "A credit of the applicable credit amount shall be allowed to the estate of every decedent against the tax imposed by section 2001." This allows a credit to be applied to the amount of tax imposed on an estate under IRC Section 2001.

the exemption was set at $5 million and it increased to $5.12 million for 2012, but further reforms in 2010 set it to revert back to its 2001 rate of 55% for amounts over $3 million and an exemption only for the first $1 million for 2013.[11] The panic among estate planners was palpable as they weren't sure Congress would agree on stopping the slide back to 2001 rates. However, fiscal cliff legislation, the American Taxpayer Relief Tax Act of 2012 (ATRA), which passed on January 2, 2013, did three important things to at least lower the height of the fiscal cliff. It permanently lowered the top gift and estate tax rate from 55% to 40%. It continued the adjustment of the annual exclusion for inflation ($13,000 in 2012 will adjust to $14,000 in 2013) and added an inflation adjustment to the unified credit as well ($5.12 million in 2012 adjusts to $5.25 million in 2013). And it made portability of the lifetime exclusion between spouses permanent, though it did not apply portability to the GST tax.

In its current form, the transfer tax regime seems to have a limited purpose as a revenue raiser since it has accounted for less than 1.5 percent of federal tax revenues in recent years. However, many have argued that it is still necessary as a way of leveling the playing field to accord with the ideals of the American dream. For an extensive discussion of other possible justifications for an estate tax, see John G. Steinkamp, *A Case for Federal Transfer Taxation*, 55 Ark. L. Rev. 1 (2002). But as we have seen historically, there is usually only the political will to pass extensive tax legislation during times of fiscal crisis. Although it is quite unlikely that we will see another year like 2010, for which the estate tax was repealed altogether (although there were some hidden costs to that benefit[12]), the current law has put in place regular adjustments of the lifetime exclusion (the unified credit) for inflation to match that of the annual exclusion. That means we cannot predict with any great accuracy the exclusion amounts for years after 2013. For 2013 the annual per person gift tax exclusion amount is $14,000[13] and the lifetime gift and estate tax exclusion is $5.25 million,[14] which are the amounts we will use throughout this chapter. However, you will need to stay on top of the actual amounts as the years pass because the numbers will adjust upwards to reflect inflation.

Then section 2010(c) tells us that the applicable credit amount is the amount of the tentative tax provided under section 2001(c). So for a taxable estate of $1 million, 2001(c) imposed a tentative tax of $345,800 in 2002 and 2003. The tentative tax is $345,800 so the 2010(c) credit will be the same amount, i.e., $345,800. Setting the credit equal to the tax, zeros out the entire tax liability on the $1 million. Because the tax liability has been erased, $1 million of the estate escapes taxation, and hence $1 million is the applicable exclusion amount. The applicable exclusion amount is the amount that can be transferred during life or at death free of federal gift or estate tax. [FEGT WGL, 3.02[1][b]]. Thus, if the decedent has no "adjusted taxable gifts" and if the value of the estate does not exceed the available "applicable exclusion amount" as determined in the year of decedent's death, the estate will incur no estate tax liability. [FEGT WGL 3.02].

[11] I.R.C. §§ 2001(c), 2502(a)(1).

[12] Taxpayers had a choice in 2010 of paying no estate taxes, but losing the benefit of the step up in basis that comes when property is inherited, or they could pay the estate tax at a rate of 35% and receive the step up in basis. We discuss the benefits of the stepped up basis below.

[13] Rev. Proc. 2012–41, 2012–45 IRB 539.

[14] I.R.C. 2010(c)(3) as amended by section 1 of Rev. Proc. 2013–15 I.R.B. 444 (released January 11,2013).

B. THE TRANSFER TAX SYSTEM

There are three elements that comprise the current federal transfer tax system: the estate tax, the gift tax, and the generation-skipping transfer tax (GST tax). To know which tax to pay, you need to know whether something is a gift or not and, if so, whether it is *inter vivos* or testamentary. You will also need to know if it is subject to the GST tax, which kicks in when you have effectively avoided the estate and gift tax by devising a scheme to skip a generation. We will not cover state inheritance taxes (taxes on the recipient of property) or state estate taxes (taxes on the donor of property) because the laws of the states are too diverse. Many states have neither. But if you are going to practice in a state with an estate or an inheritance tax, you will need to understand how those laws are coordinated with and grafted onto the federal transfer tax system. But let's start with the basics: the nature of the gift itself. Unlike the pair of socks given to your nephew, trust interests raise numerous questions about whether a gift is complete, especially if the trust is revocable.

1. WHEN IS A GIFT NOT A GIFT?

According to the Internal Revenue Code, a federal gift tax is imposed for each calendar year on the transfer of property by (completed) gift, whether the transfer is in trust or otherwise, direct or indirect, the property real or personal, tangible or intangible.[15] Two main questions arise when determining whether a transfer of property will be subject to gift taxes: (1) whether there is a *gift* for federal tax purposes? and (2) whether the gift is *complete* and thus subject to taxation in that year? If the gift is not complete in a particular year, it will be taxed in the year it becomes complete, which in many instances will be at the death of the donor. Thus, an incomplete gift will become complete no later than the death of the donor and estate taxes, rather than gift taxes, may be due.

Not surprisingly, the term *gift* is not explicitly defined within the Code, but it has come to be interpreted quite expansively, covering virtually every situation where one individual confers an *economic benefit* on another *without compensation*. Similarly, the term *property* has been expansively construed to cover nearly every type of right or interest protected by law and having some exchangeable value. For example, if Peter gives Stewie $100,000 in cash, Peter has made a direct transfer of property by completed gift and this transaction will clearly be subject to gift taxation. But what if Peter sets up a trust, making Stewie a remainder beneficiary? Or, alternatively, what if Peter gives Stewie the power to designate who will receive the remainder interest in the trust? Although Peter doesn't transfer the property directly to Stewie, he has transferred an interest in the property to him in both cases.[16] Absent some type of payment from Stewie, virtually any species of property interest transferred will be considered a gift and may give rise to current gift tax liability depending on whether the gift is complete for gift tax purposes.

As you recall from our discussion of future interests, an owner of property can make a present transfer of a right to future possession that can be

---

[15] IRC § 2501(a)(1), IRC § 2511.

[16] Whether the gift of a power is taxable or not depends in large part on whether it is a special power (non-taxable) or a general power (taxable).

vested in interest but not vested in possession. Should such a transfer be considered a completed gift? Perhaps. It depends on whether the future interest can be defeated and the likelihood of the terminating events actually occurring.

One of the most important early Supreme Court cases involving the definition of a completed gift is is the 1943 case of *Smith v. Shaughnessy, Collector of Internal Revenue.*

Smith v. Shaughnessy, Collector of Internal Revenue

63 S.Ct. 545 (1943)

In this case, the petitioner, age 72, made an irrevocable transfer in trust of 3,000 shares of stock worth $571,000. The trust income was payable to his wife, age 44, for life; upon her death, the stock was to be returned to the petitioner, if he was living; if he was not living, it was to go to such persons as his wife might designate by will, or in default of a will by her, to her intestate successors under applicable New York law.[17] *The court explained that three interests are involved here: the life estate, the remainder, and the reversion. The taxpayer concedes that the life estate is subject to the gift tax. The government concedes that the right of reversion to the donor in case he outlives his wife is an interest having value which can be calculated by an actuarial device, and that it is immune from the gift tax. The controversy, then, reduces itself to the question of the taxability of the remainder. The taxpayer's principal argument here is that . . . the value of the remainder will be included in the grantor's gross estate for estate tax purposes; and that . . . we intimated a general policy against allowing the same property to be taxed both as an estate and as a gift.* The court rejected the argument that the remainder would be taxed twice, because the payment of the gift tax is "a form of down-payment on the estate tax."

The court explained further: *Unencumbered by any notion of policy against subjecting this transaction to both estate and gift taxes, we turn to the basic question of whether there was a gift of the remainder. The government argues that for gift tax purposes the taxpayer has abandoned control of the remainder and that it is therefore taxable, while the taxpayer contends that no realistic value can be placed on the contingent remainder and that it therefore should not be classed as a gift.*

We cannot accept any suggestion that the complexity of a property interest created by a trust can serve to defeat a tax. For many years Congress has sought vigorously to close tax loopholes against ingenious trust instruments. Even though these concepts of property and value may be slippery and elusive they cannot escape taxation so long as they are used in the world of business. The language of the gift tax statute, 'property * * * real or personal, tangible or intangible', is broad enough to include property, however conceptual or contingent.

---

[17] The petitioner, under protest paid a gift tax of $71,674.22, assessed on the total value of the trust principal, and brought suit for refund in the district court. Holding that the petitioner had, within the meaning of the Act, executed a completed gift of a life estate to his wife, the court sustained the Commissioner's assessment on $322,423, the determined value of her life interest; but the remainder was held not to be completely transferred and hence not subject to the gift tax. The government appealed and the Circuit Court of Appeals reversed, ordering dismissal of the petitioner's complaint on the authority of its previous decision in *Herzog v. Commissioner,* 116 F.2d 591.

The essence of a gift by trust is the abandonment of control over the property put in trust. The separable interests transferred are not gifts to the extent that power remains to revoke the trust or recapture the property represented by any of them, or to modify the terms of the arrangement so as to make other disposition of the property. . . .   In cases such as this, where the grantor has neither the form nor substance of control and never will have unless he outlives his wife, we must conclude that he has lost all 'economic control' and that the gift is complete except for the value of his reversionary interest.

Justice Roberts dissented, stating: *I am of opinion that, except for the life estate in the wife, the gift qua the donor was incomplete. . . . It will not square with logic to say that where the donor reserves the right to change beneficiaries, and so delays completion of the gift until his death or prior relinquishment of the right, the gift is incomplete, but where he reserves a contingent interest to himself the reverse is true,—particularly so, if the criterion of estate tax liability is important to the decision of the question . . . The question is not whether a gift which includes vested and contingent future interests in others than the donor is taxable as an entirety when made, but whether a reservation of such an interest in the donor negatives a completion of the gift until such time as that interest is relinquished.*

Query: Do you think the Court held the remainder to be a gift in large part because the value of the reversion would be relatively small since the likelihood of the husband outliving his wife was so remote? Since the odds were so great that the remainder interest would vest, and the husband could not revoke the remainder (he could only defeat it by surviving his wife), it was treated as an *inter vivos* gift with taxes payable at the gift tax rate and not a testamentary gift payable at the estate tax rate. Assuming the former was higher, how should the trust have been set up to avoid the determination that the remainder was a completed gift? Moreover, if it was deemed a testamentary gift, it would be included in the husband's gross taxable estate as well as in the wife's estate.

Under the Treasury Regulations, a gift is considered complete when the owner has parted with all dominion and control of any part or interest in property so as to leave him no power to change its disposition, whether for his own benefit or another.[18] The relinquishment or termination of a power to change the beneficiaries of transferred property is regarded as the event that completes the gift, unless, of course, the relinquishment or termination occurs upon death.[19]

Conversely, a gift is incomplete in every instance in which a donor reserves the power to revest beneficial title to the property in himself and to the extent that the donor has reserved the power to name new beneficiaries or change the interests of the beneficiaries as between themselves.[20] However, when the power to revest title in the grantor is held by the trustee and is limited by a fixed or ascertainable standard enforceable by or on

---

[18] Treas. Reg. § 25.2511–2(b).

[19] Treas. Reg. § 25.2511–2(f).

[20] Treas. Reg. § 25.2511–2(c).

behalf of the grantor, the gift is considered complete but for the *ascertaina-ble* value of any rights retained by the grantor.[21] If the interest retained by the grantor cannot be valued by any recognized actuarial method, the entire gift is considered complete and no reduction in the value of the gift will be applied to account for the grantor's retained interest.[22]

In contrast, consider the situation where a trustee has the *discretionary* power to revest beneficial title to the grantor. Treas. Reg. § 25.2511–2(c) seems to point to an incomplete gift if the trustee has the power to revest beneficial title in the donor, but, if it is completely discretionary under the terms of the instrument and state law so that the donor cannot require that any of the trust assets be distributed to the donor and the creditors of the donor cannot reach any of the trust assets, then the donor has parted with dominion and control over the property transferred in trust.[23] Dealing with a corporate trustee who could not be removed by the grantor, a revenue ruling noted that "although the trustee has an unrestricted power to pay trust assets to the grantor, the grantor cannot require that any of the trust's assets be distributed to the grantor nor can the grantor utilize the assets by going into debt and relegating the grantor's creditors to the trust."

What would have been the result if the terms of the trust instrument allowed the grantor to remove the trustee and appoint himself as trustee? What if he could remove the trustee but could only appoint another independent trustee?

Furthermore, a gift is complete when the grantor merely reserves the power to change the time or manner of the enjoyment of the property, but has no power to change the interests of the beneficiaries.[24] Thus, consider the situation where A creates and funds an irrevocable trust, appoints himself as trustee, and retains the power to pay out or accumulate income for the benefit of the sole beneficiary, B. A has made a completed gift of property because although he can dictate when B will receive the benefit, B's interest as a whole will remain unchanged and he will eventually receive the entire trust corpus.

With that exceptionally clear and simple description of a completed gift in mind, consider this transfer.

Stewart v. State of California

8 Cal.App.3d 449, 87 Cal.Rptr. 672 (Cal.App. 1970)

On November 14, 1948, Cepha and Robert Sisk (Cepha and Robert), husband and wife, orally agreed that on the death of either, the survivor would succeed to all the property of the other and that such survivor would leave all property in his or her possession at the time of death to their daughter, Marian, to take absolutely at age 35. Mutual wills were executed by Cepha and Robert. Cepha died on November 17, 1957, without having changed her will. Her property, all of which was community, passed to Rob-

---

[21]   *See Estate of Holtz v. C.I.R.*, 38 T.C. 37, 38 acq., 1962–2 C.B. 3 (1962).

[22]   *See Robinette v. Helvering*, 318 U.S. 184, 63 S. Ct. 540, 87 L. Ed. 700 (1943).

[23]   *See* Rev. Rul. 77–378.

[24]   Treas. Reg. § 25.2511–2(d).

ert. An order fixing inheritance tax on his succession to her estate was entered on December 11, 1961.

On May 9, 1960, Robert revoked his mutual will by means of a holographic will. Robert died on February 25, 1964. Along with minor bequests not at issue, the bulk of Robert's estate was left in a trust from which Marian was to receive the income. Marian thereafter brought an action to impose a constructive trust on Robert's estate. Judgment in her favor was entered on August 1, 1966. The Controller sought to impose inheritance taxes on Cepha's half of the community property which passed to Marian as a result of the constructive trust action.

On May 28, 1968, the Controller determined that a gift tax was due on Cepha's half of the property. Both parties agree that Cepha retained the power and the right to revoke her mutual will until the time of her death. Appellant, therefore, contends that 'dying without having changed the terms of a prior revocable agreement can be the operative fact which fixes the rights of the donee and results in a taxable gift under the California Gift Tax Law.'

Since the California law is derived from the federal gift tax law, authorities pertaining to the federal law are relevant. It has been settled . . . that 'gift taxes will not be imposed on transactions which fall short of being completed gifts.' It is a fundamental assumption that the gift tax is confined to transfers completed by living donors. Section 15105 [of the California Revenue and Taxation Code] reads in pertinent part: "Transfer' or 'Gift' does not include any transfer of property in trust where the power to revest in the donor title to the property is vested in the donor * * *. However, 'transfer' or 'gift' does include the relinquishment or termination of any such power, other than by the donor's death * * *.' Cepha's agreement with Robert was, in effect, a revocable trust. Cepha's death did not result in the completion of a gift within her lifetime. It was a testamentary disposition.

We are satisfied that nothing was taxable in any form at the time Cepha and Robert entered into the oral agreement in 1948. Obviously, there was no gift, i.e., no transfer of any interest to Marian. There was no assurance that Marian would have received anything at any time. Nor was there any gift at the time of the tax-free transfer of one half the community property from Cepha to Robert in 1957. Here again there was no assurance that Marian would ever succeed to anything or that any property would ever come to her.

The only taxable point occurred in 1964 when Robert died, Marian being alive, and this transfer, whether by way of succession through Robert's will or impression of a constructive trust, it seems to us, clearly falls within the inheritance tax law. It is clear from the record that Robert was obligated by his contract with Cepha to transfer and will the community property to Marian, and that, if he had carried out his contract, she would have taken the property by succession under Robert's will. Whether by calculation or inadvertently, Robert ignored his obligations under his contract with Cepha as a consequence of which Marian by the device of an action to impress a constructive trust, caused him to perform the contract he had made with his wife.

It seems to us that the enforcement of the obligation to transfer by will through the device of an action to impress a constructive trust, does not change the inherent nature of the succession nor the obligation to pay an inheritance tax on the entire amount of property transferred.

Query: Why do you think Marian wanted her mother's half of the property to be considered a gift rather than an inheritance? Why, if Marian could enforce the trust on her father's estate, couldn't she enforce it on her mother's estate? There were two points of uncertainty in the completion of Marian's gift: 1) her mother not revoking her will, and 2) her father not revoking his will. Why was the court willing to undo her father's revocation but not her mother's? So did Marian receive a future interest in her mother's property at her mother's death, which only came into possession at the death of her father? If so, when should the transfer tax be payable, at her mother's death or her father's death?

Now consider the following transfer.

Holtz's Est. v. Comm'r

38 T.C. 37 (1962)

Leon Holtz, settlor/decedent, established a trust that provided the income to the settlor for his life, then to his wife if she survived him for her life, and then the principal was to be paid to her estate. If she did not survive him, the principal was to be paid to his own estate. The relevant provision, however, allowed the trustee to invade the principal for the settlor's benefit. It stated:

> *As much of the principal as Trustee may from time to time think desirable for the welfare, comfort and support of Settlor, or for his hospitalization or other emergency needs, shall be either paid to him or applied directly for his benefit by Trustee. Trustee shall keep the principal of this trust invested and shall distribute the net income therefrom and the principal thereof as follows.*

A similar provision allowed the trustee to invade the principal for the benefit of Leon's surviving spouse. The trust further provided that it was wholly irrevocable, and that the settlor shall be *without any power . . . at any time to revoke, change or annul any of the provisions herein contained; except that Settlor and others may hereafter bring other properties within the operation of this Deed of Trust.*

In determining whether Leon had made a completed gift of a future interest to the remaindermen of the trust principal, or whether he had retained enough control over it so that the gift to the remaindermen was an incomplete gift of a contingent future interest, the court explained:

> *Leon reserved no rights in himself to change the disposition of the income or principal of the trust as fixed in the trust agreement. However, the trust agreement itself gave the trustee power to pay directly to Leon or for his benefit as much of the principal of the trust as the trustee thought desirable for Leon's welfare, comfort, and support, or for his hospitalization or other emergency needs. The question is whether this discretionary power placed in*

the trustee by the settlor under the terms of the trust agreement made the gifts of the remainder interests incomplete for gift tax purposes.

The rule of thumb appears to be a reasonable application of the general rule established in the Guggenheim, Sanford, *and* Shaughnessy *cases because where there is a reasonable possibility that the entire corpus might be repaid to the settlor there can be no assurance that anyone else will receive anything in the form of a gift, and if the corpus should happen to be kept intact until the settlor's death, even though the transfer in trust was not subjected to a gift tax, the corpus of the trust will in all likelihood be subjected to the estate tax in the settlor's estate.*

Applying the above principles to the facts under consideration here, we conclude that no part of or interest in the property transferred to the trust constituted a completed gift for gift tax purposes when transferred to the trust.

Query: The Tax Court found that no gift was made of the remainder interest of the trust even though the settlor had no power of his own to revoke or withdraw the principal, and the trust was irrevocable. The trustee's power to disburse principal on the settlor's behalf was enough to render the gift to the remaindermen only a contingent future interest and therefore not subject to the gift tax. What else should have been done by the lawyer to make the gift *inter vivos*? Note the date of the case—the highest estate tax rate was 77% in 1962 and the highest gift tax rate was 57.75%. Do you see why the trustee litigated the case?

Was the settlor trying to continue to benefit from the property while still having it count as a completed *inter vivos* gift in order to receive a lower tax rate? Much of the incentive to make *inter vivos* gifts look like testamentary gifts, and *vice versa*, has disappeared with the unification of the rate tables between the gift and the estate tax that occurred in 1976. And if all things were equal, it would usually be better to wait and pay the transfer taxes at death rather than during life, especially if it's possible that the rates will go down. But despite the unified rate table, all things are not equal.

Tax Tip: Tax Exclusivity and Inclusivity

It is almost always cheaper from a tax perspective to pay the gift taxes on a transfer during life, rather than to wait and pay the estate taxes on the same gift at death. This is because the estate tax is tax *inclusive* and the gift tax is tax *exclusive*. We discuss the implications of this more fully below, but remember the exoneration case involving Charles Kuralt and his mistress, Pat Shannon? Assume the Montana property was worth $3 million, and let's say the gift tax rate for the property would be 50%, or $1.5 million. Kuralt could have given Shannon the property during life and paid the taxes at that time, for a total outlay of $4.5 million. But, by waiting until his death to give Shannon the property, the estate taxes (assuming a 50% tax rate) are compounded, meaning that he pays the $1.5 million in estate taxes. But because the money he used to pay his taxes is part of his estate and is subject to the transfer tax, he has to pay 50% on the tax, or an additional $750,000! And then he has to pay 50% on the $750,000, for an additional $375,000, and so on.[25] Kuralt will end up paying $3 million for the property and $3 million for the estate taxes if the entire property is subject to the estate tax! He could have saved $1.5 million in taxes by making the transfer to Shannon an *inter vivos* gift rather than a testamentary gift.

But the tax rate is not the only important consideration in deciding whether to make lifetime gifts or wait until death. Gifts that pass at death get what are called a "step up in basis." This means that if Kuralt only paid $500,000 for the property and it is now worth $3,000,000, it appreciated in value 600%. If Kuralt made the gift at death and paid the estate taxes on it, then Shannon receives it at its new value for income tax purposes, and can turn around and sell it without having to pay capital gains tax on the increased value. But if she received it as a lifetime gift, which does not get a step up in basis, it will be valued for income tax purposes at what Kuralt paid for it, the $500,000. That means that when she sells it, she will have to pay capital gains tax on the amount the property increased in value (the $2.5 million difference). So the donor pays a lower gift tax but the recipient will pay capital gains tax IF the recipient sells the property. And the nice thing about the step-up in basis rules is that it applies to testamentary gifts whether or not the donor had to pay estate taxes.

This means you have to pay attention to many different issues when advising someone to make a lifetime gift or wait and make a testamentary gift of high-value property. It the property has not appreciated in value, it is probably better to make a lifetime gift, but if the property has appreciated in value, it may be better to pay the higher estate taxes in order to forego having your donee have to pay capital gains tax. But it also depends on whether the donee is likely to sell the property, or simply hold onto it. A gift of a valuable family portrait might never be sold, and so capital gains taxes won't be an issue. Because the estate tax rate is usually higher than the income tax rate, it usually makes sense to substitute a future income tax liability for an immediate estate tax liability for transfers over the lifetime exclusion amount, especially if the recipient expects to hold on to the property.

You can see, now, why taxpayers argue with the IRS about whether something is a completed gift—it can mean a tax bill that is significantly lower if it qualifies as a lifetime gift. BUT, remember King Lear! A gift is only a gift if one gives up dominion and control—it's hard to change one's mind after making a lifetime gift.

2. JOINTLY OWNED PROPERTY AND GIFTS BY HUSBAND AND WIFE

As seen in Chapter Four, when property is held jointly, the primary issue for probate estate purposes is whether the property is held in a form that provides for a right of survivorship and therefore removes the property from the probate estate. For gift tax purposes, the issue is whether one makes a gift upon creation of the joint interest or at some later time, usually when the right of survivorship kicks in upon the death of the first cotenant. Consider the following examples: If Bill's grandmother Vicky opens

---

[25] Another way to think about this is that by saving $1.5 million in gift tax, Charles owns $1.5 million at death (in addition to the property), so his estate tax bill will be 50% of $4.5 million, or $2.25 million, leaving only $2.25 million to pass to beneficiaries.

a joint bank account in her and Bill's names and deposits $100,000 in the account, has she made a gift to him? What if she can regain the entire $100,000 without Bill's consent? In this case, there will only be a gift from Vicky to Bill whenever Bill draws upon the account for his own benefit.[26] However, if Vicky would be legally obligated to account to Bill for one half of the value of the bank account under state property law, the fact that Vicky had the power to withdraw the entire deposit at her option would not defeat the finding of a gift.[27]

What if instead of a bank account, Vicky purchases a house for $100,000 and takes title to the home with Bill as joint tenants with rights of survivorship? In this case, if each party has the ability to unilaterally sever their interest, there is a gift in the amount of $50,000 upon creation of the joint tenancy (1/2 the value of the property).[28] But what if Bill and Vicky had been husband and wife instead of grandson and grandmother? While the transfer is still technically a gift of property as above, I.R.C. § 2523(a) will provide a marital deduction for the full value of any gift transfers made to Bill.[29]

State property law can also have federal transfer tax implications when transfers are made by a husband or wife to a third party. For example, a gift of community property made by a husband or wife to a third party will be treated as a gift of a one-half interest by the husband and a one-half interest by the wife. To reduce disparities between the tax treatment of married couples in community property states and separate property states, § 2513 was enacted to allow for "gift splitting" by husbands and wives in separate property states.[30] To qualify under the statute, a gift must be made during a couple's marriage, each spouse must be a citizen or resident of the United States at the time of the gift, and both spouses must consent to the election to split gifts.[31] As you will see later in this chapter, gift splitting can be a useful tax planning device by utilizing the § 2503(b) annual exclusion amount and the § 2505 unified credit of both spouses.

3. FREE USE OF PROPERTY AND BELOW MARKET INTEREST LOANS

While a transfer of property constituting a gift may be easy to spot in most instances, the interest free use of money or other property can sometimes result in an unexpected taxable gift. Beginning with the Supreme Court's decision in *Dickman v. C.I. R.*,[32] interest free loans clearly result in taxable gifts of the reasonable value of the use of the property loaned. The Court explained:

> Just as a tenancy at will in real property is an estate or interest in land, so also is the right to use money a cognizable interest in personal property. The right to use money is plainly a valuable right, readily measurable by reference to current interest rates; the vast banking in-

---

[26] Treas. Reg. § 25.2511–1(h)(4).

[27] *See First Wisconsin Trust Co. v. United States*, 553 F. Supp. 26, 28 (E.D. Wis. 1982).

[28] Treas. Reg. § 25.2511–1(h)(5).

[29] See I.R.C. § 2523(d).

[30] In its current form, therefore, I.R.C. § 2513 allows gift splitting for all couples, regardless of state property rules.

[31] I.R.C § 2513(a); Treas. Reg. § 25.2513–1.

[32] 465 U.S. 330, 104 S. Ct. 1086, (1984).

dustry is positive evidence of this reality. Accordingly, we conclude that the interest-free loan of funds is a "transfer of property by gift" within the contemplation of the federal gift tax statutes.[33]

Subsequent to *Dickman,* Congress enacted I.R.C. § 7872 to statutorily create a "transfer" of property in the case of a below market gift loan. Without getting into the differences between the tax treatment of demand loans versus term loans, § 7872 essentially deems the lender as making a transfer of the foregone interest to the borrower, with the borrower subsequently retransferring the interest to the lender. Thus, the amount deemed transferred from the lender to the borrower will be treated as a transfer of property by completed gift for federal transfer tax purposes and will be taxed accordingly.

4. EXERCISE, RELEASE, OR LAPSE OF A GENERAL POWER OF APPOINTMENT

Similar to the treatment of below market loans, I.R.C. § 2514 operates to treat the exercise, release, or lapse of certain powers of appointment as transfers of property for the purposes of the transfer tax. As you recall from Chapter 4, a power of appointment over property is the power to determine who will receive beneficial ownership of that property. Although powers may not include the right to benefit personally from the property itself, they can be beneficial to the donee in many ways. In the context of a trust, a power of appointment exists where an individual has the power to alter, amend, or revoke a trust instrument and thereby affect the beneficial enjoyment of trust property. And remember, there are two kinds of powers: general and special. A general power is one in which the donee can exercise the power in favor of herself, her creditors, her estate, or creditors of her estate.[34] If the donee can exercise the power only in favor of others, she has a special power.

The tax code doesn't use the term *special* power or *non-general* power, which is a creature of the Restatement of Property. It refers only to general powers, which are treated like ownership interests andare considered transfers of property. Thus, when a donor gives a donee a general power of appointment it is a transfer of property to the donee. Furthermore, when a donee of a general power exercises or releases the power it is considered a transfer of property for transfer tax purposes. But two important exceptions to this general rule exist: powers limited by an ascertainable standard and powers exercisable only in conjunction with another may not be considered taxable transfers.

A power which is limited by an ascertainable standard relating to the health, education, support, or maintenance of the decedent is not a general power of appointment.[35] Commonly called the "HEMS" standard, a power will be considered limited to such a standard if the extent of the holder's duty to exercise and not to exercise the power is reasonably measurable in terms of the appointee's needs for health, education, maintenance, or support (or any combination of them). As explained by the regulations, the power need not be limited to merely provide for the "bare necessities of life"

---

[33] Id. at 337–38.

[34] I.R.C. § 2041(b)(1).

[35] I.R.C. § 2041(b)(1)(A).

to meet the exception, but the power should not be so expansive as to allow the holder use of property for her "comfort, welfare, and happiness."[36]

In addition to powers limited by a HEMS standard, powers exercisable only in conjunction with the creator of the power or with a person having a substantial adverse interest are not considered general powers of appointment. For instance, consider a trust in which Peter and Ricky were trustees and under the terms of the trust the income was to be paid to Peter for life and then to Mike for life, and the remainder was to be paid to Ricky. The trustees also had power to distribute corpus to Peter. Since Ricky's interest is substantially adverse to an exercise of the power in favor of Peter, Peter does not have a general power of appointment. If Mike and Peter were the trustees, Mike's interest would likewise have been adverse.[37]

After having properly identified a general power of appointment, the next relevant inquiry is deciding whether the power has been exercised, released, or has lapsed. A transfer by exercise of a general power of appointment is usually fairly easy to identify because an interest in property is actually transferring from one person to another. However, a lapse or release is also treated as a transfer because the holder of the power is effectively transferring the property to the default taker. The lapse or release of a general power of appointment is treated as though the holder exercised the power in favor of himself and then transferred the property to whomever would have received the property initially. While there are several nuances within these rules, including different treatment for powers of appointment created on or before October 21, 1942 and thereafter, the main exception from the lapse rule is the so called "5 and 5 power."

Under this exception, a lapse is treated as a transfer of property only to the extent that the amount subject to withdrawal under the general power of appointment exceeds the greater of $5,000 or 5% of the value of assets subject to the power.[38] Consider the following example: Bob creates an irrevocable trust, naming his daughters Jill and Jane as income beneficiaries for life with the remainder to his son Joe. Under the terms of the trust, Jill and Jane also have the power to withdraw $10,000 from the trust principal every year; however, they must exercise their power of withdrawal before December 1. If neither Jill nor Jane exercise the power before December 1, such power will lapse to the extent that it exceeds the greater of $5,000 or 5% of the trust principal. If the trust principal is greater than $200,000, the failure to exercise this right of withdrawal in a particular year will not constitute a gift by Jill or Jane. If, however, the trust principal were only $100,000, the failure to exercise the power will be considered gifts by Jill and Jane to the extent of $5,000, the excess of $10,000 over 5% of a fund of $100,000.[39] Notice that the 5 and 5 power exception applies on a per-beneficiary basis rather than per trust.[40]

A final exception to the general power of appointment rules exists for disclaimers. An individual can "disclaim" a general power of appointment at the time it is bestowed upon him without it being considered a release of

---

[36]   Treas. Reg. § 20.2041–1(c)(2).

[37]   Treas. Reg. § 20.2041–3(c)(2), Ex. (1).

[38]   I.R.C. § 2514(e).

[39]   Treas. Reg. § 25.2514–3(c)(4).

[40]   Rev. Rul. 85–88, 1985–2 C.B. 202.

the power for gift tax purposes.[41] Disclaimers are considered more generally in the following section.

5. DISCLAIMERS OF INTERESTS IN PROPERTY

Under the terms of I.R.C. § 2518, if a person makes a *qualified disclaimer* of any interest in property, it is treated as though the interest had never been transferred to such person for purposes of estate, gift, and GST taxes. The term qualified disclaimer is generally described in the statute as an irrevocable and unqualified refusal by a person to accept an interest in property; however, to qualify under the statute, several other specific elements must be satisfied. Thus, in order to be a qualified disclaimer:

(1) the refusal must be in writing;

(2) it must be received by the transferor of the interest, his legal representative, or the holder of the legal title to the property to which the interest relates not later than the date which is 9 months after the later of—**(A)** the day on which the transfer creating the interest in such person is made, or **(B)** the day on which such person attains age 21;

(3) such person must not have accepted the interest or any of its benefits, and

(4) as a result of such refusal, the interest passes without any direction on the part of the person making the disclaimer and passes either—**(A)** to the spouse of the decedent, or **(B)** to a person other than the person making the disclaimer

Remember Mary Hall, from Chapter 5? She wanted to disclaim her life estate in her aunt's house in order to accelerate the remainder in her children. But the court would not allow her to disclaim and cut off the interests of the contingent beneficiaries who were her siblings and their issue who would take if Mary had no issue at her death. The court distinguished disclaimer of the property rights under state law and disclaimer for tax purposes. Usually a disclaimer that qualifies for tax purposes will also constitute a disclaimer under state law, but not the other way around. Not all state law disclaimers will meet the Internal Revenue Code's requirements. Any person about to inherit a large gift, especially if the gift will likely not be touched (grandma's $8 million stock account), might well want to consider disclaiming the gift to avoid taxes accruing to her own estate.

Why, you might ask, would states pass disclaimer laws that set a longer time for a disclaimer of property under state law than the 9 months allowed by the Revenue Code? The main reason is that disclaimers serve more purposes than merely reducing tax liabilities. Creditors of the recipient of property will not be able to reach the property if a valid disclaimer is made, regardless of whether it occurs within the 9 month period, so long as your state permits disclaimers to be made at any time. And that soon-to-be ex-spouse won't be able to claim an elective share in disclaimed property either. In all instances, disclaimers have to be made before the donee of the property enjoys any benefits from the property. But that big IRA or stock account that you inherited from grandma can be effectively disclaimed so that you won't be facing transfer taxes in your own estate and your creditors can't reach the property if you disclaim within the appropriate time

---

[41]   Treas. Reg. § 25.2514–3(c)(5), (6).

period. But to get both benefits be sure you pay attention to the clock ticking away and disclaim within 9 months.

C. THE ESTATE TAX

Gifts or transfers of property that are completed during the donor's life are considered *inter vivos* or lifetime gifts. Gifts or transfers that are not complete until the donor's death are considered *testamentary* gifts. *Inter vivos* gifts require relinquishing dominion and control over the items during life. Testamentary gifts, of course, are not completed until the donor's death and allow the donor to retain control, possession, and use of property until death. Once a person has died, all property owned by the decedent at death must transfer to a living person or legal entity. So whatever you don't give away during life you must give away at death. Hence, all transfers of property will come within the gift or the estate tax regimes. Gift taxes apply to *inter vivos* gifts and estate taxes apply to testamentary gifts. And if the gift tax regime and the estate tax regime were identical and fully unified, it wouldn't matter whether people made lifetime or testamentary transfers of their property. And in fact, if they were fully unified, most people would likely hang onto their property until death. But the tax regimes are not fully unified and consistent, leaving gaps that estate planners can use to their client's advantage.

One obvious gap that existed until 1976 was the fact that *inter vivos* and testamentary gifts were taxed at different rates. Thus, when the gift tax rates were lower it made sense to make lifetime gifts and pay the taxes during life, leaving only enough property to pass at death to qualify for the estate tax exclusion.[42] If gift taxes are higher than estate taxes, it obviously made more sense to hold onto property and have it pass at death where it would be subject to the lower estate tax. The same is true if the gift tax exemption is lower than the estate tax exemption. Although Congress closed the rate loophole in 1976, it left others. One, as noted above in the tax tip at the beginning of this Chapter, is that the gift tax is estate tax exclusive and the estate tax is gift tax inclusive. This means that, at death, the estate may pay taxes on the gift taxes previously paid.[43] Hence, if I want to make a $10 million gift during life, and let's say the gift and estate tax rate on that gift would be 40%, then I would write a check for $10 million to my donee, and a check for $4 million to the Treasury for the gift taxes. Assuming the gift was made more than three years prior to my death, the value of the gift, and the gift taxes paid, are no longer considered in my gross estate. To pass that same gift at death, however, my executor would write the $10 million check to my beneficiary, and would then write a check for $6,666,667 to the Treasury because the $4 million tax to the treasury is part of my estate and subject to estate taxes as well as the $10 million gift to the beneficiary. This higher tax ultimately reduces the size of my residuary estate.

---

[42] Prior to 1976 the statuted referred to an "exemption" from estate taxes. After 1976 we refer to it as the "unified credit." The term "applicable exclusion amount" came in the 1997 Act as another term for the unified credit.

[43] This is called the gift tax gross-up rule of 2035(b). Under this provision, the federal gift tax paid by the decedent or the decedent's estate on any transfers made after 1976 and within three years of decedent's death, are pulled back into decedent's gross estate. The actual value of the gift will come back into the estate only if the requirements of I.R.C. section 2035(b) and (c) are met.

Another tax difference is the different treatment of appreciated lifetime gifts and testamentary gifts in terms of receiving a step up in basis. Testamentary gifts subject to the estate tax receive a step up in basis for the beneficiary. This is because I.R.C. 1014(a)(1) , sets the donee's basis equal to the fair market value of the property at the date of decedent's death. If the property appreciated in value during the donor's life, the donee doesn't have to pay capital gains taxes on the increase in value if it is treated as a testamentary gift when it is sold. The donee takes it with the new basis of its value at the time of the donor's death. However, under I.R.C. 1015(a) a recipient of a lifetime gift that has appreciated in value takes the gift subject to its original basis, which is whatever the donor paid for it (or the donor's cost). Because the asset has appreciated over the donor's original cost basis, gain is recognized upon subsequent sale by the donee. Thus, although making a lifetime gift removes from the donor's estate tax base any further appreciation in the value of the donated property and future income generated by the donated property, making the decision to gift appreciated property during life is counterbalanced by a loss of step up in basis at death, which for low basis assets might be reason enough to hold onto the asset.

There are other differences that are too technical to develop here. But you can be certain that so long as there are differences, there will be reasons for suggesting that certain clients make lifetime gifts rather than testamentary gifts, and *vice versa*, and you need to be knowledgeable explaining why. However, as many estate planners learned during the uncertain years of 2010 and 2012, it's hard to predict how Congress might change the estate and gift tax laws and your very clever reading of the tea leaves may actually turn out to be very bad advice for your clients.

Another important point to realize is that everything that isn't a lifetime gift will be considered a testamentary gift, even if the gift wasn't technically one that takes effect at death. The estate tax will apply to all transfers that don't count as lifetime gifts. To understand this, you need to understand the behemoth: the *gross estate*. Remember the probate estate? The probate estate consisted of all property owned by the decedent at death and subject to probate. It does not include property held in joint tenancies, revocable trusts, PODs and TODs, and other will substitutes. However, just because you can avoid probating property passing through these will substitutes doesn't mean it is not included in the decedent's estate for transfer tax purposes. The term *gross estate* is a tax term of art and, as a general matter, includes any interest in property described in §§ 2033–2044 of the Internal Revenue Code. These sections include property over which the decedent had a general power of appointment, life insurance proceeds, the decedent's proportional share of property held as a joint tenancy, as well as probate property and property held in both revocable and irrevocable trusts. The only property not included is property that was already transferred away through a completed lifetime gift. Remember homestead property, that passes automatically to surviving spouses or children? Even though homestead property may not be part of the probate estate, it is still part of the gross estate.

In many instances, property will be includible in the gross estate under more than one of the relevant provisions of the Code; however, in the event that an item is included in the gross estate under more than one of the statutory provisions, the provision providing for the greatest amount of inclusion will be applicable. Even certain gifts made within three years of death may be included in the gross estate, even though the donor considered them to be lifetime gifts. Thus, even though an individual may not "own" property at his death under state property law principles, it may still be includible in the gross estate for federal tax purposes. And remember the elective share. Few states tie the elective estate to the gross estate for federal tax purposes, so there may be subtle recalculations necessary to determine estate taxes based on the gross estate, elective shares based on the elective estate, and the probate estate. And not surprisingly, the gross estate for federal estate tax purposes will usually capture the largest amount of property. Without going into too much detail, let's consider the property that is generally included in the gross estate.

1. PROPERTY OWNED AT DEATH

Section 2033 of the Code defines the gross estate as including the value of all property to the extent of the decedent's interest at the time of his death. The regulations further clarify that the statute only includes the value of property "beneficially owned" by the decedent at the time of his death, thus excluding property legally held by a decedent at his death, but in which he has no beneficial interest.[44] Hence, property held by the decedent as a trustee or for the benefit of a minor under guardianship will not be included in a decedent's gross estate because he only holds legal (and not beneficial) title to the property. Whether a decedent beneficially owns an interest in property will necessarily be determined by reference to state property law. However, state law property principles will cede to controlling federal law. Thus, property subject to homestead or other exemptions under local law will be included in the gross estate to the extent of the decedent's interest therein at the time of his death, notwithstanding the state law homestead protections for family members, or state law exclusions from taxation.[45]

2. NEAR DEATH TRANSFERS

What do you do when grandma, lying on her deathbed, tells you she wants you to have that Renoir painting hanging above her mantel so it won't be included in her estate and won't be subject to estate taxes? Maybe you can fool all of the people some of the time, and some of the people all of the time, but Grandma can't fool the I.R.S. The Congressional tax writers weren't born yesterday, and they have certainly figured out that death-bed gifts might be a great way to keep control over property until death, but then have it taxed at the gift tax rate because it is *technically* a lifetime transfer. Not a chance—the gross estate may also include certain property that a decedent gave away before his death. Under I.R.C. § 2035(a), property is included in the gross estate of a decedent if the decedent made a transfer of an *interest* in property in the 3 years preceding death and, had the transferred interest been retained by the decedent, the value of the property would have been included in the decedent's gross estate under § 2036, § 2037, § 2038, or § 2042. Note, however, that an outright transfer of property or cash that, if retained, would have been included in the gross estate under I.R.C. § 2033 are unaffected by, and are not included by

---

[44] Treas. Reg. § 20.2033–1(a).

[45] Treas. Reg. § 20.2033–1(b). See also, Chapter Two discussion of Homestead.

§ 2035(a) because 2035(a) by its terms is limited to § 2036, § 2037, § 2038, or § 2042. Moreover, under § 2035(b), any gift tax incurred by the decedent on amounts transferred during this 3 year period will be included in the gross estate.

So what does this all mean? It means that if grandma actually gives away the Renoir, and gift taxes are paid, or if grandma hangs onto the Renoir until the day before she dies, the Renoir will not be part of her gross estate if she gives it away with no strings attached. But if she gives it away in the last three years, any gift taxes paid will be drawn back into her estate to be subject to estate taxes. And of course, if she gives it away the day before she dies, she hasn't had time to pay her gift taxes, and so the gift will be considered testamentary, and estate taxes will be due.

The moral: if you are pretty sure you are going to die in the next three years, there is no *transfer tax reason* for making a lifetime gift because it will be deemed testamentary regardless of the fact that the decedent gave up control and completed delivery of the item.

3. TRANSFERS WITH RETAINED ENJOYMENT

In some cases, a decedent may not legally own an interest in property at her death at all, but such property will nevertheless be included in the gross estate under the theory that the decedent continued to have sufficient control or influence over such property until her death. The first of such sections, § 2036, generally includes in the gross estate the value of any interest transferred by the decedent, if the decedent retained beneficial enjoyment over the property transferred. To be included in the gross estate under § 2036, three basic requirements must be met:

(1) there must be a transfer by a decedent,

(2) who retains a prescribed interest,

(3) for a prescribed period.

For this purpose, a transfer of property may include a direct transfer, an indirect transfer, imputed transfers, and even the accumulation of income in some cases.[46] The prescribed interest under § 2036 includes the possession, enjoyment of, or right to income from property, and also includes the right to designate the person who shall possess or enjoy the property or income therefrom. Finally, the prescribed period is the life of the decedent, any period not ascertainable without reference to decedent's death, or any period that does not in fact end before decedent's death. Thus, if the period of enjoyment is set for 10 years, and decedent dies in year 9, then the fair market value of the property will be included in his estate because the period of decedent's enjoyment did not in fact end before his death. On the other hand, if the decedent died in year 11, nothing would be included in decedent's estate under this section because the decedent's beneficial interst had terminated.

For example, a typical retained-interest transfer occurs when a parent gives her personal residence to a child and continues to occupy the residence (rent-free) until death. Technically, it is important that the interest or power be retained "under" the transfer (i.e., pursuant to an agreement or

---

[46] See United States v. O'Malley, 383 U.S. 627, 634 (1966).

understanding) and that the transfer be made for less than an adequate money's-worth consideration.

4. TRANSFERS TAKING EFFECT AT DEATH AND REVOCABLE TRANSFERS

What if a decedent has transferred property and has retained no enjoyment of or control over the property but only a reversionary interest? If the transferee's enjoyment of the property is conditioned upon surviving the decedent, the transfer is essentially viewed as a substitute for a testamentary disposition and the value of the property transferred will be included in the gross estate under I.R.C. § 2037. However, such inclusion is contingent upon the decedent retaining a more than *de minimis* reversionary interest in the property. This reversionary interest test requires the value of the reversion to be at least 5% of the value of the subject property immediately before the decedent's estate.[47] If this provision applies, the amount that is included in the decedent's gross estate is the value of all property interests conditioned on surviving the decedent.

Also included in a decedent's gross estate are those transfers, by trust or otherwise, over which a decedent retains a power to alter, amend, revoke, or terminate the transferee's interest in the property.[48] Even where a transfer is otherwise irrevocable, the property can be included in the gross estate where a decedent possessed the power to alter either the amount of a transfer or even merely the time of enjoyment. For example, § 2038 is applicable to a power reserved by the grantor of a trust to accumulate income or distribute it to A, and to distribute corpus to A, even though the remainder is vested in A or his estate, and no other person has any beneficial interest in the trust

However, only the *value* of an interest in property subject to a power to which § 2038 applies is included in the decedent's gross estate under this section.[49] Frequently, items will be included in the gross estate of a decedent under both § 2036 and § 2038 as both sections are concerned with powers being retained by a transferor of property; however, as noted above, when an item could be included under multiple sections, that section providing for the greatest inclusion will be applicable. The real lesson to be learned here is that there is a cost to keeping some control over property and that cost is potential inclusion in the gross estate. As succinctly put by Chief Judge Aldrich in *Old Colony Trust Co. v. United States*, "the cost of holding onto the strings may prove to be a rope burn."[50]

5. OTHER INCLUSIONS FOR CERTAIN TYPES OF ASSETS

In some instances, the concepts of property ownership and the transfer thereof are complex enough to warrant special treatment. Thus, unlike the categories of property discussed previously, which are generally always included in the gross estate, other property is treated in a more nuanced way. These include annuities, life insurance, powers of appointment, and jointly owned property.

---

[47]   See I.R.C. § 2037(a)(2).

[48]   I.R.C. § 2038.

[49]   Treas. Reg. § 20.2038–1(a).

[50]   423 F.2d 601, 605 (1st Cir. 1970).

An *annuity* is essentially an insurance product that pays income to an individual for a term of years (or life) and is frequently used in retirement planning for those who want to ensure a steady stream of income during their retirement. For estate tax purposes, the focus is on whether or not the annuity provides for survivorship benefits and whether this benefit should be included in the gross estate of a decedent. The survivorship benefit is a gift from the decedent to the survivor. In general, § 2039 includes the value of an annuity or other payment (such as a deferred compensation agreement with an employer), receivable by any beneficiary by reason of surviving the decedent, if under the contract or agreement an annuity or payment was payable to the decedent, or the decedent possessed the right to receive such annuity or payment for his life or for any period not ascertainable without reference to his death or for any period which does not in fact end before his death.[51]

Thus, by its own terms, § 2039 does not apply to the situation where an individual purchases an annuity solely for the benefit of another. The section's true aim is to include those situations where a decedent had purchased an annuity for his own benefit as well as for the benefit of another. In that case, § 2039 includes a proportion of the value of the annuity in the decedent's gross estate equal to the *decedent's contribution* to the purchase price of the annuity over the entire purchase price of the annuity. For purposes of calculating the amount to be included in the gross estate of a decedent, the value of the annuity is equal to the present value of the stream of future payments to be made *after* the decedent's death.[52] However, if an annuity or other payment is in substance the proceeds of an insurance policy on the life of the decedent, § 2039 does not apply; instead, the appropriate analysis for inclusion in the gross estate will be under § 2042 which specifically covers life insurance.[53]

There are many different ways in which *life insurance* is bought and sold. The decedent can buy a policy on his own life, payable to his estate, or payable to another. The decedent can also buy life insurance on someone else's life, payable to himself or to someone else. And a third party can buy life insurance on the decedent payable to the decedent's estate or payable to herself or someone else. Section 2042 only applies to insurance policies on the life of the decedent. Where the decedent is the owner of an insurance policy on the life of another, such ownership interest is properly includible in the gross estate under § 2033, and not § 2042. But for insurance policies owned by the decedent on his own life, any amount that is payable to an insured decedent's estate is logically included in the gross estate.[54] This makes sense because any proceeds that become part of the probate estate and are disposed of according to the probate process are nothing more than testamentary transfers. However, when another individual is named as a beneficiary, the result will depend on whether or not the decedent possessed any of the "incidents of ownership" in the policy at his death.[55]

The term "incidents of ownership" is not limited in its meaning to ownership of the policy in the technical legal sense, but includes the power to change the beneficiary, to surrender or cancel the policy, to assign the

---

[51] I.R.C § 2039.

[52] Treas. Reg. § 20.2031–8.

[53] See Treas. Reg. § 20.2039–1.

[54] I.R.C. § 2042(1).

[55] I.R.C. § 2042(2).

policy, to revoke an assignment, to pledge the policy for a loan, or to obtain from the insurer a loan against the surrender value of the policy.[56] The term "incidents of ownership" also includes a reversionary interest in the policy or its proceeds, whether arising by the express terms of the policy or other instrument or by operation of law, but only if the value of the reversionary interest immediately before the death of the decedent exceeds 5% of the value of the policy.[57] On the other hand, the mere payment of the insurance premiums or contribution to a trust for the payment of policy premiums is not considered to be an incident of ownership under § 2042.[58] Although § 2042 concentrates on whether or not the decedent possesses any incidents of ownership at death, remember that § 2035 may apply to include the value of the policy benefit where the decedent transfers any incidents of ownership in the 3 years preceding his or her death.

An individual also may effectively hold an ownership interest in property by way of a *general power of appointment* over such property. If an individual has the power to appoint trust income or principal among a designated class of beneficiaries that includes such individual (or his estate or creditors) and dies holding such power, § 2041 will include the value of the underlying property in his gross estate. Note that the power of appointment is considered to exist on the date of the decedent's death even though the exercise is subject to a condition precedent of giving notice or only takes effect upon the expiration of a stated period after its exercise, whether or not notice has been given or the power has been exercised on or before the date of death. In addition to property subject to a decedent's general power of appointment at his death, § 2041(a)(2) requires inclusion in the gross estate where the decedent exercised or released a general power of appointment that would have resulted in inclusion in the gross estate under §§ 2035–2038 if it had been a direct transfer of property.

When property is held in a form of *joint ownership* that provides for a right of survivorship, a decedent's interest in such property extinguishes upon his or her death for state property purposes. But jointly held property may be included in the decedent's gross estate depending on the relative contributions of the joint owners. Essentially, what is included in the gross estate is the ratable portion of the property equivalent to a decedent's contribution to the purchase of such property.[59] That is of course, unless such property is held by a husband and wife as tenants by the entirety or joint tenants with a right of survivorship, in which case the value included in the gross estate is one-half the value of such property.[60] The spousal exception for joint ownership between spouses is consistent with the numerous provisions in the code that provide for the free transferability of property between spouses and that attempt to provide a parity between community and separate property states.

---

[56]   Treas. Reg. § 20.2042–1(c)(2).

[57]   Treas. Reg. § 20.2042–1(c)(3).

[58]   See Estate of Headrick v. C.I.R., 918 F.2d 1263, 1268 (6th Cir. 1990); Estate of Leder v. C.I.R., 893 F.2d 237, 242 (10th Cir. 1989).

[59]   I.R.C. § 2040(a).

[60]   I.R.C. § 2040(b). The 50–50 rule for spouses applies only to joint tenancies created after 1976. Note that the surviving spouse's interest automatically qualifies for a marital deduction, so the only function of the 50-percent inclusion is to limit the basis step-up in the surviving spouse's hands.

As you can see, the Internal Revenue Code includes as part of his gross estate virtually all property that a decedent owns at death, controls at death, has an interest in just prior to death, gave away shortly before death, or in any way benefits from before death. Then, at death, everything in the gross estate transfers to others and is potentially taxable, i.e. subject to the estate tax. If a lifetime gift was made more than three years prior to death, and gift taxes were paid on that transfer, that property is not included in the gross estate. But gift taxes paid for gifts made in the three years prior to death are included in the gross estate.

Now that you know how to distinguish between a lifetime gift and a testamentary gift, and you know what property is included in the gross estate, you know all the potentially taxable transfers that have been made. But not all potentially taxable transfers will in fact be subject to either the estate or the gift tax. Exclusions, exemptions, deductions, and credits can all decrease a decedent's estate tax liability, and maximizing the use of these categories of tax-free transfers is the heart of planning for high-wealth individuals.

D. Tax-Free Transmission of Wealth: The Utilization of Deductions, Exclusions, and Credits

So far we have focused on the general tax base and the potential breadth of gift and estate taxes so that you understand the kinds of transfers that are taxable and the types of property that are typically included in either the gift or the estate tax base. With both estate and gift taxes, however, there are a realm of planning opportunities to lower potential tax liability by using *exclusions*, *deductions*, and *credits*. This section highlights the basics of how these items operate within the federal transfer tax scheme and how they may be used to effectuate a tax efficient estate plan.

1. Amounts Excluded from Gift Taxation

Certainly, every time I buy a package of legos for my kids, or I buy them ice cream cones at the beach, I am making a gift to them. But life would be a nightmare of bookkeeping if I had to keep track of every little thing I give them or what I pay on their behalf. Even their proportionate share of the utility bills, the heat for their bedroom, as distinct from the heat for mine, could conceivably come under the gift tax regime.[61] To provide administrative ease and make the gift tax regime reasonable, there are two basic categories of gifts that are exempt from tax altogether: gifts under a certain value (the annual exclusion) and gifts for certain purposes. More importantly, transfers that are excluded altogether from taxation do not get factored in to determine the tax rate. So exclusions reduce not only the tax base but the tax rate which may help with passing on my unused portion of my unified credit to my spouse.

---

[61] Admittedly, many of these expenses qualify as transfers that discharge my support obligations, and as such are deemed mad for adequate money's-worth consideration. But many incidentals and non-necessaries would count as gifts.

a.   Qualified Transfers

Under § 2503(e), certain transfers for educational or medical expenses are excluded from taxable gifts. Educational expenses paid on behalf of any individual as tuition to an educational organization are excluded from the definition of taxable gifts.[62] While the statutory language is relatively straight forward, it is important to note that gifts of these types should be made directly to the educational institutions and should not be made by depositing tuition money into Little Johnny's bank account as a court could view that as a gift of money to Little Johnny instead of a gift of tuition, which is excluded from taxation. Similarly, medical expenses paid on behalf of another to a person who provides medical care are not taxable gifts.[63] As with tuition payments, it is important that any payments go directly to the person who provided the medical care and are not given to the recipient directly.

Most importantly, there are no limitations on the size of gifts for tuition and medical care. I can send my children to Columbia University[64] or Macon State College[65] and not have to worry about gift taxes. Notably, however, the costs of room and board are not part of *tuition*. Therefore, buying a loft in New York City so your children can live while they attend Columbia may constitute a taxable gift, depending on how it is titled, who owns it, and who has primary dominion and control. And I can pay for a friend's heart transplant or a mere teeth cleaning so long as I pay the health care provider directly. Not surprisingly, some so-called medical services won't be deemed valid expenses, such as elective cosmetic surgery, over the counter aspirin, illegal drugs, the gallon of scotch to drown one's sorrows over the untimely demise of one's dog, or the trip to India to visit one's guru in the search for inner peace.

b.   Annual Exclusion Gifts

Under I.R.C. § 2503(b) , gifts up to a certain dollar value are excluded from taxable gifts on an annual basis. In 2013, an individual can give up to $14,000 to any other person, or to a hundred different people, without making any taxable gifts for the year.[66] And that amount has been gradually adjusted for inflation since 1998 and will continue to be subject to adjustment for the immediate future. In general, the annual exclusion from gift taxation is meant to exclude *de minimis* gifts made throughout the year, which would be difficult to account for administratively and would raise a negligible amount of revenue. For example, if Uncle Bob decides to buy you a steak dinner one night and your portion of the bill comes out to $60, he has technically made a gift of $60 to you. However, such a gift will not give rise to taxation unless your Uncle Bob makes other gifts to you during the taxable year that equal more than $14,000 in the aggregate. So, consider

---

[62] I.R.C. § 2503(e)(2)(A).

[63] I.R.C. § 2503(e)(2)(B).

[64] Columbia was named the most expensive college in the U.S. by U.S. News and World Report.   See   http://www.huffingtonpost.com/2012/01/24/the–10–most–expensive–col_n_1229224.html at $45,290 per year, far more than the annual gift tax exclusion.

[65] Macon State was named the cheapest public college. See http://www.huffingtonpost.com/2012/04/24/10–cheapest–public–colleges_n_1448497.html?ref=topbar#s898412   &   title=Macon_State_College.

[66] The amount subject to exclusion in any year is indexed to inflation based on cost-of-living adjustments under § 1(f)(3) and is rounded down to the nearest $1000. *See* 2503(b)(2)

the situation where your uncle buys you dinner every night of the year and the aggregate amount of these dinners equals $21,900 ($60x365).

How much of this will be subject to gift taxes? Again, assuming 2013 numbers, Uncle Bob will only be subject to taxation on $7,900 ($21,900–14,000), which is the value of gifts made to you during the taxable year in excess of the *Annual Exclusion* amount. Additionally, as the annual exclusion is applied to the amount given to each recipient and is not aggregated by transferor, Uncle Bob could give up to $14,000 to any number of individuals without making any taxable gifts. Moreover, when Uncle Bob has to pay for your triple bypass because you ate so much cholesterol-laden red meat all year, the medical costs will be excluded from gift taxes as a qualified medical expense.

However, the annual exclusion only applies to gifts of present interests in property or, more accurately, only to gifts, other than gifts of future interests.[67] Thus, whether a gift may be excludible depends on whether the property interest gifted is a present interest or a future interest for the purposes of the tax code. Under the regulations, a future interest is one that is limited to commence in use, possession, or enjoyment at some future date or time.[68]

From the perspective of tax planning, especially for an estate that is only marginally larger than the estate tax exemption, one will want to make full use of annual exclusions available on a year to year basis. And if you don't want to give $14,000 every year to your children outright, a very effective way to aggregate the annual exclusion is through a trust with what are known as "Crummey Powers." Crummey Powers, named for the famous tax case *Crummey v. Comm'r*, involve giving the beneficiary a right to withdraw principal from the trust, which converts the gift from a future interest to a present interest. When used in the context of annual donations of an amount equal to the annual exclusion, and if the beneficiary does not make a withdrawal, the trust can grow without ever triggering gift taxes.

Crummey v. C.I.R.

United States Court of Appeals Ninth Circuit. 397 F.2d 82 (1968)

[On February 12, 1962, D.C. and E.E. Crummey, husband and wife, executed, as grantors, an irrevocable living trust for the benefit of their four children. One child, J.K., was 22 on December 31, 1962 and the other three were under age 21. On December 31, 1962, another child, J.S. had reached age 21. The annual exclusion for gift tax purposes in 1962 and 1963 was $3,000 for each child, for a total for all four children of $24,000 each year ($3,000 for each child paid by the husband and $3,000 for each child paid by the wife). On December 15, 1962 the petitioners placed $49,550.00 in the trust, and on December 19, 1963 they placed $12,797.81 in the trust. Husband and wife each took four $3,000 exemptions for a total of $24,000 each year against the gifts, but the Tax Commissioner allowed only $3,000 each in 1962 because only one child was over the age of 21, and only $6,000 each in 1963. On appeal, the Tax Court allowed an additional $3,000 each for 1962 because J.S., the second oldest child, was 18 and had limited rights by California law. On appeal, the Ninth Circuit reversed.]

---

[67]   § 2503(b)

[68]   Treas. Reg. § 25.2503(b).

The key provision of the trust agreement is the 'demand' provision which states:

. . . "With respect to such additions, each child of the Trustors may demand at any time (up to and including December 31 of the year in which a transfer to his or her Trust has been made) the sum of Four Thousand Dollars ($4,000.00) or the amount of the transfer from each donor, whichever is less, payable in cash immediately upon receipt by the Trustee of the demand in writing and in any event, not later than December 31 in the year in which such transfer was made. Such payment shall be made from the gift of that donor for that year. If a child is a minor at the time of such gift of that donor for that year, or fails in legal capacity for any reason, the child's guardian may make such demand on behalf of the child. The property received pursuant to the demand shall be held by the guardian for the benefit and use of the child."

The whole question on this appeal is whether or not a present interest was given by the petitioners to their minor children so as to qualify as an exclusion under § 2503(b)(1). The petitioners on appeal contend that each minor beneficiary has the right under California law to demand partial distribution from the Trustee. In the alternative they urge that a parent as natural guardian of the person of his minor children could make such a demand. As a third alternative, they assert that under California law a minor over the age of 14 has the right to have a legal guardian appointed who can make the necessary demand. The Commissioner, as cross petitioner, alleges as error the Tax Court's ruling that the 1962 gifts in trust to Janet (then age 20) were present interests.

It was stipulated before the Tax Court in regard to the trust and the parties thereto that at all times relevant all the minor children lived with the petitioners and no legal guardian had been appointed for them. In addition, it was agreed that all the children were supported by petitioners and none of them had made a demand against the trust funds or received any distribution from them.

The tax regulations define a 'future interest' for the purposes of § 2503(b) as follows:

'Future interests' is a legal term, and includes reversions, remainder, and other interests or estates, whether vested or contingent, and whether or not supported by a particular interest or estate, which are limited to commence in use, possession or enjoyment at some future date or time.' Treasury Regulations of Gift Tax, § 25.2503–3.

This definition has been adopted by the Supreme Court. [The court then explained that there were three approaches to determining whether a gift to a minor constituted a future or a present interest when the minor was actually or legally incapacitated from demanding the property. The Tax Court's view, articulated in the case of *Stifel v. C.I.R.*, 197 F.2d 107 (2nd Cir. 1952) was that the court should look at the actual circumstances to determine if the minor could, in fact, make a demand in conjunction with the likelihood of the minor doing so, and having a guardian actually appointed was an important element. On the other extreme was the case of *Kieckhefer v. C.I.R.*, 189 F.2d 118 (7th Cir. 1951) in which the court held that so long as the minor had the legal right to make the demand, and the only disability was his underage status, the interest was a present interest, regardless of whether he was likely or not to actually make the demand. The court then identified a third approach, a blend of the "actual circumstances" v. "legal rights" views, that looked to the legal rights of the child to make a demand, which would be dependent on the laws of the jurisdiction, plus the trust instrument language. This blended view came from the case of *George W. Perkins*, 27 T.C. 601 (1956). The court then explained that so long as a parent could make a demand on behalf of a minor, and a guardian could be appointed to accept and manage the property, minority status should not defeat a child's legal right to demand the property, thus rendering it a present interest. The court then determined that all the gifts were of present interests, explaining:]

Given the trust, the California law, and the circumstances in our case, it can be seen that very different results may well be achieved, depending upon the test used. Under a strict interpretation of the Stifel test of examining everything and determining whether there is any likelihood of present enjoyment, the gifts to minors in our case would seem to be 'future interests'. Although under our interpretation neither the trust nor the law technically forbid a demand by the minor, the practical difficulties of a child going through the procedures seem substantial. In addition, the surrounding facts indicate the children were well cared for and the obvious intention of the trustors was to create a long term trust. No guardian had been appointed and, except for the tax difficulties, probably never would be appointed. As a practical matter, it is likely that some, if not all, of the beneficiaries did not even know that they had any right to demand funds from the trust. They probably did not know when contributions were made to the trust or in what amounts. Even had they known, the substantial contributions were made toward the end of the year so that the time to make a demand was severely limited. Nobody had made a demand under the provision, and no distributions had been made. We think it unlikely that any demand ever would have been made.

All exclusions should be allowed under the *Perkins* test or the 'right to enjoy' test in *Gilmore*. Under *Perkins*, all that is necessary is to find that the demand could not be resisted. We interpret that to mean legally resisted and, going on that basis, we do not think the trustee would have any choice but to have a guardian appointed to take the property demanded. . . .

We decline to follow a strict reading of the *Stifel* case in our situation because we feel that the solution suggested by that case is inconsistent and unfair. It becomes arbitrary for the I.R.S. to step in and decide who is likely to make an effective demand. Under the circumstances suggested in our case, it is doubtful that any demands will be made against the trust—yet the Commissioner always allowed the exclusion as to adult beneficiaries. There is nothing to indicate that it is any more likely that John will demand funds than that any other beneficiary will do so. The only distinction is that it might be easier for him to make such a demand. Since we conclude that the demand can be made by the others, it follows that the exclusion should also apply to them. In another case we might follow the broader Kieckhefer rule, since it seems least arbitrary and establishes a clear standard. However, if the minors have no way of making the demand in our case, then there is more than just a postponement involved, since John could demand his share of yearly additions while the others would never have the opportunity at their shares of those additions but would be limited to taking part of any additions added subsquent to their 21st birth-days.

We conclude that the result under the *Perkins* or 'right to enjoy' tests is preferable in our case. The petitioners should be allowed all of the exclusions claimed for the two year period.

———————

Query: Does it seem reasonable that a taxpayer should be able to consider a gift to a minor of a power to withdraw funds as satisfying the annual exclusion amount? What if the trust settlor is the parent who serves as the child's guardian and is the person who would elect to withdraw funds under the *Crummey* power? Does the child really have any reasonable power to withdraw the funds? If not, should the law be changed?

———————

After *Crummey* was decided, it seemed clear that a future interest of a beneficiary could be converted into a present interest by granting an immediate right of withdrawal upon contribution to the trust. However, what should be the result where the power holder lacks the knowledge necessary or the time to make the demand either because she did not receive a "Crummey Notice" or because she received it too late to effectively act on it? If you read the *Crummey* case carefully, you will notice that the withdrawal beneficiaries in that case did not receive any notice of the gifts; however, in Rev. Rul. 81–7, the Service found that if the donor's conduct makes the demand right illusory and effectively deprives the donee of the power, such a transfer to the trust will not qualify as a present interest eligible for the gift tax annual exclusion under § 2503(b).[69] In that revenue ruling, neither the grantor nor the trustee informed the beneficiary of the demand right before the demand right had already lapsed, essentially making it impossible for the beneficiary to exercise a right of withdrawal giving rise to the present interest envisioned by § 2503(b).

Sending timely and effective withdrawal notices seems to have become a necessary condition to take advantage of the principles of the *Crummey* case in creating a gift of a present interest. Recently however, the Tax Court found a gift of a present interest notwithstanding the fact that some or even all of the beneficiaries may not have known they had the right to demand withdrawals.[70] Specifically, the court found that "in distinguishing present interests from future interests for federal gift tax purposes, the test is not whether the beneficiary was likely to receive the present enjoyment of the property, but whether he or she had the legal right to demand it."[71] That being said, since the IRS has not acquiesced with this result, it would behoove the careful estate planner to ensure that beneficiaries are given reasonable notice of their withdrawal rights. After all, what good is a right that you don't know about?

Most aspects of the *Crummey* trust are concentrated on achieving tax benefits for the grantor or donor of property. However, when a beneficiary does not exercise his right to withdrawal from the trust, he has essentially

———

[69] Rev. Rul. 81–7, 1981–1 C.B. 474 (1981).

[70] *Estate of Turner v. C.I.R.*, 102 T.C.M. 214 (T.C. 2011).

[71] *Id. at 21.*

made a transfer back to the trust and to whoever would receive the funds under the terms of the trust. Thus, if one reviews the rules regarding powers of appointment discussed in Chapter Four, the lapse of such a power may properly result in a taxable gift to the other trust beneficiaries. For the same reasons discussed above, such a result can be avoided by limiting a beneficiary's withdrawal power in any year to the greater of $5,000 or 5% of the trust principal which is available to satisfy the withdrawal power.

In addition, if there are minor beneficiaries, § 2503(c) can provide yet another way to create a present interest in property for a transfer in trust and allow for utilization of the annual exclusion amount. Under § 2503(c), if gifted property and income therefrom may be expended by, or for the benefit of the donee, and will pass to the donee on his attaining 21 years of age, no part of the gift shall be considered a gift of a future interest in property. Such provision can be useful in instances where the parents or grandparents do not want to give a child or grandchild property directly, but wish to make use of the § 2503(b) exclusion amounts.

Additionally, you can aggregate the effects of the annual exclusion through some not very difficult trust transactions. Consider the following case of a settlor who owns property worth $210,000 that she wants to give to her two children. If she transfers it directly to them, she has to report $190,000 as gifts ($210,000 less the 2 annual exclusions of $10,000). So how can she use the annual exclusions of her grandchildren to make the gift tax problem for her children disappear? Keep reading.

Est. of Cristofani v. Comm'r

97 T.C. 74 (1991)

In this case the settlor created an irrevocable trust, funded with a 1/3 interest each year in unencumbered real estate worth a total of $210,000 ($70,000 was to be placed in the trust each year through a real estate deed transferring 1/3 of the property). The primary trust beneficiaries were her two children and, if both children survived the settlor by 120 days, the trust was to end and the property distributed to the two children. Each of her children had the power to withdraw an amount equal to the annual gift tax exclusion each year in the period 15 days following the contribution of the property to the trust. The settlor's 5 grandchildren were also provided for. They too had the right to withdraw from the trust an amount equal to the annual gift tax exclusion (*Crummey* Power), and they were contingent remainder beneficiaries in case one or both of the settlor's children did not survive her by 120 days. The IRS allowed the annual exclusion for the two children ($20,000 each year) but not the five grandchildren, claiming that their interest was a contingent future interest and not a present interest eligible for the annual exclusion. The Tax Court disagreed, following *Crummey*. The IRS tried to distinguish *Crummey* on the fact that in that case the beneficiaries who had the power to withdraw up to the annual exclusion amount were also the parties who would ultimately reap the final benefit by receiving the principal of the trust in the future. In this case, the grandchildren might have had the right to withdraw for 15 days, but once they didn't exercise that right, they had no further rights to the principal unless their parent died in the 120 days after the settlor. The Tax Court again disagreed, stating that so long as the grandchildren had the legal right to withdraw the property, the settlor was entitled to the gift tax exclusion.

Query: Assuming a present interest was given to each grandchild, what happens legally when that grandchild fails to withdraw his or her share? Has he or she just made a gift of a present interest to his or her parent, the person who will most likely be entitled to the principal?

The answer to the above query is yes! Notice how the settlor was able to take property worth $210,000, divide it into 3 parts worth $70,000 each, and each year put one share worth $70,000 into the trust. By giving not only her primary beneficiaries, but also her contingent beneficiaries, a *Crummey* Power to withdraw, she essentially makes 7 gifts each year of property valued at $10,000, and the five grandchildren who fail to withdraw their gifts, make 5 gifts back to their parents.[72] In the end, had the settlor lived one more year and been able to make the final contribution to the trust, she would have been able to transfer property worth $210,000 to her two children, by dividing it into 21 shares worth $10,000 each. Since no one exercised their rights to withdraw, the trust terminates and gives possession of the principal half to each child. Voila! She made a gift of $105,000 to each of her two children without triggering gift taxes, when the annual exclusion for the two children would have been only $30,000 each for the three years. By dividing the gift over time and using the exclusions of her grandchildren, she broke the gift down into 21 shares worth $10,000 each.

2. DEDUCTIONS COMMON TO ESTATE AND GIFT TAX

Crummey Powers are applicable in the context of the gift tax only, because the annual exclusion applies only to the gift tax. But some deductions apply whether they are made in the context of an *inter vivos* transfer (gift tax) or a testamentary transfer (estate tax). These deductions are the most important for estate planning because they can be used in ways that weave gift and estate tax minimization mechanisms together into a blended, coherent whole. The current tax code allows for two unlimited deductions: for charitable gifts and for transfers between spouses. The unlimited deduction means that no estate or gift taxes will be due if all of a wealthy donor's property is given for charitable purposes, or to one's spouse. Hence the popularity of charitable foundations established by the super wealthy, like Bill and Melinda Gates or Leona Helmsley or Robert Wood Johnson.

The unlimited deduction for one's spouse can be helpful for limited family planning purposes, but unless every owner keeps marrying a younger spouse and passing property to the new spouse with each death, eventually the property will be taxable. Thus, if Bill Gates predeceases his wife and he leaves his vast Microsoft fortune to Melinda, she will need to remarry (or spend it all or give it to charity) before she dies or the property

---

[72] Furthermore, the lapse of the grandchildren's powers is sheltered from gift tax (at least in part) by the 5 and 5 rule discussed *supra*. Does anyone really think the grandchildren filed gift tax returns for taxable gifts in excess of $5,000 or 5%?

will be taxable as part of her estate. If she remarries, she can pass the property to her new husband, and then her new spouse can remarry when she dies. But if she dies before she remarries, then oops—estate taxes will be due. For obvious reasons, Congress isn't too worried that people will enter into an endless cycle of marriages in order to escape estate taxes. Marriage is probably too important a decision to make solely on the basis of tax avoidance.

Note, though, that if Melinda marries a woman, even in a state that allows same-sex marriage, she cannot take advantage of the unlimited marital deduction because the federal government does not recognize them.[73] Couples in same-sex marriages face considerable tax and bookkeeping problems because once John reaches his $14,000 annual exclusion in making gifts to and supporting Steve, his further support[74] or gifts to his partner (including paying the heating bill for the house) would be considered taxable gifts.

For the seriously wealthy, therefore, the marital deduction is important but probably not as important as the charitable deduction. And the *charitable trust* is the most common mechanism for making large charitable gifts. Although I might be willing to give a million dollars here and there to a variety of charities, if I have $100 million I want to devote to charitable purposes, I will probably want to set up my own foundation to make sure that my trustees administer the money entirely according to my own wishes.

a. *Charitable Deductions and Charitable Trusts*

Certain transfers of property, whether occurring during life or at death, may give rise to deductions against the estate or gift tax respectively. First, transfers of property to a qualified charitable organization will give rise to a deduction against the gift tax under § 2522 and against the estate tax under § 2055. Although structurally similar, the main difference between making a charitable contribution during life rather than at death is related to the income tax deduction, which is only available for charitable contributions during life. If a client has concrete charitable inclinations, it would be counterproductive to forego the potential income tax deduction only to delay the inevitable contribution.

But let's spend a little time on charitable gifts because there are a number of interlocking benefits and overlapping rules that are important to grasp. First, if I want to make a gift to my favorite charity, I can just write a check. If I do it during life, the contribution is a deduction against my income to reduce my income taxes. If I do it at death, in my will, the entire value of all gifts to qualified charities is exempt from estate taxes. That means I can give $5.25 million in 2013 to private individuals exempt from

---

[73] Yet. As this book is going to press, the Supreme Court is considering an estate tax case challenging the Defense of Marriage Act (DOMA), the law that defines marriage as between a man and a woman for federal purposes. That case, *Windsor v. U.S.,* arose when the IRS assessed the executor over $300,000 in estate taxes for a decedent who left all her property to her same-sex surviving spouse. Refusing to give the decedent's estate the benefit of the unlimited marital deduction, despite the parties' marriage, the surviving spouse/executor sued to have DOMA declared unconstitutional. It was held unconstitutional in the Second Circuit. See *Windsor v. U.S.,* 699 F.3d 169 (2d Cir. 2012).

[74] Arguably, transfers in discharge of support obligations should escape gift tax (deemed made for adequate money's-worth consideration), because the rationale depends on the enforceability of an obligation under state law, not on marital status.

estate taxes, and if I give all the rest of my estate directly to my favorite charity, my estate won't pay any estate taxes at all. But direct gifts to charities are usually fairly small, unless you want to have a building named for you or you can limit the way the charity uses your money. If you are a high net worth individual and you are thinking of using charitable gifts to reduce your estate or gift tax liability, you aren't thinking about the $500.00 donation to help tsunami victims or the $50.00 you paid to enter the Cancer Society's 5K fun run.

There are two basic ways to make high-value gifts: you either give the money to the charity directly to be held in trust and used for limited charitable purposes, or you establish your own charitable trust or foundation like the Bill and Melinda Gates Foundation or the MacArthur Foundation. In both instances, you are using a trust form because, besides getting the tax benefits of your charitable gift, you will also get the favorable legal benefits of the *charitable trust*. Charitable trusts have three important benefits: 1) charitable interests in trust are not subject to the Rule Against Perpetuities like private trusts are, 2) they do not require ascertainable beneficiaries and, 3) they get the benefit of *cy pres* reformation rules when circumstances change. And using a trust will prevent your favorite entity from siphoning off some of your generous gift and using it to send the director on a cruise or buying lottery tickets when private donations are down because a trustee is keeping an eye on how the money is being spent.

But just when you thought things were making sense, it turns out that the definitions of charity, or *charitable purpose*, aren't the same when it comes to the IRS validating a tax deduction and the common law rules on *cy pres* or the RAP. And that is because the tax-privileged 501(c)(3) nonprofit status is of relatively recent origin. So we must go back and begin with the charitable trust rules. Most *private* trusts must end; that is, they must terminate and the property come out of the trust and be paid outright to remainder beneficiaries, usually no later than the end of the perpetuities period as defined by your state's RAP. A trust to "my spouse for life, then my children for life, then to my grandchildren for life, with a remainder to my great-grandchildren" will run into RAP problems. The remainder to the great-grandchildren violates the common law RAP so it will be extinguished, and replaced with a reversion in the settlor. At the end of the grandchildren's life estate the trust will end and the property will pass to the then-living heirs of the settlor. Many states interpret their RAP to void perpetual trusts or trusts of infinite duration that do not end within the perpetuities period. But a trust to "use the income from the trust to help unwanted pets find homes" can exist in perpetuity so long as the purpose of the trust is a truly charitable one.

The trust also doesn't fail because of lack of ascertainable beneficiaries. Charitable trusts don't have identifiable beneficiaries, but they are allowed to continue because the criteria for identifying beneficiaries is reasonably well articulated and the public policy reasons of promoting charitable giving justifies allowing these trusts to continue even though identifiable beneficiaries may not exist at the inception of the trust.

The most important criteria for a charitable trust is that it have a *charitable purpose*, a criteria that has been defined by judges over the centuries, and which has been overlaid by statutory definitions. The definition of charitable purpose is more expansive than simply meeting the IRS definition of a non-profit entity under IRC 501(c)(3). Consider these famous, and not-so-famous cases:

Shendandoah Valley National Bank v. Taylor

192 Va. 135, 63 S.E.2d 786 (Va. 1951)

Charles B. Henry, a resident of Winchester, Virginia, died testate on the 23rd day of April, 1949. His will dated April 21, 1949, left the testator's entire estate valued at $86,000, to the Shenandoah Valley National Bank of Winchester, in trust, to invest and reinvest the trust estate and collect the income and pay it as follows:

(1) On the last school day of each calendar year before Easter my Trustee shall divide the net income into as many equal parts as there are children in the first, second and third grades of the John Kerr School of the City of Winchester, and shall pay one of such equal parts to each child in such grades, to be used by such child in the furtherance of his or her obtainment of an education.

(2) On the last school day of each calendar year before Christmas my trustee shall divide the net income into as many equal parts as there are children in the first, second and third grades of the John Kerr School of the City of Winchester, and shall pay one of such equal parts to each child in such grades, to be used by such child in the furtherance of his or her obtainment of an education.

The will also provided that the names of the students would be determined from school records, that payment was to be as equal for each child as could be practicable, and that if the John Kerr School is discontinued the payments would be made to the children of the same grades of the school that replaces the John Kerr School. Voiding the trust as non-charitable, the Virginia Supreme Court explained:

'A charity', in a legal sense, may be described as a gift to be applied, consistently with existing laws, for the benefit of an indefinite number of persons, either by bringing their hearts under the influence of education or religion, by relieving their bodies from disease, suffering or constraint, by assisting them to establish themselves for life, or by erecting or maintaining public building or works, or otherwise lessening the burdens of government. It is immaterial whether the purpose is called charitable in the gift itself, if it is so described as to show that it is charitable. Generally speaking, any gift not inconsistent with existing laws which is promotive of science or tends to the education, enlightening, benefit or amelioration of the condition of mankind or the diffusion of useful knowledge, or is for the public convenience is a charity. It is essential that a charity be for the benefit of an indefinite number of persons; for if all the beneficiaries are personally designated, the trust lacks the essential element of indefiniteness, which is one characteristic of a legal charity.

In the law of trusts there is a real and fundamental distinction between a charitable trust and one that is devoted to mere benevolence. The former is public in nature and valid; the latter is private and if it offends the rule against perpetuities, it is void.

It is quite clear that trusts which are devoted to mere benevolence or liberality, or generosity, cannot be upheld as charities. Benevolent objects include acts dictated by mere kindness, good will, or a disposition to do good

* * *. *Charity in a legal sense must be distinguished from acts of liberality or benevolence. To constitute a charity the use must be public in its nature.*

Query: The court voided this "candy cane trust" for not being charitable because it did not limit the beneficiaries to those in need, its timing was such that it was unlikely to induce the children to focus on their education and, although it promoted general happiness, it did not advance the social interest of the community. What should Mr. Henry have done if he really wanted his property devoted to giving a small amount of ready money to the school children in his community?

Marsh v. Frost Nat'l Bank

129 S.W.3d 174 (Tex.App. 2004)

Charles Walker died on March 13, 2000, leaving a holographic will with the following provision:

> *I hereby direct my Executor to sell tract 3 of the V.M. Donigan 456.80 Partition for cash and to invest the proceeds in safe and secure tax-free U.S. government bonds or insured tax-free municipal bonds. This trust is to be called the James Madison Fund to honor our fourth President, the Father of the Constitution. The ultimate purpose of this fund is to provide a million dollar trust fund for every American 18 years or older. At 6% compound interest and a starting figure of $1,000,000.00, it would take approximately 346 years to provide enough money to do this. My executor will head the Board of Trustees. . . . When the Fund reaches $15,000,000 my Executor's function will cease, and the money will be turned over to the Sec. of the Treasury for management by the federal government. The President of the U.S., the Vice President of the U.S., and the Speaker of the U.S. House of Representatives shall be permanent Trustees of the Fund. The Congress of the United States shall make the final rules and regulations as to how the money will be distributed. No one shall be denied their share because of race, religion, marital status, sexual preference, or the amount of their wealth or lack thereof. . . .*

Quoting this famous line from *Bogert on Trusts*, the Texas court remanded the case to the trial court to consider if reformation were possible. *"Furthermore, trusts created to distribute money out of liberality or generosity, without regard to the need of the donees and the effect of the gifts, do not have the requisite public benefit necessary to a charity.*

Query: On remand, do you think the trial court will be able to reform this trust to not violate the RAP? Would it qualify as an honorary trust under the UPC? If so, will that help achieve the settlor's purpose?

Griffin v. U.S.

400 F.2d 612 (6th Cir. 1968)

George W. Griffin left $100,000 in trust to be used for the benefit of his wife, for her life, and upon her death, *the income to be used for the education of my grandchildren and for the education of deserving boys and girls in the manner hereinafter set out:*

(1) The Trustee shall use so much of the net income from this trust as may be necessary to assist any grandchild of mine who desires a four-year college education to obtain such college education in a Protestant Christian College; provided, however, that the sum so expended for or on behalf of any grandchild of mine shall not exceed $750.00 in any one school year. This trust for the benefit of my grandchildren shall termi-nate not later than twenty-one (21) years after the date of the death of the last survivor of the group composed of myself, my wife, my three children, and any of my grandchildren who are living at the date of my death; and, at the expiration of such period, the remainder of this trust estate shall be administered entirely as a charitable trust in accordance with the provisions of the next succeeding paragraph.

"(2) It is my intention and desire to make my grandchildren the prima-ry beneficiaries of this trust, and if at any time any grandchild of mine desires to avail himself or herself of the benefits of this trust, he or she shall be entitled to such benefits even to the exclusion of all other per-sons. However, if at any time the net income from this trust is in excess of the amount required to provide college educations for those of my grandchildren who then desire same, in accordance with the preceding paragraph, I direct that my Trustee shall use the balance of said net in-come to provide as many annual scholarships of Five Hundred Dollars ($500.00) each, as possible, to worthy boys or girls residing in South-eastern Kentucky who are ambitious to receive a college education at any Protestant Christian College, and who, without financial assis-tance would be unable to attend college.

The court held that the trust was not entirely charitable and therefore the entire trust corpus was not entitled to the full charitable tax deduction. But the court did allow the taxpayers to offer evidence that the value of the "private" part of the trust was less than what it would be if no charitable benefits could pay out until the death of the last of Griffin's grandchildren.

Query: The IRS allows for a partial deduction when a portion of a gift will be devoted entirely to a charitable purpose and a portion to a private purpose. How could this taxpayer have achieved better tax results and still provided for educational support for his grandchildren?

Tax Tip: The Mixed-Use Charitable Gift

What if a grantor, like George Griffin, wishes to make a mixed bequest of a single piece of property? For example, consider Uncle Bob who owns an apartment complex and would like to ultimately leave it to his favorite qualified charity, "Pet Pads," so that they can convert the complex into a housing unit for stray dogs and cats. However, Uncle Bob is concerned about the financial stability of his nephew Mike and would like to provide Mike with a stream of income for his life from the operation of the apartment complex. Under the general rule, if property is given to both a charity and a non-charity, the charitable deduction will be disallowed. This is because it can frequently be very difficult (if not impossible) to accurately value the interests that will ultimately be received by the charity, which is essential to de-termining the appropriate amount of a deduction for a contribution to a charity. However, the code provides a number of exceptions that would allow Uncle Bob to make such a mixed bequest while still receiving the charitable deduction. In a char-itable remainder annuity trust (a "CRAT") or a charitable remainder unitrust (a

"CRUT"), the non-charity beneficiary receives a fixed payment for a certain term while the charity is given the entire remainder interest in the property. In a CRAT, the non-charity beneficiary will receive a fixed amount to be paid at least annually; In a CRUT, the non-charity beneficiary receives a fixed percentage of the net fair market value of the trust principal. In addition to CRATs and CRUTs, a grantor could also switch the respective positions of the charity and non-charity through the use of the charitable lead trust (CLT). In a CLT, the annual payments are made to the charity with the remainder passing to the non-charity beneficiary. Whatever the form of contribution, it is essential to remember that a charitable deduction is only available for contributions to certain qualified organizations. No matter how grand the donor may think an organization's cause is, if the organization does not qualify under the provisions of the internal revenue code, no charitable deduction will be had. What makes CRATs, CRUTs, and CLTs work is that a fixed, identifiable proportion of the trust can be attributed to non-charitable purposes, thus making the calculation of the value of the exemption reasonably ascertainable. But if the private beneficiary's interest cannot be easily sectioned out of the rest of the trust, and assigned a reasonably accurate value, the entire trust will be deemed private for purposes of the exemption.

Est. of Kidd

479 P.2d 697 (Az. 1971)

James Kidd was a bachelor of frugal nature who came to Arizona about 1920. On January 2, 1946, he wrote a holographic will which was sealed in an envelope and placed in a safety deposit box. A few years later, Kidd disappeared without a trace. But it was not until shortly before March 6, 1964 that his will was discovered and on that date offered for probate. On proof that Kidd had absented himself from Maricopa County, Arizona for such a period as to be presumed dead, his will was admitted to probate and the First National Bank of Arizona was appointed as Administrator With Will Annexed.

Pursuant to A.R.S. s 14–641, the First National Bank filed a petition to determine heirship and subsequently moved for summary judgment, asking the court to declare that Kidd's will created a valid charitable trust. The trial court granted the motion of the bank, declaring that Kidd's will created a valid charitable trust, and set for hearing the petitions, statements of interest, and claims of those individuals and organizations who sought distribution of the estate under the terms of the will. Hearings were held which continued for a period of almost three months—the trial court taking testimony and receiving exhibits from more than sixty claimants in addition to the more than forty claims submitted without oral testimony.

After extended consideration, the court decreed that the claim of the Neurological Sciences Foundation be granted, and that the residue of James Kidd's estate, amounting to about $175,000.00, be distributed in trust to be used for the purpose of research to be performed and carried on by the Barrow Neurological Institute of Phoenix, Arizona. It rejected the petitions and statements of interest of the other 102 claimants.

Kidd's holographic will provided:

This is my first and only will and is dated the second day in January 1946. I have no heirs have not been married in my life, after all my funeral expenses have been paid and #100. one hundred dollars to some

*preacher of the gospital to say fare well at my grave sell all my property
which is all in cash and stocks with E. F. Hutton Co Phoenix some in
safety box, and have this balance money to go in a research or some scientific proof of a soul of the human body which leaves at death I think
in time their can be a Photograph of soul leaving the human at death,*

James Kidd

The Arizona Supreme Court affirmed in part and reversed in part, affirming the finding of a charitable trust, but remanding to determine which of
four possible claimants should be allowed to control the trust: two individual scientists doing research on the metaphysics of death, the American
Society for Psychical Research or the Psychical Research Foundation.

Query: Although there was no language of trust in this bequest, the court
found a charitable trust to exist. Do you think this trust meets the criteria of
charitable purpose as expounded by the Restatement?

The Restatement 3d of Trusts § 28, Charitable Purposes

Charitable trust purposes include:

(a) the relief of poverty;

(b) the advancement of knowledge or education;

(c) the advancement of religion;

(d) the promotion of health;

(e) governmental or municipal purposes; and

(f) other purposes that are beneficial to the community.

The UTC also defines *charitable purposes* for validating charitable trusts.

UTC § 405.   CHARITABLE PURPOSES; ENFORCEMENT.

(a) A charitable trust may be created for the relief of poverty, the advancement
of education or religion, the promotion of health, governmental or municipal purposes, or other purposes the achievement of which is beneficial to the community.

(b) If the terms of a charitable trust do not indicate a particular charitable
purpose or beneficiary, the court may select one or more charitable purposes or
beneficiaries. The selection must be consistent with the settlor's intention to the
extent it can be ascertained.

(c) The settlor of a charitable trust, among others, may maintain a proceeding
to enforce the trust.

Do you think the following trust meets either statute's definition of a
charitable purpose?

Est. of Breeden

208 Cal.App.3d 981 (1989)

Wilmer Breeden, an active socialist, willed the residue of his estate to the Breeden-Schmidt Foundation or, if it had not been created before his death, to Milton Lessner and Willard Sinclair, as cotrustees, for distribution "to persons, entities and causes advancing the principles of socialism and those causes related to socialism. This shall include, but not be limited to, subsidizing publications, establishing and conducting reading rooms, supporting radio, television and the newspaper media and candidates for public office." His niece and nephew, intestate heirs, petitioned to have the trust invalidated as non-charitable and/or against public policy.

The court affirmed the trust as charitable, explaining: *Although a trust to promote the success of a specific political party is not charitable (see 4A Scott, Law of Trusts (4th ed. 1989) § 374.6, p. 221; the promotion of a particular cause or doctrine remains charitable regardless whether it is embraced as well by a political party."* This finding was despite the fact that the trust document itself stated: *"Trustor specifically declares that this is not intended to be a charitable trust, although the Trustees may in the future, if they unanimously determine, apply for such designation and tax status. Unless that is done, however, the Trustees are free to use the trust assets for non-charitable purposes as long as they determine that said purposes are consistent with the purpose of establishment of this trust."*

Query: The court found the trust to meet the definition of a charitable trust, even if it did not qualify as a charitable trust under the IRC. Can you justify the court's findings in light of the settlor's own statements that the trust was not intended to be a charitable trust?

Courts have found a variety of different trusts to be charitable, even if they don't qualify for tax exempt status. Many free-speech issues can easily fit within this category. *See, e.g., People ex rel Hartigan v. National Anti-Drug Coalition*, 464 N.E.2d 690 (Ill.App. Ct. 1984) which involved the charitable nature of a group advocating for the legalization of marijuana. A good article on the inconsistencies of the laws on charitable trusts is: Mary K. Lundwall, *Inconsistency and Uncertainty in the Charitable Purposes Doctrine*, 41 WAYNE L. REV. 1341 (1995).

Whether a trust qualifies as charitable when it is for religious or political purposes can sometimes depend on whether courts feel the cause is legitimate and traditional or too far out and on the fringe. Charitable trusts for religious cults or for political causes aimed at bringing down the government do not qualify. But some pretty odd trusts have been created, such as James Kidd's trust for psychical research and a trust to prove that Francis Bacon wrote the plays attributed to Shakespeare.[75] And a trust to further the legalization of marijuana was deemed to have a charitable purpose. At the same time, some not so crazy trusts have been denied, as was a trust for "indigent widows and maiden ladies"[76] and George Bernard Shaw's alphabet trust. Shaw, who won the Nobel Prize for Literature in

---

[75] In re Hopkins' Will Trusts, 3 All. E.R. 46 (1964).

[76] McClure v. Carter, 202 Va. 191 (Va. 1960).

1925, devised the residue of his estate in trust for 21 years to develop a new alphabet of 40 letters (hoping to do away with such absurdities as the gh that can sound like an f). The Chancery Court refused to recognize the alphabet trust as a charitable trust and the proceeds of Shaw's estate went, instead, to the British Museum, the National Gallery of Ireland, and the Royal Academy of Dramatic Arts.[77]

At least one commentator thinks courts should be more willing to validate questionable charitable trusts because they can be used "to try many experiments to which it would be improper to devote the public funds, or that the public would be unwilling to support until convinced by proof of their success."[78]

PROBLEMS

9.1. You have a wealthy and eccentric client who wants her estate to be used for the following purposes. Try your hand at drafting the trust language to make these qualify as charitable gifts.

   a. She wants all her money to be used to get the *Citizens United* case overruled so that corporations and labor unions cannot fund political causes.

   b. She wants all her money to be used to get a constitutional amendment passed that will eliminate the second amendment.

   c. She wants all her money to be used to encourage people to become Vegans.

   d. She wants all her money to be used to assist in the creation of a public transportation system to take tourists to the moon.

   e. She wants all her money to be used to convince school boards to go back to teaching children that the earth is flat.

   f. She wants all her money to be used on abstinence only sex education in schools.

   g. She wants all her money to be used on comprehensive sex education in schools for children as young as age 5.

   h. She wants all her money to be used to prove that human activity is not causing climate change.

Cy Pres

Charitable Trusts also receive beneficial treatment through the application of the *cy pres* doctrine. Pronounced "see pray," the doctrine allows a charitable trust to be reformed when the specific manner of promoting the charitable intent becomes illegal, impossible, or impracticable, but the testator's general charitable intent remains. Thus, if a testator establishes a scholarship fund for nursing students at the local college, and the college is forced to close because of economic difficulties, the trust can be shifted to a nearby state college or to a parent entity of the first college that promises

----

[77] See 1 All E.R. 745 (Ch. 1957).
[78] Lundwall, 41 Wayne L. Rev. 1341, citing Scott on Trusts, 4A § 374.7.

to use the money for scholarships for nursing students. See *Est. of Craw-shaw*, 249 Kan. 388 (Kan. 1991). Or if a U.S. Senator wants to donate land for a segregated city park, *cy pres* could be available to allow for integration of the park IF the court determines that the Senator had a general charitable intent of providing for a public park, and the segregated character of the park was not central to his charitable intent. See *Evans v. Abney*, 396 U.S. 435 (1970).

The Uniform Trust Code provides for reformation under *cy pres*.

UTC § 413. CY PRES.

(a) Except as otherwise provided in subsection (b), if a particular charitable purpose becomes unlawful, impracticable, impossible to achieve, or wasteful:

(1) the trust does not fail, in whole or in part;

(2) the trust property does not revert to the settlor or the settlor's successors in interest; and

(3) the court may apply cy pres to modify or terminate the trust by directing that the trust property be applied or distributed, in whole or in part, in a manner consistent with the settlor's charitable purposes.

(b) A provision in the terms of a charitable trust that would result in distribution of the trust property to a noncharitable beneficiary prevails over the power of the court under subsection (a) to apply cy pres to modify or terminate the trust only if, when the provision takes effect:

(1) the trust property is to revert to the settlor and the settlor is still living; or

(2) fewer than 21 years have elapsed since the date of the trust's creation.

The key issue for determining whether *cy pres* will be applied to re-form a charitable trust is to compare the trust settlor's general charitable intent with his specific charitable intent. Consider the following cases that raised *cy pres* issues and whether you think the doctrine was appropriately applied or not. Consider too whether application of the UTC and *cy pres* provisions would alter the outcome of these cases.

Evans v. Abney

396 U.S. 435 (1970)

Senator Bacon left a piece of unimproved land to the City of Macon, Georgia, for use as a city park for whites only. When it became illegal to operate a segregated park, the City tried to transfer the park to private trustees but the U.S. Supreme Court determined that the park was so imbued with its public character that it could not be separated from its public ownership and reprivatized. The Georgia Supreme Court then determined that *cy pres* was inappropriate because Senator Bacon's racial criterion was foundational to his gift. Because there was no general charitable intent to benefit all people, black and white, the gift could not be separated from its discriminatory condition. Thus, the trust failed and the land reverted back to Senator Bacon's heirs. The U.S. Supreme Court affirmed the Georgia

Supreme Court's refusal to apply *cy pres*, finding there was no state action when the court enforced the implied reversion of Senator Bacon's heirs.

Est. of Buck

Unreported, but reprinted at 21 U.S.F. L. Rev. 691 (1987)

Beryl Buck was the heir to about $9 million in a privately held oil company founded by her father-in-law. When the company was bought out by Shell Oil for $260 million, the trust suddenly had significantly greater income to further Buck's charitable aims. She had directed that the residue of her estate be paid to the San Francisco Foundation to be administered as the Leonard and Beryl Buck Foundation, and to be used for "exclusively non-profit charitable, religious, or educational purposes in providing care for the needy in Marin County, California, and for other non-profit charitable, religious, or educational purposes in that county." By 1984 the trust corpus was worth over $300 million and the San Francisco Foundation sought reformation to allow it to expend the income to benefit needy residents in other counties in the San Francisco Bay area. After a public outcry, on both sides of the issue, the San Francisco Foundation withdrew as trustee and its claim for *cy pres* was dismissed. But the trial court opined on the applicability of *cy pres*, declaring that "inefficiency" or "ineffective philanthropy" was not a sufficient reason to reform a charitable trust so long as there were people in Marin County who could benefit from the trust. Despite the fact that Marin County, California had the highest *per capita* income for any county in California, and is one of the wealthiest counties in the country, the trust, now valued at over $1 billion, remains tied to serving the needs of Marin County's needy.

The Barnes Foundation

(John Anderson, Art Held Hostage: The Story of the Barnes Collection (2003))

Dr. Albert Barnes, who made a fortune by inventing a common cold medicine, invested heavily in art during the first half of the twentieth century. Described as "the greatest private art collection in American history," it is valued in the billions of dollars. Before Dr. Barnes died, he established the Barnes Foundation to further his unusual aesthetic beliefs, which included provisions that his collection would be open only to common people, the paintings were cluttered on the walls of his museum in suburban Philadelphia, and they were never to be moved or sold or loaned. Unfortunately, the endowment of the foundation was insufficient to pay the cost to maintain the spectacular art collection and the trustees were faced with either closing the museum or generating income through opening the gallery to the general public, which necessitated $12 million in renovations, charging admission, holding fundraisers, and eventually touring some of the most famous works, all of which directly conflicted with Barnes' trust terms. Even when these were allowed through *cy pres*, the foundation was foundering and sought permission to build a museum in downtown Philadelphia and move the collection to a more appropriate location to attract visitors. After much skepticism, the court allowed the move, but noted that the foundation, which was keeping its recently renovated gallery space in suburban Philadelphia, would have the most expensive administration building in the history of non-profits.

The Bishop Estate

Princess Bernice Pauahi Bishop, the last descendant of King Kamehameha of Hawaii, established a charitable trust to benefit the native peoples of Hawaii. One of the terms of the trust was to provide a school that specializes in preserving the native Hawaiian language and cultural heritage. Since 1965, it has admitted only two non-native students. The trust provided that the two schools, one for girls and one for boys, would be for the "support and education of orphans, and others in indigent circumstances, giving the preference to Hawaiians of pure or part aboriginal blood." The trust also required that the teachers be Protestants. In 1991, the EEOC sued claiming that the Protestant requirement violated the Civil Rights Act of 1964. The U.S. District Court for the District of Hawaii ruled in favor of the school, but the Ninth Circuit reversed, finding that the school was primarily secular and that the Protestant requirement violated the Civil Rights Act. Lawsuits claiming that the admissions policies are discriminatory were settled. And throughout the late 1990s and into the 2000s, controversy has raged over the selection and accountability of the trustees. Hawaii, and the Bishop Estate, have been caught up in complex controversies involving land ownership in the islands, especially where most land is unavailable for sale outright to individual homeowners. See *Hawaii Housing Authority v. Midkiff*, 467 U.S. 229 (1984), for a description of the land oligopoly in which 22 landowners owned over 72% of all fee owned land. The Bishop Trust's control over large swaths of land was one of those landowners. As the native population declines, however, and the wealth of the trust increases, should the trust be reformed to allow non-native students to attend the schools?

There are, quite literally, hundreds of cases involving charitable trusts, usually when trustees feel the need to deviate from the express terms of the donor's bequest. In *Museum of Fine Arts v. Beland*, 432 Mass. 540 (2000), William Wolcott had left 17 paintings by Boudin, Pissarro, and Monet to trustees to allow the Museum of Fine Arts of Boston to exhibit them, and that if the City of Lawrence, Massachusetts, ever has a gallery with sufficient fire and security protections to allow for their display, that the trustees should allow for an exhibition in Lawrence. The trustees also were given full discretion to manage the paintings for the purpose of facilitating the primary goal of public exhibition. Since Wolcott's death in 1911, the paintings have been housed by the MFA, but only three are on exhibit; the rest are in storage. The trustees then sought to sell some of the 14 paintings in storage because, they argued, there is little likelihood the City of Lawrence will have an appropriate space to display them, and the MFA is only displaying 3 of them. Selling them will give the public a greater opportunity to see them. The Massachusetts Supreme Court refused to amend the trust, or to allow the trustees to sell the paintings, stating that the sale violated Wolcott's underlying general intent, and that the trustees needed to find alternative ways to exhibit the 14 stored paintings.

While there may be an endless stream of needy recipients of charitable trust aid, not all charitable trusts are likely to stay relevant as the world changes rapidly around us. A 40-letter alphabet and a school for native Hawaiians may both become obsolete. And segregated parks have since become illegal. What happens when the trust purpose ends is a matter facing all trusts, charitable and private. Whether the trust should be reformed to meet modern times is a key element of the UTC and Restatement provisions on *cy pres*. As an estate planner, looking to help a client establish a charitable trust, you should be keenly aware of the legal and tax landscape for these mechanisms and, perhaps even more importantly, the implications if the trust wildly appreciates in value, or wildly depreciates. And look beyond the immediate horizon to think about the kind of world we may be living in 50 years, 100 years, or 500 years from now. Will the same charitable purposes still be viable?

b.   *Marital Deduction*

Another deduction common to both the gift and estate tax regimes involves gifts or bequests to one's spouse. As a general matter, the transfer of property to a spouse will be a non-taxable event. Very similar in language and scope, the gift tax marital deduction can be found in § 2523, while the estate tax marital deduction is found in § 2056. The idea behind the free transferability of property between spouses rests on the laurels of viewing a married couple as a single economic unit. Under this theory, whether property is owned by a husband or wife should be as inconsequential as whether an individual decides to put his money in his left pocket or his right pocket. In addition to supporting the idea of a married couple as a single economic unit, the free transferability of property between spouses also provides a parity between married couples in separate property states and community property states, where half of the marital assets are considered to be owned by each spouse.

An important exception to the marital deduction exists when one of the spouses is not a U.S. citizen. This is because the marital deduction is only designed to defer taxation until the death of the surviving spouse, at which point the property received by such surviving spouse would presumably be included in his or her estate. If the marital deduction were allowed in full for transfers to non-US citizen spouses, it is entirely possible that such amount could forever escape further US transfer taxes.

Because of the free transferability of property between spouses, much of estate planning for married couples concentrates on making the most effective use of each spouse's annual exclusion amount and unified credit. At first, however, you must understand what property is actually owned by each spouse before being able to effectively divvy up their tax attributes to achieve the most tax effective estate plan, and the answers may differ significantly between common law and community property states. In both types of states, however, spouses are entitled to own property in a joint form, and in a separate form. Thus, when each spouse dies, the wife's gross estate will include all of her separate property as well as her share of the joint property, and her husband's gross estate will include all of his separate property and his share of the joint property. If it is all held as joint property it is relatively easy to attribute half to each spouse. But if one has significantly more separate property than the other, they will want to take advantage of the unlimited marital deduction to equalize the two estates in order to maximize the effectiveness of their exclusions and credits.[79]

---

[79]   This is less important with portability.

Thus, if a couple together has, say, $15 million, then they don't want to have the first spouse pour everything into the second spouse's estate so that it all gets taxed when the survivor dies. The first $5.25 million would be exempt, but the next $9.75 million would be taxed. That is a worst case scenario. So the first spouse wants to go ahead and take advantage of his $5.25 million deduction, which means he could simply give away his half of the couple's property, or $7.5 million, which means he would pay estate taxes on the $2.25 million over his deduction, and his surviving spouse would do the same when she dies. In that scenario, they pay estate taxes on a total of $4.5 million and each pass their exempt amount to their children or other beneficiaries for a total of $10.5 million tax free. That is the most straightforward approach. But what if the surviving spouse may need access to some of her deceased husband's $7.5 million that he already gave away, perhaps to pay medical bills or to invest in a new business that may make even more money? In that case, we need to think about using trusts to allow the spouse limited access to the money in the trust, but not have it count as part of her estate when she dies.

As we discussed in Chapter 7, on Planning for the Living, when it comes to spouses, and utilizing the marital deduction, there are two common types of trusts: marital deduction trusts and qualified terminable interest trusts (QTIP) that are used in conjunction with a credit shelter trust. A credit shelter trust can be established, giving the spouse some limited interest in the trust, but in such a way that the remainder passes according to the settlor's direction to his beneficiaries, and usually to qualify for the settlor's lifetime exclusion of $5.25 million. Then, the remainder of the decedent spouse's estate is set to pass into a marital deduction trust in which the surviving spouse has a sufficient interest in the trust to count as a gift to her and qualify for the unlimited marital deduction. Upon the surviving spouse's death, however, the property in the marital deduction trust is considered part of the survivor's estate for tax purposes even though the decedent spouse/settlor designated the remainder beneficiaries.

But let's see if we can come up with a way to reduce the liability a bit more, perhaps with some *inter vivos* gifts. So the first spouse makes testamentary gifts of $5.25 million to children and grandchildren, using up his lifetime exclusion. Then he places an additional $4.5 million in trust giving the income to his spouse for life, remainder to his children. The value of the two gifts (the life estate and the remainder) must add up to $4.5 million, but no more. Let's say they are each valued, for immediate tax purposes, at 50–50. The gift of the life estate to the surviving spouse qualifies for the marital deduction so it passes tax free, and only the 50% share of the $4.5 million passing to the remaindermen is hit with estate taxes. Voila—estate taxes are now payable only on $2.25 million. And when the surviving spouse dies, her estate consists only of what's left of the couple's wealth, or $5.25 million, which she can pass to the children tax free using her lifetime estate tax exclusion.

Needless to say, Congress isn't going to make it that easy to avoid half of the couple's estate tax liability. So, in order to benefit from the marital deduction, the first spouse has to give the surviving spouse more than a mere life estate, he must give her a *non-terminable interest,* i.e. an interest that does not terminate upon the happening of a future event (like her death). A non-terminable interest is one in which the surviving spouse has greater control over the corpus than a mere life estate. Thus, giving the

spouse a life income and a general power of appointment in the trust qualifies for the marital deduction. The value of her interest in the trust will
now be higher, and the corresponding remainder interest lower, thus reducing the potential estate taxes even more, to 60–40 perhaps. Then, if the
surviving spouse does not exercise the power of appointment, the trust corpus will pass to the remainder beneficiaries.

Thus, the most common marital deduction trust is called the QTIP
trust, for *qualified terminable interest property*. The I.R.C. recognizes certain terminable interests as qualifying for the marital deduction, and the
life estate with a general power of appointment is the quintessential QTIP.
The pervasive use of the QTIP and credit shelter trust scheme makes sense
if the sole goal of your clients is to minimize tax liabilities. But structuring
the marital deduction trust to be especially restrictive to the surviving
spouse may hamper the surviving spouse's ability to make tax-
advantageous lifetime gifts or other financial decisions, and may ultimately
result in greater tax liabilities. Thus, once again, building flexibility into
trusts is important, so long as the tax objectives are not defeated by giving
the spouse too much or too little control. This is most commonly accomplished by giving a third-party trustee broad discretion to distribute
property to the spouse.

A big advantage of the marital deduction is the step up in basis. Let's
say a couple purchases land in Montana for $500,000. Forty years later,
when the first spouse dies, the land is now worth $3 million and will be
subject to income taxes on the appreciated value of $2.5 million when it is
sold. But the first spouse devises the property to the surviving spouse, taking advantage of the unlimited marital deduction. The surviving spouse
then sells the land just before her death for $3 million but pays no income
taxes on the increased value because when she received it she benefitted
from its step up in basis. Now the $3 million is part of her estate and she
can either make a lifetime gift of the cash to the couple's children, which
will be taxed at the gift tax rate, or it can pass through her estate and it
will pay estate taxes. But no income taxes will be due regardless of whether
the cash is given during life or at death. But if the first spouse had gifted
the property directly to the children during life, they would have paid the
income taxes on the appreciated value and he would have paid the gift taxes. By passing it through the spouse, the couple receives the step up in
basis when it is gifted to the children and no income tax will be due.

For our purposes here, it is important that you understand the basic
effects of marital deduction trusts and QTIP trusts for estate planning. But
how to deal with appreciated property, whether the surviving spouse is
capable of making lifetime gifts with the property passed from the first
spouse, whether the surviving spouse is likely to get remarried, and whether the gift or estate tax rates favor different types of giving are all complex
interconnected considerations for estate planning for high wealth clients.
You will need a special course in transfer tax before you can competently
structure different mechanisms for minimizing tax liabilities. We have already covered certain aspects of these spousal provisions in Chapter 7,
when tax considerations were not on the top of our radar screen. Here, just
realize that marital deduction and QTIP trusts, like elective share trusts,
serve additional purposes besides tax minimization.

3. ADDITIONAL DEDUCTIONS AGAINST THE ESTATE TAX

Unique to the estate tax regime, § 2053 provides a deduction against the taxable estate of a decedent for funeral expenses, administration expenses, claims against the estate, and for debt against property included in the gross estate. Seemingly simply at first glance, the breadth of such deduction may be somewhat larger in scope than originally anticipated. For example, under the regulations, funeral expenses extends to include any reasonable expenditure for a casket, plot, service, and all expenses incurred to dispose of the decedent's bodily remains including tombstone, monument, or for burial lot—either for the decedent or his family—including a reasonable expenditure for future care so long as the expenditure is allowable under local law.[80] Administration expenses include expenses that are actually and necessarily incurred in the administration of the decedent's estate (i.e. the collection of assets, payment of debts, and distribution of property).[81] Such expenses may include court costs, surrogates' fees, accountants' fees, appraisers' fees, attorneys' fees, and trustee fees; as well asexpenses incurred in preserving and distributing the estate, such as the cost of storing or maintaining property of the estate, expenses incurred in the sale of property, and even expenses incurred in defending the estate against claims.[82] While the details of § 2053 are far beyond the context of this book, it is important to remember that many of the "transactional costs" of death and the administration of the estate may ultimately be deductible against the taxable estate of a decedent. So you can explain to your executor client that even if she now is having to pay your steep attorney fees to administer her deceased husband's estate, at least she won't also have to pay estate taxes on those fees.

And while you might not think these fees are worth paying a lot of attention to, fees for the maintenance and sale of property can add up, costing as much as 10% of the value of the property itself. Thus, if you instruct the executor to sell your Palm Beach mansion and distribute the proceeds between your children, the costs of sale will be deducted before estate taxes are assessed. But if you simply devise the mansion directly to your children, and they have to sell it and divide the proceeds, the costs of the sale are not deductible against the estate tax. If you are looking at a tax rate of 40%, you could save up to or perhaps more than 4% of the value of your house by instructing the executor to manage the sale.

4. UNIFIED CREDIT AGAINST ESTATE AND GIFT TAXES

Under the unified credit system, an individual receives a fixed amount of credit against any taxes imposed during one's life (in the form of the gift tax) as well any taxes imposed at death (in the form of the estate tax). First, it is necessary to explain the difference between a deduction and a credit. A deduction is something that is subtracted from the tax base before the tentative tax liability is calculated and before the tax rate is applied to the tax base; whereas a credit is applied after calculating the tentative tax liability and merely serves to reduce the amount of taxes owed. The amount of the credit is equal to the tentative tax under § 2001(c) on the applicable

---

[80] Treas. Reg. § 20.2053–2.

[81] Treas. Reg. § 20.2053–3(a).

[82] Treas. Reg. § 20.2053–3.

exclusion amount.[83] For 2013, the $5,250,000 applicable exclusion amount would produce a credit of up to $2,045,800. Thus, in simplified terms, one can give up to $5,250,000 away during one's life or at death without incurring any gift or estate tax liability. Unlike the annual exclusion amount seen earlier, which effectively resets each year, the unified credit amount is only available to the extent that an individual has not already used it to decrease his gift tax liability. This means that if you made $5.25 million in lifetime gifts, your estate tax liability will begin with the first $1.00 of your gross estate because you used up your unified credit during life.

So I'm sure you are thinking: "hmmmm—why should I make lifetime gifts at all, especially if I'm getting close to reaching my unified credit limit and another gift will put me over and I'll have to pay gift taxes, but if I wait the credit amount may increase and I won't have to pay taxes at all?" This, of course, was the thinking of every estates and trusts attorney during 2009 and 2012, when big changes to the amount of the credit were possible in the upcoming year. As it turned out, there was an unlimited credit for 2010,[84] and Congress has reasonably firmly set the unified credit in 2013 and forward to be $5.25 million with annual adjustments for inflation, which stopped the backward step the tax was going to make if Congress didn't act. While it is unlikely that the lifetime exclusion amount will go down anytime soon, one does need to keep an eye on the rates and the credits, as well as the tea leaves, in recommending anyone make lifetime gifts over the unified credit amount. But even if the rate benefits don't exist, there is always the benefit of tax exclusivity to the gift tax to consider. However, the nitty-gritty details are best left to a course dedicated to the transfer tax system.

An additional consideration is that, in the case of a husband and wife, the surviving spouse may be entitled to make use of the deceased spouse's unused exclusion amount under the relatively new "portability" provisions.[85] Assuming that a proper election is made on the first deceased spouse's estate tax return, any unused exclusion will carry over to the surviving spouse for both gift and estate tax purposes (but not GST tax purposes). Thus, if the first deceased spouse made no taxable gifts during his life and died without a taxable estate, the surviving spouse could subsequently make lifetime or testamentary transfers of up to $10,500,000, which is the sum of the deceased spouse's unused exclusion amount plus the surviving spouse's own basic exclusion amount, before generating any gift or estate tax liability.

5. GENERATION SKIPPING TRANSFER TAXES

Prior to 1986, individuals could partially avoid the imposition of estate or gift taxes on the transmission of wealth by transferring property to their grandchildren (and other successive generations) instead of their children. Although a gift or estate tax would be imposed on the initial transfer, the

---

[83] I.R.C. §§ 2505, 2010.

[84] More accurately, the estate tax exclusion amount was $5 million (with a 35% rate on the excess). The executor could elect out of the estate tax (in effect getting a zero estate tax rate), but only by accepting carryover basis. This may have sounded like a good bargain, but while relieving the executor from the duty of paying estate taxes, it imposed on donees the burden of foregoing the stepped up basis and thus paying capital gains taxes if the property were liquidated.

[85] I.R.C. §§ 2010(c)(2)(B), (c)(4), (5).

property would escape taxation at their children's generational level. Thus, the generation-skipping transfer ("GST") tax was enacted to ensure that some type of federal transfer tax would be imposed roughly with each generation. Like the alternative minimum tax, the GST taxwas passed to fill a gap that tax advisors and estate planners had been exploiting. With the gradual decline in the RAP, trust interests could be set to pass directly to distant generations, thus avoiding transfer tax liabilities at each intervening generation. If the RAP had remained intact, and private trusts could only effectively skip one or at most two generations, most estate planners would structure trusts to avoid the GST tax. But with the never-ending potential of dynasty trusts, the GST tax will be a far more important factor in estate planning, even if it can't be successfully avoided.

The GST tax is simple. Assume Grandpa Joe creates an irrevocable trust that gives a life estate to his daughter, Doris, with a remainder to his grandchild, Li'l Joe. Prior to the GST tax, Grandpa Joe would pay a gift tax on the interests transferred to Doris and Li'l Joe, but the property would not be subject to estate taxes when Doris dies because Doris's life estate would not be included in her gross estate. To compensate for the tax avoidance, an additional GST tax is imposed upon the original transfer from Grandpa Joe to the trust to account for the missed estate taxes when the property is passed from Doris to Li'l Joe at Doris's death.

Although the example only deals with 3 generational levels, the same result would occur if additional generations down the line were given interests under the trust instrument. Essentially, without the GST tax regime, an individual could place property in trust for the benefit of several generations for the maximum period allowed by the locally applicable RAP, while at the same time avoiding transfer taxes and diminution of trust assets at each successive generation level.

The GST tax exemption is the same amount as the lifetime exclusion. So how can a settlor minimize the potential taxes? Imagine that a decedent has a $15 million estate that he wants to pass to his children and grandchildren. He first establishes a trust for the benefit of his grand-children, who would count as a skipped generation. He puts $5.25 million in the trust and uses both his lifetime exclusion and GST exemption for this money. Then he gives the remainder of his estate to his children and pays the estate tax on all of it. When the grandchildren finally are old enough to take their shares of the GS trust, the principal may have tripled in value, allowing them to take perhaps as much as $15 million tax free (more if the trust exists for longer and the beneficiaries are great-great grandchildren). His beneficiaries thus receive a total of $24.75 million but his estate only paid taxes on $9.75 million.

On the other hand, if he had allocated his $5.25 million lifetime exclusion to the gifts to his children, and given the rest of his estate to his grandchildren, he would pay both estate taxes and GST taxes on the $9.75 million to his grandchildren. He would pay 40% in estate tax, and an additional 40% of the remainder in GST tax, thus passing only $3.51.[86]

---

[86] This GST exemption amount may be allocated by the individual donor or the executor of the individual's estate, to any property transferred by the individual. I.R.C. § 2631(a); Treas. Reg. § 26.2632–1(a). Thus, the GST exemption may be used by a person during life [I.R.C. § 2652(a)(1)(B)] or at death [I.R.C. § 2652(a)(1)(A)]. Once an allocation is made, it is irrevocable. I.R.C. § 2631(b). The person responsible for making sure the IRS gets its tax revenue differs depending on the type of transfer made. The transferee of the property is

The details of the GST tax are way beyond the scope of this chapter, but it is important to realize that any time you are dealing with beneficiaries who are more than one generational level away from the donor (or decedent), there are potential GST tax consequences that must be considered. Similar to the unified credit against estate and gift taxes, an individual can shield a certain amount of transfers from the GST tax through the use of the GST exemption amount. Under I.R.C. § 2631 the GST exemption amount is equal to the basic exclusion amount under I.R.C. § 2010(c), or $5.25 million for 2013.

And just because most people set up generation-skipping trusts to benefit their descendants, the GST has a provision for non-relatives. Thus, transfers to non-relatives more than 37.5 years younger than the donor may be subject to the GST tax as well.[87]

6. VALUATION BASICS

In addition to the utilization of exempt amounts, deductions, and credits discussed above, a taxpayer may lower his potential transfer tax liability by decreasing the value of his property before transfer (at least for federal transfer tax purposes). We don't recommend setting fire to the valuable Picasso or hammering holes in the roof of the Palm Beach mansion to do this. Rather, most property held outright, with no strings attached, in fee simple absolute will hold the highest value for such items, while life estates, partnership shares, or lesser interests in the same item may be valued much lower. To the extent you can lower the valuation of particular property without actually harming it, you may be able to achieve a corresponding reduction in transfer tax liabilities.

The valuation of property for transfer tax purposes is determined by calculating the fair market value at the time of the transfer.[88] Fair market value is defined as the "price at which the property would change hands between a willing buyer and a willing seller, neither being under any compulsion to buy or to sell and both having reasonable knowledge of relevant

---

personally liable for paying the tax in the case of taxable distributions. I.R.C. § 2603(a)(1); Treas. Reg. § 26.2662–1(c)(1). The trustee is responsible for paying the tax for taxable terminations or a direct skip from an explicit trust agreement, I.R.C. § 2603(a)(2); Treas. Reg. § 26.2662–1(c)(1), and in the case of a direct skip (other than for direct skips from a trust), the tax is paid by the transferor or estate executor. I.R.C. § 2603(a)(3); Treas. Reg. § 26.2662–1(c)(1). Now from what source is the GST tax paid? The code directs the tax to be paid from the very property transferred. I.R.C. § 2603(b). For example, Trustee pays skip person, Grandchild, $100,000. Assuming a 40-percent GST tax rate, Grandchild pays GST tax of $40,000 and is left with $60,000. A transferor can override this default rule and prevent depletion of the gift by GST tax paid, by providing a specific instruction in the governing instrument to pay GST tax from a different source. I.R.C. § 2603(b). The $3.51 million comes from multiplying $9.75 million by 40% to determine the estate tax ($3.9 million) and then multiplying what is left ($5.85 million) by 40% to determine the GST tax.

[87] I am sure there is a good reason for 37.5 and not something simple, like 40 years. But that one is beyond me. Assuming it is based on some actuarial table, is it likely Congress will change the number as life expectancy increases? Also, note that the GST tax regime does not provide a portability mechanism from spouse to spouse, so that is something else to keep in mind.

[88] *See* I.R.C. § 2031(a); Treas. Reg. § 20.2031–1(b) (providing that a decedent's gross estate includes the 'value' of all of his property, defined in the regulations to mean fair market value). *See also* I.R.C. § 2512(a); Treas. Reg. § 25.2512–1 (giving an identical definition for gift valuation).

facts."[89] Although the fair market value standard seems rather logical for determining the value of a property interest transferred, it has run into some confusion when tax planning enters into the scheme. Say Homer owns 1000 shares of stock in Google and wishes to make a gift of 250 shares to his son Bart. If he were to gift the shares directly to Bart, the fair market value could easily be identified by simply looking up the trading price of Google shares on the day the gift is made.

However, what if Homer transfers the 250 shares of Google stock into a trust, retaining a life income interest for himself, with a remainder interest in his son Bart? Now the gift to Bart is less easily valued, although the combined value of the trust cannot exceed the value of the 250 shares on the day they were transferred into trust. What happens when he imposes a condition precedent on Bart's share that he reach a certain age, marry wisely, or finish law school? Then the contingent remainder interest may be valued even lower. But even though Bart's share may be lower, Homer will still have to include the value of the life estate in his gross estate for tax purposes. Thus, although the value of the shares can be split between Bart and Homer, the full value will show up somewhere. If Homer is likely to have a large enough estate to face transfer tax liabilities, he hasn't accomplished much by gifting half now to Bart and the other half at his death.

Now consider if Homer transfers the shares to a family limited liability company or limited partnership, and then he gifts Bart a 25% interest in the LLC or partnership? Isn't the result the same in either case? The short answer is no. The task of valuing an interest in a closely held entity can be divided into two main steps; first, valuation of the entire closely held entity and, second, valuation of the particular interest in such business. The second step in the valuation process involves significantly different considerations than are involved when the entire business is being valued, such as whether the interest has a ready market of potential buyers, the ability of the owner to sell such interest, whether the owner has a minority or majority interest, the amount of control the owner has over the closely held entity, and whether any discount is appropriate considering these factors. In an area rife with litigation, it now appears firmly established that an interest in a closely held entity will be discounted to reflect lack of marketability or lack of control if corporate formalities are duly observed. More fully described in Rev.Rul. 93–12, this discount can dramatically lower the overall tax liability.

To see how this might work, consider that Homer has two children, Bart and Lisa. Homer contributes $99 million worth of investment securities to a newly formed partnership (The Simpson Family LLP) in exchange for a 99% limited partnership interest, and B & L, a limited liability company owned equally by Bart and Lisa, contributes $1 million in exchange for a 1% general partnership interest. Although the partner's capital accounts are initially kept proportional to the value of their initial contributions, subsequently, by gift or by will, Homer transfers his 99% limited partnership interest in equal shares to Bart and Lisa. But this subsequent transfer will be valued at only $66 million, reflecting a one-third discount from liquidation value due to lack of marketability and/or lack of control. The end result is that Homer will have transferred assets worth

---

[89]   United States v. Cartwright, 411 U.S. 546, 551 (1973), see. e.g. Treas. Reg. 20.2031–1(b) and Treas. Reg. 25.2512–1.

$99 million for a reported value of only $66 million and the remaining $33 million will be effectively shielded from inclusion in the transfer tax base.

So if a client ever asks how an asset can be valued differently if given away during life, rather than being held until death, the valuation discount is how. For instance, if Homer held on to the securites until he died, he would have to pay estate tax on 100% of the value because, at death, Homer would own the whole company. But if given away during life, Homer pays tax on interests retained depending on the factors listed above. Essentially, the discounts are a legislative gift from Congress, allowing the transferred asset to be valued differently (lower) for gift tax purposes, than for estate tax purposes.

As with many of the subtleties of this subject, discounting the value of property interests for transfer tax purposes can get into complex calculations that are beyond the scope of this course. The point here is to realize that just as decedents can spread their wealth among a variety of different trust or partnership interests, with different beneficiaries, structured to minimize transfer tax liabilities, the value of those interests can change depending on the amount of dominion and control, and the market for such interests, that the client retains or gives away. The more strings attached, the less the value because the less likely it is that someone would pay full value for property that is not freely marketable. But of course, the more strings attached, the more strings are attached. That means that the property is less liquid and less marketable for the donor as well.

E. EFFECTIVE ESTATE PLANNING

1. TAX BENEFITS OF MAKING LIFETIME GIFTS

Lifetime gifting is an essential component of any estate plan because (1) the gift tax is tax-exclusive, (2) the donor may take advantage of tax-free gifting through the use of the annual exclusion amounts discussed above (*Crummey* powers), and (3) income on and appreciation of the gifted property is removed from the donor's estate.

Gift tax is tax exclusive or, said another way, the amount of the taxable gift does not include the donor's gift tax liability.[90] Conversely, the estate tax is tax inclusive and will be paid by the executor prior to the distribution. Essentially, the estate tax is calculated by including the amount that will ultimately be paid to the government as taxes while the gift tax is calculated according to the value of the gift only. Thus, by failing to give away property during life one is basically made to pay tax on the tax—a dubious honor at best.

One of the most basic (and hopefully apparent) benefits of making gifts during life is the utilization of the annual exclusion amount. By giving away just a little bit each year, an individual can avoid transfer taxes, while removing a portion of her potential taxable estate and without using up her unified credit against gift and estate taxes, and GST taxes for outright transfers (i.e., transfers not in trust) to persons more than one generation from the transferor.[91] While $14,000 may seem like somewhat of

---

[90]   Treas. Reg. § 25.2511–2(a).

[91]   I.R.C. 2642(c)(1) provides there is no GST tax on the 2503(b) annual exclusion amount in the case of an outright direct skip which is a nontaxable gift. So if grandpa gives $14,000

an insignificant figure in the grand scheme of things, this amount is renewable annually per person and can definitely add up over the course of a transferor's lifetime, especially when combined with wealth transfer vehicles that make use of valuation discounts (discussed above). Additionally, if a married couple work together to maximize the effects of their annual exclusions, they could make lifetime gifts of hundreds of thousands of dollars every year by jointly giving $28,000 to each child, spouse of a child, grandchild, niece and nephew, neighbor, spouse of a neighbor, family friend, or esteemed law professor.

Finally, by gifting away property during life, an individual is able to avoid having to include any future appreciation or income from an asset in her gross estate. Consider the following example. In year 1, Harry's second home, which he rents out for $20,000 per year, is worth $1,000,000. In year 10, when Harry dies, the house is worth $1,500,000 and Harry has $200,000 in his bank account from the rental receipts. Thus, $1,700,000 will be included in Harry's taxable estate. On the other hand, if Harry had gifted away the property in year 1, he would only have to pay gift taxes on the value of the home at the time of the gift, $1,000,000, and the future appreciation and income from the property would be shielded from any future transfer taxes assessed against Harry. Of course, the recipient of the property could be on the hook for income or capital gains taxes, but many donees will happily pay the taxes in exchange for a new house. Even the acceleration of an inherited gift carries with it benefits due to the time value of money. It is tacky at best to look a gift horse in the mouth. I may be annoyed that dad is reducing his estate taxes to my detriment as his beneficiary, but this is better than being completely disinherited if I complain. Ideally, families will work together to lessen their total tax liabilities and share profits if one way of transferring makes more sense than another way. But regardless of the family dynamics, your duty will most likely be only to your client, and if the kids have to worry about the taxes that you saved, at least they will have a larger inheritance from which to do so.

2. CHOOSING PROPERTY TO GIVE AWAY—BASIS AND RECOGNITION OF GAIN

When an individual sells a piece of property, he is usually taxed on the difference between the amount realized[92] and his *basis* in the property.[93] Amount realized can best be explained as whatever an individual receives for the property. So, if you sell stock on the open market for $20,000—this will be the amount you realized. The concept of basis, however, tracks an individual's historic "cost" for the asset. If, in the previous example, you had purchased the stock for $10,000, this "cost" of the stock would be your basis.[94] However, when an individual receives property by gift or bequest

---

outright to grandchild (a direct skip), 2503(b) says there is no gift tax. To provide consistency, since grandchild gets the gift free of gift tax, the transfer is also excluded from GST tax by 2642(c)(1). So gifts equal to the annual exclusion amount are totally tax free; there is no gift, estate or GST tax. Note, a transfef in trust made in compliance with 2642(c)(2) can also be made GST tax free.

[92]   I.R.C. §1001(b), Treas. Reg. § 1.1001–1(a).

[93]   I.R.C. § 1001.

[94]   See § 1012.

instead of by purchase, special basis rules apply. In general, for property acquired by *inter vivos* gift, § 1015 provides the recipient with a transferred basis; i.e. the basis in the hands of the recipient will be the same as it was in the hands of the donor. Conversely, for property acquired by bequest, § 1014 provides the recipient with a fair market value basis; i.e. the basis of the recipient will be the fair market value of the property at the donor's death without regard to the donor's basis.

With these basic principles in mind, we can begin to see the potential interplay between basis and choosing which property to gift away. With regard to testamentary gifts, therefore, the recipient receives what is called a "step up in basis." This means that the donee's basis in the property will be its worth when it was inherited, not the cost of the property when it was originally acquired by the donor. But property acquired by lifetime gift will not receive this step up in basis, and if the recipient turns around and sells the item, she may owe some capital gains taxes on its appreciated value from the time it was originally acquired by the donor.

Special considerations must be made when gifting appreciated Property. For instance, in making intra-family gifts, individuals will generally prefer to give appreciated property rather than cash or property which has declined in value. When the donees are in a lower tax-bracket than the donor, it may be advantageous to give property with more built in gain, especially if the donees are not expected to sell the property within a short time. Another advantage is that the capital gain that may be recognized by the donor on the sale of property retained will be smaller if he has retained assets that have appreciated less in value. On the flip side, however, where the donor is very elderly or in failing health, highly appreciated property might be retained in order to take full advantage of the tax-free step up in basis at death for property includible in his gross estate.

For depreciated Property, though a donor's basis in an asset generally carries over to the donee under § 1015, for the purposes of determining loss the basis cannot exceed the fair market value of the property on the date of the gift. Accordingly, a donor should not make a gift that involves losing the tax benefit of a loss. Instead, she should consider selling the depreciated property, taking advantage of the loss, and making a gift of the proceeds or other property. The one exception to this general rule is where the donee is unlikely to part with the asset (such as a family heirloom with special meaning) or is planning to hold onto the property for a significant period of time so that the value will once again increase, in which case the tax benefit of the loss will not be foregone.

These are not the only considerations that would affect a comprehensive estate plan for high tax individuals, but they form the foundation for effective planning for tax minimization. Making judicious uses of *inter vivos* gifts that take advantage of the recipient's income tax bracket or likelihood of selling the property can reduce tax liabilities for certain kinds of gifts. *Inter vivos* transfers can also be used to tie up property with sufficient strings to reduce the value of the property for transfer tax purposes. Lifetime gifts also receive the benefit of tax exclusivity. Testamentary gifts, however, get the benefit of the stepped up basis which is very important for gifts that have appreciated greatly during the donor's lifetime, or gifts which are likely to be sold by the recipient.

F. CONCLUSION

As the preceding material has shown, there is an intricate body of laws dealing with the taxation of gratuitous transfers, whether made during one's life by gift or at death by bequest. However, as you've hopefully realized, the careful and meticulous estate planner is afforded many opportunities to minimize the burden of transfer taxes for a client. While tax avoidance will not typically be the primary consideration of the client, the good estate planner should be able to effectuate the personal goals of the client in the most tax efficient way possible. If you enjoyed reading this chapter, and were eager to learn more about the nuances of the GST or how to use CRATs and CRUTs more effectively, or if you have the mobile app on your phone of the entire Internal Revenue Code, then you are hooked. You will want to take additional courses on income tax, taxation of trusts and estates, transfer tax, and even partnership tax to understand how the complex tax code works together in all aspects of economic life.

As you become more adept at maximizing the effects of credits, deductions, and exclusions, you will learn how to set up transfer mechanisms that maximize benefits for your clients during life and at death. But lest you get too mired in the Internal Revenue Code, remember that with the unified credit at $5.25 million, continually ratcheting upwards each year, roughly 99.8% of estates will pass without any transfer tax liabilities at all. Don't let the tax concerns of the remaining .2% dominate your estate planning priorities. Planning for tax minimization can be fun, challenging, and exhilarating—but most people simply won't need it. You have far more important concerns to make sure that family members are properly provided for, surviving spouses have adequate means to live out their final years, your clients are protected from scam artists or unscrupulous creditors and their estates are smoothly administered. The technical details of this chapter are important, but the true value of the good estate planner is to have client who leave your office feeling good about what you have accomplished together, whether or not it involves a CRAT, a QTIP, or a *Crummey* power.

Changing the Plan, Litigating the Plan, and Attorney Duties

CHAPTER 10

REVOCATION, MODIFICATION, AND TERMINATION OF TESTAMENTARY DOCUMENTS

All testamentary documents must provide for the eventual transfer of the property from the transferor to the transferees. In most instances, the dead hand cannot persist in perpetuity. Eventually the dead hand lets go, and the new takers of the property can acquire full control to do with it as they wish (except perhaps in the case of dynasty trusts). This can occur when a will is probated, the property is administered, and the estate is closed or when the trust corpus is paid out by the trustee to the remainder beneficiaries. These documents and mechanisms can also be revoked during the testator's life, by the testator and by others, and some can be modified or terminated by the beneficiaries after the death of the decedent, before the natural termination point established by the donor.

In this chapter we look first at statutory mandates that terminate the donor's control over property, besides those already covered such as the elective share, pretermission statutes, and the Rule Against Perpetuities. These are statutory and/or common law rules that prevent a decedent from fully controlling the descent or devise of her property. The Rule Against Perpetuities and the Rule Against Unreasonable Restraints on Alienation are the most well-known, but other legislation can revoke a will or portions of a will or other testamentary documents, despite a testator's apparent intent. Usually these work to effectuate the likely intent of most testators, including the revocation of provisions for a spouse upon divorce and revocation of gifts to persons who kill the decedent, or contribute to his death (slayer statutes). Such laws also can work against testamentary intent, like the RAP, as well as mortmain statutes that invalidate certain gifts to charities.

Second we look at revocation and modification by the testator herself, and the various ways a testator can revoke a will or trust and the effects of ineffective or partial revocation. There has been a gradual shift from requiring strict formal steps to revoke a will, to the liberal approach taken by the UPC to validate revocations that are intentional, even if they don't meet the formal requirements of obliterating every word or defacing the entire document. Like the formalities, however, the law on revocation varies greatly across the different states and requires close attention to your state's probate code.

Third, we look at modification by judges or trustees, usually based on administrative difficulties or costs, and revocation based on frustration of purpose. Fourth, we briefly examine modification or termination by beneficiaries after the death of the settlor or testator. Although these issues are more likely to arise in the context of trust or probate administration, and are covered in much greater detail in a course on fiduciary administration, it is important to understand the basic outlines of how testamentary documents can be modified, revoked, or terminated *after* they are in effect. You may need to plan to avoid beneficiary termination of a trust, or you may need to plan to ease beneficiary modification, depending on your client. Understanding the basic parameters of modification, revocation, and termination is critical to good planning.

A. SLAYER STATUTES

Most states have statutes, or have developed case precedents, that revoke gifts to people who kill their benefactors, regardless of whether the killing was motivated by a desire to accelerate an inheritance or was from simple malice or sometimes even negligence. We assume that most people, if they knew their beneficiary was going to kill them, would have revoked their will or trust to omit any gifts to their killer. But not every case involves the timely administration of arsenic just as grandpa is about to change his will. Cases can involve murder/suicides, car crashes, the victims of domestic violence who fight back against their abusers, and the mercy killing of the prize fighter after she is paralyzed.[1]

Some slayer statutes rely on the murder/manslaughter distinction, while others rely on criminal intent to determine if a gift will be revoked. In all states, conviction of intentional murder is enough to revoke gifts to the murderer. And most states will also revoke gifts to persons who commit a lesser offense, like intentional manslaughter. Persons convicted of manslaughter are likely to lose their gifts, though accidental killings usually don't trigger the revocation. Some states prohibit not only the killer, but anyone who would inherit through the killer from inheriting.[2] Other states void gifts to anyone who commits any intentional act that results in death, even if there was no intent to accelerate an inheritance. In states that do not have slayer statutes, equitable doctrines holding that a wrongdoer should not benefit from his wrong are relied upon to prevent inheritance.[3] Other state courts, faced with a killer and no slayer statute, have allowed the killer to take in the hopes that the outcome would spur the legislature into passing a slayer statute.[4]

Some states have a slayer statute that applies to wills but no provisions for trusts or other will substitutes, which means courts in that state have to apply equitable doctrines to void gifts from trusts. Also, rights like homestead, exempt property, and family allowance often are not explicitly

---

[1]   *Million Dollar Baby.* Dir. Clint Eastwood. Perf. Hilary Swank, Clint Eastwood and Morgan Freeman. Warner Bros. Pictures, 2005. Film.

[2]   Cook v. Grierson, 380 Md. 502 (2004).

[3]   Texas, for instance, has no statute. Only 42 states have them, and only 11 follow the UPC. For recent slayer articles, see generally: Julie Waller Hampton, *The Need for a New Slayer Statute in North Carolina*, 24 CAMPBELL L. REV. 295 (2002); Diane J. Klein, The Disappointed Heir's Revenge, Southern Style: Tortious Interference with Expectation of Inheritance—A Survey with Analysis of State Approaches in the Fifth and Eleventh Circuits, 55 BAYLOR L. REV. 79 (2003); Bradley Myers, The New North Dakota Slayer Statute: Does it Cause a Criminal Forfeiture, 83 N.D. L. Rev. 997 (2007); Laurel Sevier, Kooky Collects: How the Conflict Between Law and Psychiatry Grants Inheritance Rights to California's Mentally Ill Slayers, 47 SANTA CLARA L. REV. 379 (2007); Robert F. Hennessy, Note, Property—The Limits of Equity: Forfeiture, Double Jeopardy, and The Massachusetts "Slayer Statute", 31 W. NEW ENG. L. REV. 159 (2009); Sara M. Gregory, Note, Paved with Good "Intentions": The Latent Ambiguities in New Jersey's Slayer Statute, 62 RUTGERS L. REV. 821 (2010); Mark Adam Silver, Note, Vesting Title in a Murderer: Where Is the Equity in the Georgia Supreme Court's Interpretation of the Slayer Statute in Levenson?, 45 GA. L. REV. 877 (2011).

[4]   Shellenberger v. Ranson, 59 N.W. 935 (1894); Bird v. Plunkett, 95 A.2d 71 (1953).

revoked. And as you saw in Chapter 2, ERISA may pre-empt the application of slayer statues to retirement and pension plan benefits.

The UPC slayer statute tries to balance as many of these policies as possible:

UPC § 2–803. Effect of Homicide on Intestate Succession, Wills, Trusts, Joint Assets, Life Insurance, and Beneficiary Designations.

(a) **[Definitions.]** In this section:

(1) "Disposition or appointment of property" includes a transfer of an item of property or any other benefit to a beneficiary designated in a governing instrument.

(2) "Governing instrument" means a governing instrument executed by the decedent.

(3) "Revocable," with respect to a disposition, appointment, provision, or nomination, means one under which the decedent, at the time of or immediately before death, was alone empowered, by law or under the governing instrument, to cancel the designation, in favor of the killer, whether or not the decedent was then empowered to designate himself [or herself] in place of his [or her] killer and whether or not the decedent then had capacity to exercise the power.

(b) **[Forfeiture of Statutory Benefits.]** An individual who feloniously and intentionally kills the decedent forfeits all benefits under this Article with respect to the decedent's estate, including an intestate share, an elective share, an omitted spouse's or child's share, a homestead allowance, exempt property, and a family allowance. If the decedent died intestate, the decedent's intestate estate passes as if the killer disclaimed his [or her] intestate share.

(c) **[Revocation of Benefits Under Governing Instruments.]** The felonious and intentional killing of the decedent:

(1) revokes any revocable (i) disposition or appointment of property made by the decedent to the killer in a governing instrument, (ii) provision in a governing instrument conferring a general or nongeneral power of appointment on the killer, and (iii) nomination of the killer in a governing instrument, nominating or appointing the killer to serve in any fiduciary or representative capacity, including a personal representative, executor, trustee, or agent; and

(2) severs the interests of the decedent and killer in property held by them at the time of the killing as joint tenants with the right of survivorship transforming the interests of the decedent and killer into equal tenancies in common.

(d) **[Effect of Severance.]** A severance under subsection (c)(2) does not affect any third-party interest in property acquired for value and in good faith reliance on an apparent title by survivorship in the killer unless a writing declaring the severance has been noted, registered, filed, or recorded in records appropriate to the kind and location of the property which are relied upon, in the ordinary course of transactions involving such property, as evidence of ownership.

(e) **[Effect of Revocation.]** Provisions of a governing instrument are given effect as if the killer disclaimed all provisions revoked by this section or, in the case of a revoked nomination in a fiduciary or representative capacity, as if the killer predeceased the decedent.

(f) **[Wrongful Acquisition of Property.]** A wrongful acquisition of property or interest by a killer not covered by this section must be treated in accordance with the principle that a killer cannot profit from his [or her] wrong.

(g) **[Felonious and Intentional Killing; How Determined.]** After all right to appeal has been exhausted, a judgment of conviction establishing criminal accountability for the felonious and intentional killing of the decedent conclusively establishes the convicted individual as the decedent's killer for purposes of this section. In the absence of a conviction, the court, upon the petition of an interested person, must determine whether, under the preponderance of evidence standard, the individual would be found criminally accountable for the felonious and intentional killing of the decedent. If the court determines that, under that standard, the individual would be found criminally accountable for the felonious and intentional killing of the decedent, the determination conclusively establishes that individual as the decedent's killer for purposes of this section.

Note that under the UPC, the effect of revocation is that the killer is treated as though he *disclaimed* all interest in the property. Why does the UPC use disclaimer, rather than predeceasing, as do most slayer statutes? The answer has to do with the special provisions of the disclaimer statute and its interplay with the *Per Capita* by Generation scheme of intestate distribution. Go back and think about the discussion of disclaimer in Chapter 5.

Consider the following slayer cases and the variety of factors that come into play in deciding not guilt or innocence, but the right to inherit:

In re Est. of Mahoney

126 Vt. 31, 220 A.2d 475 (1966)

Charlotte Mahoney shot her husband, Howard Mahoney, and was convicted of manslaughter. Vermont did not have a slayer statute at the time, and the court opined that in the absence of a statute, most courts either 1) allow legal title to pass to the killer,[5] 2) deny any benefit to the killer under equitable principles that a wrongdoer should not benefit from his crime,[6] or 3) impose a constructive trust on the beneficiary for the heirs or next of kin of the victim. The court adopted the third alternative, reasoning that the first option would allow a killer to benefit from his crime which is counter to public policy, and the second would engraft an exception onto the statutes of descent and devise which should be left to the legislatures. Imposing a constructive trust would prevent the killer from benefitting from her wrong but would not effectively legislate a new rule for all time. But because probate courts did not have equity powers in Vermont in 1966, the probate decree was stayed to allow the heirs or next of kin to petition for a constructive trust in the Chancery.

---

[5]   See In re Carpenter's Est., 32 A. 637 (Pa. 1895); Wall v. Pfanschmidt, 106 N.E. 785 (Ill. 1914); Bird v. Plunkett, 95 A.2d 71 (Conn. 1953).

[6]   See Riggs v. Palmer, 22 N.E. 188 (N.Y. 1889); Price v. Hitaffer, 165 A. 470 (Md. 1933); Slocum v. Met. Life Ins., 139 N.E. 816 (Mass. 1923).

Query: Should it matter if the killer acted in self defense? Is there a functional difference between the second and third options the court identified? Should probate courts be able to declare probate rules in the absence of legislative action?

In re Est. of Schunk

314 Wis. 2d 483, 2008 WI App 157, 760 N.W.2d 446 (Ct. App. 2008)

Edward Schunk died from a self-inflicted gunshot wound. At the time of his death he was terminally ill with non-Hodgkin's lymphoma. He lived with his wife, Linda, and their daughter, Megan. Edward had six older children who are not Linda's children. Edward left a will that provided bequests for both Linda and Megan. The six older children claimed that Linda and Megan knew that Edward wanted to commit suicide and brought him home so that he could do so. *They drove him to a cabin on their property, helped him inside, gave him a loaded shotgun, and left.* Viewing the evidence *most favorably to Linda and Megan, the evidence shows that Edward drove himself to the cabin, taking his gun and hunting bag, and they did not know that he intended to commit suicide. It is undisputed that Edward's son and grandson found him later that day in the cabin, dead from a single gunshot wound to the chest.* The court admitted that it did not know what truly happened except that the wound was self-inflicted.

The Wisconsin Slayer Statute provides:

2) Revocation of benefits. Except as provided in sub. (6), the unlawful and intentional killing of the decedent. . . .

[P]rovisions of a governing instrument that are revoked by this section are given effect as if the killer disclaimed all revoked provisions. . . .

The court sided with Linda and Megan that even providing the means with which another takes his own life is not the "unlawful and intentional killing" intended by the plain language of the statute.

Query: What if Linda and Megan had withheld the decedent's medicines at his request, or been careless in leaving them at hand so he could take an overdose? Should assisting someone's suicide be deemed an intentional killing? How would the case be resolved under the UPC § 2–803(f)?

Bell v. Casper

282 Va. 203, 717 S.E.2d 783 (2011)

Collette Lynn Lockard was shot and killed by her only child, Clayton Devoy Lynn in 2005. Clayton had two daughters who sought to take their grandmother's entire estate, which she had devised entirely to her son. The case was opposed by the victim's mother, who was the sole heir under the Virginia slayer statute at the time of the killing. At that time, anyone who would take *through* the killer was also precluded from inheriting. In 2008, Virginia amended its slayer statute to allow that "an heir or distributee who establishes his kinship to the decedent by way of kinship to a slayer shall be deemed to be claiming from the decedent and not through the slayer." (Code § 55–403). The daughters argued that because their father was not convicted of the slaying until after passage of the 2008 amendments he should not be deemed a slayer until the date of his conviction. The Virginia

Supreme Court ruled that the relevant time for application of the statute was the death of the victim when the property rights vested in the beneficiaries. Therefore, the victim's mother was deemed the sole heir.

The court also rejected the daughters' arguments that the earlier slayer statute violated Virginia's prohibition against corruption of blood. The court stated that: *the Slayer Statute, as it existed in 2005, does not work a corruption of blood because it does not deprive a "slayer's" heirs the right to inherit from the "slayer" property properly belonging to the "slayer." Neither does it work a forfeiture of estate because it does not require a "slayer" to forfeit his property. Rather, former Code § 55–402 (2003) merely prohibited a slayer from acquiring additional property rights as a result of his wrongdoing, which his heirs could subsequently claim "through him."*

Query: Are the granddaughters claiming additional property *through* their father the killer, or are they claiming a right to take in their own name? What does the Virginia statute mean when it disallows beneficiaries to take "through" the killer?

Newton v. Newton

365 S. W. 3d 565 (Ky. Ct. App. 2011)

On May 20, 2007, [Clara] Sanders was on the premises she and [James] Newton owned in joint tenancy with right of survivorship. The two had lived on the property together as unmarried cohabitants for some time. On that date, they had thrown a party for Sanders's grandchild. According to Newton, Sanders became intoxicated and belligerent, and Newton attempted to restrain her. While doing so, Newton recklessly choked and held Sanders down, resulting in her death. Newton was criminally charged in her death and subsequently pled guilty to reckless homicide, a class D felony. Newton was sentenced to five years' imprisonment, which he has now served.

Sanders' estate argued that the slayer statute causes Newton to be treated as though he predeceased Sanders, his joint tenant, and that therefore her estate should take the premises through the right of survivorship. Newton, argues, however, that his half share of the property should not be forfeited, though he agrees that he forfeits Sanders' half share under the slayer statute. The court agreed with Newton that he gets to keep his half of the joint tenancy property.

Query: Does it make sense to allow a killing to effectively sever a joint tenancy and turn it into a tenancy in common? If we treat a killer as disclaiming, would there be Fifth Amendment takings implications if a court were to give his share of the jointly held property to his victim's estate?[7]

---

[7] The Fifth Amendment provides that private property shall not be taken for public use without just compensation. The flip side is that private property cannot be taken for private use at all. Assuming that the parties each paid half for jointly held property, how should a slaying affect the question of severance and survivorship?

In re Estate of Kissinger

166 Wash.2d 120, 206 P.3d 665 (2009)

On January 13, 2000, Joshua Hoge was found not guilty by reason of insanity for the murder of his mother, Pamela Kissinger, and stepbrother, James Zachary Kissinger. After obtaining a settlement in a wrongful death action, the personal representative for Pamela's estate brought a motion for a determination of statutory beneficiaries in King County Superior Court, arguing that Hoge was a "slayer" and that he was therefore barred from receiving any portion of the settlement. Washington's slayer statute prohibits individuals who have participated in the "willful and unlawful" killing of another person from receiving any benefit as a result of their acts. Ch. 11.84 RCW. We are asked to decide if a finding of "not guilty by reason of insanity" is a complete defense to the slayer statute. We conclude that it is not. An action under the slayer statute is civil, and the determination of whether a slaying was willful and unlawful must be made in civil court notwithstanding the result of any criminal case. A finding of not guilty by reason of insanity does not make an otherwise unlawful act lawful. We agree with the Court of Appeals that willful under the slayer statute means intentionally and designedly. However, we also conclude that even under this definition, the trial court's findings of fact clearly establish that Hoge acted willfully when he killed his mother and stepbrother. Hoge is barred from recovery under the slayer statute.

Query: How appropriate is it for a probate court or civil court, applying civil standards, to hold that "willful and unlawful" is defined differently for their purposes than for a criminal conviction? Should the standards be the same?

Ford v. Ford

307 Md. 105, 512 A.2d 389 (1986)

Pearl Rose Ford murdered her mother, Muriel L. Holland, by stabbing her some 40 times. She wrapped the body in plastic garbage bags and deposited it in the backyard of her home. She now seeks to obtain the property left her under her mother's will. George Benjamin Ford, Jr., her son, asserts that Pearl forfeited her entitlement to the property by the matricide and claims the property as the alternative beneficiary named in the will. The Orphans' Court for Anne Arundel County, in which the will was admitted to probate, ruled that George "be declared the heir" of the estate. The Circuit Court for Anne Arundel County, on appeal by Pearl to it, decided that Pearl was entitled to the property. We ordered that a writ of certiorari be issued to the Court of Special Appeals, to which George appealed, before decision by that court.

The Maryland Legislature has not enacted a "slayer's" statute establishing what principles govern when a person kills another and would be tangibly enriched by the death. This Court, however, has addressed the matter in three of its decisions: [citations omitted]. Through these cases the Court has created in the common law of this State, the equivalent of a "slayer's" statute, which we shall refer to herein as the "slayer's rule." . . .

It is not disputed that Pearl killed her mother and that under the criminal law she was guilty of first degree murder in that the homicide was "willful, deliberate and premeditated." Were this the posture of the case, it is

*clear that under the "slayer's rule" . . . Pearl would be precluded from shar-
ing in the estate of her victim; her conduct would be both felonious and
intentional. But in addition to the fact that Pearl was the criminal agent of
a first degree murder, it is also undisputed that at the time the crime was
committed, she was not criminally responsible by reason of insanity. In
short, she stands as guilty of murder in the first degree but insane. . . .*

*It is at this point, upon a finding that the claimant was not criminally
responsible for his criminal conduct, that the question we noted supra, arises, namely what impact does the fact that the claimant was "insane" at the
time of the commission of the crime have on the slayer's rule. The answer is
that the slayer's rule is simply not applicable when the killer was not criminally responsible at the time he committed the homicide.*

Query: Can you reconcile *Ford* with *Kissinger*? Should criminal responsibility
be the standard, or something else? If something else, what?

Unfortunately, slayer statute cases are often media sensations. See:

- Dennis Wagner, "$4.5 Million Life-Insurance Battle Following
  Woman's Murder Takes a New Twist," *AZ Central*, Sept. 30, 2011
  (about a surviving widower who seems to have a knack for being
  connected to other murder victims with large life-insurance policies—according to his step-children, who allege he murdered their
  mother and are invoking the slayer statute to prevent his taking
  the life insurance).
- Kieran Crowley, "Murderer to Inherit fortune from Victim," *New
  York Post*, Jan. 3, 2011 (about Brandon Palladino, 24, who killed
  his wealthy mother-in-law after she caught him trying to steal
  jewelry from her Long Island home. Palladino entered into a plea
  deal to serve 25 years in prison and was serving his sentence when
  his wife, the victim's daughter, died, devising all her property to
  her husband, property she had inherited from her mother the victim. Here the killer would be taking through an intermediary who
  could have taken steps to limit his gain, though as a surviving
  spouse Palladino would be entitled to an elective share.)
- Julie Brown, "Narcy Novack may seek Separate Trial," *Miami
  Herald* (Oct. 5, 2011) (about Narcy Novack, accused of killing her
  husband Ben Novack, Jr. and her mother-in-law, Bernice Novack,
  the son and wife of the founder and builder of the Fountainbleu
  Hotel in Miami Beach. Because hit men were hired to kill both victims, the police were slow to charge Narcy and her brother with
  masterminding the killings, and at least one Florida court ordered
  Narcy was entitled to her inheritance since no charges had been
  filed against her. But the order was stayed on appeal, pending further police investigation, and she was eventually charged and
  convicted.)

As the slayer statute cases show, complex disputes often arise in the
context of mercy killing, insanity or diminished capacity, assisted suicide,
unintentional or reckless manslaughter, or rights to property held in joint
tenancy or tenancy by the entirety. Few slayer cases actually involve killers

who acted in order to accelerate their inheritances. Most kill for other reasons. Ultimately, most states will prohibit a convicted murderer from taking under a testamentary devise or intestate succession, but where the facts become less clear, so does the law.

Technology Trend

As you can see from the cases discussed above, the slayer statute is a blunt weapon for dealing with the problem of beneficiaries trying to accelerate an inheritance. Many people kill by accident, and a significant number of people who kill family members do so because of abuse, neglect, or trauma within the family. Professor Carla Spivack suggests that in the vast majority of cases the traditional slayer statute metric needs to be recalibrated to recognize the contributing factors of family dysfunction.[8] The idea that there is a bright line between guilt and innocence makes about as much sense in the area of Trusts and Estates as it does in criminal law. There are varying shades of guilt and an infinite variety of exculpatory causes to many actions that result in death. With better and better medications for dealing with mental illness, is it going to become easier or more difficult to prove culpability for purposes of a slayer statute? Are we going to see family members who choose to pull the plug on grandma who is on life support denied their inheritance? If we can medicate to correct for all mental imbalances, will the failure to medicate lead to greater culpability? Considering the obesity epidemic in this country, should family members who facilitate another's bad eating habits by providing the Cheetos and Big Macs lose their inheritances? Technology has enabled us to uncover the basic genes for obesity and mental illness. Do you think medical advances that can connect diabetes and death to drinking too much coca cola will result in more efforts to limit inheritances by people who facilitate people's bad habits? Will we be required to do an intervention if we want to not risk our inheritances?

The slayer statute is a salvage doctrine designed to fix the problem of a killer potentially inheriting his victim's estate and, therefore, it is not something we usually plan for. But can you imagine the ways to better plan for both simultaneous death and revocation under the slayer staute? You might find it difficult to ask your clients how they would want their estates to pass if their beloved child and heir is another Lizzie Borden. But you certainly can create an alternate bequest for any gift that is revoked by law without having to mention the unmentionables like murder and divorce, thus passing property to grandchildren or charities even if the parents get knocked out of the will.

PROBLEMS

Consider the likely outcomes under the UPC and the slayer statute of your state in the following circumstances:

10.1. Your clients are Lizzie Borden's father and stepmother (Andrew and Abby) and they have left their entire estate to each other, and upon the survivor's death the estate is to pass in equal shares to Andrew's two children, Lizzie and

---

[8] Carla Spivack, *Killers Shouldn't Inherit From Their Victims ... Or Should They?* (2012) (unpublished paper) *available at* http://works.bepress.com/carla_spivack/26.

Emma. Lizzie is accused of killing her father and stepmother with an ax and is tried for murder. She is acquitted, but at the trial information comes out that Lizzie's mother's brother visited the family the night before with complaints that Andrew's will leaves too much of his first wife's property to Abby and not to Lizzie and Emma. After the trial Lizzie and Emma continue to live together as spinster sisters, but Emma dies intestate shortly thereafter from pneumonia.

10.2. Professional wrestler Chris Benoit, suffering from brain lesions and dementia, killed his wife, his son, and then himself, over a three-day period. Because he killed himself, the state did not formally charge him with murder. In a suit by his wife's brother alleging that Chris's estate should not inherit anything from his deceased wife's estate, Chris's executor countered that since the state had not adopted a 120 hour waiting period for simultaneous death, that Chris is entitled to all of his wife's property under intestacy.

B. MORTMAIN STATUTES

Mortmain statutes originally prevented people in the last few years before death, when they were presumed to be more susceptible to undue influence or were of weakened sensibilities, from devising property over a certain amount (usually around 10%) to charitable or religious causes. Most states today have abolished mortmain statutes, but not all. The English statutes of mortmain, of 1279 and 1290, were originally aimed at preventing people from leaving real property to the Church, which removed the land from the feudal land roles and avoided the services and incidents of military tenure. By the eighteenth and nineteenth centuries, however, the fear was not using collusive agreements with Church members to avoid feudal services, but with overreaching by Church officers that resulted in disinheriting family members. The fear was that the presiding clergyman, using threats of eternal damnation, would prey upon the weakened intellect of the dying, to urge them to leave large bequests to the Church and disinheriting dependents who would then fall on the welfare rolls. Parliament, in 1736, passed a mortmain act requiring that gifts to charities be made at least twelve months before death, witnessed by at least two disinterested witnesses, and registered in the Court of Chancery. Parliament referred to the "publick mischief" that is caused by the improvident alienations to charitable uses to the disherison of the legitimate heirs. Further legislation in 1881 amended the mortmain laws, but they were not abolished until 1960 in England.

Most states in the U.S. adopted mortmain statutes during the colonial and early republic years, usually modeled on the English law of 1736. Over the twentieth century, however, as written wills and estate planning became more common, and as charitable giving received preferential tax treatment, most states abolished their mortmain laws. In 1970, ten states still retained mortmain legislation, and by 1992, only three did.[9] Since then, the Virgin Islands, Georgia and Idaho have repealed their mortmain law and Mississippi held theirs unconstitutional.

---

[9]   Georgia, Mississippi, and Idaho retained mortmain statutes, along with Guam and the Virgin Islands. See generally Mary Radford, "The Case Against the Georgia Mortmain Statute," 8 GA. ST. L. REV. 313 (1992).

The term mortmain is Latin and French and means dead hand, or inalienable hand. It was the passing of real property to the Church, which then never alienated it again, that made the property dead. We generally refer to the term dead hand in reference to testamentary control over property that lasts far beyond the testator's death. Here the fear was that the testator would pass property in ways that would take it out of the market by giving it to a religious order. Mortmain, therefore, could appropriately apply in the context of dynasty trusts, asset protection trusts, and corporate holdings of property today, as well as its usual meaning of limitations on charitable gifts. It is ironic that mortmain statutes cast such a negative eye on the clergy and the Church, when modern mechanisms of mortmain are far more readily available and socially acceptable than in the thirteenth or the eighteenth centuries. Despite the virtual disappearance of mortmain statutes, however, I wonder if mortmain will become of greater and greater concern as states continue to repeal or extend their Rule Against Perpetuities.

C. REVOCATION UPON DIVORCE

Besides revocation by operation of law in the case of slayers or overreaching clergy, every state also has a statute that revokes gifts to a spouse upon divorce. Some statutes even revoke gifts in trusts, life insurance, or other will substitutes, and some revoke gifts to kin or relatives of an ex-spouse. But, as you saw in Chapter 4, ERISA may preempt these kinds of revocation statutes in the context of retirement and pension plans. Consider the UPC revocation provisions:

UPC § 2–802. Effect of Divorce, Annulment, and Decree of Separation.

(a) An individual who is divorced from the decedent or whose marriage to the decedent has been annulled is not a surviving spouse unless, by virtue of a subsequent marriage, he [or she] is married to the decedent at the time of death. A decree of separation that does not terminate the status of husband and wife is not a divorce for purposes of this section.

(b) For purposes of Parts 1, 2, 3, and 4 of this Article, and of Section 3–203, a surviving spouse does not include:

(1) an individual who obtains or consents to a final decree or judgment of divorce from the decedent or an annulment of their marriage, which decree or judgment is not recognized as valid in this State, unless subsequently they participate in a marriage ceremony purporting to marry each to the other or live together as husband and wife;

(2) an individual who, following an invalid decree or judgment of divorce or annulment obtained by the decedent, participates in a marriage ceremony with a third individual; or

(3) an individual who was a party to a valid proceeding concluded by an order purporting to terminate all marital property rights.

UPC § 2–804. Revocation of Probate and Nonprobate Transfers by Divorce; No Revocation by Other Changes of Circumstances.

(a) **[Definitions.]** In this section:

(1) "Disposition or appointment of property" includes a transfer of an item of property or any other benefit to a beneficiary designated in a governing instrument.

(2) "Divorce or annulment" means any divorce or annulment, or any dissolution or declaration of invalidity of a marriage, that would exclude the spouse as a surviving spouse within the meaning of Section 2–802. A decree of separation that does not terminate the status of husband and wife is not a divorce for purposes of this section.

(3) "Divorced individual" includes an individual whose marriage has been annulled.

(4) "Governing instrument" means a governing instrument executed by the divorced individual before the divorce or annulment of his [or her] marriage to his [or her] former spouse.

(5) "Relative of the divorced individual's former spouse" means an individual who is related to the divorced individual's former spouse by blood, adoption, or affinity and who, after the divorce or annulment, is not related to the divorced individual by blood, adoption, or affinity.

(6) "Revocable," with respect to a disposition, appointment, provision, or nomination, means one under which the divorced individual, at the time of the divorce or annulment, was alone empowered, by law or under the governing instrument, to cancel the designation in favor of his [or her] former spouse or former spouse's relative, whether or not the divorced individual was then empowered to designate himself [or herself] in place of his [or her] former spouse or in place of his [or her] former spouse's relative and whether or not the divorced individual then had the capacity to exercise the power.

(b) **[Revocation Upon Divorce.]** Except as provided by the express terms of a governing instrument, a Court Order, or a contract relating to the division of the marital estate made between the divorced individuals before or after the marriage, divorce, or annulment, the divorce or annulment of a marriage:

(1) revokes any revocable (i) disposition or appointment of property made by a divorced individual to his [or her] former spouse in a governing instrument and any disposition or appointment created by law or in a governing instrument to a relative of the divorced individual's former spouse, (ii) provision in a governing instrument conferring a general or nongeneral power of appointment on the divorced individual's former spouse or on a relative of the divorced individual's former spouse, and (iii) nomination in a governing instrument, nominating a divorced individual's former spouse or a relative of the divorced individual's former spouse to serve in any fiduciary or representative capacity, including a personal representative, executor, trustee, conservator, agent, or guardian; and

(2) severs the interests of the former spouses in property held by them at the time of the divorce or annulment as joint tenants with the right of survivorship transforming the interests of the former spouses into equal tenancies in common.

(c) **[Effect of Severance.]** A severance under subsection (b)(2) does not affect any third-party interest in property acquired for value and in good faith reliance on an apparent title by survivorship in the survivor of the former spouses unless a writing declaring the severance has been noted, registered, filed, or recorded in records appropriate to the kind and location of the property which are relied upon, in the ordinary course of transactions involving such property, as evidence of ownership.

(d) **[Effect of Revocation.]** Provisions of a governing instrument are given effect as if the former spouse and relatives of the former spouse disclaimed all provisions revoked by this section or, in the case of a revoked nomination in a fiduciary or representative capacity, as if the former spouse and relatives of the former spouse died immediately before the divorce or annulment.

(e) **[Revival if Divorce Nullified.]** Provisions revoked solely by this section are revived by the divorced individual's remarriage to the former spouse or by a nullification of the divorce or annulment.

(f) **[No Revocation for Other Change of Circumstances.]** No change of circumstances other than as described in this section and in Section 2–803 effects a revocation.[10]

UPC § 2–802 revokes a spouse's rights to elective share, intestate succession, and the statutory rights like homestead, exempt property, and family allowance upon dissolution of the marriage. Section 2–804 revokes provisions for a spouse in a will, trust, joint tenancy, life insurance, or other will substitute. But not all divorce revocation statutes are as thorough as the UPC.

Two things to pay attention to when applying these revocation statutes are: 1) the effect of the statute on non-will documents (trusts, life insurance, joint tenancies, and the like) and 2) the effect on relatives of the ex-spouse. Under the UPC, both the ex-spouse and relatives of the ex-spouse are excluded from taking any benefits under a decedent's will or will substitute. Many other state statutes only exclude the ex-spouse, and some states only apply the rule of revocation to the will itself, though the revocation statutes may be extended to cover will substitutes if equity demands it. Consider these three cases you have already studied in earlier chapters. Go back and review the facts of each one and then decide whether or not you think the court got the legal issues right.

Clymer v. Mayo

393 Mass. 754, 765 (1985) (Chapter 4)

During her lifetime, the decedent retained power to amend or revoke the trust. Since the trust was unfunded, her co-trustee was subject to no duties or obligations until her death. Similarly, it was only as a result of the decedent's death that Mayo [husband] could claim any right to the trust assets. It is evident from the time and manner in which the trust was created and funded, that the decedent's will and trust were integrally related components of a single testamentary scheme. For all practical purposes the trust, like the will, "spoke" only at the decedent's death. For this reason Mayo's interest in the trust was revoked by operation of G.L. c. 191, § 9, at the same time his interest under the decedent's will was revoked.

---

[10] UPC § 2–508 also provides "Except as provided in Sections 2–803 and 2–804, a change of circumstances does not revoke a will or any part of it."

It has reasonably been contended that in enacting G.L. c. 191, § 9, the Legislature "intended to bring the law into line with the expectations of most people. . . . Divorce usually represents a stormy parting, where the last thing one of the parties wishes is to have an earlier will carried out giving everything to the former spouse." To carry out the testator's implied intent, the law revokes "any disposition or appointment of property made by the will to the former spouse." It is indisputable that if the decedent's trust was either testamentary or incorporated by reference into her will, Mayo's beneficial interest in the trust would be revoked by operation of the statute. However, the judge stopped short of mandating the same result in this case because here the trust had "independent significance" by virtue of c. 203, § 3B. While correct, this characterization of the trust does not end our analysis. For example, in Sullivan v. Burkin, 390 Mass. 864, 867, 460 N.E.2d 572 (1984), we ruled prospectively that the assets of a revocable trust will be considered part of the "estate of the decedent" in determining the surviving spouse's statutory share.

Treating the components of the decedent's estate plan separately, and not as parts of an interrelated whole, brings about inconsistent results. Applying c. 191, § 9, the judge correctly revoked the will provisions benefiting Mayo. As a result, the decedent's personal property—originally left to Mayo—fell into the will's residuary clause and passed to the trust. The judge then appropriately terminated Trust A for impossibility of purpose thereby denying Mayo his beneficial interest under Trust A. Yet, by upholding Mayo's interest under Trust B, the judge returned to Mayo a life interest in the same assets that composed the corpus of Trust A—both property passing by way of the decedent's will and the proceeds of her TIAA/CREF annuity contracts. . . .

Query: The Massachusetts statute revoking testamentary gifts to a spouse upon divorce spoke only of wills, not trusts or other will substitutes. The trial court applied the statute literally and revoked Mayo's interest in the will, but not in the trust, which ironically then received the residue and all lapsed property from the will. On appeal, the Court of Appeals expanded the application of the revocation statute to the trust on the grounds that the will and trust were part of an integrated estate plan. Did the Massachusetts court go too far? Note, too, that the court here did not revoke Clara Mayo's gifts to her ex-husband's nieces, even though some state statutes and the UPC revoke gifts to all the relatives of an ex-spouse as well.

Egelhoff v. Egelhoff

532 U.S. 141, 148–149 (2001) (Chapter 4)

In 1994 Donna and David Egelhoff divorced and David died two months later. Donna was his designated beneficiary under his Boeing pension plan. The U.S. Supreme Court held that the Washington revocation statute did not apply to the pension plan and Donna was able to take as his beneficiary despite their divorce. The Court explained:

The Washington statute also has a prohibited connection with ERISA plans because it interferes with nationally uniform plan administration. One of the principal goals of ERISA is to enable employers "to establish a uniform administrative scheme, which provides a set of standard procedures to guide processing of claims and disbursement of benefits." Uniformity is impossible, however, if plans are subject to different legal obligations in different States.

The Washington statute at issue here poses precisely that threat. Plan administrators cannot make payments simply by identifying the beneficiary specified by the plan documents. Instead they must familiarize themselves with state statutes so that they can determine whether the named beneficiary's status has been "revoked" by operation of law. And in this context the burden is exacerbated by the choice-of-law problems that may confront an administrator when the employer is located in one State, the plan participant lives in another, and the participant's former spouse lives in a third. In such a situation, administrators might find that plan payments are subject to conflicting legal obligations. . . .

Finally, respondents argue that if ERISA pre-empts this statute, then it also must pre-empt the various state statutes providing that a murdering heir is not entitled to receive property as a result of the killing. In the ERISA context, these "slayer" statutes could revoke the beneficiary status of someone who murdered a plan participant. Those statutes are not before us, so we do not decide the issue. We note, however, that the principle underlying the statutes—which have been adopted by nearly every State—is well established in the law and has a long historical pedigree predating ERISA. And because the statutes are more or less uniform nationwide, their interference with the aims of ERISA is at least debatable.

Query: The Court claimed that the variability of the revocation upon divorce laws among the different states justified their preemption. Is this a valid reason, or simply a matter of the laws not yet catching up to the complexities of modern daily life? Given the U.S. statistics that nearly 50% of marriages end in divorce, is the Court solving a problem, avoiding it, or making it worse by preempting state revocation laws?

In *Est. of Maxey v. Darden*, 124 Nev. 447, 450 (2008) (Chapter 6) Avis Maxey died from ingesting over 200 prescription pills in a suicide attempt. Theodore, her ex-husband, with whom she resided, authorized the withdrawal of life support after she was taken to the hospital and no one challenged his right to do so. Even the UPC does not mention revocation in the context of health care proxies. The same thing happened with the ex-wife of Gary Coleman who authorized the withdrawal of life-saving treatment after he suffered a seizure and fell down the stairs of his home, resulting in an epidural hematoma. No one challenged her legal right to withdraw medical treatment. Courts generally have been willing to expand will-based statutes to trusts and other will substitutes on the theory that they are all part of a comprehensive estate plan. But should medical proxies, living wills, or powers of attorney also be revoked upon divorce?

Compare the Illinois revocation statutes with the UPC. What is missing?

---

755 ILCS 5, Sec. 4–7. Revocation—revival.

. . .

(b) No will or any part thereof is revoked by any change in the circumstances, condition or marital status of the testator, except that dissolution of marriage or declaration of invalidity of the marriage of the testator revokes every legacy or interest or power of appointment given to or nomination to fiduciary office of the testator's former spouse in a will executed before the entry of the judgment of dissolution of marriage or declaration of invalidity of marriage and the will takes effect in the same manner as if the former spouse had died before the testator.

---

760 ILCS 35 Sec. 1 Trusts and Dissolution of Marriages Act

(a) Unless the governing instrument or the judgment of judicial termination of marriage expressly provides otherwise, judicial termination of the marriage of the settlor of a trust revokes every provision which is revocable by the settlor pertaining to the settlor's former spouse in a trust instrument or amendment thereto executed by the settlor before the entry of the judgment of judicial termination of the settlor's marriage, and any such trust shall be administered and construed as if the settlor's former spouse had died upon entry of the judgment of judicial termination of the settlor's marriage.

---

755 ILCS 45 Sec. 2–6. Effect of Disability—Divorce [On Powers of Attorney].

. . .   (b) If a court enters a judgement of dissolution of marriage or legal separation between the principal and his or her spouse after the agency is signed, the spouse shall be deemed to have died at the time of the judgment for all purposes of the agency.

No problem, you might think. Any good family lawyer will make sure that spouses waive their inheritance rights as part of a divorce decree, and the waiver will shore up any inadequacies in state probate law. But family lawyers are often not estates lawyers. Consider this case involving insurance benefits:

Williams v. Gatling

186 Ill.App.3d 23, 542 N.E.2d 121 (Ill. App. Ct. 1st Dist. 1989)

Andrew Ware and Marguerite Gatling were married on August 10, 1974. Ware named Gatling as beneficiary of his Metropolitan Life insurance policy and General Motors Corporation Employees Stock Ownership Plan (ESOP) account. On September 27, 1982, Ware and Gatling were divorced. The property settlement portion of the divorce decree did not contain specific provision of the insurance policy or ESOP account. After Ware's death on November 20, 1986, the proceeds of the policy and ESOP account were paid to Gatling as named beneficiary.

The executor of Ware's estate sought to recover the insurance proceeds from Gatling, which was denied by the circuit court. On appeal, the decision was affirmed, despite the existence of the following waiver in the divorce decree:

> *[E]ach of the parties does hereby forever relinquish, release, waive and forever quitclaim and grant to the other * * * all rights of maintenance, dower, inheritance, descent, distribution, community interest and all other right, title, claim, interest and estate as Husband and Wife, widow or widower, or otherwise, by reason of the marital relations existing between said parties hereto * * * or which he or she otherwise has or might have or be entitled to claim in, to or against the property and assets of the other, real personal or mixed, or his or her estate whether now owned or hereafter in any manner acquired by the other party, or whether in possession or in expectancy, and whether vested or contingent.*

In upholding Marguerite's rights to take the insurance proceeds of her exhusband, the court explained: *Illinois follows the majority rule that a decree of divorce in no way affects the rights of the divorced wife as a beneficiary in a husband's life insurance policy. Only if a property settlement agreement should specifically include a termination of the beneficiary's interest, will the right to the proceeds of a policy on the life of the husband be affected, unless the policy itself or a statute provides otherwise.*

> *[I]n the instant case, the decree, despite the broadly worded waiver of claim to property contained in paragraph 2(k), makes no mention of Ware's insurance policy or ESOP account and, therefore, cannot defeat Gatling's interest. In fact, we believe circumstances here present an even more compelling factual situation for affirming award of the proceeds to Gatling as named beneficiary. . . . We note that Ware died over four years after his divorce from Gatling. During that period, Ware retained the sole power, and had ample opportunity, to designate a different beneficiary than his former wife. He did not do so nor attempt such effort.*

> *Further, we are not persuaded by any argument that we should extend provisions of the Probate Act to govern over what is, essentially, a contract to pay Ware's designee. Such an argument is properly directed, instead, to the legislature, not this court.*

Query: In this case the court held that even a fairly explicit waiver of inheritance rights did not revoke beneficiary designations of ex-spouses in insurance or pension plans. And you can see why states haven't been all that motivated to change their statutes given ERISA pre-emption. So what is a good attorney to do?

PROBLEMS

10.3. Compare the UPC's revocation statute with the revocation provisions of your state to determine, under both, if Wilma is prohibited from taking any part of the following property after her divorce from her husband, Herman:

1. Herman's will

2. Herman's revocable living trust giving Wilma a life estate upon his death

3. A trust established by Herman's mother, giving him a life income, followed by a life income for "his widow, Wilma, if she survives my son Herman"

4. A stand-alone presently exercisable special power of appointment Herman gave Wilma over property in his father's estate when Herman joined the military

5. Life insurance proceeds naming Wilma a beneficiary

6. POD designations naming Wilma a beneficiary of his stock and mutual fund accounts

7. Beneficiary designations naming Wilma a beneficiary of his state employees' retirement fund

8. Herman's irrevocable asset protection trust naming himself the principal beneficiary, followed by a life estate in Wilma, then a life estate in their children.

9. Herman's durable power of attorney naming Wilma his agent for property transactions in case he becomes incapacitated

10. Herman's health care proxy allowing Wilma to make medical decisions for him

11. Real estate Wilma and Herman owned as joint tenants with rights of survivorship

12. Real estate Herman owned with a TOD designation giving the property to Wilma upon his death

13. Bank accounts held by Herman and Wilma as joint tenants with rights of survivorship

14. Homestead property that Herman devised to Wilma in his will

15. The proceeds from a wrongful death action against British Petroleum when Herman was killed in the Gulf of Mexico from the explosion of the Deepwater Horizon platform

16. The tax refund that Herman and Wilma received the year before when they were still married and they filed a joint tax return but which was deposited into Herman's individual checking account

17. The Picasso painting hanging above Herman's mantel given them by Herman's parents as a wedding present

---

As you can see, married spouses can have extensive commingled assets, as well as beneficiary designations, that they acquired and established on their own, or that were given them by relatives. We would like to think that a property settlement upon divorce would appropriately divide up all the assets, including rights in future property like earnings made possible because one spouse put the other through law school, or like pension funds and annuities that don't vest until many years after the divorce. Divorce lawyers are getting much better at figuring out ways to divvy up the marital property, but most divorce lawyers are not estates lawyers. They think that simply waiving future rights to *inheritance* will cover all the bases as in *Williams v. Gatling*. But that isn't always the case. And even if they write into a property agreement that a spouse waives rights to pension funds, ERISA might pre-empt the settlement if the beneficiary designations are not changed. Consider the property in question 10.3 above and whether the waiver used in *Williams v. Gatling* would take care of all the likely disputes.

Now take the issue one step further and think about the complexities that can arise with same-sex relationships, especially where the parties might be legally married in one state, but may have moved to a different state. If they end their relationship but don't amend their estate documents, they may wind up with absolutely no protection under state revocation laws. The estranged partner may take everything in the will, trust, insurance, pension plan, and joint accounts. Statutes that provide for revocation upon divorce protect the average testator who would not want an ex-*spouse* to share in his or her estate, but offers no protection for same-sex couples or non-traditional unmarried couples in functional relationships. After you do all of the estate planning we have talked about in the book that is necessary to have your non-traditional couple be treated as though they were married, you need to undo all of those mechanisms upon their break-up and cannot rely on the quick-fix of a statute.

Tax Tip: Oops, What About That QTIP?

Now that you are aware of the many tax benefits to marriage, and you have established that nice marital deduction trust for your clients, you need to have in the back of your mind what will happen if they divorce. In *Clymer v. Mayo* the court simply held the marital trust to be ineffective because, upon divorce, the estate tax benefits disappeared and thus the whole point of the trust disappeared. But what happens to that property that now isn't going to pass into the nifty tax avoidance trust? You will want to be sure that it doesn't just go into the residue or pass directly to children if doing so will lead to additional taxes. When one leg of the plan fails, and the entire plan is set up to take advantage of the unlimited marital deduction, you need a back-up plan, and you need to channel the property in the appropriate direction in the original documents and not wait for your client to execute a new estate plan. Your client may be uncomfortable with a provision in her will or her trust that if she gets a divorce all property to the now-ex-spouse will pass into a charitable trust or to some other beneficiary. But a generally worded provision that "if any trusts or gifts fail by operation of law, the property is to pass . . ." (in a particular way) can avoid making it look like you are planning for the divorce that you in fact are planning for. And do not be fooled into thinking that your sane, rational client will come to you to revise her estate documents after her divorce just because she was quick to revise them upon her marriage. Divorce is one of the most stressful events in a person's life, and it can take months or even years before the pain has worn off such that the person can go on with his or her life. You want to be sure that any estate plans that take advantage of marital status have alternate dispositions in case of divorce, even if they aren't explicitly worded that way, for not all state revocation statutes are comprehensive, and many plans can become quite lopsided if the marital provisions are voided.

PROBLEMS

10.4. Your client, Eva, can't stand her husband, Steve, and comes to your office to inquire about a divorce. Steve has diabetes and heart disease, drinks excessively, and is grumpy all the time. Eva seems to be healthy. Currently each has a will giving all their property to the survivor. Assuming Eva has little property of her own, and Steve has extensive property he inherited from his family, how would you counsel her if she and Steve are both in their 30s? Would your answer change if they are both in their 80s?

10.5. Tim and John were married in California during the window when same-sex marriages were allowed to stand. But they moved to Mississippi, which prohibits same-sex marriage, and therefore they had to redo their wills and trusts to try to replicate the rights each would receive if they were deemed married. Each gave the other the equivalent of homestead, exempt property, family allowance, and elective share, and then devised the rest of their property to nieces and nephews. A year later, however, John discovered that Tim had been secretly involved in a relationship with a woman, Sally, who he had married in a civil service the month before. Distraught at Tim's infidelity, John drank a bottle of 40-year old Glenfiddich single malt scotch and then decided to stay in a motel downtown. On the way, he spun out and crashed the car into a tree, dying instantly. Can Tim take his bequests under John's will. What if it was Tim who crashed the car into a tree and died? Would John be entitled to any of Tim's property?

So far, we have been talking about revocation by operation of law—circumstances in which a will provision, or the will or trust itself, simply won't be given effect. More likely, however, is the case where the testator herself decides to revoke her will or trust document. As with revocation by law, not all state statutes governing revocation apply equally to will substitutes.

D. REVOCATION BY THE TESTATOR

Usually a testator does not intentionally rely on the above statutes revoking bequests by operation of law because testators either don't know their beneficiaries are going to kill them, or because they simply didn't re-execute their wills and other testamentary documents after a divorce. Of course, if the testator does have time, and thinks about it, the testator should rewrite his will if he suspects foul play is afoot or gets a divorce. Still, even the most responsible testator may be caught off guard. Revocation by operation of law is for managing the *unexpected* circumstances of life and death; it should not be relied on by planners or clients. But a testator can also voluntarily revoke a will at any time and for any reason. Under the law of every state, she can do so in one of two ways, either by *writing* or by *physical act.* She can also revoke a trust if it is revocable, she can change a beneficiary designation on her life insurance or her POD, but she cannot revoke a gift of a joint tenancy with right of survivorship. She may not be able to revoke a presently exercisable power depending on its terms. Most states, however, only have laws on revocation of wills, and they leave the revocation of will substitutes up to the express terms of the trust or power, or to common law rules regarding conditional gifts.

Historically, revocation of a will was almost as complex as execution of a will, often requiring witnesses or the complete obliteration of the document. But over time, the complex cancelling or destroying that was necessary under the Statute of Frauds was relaxed so that a variety of revocatory acts would be effective to revoke a will. The UPC revocation provision, as we have come to expect, is even more liberal than the laws of many states in allowing for intent to overcome the need for unambiguous physical revocatory acts.

UPC § 2–507. Revocation by Writing or by Act.

(a) A will or any part thereof is revoked:

(1) by executing a subsequent will that revokes the previous will or part expressly or by inconsistency; or

(2) by performing a revocatory act on the will, if the testator performed the act with the intent and for the purpose of revoking the will or part or if another individual performed the act in the testator's conscious presence and by the testator's direction. For purposes of this paragraph, "revocatory act on the will" includes burning, tearing, canceling, obliterating, or destroying the will or any part of it. A burning, tearing, or canceling is a "revocatory act on the will," whether or not the burn, tear, or cancellation touched any of the words on the will.

(b) If a subsequent will does not expressly revoke a previous will, the execution of the subsequent will wholly revokes the previous will by inconsistency if the testator intended the subsequent will to replace rather than supplement the previous will.

(c) The testator is presumed to have intended a subsequent will to replace rather than supplement a previous will if the subsequent will makes a complete disposition of the testator's estate. If this presumption arises and is not rebutted by clear and convincing evidence, the previous will is revoked; only the subsequent will is operative on the testator's death.

(d) The testator is presumed to have intended a subsequent will to supplement rather than replace a previous will if the subsequent will does not make a complete disposition of the testator's estate. If this presumption arises and is not rebutted by clear and convincing evidence, the subsequent will revokes the previous will only to the extent the subsequent will is inconsistent with the previous will; each will is fully operative on the testator's death to the extent they are not inconsistent.

The UPC recognizes that a later *testamentary writing* may revoke a will in its entirety, even if the later writing merely states: "I hereby revoke the will I executed on ___ date." One doesn't have to execute an entirely new will just to revoke an old one. However, most people who die testate will have executed more than one will in their lifetimes, thus revoking an earlier will through the execution of a later one. But the key element to any revocation by writing is that it must be *executed with the will formalities*. In other words, simply writing on a post-it note "this will is hereby void" and attaching it to a validly executed testamentary document will not meet the requirements of revocation by writing.

Also, it is not necessary that a later will state that it is revoking all prior wills, although it is always a good idea to state the obvious, especially if one or both wills do not expressly provide for all of a testator's property. For instance, if a testator, in will 1, gives all of his proeprty to his daughter, and in will 2 gives his house to his son, the son will take the house so long as the second will was validly executed, regardless of whether there are other differences in the wills or whether will 2 only devises the house. In the latter circumstance, will 2 would most likely be deemed a codicil because it only made provisions for the house and not the remainder of the testator's property. By interpreting will 2 to be a codicil, its execution has no effect on the rest of will 1; it merely revokes the inconsistent gift of the house to the daughter. Thus, the rest of will 1 stands. Remember, a codicil revokes whatever provisions of the earlier will are inconsistent with it, but not other provisions that are unaffected by the second writing.

Revocation by *physical act*, on the other hand, can be effected by writing on, or by defacing, burning, obliterating, or destroying the actual will itself. Thus, a testator may write "VOID" across the face of every page, and the will would be deemed revoked by physical act, not by writing. The testator may also tear the pages up and flush them down the toilet, burn the pages, or crumple them and throw them away. Most of these acts, especially if done in the presence of witnesses, and with a declaration by the testator that she is revoking her will, are effective revocations, so long as the testator has the intent to revoke. Of course, if she thought she was tearing up the utility bill, or her draft notes from her meeting with the lawyer, the actions will not be effective to revoke her will.[11]

Consequently, there are four general areas in which litigation over revocation tends to occur:

1.   Did the testator understand the meaning of her act and do so with proper revocatory intent or did she think she was tearing up the utility bill?

2.   Are the testator's actions sufficient forms of defacing, burning, obliterating, or other destruction to satisfy the statute, or are they marginal, vague, or ambiguous as to the testator's revocatory intent?

3.   What is the effect on the rest of the will if only certain portions are defaced and it appears the testator wanted to make a change to a single provision and not revoke the entire will, but partial revocation by physical act is not allowed in your state?

4.   What do we infer from a missing will, what evidence is necessary to rebut the presumption that the testator revoked her will, and how do we discover the true contents of a missing will?

In analyzing a testator's revocatory intent, we are in the same position as when analyzing a testator's intent to make a will, i.e., the testator is deceased and we can only infer actual intent from evidence of the testator's actions and statements. If the testator destroys her will in front of witnesses, appears to have full mental capacity and understanding, and expresses intent to revoke, there will probably be no questions about the legal effect

---

[11]   Evidentiary issues may arise if the only copy of a will is destroyed by accident or natural disaster. Wills drafted by a lawyer however, can be pieced together from the lawyer's notes or even the computer file on which it was created.

of her actions. But consider these cases dealing with a variety of revocation problems:

Peterson v. Harrell

286 Ga. 546, 690 S.E.2d 151 (2010)

Testator Marion E. Peterson died in 2008. She was survived by her two siblings, Arvin Peterson and Carolyn Peterson Basner (caveators). After testator's death, Vasta Lucas, testator's longtime companion and executor of testator's estate, filed a petition to probate testator's will in solemn form. Lucas died during the pendency of this appeal, and appellee Richard Harrell was appointed as successor executor and trustee for the estate. Caveators filed a caveat to the petition to probate alleging the will was not properly executed or had been revoked due to obliterations. The trial court admitted the will to probate and caveators appealed. We affirm.

1. . . . [T]he evidence supports the trial court's finding that the will was duly executed.

2. The will contained a bequest to Lucas in the form of a trust and provided that upon Lucas' death the trustee shall distribute any remaining assets to four beneficiaries, including caveators. Some time after the will was executed, testator struck through with an ink pen the names of all successor beneficiaries of the trust estate, as well as language in the will nominating Richard Harrell as successor executor and trustee. None of the strike-throughs were witnessed or attested to. Near the end of the will, testator wrote, "My executrix is Julie Peterson."[1] Caveators contend these alterations constitute material cancellations that effect a revocation of the will.

To effect a revocation of a will by obliteration, caveators must show that testator made material obliterations to her will or directed another to do so and that testator intended for this act to revoke the will. Joint operation of act and intention is necessary to revoke a will. The intent to revoke the will in its entirety shall be presumed from the obliteration or cancellation of a material portion of the will, but such presumption may be overcome by a preponderance of the evidence. "Revocation pro tanto by obliteration, canceling, or destroying such part is not authorized in Georgia." Price v. Hill, 184 Ga. 191, 195, 190 S.E. 575 (1937).

Even assuming, arguendo, that the alterations to testator's will constituted a material cancellation, we find no error in the trial court's conclusion that testator did not intend to revoke her entire will. The record supports the trial court's findings that caveators had no knowledge of the circumstances surrounding what they allege to be the revocation of the will, that testator never discussed revoking her will with caveators, and that caveators were not present when testator made the alterations to the will. Caveators presented no evidence of testator's intent other than the alterations themselves, and they satisfied their initial burden only by proving that testator made alterations to the will.

The record also shows, however, that the will was found in good condition on testator's desk among her personal papers. It bore the signatures of both testator and her subscribing witnesses and set out a primary bequest to Lucas which remained intact. Handwritten alterations crossing out the

---

[1] The parties do not dispute that these handwritten alterations were made by testator.

names of the successor beneficiaries with a single line were initialed by testator and she added language to the will indicating her desire to substitute Julie Peterson as her executrix. As found by the trial court, this evidence clearly indicates testator's intent to cancel only certain provisions of the will, not an intent to revoke the will in its entirety as required for revocation under OCGA § 53–4–44.

We have found similar evidence of a testator's intent to cancel certain provisions of a will sufficient to overcome the statutory presumption of intent. [The court explained that an intent to effect a partial revocation is not allowed in Georgia.]

[T]he record here demonstrates by a preponderance of the evidence testator's intent to cancel or amend only certain provisions of her will. Caveators thus failed to prove a cancellation by obliteration under OCGA § 53–4–44, and the petition to probate in solemn form was properly granted.

■ *CARLEY, PRESIDING JUSTICE, dissenting.*

I cannot agree with the affirmance of the trial court's admission of Testatrix Marion Peterson's alleged will to probate. Even assuming that the will was duly executed in 1976, the cancellation of a material portion of the will raises the presumption, which has not been rebutted, that Testatrix intended to revoke the entire will. Although the majority purports to assume the existence of a material cancellation, it actually conflates the separate issues of what constitutes an obliteration or cancellation, what is a material portion of the will, and how the intention to revoke is determined. Thus, I respectfully dissent.

An express revocation may be effected by any destruction or obliteration of the will done by the testator with an intent to revoke or by another at the testator's direction. The intent to revoke shall be presumed from the obliteration or cancellation of a material portion of the will, but such presumption may be overcome by a preponderance of the evidence.

Thus, an intention to revoke will be presumed from either "the obliteration or canceling of a material portion of the will. In Georgia, the drawing of [even] pencil lines through provisions of a will is a sufficient 'canceling.' [Cit.]" In this case, the names of all successor beneficiaries were stricken through by a single ink line. Under Georgia law, this constituted an actual cancellation of a portion of the will and, contrary to the majority, was not a mere unsuccessful attempt.

Because there was an actual cancellation of the names of all successor beneficiaries, the next question presented is whether that cancellation "is 'material' within the meaning of the statute. . . . Whether [it] is material such as will invoke the statutory presumption that the testator intended to revoke his will is a question of law for the court.

Under the code it is provided that an intention to revoke the will will be presumed from the obliteration or cancellation of a material portion of it. It was argued that the word "material" meant essential. But the language of the code indicates that it does not use the word in so restricted a meaning. . . . In Black's Law Dictionary the word "material" is defined to mean "important; more or less necessary; having influence or effect; going to the merits; having to do with matter, as distinguished from form."

The will provided that the entire estate was to be held in trust for the primary beneficiary during her lifetime and that, upon her death, the entire remaining estate would be distributed to the successor beneficiaries in a specified manner. The cancellation of all of their names "was material because it directly affected the distribution of all property in the estate."

Because the striking of the beneficiaries' names was a material cancellation, it "gave rise to a rebuttable presumption under OCGA § 53–4–44 that [Testatrix] intended to revoke [her] entire will. Furthermore, as the majority recognizes, Testatrix's will was found on her desk among her personal papers. Where, as here, a will containing cancellations or obliterations is found among the testatrix's effects or in her custody, a common law presumption arises that she made the obliterations or cancellations. As a result of the evidence supplied by the presumption in OCGA § 53–4–44 that Testatrix intended to revoke her will, supported by the presumption that she made the cancellations, Caveators Arvin Peterson and Carolyn Peterson Basner clearly met their burden of coming forward with some evidence that Testatrix intended to revoke her will by material cancellations.

Neither the majority nor Appellee Richard Harrell points out any evidence in rebuttal. There is no parol evidence as to the acts and declarations of Testatrix, although such evidence is admissible. The nature of the cancellations themselves obviously does not rebut the very presumption which they raise. The fact that Testatrix also cancelled another, less material provision, by altering the appointment of an executrix, is simply evidence of even more extensive cancellation than is necessary to raise the presumption of intent to revoke the entire will. . . .

Accordingly, contrary to the majority opinion, evidence of a material cancellation and an intent thereby to revoke the entire will arises from the face of the will and from the correct application of presumptions long established by Georgia law, and there is a total absence of any evidence to the contrary. The rationale and operation of the presumption in OCGA § 53–4–44 have been extensively considered and well settled, and any change therein should be solely a matter for the legislature. Therefore, the trial court's judgment against Caveators should be reversed.

Query: Do you think Marion Peterson intended to revoke her entire will by physical act or do you think she wanted to revoke one or two specific portions? Assuming partial revocation by physical act is not permissible in Georgia, and holographic codicils are also not permissible, do you think Marion would have preferred that the will stand unchanged, or that it be entirely revoked as suggested by the dissent? Note how the majority imposes the burden on the caveators (opponents) to prove that the testator intended to revoke her entire will and the dissent would impose the burden on the proponents of the will to prove she did not intend to revoke the entire will. Which makes more sense? Who stands to take under the various scenarios?

Taft v. Zack

830 So.2d 881 (Fla. Dist. Ct. App. 2d Dist. 2002)

Dale Monroe Taft appeals a circuit court order that held the last will executed by Sarah Zack Taft (the decedent) had been revoked and the decedent died intestate. We reverse.

The decedent died on August 3, 2000. Her last will, dated January 26, 2000, was filed for probate. The will named her husband, Dale Monroe Taft, as the primary beneficiary. The will provided that if Mr. Taft did not survive the decedent, her five children (the appellees) would be the beneficiaries.

The children contested the will, and they filed a counterpetition for administration seeking to have an earlier will of the decedent admitted to probate. The children alleged that the last will had not been properly executed; that decedent's marriage to Mr. Taft was void at its inception; that the decedent lacked the requisite testamentary capacity; that the will was void as it had been procured through fraud, duress, mistake, or undue influence; and that the decedent had intended to remove Mr. Taft from the will and to leave her estate to the children.

At trial, the primary issue that was addressed was whether the will had been revoked. The will had been altered in two places: the devise to Mr. Taft and the sentence naming Mr. Taft as the personal representative were each lined through. The word "void" and the initials "SZT" were written next to each line-through. Other than the attempt to delete the references to Mr. Taft, the will was otherwise unmarked in any manner to indicate that the decedent intended to completely revoke the will. Also, there was nothing marked on the will to indicate that, after the alterations, the will had been executed with the requisite formalities to constitute a valid modification of the will.

In order to revoke a valid will, there must be both an act and an intention to revoke. Clear evidence is required to prove the intent to revoke a properly made will.

The record does not support the conclusion that the decedent intended to revoke the will. While there was some evidence that the decedent did not want Mr. Taft to get her property and that she had been contemplating the possible dissolution of her marriage to Mr. Taft, the record reflects that she did not revoke the will by an act as contemplated by section 732.506 or by a codicil or other writing as contemplated by section 732.505.

At best, the evidence reflects an attempt to partially revoke the will. That attempt failed because Florida law does not allow the partial revocation of a will in the absence of compliance with the statutory requirements for revocation. . . .

Because the decedent did not comply with the statutory requirements governing revocation of a will, the attempted revocation was a nullity. The will, as originally written, was entitled to be admitted to probate. . . .

Query: Again, the testator attempted to partially reform her will, and, like Georgia, Florida does not allow partial revocation by physical act. The strike-outs either have no effect or the entire will fails under the theory that a material cancellation has occurred. Do you think the testator in this case would have preferred her entire will fail if the strike-outs could not be given effect? In *Peterson* the testator struck out the remainder beneficiaries; in this case she struck out the primary. Should that difference matter?

Strike-outs and interlineations are perhaps one of the most common sources of litigation over revocation and revocatory intent. Testators seem to think that the changes are effective, which is true in only a small minority of states that have adopted rules allowing partial revocation by physical act and the use of holographic codicils or the UPC's dispensing power to give effect to the rewritten provisions. Or, if testators know the changes are not effective, they are usually taking notes on their current will with the intention of writing a new will in the near future. Scratching out names and adding others is a good way to tell one's lawyer what changes to make. But despite the testator's desires that the new beneficiaries take the gifts, very few of these changes will be given legal effect. Similar to the *List*, the *Strike-Out* seems to be such a common problem that perhaps states should draft legislation allowing certain changes to be valid if accompanied by clear and convincing evidence of intent and adequate evidence that thetestator herself made the changes (as many states have done with the separate writing doctrine to deal with the list).

But in the absence of liberalizing rules on revocation, what can you do as a lawyer to prevent the kind of litigation that occurred in these two cases? Clearly, the people whose names are being struck are going to be annoyed, probably enough to file an objection to the will. Can you figure out a way to ensure that if your client starts tinkering with her will, she can direct what the final interpretation will be? Consider now whether you think the following actions should be sufficient to deem the entire will revoked:

Dowdy v. Smith

818 So.2d 1255 (Miss. Ct. App. 2002)

The testatrix, Zula Dowdy, died on January 3, 2000, at the age of eighty-nine . . . Dowdy made several wills during her lifetime. Each of the wills left the bulk of her estate to her son, Elgie Smith, and to her nephew, Tommy Smith. She apparently considered the latter as almost her second child. . . . Elgie Smith died in 1997. Subsequently Dowdy entered into an agreement with Tommy and Dorothy Smith, who were separated at the time, that if they would reunite as husband and wife and take care of her, she would leave her estate to them. This agreement was followed by the execution of a new will on August 4, 1997, in which Dowdy left her entire estate to Tommy and Dorothy Smith . . . Malone was Dowdy's brother. He contends that before Dowdy died, she destroyed her will and that it was her desire to die intestate. Upon Dowdy's death her original will of August 4, 1997, could not be located. Evidence was presented that Dowdy's brother, Malone, had presented her with a power of attorney while she was in a nursing home having been diagnosed with dementia and suffering from depression. After Dowdy signed it, Malone went to the bank and took Smith's name off all accounts and certificates of deposit. In ruling that the testator had not revoked her will, the court explained:

A testator's intent to revoke a will must be shown to be clear and unequivocal. Malone never established that Dowdy actually burned her will. However, "a rebuttable presumption of destruction of a will with intent to revoke arises when the evidence shows (a) the testator made a will, (b) which was last shown to have been in its maker's possession, but (c) it was not found after death despite a reasonably diligent search." This presumption was established by evidence. It is undisputed that Dowdy had the will in her possession prior to her death; the original has yet to be found. However, this presumption can be defeated with slight evidence when it can be shown that contestants of the will had access to it. There was testimony that Malone took Dowdy to the safety deposit box in which her will was kept. Further testimony revealed that after Dowdy retrieved her will from the safety deposit box, that she began keeping the will in her home. Shortly after Malone obtained the power of attorney from Dowdy, he had all the locks to her home changed. That gave him complete access to her home. We find that these facts are more than slight evidence to rebut the presumption that Dowdy intended to revoke her will.

Query: This case raises the problem of the missing will. Is this court simply relying on an assumption that once Zula Dowdy reached a certain age and was in a nursing home she could not ever again attain a level of mental capacity necessary to form the requisite revocatory intent? Or is the court suspicious of her brother Malone, who seemed to have been acting in self-serving ways in other matters?

In re Estate of Martinez

985 P.2d 1230 (1999)

On June 6, 1984, Jose C. Martinez (the decedent) executed a will appointing his daughter, Cristina Sanchez (Appellant), as his personal representative, and directing, among other things, that certain realty owned by him and located in Valencia County, New Mexico, be devised to two of his children, Juan Martinez and Consuelo Martinez.

On January 23, 1995, prior to his death, the decedent executed a document entitled "Revokation [sic] of Last Will and Testament of Jose Martinez." The instrument recited, in applicable part:

> *I, the undersigned JOSE MARTINEZ, a legal resident of the City of Los Lunas, County of Valencia, State of New Mexico, being of very sound and disposing mind and memory, and not under any restraint or undue influence of any kind, do hereby make, publish and declare hereby revoking a previous WILL which was executed approximately __ Twelves [sic]__ years ago, which I had named my daughter, Cristina Sanchez as Personal Representative, where as [sic] this said aforemention [sic] Last Will and Testament I am revoking on this date of January 23, 1995.*
>
> *Also there was [sic] additional names; Consuelo Martinez and Juan Martinez.*
>
> *Witness my hand and seal on this 23rd. day of January 1995.*

The instrument bore an illegible signature which the trial court found to be that of the decedent. The instrument also contained the signature of Consuelo Martinez and the recording stamp of the county clerk of Valencia County. . . .

Generally, the question whether a will can be revoked by a writing not testamentary in character depends upon the provisions of the governing statute. In most states, the statute relating to wills usually provides that a will may not be revoked otherwise than by a subsequent will or codicil or "some other writing of the testator declaring such revocation," executed with the same formalities required of wills. . . . But where the statute omits the clause "some other writing" or its equivalent, and simply states that no will shall be revoked except by some other "will, testament or codicil in writing, declaring the same," it has been held that a will may not be revoked by a writing not testamentary in character. The court held the will was not revoked because the "later instrument would have taken effect immediately, not after the death of the decedent" and because it was not properly executed since it was signed only by a notary public.

Query: Should a beneficiary under a will be estopped from benefitting in a case like this, where the decedent clearly had the intent to revoke but did not use the proper testamentary writing? Jose Martinez would have been better served to tear the old will up and throw it away, or deface it. Is the New Mexico court correct that the later instrument was invalid because it was designed to take effect immediately? Wouldn't a revocatory act take effect immediately too? What was the problem here?

Southtrust Bank of Alabama v. Winter

689 So.2d 69 (Ala. Civ. App. 1996)

Marcella Baldwin, died on January 3, 1992, at the age of 89. She was survived by her adopted daughter, Winter, who lived in Oregon with her family. Baldwin had lived alone in her home since her husband's death in 1968. According to the testimony, Baldwin and Winter's relationship was tenuous, at best, most of their lives. Baldwin visited Winter on several occasions until on one visit Winter's husband told Baldwin she had outstayed her welcome. Baldwin was very angry and never traveled to Oregon to visit Winter again. Winter did visit with Baldwin several times between that visit and her mother's death in 1992. Winter's children did not visit Baldwin except on one occasion when Winter, accompanied by her 15-year-old son, visited Baldwin. Baldwin had requested that Winter send her daughter to live with Baldwin and attend school in Alabama, but Winter refused this request.

Several of the witnesses described Baldwin as "manipulative." These witnesses also testified that Baldwin would tell people she intended to leave them something in her will in exchange for these person's performing some service for Baldwin. These witnesses also acknowledged that although Baldwin was manipulative, she could not be manipulated.

Baldwin's grandnieces, Andrea and Susie Brown, testified at the trial. Both nieces had fond memories of Baldwin and related a visit they had with Baldwin in the spring of 1975. They visited Baldwin at her home in Birmingham for two weeks. They testified that Baldwin was like a grandmother to them. Both nieces corresponded with Baldwin, one more frequently than the other. While they were visiting with Baldwin, Baldwin inquired what items of Baldwin's property they might want upon Baldwin's death. Andrea commented that she loved Baldwin's house.

On September 23, 1975, Baldwin executed her will. Paul Woodall prepared the will and witnessed its execution. The will left three-fourths of the residuary estate to Winter and her family. The remaining one-fourth of the residuary was left to the Industrial Design Laboratory of Auburn University. Baldwin's residence was bequeathed to Herbert Darnell for one year and then to Andrea and Susie Brown. The will also provided for specific bequests of personalty to certain of Baldwin's friends.

In 1980, Baldwin executed a codicil, which was prepared and witnessed by Anne Mitchell. Mitchell testified at trial that she discussed the terms of both the will and the codicil with Baldwin at the time the codicil was executed. Mitchell stated that Baldwin had reasons for every disposition of property that she made. Mitchell also testified that she had no doubts regarding Baldwin's testamentary capacity. Mitchell testified that the codicil provided that Andrea and Susie Brown were to receive Baldwin's home immediately upon Baldwin's death. Pursuant to the codicil, Winter and her family received three-fourths of the residuary, with the remaining one-fourth to go to Lindenwood College in Missouri.

Baldwin's will was not located until several days following her death. Roberta Harkins testified at trial that she found the will while she was organizing and appraising items in Baldwin's estate for the county administrator. The will and codicil were located in a paper sack in a hallway closet area that Baldwin referred to as "trash alley."

Felix Yarboro, the director of community ministries at Independent Presbyterian Church, testified at trial that he began visiting Baldwin and assisting her in her personal affairs in 1989. Yarboro testified that Baldwin told him that she did not intend for her grandnieces to receive the house, but that she had bequeathed the house to them to make Marcia (Winter) mad. Yarboro also testified that Baldwin told him that she had "thrown away" her will and that she needed a new one. She provided Yarboro with a handwritten list of her property and specific bequests of personalty. Yarboro then typed the list and mailed it to an attorney, Vernon Patrick. Baldwin, however, never got a new will drafted and signed. With regard to the "trash alley," Yarboro stated that most of the items in there were to be discarded. Yarboro disposed of only the papers Baldwin instructed him to discard. Yarboro testified that two sacks remained in the "trash alley" the entire time he assisted Baldwin with her personal affairs. . . .

Following the presentation of all the evidence, the trial court determined that Baldwin had revoked her will because, it found, she effectively canceled the will and took steps toward making a new will. The trial court held that the act of placing the will in the "trash alley" was an act of "cancellation" or "abandonment," as those words are defined in Black's Law Dictionary. The trial court found that Baldwin abandoned her will by placing it in the trash and taking steps toward making a new will. The trial court further found that the evidence clearly supported a finding that Baldwin intended to revoke the will and codicil and to make new provisions for the disposition of her property. We must determine if the trial court correctly concluded that, as a matter of law, the placement of the will in a paper sack located in an area referred to as a "trash alley" constituted an act of revocation. We conclude that the court erred . . .

Baldwin's will was located intact. The signature page was not removed, nor was the signature erased. Baldwin had not written any words on the document to indicate an intent to revoke the will. Essentially, nothing was done to the will except that it was placed in a paper sack with other documents. Baldwin never instructed anyone to discard this particular paper sack, as she did with regard to the other paper sacks kept in "trash alley." The cases all support a rationale that some act of revocation must be accomplished in order for the will to be revoked. The intent to revoke, alone, is insufficient to establish revocation. No act was done to Baldwin's will. Therefore, we must conclude that, as a matter of law, the mere placement of

*the will in the paper sack did not "materially and permanently destroy the
efficacy of the document." Accordingly, placing the will in the paper sack
was not an act of cancellation or abandonment and did not constitute a
revocation of the will.*

Query: As with making a will, should courts trend toward the UPC's dispensing power and find revocation regardless of the statutory requirements if there
is clear and convincing evidence that a testator intended that a particular will
or will provision not have dispositive effect?

These cases all raise a number of important issues in determining
whether a will has been revoked or not. Many testators may have the intent to disinherit someone named in a will, and may make comments to
witnesses to that effect, but fail to take the actual steps to do so. Should
those statements be given effect? Assuming no, what if the testator
scratches the person's name out of the will and writes another in. Should
that be enough? Clearly, if the testator resides in a state that does not recognize partial revocation by physical act, the courts will have to determine
if partial deletions affect enough material portions of the will to constitute
total revocation, or if the partial deletions should not be given any legal
effect whatsoever.

If partial revocation by physical act is permissible, as under the UPC,
what effect should be given to the replacement names? If the testator
scratches out her son, John, and writes above the deletion her daughter's
name, Sallie, should John, Sallie, or the residuary beneficiary take the gift?
Sallie can only take if holographic codicils are allowed and the testator
signs the change, or the UPC's dispensing power has been adopted. What is
clear is that a testator could certainly scratch out names and write in others and then re-execute the will with new witnesses. How often do you
think this actually happens? Assuming it is quite infrequent, do you think
there is a public policy imperative to devise new laws or judicial remedies
to deal with the ubiquitous strike-out?

**Practice Point: Could You Just Tear Up That Will for Me? and
Other Reasons Why We Love the Paper Shredder**

As you can see, the concept of revocation *should* make it easy for a testator to
change or destroy her will. However, if not done with proper care, as evidenced in
Peterson v. Harrell, it can be extremely difficult after death to determine what a
testator actually meant to do when she struck through all or part of her will. It is
important to realize that this is actually a fairly common occurrence in practice.
Despite the painstaking written and verbal instructions you will give a client at the
execution meeting, you are bound to be startled into quick action when she shows
up for the client review meeting with the perfectly executed will you drafted 5 years
ago now covered in ink. More likely than not, she will feel proud that she was so
clever and efficient in identifying her new preferences.

Yet, you can help remedy that situation, of course, by simply drafting a new
will for the client and getting it promptly executed. Because we all live with our
electronic files, this may be a pretty simple matter for you. Consider, however, a
potential problem that is worth a bit of forethought: that is, what are you, as the

attorney, going to do with all those old wills that are now revoked by writing since a new one has been signed and properly executed? Do you just tear them up? Throw them away? Come to think about it, don't you have oodles of trash from prior drafts and notes that you might be tempted to throw away as well?

Some of you may ultimately be practicing in large firms that have an established procedure for this very situation. But, many of you may run the route of the solo or small firm estate planner, so you will be creating your procedure as you go. Enter the beauty of the paper shredder. Of course, you will be keeping your office running efficiently in accordance with your Rules of Professional Responsibility (which will help guide you in matters of file retention and safety), but I have found that in estate planning, there are a lot of documents that have so much potential power (ranging from now-revoked wills to trust funding instructions) that it is worth just placing the paper shredder in the hallway right outside the conference room door.

You and your staff will be using that shredder a lot. So, go ahead, invest in a powerful one. Also, don't forget to remind your clients to make sure to bring their old wills with them to the new execution meeting to eliminate the possibility that cousin Sarah might just snatch up that revoked will after death and try to probate it because it actually left the china set to her.

PROBLEMS

10.6. Janice executed a will in 1984 which left her entire estate to her husband and, if he predeceased her, then to her three sisters, equally. A remote contingency provision provided that if there were no living beneficiaries at the time of Janice's death, then the estate should go to the Humane Society. In 2010, Janice executed a codicil which amended the distribution pattern entirely (her husband and three sisters had all died, leaving no issue) and instead directed that the estate be distributed equally to her friends Elliot and Mona. Janice dies in 2011. When her will is found, the codicil has a line through every page and "Revoked—Fair weather friends" written across the top of each page. Janice's caregiver, Alice, tells you that she was present when Janice crossed out the pages of the codicil and that she stated "It would be horrible to give everything I have worked for to these lousy people." To whom does Janice's property pass?

10.7. Virgil and Margareta executed reciprocal wills in 2005, leaving everything to the survivor, or if both spouses were gone, then to a Trustee of a common trust established to benefit their minor children. When Virgil dies suddenly in 2009, his will is found with the provision to Margareta crossed out and an expletive written beside it. Underneath the crossed out section is what appears to be Virgil's signature and the date May 2, 2007. Margareta tells you that Virgil probably did this after he found out that she had an affair in 2006, because he filed for divorce shortly thereafter. The couple later reconciled, however, and he withdrew his petition for dissolution of marriage. Assume that partial revocation by physical act is permissible in your state. What do you think the result would be?

Revocation by physical act raises many questions about whether the physical acts are enough to evidence revocatory intent. In states that strictly interpret their revocation statutes, simply writing across the top of the will "this will is void" may not be enough if the statute requires that the defacing touch the actual words. Although the UPC continues the trend toward relaxing the rules of revocation if there is adequate evidence of revocatory intent, as it has with the will formalities, not all states have followed along. The majority of litigation occurs over issues of strike-outs and interlineations, or missing wills that were in the control of the testator shortly before death, but could not be found later.

The latter circumstances raise the issue of lost or destroyed wills, which can be proved through copies or even attorney notes if a probate court determines that the testator did not intend to revoke the will. The real question is figuring out if a lost or missing will was intentionally revoked or accidentally lost. Since everyone's situation is unique, there are no easy solutions.

In the case of a missing will, there is a presumption that a testator intended to revoke her will if there is evidence that:

1. the testator was in possession of the will shortly before her death,

2. the will was not found after her death, and

3. no other person with sufficient motive had access to the will.

But imagine how easily the will could have been thrown away after it was placed in the trash bag in the "trash alley" in *Southtrust Bank v. Winter* and then we would not have known whether the testator actually obliterated the words, or accidentally caught the will up with the rest of her trash. Would its having been thrown out change the outcome? Should it have? Commentators have suggested that the testator in *Winter* did not do any *act* on the will itself other than place it, or allow it to be placed, in the trash alley. For that reason, the statutory requirements of *physical act* were not met. For physical revocation to occur, the testator must have the intent to revoke and must do some act upon the will manifesting that intent. One without the other is not sufficient (intent and no act in *Est. of Martinez*, and act and no intent in *Winter*). Without some physical marks, obliterations, crumpling, or defacing we cannot be sure whether the testator intended to throw the will away or accidentally caught it up by mistake

If Marcella Baldwin did intend to revoke her will by putting it in the trash, should the outcome depend on whether she got around to taking the trash out to the curb before she got sick and died? Without the actual will to observe, to see if there are marks or tears or cancellations, we are often walking a tightrope when trying to determine if a missing will was actually revoked or accidentally was lost or destroyed. Evidence that a hurricane had recently flooded the testator's house is helpful in tipping the balance that a will was merely lost and not revoked. Without a well-timed natural disaster, we have to rely on presumptions and, in many cases, evidence from the lawyer.

A sample Lost and Destroyed Wills Act is this one from New York:

N.Y. Surr. Ct. Proc. Act § 1407. Proof of Lost or Destroyed Will

A lost or destroyed will may be admitted to probate only if

1.   It is established that the will has not been revoked, and

2.   Execution of the will is proved in the manner required for the probate of an existing will, and

3.   All of the provisions of the will are clearly and distinctly proved by each of at least two credible witnesses or by a copy or draft of the will proved to be true and complete.

Recall the case of *Smith v. DeParry*, 86 So. 3d 1228, (Fla. 2d DCA 2012) (Chapter 2) in which the Orlando lawyer, Mr. Allen, lost the codicil of the decedent, Scott Smith, after travelling to St Petersburg to supervise its execution. The codicil established a pet trust for Smith's two dogs, and named his co-personal representative, Lance Smith, as trustee. The Florida lost wills statute provided that:

> Fla. Stat. § 733.207. Any interested person may establish the full and precise terms of a lost or destroyed will and offer the will for probate. The specific content of the will must be proved by the testimony of two disinterested witnesses, or, if a correct copy is provided, it shall be proved by one disinterested witness.

The Florida District Court of Appeals first held that a computer copy of the codicil was a sufficiently correct copy to satisfy the statute. That meant that Allen and Smith, the personal representatives, needed to provide only one disinterested witness since the computer copy was correct and complete. The court held that Smith, as designated trustee, was not disinterested, and it further held that Allen, the lawyer, was not disinterested because of the potential for malpractice liability arising from his misplacement of the codicil. Because there was no disinterested witness to prove the contents of the missing codicil, it failed. Would this case have come out the same way under the New York missing will statute?

As you can imagine, there are countless instances where wills and other testamentary documents will be lost or destroyed by acts of nature or human intervention. Two factors then have to be addressed. The first is proving the actual contents of the will, which is usually done with lawyer testimony. In fact, in most cases, the lawyer is the only person who can bridge the gap between the clerk, typist, secretary, or assistant in the lawyer's office who actually prepared the will and therefore has some knowledge of its contents and the witnesses who were present at its execution and can testify that the will was properly executed. Thus, the Florida statute's requirement that only one disinterested witness is needed to prove a lost will if the court has a correct copy is a recognition that, in 99% of such cases, the lawyer will be that witness. The *Smith v. DeParry* case, however, may throw a big wrench into the practice of having the lawyer prove the will, or else it will create a huge disincentive for the lawyer to retain any original documents for fear of losing them. What if Lawyer Allen's office burned due to an electrical storm and his files and computers were lost? How should the law protect innocent testators in such cases?

The second factor arises when the will is mysteriously missing, not attributable to Hurricane Katrina or a Kansas tornado, and the court has to determine if the testator revoked it or it was simply lost. The presumption discussed above, that the testator revoked it unless there is evidence that an interested beneficiary had access to the will shortly before or after the testator's death, is the starting point, but by no means is the final word on whether to allow the probate of a missing will. As you saw from the case of *Dowdy v. Smith*, the mere evidence that a beneficiary had access to the decedent's financial accounts and safe deposit box can be enough to defeat the presumption of revocation. And if the presumption is defeated, then you are back at the first issue, of trying to prove the contents of the lost will.

Controversies also can arise when a testator destroys a *copy* of a will, perhaps thinking it is the valid will. In general, physical acts done to copies of wills are ineffective. The Restatement disagrees with this general rule, however, and would allow a testator's revocatory act on a copy to be effective *if* the testator mistakes the copy for her original *and* has the appropriate intent. See Restatement 3d Property, § 4.1, cmt. f. Under UPC § 2–503, the Harmless Error provision, many of the execution and revocation formalities may be dispensed with if there is adequate evidence of intent, thus allowing the clumsy or partial revocation of a copy to be effective.

Some testators execute what are called *duplicate original wills*. These are two or more fully executed originals, which the testator may give to friends or family for safe-keeping. The general rule about duplicate originals is that the testator must destroy both in order to fully revoke her will. Revocation of only one original will be ineffective unless the testator was physically unable to retrieve the other will.[12] As with most will formality issues, however, the states are beginning to adopt more liberal rules to effectuate testator's intent where there is clear evidence testator did not want that will anymore. Good lawyers, however, allow a testator to execute only one will, and they instruct their clients carefully to safeguard the original. Copies are handy if the original is lost, but you can be sure there will be litigation whenever survivors try to probate copies claiming the original is lost, unless the loss was understandable, like fire, earthquake, or hurricane damage to the decedent's home. If there is an unrevoked duplicate original, and the other is missing, you can have a very messy will contest case on your hands.

Technology Trend: Formalities and Revocation in the Digital Age

As you saw from the material above, in many cases revocation can be as tricky as execution, with lawyers and clients falling into a variety of traps laid for the unwary. So is practice going to be easier or more difficult when we go to paperless wills? Assuming you have a valid digital will, should the law impose some kind of extra step to ensure that your revocation is intentional? The last thing you want is an accidental slip of the delete key to work a revocation that is unintended. At the same time, you also don't want copies going viral that are indistinguishable from the original, making it near impossible to revoke a will. It could become as difficult to revoke a will as getting that embarrassing picture of you dancing with the

---

[12] But see *Horton v. Burch*, 267 Ga. 1 (1996) holding that it is not possible to execute duplicate originals because there can only be one version in existence at a time. The first one executed was the only valid will.

lampshade off the internet. Furthermore, how would one revoke by *physical act* a digital will if one can't obliterate, deface, tear, or destroy the will itself? If the will is digital, can a message left on an answering machine or posted to Facebook constitute a revocation by digital media?

Usually testators go home with the actual will in their hands, which they can destroy if they feel so inclined. Digital wills can be both more durable and less durable than paper. A number of companies are offering to maintain authenticated digital records that can be validated by the company. Usually there is fairly complex software necessary to allow someone to go into a file and electronically sign official legal documents, as is being done with real estate closings, mortgage applications, and other contracts. But if you need a user name and PIN to change, delete, or revoke your documents, are they safer than they are in the safe deposit box at the bank? I for one have so many PINs that I can't keep track of them and I constantly have to reset them. Some require 8 characters, some 12, some want numbers and punctuation marks, others are fine with just lower case and capital letters. How much safer, if at all, are digital documents when they are protected by encryption or various security questions, like my mother's maiden name or the name of my first pet? Moreover, as technology changes so rapidly, some of the security mechanisms we rely on today will be passé in just a couple of years. How do we maintain the integrity of the digital media when things are changing so rapidly? Given these questions, do you think wills are going to be some of the last legal documents to give up their ephemeral paper form?

PROBLEMS

10.8. Andrew executed a will at his lawyer's office, where it was witnessed by the lawyer's paralegal and secretary. He went home with the original will and promptly made three copies, one for each of his three children. The original he placed in a fancy envelope entitled *Last Will and Testament* and put it in his filing cabinet drawer in a folder labeled *Will*. He told all three of his children where the will was located and he reminded them when he got sick and went into the hospital where the will was. Andrew died in the hospital during tricky brain surgery to remove a tumor that was making him act erratically. After his death his children could not find the will in the filing cabinet and, after a lengthy search, they found it in a trash bag out in the garage with a bunch of old papers, like Andrew's high school term papers and 1973 utility bills. The will had a large X scratched across each page, the pages were crumpled, and there was a big coffee stain where it looked like someone had set coffee on it for many days. What effect?

10.9. Jessica and Balthazar, a married couple, executed reciprocal wills giving all to the other, and if either failed to survive, then to the Red Cross. They had no children, but had nieces and nephews. They also executed duplicate original wills, leaving one will with their lawyer, and taking the other will home to put in the desk drawer. One day they were talking about how one of their nephews, Sebastian, had become a drug dealer and was running with a fast crowd and they worried that he might somehow inherit some of their property. They decided they should revise their wills to leave a little something to the other nieces and nephews, omitting Sebastian, and include a no contest clause to prevent anyone from challenging their wills. The next day they called their lawyer and asked him to tear up the wills he had in his file and made an appointment for a week later to visit him to redraft new wills. That night, however, Sebastian and his gang, thinking they were in the home of a rival drug lord, broke in, shot Jessica and Balthazar, and set the house on fire. Both died, apparently simultaneously, and their house burned to the ground. How should their estates be distributed?

E. REVIVAL AND DRR

One of the most common misconceptions held by testators is that revocation of a later will can revive a prior will, especially if the prior will was spared the paper shredder and the later will was flushed down the toilet. This misconception has led to countless lawsuits and the development of equitable remedies, notably *dependent relative revocation* (DRR), to try to ease the effects of the non-revival rule.

Under the English common law, the revocation of a second will revived a prior will on the theory that neither will was truly effective until death— thus, the first was not truly revoked until the testator died with the second will in existence. At death, we would see which will, if any, was in existence. This presumption was changed as a result of the 1837 Wills Act, which created a rule of non-revival. The non-revival rule was adopted in a majority of states, even so far as to become absolute in many despite clear and convincing evidence of contrary intent.

Under non-revival rules, if a testator executes a will that expressly, or by implication, revokes a prior will, that prior will cannot be revived without re-execution following the will formalities. Simply destroying the later will cannot revive a will that had already been revoked. To further confound the issue, however, most statutes provide that the revocation of a codicil does revive elements from the primary will that were revoked by the codicil, and that revocation of a will revokes all codicils to that will. Thus, figuring out if a testamentary document is a will or a codicil may be profoundly important.

If testator left all her property to her two children in her will, then executed a codicil leaving her car to her niece, upon revoking the codicil the car will pass to the children according to the will. If the revocation of the codicil did not revive the relevant provision in the will, the car would pass outside the will by intestacy. Likewise, if testator revokes the will and not the codicil, the car would not pass to the niece. Instead, the entire estate passes by intestacy because the codicil fails with the revoked will.

The Florida provision on revocation and revival are typical of most states.

Fla. Stat. § 732.508 Revival by revocation.—

(1) The revocation by the testator of a will that revokes a former will shall not revive the former will, even though the former will is in existence at the date of the revocation of the subsequent will.

(2) The revocation of a codicil to a will does not revoke the will, and, in the absence of evidence to the contrary, it shall be presumed that in revoking the codicil the testator intended to reinstate the provisions of a will or codicil that were changed or revoked by the revoked codicil, as if the revoked codicil had never been executed.

The New York statute takes a more nuanced approach.

N.Y. E.P.T.L. § 3–4.6 Revocation or alteration of later will not to revive prior will or any provisions thereof

(a) If after executing a will the testator executes a later will which revokes or alters the prior one, a revocation of the later will does not, of itself, revive the prior will or any provision thereof.

(b) A revival of a prior will or of one or more of its provisions may be effected by:

(1) The execution of a codicil which in terms incorporates by reference such prior will or one or more of its provisions.

(2) A writing declaring the revival of such prior will or of one or more of its provisions, which is executed and attested in accordance with the formalities prescribed by this article for the execution and attestation of a will.

(3) A republication of such prior will, whether to the original witnesses or to new witnesses, which shall require a re-execution and re-attestation of the prior will in accordance with the formalities prescribed by 3–2.1.

And, revocation of a will usually revokes codicils to that will.

Fla. Stat. § 732.509 Revocation of codicil

The revocation of a will revokes all codicils to that will.

Not surprisingly, the liberal-minded UPC has amended its revival statutes to allow for revival if there is clear evidence the testator wanted to revive a previously revoked will, thus making a partial return to the old common law rule.

UPC § 2–509. Revival of Revoked Will.

(a) If a subsequent will that wholly revoked a previous will is thereafter revoked by a revocatory act under Section 2–507(a)(2), the previous will remains revoked unless it is revived. The previous will is revived if it is evident from the circumstances of the revocation of the subsequent will or from the testator's contemporary or subsequent declarations that the testator intended the previous will to take effect as executed.

(b) If a subsequent will that partly revoked a previous will is thereafter revoked by a revocatory act under Section 2–507(a)(2), a revoked part of the previous will is revived unless it is evident from the circumstances of the revocation of the subsequent will or from the testator's contemporary or subsequent declarations that the testator did not intend the revoked part to take effect as executed.

(c) If a subsequent will that revoked a previous will in whole or in part is thereafter revoked by another, later, will, the previous will remains revoked in whole or in part, unless it or its revoked part is revived. The previous will or its revoked part is revived to the extent it appears from the terms of the later will that the testator intended the previous will to take effect.

California has similarly moved back toward revival under certain circumstances.

> **Cal. Prob. Code § 6123.**
>
> (a) If a second will which, had it remained effective at death, would have revoked the first will in whole or in part, is thereafter revoked by acts under Section 6120 or 6121, the first will is revoked in whole or in part unless it is evident from the circumstances of the revocation of the second will or from the testator's contemporary or subsequent declarations that the testator intended the first will to take effect as executed.
>
> (b) If a second will which, had it remained effective at death, would have revoked the first will in whole or in part, is thereafter revoked by a third will, the first will is revoked in whole or in part, except to the extent it appears from the terms of the third will that the testator intended the first will to take effect.

Revival, like the List and the Strike-out, is an area of relatively great disconnect between law and practice. States that have adopted the strict anti-revival rule, by statute or by common law, are often faced with difficult cases when a testator destroys a subsequent will in the mistaken belief that she can revive a previous will. In that case, unable to give effect to the previously revoked will, courts have sometimes used their equitable powers to hold the testator's hand, so to speak, and prevent the revocation of the second will if it appeared that the testator would have preferred that will to intestacy. This doctrine is called *dependent relative revocation* and is essentially a doctrine of second best alternatives. DRR permits a court to disregard the revocation of the second will if it was based on a mistake of fact or law (in many cases the mistake of law as to the effect of revival) AND the testator would have preferred the intervention over the alternative: intestacy. Consider the following case and the court's decision not to apply DRR.

Kroll v. Nehmer

705 A.2d 716 (Md. 1998)

Margaret Binco died on December 19, 1994, leaving four wills—one dated July 24, 1980, a second dated April 12, 1985, a third dated June 28, 1990, and a fourth dated October 27, 1994. We are concerned here only with the second will—the 1985 will.

The 1980 will, it appears, had been altered, and, although it was at one time offered for probate, no one now contends that it has any validity. When Ms. Binco drew the 1990 will, she wrote on the back of her 1985 will "VOID—NEW WILL DRAWN UP 6–28–90." The 1990 and 1994 wills, all parties agree, are ineffective because they lack the signatures of attesting witnesses, as required by Maryland Code, Estates and Trusts Article, § 4–102. Accordingly, if the 1985 will was effectively revoked by Ms. Binco, she would have died intestate, in which event appellant, her brother and closest surviving relative, who was not named as a beneficiary under the 1985, 1990, or 1994 wills, would inherit. The dispute now before us is therefore between appellant, urging that the 1985 will had been revoked, and appellee, the person who offered that will for probate and who was appointed as personal representative to administer the estate under the will, who contends that the 1985 will had not been effectively revoked.

Over appellant's objection, the Orphans' Court for Baltimore County, apparently applying the doctrine of dependent relative revocation, admitted the 1985 will to probate, notwithstanding its apparent revocation by Ms. Binco. The Circuit Court for Baltimore County affirmed that decision. We granted *certiorari* on our own initiative before any proceedings in the Court of Special Appeals to consider whether the lower courts erred in applying the doctrine and finding the 1985 will to be valid. We believe that they did err and shall therefore reverse.

Dependent Relative Revocation

Section 4–105 of the Estates and Trusts Article permits a will to be revoked by "cancelling . . . the same, by the testator himself. . . . " It is clear, and neither party now suggests otherwise, that, by writing on the 1985 will "VOID—NEW WILL DRAWN UP 6–28–90" and retaining the will, so marked, among her papers, Ms. Binco intended to revoke that will and that, unless saved by the doctrine of dependent relative revocation, that will was effectively revoked.

The doctrine, in its most general form, is described in 2 WILLIAM J. BOWE & DOUGLAS H. PARKER, PAGE ON THE LAW OF WILLS § 21.57 at 446 (rev. ed.1960):

> In general the doctrine of dependent relative revocation applies to invalidate the revocation of a will where it is shown that the revocation was conditioned on the occurrence of certain facts which never came to pass or upon the existence or nonexistence of circumstances which were either absent or present contrary to the condition.

As most commentators, including the revisors of Page's opus, point out, in applying the doctrine, courts often speak in terms of a *conditional* revocation, regarding the revocation as conditioned on the existence of a set of facts or circumstances that the testator assumes to exist, when, in reality, the revocation is itself unconditional but is rather based on a mistaken frame of mind—a mistake of either fact or law. They give as an example of a mistake of fact the circumstance in which a testator physically destroys his will believing that the document he is destroying is not his will but some other instrument. In that circumstance, they suggest, the necessary intention to revoke the will is clearly lacking, and a "mistake of this sort prevents revocation, although all the other elements are present." *Id.* at 448. There is no need in that situation to construe the revocation as a "conditional" one—the presumed condition being that the document being destroyed is not the testator's will—for a mistake of that kind suffices on its own to justify granting relief.

The more troublesome branch of the doctrine is where the mistake is not in the act of revocation itself but in the inducement for the act, arising from facts or circumstances extrinsic to the instrument revoked. This often takes the form of a mistake of law or of legal consequences. The most common instance of this form is "where a testator revokes a later will in the belief that he can thus put a prior will into effect, or where he revokes a prior instrument thinking that a later instrument has been executed in due form and that no other facts exist which will prevent such instrument from operating as a later will." *Id.* at 448.

It is possible, of course, for a testator to make clear that his revocation of an existing will is conditioned on the legal validity or effectiveness of some other instrument, but, as the Page authors note, in most instances the testator has simply assumed that state of affairs and has articulated no such condition. In such cases, the revocation is really less of a conditional one than one based on a mistake of law which, if regarded in that manner, would not normally suffice to avoid an otherwise deliberate act. Some courts, in an effort to effectuate what they presume would have been the testator's intent had he known the true circumstances, have thus constructed the fiction of a conditional, or dependent relative, revocation, as a more plausible theory upon which to provide relief. *See* George E. Palmer, *Dependent Relative Revocation and its Relation to Relief for Mistake,* 69 Mich. L.Rev. 989–90 (1970–71):

> The one part of the law of wills in which courts often do give relief for mistake is in connection with revocation by holding that an apparent revocation was ineffective because of mistake in underlying assumptions. Rarely, if ever, however, does a modern court rest its decision squarely on its power to relieve for mistake. Instead, the testator's intent to revoke is regarded as conditioned upon the truth of the matter in question; since the condition has not been met the conclusion is reached that there was no revocation for lack of the requisite intent. This is the doctrine of dependent relative revocation. *It rests upon an analysis that, with few exceptions, is found nowhere else in the law relating to mistake in underlying assumptions.*(Emphasis added.)

This theory, almost peculiar to revocations of wills, gained initial currency in English decisions. As Page, and increasingly many courts, have warned, however, the testator's true intentions in a mistake of law-implied condition context are often ambiguous—harder to discern with real clarity and authority—and, before applying legal fictions based on undocumented presumptions to accept as valid a will that has otherwise been facially revoked in accordance with all legal prerequisites, courts need to examine the circumstances with great care and caution. We shall turn now to those circumstances, as they appear in this case.

The Four Wills and the Proceedings Below

When Ms. Binco died, her only heir was her brother, Henry J. Kroll, the appellant. Mr. Kroll was not mentioned as a beneficiary in any of the three later wills; the 1980 will is not in the record before us, but, from a comment made during the hearing in the circuit court, it appears that he was left a car in that will. The 1985 will was drawn by an attorney and made a complete disposition of Ms. Binco's estate. . . .

The 1990 will, which was handwritten and contained a number of margin notes and interlineations, had no residuary clause, so it is not clear whether that will made a complete disposition of Ms. Binco's estate. . . . The 1994 will is also a handwritten document, containing no residuary clause. At the top, Ms. Binco declares it as her Last Will and Testament and states that she "would like to designate the following items to those mentioned below." . . . Neither the 1990 will nor the 1994 will make any reference to any earlier will, and, as noted, neither contains the signatures of any attesting witnesses, although the 1990 will has a place designated for witnesses. . . .

The sole question presented to the circuit court was whether the orphans' court erred in applying the doctrine of dependent relative revocation and admitting the 1985 will to probate, notwithstanding its apparent revocation. After a brief evidentiary hearing, the court entered an order affirming the admission of the 1985 will to probate. The basis of its ruling was that "the revocation of the April 12, 1985 Will was so related to the making of the June 28, 1990 Will as to be dependent on it. Therefore, since the June 28, 1990 Will was invalid, the April 12, 1985 Will, whose contents can be ascertained, should be given effect."

Application of Dependent Relative Revocation

At issue here is the branch of the dependent relative revocation doctrine that, in effect, disregards conduct otherwise qualifying as a revocation of a will when that conduct, in the court's view, was based on an assumption by the testator that the will being revoked would be immediately replaced by a valid new will. It is the "mistake of law" branch of the doctrine. Two overlapping and confluent assumptions underlie the theory. One was expressed in a 1929 Annotation, A.G.S., *Effect of Testator's Attempted Physical Alteration of Will After Execution,* 62 A.L.R. 1367, 1401 (1929):

> It is based upon the presumption that the testator performed the act of revocation with a view and for the purpose of making some other disposition of his property in place of that which was canceled, and that there is, therefore, no reason to suppose that he would have made the change if he had been aware that it would have been wholly futile, but that his wishes with regard to his property, as expressed in his original will, would have remained unchanged, in the absence of any known and sufficient reason for changing them.

A second, or perhaps simply a different articulation of the same, theory offered in support of the doctrine comes into play when, as is often the case, the effect of not disregarding the revocation is for the decedent's estate, or some part of it, to pass intestate. *See In re Macomber's Will,* 274 A.D. 724, 87 N.Y.S.2d 308, 312 (1949): "The rule seeks to avoid intestacy where a will has once been duly executed and the acts of the testator in relation to its revocation seem conditional or equivocal." The law disfavors intestacies and requires that, whenever reasonably possible, wills be construed to avoid that result. Courts have made it clear, however, that the law's preference for a testate disposition is always subordinate to the intention of the testator, whether ascertained or presumed.

[The court then discussed prior cases where the doctrine arose but was not applicable.] This case presents for the first time a situation in which the doctrine *might* be applied and in which other courts have applied it. It is not a situation, however, in which we believe it appropriate to apply the doctrine.

It is important to keep in mind that, in the context now before us, the doctrine rests on a fiction that is, in turn, supported only by an assumption as to what Ms. Binco would have done had she known that her 1990 will was invalid. As Professor Warren observed in his law review article, "[t]he inquiry should always be: What would the testator have desired had he been informed of the true situation?"[13] The most rational and obvious answer to that question, of course, is that the testator would have desired to make the new instrument effective, and, if presumed intent were to control,

---

[13] Joseph Warren, *Dependent Relative Revocation,* 33 HARV. L. REV. 337, 345 (1920).

the court would simply overlook the statutory deficiency and probate the new will, rather than overlook the legal effect of an otherwise deliberate revocation and probate the old one. That is an option the law does not permit, however. We thus must look for secondary, fictional intentions never actually possessed by Ms. Binco. The real question is what Ms. Binco would have wanted to do if she had been told that she was unable to make a new will: would she have preferred her estate to pass under the existing (1985) will to persons she had decided to remove as beneficiaries, or would she have preferred that her estate pass intestate to her brother?

In attempting to arrive at a reasonable answer to that kind of question, courts have considered all of the relevant circumstances surrounding the revocation—the manner in which the existing will was revoked, whether a new will was actually made and, if so, how contemporaneous the revocation and the making of the new will were, parol evidence regarding the testator's intentions, and the differences and similarities between the old and new wills. The courts recognize that the question is always one of presumed intent. In many cases, because the other evidence is either inconclusive or nonexistent, the principal focus is on the differences and similarities between the two instruments. In that regard, the courts have generally refused to apply the doctrine unless the two instruments reflect a common dispositive scheme.

Conversely, courts that have applied the doctrine have looked to the similarity of the new and old dispositive schemes as a basis for concluding that the testator indeed intended the revocation to be conditional and that he would have preferred to have his estate pass under the old will rather than through an intestacy.

In the case before us, Ms. Binco indicated a clear intent to revoke her 1985 will by writing VOID on the back of it. [T]here is nothing ambiguous about her intent to revoke that will. Also unlike that case . . . , however, she did contemporaneously handwrite a new will, thereby indicating with some clarity that her act of revocation was based on her mistaken belief that the new will was valid and would replace the old one. The confluent inference, that she intended to revoke the 1985 will based on her belief that it would be superseded by the 1990 will, does not alone justify application of the doctrine of dependent relative revocation. We must still search for that fictional presumed intent of what she would have done had she been informed that she could not make a new will. There was some evidence that Ms. Binco did not have a good relationship with her brother and would not have desired that he take any part of her estate. That evidence was contradicted, however, by testimony that appellant and his sister did have a cordial relationship.

We turn, then, to a comparison of the 1985 and 1990 wills and, as noted, we find two very different dispositive schemes. Apart from the fact that the 1990 will did not contain a residuary clause and may not have effected an entirely testate disposition, the fact is that, with the possible exception of the First Church of God, whose status under the 1990 will is, at best, unclear, none of the beneficiaries under the 1985 will were named in the 1990 will. The 1990 will replaced them all, indicating that Ms. Binco did not wish any of them (again with the possible exception of the First Church of God) to be benefitted. The effect of applying the doctrine and disregarding her revocation, however, is precisely to do what she clearly did not want done—to leave her estate to people she had intended to disinherit. We cannot fairly presume such an intent on her part; nor should the lower courts have done so.

We need not decide in this case whether the doctrine of dependent relative revocation, as articulated above, is part of Maryland law and, if it is, the circumstances under which it may properly be applied. It cannot be applied under the circumstances of this case.

Query: What had Ms. Binco done to the 1985 will to revoke it? Do you think she did that based on a mistaken assumption of fact or law? The court refused to apply DRR because it did not appear that Ms. Binco would have preferred the 1985 will over intestacy. Do you see why that is the relevant question?

DRR has not been adopted in all states, and where it has been adopted it has been used sparingly. In many cases, however, it isn't necessary to apply the doctrine. The following chart helps explain the different circumstances in which DRR applies and those in which it does not.

Will 1	Will 2	Mistake of Fact or Law	Does DRR Apply?
Validly executed	Validly executed, thus revoking Will 1	T tears up Will 2 on mistaken assumption that Will 1 is revived	Yes—only if there is clear evidence that testator would prefer Will 2 to intestacy
Validly executed	Invalid b/c lacking formalities—or technical error	T tears up Will 1 on mistaken assumption that Will 2 is valid	Yes—only if there is clear evidence that testator would prefer Will 1 to intestacy
Validly executed	Invalid b/c lacking formalities—or technical error	T tears up Will 2 on belief that Will 1 is revived	No—don't need it because Will 1 was never revoked by Will 2
Invalid b/c lacking formalities—or technical error	Validly executed	T tears up Will 2 on belief that Will 1 is revived	Yes—only if there is clear evidence that testator would prefer Will 2 to intestacy
Invalid b/c lacking formalities—or technical error	Validly executed	T tears up Will 1 on belief that Will 2 has revoked Will 1	No—don't need it because Will 1 was not revoked since it was never valid

From this chart, can you tell which scenario was operating in *Kroll*. The important point to remember about DRR is that in analyzing the sequence of events, the law can only intervene at the point where the testator is about to revoke a *valid* will on the basis of a *mistaken* assumption. Thus, the typical scenario is that described in example 1 of the chart. The testator validly executes Will 2, which revokes Will 1, and at that time has the intent to replace Will 1 with Will 2. Only later, when testator tries to tear up Will 2 in the hopes of reviving Will 1 can we say that the testator's actions are based on a mistake. At that point equity can step in to hold the testator's hand and prevent her from revoking Will 2. There is nothing we can do to give her back Will 1 because at the time she revoked Will 1 she had the appropriate revocatory intent and followed through by executing a valid testamentary writing.

Of course, the key to whether a court should even apply DRR is whether the second best alternative (the other will) would be preferable to intestacy. Once we have analyzed the mistake and determined that equity *could* step in to prevent the testator, as in *Kroll*, from revoking her 1985 will by physical act on the mistaken belief that the 1990 will was valid, we then must determine whether she would prefer the 1985 will to intestacy. In *Kroll*, do you see why the court did not apply the doctrine? Do you think the court was right?

DRR can also be helpful in those cases involving the ubiquitous strike-outs and interlineations. If a court cannot give effect to a handwritten change, it can choose not to accept a strike-out if it seems that the testator would have preferred the original bequest over failure of the devise altogether. Consider the following case:

In re Estate of Carpenter

34 So.3d 1230, (Miss. Ct. App. 2010)

Following the death of Lura Foster Carpenter (Lura), her three surviving children—Bobby Dean Carpenter (Bobby), Jerry Wayne Carpenter, and Nancy Lynn Carpenter Dempsey—filed a petition to probate Lura's will, which contained several handwritten interlineations and markings. Autumn Cosby (Autumn), the daughter of Lura's deceased child, challenged the probate of the will claiming that the handwritten markings showed that Autumn was to receive a child's share of the estate. The chancellor found that, based upon the handwritten changes to the will, Lura's original will was totally revoked and that Autumn should inherit a child's share through the laws of intestacy. Bobby now appeals the chancellor's judgment. Finding error, we reverse and remand for further proceedings by the chancery court consistent with this opinion.

Upon her death on May 27, 2007, Lura left a last will and testament, which was dated February 26, 1999. The will contained numerous deletions and added language handwritten by Lura. Paragraph III of the will states:

> *I have three children now living; my son, Jerry Wayne Carpenter; my son, Bobby Dean Carpenter; and my daughter, Nancy Lynn Carpenter Dempsey. It is my specific intent that my deceased daughter, Sandra Gwyn Carpenter McSheffrey, and her daughter, Autumn Cosby, **will** ~~will not~~ inherit anything under my Last Will and Testament except as specified herein. Any references to my children shall mean my three living children or their issue. (Emphasis added).*

In paragraph VII, Lura bequeathed a bedroom suite to another granddaughter, Tammy Maycock; however, she marked through a small portion of the sentence. This marking did not affect the above-stated bequest. Paragraphs VIII, IX, X, and XI were completely marked through, rendering them illegible. Finally, in paragraph XIII, Lura made another handwritten addition. Paragraph XIII reads:

> *I will, devise and bequeath any real property, including my residence, in equal shares to my children, Jerry Wayne Carpenter, Bobby Dean Carpenter and Nancy Lynn Carpenter Dempsey. In order to accomplish this, it is my desire that my real property, including my residence, be sold and the net proceeds divided equally between Jerry Wayne Carpenter, Bobby Dean Carpenter and Nancy Lynn Carpenter Dempsey **[and] Autumn Crosby.** If one of my children wants the real property, then that child shall pay the fair market value as determined by a duly licensed appraiser, whose name will be drawn from three appraisers; and the proceeds will be distributed between the other two children.*

[The chancellor had held that Lura's will was entirely revoked and her estate passed by intestacy, rather than holding that only the marked up paragraphs were revoked and all property purportedly passing by those paragraphs passed by the residuary clause to Lura's living children. In explaining the chancellor's errors, the court explained:]

In the present case, the chancellor seized upon the italicized language to find that the will was totally revoked in accordance with Estate of Lyles. We find this analysis misplaced. In Estate of Lyles, since the testatrix deleted the number of acres devised to both Howell and Mothershed, the effect of these cancellations was that the land passed by intestate succession because there was not a valid clause remaining in the will concerning the real property. In the case before us, however, when the cancellations are taken into account, there still exist both a valid devise of the land "in equal shares to my children, Jerry Wayne Carpenter, Bobby Dean Carpenter and Nancy Lynn Carpenter Dempsey" and a residuary clause reading, "[a]ny items other than the above mentioned items may be disposed of as necessary and the net proceeds divided as equally as possible among my surviving children, per stirpes." The revocation in this case, therefore, cannot result in intestate succession.[6] The language in Estate of Lyles relied upon by the chancellor, while appearing broad, was, in fact, case specific. Accordingly, we find that the chancellor erred in her holding that Lura revoked her entire will.

Proper application of the doctrine of dependent relative revocation would only result in re-inserting the cancelled clauses, which might have left certain items of the estate to Autumn. As the general doctrine states: "[I]f the testator by . . . physical act, revokes a portion of a prior testamentary instrument and makes a substituted disposition under a mistake of fact or of law with the result that the later disposition is invalid, the prior disposition is revived[.]" Estate of Lyles, 615 So.2d at 1190 (quoting Crosby, 276 So.2d at 666). We do not agree with Bobby's contention that any claim by Autumn

---

[6] Further, as a result of the total revocation of Lura's will, Autumn would receive one-fourth of the *entire* estate, an outcome that we find to be clearly inconsistent with both the original will and Lura's handwritten changes. This is apparent when we look at ineffectual additions to paragraphs III and XIII, which express an intent for Autumn to inherit only a share of Lura's real property. Further, specific bequests of personal property to Lura's three children and, in paragraph VI, a specific bequest of bedroom furniture to her granddaughter, Maycock, would be cancelled if the entire estate were to descend by intestate succession. Autumn would own one-fourth interest in each item of personal property in her grandmother's estate. Furthermore, we find that the inclusion of a residuary clause in the will, which Lura left unaltered, bolsters the presumption against intestacy.

as a beneficiary under the original will may not be revived under the doctrine of dependent relative revocation. As noted, since Lura's additions to paragraphs III and XIII were not attested to by any witnesses, or by a holographic instrument, these changes were ineffectual. It is not clear from the record whether the cancelled portions of the original will, paragraphs VIII through XI, devised any portion of Lura's estate to Autumn. Paragraph VIII mentions a granddaughter, and paragraph XI contains a name that begins with an "A," but for the most part, these paragraphs are illegible. However, paragraph III under the original will states that Autumn was not to inherit "except as specified herein," suggesting that there was a specific bequest to Autumn contained in the deleted provisions. Regardless, it is apparent that Lura revoked those paragraphs under the mistaken assumption that Autumn would receive a devise under the invalid amendments to paragraphs III and XIII.

Accordingly, we remand this case to the chancellor to determine whether Autumn would have received any bequests under the deleted portions of the original will, which should be reinstated under a proper application of the doctrine of dependent relative revocation.

Query: Do you think Lura would have preferred intestacy over the original, unchanged version of her will? You can see why different beneficiaries hotly contest these changes and why courts are reluctant to adopt equitable doctrines like DRR unless there is clear evidence of a testator's most likely intentions.

Practice Point: The Natural Objects of Whose Bounty?

As you can see in the context of DRR, the courts are going to look very carefully at the actual bequests made in various wills or other testamentary documents. In deciding whether to apply equitable doctrines like DRR, the court has to make a judgment (or the jury does) about whether the testator would have preferred the will she is about to revoke (or the individual bequests), or would she have preferred lapse and intestacy since she can't have her first choice, which might be the previously revoked will or an invalidly executed will. This means going through the actual dispositions to see if there is a pattern of always wanting to benefit certain persons, or if there is an abrupt change disinheriting someone. When your client calls you up and asks to meet to revise her will, you will be watching out for erratic changes that could cause a court to look suspiciously at a particular dispositive scheme. Courts assert that testamentary freedom is the touchstone, and yet when clients have multiple documents with very different bequests, it is hard to determine which one represents the client's actual and final wishes. In the absence of clear guidance from the documents, courts often have to look at extrinsic evidence about how much Aunt Ethel liked cousin Fred or spoke disparagingly about cousin Floyd's adultery. This means lots of weepy testimony about how much each of the potential beneficiaries loved Aunt Ethel and sent her birthday cards and thank you notes every year. Your job is to cut through the family dramas and recriminations to discover who your client really wants to benefit, to counsel your client about the possibility of challenges from disappointed family members, and devise an estate plan that minimizes the likelihood of litigation. You also need to offer the court a rationale for an estate plan that deviates from one that judges and the jury are likely to think should benefit the testator's natural objects of her bounty. A good estates attorney is one who asks a lot of questions, tries to discover the family skeletons, keeps in touch with clients and their changing needs, and ultimately understands the family dynamics behind the client's decisions.

PROBLEMS

10.10. Applying the revocation and revival laws of your state, and considering your state's willingness to apply DRR, determine the likely disposition if Lulu Smith's will had the following provisions/changes (the provisions in bold were added later and were not validated through re-execution of the will):

   a.   I give ~~$7,000~~ **$10,000** to my brother Fred for being such a good brother.

   b.   I give my car to my niece, ~~Jessica~~ (**Jason**), because she needs a car.

   c.   ~~I give my house to my beloved husband Will, because he was such a good husband to me~~. **My husband Will is a worthless scoundrel and I want him to have nothing but regrets about his lousy worthless life.**

   d.   I give ~~$10,000~~ **$2,000** to my son, Andrew, so he can pay off his student loans.

   e.   I give the residue of my estate in equal parts to my two best friends, ~~Stephanie and Grace~~ **the Church of Billy Bob**.

F. MODIFICATION OF TESTAMENTARY DOCUMENTS FOR MISTAKE

Under the common law, courts generally had little ability to reform or modify testamentary documents because the wills act required that all relevant provisions be executed with the proper formalities. Thus, courts might be able to delete a phrase or word if there was an ambiguity or a mistake and deletion would solve the problem. However courts could not add new words because the new words had not been properly executed. This led to a variety of unusual outcomes, as when a husband and wife drafted reciprocal wills, each leaving their estates to the other, but then accidentally signed the wrong wills. The husband, thus, would be leaving his estate to himself, and the wife would be doing the same. Arguably, if the names were deleted and the will used the term spouse rather than husband or wife, then the will might be allowed to stand.[14] You have also seen arguments in earlier chapters where a provision for "my son's widow, Ann Burke" should be interpreted to mean whoever the son's widow is at the relevant time, even if he has divorced Ann and is married to Sally at his death.

These legal manuevers came under steady attack by scholars and judges who thought it made no sense to allow for reformation in contracts on the basis of mistake but not in wills. Consequently, the UPC and many states adopted provisions allowing for modification when important trust and will purposes would be frustrated otherwise. In essence, this simply

---

[14] *But see In re Estate of Pavlinko,* 394 Pa. 564, 148 A.2d 528 (1959), where the Supreme Court of Pennsylvania declined to reform mutual wills where a husband and wife mistakenly signed each other's will.

extended *cy pres* doctrines to private trusts and wills, but with slightly different criteria.

As discussed more fully in the next chapter, courts have become more willing to reform a will on the basis of mistake if the jurisdiction has adopted a reformation provision, like that of UPC § 2–805. And the UPC pro-provides for reformation not only of wills, but all other will substitutes.

UPC § 2–805. Reformation to Correct Mistakes.

The court may reform the terms of a governing instrument, even if unambiguous, to conform the terms to the transferor's intention if it is proved by clear and convincing evidence that the transferor's intent and the terms of the governing instrument were affected by a mistake of fact or law, whether in expression or inducement.

Frequently, reformation has been necessary when testamentary documents were drafted and executed to take advantage of a particular legal regime, and the laws changed, making the document inefficient or impracticable. Similarly, if a will was drafted to take advantage of a particular tax exemption, it made little sense to blindly enforce the provision when the tax law had changed. The UPC again offered the power to correct will provisions in the case of changing tax law.

UPC § 2–806. Modification to Achieve Transferor's Tax Objectives.

To achieve the transferor's tax objectives, the court may modify the terms of a governing instrument in a manner that is not contrary to the transferor's probable intention. The court may provide that the modification has retroactive effect.

Nonetheless, most jurisdictions have not adopted these reformation provisions in their probate codes. Thus, in the context of wills, the ability to modify or reform testamentary bequests is often quite limited. Ironically, however, the law of trusts is more flexible, and the Uniform Trust Code has adopted a number of provisions for dealing with mistakes, changing circumstances, and changing legal regimes in the context of trusts. The UTC thus provides for reformation or modification because of unanticipated circumstances (§ 412), economic inefficiency (§ 414), to correct for mistakes (§ 415), and to achieve the settlor's tax objectives (§ 416).

UTC § 412. Modification or Termination Because of Unanticipated Circumstances or Inability to Administer Trust Effectively.

(a) The court may modify the administrative or dispositive terms of a trust or terminate the trust if, because of circumstances not anticipated by the settlor, modification or termination will further the purposes of the trust. To the extent practicable, the modification must be made in accordance with the settlor's probable intention.

(b) The court may modify the administrative terms of a trust if continuation of the trust on its existing terms would be impracticable or wasteful or impair the trust's administration.

(c) Upon termination of a trust under this section, the trustee shall distribute the trust property in a manner consistent with the purposes of the trust.

UTC § 414. Modification or Termination of Uneconomic Trusts.

(a) After notice to the qualified beneficiaries, the trustee of a trust consisting of trust property having a total value less than [$50,000] may terminate the trust if the trustee concludes that the value of the trust property is insufficient to justify the cost of administration.

(b) The court may modify or terminate a trust or remove the trustee and appoint a different trustee if it determines that the value of the trust property is insufficient to justify the cost of administration.

(c) Upon termination of a trust under this section, the trustee shall distribute the trust property in a manner consistent with the purposes of the trust.

(d) This section does not apply to an easement for conservation or preservation.

UTC § 415. Reformation to Correct Mistakes.

The court may reform the terms of a trust, even if unambiguous, to conform the terms to the settlor's intention if it is proved by clear and convincing evidence what the settlor's intention was and that the terms of the trust were affected by a mistake of fact or law, whether in expression or inducement.

UTC § 416. Modification to Achieve Settlor's Tax Objectives.

To achieve the settlor's tax objectives, the court may modify the terms of a trust in a manner that is not contrary to the settlor's probable intention. The court may provide that the modification has retroactive effect.

But as we discuss in more detail in Chapter 11, figuring out what the mistake is, how to reform a testamentary document in light of a mistake, and how to distribute the property afterwards are quite difficult issues, especially when the parol evidence rule prohibits the admission of certain extrinsic evidence. Although courts try to glean the settlor's intent, sometimes it is no easy task figuring out how to distribute the property once the mistake is corrected. Where there is clear and convincing evidence for a particular solution, however, the modern trend is to allow for reformation.

G. MODIFICATION OR TERMINATION BY THE SETTLOR

The trust settlor may always modify a trust *if* she has retained a power to revoke or amend. Even with such a power a settlor may still go too far and violate the trust terms by revoking in a manner not allowed in the trust documents or amending the trust in ways prohibited by law. Trust beneficiaries may enforce the trust terms, requiring the settlor to go back and properly revoke or modify the trust, or risk having any unauthorized changes voided. Think back to *Farkas v. Williams* in Chapter 4. In that case the trust settlor had purchased securities in his name as trustee for his beneficiary, a young veterinarian who worked for him. The court upheld the trust, even though Farkas was settlor, trustee, and principal beneficiary, on the grounds that Williams, the secondary beneficiary, could enforce the trust terms, especially the steps required for revoking the trust, if Farkas were to violate them.[14] This power to enforce meant that Farkas did not have sole, unfettered control over the property, and consequently the trust was held to be valid. He had transferred a tiny sliver of a property stick to Williams.

What if Farkas didn't follow his own trust procedures if he sought to modify or revoke the trust. That is exactly what happened in *Heaps v. Heaps*, also from Chapter 4. The court held the revocation invalid and then, when one of the settlors died, the trust became irrevocable, and all further transactions were voided. Where trust settlors are still living and seek to modify the terms of their trusts, you would think that courts would be receptive to such changes. But of course, they are not always. Why? Because the whole premise of the legal fiction of the trust is that the settlor has parted with sufficient dominion and control to justify a finding that a property right has been transferred to the beneficiaries. Without the transfer of the property right, the trust itself is illusory and void. That means there are beneficiaries out there whose interests will be reduced if the settlor is allowed free rein to modify or terminate a trust, or certain provisions of a trust, however she chooses, in violation of the trust terms. While a testator may revoke a will at any time up until death, the same is not true of trusts, unless the settlor has retained broad revocation powers. As you now realize, the retention of broad revocation powers has led the IRS to tax such trust interests as though they are entirely the full property of the settlor.

Under the UTC, the settlor may always petition for reformation on the basis of changed circumstances, changing tax law, or mistake. More often than not, however, it isn't the settlor who wants to modify or terminate a trust, but rather the beneficiaries. Most beneficiaries would much rather have all the property outright, free of trust, than have to wait for quarterly payments of income, or until they reach 25 or graduate from college, or whatever completely unreasonable constraint the settlor has placed on the principal.

H. MODIFICATION OR TERMINATION OF TRUSTS BY THE BENEFICIARIES

In 1889, a trust beneficiary sought permission to terminate a trust his father had established that gave him $10,000 when he reached age 21, $10,000 when he reached age 25, and the remainder of his inheritance when he reached age 30. Quite annoyed that his father obviously didn't feel that his son could handle his entire inheritance when he reached the age of majority, the son brought suit to terminate the trust. The Massachusetts Supreme Court, presumably composed of a bench of fathers, refused the son's request, explaining that no unusual circumstances had occurred that undermined the father's intentions in establishing the trust, and it certainly wasn't against public policy to postpone receipt of large sums of money. The court explained: "It cannot be said that these restrictions upon the plaintiff's possession and control of the property are altogether useless, for there is not the same danger that he will spend the property while it is in

---

[14] The fact that Williams didn't even know about the trust makes this a bit fishy, but the point remains valid as a matter of law. The beneficiary can enforce trust provisions, including provisions restricting or limiting the settlor's ability to revoke or modify the trust.

the hands of the trustees as there would be if it were in his own."[15] Respecting the father's judgment about his son's spendthrift habits, the court refused to terminate the trust and accelerate the inheritance for the beneficiary, even though the son was the sole beneficiary.

That case, *Claflin v. Claflin,* is the origin of the cleverly-named *Claflin Doctrine,* which holds that even if all the beneficiaries consent, a trust will not be modified or terminated so long as a material purpose of the trust remains. The opposite is generally applicable as well. If the beneficiaries all consent and no material purpose remains, a trust can be modified or terminated. The requirement of unanimous consent, however is necessary for modification or termination, although a trustee who resists termination because of the mere possibility of additional class members who might qualify as remote beneficiaries may be scrutinized by the court, especially if the trustee is resisting termination in order to retain trustee fees. In one case the trustee resisted termination of a trust that was set to terminate when all of the settlor's grandchildren reached age 30. At the time of the petition, all the living grandchildren had reached age 30, and the settlor's two daughters were then aged 65 and 70 and unlikely to have any more children. Nevertheless, the trustee argued that "the presumption that the birth of a child is possible throughout the life of a woman" should prevent termination. The court disagreed.[16]

Courts are skeptical when parties claim that they aren't going to have any more children in order to terminate a trust early.[17] Obtaining consent of all beneficiaries is easy when they are all in the same family, all in being, all get along, and all get more if the trust terminates now rather than later. On the other hand, when trust interests pass to open classes, or type 2 classes like heirs or issue, it can be difficult to obtain the consent of all beneficiaries. Some states disregard the interests of remote beneficiaries, especially those who would take only as alternates or on the basis of a remote contingency.[18] Where the class of takers cannot be determined until the death of a person then living, courts will not terminate the trust even though the Rule in Shelley's case or the Doctrine of Worthier Title would have permitted the termination of the future interests. Because these rules have been abolished in many states, it is now more difficult to terminate trusts with open classes.

Usually guardians *ad litem* are appointed to represent the interests of minor or unborn beneficiaries, and in most cases they are precluded from approving the termination of a trust if doing so would disadvantage the persons they represent. Yet if beneficiaries disapprove modification or termination of a trust, but their interests would not be affected by the change, courts may ignore their decision.[19]

The more common subject of litigation surrounding modification and termination of trusts is over the existence or lack of a remaining material purpose. Although the majority rule remains that trusts may not be terminated early simply on the request of the beneficiaries, most courts

---

[15]   Claflin v. Claflin, 20 N.E. 454 (Mass. 1889).

[16]   Korten v. Chicago City Bank and Trust Co., 533 N.E.2d 102 (Ill. App. Ct. 1st Dist. 1988).

[17]   In re Testamentary Trust of Hasch, 721 N.E.2d 1111 (Ohio App. 1999).

[18]   CAL. PROB. CODE § 15404(c) (West 1991); N.C. GEN. STAT. Ann. § 41–6 (West 2012).

[19]   See, e.g. Musick v. Reynolds, 798 S.W.2d 626 (Tex. App. Eastland 1990).

recognize the corresponding doctrine that if no material purpose exists for retaining property in trust, the trust can be terminated. See the UTC §§ 410 and 411 and the Restatement 3d of Trusts § 65.

UTC § 410. Modification or Termination of Trust; Proceedings for Approval or Disapproval.

(a) In addition to the methods of termination prescribed by Sections 411 through 414, a trust terminates to the extent the trust is revoked or expires pursuant to its terms, no purpose of the trust remains to be achieved, or the purposes of the trust have become unlawful, contrary to public policy, or impossible to achieve.

(b) A proceeding to approve or disapprove a proposed modification or termination under Sections 411 through 416, or trust combination or division under Section 417, may be commenced by a trustee or beneficiary, [and a proceeding to approve or disapprove a proposed modification or termination under Section 411 may be commenced by the settlor]. The settlor of a charitable trust may maintain a proceeding to modify the trust under Section 413.

UTC § 411. Modification or Termination of Noncharitable Irrevocable Trust by Consent.

[(a) [A noncharitable irrevocable trust may be modified or terminated upon consent of the settlor and all beneficiaries, even if the modification or termination is inconsistent with a material purpose of the trust.] [If, upon petition, the court finds that the settlor and all beneficiaries consent to the modification or termination of a noncharitable irrevocable trust, the court shall approve the modification or termination even if the modification or termination is inconsistent with a material purpose of the trust.] A settlor's power to consent to a trust's modification or termination may be exercised by an agent under a power of attorney only to the extent expressly authorized by the power of attorney or the terms of the trust; by the settlor's [conservator] with the approval of the court supervising the [conservatorship] if an agent is not so authorized; or by the settlor's [guardian] with the approval of the court supervising the [guardianship] if an agent is not so authorized and a conservator has not been appointed. [This subsection does not apply to irrevocable trusts created before or to revocable trusts that become irrevocable before [the effective date of this [Code] [amendment].]]

(b) A noncharitable irrevocable trust may be terminated upon consent of all of the beneficiaries if the court concludes that continuance of the trust is not necessary to achieve any material purpose of the trust. A noncharitable irrevocable trust may be modified upon consent of all of the beneficiaries if the court concludes that modification is not inconsistent with a material purpose of the trust.

[(c) A spendthrift provision in the terms of the trust is not presumed to constitute a material purpose of the trust.]

(d) Upon termination of a trust under subsection (a) or (b), the trustee shall distribute the trust property as agreed by the beneficiaries.

(e) If not all of the beneficiaries consent to a proposed modification or termination of the trust under subsection (a) or (b), the modification or termination may be approved by the court if the court is satisfied that:

> (1) if all of the beneficiaries had consented, the trust could have been modi-fied or terminated under this section; and
>
> (2) the interests of a beneficiary who does not consent will be adequately protected.

In order to determine if a material purpose remains, a court must care-fully consider why a trust is established and whether the reasons for termination outweigh the reasons for continuation. A trust that is merely in place to postpone distribution until the last possible moment under the RAP has been allowed to terminate when an intervening future interest was void.[20] Where a court has determined that the trust form was intended to provide a steady stream of income to the beneficiaries, it held that a ma-terial purpose existed so as to prevent termination. Spendthrift trusts and discretionary trusts generally have an additional purpose that would pre-vent early termination, as would a QTIP or marital deduction trust. Trusts that have tax advantages, or seek to benefit from the extended RAP, thus could not be terminated so long as those advantages remained.

Consider whether the following trusts should have been terminated or not:

In re Estate of Brown

528 A.2d 752 (1987)

Andrew Brown died, leaving his entire estate in trust to provide an education "particularly a college education, for the children of my nephew, Woolson S. Brown." The trustee was directed to use the income and such part of the principal as may be necessary to accomplish that purpose. Once the purpose has been accomplished, in the trustee's discretion, then the income and such part of principal as may be necessary was to be paid for the care, maintenance, and welfare of Woolson Brown and his wife, Rose-mary Brown, "for and during the remainder of their natural lives." At their death, the principal was to be paid to their then living children in equal shares. Once the trustee determined that the educational purpose had been accomplished, he began paying the income to Woolson and Rosemary Brown. After some time, Woolson and Rosemary petitioned for termination of the trust and the payment of the entire principal to them, claiming that the entire remaining assets were necessary to maintain their lifestyle. The remaindermen, their children, consented, but the probate court denied the petition to terminate.

On appeal, the superior court reversed, concluding that continuation of the trust was no longer necessary because the only material purpose, the education of the children, had been accomplished. Noting that this was not a support or a spendthrift trust, the Vermont Supreme Court reversed, finding that the trust had two purposes, the education of the children AND the assurance of a life-long income for the nephew and his wife. Quoting the relevant language of the trust, the court emphasized that the trust was for the "care, maintenance and welfare" of the lifetime beneficiaries, "so that they may live in the style and manner to which they are accustomed, for and during the remainder of their natural lives." Finding the life-long

---

[20] Conn. Bank and Trust Co. v. Brody, 174 Conn. 616, 392 A.2d 445 (1978).

income stream was a material purpose, the court refused to allow termination of the trust, even though the trust would be responsible for continuing trustee fees.

Query: When should an income stream be deemed a material purpose? Additionally, what happens if, as in the instant case, the trustee fees were eating into the income of the trust to such an extent that the beneficiaries thought it made sense to terminate it and apply all the principal to the life beneficiaries' support? Should the mere right of the trustee to exercise discretion be enough to prevent termination of the trust?

American Nat'l Bank of Cheyenne v. Miller

899 P.2d 1337 (Wyo. 1995)

Evelyn Plummer established a trust at his death that provided the income would be payable to his wife for her life, then to his only daughter and her husband for their lives, and then at their death to divide the property into three shares for his only grandchildren. The trustee was then to pay 20% to each child at age 23 or college graduation, 20% to each child at age 28, and 20% to each child at age 35. When the last grandchild's share was paid, the remainder was to be distributed to the University of Wyoming for scholarships. After the death of the settlor's wife, and daughter, however, all three grandchildren had already reached age 35. The son-in-law disclaimed his interest in the income and the grandchildren sought termination of the trust. The University of Wyoming agreed and the trial court ordered termination over the trustee's objection. The trustee claimed that until the son-in-law actually died, the trust had a material purpose, but the Supreme Court of Wyoming disagreed. It determined that since the trust had no spendthrift provisions, that the educational support terms of the grandchildren's shares had already become moot, and the postponement of the trust was principally aimed at the grandchildren reaching age 35, not the son-in-law's death, therefore, the trust retained no material provisions to foreclose termination.

Query: Should a beneficiary be able to disclaim a life interest with the sole motive of accelerating the remainder beneficiary's distribution? Should a trustee be able to withhold consent to termination solely to continue managing the trust and receiving trustee fees? Should the trust have to pay for the litigation to terminate a trust when everyone but the trustee consents?

Claffey v. National City Bank

2011 WL 4477315 (Ohio App. Ct. 10 Dist. 2011)

The trust at issue was established in June 1989 by Lynne Claffey. Upon the death of Lynne Claffey, the trust was divided into two equal halves. National City Bank ("NCB") was later appointed as successor trustee. The purpose of the first half of the trust, Trust #1, was to make distributions to Lynne Claffey's son, Joel Claffey, at ages 25 and 30 with the balance of the corpus being distributed when he reached 35. The purpose of the second half of the trust, Trust #2, was to provide a source of benefits for the life of Lynne Claffey's daughter, Dena Claffey.

The trust estate holds title to two adjacent parcels of property. The real subject property consists of approximately 15 .4 acres of primarily undeveloped real estate, including a 6.9 acre pond. Complaints were submitted to the U.S. Army Corps of Engineers ("USACE") alleging illegal dumping or filling of solid waste material by Joel Claffey into the pond. USACE investigated and, as a result, sent an order dated December 20, 2002 to Joel Claffey requiring him to: cease and desist his unlawful fill activities; within 15 days to provide certain information; to take steps to restore the area; and to apply for an after-the-fact permit for the dumping that had already taken place. Joel Claffey believes that the USACE does not have jurisdiction over the pond.

NCB claims it did not become aware of any problem until two years later when, on May 19, 2005, a letter was sent from the U.S. Environmental Protection Agency ("USEPA") asking NCB to assist Joel Claffey in cooperating with the USACE. The letter warned that failure to comply could result in administrative penalties of $157,500, civil penalties of up to $27,500 per day of violation, and criminal prosecution.

Once NCB learned of these environmental issues, they retained legal counsel and environmental consulting services to defend the environmental claims on behalf of the trust. The environmental consulting firm opined that the pond is under federal jurisdiction due to its emptying into Alum Creek and that additional dumping had occurred since the initial cease and desist order. Based upon the consultant's advice, NCB submitted a restoration plan in order to resolve the issue.

In April 2006, after his 35th birthday, Joel Claffey, through counsel, asked that NCB terminate Trust #1 (his portion of the trust) and stated that he would deal with the USACE. NCB responded explaining that both USACE and USEPA made it clear that remedial action must be taken to address the violations committed. Further, NCB stated that they had an obligation to preserve and restore the trust property for the benefit of both beneficiaries, Joel and Dena Claffey.

The trial court ruled against Joel and held that NCB had an obligation to both Joel and Dena Claffey as beneficiaries, and that NCB's actions were reasonable and prudent. On appeal, the court affirmed, explaining:

The trust for the benefit of Dena Claffey was intended to be an on-going income stream for Dena. The corpus of the trust had to be administered in a way to provide that income. Simply turning the responsibility for caring for the real estate over to her brother could not guarantee that the real estate and trust corpus would guarantee her any income in the future. NCB needed to protect the real estate for the benefit of both trusts and acted appropriately in attempting to protect the pond and surrounding area.

Query: This is a typical case of a relatively small piece of property being placed into a revocable living trust that would become irrevocable upon the death of the settlor, Lynne Claffey. The settlor and her children most likely assumed that they could do whatever they wanted on the property (legal actions anyway), but when Joel began filling the pond the trustee had an obligation to ensure that the property was not devalued or injured. Does the trustee in this case have a valid duty to make sure that no changes are made to the property, or is the trustee overreacting? Is there an ongoing material purpose here?

Shepard v. Barrell

935 N.E.2d 391 (Mass.App.Ct. 2010)

John Shepard and his daughters brought an action seeking partial termination of a trust established by his great-grandparents which provided that the principal was to be divided into two shares, one for the settlors' daughter and her descendants, and one for the settlors' son and his descendants. The trusts were then to terminate 20 years after the death of the last of the named beneficiaries, all of whom were living when the trust was created, and the principal was to be payable to the settlors' then living issue. Before termination, the issue would receive the income from the trust. John Shepard's mother was a named beneficiary, and she died in 1989, but two other named beneficiaries were still alive in 2010. Thus, the trust would not terminate until 20 years after the death of those two named beneficiaries. John Shepard sought early termination on the grounds that *(1) the trusts have no remaining purpose; (2) John Shepard's interest in the principal of the trusts is vested; (3) his interest is severable from the other interests; and (4) all of the beneficiaries have consented to termination of his portion of the trusts. The plaintiffs also argue that there is a risk that John Shepard's share of the principal will be subjected to the Federal generation-skipping transfer tax (the GST tax) and that the risk will be avoided if his share is disbursed in 2010.*

The trial court dismissed the complaint, determining that the trusts have *"a remaining purpose, namely to continuously provide for the financial needs of the Settlors' descendants by investing the property and funds of the Company and distributing the dividends to the Trusts."* The trial court found that John Shepard has contingent interests, which are not severable, and which will not vest *"until twenty (20) years after the death of the last life in being . . . [and] only if he is living at the time of the Trusts' termination."* The court also *concluded that the other beneficiaries have not consented to termination of the trusts. Finally, the judge ruled that there is no tax advantage that would warrant early termination.*

On appeal, the court affirmed, explaining: *On this record, it is clear that the settlors fixed the time for termination of the trusts and it is equally clear that the purposes of the trusts are ongoing. The settlors intended to provide continuous financial support and long-term financial stability for their descendants until the time for termination of the trusts arrived. That much is plain not only from the way the trusts are structured but also from the spendthrift provisions five of the trusts contain.* The court also agreed that there was no GST tax liability.

Query: Do you think a change in tax regime that would have created estate or GST tax liability should override a settlor's intent to provide an income stream for as long as possible for his descendants? What do you think these settlors would have done had Massachusetts abolished the RAP before they established this trust? If there were no RAP, and the trust was established to continue in perpetuity, could the beneficiaries ever terminate the trust? Should they be able to?

If the settlor is still alive and consents to the termination of an irrevocable trust, even if a material purpose exists, the Claflin Rule will not bar the action. So long as the settlor and all the beneficiaries agree, the trust can be terminated.[21] Once the settlor has died, the Claflin Rule will generally bar termination of trusts that continue to have a material purpose. Thus, the thoughtless insertion of a spendthrift provision may cause a trust not to be terminated when it probably should be. Litigation over trust termination, like most litigation we've seen, is an estate planner's failure. If the settlor absolutely does not want a trust terminated until the absolute last moment in time that it can legally exist, then you want to include clear language of material purpose to fit the trust within the Claflin Rule. But if the settlor would want termination if circumstances change, or the property warrants the removal of the trust, then there should be some provision allowing for termination and setting out the steps necessary to accomplish that end. A settlor could give a limited set of beneficiaries the power to terminate or modify a trust, without forcing them to appoint guardians *ad litem* for unborn or minor beneficiaries.

As with everything we have studied so far, understanding the rules allows you to effectuate your client's intentions with regard to future control over the property. Not all trusts should continue in perpetuity. Trusts of relatively small value, trusts with volatile property, and trusts with complex administration duties may be better off terminated, even if that may result in estate taxes being due. However, remember that trustees will almost always resist terminating a trust if doing so deprives them of their trustee fees. How you manage the possible conflicts to avoid litigation is another sign of good planning.

I. CONCLUSION

Wills and trusts, or portions of them, may be revoked for any of a number of important reasons—by operation of law such as the divorce of the settlor or by slaying; by voluntary act of the testator such as tearing it up and flushing it down the toilet; as a result of mistake or changing legal rules; and by consent of all the parties. But American courts have not adopted the English rule that mere consent of the beneficiaries is enough to terminate a trust. The Claflin Rule prevents termination of trusts that continue to have a material purpose. Furthermore, where provisions exist for possible future takers (as when the issue of a trust beneficiary is to take in case the beneficiary predeceases the distribution), it will be very difficult to terminate a trust. Are the policy reasons in favor of free alienation and unencumbering property enough to defeat the dead hand of the settlor? Should they be? Settlors can certainly make it very difficult to terminate a trust early by giving the trustee discretion, making clear that there are multiple important purposes, and giving interests to unborn beneficiaries who can't give consent to early termination. But is it wise to do so? The answer to that question is, it depends. It depends on the needs of the client, and the purposes of the trust. At what point, therefore, should the dead hand be lifted and the living be allowed to take control? And remember, that paper shredder will come in handy if you have clients who frequently modify their estates documents.

---

[21]   Hein v. Hein, 543 N.W.2d 19 (Mich.App. 1995).

CHAPTER 11

LITIGATING TESTAMENTARY DOCUMENTS

One important goal of this book has been to focus on proper planning, that is, doing things right the first time, to avoid the cost and delay of probate litigation. No one is well served by complex litigation that generally leaves bad feelings and needless bills to pay. But as survivors bitterly dispute who should get grandma's doily collection, the most common allegation, behind lack of proper will execution, is lack of mental capacity. Unfortunately, claims of undue influence, fraud, delusion, mistake, and incapacity often leave nothing but emotional scars in the surviving family while doing little to promote testamentary intent or protect testators from the kinds of overreaching that are most likely to occur.

The execution of donative documents like wills, trusts, joint tenancies, powers, PODs and TODS, and other financial instruments all require intent and a certain level of mental capacity to understand the implications of one's actions. In the context of *inter vivos* gifts, most people understand the implications of their gift when they give up actual possession. But in the context of testamentary gifts, or gifts that transfer upon death, the transferor is able to retain complete control during life and does not suffer the loss of possession that brings home to her the implications of her act. Because of important differences in the ability to obtain proof after the donor's death and the presumption that people don't usually give away property they need, the mental capacity necessary to execute a will is generally less than that required to make an *inter vivos* gift. Does that make sense to you?

Litigation is very often the result of poor lawyering or poor drafting, but it can also be necessary to protect the testator, her family, or her estate from overreaching or to correct estate plans when laws or family circumstances change. Historically, the laws on mental capacity, undue influence, insane delusion, and the like, evolved in the context of will challenges, but with the popularity of will substitutes they have been incorporated into the broader area of donative transfers. Some commentators have argued that the rules in this area are fraught with inconsistencies and often permit second-guessing by judges and juries who don't like a donor's life-style, value choices, or estate plan. Some have also argued that the doctrines don't adequately protect testators or their intended beneficiaries, especially when they apply only to wills and not to other will substitutes. Someone who wants to unduly influence a trust, for example, can do so more easily than a will, because the will must be executed with appropriate witnesses. But most kinds of undue influence are far more subtle than the doctrine recognizes, aren't they? It is only the crude defrauder who holds a gun to the testator's head during the will execution ceremony; most are more savvy, and the laws on extrinsic evidence and presumptions in favor of donative freedom are often too inexact to be particularly effective except in the most egregious cases.

Sometimes the donor is still alive and judges and juries can evaluate the donor personally. Other times, the donor is deceased and the only evidence available is circumstantial. Who has standing to challenge estate documents, what kinds of evidence can be offered, and to show what kinds of incapacities are all complex questions that could easily occupy an entire course on probate litigation. In this chapter we will examine the basic requirements for mental capacity, different rules on the kinds of evidence that will be allowed to challenge the four corners of a properly-executed document, and who has standing to bring suit. We begin with mental capacity because that is necessary for the proper execution of all donative documents. Then we move to the various things that can interfere with the exercise of a donor's intent, like undue influence, fraud, misrepresentation, and mistake. Then we will briefly cover the tort of intentional interference with an expectancy, and finally the effects of *in terrorem* clauses that are often standard boilerplate in many wills and trusts.

Most of the rules you will learn about in this chapter are the product of case law, not statutes. Therefore, in this chapter we will be reading numerous cases that all deal with unique factual circumstances. As you progress, try to make sense of the different cases and the rules they articulate by looking for the overarching principles that underlie the basic causes of action. Ponder, too, why these topics have generally not been the subject of codification.

A. MENTAL CAPACITY

The UPC § 2–501 requires that a testator be at least 18 years of age and of *sound mind*, but the UPC does not attempt to define what being of sound mind entails. The common law has defined sound mind as requiring that the testator be capable of knowing and understanding:

- the nature and extent of her property
- the natural objects of her bounty
- the disposition that she is making of that property
- the relationship between these elements and the disposition she is making of her property.

The requirement of mental capacity is one of ability, not actual knowledge. Some states require greater capacity in the making of *inter vivos* gifts than testamentary gifts. In those states a donor of an *inter vivos* gift must have the capacity necessary to make or revoke a will and also be capable of understanding the effect of the gift on the donor's financial security or the security of anyone dependent on the donor. See Restatement 3d of Property, § 8.1.

Few states are like California, however, that has defined its mental capacity requirement by statute.

Cal. Prob. Code § 6100.5.

(a) An individual is not mentally competent to make a will if at the time of making the will either of the following is true:

(1) The individual does not have sufficient mental capacity to be able to (A) understand the nature of the testamentary act, (B) understand and recollect the nature and situation of the individual's property, or (C) remember and understand the

individual's relations to living descendants, spouse, and parents, and those whose interests are affected by the will.

(2) The individual suffers from a mental disorder with symptoms including delusions or hallucinations, which delusions or hallucinations result in the individual's devising property in a way which, except for the existence of the delusions or hallucinations, the individual would not have done.

(b) Nothing in this section supersedes existing law relating to the admissibility of evidence to prove the existence of mental incompetence or mental disorders.

(c) Notwithstanding subdivision (a), a conservator may make a will on behalf of a conservatee if the conservator has been so authorized by a court order pursuant to Section 2580.

Any document executed without the requisite mental capacity is void and of no effect. Thus, challengers who don't like the disposition of a relative's will may be tempted to argue that the testator lacked capacity altogether. If successful, a prior will may be deemed controlling, or the estate will pass by intestacy if there is no prior will. And challengers who don't like certain portions of a relative's will are likely to argue *undue influence* or *insane delusion*, sub-categories of the capacity requirement that will void only the tainted elements of the will. *Fraud, duress, misrepresentation*, and sometimes *mistake* can also taint a will, or portions of it.

Insane delusion is a form of mental incapacity that voids all or part of a will. Sometimes defined as monomania, and sometimes requiring evidence of mental illness, insane delusion is usually a belief in things impossible or so improbable that no person of sound mind could give them credence AND such firm conviction by the testator as to the truth of the delusion that even the production of facts disproving the belief will not alter the testator's conviction. The testator's mind must not be open to correction through argument or evidence. And, the donative instrument must have been influenced by the delusion, in which case any tainted parts will be voided. Just because I am convinced that the FBI is monitoring my every move and that my television is controlled by aliens doesn't mean I am incapable of executing a valid will. On the other hand, if I am convinced beyond all evidence and reason that my spouse is having an affair, despite proof to the contrary, and therefore omit him from my will, it may be stricken on the ground of insane delusion. The delusion must affect the will to render any parts void.

We should think of mental capacity as a basic threshold requirement for execution of a valid testamentary document. But many things can interfere with one's mental capacity. One can suffer delusions, be mentally unstable, have dementia, or be so drugged as to not understand one's actions at all. In such a case, the entire will or will substitute will be deemed void. Or, one could suffer from an insane delusion that affects only a part of a will. Or, one could be perfectly capable of understanding one's actions but be forced through undue influence, duress, or fraud to execute a document against one's will. Again, depending on the disposition, all or merely a part of the document will be voided. Finally, misrepresentation or mistake could taint one's intentions. A testator can be perfectly capable of understanding her actions but simply make a mistake about a material fact that ultimately alters a disposition inappropriately. These rules apply to revocations as well. Thus, a testator needs to have the capacity and intent to revoke a will or trust just as she does to execute one.

Often these categories blend into one another, making it difficult to know whether the lack of intent is cause by incapacity, delusion, fraud, or undue influence. Although treatises and the Restatement imply that these common law categories might seem to have clear elements and bright line boundaries, litigants and judges often use them interchangeably, leading to confusion compounded. Lawyers for challengers plead all the infirmities hoping that one will stick, and judges affirm one or more when they feel there is something fishy about the will and its execution, even if the facts don't quite fit the doctrine being used. This, of course, leads to an endless cycle of inconsistencies when there is any chance that a will contest can be successful.

Challenges alleging any of these infirmities can be quite messy, requiring circumstantial evidence and second-guessing of deceased testators. When the categories are not coherently developed, the difficulties increase even more. Consequently, proponents will often choose to settle rather than have grandpa's idiosyncrasies and obsessions exposed in great detail in public hearings. But we can make some sense of the variety of doctrines by focusing on whether the situation involves a defect in the testator's capacity, wrongdoing by a third person, or both.

Lack of capacity, either total incapacity or insane delusion, are defects in the testator's state of mind. They can be caused by mental illness, injury, drugs, age, or a variety of these and other circumstances. Some testators can suffer from depression or alcoholism or other infirmity and still maintain the capacity to execute a will. Others might be perfectly rational in most respects, including an understanding of one's property and disposition, and yet suffer an insane delusion that a sibling is stealing from them or a spouse is unfaithful. If the delusion infects the will, or a portion of the will, those infected portions will be stricken. Understanding the nature of the incapacity and then determining whether it infected the will, or whether the testator executed the will during a lucid interval, is a difficult undertaking, especially when the testator is not available to be examined.

Persons with weakened mental capacity, though perhaps not so weak as to be lacking altogether, can also be taken advantage of by unscrupulous friends, relatives, or strangers. Undue influence, fraud, and duress usually involve testators of *weakened capacity* who are taken advantage of by someone in a *confidential relationship*. Thus, these infirmities require proof of both the weakened capacity of the testator as well as the wrongdoing of a third party. And clearly the boundaries are not always bright and distinct. A person may suffer from an insane delusion and another might exploit that delusion to benefit personally. In such a case, insane delusion or undue influence might both apply.

Persons of strong mental capacity, however, can also be taken advantage of, either by fraud, duress, misrepresentation, or they might even make mistakes. In these cases the mental capacity of the testator is not the issue so much as the effects of the mistake, misrepresentation, or duress. A wrongdoer who interferes with a will may find that a court will invalidate any benefits going to the wrongdoer or made in reliance on the influence or misrepresentation. And the wrongdoer may also find herself subject to a tort suit for *tortious interference with expectancy* from the beneficiary who would have benefitted had the wrongdoer not intervened. As you can imagine, the proof issues in such cases are terribly difficult because the testator is gone. And even if a contestant can show that a testator had weakened capacity and made a will to benefit someone who was unduly influencing the testator, it's not always clear who the testator would have benefitted had her will not been taken over.

The Restatement 3d of Property, § 8.3, provides that a donative transfer is invalid if it was procured by undue influence, duress, or fraud. They are defined as follows:

- Undue influence occurs "if the wrongdoer exerted such influence over the donor that it overcame the donor's free will and caused the donor to make a donative transfer that the donor would not otherwise have made."

- Duress occurs "if the wrongdoer threatened to perform or did perform a wrongful act that coerced the donor into making a donative transfer that the donor would not otherwise have made."

- Fraud occurs "if the wrongdoer knowingly or recklessly made a false representation to the donor about a material fact that was intended to and did lead the donor to make a donative transfer that the donor would not otherwise have made."

Mistake can often infect a will or a provision of a will as well, but courts historically would not correct for mistakes. If the testator was mistaken about an item of property, about the identity of a beneficiary, or whether someone was alive or dead, and made a testamentary provision based on that mistake, the courts would not intervene to correct the mistake. But it seemed unfair that drafting errors could not be corrected, or that dispositions based on a particular statutory scheme could not be changed if the statute had been repealed before the will was executed. These were mistakes that did not affect the testator's intentions at all. And it certainly seemed unfair to allow a beneficiary to keep a bequest that was based on a mistake when the person the testator wanted to benefit takes nothing. Courts of equity, therefore, over time, began to reform wills on the basis of mistakes in some limited circumstances, but the doctrine still has not been wholly adopted across the states.

There is a tremendous amount of scholarship criticizing the case law on mental capacity, insane delusion, and undue influence. Commentators argue that in most cases wills are stricken simply because they do not conform to juries' and judges' notions of what an appropriate testamentary distribution should be. Thus, many judges struck wills by lesbian and gay testators on the grounds of undue influence if they left the bulk of their estates to their partners. Testators who left their property to special causes rather than to family were often held to have suffered from insane delusion. And testators with weakened capacity, symptoms of mental illness like Alzheimers or dementia, or testators on high doses of medications that affect mental alertness had their testamentary plans set aside on the claims of disinherited relatives that the unnatural disposition was the product of their mental state and not a result of neglect by the persons now claiming to be the natural objects of their bounty. The actual disposition being made, therefore, is often evidence of incapacity or undue influence, thus opening doors to judges and juries who might be uncomfortable with certain dispositions and a finding of incapacity would allow them to strike wills and other donative documents that don't conform to traditional expectations.

Most of these will challenges hinge, as well, on the argument that the executed will does not reflect the *true intent* of the testator, either because of incapacity, wrongdoing by an interloper, or mistake. Thus, they go to the most important of the elements of a valid will: intent that this document be one's will. I might intend that the document I am signing be my will, but lack intent if the provisions made in the will are not the ones I intend to make. This may seem like a distinction without a difference, but it is not. Intent that the physical document I am signing be my will is one thing. Intent to benefit the persons identified in the document, in the way expressed, is another. If the dispositions made in the document are not what I would intend, either because I lack capacity to understand the dispositions, or I have been unduly influenced to benefit one person at the expense of another, the will should be deemed invalid. But exactly how one proves lack of intent, especially when faced with a duly executed document and witnesses claiming the testator was of sound mind, is quite a difficult matter.

Consider the facts of the following cases and whether you think the testator showed evidence of mental incapacity or delusion, what the appropriate legal doctrine should be, and whether the court got it right.

Barnes v. Marshall

467 S.W.2d 70 (Mo. 1971)

Dr. A.H. Marshall died on July 29, 1968, leaving a will that completely excluded one of his three daughters and her issue, instead leaving the bulk of his property in trust, payable to many relatives and religious, charitable, and fraternal organizations. On a petition by the daughter (plaintiff) that her father's will was the product of an unsound mind, the jury determined that Dr. Marshall lacked mental capacity. The testamentary devisees (defendants) appealed. The judgment of unsound mind was affirmed on the following evidence:

Ward Barnes, husband of plaintiff, testified that he visited in the Marshall home frequently from the time of his marriage in 1930 until Dr. Marshall's death; that Mrs. Marshall was a very cultured, refined, patient, and accommodating woman; that he spent a great deal of time with testator and soon learned that testator would dominate the conversation in accordance with a certain pattern; that testator told him that he discontinued his medical practice at the command of the Lord so that he might use his time in saving the nation and the world; that testator had told him 'that the Lord had revealed to him the secrets of heaven; that he was the only man on earth to whom the Lord had revealed these secrets; that he had told him that heaven was a glorious place and that when he went to heaven he would have a beautiful crown and a wonderful throne sitting next to Thee Lord. He said that there were three powers in heaven, the Lord, Thee Lord, and God, and he said that this throne that he would have would be on the right hand side of Thee Lord in heaven. He said that heaven was a wonderful place, Thee Lord had revealed to him that whatever pleasures man had on earth he would have in heaven. If it was whiskey, if it was gambling, if it was women, that these would be provided him.' He stated that testator had also told him that the Lord had given him a special power of calling upon the Lord to right the wrongs which people had done to him; that many times he related instances of various people whom he had 'turned over to the Lord' and the Lord had meted out justice at his instance by taking away the person's wealth, and usually that the person lost his health, had a long period of suffering, and eventually died; that when testator related stories about the men he had turned over to the Lord he would become highly emotional, would pound on the table with his fists, would call these men dirty profane names, his face would become flushed, and the veins in his neck would stand out; that testator had told him that he (testator) had run for Congress on two occasions and had run for President of the United States (although apparently never nominated by any party) on two or three occasions; that he had told him that 'if he were made President of the United States he would cancel all public debt, that he would call in all government bonds and discontinue the interest on all of these obligations, and that he would then print money and control the currency, and that he would kill the damn bankers and the crooks and the thieves that were robbing the people in political office and that the world would then be able to settle down and live in peace.' He stated that on one occasion testator took him to his office and showed him a number of young women who were mailing out material in the interest of his candidacy; that he had said it was costing him 'thousands of dollars to mail this material out, but the Lord had told him to do it and he had no right to go counter to what the Lord had told him to do.' He further stated that in one of his campaigns for President testator had purchased a new car and had many biblical quotations and sayings of his own printed all over the automobile; that he had observed him, campaigning from this car, at the corner of Grand and Lindell Boulevard in St. Louis.

Numerous other witnesses testified to similar behaviors. The court then explained: *As we have indicated, we do not agree with defendants' contentions. We have stated a portion of the evidence and it need not be repeated here. It is sufficient to say that we think testator's stated views on government, religion, morals, and finances go beyond the classification of peculiarities and eccentricities and are sufficient evidence from which a jury could reasonably find he was of unsound mind. When we add the strong medical testimony to that of the lay witnesses there would seem to be no doubt that a submissible case was made.*

Defendants also point out that there is evidence that a person suffering from manic-depressive psychosis has periods of normalcy between the abnormal periods of elation or depression and that testator was in a normal period at the time the will was executed. The mental condition of testator at the precise time the will was executed was a question for the jury to decide. The jury was obviously persuaded that he was not of sound mind and since there was evidence to support that verdict it is conclusive.

Query: From the evidence quoted here, do you think Dr. Marshall lacked the 4 requirements of mental capacity? Did he understand his property, the natural objects of his bounty, the disposition he was making, and the relationship of his disposition to these other elements? If not, do you think a different infirmity would have been more appropriate? What was the disposition he made? What now happens to his property?

In re Strittmater

53 A.2d 205 (N.J. App. 1947)

This is an appeal from a decree of the Essex County Orphans' Court admitting to probate the will of Louisa F. Strittmater. Appellants challenge the decree on the ground that testatrix was insane. 'The only medical witness was Dr. Sarah D. Smalley, a general practitioner who was Miss Strittmater's physician all her adult life. In her opinion, decedent suffered from paranoia of the Bleuler type of split personality. The factual evidence justifies the conclusion. But I regret not having had the benefit of an analysis of the data by a specialist in diseases of the brain.

The deceased never married. Born in 1896, she lived with her parents until their death about 1928, and seems to have had a normal childhood. She was devoted to both her parents and they to her. Her admiration and love of her parents persisted after their death to 1934, at least. Yet four years later she wrote: 'My father was a corrupt, vicious, and unintelligent savage, a typical specimen of the majority of his sex. Blast his wormstinking carcass and his whole damn breed.' And in 1943, she inscribed on a photograph of her mother 'That Moronic she-devil that was my mother.'

Numerous memoranda and comments written by decedent on the margins of books constitute the chief evidence of her mental condition. Most of them are dated in 1935, when she was 40 years old. But there are enough in later years to indicate no change in her condition. The Master who heard the case in the court below, found that the proofs demonstrated 'incontrovertably her morbid aversion to men' and 'feminism to a neurotic extreme.' This characterization seems to me not strong enough. She regarded men as a class with an insane hatred. She looked forward to the day when women would bear children without the aid of men, and all males would be put to death at birth. Decedent's inward life, disclosed by what she wrote, found an occasional outlet such as the incident of the smashing of the clock, the killing of the pet kitten, vile language, etc. On the other hand,—and I suppose this is the split personality,—Miss Strittmater, in her dealings with her lawyer, Mr. Semel, over a period of several years, and with her bank, to cite only two examples, was entirely reasonable and normal.

Decedent, in 1925, became a member of the New Jersey branch of the National Women's Party. From 1939 to 1941, and perhaps later, she worked as a volunteer one day a week in the New York office, filing papers, etc. During this period, she spoke of leaving her estate to the Party. On October 31, 1944, she executed her last will, carrying this intention into effect. A month later, December 6, she died. Her only relatives were some cousins of whom she saw very little during the last few years of her life.

The question is whether Miss Strittmater's will is the product of her insanity. Her disease seems to have become well developed by 1936. In August of that year she wrote, 'It remains for feministic organizations like the National Women's Party, to make exposure of women's 'protectors' and 'lovers' for what their vicious and contemptible selves are.' She had been a member of the Women's Party for eleven years at that time, but the evidence does not show that she had taken great interest in it. I think it was her paranoic condition, especially her insane delusions about the male, that led her to leave her estate to the National Women's Party. The result is that the probate should be set aside.

Query: Admitting that this case is quite old, do you think the result would have been different today? Did Louisa Strittmater lack mental capacity, suffer from insane delusion, or undue influence? Should a person with no spouse or children, whose only relatives are remote cousins, not be able to leave her property to whatever organization she wants, even if she has insane delusions about men? Was this an unnatural disposition? Did her insane delusion affect the disposition of her property?

Breeden v. Stone

992 P.2d 1167 (Colo. 2000)

This case involves a contested probate of a handwritten (holographic) will executed by Spicer Breeden, the decedent. Mr. Breeden died in his home on March 19, 1996, from a self-inflicted gunshot wound two days after he was involved in a highly publicized hit-and-run accident that killed the driver of the other vehicle.

Upon entering the decedent's home following his suicide, the Denver police discovered on his desk a handwritten document that read: "I want everything I have to go to Sydney Stone—'houses,' 'jewelwry,' [sic] stocks[,] bonds, cloths [sic]. P.S. I was Not Driving the Vehical—[sic]." *At the bottom of the handwritten document, the decedent printed,* "SPICER H. BREEDEN" *and signed beneath his printed name.* Breeden did not leave any of his property to his family (siblings and his father), who contested the will, and who provided extensive evidence that he used alcohol and cocaine in the two days prior to his death. He had no spouse or children. *Based on the testimony of a number of the decedent's friends, the court found that the decedent's moods were alternately euphoric, fearful, and depressed, and that he was excessively worried about threats against himself and his dog from government agents, friends, and others.* The Colorado Supreme Court affirmed the probate court's finding that the decedent did not lack mental capacity nor did he suffer from an insane delusion that infected any part of his will.

Query: Is it reasonable to say that anyone who commits suicide is lacking some important mental capacity? Is that especially true here where the anxiety and stress of the accident, and the use of alcohol and drugs, preyed on the decedent's mind and perhaps induced him to take his own life? Would your opinion change if Breedon left everything to the surviving family of the hit and run victim?

Paine v. Sullivan

950 N.E.2d 874 (Mass. App. 2011)

John and Odette Sullivan were married for 47 years. *Odette owned and operated her own beauty salon in Brookline. The overall evidence supported the judge's findings that, at home, Odette was the "boss" and John happily acceded to her wishes in most areas throughout their marriage. In particular, Odette always took the lead on the couple's estate planning. Odette was diagnosed with melanoma in late 2001. In 2002, she asked the same attorney (attorney) who had drafted the couple's 1995 wills to draft new reciprocal wills for her and John, leaving their estates to one another but, in the event that one predeceased the other, leaving Valerie [adopted daughter that Odette had quarreled with] one dollar and the residuary of their estates to friends of Odette. John executed a will on January 14, 2002, consistent with this request. Paine was named executor of the will if Odette did not survive him. Paula Miller, Odette's assistant for over twenty years and a personal friend of Odette and John, was named as one of the residuary beneficiaries of the will. New wills were executed on February 1, 2003, February 3, 2004, and June 26, 2004, in which minor changes to the residuary beneficiaries were made, but Paine remained the alternate executor. The [probate] judge allowed the June 26, 2004, will.*

The medical records contained in the record appendix leave little doubt that John suffered from some degree of dementia during the time period that the 2002–2004 wills were executed. A June 25, 2001, neurology note concludes that John had "significant frontal dysfunction with poor insight and judgment, difficulty changing set and mild recent memory difficulties." The neurologist indicated that he discussed with John and Odette that John's insight and judgment difficulties made it difficult for him to appreciate his "gait instability." While there was some suspicion that a vitamin B12 deficiency was the cause of some of his symptoms, a full neuropsychological evaluation was recommended, which John underwent on October 15, 2001. The [probate] judge acknowledged the report of the October 15, 2001, evaluation, noting only that it revealed "mild cognitive slowing."

In fact, the history portion of the report of the October 15, 2001, evaluation reflects that Odette had observed some memory impairment over the past three years and more recent word-finding difficulty. The report reflects that before January of 2001, John had managed their financial affairs, but that he had become "confused" about the taxes and thereafter Odette took over the finances. In addition, John was receiving personal care assistance when his wife was at work. The report further reveals "evidence of significant cognitive impairment. Specifically, testing revealed mild disorientation (time), mild cognitive slowing, moderate anomia, moderate amnesia, and less pervasive frontal lobe deficits." Although it was felt that incompletely treated vitamin B12 deficiency could contribute to some of John's symptoms, the report concluded that a vitamin B12 deficiency did not explain all of them and that the "anomia and amnesia combined with less pronounced deficits in frontal lobe functioning [were] highly suggestive of a diagnosis of Senile Dementia of the Alzheimer's Type (SDAT)." The neuropsychologist concluded that "[u]nless his mental status improves appreciably, [John] will continue to need close supervision. Driving is contraindicated." The medical records do not reflect that John's mental status improved appreciably thereafter.

In July of 2002, John was seen by his primary care physician, and with regard to dementia, he was "strongly encouraged to followup with the neurologist for additional evaluation." There is no evidence that John followed this advice; the next neurology note is in 2004, after his wife died and Valerie was caring for him. When John was seen in the emergency room on June 7, 2003, a week or two after a motor vehicle accident, he was described in a neurosurgery consult as "bright and oriented x 4," and the [probate] judge relied on this portion of the note in support of her finding that he had testamentary capacity when the 2004 will was executed. The next sentence of the note stated, however, that "[t]here are obvious gaps in his short-term memory but this is of a chronic nature, as his wife was present during the interview." In addition, the emergency room physician noted that John was able to tell him he was in the hospital, but not which one, and that John was able to identify the month and day of the week, but could not tell him the date or the year. It was further noted that Odette reported "more of a significant problem with some baseline confusion and this was confirmed by. . . his primary care physician."

The medical records reflect that by July 3, 2003, John had a personal care attendant twenty-four hours per day. Notwithstanding his need for twenty-four-hour care, the judge credited a September, 2004, note of his primary care physician that refers to John's dementia as "mild." The complete statement is that "[t]he patient also has ongoing progressive mild dementia and this has been an ongoing symptom that was first noted in 2001. The patient also had neuropsychological exam and testing in 2001 as well. Progressively, this has been monitored and certainly has noticed...increasing forgetfulness." In the assessment and plan section of the note, the doctor states, "Regarding his dementia, the patient will be scheduled to follow up with the neurologist for additional followup evaluations. He will continue with his Zyprexa and continue to have supervision at all times with monitoring of his medications and activities." On August 3, 2004, his primary care physician signed a document saying that John suffered from senile dementia and was unable to live alone. A November 2, 2004, neurology note reflects poor orientation, "poor recall memory, poor working memory and poor visual spatial construction."

The [probate] judge essentially adopted the opinion of the proponent's expert, Dr. Barry Roth, who identified medical records that described John's dementia as mild, and noted that medical providers continued to direct their reports to John and explained test results to John, and that John continued to be involved in making treatment decisions for himself. From this evidence, Dr. Roth concluded that "[a]s a physician, the preponderance of evidence indicates that [John] had capacity to know his property, who were the natural heirs to his bounty, that he was in the process of making a will to make distribution with respect to those elements, and that he was in fact making such a plan."

On appeal, the court disagreed, and found that John lacked testamentary capacity and that the proponent of the will failed to put forward adequate evidence to show that when John executed his will in 2004 he had testamentary capacity.

Query: Do you think John lacked testamentary capacity, or did he simply have a relationship with his wife in which she made all financial decisions? What should courts do when faced with conflicting testimony from doctors as to the physical and mental state of their patients? When should the burden shift from the proponent to the opponent and back? If his 2004 will was invalid, which will should be probated?

Parish v. Parish

704 S.E.2d 99 (Va. 2011)

The decedent, Eugene Neal Parish ("Eugene"), suffered a head and spinal cord injury in 1982 due to being struck in the head with a metal pipe while at a bar. The injury left him paralyzed in his legs and right arm. Eugene sued the bar and the person who attacked him and recovered $3.5 million. At the time of his injury, Eugene's only child, David M. Parish ("David"), was eleven months old.

In 1983, Eugene was declared incompetent in Florida due to encephalopathy.[1] His wife was appointed as guardian. For the court to make such an appointment, Eugene had to be shown "incapable of caring for himself or managing his property or . . . likely to dissipate or lose his property or in-

---

[1] Encephalopathy is "[g]eneralized brain dysfunction marked by varying degrees of impairment of speech, cognition, orientation, and arousal. In mild instances, brain dysfunction may be evident only during specialized neuropsychiatric testing; in severe instances, . . . the patient may be unresponsive even to unpleasant stimuli." *Taber's Cyclopedic Medical Dictionary* 761 (21st ed.2009).

flict harm on himself or others." Later, Eugene's mother assumed the duties as his guardian.

In 1989, Eugene moved to Tennessee and resided at a nursing facility near Memphis. David Wayne Parish ("David Wayne"), Eugene's brother, lived approximately 40 to 50 miles from Eugene's nursing facility. Diane E. Parish ("Diane") and David Wayne were married in 1998. Eugene's mother, who had acted as his conservator, remained in Florida. She agreed to transfer the conservatorship to David Wayne and Diane in Tennessee.

In 2000, David Wayne and Diane petitioned to be appointed as Eugene's co-conservators in Tennessee. They described the reason for the appointment as Eugene's encephalopathy. Tennessee law required that David Wayne and Diane show that Eugene was a "[d]isabled person," which "means any person eighteen (18) years of age or older determined by the court to be in need of partial or full supervision, protection and assistance by reason of mental illness, physical illness or injury, developmental disability or other mental or physical incapacity." The Tennessee court granted the petition, and David Wayne and Diane became Eugene's conservators.

In the fall of 2002, David Wayne assisted Eugene in preparing a Last Will and Testament (the "will"). David Wayne testified at trial that Eugene had informed him "out of the blue" that he wanted a will. During Eugene's meeting with the paralegal who drafted the will, David Wayne acted as a translator because Eugene, who spoke through a voice box due to a tracheotomy, was difficult to understand. David Wayne was present in the room with the witnesses and the notary when the will was executed and witnessed on October 2, 2002.

In the will, Eugene bequeathed 25% of his estate to David Wayne, 25% to Diane, 25% to David, and 25% to other family members. Eugene's will appointed David Wayne as executor and Diane as substitute executor. Neither David Wayne nor Diane informed David that Eugene had executed a will.

Eugene died in 2006. David qualified as his administrator. Diane then petitioned the circuit court to have David removed as administrator and herself appointed as executor pursuant to Eugene's will. David filed a counterclaim to impeach the will. David claimed that Eugene lacked testamentary capacity to execute a will due to encephalopathy. He further claimed that David Wayne and Diane subjected Eugene to undue influence. At trial, the court found that Diane had proved by clear and convincing evidence that Eugene had testamentary capacity, and that Eugene was not subjected to undue influence.

Affirming the trial court's finding that Eugene had testamentary capacity, the Virginia Supreme Court explained: *Mental weakness is not inconsistent with testamentary capacity. A less degree of capacity is requisite for the execution of a will than for the execution of contracts and the transaction of ordinary business. One may be capable of making a will yet incapable of disposing of his property by contract or of managing his estate. Mental strength to compete with an antagonist and understanding to protect his own interest are essential in the transaction of ordinary business, while it is sufficient for the making of a will that the testator understands the business in which he is engaged, his property, the natural objects of his bounty, and the disposition he desires to make of his property. The condition of being unable, by reason of weakness of mind, to manage and care for an estate, is not inconsistent with capacity to make a will.* Citing another case, the Court further explained: *Neither sickness nor impaired intellect is suffi-cient, standing alone, to render a will invalid. If at the time of its execution the testatrix was capable of recollecting her property, the natural objects of her bounty and their claims upon her, knew the business about which she was engaged and how she wished to dispose of her property, that is suffi-cient.'*

Query: Can you reconcile *Parish* and *Paine*? What kind of medical evidence supports a finding of incapacity and what evidence seems irrelevant? Does it matter that David was bereft of his father at the age of eleven months, proba-bly rarely visited, if at all, and then complained about receiving only 25% of his estate (which was probably reasonably large despite Eugene's extensive medi-cal bills)? Or does it seem unreasonable that Eugene did not provide primarily for his only child, despite not having been there to help him grow up? Was this an unnatural disposition?

Matter of Turner

56 A.D.3d 863 (N.Y. A.D.3 2008)

At issue in this probate proceeding is the validity of Mary C. Turner's *last will and testament, executed in December 1999. In previous wills, dece-dent bequeathed her estate in equal shares to her daughters—petitioner* Mary Kay Turner *and respondent Kerry A. Corrigan (hereinafter respond-ent)—and her only son, John Turner. In the most recent will, decedent distributed her assets to her son, petitioner, petitioner's daughter, and peti-tioner's granddaughter, making no provision for respondent or respondent's issue. After decedent's death in 2002, petitioner sought to admit the will to probate and respondent objected. Petitioner moved for, and obtained, sum-mary judgment. Respondent now appeals.*

We affirm. Respondent does not challenge decedent's capacity, in gen-eral, to make a will, but asserts that the will was the product of an insane delusion or petitioner's undue influence. To set forth a prima facie case to invalidate the will based on insane delusion, it was incumbent upon re-spondent to establish that decedent exhibited a "persistent belief in supposed facts, which have no real existence coupled with conduct taken upon the assumption of their existence." Notably, the belief " 'may be illogical or ab-surd, but it is not an insane delusion if there was the slightest basis for the testator's belief' "

Here, the basis of respondent's insane delusion claim is that decedent believed that respondent was stealing from her. When decedent's husband died in 1998, his will created a credit shelter trust of which decedent was the sole beneficiary and respondent was trustee. As trustee, respondent was in-structed to pay decedent "so much of the net income as [respondent] shall deem advisable," as well as discretionary payments from principal in order to maintain decedent's standard of living. Prior to her execution of the new will, decedent received all the income from the trust, but respondent declined to invade the principal as she believed her mother had sufficient other re-sources. Decedent apparently did not fully appreciate the benefits of creating the trust and frequently expressed dissatisfaction with the loss of control over her late husband's assets and with respondent's administration of the trust. Although respondent testified that she endeavored to explain the trust to decedent, decedent persistently demanded greater access to the money and, as a result, the relationship between respondent and decedent deteriorated.

In January 1999, decedent called a family meeting at her home with her children, ostensibly to address the trust and her difficulties with respondent. According to respondent, decedent demanded to know where her money was and how much there was. When respondent answered that the money was in trust and decedent would get it as she needed it, decedent accused her of lying and lunged at her across the room. When petitioner then said that respondent was stealing petitioner's money, respondent left. Following this meeting, decedent no longer allowed respondent into her home or took telephone calls from her. However, she continued to have lunch with respondent once a week at the hospital where respondent worked and decedent volunteered, where mother and daughter interacted socially in a positive manner, but did not discuss finances.

Even crediting respondent's version of events as true—as we must in considering petitioner's motion for summary judgment we agree with Surrogate's Court that respondent has alleged insufficient evidence to make a prima facie case of incapacity by insane delusion. The only evidence proffered that decedent ever—much less persistently—accused respondent of stealing is the deposition testimony of her former attorney who stated that decedent was confused by the trust and "believed that [respondent] had taken her money." Respondent testified only that petitioner accused her of stealing in front of decedent, but not that decedent ever expressed that belief. Although this evidence could establish that decedent had developed an unfounded distrust in respondent and that she did not understand the nature of a trust, misunderstandings and unjust opinions—standing alone—are insufficient to establish insane delusion. Indeed, "if there are facts, however insufficient they may in reality be, from which a prejudiced, or a narrow, or a bigoted mind might derive a particular idea, or belief, it cannot be said that the mind is diseased in that respect. The belief may be illogical, or preposterous, but it is not, therefore, evidence of insanity in the person." Here, the apparently unfounded perception by decedent that respondent was mishandling—or even misappropriating—her money, even though persistent and contrary to the record evidence that respondent was not guilty of any misconduct, could readily have stemmed from decedent's frustration over the loss of control of the assets, rather than some form of insanity. Indeed, we cannot say that decedent's failing opinion of respondent, even if illogical and unfair, is so devoid of reason to establish a basis upon which a finding could be made that decedent suffered from an insane delusion.

Here, respondent's allegations, if credited, could establish that petitioner had motive and opportunity to influence decedent's testamentary decisions, but these allegations fail to demonstrate that any undue influence was actually asserted. By all accounts, decedent was exceptionally independent up to and until the time she made her last will. She lived alone, drove her own automobile, was involved in her church, and continued to do volunteer work. She directly addressed her wishes to her new attorney with respect to her will. Although decedent suffered a stroke in October 2000 at which point she went to live with petitioner and, allegedly at times thereafter, petitioner excluded other family members from seeing decedent, this occurred nearly a year after the will was executed. The only allegations of undue influence by petitioner during the relevant time period are that petitioner accused respondent of stealing at the January 1999 family meeting, and that she recommended a new attorney for decedent, accompanied dece-

dent to the attorney's office, and was present when the will was executed. In our view, this circumstantial evidence supports conflicting inferences "such that a conclusion of undue influence may not be drawn."

Query: The court here found no insane delusion that her daughter was stealing from her because the decedent's frustration over the trust arrangement was not so unreasonable as to constitute a mental disease or form of insanity. Does it seem that perhaps the lawyers who arranged the decedent's husband's trust should have done more homework on the rifts it might create in the family that would later lead to this litigation? Or should that not be a concern of the lawyers? Isn't the point of the credit shelter trust to give the surviving spouse as much property as possible without it looking like she received it? If Mary Turner was not good at understanding the finances, perhaps a corporate trustee would have been a better idea.

As you can see, there are countless reasons why a person might lack mental capacity, from the effects of dementia, to drugs, to brain injuries, to age and frailty, to simple orneriness. If we keep our focus on the relevant criteria—knowledge of one's property, the natural objects of one's bounty, and the disposition one is making—would most of these cases be easily resolved? To what extent do you believe courts are, as some commentators have claimed, using testamentary capacity and insane delusion to void wills that the judges believe are unreasonable or unnatural?[22]

Insane delusion, as the court in *Turner* explained, requires a belief in something so preposterous that no rational person could believe as the decedent believed. Should this be the more appropriate theory of *Strittmater* and, if so, do you believe Louise Strittmater was deluded?

A few states (Arkansas, North Dakota, and Ohio[23]) permit the probate of a will while the testator is still living in order to prove its validity and the testator's capacity. Known as "living probate," or "ante-mortem probate," this adversarial procedure allows a person with standing to petition a court to declare the validity of a will so long as all named beneficiaries and all intestate heirs are made parties to the suit. Other states permit the video-taping of the will execution ceremony to be used as evidence in a will contest challenging the testator's capacity. If a testator appears drugged, has trouble understanding what he is doing, or appears to be taking direction from another, a video can be useful evidence of a capacity problem. What it doesn't do, however, is tell us what a testator really wanted.

---

[22] Numerous studies have shown that juries are particularly likely to favor will contestants, even when the evidence was not legally sufficient to overcome the presumption in favor of validity. See, e.g. Jeffrey Schoenblum, *Will Contests—An Empirical Study*, 22 Real Prop., Prob. & Tr. J. 607 (1987).

[23] Ark. Code Ann. § 28–40–202; N.D. Cent. Code § 30.1–08.1–01; Ohio Rev. Code Ann. § 2107.081.

Practice Point: Being a Zealous Advocate for the Client Who Marches to the Beat of a Different Drummer

By now, the plethora of unfortunate cases you have digested should leave no doubt that estate planning clients are, in many ways, like proverbial snowflakes, each having a unique set of life circumstances that warrant careful planning. Yet, even with this perspective, you will, on occasion, encounter clients who are, well, just different in a fundamental way from the majority of clients with whom you work. They may have backgrounds as artists, musicians, scientists or training in religious practices outside of the major religions and your mission, should you accept it, will be to make sure that these clients' plans are just as sound and solid as their average-Joe-counterparts' plans would be.

In my practice, these sorts of clients announce their presence by asking if they could include things in their plans that most clients just do not. Some examples of these requests have included: the desire to be referred to by an "Angel Name" in all written documents, in lieu of the client's legal name; incorporation of a list of more than one hundred sex toys as specific bequests to more than one hundred individuals; a request by a patient in a nursing home that as dementia progressed that someone be hired to come and end the client's life; as well as the desire to leave a specific bequest of one's skull to a life partner.

And, just in case you are wondering, no, I did not actively seek these sorts of cases. They just happened to come along, nestled right in between the numerous plans where mom and dad, married for 45 years, wanted to leave everything equally to their three children, end of story.

So, as a planner, how will you deal with the sorts of "special requests" that you may encounter? Of course, the first thing that you will need to evaluate is whether your client is of sound mind, because if the answer to that is "No," then you will be moving in an entirely different direction all together. If the answer is "Yes," but with the added "and this client is just a little different from her peers," then get ready to play the game, because it is all about balancing the client's short term goals (the desire to put a plan together) and her long-term goals (the desire that the plan actually work when it is set into motion).

Of those that I mentioned above, one is pretty easy to address: the hiring of someone to end the client's life. A candid discussion that in my state euthanasia, physician assisted suicide and, of course, murder were all illegal and therefore the request had no place in the plan was all it took, along with a discussion of various avenues in which the client might find appropriate medical and psychological support. Similarly, the client wishing to pass along the skull agreed to omit the provision because the client's family had a very contentious relationship with the partner and the client decided it wasn't worth putting the will in jeopardy—not to mention that there were questions about whether or not the gift would be legally allowed. The other two situations were more open to creative approaches and I will leave it up to your imagination to envision how those solutions might be crafted into a plan.

The take-away here is to start thinking of planning as a means of avoiding controversy. And, if your client's particular personality, preferences, or lifestyle is likely to *invite* controversy, you will be truly planning with the end in mind to effectuate the all important balance of being a zealous advocate for your client today, so that the plan has the greatest likelihood of accomplishing your client's goals later.

PROBLEMS

11.1. Carol, a 54-year old woman, visits your office and asks you to draft a will for her mother-in-law, Martha (age 80), who is residing with her and her husband John. Carol tells you that Martha was forgetting where she lived and sometimes took herself on long walks and got lost, thus necessitating her being moved into their home. Carol tells you that Martha has often expressed dismay that her other children have not come to visit nor asked her to move in with them. Carol gives you three sheets of handwritten notes about Martha's property and how she wants it devised, and asks you to write up the will according to the notes. When you inquire about the notes, she tells you that she and John took the notes at Martha's direction. She also tells you that Martha has been spending a lot of time watching TV, especially a daily show by a prominent televangelist. When you meet with Martha after drafting the will, you find her to be perfectly competent and mentally aware, though you have to explain the details to her two or three times as she claims to have trouble understanding all the legal and financial mumbo-jumbo. When you ask her about the dispositions she is making, Martha is adamant that this is how she wants to leave her property. Consider whether Martha has the appropriate mental capacity if the will makes the following dispositions:

1. Martha leaves all her property to Carol and John, excluding entirely her other three children and their spouses and children, including her son Jason who was born with severe birth defects and requires round-the-clock nursing care.

2. Martha leaves all her property to the Rev. Billy Bob's Church of the Angels of Recycling.

3. Martha leaves all her property to her husband, Charles, who has been dead for the past 10 years.

4. Martha leaves all her property to a neighbor she hasn't seen in 10 years but who took care of her after her husband died.

5. Martha leaves all her property to her lesbian lover of her youth who she hasn't seen in 30 years.

6. Martha leaves all her property to her alma mater in trust to provide scholarships only for Caucasian girls.

7. Martha leaves her property 1/6th to each of the above mentioned parties.

As you can see, a perfectly natural disposition might be the product of insane delusion, and a seemingly unnatural disposition might be the product of a perfectly rational desire by the testator. Although the disposition itself does not necessarily determine whether the testator has the appropriate mental capacity, it could be compelling evidence as to the testator's state of mind. Make an argument for and against mental capacity for each of the 7 scenarios listed above.

Commentators and courts spend a lot of time discussing the capacity requirement, listing reasons as diverse as equity toward beneficiaries and psychiatric theories that a person lacking capacity isn't really a person to determine how to balance different interests when capacity is challenged. These include arguments that law must require capacity in order to be legitimate and testators can feel comfortable knowing that their true wishes will be carried out even if they later become delusional or incapacitated.[24] They also include arguments that we are all ultimately creatures of influence and we cannot determine when influence is truly undue or perfectly normal. In some cases a capacity challenge is undertaken only to blackmail the survivors into settling, rather than allowing public testimony about the deceased's idiosyncrasies. Whether we want to insist on capacity so that we feel confident in the decisions of the probate process, or because we want to honor the decedent's true wishes, whatever they might be, capacity is the most important element of will execution and, as an estate planner, you need to be thinking of ways to protect your clients against allegations of incapacity, whether they walk to the beat of a different drummer or seem as sane as you and I.

B. UNDUE INFLUENCE

Undue influence is a more complicated issue than mental capacity because most of us influence others in some way or other. If I ask my spouse to provide for a beloved niece I am influencing her. If I extol the virtues of the Red Cross and my best friend leaves a large bequest to the Red Cross then I have influenced her. If I tell someone I won't marry him unless he leaves me all of his property, I am certainly influencing him. But are any of these examples of *undue* influence? The answer is: it depends. It depends on whether I have replaced the testator's *intentions* with mine. In other words, has the testator been deprived of her own volition in making decisions about the disposition of her property? Or, has she simply valued my judgment about the Red Cross and decided, on her own, to leave a bequest that she knows I will approve? The key is whether the influencer has replaced the donor's free will with his own.

The common law developed a number of factors for determining "if the wrongdoer exerted such influence over the donor that it overcame the donor's free will and caused the donor to make a donative transfer that the donor would not otherwise have made."[25] These include

- whether a *confidential relationship* existed between the donor and the wrongdoer;
- whether *suspicious circumstances* exist tending to show that the will was not the donor's free and independent decision;
- whether the donor was *susceptible to influence* because of the physical and mental condition of the donor was weakened;
- whether an *unnatural or unjust gift* was made;
- whether the unnatural or unjust gift was the *result of the influence;*

---

[24] See Dukeminier, Johanson, Lindgren, Sitkoff, WILLS, TRUSTS AND ESTATES, 7th ed. (2005) at 146–148 (hereinafter DUKEMINIER).

[25] Restatement 3d of Property, § 8.3 (b).

- whether the *beneficiary participated* in the procurement of the will or whether the donor had independent legal advice;

- whether there was *secrecy and haste* attendant on the making of the will; and

- whether there was a *change* in the decedent's attitude toward others and/or a change in the decedent's plan for disposing of his property.

Some states have determined that the mere existence of a confidential relationship is enough to shift the burden of proof from the opponent of the will to the proponent who benefitted from the alleged undue influence. There is no presumption of undue influence if the confidant is a spouse, and the Restatement 3d of Property is seeking to have domestic partners, particularly same-sex domestic partners, receive the same presumption of validity if they are the primary beneficiaries of their partners' bequests. But states are slow to recognize that parties in same-sex partnerships view their own relationships as equivalent to marriage and expect the same privileges and presumptions to apply as do in the case of heterosexual marriage. And a confidential relationship is not always required as an element of proving undue influence.

Courts also usually require some proof of suspicious circumstances to raise a presumption of undue influence. The Restatement 3d of Property has identified numerous factors that may be considered in determining whether there are suspicious circumstances. These include:

- the extent to which the donor was in a weakened condition, physically, mentally, or both, and therefore susceptible to undue influence;

- the extent to which the alleged wrongdoer participated in the preparation or procurement of the will or will substitute;

- whether the donor received independent advice from an attorney or from other competent and disinterested advisors in preparing the will or will substitute;

- whether the will or will substitute was prepared in secrecy or in haste;

- whether the donor's attitude toward others had changed by reason of his or her relationship with the alleged wrongdoer;

- whether there is a decided discrepancy between a new and previous wills or will substitutes of the donor;

- whether there was a continuity of purpose running through former wills or will substitutes indicating a settled intent in the disposition of his or her property; and

- whether the disposition of the property is such that a reasonable person would regard it as unnatural, unjust, or unfair, for example, whether the disposition abruptly and without apparent reason disinherited a faithful and deserving family member.[26]

Considering these factors, do you think the courts were correct in their analysis of the following undue influence claims?

---

[26] Restatement 3d Property (Wills & Donative Transfers) § 8.3 comment h.

Latham v. Father Divine

85 N.E.2d 168 (N.Y. 1949)

The amended complaint herein has, in response to a motion under rule 106 of the Rules of Civil Practice, been dismissed for insufficiency. Its principal allegations are these: plaintiffs are first cousins, but not distributees, of Mary Sheldon Lyon, who died in October, 1946, leaving a will, executed in 1943, which gave almost her whole estate to defendant Father Divine, leader of a religious cult, and to two corporate defendants in some way connected with that cult, and to an individual defendant (Patience Budd) said to be one of Father Divine's active followers; that said will has been, after a contest instituted by distributees, probated under a compromise agreement with the distributees, by the terms of which agreement, to which plaintiffs were not parties, the defendants just above referred to will receive a large sum from the estate; that after the making of said will, decedent on several occasions expressed 'a desire and a determination to revoke the said will, and to execute a new will by which the plaintiffs would receive a substantial portion of the estate', 'that shortly prior to the death of the deceased she had certain attorneys draft a new will in which the plaintiffs were named as legatees for a very substantial amount, totaling approximately $350,000'; that 'by reason of the said false representations, the said undue influence and the said physical force' certain of the defendants 'prevented the deceased from executing the said new Will'; that, shortly before decedent's death, decedent again expressed her determination to execute the proposed new will which favored plaintiffs, and that defendants 'thereupon conspired to kill, and did kill, the deceased by means of a surgical operation performed by a doctor engaged by the defendants without the consent or knowledge of any of the relatives of the deceased.'

In this case the New York Court of Appeals allowed the plaintiffs' suit to go forward and affirmed the propriety of a constructive trust, if the appropriate facts are established at trial, showing that Father Divine had unduly influenced the decedent, held her under duress, or participated in her death.

Query: The allegations in this case, that Father Divine and his followers had interfered in the revocation and making of a new will after Mary Lyon got out from under their influence, was held to be a sufficient ground for intervention by an equity court. But what can an equity court do? The testator is dead and we don't know how she wanted to change her will. If the court finds that Father Divine did unduly influence the testator, should her will be voided and her estate pass by intestacy, or should other beneficiaries be allowed to put forward evidence that she wanted her property to go to them? If the latter, are we allowing property to pass to the intended beneficiaries in the absence of a formally executed document required under the statute of wills? Do you think this case would have come out differently had Father Divine been a clergyman in an established religion?

Will of Moses

227 So.2d 829 (Miss. 1969)

Mrs. Fannie Traylor Moses died on February 6, 1967. An instrument, dated December 23, 1957 and purporting to be her last will and testament, was duly admitted to probate in common form in the Chancery Court of the

First Judicial District of Hinds County. Thereafter, on February 14, 1967, appellant, Clarence H. Holland, an attorney at law, not related to Mrs. Moses, filed a petition in that court tendering for probate in solemn form, as the true last will and testament of Mrs. Moses, a document dated May 26, 1964, under the terms of which he would take virtually her entire estate. This document contained a clause revoking former wills and Holland's petition prayed that the earlier probate of the 1957 will be set aside.

The beneficiaries under the 1957 will (the principal beneficiary was an elder sister of Mrs. Moses) responded to Holland's petition, denied that the document tendered by him was Mrs. Moses' will, and asserted, among other things, that it was (1) the product of Holland's undue influence upon her, (2) that at the time of its signing, Mrs. Moses lacked testamentary capacity, and, (3) that the 1957 will was Mrs. Moses' true last will and testament and its probate should be confirmed.

Mrs. Moses died at the age of 57 years, leaving an estate valued at $125,000. She had lost three husbands in less than 20 years. Throughout the latter years of her life her health became seriously impaired. She suffered from serious heart trouble and cancer had required the surgical removal of one of her breasts. For 6 or 7 years preceding her death she was an alcoholic.

The exact date on which Holland entered Mrs. Moses' life is unclear. There is a suggestion that she had met him as early as 1951. Their personal relationship became what the chancellor, somewhat inaccurately, characterized, as one of 'dubious' morality. The record, however, leaves no doubt as to its nature. Soon after the death of Mrs. Moses' last husband, Holland, although 15 years her junior, began seeing Mrs. Moses with marked regularity, there having been testimony to the effect that he attended her almost daily. Holland was an attorney and in that capacity represented Mrs. Moses. She declared that he was not only her attorney but her 'boyfriend' as well.

After Mrs. Moses died, the 1964 will was brought forward by another attorney, also an associate of Holland, who said that it had been entrusted to him by Mrs. Moses, together with other papers, for safekeeping. He distinguished his relation with Holland from that of a partner, saying that he and Holland only occupied offices together and shared facilities and expenses in the practice of law. He also stated that he saw Mrs. Moses on an 'average' of once a week, most often in the company of Holland.

Throughout this period, Mrs. Moses was a frequent visitor at Holland's office, and there is ample evidence to support the chancellor's finding that there existed a continuing fiduciary relationship between Mrs. Moses and Holland, as her attorney.

The evidence supports the chancellor's finding that the confidential or fiduciary relationship which existed between Mrs. Moses and Holland, her attorney, was a subsisting and continuing relationship, having begun before the making by Mrs. Moses of the will of August 22, 1961, under the terms of which her jewelry had been bequeathed to Holland, and having ended only with Mrs. Moses' death. Moreover, its effect was enhanced by the fact that throughout this period, Holland was in almost daily attendance upon Mrs. Moses on terms of the utmost intimacy. There was strong evidence that this aging woman, seriously ill, disfigured by surgery, and hopelessly addicted to alcoholic excesses, was completely bemused by the constant and amorous attentions of Holland, a man 15 years her junior. There was testimony too indicating that she entertained the pathetic hope that he might marry her.

Although the evidence was not without conflict and was, in some of its aspects, circumstantial, it was sufficient to support the finding that the relationship existed on May 26, 1964, the date of the will tendered for probate by Holland.

The chancellor's factual finding of the existence of this relationship on that date is supported by evidence and is not manifestly wrong. Moreover, he was correct in his conclusion of law that such relationship gave rise to a presumption of undue influence which could be overcome only by evidence that, in making the 1964 will, Mrs. Moses had acted upon the independent advice and counsel of one entirely devoted to her interest.

Appellant takes the position that there was undisputed evidence that Mrs. Moses, in making the 1964 will, did, in fact, have such advice and counsel. He relies upon the testimony of the attorney in whose office that document was prepared to support his assertion.

This attorney was and is a reputable and respected member of the bar, who had no prior connection with Holland and no knowledge of Mrs. Morses' relationship with him. He had never seen nor represented Mrs. Moses previously and never represented her afterward. He was acquainted with Holland and was aware that Holland was a lawyer.

The attorney's testimony supports the chancellor's finding that nowhere in the conversations with Mrs. Moses was there touched upon in any way the proposed testamentary disposition whereby preference was to be given a nonrelative to the exclusion of her blood relatives. There was no discussion of her relationship with Holland, nor as to who her legal heirs might be, nor as to their relationship to her, after it was discovered that she had neither a husband nor children.

It is clear from his own testimony that, in writing the will, the attorney–draftsman, did no more than write down, according to the forms of law, what Mrs. Moses told him. There was no meaningful independent advice or counsel touching upon the area in question and it is manifest that the role of the attorney in writing the will, as it relates to the present issue, was little more than that of scrivener. The chancellor was justified in holding that this did not meet the burden nor overcome the presumption. . . .

The chancellor's finding that the will was the product of Holland's undue influence is not inconsistent with his conclusion that 'Her (Mrs. Moses) mind was capable of understanding the essential matters necessary to the execution of her will on May 26, 1964, at the time of such execution.' A weak or infirm mind may, of course, be more easily over persuaded. In the case under review, Mrs. Moses was in ill health, she was an alcoholic, and was an aging woman infatuated with a young lover, 15 years her junior, who was also her lawyer. If this combination of circumstances cannot be said to support the view that Mrs. Moses suffered from a 'weakness or infirmity' of mind, vis-a-vis Holland, it was hardly calculated to enhance her power of will where he was concerned. Circumstances in evidence, both antecedent and subsequent to the making of the will, tend to accord with that conclusion.

The sexual morality of the personal relationship is not an issue. However, the intimate nature of this relationship is relevant to the present inquiry to the extent that its existence, under the circumstances, warranted an inference of undue influence, extending and augmenting that which flowed from the attorney–client relationship. Particularly is this true when viewed in the light of evidence indicating its employment for the personal aggrandizement of Holland. For that purpose, it was properly taken into consideration by the chancellor.

The Court upheld the lower court's finding of undue influence, over a strong dissent.

Query: The dissent points to numerous factors that support Fannie Moses' testamentary independence. She made the appointments herself to seek a different lawyer to have her will drafted, she made numerous changes to the first draft, and she went to his office to execute the will. What else should she have done to ensure that her testamentary wishes would be followed? What did the lawyer do wrong? Would this case have come out the same way if the genders had been reversed and the testator was a man who had the same infirmities and had undertaken the same actions to execute his will?

Bell v. Hutchins

268 S.W.3d 358 (Ark.App. 2007)

Appellant Connie Bell appeals the June 28, 2006 judgment, of the Union County Circuit Court, finding that the last will and testament of decedent Alvin R. Hutchins, dated September 15, 2005, is invalid and setting aside the order admitting it to probate. Appellant contends that the circuit court erred in finding that she procured the will and that she had unduly influenced Alvin R. Hutchins to make the will. We reverse the circuit court's finding of procurement and remand for proceedings consistent with this opinion.

Mr. Alvin R. Hutchins lived in Arkansas for fifteen years prior to his death. During that time, his daughter, who lives out of state, did not visit him, but Mr. Hutchins made it known that his daughter would inherit all that belonged to him upon his death. Mr. Hutchins hired appellant Connie Bell to be his housekeeper in early 2005 after he had suffered some falls and had become too feeble to care for himself and his home. Mr. Hutchins did not own a washing machine or dryer prior to his hiring appellant, but bought a set and had them installed in appellant's home in order that she might wash his clothes. Mr. Hutchins did not drive, but after he hired appellant, he bought a brand new GMC pick-up truck, which appellant drove. Mr. Hutchins also loaned appellant money for a deposit and first-month's rent on a house.

According to trial testimony, these purchases and financial transactions were out of the ordinary for Mr. Hutchins, who was said to have been frugal. His small house had no running hot water and no toilet facilities indoors. A wood-burning stove provided heat for the house. However, it was established at trial that Mr. Hutchins was generous with his church and helped people in need. Friends became concerned about Mr. Hutchins's spending when the washing machine, dryer, and truck were purchased.

Appellant made an appointment for Mr. Hutchins with attorney Teresa Wineland for September 15, 2005. On that date, appellant drove Mr. Hutchins to Ms. Wineland's law office and waited in the truck. Mr. Hutchins asked Ms. Wineland to draft a new will, leaving the washing machine, dryer, truck, and half of the remainder of his estate to appellant, with the other half of the estate going to his daughter. After Mr. Hutchins executed the will, appellant kept it in her possession.

Friends who picked Mr. Hutchins up for church on Sunday mornings testified that appellant would help him get dressed for church. However, the last few Sundays of his life, appellant did not help Mr. Hutchins get ready for church. On Sunday, October 2, 2005, Mr. Hutchins was found on the floor of his home by a friend. He had apparently fallen and had lain on the floor for several days. He was taken to the hospital where he died a week later. Three days after his death, appellant filed a petition to probate the September 15, 2005 will. The will was admitted to probate on October 12, 2005, and a motion to contest the will's admission was filed on November 28, 2005, by Merrie Hutchins, Mr. Hutchins's daughter.

After a hearing, the trial court found that appellant had procured the will, effectively shifting the burden from the will challenger, Merrie Hutchins, to the proponent of the will, appellant. Because of the finding of procurement, the trial court found that a rebuttable presumption of undue influence arose and that the burden of proof was on the appellant to prove beyond a reasonable doubt that the testator had both the testamentary capacity and the freedom from undue influence to execute a valid will. The trial court found that Mr. Hutchins had the mental capacity to execute the will on September 15, 2005. However, the trial court found that, based upon the facts, appellant failed to rebut the presumption of undue influence and declared the will invalid. This appeal follows. After explaining the law of testamentary capacity and undue influence, the court held:

Here, appellant merely called the lawyer's office to make the appointment for Mr. Hutchins. Subsequently Ms. Wineland, the attorney, contacted Mr. Hutchins personally to make sure he wanted the appointment. Appellant was not present in the office when the will was executed. Further, Ms. Wineland testified that Mr. Hutchins explained to her the reasoning behind dividing his estate between his daughter and appellant. Ms. Wineland stated that she was convinced that Mr. Hutchins had the proper mental capacity to do what he did. Therefore, . . . we hold that the trial court erred in finding that appellant procured the will and shifting the burden of proof to her.

Further, we hold that the trial court made a proper finding of testamentary capacity as follows:

As to testamentary capacity, the testimony of Teresa Wineland, who prepared and witnessed the Will, and Martha Kellum, the second witness, clearly established that Alvin Hutchins possessed the capacity to execute the Will on September 15. Decedent knew what he wanted to do, appeared coherent, and answered counsel's questions in a manner that indicated sufficient capacity on that day. The testimony of Martha Kellum confirmed the observations and conclusions of counsel.

Once testamentary capacity is established, the question of whether the testator was unduly influenced must be answered. We do not find error in the trial court's finding that Mr. Hutchins had the testamentary capacity to execute a will; however, because the trial court erroneously shifted the burden of proof to appellant, we reverse and remand for the trial court to act consistently with this opinion.

Query: Do you think a more stringent standard should be applied to friends, caregivers, or non-relatives who take an interest in an elderly decedent and are rewarded through testamentary bequests than is applied in the context of children, spouses, or other relatives? If so, why?

Hoffman v. Kohns

385 So.2d 1064 (Fla.App. 1980)[26]

On January 16, 1969, [Herbert L.] Kohns, then over seventy years old, established a revocable trust of which he and appellant [his niece Dorothy Hoffman] were cotrustees. The trust provided that after Kohns' death forty per cent of the trust assets would be distributed to appellant's two children and appellant would have a life estate in the other sixty per cent with the remainder to her children. The assets Kohns then owned were transferred to the trust. On July 2, 1969, Kohns executed a pour-over will devising most of *his probate estate into the 1969 trust to be distributed under its terms.*

After 1969, Kohns' mental and physical condition gradually deteriorated. He became extremely forgetful, paranoid, and suspicious, expressing distrust of all banks, doctors, trust officers, and others. From 1968 to 1975, Kohns lived alone in rental apartments. Until his stroke in October, 1974, he was able to drive an automobile, but had to have a woman at his bank make deposits and reconcile his checkbook.

In early October, 1974 Kohns and Hoffman met with Kohns' long-time attorney, Curtis Timm, about minor changes to the trust. *Timm had been Kohns' attorney for almost ten years. An appointment was set up for execution of the documents the next day* but was cancelled after Kohns and Hoffman disagreed about Hoffman buying food and cooking for Kohns.

On October 25, 1974, Kohns, then age eighty-two, was admitted to the hospital for cerebral arteriosclerosis and senility. It was determined *that Kohns had acute organic brain syndrome. A patient with this condition is not usually considered competent to perform normal tasks or to make decisions. After his discharge from the hospital, Kohns entered a nursing home.*

In December 1974, Kohns refused to stay in the nursing home and was returned to his apartment, but required nurses twenty-four hours a day. Kohns' housekeepers provided him transportation, purchased all of his food, made meals, kept house, wrote checks for his signature, and generally handled his personal and routine financial matters. Kohns was frail and feeble, disoriented at times, forgetful, sometimes hostile and irate, suspicious and paranoid. He was withdrawn at times, sitting for hours staring into space. Appellant telephoned Kohns monthly, and he was on pleasant terms with her. Appellant's last conversation with Kohns was on September 3, 1975.

In the last week of August 1975, appellee, age fifty-five, was hired as Kohns' housekeeper. On September 1, 1975, appellee took Kohns to his bank, and his safety deposit box was closed. The box contained all of Kohns' assets, including at least $40,000 worth of bearer bonds. On September 9, 1975 appellee took Kohns to Timm's office to be paid and Timm asked Kohns if he wanted to execute the revised documents from 1974. Kohns agreed and the documents were executed. Timm certified that Kohns was competent at this time. *On September 19, 1975, appellee drove Kohns to Wauchula, applied for a marriage license, and obtained the required blood tests for both of them. On Monday, September 22, 1975, appellee drove Kohns back to Wauchula and had a marriage ceremony performed there by a notary public.*

---

[26] This case was disagreed with by the Florida Supreme Court in a case involving the undue influence in the revocation of a revocable trust. The court held that a competent settlor can revoke a trust even if she is under the undue influence of another because undue influence is a doctrine that simply does not apply in the context of revocable trusts. See Fla. Nat'l Bank of Palm Beach County v. Genova, 460 So.2d 895 (Fla. 1984).

The next day, September 23, appellee took Kohns to attorney Dick Lee to have a new will drawn making her the sole beneficiary. She had previously used Lee as her attorney, whereas Timm had been Kohns' attorney for ten years. The new will was executed in her presence on September 26, 1975. The attorney who witnessed the will testified that Kohns was alert and responsive. The other subscribing witness testified that Kohns was in command of his faculties and knew what he was doing.

Immediately after the marriage, appellee moved Kohns out of his apartment into a room in her home. Within a week after the marriage, appellee had arranged for the withdrawal of all of Kohns' cash from his savings account or certificates of deposit and placed them into joint accounts.

At that time, it was discovered that the securities in the 1969 trust could not be transferred without the consent of the cotrustee or an amendment or revocation of the trust. On October 3, 1975, appellee took Kohns back to Lee's office, at which time Kohns signed a one-paragraph revocation of the 1969 trust. Marion Eichler, a secretary with the law firm, testified that in her opinion Kohns was in command of his faculties.

During October, November, and December, 1975, all but two issues of securities owned by Kohns individually or in the trust were transferred either to appellee or to appellee and Kohns as tenants by the entireties or joint tenants with right of survivorship.

The Hoffmans attempted to contact Kohns periodically through the last months of 1975 but were told he was indisposed or out walking, but appellee assured them he was feeling better.

In late November, 1975, Kohns was hospitalized for prostate surgery. The nurses' notes, both those made before and those made after the operation, indicate that he was in a confused mental state. In July, 1976, Kohns underwent a hernia operation. During the operation, he had a stroke and lapsed into a coma. He was comatose thereafter until he died on September 13, 1976. The death certificate indicated that Kohns had suffered from hardening of the arteries of years duration.

The trial court found that the September 26, 1975 will was procured by undue influence but found the marriage and the revocation of the trust and subsequent transfer of trust assets to be not subject to undue influence. The Florida Supreme Court reversed in part, agreeing that *the Respondent did engage in a course of conduct before the marriage and continued it thereafter so as to unduly influence said Herbert L. Kohns so as to completely ignore his prior wishes, his relations to the persons who were or should or might have been the objects of his bounty. Such conduct completely dominated the thinking of the deceased, kept him isolated and out of contact with his family, and the resulting persuasion, coercion and excessive influence dominated his willpower so that he provided only for the Respondent in the will in question.*

The Supreme Court also found that although there are no Florida cases directly referring to the revocation of a living trust, a lifetime transfer to a nurse was held invalid as having been procured by undue influence and that the degree of proof necessary to invalidate a lifetime gift is lower than that to invalidate a will. Because the revocation of the trust was done just seven days after the execution of the will found to have been procured by undue influence, the court voided the revocation as well. The Court explained:

The evidence establishes that appellee completely dominated Kohns both before and after September 26, 1975, the date the new will was executed, by taking control of all of his business affairs, taking over the writing of checks and balancing of his checkbook, and changing his attorney, doctor, accountant, and stockbroker. The systematic transfer of all of Kohns' assets to appellee or into joint tenancy is further evidence of her undue influence. There is no evidence that Kohns made a single independent decision after the marriage.

Kohns' marriage to a woman thirty years younger than he, whom he had known for less than a month; the complete cancellation of his entire long-standing estate plan; and the changing of his doctor of over fifteen years, his lawyer of ten years, his accountant, and his stockbroker, all within a few weeks, are highly unusual, and the trial court quite properly found that these actions were taken as a result of the undue influence of appellee. The revocation of the trust was part of a continuing pattern begun immediately after the marriage. The trial court could not reasonably find otherwise.

Our holding with respect to the revocation of the trust does not affect the validity of the Kohns' marriage. A marriage to which the consent of one of the parties is obtained by undue influence is merely voidable. Consequently, it cannot be attacked upon this basis after the death of either of the parties. Cf. Savage v. Olson, 151 Fla. 241, 9 So.2d 363 (1942), which held that a showing of gross fraud could be a basis for declaring a marriage void after the death of the defrauded spouse. On the other hand, a marriage may be posthumously set aside as being void because of the mental incompetency of one of the marriage partners. Here, however, while the evidence was conflicting, it was sufficient to support the court's conclusion that Kohns was competent to marry appellee.

This leaves remaining the question of whether appellee was entitled to those of the decedent's assets which were not already in the trust before he died. The answer appears to lie in the application of Florida's Pretermitted Spouse Statute which would give appellee Kohns' entire intestate estate.

Because the court set aside Kohn's September 26, 1975, will, his last valid will was the one which he executed on September 9, 1975, prior to his marriage to appellee. Even though she improperly influenced him to execute the September 26 will, once that will was revoked they were in the same posture as if no will had been made following the marriage. Therefore, since there was no marriage contract and no reference to appellee in the September 9 will, she was entitled under the statute to her intestate share, which would be Kohn's entire estate because he died without lineal descendants.

Query: Does it make sense to you that the court would find no capacity to make a will or to revoke the trust because of undue influence but sufficient capacity to marry? Since a spouse will be entitled to an elective share or a pretermitted spousal share, what was the point of all of this litigation? If you were worried that an elderly client might be inveigled into marriage, what could you do? Can you distinguish between the behavior in *Bell v. Hutchins* and *Hoffman v. Kohns*? In Florida at this time the surviving pretermitted spouse was entitled to the entire *probate* estate. Would you feel better about the outcome if you knew that Kohns had significant non-probate property? Should such a thing matter?

There are, quite literally, hundreds of undue influence cases, some finding egregious violations, and others finding no adequate proof of influence in circumstances that might raise eyebrows on even the most jaded observers. Some courts are particularly careful to require the opponent meet the burden of proving undue influence. Others shift the burden quite easily upon evidence of a confidential relationship and an unnatural disposition of the property. Considering the factors cited earlier, could you devise a rule on undue influence that would help ferret out situations of *undue* influence from those of *regular* influence?

Unfortunately, too, will contest litigation plays on many stereotypes and expectations that may not be relevant to the actual issue of replacing a testator's free will. Consider what, if any, duty you as a lawyer have in the representation of clients to ensure that influence by friends, family, spouses, caretakers, neighbors, and strangers is not undue. And consider too your ethical responsibilities in zealously representing your client. Does that duty rise to the level of using stereotypes against your opponent? Consider the case of Fannie Moses. If you represented her distant heirs, arguing against her younger male lover's claim to her estate, should you exploit the facts of her disfigurement, her age, or her gender to imply that she was a pathetic old woman grasping at youth? Should you urge the court to find undue influence hoping the judges hold similar stereotypes about fortune hunting men and desperate women?

There are numerous circumstances in which a confidential relationship can arise. Obvious examples are the lawyer/client, doctor/patient, and pastor/parishioner relationships. But other confidants can be one's financial advisor, teacher, boss, lover, child, parent, swim coach, car mechanic, neighbor, or friend. Should the rules be different about burden of proof and presumptions of influence in some or all of these relationships?

Practice Point: The Aging Client and the Overly Eager Helper

In *Bell v. Hutchins*, the court found that Mr. Hutchins possessed the testamentary capacity necessary to make a will but that the trial court erroneously shifted the burden of proof from the will challenger to Ms. Bell regarding the issue of undue influence. The court relied heavily on the testimony of the attorney in determining the issue of testamentary capacity. But, what if the attorney *had* noticed that Mr. Hutchins was being heavily persuaded by Ms. Bell?

One of the great benefits an estate planning practice provides is the opportunity to have a longstanding relationship with many of your clients. Of course, this was not the case in *Bell*, where the attorney–client relationship consisted of a phone call and execution meeting. But, contrast that sort of relationship with the numerous other estate planning clients that you will meet with every few years or so in order to review their plans? Of course, the clients do not have any duty to follow up with you as time goes by, but many will get attached to you and actually like to come and see you every once in a while. If you are a people-person, this will be a great perk for you, and if you are a numbers person, it might be a bit of an annoyance, particularly if nothing has changed in the client's life to legally necessitate the review meeting.

But, this preference of meetings staged at intervals can provide you with a unique perspective as your client ages, particularly in matters relating to undue influence. For example, if a client you have known for many years, who is recently widowed, suddenly comes into her review meeting with a new person who insists on asking you questions about your client's legal situation and is trying to "run the show," you may be tipped off that something has gone awry. Since you know (and your Engagement Letter clearly states, of course) who is your client, in these sorts of situations, you can pretty easily assert the attorney–client privilege and ask the other party to step out to the waiting area while you discuss the estate plan—and, hopefully, the nature of your client's new relationship—with your client. But if that person refuses to leave or, as has happened several times in my practice, begins to get aggressive or say nasty things to you like "I told her that attorneys are always looking out for themselves and that she shouldn't trust what you have to say," then you have an entirely different set of circumstances, don't you?

Another clue that your client is falling under the influence of another is when she begins to fire her other longstanding advisors like financial planners, accountants, and life insurance agents. Of course she has the RIGHT to fire anyone who she wishes—including you—but sometimes you will notice that the new, sometimes creepy, person in her life is actually the one calling the shots. And what can you do as you watch these events progress?

Of course every case and every state requires a different course of action but, generally speaking, you certainly owe your client the duty of representing her honestly. If she is asking for your legal advice, give it to her, even if she doesn't like to hear it. Keep in mind that this ultimately may get you fired. However, practicing with a clear conscious, in my experience, far outweighs any financial gain that you might receive if you continue representing a client you cannot truly fight for—and under circumstances that might get you, as attorney, in hot water later. But in all of these circumstances, revisit your rules of professional responsibility—and don't be afraid to ask for advice if you need it. Things can get tricky when someone starts trying to control your client and turning to other lawyers can help you see your way clear.

PROBLEM

11.2. Imagine you are the lawyer for the testator in any one of the cases above. What would you advise your client and how could you protect your client's testamentary plan from undue influence and expensive litigation?

C. MISTAKE

Testators often make mistakes in planning the disposition of their assets at death. They may believe that someone has died who hasn't, or that someone is alive who isn't. They may believe that they have more wealth than they do. Or they may believe that the organization that provided such great benefits to the world was the Red Cross of America, not realizing that it was the Red Cross of North America, and inadvertently leave their property to the wrong entity. They have been known to leave their house, located at 123 Main Street, to their children, only accidentally written it 132 Main Street, which could result in the gift of the house being adeemed.

All manner of mistakes can arise in the context of a will, which can be problematic if the statute of wills requires strict execution according to the formalities in order for a testamentary gift to be given effect. If the wrong house is given to the wrong person in a document executed with the formalities, the gift is simply ineffective because there is no house at 132 Main Street in the testator's estate. But what should an administrator, or a court, do with the actual house that is located at 123 Main Street and is not, apparently, disposed of to anyone? Should it fall into the residuary? Unless a court chooses to reform the donative documents to purge the mistake, all kinds of unplanned consequences can occur.

But courts are hesitant to reform on the basis of mistake because mistakes are errors that the testator could have corrected and didn't. Why should the court fix a problem the testator had many years to fix? Perhaps more importantly, evidence of mistakes usually arise after the testator has died and someone challenges the provisions of the will or trust claiming they don't adequately reflect the testator's true intentions. But what are the testator's *true* intentions if not what is in writing on the testamentary document? As between a properly executed will, with all the formalities, and evidence from a bunch of interested parties about death bed clarifications or intentions that contradict the language of the will, courts are understandably leery about the quality of evidence that forms the basis of any claims of mistake. At the same time, however, lawyers make clerical and drafting errors all the time, errors that could be corrected fairly easily if they are caught early enough. But in testamentary litigation, someone will always win and someone will always lose by not correcting the mistake or by correcting it, which sets up incentives to probate litigation.

Historically, courts would not reform wills that contained mistakes, regardless of the strength of the evidence, because correcting usually meant negating a properly executed bequest and substituting a different provision that was not properly executed. Since courts could not rewrite someone's will, the property would either pass to the mistaken beneficiary or to unintended beneficiaries, like the intestate heirs. Since neither avenue could get the property to the intended beneficiary, and evidence of who the intended beneficiary was can be quite sketchy, courts generally would not bother reforming a will for mistakes. For how could the court be sure that the testator's niece or grandson was supposed to get the house when the will gave it to someone else? Moreover, giving the house to the intended beneficiary meant disposing of property to persons without satisfying the statute of wills and the requisite formalities.

Although courts would not reform wills, because of the strict requirement of execution according to the formalities, they would often use their equity powers to correct trusts or other *inter vivos* documents that contained clear mistakes, usually by imposing a constructive trust on the mistaken beneficiary to hold the property for the intended beneficiary on the basis of unjust enrichment. Before invoking their equity powers, however, courts generally require clear and convincing evidence of contrary intent before voiding a donative provision on the basis of mistake and before imposing a constructive trust.

But again, in keeping with the liberalizing trend of the UPC, and in conjunction with rules allowing for correction of mistakes in contracts and other legal documents under state law, the trend is to allow for reformation of wills and will substitutes on the basis of mistake, both in the expression or in the inducement. The UPC provides for general reformation power in the case of mistake.

UPC § 2–805 Reformation to Correct Mistakes

The court may reform the terms of a governing instrument, even if unambiguous, to conform the terms to the transferor's intention if it is proved by clear and convincing evidence that the transferor's intent and the terms of the governing instrument were affected by a mistake of fact or law, whether in expression or inducement.

So too does the Restatement 3d of Property. It provides:

---

§ 12.1 Reforming Donative Documents to Correct Mistakes

A donative document, though unambiguous, may be reformed to conform the text to the donor's intention if the following are established by clear and convincing evidence:

(1) that a mistake of fact or law, whether in expression or inducement, affected specific terms of the document; and

(2) what the donor's intention was.

Direct evidence of intention contradicting the plain language of the text as well as other evidence of intention may be considered in determining whether elements (1) and (2) have been established by clear and convincing evidence.

Many states also have adopted reformation statutes like this one, from New Jersey. It provides:

N.J. St 3B: 3–33.1. Testator's intention; settlor's intention; rules of construction applicable to wills, trusts and other governing instruments

a. The intention of a testator as expressed in his will controls the legal effect of his dispositions, and the rules of construction expressed in N.J.S.3B:3–34 through N.J.S.3B:3–48 shall apply unless the probable intention of the testator, as indicated by the will and relevant circumstances, is contrary.

b. The intention of a settlor as expressed in a trust, or of an individual as expressed in a governing instrument, controls the legal effect of the dispositions therein and the rules of construction expressed in N.J.S. 3B:34 through N.J.S.3B:3–48 shall apply unless the probable intent of such settlor or of such individual, as indicated by the trust or by such governing instrument and relevant circumstances, is contrary. For purposes of this Title, when construing each of these rules of construction the word "testator" shall include but not be limited to a settlor or a creator of any other governing instrument; the word "will" shall include a trust or other governing instrument; the word "devise" shall include any disposition in a trust or other governing instrument; and the word "devisee" shall include a beneficiary of a trust or other governing instrument.

Consider the three different rules cited above and see what, if any, differences you discern in the statutes. Can you think of any situations in which reformation would be provided under one of these rules but perhaps not the others?

Now consider the following cases and whether you think the evidence was sufficient for a court to have reformed the testamentary document or not:

Brinker v. Wobaco Trust Ltd.

610 S.W.2d 160 (Tex.Civ.App. 1980)

Norman and Maureen Brinker, husband and wife, established an *inter vivos* trust funded primarily through life insurance and pour over from each spouse's will. The trust beneficiaries were "the issue of the settlor." The settlor was identified in the trust documents only as Norman, even though Maureen helped fund and establish the trust, and would serve as co-trustee if she survived Norman. Norman and Maureen had two children, Cynthia and Brenda. After Maureen's death, and the funding of the trust from her residuary estate, Norman remarried and subsequently had two additional children, Christina and Mark. During his second marriage, Norman withdrew some of the property from Maureen's residuary estate that was in the trust and placed it in different trusts, benefitting Christina and Mark. After his divorce from his second wife, Norman had second thoughts about using Maureen's property to benefit Christina and Mark, and so he told Cynthia and Brenda what he had done. They brought suit to impose a constructive trust on the assets of their mother's estate and to reform the trust to reflect that Norman and Maureen's intentions in creating the trust had been to benefit only THEIR issue, not Norman's subsequent issue.

Cynthia and Brenda's evidence consisted of the testimony of their father, Norman, and his tax lawyer, to the effect that the understanding of the parties, including Maureen, had been to benefit only their own issue. But there was also evidence that the lawyer used the singular of the terms "trustee" and "settlor" intentionally though he claimed he meant to include both Maureen and Norman as settlors, and the trust did benefit Cynthia and Brenda in other provisions, thus implying that there was no mistake—the document reflected what the lawyer dictated, and the intention to benefit Cynthia and Brenda individually was also reflected by using their names. The use of the term *issue*, therefore, implied the possibility of additional beneficiaries because it was class gift terminology. The court remanded for a new trial, explaining:

If, by mistake, an instrument as written fails to express the true intention or agreement of the parties, equity will grant reformation of the instrument so as to make it correctly express the agreement actually made. The rule applies to express inter vivos trusts as well as to other written instruments. The mistake may be shown by parol evidence. And although a mutual mistake of the parties is required in most instances, if a settlor of a trust receives no consideration for the creation of the trust, a unilateral mistake on his part is sufficient. It is immaterial whether the mistake be one of fact or law. Any mistake of the scrivener which could defeat the true intention may be corrected in equity by reformation, whether the mistake is one of fact or law.

Query: The Brinker court was willing to reform this trust, in large part, because it was not a will, and it also rejected the argument that it could not reform the trust because it had become irrevocable upon Maureen's death. But where exactly did the mistake lie? Is it that Norman didn't intend the trust to benefit all of his issue, or that Maureen didn't intend the trust to benefit all of Norman's issue? Can we read the trust, realistically, to benefit only Maureen's issue when the trust is called the "Norman Brinker Family Trust," Norman is identified in the trust as the settlor, and the designated beneficiaries are "the settlor's issue" and not "the settlors' issue?"

Mahoney v. Grainger

186 N.E. 86 (Mass. 1933)

The residuary clause of Helen Sullivan's will gave "all the rest and residue of my estate, both real and personal property, . . . to my heirs at law living at the time of my decease, absolutely; to be divided among them equally, share and share alike." At her death, her closest living heir was her maternal aunt. She also had about twenty-five first cousins. The trial judge dismissed a claim by some cousins for a share of the estate on the grounds that the term "heir at law" had a specific meaning that did not give rise to an ambiguity that would allow the admission of extrinsic evidence as to the testator's intent to benefit more people than her aunt. On appeal, the Massachusetts Supreme Court affirmed, stating: *A will duly executed and allowed by the court must under the statute of wills be accepted as the final expression of the intent of the person executing it. The fact that it was not in conformity to the instructions given to the draftsman who prepared it or that he made a mistake does not authorize a court to reform or alter it or remold it by amendments.*

Query: The rule applied in *Mahoney* is the plain meaning rule, which prohibits deviation from the will if the terms have a plain meaning, regardless of whether the testator understood or intended the plain meaning. So what did the lawyer do wrong in this case? As in the *Est. of Moses*, discussed above, should a lawyer be held liable to the intended beneficiaries when she fails to explore the full range of potential heirs and beneficiaries and thus drafts a will that doesn't effectuate the testator's true intentions?

In re Est. of Flores

76 S.W.3d 624 (Tex.App. 2002)

In 1968, the decedent, Jimmy Flores, had a non-marital son, Roman De Luna. Thirteen years later, Jimmy filed a legitimation suit seeking to have Roman declared his son and to change Roman's last name to Flores. The suit was granted. Three years later he married appellee, Rosa Flores and they had four children. In Jimmy's will, he acknowledged that he was married to appellee, that he had four living children, and that he had no deceased children. Roman was not mentioned anywhere in the will or acknowledged as Jimmy's child. After Jimmy's death, Roman filed a will contest asserting that the will was not valid because not executed with the formalities, that it was a forgery and had been altered, and alternatively that it was executed while Jimmy was mistaken as to its contents. Roman later amended the petition to allege that Jimmy lacked testamentary capacity and that the will was procured by misrepresentation or fraud. Under any of these theories the will would not be entitled to probate and Jimmy would be deemed to have died intestate and, as Jimmy's natural child, Roman would be entitled to a share. The court ruled against Roman on all points, finding that there was no evidence that Jimmy lacked testamentary capacity at any time during his life, much less at the time the will was executed. There was also no probative evidence as to the forgery, misrepresentation, fraud, or lack of will formalities. As to the issue of mistake, the court stated: *Appellant also contended that Jimmy was mistaken as to the contents of the will when he signed it. A competent testator is presumed to know and understand the contents of the testamentary instrument he has signed, unless circumstances exist that cast suspicion on the issue.*

Appellant points to the inclusion in the will of a statement that Jimmy had no other children, living or dead, besides those named in the will, and adduced evidence of the birth of a daughter to Jimmy and his wife in 1956; this child died at the age of one month. While this evidence may be relevant to the issue of mistake as to the fact of the deceased child, it does not constitute evidence of mistake of fact regarding the crux of this case, Jimmy's intent to disinherit appellant.

Appellant also points to the affidavits of two witnesses, Rosie Dominguez and Jesus Munoz, which state that Jimmy told them in 1996, some three years after the signing of the will in 1993, that he had left property in his will to appellant. However, appellant adduced no evidence concerning Jimmy's intent, if any, to leave property to appellant on the date of the execution of the will. We agree with the trial court that the affidavits of Dominguez and Munoz do not constitute probative evidence; they are not probative as to the relevant date, and amount to no more than a bare suspicion of wrongdoing. We hold the trial court did not err in granting summary judgment on this issue.

Query: What should a court do in a case like this? The decedent was the one who insisted on asserting paternal rights through the legitimation suit and by having his illegitimate son's name changed to his, yet, in his will he claimed to have only four living children when he in fact had five. Of course Jimmy was entitled to disinherit Roman, or any of his other children. But his omission of Roman left his will open to challenge. Do you think the evidence from the friends that Jimmy had provided for Roman in his will is credible? If so, what was the mistake and how could a court fix it?

In re Est. of Patrick

188 Misc.2d 295 (N.Y. Sur. 2001)

The decedent, Charles Patrick, executed a will which left his residuary estate, consisting solely of his residence, to his daughter Lisa Patrick. On the day he executed his will, he signed an affidavit stating that he was leaving his entire estate to Lisa because she was the only one of his four children who did not own her own home. After Charles' death, two of his other children, David and Joyce, challenged the will contending that the testator was under the mistaken belief that his other three children owned their own homes, when in fact David and Joyce also did not own their homes. The court denied the challenge and affirmed the will as written, stating: *The situation before the Court is unfortunately difficult on the facts, but uncomplicated on the law. The body of decedent's will is simple and straightforward. The residuary bequest to petitioner is not contingent on her not owning a home and his other children having homes. There is no qualification of any kind regarding his children's home ownership in the will itself.*

The Courts have held that "[w]hen the purpose of a testator is reasonably clear by reading his words in their natural and common sense, the courts have not the right to annul or pervert that purpose upon the ground that a consequence of it might not have been thought of or intended by him." Moreover, when the will itself is clear, any alleged mistake must be evident on the face of the document itself. It is elemental that the remedy of reformation of a testamentary instrument is to be applied sparingly if at all.

In the present situation, the words used in the will are clear, definite and unambiguous. The alleged mistake imputed from decedent's affidavit is not evident on the face of the document. Moreover, the will and the affidavit were executed more than ten years prior to decedent's death. It appears that his children were aware of the terms of decedent's will as presumably was decedent himself who made no attempt to change its terms during those ten years.

Although the affidavit was signed at the same time as the will, it was not referred to therein. Addressing extraneous matters put forth by objectants in this regard is fraught with difficulty and mischief. To sustain the objections would substantially alter decedent's express testamentary scheme and result in a deviation from his clearly stated wishes. In short to reform a will that has no ambiguities results in a will that is not that of the decedent. When the words used in a will are clear and definite there is no power to change them.

Query: Courts often distinguish between a mistake of fact and a mistake of judgment, correcting only for the former and not the latter. It is assumed that a testator might have changed her will had she known of the mistake of the first kind, but not of the second kind (like a belief that her son-in-law is a criminal and a drunkard[27]). Is the mistake alleged in this case a mistake of fact or of judgment?

Matter of Est. of Smelser

818 P.2d 822 (Kan.App. 1991)

The decedent, Martha Smelser, owned a 160 acre tract of land at her death. In 1983 she had executed a will leaving the north half of the land to her son Lloyd and the south half to her other two sons, Frank and John. In 1989 she executed a codicil revoking the paragraph of her 1983 will that devised the 160 acre tract of land and making other amendments to her will. After her death, Lloyd filed the 1983 will for probate but objected to probate of the codicil on the ground that it did not reflect the testamentary intent of Martha because of a scrivener's mistake. Testimony showed that Lloyd and his wife lived close to the decedent and assisted them in their farming and cattle operations and that 2 acres of the north lot had been conveyed to Lloyd and his wife to build a house so they could be close to the decedent. Testimony also showed that Lloyd had purchased the south half of the land in order to keep it intact for farming, and that the proceeds of the sale were to go to Frank and John at Martha's death, but that the devise of the north half to Lloyd was not supposed to have been revoked. The codicil thus erroneously revoked the bequests for both the north and south parcels, and correctly replaced the south gift with cash to Frank and John. The probate court admitted the will and codicil to probate except for the provision revoking the bequest to Lloyd of the north half on the basis of a scrivener's error. In affirming, the court of appeals stated: *John and Frank rely on the well-established rule that where the language of a will is clear and unambiguous, a court cannot go beyond that document to determine testator intent. However, this rule is applied only where the action is to construe or interpret the will after it has been admitted to probate. This case involves an action not to construe Martha's codicil, but to determine whether*

27　See Joseph v. Grisham, 482 S.E.2d 251 (Ga. 1997).

it is a valid expression of her testamentary intent and thus admissible to probate. The validity of a will or codicil does partly depend on whether it accurately expresses the testator's true testamentary intent. A corollary to this rule is the requirement that the testator have knowledge of the will's contents at the time of its execution for the will to be valid. Execution of the will establishes a rebuttable presumption that the testator has this knowledge. Clear and convincing evidence must be presented to rebut this presumption.

We believe the district court here properly admitted the testimony of Martha's attorney and Margaret [Lloyd's wife] on the issue of whether Martha's codicil as written accurately reflected her testamentary intent regarding the devise of the north half. We are satisfied this testimony provides substantial competent evidence to support the district court's factual finding that the scrivener erred in inserting a statement into the codicil which resulted in the revocation of the devise of the north half to Lloyd.

The effect of this scrivener mistake on the validity of the revocation of the devise to Lloyd must next be determined. Testator knowledge of the scrivener's mistake is an important factor in the determination of whether a will is a valid expression of the testator's testamentary intent. Some jurisdictions have held that where affirmative proof was presented that the testator was made aware of the contents of the will as written, the will is not invalid.

Other jurisdictions, however, have held to the contrary, finding a will containing scrivener error invalid despite the testator having been made aware of its contents or having had the opportunity to become aware of its contents.

Here, the district court found that Martha believed the codicil accurately expressed her testamentary intent. The court's finding that the codicil was not read at its execution and that it was not read to or by Martha is supported by the record. However, while Margaret did testify that she did not read the codicil to Martha after Martha received it in the mail, there is no affirmative evidence showing that Martha did not read the codicil herself at some time before it was executed. On the other hand, there is no affirmative evidence that she did read the codicil and was thus familiar with its contents before executing it. There is undisputed, substantial and credible evidence that Martha intended to devise the north half to Lloyd and to bequeath the sale proceeds from the south half to Frank and John. We conclude there is no affirmative evidence that Martha actually knew the codicil revoked the devise to Lloyd when she executed it. The codicil's revocation of that devise is not a correct expression of her testamentary intent which allows the fulfillment of Martha's actual testamentary wishes.

Finally, we must decide if, despite the lack of affirmative evidence that Martha was aware of the contents of the entire codicil, the district court properly refused to probate only that part which revoked the devise of the north half to Lloyd. In cases where the testator's lack of knowledge of the will's contents is due to scrivener mistake, deletion of only the portion inserted by error has been established as a proper method of correcting the error. Kansas also follows the rule that where a provision of a will is invalid for any reason and the testamentary scheme of the testator can be carried out regardless of the void provision, that provision will be stricken and the testamentary plan given effect. We conclude striking from the codicil only the revocation of the devise of the north half to Lloyd does not destroy the testamentary scheme remaining in Martha's will and codicil.

Query: The supposed mistake in this case was the lawyer simply revoking the entire paragraph of the will in the codicil rather than just the provision of the south half to Frank and John. Note how the court relied more on notions of lack of testamentary intent for that aspect of the codicil rather than mere mistake. Is there an important difference between intent and mistake and, if so, what is it? Also, note how easy it was for the court to simply scratch out the revocation of the north half of the land and allow that property to pass according to the original will provision? The court did not have to write in a new provision based on extrinsic evidence of testamentary intent.

Courts often have a difficult time determining whether or not to admit evidence that would support a claim of mistake. Obviously, the will says one thing and a challenger is claiming that it should say something different. When can courts admit extrinsic evidence to prove lack of intent or mistake, and when must they simply rely on the plain language of the document? That is the subject of the next section, which is important for any kind of testamentary challenge, whether to a will or other donative document, and whether the challenge is based on lack of capacity, undue influence, insane delusion, mistake, fraud, or misrepresentation. For we cannot know of the error unless there is evidence that the testator had a different testamentary scheme in mind, and that usually requires the admission of extrinsic evidence.

PROBLEM

11.3. Go back through the five cases discussed above and apply the UPC, Restatement, and the rule from your state to each to determine whether the different rules would affect the outcome of any of these cases.

D. AMBIGUITIES (LATENT AND PATENT) AND ADMISSION OF EXTRINSIC EVIDENCE

Under the *Parol Evidence Rule*, extrinsic evidence is not admissible to contradict clear language of a written document, especially a document under seal or, as in the case of a will, executed with the legal formalities. This is even more so when the drafter of the document, the testator, has died and cannot give evidence as to intent. Litigation could quickly turn into a "he said/she said" of disgruntled relatives and friends all claiming that Grandpa told them they were going to inherit his 8-track tape collection and extra used tractor fenders. But when Grandpa's will purports to leave his house at 123 2nd Street to his daughter, and his house is actually located at 123 2nd Avenue, a court will allow extrinsic evidence to clarify the testator's true intention. He certainly wouldn't want his executor to sell his house on 2nd Avenue and buy the house on 2nd Street just so the devise can be given effect. Nor, of course, would Grandpa or his daughter want the court to treat the gift as adeemed simply because it was incorrectly identified. On the other side of the spectrum, does a devise of "living room furniture" include lamps, vases, statues, and candlesticks or just the sofa, coffee table, and easy-boy chairs? What about the television?[28] Ambiguities come in all flavors and sizes.

---

[28]   See Kelly v. Est. of Johnson, 788 N.E.2d 933 (Ind.App. 2003).

Drafting errors, or simple human mistakes (like leaving your estate to your favorite charity, the National Society for the Prevention of Cruelty to Children when you really meant to leave it to the Scottish National Society for the Prevention of Cruelty to Children)[29] can happen to the best of us. So when should courts admit extrinsic evidence to try to clarify the testator's true intent, and when should they not? Not surprisingly, the rules are complex and vary from jurisdiction to jurisdiction. Some courts are quite rigid, refusing to permit extrinsic evidence to contradict the language of a properly executed will. One court put it this way: "A will cannot be reformed to conform to any intent of the testator not expressed in it, no matter how clearly a different intent may be proved by extrinsic evidence . . . [I]f the rule were otherwise, . . . property would pass without a will in writing, which the law demands."[30]

But other courts, following the lead of the Restatement 3d of Property (Donative Transfers) and the Uniform Trust Code, which have fairly liberal provisions for reforming donative documents, have relaxed their concern about the risks of false testimony. Naturally, the relaxing trend has occurred in jurisdictions that tend to have moved away from strict compliance to substantial compliance or the UPC's dispensing power in determining the validity of will execution. With the tremendous increase in will substitutes that are not subject to the will formalities, and therefore are more open to reformation or admission of extrinsic evidence, the requirement of a higher standard of proof in wills, and the hair-splitting necessary to judge between different types of ambiguities, has led many courts to allow extrinsic evidence to further the overarching goal of promoting testamentary intent in respect to all testamentary documents.

The common law has generally drawn a number of arcane yet important distinctions between types of ambiguities and types of evidence that is admissible for different types of mistakes and ambiguities. First, there is the distinction between *patent* and *latent* ambiguities. *Patent ambiguities* are those that are evident on the face of the will. Thus, a devise that instructs the administrator to divide the "rest and residue of my estate into three equal shares for my nephews, John Smith and Paul Smith" raises an immediate question. What does the testator mean in this case? Are John and Paul to each take half? Are John and Paul to each take one-third and the remaining one-third is to pass by intestacy? Or is the remaining one-third to pass to Herman Smith, the testator's other nephew whose name may have simply been omitted by the drafter or may have been omitted intentionally? Patent ambiguities appear on the face of the will, and you don't need to know anything about the testator's individual circumstances to realize there is something wrong.

Latent ambiguities, on the other hand, arise when something seemingly clear on the face of the will turns out to be confusing only when the facts of the testator's property or her relationships become known. The devise of the house at 123 2nd Street is a latent ambiguity, realized only when the administrator is compiling the testator's property and realizes that the house is located on 2nd Avenue. The term "heirs at law" seems unambiguous until you discover that the testator was thinking of all of her cousins, and not just her elderly aunt who turns out to be her only heir at law, as in *Mahoney v. Grainger*, above. Bequests to "nieces and nephews" may be

---

[29] See National Society for the Prevention of Cruelty to Children v. Scottish National Society for the Prevention of Cruelty to Children, A.C. 207 (H.L.) (1915).

[30] Est. of Frietze, 966 P.2d 183, 186 (N.M.App. 1998).

ambiguous if the testator intended to include his wife's nieces and neph-ews,[31] or step-nieces.[32]

Ironically, courts were more willing to admit extrinsic evidence to re-solve latent ambiguities than patent ambiguities, because resolving patent ambiguities would require, in most instances, adding words to the will, something courts are loath to do. Latent ambiguities often don't require changing anything in the actual will itself; they simply require additional information to clarify a bequest that was not as clear as it should have been. But many modern courts have rejected the latent/patent distinction as a hold-over from the formalistic days of strict compliance, a policy that no longer meets the important policy goal of promoting testamentary intent or minimizing the disparity of rules between wills and will substitutes.

Courts also distinguish between types of evidence, between evidence of the *circumstances* and evidence regarding *statements* or *declarations* of the testator. Evidence of the circumstances concern readily-verifiable facts, like the name and ages of children, the identity of other relatives, or the street address of the testator's home. More complicated circumstantial evidence may be offered when, for instance, a husband executed his wife's will and *vice versa*. Evidence that the two wills were signed at the same time in a joint meeting suggests that they simply signed the wrong wills. Had they been executed at different times, or been drafted by different attorneys, we might draw different conclusions. These are still examples of evidence of the circumstances.

Declarations of the testator, like "I don't want my good-for-nothing son to have any of my property," may be important evidence, but isn't likely to be admitted if the testator's will leaves all of his property to his "children." Declarations of the testator are open to misremembering by witnesses, mis-interpretation, and can't be validated easily because it is hard to know if the testator changed her mind or made a mistake in the drafting of her will. Declarations of the testator may also be subject to the *Dead Man's rule*[33] and evidence rules against hearsay that prohibit the admission of certain evidence.

Finally, some witnesses and evidence may be deemed more reliable than others. Lawyers who draft wills, and their file notes, are generally deemed more reliable than a potential beneficiary who claims Grandma wanted her to have everything to the exclusion of the rest of her siblings. Some courts have created rules that certain types of ambiguities can result in the admission of limited testimony while others types of ambiguities result in the admission of any and all relevant testimony. Much of the hair-splitting about types of evidence are better covered in an evidence class. But for our purposes, it is best to keep in mind two things: the rule against *no reformation of a will* and the *plain meaning rule* are designed to pro-mote the protective and the channeling functions of the will formalities. But the liberalizing trend that permits reformation for mistake (which is of relatively new origin), as well as for fraud or undue influence, promotes that lodestar of the field, testamentary intent while, coincidentally, reduc-ing claims against drafters for malpractice liability and preventing unjust enrichment. So what's not to like about the trend?

---

[31] Est. of Anderson, 359 N.W.2d 479 (Iowa 1984).

[32] Clymer v. Mayo, 473 N.E.2d 1084 (Mass. 1985).

[33] About half the states have statutes prohibiting an interested party to an estate from testifying about statements made by the now-deceased testator.

As with all such changes, strict formalities and unjust outcomes are replaced with fuzzier standards, more litigation, and greater accusations of judicial activism. Whenever courts, either judges or juries, are asked to second-guess a testator's state of mind, opportunities always arise for them to impose their own ideas of what they think the testator should have done. Think about *Barnes v. Marshall* or *Est. of Strittmater*. Then consider these cases involving evidence that the decedent's testamentary documents do not reflect her intent, and what should be done about that.

In re Est. of Camas

2012 WL 612541 (N.D. 2012)

Eugene Camas died on March 23, 2011, leaving a will that provided, in pertinent part:

> *I hereby leave an undivided one-half (1/2) interest in and to the personal property located in my personal residence which I own at the time of my death to my daughter, SHERRY NESEMEIER.*
>
> . . . .
>
> *I give all of the rest, residue and remainder of my property and estate of every kind and character whatsoever, and wheresoever situated to my son, KEVIN CAMAS.*

Sherry Nesemeier, nka Sherry Jensen, argues that the term "personal property" includes intangible and tangible property, not just the tangible property located in the residence. Kevin Camas argues the contrary. The Supreme Court of North Dakota ruled in favor of Kevin, explaining:

> *From the unambiguous language of the will, it is clear Eugene Camas intended the popular meaning of "personal property" to apply to the bequest to Jensen. Eugene Camas limited the bequest to Jensen to one-half of his personal property "located in my personal residence[.]" By including this qualifying language, Eugene Camas demonstrated his intent to only include personal property that was physically located within his home. Intangible property "lacks a physical existence." Because intangible property cannot be "located" within a home, Jensen is entitled to a one-half interest in the tangible personal property located in Eugene Camas's residence. Courts in other jurisdictions have noted language describing the location of personal property indicates the property is limited to tangible personal property.*
>
> *Jensen also argues the district court erred in relying on the residuary clause to conclude the bequest to Jensen was limited to a one-half interest in the personal property found in Eugene Camas's residence. When interpreting a will, the court must, if possible, harmonize all parts of the will so every word and phrase is given effect. The bequest to Jensen disposed of only one-half of Eugene Camas's personal property located in his home. Therefore, the district court had to look to the other provisions of the will to determine the proper distribution of the estate. The will's residuary clause gave "the rest, residue and remainder of my property and estate of every kind and character whatsoever, and wheresoever situated" to Kevin Camas. The district court noted the residuary clause did not contain a qualifying phrase to describe property as the bequest to Jensen did. When construing the bequest to Jensen and the residuary clause together, the district court determined Eugene Camas intended to leave all of his property of every kind to Kevin Camas, except for the one-half interest in the tangible personal property located in his residence, which was left to Jensen. Because the bequest and*

the residuary clause can each reasonably be given effect, the district court did not err in considering both phrases to interpret the will.

Query: The court found the term *personal property* to be unambiguous. Would you agree? What kind of ambiguity did Sherry Jensen argue it to be? Should Sherry Jensen be entitled to half of the stock certificates located in Eugene's home? What about half the money in his bank accounts, where the checkbook and bank statements are all located in his home? Personal property usually means intangible property too. Why didn't it mean that here?

In re Est. of Flood

417 N.J. Super. 378 (N.J. Super.A.D., 2010)

Margaret A. Flood was survived by four children. Two of her children are disabled and the beneficiaries of supplemental security income and Medicaid programs; one of those two receives special residential services and other benefits from the Division of Developmental Disabilities (DDD). When judgment was entered, DDD's statutory lien exceeded $1,000,000; the lien has since grown at a rate in excess of $300 per day.

Margaret first considered estate planning following her husband's death in 2004. Margaret's daughter-in-law, who is an attorney, certified that Margaret was concerned about protecting the inheritances of her disabled daughters from any obligations to reimburse the governmental entities that had provided benefits and services. Although in late 2004 Margaret expressed these concerns and her desire to retain an attorney, it appears she did not consult an attorney until March and April 2008. Thereafter, Margaret's plans were interrupted first by the illness of one of her daughters and then by an injury she sustained in April 2008. Margaret died on May 24, 2008, with an estate valued at $480,000. She never executed a will or testamentary trust.

The estate's administrator filed this action, seeking the court's authorization to establish and fund the trusts he claims would have been created had Margaret's death not intervened. The matter came before the trial court on the return date of the initial order to show cause; DDD opposed the relief sought.

The bone of contention . . . turned on whether a court may animate such an intention in the complete absence of a will or testamentary trust. The trial judge rejected DDD's arguments and held that the doctrine of probable intent could reach that far.

We conclude that the trial judge's well-intended decision was based on a mistaken understanding of the applicable law. In the absence of a testamentary disposition, Margaret's estate passed by way of the laws of intestacy, and her children's interests vested immediately upon her death. The doctrine of probable intent—utilized here to do what Margaret failed to do in life—has no application in the absence of a will. Certainly, as the administrator argues, the doctrine of probable intent has evolved; it now represents, as our Supreme Court has held, a "broader and more liberal approach to will construction" than the prior insistence on formalistic results.

The doctrine permits the reformation of a will in light of a testator's probable intent by "searching out the probable meaning intended by the words and phrases in the will." Moreover, extrinsic evidence may be offered not only to show an ambiguity in a will but also, if an ambiguity exists, "to shed light on the testator's actual intent." . . .

Although there has been a progression from an era that exalted and enforced more formalistic limits, the doctrine of probable intent has never been applied to create a testamentary disposition when the decedent failed to execute a will. It "cannot be used to write a will that the testator did not write."

In essence, the doctrine of probable intent is a rule of construction or interpretation and, therefore, presupposes an existing testamentary disposition. Where there is no will there can be no will construction.

Query: What if Margaret had drafted extensive notes but not executed any will? What if a formal will was drafted but it was unexecuted? What if the formal will was drafted and executed, but it didn't have the correct number of witnesses? When should we draw the line in applying reformative doctrines and not applying them, allowing the estate to simply pass according to the default rules? What was Margaret's mistake?

In re Est. of Sherry

158 Wash.App. 69, 240 P.3d 1182 (Wash.App. Div.3 2010)

Audrene and Fred Sherry died in late 2007 and early 2008, respectively, each leaving wills that disposed of two major items of property to their three children Barbara, Mark, and Beverly. The first piece of property was shares of Fred Sherry Farms, Inc, a family farm corporation, and the other was fee ownership of additional farmland. Both wills provided that Mark, who was active in farming, be given his parents' shares in the farm corporation, including the real estate and personal property of Fred Sherry Farms. But Beverly and Barbara also owned shares in the corporation. Hence, to encourage them to give Mark their shares in order to consolidate them, both wills provided that Mark, as personal representative, is to "allocate and divide the farmland equally between my children," except that Mark is to receive shares in the corporation in lieu of other assets. Fred Sherry's will also added that "it is my desire for my three children to inherit assets of nearly equal value." Mark then distributed the farmland to himself and his two sisters as tenants in common and Barbara filed suit, claiming that the wills unambiguously required that Mark divide the property into separate fee simple parcels for each sibling. The trial court ruled that the wills were unambiguous and concluded that the terms *allocate and divide* did not require Mark to distribute separate property in fee simple. Barbara appealed, arguing that the wills were unambiguous in requiring distribution in fee simple, or in the alternative, that they are ambiguous and extrinsic evidence should be allowed to consider the intention of the testators regarding division of the farmland.

On appeal, the court found the wills to be ambiguous and reversed for additional extrinsic evidence, but explained as follows:

In support of Barbara's position that the wills require distribution of separate farmland in fee, she first points to the terms "divide" and "allocate," which she contends have a plain meaning that is opposite of tenancy in common, the essential attribute of which is unity of possession, . . . Mark responds that if a technical reading of the several words emphasized by Barbara conflicts with the remainder of the wills, then the meaning of those words yields to the meaning and legal effect of the wills as a whole. We agree with Mark, and begin by addressing whether the testators' intent is clear from the remaining language of the wills.

Both wills are clear that a principal objective of the Sherrys was to treat their children equally, or as close to equally as ble. . . . Equally clear is that both wills treat ownership of the stock of Fred Sherry Farms, Inc. as more important to Mark than to his sisters, and accommodate Mark's interest in two ways. Each will specifically bequeaths to Mark all of the parent's stock in Fred Sherry Farms in lieu of assets of equal value. In addition, both wills encourage the daughters to exchange their stock in the farm corporation with Mark for other assets, so that Mark can become the sole shareholder. . . . Finally, the Fred Sherry will reflects an intent, with respect to the farmland in his estate, to give Mark a limited prerogative in the event of a sale of farmland by Barbara or Beverly, granting Mark a 15-year right of first refusal.

In interpreting the wills, we are obliged to give effect to every part. The difference between the parents' treatment of stock in Fred Sherry Farms, Inc. and the farmland owned outright is clear, and cannot be ignored. When it comes to the farm corporation, the wills reflect Fred and Audrene Sherry's intentions that Mark receive all of their stock (with the daughters taking other assets) and a hope that, by exchanging other assets, Mark can become the sole owner. But when it comes to the farmland owned outside the corporation, neither will gives the land to Mark to the exclusion of the daughters, nor does either will grant Mark an option to acquire the farmland.

With respect to the farmland, equal treatment is the rule. It is to be allocated and divided "equally." . . . Having identified this intent, we next consider whether it compels us to construe "allocate and divide" to permit Mark to distribute undivided interests in the farmland. Allowing him to distribute undivided interests is consistent with his parents' recognition of his interest, and their evident desire, that he continue to farm—but a requirement that he allocate the farmland and distribute parcels in fee to his sisters is consistent with that intent as well. Reading the wills to require that Mark divide the farmland into separate parcels and allocate them among his sisters and himself allows him, subject to his fiduciary duty as personal representative, to allocate to himself that equal third of the farmland which, by location or type, best complements his farming operation. This is an advantage he would not have in a separate partition action. . . .

To allow distribution of undivided interests is a further and even more material departure from equal treatment. Undivided fractional interests in land have diminished value in light of the difficulty in finding a willing buyer. The court then reversed the trial court's ruling that the wills unambiguously allowed Mark to allocate joint interests, and instead held that the Audrene Sherry will unambiguously required distribution in fee simple. But the court also held that changes Fred Sherry made to his will after his wife's death, giving Mark a right of first refusal, made the allocate and divide language in Fred Sherry's will ambiguous. The court then remanded for consideration of extrinsic evidence.

Query: As you can see, even relatively simple directions, like "allocate and divide" can be quite difficult to construe, and courts will first look to the terms themselves. They can follow the plain meaning rule or, if the terms have specific legal meaning, follow the legal meaning. If simply looking at the words won't resolve the problem, then the courts will look to the will as a whole, trying to use different meanings/interpretations to harmonize the whole. If they still aren't sure, then the ambiguity allows for consideration of extrinsic evidence. Do you think Fred and Audrene's choice of Mark as personal representative, with the power to make the allocation decisions, indicated that he should have the power to distribute the property in undivided shares? Was this a case of Mark taking more than he should have, or was Barbara just angry that she wasn't given the power of deciding which farmland she would get? Should the Sherrys have simply divided up the farmland and let the kids negotiate so Mark could buy the corporate shares by exchanging farmland with his sisters? Would you have anticipated litigation over this issue? How would you have counseled Fred and Audrene?

Est. of Gill ex rel. Grant v. Clemson University Foundation

2012 WL 720378 (S.C.App. 2012)

Caroline Gill, in her will, bequeathed $100,000 to Clemson University to establish a scholarship for deserving football players. Then, to fund the $100,000 bequest, one year later, in an *Agreement*, Gill designated the scholarship and her estate as the beneficiary of $100,000 contained in her I.R.A. account with Morgan Stanley. After her death, Clemson claimed the $100,000 in the I.R.A. and then also requested $100,000 from Gill's estate pursuant to the provision in her will. The estate disagreed and the special referee, in a non-jury trial, found the will unambiguous and therefore refused to admit extrinsic evidence about how the will provision was to be funded. The estate appealed.

The Estate argues the special referee erred in failing to consider extrinsic evidence of Gill's intent because the terms of the Will and IRA beneficiary designation, as they pertain to the establishment and funding of the Scholarship, were ambiguous. We disagree.

The court explained that the paramount rule of will construction is to determine the testator's intent and that a will must be read in the ordinary and grammatical sense of the words employed. If the terms are ambiguous a court may look to extrinsic evidence to resolve the ambiguity and a court may admit extrinsic evidence to determine whether a latent ambiguity exists, and if the court finds a latent ambiguity, extrinsic evidence is also permitted to help the court determine the testator's intent.

At trial, the Estate asserted the Scholarship did not exist prior to the Will, and that fact alone created an ambiguity that required the special referee to resort to extrinsic evidence. On appeal, the Estate asserts a latent ambiguity in the Will provided the special referee with the legal authority to look beyond the "four corners" of the Will to extrinsic evidence to ascertain Gill's intent. Specifically, the Estate argues "a latent ambiguity exists when considering the circumstances as a whole and the documents that were executed to carry out [Gill's] intent." Thus, the Estate asserts the special referee should have considered "both [the] Will and the [Agreement] as part of her overall plan and scheme and construe the two together to determine her intent." The extrinsic evidence offered by the Estate consisted of the Agreement and witnesses presented by the Estate. Grant [her lawyer] testified he instructed Gill that if she designated a portion of her IRA to Clemson, she would get a charitable deduction of $100,000 and not have to pay ordinary income taxes on the $100,000. Linda Fraser, a financial advisor at Morgan Stanley, testified she went to Gill's home to meet with her, and Gill signed *the Agreement. Fraser said she was not familiar with the terms of the Will, and Grant told her the Agreement was for estate planning reasons to establish the Scholarship. She further testified that nothing in the Will states the IRA account was to satisfy the bequest to Clemson. Thomas Baldwin, co-personal representative, testified Gill told him she was going to set up the Scholarship, but he did not know about the Agreement until after her death.*

At trial, Clemson objected to parts of Grant's testimony as being hearsay and violative of the dead man's statute. The Estate argued his testimony was admissible as an exception to the hearsay rule under Rule 803(3), SCRE. The court sustained Clemson's hearsay objection, and Grant proffered testimony that Gill told him she intended for the IRA designation to fulfill the Clemson bequest created in the Will. The Estate asserts Grant's testimony should have been admissible to show that "the IRA Beneficiary Designation was part of [Gill's] overall scheme and that the designation was part of the plan to fund the gift expressed in [the] Will" and the "testimony is relevant because it goes to [Gill's] intent."

However, Grant's testimony related to a statement made by Gill almost a year after she created the Will; therefore, her statement was not made at the time of the making of the Will to show her belief at that time, and the hearsay exception provided in Rule 803(3) does not apply to the testimony. Accordingly, we hold the special referee did not err in prohibiting Grant's proffered testimony because it was not admissible under Rule 803(3), SCRE, as an exception to the hearsay rule.

The Estate argues the special referee erred in refusing to make a factual finding that Gill intended to make a single bequest of $100,000 to Clemson. We disagree.

The Estate asserts the testimony confirms this fact and, even if the special referee found the extrinsic evidence was not admissible, he could have found it was Gill's intent to leave a single bequest of $100,000. We already determined the special referee was correct in finding the Will was unambiguous, giving Clemson a bequest of $100,000. Because the IRA account was a non-testamentary asset that passed outside the Will, it would have been error for the special referee to make a finding that Gill only intended to make a single bequest of $100,000.

The Estate argues the special referee erred in failing to find the written beneficiary designation in the Agreement satisfies the contemporaneous writing requirement of S.C.Code Ann. § 62–2–610. We disagree.

Section 62–2–610 of the South Carolina Code provides:

Property which a testator gave in his lifetime to a person is treated as a satisfaction of a devise to that person in whole or in part, only if the will provides for deduction of the lifetime gift, or the testator declares in a contemporaneous writing that the gift is to be deducted from the devise or is in satisfaction of the devise, or the devisee acknowledges in writing that the gift is in satisfaction.

At trial, Clemson argued the Estate's claims were barred by this section. In its supplemental memorandum of law, the Estate argued in response that section 62–2–610 only contemplates lifetime gifts, and the IRA was not a gift during Gill's life because it did not pass until her death. In the alternative, the Estate asserted . . . that if the Agreement form was itself a lifetime gift, then it satisfied the contemporaneous writing requirement because it designated Clemson as the beneficiary. It also asserted Fraser's testimony regarding her meeting with Gill, and the fact that the Morgan

Stanley check was restricted to Clemson for the benefit of the Scholarship, when taken together with the Agreement, was sufficient to satisfy the statute's requirements.

Although Gill designated Clemson as a beneficiary on the IRA Agreement, the Will did not provide for the deduction of the money. Also, the Agreement did not state the IRA amount was to be deducted from the $100,000 devise or was in satisfaction of the devise. Further, Clemson did not acknowledge in writing that the IRA account was in satisfaction of the $100,000 devise. Therefore, we find the special referee correctly found the written beneficiary designation in the Agreement did not satisfy the contemporaneous writing requirement of section 62–2–610. The court affirmed the special referee's findings that there was no latent ambiguity in the will and that Clemson should receive $200,000, half from the will and half from the IRA.

Query: Assuming that Gill intended that Clemson receive only $100,000 for the scholarship identified in the will, and that the funds in the IRA were to be used to satisfy the bequest, what went wrong? Was there malpractice involved in the drafting of the will or was there improper review of the beneficiary designations under the IRA?[34] Can there ever be a latent ambiguity in a situation like this? Think back to our study of ademption and the contemporaneous writing doctrine. A devise will be judged adeemed by satisfaction if there is a contemporaneous writing that a life-time gift is intended to satisfy a will bequest. What went wrong here? Should there have been a codicil after the IRA designation was made to reflect the testator's intention that the IRA be used to fund the will bequest?

Est. of Mousel

271 Neb. 628, 715 N.W.2d 490 (Neb. 2006)

Opal [Mousel] died on December 18, 2003, leaving a last will and testament dated October 27, 1986. Opal was survived by [her husband] George, but George died on January 6, 2004, which was within 60 days of Opal's death. The will contained the following relevant provisions:

> *SECOND, after the payment of such debts and funeral expenses, I give, devise and bequeath our home residence, family automobile, household goods and personal effects to my husband, George A. Mousel, together with a life estate in my ranch real estate.*
>
> *THIRD, My interests in my ranch real estate I devise in the following shares: to George's brothers Paul—1/5th interest; to Charles—1/5th interest; to sister Madelene Coder—1/5th interest; to brother Ashur— 1/5th interest and to the two children of George's deceased sister, Lucille Haas: each a 1/10th interest in nephew Walter Haas and niece, Carolyn Knehans.*
>
> *FOURTH, I give devise and bequeath my interest in the West Half of the Southeast Quarter of 30–14–25 in Roger Mills County, Oklahoma to the children of my deceased brother, Orville Gaines, in equal shares*

---

[34] Problems often arise when brokers fill in beneficiary designations, not understanding that the particular wording is CRUCIAL to the plan. Therefore, in practice, an attorney either fills in the blank form with the client or reviews the completed form. But, the attorney can't actually establish the IRA in most jurisdictions.

who are Margie Gaines Bagley, Jerry Gaines, Jon Gaines and Susan Gaines subject to the life estate in my husband, George Mousel.

FIFTH, in the event that my husband and I meet simultaneous death in an accident or if he does not survive me for 60 days, I direct that the provisions for him shall lapse and my estate shall pass under paragraph Four, together with my residuary estate.

On September 16, 2004, Appellants [two children of Opal's deceased brother Orville Gaines] filed a petition for construction of the will. They asserted that the heirs named in paragraph "THIRD" (known hereinafter as George's relatives) and the heirs named in paragraph "FOURTH" (known hereinafter as Orville's children) were unable to agree as to the proper distribution of the interests in the ranch real estate described in paragraph THIRD. George's relatives filed a response to the petition, in which they asserted that paragraph THIRD showed Opal's intent that the ranch real estate pass to them, whether or not George survived 60 days after her death. Orville's children argued that because George died within 60 days after Opal's death, paragraph "FIFTH" controlled and that paragraph FIFTH provided that Opal's entire estate, including the ranch real estate, was to pass to them as the heirs named in paragraph FOURTH.

The trial court determined that the will was ambiguous and, in looking at the will as a whole, determined that the ranch real estate should be distributed according to article three, and the rest of her property according to article four. On appeal the court identified the ambiguity as patent and concluded that patent ambiguities cannot be resolved by recourse to extrinsic evidence. However, it affirmed the trial court, explaining:

Examining the will in its entirety and considering every provision, we conclude that Opal intended the interests in the ranch real estate should pass to George's relatives under paragraph THIRD whether or not George survived her for more than 60 days. Paragraph THIRD indicates a specific devise of the ranch real estate to George's relatives. Because the will makes a specific devise of the ranch real estate, the ranch real estate is not part of the residuary estate.

Although in isolation a reference to "my estate" might, as urged by Appellants, indicate the entire estate, we conclude that in the context of the entire will and giving consideration to all provisions of the will, Opal intended the interests in the ranch real estate to pass under paragraph THIRD to George's relatives and that her reference to "my estate" in paragraph FIFTH excluded this specific devise of the ranch real estate to George's relatives.

Query: The court concluded that the ambiguity here was patent and that patent ambiguities do not allow for examination of extrinsic evidence? Does that rule make sense to you? Can you think of a patent ambiguity that could be resolved by, for instance, reference to the scrivener's notes?

As you can see, ambiguities are very often in the eyes of the beholder. A term like "allocate and divide" seems unambiguous when referring to cash in a bank account, but could be ambiguous when referring to land. And the same term was held to be ambiguous in Fred Sherry's will but not in his wife's will. Does that make sense to you? The most important policy is toward discovering and effectuating the intent of the testator, but sometimes testators have an intention that is counter to the written terms of the will. In one crazy case the testator's son and daughter had quarreled about a partnership interest they shared, which the son convinced the daughter to surrender to him through fraud or misrepresentation. So the daughter sued the son. The testator then executed a phony will as a bluff disinheriting his daughter just to pressure her to accept her brother's offer of a cash settlement in the lawsuit. The court upheld the will even though the daughter had plenty of evidence suggesting that her father went through with the execution simply to pressure her to make up with her brother but he died before he could revoke it.[35] The moral: don't mess with legal documents unless you intend them to take effect.

Practice Point: Coordinating with Other Planners

In *Est. of Gill*, we see a stunning example of how important the beneficiary designation of an IRA can be to an estate plan. As a matter of review, IRAs generally will pass *outside* of the probate estate because they pass by operation of law to the beneficiaries designated by the agreement. And usually we think of named individuals being the best beneficiaries (as opposed to "my Estate") of those contracts since individuals can more easily take full advantage of the tax and distribution options provided by the IRA. But, this is not always the case. And you, as attorney, will be providing the advice on how the estate plan should line up; but keep in mind that another professional will most likely be establishing the very tools that will flow *with* your plan.

And, don't take it for granted that your non-attorney peers will have a detailed understanding of estates and trusts. As you can already see, this is a dense area and, in my experience, planners are very open to discussing concepts that might be a little bit fuzzy to them.

On more than one occasion, I have encountered contracts where the agent failed to correctly identify the client's trust as beneficiary. Take, for example, the case where your client tells his agent that he wants to name his trust as beneficiary of a certain policy but forgets to bring along the specific instructions that you gave him to the meeting. The agent, in turn, names "The Smith Trust" as beneficiary. Do you see a problem here? Only a Trustee can hold property, for one thing. For another, no date or context is provided to properly identify the trust. We can easily fix the designation by revising it "To Terry Smith, as Trustee, and to the Successor Trustees, of The Terry Smith Revocable Living Trust dated April 2, 2011, and any amendments thereto" but you will only know to do this if you stay on top of things.

For this reason, among others, estate planning attorneys often develop close relationships with their clients' accountants, financial planners, stock brokers and life insurance agents, often coordinating trust funding with all relevant parties. And, part of the many "review" meetings over time involves the examination of those beneficiary designations to ensure that the plan stays consistent with the clients' goals as they age.

---

[35] Est. of Duemeland, 528 N.W.2d 369 (N.D. 1995).

PROBLEMS

Consider the following situations and identify whether they involve latent or patent ambiguities. Also identify what, if any, evidence you think should be allowed in to resolve the ambiguity.

11.4. Mary's will leaves her "collection of 43 Amish quilts" to her sister Suzy and the residuary of her estate to her sister Aileen. After Mary's death, her Executor discovers that all 43 of Mary's quilts have labels identifying that they were made in China, even though she purchased them in Edinburgh, Indiana, known for its Amish communities. Suzy and Aileen both *really* want the quilts.

11.5. Tom wishes to leave his estate to his wife Teresa and, if she predeceases him, then to his two children equally. His will names Teresa as his wife in a section titled "My family" but in the distribution section, it reads that all property shall pass "to my husband."

11.6. Meika, a childless widow, asks an attorney to draft a will for her. Inttempting to save time on an "easy" plan, the attorney takes an existing will that he drafted for another widowed client, and switches out a few names. Meika executes the will later that day and dies the following year. The will gave her entire estate to Meika's brother, Ford, and if he predeceased her then to "my children in equal shares." Meika's other siblings contend that the word "children" was mistakenly used instead of "siblings" and her nieces claim the grant was to "his" children in equal shares instead of "my" children.

11.7. Jordan leaves his home, located at 222 Central Boulevard, to the Center for Creative Child Growth. Upon admission of the will to probate, it surfaces that Jordan's address was 222 Central Avenue and that there is no Center for Creative Child Growth in his town. There is, however, a Center for Creative Child Development, where Jordan spent many years volunteering.

E. FRAUD AND MISREPRESENTATION

If someone dressed as Mother Teresa approaches your elderly grandmother and convinces her to leave her entire estate to Mother Teresa's Missionaries of Charity, and you discover that Mother Teresa died in 1997, can you challenge your grandmother's will? The answer is, "it depends." Fraud and misrepresentation generally arise in two ways in the context of donative documents—fraud in the *execution* (where testators are defrauded about the nature of the documents or the contents of the documents they are executing) and fraud in the *inducement* (where testators are defrauded into making testamentary dispositions that they would not otherwise make). If the Mother Teresa lookalike never claimed to be Mother Teresa and simply asked your grandmother to leave her residuary estate to the Missionaries of Charity, she is doing nothing more than all charities do when they make pleas for financial assistance. But if she lied to your grandmother, telling her that she is Mother Teresa, and that she will damn your grandmother's soul for all eternity if she doesn't pay a price for her good prayers, than your grandmother has been defrauded.

The common law rules on fraud in the context of testamentary documents require that the misrepresentation be made with the *intent* of deceiving the testator and the *purpose* of influencing the devise, and the misrepresentation *must in fact influence* the disposition. Despite the simplicity of the rule, however, the law on fraud and misrepresentation is particularly thorny. Consider the following examples:

1.   O's beneficiary, A, convinces O not to change her will in favor of B, by claiming that he will convey his inheritances to B after O's death. As a result, O does not change her will and A does not give anything to B.

2.   O asks A to pick up her new will from the lawyer's office and bring it home for her to sign. On the way home, A substitutes a will he wrote leaving everything to himself. O signs the substitute will thinking it is her will.

3.   A is O's caregiver and tells O that he will only fix her creamed spinach every meal unless O buys A a car and agrees to leave the car to A in the will.

4.   O's favorite charity, the Red Cross, is racked by scandals one year and so O decides to leave her estate to A's favorite charity, the Sisters of Perpetual Indulgence. A explains how the sisters are a very pious organization that feeds and clothes the poor, when in fact they are a social organization that does nothing but party.

5.   The director of the Red Cross asks O to leave all her estate to the Red Cross, explaining that 95% of donations go to help those in need. O leaves her estate to the Red Cross because she wants to help tsunami victims, but after her death it is discovered that only 85% of donations go to help those in need.

6.   O learns from B that her favored niece, A, has started smoking again, and so she changes her will to leave everything to B instead. A has not started smoking again.

7.   O is on her deathbed and wants to make a will leaving everything to her favorite niece, A. B, who is A's only child, knows that A just died in a car accident but doesn't want to tell O this because the shock may make her medical situation worse. O goes through with her plan and makes a will leaving everything to A, and B takes A's share under the anti-lapse statute of their state. B would take nothing if O died intestate.

8.   O has a will leaving everything equally among her five children. Shortly before her death, O moves in with her oldest daughter, A who complains all the time about how much it is costing her to take care of O, and how her brothers and sisters are rolling in money and don't bother to help out at all. O changes her will to leave everything to A. All along, however, A's siblings have been writing checks to help pay for O's expenses and whenever they want to visit O, A tells them that O is too sick to see them.

9.   O has early stage Alzheimers and wants to make a will before her condition gets worse. She asks her caregiver, A, to call the lawyer but the caregiver stalls and stalls, meanwhile telling O that her family is neglecting her and wants to put her in a nursing home so they can be rid of the bother and expense of taking care of her. After O is convinced that her family doesn't care about her, A calls the lawyer who prepares O's will, leaving everything to A.

10. O died leaving everything to her husband, A, who had participated in a marriage ceremony with O three years before her death. At the time of the marriage, A was married to someone else and not free to marry O.

As you can see from these examples, fraud can be a tricky issue. Not only must there be intent on the part of the defrauder to influence the donative act, but the fraud must cause the testator to act in reliance on the misrepresentation. If the will is not the product of the fraud, then the will won't be set aside.

Another tricky issue is figuring out what to do if fraud or misrepresentation are proved. Though it is easy to impose a constructive trust on the defrauder to hold the property for the intended beneficiary, it isn't always easy to determine to whom the testator would have wanted the property to go. Go back over the examples above and see who you think should be entitled to the property in any cases where fraud or misrepresentation were present. If it's impossible to determine who the testator would have preferred had there been no fraud, then the will may be stricken and the estate will pass by intestacy, which may be a worse solution than allowing the defrauder to take the property. Once fraud has infected an estate plan, it is almost impossible to put the genie back in the bottle. The same is true of undue influence, which is present in some of the above examples.

Consider the following fraud cases and whether you think some equitable remedy should be available for the person who should have gotten the property.

McDaniel v. McDaniel

707 S.E.2d 60 (Ga. 2011)

Mary Agnes Royster McDaniel and Luther Lee "Mutt" McDaniel were married for over 60 years and had two sons, Charles and Jerry. They had executed joint reciprocal wills in 2002 leaving everything to their surviving spouse, and when the second spouse died all was to pass to their two sons equally. As the two approached their 90s, they began showing signs of dementia, and Charles and his wife moved into their home to help take care of them. Over the next few years, Charles' name was added to all their bank accounts, although on weekends Jerry would stay with the couple to give Charles a break in the caregiving. After the death of Mary Agnes in early 2007, Jerry suggested that Charles take a long vacation in Florida. While they were away, Jerry became convinced that Charles had stolen over $600,000 that he estimated was in the joint bank accounts. Jerry then convinced Mutt that Charles had stolen his money and had moved to Florida and wasn't coming back. Jerry then drove Mutt to all the banks to remove Charles' name from the joint accounts, called the lawyer to make an appointment to have the will changed, and changed the locks on the doors to the house all while Charles was in Florida. Jerry insisted at the meeting with the lawyer that a new will be drawn up leaving everything to himself, but the lawyer insisted on meeting with Mutt privately. At the meeting, Mutt told his lawyer that Charles had "gotten all the money from me he's going to get." When Jerry and Mutt went back to execute the new will the following day, Mutt also executed a durable power of attorney authorizing Jerry to take full control of all financial affairs and they instructed the lawyer to get a restraining order to keep Charles from coming back to his father's house. Over the next two years Charles was not allowed to see his father, except in Jerry's presence, and Mutt was soon moved into Jerry's basement, where he lived until his death. When Jerry offered the 2007 will for probate, Charles opposed it and offered the 2002 will leaving everything equally between the two sons, and he alleged fraud and undue influence in the drafting of the 2007 will. The jury found both fraud and undue influence and the court denied probate of the 2007 will. On appeal, the Georgia Supreme Court affirmed, stating:

> *Undue Influence: [T]he 2007 will radically changed the distribution of the estate envisioned by the testator's 2002 will, which would have divided the estate equally between the testator's two grown sons, to a scheme award-ing 89% of the estate to [Jerry] and nothing to [Charles]. See Holland v. Bell, 148 Ga. 277, 279, 96 S.E. 419 (1918) ("[W]here probate of the will is contested . . . for fraud and undue influence, 'it is always proper to inquire whether the provisions of the will are just and reasonable, and accord with the state of the testator's family relations, or the contrary.' " (citation omit-ted)). We therefore conclude that evidence regarding "the circumstances and surroundings of the testator and his associations" authorized the jury's find-ing that the 2007 will was the product of undue influence.*

> *Fraud: There was also sufficient evidence to support the jury's finding that the will was procured by fraud. See Edwards v. Shumate, 266 Ga. 374, 375–376, 468 S.E.2d 23 (1996) ("The type of fraud that 'will invalidate a will must be fraud which operates upon the testator, i.e., a procurement of the execution of the will by misrepresentations made to him. It exists only when it is shown that the testator relied on such a representation and was deceived.' "). The evidence showed that after [Jerry] and his wife encouraged [Charles] and his wife to go on vacation in Florida, they embarked on a campaign to convince the testator that [Charles] had stolen all his money, left him broke, and abandoned him by moving to Florida. These were mis-representations, but they worked; the testator changed his will to disinherit [Charles] completely. As a result of these misrepresentations, the [testator] went into the meeting with the attorney who drafted the 2007 will intending to leave his entire estate to [Jerry] . . . Accordingly, we conclude that the evidence supports the jury's finding that the 2007 will was procured through "misrepresentation" and "fraudulent practices upon the testator's fears, af-fections, or sympathies."*

Query: Did the lawyer have any duty to investigate the testator's claims that Charles had already gotten all the money he was going to get? Is there any-thing Charles could have done to stop Jerry's plan to brainwash their father?

In re Coviello

870 N.Y.S.2d 369 (N.Y.App.Div. 2d Dept. 2008)

The decedent, Pasquale Coviello, died unexpectedly in 2004, survived by his estranged third wife Isabel and his three daughters. One daughter, Angela, offered for probate a will drafted in 2003 by Michele Okin. Okin met the decedent when he and his wife first came to her office to have a post-nuptial agreement drafted for them in 1998. She continued to repre-sent them in various estate planning matters, but became intimately involved with the decedent in 2002, and they began living together in Jan-uary, 2003. The 2003 will appoints Okin as executor and bequeathed her the residue of his estate in a sentence placed at the end of a list of specific bequests to the decedent's children and other family members. The surrogate found both fraud and undue influence and the appellate division affirmed, stating: *While the proponent held herself out as a tax and estate expert prior to her disbarment in June 2004, she drafted Article VIII of the will to impose the entire burden of the estate tax on the specific bequests, contrary to the decedent's stated intention for the entire estate to bear the taxes "across the board." Moreover, given that an estate tax in the sum of $2 million was imposed on the estate subsequent to the decedent's death, the tax allocation virtually nullified the specific bequests despite the decedent's intention to provide for his family as well as Okin....   The Surrogate properly found that the proponent intentionally misrepresented the terms of the propounded will, which caused the decedent to dispose of his property in a manner different from that which he intended.*

Query: Was this an example of fraud and undue influence, or rather an example of bad lawyering? Although perhaps it is never a good idea to draft your lover's will, can a fiancée or spouse ever draft a partner's will without it raising some red flags? Okin and the decedent were engaged, even though he was still married to his third wife at the time of his death. Is his third wife entitled to an elective share? How should this estate be disposed of?

In re Est. of Richmond

701 N.W.2d 897 (N.D. 2005)

Lois Bristol, the decedent, was a widow with one child, Karen Black. During the fall of 1976 Lois started dating Donald Richmond who was married and had three children, but who then separated from his wife in 1978. Although Richmond had not sought a divorce when he moved in with Lois, he told Lois that his wife had begun divorce proceedings. In 1982, while at a trade show in Chicago, Lois met with Donald's wife and was allegedly told that the divorce had gone through. Donald was not present at the meeting between Lois and his wife, but testified that Lois returned from the meeting and told him *"Henrietta said the divorce is complete. She showed me some papers, and she's going to send me copies of them. So she said, You're divorced. She said, No sense in putting it off. Let's get married. So we got married."* After the marriage, Lois executed a will bequeathing everything to Donald, but if he failed to survive her, then everything to Karen Black. After Lois's death, one of Donald's children contacted Karen informing her that Donald and his first wife, Henrietta, had not divorced as no records could be found of any divorce proceeding. Karen Black then filed a petition contesting her mother's will alleging that Donald "knowingly and willfully misled the decedent into an unlawful void marriage by misrepresenting to decedent that he was divorced from his first wife." The trial court granted summary judgment in favor of Donald and Karen Black appealed. In affirming the trial court, the North Dakota Supreme Court stated:

Because fraud must be proven by clear and convincing evidence, the actual quantum and quality of proof necessary to support liability must be considered in determining whether a genuine factual issue as to fraud exists. If the evidence presented is of insufficient caliber or quantity to allow a rational finder of fact to find fraud by clear and convincing evidence, there is no genuine issue of material fact.

Actual fraud is defined in N.D.C.C. § 9–03–08 as:

1. *The suggestion as a fact of that which is not true by one who does not believe it to be true;*

2. *The positive assertion, in a manner not warranted by the information of the person making it, of that which is not true though he believes it to be true;*

3. *The suppression of that which is true by one having knowledge or belief of the fact;*

4. *A promise made without any intention of performing it; or*

5. *Any other act fitted to deceive.*

The burden is on the party asserting fraud to establish the elements of fraud, including an intent to deceive. Fraud is never presumed, even under circumstances that give rise to a suspicion of fraud. Although fraud actions are not usually suited for disposition by summary judgment, if the plaintiff fails to support her opposition to a summary judgment motion with sufficient facts to show that there is a genuine issue for trial, then summary judgment is appropriate.

Black's theory is that Donald deceived Lois into believing he was divorced from Henrietta so Lois would marry him and name him as a devisee in her will. Consequently, to prevail, Black has the burden of proving by clear and convincing evidence that Donald fraudulently induced Lois into marrying him and that Lois would not have devised property to Donald in her 2001 will had she known that Donald and Henrietta were not divorced. We believe Black has failed to raise a genuine issue of material fact regarding either allegation.

Query: Ironically, a well-known California case of 1920, *Est. of Carson* (194 P. 5) discussed precisely this issue as a hypothetical, whether the marriage should be treated as fraud by a "marital adventurer" or as a happy relationship of 20 years such that knowledge of the truth would not have changed the disposition. In *Carson*, the court easily concluded that the marriage was a fraud. The issue in *Richmond* is the same: was the will the fruit of the fraud, or would the will have been made even if the truth about the invalidity of the marriage were known. Do you think the outcome would have been the same in either *Richmond* or *Carson* had the decedent been the husband, and the proponent of the will the widow?

Mysterious Case of Huguette Clark[2]

Huguette Clark, the heiress to a copper mining fortune amassed by her father, Senator William Andrews Clark, died at the age of 104, a recluse for the last 70 years of her life, living in a hospital room for the last 20 years under various pseudonyms. She was attended by a nurse who benefitted handsomely during life and received $30 million in Clark's will for her devotion. And her attorney and accountant, who had managed her affairs for years, also benefitted during life to the tune of gifts worth several millions of dollars. They each received $500,000 at her death. Roughly 75% of her estate went to charitable causes. But her attorney and account-

---

[2] *Huguette Clark Estate: More Than $300 Million At Stake In Legal Battle Over Properties*, **HUFFPOST N.Y.**, (Oct. 5, 2012), http://www.huffingtonpost.com/2012/10/05/huguette-clark-estate-300-million-legal-battle_n_1942592.html.

ant, Wallace Bock and Irving Kamsler respectively, were appointed trustees of the charitable foundation which would generate millions in fees for them and their successors. A criminal investigation is underway to determine if Clark was unduly influenced and whether Bock or Kamsler mismisappropriated any of her vast fortune. Clark executed two wills within six weeks of each other in 2005, the first leaving most of her property to her extended family; the second left most of her property to her charity, her nurse, doctors, and other friends, stating explicitly that none was to go to her family. Currently the New York Public Administrator is handling her estate, but there will no doubt be litigation over the table scraps of her half a billion dollar fortune.

Fraud, misrepresentation, and undue influence all tie together in many instances. Fraud is a subset of misrepresentation, consisting of misstatements made with the intent to deceive. Misrepresentation can be innocent and unintentional. Undue influence might not involve any misstatements or fraudulent acts, but in many circumstances misstatements are made. Undue influence can rise to the level of duress if extreme pressure is put on a testator to overwhelm her true wishes. The fine lines between each of these doctrines are a product of state common law, and you should study those distinctions carefully if you are going to practice in this area. Although all of these acts can occur in the context of commercial transactions between arms-length sophisticated negotiators, they are far more likely to occur in the context of donative transfers where testators are susceptible to overreaching by marital adventurers, fortune hunters, disgruntled relatives, or anyone hoping to be on the receiving end of a sizable gift.

We have already studied the issues of mental capacity and insane delusion that can cause a testator's will or other testamentary documents to be voided. When testators have some kind of mental infirmity they may make decisions about their property that don't comport with their truententions, intentions that were formed when their minds were capable and strong. Weakened testators are often the prey of overreaching by those seeking to obtain property belonging to others. But even strong and vital testators can be duped by fraud or misrepresentation, or can give in to undue influence or duress. Proving that the victim was of sound and able mind is not enough to defeat an allegation of wrongdoing. But as you can see from the many cases we've covered so far, most of the cases involving wrongdoing occurred against testators who were of a weakened physical or mental state. Consequently, it's not always clear whether the proper claim should be incapacity or misrepresentation. Even the relatively simple case of mistake might be better litigated under a theory of misrepresentation if appropriate.

So far we have studied what happens when there is a problem and the will, or portions of it, are voided. The wrongdoer will not receive her gift or, in the case of incapacity, the infected will is thrown out and the property passes according to an earlier will or intestacy. In all of these cases, someone wins and someone loses. What often happens, however, is that the effect of someone's wrongdoing causes an innocent person to lose, and the laws of the state won't permit rewriting a will or following the testator's clear intent. In that case, the wrongdoer may be prevented from winning, but the loser still loses. If the courts cannot devise a remedy to effectuate the testator's true intent, usually through a constructive trust, and the estate passes by intestacy or according to a prior will that the testator really didn't want, the intended beneficiary is generally out of luck. But thanks to liberalizing trends in evidence, and in furthering testamentary intent, a new tort claim can sometimes come to the aid of the loser through the tort of tortious interference with expectancy.

F. TORTIOUS INTERFERENCE WITH EXPECTANCY

A relatively new theory of tort liability has arisen to deal with the wrong done to an intended beneficiary by someone who, through fraud, duress, or undue influence, causes a testator to change an estate plan, but a constructive trust or other remedy cannot make the intended beneficiary whole. Called *Tortious Interference with an Expectancy,* or *Wrongful Interference with an Inheritance*, this cause of action allows for a tort suit against the wrongful beneficiary, even if the wrongdoer does not benefit from her misdeeds.

Imagine a case where a testator wrote a will 40 years ago leaving everything to her husband, but he died 15 years ago. Since his death, her favorite niece has been taking exceptional care of her and the testator decides to make a new will, leaving all to the niece. But just as she is about to make the new will, her estranged son arrives on the scene and tells her that the niece has just been killed in a car accident, which he knows is untrue. The shock of the news causes the testator to have a heart attack from which she never recovers, and she dies intestate since the bequests in the 40-year-old will lapsed. Her estate passes by intestacy to her five children, including the estranged son, none of whom have taken any interest in her for the past 10 years. Certainly the four siblings did nothing wrong, and a court would be unlikely to take their inheritances away. And even if the guilty son loses his inheritance, it is unlikely that a court would grant the testator's estate to the niece since the testator did not actually complete a will giving the niece any of her property. (Remember *Est. of Flood*?) But if the niece can prove that the estranged son acted with the intent to wrongfully interfere with the niece's inheritance, she may be able to recover against him in tort.

Many states still do not recognize the tort claim, and those that do have sometimes hedged the doctrine with certain other limitations. For instance, some states rule that if a person challenges a will for fraud or undue influence and loses, she is barred from suing in tort under the doctrine of *res judicata*. But even if she is successful in the fraud suit, and the will is thrown out, the new beneficiaries may be heirs at law, not the victim of the fraud.

Consider again the case of Anna Nicole Smith and J. Howard Marshall. J. Howard was an immensely wealthy Texas oil tycoon who met Anna Nicole at a strip club in Houston when he was 86 and she was 28. After seeing her dance, he asked her out to lunch and then began to bestow lavish gifts on her. He proposed many times, declaring that she was the "light of his life" and that he wanted to marry her. He allegedly offered her half his fortune if she would accept. After three years of courtship, during which time Anna appeared in *Playboy Magazine* and landed a gig advertising Guess Jeans, Anna Nicole finally agreed and they were married. Eighteen months later, J. Howard died at the age of 90. He was survived by two sons and his wife, Anna Nicole.

During the courtship and later marriage, J. Howard's oldest son, E. Pierce Marshall, restricted Anna Nicole's access to J. Howard's accounts to such an extent that she ended up in bankruptcy court. During the bankruptcy hearing, it was established that E. Pierce had siphoned off much of J. Howard's assets, he had purchased annuities on J. Howard's life that could only be justified if he was expected to live at least five more years (which given his health was unlikely) and E. Pierce and his lawyer backdated, destroyed, or altered documents. They presented documents to J. Howard for his signature and lied about their effect. The bankruptcy court found that this was done to prevent Anna Nicole from receiving any of J. Howard's money and to prevent J. Howard from making a will to benefit Anna Nicole.

The bankruptcy court applied the following test for tortious interference with an expectancy:

A plaintiff must prove

(1) the existence of an expectancy;

(2) a reasonable certainty that the expectancy would have been realized but for the interference;

(3) intentional interference with that expectancy;

(4) tortious conduct involved with the interference; and

(5) damages.[36]

The bankruptcy court found that E. Pierce was guilty of interfering in Anna Nicole's expectancy and also imposed punitive damages. But with over $1.5 billion at stake, E. Pierce did not accept the bankruptcy court's ruling and appealed to the U.S. District Court, which reviewed the case de novo and affirmed. The District Court awarded Anna Nicole some $44.3 million in compensatory damages and, based on "overwhelming" evidence of E. Pierce's willfulness, maliciousness, and fraud," an equal amount in punitive damages. E. Pierce then appealed to the Ninth Circuit which reversed, holding that the probate exception to federal jurisdiction precluded the claim.[37] On appeal by Anna Nicole, the U.S. Supreme Court reversed the Ninth Circuit, holding that the District Court's jurisdiction was proper, and reinstating the District Court's ruling.[38]

On remand the Ninth Circuit found that the tortious interference claim was not a core proceeding in the bankruptcy court and that the state court judgment in favor of E. Pierce was entitled to preclusive effect.[39] The Ninth Circuit reversed and remanded the issue to the District Court, but Anna Nicole appealed the decision again to the U.S. Supreme Court, which upheld the Ninth Circuit decision that found the matter was beyond the constitutional scope of the bankruptcy court.[40] During all of this time, litigation was proceeding in Texas state courts regarding the probate of the estate, Anna Nicole's alleged defamation of E. Pierce, and E. Pierce's alleged tortious interference with Anna Nicole's expectancy. E. Pierce prevailed in most of the state court litigation. And ironically, much of this litigation occurred after the death of E. Pierce, who had died in 2006 and

---

[36]   See Doughty v. Morris, 871 P.2d 380 (N.M. 1994).

[37]   In re Marshall, 392 F.3d 1118 (9th Cir. 2004).

[38]   Marshall v. Marshall, 547 U.S. 293 (2006).

[39]   In re Marshall, 600 F.3d 1037 (9th Cir. 2010).

[40]   Stern v. Marshall, 131 S.Ct. 2594 (2011).

was carried on by his executor, his wife. The rest is tabloid fodder. Anna Nicole's son by her first husband, Daniel Smith, died at age 20 from a drug overdose while visiting his mother in her hospital room, just after she had given birth prematurely to her daughter, Danielynn in September, 2006. In February, 2007, Anna Nicole died from a drug overdose in her hotel room in Hollywood, Florida, and thus commenced a media frenzy about the parentage and future of the infant Danielynn and, more importantly, her estate. If Anna Nicole's estate is successful in getting her share of J. Howard's estate away from E. Pierce's estate, then Danielynn will be a very wealthy child and her guardian will be entitled to a sizable allowance for her upbringing.

State courts have taken quite divergent approaches to whether or not a tortious interference with expectancy claim can be maintained outside of the probate process. It seems only fair, if a contestant has shown that an undue influencer produced a will through fraud and misrepresentation that resulted in the loss of an inheritance, that she should be able to recover. But the fly in the ointment is trying to figure out, as with J. Howard and Anna Nicole, what she would have received had the wrongdoer not interfered. Would J. Howard really have written a will giving her half of his estate? Should evidence and statements from witnesses that he said he would give her half his estate permit a court to give it to her, despite the fact that he never wrote a new will and never took actual steps to make the testamentary gifts happen? Did J. Howard not keep his half of the bargain after Anna Nicole married him? This is the kind of case where settlements usually come into play, although people can get very adamant about their entitlements when messy marriages, divorces, or other family dynamics get in the way.

Consider the following cases and whether you think the courts properly considered the interests of the various parties and the equities that come into play:

Peralta v. Peralta

139 N.M. 231 (Ct.App. N.M., 2005)

After the death of her husband in 1979, Helen Peralta [decedent] executed a will leaving her estate to her three children [Nora, Manfred and Ruby] or their survivors equally. At that same time, Nora was living with Helen and, together with Delores Valdez, providing care for Helen when it was needed. In December 1994, Manford removed Helen from her residence and moved her to live with him and/or Ruby. Shortly thereafter, in March 1995, Helen's bank accounts were changed to payable-on-death accounts for the benefit of Manford and Ruby. At the same time, Helen executed a codicil to her 1979 will that excluded Nora and divided her estate between Manford and Ruby. In January 1996, Helen transferred by quitclaim deed the sole remaining asset in her estate, a piece of property with a house and apartments, to Manford and Ruby and their respective spouses.

During this time, Manford and Ruby maligned Nora to Helen, telling her that Nora had no use for her and would not take care of her. The transfer of the assets of the estate were concealed from Nora for several years. Helen died on August 2, 1999, at the age of 94. There was no probate of her estate.

Nora Peralta then filed suit against her brother Manford Peralta and her sister Ruby Archuleta seeking to recover assets of their mother . . . that had been diverted prior to Helen's death by Manford and Ruby

(Defendants). The district court granted summary judgment to Manford and Ruby on the basis that Nora's action should have been brought in a probate proceeding on behalf of the estate. Nora appeals the order granting summary judgment.

Nora first claimed that Manford and Ruby unduly influenced their mother to cut her out of the inheritance. In a summary judgment hearing, the district court *expressed concern that the estate had not been included in Nora's suit and that her claim had not been made in connection with probate. The district court granted the motion for summary judgment on grounds different from those argued by Defendants, ruling:*

> *There is no case. There is absolutely no case because if there was any undue influence, it was exerted on the senior Mrs. Peralta, who is dead; and the damage, if any, was done to her or her estate. . . . Without an estate, you don't have a case. It wasn't brought in the name of the estate or against it but, more importantly, in the name of the estate, which is something your client could have undertaken to do, is open up an estate and say, I'm suing on behalf of my mother; it has been dissipated by the following misconduct on the part of these putative heirs. Maybe you have a case there, but you don't now.*

The court of appeals reversed and remanded, explaining: *We must decide whether Nora was required to proceed on her claim in probate.*

In 1994, we recognized a cause of action against those who intentionally interfere with an expected inheritance. Doughty v. Morris, 117 N.M. 284, 287, 871 P.2d 380, 383 (Ct.App.1994). In that case, a will beneficiary alleged that her brother had tortiously interfered with her inheritance by coercing their ailing mother into making certain inter vivos transfers of property, which resulted in no property remaining in the estate to divide as the will specified. Relying on the Restatement (Second) of Torts, § 774B (1979), we recognized the tort of interference with a prospective inheritance. Thus, we allowed the cause of action where an inter vivos transfer of property depleted the estate and left nothing to be transferred in probate. The elements of the cause of action are: "(1) the existence of an expectancy; (2) a reasonable certainty that the expectancy would have been realized, but for the interference; (3) intentional interference with that expectancy; (4) tortious conduct involved with interference, such as fraud, duress, or undue influence; and (5) damages."

In 2002, we were asked to decide whether the tort of intentional interference with expected inheritance would lie where probate proceedings were available to address the distribution of disputed assets and would otherwise provide an adequate remedy. [In that case] the plaintiffs were beneficiaries of a trust that would have allowed each of them to receive one-third of their uncle's estate. About five years later, the uncle drastically changed the testamentary plan on the urging of a third party so that the plaintiffs' share of the estate was distributed to a nursing home. When their uncle died, the plaintiffs indicated that they were challenging the revised testamentary plan. No formal probate proceeding was instituted. However, the trustee filed an interpleader and informal probate proceeding, which eventually resulted in a settlement where plaintiffs each received 18.7875 percent of the estate. Sometime thereafter, the plaintiffs filed a lawsuit alleging that the defendants had tortiously interfered with their inheritance.

We decided, following the majority of our sister states, "that a cause of action for tortious interference with an expected inheritance will not lie when probate proceedings are available to address the disposition of disputed assets and can otherwise provide adequate relief." We determined that "when property passes subject to a testamentary instrument, it is preferable to conclude the dispute at one setting, which ordinarily will afford injured parties an opportunity for substantial relief." We stated that the preferred proceeding was in probate because the legislature had enacted the Probate Code to deal with such matters and we did not want to undermine the legislative intent in enacting the Probate Code.

We are now faced with a case falling between Doughty *and* Wilson. *Defendants argue that the proper forum for resolution of the issues raised by Nora is pursuant to the Probate Code. It is true that any action attacking the testamentary capacity of the decedent should be brought pursuant to the Probate Code. Defendants argue that Nora placed the validity of her parents' will and Helen's codicil into issue, thus putting this case squarely within the holding of* Wilson. *Nora counters that her case falls within the holding of* Doughty *because she is attacking the inter vivos transfers of all the property in Helen's estate before she died. Contrary to the arguments of the parties, we believe this case does not fall precisely within the holding of either* Doughty *or* Wilson *because there was both an inter vivos transfer of all the property in Helen's estate as well as a claim of improper influence in the revision of Helen's will to exclude Nora.*

Although a probate proceeding would be the proper place to attack the codicil, such an attack does not provide an adequate remedy here. If Nora were to prevail and have the codicil set aside, she is placed in the same situation as the Doughty *plaintiff. There is no estate left to distribute under the will. It is this injustice that the tort of intentional interference with inheritance was meant to remedy. We conclude that in a situation where the estate has been depleted so that there could be no remedy in probate, proceeding in a civil action is appropriate.*

While a probate proceeding would have been futile for Nora to pursue, in order to establish her claim for tortious interference with expected inheritance, she would nonetheless have to challenge the validity of Helen's codicil in order to establish the existence of an expectancy that she would inherit from Helen if Manford and Ruby had not interfered with that expectancy, which is an element of her tort cause of action. Under our holding, on remand Nora may attack the codicil in an attempt to prove her tort claim.

The court then recognized the different burdens of proof that Nora may face in proving undue influence by a clear and convincing standard while tortious interference need only be proved by a preponderance of the evidence standard. But it felt confident the district court could apply the different standards to the different elements of Nora's claim.

Query: The New Mexico court held that there would be no cause of action for tortious interference with an expectancy if the claimant had a remedy in the probate court. But assuming a tort claimant should be entitled to full damages for the interference, will a probate judgment ever provide a full remedy? And assuming a claimant can challenge a will or codicil that was not even probated, are we at risk of making probate irrelevant?

Economopoulos v. Kolaitis

528 S.E.2d 714 (Va. 2000)

Michael A. Kolaitis died on April 21, 1997. He had four children, Anastasia Economopoulos, Aphroditi Kolaitis, Fereniki Kolaitis, and Andrew M. Kolaitis. By separate four-count motions for judgment, Anastasia Economopoulos, Aphroditi Kolaitis, and Fereniki Kolaitis (the Plaintiffs) sued Andrew M. Kolaitis (the Defendant). Each Plaintiff sought to recover $262,500 in compensatory damages and $50,000 in punitive damages arising from the redemption of certain Treasury bills. The Plaintiffs alleged conversion and misappropriation in Count I, constructive fraud in Count II, unjust enrichment in Count III, and "tortious interference with inheritance" in Count IV. The Plaintiffs also sought certain equitable relief, including the imposition of a constructive trust.

The facts showed that the decedent, Michael, had operated a Parkington Sleep Center in Arlington County, Virginia and that, in 1966, his son Andrew began working at the business. Over time, Andrew took over the business and the two had extensive intermingled assets until 1990 when the business was sold for $3 million. *Michael invested his portion of the sale proceeds in five Treasury bills: three $200,000 bills, each titled jointly with a daughter; a $50,000 bill titled jointly with Andrew; and a $250,000 bill titled solely in Michael's name. From April 1990 until May 1996, Michael renewed the Treasury bills quarterly. In 1994, Michael executed a codicil to his 1992 will, directing his executor (Andrew) to divide into three equal shares $600,000 of the Treasury bill funds and to pay the shares to his three daughters.* After being diagnosed with kidney failure, *Michael directed Andrew to retrieve Michael's NationsBank checkbook from his house. On May 16, 1996, Andrew brought the checkbook to the hospital, and Michael instructed Andrew to prepare a check, which Michael signed, payable to Andrew and in the amount of $300,000. At that time, Michael's account did not contain sufficient funds to cover the check.*

On May 17, 1996, while Michael was hospitalized, Andrew went to Michael's home and retrieved Michael's mail, including renewal notices for the Treasury bills. Michael, however, had decided to redeem all of the Treasury bills so that he would have control over his funds. Consequently, Michael directed Andrew to hold the $300,000 check until June 27, 1996, the day the Treasury bills were to be redeemed and the funds deposited in Michael's NationsBank account. Michael also directed Andrew to place the funds represented by the check in an account in Andrew's name and to hold the funds until further notice. Andrew did as directed.

In early July 1996, Michael told Andrew that he wanted $140,000 of the $300,000 returned to him and that the $160,000 balance was a gift to Andrew. Consequently, at Michael's direction, Andrew drew two checks, payable to Michael, each in the amount of $70,000. Thereupon, Michael deposited one of the checks in a new Signet Bank account, and he deposited the other $70,000 check in his existing account at Chevy Chase Bank. The funds remained in these two accounts, subject to Michael's control, until his death. Upon Michael's death, the funds were paid to Andrew.

On July 11, 1996, Michael executed a new will by which he divided his residuary estate equally among his four children. By his new will, Michael also revoked all prior wills and codicils. This will was admitted to probate upon Michael's death.

The Virginia Supreme Court found there was insufficient evidence to show a confidential relationship or to meet the prima facie elements of fraud. The Court also agreed that the plaintiffs had not met their burden in proving conversion, tortious interference with inheritance, or unjust enrichment explaining: *the failure to renew the Treasury bills cannot be a conversion because, even assuming that Andrew Kolaitis was involved in the fact that they were not renewed, the monies from the T-bills went into an account in Michael Kolaitis' name.*" Because the uncontradicted evidence showed that Michael intended to make the $160,000 gift to Andrew, there was no unjust enrichment. About tortious interference, the court explained:

> *We also agree with the trial court that a cause of action for "tortious interference with inheritance" is not recognized in Virginia. A person who is mentally competent and not subject to undue influence may make any disposition of his property he chooses during his lifetime or by will at his death. Moreover, the Plaintiffs had only an expectancy in the Treasury bills while Michael was alive and in control of them.*

Query: What do you think Michael was thinking in the hospital when he wrote the $300,000 check to Andrew? Do you think Andrew was simply doing his father's bidding, or was he subtly controlling Michael? Did Andrew tell Michael that he would distribute the $160,000 among the four siblings or did Michael want Andrew to keep the entire amount, knowing it would reduce the inheritances of the other three children? Assuming the court is correct that there is no cause of action for tortious interference in Virginia, what remedy would the daughters have if Andrew had in fact been unduly influencing their father? Is this another case of wrongful *inter vivos* transactions reducing the size of the probate estate so that the will beneficiaries take less? Can undue influence be used to set aside *inter vivos* transfers?

Allen v. Hall

974 P.2d 199 (Or. 1999)

> *The underlying case arises out of a tort action that was filed in the United States District Court for the District of Oregon under 28 USC § 1332 (diversity of citizenship). The case was assigned to a magistrate judge. In that action, plaintiffs Kristine Sandoz Allen and Eric Sandoz alleged the following facts, as summarized by the magistrate judge:*

> "Following heart transplant surgery in 1984, Gregory Putman developed a number of serious medical problems. As his illness advanced, Putman became increasingly dependent on [defendants Sheryl and Daniel] Hall[ ] for assistance in managing his medical and financial needs. During the last four years of his life, Putman gave the Halls possession of various wills he had executed, placed Sheryl Hall's name on his bank accounts, and placed title to various motor vehicles in the Halls' names.

> "On October 9, 1995, Putman executed a will devising substantially all of his assets, including homes in Pacific City, Oregon, and Oregon City, Oregon, to the Halls. That will, prepared on Putman's home computer, devised nothing to plaintiffs. Putman gave the Halls the original of this will.

> "Putman drafted a second will on his home computer on October 13, 1995. This will, unlike the will executed four days earlier, left Putman's Oregon City home to plaintiffs.

"Putman met with an attorney, Stephanie Barrie, on October 19, 1995, in order to draft and execute a new will. Putman brought a copy of the October 13, 1995 draft with him to that meeting, and told Barrie that he wanted to leave his Oregon City home to plaintiffs. Putman told Barrie that his illness required that the new will be prepared immediately. Barrie prepared a will according to these instructions.

"Defendant Sheryl Hall became aware of Putman's efforts to change his will, and brought Putman for admission to Good Samaritan Hospital in Portland, Oregon, on October 30, 1995. At the hospital, Sheryl Hall falsely stated that Putman had been confused during the previous two weeks.

"Putman telephoned Barrie's office from the hospital on October 31, 1995, asking Barrie to return his call on his pager. Sheryl Hall telephoned Barrie the same day, asking Barrie to call her on Putman's pager regarding Putman's will.

"The next day, Barrie spoke with Sheryl Hall by telephone. Sheryl Hall told Barrie that Putman could not execute a new will because he was not lucid, and agreed to inform Barrie when he was lucid enough to sign a will. Sheryl Hall never telephoned Barrie with such information.

"On November 3, 1995, Sheryl Hall falsely claimed to have a power of attorney to decide whether Putman should be given life support, and instructed the Good Samaratin Hospital staff not to provide such support to Putman. Putman died two days later, deprived by Sheryl Hall's conduct of the opportunity to execute the will Barrie had prepared."

The Plaintiffs alleged that but for the Halls' intentional interference, they would have inherited the Oregon City home. They sought $245,000, the value of the home, in damages. On the Halls' motion, the district court dismissed the action for failure to state a claim. The magistrate judge opined that, although some jurisdictions have recognized a claim for intentional interference with prospective inheritance, Oregon courts have not, and most likely would not, follow that trend. On plaintiffs' appeal, the Ninth Circuit concluded that, in the absence of controlling precedent from the courts of this state regarding the existence or elements of the tort of intentional interference with prospective inheritance, certification of the existence of the cause of action was appropriate. The Oregon Supreme Court then explained:

1.   Does Oregon recognize the tort of intentional interference with prospective inheritance?

On the facts presented, this case does not afford this court a reason to resolve that specific question. It is true that this court to date has not recognized a separate and distinct claim of intentional interference with a prospective inheritance. The reason that the issue need not be answered now (or, perhaps, ever) is that, under Oregon law, an intentional interference with a prospective inheritance may be actionable under a reasonable extension of the well-established tort known as intentional interference with economic relations. Although, heretofore, this court has applied that tort only to contractual and business relationships and prospects, we are persuaded that the tort also may, by a reasonable and principled extension, be made applicable to some noncommercial relationships and prospects, such as the one alleged by plaintiffs in the present case.

Our cases to date have stated the elements of the tort of intentional interference with economic relations as follows: (1) the existence of a professional or business relationship (which could include, e.g., a contract or a prospective economic advantage); (2) intentional interference with that relationship or advantage; (3) by a third party; (4) accomplished through improper means or for an improper purpose; (5) a causal effect between the interference and the harm to the relationship or prospective advantage; and (6) damages. As noted, this court heretofore has applied those elements only to business and contractual relationships and prospects. It follows that, before we attempt to relate the allegations in the present complaint to the elements of that tort, we must explain why the tort may, by a reasonable and principled extension, be made applicable to a prospective inheritance— typically a noncommercial expectancy.

The answer lies in the very close analogy that exists between an expectancy of inheritance and those other interests to which this court already has extended the protections of the tort of intentional interference with prospective economic advantage. Although an expectancy of inheritance is, by definition, purely prospective, so are many of the commercial interests that have been associated with and are protected by the tort. Moreover, prospects of inheritance long have been recognized as interests that are worthy of common-law protection. Ultimately, an expectancy of inheritance is an interest that fits by logical extension within the concept underlying the tort of intentional interference with prospective economic advantage and, absent some legitimate reason for excluding it, may be deemed to be covered by that theory of recovery.

Defendants . . . argue that recognizing any liability in tort for the kind of interference alleged here could undermine a central element of this state's common law and statutory system of probate—the so-called "testamentary intent" rule. That rule holds that, for purposes of disposing of a decedent's estate, the decedent's intent is to be ascertained only from the four corners of a validly executed will, if one exists. Defendants contend that recognizing tort liability for intentional interference with a prospective inheritance could violate that rule by, in essence, permitting a plaintiff to obtain relief that is contrary to a will's clear import by alleging and proving facts outside of the will. They suggest, in fact, that that potential exists in the present case.

We disagree. We are considering a tort action, not an action to set aside a will. Although the testamentary intent rule clearly is controlling in a will contest, it does not follow that the rule must be followed in the tort context. If, as alleged here, a party has obtained the benefit of the testamentary intent rule by committing a tort against a third party, the policy of the law should be to provide an avenue for relief from the tortious act. To do so here still would give defendants all the benefits that the testamentary intent rule calls for them to receive. Once possessed of those benefits, however, defendants would be liable to respond in damages for torts that they may have committed—a separate legal inquiry with its own societal justifications.

Defendants ascribe a breadth of purpose to the Oregon Probate Code that is not borne out by the statutes. Although it is true that that code strictly controls the kinds of issues that can be litigated in a proceeding to probate a will, and presumably requires plaintiffs to pursue those issues in the probate system where possible, that fact does not necessarily translate into a broader legislative purpose to deny legal significance to any other issue that might arise out of a decedent's making of, or failure to make, a will. Whether or not the probate code is or may be a "complete" legislative scheme, it is complete only within the confines of its subject matter, i.e., will contests. A tort claim does not become a will contest simply because it arises out of facts relating to the making or unmaking of a will.

We turn, now, to the complaint that is at issue in this case. As noted, plaintiffs have alleged facts that satisfy the first element of the tort, viz., the existence of a prospective economic advantage in the form of a prospective inheritance. They also have alleged the second and third elements, viz., an intentional interference by a third party: They have alleged that, after learning that Putman intended to change his will, Sheryl Hall—a third party— took steps to prevent that eventuality by having Putman admitted to the hospital under false pretenses, by contacting Putman's lawyer and falsely informing her that Putman could not execute a new will, and by falsely claiming a power of attorney to stop life support, thereby depriving Putman of the opportunity to execute the new will that his lawyer had prepared.

Turning to the fourth element, we must consider whether Sheryl Hall's interference allegedly was accomplished through improper means or for an improper purpose. In Top Service, *we stated that that element is satisfied*

> *"when interference resulting in injury to another is wrongful by some measure beyond the fact of the interference itself. Defendant's liability may arise from improper motives or from the use of improper means. They may be wrongful by reason of a statute or other regulation, or a recognized rule of common law."[41]*

. . . . In a claim of improper interference with plaintiff's contractual relations, it is not necessary to prove all the elements of liability for another tort if those elements that pertain to the defendant's conduct are present. For instance, fraudulent misrepresentations made to a third party are improper means of interference with plaintiff's contractual relations whether or not the third party can show reliance injurious to himself."[42]

Under the foregoing standard, the conduct alleged in the present case was improper.

To state a claim, plaintiffs also must allege facts that establish a causal relationship between the interference and the loss of the prospective advantage. They have done so.

As to the final element of the claim, damage, plaintiffs have alleged that the interference resulted in the loss of the intended bequest, Putman's home, valued at approximately $245,000.

We have shown that, under Oregon law, plaintiffs' complaint states a claim under an appropriate extension of the tort of intentional interference with economic relations. Before we conclude our analysis, however, we note one final argument offered by defendants—that the elements of the traditional intentional interference economic relations tort are insufficiently demanding in the prospective inheritance context, particularly when compared to the elements of the tort of intentional interference with prospective inheritance, as it has been recognized by the Restatement (Second) of Torts § 5774B (1979) and other jurisdictions.[3]

The jurisdictions that recognize the tort of intentional interference with prospective inheritance either repeat that wording, or require that the interferer's conduct be "independently tortious."

---

[41] 283 Or. at 209–10, 582 P.2d 1365.

[42] *Id.* at 210 n. 11, 582 P.2d 1365.

[3] The *Restatement (Second) of Torts,* section 774B (1979), provides:

"One who by fraud, duress or other tortious means intentionally prevents another from receiving from a third person an inheritance or gift that he would otherwise have received is subject to liability to the other for loss of the inheritance or gift."

We decline to involve ourselves in that argument. The question whether there is, in fact, a difference between the "independently tortious" and "reasonable certainty" of realization elements of the intentional interference with a prospective inheritance tort, as that tort is recognized by the Restatement and other jurisdictions, and the "improper means or purpose" and "causal effect" elements of Oregon's economic relations tort, is a purely abstract one for the purposes of this case. That is so because, as we have explained, plaintiffs' allegations are sufficient to meet the requirements of a tort presently recognized in Oregon. Because a reasonable and principled extension of that tort can encompass the facts that plaintiffs allege, Oregon law demands no more.

In summary: The answer to the questions propounded to us by the Ninth Circuit, as we have reformulated them, is that there is no need, in the case before us, to decide in the abstract whether to recognize a separate and distinct claim for intentional interference with prospective inheritance in this state. We hold that the complaint in the present case states a claim under a reasonable extension of the scope of the tort of intentional interference with economic relations.

Query: The plaintiffs were the niece and nephew of the decedent but the court does not tell us the relationship of the Halls to Putnam. Assuming they were unrelated caregivers, did the plaintiffs have a cause of action in undue influence? The Oregon Supreme Court did not directly adopt tortious interference with expectancy, holding that tortious interference with economic relations provided a sufficient remedy. Do you agree? Can you foresee circumstances where the latter would not be sufficient?

———————————

Tortious interference with an inheritance is still very much evolving in different jurisdictions. Where it has been accepted, there are questions about differing standards of proof between tort and probate actions that will require careful attention to the elements and allegations. Where it has not been accepted, it is usually because of a fear of interfering with probate jurisdiction. And where it has been accepted in some other form, as in Oregon, lawyers must be careful to properly recognize the differences and argue the elements well. If it has not been adopted in a particular jurisdiction, it will most likely take a very compelling case to get a court to adopt it. The *Kolaitis* case was not particularly compelling. Do you think the Virginia Supreme Court would have ruled differently had the *Allen* case been brought before it?

G. IN TERROREM CLAUSES

Game theorists have spent a lot of time analyzing how the final round in the popular game show, *Jeopardy!*, should be played, whether the leading scorer should bet her entire winnings, or should only bet enough to beat the second closest player in case that player also successfully answers the *Final Jeopardy!* question. Of course, all three players also want to go home with some winnings, but the chance of winning more the next day drives each player to balance the risk of losing known winnings with the chance of greater winnings if the bet pays off. *In terrorem* clauses in wills put all beneficiaries in a *Final Jeopardy!* round. The clause tells a potentially disgruntled beneficiary to take what is given her under the will, or risk losing it all if she files a will challenge suit. Called *no contest* clauses, or *in terrorem* clauses, these provisions are designed to scare a potential opponent away from contesting a will for fear of losing an inheritance. But a will contest suit may be successful even with an *in terrorem* clause in the will, thus netting greater benefit to the challenger than was provided to her under the will. So not only does the potential contestant to a will have to make a risk assessment before deciding to challenge a will, but the testator needs to assess the likelihood of a will contest suit being brought, the cost of the suit to his or her estate, and the size of the bequests that will be sufficient to discourage the challenge.

To be effective, a bequest must be large enough to make the challenger pause. If an estranged daughter is given $5.00 by her mother's will, while her siblings split the rest of mom's $10 million estate, the daughter has no incentive not to challenge the will and hope for an intestate distribution in which she will receive an equal share to that of her siblings. On the other hand, if she is given $1 million of her mother's $10 million estate, and she risks losing it if her challenge to mom's will is unsuccessful, she will likely think twice, especially if she will only get $1.5 million if her suit is successful. Thus, any deviation from a strict intestate distribution will give someone, somewhere, an incentive to challenge a will. Hence the frequent use of *in terrorem* clauses.

Do no-contest clauses work? Yes and no. Brooke Astor, the New York philanthropist, had one in her will that seems not to have worked. Michael Jackson had one in his trust which made his mother at least pause; she had to ask a judge whether the clause was enforceable in regard to her potential challenge of the people he named as executors and trustees of his estate.[43] The judge ruled the clause did not apply, paving the way for a challenge suit. No contest clauses do not penalize challenges to the actions of trustees, executors, or other fiduciaries. But they can be effective, as Leona Helmsley's executors discovered. The *in terrorem* clause in her will did not prevent her disinherited grandchildren from challenging her will, but it did prevent the ones who received bequests from doing so.

Most states will permit *in terrorem* clauses to be inserted in a will, and most states will enforce the clause against beneficiaries who challenge the will on grounds like incapacity or undue influence. But what if the will was not properly executed? If the will does not conform to the will formalities, then the will is invalid, and the *in terrorem* clause is therefore invalid as well. So should a potential beneficiary be able to challenge a will for lacking the formalities if it includes an *in terrorem* clause? The answer is generally yes. And the challenger does not lose her inheritance if the court determines the will was properly executed, even though she brought a will challenge suit? So how do we know when a will challenge suit is permissible despite the presence of an *in terrorem* clause, and when will it be enforced to deprive a beneficiary of a bequest? The answer, not surprisingly, is "it depends."[44]

---

[43] Deborah L. Jacobs, *Clauses Aimed at Keeping the Heirs Quiet*, THE NEW YORK TIMES (Octdober 28, 2009), available online at: http://www.nytimes.com/2009/10/29/your–money/estate–planning/29ESTATE.html?_r=0

[44] See T. Jack Challis and Howard Zaritsky, *State Laws: No Contest Clauses*, ACTEC Publication available at: http://www.actec.org/public/Documents/Studies/State_Laws_No_Contest_Clauses_–_Chart.pdf

Florida and Indiana are the only states that, by statute, will not enforce an *in terrorem* clause in a will.[45] Vermont has no law on their enforceability, and Alabama has not yet enforced one, though it purports to permit them. The vast majority of states will enforce *in terrorem* clauses, but they do so under a variety of conditions. Under the UPC, *in terrorem* clauses will be enforced unless the contest is based on probable cause. A version of the UPC, or a similar rule, has been adopted in nearly half of states.

UPC § 2–517. Penalty Clause for Contest

A provision in a will purporting to penalize an interested person for contesting the will or instituting other proceedings relating to the estate is unenforceable if probable cause exists for instituting proceedings.

Fourteen states enforce *in terrorem* clauses without reference to probable cause or good faith. And a handful of states require both probable cause and good faith. New York has an even more complex statute, limiting the enforceability of *in terrorem* clauses to certain types of actions. Delaware will enforce an *in terrorem* clause unless the contest is successful.

NY EPTL § 3–3.5 Conditions qualifying dispositions; conditions against contest; limitations thereon

(a) . . .

(b) A condition, designed to prevent a disposition from taking effect in case the will is contested by the beneficiary, is operative despite the presence or absence of probable cause for such contest, subject to the following:

(1) Such a condition is not breached by a contest to establish that the will is a forgery or that it was revoked by a later will, provided that such contest is based on probable cause.

(2) An infant or incompetent may affirmatively oppose the probate of a will without forfeiting any benefit thereunder.

(3) The following conduct, singly or in the aggregate, shall not result in the forfeiture of any benefit under the will:

(A) The assertion of an objection to the jurisdiction of the court in which the will was offered for probate.

(B) The disclosure to any of the parties or to the court of any information relating to any document offered for probate as a last will, or relevant to the probate proceeding.

(C) A refusal or failure to join in a petition for the probate of a document as a last will, or to execute a consent to, or waiver of notice of a probate proceeding.

(D) The preliminary examination, under SCPA 1404, of a proponent's witnesses, the person who prepared the will, the nominated executors and the proponents in a probate proceeding and, upon application to the court based upon special circumstances, any person whose examination the court determines may provide

---

[45] Fla. Stat. 732.517. Penalty clause for contest.—A provision in a will purporting to penalize any interested person for contesting the will or instituting other proceedings relating to the estate is unenforceable. See also Ind. Code § 29–1–6–2.

information with respect to the validity of the will that is of substantial importance or relevance to a decision to file objections to the will.

(E) The institution of, or the joining or acquiescence in a proceeding for the construction of a will or any provision thereof.

After determining how your state handles *in terrorem* clauses, you next need to determine if it has coordinated its *in terrorem* clause legislation to apply to both wills and trusts. Again, in roughly half the states the same rules apply to both; unenforceable in both wills and trusts in Florida and Indiana, and enforceable in both wills and trusts in 19 other states. No states have expressly adopted different rules for wills and trusts. But most states that enforce them do so strictly and narrowly because they work a forfeiture.[46] Thus, many states will allow suits to challenge fiduciary actions, to construe the governing instrument, and even to determine if a no contest clause is enforceable without resulting in forfeiture of the devise.

Michael Jackson's mother had to ask a court to rule on whether an *in terrorem* clause was enforceable, thus giving her the benefit of knowing what her exact risk would be if she challenged his trust. Imagine being able to ask Alex Trebek how the other contestants are going to play before making your wager. Ironically, a suit to determine whether an *in terrorem* clause is enforceable is generally not seen as a will challenge. A well plead declaratory judgment action, therefore, can help a disgruntled beneficiary steer clear of claims that would trigger the forfeiture while also making life difficult for the administrator and imposing litigation costs on the estate.

Most states follow one of three common law approaches to *in terrorem* clauses:

1. Apply the clause but strictly construe it to prevent forfeiture if possible, limiting the scope of the clause only to give effect to the testator's intent.
2. Apply the clause only to will challenge suits that actually contest the will provision itself, but not to suits seeking to construe the will or to determine the testator's true intent, mental capacity, or the administrator's actions.
3. Enforce the clause against will contest suits only if they lack probable cause or are brought in bad faith.

Consider the following cases and whether you think the *in terrorem* clause was properly interpreted by the court and what, if any, common law rule the court seemed to adopt.

Hallman v. Bosswick

899 N.Y.S.2d 233 (NY App. Div. 1st Dept. 2010)

Seymour Cohn left his entire estate in trust for the benefit of his two children and his grandchildren, naming his two children as co-executors along with two of his legal and financial advisors, Mark Bosswick and Charles Goldenberg. One child, Paula Hallman, brought a will construction suit to determine if the *in terrorem* clause would be enforceable against her interest in her father's estate if she challenged Bosswick and Goldenberg's appointment as co-executors on the grounds that they did not divulge to the

---

[46] New Hampshire, however, provides that no contest clauses are to be construed expansively to fulfill testamentary intent. See N.H. Rev. St. § 521:22(11).

testator the financial benefits they would receive by acting as executors and trustees. Hallman wanted to challenge Bosswick and Goldenberg's appointment under SCPA§ 711 which allows for the revocation of letters testamentary that had been granted an executor or trustee upon the occurrence of certain events, like wasting the property or where the fiduciary has a conflict of interest. In enforcing the *in terrorem* clause, the court explained: *As the proposed proceeding does not fall within the safe harbor provisions of EPTL 3–3.5 (b), the applicability of the in terrorem clause is a matter of the decedent's intent (see Matter of Singer, 13 NY3d 447, 451 [2009]). We reject petitioner's argument that because the decedent bequeathed his estate only to his children and grandchildren, and gave nothing to respondents, he must have intended to limit the scope of the in terrorem clause to challenges against his family members. The decision of decedent not to leave his estate outright to his children and grandchildren, but set up lifetime trusts for their benefit, is consistent with an intent that they not have unfettered control over his fortune. Such an intention would be furthered by the nomination of two nonfamily members as coexecutors and cotrustees, preventing the children from having a majority vote.*

Petitioner also contends that even if the testator intended the in terrorem clause to operate with respect to the proposed proceeding, public policy considerations dictate that it not be enforced. This argument assumes that the safe harbor provisions of Estates, Powers and Trusts Law § 3–3.5 (b) are not exhaustive. Although a recent decision of the Court of Appeals expressly so states (Matter of Singer, 13 NY3d 447, 449, 452 [2009]), that statement appears to be dictum as the Court held that the testator did not intend the clause to operate on account of the conduct of his son (id. at 452– 453). In any event, we reject petitioner's additional argument on the ground that a judicial expansion of the safe harbor provisions specified by the Legislature should originate with the Court of Appeals rather than with the trial or intermediate appellate courts.

Query: Why did Hallman want to have the letters testamentary revoked on behalf of Bosswick and Goldenberg? Go back through the New York statute cited above to determine why this challenge did not fit within the statute's exceptions and therefore would lead to forfeiture of the daughter's gift. The daughter argued 1) that challenging the co-trustees for failing to disclose their conflict of interest is not a will challenge, 2) even if it is, the applicability of the *in terrorem* clause is a matter of testamentary intent and her father would not have intended it to apply in this context, and 3) even if he intended it, public policy should not allow it to apply. If the co-trustees did breach their duty to the testator by failing to disclose the conflict of interest, how should the court have ruled on this case?

Haynes v. First Nat'l State Bank of New Jersey

87 N.J. 163 (NJ 1981)

Isabel Dutrow, the testatrix, had lived with her daughter Betty and her grandsons for 30 years in York, Pennsylvania, until the grandsons grew up and moved away, and Betty died in 1973. At that time, she moved in with her other daughter, Dorcas Cotsworth and her husband John, in New Jersey. Over the next four years, Dorcas and John pressured Isabel into dramatically changing her estate plan, they hired their own lawyer to prepare her testamentary documents, and she was encouraged to add *in terrorem* clauses to her will and codicils. Prior to Betty's death in 1973, Isabel had drafted a number of wills and trust provisions, all of which treated her grandchildren fairly equally, and which gave Betty and Dorcas life interests only in trust property. After the four years of pressure and persuasion, Isabel's last set of will and trust documents gave Dorcas all of her property outright at her death, with small bequests of $10,000 to each of her grandchildren. Betty's two sons contested the will alleging undue influence, and asked that the *in terrorem* clauses not be enforced.

The New Jersey Supreme Court remanded the case to the trial court after clarifying the evidentiary standard for proving undue influence, and then held the *in terrorem* clause unenforceable, explaining: *In Alper v. Alper, 2 N.J. 105, 65 A.2d 737 (1949), the Court said that the existence of probable cause to bring the challenge to the will should result in nonenforcement of an in terrorem clause "where the contest of the will is waged on the ground of forgery or subsequent revocation by a later will or codicil." However, where typical grounds of challenge were advanced "fraud, undue influence, improper execution or lack of testamentary capacity" the clause was deemed to be enforceable, notwithstanding probable cause, as a safeguard against deleterious, acrimonious and wasteful family litigation. [A new statute passed a year after the testatrix's death] abolishes the distinction drawn by the Court in* Alper *between cases in which in terrorem clauses in wills shall be enforced, and those in which they shall not, stating quite simply that whenever there is probable cause to contest a will, the clause should not be enforced. While the statute applies neither to the will in this case, which was probated prior to the statute's effective date, nor to the trust agreement, since the statute applies only to wills, the statute is indicative of a legislative intent to create a policy less inhibitory to the bringing of challenges to testamentary instruments. There does not appear to be any logical reason why the purpose of the statute should not be presently recognized and be applied equally to trust instruments or should not be applied in the circumstances of this case.* Recognizing that enforcement reduces vexatious litigation, and non-enforcement where probable cause exists advances equitable considerations, the Court refused to enforce the clause even though the statute itself was not *binding upon the judiciary's decisional authority in a matter not governed by such enactments. Nevertheless, the legislative handling of the subject is, and should be, strongly influential in the judicial quest for the important societal values which are constituent elements of the common law and find appropriate voice in the decisions of the court expounding the common law. We therefore decline to enforce an in terrorem clause in a will or trust agreement where there is probable cause to challenge the instrument.*

Query: Under the law in New Jersey, prior to the passage of the statute, a will contest claiming undue influence, fraud, or incapacity would be subject to a valid *in terrorem* clause, while a suit based on forgery or revocation would not trigger application of the *in terrorem* clause. The statute abolished the distinction, and would permit any challenge to go forward if there was probable cause. Certainly one should be able to claim that the insertion of the *in terrorem* clause was the result of undue influence and have it stricken, argued the grandsons. But Mrs. Dutrow died before the statute was passed. Do you think the existence of the statute affected the court's decision? Why or why not? Assuming your clients want to make a strong public policy argument that the law is unfair or should be changed, would you recommend they bring a will challenge suit to do so if there is an *in terrorem* clause? Do these clauses stifle the kind of innovation that underlies the common law?

Savage v. Oliszczak

928 N.E.2d 995 (Mass.App. Ct. 2010)

Georgenia Hatch died leaving a will that poured all of her property into the Georgenia Hatch Living Trust. The will had no *in terrorem* clause, but the trust did, stating that "if any person . . . shall . . . contest or oppose the validity of this agreement . . . such person shall forfeit his or her share." Three of the trust beneficiaries contested Hatch's will on the grounds of incapacity, duress, and undue influence, but later withdrew their challenge to the will. The executors to Hatch's will then brought suit to determine if the trust *in terrorem* clause applied against the trust beneficiaries for filing the will contest suit. The court explained that: *'A provision forfeiting the interest of a beneficiary who contests a will is valid.' However, the will in the present case contains no such provision. The trust is a separate instrument from the will, with independent legal significance. The trust was not a testamentary trust created by the will, and the will did not incorporate the terms of the trust by reference. The defendants' challenge was directed to the will, rather than the trust, and accordingly did not implicate the in terrorem clause by the terms of either the will or the in terrorem clause itself.*

As a threshold matter, the plaintiffs overstate the interrelationship between the will and the trust. Though it appears that the trust was in fact only nominally funded during Georgenia's life, there is nothing in the terms of either the will or the trust that prevented more significant funding during her life. The trust could have been funded by any number of sources wholly independently of the will.

We also note that the purpose of an in terrorem clause is to deter challenges to a will. In the present case, the defendants filed their challenge to the will in response to the filing of the will for probate; the trust was not required to be submitted with the will, and was in fact not so filed. As the defendants observe, there can be no deterrent value to a clause contained in an instrument that is not made public incident to the proceeding in which the challenge arises (and thus not thereby disclosed to all beneficiaries); indeed it would be draconian to invoke a forfeiture clause against beneficiaries who challenge a will that does not contain an in terrorem clause, based on the inclusion of such a provision in a separate but undisclosed instrument. We likewise observe that, "because equity does not favor forfeitures, [in terrorem] clauses have been construed narrowly." Bogert, Trusts and Trustees, § 181.

Query: After the Massachusetts Supreme Court applied will statutes to trusts established at the same time, especially a pour over trust, in *Clymer v. Mayo*, as discussed in Chapters 4 and 10, do you think the court was correct here to keep the documents distinct and strictly apply the *in terrorem* clause only to trust challenges? Does the forfeiture provision of the trust support the court's decision?

Schwartz v. Schwartz

84 Cal.Rptr.3d 387 (Cal.App. 5 Dist. 2008)

Adolf Schwartz died, leaving a complex array of testamentary documents, including three trusts with amendments, a will, and numerous codicils. But his final holographic codicil increased bequests to his surviving second wife, affirmed bequests of the house to his second wife, recited that certain *inter vivos* cash gifts to his son were to be treated as part of his inheritance, and made some specific distributions to his daughter. The rest of the trust assets were to be divided equally between his son and daughter. His daughter was appointed successor trustee. The testator's son filed an application for determination of whether a petition for order directing distribution of property from the *inter vivos* trust would be a "contest" under Probate Code § 21320 and he attached a proposed petition for order directing distribution of the trust property. Without waiting for a ruling on his application, the son filed his petition for distribution of the trust property. The daughter opposed the petition and claimed that it was a contest under the terms of the trust. After a hearing at which the court continued the matter until other beneficiaries had been notified, the son withdrew his petition, stating:

> The Petition was filed subsequent to the filing of an Application which seeks a judicial determination as to the effect, if any, pursuing legal action on the Petition will have on Petitioner under the no contest clause of the Adolph W. Schwartz and Chris Edda Schwartz Living Trust of 1987, as amended and restated (the 'Trust'). The Petition was filed with the understanding that the Court's initial determination on the Application could affect Petitioner's decision as to whether or not to move forward on the Petition. To avoid any confusion or argument, Petitioner is simply withdrawing the Petition without prejudice to subsequent filing.

At subsequent hearings, the son claimed that by withdrawing the petition he had not triggered the no contest clause, and the daughter disagreed. Her counsel explained: *"That makes no sense, your Honor. Because, again, at what point can a contestant withdraw a petition and say, Well, I was just kidding? I'm sorry I exposed the trust or will probate estate to litigation expenses. But I don't like how the outcome is looking so I'm gonna withdraw the petition."*

In affirming the application of the no contest clause and causing the son to forfeit his bequests, the court explained:

> Whether there has been a "contest" within the meaning of a particular no-contest clause depends upon the circumstances of the particular case and the language used. No-contest clauses are valid and favored by the public policies of discouraging litigation and giving effect to the testator's intent. Nevertheless, they are also disfavored by the policy against forfeitures, are strictly construed, and may not extend beyond what plainly was the testator's intent. The testator's intentions control, and a court must not rewrite an estate planning document in such a way as to immunize legal proceedings plainly intended to frustrate the testator's unequivocally expressed intent from the reach of the no-contest clause. Appellant's petition prayed for an order directing respondent to divide the property of the survivor's trust equally between himself and respondent "as required under the terms of the Survivor's Trust without giving any force or effect to the Holographic Will [the third codicil]." . . .

In the instant case, appellant knowingly filed a petition that took him outside the safe harbor provisions of Probate Code section 21320. The clear purpose of appellant's petition was to defeat Schwartz's testamentary and donative intent by nullifying his third codicil and giving equal shares of the survivor's trust to appellant and respondent, something that was neither contemplated nor specified in the settlors' estate plan. Appellant used the mechanisms of the court in attempting to achieve this goal. By filing his petition, appellant compelled respondent to respond to the petition, attempted to negotiate with respondent while his petition was pending, and caused the court to conduct [three] hearings . . .

As respondent correctly points out, "Robert cannot now escape the no-contest clause after he has dragged the trust, will, and codicils through the court and attempted to gain an advantage by thwarting Dr. Schwartz's intent. No-contest clauses are put in testamentary documents specifically to prevent behavior like Robert's. Robert has wasted trust resources and attempted to defeat Dr. Schwartz's intent. Robert cannot now escape the consequences by merely withdrawing the Contest—this would defeat the purpose of the no-contest clauses."

Query: Robert ended up losing his entire inheritance under the will and trust of his father, besides creating bad feelings between himself and his sister and step-mother. Do you think Robert would have a cause of action against his attorney who presumably decided to, or agreed to, file the petition for distribution without waiting for a determination of whether such a petition would violate the no-contest clause? Could this case have been avoided with better estate planning by Adolf and his lawyer?

Practice Point: That Boilerplate No-Contest Clause

One thing you are likely to learn very quickly in your practice is that clients tend to get very worked up when you bring up the matter of will contest suits. "This is MY plan, d—n it, and anyone who challenges it should be cast off without a farthing for the audacity of questioning my decisions. Who do they think they are?" And most practitioners will tell you that they use *in terrorem* clauses as boilerplate in every will, even if they practice in Indiana or Florida. Wills are ambulatory, so you never know if your Indiana client is going to move to Alabama or the Bahamas and take her will with her. And all those public policy reasons of promoting testamentary intent and minimizing fractious family litigation support strict enforcement of these clauses. But step back a moment and think about all the things that can go wrong with an estate plan. Of course, you would not participate in the execution of a will or trust if you know your client lacks the appropriate mental capacity. But are you certain your client isn't under someone's undue influence, or is not in any way mistaken about his or her property and appropriate beneficiaries? Are you certain that the executors, administrators, trustees, and other fiduciaries are of impeccable moral character? Some beneficiaries will certainly challenge a will if they are annoyed that dad didn't leave them the property they were expecting outright, but instead gave it to his second wife, put it in trust, or is making him share it with his sister. But many beneficiaries are truly concerned about improprieties in the creation and management of a relative's estate. If you can't count on your state to have legislation in place that wisely distinguishes between sound and frivolous will challenges, you need to think more carefully about how you word that boilerplate no-contest clause. Every case we have read in this book involves litigation; i.e. a challenger who thought something was fishy. And in at least half of them, something fishy was going on. If every one of those wills and trusts had a no-contest clause, would the suit have been brought and the fishiness exposed? Probably not. There are very sound reasons for including no-contest clauses in certain situations, and equally sound reasons for not including them in others. The moral of the story: nothing should be boilerplate. Each client is unique and each client's estate plan documents should be unique. The only way you will know whether a no-contest clause is appropriate is by getting to know your client's unique circumstances and that of his family members. You don't have to take each one out to lunch to judge their likelihood of filing a frivolous will contest suit, but you do need to discuss these matters very carefully with your client, and you will ultimately have a lot of influence in recommending whether or not a no-contest clause should be inserted. How well you can sniff out the likely bad apples will determine how well you use no-contest clauses to the benefit of your client.

H. CONCLUSION

In most books you will use in law school, you will study cases which are, by definition, examples of things that went wrong. We have tried to focus in this book on the cases only to give you a sense of how things can go wrong so you don't fall into the same traps, as Robert's lawyer did in *Schwartz v. Schwartz*. The court in that case held that simply holding a hearing that requires the trustee to respond to an application costs the estate or the trust resources and thus triggered the forfeiture of the *in terrorem* clause. Litigation is expensive! And to the extent testators justifiably want to avoid needless costs that waste estate resources, they are wise to include *in terrorem* clauses. But the most important way to avoid litigation is to make sure that all potential beneficiaries understand the testator's decisions and feel that the testator has good reasons for her decisions. We have seen too many examples of situations in which brothers and sisters, or grandchildren and second spouses, have become estranged because they are at odds about the testamentary plans of their relative. Avoiding litigation requires doing things right in addition to understanding the family dynamics that can lead to conflicts.

As we have also emphasized throughout the book, it is always cheaper and easier to do things right the first time, even if that means re-executing the will, or setting up a trust, or holding a family meeting, or drafting lengthy explanations of why the testator made certain bequests, than it is to litigate these issues after the fact. Many of the issues that get litigated depend on rules of construction, presumptions, and evidentiary standards that have little to do with a testator's true intent. So if there is any moral here, it is that a good estate planning attorney has usually failed if her client's estate plan gets litigated for any reason. Although some litigation simply cannot be avoided, the vast majority can be. Knowing the law, however, is only half the job; you also need to know your clients, their situations, their relatives, their property, their financial advisers, their aspirations, and ultimately their secrets. You should also be sure to take Family Law, Evidence, Taxation of Estates and Trusts, and Probate Administration if they are offered in your law school. And always remember, form books may be good places to start, but they are not the end.

CHAPTER 12

PROFESSIONAL RESPONSIBILITY

Throughout this book you have encountered numerous situations involving lawyers who seem not to have met the basic requirements of professional ethics, from the lawyer who married her client to get his money, to the lawyers who drafted estates documents without determining if their clients were under duress or lacked mental capacity, and even to the lawyer who lost his client's codicil. Yet, considering the number of cases involving overreaching by relatives, caregivers, and friends, the misbehavior of lawyers was relatively modest. As the case should be, lawyers are held to a higher standard. There are laws prohibiting testamentary gifts to lawyers and limiting a lawyer's investment in a client's business. Conflicts of interest certainly arise when you are advising a client about an estate plan and the client wants you to act as trustee, a position in which you will be able to earn perhaps significant fees. In many instances, you will be the most trusted, knowledgeable, and objective person in your client's life, and you will be asked to take on fiduciary obligations that may raise some eyebrows if you are also drafting the documents and advising the client about her plan.

Remember Lawyer Farr, from *Marsman v. Nasca* in Chapter 4? He drafted the will and trust for his client, Sara Marsman, which provided a life income interest to her husband Cappy with a remainder over to her daughter, Sally. Lawyer Farr also included an exculpatory clause in the will that relieved the trustee from liability for all but willful neglect or default, and Sara named him the trustee. Now we don't know what went on in the office when Sara and Lawyer Farr were discussing who would serve as trustee and whether the trustee should be relieved of liability for breaches of fiduciary duty, but I suspect it went something like this:

Lawyer Farr: Now Sara, if we are going to set up a trust you need to appoint a trustee. Do you want Cappy to be the trustee?

Sara: Oh no, Cappy is a dear sweet man, but he has absolutely no financial savvy. He can't even balance his own checkbook. If he had control, the money would be gone in a year.

Lawyer Farr: What about your daughter?

Sara: No, she and Cappy don't get along that well, plus her husband is kind of a jerk. I don't trust him.

Lawyer Farr: Well, do you have any other family who could serve as trustee? It's not a large trust so most banks or trust companies won't want to mess with it—the fees just aren't substantial enough. What about a trusted family friend?

Sara: Well, I do have a good friend, Rita, but she's retiring and moving to Florida, and I have a favorite aunt I trust with everything, but she's almost 90 and may have to move into a nursing home. I need someone younger than we are, someone trustworthy who understands the financial responsibility, and someone who isn't going to just up and move to Florida before Cappy dies. In fact, I need someone like you. Can you do it?

Lawyer Farr: Yes, I can do it, and I have done it for other clients, but we would need to discuss the potential conflict of interest that it creates and you would have to understand that my loyalties to you as my client may conflict with my loyalties to the trust and the trust beneficiaries.

Sara: Oh, I can't see any problems with that. You know Cappy and Sally, you know what they are like and they trust you, and you understand all this stuff about duties and filing the right papers. And it's just the house and a small bank account. All you would have to do is write checks to Cappy or pay some bills, and I would gladly pay you for your time to do that. It would be a huge relief to me to know that you are taking care of this because you understand all my property and you have arranged my estate plan so well. Why, you are the perfect trustee. Besides, in this small town, where everyone knows everyone's business, you are the only one who can keep his mouth shut. You'll do it, won't you?

Lawyer Farr: Yes, I'm happy to do it, but you will need to carefully read a disclosure form and sign it, acknowledging that you understand the conflict if I have to make decisions as trustee that could be counter to your interests as my client. It's a long form and I need you to read it carefully. Unfortunately, I don't have something appropriate right here because I will need to draft it and fill in all the right information. I will need to do some research and make sure that we modify the retainer agreement so that everything is clear about my responsibilities and that you understand and waive the potential conflicts of interest.

Sara: Oh no—how long will that take? I'm here ready to execute all my estate documents and I don't want to come back in a month when you've gotten that all worked out. Can't we just say that you explained it all to me and I understand it and trust you? Nothing is going to go wrong—it's a simple trust.

Lawyer Farr: Well, if we don't execute a new retainer agreement with an appropriate disclosure then I would need to put an exculpatory clause in the trust or the will just so that all of our "I"s are dotted and our "T"s are crossed.

Sara: Oh yes, that is fine. Can you do that right now? Can't your assistant just retype that last page of the will while I'm sitting here and we can get this all done right now? That is perfect. I am so happy that you will be trustee and I feel such relief knowing that I can go home today and everything is all set.

It is highly unlikely that Sara said to Lawyer Farr, "Oh, please put an exculpatory clause into the will so that you will only be liable for breaches of fiduciary duty if you are willfully negligent, not if you are merely negligent." How many clients would understand that such a clause relieves the lawyer from liability for certain breaches but not all, and how many understand the complex decisions that have to be made in which potential ethical traps might lie? A sophisticated client, like another lawyer, might understand the language of such a clause, but most lay people do not.

On the other hand, do you think Lawyer Farr put that clause in the will because he expected to breach his fiduciary duties? Probably not. Most likely, he recommended it as a way to get around a different problem and he and his client couldn't imagine that the clause would ever come into play. He certainly didn't intend to breach his fiduciary duties to the beneficiaries. But he, like many well-intentioned lawyers, was wrong.

The practice of estate planning is somewhat unique in the lawyering world because you will very likely have loyalties to more than one person. Often, a married couple will come to you to draft their wills, telling you that they are in full agreement about how their property is going to be distributed upon their respective deaths. In most cases you will be able to represent both, in part because they will waive their rights to your sole loyalty, and because their interests will dovetail. In other cases, you will be the family lawyer representing many clients in the same family, and you will have loyalties to them all. Most of the time, you can appropriately serve them all without running afoul of your state's ethics rules.

Inevitably, however, a situation will arise in which you realize, even if your clients don't, that their interests are diverging and that you cannot properly represent both. If you say something, you will potentially breach your loyalty to one client, and if you don't say something you will potentially breach your loyalty to the other. Once you are in that kind of situation it is very hard to extricate yourself without causing even more problems. So the best solution is to avoid the conflict in the first place. But how do you do that? When your client is in your office, like Sara and Lawyer Farr, and she is telling you that she trusts you and it doesn't matter what you write into her will so long as it will get the job done, you can easily find yourself falling into an ethics trap.

Because the practice of law in this field is relatively unique, with its own pressures and unusual situations that don't generally arise in the practice of criminal law or corporate law, the American College of Trusts and Estates Counsel (ACTEC) has promulgated a set of *Commentaries* to the *Model Rules of Professional Conduct* (MRPC) that reflect the unique circumstances of the trusts and estates practice. Most of the differences lie in recognizing the more complex conflicts of interest that can arise in estate planning for multiple members of a family and duties lawyers often owe to multiple generations. As ACTEC explains:

> *Basic Themes of Commentaries.* The main themes of the Commentaries are: (1) the relative freedom that lawyers and clients have to write their own charter with respect to a representation in the trusts and estates field; (2) the generally nonadversarial nature of the trusts and estates practice; (3) the utility and propriety, in this area of law, of representing multiple clients, whose interests may differ but are not necessarily adversarial; and (4) the opportunity, with full disclosure, to moderate or eliminate many problems that might otherwise arise under the MRPC. The Commentaries additionally reflect the role that the trusts and estates lawyer has traditionally played as the lawyer for members of a family. In that role a trusts and estates lawyer frequently represents the fiduciary of a trust or estate and one or more of the beneficiaries. In drafting the Commentaries we have attempted to express views that are consistent with the spirit of the MRPC as evidenced in the following passage: "The Rules of Professional Conduct are rules of reason. They should be interpreted with reference to the purposes of legal representation and of the law itself." MRPC, Scope.

In a trusts and estates practice, you are generally trying to facilitate the smooth transmission of property between family members, all of whom have the same basic goal. They all want to transfer property upon death to survivors with the least amount of hassle, cost, and bad feelings. What's not to like about that? Unless you go into probate litigation, which can be quite adversarial, you are unlikely to even be involved in a will contest suit. Only a tiny fraction of wills are ever contested. So it can be easy to become complacent about the ethical issues of serving numerous individuals and maintaining your loyalty to all. But as an estate planner you may very well be conflicted out of later serving as a lawyer for the personal representative, or representing one of the family members who wants to contest the will because the lawyer who prepares the estate documents is likely to be called as a witness in contests questioning the will formalities, capacity, or undue influence. For that reason, there tends to be a divide between estates lawyers who work primarily in the planning side, and those that litigate or represent fiduciaries and beneficiaries.

In addition, there are some pretty significant differences between the states on certain aspects of multiple representation in the estates and trusts context. For example, states differ widely on whether an attorney for a fiduciary, like the personal representative or a trustee, owes a duty to the beneficiaries of the estate or the trust. As the ACTEC Commentaries again explain:

> *Duties of Trusts and Estates Lawyers Incompletely and Inconsistently Described.* In large measure the duties of trusts and estates lawyers are defined in many states by opinions rendered in malpractice actions, which provide incomplete and insufficient guidance regarding the ethical duties of lawyers. Compounding the problem, the decisions in malpractice actions and the legal principles upon which they are based vary considerably from jurisdiction to jurisdiction. Courts have perhaps had the most difficulty in defining the role and duties of the lawyer who represents a fiduciary in the fiduciary's representative capacity with respect to a fiduciary estate (who might be said to represent the fiduciary generally). For example, in a malpractice action brought by the beneficiaries of a fiduciary estate against the lawyer for the fiduciary, a California appellate court stated that the lawyer owed no duty to the beneficiaries of the estate. *Goldberg v. Frye*, 266 Cal. Rptr. 483 (Cal. App. 1990); Other appellate courts have reached the opposite conclusion, including courts in California. Thus, in *In re Estate of Halas*, 512 N.E.2d 1276, 1280 (Ill. App. 1987), the court stated that, "The attorney for the executor, therefore, must act with due care and protect the interests of the beneficiaries". Similarly, in *Charleson v. Hardesty*, 839 P.2d 1303 (Nev. 1992), the court wrote that the lawyer for a personal representative owes the beneficiaries "a duty of care and fiduciary duties." *Id.* at 1307. See also *Fickett v. Superior Court*, 558 P.2d 988 (Ariz. App. 1976), in which the court held that the lawyer for the guardian owed a duty directly to the ward to protect the ward's interests.

Since there are few situations in which your average lawyer will be deemed to owe a duty to third parties who are not the client, the generic ethics rules and guidelines don't adequately address the realities of an estates and trusts practice. However, as in all areas of the practice of law, your clients can waive certain rights and, with proper disclosure, the usual conflicts can be managed. Attorneys and clients are free to define the scope of their professional relationship—but this usually means that the lawyer has to be proactive in identifying possible conflict situations, discussing them with the clients, realizing that certain privileged documents may have to be shared, and informing the client that her duties may extend beyond the individual client. Assuming the lawyer and client can work together to define the scope of the representation, a well-drafted retainer agreement and client letter must be executed. While clients may become impatient with the need to reduce everything to writing, it is necessary so long as you are going to deviate from the traditional standards of professional practice that were developed in the context of adversarial litigation.

Because many of you may yet not have taken Professional Responsibility, and because of limited space in the typical Trusts and Estates course, we will focus on only four areas of lawyer ethics here: Conflicts of Interest, Disclosure of Confidential Information, Fiduciary Duties to Beneficiaries, and Gifts to Lawyers. We end the chapter with two sample retainer letters to give you a sense of the kinds of detail you probably should reduce to writing and explain to your clients.

A. CONFLICTS OF INTEREST

The ABA Model Rules of Professional Conduct (MRPC) recognize that conflicts of interest arise, and so they must be managed well in order for the conflict not to get in the way of ethical representation. Clients can waive their rights to undivided loyalty if they have appropriate information, and the parties can define the scope of their representation as they choose. As you can see, in most instances, disclosure to the client and obtaining the client's permission is enough to manage a typical conflict reasonably well. The Conflict of Interest provision of the Model Rules states:

MRPC Rule 1.7 Conflict of Interest: Current Clients

(a) Except as provided in paragraph (b), a lawyer shall not represent a client if the representation involves a concurrent conflict of interest. A concurrent conflict of interest exists if:

(1) the representation of one client will be directly adverse to another client; or

(2) there is a significant risk that the representation of one or more clients will be materially limited by the lawyer's responsibilities to another client, a former client or a third person or by a personal interest of the lawyer.

(b) Notwithstanding the existence of a concurrent conflict of interest under paragraph (a), a lawyer may represent a client if:

(1) the lawyer reasonably believes that the lawyer will be able to provide competent and diligent representation to each affected client;

(2) the representation is not prohibited by law;

(3) the representation does not involve the assertion of a claim by one client against another client represented by the lawyer in the same litigation or other proceeding before a tribunal; and

(4) each affected client gives informed consent, confirmed in writing.

The MRPC have also identified a number of specific instances that often give rise to conflicts, like having sexual relations with your client or investing in your client's business. The one most linked to the practice of trusts and estates is MRPC 1.8(c), involving gifts, especially testamentary gifts, to the lawyer. But other specific conflicts can easily arise in a trusts and estates practice, and we have seen examples of them in many of the cases in this book. Consider how the specific rules of the MRPC 1.8 interact with the general rule just presented.

MRPC Rule 1.8 Conflict of Interest: Current Clients: Specific Rules

(a) A lawyer shall not enter into a business transaction with a client or knowingly acquire an ownership, possessory, security or other pecuniary interest adverse to a client unless:

(1) the transaction and terms on which the lawyer acquires the interest are fair and reasonable to the client and are fully disclosed and transmitted in writing in a manner that can be reasonably understood by the client;

(2) the client is advised in writing of the desirability of seeking and is given a reasonable opportunity to seek the advice of independent legal counsel on the transaction; and

(3) the client gives informed consent, in a writing signed by the client, to the essential terms of the transaction and the lawyer's role in the transaction, including whether the lawyer is representing the client in the transaction.

(b) A lawyer shall not use information relating to representation of a client to the disadvantage of the client unless the client gives informed consent, except as permitted or required by these Rules.

(c) A lawyer shall not solicit any substantial gift from a client, including a testamentary gift, or prepare on behalf of a client an instrument giving the lawyer or a person related to the lawyer any substantial gift unless the lawyer or other recipient of the gift is related to the client. For purposes of this paragraph, related persons include a spouse, child, grandchild, parent, grandparent or other relative or individual with whom the lawyer or the client maintains a close, familial relationship.

* * *

(h) A lawyer shall not:

(1) make an agreement prospectively limiting the lawyer's liability to a client for malpractice unless the client is independently represented in making the agreement; or

(2) settle a claim or potential claim for such liability with an unrepresented client or former client unless that person is advised in writing of the desirability of seeking and is given a reasonable opportunity to seek the advice of independent legal counsel in connection therewith.

* * *

Note how some of these activities listed in MRPC § 1.8 are absolutely prohibited, and others are prohibited unless certain things happen, like the business relationship is fair or the client consents. Consider the ACTEC Commentary on MRPC 1.7 involving multiple representation.

General Nonadversary Character of Estates and Trusts Practice; Representation of Multiple Clients. It is often appropriate for a lawyer to represent more than one member of the same family in connection with their estate plans, more than one beneficiary with common interests in an estate or trust administration matter, co-fiduciaries of an estate or trust, or more than one of the investors in a closely held business. See ACTEC Commentary on MRPC 1.6 (Confidentiality of Information). In some instances the clients may actually be better served by such a representation, which can result in more economical and better coordinated estate plans prepared by counsel who has a better overall understanding of all of the relevant family and property considerations. The fact that the estate planning goals of the clients are not entirely consistent does not necessarily preclude the lawyer from representing them: Advising related clients who have somewhat differing goals may be consistent with their interests and the lawyer's traditional role as the lawyer for the "family". Multiple representation is also generally appropriate because the interests of the clients in co-operation, including obtaining cost effective representation and achieving common objectives, often clearly predominate over their limited inconsistent interests. Recognition should be given to the fact that estate planning is fundamentally nonadversarial in nature and estate administration is usually nonadversarial.

A typical example often offered in ethics courses involving conflicts of interest is the husband and wife who come to your office and ask you to draft reciprocal wills. At the end of the client meeting, the wife whispers to you as you are escorting them to the door, that she has a lover who she wants to benefit and that as soon as they have all executed the reciprocal wills, she wants you to draft a new will to benefit her lover. What do you do? Can you follow through with drafting any of the wills? If you decline to do so, does that plant a seed in the husband's mind that something is amiss? If so, should you be liable when the husband now decides not to leave his wife anything or, in fact, petitions for a divorce? Have you breached your duty to the wife?

Other situations arise when you serve as the trustee for both spouses' trusts, and there are conflicts about which trust is to pay the estate taxes or whether you should exercise discretion and make a payout from one trust rather than another, especially if there are different remainder beneficiaries to the different trusts. Conflicts can arise if you represent the personal representative in her official capacity, and also in her personal capacity as a beneficiary of the estate. Conflicts can certainly arise as in the *Marsman v. Nasca* situation, where the lawyer drafts the estate documents and then names himself or herself trustee or executor. Although no state prohibits this dual service, courts will look closely at how well the client understood the conflict and approved it.

Consider the following cases and ethics opinions on general conflicts of interest involving representation of multiple parties. As you read through them, ask yourself if the lawyers should have seen the conflict coming, or whether unforeseen circumstances cropped up to put them in an ethical quandary.

Bishop v. Maurer

823 N.Y.S. 2d 366 (N.Y.A.D. 1 Dept., 2006)

Husband and wife hired the law firm of Goodkind Labaton Rudoff & Sucharow to represent them in their estate planning. In doing so they signed a standard retainer agreement acknowledging that any *relationship between a lawyer and a client is subject to Rules of Professional Conduct. In estate planning, ethical rules applicable to conflicts of interest and confidentiality are of primary concern. By countersigning a copy of this letter, you each acknowledge that you have had the opportunity to consult independent legal counsel with respect to your estate planning, and you each affirmatively waive with full understanding any conflict of interest inherent in your both relying on the advice of this firm and its attorneys.* The firm then drafted wills and trusts for both husband and wife which gave the house and an apartment building to the wife, to the exclusion of the husband's children. In a later malpractice action, the husband claimed that he suffered from mild cognitive impairment, did not read the complex trust documents, and relied on the firms' statement that the wife was only receiving a life estate in the property, which the document apparently did not reflect. The husband alleged that the wife had been badgering him for quite some time and demanded that she have the properties in her own name and that she hired the law firm and met with them in advance before he did. When he later realized that the documents he signed had irrevocably transferred his properties into the trust, he tried to rescind them, claiming fraud, misrepresentation, and legal malpractice. The court dismissed the malpractice claim because the retainer letter was clear about the conflict, and because the trust documents clearly showed what interests in his property the husband was giving up.

A strong dissent, however, argued that on a motion to dismiss, the court should take the facts to be as alleged, and that if the firm misrepresented that the trust documents only gave the wife a life estate, when they in fact gave her more, the allegations should be sufficient to withstand a dismissal. The dissent was particularly skeptical of the majority's reliance on the *clarity* of the trust documents and retainer agreements and their willingness to so quickly rely on the presumption that a person who signs documents understands their import. The dissent asserted that the failure to understand the trust documents was allegedly the result of erroneous advice by the attorneys, which should be a sufficient claim to sustain the motion to dismiss.

Query: In this case the husband faulted the lawyers for 1) not recognizing that he and his wife had different opinions about the property and that the wife was badgering him to get their estate plan done, 2) that when the lawyers said they were establishing the trust for managing estate taxes, they didn't clearly tell him that the wife would have a general power of appointment (typical of a QTIP) after his death and thus could take control over all the property to the exclusion of his children, the remaindermen, and 3) the trust documents were so long and complex that he didn't read them and instead relied on their statements about their meaning. Do you think the court was correct in dismissing the malpractice claim? Do you think an insurmountable conflict arises when one spouse wants to do tax-effective estate planning and the other keeps avoiding it altogether? And do you think the firm was negligent in not explaining in extra detail how these complex trusts work?

In re Estate of Klarner

98 P.3d 892 (Colo. Ct. App., 2003), rev'd in part 113 P.3d 150 (Colo, 2005)

Marian and Albert Klarner were married, each with two children from previous marriages, when they did their first estate planning. In 1979 Albert established a revocable living trust which provided for the creation of a marital trust and family trust at his death. In 1982 he amended the trust to provide that the marital trust would be split into two trusts at his death; in one Marian had the right to demand principal at any time and in the other the trustee could make distributions only for her health, education, maintenance and support (QTIP). Because of the QTIP character of the trust, the assets in the trust were included in the spouse's gross estate for estate tax purposes, and the estate was reimbursed from the QTIP trust's assets enough to offset the extra taxes due by reason of the trust being included in the estate. The trust beneficiaries, Albert's two children, complained, however, at the trust having to pay its share of estate taxes (both federal and state). On appeal to the Colorado Supreme Court, the trust was required to pay both the federal and state taxes even though the federal QTIP statute only mentions federal taxes. Albert's daughters also alleged, however, that the law firm and Marion's sons had an inherent conflict of interest as trustees of the QTIP and of Marian's trust. In finding a conflict, the court explained:

Here, Marian's sons are trustees of the QTIP Trust and, accordingly, owe a duty of loyalty to Albert's daughters as beneficiaries of the QTIP Trust. Consistent with that duty of loyalty, and pursuant to the QTIP Trust documents, Marian's sons have a duty to pay only those taxes that are necessary and advisable from the QTIP Trust. Marian's sons are also trustees of Marian's Trust and beneficiaries of Marian's estate, giving them a financial interest in maximizing the contribution of the QTIP Trust's assets to Marian's estate. Therefore, we conclude as a matter of law that Marian's sons have a conflict of interest in serving as trustees of the QTIP Trust.

The Law Firm is also a trustee of the QTIP Trust and owes a fiduciary duty to Albert's daughters. Simultaneously, the Law Firm is a trustee of Marian's Trust and represents the cotrustees, Marian's sons, in this litigation. Therefore, the Law Firm owes fiduciary duties to its clients, Marian's sons, while also owing fiduciary duties to Albert's daughters. The Law Firm is in the precarious position of advocating in this litigation an advantageous position for its clients, Marian's sons, that, if successful, would operate to the detriment of the beneficiaries to whom it owes a duty of loyalty. Therefore, we conclude as a matter of law that the Law Firm has a conflict of interest in serving as trustee of the QTIP Trust.

Query: Remember all of the estate planning ideas we discussed in Chapter 7, especially the Marital Deduction Trust and the QTIP? Many estate plans today involve multiple trusts for maximizing estate tax exemptions and deductions. How often will the same trustees serve in that capacity for all the trusts? Often! So how does one manage the conflict that might exist between the trusts? A trustee who is also a remainder beneficiary may be disinclined to use discretion to make payments to a life tenant, or to pay expenses like estate taxes unless the documents are excruciatingly clear as to which trust pays what fees. Assuming the law firm does a good job articulating all the details, does one then run into the *Maurer* problem from the case above of making the documents too complicated for the average person to read and comprehend?

Baker Botts, LLP v. Cailloux

224 S.W.3d 723 (Tex.App., 2007)

Floyd and Kathleen Cailloux hired Baker Botts, L.L.P., to devise an estate plan for their multimillion dollar estate. Floyd died before Baker Botts could finish all stages of the Caillouxes' estate plan. Baker Botts designed a revised estate plan for Kathleen immediately following her husband's death. Under the revised plan, Kathleen voluntarily disclaimed her right to her husband's share of the marital estate. As a result of Kathleen's disclaimer, $65.5 million vested immediately in various charitable organizations Floyd had designated in his will.

Kathleen subsequently became incapacitated by Alzheimer's disease, and her son, Ken Cailloux, took over her affairs. More than six years after Kathleen disclaimed her husband's estate, Ken, as next friend of Kathleen, sued Baker Botts as well as the executor of Floyd's estate, Wells Fargo Bank, N.A., for, among other things, breach of fiduciary duty relative to Kathleen's execution of the disclaimer. A jury found that both Baker Botts and Wells Fargo had breached their fiduciary duties to Kathleen. The jury further found that $65.5 million is the value Kathleen would have received in trust had she not disclaimed her right to Floyd's estate, but determined that Kathleen had zero "lost income" damages and zero "economic loss" damages as a result of executing the disclaimer. Based on the jury's findings, the trial court, relying on its equitable powers, created a $65.5 million "equitable trust" through its judgment to benefit Kathleen. This "equitable trust" was to be funded by Baker Botts and Wells Fargo and was similar to the trust that would have existed had Kathleen not executed the disclaimer.

On appeal, the court reversed the jury verdicts in favor of Ken, finding that there was insufficient evidence that the breaches of duty caused Kathleen to disclaim her rights to Floyd's estate. The court explained further: *As additional support for his assertion that causation was established as a matter of law, Ken argues that Kathleen's decision to disclaim was "inapposite with logic and human nature" because no individual, given the choice of "keeping their money and the power over it and paying no taxes" or "giving away their money and the power over it and paying no taxes" would choose to divest. Ken's argument, however, ignores that the probate court accepted Kathleen's disclaimer. Although Ken may have made a different decision than his mother did, such does not render his mother's decision unreasonable as a matter of law. Kathleen was independently wealthy and made a choice to support her husband's charities now, rather than later. We therefore cannot say this particular evidence establishes causation as a matter of law.*

Query: Despite a lengthy recitation of all the ways in which multiple parties involved with Wells Fargo and Baker Botts were aware of the conflicts and were negligent in failing to inform Kathleen of the estate planning moves that were being suggested, the court of appeals dismissed a jury finding of liability. Why? Floyd's estate plan gave Kathleen a testamentary power of appointment over Floyd's property as well as a 5X5 power to withdraw principal. Because of the disclaimer, she could not benefit from any of those powers. Assuming the jury was correct that the corporate actors breached their fiduciary duties, shouldn't she be entitled to damages at least equal to that amount? What should corporate trustees and estate planners do when faced with the complexity of the Cailloux' estate, especially when one of them dies before the estate plan is completed? Do they do as they did here, essentially consult among themselves and decide what they think is best and present it to the family as the most logical choice, or involve the family at each stage, educating them about the implications and possibilities of different choices which will take time and money chargeable to the estate?

These cases raise at least two important points. The first is the conflict that exists when more than one person walks into your office and wants estate planning work done. You owe duties to both, and perhaps to others as well. When things start going badly, you may very well have to extricate yourself from representing at least one, if not both, parties. If you sense any potential for conflict between them, you need to be sensitive to how you are going to handle it.

The second is the conflict that inevitably arises when the same fiduciaries are trustees for multiple trusts, and the remainder beneficiaries of the trusts themselves are in conflict. Thus, in complex estate planning involving marital and family trusts, very often the remainder beneficiaries and the life beneficiary are going to be in conflict if they are different people, and if one trust prefers one set of beneficiaries over the other, and a different trust has the opposite preferences, competing trust terms may very well put the trustees into conflicts. As lawyers who establish these trusts, and then serve as trustees, you are quite likely to get into a conflict situation.

We will discuss below some of the special circumstances that can arise with these conflicts. For now, be aware that the estate plans you create can very likely create conflicts that will require multiple lawyers if the family relationships get fractious. You may also be conflicted out from later representing any of the parties if litigation ensues. So consider now the special cases of divorce, the lawyer as planner and fiduciary, and the lawyer as planner and witness.

Practice Point: The Importance of Saying No

The practice of estate planning often takes one of two paths when it comes to how new clients will find their way to your door. If you take a position in a large law firm, your calendar may be booked out well in advance with existing firm clients and their family members/referrals who are in need of estate planning, so going out and "hoofing it" to wrangle in new business may not be necessary. You may well be salaried and not worrying about how your bills will be paid that month. If, however, you take the small or solo firm route, rest assured that finding new clients will ALWAYS be an issue, as every month you are essentially starting from scratch with new cases, and the revenue from those cases may dictate your monthly compensation. In this light, it is especially tempting to say "Yes!" to prospective clients who are eager to hire you to do their work. This is why you are there, right—to do the work?

Sometimes, however, the answer may be no. Of course you will want to take on new and challenging cases. You will, however, always be balancing your workload with the inherent conflict checks that are necessary to the practice of estate planning. I was told in law school that potential conflicts in estate planning are everywhere. In practice I found this was definitely the case. My very first week as an attorney, I faced a situation where an adult daughter, in the presence of her mother, who was an existing client of the firm, asked me to do her will. She then casually mentioned that her mother also wished to change her own will as well, making the adult daughter the sole beneficiary (specifically disinheriting the mother's other two children and grandchildren). Mom looked uncomfortable and wasn't saying much at all. Conflict? Needless to say, at that point, an attorney has to go back to the very basic of ethical rules that a duty of loyalty is owed to every client. Mom needed zealous representation. So did daughter. The trick is discovering which hats, if any, you can wear. So what did I do? I did what all fresh, young attorneys should do—I called someone more seasoned in the practice and asked for help.

One of the best protections that you can give to yourself is a well-armored Engagement Letter, which spells out to your clients what your duties are as a lawyer, drafted in accordance with your state's ethical rules. Just seeing the numbers of happy couples who divorce/split just years after those loving estate planning meetings is enough to convince many lawyers to explain in very clear language how changes in relationships between existing clients can create future conflict situations for the attorney. But, be prepared. If they really liked and trusted you as their estate planner, they may well call you anyway—right when they are in the midst of a new relationship which places you in a conflict. And then you will have to say no. Remember that well-seasoned mentor? Developing relationships with other practicing attorneys also allows you to refer clients to other trusted professionals when you are in a conflict. So, stay current on your CLEs, speak frankly, don't forget to put it in writing, and most important, reach out to others in the field.

PROBLEMS

12.1. A husband and wife seek your legal counsel to draft their wills. You have previously represented the wife by drafting a prenuptial agreement, which her fiancee (now her husband) signed after review by independent counsel. The prenuptial agreement designates her sizable estate as separate property and, by signing it, he agreed to forfeit any current or future interest or elective share he might otherwise be entitled to upon divorce or her death. Are you in a conflict situation?

12.2. You represent a client and his son in various matters involving their joint ownership of an auto dealership. The client comes to your office for estate planning and tells you that he wants to leave all of his property, including his share of the auto dealership, to his son, and to the exclusion of his other three children. He tells you that his son is the only one who has stayed in their small town and continued to take an interest in your client's life. The others all moved away and visit only on holidays. You are good friends with the son, however, and you have heard him talk about his siblings and how much he likes them and is proud of them for striking out on their own. After the dad has mentioned that he is going to disinherit the other three children, the son has talked with you about how terrible he would feel if dad actually did that, and how he would want to make sure that his siblings got their fair share. You know that if dad actually follows through with his plan, and the son gives 3/4ths of the estate to his siblings, that they will be facing significantly greater transfer tax liabilities than if dad just gave the property equally to all four children. What are your responsibilities here?

1. THE SPECIAL CASE OF DIVORCE

Conflicts are very likely to arise when you represented a married couple to draft their estate plans and they later divorce. You certainly cannot represent them both in the divorce action, and I'm sure they would not want you to. Assuming the wife gets to you first and asks you to represent her in the divorce, are you conflicted because of your prior representation of the husband? It is probably best not to represent either, especially if by representing one you open yourself up to a challenge that will take your time away from other matters. Remember, even if there is no impropriety because you don't know anything about their property situation that both don't already know, even the appearance of impropriety can be trouble, especially if you end up making an enemy of the other spouse. You might very well be better served declining to represent either in the divorce and then attracting both as future clients when they redraft their estate plans after their divorce. That's when you can always use that valuable line: "I'm really an estates and trusts practitioner and don't feel comfortable venturing into the complex and adversarial world of family law (criminal law, business law, antitrust, or any other area that a client may have fallen into)."

Representing one divorcing spouse in the divorce, which may not be a conflict, is not the only situation that tests the ethical waters. Consider these cases as well:

Oregon Ethics Opinion

2005–148

In this case the lawyer represented a husband and wife in their estate planning, drafting wills for both. A few years later, the wife hired the lawyer to represent her in a divorce proceeding. Can the lawyer represent the wife? The ethics board explained:

In this scenario, Wife is a potential current client and Husband is a former client. It is necessary to determine whether the proposed representation would constitute a former client conflict under Oregon RPC 1.9(a). We do this by determining whether the current and former matters are the same or substantially related within the meaning of the rule.

On the limited facts presented, it does not appear that Lawyer would be in possession of information relating to the representation of Husband that would not already be known to Wife or to which Wife would not otherwise have access. If this is so, no information-specific former client conflict would exist.

Are the estate planning and the marital dissolution the same or substantially related matters because they are "matter-specific"? Without more, it cannot be said that estate planning on the one hand and marital dissolution on the other constitute the same matter.

The key question, then, is whether Lawyer's representation of Wife in the marital dissolution is a matter-specific conflict because it will work to Husband's injury or prejudice in connection with the estate planning that Lawyer did for him. Even though it may generally be true, pursuant to ORS 112.315, that a divorce revokes all provisions in a will in favor of the testator's former spouse, the revocation of wills in that manner is not sufficient to create a conflict of interest unless the parties are legally bound not to revoke or change their wills. Cf. ABA Formal Ethics Op No 05–434 (absent addi-

tional factors, there is no conflict in representing testator in disinheriting beneficiary who is also client, because testator is free to change will at any time).

Query: Why is there no conflict here when clearly the lawyer knows everything about the husband's property? What would the husband need to show to convince a court that there is an information-specific conflict? Would the decision change if the laws of your state did not provide for the revocation of trust interests, powers of attorney, or health care proxies upon divorce?

Smith v. Hastie

367 S.C. 410 (S.C. Ct. App. 2005)

In this case, Berrien and Everett Smith, husband and wife, were having marital difficulties in the early 1990s. They began marriage counseling, and during the counseling met with J. Drayton Hastie, a lawyer who had become known to Everett, to establish a family limited partnership. The partnership was formed and Berrien assigned her share of jointly held property as well as some sole-owned properties to the partnership, under assurances by Hastie that both she and Everett would have access to the assets during their lifetimes and, if she divorced Everett, she would be "fine." In 1997, however, Everett filed for divorce and Berrien signed numerous documents prepared by Hastie that amended the partnership in an effort to settle the marital property division. Berrien retained counsel after a meeting with Hastie where he purportedly told her he intended to file a petition to force her to relinquish her shares in the family partnership. Everett and Berrien then executed a marital settlement agreement in which Berrien relinquished her shares in the family limited partnership upon Everett's representations that her shares would be gifted to their three children. A year later Berrien sued Hastie for breach of fiduciary duty, professional negligence, civil conspiracy, and fraud. The court dismissed the civil conspiracy and fraud charges but upheld the breach of fiduciary duty and negligence claims, explaining: *Smith alleged Hastie was liable for negligence and breach of fiduciary duty in the following particulars: (1) improperly undertaking joint representation of her and Everett; (2) failing to inform her of any potential conflict; (3) failing to recommend that she seek independent counsel; (4) failing to advise her about the consequences of the transfer of assets to the partnership in the event of a divorce between her and Everett; (5) improperly attempting to force her to relinquish her shares in the partnership; (6) improperly attempting to negotiate a settlement of the domestic dispute between her and Everett; and (7) acting solely on Everett's behalf.* The court admitted the affidavit of an estates and trusts attorney, H. Dewain Herring, who explained the standard practice for dealing with conflicts in this kind of case.

In the affidavit, Herring stated that, even if Hastie had no initial knowledge of marital problems between Smith and her husband, he should have advised her of the ramifications of the family limited partnership in the event of a divorce and should have advised her to seek at least a second opinion because he had represented her husband substantially in the past. In conjunction with this opinion, Herring also stated that Hastie "should have probed further into existing conflicts between the spouses" and suggested that this could have been done by an engagement letter asking the clients to identify any conflicts that exist at the outset of joint representation. Her-

ring was emphatic that the present case called for such a letter, noting this precaution was advisable in cases in which one spouse has most of the financial wealth, tends to be the dominant person in the planning process, or is the client of longer standing with the lawyer.

Herring further stated the following: (1) devices such as family limited partnerships could be used to "freeze out" unit holders and devalue assets because of the lack of marketability and closely held nature of the unit; and (2) there was no written documentation showing that Smith was informed of this possibility. In addition, Herring opined that, based on his review of the case, Smith's participation in the family limited partnership caused her to lose control over the assets placed in the partnership while her estranged husband, because of his control of the Broughton Corporation, seized control over these assets.

The trial court granted summary judgment to the lawyer, dismissing Berrien's negligence and malpractice claims. On appeal, however, the court reversed and remanded for a new trial, noting that Berrien had alleged adequate facts to support her claim.

Query: Assuming Hastie was a commercial lawyer and not a trusts and estates lawyer, what was he thinking? Trusts and estates lawyers know that when a married couple walks in their door there is a potential conflict that must be managed. A commercial lawyer should know this even better, because joint representation is rarer in the commercial context. Even assuming Hastie didn't know of Berrien and Everett's marital difficulties, should a trusts and estates lawyer doing any work for a married couple always, as Herring claimed, be thinking about the effects of divorce? Herring's affidavit suggested numerous steps that Hastie should have taken to manage the conflict between Berrien and Everett. Do you think all of those steps are reasonable? Do you think all trusts and estates lawyers who represent couples take all of those steps?

Tensfeldt v. Haberman

319 Wis.2d 329, 768 N.W.2d 641 (2009)

Robert Tensfeldt and his first wife, Ruth, had three children—Christine, Robert William, and John. When Robert and Ruth divorced in 1974, they entered into an agreement stipulating to various terms of the divorce. The divorce court determined that the stipulation was "fair and reasonable" and incorporated the stipulation into the divorce judgment. One of the terms of the stipulation provides that Robert would make and maintain a will leaving two-thirds of his net estate to the children.

Robert married his second wife, Constance, in 1975. They remained married until Robert's death in 2000. Robert and Constance had no children together, although Constance had three children from a previous marriage. In 1978, Robert executed a will that was compliant with the stipulation and order—one-third of the net estate went to Constance, and two-thirds of the net estate went to his children or their issue.

In 1980, Robert retained Attorney LaBudde (LaBudde) of Michael Best & Friedrich, LLP to provide estate planning services. It is undisputed that Robert made LaBudde aware of his obligation to his children from the outset. When Robert initially met with LaBudde, he gave the attorney a copy of the divorce judgment and stipulation. LaBudde told Robert that he had three choices: comply with the stipulation; negotiate with the children to alter his obligation; or ignore the stipulation, knowing that the children might contest Robert's will upon his death. Robert chose the third option, and in 1981, LaBudde drafted an estate plan that did not leave two-thirds of the net estate outright to the Tensfeldt children.

In addition, Robert consulted Attorney Haberman of LaBudde's office when the latter retired and moved to Florida, and Haberman continued to represent Tensfeldt and Constance. Robert died in 2000 in Florida and Robert's son and Constance were appointed personal representatives of the estate. At that point they learned of a Florida decision allowing a surviving spouse to elect against an estate and continue to receive income from an *inter vivos* trust, a decision that Haberman should have known about and warned Robert that, under the new rule, Constance would get even more than Robert originally provided her. After his death, Constance then elected against the estate and Robert's children sued in Florida to enforce the divorce stipulation and order promising them two-thirds of Robert's estate outright. The Florida courts held that Constance's 30% elective share would be calculated before the children's claim for two-thirds, giving the children only 2/3rds of 70% of Robert's net estate.

The children then returned to Wisconsin and sued Attorneys LaBudde and Haberman for various intentional torts. On certification to the Wisconsin Supreme Court, the Court affirmed summary judgment against LaBudde for intending to draft a will that violated a court judgment and found he had no immunity or privilege to draft a will in violation of the court judgment. The court did not find LaBudde liable to the Tensfeldt children for negligence in the drafting of Robert's estate plan. Even though they were not in privity of contract with him, the Court noted that third party beneficiary doctrines could hold an attorney liable for negligence in drafting estates documents IF the children could establish that the attorney's negligence thwarted the testator's clear intent. Here, because it was clear that Robert wanted to thwart the judgment of the divorce court, LaBudde was entitled to summary judgment on the negligence claim because his actions were directed by Robert, and were not due to his own negligence.

The children also sued Attorney Haberman for negligence in failing to inform Robert about the likely consequences of the Florida decision. The court upheld the summary judgment dismissing the claim against Attorney Haberman on the grounds that there was no evidence that Robert would have altered his estate plan had he realized the likely impact of the Florida decision.

The dissent would have relieved Attorney LaBudde from liability for intentionally violating the divorce judgment on the grounds that the divorce court did not have jurisdiction to order the estate plan, that LaBudde was immune from liability because he proceeded in a good faith belief that the provision in the divorce judgment was void, and that the statute of limitations precluded actions on the divorce judgment.

Query: As we have mentioned numerous times throughout this book, divorce lawyers need to be thinking about estate matters when they draft a property settlement and divorce agreement. Do divorce lawyers potentially commit malpractice if they don't consult with estates lawyers at divorce, and do estates lawyers potentially commit malpractice if they don't consult with divorce lawyers when drafting estate plans for divorced individuals? Should the lawyers get off just because the client is insistent on violating court judgments? And should the lawyers get off when the third party beneficiaries, who have standing to sue for negligence, cannot prove that the client would have altered his plan had the lawyer done his job properly?

These cases pinpoint numerous places where ethical conflicts can arise in representing couples through and after divorce. If you have learned anything in this course it is that spouses occupy a privileged position in the law of trusts and estates. That means that spouses have legal and equitable claims on the property of their partners. As couples divorce, those legal and equitable claims get partitioned in ways that often require adjustments to estate planning instruments. It would be ideal if all divorces occurred with the assistance of an estate planning expert. This, however, is unlikely to happen. In the meantime, as an estate planning and probate attorney, you probably need to do what Attorney Herring suggested, which is to plan with the possibility of divorce in the back of your mind at all times.

Another note to keep in the back of your mind is the potential ethical conflict that can arise if you draft estate plans that call for you to act further in managing, probating, or distributing the estate. Just as it makes sense for an estates client to ask you to represent them in their divorce, they will also want you to manage matters after their death. Can you do so ethically?

2.   THE LAWYER AS PLANNER AND FIDUCIARY

As with Sara and Lawyer Farr, there will be countless opportunities in which the lawyer who drafts the estate plan will be asked to serve as a trustee, or as a lawyer for the personal representative, or as a lawyer for the surviving spouse who may have also been a client. It makes perfect sense for the lawyer who drafted all the documents and met with mom and dad about how they wanted their estates to pass at their deaths to also be the lawyer who helps make that happen. The details of how to competently probate their estates is usually covered in a course on Probate or Fiduciary Administration and there are numerous excellent books that discuss the fiduciary obligations of administrators in the actual process of handling the estate. Here we will focus exclusively on the potential conflict that exists when the lawyer who drafts the estate plan drafts a plan that appoints himself as a fiduciary (trustee or personal administrator) for an estate. Remember the Florida lawyer who lost the codicil?[1] He was also appointed one of the executors of the decedent's estate. The court held that he was no longer a disinterested witness to the execution because he had a financial stake in how the lost codicil issue was resolved. Because he risked being sued for malpractice or negligence, his independence was successfully challenged.

There are countless ways in which the planner's loyalties to the clients can diverge from the lawyer's loyalties to the estate, the trust, or beneficiaries. As you will see from the next section, lawyers often have duties to beneficiaries, even though the privity only exists between the lawyer and

---

[1]   Smith v. DeParry, 86 So.3d 1228 (Fla.App. 2 Dist. 2012).

the testator. Consider the ACTEC Commentaries on conflicts between the lawyer as planner and the lawyer as fiduciary.

Selection of Fiduciaries. The lawyer advising a client regarding the selection and appointment of a fiduciary should make full disclosure to the client of any benefits that the lawyer may receive as a result of the appointment. In particular, the lawyer should inform the client of any policies or practices known to the lawyer that the fiduciaries under consideration may follow with respect to the employment of the scrivener of an estate planning document as counsel for the fiduciary. The lawyer may also point out that a fiduciary has the right to choose any counsel it wishes. If there is a significant risk that the lawyer's independent professional judgment in the selection of a fiduciary would be materially limited by the lawyer's self interest or any other factor, the lawyer must obtain the client's informed consent, confirmed in writing.

Appointment of Scrivener as Fiduciary. An individual is generally free to select and appoint whomever he or she wishes to a fiduciary office (e.g., trustee, executor, attorney-in-fact). None of the provisions of the MRPC deals explicitly with the propriety of a lawyer preparing for a client a will or other document that appoints the lawyer to a fiduciary office. As a general proposition lawyers should be permitted to assist adequately informed clients who wish to appoint their lawyers as fiduciaries. Accordingly, a lawyer should be free to prepare a document that appoints the lawyer to a fiduciary office so long as the client is properly informed, the appointment does not violate the conflict of interest rules of MRPC 1.7 (Conflict of Interest: General Rule), and the appointment is not the product of undue influence or improper solicitation by the lawyer.

The designation of the lawyer as fiduciary will implicate the conflict of interest provisions of MRPC 1.7 when there is a significant risk that the lawyer's interests in obtaining the appointment will materially limit the lawyer's independent professional judgment in advising the client concerning the choice of an executor or other fiduciary. See ACTEC Commentary to MRPC 1.8. (addressing transactions entered into by lawyers with clients).

For the purposes of this Commentary a client is properly informed if the client is provided with information regarding the role and duties of the fiduciary, the ability of a lay person to serve as fiduciary with legal and other professional assistance, and the comparative costs of appointing the lawyer or another person or institution as fiduciary. The client should also be informed of any significant lawyer–client relationship that exists between the lawyer or the lawyer's firm and a corporate fiduciary under consideration for appointment.[2]

Do you think Sara Marsman and Lawyer Farr had an appropriate conversation about the comparative costs of appointing a lay person rather than a lawyer as the trustee of her estate? What about the costs? Do you think Lawyer Farr adequately understood in advance the costs of serving as trustee to a small estate that had a fairly small amount of property in it? Remember, too, that executors and personal administrators are appointed by a court. There will be a judge looking over the will and estate documents

---

[2]   See ACTEC Commentaries at: http://www.actec.org/public/Commentaries1.7.asp (emphasis added).

at the time Letters Testamentary are issued. Not so with trusts. No one supervises, or even might know, that a lawyer is serving as a trustee unless the trust is testamentary or someone challenges some aspect of the trust and its administration. Should that difference matter?

Consider the following cases involving lawyers who drafted the plans that nominated them to fiduciary positions and ask if there was overreaching by the lawyers, or if the lawyers breached their ethical responsibilities in doing as their clients apparently asked them to do:

In re Estate of Lowenstein

600 N.Y.S.2d 997 (N.Y. Sur. Ct. 1993)

Toni Lowenstein and her husband went to Lawyer Fred Sichel in December, 1984, for estate planning. In the course of the representation, they signed an agreement that read:

> We appoint *FRED J. SICHEL* as executor and trustee herein since we have known him and his family for over 40 years and trust his business judgment and fairness.

Upon the death of Lowenstein's husband in 1987, his wife offered for probate an earlier will dated August, 1984, in which she and another person were named executors. Mr. Sichel cross-petitioned for probate of the will he drafted and he produced the agreement by which the husband had agreed to nominate him as executor. *The resulting probate contest was settled by the payment of $25,000 to Mr. Sichel in consideration of his renunciation as executor and trustee. Thereafter, Mrs. Lowenstein executed a new will, dated July 6, 1987, naming her daughter, Hilda Straus, as executrix. That will was admitted to probate by this court on July 10, 1991 and letters testamentary issued to Mrs. Straus. Mr. Sichel seeks damages of $64,894, which he alleges he would have earned as commissions for serving as executor.*

Sichel claimed that a contractual agreement to name an attorney as fiduciary is enforceable if reduced to writing. But the court disagreed, noting that *when the nominated executor . . . is also the draftsman, even a writing to such effect would be of doubtful value.* The court cited the Code of Professional Responsibility, EC 5–6, which states in relevant part: *A lawyer should not consciously influence a client to name him as executor, trustee or lawyer in an instrument. In those cases where [the] client wishes to name [a] lawyer as such, care should be taken . . . to avoid even the appearance of impropriety.* Refusing to enforce the contract, the court explained: *The contract in question, drafted by an attorney and purporting to bind the testatrix to appoint him as fiduciary, presents at least the appearance of the very type of improper behavior prohibited by the Code of Professional Responsibility. Such a contract, unlike a will, may not be unilaterally revoked or amended by the testatrix. This irrevocability is particularly important here, since the contract under consideration makes no provision for future changes in circumstances. The contract purports to mandate the appointment of the attorney regardless of his health, age, competency or geographic location. Such a requirement would make no sense for most testators and there do not appear to be any special circumstances here which would lead the court to hold otherwise.* The court articulated the rule that: *a contract provision requiring the nomination of the attorney draftsman as fiduciary of the testator's estate is unenforceable unless it is clearly demonstrated to the satisfaction of the court that special circumstances required the services of the attorney draftsman and that the nomination was not the product of overreaching.*

Query: Do you think Fred Sichel decided to forego his fees for drafting the estate documents in exchange for a binding contract that he would serve as executor? If he did, would he have also created a conflict? This is a case in which the lawyer's duty to his clients seems to have been overpowered by his own desire to financially benefit himself at his clients' expense. Should this kind of contract ever be enforceable?

In re Matter of Ryan

594 N.Y.S.2d 168 (App. Div. 1993)

In this case, Attorney Ryan, a graduate of Columbia University and Georgetown Law Center, was in practice with his father for many years engaged in an estates and trusts practice. In that context, they began to represent Caroline Becker and her husband. They drafted the couple's estate plans, and Ryan served as attorney for Mr. Becker's estate. After her husband's death, Caroline Becker was admitted to a nursing home where she lived for five years, until her death at age 92. During that time, attorney Ryan was summoned numerous times to execute new wills, new codicils, and to deal with Chase Manhattan Bank, the corporate trustee of Mrs. Becker's property. Over time, Caroline grew frustrated with Chase and signed documents adding Ryan as co-trustee and co-executor of her estate. Also, Ryan's wife, Viviane Ryan, began to meet with Caroline frequently, helping her to deal with her room or her aides. Caroline was impressed with Viviane's handling of her matters, and knew that Viviane worked in her husband's office (she had a year of law school besides a PhD in French Literature). Caroline purportedly asked Ryan to amend the trust agreement and her will to name Viviane a co-trustee and co-executor as well. Over time Caroline also reduced many of her bequests to her children and grandchildren, and increased the bequests to nurse's aides. Ryan also drafted, and Caroline executed, a Codicil that granted Ryan and his wife the power to remove Chase, the corporate trustee, *in their sole, absolute, and uncontrolled discretion* but they never did so. Upon Caroline's death in 1977, letters testamentary were granted to Ryan, Viviane, and Chase. Objections were filed by a grandson of Caroline, and the Surrogate found that all the propounded instruments had been duly executed and that the decedent was in all respects competent to make a will, except as regards the appointment of Ryan and his wife as executors and trustees. In a disciplinary hearing, Ryan was found not to have acted in a fraudulent, venal, or deceitful manner, but he was given a public censure for the appointment of his wife, who the board felt was *unqualified* because "*she had never owned stocks and had no expertise in financial investments.*" Declining to articulate a general rule about appointing relatives as executors or trustees, the court stated: *in cases such as this, the burden is on the attorney to prove that the client is cognizant of all the circumstances. While bringing in another lawyer to counsel the testator and provide an affidavit that the testator was fully apprised of the relevant facts would allow an attorney to easily meet his burden should such transaction be questioned, sufficient cause has not been demonstrated which would warrant making such procedure a formal requirement.*

Query: This is a case in which an elderly client, living in a nursing home and being dependent on family and friends, turned to her lawyer and his wife, more and more, for assistance. Over time, she logically found them to be efficient and caring, able to resolve problems with her room, her medical care, and her property. Is it surprising that she asked them to serve as trustees since they were far more likely to be responsive than Chase Manhattan Bank? Although Caroline Becker had children and grandchildren, would it surprise you that she preferred calling the Ryans to take of things rather than her family? Was the appointment of Viviane Ryan a violation of Ryan's duty to his client or a conflict of interest?

Estate of Devroy

109 Wis. 2d 154, 325 N.W.2d 345 (Wis. 1982)

Mr. Dave Devroy died testate on January 19, 1981. His will datedNovember 7, 1979, was drafted by attorney Todd Schmeling. Article XI of the will provided:

ARTICLE XI

I hereby nominate Ray Devroy as Personal Representative of this Will, on the condition that he retains Todd J. Schmeling, if living and willing to so act, as the attorney for the performance of all legal services required in the probate of my estate and in the fulfillment of the terms of this Will. If for any reason Ray Devroy is unwilling or unable to act as my Personal Representative, then I nominate James Devroy as Personal Representative of this Will, on the condition that he retains Todd J. Schmeling, if living and willing so to act, as the attorney for the performance of all legal services required in the probate of my estate and in the fulfillment of the terms of this Will. If for any reason both Ray Devroy and James Devroy are unable or unwilling to act as my Personal Representative, I request that the Circuit Court appoint a personal representative who will retain Todd J. Schmeling as such attorney. This preferential designation of Todd J. Schmeling as the attorney to probate my estate is made as an expression of my intent and desire as to the manner in which I wish my affairs to be settled, and without any solicitation, suggestion or influence on the part of Todd J. Schmeling whatsoever. Todd J. Schmeling has represented and advised me during several years preceding the execution of this Will, has an intimate knowledge of my business affairs and property, and knows my views and wishes respecting many matters that may arise in the probate of this instrument. Should either Ray Devroy or James Devroy act as my Personal Representative, I request that he not be required to furnish a bond.

On January 30, 1981, Raymond Devroy petitioned the Circuit Court for Brown County for the probate of the will. Because he did not wish to retain Mr. Schmeling as attorney for the estate, Mr. Devroy petitioned the court for a Declaratory Judgment determining his rights and responsibilities under Article XI of the will. In discussing the law on will provisions requiring the appointment of a particular attorney, the Wisconsin Supreme Court stated:

Wisconsin is unique among the states in holding that the right to make a will and have its provisions enforced is constitutionally guaranteed. In order to give effect to this right this court has on numerous occasions stressed that it is the intent of the testator which governs in construing will provisions. This court has also stated repeatedly that "Anything designed to defeat the intent of the testator is against public policy." Thus, in determining the enforceability of Article XI of the will of Dave Devroy, we must give great weight to the intent of Dave Devroy as expressed in the provision of his will in question.

In previous cases where this court has considered the enforceability of a will provision directing that a named attorney be employed by the personal representative, the will itself did not state what the testator's intent would be if the personal representative refused to work with the named attorney.

In the present case we have such a statement. Article XI of the will of Dave Devroy is clear in expressing the testator's preference that attorney Schmeling be employed rather than either of the named personal representatives should the personal representatives not retain attorney Schmeling. Not only did the testator make explicit his preference for attorney Schmeling but he also provided a mechanism whereby an alternate personal representative would be chosen if neither of the named personal representatives was willing to retain attorney Schmeling. Where the language of the challenged will provision explicitly expresses the testator's intent that an attorney be retained even at the cost of the nominated personal representative not being employed, this court will give effect to that which the testator intended absent some overriding public policy reason to the contrary.

In his decision the trial judge said "better jurisprudence dictates that rational principles of public policy supercede that of the testator's intent." But public policy is not balanced against the testator's intent. Rather, competing policies—one protecting the constitutional right to make a will and have its provisions enforced and the others discouraging client solicitation and protecting the right of a client, in this case the designated personal representative, to select an attorney—must be balanced to yield a result that best carries out the purposes behind each policy.

The fact that Dave Devroy provided a mechanism in his will which guaranteed that the attorney he selected to probate his estate would not be forced on an unwilling personal representative disposes of that public policy problem.

There is no public policy that requires that a testator place his personal representative's preferences above his own when attorney selection is the issue. A testator may very well conclude that selection of the attorney is more important to him than who serves as the personal representative. The fact is that testators frequently choose relatives or friends for the position as a token of honor or esteem even though they may have little qualifying experience. The testator knows the attorney will see to it that the job is properly carried out.

A provision which directs that nomination of a personal representative is conditioned on the willingness of that person to retain a specific attorney may arouse suspicion that the named attorney improperly solicited the business. Such a suspicion will often be unfounded. A testator may well believe it important that the attorney who handled his personal and business affairs during his lifetime also be the one who provides legal services to his estate.

It is evident to this court that Mr. Schmeling has avoided even the appearance of solicitation. To require more of any attorney or firm would have the effect of saying that an attorney could under no circumstances draft a will provision which designated his employment by the testator's estate.

Query: Do you think an absolute bar is the best rule, or should an attorney draftsman be permitted to draft language appointing him or herself as executor, trustee, or lawyer for the estate? When you read the reasons why the law-lawyer is appointed trustee or executor are you suspicious? Who do you think drafted the actual words used? Assuming there is no bar to a lawyer serving in a fiduciary capacity, is the real question a court should probe whether undue influence or incapacity existed? If the answer is yes, is the solution attorney discipline or nonprobate of the will, or both?

Massachusetts Bar Association Ethics Opinion

#06–01

A lawyer asks whether she can draft a client's will that names the lawyer as executrix and whether as executrix she can retain herself as counsel

Discussion: *Massachusetts has no [formal] requirement, and lawyers under wills that they have drafted often serve as fiduciaries and counsel to fiduciaries. The Supreme Judicial Court has held that there is no* per se *bar to a lawyer's qualifying as executor under a will that he drafted. Nevertheless, it is important that the lawyer consider carefully with the client if alternative fiduciaries might be better equipped to handle the estate, whether because of the nature of the assets involved, the personal experience of the lawyer, or other reasons. If the lawyer represents, in addition to the testator, members of the testator's family who may benefit from the estate, the lawyer should discuss this with the testator, provided that the representation of the family member is not in itself a confidence that should not be disclosed to the testator. If such were the case, in some circumstances the lawyer might have to refrain from acting as executrix or counsel to the executrix. The lawyer should also discuss the intended methods of calculating fees as fiduciary and as counsel and that the probate court would review total fees for reasonableness.*

Query: The Massachusetts Opinion references a Formal Advisory Opinion #91–1 from the Supreme Court of Georgia that prescribes the actual form a client must sign before a lawyer drafting a will can be designated as executor or trustee. In Georgia, therefore, a lawyer is barred from serving as fiduciary unless the lawyer obtains the client's consent in advance in writing. Why doesn't Massachusetts require a similar writing? Note the myriad alternatives the lawyer needs to explain to her client before drafting a will naming herself as a fiduciary. Do you see how it is easy to cut corners when your client is in your office and simply wants all the paperwork to be done? In *Estate of Peterson*, 465 S.E.2d 524 (Ga. Ct. App. 2002) the attorney who drafted a will under which he was named as executor was disqualified from acting because, although he had informed testator orally of the potential conflicts of interest, he failed to either obtain client's consent in writing or to give the client written notice as required by the applicable Georgia ethics opinion.[3]

---

[3]   For a thorough discussion of these issues, see the ABA Formal Opinion No. 02–426, and New Hampshire Ethics Opinion, 2008–09/1, available at: http://www.nhbar.org/legal-links/Ethics–Opinion–2008–09_01.asp.

There is obvious potential for conflict when an attorney draftsman drafts an instrument nominating himself to a fiduciary position, especially a remunerative position. Assuming the attorney was paid to draft the estates documents, should he be barred from accepting the paid position of personal representative or trustee? No state prohibits the practice altogether, for the very sound reason that lawyers do a good job in fiduciary capacities. Lawyer Farr may very well have been the most appropriate person to serve as trustee for Sara Marsman's trust. But other situations are not so clear-cut. Lawyer Sichel certainly raised some eyebrows when he drafted an agreement for his clients in which they agreed to bind their estates to hire him to be executor. How do you think that conversation went in the office? Was it illegal, against public policy, unethical, or simply bad taste to sue the estate for lost damages when he was not appointed executor?

There is nothing wrong with drafting documents that appoint yourself to a future fiduciary position. However, as the rules clearly mandate, the conflict must be managed by 1) informing your client of the existence of the conflict, 2) informing your client of the fees that you might earn in that position, 3) adequately discussing the possibility of appointing lay persons or other professionals as fiduciary, 4) revealing any relationships between you the lawyer and others under consideration for the appointment. Go back and consider each of the cases above in light of these requirements. Picture whether you think these were met, or could have been met. Did Caroline Becker have the testamentary right to appoint Viviane Ryan as trustee, even if she was unqualified?

Whether or not the lawyer–draftsman has written a plan that nominates herself to a fiduciary position, or nominates herself to serve as a lawyer for the fiduciary, she may still be conflicted out of serving in that capacity if the estate is contested, even if she obtained the client's consent to the nomination. This can occur when there are challenges to the will or other testamentary documents and the lawyer is going to be a material witness in the contest litigation. Not only do you want to be extremely careful in the execution of estates documents, but you will need to keep good notes and be prepared to testify that the process was done correctly. This obligation to your client may very well conflict you from serving as a fiduciary, or as a lawyer for a fiduciary to the estate.

3.   THE ATTORNEY WITNESS RULE

In addition to being precluded from serving as a fiduciary in certain circumstances, the lawyers who draft estates documents are often precluded from litigating will contest suits because they are likely to be called as witnesses, especially in cases involving incapacity or undue influence. The MRPC § 3.7 on lawyer witnesses provides:

> **MRPC § 3.7 Lawyer as Witness**
>
> (a) A lawyer shall not act as advocate at a trial in which the lawyer is likely to be a necessary witness unless:
>
> (1) the testimony relates to an uncontested issue;
>
> (2) the testimony relates to the nature and value of legal services rendered in the case; or
>
> (3) disqualification of the lawyer would work substantial hardship on the client.
>
> (b) A lawyer may act as advocate in a trial in which another lawyer in the lawyer's firm is likely to be called as a witness unless precluded from doing so by Rule 1.7 or Rule 1.9.

The ACTEC Commentaries to this rule elaborate further:

> MRPC 3.7 is intended to avoid or eliminate not only possible conflicts of interest between lawyer and client but also situations in trial that may prejudice the opposing party when the lawyer combines or intermingles his or her role as an advocate with that as a witness.
>
> The first two exceptions to acting as an advocate at trial when the lawyer is "likely to be a necessary witness" are straightforward and uncontroversial. Exception two is commonly encountered in estate, trust and protective proceedings where the reasonableness of the attorney's compensation for legal services may be an issue and testimony by the lawyer(s) involved is required to resolve the dispute. The third or "substantial hardship" exception involves a balancing of the interests of the client in keeping his or her counsel (despite counsel's involvement as a witness) and the possible prejudice to the opposing party. In determining prejudice, the trier of fact will look to the nature of the case, the importance and probable tenor of the lawyer's testimony and the probability that the lawyer's testimony may conflict with that of other witnesses. However, even if a risk of prejudice to the opposing party exists, the court will nevertheless consider the negative effects of disqualification on the lawyer's client. In applying this Rule, the principle of imputed disqualification (MRPC 1.10: Imputation of Conflicts of Interest; Disqualification: General Rule) does not apply.[4]

As you can imagine, the lawyer who represents the personal administrator of an estate should not be testifying in court that the testator was of sound mind during the execution of the will that purportedly appoints the personal administrator. This would create a clear conflict of interest, although it is one that is very likely to arise in the context of an estates and trusts practice. As a lawyer drafting wills for your clients, you can easily imagine that you will be asked to help with the probate of the wills that you drafted. Certainly you could not represent an opponent of the will challenging it on incapacity grounds if you are the lawyer who supervised the execution as you would be violating your duty to your client the testator by challenging her will. However, if you represent the proponent of the will, you may still be in a conflict situation and be forced to step aside from representing any of the parties to a contest suit. Consider the following cases in this context:

---

[4]   See http://www.actec.org/public/Commentaries3.7.asp.

Estate of Waters

647 A.2d 1091 (Del. 1994)

Elizabeth Waters executed a will in December, 1988, after being pressured to do so by the family of her cousin, Lillian Young, with whom Waters lived after her health began to decline in 1983. Lillian's sister, another cousin, contacted Attorney Brian Murphy to prepare a will for Waters leaving the only major asset, a house, to Lillian for life, remainder to Waters' granddaughter and next of kin, Claire Trent. Without ever meeting with Waters, Murphy drafted a will according to instructions from Lillian's sister, and went to Waters' house for the execution. The Master made the following findings of facts and conclusions of law with regard to Murphy's testimony about the execution:

He had prepared a will for a client he never met or spoke with until the time he asked her to sign the will. The woman he met was debilitated from disease: a stroke had impaired her ability to hear him and to hold and sign a piece of paper, and the pain of cancer had caused her to be medicated with a narcotic. He never met with the client privately to ascertain from her the nature of her wishes, as opposed to her wishes as related by the sister of the principal beneficiary of the will. The effect of the will is to disinherit, for all practical purposes, the client's next of kin, her granddaughter. The statutory law of Delaware may not spell out in so many words the practice to be followed by a lawyer in drafting a will for a client who is a stroke victim and whose ability to comprehend may be diminished by medication, but the case law, [citations omitted] clearly indicates that a lawyer has a duty to proceed with caution when preparing a will for a client who is in very bad health and perhaps near death. I do not believe the necessary degree of caution was exercised in this case such as to allow me to give any weight to the lawyer's testimony that Elizabeth Waters understood what she was doing when she signed her will. He saw her only once, it is undenied that her ability to hear was impaired, and she could not speak. All she could do was gesture with her head and, with difficulty, make a mark on a piece of paper. This is not enough when one has had no prior opportunity to learn from the testator his wishes in connection with his estate. (emphasis added).

The Master then refused to allow the will to probate. Despite that, Brian Murphy continued to act as trial attorney for the estate in the proceedings contested in Chancery by Claire Trent. The Court of Chancery then declined to follow the Master's report and allowed the will to be probated. Upon appeal by Trent, Murphy continued to represent the estate.

During the Chancery litigation, Trent's lawyer sent the following letter to Murphy:

Dear [Mr. Murphy]:

As we discussed on the phone, it is my opinion that you should be disqualified from acting as an attorney in the above matter because you are a necessary witness concerning the circumstances surrounding the preparation and execution of Elizabeth Waters' Last Will.

In particular, your deposition testimony concerning the events leading to your preparation of the Will is in direct conflict with the testimony of Mildred Young. Also, your testimony is relevant to the issue of Elizabeth Waters' testamentary capacity, as well as the issue of undue influence.

> *By reason of the above facts, your disqualification to act as attorney in this matter appears to be clearly prohibited under Rule 3.7 of the Delaware Rules of Professional Conduct. I would prefer to avoid filing a formal motion with the Court concerning this matter. However, I will do so if you do not voluntarily withdraw as attorney in this matter.*

Murphy replied by letter as follows: "I see no conflict of interest. Lawyers witness wills all the time."

Trent's lawyer did not move to disqualify Murphy at that time under a mistaken interpretation that his client lacked standing to do so. However, the Supreme Court of Delaware held that this was precisely the kind of circumstance in which a non-client litigant has standing to move to disqualify a lawyer. The Court explained the law as such:

> *The duty of a witness to state the objective truth when testifying is fundamentally different from the duty of a trial advocate to represent his or her client zealously within the bounds of the law. The personal credibility of a witness is always at issue and often subjected to vigorous cross-examination for purposes of impeachment. A trial advocate may not vouch for the credibility of a witness or state a personal belief in the merit of his or her client's position.*

> *In fact, one of the rationales for prohibiting the dual lawyer–witness situation in a contested proceeding is to prevent confusion by the trier of fact with regard to the separate roles of an advocate and a witness. That rationale is explained as follows:*

>> *Combining the roles of advocate and witness can prejudice the opposing party and can involve a conflict of interest between the lawyer and client.*

>> *The opposing party has proper objection where the combination of roles may prejudice that party's right in the litigation. A witness is required to testify on the basis of personal knowledge, while an advocate is expected to explain and comment on evidence given by others. It may not be clear whether a statement by an advocate–witness should be taken as proof or as an analysis of the proof.*

Delaware and Model Rules of Professional Conduct Rule 3.7 (commentary).

"The interest of the opposing party protected by Rule 3.7 is parallel to that protected by Rule 3.4(e), which forbids an advocate from voicing personal opinions about the merits of a cause." Geoffrey C. Hazard, Jr. & W. William Hodes, The Law of Lawyering: A Handbook on the Model Rules of Professional Conduct 680 (2d ed. 1993). Rule 3.7 and Rule 3.4(e) both prohibit the mixing of advocacy and testimony. Id. There are multiple threats to the integrity of the judicial proceedings if a trial advocate also testifies as a trial witness regarding a contested issue, e.g., (i) the attorney may either be accused of distorting the truth for the client's benefit or testifying truthfully to the client's detriment; (ii) the attorney may, perhaps even inadvertently, interject unsworn testimony into the cross-examination of other witnesses; (iii) the attorney may be called upon by other evidence to argue his or her own credibility to the trier of fact; (iv) the attorney may, in effect, give "unsworn" testimony during arguments to the trial judge and/or jury.

Query: It makes perfect sense that the lawyer who drafted the will should help with its probate. Yet does it make sense that every time a will is contested the lawyer/draftsman has to step aside? If not, what rule should the court adopt for when the attorney can continue to represent the estate and when she must step aside? Do you think Brian Murphy breached his ethical duty to his client in this case? Who was his client? Do you think he had a client retainer letter setting out his duties and the work expected of him?

Pew Trust (No. 2)

16 Fiduc. Rptr.2d 80 (Montg. Cty. PA., 1995)

Corporate trustees of the Pew Trust were represented by a large Pennsylvania law firm. Trust beneficiaries petitioned to disqualify the firm's lawyers because some of them had participated in the issuance of a tax opinion that allegedly encouraged the corporate trustee to participate in a $1.36 billion stock transaction. The Orphan's court explained: *A key document in this litigation, which forms the basis for our position, is a tax opinion authored by the ___ firm in September of 1990. Pursuant to this opinion, (law firm) is alleged to have encouraged (corporate trustee) to participate in the $1.36 billion dollar stock transaction. There can be no question that ___, Esquire, as the head of the Probate, Estates and Trusts Department at (law firm) and as attorney to (corporate trustee), and ___, Esquire, as former counsel to (corporate trustee) for nearly twenty (20) years and as the current managing/executive partner (and partner in 1990) for (law firm), have knowledge of the stock transaction, and of its structuring and consummation. Such knowledge makes them likely candidates to be deposed and to be called as witnesses in the instance action. (Law firm) further admits that at least nine other lawyers from its Corporate, Tax, and Probate, Estates and Trusts Departments, also had certain involvement and knowledge of this deal.* The court then explained that the likelihood the lawyers will be called to testify to the terms and circumstances surrounding the stock transaction was sufficient to disqualify the entire law firm from representing the corporate trustee in a suit by the beneficiaries.

Query: This case involves a suit by the beneficiaries of a trust against the corporate trustee who acted pursuant to a tax opinion provided by its legal counsel. How likely is it that counsel for the trustee will advise the trustee on certain financial transactions? Will that advice always lead to the lawyer being disqualified if the lawyer represents the trustee in actions brought by beneficiaries who disagree with the trustee's actions? Where does the attorney/client privilege come in here? Although you don't probably know a lot about law firm life yet, should the entire firm have been disqualified just because someone in the tax department issued an opinion on which the corporate trustee acted?

Eccles v. Nelson

919 So.2d 658 (Fla.App. 2006)

Beverly Nelson filed a petition for administration of her mother's estate, Elfreda Eccles, who died in 2004. She sought administration of a will dated 2001. Karen Eccles, another daughter, then filed an objection to the 2001 will and submitted a will purportedly executed in 2004. Attorney George Salter prepared and notarized the 2004 will. Mr. Salter and Karen Eccles had had a fourteen-year relationship and Eccles worked in Salter's office. There were allegations that the signature on the 2004 will was markedly different from the signature on the 2001 will, and undue influence and questions about the decedent's mental capacity were all raised in trial documents. Nelson then moved to disqualify Salter because, based on his drafting of the 2004 will, he would be a witness to many of the issues in dispute. The court affirmed his disqualification and noted the likely conflict of interest if he represented Eccles in the litigation given his romantic involvement with her. In affirming the trial court's disqualification, the court of appeals explained the Florida rules on lawyer witnesses:

> *Rule 4–3.7 reads in pertinent part, as follows:*
>
> *(a) **When Lawyer May Testify.** A lawyer shall not act as advocate at a trial in which the lawyer is likely to be a necessary witness on behalf of the client except where:*
>
> *(1) the testimony relates to an uncontested issue;*
>
> *(2) the testimony will relate solely to a matter of formality and there is no reason to believe that substantial evidence will be offered in opposition to the testimony;*
>
> *(3) the testimony relates to the nature and value of legal services rendered in the case; or*
>
> *(4) disqualification of the lawyer would work substantial hardship on the client.*

In the present case the issues of mental incapacity, undue influence and genuineness of the signature are obviously contested matters of substance, and Mr. Salter's testimony is well beyond a mere formality.

The court also dismissed Eccles' claim that the disqualification of her lawyer violated her constitutional right to freedom of association. The court explained: *The petitioner argues that she has an associational right to choose her own counsel, and that the state courts may not interfere with that selection. State courts, however, have a valid governmental interest in protecting the integrity of litigation taking place within it, and may certainly in the exercise of that interest enact rules governing when and how lawyers may act vis-à-vis that litigation.*

Query: The court acknowledges that the lawyer who drafts estates documents is not automatically excluded from representing a party to the suit and providing testimony about the drafting. So why was Lawyer Salter disqualified?

———————

Courts that disqualify lawyers from serving as advocates if they are likely to be called as witnesses point primarily to the duty the lawyer owes to his client in the litigation. That duty can be breached if the lawyer then has to provide testimony that might conflict with the position he is taking as an advocate. In the *Eccles* case, Lawyer Salter owed a duty to his girlfriend, Beverly Nelson, to advocate solely on her behalf. Why, if she understood the conflict, would the court not allow him to represent her? What about his duty to Elfreda? Is there a public policy protecting the integrity of litigation that supersedes the client's right to waive the conflict and choose her own attorney?

Practice Point: Stranger than Fiction

Consider this sequence of events: Husband and wife have been clients for many years. He is a millionaire many times over and a savvy business person. You drafted husband's trust and prenuptial agreement when he married his new wife. She hires you to draft her will, as well, and also signs a conflict of interest disclosure which you have carefully drafted. Some time later, husband dies, and you are hired to administer his estate, which is largely to be divided among his surviving lineal descendants, with a life estate in certain real property granted to his wife. During that administration, wife also dies, suddenly. You are stunned when her adult daughter then files a motion with the court claiming that her mother's signature on the will was forged. Even though you are not administering the mother's estate, you can hardly believe this move, because you have specific knowledge that not only was the will not forged (you were there at signing), but you also know that daughter was present at the time of signing. Your day gets even more strange when you receive a phone call from a police detective, stating that the wife appeared to have died from blunt trauma and that members of the family were suspects. The detective saw your card on a magnet on the fridge and asks you what you know about the situation regarding the daughter's interests in the mother's estate.

Conflict? Where? To Whom? Duty? To whom? Stranger than fiction? Yes! And if you practice in this area long enough, one thing is certain—you WILL face these sorts of strange scenarios. Wrestling with the rules is crucial when they surface. Asking for the opinions of other lawyers is also critical. Also, don't forget that your malpractice carrier may want to know about the situation, as well. In this particular case, the tension eased significantly when the daughter withdrew her petition. But what if she hadn't? Can you think of ways this would play out if you were called to be a witness?

As you can see, the potential for conflicts of interest abound in this area of law. You may have conflicts because you will be required to testify, because you have a financial stake in the administration of the estate, or simply because you represented parties whose interests are now adverse to one another. There is no end to the potential conflicts that can arise because you are very likely to have some kind of relationship with members of the family beyond your client. You can manage most of those conflicts through adequate disclosure and a well-drafted engagement letter. The practice point above, however, illustrates just how complicated and unexpected certain conflicts may be. In reviewing the material in this section, go back over the cases and think about how, if at all, these cases would be different if they arose in the context of a criminal law, family law, or business law practice. In other words, what is it about the practice of estates and trusts that generates these kinds of ethical situations?

B. DISCLOSURE OF CONFIDENTIAL INFORMATION

A second area of potential conflict involves the disclosure of confidential information. Obviously, if you represent a husband and wife in the drafting of their wills and estates documents you will most likely have to disclose the contents of these documents to both clients. In most cases, that won't be a problem as they will know each other's assets and have no secrets from each other. But not all clients are as open with their information as others, and you are prohibited from disclosing confidential information to others without your client's consent, even to a spouse, personal representative, or fiduciary. As with the conflicts arising from multiple represen-representation, you can manage the disclosure issue with a well drafted consent form. It is imperative that you know what information might need to be shared to further your client's representation (like to insurance providers or financial planners) and what information must be kept secret, perhaps including the very fact of your representation.

The MRPC § 1.6 addresses the disclosure of confidential information.

Rule 1.6 Confidentiality of Information

(a) A lawyer shall not reveal information relating to the representation of a client unless the client gives informed consent, the disclosure is impliedly authorized in order to carry out the representation or the disclosure is permitted by paragraph (b).

(b) A lawyer may reveal information relating to the representation of a client to the extent the lawyer reasonably believes necessary:

(1) to prevent reasonably certain death or substantial bodily harm;

(2) to prevent the client from committing a crime or fraud that is reasonably certain to result in substantial injury to the financial interests or property of another and in furtherance of which the client has used or is using the lawyer's services;

(3) to prevent, mitigate or rectify substantial injury to the financial interests or property of another that is reasonably certain to result or has resulted from the client's commission of a crime or fraud in furtherance of which the client has used the lawyer's services;

(4) to secure legal advice about the lawyer's compliance with these Rules;

(5) to establish a claim or defense on behalf of the lawyer in a controversy between the lawyer and the client, to establish a defense to a criminal charge or civil claim against the lawyer based upon conduct in which the client was involved, or to respond to allegations in any proceeding concerning the lawyer's representation of the client;

(6) to comply with other law or a court order; or

(7) to detect and resolve conflicts of interest arising from the lawyer's change of employment or from changes in the composition or ownership of a firm, but only if the revealed information would not compromise the attorney–client privilege or otherwise prejudice the client.

(c) A lawyer shall make reasonable efforts to prevent the inadvertent or unauthorized disclosure of, or unauthorized access to, information relating to the representation of a client.

The ACTEC Commentaries have explained some of the special circumstances facing the estates and trusts practitioner in this regard.

> *Consultants and Associated Counsel.* The lawyer should obtain the client's consent to the disclosure of confidential information to other professionals. However, the lawyer may be impliedly authorized to disclose confidential information to other professionals and business consultants to the extent appropriate to the representation. Thus, the client may reasonably anticipate that a lawyer who is preparing an ir-

revocable life insurance trust for the client will discuss the client's affairs with the client's insurance advisor. Additionally, in order to satsatisfy the lawyer's duty of competence, the lawyer may, without the express consent of the client, consult with another professional regarding draft documents or the tax consequences of particular actions, provided that the client's identity and other confidential information is not disclosed. In such a case the lawyer is responsible for payment of the consultant's fee. As indicated in the ACTEC Commentary on MRPC 1.1 (Competence), with the client's consent the lawyer may associate other professionals to assist in the representation.

Implied Authorization to Disclose. The lawyer is also impliedly authorized to disclose otherwise confidential information to the courts, administrative agencies, and other individuals and organizations as the lawyer believes is reasonably required by the representation. A lawyer is impliedly authorized to make arrangements, in case of the lawyer's death or disability, for another lawyer to review the files of his or her clients. As stated in ABA Formal Opinion 92–369 (1992), "[r]easonable clients would likely not object to, but rather approve of, efforts to ensure that their interests are safeguarded."

Obligation After Death of Client. In general, the lawyer's duty of confidentiality continues after the death of a client. Accordingly, a lawyer ordinarily should not disclose confidential information following a client's death. However, if consent is given by the client's personal representative, or if the decedent had expressly or impliedly authorized disclosure, the lawyer who represented the deceased client may provide an interested party, including a potential litigant, with information regarding a deceased client's dispositive instruments and intent, including prior instruments and communications relevant thereto. A lawyer may be impliedly authorized to make appropriate disclosure of client confidential information that would promote the client's estate plan, forestall litigation, preserve assets, and further family understanding of the decedent's intention. Disclosures should ordinarily be limited to information that the lawyer would be required to reveal as a witness.

Does a lawyer have to disclose a client's will to the family or to the court? Presumably a client asked for a will or other testamentary document because he wants it to be effective, and to do that you will ordinarily have to produce the documents. The same is not necessarily true with trust documents, which can be kept strictly secret (of course, not from the trustee) from nonparties. Nonetheless, even certain terms of the trust may have to be revealed to beneficiaries or the court if there is a challenge. Thus, determining what information must be kept secret, what information must be shared, and what information lies in between is far from straightforward, and it can change depending on the wishes of your client.

Clearly, if you are sitting in your office with a married couple and one of them produces a bank statement for you to copy for your file, the existence of the bank account and probably the balance is not confidential as between those two clients anymore. On the other hand, disclosing facts or information learned in private from one client to another client may be a violation of the Rule. Consider the ACTEC Commentaries on the common example of the lawyer representing a husband and wife who learns that one has committed an affair or wants to divorce the other.

Confidences Imparted by One Joint Client. A lawyer who receives information from one joint client (the "communicating client") that the client does not wish to be shared with the other joint client (the "other client") is confronted with a situation that may threaten the lawyer's ability to continue to represent one or both of the clients. As soon as practicable after such a communication the lawyer should consider the relevance and significance of the information and decide upon the appropriate manner in which to proceed. The potential courses of action include, inter alia, (1) taking no action with respect to communications regarding irrelevant (or trivial) matters; (2) encouraging the communicating client to provide the information to the other client or to allow the lawyer to do so; and, (3) withdrawing from the representation if the communication reflects serious adversity between the parties. For example, a lawyer who represents a husband and wife in estate planning matters might conclude that information imparted by one of the spouses regarding a past act of marital infidelity need not be communicated to the other spouse. On the other hand, the lawyer might conclude that he or she is required to take some action with respect to a confidential communication that concerns a matter that threatens the interests of the other client or could impair the lawyer's ability to represent the other client effectively (e.g., "After she signs the trust agreement I intend to leave her"; or, "All of the insurance policies on my life that name her as beneficiary have lapsed"). Without the informed consent of the other client the lawyer should not take any action on behalf of the communicating client, such as drafting a codicil or a new will, that might damage the other client's economic interests or otherwise violate the lawyer's duty of loyalty to the other client.

In order to minimize the risk of harm to the clients' relationship and, possibly, to retain the lawyer's ability to represent both of them, the lawyer may properly urge the communicating client himself or herself to impart the confidential information directly to the other client. See ACTEC Commentary on MRPC 2.1 (Advisor). In doing so the lawyer may properly remind the communicating client of the explicit or implicit understanding that relevant information would be shared and of the lawyer's obligation to share the information with the other client. The lawyer may also point out the possible legal consequences of not disclosing the confidence to the other client, including the possibility that the validity of actions previously taken or planned by one or both of the clients may be jeopardized. In addition, the lawyer may mention that the failure to communicate the information to the other client may result in a disciplinary or malpractice action against the lawyer.

If the communicating client continues to oppose disclosing the confidence to the other client, the lawyer faces an extremely difficult situation with respect to which there is often no clearly proper course of action. In such cases the lawyer should have a reasonable degree of discretion in determining how to respond to any particular case. In fashioning a response the lawyer should consider his or her duties of impartiality and loyalty to the clients; any express or implied agreement among the lawyer and the joint clients that information communicated by either client to the lawyer or otherwise obtained by the lawyer regarding the subject of the representation would be shared with the other client; the reasonable expectations of the clients; and the nature of the confidence and the harm that may result if the confidence is, or is not, disclosed. In some instances the lawyer must also consider whether the situation involves such adversity that the lawyer can no longer effectively represent both clients and is required to withdraw from representing one or both of them. See ACTEC Commentary on MRPC 1.7 (Conflict of Interest: General Rule). A letter of withdrawal that is sent to the other client may arouse the other client's suspicions to the point that the communicating client or the lawyer may ultimately be required to disclose the information.

There are no easy answers to how an attorney must manage confidential information, be it the terms of a trust agreement, the fact of an extramarital affair, or the contents of a safe deposit box. Consider these ethics opinions in this regard.

Washington Ethics Opinion

#2188 (2008)

I.   QUESTION PRESENTED

This inquiry concerns whether and to whom a lawyer may deliver funds held for a deceased client; and also the duty of confidentiality owed to the deceased client. The lawyer held an initial consultation with the client to discuss representation in a legal separation from her husband. The client agreed to retain the lawyer, signed a representation agreement, and paid a fee deposit out of a bank account that appeared to be in the client's name only. Shortly thereafter, the client died.

The attorney posed the following questions: (1) To whom should the lawyer report that she holds the client's funds in her trust account? (2) To whom should the funds be paid? (3) If obligated to talk to the client's husband, what, if anything, can the lawyer reveal about the nature of the representation? (4) What fees may be collected from the client's fee deposit in the lawyer's trust account? (5) What mechanism is there for collecting fees from the client's fee deposit? (6) Would it just be easier to turn the funds over to the state as unclaimed property?

II.   RESPONSE

The lawyer has a duty to take reasonable steps to locate a client or third person for whom the lawyer is holding funds or property. See RPC 1.15A, Cmt. 6. Then, the lawyer must promptly pay or deliver the funds to which the client or third person is entitled. See RPC 1.15A(f); see also Informal Opinion 1313 (lawyer could deliver deceased client funds to client's mother if she was entitled).

C.   Duty of confidentiality

In general, the lawyer's duty of confidentiality continues beyond the client's death. See Formal Opinion 175 (an attorney's duty to preserve confidences continues after the client's death). See footnote 1. Although limited in what she can reveal, the lawyer can disclose information that would facilitate a satisfactory conclusion to the matter and thus potentially revealing to the husband or another person found to have an interest that she holds funds in trust would not be prohibited. See RPC 1.6(b)(6). In the event the lawyer decides to file an interpleader or join in a probate action, she would be permitted to reveal client confidences to the extent determined by the court.

Query: In this case the lawyer holds money that is due to her client's estate, money that the client's husband will certainly have an interest in as surviving spouse. Can she disclose what the money was to be used for? What is the harm of her sending a check to the husband with a note that says "your wife came to me to begin divorce proceedings and made a payment on fees, but her death intervened so I am returning the unused fees"? Can she ethically keep the funds?

Maine Ethics Opinion

#192 (2007)

Bar Counsel has asked whether it is a violation of M. Bar R. 3.6(h) for an attorney to disclose confidential information of a deceased client ("Decedent") to the Decedent's court-appointed Personal Representative ("PR") in circumstances where the PR has requested the information, citing M. R. Evid. 502(c) as the source of authority for waiving the lawyer–client privilege on behalf of the Decedent.

Opinion

Like many questions that are presented to this Commission, Bar Counsel's question leads us to set forth a framework for guiding attorneys in their conduct, rather than to provide an unequivocal answer.

The [Me Bar R. 3.6(h)] recognizes that attorneys are obligated to refuse to disclose three categories of client information: (1) information that would be considered privileged under applicable rules of evidence; (2) information that may not be privileged but that the client has asked to be kept confidential; and (3) information that would be detrimental to the client if it were disclosed. Notwithstanding this broad prohibition, however, the Rule provides two safe harbors that allow attorneys to disclose information "when authorized to carry out the representation" or "as required by law or order of the court." Id.

The general privilege provided by M. R. Evid. 502(b) permits "[a] client . . . to refuse to disclose and to prevent any other person from disclosing confidential communications made for the purpose of facilitating the rendition of professional legal services to the client," provided that those communications are made between and among a select group of individuals, including "the client or the client's representative and the client's lawyer or the lawyer's representative." Me. R. Evid. 502(b).

For the purposes of the Rules of Evidence, "[t]he privilege may be claimed by the client, the client's guardian or conservator, the personal representative of a deceased client, or the successor, trustee, or similar representative of a corporation, association or other organization, whether or not in existence." M. R. Evid. 502(c). Recognizing that a client's attorney may be in the best position to assess the risks and benefits of claiming the privilege on the client's behalf and perhaps recognizing the ethical obligationsimposed upon attorneys by the provisions of M. Bar R. 3.6(h) of the Maine Code of Professional Responsibility, the Rules of Evidence also provide that "[t]he person who was the lawyer or the lawyer's representative at the time of the communication is presumed to have authority to claim the privilege but only on behalf of the client." Id.

In the situation presented by the Question, the PR has decided not to "claim" the attorney–client privilege on behalf of the Decedent, but has instead decided to waive the privilege. In such a situation, we believe the attorney from whom the confidential information is sought may not rely exclusively upon the waiver by the PR, but must undertake an independent analysis pursuant to M. Bar R. 3.6(h) as to his or her own obligations with respect to the requested disclosure.

In many cases, the attorney's disclosure of information at the request of a PR will fall within the first safe harbor of M. Bar R. 3.6(h). For example, disclosure of information regarding a will's execution or a decedent's testamentary intent would ordinarily further the attorney's representation of the client. See In re Greene's Estate, 102 Me. 455, 460, 67 A. 317, 319 (1907) (holding that a PR may waive the attorney–client privilege on behalf of a decedent, because the PR is interested in the protection of the decedent's estate and "would consent to the waiver of the privileged communication only for the purpose of securing that end").

If, however, the attorney believes that the information sought to be disclosed would not further the client's purpose or would be detrimental to a material interest of the client, the attorney may waive the privilege only as required by law or by court order. Thus, despite a PR's waiver of the attorney–client privilege, the attorney may still be ethically obligated to claim the privilege on behalf of his former client if, for example, the information had been specifically sought to be kept unqualifiedly confidential by the client or if disclosure of the information would embarrass or otherwise be detrimental to a material interest of the client. See M. R. Evid. 502(c). The only safe harbor available to the attorney in that case would be a court order allowing disclosure of the information requested by the PR. See M. Bar R. 3.6(h)(1). Because the PR is the one seeking disclosure of the information, the PR will likely be the one seeking the court order compelling disclosure.

Query: The ethics board in this case did not give a clear answer as to whether the attorney should or should not disclose confidential information of a deceased client to the personal representative. Even though the representative may waive the attorney–client privilege, the attorney must do an independent analysis of whether the disclosure is in the client's best interests. Assuming the attorney discloses information detrimental to the client, who has standing to complain? On what would the attorney base his independent decision whether or not to disclose? What if the confidential information was the fact that the client had been diagnosed with dementia and was being treated for it?

South Dakota Ethics Opinion

#2007–3

I. Facts.

Attorney drafted a Will and Power of Attorney for Client, who executed them in 2002. In 2006, a niece of Client ("Niece") requested a copy of Client's Will. Attorney advised Niece that Attorney could not furnish a copy of the Will because it is a private document.

Thereafter, in October of 2006, Attorney conferred with the Client about Client's will. The Client is 90 years old, has never been married, is residing in an assisted living center, and recognizes problems with his health. The Client stated that the Will expresses his wishes, and that no one should be permitted to see the Will during his lifetime. Client confirmed those instructions in writing.

In April of 2007, Niece again demanded a copy of Client's will. The demand included a copy of a Durable General Power of Attorney that Client executed on March 30, 2007. Attorney informed Niece of Client's instructions, and declined to furnish the will to the niece.

On April 16, 2007, the lawyer for Niece sent a letter to Attorney, threatening either to sue Attorney, or file a complaint with the South Dakota Bar Association "Grievance Committee" if it Attorney failed to provide the Client's Will to the Niece. On April 22, 2007, Attorney consulted the Client. Client confirmed that he does not want his Will changed, or for any person to know its contents during his lifetime. Client further stated that his assets are to remain in his name, and are to be distributed under the provisions of the Will as written.

Attorney asks whether he must provide a copy of the Client's Will to the Niece.

II. Discussion

An attorney must keep a client's communications confidential unless an exception applies. Rule 1.6. There is no exception in the facts presented to the Committee. Therefore, Attorney cannot give the Niece the Will.

Niece's lawyer asserts, in essence, that the POA makes the Niece a "co-client" in the shoes of Client. The Committee disagrees. Who is the "client" is a question of substantive law. "Whether a client–lawyer relationship exists for any specific purpose can depend on the circumstances and may be a question of fact." Preamble to South Dakota Rules of Professional Conduct ¶ 17, SDCL 16–18 Appendix. "The existence of an attorney–client relationship is usually a question of fact dependent upon the communications and circumstances." Keegan v. First Bank of Sioux Falls, 519 NW2d 607, 611 (SD 1994).

The Committee believes that, under the "communications and circumstances," the Niece is not a "client" for the "specific purpose" of reviewing Client's Will. First, absent a guardianship, conservatorship or other legal limitation, Client can revoke or modify the attorney-in-fact's authority. Second, if the general POA ever gave the Niece the authority to review the Will, the April 22, 2007 communication from Client to Attorney revoked it. Attorney believes that Client is slipping, but, until he is adjudicated unable to make such decisions, Rules 1.6, and 1.14(a) & (c) require that Attorney continue to protect Client's confidences.

Query: Go back and review the material in Chapter 6 on Powers of Attorney. Should an agent have the legal right to request disclosure of information in a principal's will? Won't the agent have a fiduciary duty to act in ways that preserve the principal's estate and property, and won't knowing the disposition of that property be relevant in certain instances? Can you think of cases in which it would be relevant and cases in which it would not be? Why do you think the niece was so insistent on seeing the will?

California Bar Formal Opinion

§ 2007–173

Statement of Facts

In 1973, Attorney drafted a will for Client. At the time, Attorney and Client agreed that Attorney would retain possession of the executed original will. By 2003, Attorney is contemplating retirement and would like to terminate the deposit. However, Attorney has not heard from Client for 25 years, and recent efforts to locate the client have been unsuccessful. Attorney wants to ensure that Client can obtain access to his will at a future time or, in the event of his death, that the client's heirs can locate the will. Therefore, Attorney is considering either depositing the original will with a private will depository and/or registering certain information about the will with a private will registry. Attorney's file contains no notes regarding communications with Client, Attorney has limited recollection of Client, and has no independent recollection of any communications with Client.

DISCUSSION

1. May an attorney ethically deposit a will with a commercial will depository without the client's express consent?

Because the Probate Code provides the exclusive legal means for disposition of wills and other estate planning documents held on deposit by an attorney, an attorney may not ethically deposit estate planning documents with a private will depository absent consent of the client pursuant to Probate Code section 731(c). To do so would, at the very least, constitute a violation of Business and Professions Code section 6068(a), which requires lawyers to support the laws of this state, and the prohibition against intentionally or recklessly failing to perform legal services with competence. (See Rule of Professional Conduct 3–110.)

2. May an attorney ethically register a will with a commercial will registry without the client's express consent?

Registering a client's will with a registry would typically require disclosure of the testator's name, the present location of the will, the name of the attorney who drafted the will, and often the date of execution of the will as well.

A client's identity and address is not typically considered privileged information. There are, however, several important (but narrowly construed) exceptions to this rule. Specifically, if disclosure of a client's identity would itself reveal the nature of the client's legal problems for which the attorney was hired, the client's name may be privileged information.

Disclosure to the will registry of the client's name as well as information about the documents being registered inescapably reveals the nature of the matter for which the lawyer was retained. However, unlike other cases that have held the identity of the client to be privileged (where criminal conduct or private medical issues are at stake), the mere execution of testamentary documents may or may not be considered "private information."

Like the evidentiary attorney–client privilege, the attorney's ethical duty of confidentiality is considered fundamental to the attorney–client relationship, involving policies of paramount importance. However, as noted, while the attorney–client evidentiary privilege covers only confidential communications between the attorney and the client, the broader ethical duty of *confidentiality requires the protection of all client secrets. In this regard, it is important to keep in mind that the decision whether to apply the privilege is made by judges or other arbiters in judicial or quasi-judicial proceedings. The duty of confidentiality is necessarily broader because it applies in non-litigation contexts where judicial protection may not be present.*

The identity of a client who has executed a will, trust or other legal document may or may not be protected by the evidentiary attorney–client privilege. The client's identity may nevertheless be a client confidence or secret protected by Business and Professions Code section 6068, subdivision (e) and rule 3–100, or be deemed confidential information protected by the client's Constitutional right of privacy. In any event, if information about the will or its execution would be embarrassing to the client or likely be detrimental to the client's interests, the attorney (absent express consent of the client) should protect the confidentiality of that information.

Thus, before registering testamentary documents with a will registry without client consent, a lawyer must determine, from a review of the client's file and any independent recollection of communications with the client, whether registration would further the client's objectives as communicated to the attorney during the course of the attorney–client relationship or whether registration would breach the duty of confidentiality either because the client would want to keep the information private, or registration would embarrass the client or likely be detrimental to the client's interests. In the context of the hypothetical facts presented in this opinion, the attorney must also consider the effect of the substantial lapse of time on whether disclosure would be embarrassing or likely be detrimental to the client. As there can be no bright-line rule applicable in all circumstances, the attorney who registers a will without the client's express consent acts at his or her peril.

Query: Note that even revealing that you represent a client, or that it is an estates and trusts matter, can be a breach of client confidentiality. What do you think this lawyer should have done to keep in better contact with his clients? Should he have sent the will home with the client where anyone snooping through the filing cabinet could find it? Is it likely that the client's reason for leaving it with the attorney was to maintain confidentiality? Where do you think this client is? Do you think he has likely made a new will and didn't bother to tell his old attorney?

Maintaining a client's confidences has both an evidentiary and an ethical dimension. Certain information must be kept confidential under applicable rules of evidence. Other information might not rise to the level of evidentiary privilege, but must be kept confidential nonetheless. This includes information that the client has asked be kept secret, and information that would be detrimental to the client if it were disclosed. There are two exceptions, however: when disclosure is required by law or order of a court and when disclosure is necessary to carry out the representation. Go back and consider the fact situations of the above ethics opinions in light of these three categories of confidential information and the two safe harbors.

As you can imagine, revealing the will or portions of a trust is necessary to carrying out the representation of a client. It's impossible to probate a will if the attorney is prohibited from disclosing it. Additionally, guardians and conservators are generally entitled to claim the privilege of disclosure or waive it in order to fulfill their fiduciary duties to their wards. Certainly as between joint clients, or clients and their beneficiaries, there is a duty to protect confidential information requested by the client.

Once you've got a handle on the conflict of interest rules and the confidentiality rules as they apply in the trusts and estates context, you also must consider carefully your duty, if any, to the beneficiaries of the instruments you draft. If you draft a will that violates the RAP and a remainder interest in grandchildren is voided, are you liable to them for your error? They are not your clients and you have no ethical duty towards beneficiaries, but you certainly have a duty to your client and your client's estate not to commit malpractice. The $100,000 question in many states, however, is whether you also owe a duty to those beneficiaries to effectuate your client's intent effectively?

C. MALPRACTICE AND DUTY TO BENEFICIARIES

It seems quite simple: a client walks into your office to draft her will, you do so, you get paid, and you go on with your life. Simple. But when she dies, her will is probated, and in the course of probate it is discovered that you drafted a provision that violates the Rule Against Perpetuities and now the remainder beneficiaries who just lost their big inheritance sue you. Remember *Lucas v. Hamm*?[5] In that case the lawyer was not held liable, not because he didn't owe a duty to the beneficiaries, but because getting the RAP wrong was understandable. While I have a hard time excusing any errors involving the RAP, there are certainly situations where human errors should not give rise to liability, especially to persons who are not your clients. But most people draft estates and trusts documents precisely in order to benefit others—and there is no particularly good reason for denying lawyer liability to those beneficiaries in the case of gross negligence or malfeasance. So where does privity end and a duty to third party beneficiaries begin?

The states diverge dramatically on duty to beneficiaries. As the ACTEC Commentaries explain:

> Courts have perhaps had the most difficulty in defining the role and duties of the lawyer who represents a fiduciary in the fiduciary's representative capacity with respect to a fiduciary estate (who might be said to represent the fiduciary generally). For example, in a malpractice action brought by the beneficiaries of a fiduciary estate against the lawyer for the fiduciary, a California appellate court stated that the lawyer owed no duty to the beneficiaries of the estate. Goldberg v. Frye, 266 Cal. Rptr. 483 (Cal. App. 1990); Other appellate courts have reached the opposite conclusion, including courts in California. Thus, in In re Estate of Halas, 512 N.E.2d 1276, 1280 (Ill. App. 1987), the court stated that, "The attorney for the executor, therefore, must act with due care and protect the interests of the beneficiaries". Similarly, in Charleson v. Hardesty, 839 P.2d 1303 (Nev. 1992), the court wrote that the lawyer for a personal representative owes the beneficiaries "a duty of care and fiduciary duties." Id. at 1307. See also Fickett v. Superior Court, 558 P.2d 988 (Ariz. App. 1976), in which the court held that the lawyer for

---

[5]   364 P.2d 685 (Cal. 1961).

the guardian owed a duty directly to the ward to protect the ward's interests.

There are two factors that generally come into play in considering liability for malpractice. The first is whether the estate itself suffers harm, or whether the harm accrues solely to certain beneficiaries. Thus, if malpractice causes the estate to incur excessive estate tax liabilities, the estate itself is harmed, and the attorney will likely be held liable to the estate. If the estate is unharmed, and the malpractice simply means that the property will pass to intestate takers rather than the intended beneficiaries, courts are split on whether the attorney will be liable. Generally, where the malpractice consists of dilatoriness that results in a will being drafted but not executed in time, courts will not allow the will beneficiaries to recover. However, where the malpractice consists in drafting a will with a clear error, or which patently violates the testator's intent, recovery has been allowed.

The second factor that comes into play is whether liability should be allowed for mere negligence or unintentional harms as well as for gross malfeasance, or only for the latter. Here the states are split, some allowing recovery for mere negligence and others not. As you read the following cases, consider what the attorney did wrong, whether it was intentional or unintentional, and whether there was harm only to the beneficiaries, or harm to both the beneficiaries and the estate.

Babcock v. Malone

760 S.2d 1056 (Fla. Dist. Ct. App. 4th Dist. 2000)

Appellants, who were plaintiffs in the trial court, alleged in a complaint that the appellee, a lawyer, was negligent in failing to timely prepare a new will for their uncle. As a result, their uncle died before executing the new will under which plaintiffs would have inherited, and instead they were left nothing. The trial court dismissed the complaint for failure to state a cause of action. The court of appeal affirmed, explaining: "*standing in legal malpractice actions is limited to those who can show that the testator's intent as expressed in the will is frustrated by the negligence of the testator's attorney.*" Even though the draft will was completed and mailed to the uncle, along with a statement of services, which would confirm what the testator's intentions were, the court refused to allow the nieces standing.

Query: The court refused to allow the nieces to sue for malpractice because the Florida rule requires a showing of testamentary intent "as expressed in the will." This means that negligence in drafting a will that is actually executed can lead to liability, but negligently failing to get the will executed will not. Does that make sense to you? Many states allow standing only to beneficiaries named in a will or trust in order to avoid all the evidentiary problems of figuring out what grandpa intended when there is no actual will from which to determine it. Does that seem like the proper line to draw? Shouldn't a draft will be sufficient?

Jenkins v. Wheeler

69 N.C.App. 140, 316 S.E.2d 354 (1984)

Plaintiff Jenkins is the sole heir of her natural mother, Louella Wheeler. Louella Wheeler was a passenger in a truck driven by her husband, Austin Wheeler, which was involved in a one vehicle accident on 19 May 1980. Louella Wheeler died 20 August 1980. Austin Wheeler, Louella Wheeler's second husband and no blood relation to Jenkins, renounced the administratorship in favor of his sister, Ava Wheeler who qualified as administratrix of Louella Wheeler's estate. Austin Wheeler committed suicide at some point thereafter, and Ava Wheeler qualified to administer his estate as well. At the time of the accident, Austin Wheeler had an automobile liability insurance policy with Nationwide Mutual Insurance Company with a policy limit of $25,000.

On 18 August 1982 Jenkins filed this action against Ava Wheeler, her attorney, James Wilson, and Nationwide. In essence, the Complaint alleged that defendants had breached various fiduciary duties and conspired to deprive Jenkins of any recovery on the Nationwide policy. As to attorney Wilson, the Complaint alleged that he failed to advise Ava Wheeler to list the wrongful death action as an asset of Louella's estate, that he improperly continued representation of conflicting interests, and that he wilfully refused to proceed with the wrongful death action despite Jenkins' insistence and offers to pay all costs, thus breaching the applicable standards of professional skill and ethics.

The Complaint alleged that Wilson's acts of professional malpractice resulted in the administratrix's failure to sue Nationwide and the consequent loss of Jenkins' right to any recovery based on Austin Wheeler's negligence. Since ordinarily on Ava Wheeler, the administratrix, could properly bring suit for Louella Wheeler's wrongful death, and since any such recovery would have inured only to the benefit of Jenkins, Jenkins now seeks to recover the lost award from Wilson. Wilson argues (1) that Jenkins has no standing to bring the action, (2) that she has alleged no negligence, and (3) that she is barred by her own contributory negligence as a matter of law. We disagree.

North Carolina now recognizes a cause of action in tort by non-client third parties for attorney malpractice. United Leasing Corp. v. Miller, 45 N.C.App. 400, 263 S.E.2d 313, disc. rev. denied, 300 N.C. 374, 267 S.E.2d 685 (1980). We established a general balancing test in United Leasing:

> *Whether or not a party has placed himself in such a relation with another so that the law will impose upon him an obligation, sounding in tort and not in contract, to act in such a way that the other will not be injured calls for the balancing of various factors: (1) the extent to which the transaction was intended to affect the other person; (2) the foreseeability of harm to him; (3) the degree of certainty that he suffered injury; (4) the closeness of the connection between the defendant's conduct and the injury; (5) the moral blame attached to such conduct; and (6) the policy of preventing future harm.*

First, harm to Jenkins as a result of Wilson's failure to press a meritorious claim was eminently foreseeable: Jenkins was the sole heir of Louella Wheeler's estate and any recovery would have inured to her benefit. Second, it is reasonably certain, again taking the complaint as true, that Jenkins suffered injury, since the complaint properly alleges facts regarding Austin Wheeler's negligence which would have entitled Jenkins to recovery, if the

*suit had been brought. Third, there were no intervening circumstances be-
tween Wilson's allegedly negligent conduct and Jenkins' loss, except the
possibility of no recovery on the suit not filed. Since the complaint alleges
facts which, if true, would entitle Jenkins to recovery, this connection is sufficiently close. Fourth, if plaintiff's allegations of conflict of interest and
collusion are correct, Wilson's position is not morally sustainable under
current conceptions of professional responsibility. And, finally, public policy
has always required that attorneys represent their clients zealously. When
the client merely represents a class of beneficiaries, the attorney should consider the beneficiaries' interests, without undue concern for the interests of
the legal representative. We therefore hold that Wilson owed Jenkins a duty
to use reasonable care in representing Louella Wheeler's estate, and that
Jenkins had standing to sue Wilson in tort.*

Query: North Carolina has held that a lawyer is liable in malpractice for for-
seeable harms to beneficiaries caused by malpractice. Does this seem like a
good rule? Why do you think Wheeler failed to bring the wrongful death action?
Was it laziness, incompetence, neglect, or a belief that the action was not viable? Note that the court said that when a lawyer represents a fiduciary who
represents a class of beneficiaries (i.e. the executor or trustee of an estate), the
lawyer has to think of the beneficiaries as well. Would this apply to the lawyer
who drafts a poorly worded will or trust?

Jones v. Wilt

871 A.2d 210 (Pa. Super., 2005)

In 1991 Gail Jones retained attorney Walter Wilt to prepare a will and
trust agreement on her behalf. At the time, Jones was expecting to receive
a large inheritance from her father's estate. The trust Wilt prepared provides that the entire corpus passes to Jones' sister, Carolyn Leech, upon
Jones' death. The will directs most of the probate property will pass to her
surviving husband, Benjamin Jones. The will also had a tax clause directing that all estate taxes be paid from the residuary estate. After Jones'
death in 1999, the estate paid over $200,000 in estate and inheritance tax-
es from the residuary estate. Jones' husband, Benjamin, asserted
malpractice in the failure of Wilt to utilize certain estate tax planning
methods that would have minimized estate taxes. Benjamin, as executor
and primary beneficiary, claims Wilt committed malpractice by failing to
determine the full nature and value of Jones' property (especially from the
inheritance), by failing to adequately advise her on the potential tax implications, and by failing to use common tax reduction techniques. The trial
court granted summary judgment to Attorney Wilt. On appeal, the court
affirmed, explaining that the executor has no grounds to sue if there is not
harm to the estate:

> *We therefore turn to the question of whether the estate could sue the
> drafting attorney for malpractice and receive damages for the failure of the
> instrument to effectuate testator's intent. In any cause of action for malprac-
> tice, some harm must be shown to have occurred to the person bringing suit.
> In the case of a failed legacy, the estate is not harmed in any way. Califor-
> nia, the first state to find a cause of action in malpractice for beneficiaries
> has held that the executor has no standing to bring an action.*

> *Indeed, the executor of an estate has no standing to bring an action for
> the amount of the bequest against an attorney who negligently prepared the*

estate plan, since in the normal case the estate is not injured by such negligence except to the extent of the fees paid; only the beneficiaries suffer the real loss. Even if the estate would have standing to bring the suit, the fact that no harm had occurred to it and the estate has nothing to gain would remove any incentive for suit.

But the beneficiary does have standing under third party beneficiary doctrines. Appellant claims that he cannot possibly prove that Appellee "breached his contract to provide legal services without resorting to extrinsic evidence." We agree. "To limit a[ ]cause of action by a non-client to the face of the testamentary document that does not reflect the testator's true intent would render the recognition of [this] cause of action meaningless." In order to permit a party to properly pursue the cause of action . . . , we must permit the introduction of extrinsic evidence. Yet while certain types of extrinsic evidence should be admitted to prove such claims, we conclude that the trial court properly excluded Appellant's expert's opinion.

As part of discovery, Appellee was deposed and was questioned regarding his representation of Decedent and his drafting of her will. He testified that Decedent told him that "she did not want her husband to have" "the assets that she had received from her father . . . She wanted those assets to go to her sister." Repeatedly, Appellee stated that this was her primary intent and that she did not care about the tax consequences so long as Leech received the assets upon Decedent's death.

In responding to Appellee's motion for summary judgment, Appellant provided an expert opinion by Kirby G. Upright, LLM, CPA, which states that Appellee was negligent in not advising Decedent of the utilization of a Qualified Terminable Interest Property Trust (QTIP Trust). This is the "extrinsic evidence" that Appellant claims the trial court erred in not considering. According to the expert opinion, by utilizing a QTIP trust, the "assets could have passed into the trust at Mrs. Jones' death, tax-free and, by Mrs. Jones' direction in the trust, passed to Carolyn B. Leech upon the death of Mrs. Jones' surviving husband." However, Appellant has absolutely no evidence that shows that Decedent intended to delay the passing of these assets until after Appellant's death. The entire expert opinion is premised on the fact that Decedent intended to leave these assets for the benefit of Appellant during his lifetime, and that only after his death would the assets then pass to Leech. As there is absolutely no evidence to support this fact, we conclude that the opinion is without a proper foundation and therefore, the trial court did not err in not considering it.

Query: This case raises two important points. The first is that executors do not have standing on behalf of the estate to raise malpractice issues if there is no harm to the estate. Do you see why that is the rule? Is it a good rule? The second is that beneficiaries have standing, but only certain extrinsic evidence is admissible to prove testamentary intent. Does it seem reasonable to you that the lawyer who drafted the will (and is charged with malpractice) is permitted to provide testimony to what the client purportedly wanted, but that the beneficiary is not permitted to provide testimony to what a client would have likely intended had she been presented with the information that was withheld through the malpractice? Does that rule seem overly lopsided to you? If so, how would you draw the line?[6]

Some states have ruled that attorneys owe no duties whatsoever to beneficiaries of wills and other estates documents under strict privity doctrines. Others have held that there is liability under certain limited circumstances, often constrained by evidentiary rules. Others have held that there is a general duty to beneficiaries not to be negligent under standard third party beneficiary doctrines. Obviously, the best strategy is to be responsible to the interests of all parties, so long as doing so is consistent with your primary responsibility to your client. But be aware that errors on the face of the documents are more likely to be grounds for malpractice than dilatory or negligent representation. The moral, therefore, is: learn the proper ways to draft future interests, understand the Rule Against Perpetuities, know the details of tax minimization mechanisms, and learn fully about your client's property and intentions. You don't want to be on the other end of an affidavit by an estates and trusts expert opining on your incompetence in drafting estates documents.

There are hundreds of cases on attorney malpractice, to their clients and to third party beneficiaries. You need to study the law of your state well to steer clear of the shoals. Even if your state does not impose any liability for malpractice to beneficiaries, you don't want to be the lawyer whose case changes the law. It is fine to rely on your client's statements that he wants his estate to pass a particular way, even if that means additional estate taxes might accrue. But if you detect a potential conflict between your client's wishes and the likely interests of beneficiaries, you will want to document your client's intentions well so that you aren't sitting across the table from disgruntled heirs accusing you of not understanding the tax effect of the plan you drafted, without the backing of evidence to support your client's actual intent. Now you understand one of the important reasons for taking all of those detailed notes during your client meetings.

D. GIFTS TO LAWYERS

So what do you do when your client, who happens to be your best friend's mother, wants to give you that bike tool kit you and your friend played with so often, or some of her favorite jewelry that you dressed up with as kids? If you are drafting the will and she says she wants to give you a little something, like a small Picasso or Renoir, what do you say? Many lawyers are relatives or family friends and it only makes sense that the testator would want to include them in their bounty. Yet gifts to lawyers are strictly scrutinized and outright prohibited in most states. The MRPC Rule 1.8 provides specifically that:

---

[6]   Ohio does not recognize a cause of action in malpractice against an attorney who in good faith executes estates documents that result in higher tax liabilities. *Shoemaker v. Gindlesberger*, 118 Ohio St.3d 226 (Ohio, 2008).

> **MRPC § 1.8**
>
> (c) A lawyer shall not solicit any substantial gift from a client, including a testamentary gift, or prepare on behalf of a client an instrument giving the lawyer or a person related to the lawyer any substantial gift unless the lawyer or other recipient of the gift is related to the client. For purposes of this paragraph, related persons include a spouse, child, grandchild, parent, grandparent or other relative or individual with whom the lawyer or the client maintains a close, familial relationship.

Unlike many of the rules we have covered so far, this rule is an outright prohibition unless the lawyer is related to the client. Even close functional relationships can get dicey. So what is the answer? If you really want the bike tool kit, the costume jewelry or the Picasso, another lawyer must draft the will. But what if that lawyer costs a lot more and the client doesn't feel close to the other lawyer? Remember that advice about maintaining professional friendships with other lawyers. You can certainly recommend that your client use a different lawyer, and that lawyer can recommend that her clients come to you if there is a conflict, and you can agree to charge what the referring lawyer charges on condition that you each act independently and pursuant to strict ethical rules. Thus, if your lawyer friend down the hall recommends a client to you for a will which leaves everything to him, you will want to independently ensure that the client is not under any undue influence, is comfortable with your drafting the will, and understands that your duty is to the client, and not your friend. If the client understands why the friend can't draft the will and consents, you can certainly draft a will leaving property to another lawyer.

The rule against gifts to lawyers can be enforced in different ways. The gift itself can be deemed revoked by operation of law, in which case the gift lapses and passes to the residuary or by intestacy, depending on the instrument. Or, the entire will itself may be deemed void due to the presumption of undue influence, in which case a prior will or intestacy may operate. Assuming there is no overreaching by the attorney, however, many courts allow the gifts to stand if they are prepared by a different attorney. Consider the ACTEC Commentaries on gifts to lawyers:

> *Gifts to Lawyer.* MRPC 1.8 generally prohibits a lawyer from soliciting a substantial gift from a client, including a testamentary gift, or preparing for a client an instrument that gives the lawyer or a person related to the lawyer a substantial gift. A lawyer may properly prepare a will or other document that includes a substantial benefit for the lawyer or a person related to the lawyer if the lawyer or other recipient is related to the client. The term "related person" is defined in MRPC 1.8(c) and may include a person who is not related by blood or marriage but has a close familial relationship. However, the lawyer should exercise special care if the proposed gift to the lawyer or a related person is disproportionately large in relation to the gift the client proposes to make to others who are equally related. Neither the lawyer nor a person associated with the lawyer can assist an unrelated client in making a substantial gift to the lawyer or to a person related to the lawyer. See MRPC 1.8(k).
>
> For the purposes of this Commentary, the substantiality of a gift is determined by reference both to the size of the client's estate and to the size of the estate of the designated recipient. The provisions of this rule extend to all methods by which gratuitous transfers might be

made by a client including life insurance, joint tenancy with right of survivorship, and pay-on-death and trust accounts. As noted in ABA Formal Opinion 02–426, the client's appointment of the lawyer as a fiduciary is not a gift to the lawyer and is not a business transaction that would subject the appointment to MRPC 1.8. Nevertheless, such an appointment is subject to the general conflict of interest provisions of MRPC 1.7.

Now consider the situations facing the lawyers in these cases and think about how you would have handled the matter:

Sandford v. Metcalfe

110 Conn.App. 162, 954 A.2d 188 (2008)

Five days before the decedent's death, on February 5, 2000, she asked [Irene] Sandford, a friend who lived in Armonk, New York, to come to her house in Greenwich.[1] Sandford, an attorney licensed to practice law in New York but not in Connecticut, arrived at the decedent's home after work that evening. Sandford found the decedent in her bed and suggested that the decedent should be seen by a physician.

The decedent asked Sandford to draft her a new will, continually insisting that she would discuss no other subject until Sandford did as she requested. The decedent's prior will had been executed in December, 1962, and left her estate to her now deceased mother and husband with a contingent beneficiary of her cousin, Watson B. Metcalfe. Sandford explained to the decedent that she was not licensed to practice law in Connecticut and, upon learning that the decedent wanted to name her as a beneficiary, told the decedent that she could not prepare the will. The decedent, however, insisted that she prepare the will. Sandford relented and complied with the decedent's wishes by handwriting a will that, in accordance with the decedent's instructions, left the estate in equal shares to Sandford and to the decedent's handyman, Robert Peterson, who was also present in the decedent's home that evening. No provision was made in the will for residuary beneficiaries. After the will was signed and witnessed, the decedent was taken to a hospital where she died five days later.

The probate judge admitted the 2000 will to probate and Metcalfe failed to appeal in a timely manner. Later, he sought to have the gift to Sandford revoked by operation of law, as a result of which it would pass by intestacy to himself and others. For technical reasons the unauthorized practice of law issue was not addressed in this appeal. In upholding the gift, the court explained: *The issue before this court, therefore, is not whether there should be a distribution in accordance with the will, because that issue was decided by the decision of the Probate Court and unsuccessfully appealed, but whether there should be a forfeiture of the bequest to Sandford, the attorney who drafted the will, on the basis of public policy. We* conclude that there should not be a forfeiture. The court explained its reasons why: *The law governing descent and distribution emanates from the legislature and is purely statutory. . . . The legislature has, by statute, carved out exceptions to the statutes governing descent and distribution to deprive an ostensibly rightful heir, falling within the ambit of those exceptions, of an otherwise lawful inheritance. Under [General Statutes] a person*

---

[1]   Sandford was related to the decedent's deceased husband, and she and her family were friendly with the decedent.

who, without sufficient cause, abandons his or her spouse is foreclosed from receiving a statutory share of the estate of the deceased spouse as well as a person finally convicted of murder is precluded from inheriting any part of the estate of the deceased victim. There is, however, no statute barring an attorney who drafted a testamentary instrument from inheriting by the instrument she drafted. Although we agree that it is ill-advised, as a matter of public policy, for an attorney to draft a will in which she is to receive a bequest, in the absence of statutory provisions to the contrary, there is no bar against the right of Sandford to inherit from the decedent's estate under the statutes governing descent and distribution. If the law is to be changed to make provision for the situation at hand, it is for the legislature to make the change, not the court.

Query: Because there was no statute barring an attorney from inheriting, the court allowed the gift to stand, stating that the opponents should have appealed the admission of the will in a timely manner. How do the model rules fit into this statutory scheme? Would the Connecticut court have considered Sandford to be related to the decedent under the model rules?

Estate of Rohde

158 Cal. App. 2d 19, 323 P.2d 490 (Cal. App. 1st Dist. 1958).

Mary Rohde had no children, no relatives in the United States, and no husband when, at 82, she called a friend to drive her to the office of Mr. Magee, a lawyer. During a meeting of less than an hour, a will was drafted and executed giving all of her property to Mr. Magee and nominating him to be executor. When Magee asked a lawyer who worked in the office next door to witness the will, that lawyer insisted on meeting privately with Rohde where he read the will, word for word, to her and she answered that it was her will. Magee was not present when the will was executed. Magee's mother and Rohde were acquaintances through a war veteran's association but Magee and Rohde had no prior acquaintanceship. Rohde's closest relative, a niece of her predeceased husband, challenged the will, claiming incapacity and undue influence. A jury found in favor of the niece and the will was refused probate. On appeal, Lawyer Magee challenged the jury's finding, including the judge's refusal to submit a jury instruction that stated: *any decree of influence resulting from kindness and attention to the testatrix can never constitute undue influence within the meaning of the law. Mere acts of kindness and solicitude performed with honest motives without regard for monetary gain should not be regarded by you as undue influence.* The court of appeals agreed that the jury instruction should not have been given and affirmed the jury's finding of undue influence.

Query: There are two very different narratives for what happened in Lawyer Magee's office. A widow with no close relatives decided to leave all her property to the fine, upstanding son of a friend, who happened to be a lawyer who had helped her on occasion; or, a widow of weakened intellect went to a conniving lawyer to deal with a real estate sale and left with a will giving the lawyer everything. What do you think happened in the office for the fifteen minutes they met, before the lawyer emerged with notes for Rohde's will that he gave to his secretary to type up? There is a presumption of undue influence when a client leaves significant gifts to her lawyer, a presumption arising from the attorney/client relationship. Do you think the jury should have been given the alternate instruction about kindness? Is the allegation of undue influence too outrageous to be believable? Do you smell a rat here? Do you think the jury smelled a rat just because a lawyer was the alleged influencer and the beneficiary? Was it enough for Lawyer Magee to have his neighbor lawyer supervise the execution of the will? Did the neighboring lawyer breach any rules by not actually drafting the will?

In re Est. of Southwick

66 Mass. App. Ct. 740, 850 N.E.2d 604 (2006)

In this case, the decedent, Nathan Southwick, had no legal heirs at law. His will, executed in 1994, gave all of his stock in General Electric to Bentley College, his alma mater, and the residue of his estate to his lawyer. The decedent and the lawyer had become acquainted in 1986 when the lawyer represented Southwick in a real estate purchase. Then, in 1991, the lawyer was contacted by neighbors to visit Southwick in the hospital. Over the next few years the lawyer assisted Southwick in recovering the proceeds of a travel insurance policy, arranging for his discharge from the hospital to a nursing facility, then discharge to his home which the attorney arranged to be renovated. The lawyer also purchased a motorized wheelchair for Southwick so he could move around his neighborhood. In 1994, Southwick asked the attorney to draft his will, which he did. At the time of drafting, there was no ethics rule prohibiting the drafting of a will in which the attorney is a beneficiary. That rule was changed in 1995 with the adoption of a new ethics rule prohibiting a lawyer from drafting an instrument that gives the lawyer any substantial gift. The lawyer continued to check on Southwick weekly and take care of his financial and personal affairs.

After Southwick's death, the lawyer followed all legal requirements for publication and locating heirs, but was unsuccessful. The probate judge, however, felt that the lawyer's actions were questionable in light of the changed ethics rule and concluded that *the changes in bar disciplinary rules subsequent to execution of the decedent's will imposed a duty on the attorney to contact his client, advise him of the change, and notify him that if he still wished to benefit the attorney on his death, he should seek out independent counsel and draft a new will to that effect. Predicated on this finding, and the implicit conclusion that the attorney's conduct constituted a breach of professional duty, the judge reported the question whether that breach of duty rises to such level as to invalidate the residuary bequest to the attorney and preclude approval of the first and final accounting. Because the decedent apparently died leaving no heirs at law and next of kin, the residuary estate would escheat to the Commonwealth should the decedent's bequest of the residue to the attorney be invalidated.*

The court of appeals commented on the unusual posture of the case, that it was brought forward upon a question by the judge in the absence of anyone challenging the will. However, in affirming the gift to the lawyer, the court explained: *Because of the peculiar procedural posture of the case and the absence, at present, of objection by anyone other than the judge, we are unable to resolve definitively whether the judge would be warranted in refusing to allow the account and invalidating the bequests to the attorney under the will. Nevertheless, because we consider the reported question to rest on a flawed premise, we state our views on whether the enactment of Mass.R.Prof.C. 1.8(c) imposed a retroactive obligation on the attorney, the violation of which would constitute a breach of fiduciary duty that would invalidate the residuary bequest to the attorney*

Disciplinary rules operate prospectively, not retroactively. Nothing in the amendments to the disciplinary rules or rules of professional conduct suggests or imposes a retroactive prohibition on the attorney's drafting of such an instrument or an obligation to revisit with the client the circumstances of an already executed document. Moreover, even if the attorney's conduct and failure to advise the client subsequently regarding an already-executed will may be said to have violated an applicable disciplinary rule, such a violation is only evidence of a breach of professional duty, not, ipso facto, a determination that the lawyer has breached his professional duty and that the transaction must be undone.

Absent a challenge by an adversary party, on the present record and the facts found here, we discern no basis for concluding that the testator did not make the bequest with full knowledge and intent. However, we are also unable to conclude that he did. We would have greater confidence that there is no basis for such a challenge were a disinterested neutral without a direct financial interest in the estate to have made the determination that there are no heirs at law or next of kin who wish to challenge the attorney's status as executor and residuary beneficiary. Such a determination would provide assurance to the judge considering allowance of the account, and to this court, that reasonable efforts have been made to ascertain whether a potential challenger exists by a disinterested person who, unlike the attorney here, has no direct financial interest in the estate. On the other hand, the alternative suggested by the judge, invalidating a residuary bequest and escheating the residue to the Commonwealth, risks operating in derogation of the expressed wishes of a competent testator.

Query: The ethics rules do not require lawyers to neglect clients or refuse to assist them in the personal aspects of their lives. When they do reach out a hand and help, they are often much more capable than relatives or friends who might have little knowledge of the complex issues surrounding aging, or who live far away and only visit periodically. Consequently, lawyers are often found checking in on people and doing nice things for them, things that often lead to testamentary gifts or remembrances. Is it reasonable to completely prohibit a lawyer from drafting a will in which a substantial gift is made to the lawyer? Can we count on the judge to keep an eye on questionable situations? If there are no legal heirs to challenge a will, are these elderly clients at risk of overreaching or are they acting quite reasonably when they leave their estates to their lawyers? How would a neutral participant who can verify that there are no kin make the gift to the lawyer permissible after the fact?

California and Texas have adopted specific statutes for dealing with gifts to lawyers.

Cal. Prob. C. § 21350

(a) Except as provided in Section 21351, no provision, or provisions, of any instrument shall be valid to make any donative transfer to any of the following:

(1) The person who drafted the instrument.

(2) A person who is related by blood or marriage to, is a domestic partner of, is a cohabitant with, or is an employee of, the person who drafted the instrument.

(3) Any partner or shareholder of any law partnership or law corporation in which the person described in paragraph (1) has an ownership interest, and any employee of that law partnership or law corporation.

(4) Any person who has a fiduciary relationship with the transferor, including, but not limited to, a conservator or trustee, who transcribes the instrument or causes it to be transcribed.

(5) A person who is related by blood or marriage to, is a domestic partner of, is a cohabitant with, or is an employee of a person who is described in paragraph (4).

(6) A care custodian of a dependent adult who is the transferor.

(7) A person who is related by blood or marriage to, is a domestic partner of, is a cohabitant with, or is an employee of, a person who is described in paragraph (6).

(b) For purposes of this section, "a person who is related by blood or marriage" to a person means all of the following:

(1) The person's spouse or predeceased spouse.

(2) Relatives within the third degree of the person and of the person's spouse.

(3) The spouse of any person described in paragraph (2).

In determining any relationship under this subdivision, Sections 6406, 6407, and Chapter 2 (commencing with Section 6450) of Part 2 of Division 6 shall be applicable.

(c) For purposes of this section, the term "dependent adult" has the meaning as set forth in Section 15610.23 of the Welfare and Institutions Code and also includes those persons who (1) are older than age 64 and (2) would be dependent adults, within the meaning of Section 15610.23, if they were between the ages of 18 and 64. The term "care custodian" has the meaning as set forth in Section 15610.17 of the Welfare and Institutions Code.

(d) For purposes of this section, "domestic partner" means a domestic partner as defined under Section 297 of the Family Code.

  Exceptions apply if the beneficiary is related by blood or marriage to, is a cohabitant with, or is the registered domestic partner of the transferor or if the instrument is reviewed by an independent attorney.[7]

---

  [7] *See* Cal. Prob. C. § 21351.

Texas takes an even more straightforward approach:

Tex. Prob. Code § 58b. Devises and Bequests that are void.

(a) A devise or bequest of property in a will is void if the devise or bequest is made to:

(1) an attorney who prepares or supervises the preparation of the will;

(2) a parent, descendant of a parent, or employee of the attorney described by Subdivision (1) of this subsection; or

(3) a spouse of an individual described by Subdivision (1) or (2) of this subsection.

(b) This section does not apply to:

(1) a devise or bequest made to a person who:

(A) is the testator's spouse;

(B) is an ascendant or descendant of the testator; or

(C) is related within the third degree by consanguinity or affinity to the testator; or

(2) a bona fide purchaser for value from a devisee in a will.

Apply the California and Texas statutes to the cases above and see if the outcomes would be any different.

Gifts to lawyers can run the gamut from an entire estate to a token gift. The same factors come into play, however, when a lawyer drafts a will nominating herself as a fiduciary. So why are gifts absolutely prohibited, when the nomination of oneself as a fiduciary is permissible, especially when trustee or executor fees may more than eclipse the value of the outright gift to a lawyer? As you can see, there is no prohibition against you drafting a will for your parents or siblings, and including in that will gifts to yourself. You can even do it for great Aunt Edna, your remote cousin Al, or your spouse's great Aunt Edna or your spouse's remote cousin Al. But if you are unrelated by marriage or blood to the donor of the gift, you will need to have another lawyer draft the will and oversee its execution, being sure to independently determine the testator's capacity and freedom from undue influence or duress.

E. SAMPLE ENGAGEMENT LETTER

We have talked extensively in this chapter about managing conflicts by negotiating and memorializing an understanding between multiple clients that conflicts can arise. Here is one sample engagement letter. As you read through it, can you think of provisions you would change, based on some of the cases you have read in this chapter.

Sample Engagement Letter—Married Couple as Clients[8]

[Date]

Mr. and Mrs. [Husband's Name]

[Client's Address]

Re: Agreement for Legal Services

Dear Mr. and Mrs. [Client Last Name]:

The purpose of this letter is to set forth the terms of my legal representation of you.

1. *Scope of representation.* You have asked me to help you with planning your estate. This representation will include the following:

a. Drafting your estate planning documents based on the information you have provided to me. Your estate planning documents will include the following documents for each of you:

(1) A will, which provides (among other things) for the creation of a "Bypass Trust" as a means to preserve the estate and gift tax credit of the first spouse to die. This credit, which is currently equivalent to $_____ in assets, may allow the two of you to pass more of your combined marital wealth to your descendants or other estate beneficiary free of the estate tax. **[Option 1:** The Bypass Trust in each will is funded by means of a disclaimer by the surviving spouse. This method of funding permits the surviving spouse to wait until the death of the first spouse to die to decide to what extent the Bypass Trust is to be funded. The surviving spouse could choose to disclaim nothing, meaning that the surviving spouse would receive the entire estate and nothing would be placed in the Bypass Trust. Or the surviving spouse could decide to disclaim up to $_____ worth of property, causing the property so disclaimed to pass into the Bypass Trust. Thus, the estate tax savings under each will is totally dependent upon the decision of the surviving spouse to disclaim or not to disclaim.**] [Option 2:** The Bypass Trust in each will is funded by means of a formula. This formula contains language which is intended to maximize the amount of property passing into the Bypass Trust without causing there to be any tax due on the death of the first spouse to die. Funding of the Bypass Trust pursuant to this formula is mandatory on the death of the first spouse—the surviving spouse has no power to choose whether or not to fund the Bypass Trust.**]**

(2) A statutory durable power of attorney.

(3) A durable power of attorney for health care.

(4) A declaration of who you want your guardian to be if the need for one ever arises in the future.

(5) A directive to physicians (often called a "living will").

b. Providing you with instructions on how to coordinate your life insurance and retirement plan beneficiary designations with your estate planning documents.

---

[8] Copyright 1997–2007 by Glenn M. Karisch, all rights reserved.

    c.   Sending these drafts to you and answering any questions that you may have.

    d.   Preparing final drafts of the documents for signing.

    e.   Supervising your execution of these final documents in my office.

    f.   Sending you the completed, signed documents for your records.

2. *Excluded from representation.* My representation of you is limited to matters described above, and I owe you no duty of ongoing representation in this or other matters. My duties to you under this agreement will end when I have sent you your completed documents and you have had two weeks to review them for accuracy. After that time, my representation of you will cease, and I will owe you no duty to update your plan or to notify you of law changes which may affect you. Any future representation is not a part of this engagement and will be covered by a separate agreement.

3. *Planning objectives.* In helping you with your estate plan, my objective will be planning for the death or disability of either or both of you; I will not be considering the effects of a possible divorce. Either or both of you may be adversely affected by your estate plan in the event your marriage ends in divorce. If you have any questions about how this plan may affect you in the event of a divorce, please consult with an attorney experienced in family law matters. In addition, you have indicated that you want your estate plan to include provisions designed to save your family estate and/or gift taxes. By including these provisions, you should recognize that (a) your estate planning documents are likely to be more complex than they would have been if tax savings was not an objective and (b) restrictions may be placed on your beneficiaries (including the surviving spouse) that may make it more difficult to fully utilize and enjoy the property free from interference by and/or liability to others. This will confirm that we have discussed these issues at some length and that you have decided that the potential tax savings to be gained from this plan take priority over these potential detriments.

4. *Fees.* I will perform the services described above for a fee of $[Flat Fee], which fee includes up to [Hours in Flat Fee] hours of attorney time. If this project takes more than this amount of time, you agree to pay for time in excess of [Hours in Flat Fee] hours of attorney time at the hourly rate of $[Attorney Rate] per hour of attorney time. I will keep track of all time that I spend on this matter, and all of that time will count this limit. This will include the time that I or other office personnel may have already spent discussing this matter with you, time that I or other office personnel spend talking to you on the telephone or in person, time that I or other office personnel spend talking to each other or to third parties (your advisors, other attorneys, etc.) about your matter, time that we spend doing research on your matter, time that we spend drafting, revising and reviewing your documents, time that we spend drafting and reading correspondence, and time that our attorneys or other office personnel spend supervising your execution of documents. It has been my experience that I and my staff have been able to prepare estate plans like the one you have indicated you want for the majority of my clients within this time frame. Therefore, I have priced my services so that the majority of my clients can get a fair price for their plans and have a good idea of what those plans will cost. If I exceed the time limit in your case, I will charge you a larger fee based on the hourly rate stated above. Reasons why the time limit may be exceeded are: the need to make more revisions than usual; the need to spend more time than usual explaining provisions or answering questions; and delay in providing me with requested information. We mention these reasons not to discourage you from asking questions or having your documents be just the way you want, but to explain to you the effect this may have on the fee I charge so that you are in a position to control costs if you wish to do so.

5. *Expenses.* In addition to the fee described above, you agree to pay all expenses related to this matter. These expenses include, but are not limited to, postage, long distance telephone, photocopying, overnight messenger charges and filing fees. It has been my experience that, if there is only one overnight messenger charge and no long distance charges, the expenses associated with a plan such as yours will be approximately $[Flat Expenses]. Since these expenses usually are not known precisely until after you sign your documents, I probably will bill you the estimated amount stated above. This allows you to pay your bill in full and complete your business with my firm without having to wait a month or two to pay the expenses.

6. *Billing procedure.* Payment for fees and expenses is due at the *earlier* of (1) the time you sign your documents; or (2) 45 days from the date of this letter. Please be ready to pay when you come in to sign your documents.

[Option 7:A *You are my clients.* You, and you alone, are my clients. I owe no duty to your family members or to your potential estate beneficiaries. Since there are two of you, the possibility of a conflict between you exists. You acknowledge and understand that, since I am representing both of you, no communication either of you has with me can be kept confidential from the other of you. If a conflict develops between the two of you, I may decline to continue to represent you.]

[Option 7:B. *Multi-party representation.* My representation of you in this matter requires me to represent each of you as clients at the same time. Of course, you could each retain your own attorney to prepare your estate planning documents, but you have indicated that you prefer to have me prepare estate planning documents for both of you. I am happy to do this, subject to the following conditions regarding multi-party representation:

    a.   Since there are two of you, the possibility of a conflict between you exists. You acknowledge and understand that, since I am representing both of you, no communication either of you has with me can be kept confidential from the other of you. If a conflict develops between the two of you, I may decline to continue to represent you.

    b.   When I am advising [Husband] and preparing [Husband]'s documents, [Husband] is my only client, and I owe no duty [Husband]'s family members or potential estate beneficiaries.

    c.   When I am advising [Wife] and preparing [Wife]'s documents, [Wife] is my only client, and I owe no duty [Wife]'s family members or potential estate beneficiaries.]

8. *Termination of Representation.* Either of us can terminate this relationship at any time for any reason by giving written notice to the other party. My representation of you will terminate immediately upon the giving of this notice by either party, except that, if you are involved in a court proceeding (such as a lawsuit or probate proceeding) at the time of termination and I am the attorney of record, my representation will continue until I am sure that my immediate withdrawal as your attorney will not jeopardize your interests in the proceeding. Upon termination by either party for any reason:

    a. You agree to pay my fees through the date of termination calculated at the hourly rate or rates stated above;

    b. You agree to pay expenses incurred through the date of termination; and

    c. You are entitled to the file I maintain on your matter if you request it, provided that I am entitled to photocopy the file contents at your expense prior to delivery of the file to you.

9. *Grievances.* The State Bar of Texas investigates and prosecutes professional misconduct committed by Texas attorneys. Although not every complaint against or dispute with a lawyer involves professional misconduct, the State Bar Office of General Counsel will provide you with information about how to file a complaint. For more information, please call 1/800/932–1900. This is a toll-free phone call.

I look forward to working with you on this matter. If you want me to represent you, and if you agree to the terms of this letter, please sign one copy of this letter and return it to me. (The other copy is for your records.)

Very truly yours,

[Law Firm]

Accepted and Agreed:

_____

[Husband's Name]

_____

[Wife's Name]

_____

    Think about the will that Irene Sandford drafted in Connecticut[9]. An elderly friend/relative/client calls and asks you to come to her home. You do so and she asks you to draft her will, on the spot. Although there was no multiple representation in that case, think about the attorney's ability to memorialize the terms of the representation in that instance with an appropriate client letter. Though the ethics rules do not require that all client agreements be in writing, it is certainly better if they are. For instance, how many clients are capable of understanding the turgid prose and technical terms of a client letter like this one? Is it enough to simply state: "Dear clients—You have asked me to draft multiple estates documents for you and I am happy to do so. You understand that in the context of doing so I will have a loyalty to both of you, and will have to disclose confidential information relating to your property and estate plan to both of you. If my loyalties to either indicate that an insurmountable conflict has arisen, I will withdraw from representing both of you. Your signature on this letter confirms your understanding of my representation." Do you think a simple letter such as this would be sufficient? Why or why not?

    Consider now the ACTEC sample retainer letter.[10] How does it compare to the one you just read:

---

    [9]   *Sandford, supra* note 7, at 162, 164–165.

    [10] http://www.actec.org/public/EngagementLettersPublic.asp#INTRO.1

[Date]

[Name(s) and Address(es)]

Subject: [Subject Matter of the Engagement]

Dear [Clients]:

You have each asked me to [scope of representation]. I have agreed to do this work and will bill for it on the following basis: [DESCRIBE ARRANGEMENTS PERTAINING TO FEES, BILLING, ETC.]. If I am asked to perform tasks not described in this letter, an additional engagement letter may be required for that work.

It is common for a husband and wife to employ the same lawyer to assist them in planning their estates. You have taken this approach by asking me to represent both of you to [scope of representation]. However, each of you wants to maintain your right to confidentiality and the ability to meet separately with me. I have agreed to do this work on this basis and will bill for it on the following basis: [DESCRIBE ARRANGEMENTS PERTAINING TO FEES, BILLING, AND WHICH OF THE PARTIES, IF NOT BOTH, WILL BE RESPONSIBLE FOR PAYMENT.]. If I am asked to perform tasks not described in this letter, an additional engagement letter may be required.

I will represent each of you separately and will not discuss with either one of you what your spouse has disclosed to me. Each of you releases me from the obligation to reveal to you any information I may have received from the other that is material and adverse to your interest. Furthermore, I will not use any information I obtain from one of you in preparing the other's plan, even if the result is that the two plans are incompatible or one plan is detrimental to the interests of the other spouse. In short, the representation will be structured so that each of you will have the same relationship with me as if each of you had gone to a separate lawyer for assistance in your planning.

While I have agreed to undertake this representation on a separate and confidential basis, you should be aware that there might be disputes between you now or in the future as to your respective property rights and interests, or as to other issues that may arise between you. Should this occur, I would not be able to represent either of you in resolving any such dispute, and each of you would have to obtain your own representation. After considering the foregoing, if each of you consents to my representation of each of you separately, I request that each of you sign and return the enclosed copy of this letter. If you have any questions about anything discussed in this letter, please let me know. In addition, you should feel free to consult with another lawyer about the effect of signing this letter.

Sincerely,

[Lawyer]

CONSENT

We have read the foregoing letter and understand its contents. We consent to having you represent each of us on the terms and conditions set forth.

Signed: _____, 20___   _____ (Client 1)

Signed: _____, 20___   _____ (Client 2)

Take a stab at drafting your own client letter that complies with the ethics rules we have discussed in this chapter. What would you say to your clients if you sent them a letter like the one above? Would you tell them that the tone is formal and professional because you insist that all client relationships be formal, or that it is simply in legaleze? What if they took longer than two weeks to finish reviewing and executing the documents? Does your responsibility end when the two weeks have elapsed or when the work is concluded? What parts of this letter do you think would be binding in court if one of the clients complained that you disclosed privileged information or should be disqualified because of a conflict?

F. CONCLUSION

There are many more ethics issues that can arise in the typical trusts and estates practice, and we urge you to familiarize yourself with the ACTEC Commentaries as well as the Professional Rules applicable in your state. You may have already taken, or will take, a course on lawyer ethics. Many students often fail to take that course as seriously as they should, imagining that they would never run afoul of the rules. To the contrary, and as every estates and trusts practitioner will tell you, you will encounter potential conflicts on your first day of practice in this field and they won't stop until years after you have retired.

This has been a very long book and you have come a long way in learning about the intricacies of planning and litigating estates and trusts. You have been bombarded with warnings of things not to do, and your mind is probably completely muddled with all of the different rules and complex issues that go into drafting even a simple will. Just the tax matters are enough to possibly convince you that maybe being a taxi driver isn't such a bad career after all. However, being an estates and trusts lawyer can be one of the most rewarding career choices you can make. No, you won't likely be rescuing people from death row or ensuring that they have visitation rights with their children, but you will give them peace of mind throughout their lives that they have adequately taken care of their loved ones. And perhaps most importantly, you will help them go out of this world gracefully and respected. As age makes us frail and even bitter sometimes, the staunch support of our estates lawyer/professional will ease many minds. At the end of the day, you can go to sleep knowing you have helped a family meet its needs and, now and then, you will have made friends and done many good deeds.

APPENDIX

ANSWERS AND EXPLANATIONS

The answers to the questions presented here are not, as you should know by now, definitive and absolute. In some states, the rules to be applied may result in contrary outcomes. We have tried to be somewhat general in our answers in order not to run afoul of state law differences. As a result, these answers are intended to facilitate your studying of the material in this course. It is intended that you will attempt to answer the questions on your own as you study, then look back to these answers and explanations to see if you are on the right track, or are forgetting important considerations. If you don't understand how we got to a particular answer after reading the answer, go back and review the material in the book that precededed the question. If you are still not sure, then ask. The point of giving answers is to help you in your studying, not to try to trip you up. Because few professors have time to cover all the problems in class, these should give you a start on thinking about how you would prepare for your exam, and ultimately how you will prepare to practice in this area.

Chapter One

Answers

1.1. Marcus will most likely get the necklace since it was in Grandma's possession at the time of her death and her will left her entire estate to Marcus. The package appeared to be intended as a gift (Grandma mailed it to Sasha) and it was delivered (the shipper received a signature); however, the problem arises in the area of acceptance. Since Sasha returned the package, unopened, the most likely interpretation is that Sasha rejected the gift. The fact that she called and said she changed her mind, when the package was back in the possession of the giver, would not automatically re-trigger the intention to gift by Grandma. How would your answer change, if at all, if Sasha had been out of town and the shipper had returned the package to the sender?

1.2. No, the children cannot force their dad out of his home because their father did not make a present gift to them of any interest in the home. A will is revocable up until the time of death; therefore, Bill still retains full ownership and control of his home. It is likely, however, that he may be looking to amend the beneficiary portion of his will in the near future. What if, instead of a will, Bill had executed a deed transferring the property to his children?

1.3. Tom would make a good argument for a gift *causa mortis*; however, there was no delivery before Keri's death. Assuming that she was in possession of the motorcycle when she died, she obviously never gave up dominion and control. However, perhaps she gave up a future interest before her death since she intended to retain physical possession at least for the duration of the race. Steve's testate or intestate heirs, rather than Kevin, would most likely be the recipients of Steve's bikes because he did not die from the anticipated cause. Depending on medical evidence, however, Kevin might be able to make a convincing argument that Steve's fatal heart attack was actually triggered by (and therefore a related part of) the accident on the track. In that case, Kevin might have a better argument that he was the donee of Steve's bikes. Both clearly had donative intent but none gave up possession. However, what if Keri handed Tom the key to her shed where she kept her extra motorcycles just before she began the race?

1.4. Pat will make the argument that the money is a gift *causa mortis*, that Clarence had intent, constructive delivery was made, and Pat certainly accepted, even if it wasn't during Clarence's lifetime. Perhaps a court would be willing to overlook the short gap in the acceptance and deem it constructive acceptance. But what about delivery? One issue is whether delivery to the doctor constitutes constructive delivery. Although Clarence certainly gave up dominion and control, which is the usual requirement for delivery of personal property, did he really? If he miraculously recovered couldn't he still call his bank and tell them not to honor the check up until the time Pat cashes it? Should the delivery rule look to the time the physical piece of paper is out of the donor's hands or when the money it represents is in the hands of the donee? This question illustrates one of the most confounding difficulties with using checks as gifts. Even if Pat's argument is successful, however, banking rules might come into play. Pat could not cash a check from Clarence's account after Clarence's death; therefore, the claim would have to be made against Clarence's estate.

1.5. Minka's intestate heirs would receive the coffee shop, rather than the three friends. Minka's email does not follow the rules necessary to make her statement a testamentary gift (no witnesses, signature, etc) and her statement "if something happens to me" is too vague to cover her accidental death as triggering a gift *causa mortis*. Plus, there was no delivery or acceptance.

1.6. Kylie gets the grill. Although Ted expressed the intent to make an *inter vivos* gift on the phone to Garrett, the grill was not delivered or accepted by Garrett. Therefore, it would be distributed to Kylie as a specific bequest under Ted's will since it was still in Ted's possession at the time of his death (and therefore, part of his estate). It cannot be a gift *causa mortis* because Ted had no expectation of dying.

1.7. The most likely result would be that the three daughters could challenge the will based on undue influence or fraud, thereby invalidating their disinheritance. Since Marta did not seem to understand what she was signing or specifically what the document said, the fact that she merely signed a document when asked to by her son would most likely be viewed as insufficient evidence that she actually intended to disinherit her three children in favor of the one child who presented her with the documents while she lay in critical care. Depending on her medical record and medication history, the daughters could also attempt to argue that their mother was not of sound mind at the time that she signed the document, which would also invalidate the will.

1.8. The niece is not entitled to the money in the account. Under *Samuel*, the court found that delivery must be made in such a way that "the donor parts with all control over it". Under these facts, merely giving a debit card to her niece does not show Aunt Alex parted with all control over her account. She still could arguably exert control by writing checks or making online transfers up until the moment of her death. Further, Alex did not provide the PIN to the account (which the niece may not be able to legally use, anyway).

1.9. Chen's written disposition of property to his wife would be voided by operation of law because he divorced his wife after the will was drafted and, of course, prior to his death. Instead, the property would pass to his contingent beneficiaries or by intestacy. But a good argument could be made that if he did not bother to change his will in the two years between his divorce and his death, that is sufficient evidence that he wanted his ex-wife to receive his estate. It is a dangerous argument, however, and one that doesn't often work. Can you see why?

1.10. Drake could freely make a new will in 2011, which, assuming proper execution, would revoke the first will; however, since Drake was still married at the time of his death, his spouse may still make a claim against the estate for an elective share.

1.11. The children could claim against Tera's will as pretermitted heirs (discussed in more detail in the following chapters) since they were born after her will was drafted.

1.12. Brad has been instrumental in the death of Ashley and therefore would be excluded from taking any property in Ashley's estate under the state's slayer statutes. A criminal conviction of murder is not necessary; most states rely on the intentional/unintentional homicide distinction in triggering the application of the slayer statute. To date mercy killing has not been recognized as an exception, even though clearly Ashley would want Brad to have everything.

1.13. Clearly these intentions are all against public policy and would not be affirmed. On the other hand, can you think of less egregious devises that might be upheld but which most of us might consider against public policy as well?

Chapter 2

Answers

2.1. Individuals with standing include: Noel, who could possibly claim both homestead and spousal election; American Express and Shannon, as creditors; Michael, as named trust beneficiary of a life estate; Vita, as named trust beneficiary of a life estate; Austin, as Trustee; and Thomas, as residuary beneficiary of a life estate. The terms of the trust share for the benefit of Vita would determine who the residuary beneficiaries are after Vita's death under that share, giving possible standing to the same.

Individuals with no standing: Neither Carla's sister Judy nor the elementary school would have standing as they are not parties to the will nor creditors of the estate. Absent evidence to the contrary, Carla's sister is disgruntled and the school had, at most, an unenforceable promise to make a gift.

2.2. Tyra's state operates on a limited value homestead protection tied to particular real estate and therefore the creditors could only force the sale of the home if the property is valued over the statutory limitation ($300,000 in this example).

2.3. Doris's state offers homestead protection tied to particular real estate with limitations on descent and devise, therefore, she cannot chose to leave her house to another party.

2.4. Gordon and Melissa's state provided a cash amount/homestead allowance in accordance with the UPC Homestead Allowance which provides that each of the minor children (since no spouse survived) is entitled to an equal share of the $22,500 homestead allowance.

2.5. Under the UPC, the set-asides consist of $22,500 homestead, $27,000 maximum family allowance, and $15,000 exempt property, for a total of $64,500. Deduct that from the $300,000 estate and you have $235,500 left to pay debts, costs, and devises.

2.6. Using the first example of $100,000 homestead, $18,000 family allowance, $15,000 exempt property, and $30,000 debts and costs, the net probate estate is $137,000. If the decedent devises one-half to the spouse, he will take by will: $68,500. In the first scenario, therefore, the surviving spouse takes a total of $201,500 (or 67% of the total estate). If the decedent died testate and the surviving spouse takes a one-third elective share, that amount is: $55,667. Thus, the surviving spouse's total share if using the elective share amount is: $188,667 (or 63% of the total estate).

Using the UPC, with $22,500 homestead, $27,000 family allowance, $15,000 exempt property, and $30,000 debts and costs, the net probate estate is 205,500. If the decedent devises one half to the surviving spouse, he will take by will: $102,750. In this scenario the surviving spouse takes a total of $167,250 (or 56% of the total estate). If the decedent dies testate and the surviving spouse takes a one-third elective share, that amount is $68,600. Thus, the surviving spouse's total share of set-asides and elective share is $133,000 (or 44% of the total estate).

2.7. Of course, state law varies widely but, generally speaking, in a community property state, Raj and Arti may be considered joint owners of all of the property and income acquired during the marriage, regardless of title and so Arti could only devise her half of her bank account. But she also owned half of Raj's business and could conceivably devise half of it at her death as well. A few community property states treat community property as joint tenancies with a right of survivorship, in which case Raj would own the bank account and the business in full at Arti's death. In contrast, in common law states, ownership of assets between spouses is determined by title—and the spouse could elect against the estate at death for a share of the decedent spouse's estate. Raj would have to make a decision to elect against her estate. In a common law state, Arti and Raj could keep their property separate during life, manage it separately, and make unilateral decisions to spend or save it. In a community property state, however, the other would be entitled to a say in how the property is managed and spent. Of course, if Arti spent the money in her bank account and Raj didn't say anything about it, he could be held to have acquiesced in her management decisions.

2.8. Since Luke revoked his will, his probate estate will pass to his heirs through the operation of his state's intestacy statute. His spouse, Lena, could certainly seek homestead, family allowance and exempt property, in addition to her spousal share (covered in more detail in the next chapter), and his genetic children would be considered heirs for the remaining portion. Gina's son could also inherit as a child, if paternity can be established, since children born outside of marriage may also inherit as children through intestacy. But Lucy might not be able to inherit if it is determined that Luke was not her genetic father. Under UPC §2–120, once Lena gives birth, the child conceived through in vitro fertilization should also be able to inherit because the child was *in utero* not later than 36 months after Luke's death and would be born not later than 45 months after Luke's death. This might allow for future children to be born, as well. But beware of some parent/child statutes that prohibit post-mortem judicial determinations of paternity. Gina's son might be precluded from proving paternity and thus sharing in Luke's estate, and Lucy might inherit as his child if the paternity action to disprove her relationship with Luke fails.

2.9. Upon Lena's death, her heirs would be her surviving spouse, Luke, and her genetic children, Lucy, Lacey, and Lewis. Gina's son would be irrelevant because he is not related to her, and we know Lucy is her daughter. The question arises about the fertilized embryos. Gestational surrogates don't have parental rights, but the rights of genetic donors depends on intent. Lena may have intended the in vitro be used to help her carry a fourth child, not a stranger. Should that matter under UPC §2–121(e)?

Chapter 3

Answers

3.1. Calculate the Homestead, Exempt Property, and Family Allowance allocations for your state.

3.2. Using the UPC as an example, Wila would be entitled to 100% of Herman's net probate estate (NPE) if Seth and Doris are descendants of both Herman and Wila. Thus, her total share would be $964,500, Seth and Doris would each take $50,000 from the stock brokerage account, but would take nothing from his net probate estate, and the debts of $115,500 would be paid. If Seth and Doris are Herman's children, Wila would take the first $150,000 plus half of the remaining $200,000 for a total of $250,000 from Herman's NPE (leaving $100,000 to pass to Seth and Doris). If Seth and Doris are Wila's children, and Herman has no children, then 100% of the NPE passes to Wila.

3.3. a. 100% or $350,000; b. first $150,000 plus half, for a total of $250,000; c. 100% or $350,000.

3.4. Calculate the intestate distributions for this estate under the intestacy laws of your state.

3.5. Janice's total spousal share is $350,000. She in entitled to all $100,000 of the homestead, family allowance and exempt property, leaving $350,000 after debts as the net probate estate for UPC intestate calculations. From that amount, her UPC share is calculated as follows: $150,000 plus ½ of the remainder, which is $100,000 (200,000/2 = 1,000) for a total UPC share of 250,000, and thereby making Janice's total distribution $350,000.

3.6. Tamika's spousal share is $462,500. She is entitled to all $200,000 of the homestead, family allowance and exempt property, leaving $300,000 in the estate after debts for UPC intestate calculations. From that amount, her UPC share is calculated as follows: $225,000 plus ½ of the remainder, which is $37,500 (75,000/2 = 37,500) for a total UPC share of $262,500, and thereby making Tamika's total distribution $462,500.

	Classic Per Stirpes	Per Capita by Generation	Per Capita with Representation
3.7.	E & F = 1/6 each G, H & I = 1/9 each J = 1/3 D has no living issue	E, F, G, H, I & J = 1/6 each	E, F, G, H, I & J = 1/6 each
3.8.	A & J = 1/3 each G & I = 1/9 each M & O = 1/18 each	A = 1/3 G, I & J = 1/6 each N & O = 1/12 each	A & J = 1/3 each G & I = 1/9 each M & O = 1/18 each
3.9.	D & J =1/4 each K, L & M = 1/24 each P, Q, R & S = 1/32 each G & I = 1/12 each N & O = 1/24 each	D = 1/4 G, I & J = 1/8 each K, L, M, N, O, P, Q, R & S = 1/24 each	D & J = 1/4 each K, L & M = 1/24 each P, Q, R & S = 1/32 each G & I = 1/12 each N & O = 1/24 each
3.10.	D & J = 1/4 each K, L & M=1/24 each P, Q, R & S = 1/40 each G & I = 1/12 each N & O = 1/24 each U & V = 1/80 each	D = 1/4 G ,I & J= 1/8 each K, L, M, N, O, P, Q, R & S = 3/80 each U & V = 3/160 each	D & J = 1/4 each K, L & M = 1/24 each P, Q, R & S = 1/32 each G & I = 1/12 each N & O = 1/24 each U & V = 1/80 each
3.11.	J = 1/3 E & G = 1/6 each K, L & M = 1/18 each N & O = 1/12 each	E, G & J = 1/5 each K, L, M, N & O = 2/25 each	E, G & J = 1/5 each K, L & M = 1/15 each N & O = 1/10 each
3.12.	All to parent*	All to parent under UPC	All to parent*
3.13.	C = 1/3 E & G = 1/6 each K, L & M = 1/18 each N & O = 1/12 each	C = 1/3 E & G = 1/6 each K, L, M, N & O = 1/15 each	C = 1/3 E & G = 1/6 each K, L, M, N & O = 1/15 each
3.14.	J = 1/3 K, L & M = 1/18 each P, Q, R & S = 1/30 each U & V = 1/60 each G & I = 1/9 each N & O = 1/18 each	G, I & J = 1/6 each P, Q, R, S, K, L, M, N & O = 1/20 each U & V = 1/40 each	G, I & J = 1/6 each K, L & M = 1/18 each N & O = 1/12 each P, Q, R & S = 1/30 each U & V = 1/60 each

* Most states, like the UPC, would give all to a parent if no spouse or descendant survives.

3.15   3.13

    C = 2/5
    E = 1/5
    K, L & M = 1/15 each
    G = 1/10
    N & O = 1/20 each

3.14

    J = 2/5
    K, L & M = 1/15 each
    P, Q, R & S = 1/25 each
    U & V = 1/50 each
    G = 1/10
    N & O = 1/20

3.16. First, we do hotchpot, which is the same for all intestacy schemes. We omit A's and B's gifts because they predeceased the testator. Then we add D's and E's gifts to the net probate estate for a total of $240,000 ($40,000 + $20,000

+ $180,000). We divide the total by 4 for the 4 children (either living or deceased with issue surviving), entitling each child to $60,000. Thus, D gets $20,000 to account for her advancement under all three schemes.

At this point the three schemes would lead to different results. Under classic *per stirpes* J takes C's $60,000 by representation; G, N & O take B's share by representation (G gets $30,000, N & O get $15,000 each); and E, K, L, & M take A's share by representation but E's share is reduced by $20,000 to account for the advancement to E (E gets $10,000, and K, L, & M get $10,000 each).

Under *Per Capita* by Generation, D would also take her $20,000 ($60,000 share reduced by D's advancement). But the remaining $180,000 (E's $20,000 advancement + the $160,000 left in the probate estate after taking out D's share) is recalculated at the next level for division and distribution to the grandchildren. Because there are 5 living grandchildren, or deceased grandchildren with living issue, each grandchild would be entitled to $36,000. Thus, G and J would each take $36,000 and E would take only $16,000 to account for the $20,000 advancement to E. Then F and H's shares would be added together for a total of $72,000 and divided 5 ways for the great-grandchildren, giving K, L, M, N, & O each $14,500 each.

Under *Per Capita* with Representation, the distribution would be the same as for classic *per stirpes* in the above example because there is a living heir at the initial level of distribution. However, if D also predeceased X leaving no issue, the distribution would be as follows: E gets $20,000; G & J get $40,000 each; K, L, & M get $13,333 each; and N & O get $20,000 each. Can you arrive at the same answers?

3.17. Classic *Per Stirpes*: D=0; J=$30,000; G=$15,000, N & O=$7,500 each; E=0; K, L, & M= $3,333 each.

Per Capita by Generation: D=0; G & J=$17,500 each; K, L, M, N, & O=$7,000 each.

Per Capita with Representation: Same as classic *per stirpes*.

3.18. Classic *Per Stirpes*: J=$30,000; G=$15,000; N & O=$7,500 each; K, L, & M = $3,333 each.

Per Capita by Generation: E=0; G&J=$17,500 each; K, L, M, N, O=$7,000 each.

Per Capita with Representation: E=0; G&J=$17,500 each; N & O=$8,750 each; K, L, & M=$5,833 each.

Chapter 4

Answers

4.1. His children, equally, inherit the estate. The email to his attorney does not meet the execution and witness requirements to be considered a will or an amendment, nor does it serve as a revocation of the prior will. Because the first will was properly executed and not revoked by Charlie prior to his death, the will is still valid at his death.

However, if UPC § 2–503 is applicable, Carol could argue that Charlie intended the email to serve as an alteration to his will. His children could contend, however, that if 2–503 applies as a Harmless Error, that Charlie only intended Carol to inherit in the capacity as "my fiancé". Because she ended the relationship just prior to Charlie's death, the descriptive language in the email may become relevant to whether Carol could still inherit if she were no longer Charlie's fiancée.

4.2. Concerns include, first and foremost, does the will as it stands conform in formalities to meet the state's will requirements? If so, your role will be to advise the client on the will he brought you. Most attorneys find that drafting language is a particular art, and that they feel the most comfortable drafting their own documents, rather than signing off on someone else's work. It would be unethical to assist a client in drafting a document that is known to be ineffective. But if you realize the document doesn't actually effectuate your client's intentions, you will also need to do a client intake to ensure that the will actually functions to accomplish the client's desires. Also, a powerful, clear engagement letter will be in order identifying exactly what services you are providing and what services you are not providing.

4.3. The will was clearly executed with testamentary intent and the witnesses observed the testator sign, but not all witnesses observed each other sign and the testator did not see at least the second and third witness sign. Under the line-of-sight test the will may be voided because the first witness did not see the second witness sign. Under substantial compliance or conscious presence tests, the first and second witness signatures would be sufficient. Even the signature of the third, Professor Plum, would be valid since the address is not required by the wills statutes. Finally, if the Colonel was suffering the effects of the poison at the time Professor Plum was signing, could the Colonel have seen this third witness sign? It is likely his mind was pre-occupied with dying and one could reasonably argue that even in a conscious presence state the Colonel was not aware that the Professor was signing as a witness. If the state only requires two witness signatures, that may be irrelevant. But if the third is needed, the will might be voided.

4.4. Many states allow a witness to sign some days or even months after the testator signs, so long as the witness actually saw the testator. This would not be permissible in a strict compliance state, but has been allowed in both substantial compliance and dispensing power states. The question, however, is whether the state would allow a witness to ascribe his signature after the death of the testator, which is often used as a cut-off. Of course, if the state only requires the signatures of two witnesses, Professor Plum's may not be required and the will can stand.

4.5. Despite all three witnesses having seen the testator sign the will, this will would most likely not be valid because the testator did not see any of the witnesses sign the will. Though if a state has adopted the UPC's dispensing power it could be argued that the requirements were met so long as there is clear and convincing evidence of testamentary intent.

4.6. The reasons for client requests can be somewhat startling when you take the time to ask: some might have signing "stage fright" and feel that they need more time to read and think it over. This might be a valid concern, or an opportunity to discuss the benefits of "revocable" documents. Some might have driven a long way to see you (out of concern that their small town might be too nosy in their business, for example) and want to show the document to their children before they sign, not wanting to make the trip again.

This brings up a concern that should be discussed with your clients: that of course they are free to show their will to anyone that they wish, but that it may be inadvisable because the document is revocable—and that they might want to emotional freedom to change it later. It is usually a more effective strategy for many parents to just tell their children that the will has been created and, if they desire, to explain relevant provisions, rather than to have the parents show them a draft, which can invite "eager hands" to get overly involved in the process.

Finally, other clients may claim that the person they are naming as guardian or executor wants to read the will. This brings up the same notion of confidentiality as in the prior example, but also provides another counseling opportunity with clients: that they are not binding anyone to do anything in a will because the guardian or executor can always say "no thanks" when the time comes if they do not wish to serve.

4.7. First, if you are on the board of the charity that is a beneficiary under the will, you would most likely be considered an interested witness, even if you have little to do with the day-to-day operations of the organization. But you can still serve as a notary, since the notary function is different from the witness function. If the gift to the charity is purged, it will lapse and pass to the residuary clause to then pass to Wila, Seth, and Doris. In a state that simply purges the gift to interested witnesses, either Wila or Seth would lose his or her share altogether. But, as you will learn in Chapter 7, Wila is entitled to a spousal share regardless of whether she is provided for in a will. Thus, if Wila signs and her gift is purged, she can reclaim it under most state's elective share statutes. If Seth signs and his gift is purged, he is out of luck. Under the UPC, assuming Seth and Doris are the children of both Wila and Herman, Wila would be entitled to all of Herman's intestate estate. Thus, there would be no effect in a state that purges only the amounts greater than their intestate share. But obviously if Seth served as the witness, his entire share would be voided because he would not be entitled to any intestate share if Wila is his mother.

4.8. Even under the UPC's dispensing power, the 2005 completely unexecuted will cannot stand alone for there is no evidence that Coleman had anything to do with its creation, much less wanted it to revoke his earlier will and dispose of his property. Assuming the 2007 holographic will is not stricken for being unduly influenced by Shannon Price, the question is whether stapling it to the 23 page 2005 unexecuted will is sufficient to validate the latter. It is very unlikely to be the case, primarily because of the internal inconsistencies. The 2005 document makes provisions for trusts, charities, and a host of other bequests that are completely irrelevant in light of the 2007 will which gives everything outright to Shannon. Perhaps the executor or trustee or funeral provisions could stand IF it were shown that Coleman himself stapled the 2005 will to the 2007 holograph AND intended it to execute the former. Since he clearly understood the will execution requirements and failed to execute the 2005 will at all, it is unlikely he had testamentary intent with regard to that document in 2005, even if he later acquired it in 2007. But we have no evidence that Coleman actually stapled the two documents together, which would be the only evidence that he had testamentary intent in 2007 with regard to the 2005 document.

4.9. There are problems with both attempts by Wila. The first, of course, is that Seth and Doris do not meet the criteria of "my two children. . .by my first marriage." This ambiguity could cause problems. Second, although Wila intends for the actual page of Herman's will to become integrated as part of her will, any integrated will requires a certain amount of internal coherence which this document lacks. More often people will instruct that their property is to be disposed of according to the terms of someone else's will, and as we will learn below under Acts of Independent Significance and Incorporation by Reference, this is permissible so long as the document or act has either been in existence (which this has) or serves some purpose besides disposing of her property. Although Herman's will *used* to have an independent significance, it no longer does, making it questionable whether the Acts of Independent Significance doctrine can save it. Furthermore, all the attempts purport to give the property to her first and only to the kids if she predeceases Herman, which she did not do. The whole bequest becomes circular if she is giving it to herself.

4.10. This provision could prevent the problem of constant bickering as it relates to property distribution (a problem notorious among siblings), especially when there exists an odd number of beneficiaries and the possibility of a stubborn hold-out. Of course, this provision will only work if the Executor is actually able to put her foot down and sell the items. Therefore, if the Executor is a child of the testator in this example, there could be some disagreements and friction.

4.11. Be as clear as possible in drafting. Language such as "For purposes of this will, "my children" shall include not only those children naturally born to me or adopted by me, but also, specifically, (stepchild's name), and that such relationship shall not be affected by any change in my marital status." Can help to clarify the first situation. The opposite language can be used to effect that latter, but clear disinheriting language may also be warranted.

4.12. Note that, like *Tipler's Will*, if Wila simply intends to benefit whoever Herman had benefitted, then the Independent Significance doctrine can be used. But if Wila intends to benefit the particular people that Herman identified (so that if Herman had listed different beneficiaries Wila would not have wanted Herman's will to guide hers) then Independent Significance would not apply. If she is using the sentence from Herman's will to function as a separate document, so long as it was in existence before she wrote her will, Incorporation by Reference might apply. This kind of estate planning, besides being a litigator's dream and a court's nightmare, shows how the doctrines don't always fix all problems—they are good for lists and having someone else's will guide the testator's dispositions, but they can't always deal with the letter, the cut and pasted page from someone else's will, or even the will that consists of multiple documents not always stapled together.

4.13. It depends. If Carmen's state has a statute on separate writing, then the letter is sufficient so long as Carmen has made some provision in her will that separate writings may exist. If the will does not refer to the separate writing, however, that doctrine won't save it, and neither will Incorporation by Reference. Could the writing serve as a holographic codicil, however? In a state that has adopted the dispensing power, a letter might be sufficient. In a strict compliance state, however, a letter does not meet the will formalities and would not be sufficient.

4.14. Yes, so long as the trust instrument was in existence at the time the will was drafted, and no changes were subsequently made, Incorporation by Reference can save it. But (F)acts of Independent Significance cannot because until it is funded the trust has no separate existence.

4.15. Settlor: Mary Lenny; Trustee: Lorie Lenny; Successor Trustee: Bob Starks; Beneficiary: Carol Troy; Contingent Beneficiary: Terrance Troy.

4.16. Settlors: Sam and Margaret; Trustee: Seasons Bank; Successor Trustee: None Named; Beneficiaries (at death): Anne and Tommy, equally, assuming that they are both living; Contingent beneficiaries: if either Anne or Tommy predeceases their parents, their living children would receive a ½ share to divide equally among themselves.

4.17. Bill Gates is the settlor, trustee, and primary beneficiary of this revocable *inter vivos* trust. The Bill and Melina Gates Charitable Trust is the successor beneficiary with the power to enforce the duties of a trustee against Bill if he fails to act with due concern for the BMGCT's interests.

4.18. This trust is mandatory because the conditions that would cause various different outcomes are not within the trustee's discretion, but are spelled out in the trust. There is precatory language but it is directed at the spouse and the children, not at the trustee.

4.19. This trust has one small discretionary element, but the rest is mandatory. Income to spouse is mandatory, the remainder must be distributed at the spouse's death. The only discretion is how much of the remainder to pay to each living child, but the entire amount must be paid out. The spouse has the discretion to invade the principal but the trustee does not have the discretion to prevent it.

4.20. This trust is entirely mandatory—there is no discretion anywhere to pay more or less or to distribute different amounts to different beneficiaries.

4.21. This trust is also mandatory because there is no option *not to pay out*. The residue must either be paid to the children or for their benefit. Even though the trustee has the discretion to choose among charities, the trust is not discretionary, especially since the actions of the children can eliminate whatever discretion the trustee may have.

4.22. This designation raises questions of whether "all of the people who have Friended me on Facebook" is an ascertainable beneficiary. Assuming that Facebook is still in existence at the death of the Settlor, the term "Friends" may be clear, since it could be found as a definable term on Facebook. However, a date to determine exactly which friends to include would be important (such as "the Friends I have on Facebook as of the date of my death"). And Facebook has made it possible for there to be different levels of Friends and that must be clarified. Eminem had something like 38 million friends as of the date of writing this, and Michael Jackson had in the neighborhood of 32 million. Thus, there are Friends and there are Friends. But, other problems could arise: what if Facebook is not in existence at the Settlor's death? Or what if the account has been deleted? Here, a detailed clause would be in order which would name a contingent beneficiary under those circumstances.

4.23. This raises the problem of the semi-secret beneficiary. Who determines what is being said and whether it is nasty? A good solution here would be to avoid the ambiguity all together and just name beneficiaries (or specifically exclude individuals). Another solution could be to use the Power of Appointment instead of the trust. Powers of Appointment are discussed in more detail in the following sections.

4.24. Under the Uniform Trust Code and the UPC, Pet Trusts are allowed. However, depending on the size of the trust principal, 5% may be an amount in excess of what is needed to actually care for the pet. Furthermore, there is no person named as trustee to receive the income and care for the pets. Although a trust won't fail for lack of a trustee, it would be better to identify the trustee. It would further be a good idea to detail what is meant by "housing" and also how the pet is to be cared for in the event that the trust principal is distributed in full (and therefore, no income is available to care for the pet).

4.25. Here there is a clear problem of ascertaining the beneficiaries. This could raise tax concerns if the party is a huge bash, as well as open up the trust to challenges by people who might like to be part of the annual party but who aren't invited. A solution would be to craft a list of named beneficiaries, or a class considered to be an ascertainable beneficiary like "all those who attended my funeral," or "all the people on my Christmas Card list." And to avoid potential tax traps, specify an amount so the trustee isn't flying everyone to Hawaii for a week-long junket that exceeds the annual gift tax exemption.

4.26. Tina and Jessica are contingent beneficiaries under the trust. Since during the lifetime of the Settlors the trust is revocable and for the benefit of only Tom and Linda, Tina and Jessica have no enforceable interest in the trust. Mom and dad can rest easy knowing that they can spend their own money however they wish.

4.27. Even though the language does not use the words "power to appoint", Bob has been given an unfettered ability to consume the property during his lifetime, and, therefore a general power of appointment coupled with a life estate for Federal Estate Tax purposes.

4.28. Aunt Susan's will granted Harriet a presently-exercisable general power of appointment, because Harriet could use the property for herself or anyone else during her life or at death; therefore, legally, Harriet was under no imperative to conserve Aunt Susan's property and most likely Clara is out of luck If Aunt Susan had wished for Harriet's powers to be narrowed, a better mechanism would have been to grant her a limited power of appointment over all or some of the estate, with the permissible objects being Harriet's siblings, or use a discretionary trust. Clara might have a claim if she could argue that the power was non-exclusive and thus required that at least some portion of the estate be bestowed on each sibling. Although courts grapple with how much has to be distributed to each appointee, the amount is usually something more than a mere pittance.

4.29. The majority approach in this scenario would be that the residuary clause alone is insufficient to capture the property from Scott's estate and pass it to the school. The Restatement's broader approach may allow the capture if, under Scott's father's will, there are no default takers. Under UPC § 2–608, the school may prevail, as well under UPC § 2–608 if Scott's father's will listed no default takers.

4.30. Claire is not a permissible appointee under the power of appointment, because the power specifically names Angus's living siblings and she is a widow of a deceased sibling. Mary and Scott are permissible appointees, however. Therefore, Mary and Scott would receive the property subject the power of appointment, in 2 equal shares.

4.31. Yes, Tom may include a portion of the portfolio because Tom has a presently-exercisable general power of appointment. Therefore, he may exercise it immediately in favor of his wife as part of the property settlement or he may make a contract to exercise it in the future.

4.32. Ann will need Tyler's written consent to convert the farm from joint tenancy with rights of survivorship to tenancy in common. A new deed, signed by both parties, which reflects the change in status must be recorded. Then the codicil to Ann's can be effective to pass Ann's interest to her children at her death. Joint tenancies may not be severed by a will, for that operates as a fraud upon the other joint tenant. The severance must occur before the will can be effective.

4.33. Upon dissolution of marriage, the ownership of the home was changed by operation of law to tenancy in common. Therefore, Meg's brother, as Trustee for the trust share established for Meg's children, would receive Meg's interest in the home.

4.34. Sarah is entitled to the home in fee simple. In order to successfully attach a claim to John's interest, his creditors must have done so prior to his death.

4.35. No, under the UMPAA, no present or future interest of a gift occurs with an agency account and therefore there is no interest to which Tim's creditors may attach.

4.36. The chances are quite good that the cash in the suitcase would not be deemed subject to a TOD designation unless the note was executed with the will formalities. Because Mildred presumably retained complete physical control over the suitcase, there was no transfer of any property right to Ellen. A POD or TOD designation is always made in the context of an institution that controls access to the account, or title documents that are recorded to put the public on notice of the designation. Assuming the TOD designation is not effective, the cash would remain part of Mildred's estate at her death. If Mildred had declared herself the trustee, however, of a revocable trust, for the benefit of her daughter Ellen, and appropriate documents were available, perhaps a trust could be proved to help avoid probate.

Chapter 5
Answers

	UPC	Maryland	DC
5.1.	Harold's share lapses—all to Wilma	Harold's share passes to his testate or intestate takers; Wilma takes her share	Harold's share passes to his issue under anti-lapse statute; Wilma takes her share
5.2.	Both lapse and the property passes by intestacy	Each half pass to their respective testate or intestate takers	Both shares pass to their issue under anti-lapse statute
5.3.	Wilma takes half, Harold's half passes to his issue according to testator's will	Wilma takes half, Harold's half passes to his issue according to testator's will	Wilma takes half, Harold's half passes to his issue according to testator's will
5.4.	The niece's share passes to her children by application of the anti-lapse statute	The niece's share passes to her testate or intestate takers; the other kids keep their share	The niece's share passes to her issue by application of anti-lapse statute; the other kids keep their share
5.5.	The niece's share passes to the Red Cross	The niece's share passes to the Red Cross	The niece's share passes to the Red Cross
5.6.	Two nephews' shares go to their issue under anti-lapse; unclear whether Carol's issue also take as members of class	Two nephews' shares go to their testate or intestate heirs; unclear whether Carol's issue also take as members of class	Two nephews' shares go to their issue under anti-lapse; unclear whether Carol's issue also take as members of class
5.7.	Because issue is a class that is excluded from application of the anti-lapse statute, all living issue take a share in their own right and no predeceased issue take a share	Usually the term issue precludes application of the anti-lapse statute since the descendants of the predeceased issue take in their own right—but the statute is not clear on this	Usually the term issue precludes application of the anti-lapse statute since the descendants of the predeceased issue take in their own right—but the statute is not clear on this

5.8. According to identity theory, the only named motorcycle, the Paul Smart, was undoubtedly in the estate at the time of death, so this does not shed light on our problem. Arguments can be made both for and against Paulo's actions under the intent theory (i.e. The testator knew his sons and how contentious they were but still told Paulo he could have ANY bike, therefore, he intended that the Paul Smart could be one of those bikes; and, alternatively, the testator intended for the Paul Smart to go to Julian because he specifically identified it and set it apart for him in the will); Assuming, however, that Paulo does take the Paul Smart, one could use the intent theory to get Julian another one of his father's bikes by arguing that his language "Because I know that my sons will always love to ride" indicated that he desired for Julian to be in possession of a motorcycle at his death, even if it was not the Paul Smart.

5.9   a.   The issue here is whether or not the testator intended to pass along the cash with the books to Shantel. This will be important not only to the beneficiaries, but also to the estate in the event that inheritance taxes are applicable. Intent theory could be applied to look at the estate as a whole (Did the testator hide money in any items other than books? Did she seem to use the money as bookmarks?). Because money does not normally attach in a gift of books and music, Shantel should get the money unless Shauna can show a contrary intent.

     b.   This is a demonstrative devise because it is a cross between a specific and a general devise. Because the truck has been sold, the gift may be considered adeemed and Sally will take the proceeds. However, when looking at the will/facts as a whole, the intent theory could be applied to argue that the testator wished for Tom and Jim to have the $3,000, regardless of the source.

5.10. Testator made a specific devise of the house and a demonstrative devise of the personal property and the money in her accounts; thus the house and the personal property will abate together because demonstrative gifts out of specific property are treated as specific bequests. That means that only the $50,000 in the financial accounts will be available for debts before having to abate the specific bequests. Ben will argue that the $25,000 sewer bill should come entirely off the house since Agnes is getting the benefit of the upgrades and, as we discuss in the next section on exoneration, he is likely to succeed. That means he takes the $100,000 personal property, Agnes takes the house with the $25,000 debt, and the Red Cross gets nothing.

5.11. Agnes gets the house, Ben gets the personal property and the $50,000 in her financial accounts. The Red Cross will get the $100,000 left from the condemnation judgment after the credit card debts are paid.

5.12. In this case Agnes and Ben will have to apportion the payment of the $50,000 credit card debt between them. If the value of the house was $150,000, then each would pay half of the debt out of their bequests because the testator directed that all bequests abate ratably. Even without the debts, there would be no residuary devise to the Red Cross, so they are out of the picture.

5.13. The executor's sale of the house under the UPC would entitle Agnes to the proceeds, although it might be adeemed in states that don't follow the UPC. With the sale of the house, the executor would be required to pay the $50,000 mortgage, leaving only $125,000 from the sales proceeds. Agnes might argue that the estate should pay the mortgage and she should not take the hit, but under most modern exoneration rules, she will lose. That leaves $125,000 cash from the house to which Agnes is entitled. Assuming the house was worth $190,000, she can try to get the full value from the estate, which would come out against the $50,000 in the financial accounts and the personal property. That leaves the $20,000 credit card debt to come out of the estate. Normally, it would come out of the general devise of the $50,000 in the financial accounts, leaving Ben only $30,000. You can see that there are different outcomes depending on whether the house is judged to be adeemed, in which case the cash proceeds of the sale of the house will pay the debts and the remainder will pass to the Red Cross. On the other hand, if Agnes gets the proceeds as replacement for the house and it isn't adeemed, then the question arises how to allocate the mortgage. Usually that will go against the devisee of the property to which it is attached, but Agnes could argue otherwise. Depending on the outcome of that argument, she can also argue for the full value of the house, not the reduced amount accepted by the executor. Finally, the credit card debt will be offset against general devises first, but if there aren't any, then it will be offset against the specific bequests.

5.14. UPC 2–607 states that a specific devise passes subject to any mortgage interest regardless of a general directive in the will to pay debts. Therefore, the home would pass subject to the mortgage, unless an argument could be made that the language "in fee simple" expressed the testator's desire that the property pass without the mortgage. Without more it is unlikely a court would find that the wish to treat her children equally will justify paying off the mortgage, especially because paying off the mortgage means George will take significantly less than Bella. But a clause instructing the executor to sell the assets and split the proceeds if the estate otherwise won't result in equal treatment could save the day.

5.15. Since Luther's share of the joint tenancy property is part of his taxable estate, the farm will have to pay its share of Luther's estate tax liability. This may require the sale of Luther's share even though it has passed to Thorn by right of survivorship because the property is encumbered with the tax liability.

5.16. The UETAA and the UPC state that taxes will be apportioned however the testator indicates with explicit directions. It also states that where two or more conflicting directions appear in different amendments to a revocable trust, the latter will prevail. However, the statutes provide that trust instructions prevail only in the absence of will instructions. Therefore, the will provision will prevail even though doing so completely violates the testator's intentions. See UPC § 3–9A–103(a). Because the probate estate is not sufficient to pay the tax liabilities, the revocable trust will have to cover the tax liability beyond what is paid for by the probate estate. Some courts might, however, interpret the will provision to direct tax liability for the probate property and the trust provision to direct tax apportionment for the trust property so as not to entirely wipe out the probate estate in a case like this. But unfortunately, the statute leaves little wiggle room.

5.17. At issue is whether or not Karl's moving into the beachfront home with his wife is sufficient to show that he has "exercised dominion and control over the property." Most likely it is. He has certainly benefitted from the property by being able to live there and therefore won't be able to disclaim. He should have stayed at a hotel.

5.18. If Sally has not accepted any benefit from the horse she can wait until he runs the Derby to decide whether or not to disclaim. Of course, she will need to do this within 9 months if she wants to reap any tax benefits. It is unlikely that the interview would be considered an acceptance of the benefits of ownership, especially since she is both a primary and an alternate beneficiary and has had connections with the horse without any ownership interest. Her share of the horse will pass to her children if she disclaims.

5.19. Assuming the order of the deaths cannot be ascertained, Anne's property will be administered as though Tim predeceased her, and Tim's property will be administered as though Anne predeceased him. If Shawn's estate sues Anne's estate, Tim's property will be protected from any judgment because it won't have passed to Anne.

5.20. First, if it can be determined that the wife survived the son, she would inherit from her son, and vice versa if he survived her. But then of course, we need to determine where the second estate would go. Thus, if the wife survived and received the son's estate, it would pass to her will beneficiaries or to her parents if alive, or to her siblings if her parents were deceased under intestacy since her husband would be unable to take under the slayer statute, despite Chris having survived her. The son was only 7. Thus, he would be unable to write a will and, if he survived and inherited his mother's property, it would pass most likely to his grandparents equally (50% to his mother's parents and 50% to his father's parents). In that way, it is conceivable that his paternal grandparents would receive some of his mother's property. If Chris were deemed mentally incapacitated or suffering from some kind of insane delusion by which he would not be held accountable for the murders, he would inherit from both his wife and son, and his parents would likely share his estate with his two children by his prior marriage. Problems do arise when property is held in different states. Thus, the real property owned in a different state could be distributed under one set of laws and the rest of the estate under a different set of laws, each resulting in a different outcome.

Chapter 6

Answers

6.1. Gates is certainly looking at extensive estate taxes with an estate of that size. He has already established a charitable foundation and it is likely that most of his estate will roll into the foundation at his death. But he will want to provide reasonable assets for his surviving spouse and children. He also will want access to plenty of money for desired lifetime spending. Thus, he will want the usual joint checking accounts to pay the bills, he will probably want to establish TTs for his minor children to cover their education and to get them established in their careers. Additionally he will want a trust for his surviving spouse to cover all of her lifetime needs. Gates will probably want to pass the remainder to his charitable foundation. A GPA could be effective by giving his surviving spouse control over $10 or $15 million for the kids and herself in case he dies while they are minors.

6.2. Ruth's main concern at this point is her end of life expenses, including medical expenses and the possibility of short or long term periods of incapacity. She needs to be getting her financial house in order by taking advantage of PODs and TODs and even joint tenancies with her adult children. Assuming she isn't looking at estate taxes, probate avoidance should be her main concern. But because of her health needs, she wants to make sure she has full control over the assets she will need. A GPA or a revocable trust can accomplish Ruth's goals. However the revocable trust includes the added benefit of appointing a successor trustee in case she becomes incapacitated.

6.3. Tom has a large, extended family who will expect to share in his wealth at his death, including his minor child. His first priority will be to her. But, because he may want to minimize the amount of money he has to give to his estranged wife, he may want to consider an IIT benefitting himself and then his children. He also will be looking at estate taxes and, of course, the Church would be happy to have as much as he will donate in order to use the unlimited charitable deduction. As a lawyer for Tom you may be worried about over-reaching by the Church and so will want to establish trusts that limit Tom's ability to be unduly influenced by Church officials. At the same time, Tom may want to benefit the Church rather than his family at his death, and you will need to respect his decisions. Tom will most certainly want a trust to continue to receive and manage royalties from his films. But you will want to limit Tom's access to some of the trust property if you want to reduce Katie's claims to the property.

6.4. Jerry's main issue is having his estate depleted by tort claimants, leaving nothing for his surviving spouse and issue. Because he won't need to worry about managing his property or having access to it while he is in jail, and he won't need to worry too much about incapacity, he may want to consider giving it all away now, through lifetime giving and the use of an IIT. Tying it up for the benefit of his spouse and children makes sense, though he might want to continue to make some portion of it available for his legal defense expenses and for incidentals while he is in prison.

6.5. Like Jerry Sandusky, Ted doesn't need to worry about access to his money for living expenses or health care expenses, since those expenses are generally on the government. The government does however have a policy of extracting assets from wealthy prisoners to help pay for their incarceration, so Ted may be on the hook for a portion of his expenses. He also isn't likely to be worrying about estate taxes, though income taxes are an issue. Ted should probably put his royalties into a trust, perhaps with charitable purposes, to be managed by a corporate trustee.

6.6. Barney clearly isn't concerned with estate taxes, but first and foremost he does want to be able to provide adequately for himself and his partner. Since he has no children, he may want to have what residue is left go to his sister or to charity. His estate is probably too small to require a trust. Rather, he can use a TOD deed for the house and have PODs for his various bank accounts. Because his marriage to Jim is not recognized under federal law, however, any lifetime gifts at this time may require a gift tax return. A power of attorney may be sufficient in case he is incapacitated, but he must face the very real possibility that both he and Jim will be incapacitated together. Thus, a trusted sister would make a good successor trustee or donee of a SPA. He may want to look to a niece or nephew, in case his sister is also at risk of predeceasing him or becoming incapacitated.

Chapter 7

Answers

7.1. Clyde and Helga's state law retains dower. Therefore, even though only Helga's name is on the deed, her spouse must consent to the transfer of the home because it was purchased during the marriage.

7.2. As a tenant in curtesy, Franklin would be entitled to a life estate in the farm and any other real property that Angelica owned. He would further be the presumed owner of all of her personal property, in the house and otherwise located, through coverture. He can sell it if the remaindermen agree—as if he sold it to the remaindermen or they joined the conveyance.

7.3. The answers to this question are in the text, but see if you can work it out on your own with just the information about the different types of property Herman has in his estate.

7.4. The answers to this question are also in the text.

7.5. Calculate Wilma's elective share by using the elective share laws of your state. If you live in a community property state, calculate how much of Herman's property is likely to be deemed community property and how much of it will Wila be entitled to?

7.6. We would deduct the $300,000 from the elective estate because the decedent spouse did not have a general power of appointment, making his total wealth upon death $1,400,000 and the surviving wife's elective share only $420,000. She would receive the $300,000 life insurance, and the remaining $120,000 would be taken from his NPE and his revocable trust ($20,000 from his NPE and $100,000 from the trust).

7.7. Answers are in the text.

7.8. We begin by calculating the different types of property.

Harry's probate property

House titled in Harry's name worth	$500,000
Bank accounts titled in Harry's name only	$50,000
Harry's car titled in his name	$25,000
Property in Harry's mother's estate over which Harry has a general power of appointment*	$500,000
Personal property of Harry	$100,000
Harry's share of business	$500,000
Total of Harry's probate property	**$1,675,000**

Assume that Harry captured the property from his mother's estate and added it to his residuary, which he devised to his children.

1. To calculate the elective share under the DC statute (a net probate estate elective share statute), we first subtract

Funeral expenses	$5,000
Homestead	$15,000
Exempt Property	$10,000
Family Allowance	$18,000
Remaining debts	$95,000
TOTAL Offsets	**$143,000**

$1,675,000 – $143,000 = $1,532,000 is the NET probate estate (NPE).

In the District of Columbia, the elective share equals the intestate share which, under §19–302(5), is one-half of the NPE. So we take ½ of $1,532,000 which equals $766,000

Thus, Wilma is entitled to the $43,000 (homestead, exempt property, family allowance) + $766,000 in elective share for a total of $809,000. If Harry did not devise Wilma at least $766,000, she could renounce what is devised to her and take her elective share.

Note that some net probate estate regimes do not consider how much of the decedent's property is passing outside of probate to the surviving spouse. Others offset the elective share entitlement by deducting amounts passing to the surviving spouse. So let's be sure to determine how much property is passing to the surviving spouse outside of the probate estate.

Property that passes outside probate to the surviving spouse

Bank accounts titled in both Harry and Wilma's names (Harry's half)	$25,000
Yacht Harry bought so they could travel in their retirement titled in both names—paid entirely by Harry	$100,000
Life insurance bought by Harry payable to Wilma	$1,000,000*
Gifts to Wilma made by Harry in the year before his death—jewelry	$100,000
Condo in New York City they bought just after their marriage titled in both names as joint tenants with right of survivorship (each paid half)	$250,000
Total of non-probate property passing to Wilma	**$1,475,000**

Note that if the elective share in the relevant state is reduced by nonprobate transfers to the surviving spouse. In our instance here Wilma may not elect because she is receiving more than her $766,000 elective share entitlement through nonprobate transfers. In that case, the estate will pass exactly as the husband had provided. In the District, however, non-probate transfers do not count against the elective share.

So what lessons can we take from a NPE elective share state? If nonprobate transfers are not taken into account, a decedent spouse need only leave an amount equal to half of his net probate estate in some form to his surviving spouse. In that case, a decedent who wants to minimize his elective share need merely put 99% of his property into a non-probate mechanism, and then give his surviving spouse half of his probate property or life insurance equal to half of the remaining 1%. For an estate that doesn't use many non-probate mechanisms, however, the decedent will need to be sure that his surviving spouse is bequeathed half of his net probate estate. For smaller estates, the homestead, exempt property and family allowance may eat up a significant portion of the estate, leaving a fairly small elective share to which the surviving spouse is also entitled.

2. Now let's calculate the elective share using the Augmented Estate (but without taking varying percentages for length of marriage or accounting for surviving spouse's wealth—this is the rule in Florida). To do this, we determine the DECEDENT's augmented estate only, which consists of his probate estate (NPE), property that passed from him to the surviving spouse outside of probate (NPTSS), and property from him that passed to others outside of probate (NPTO).

Harry's probate estate is the same as we determined earlier: $1,675,000.

Then we remove the usual offsets from the probate estate (remember this is Florida and thus has different amounts for the offsets):

Funeral expenses	$5,000
Homestead	$500,000*
Exempt Property	$20,000
Exempt Property—car	$25,000
Family Allowance	$18,000
Remaining debts	$95,000
TOTAL Offsets	**$663,000**

*In Florida, the homestead (if not devised outright to the spouse) cannot be devised at all, and must descend as a life estate in the surviving spouse with a remainder in he decedent's children. For purposes here, the house will pass entirely outside of the probate process and is not included for elective share or intestacy purposes at all.

Harry's NPE is his probate estate of $1,675,000 minus the offsets of $663,000 for a total of $1,002,000.

Then we need to calculate all of the decedent's property that passes outside probate to others.

Property that passes outside probate to others (NPTO)

Harry's stock portfolio POD his daughter and son	$500,000
Harry's daughter's house in joint tenancy with right of survivorship with Harry—paid entirely by Harry*	$250,000
Term Life insurance bought by Harry payable to his daughter and son	$500,000
Property in revocable trust established by Harry in 2006 giving him a life interest and his daughter and son the remainder interest	$1,000,000
Gift Harry made to a niece 6 months before he died	$50,000
Total property given to others	**$2,300,000**

Assume H paid the full value for the daughter's house.

So, to calculate Wilma's elective share we do the following (Fl.Stat. 732.2035):

Add probate property	$1,675,000
Add property passing to Wilma	$475,000 (omit life insurance policy*)
Add property passing to others	$1,800,000 (omit life insurance policy*)
Subtract offsets	<$663,000> (debts, homestead, etc)
Total of Augmented Estate	$3,287,000
Take 30% to determine wife's elective share	**$986,100**

In Florida, only the cash surrender value of life insurance policies is included in the augmented estate—term life policies have no cash surrender value.

To calculate the property from which the Elective Share is payable, look to the statute again (Fl.Stat. §732.2075) which gives the following priorities:

- Property that passes to the spouse (either outside probate or in the will)
- retirement benefits for benefit of spouse (not social security but private retirement funds)
- decedent spouse's half of joint tenancy property passing to spouse
- life insurance benefits
- then if there is still a deficit, apportion equally between beneficiaries of the probate estate and revocable trusts

Because the life insurance alone in this example covers the entire elective share, Wilma would take the life estate in the home, the exempt property and family allowance, the life insurance proceeds, all property passing to her through non-probate transfers, and any property devised to her in the will. Because she already has more than the $986,100 allowed for her elective share, she would be unable to elect against the estate, even if Harry left her nothing in his will.

What if Harry hadn't bought life insurance payable to Wilma? She would be receiving only $475,000 in non-probate transfers to her but would be entitled to $986,100 for her elective share. The estate is short $511,100 that would have to be made up from the NPE ($1,002,000) and the revocable trust property ($1,000,000) proportionally. Wilma would therefore take approximately one-quarter of each or 511,100/2,002,000 = 25.52%

What lessons have we learned about the augmented estate model of the elective share?

- First, notice the role of life insurance, both in calculating the elective share and in totaling up the non-probate transfers to the surviving spouse. The Florida rule may be unusual, but you need to pay attention to whether the policy is a term or whole-life policy and how it is included in the augmented estate.

- You also need to pay attention to large gifts made in the year or two before death. Some of those gifts may be included in either the NTPO or the NPTSS.

- Third, Harry had made Wilma the beneficiary of the revocable trust, giving her a life income at his death, and then the remainder over to his children at Wilma's death, the valuation of that life estate would have to be added to the NPTSS. These usually require the use of complex mortuary and annuity tables.

- Fourth, a number of these assets could have been structured to get them out of the elective estate. The revocable trust could have been irrevocable without the life interest payable to Harry. In that case the trust would not be included as a NPTO, but would have been a lifetime gift perfected before his death.

- Also, if Harry's mother had only given him a special power of appointment, her property would not be included in Harry's probate estate.

- If Harry had put his daughter's house in a trust, which would become revocable by him only if his daughter predeceased him, the joint tenancy property would be removed from his NPTO.

- Finally, perhaps Harry's share of the business should have been held in a corporate form, with Harry's stock in the corporation held in a trust that would pass outside probate to his designated beneficiaries.

If just a few of these items of property had been differently structured, the elective share would have been dramatically reduced.

Now, go back through the property listed in this problem and redo the elective share calculation taking out the daughter's house, the revocable trust property, the property from Harry's mother's estate, and Harry's share of the business.

3. Now let's use the graduated super-augmented estate scheme of the 2008 UPC.

First, calculate the offsets and debts under the UPC.

Funeral expenses	$5,000
Homestead	$22,500
Exempt Property	$15,000
Family Allowance	$27,000
Remaining debts	<u>$95,000</u>
TOTAL Offsets	**$164,500**

Under the UPC we need to also factor in the surviving spouse's property and nonprobate transfers to others (all property that would be in her augmented estate were she the decedent).

Property of spouse (SSP & SSNPTO)

Bank accounts titled in both Harry and Wilma's names (Wilma's half)	$25,000
Bank accounts titled in only Wilma's name	$50,000
Wilma's car titled in her name only	$20,000
Wilma's stock portfolio PoD her three children	$250,000
Life insurance on Harry's life bought by Wilma payable to Wilma	$500,000
Personal property of Wilma	$50,000
RV Wilma bought just after their marriage titled in both names as joint tenants with rights of survivorship	$100,000
Condo in New York City they bought just after their marriage titled in both names as joint tenants with right of survivorship (each paid half)	<u>$250,000</u>
Total of Wilma's property	**$1,245,000**

Then add all the following property:

Harry's probate estate	$1,675,000
Harry's property passing to Wilma	$1,475,000 (do not omit life insurance policy*)
Harry's property passing to others	$2,300,000 (do not omit life insurance policy*)
Add Wilma's property	$1,245,000 (do not omit life insurance policy*)
Subtract offsets	<u><$164,500></u> (debts, homestead, etc.)
Total of *Super Augmented* Estate	**$6,530,500**

*The UPC includes all life insurance property in the determination of the elective share.

Next determine the *marital property portion* of this super augmented estate. For a marriage of 2 years, it is 12% of $6,530,500 or **$783,660**.

Next take 50% of the marital property portion to determine the elective share. In this case, 50% of $783,660 is **$391,830**.

To pay the elective share we credit first:

- Property passing to spouse under the will or intestacy

- Non-probate property passing to Wilma (including life insurance)

- Percentage of Wilma's property attributable to the marriage (12% of SSP's property = $149,400 in this case). This is important!

- Then equitably apportion the rest of the probate estate plus certain non-probate property passing to others (See UPC §2–209).

- As you can see, because the marriage was of relatively short duration, Wilma is entitled only to $391,830, which was more than covered by Harry's non-probate transfers to Wilma and the life insurance. Note also how the amount of Wilma's property that is credited back against the elective share is also calculated at 12%.

- Now let's assume they had been married 15 years rather than 2 years. The property otherwise remains the same.

- Begin with the super augmented estate of $6,530,500 (total estate minus offsets). The *marital property portion* is 100% and the elective share would be half of that amount, or **$3,265,250.**

Now let's see how we pay this amount. Assume Harry's will left none of his probate estate to Wilma.

We add the following property to pay the elective share amount.

Non-probate property passing to spouse	$1,475,000
Percentage of spouse's own property (100%)	<u>$1,245,000</u>
Total covered by UPC 2–209(a)	$2,720,000

That leaves a deficit of ($3,265,250 minus $2,720,000=) $545,250 to be made up by equitably apportioning the probate estate with certain non-probate transfers to others. In this case, all the rest of the property is to be equitably apportioned so we would take $1,510,500 (probate property minus the offsets) + $2,300,000 (property passing to others) = $3,810,500. To apportion, we divide $545,250/$3,810,500 to get the percentage each is reduced to make up the elective share = 14.3%. So each probate gift and non-probate transfer is reduced by 14.3% to make up the remainder of the elective share. Of course, the decedent needed to only leave the house and a bit more of his probate property to his surviving spouse and he would have avoided the apportionment altogether. Often, this is where a disclaimer by some beneficiaries, or a settlement, will help to avoid the apportionment of ALL other dispositions.

7.9. First, calculate the offsets and debts under the UPC.

Funeral expenses	$5,000
Homestead	$22,500
Exempt Property	$15,000
Family Allowance	$27,000
Remaining debts	$95,000
TOTAL Offsets	**$164,500**

Then calculate each category of property (NPE, NPTO, NPTSS, SSP):

Harry's probate property

House titled in Harry's name worth	$500,000
Bank accounts titled in Harry's name only	$50,000
Harry's car titled in his name	$25,000
Personal property of Harry	$100,000
Total of Harry's probate property	**$675,000**

Property that passes outside probate to others (NPTO)

Harry's stock portfolio POD his daughter and son	$500,000
Term Life insurance bought by Harry payable to his daughter and son	$500,000
Gift Harry made to a niece 6 months before he died	$50,000
Total property given to others	**$1,050,000**

Non-Probate Property Given to the Surviving Spouse (NPTSS)

Bank accounts titled in both Harry and Wilma's names (Harry's half)	$25,000
Yacht Harry bought so they could travel in their retirement titled in both names—paid entirely by Harry	$100,000
Life insurance bought by Harry payable to Wilma	$1,000,000*
Gifts to Wilma made by Harry in the year before his death—jewelry	$100,000
Condo in New York City they bought just after their marriage titled in both names as joint tenants with right of survivorship (each paid half)	$250,000
Total of non-probate property passing to Wilma	**$1,475,000**

Property of spouse (SSP & SSNPTO)

Bank accounts titled in both Harry and Wilma's names (Wilma's half)	$25,000
Bank accounts titled in only Wilma's name	$50,000
Wilma's car titled in her name only	$20,000
Wilma's stock portfolio POD her three children	$250,000
Life insurance on Harry's life bought by Wilma payable to Wilma	$500,000
Personal property of Wilma	$50,000
RV Wilma bought just after their marriage titled in both names as joint tenants with rights of survivorship	$100,000
Condo in New York City they bought just after their marriage titled in both names as joint tenants with right of survivorship (each paid half)	$250,000
Total of Wilma's property	**$1,245,000**

Then add all the following property:

Harry's probate estate	$675,000
Harry's property passing to Wilma	$1,475,000 (do not omit life insurance policy*)
Harry's property passing to others	$1,050,000 (do not omit life insurance policy*)
Add Wilma's property	$1,245,000 (do not omit life insurance policy*)
Subtract offsets	<$164,500> (debts, homestead, etc.)
Total of *Super Augmented* Estate	**$4,280,500**

The UPC includes all life insurance property in the determination of the elective share.

Next determine the *marital property portion* of this super augmented estate. For a marriage of 15 years, it is 100% of $4,280,500.

Next take 50% of the marital property portion to determine the elective share. In this case 50% of $4,280,500 is **$2,140,250**.

To pay the elective share we credit first:

- Property passing to spouse under the will or intestacy
- Non-probate property passing to Wilma (including life insurance)
- Percentage of Wilma's property attributable to the marriage (100% of SSP's property = $1,245,000 in this case). This is important!

- Then equitably apportion the rest of the probate estate plus certain non-probate property passing to others (See UPC §2–209).

To reach our elective share amount let's see what Wilma is already getting and the credit of her property.

Probate property passing to Wilma	$0
Non-probate property passing to Wilma	$1,475,000
Wilma's property offset against elective share	$1,245,000
Total property **passing to Wilma under estate plan**	**$2,720,000**

Because the estate plan already credits Wilma with $2,720,000, which is greater than what she is entitled to as an elective share, she may not elect. Wilma will also receive her $64,500 homestead, exempt property, and family allowance in addition to the $1,475,000 non-probate transfers Harry gave to her.

7.10. The first thing Harry needs to do is get Winifred's name on half of their joint assets. Then, because Harry and Winifred can't be sure about the longevity of the portability of the estate tax exemption, they will need to be sure that they use a credit shelter trust to give the survivor significant access to the property in the trust but have it set up so it passes to the children upon the survivor's death. Rather than use a QTIP, however, it makes sense to have the remainder of the first spouse's property pass directly to the survivor, who can then make lifetime gifts with the property, or use it for his/her end-of-life medical expenses. The survivor might want a revocable living trust, however, to deal with incapacity and probate avoidance, but assuming there's no fear that the survivor is likely to remarry, squander the money, or have huge debts, the property can pass directly to the survivor at this point. They are looking at possible estate taxes on the additional $2 million from Harry's mother, which they could certainly disclaim if they don't need it. In that case it would probably pass directly to the children or to the mother's intestate heirs and they could avoid estate tax altogether. If they want to keep the money they should go ahead and make lifetime gifts with it to avoid the compound nature of estate taxes. They have sufficient property that they don't need Medicaid trusts, as they can pay for their own medical care. It would be advisable for each to waive their elective share in the other's estate in order to maximize the use of the first spouse's exemption. You don't want to set up all of this estate planning, only to have the surviving spouse's guardian be forced to elect against the first spouse's estate, thus reducing the amount in the credit shelter trust, and increased the likelihood that the second spouse's estate will be hit with estate taxes.

7.11. Because Sally and Joan are not married, they don't have the benefit of the unlimited marital deduction, nor are they subject to an elective share. Thus, Sally and Joan's estates should be handled somewhat separately. Each should have credit shelter trusts giving the survivor as much access as possible to the assets in the trust, remainder to their children. However any gifts between them are taxable transfers. Thus, unless the survivor is likely to need grandma's $2 million, Sally should disclaim it now or, if she keeps it, should put it in trust now for the benefit of Joan rather than give it to Joan at death.

7.12. Assuming Seamus did not provide any more information about the circumstances under which it is appropriate to invade principal for the benefit of Irene, you first need to realize that the trust is there to benefit Irene, not necessarily Lionel. But they are also married, and spouses have a legal obligation to support their spouses. So you would need to determine their income, expenses, and assets to see if her basic maintenance and support needs are being met. Assuming they are not, it is reasonable to expect Irene and Lionel to take advantage of all sources of income. Your duty to the remaindermen of the Seamus trust means you can't just ignore Lionel's access to trust funds from his mother's trust and he has an obligation to support Irene as his lawful spouse. Although you could argue that since most of the additional expenses are because of Lionel's injuries his mother's trust should pay more of their expenses, hat may not be entirely reasonable since Irene and Lionel are now married. But it would also be unreasonable to expect Seamus' trust to pay all the additional expenses. You will also need to be aware of the standard of living Irene had been used to while married to Seamus, because that is usually the standard for support trusts. So if Irene's standard of living has gone down dramatically, there may be more of an obligation to provide disposable funds that Irene can choose to spend on Lionel's health care or on charitable gifts.

7.13. You may very well have abused your discretion in both instances. You aren't required to use trust funds to keep Jason and his wife in luxury and Junie and her husband barely afloat, but you do have an obligation as trustee to be familiar with your beneficiaries' situations. You also have an obligation to keep appropriate paperwork documenting their circumstances. Learning over the phone or flipping through Junie's mail is not an appropriate way to discover her financial status, but neither is simply sitting back and waiting to hear the news of Jason's lost job. As trustee you owe multiple loyalties and taking care of them all can be difficult. But to the extent that either Junie or Jason are truly strapped, you certainly have an obligation to dispense trust funds to keep them from losing their house or being evicted or going hungry. Trustees generally don't get to play Santa Claus, however.

7.14. The first thing you need to discover is what powers must be given to a spouse under an elective share trust. If the spouse must have the 5/5 power, then it has to be available and Wilma cannot set it up so that Harry can only exercise his power at 11:45 p.m. on the night of the first full moon after the second consecutive week of average daytime temperatures above 90°. It has to be reasonably available. But if she tries to get too stingy she may run afoul of the elective share statute, which is designed to give a surviving spouse a minimum of support for the rest of his life. If Harry can sell the life interest in the trust he loses the support aspect of the trust, which may militate in favor of the spendthrift provisions, even if the greater restrictions on the trust militate against it. There is no clear answer because each state has its own unique elective share statute that must be understood very carefully. But as a general matter there is no overarching policy against putting a spendthrift provision in an elective share trust.

7.15. The first question is to decide who the primary beneficiary is and who the secondary beneficiaries are (unless the trust is large enough to provide adequately for both). Assuming Jackson and the other two children are the primary beneficiaries, the settlor will want to tie up Jackson's trust share with some pretty tight strings. Jackson could be given a life interest but subject to the trustee's discretion to use the property only for his necessary support and maintenance. He could also be given discretion to reward Jackson if he gives up some of his bad habits. One generally cannot impose such restraints on legal interests (like Jackson can have the property but he can't use it unless he gives up smoking), but one has far more flexibility to use carrots and sticks to affect behavior in the context of a trust. You will also certainly be looking at a spendthrift provision for Jackson's share, and probably also for the shares of the grandchildren. You would then want to also give the trustee broad discretion to use the trust property, including principal perhaps, to benefit the grandchildren in a variety of ways—basic child support, college tuition, giving them a down payment on a house, etc. You could state that only the grandchildren alive at the settlor's death are entitled to a share, which might discourage Jackson from having more children, or you could state that if Jackson has any more children out of wedlock his interest will terminate. But you run into public policy issues with restraints on marriage and on Jackson's liberty and privacy interests in reproductive rights if you aren't careful. Mandatory income trusts for the grandchildren until they reach a particular age would be good support for them, but usually it's better to build flexibility into the trust with trustee discretion in case Jackson's children grow up to be chips off the old block.

7.16   a.   Yes, Ellen would be entitled to a pretermitted spousal share but she would also be entitled to an elective share against George's augmented estate. Depending on the size of George's probate estate (from which the pretermitted spousal share is calculated) and his augmented estate (from which the elective share is calculated), Ellen will want to elect the better of the two.

       b.   Under UPC 2–302, Caleb and Joe would qualify as omitted children and would share equally with Gloria and Kaley. That is, once it is established what Gloria and Kaley's share would be, all 4 children would actually divide that share equally.

Chapter 8

Answers

8.1. Wila has a fee simple subject to an executory limitation and Seth and Doris have shifting executory interests.

8.2. Wila has a fee simple subject to an executory limitation and the trustee has a shifting executory interest.

8.3. Wila has a fee simple subject to an executory limitation and the trustee has a springing executory interest.

8.4. Wila has a fee simple determinable with a possibility of reverter in the grantor's heirs. The reason this is a reverter interest is because the estate has to come back to the grantor to determine his heirs at law. The possibility of reverter then descended to the grantor's heirs during the time of Wila's estate.

8.5. Wila has a fee simple determinable with a possibility of reverter in the grantor. Whenever a future interest is unspecified, it is filled in by operation of law as a reversionary interest.

8.6. Wila has a fee simple subject to an executory limitation and Seth and Doris have springing executory interests.

8.7. This is a fee simple determinable with a possibility of reverter in the grantor.

8.8. The children have a fee simple absolute in their shares, except for the share belonging to Ashley. For that share, the grantor has retained a defeasible term of years, with a contingent remainder in Ashley and an alternate contingent remainder in the other surviving issue.

8.9. The two sisters have a joint life estate and Texas A & M has a vested remainder subject to divestment in a fee simple determinable. If the college uses the property as an experimental farm for 50 years, the fee simple determinable will become a fee simple absolute as the limitation will terminate.

8.10. The City has a fee simple determinable and the grantor has a possibility of reverter. Note, however, that while the use restriction may be permissible, the restraint on alienation may not be enforceable.

8.11. Wila has a life estate and the Red Cross has an absolutely vested remainder in fee simple.

8.12. Wila has a defeasible life estate and the Red Cross has an absolutely vested remainder in fee simple as well as a shifting executory interest in fee.

8.13. Wila has a term of years, and Seth and Doris have a contingent remainder on a conditional event in a fee simple, and the grantor has a reversion in case Seth or Doris do not reach age 21.

8.14. Wila has a life estate, and the grandchildren have a contingent remainder on an unascertained person in fee simple if there are no grandchildren alive, otherwise they have a vested remainder subject to open in fee simple if there are some grandchildren, and the children are still alive. They could have an absolutely vested remainder if there are grandchildren and no living children.

8.15. Wila has a life estate, and the children have vested remainder subject to divestment in fee simple subject to an executory limitation, and the grandchildren have a shifting executory interest.

	Cain	Dunkel	Cooley	Guilliams
8.16.	An FSD seems most likely because there is no gift over language, no mention of the term "for life" and no indication that the testator wanted the property to go any-	The most logical seems to me to be an FSEL. The fee simple language does not have to indicate an FSA, and the clear gift over language indicates an intent to create a future interest.	The most likely seems to be to be a traditional LE in the husband with an AVR in Jabbia. There is no language giving the husband a power to consume and giving	It almost sounds like he is trying to create a fee tail in the son, then in the son's children. But the most likely would seem to be a life estate followed by alternate contingent

	Cain	Dunkel	Cooley	Guilliams
	where else if she did remarry and the *so long as* language indicates an FSD.	The closest is probably an FSEL.	possessions in a life estate is no different than in a fee simple.	remainders in the son's children or, if none, in the other son and daughter.
8.17.	It could be an LE based on her actions, an FSA based on lack of gift over language, or an FSEL if we assume his children were to be the takers if she did remarry. If she did not remarry, then it should vest indefeasibly in Blanche.	It could also be an LE with a power to consume, or an FSA as the court determined. Except for the fee simple language, an LE with a power to consume would make the most sense.	It could also be an FSA in the husband, or an FSEL as the court found. Although there is no mention of "for life," the remainder over to Jabbia indicates some limitation on the present estate.	The trial court held this to be an FSEL, which is plausible. It could also be an FSA in the son, with an alternate gift in his children if he fails to survive the testator. It could also be a joint tenancy between the son and his children.
8.18.	If an LE, the estate will pass back to C.E.'s estate upon Blanche's death. If an FSA, FSD, or FSEL, it will pass to Blanche's estate since she died without remarrying.	If an LE with a power, the unused property should go to the brother. If an FSEL, the SHEI would lie with the brother, though it could be divested if he fails to survive. If an FSA, the property will pass to Eloise's estate.	If an LE or FSEL, the estate goes to Jabbia upon the husband's death. If an FSA, it passes to the husband's estate.	If an LE, the children get it next. If an FSA, it passes to the son's estate. If a joint tenancy, it would either go to co-tenants by a right of survivorship or the son's share would pass to his estate. If an FSEL, it would pass to his children if he died with issue, or to his brother and sister if he died without issue. Do you see why the FSEL makes no sense —and why for the same reason it makes no sense in Cooley?

	VRSD	**CRCE**
8.19.	To A for life, remainder to my children. However, if any child of mine is divorced at the death of A, or divorces at any time, that child's interest shall be distributed to the Red Cross.	To A for life, remainder to any of my children who are married at the time of A's death. If there are no children married at A's death, then the estate is to pass to the Red Cross.
8.20.	To A for life, remainder to B, but if after B takes possession B fails to maintain the fence between our two houses, then the property shall go to the Red Cross.	To A for life, then if the fence between our two houses is still maintained, the property shall pass to B; if it is not maintained at A's death, then the property goes to the Red Cross.
8.21.	To A for life, remainder to B, but if B gets divorced at any time after my death, then the property shall go to the Red Cross.	To A for life, remainder to B, but only if B is unmarried at A's death. If B is unmarried, the property goes to the Red Cross.
8.22.	To A for life, remainder to my nieces and nephews. However, if any niece or nephew is not 21 at A's death, that person's share is to be postponed until he or she reaches age 21. If that person fails to reach 21, then that person's share shall pass to his or her legal heirs.	To A for life, remainder to my nieces and nephews who have reached age 21 by A's death If any nieces and nephews have not reached age 21 at A's death, then that person's share shall be held in trust until they reach 21. If they fail to reach 21, then that person's share shall pass to his or her legal heirs.
8.23.	To A for life, then to B and his heirs. However, if my portrait is ever removed, then to C.	To A for life, then so long as my portrait is hanging on the mantel at A's death, the property shall go to B and his heirs.
8.24.	To A for life, then to the children of B. However, if any child of B eventually decides not to live on the farm, or moves off the farm, that child's share shall pass to the others.	To A for life, then to whichever children of B are living on the farm and agree to remain on the farm at A's death. If there are none, the property shall pass to the Red Cross.

8.25. Yes, the grandson is entitled to his half of the residuary property in his own right. But the house has been adeemed by extinction since the testator herself sold the property. The real question is whether the direction in the residuary clause that she wants the daughter and son treated equally means that the grandson should take a larger percentage of the residuary property to cancel out the adeemed house. Or, is the desire to treat them equally one that applies only to the children and not the grandchildren. The son will surely say that mom's desire to treat the kids equally does not extend to the grandson who now stands in his mom's shoes since there was no instruction to treat alternate takers equally. See Roley v. Sammons, 170 P.3d 1067 (Or.App. 2007).

8.26. Bessie's foster son will take unless Bessie and Sylvia made some other arrangement after the testator's death. We can assume that the testator gave his wife and daughter joint life estates with alternate contingent remainders. Because they are the only relevant parties with a property interest, they could agree to resettle the property differently. We could also assume that the testator gave his wife and daughter a joint tenancy with rights of survivorship which could be severed by either party. We would need to know if either did anything to change the testator's arrangement. But think about what would happen if both died simultaneously. Would the property revert back since neither condition occurred (the wife didn't survive the daughter and the daughter didn't survive the wife.) See McGirt v. Nelson, 599 S.E.2d 620 (S.C.App. 2004). Or the property would be split equally between their estates per the simultaneous death statute.

8.27. Assuming the state's antilapse statute does not apply to step-children, then the question is whether Al intended the gift to the children to be a class gift or gifts of 1/3 to each child. If he intended a class gift, then Alice's share lapses and is redistributed to the other class members (Bob and Carol). But if he intended individual gifts, then Alice's share would normally fail and pass by intestacy under the no residue of a residue rule.

8.28. a. A has a life estate; C, D, and E have a remainder in a life estate; F, G, H, and I have contingent remainders in fee simple absolute, contingent on surviving to possession.

b. E now has the life estate; F, G, H, I, J, and K have contingent remainders in fee simple absolute, contingent on surviving to possession.

c. At E's death, H, J, and K each take one-third and the issue of F, G, and I take nothing. O's intent that the antilapse statute not apply will prevent the issue from taking their parents' share of the remainder.

8.29. Because the gift of the remainder is to a type 2 class, it is contingent on surviving to possession. Thus, A has the life estate and the issue have contingent remainders on surviving to possession. Assuming there are no other births and deaths before A dies, upon A's death Blackacre will be split with D, E, F, & G each taking 1/5th, and H & I taking 1/10th, unless the state follows *per capita* by generation, in which case D, E, & F each take 1/5th and G, H & I each take 2/15ths.

8.30. This question requires application of the Rule of Convenience. Although C reaches 21 before A dies, the estate is not distributable at that time, but C's interest has now fully vested in interest. That means that C's share will pass to C's estate. E's share never vested because E failed to reach age 21, so E's share is redistributed to the rest of the class members. F, however, is a member of the class and will be entitled to take if F reaches age 21. At A's death, when the remainder becomes possessory, C's estate is entitled to immediate possession. Thus, the class closes at A's death. Neither G nor H are entitled to a share because they came into being after the class had closed. Thus, at A's death C's estate takes C's share, and the remaining 2/3rds of the property is held in trust until D reaches 21 and takes her share, and until F reaches 21 and takes her share.

8.31. *Walker v. Bogle:* The present estates pass to the sons; each son's lineal descendants have contingent remainders on unascertained persons for a term of years (which are valid); then the surviving lineal descendants who reach age 30 have contingent remainders on a conditional event, with an alternate contingent remainder in the descendants of the lineal descendants who don't reach age 30 or in the other son's lineal descendants. The condition that causes the violation of the Rule is the 30 year age requirement. Although the sons are lives in being, and are the validating lives for the class of lineal descendants who will take the income at their deaths, the possibility of a lineal descendant reaching age 30 after the death of all other lives in being voids the remainder interest in those who survive to age 30.

Dickerson v. Union Nat'l Bank of Little Rock: There are a number of problems here. The first is that the trust isn't established (and therefore no interests vest) until administration is complete. This could take longer than 21 years. Also, there is an unborn widow problem. Assuming the trust is established, Nina's sons' present estates are OK. At the death of Martin, we will know his widow, and since Martin is a life in being, the widow's remainder in a life estate is OK. Presumably at the death of Cecil, his life income interest is to pass to his children until the youngest reach 21, and at the death of Martin or his widow, their life income interest is to pass to their children until the youngest reach 21. Because both sons are still alive after the creation, the class of their children is open and we won't know which ones will reach age 21 within 21 years of the death the widow because she may not have been a life in being. We will know which of Cecil's children will reach 21 years within 21 years of Cecil's death, but not Martin's because of the widow's intervening life estate. Thus, the remainder interests in the lineal descendants to pay out 21 years after the death of Martin, and the widow violates the Rule, although the remainder in Cecil's lineal descendants is probably OK

Nelson v. Kring: The Hospital has the present estate subject to an indefinite condition (failure to use for hospital purposes). George Greene has the executory interest or, if he is not alive when the event occurs, then the trust passes to his legal heirs. George's executory interest is valid because it will fail if he does not survive until the property is no longer used as a hospital, and so his interest terminates upon his death. Thus, if the hospital fails before he dies, he can take the property. But if he dies before the condition is violated, his interest terminates and the interest in the lineal descendants is the one that would take the property. But because the condition is uncertain ever to occur, their interest violates the RAP.

Kennewick Public Hospital Dist. v. Hawe: The Kennewick Public Hospital owns the present estate subject to an executory interest in the County or the State of Washington. Washington apparently applies the Rule to future interests held by charities, even though many states do not. Thus, because the condition of using it for non-hospital purposes and retaining ownership are uncertain to occur, the executory interest violates the RAP, resulting in this case in the removal of the condition altogether. Thus, the hospital receives a fee simple absolute.

Security Trust v. Cooling: The present estate lies in the two sons for their lives and is certainly valid. But after that the devise is quite problematic. Upon the death of the sons, the property is to pass to their *issue* for and during their lives. Although we will know who the issue are at the death of the sons, it is possible that more issue will be born immediately afterwards who could share in the life interest. This would not be a problem if the testator had used the term "children" instead of "issue." The court in the case, however, treats the devise as using the term children and allows a life interest to pass to the children of the two sons. Following the life estate in the grandchildren (or the first generation of issue), the devise provides that the remainder is to be paid out to the issue of the grandchildren in equal shares and, alternatively if there aren't any issue, to the issue of any survivor. To take the remainder, therefore, issue have to survive to the death of the last grandchild, and because the class of grandchildren doesn't close within the perpetuities period, the remainder after is void. At the death of the last grandchild, therefore, the estate passed out of trust via intestacy.

Meduna v. Holder: The grantors retained the present estate, followed by remainders in life estates in the three children. These are all valid as the remainders in the children will vest upon the death of the grantor and his wife who are lives in being. At the death of the three children, however, the property is to pass in life estates to Gary's children, followed by a contingent remainder in Gary's living descendants. Because we won't know the identity of the living descendants until the death of the last of Gary's children, which person might not have been a life in being, the remainder to the descendants is void. But the interests in Gary's children for life is valid because we will know their identity at Gary's death, and Gary was a life in being.

Hagemann v. National Bank & Trust Co.: Mildred's will created two trust funds from the residuary of her will, one for each of her two sons and their descendants. Thus, Fletcher and Malcolm have the present estates, which are of course valid. Note that these present estates are terms of years (they last until the youngest grandchild reaches age 25). When the youngest child reaches 25, time the trust will either pay to the son if he is still alive, or to the living issue of the son. Because 25 is not 21, it is possible that the date of the payout will occur more than 21 years after the death of all lives in being when the interest is created. Thus, the remainder interest violates the RAP. However, paragraph 8 was used as a savings clause to try to save any remainders that might violate the Rule, but the court found the savings clause ineffectual because it isn't triggered until a point in the future, a point that can't be known until we know if in fact the youngest child won't reach age 25 within the perpetuities period. Thus, because the savings clause was dependent on a time determined in reference to the void future interests, it could not save that which it relied on to trigger its application.

Rogers v. Rooth: The wife Cleone has a defeasible life estate which is the valid present estate. The daughter Dorothy then has a remainder in a life estate that is valid. The son Floy then has a remainder in a life estate that is also valid since he is a life in being. At Floy's death the property passes to Floy's children in a life estate which is valid since they will be identified at Floy's death and Floy was a life in being. But the remainder over to the children's children is void because we won't know for sure who they are until the death of the last of Floy's children, and that person might not have been a life in being. This is a standard open class following an open class. The alternate contingent remainder in the sons of O.C. is also void because we don't know that their interest will vest until the same point when the grandchildren of Floy's interest will vest.

8.32. This trust has a number of problems but it can be interpreted not to violate the RAP. The class of grandchildren is an open class that will close upon the death of the last of the testator's children who are all lives in being. Thus, the grandchildren's interest is valid because we will know the entire class membership at the death of the last child. However, there is no indication what happens when each grandchild dies or what kind of interest each grandchild is supposed to have. Assuming that the trust corpus is to be used only for the education of the grandchildren, will the trust end when the grandchildren reach a certain age, or not until they die. And when they have all died, we would assume the corpus would pass back to the testator to pass to his heirs, and not to the grandchildren's estate.

8.33. No—the bequest does not violate the RAP because it is a general *inter vivos* power of appointment that is exercisable during A's lifetime, and A is a life in being. Because it is a presently exercisable general power of appointment, the RAP period starts all over again once A appoints the property. Thus, the trust to B, remainder to B's children is fine because B is a life in being at A's death.

8.34. A's life estate is valid as the present estate, but the special testamentary power of appointment MUST be exercised within the perpetuities period. Because it will be exercised during A's lifetime (or will fail), the power itself is valid. Once exercised, however, the relation back doctrine treats the exercise as relating back to the period when the power was created (in O's will and not in A's will). Thus, the trust interests are calculated as though they were created in O's will. D is a life in being when O died, so the trust interest for D is valid under the RAP. D has a presently exercisable general power of appointment which need merely be exercisable within the RAP period to be valid. It is, and was in fact exercised during D's lifetime in favor of M. Although M is not a life in being at O's death, M is a life in being at D's death, and the identity of M is determined within a lifetime of O's death. Thus, none of the interests violate the RAP.

Chapter 9
Answers

9.1. I am not providing answers here because I want you to think about how you would draft these provisions yourself. Work with a study group and read each other's drafts.

Chapter 10
Answers

10.1. Although Lizzie is not convicted of murder, she may have feloniously and intentionally killed her father and step-mother. Assuming a court finds her criminally accountable, then her devises will be voided as though she disclaimed them. The estate will pass solely to Emma. Upon Emma's death, Lizzie will be her principal heir and will inherit all of the property unless UPC §2–803(f) is called in to void any gifts to Lizzie from Emma. If Emma has substantial property of her own, there would be no reason for Lizzie not to inherit that property. But if it could be shown that Emma's property came from her father and step-mother, and that she had no time between their death and hers to write a will, equity might prevent Lizzie from inheriting through Emma.

10.2. The wife's brother would need to bring suit challenging the right of Chris's estate to take any property from his wife, alleging that Chris was guilty under the state's slayer statute. Assuming that there is no question Chris committed the killings, the issue will come down to whether Chris is criminally accountable. If the medical evidence of his dementia is sufficient to excuse him of the crimes, then as with *Ford v. Ford*, Chris's estate should be entitled to inherit from his wife's estate.

10.3. Under the UPC, property Herman gave Wilma that is revocable would be revoked. That includes the probate property given to Wilma in the will (1), the life estate in the trust property (2), the life insurance (5), the POD designation of his stock and mutual fund accounts (6), the power of attorney (9), the health care proxy (10), the real estate with the TOD (12), the homestead property (14), and the wrongful death proceeds assuming Herman died after the divorce (15). The UPC also works a severance and equal division as tenants in common of jointly owned property, including the real estate (11) and the bank account (13). Assuming the tax refund was placed entirely in Herman's account, Wilma would have an equitable claim on that property (16). Non-revocable property would not be affected by the divorce, including the interest from Herman's mother's trust (3), the special power of appointment (4), the irrevocable asset protection trust interest (8), and the Picasso painting (17). The beneficiary designation naming Wilma of Herman's retirement fund (7) would be revoked unless it is pre-empted under ERISA.

10.4. Assuming that Eva wants to maximize her likelihood of receiving some portion of Steve's property, she needs to first decide whether she is likely to get more if she divorces or if Steve dies. Since Steve's health is not very good, it is likely he will die before her, but he could certainly outlive her. So she needs to understand the risk. If she divorces, she can be rid of his presence quite quickly, and the court will give her some share of his property, though it is unlikely that she will be entitled to any property that he acquired through inheritance. Only marital property is usually subject to equitable distribution at divorce. If she outlives him she could get it all, but at what cost? If she does divorce him, however, she might want to look at the state's revocation statute to see if any pension benefits, life insurance, or other will substitute designations will also be revoked. If so, she will want to be sure her divorce lawyer gets her a satisfactory property settlement.

10.5. Obviously, neither Tim nor John will get the benefit of the revocation statute, which means that unless Mississippi wants to apply some equitable principle to defeat the various will designations, Tim will be entitled to take under John's will. John's executor could try to argue the application of the slayer statute but there is a proximate cause problem here. On the flip side, John could argue that Tim's marriage to Sally is null due to bigamy and that he should be able to take Tim's property to the exclusion of Sally. Sally, of course, will claim her homestead, exempt property, family allowance, and pretermitted spousal or elective shares. To the extent the court has to choose between them, it is likely the court will side with Sally, the legal spouse. But if the property is devised to John, and Sally is claiming it as the legal spouse, Sally will prevail and the estate will be abated to provide for Sally's legal share. But there would be no reason to revoke all the gifts to John since they weren't legally married in Mississippi and so he would be entitled to share the estate with Sally.

10.6. It is likely that Janice's estate would pass to the Humane Society, as provided in the Remote Contingency Section of the 1984 will, because not only was the 2010 codicil revoked by physical act (the crossing out and writing on the codicil), but also because Alice can provide testimony that Janice intended to revoke the provisions by stating that "it would be horrible to give everything I have worked for to these lousy people." As discussed earlier, a revoked codicil does not revoke the original will, and since the 1984 will was left untouched, it would likely be probated and distribution of the estate made to the only named and living beneficiary: the Humane Society.

10.7. Because the provision has been crossed out, along with Virgil's signature, and because your state recognizes partial revocation by physical act, the testamentary disposition to Margareta would likely fall out of the will, leaving the entire estate to the Trustee for the common trust established for the minor children. Of course, in lieu of a valid prenuptial agreement, Virgil can't simply disinherit his spouse; therefore, Margareta could still claim homestead/family allowance/exempt property as well as elect against the will for her spousal share.

10.8. The ultimate question is whether Andrew intentionally defaced the will and threw it away, threw it away but did not have the requisite intention, or someone else attempted to revoke the will. Because there was no writing on the pages, it is impossible to know if Andrew wrote the big Xs or if someone else did. Assuming the children had no motive to destroy the will, and none had access to the house, the question is whether Andrew understood that he was destroying his will when he used it for a coaster and threw it away. If the brain tumor gave him spells of incapacity, he might have destroyed the will either not knowing it was his will, or in a fit of pique driven by the tumor and not by his rational self. His reference to his children that his will was still in the filing cabinet implies that he was not aware he had thrown the will away. The coffee stains are the most curious because they imply that the will was out, on his desk, for days, and that he set his coffee on it, perhaps not knowing it was his will. In the end, the question will be whether Andrew was the most likely person to have thrown it away, and did he do so with the requisite intent.

10.9. There is no evidence that Jessica and Balthazar revoked the duplicate original will that was in their possession, although they intended to revoke the will in the lawyer's office. Assuming they did intend to revoke it, and they had failed to write new wills, their estate will pass by intestacy to all their nieces and nephews. The question then is whether the slayer statute will operate to deny Sebastian his share of their estate. Although Sebastian participated in their murder, he was planning on murdering someone else. In that sense his crime against his aunt and uncle was unintentional, although he is criminally liable. Assuming he is prevented from taking a share, the rest will be distributed to the other nieces and nephews as Jessica and Balthazar planned. However, if they had not revoked the will in their desk, their estate will pass to the Red Cross.

10.10. If your state does not allow partial revocation by physical act, then none of the changes will be deemed valid, unless a court were to determine that the changes affected such material portions of the will (as if they were changes to every substantive provision) as to constitute revocation of the entire document. If the latter were the case, the entire estate would pass by intestacy. If there were enough other unchanged provisions, these changes would simply be deemed ineffective. But what if the strike-throughs could be given effect, but not the additional write-ins? In that case, DRR could be used to either hold the testator's hand and not validate the strike-outs, or validate them and cause those bequests to lapse or pass by intestacy or to the residue. In such a case you would need to analyze each provision as to whether the testator would prefer the original bequest or nothing. Thus, in provision a, the testator would likely prefer Fred receive at least the $7,000 if we cannot validate the full $10,000. But in provision d, the testator would likely prefer Andrew get nothing rather than the full $10,000. In provision c, the testator would probably prefer that the bequest fail altogether; however, the husband will be entitled to an elective share. If the elective share might mess up the estate plan, it would make sense to give the husband the house despite the testator's attempt to disinherit her husband. The residuary bequest is difficult. Assuming we can't give effect to the Church bequest, the question is whether she would prefer Stephanie and Grace take the residue or it pass by intestacy, where the latter might result in greater property passing to her husband. We can look to the four corners of the document to determine likely intent, and if there is clear evidence of a desire to disinherit a particular person, and that person would take more under intestacy than under the original bequests, it would make sense to apply DRR.

On the other hand, if your state does allow partial revocation by physical act, as with application of the UPC, then all the changes could be given effect.

Chapter 11

Answers

11.1. Try your hand at making these arguments.

11.2. There are numerous steps you can take to protect your client. The first is to emphasize to your client, and her family, that you represent only her interests and are watching out for her. You want to have an opportunity to satisfy yourself that the plan you are being asked to draft is what she truly wants. If you are unsure, you owe a duty to your client to not draft a plan that is contrary to her wishes. But there is little you can do to get her out from under the influence of the fortune hunter. You cannot call her other relatives and tell them that she is seeking to make a new will without violating her right to confidentiality. And if you simply refuse to write the new will, she is likely to go elsewhere. You may, and certainly should, try to speak candidly with your client in private, without the influencer around to discover if she is being urged to do something against her wishes. Many elderly clients may say something like this: "yes, I want to make a new will because that way they'll stop pestering me." When you are concerned that your client is being unduly influenced you may certainly offer her suggestions about contacting other family, resisting their influence, or getting away from them. You might even be able to come up with a plan that gives them some of what they want without jeopardizing the main elements of your client's plan.

There are also numerous steps you can take to avoid litigation, besides writing a sound estate plan. An in terrorem clause which cancels any gift to a beneficiary who challenges a will is one step, which we discuss later in this chapter. Another is to use a trust that is less public and therefore less likely to be litigated. Another is to video tape the execution ceremony, or specifically ask your client questions about her mental state and intentions during the execution ceremony so the witnesses can feel confident about her intentions.

Can you think of other steps to make sure likely contestants either won't sue or will lose if they do?

11.3. Both the UPC and Restatement would allow reformation if there is clear and convincing evidence of the donor's true intent and the error is based on a mistake. Whether the evidence adduced in these cases is sufficient is the first question to be answered, as well as whether there actually is a mistake. Sometimes it may appear that the document reflects the donor's intent at the time, but that intent changes later, as perhaps occurred in *Brinker*. It would seem likely that the mistake in Mahoney could be reformed, although it is unclear that Helen Sullivan would have wanted all her nieces and nephews to share equally. It is unlikely there would be sufficient evidence of a mistake in *Est. of Flores* or in *Patrick* as both wills clearly manifested an intent to disinherit certain beneficiaries. And in *Est. of Smelser* both the UPC and Restatement would permit reformation as there appears to be clear evidence of mistake and what the donor's true intentions were. What about under the laws of your state?

11.4. This is an example of a latent ambiguity because the will is clear in its language, and only upon examination of the property do we realize that Mary's quilts were actually not made by the Amish but instead by workers in China. In this case, evidence that these quilts comprise Mary's collection—and have over time—as well as the fact that she bought them in Amish country should likely be admitted to resolve the ambiguity.

11.5. This is an example of a patent ambiguity because we can see immediately, from the face of the will, that there is a problem—Tom cannot have both a wife and husband. Evidence showing that Teresa was still married to Tom at the time of Tom's death could be provided to resolve the ambiguity.

11.6. This is a latent or a patent ambiguity, depending on the will. If Meika says in the will, which most people should do, that she has no children, it becomes patent. But if she doesn't mention children either way, it is a latent ambiguity that comes to the fore only when we realize that she never had any children. In order to resolve the contests, testimony by the attorney may be allowed to clear up Meika's intentions. But, this is a lesson to NEVER fall into the trap of over-writing an existing client's will!

11.7. Both the mistaken address as well as the mistaken name are examples of latent ambiguities since only upon examination of Jordan's property does it become clear that there is a problem with the distribution. Evidence of Jordan's real estate deed as well as his volunteer records could be admitted, along with attorney testimony, if applicable, to help resolve the ambiguities.

Chapter 12

Answers

12.1. As in many estate planning situations, because family situations often involve potentially competing interests, conflicts do arise. It would be prudent to accept that this situation places you in conflict because "the representation of one client will be directly adverse to another client" in that the couple's wills by their very nature, direct what property, if any, passes between your clients at death. You also certainly have a duty to maintain the wife's confidences which were made to you previously as part of the attorney–client privilege. However, as noted in the rules, the clients may still give informed consent for your representation, provided it is not prohibited in your jurisdiction. Be aware, however, that this situation, like many others in estate planning, would likely knock you out as representative in the event that future litigation arises.

12.2. You owe no duties to the other three children, so their interests are irrelevant. However, because the son would have to pay the transfer taxes on the second set of transfers, you might feel inclined to want to pressure dad to structure his estate differently. But you also can't be sure that the son would really give 3/4ths of the inheritance away, and it would be inappropriate to pressure dad to give the son less than he wants to, which would disadvantage the son. You are not prohibited from doing dad's estate plan, and you certainly can suggest to dad that the unnatural disposition may cause bitter feelings and extra taxes. If dad wants to leave his property all to his son, that is ultimately his decision, so long as he fully understands the consequences. But watch out, if you have acquired confidential information in the representation of dad that might affect the son's business interests, you may be in a conflict situation.

INDEX

References are to Pages